Executive Editor: Susan Badger

Series Editorial Assistant: Laura Lynch

Production Administrator: Mary Beth Finch

Production Coordinator: Barbara Gracia

Editorial-Production Service: Woodstock Publishers' Services

Text Designer: Karen Mason

Cover Administrator: Linda K. Dickinson

Cover Designer: Susan Slovinsky

Manufacturing Buyer: Megan Cochran

A Division of Simon & Schuster, Inc.
160 Gould Street
Needham Heights, MA 02194-2134

Library of Congress Cataloging-in-Publication Data

Carlson, Neil R.,
Foundations of physiological psychology / Neil R. Carlson. — 2nd ed.
p. cm.
Includes bibliographical references and index.
ISBN 0-205-13111-5
1. Psychophysiology. I. Title.
[DNLM: 1. Behavior—physiology. 2. Nervous System—physiology. 3. Psychophysiology. WL 102 C284p]
QP360.C352 1992
612.8—dc20
DNLM/DLC
for Library of Congress 91-26204
CIP

Printed in the United States of America
10 9 8 7 6 5 4 3 2 97 96 95 94 93 92

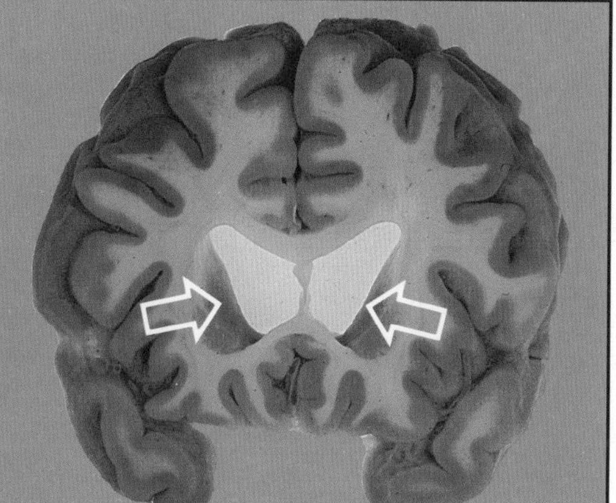

COLOR PLATE 7.1

A slice through the brain of a person [illegible] Huntington's chorea. The arrowheads [illegible] the location of the caudate nuclei, which are severely degenerated. As a consequence of the degeneration, the lateral ventricles (open spaces in the middle of the slice) have enlarged. Compare the caudate nuclei and lateral ventricles of this plate with those shown in Color Plate 7.2. (Courtesy of Anthony D'Agostino, Good Samaritan Hospital, Portland, Oregon.)

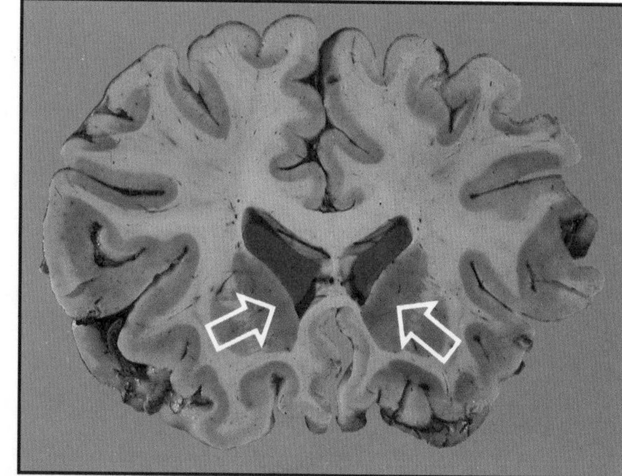

COLOR PLATE 7.2

A slice through a normal human brain, showing the normal appearance of the caudate nuclei (arrowheads) and lateral ventricles. (Courtesy of Harvard Medical School/Betty G. Martindale.)

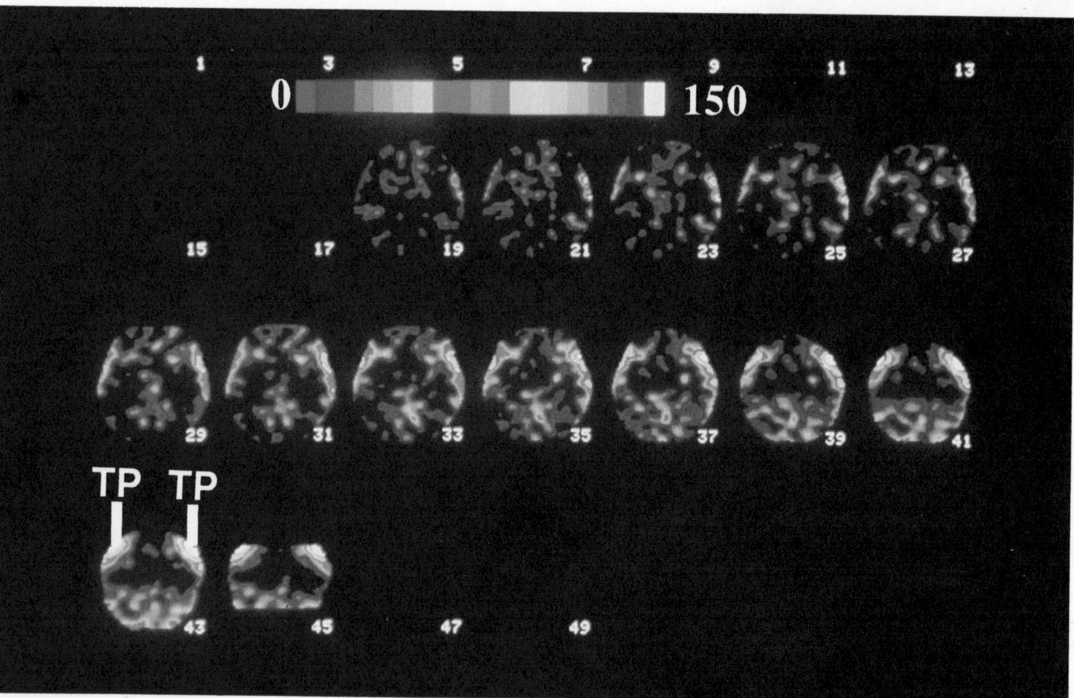

COLOR PLATE 16.1

PET scans of regional blood flow during anticipatory anxiety in normal patients awaiting a painful shock (which was not delivered). The scans are sequential horizontal sections, with rostral toward the top. The increased activity of the anterior temporal lobes is marked with the lines labeled TP (temporal pole). (From Reiman, E. M., Fusselman, M. J., Fox P. T., and Raichle, M. E. *Science,* 1989, *243,* 1071–1074. Copyright © 1989 by the American Association for the Advancement of Science. Reprinted by permission.)

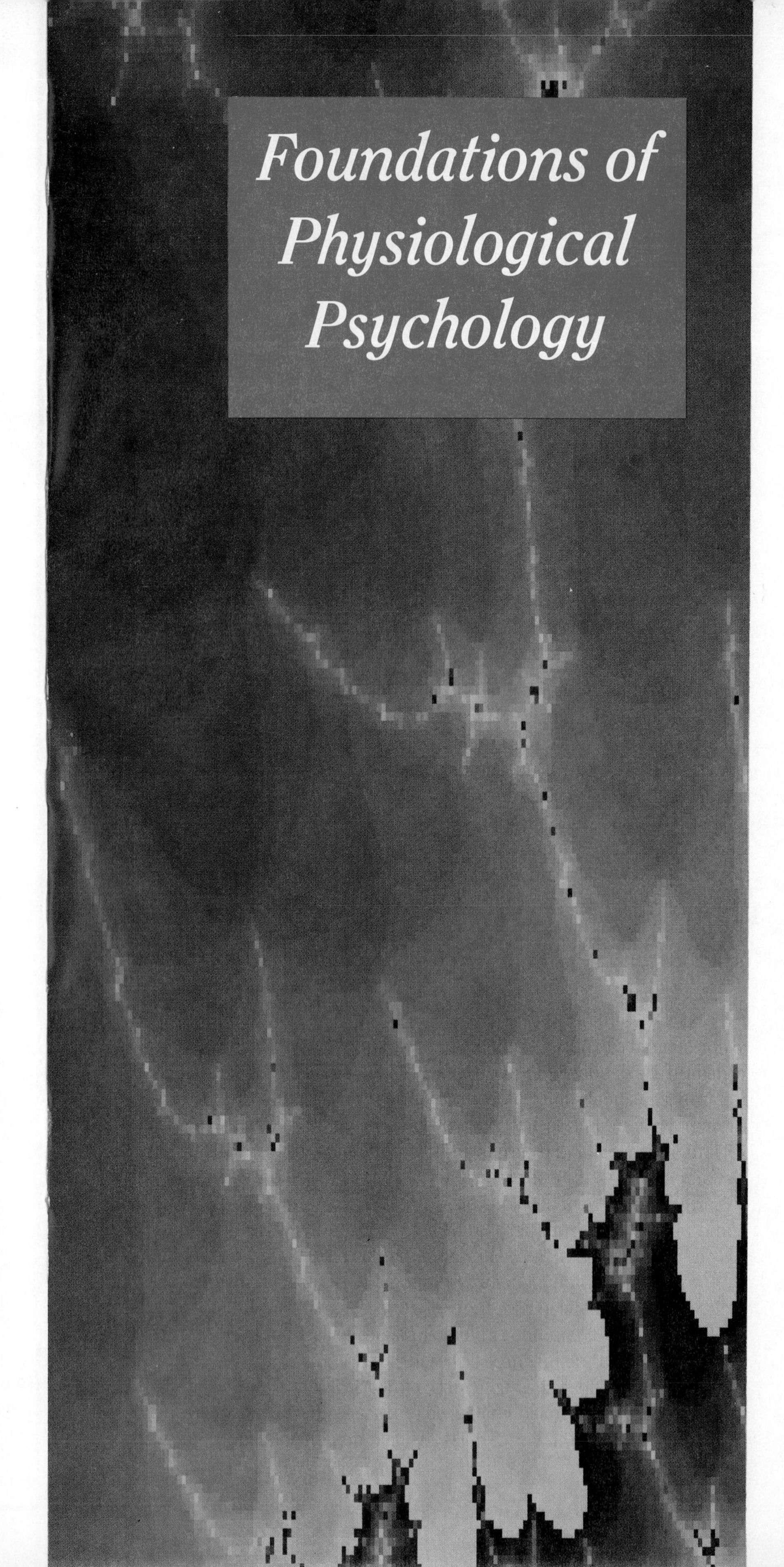

SECON
EDITIC

*N*eil *R*. *C*a

University of Massa
at Amherst

ALLYN AND B

Boston • London •
Sydney • Tokyo •

Contents

Preface

All my life I have wanted to know how things work. When I was a boy I took apart alarm clocks, radios, my mother's sewing machine, and other interesting gadgets, to see what was inside. Much to my parents' relief, I outgrew that habit (or at least got better at putting things back together), but my curiosity is still with me. Since my college days, I have been trying to find out all I can about the workings of the most intricate piece of machinery that we know of: the human brain.

The field of neuroscience research is a very busy and productive one today. A large number of scientists are trying to understand the physiology of behavior, using more and more advanced methods, yielding more and more interesting results. Their findings provide me with much to write about. I admire their dedication and hard work, and I thank them for giving me something to say. Without their efforts I could not have written this book.

I wrote the first edition of this book at the request of my colleagues who teach the course and who wanted a briefer version of *Physiology of Behavior* with more emphasis on research related to humans. Those of you who are familiar with that book will recognize its parentage in this one. Both books cover the same topics, in roughly the same order. The first part of this book is concerned with foundations: the history of the field, the structure and functions of neurons, neuroanatomy, and psychopharmacology. The second part is concerned with inputs and outputs: the sensory systems and the motor system. The third part deals with what might be called "motivated" behavior: reproduction, sleep, emotion, ingestion, and aggression. The fourth part deals with learning and with verbal and nonverbal communication. The final part deals with neurological and mental disorders.

There are some important differences between this book and *Physiology of Behavior.* The text of this book is not simply a shorter and denser version of its predecessor. I retained the illustrative examples, especially those dealing with human disorders, and added explanations of phenomena to be sure that students without much background in biology could understand what I was saying. Although I have simplified some of the detailed explanations, I have retained the important principles.

This book contains an expanded discussion of drugs. Research methods are covered in Chapter 1, along with history. Learning and memory are covered in one chapter. I have added a new chapter on emotion and stress (including a discussion of psychoneuroimmunology) and one on reinforcement and addiction. Like the first edition, this edition contains a chapter on neurological disorders. I have added more applied and clinical examples throughout the book, some of which are contained in prologues and epilogues. A *Prologue,* which contains the description of an episode involving a neurological disorder or an issue in neuroscience, opens each chapter. An *Epilogue: Application* resolves the issues raised in the Prologue, discussing them in terms of what the student has learned in the chapter. Interim summaries follow each major section of the book and provide useful reviews. When new terms are introduced, they are listed in the margin. Each chapter ends with a list of key concepts, new terms, and suggested readings. An expanded glossary defines all the terms listed in boldface.

Trying to keep up with the rapid progress being made in neuroscience research poses a challenge for teachers and textbook writers. If a student simply memorizes what we believe at the time to be facts, he or she is left with knowledge that quickly becomes obsolete. In this book I have tried to give students enough background material and enough knowledge of basic physiological processes so that they can revise what they have learned when research provides us with new information.

Writing is a difficult, time-consuming endeavor, and I find that I am still learning how to do it well. If I have at least partly achieved what I set out to do, readers will find that they can understand what I have said and will remain interested in what they are reading. I agree with Graves and Hodge (1947), who say that "good English is a matter not merely of grammar and syntax and vocabulary, but also of sense." "Readability" is not to be determined by counting syllables in words or words in sentences; it is a function of the clarity of thought and expression.

I designed this text to be interesting and informative. I have endeavored to provide a solid foundation for further study. Those students who will not take subsequent courses in this or related fields should receive the satisfaction of a much better understanding of their own behavior. Also, they will have a greater appreciation for the forthcoming advances in medical practices related to disorders that affect a person's perception, mood, or behavior. I hope that students who carefully read this book will henceforth perceive human behavior in a new light.

ACKNOWLEDGMENTS

Although I must accept the blame for any shortcomings of the book, I want to thank colleagues who helped me. I thank James W. Moore, Jr. for his work on the instructor's manual and the test bank. Several colleagues have reviewed the manuscript of parts of this book and made suggestions for improving the final drafts. I thank the following reviewers:

James Ackil, Western Illinois University
Clint Anderson, Providence College
Kent Berridge, University of Michigan, Ann Arbor
Jay Braun, Arizona State University
John Broida, University of Southern Maine, Portland
Lynn Tondat Carter, Southeastern Massachusetts College
Mark Cloud, Lock Haven University
Verne Cox, University of Texas, Arlington
Steven Fallenberg, Eastern Kentucky University
Owen Floody, Bucknell University
Robert Frank, University of Cincinnati
William Gibson, Northern Arizona University
Mary Gotch, Solano Community College
Kenneth Green, California State University, Long Beach
Stephen Kiefer, Kansas State University, Manhattan
Richard King, University of North Carolina, Chapel Hill
Paul Kolkosky, University of Southern Colorado
Robert Lansing, University of Arizona, Tucson
Michael Levine, University of Illinois, Chicago
Wesley Lynch, Montana State University, Bozeman
Richard Marrocco, University of Oregon, Eugene
Mark McCourt, University of Texas at Austin
James Moore, Marshall University
Linda Noble, Keenesaw State College

Edward Pollak, West Chester University
David Robbins, Ohio Weslyan University
A.M. Rosenwasser, University of Maine, Orono
Margaret Ruddy, Trenton State College
John Salamone, University of Connecticut, Storrs
Gary Schaumburg, Cerritos College
Frederic Shaffer, N.E. Missouri State University
Harold Siegel, Rutgers University
R.W. Skeleton, University of Victoria, Canada
Michael Stoloff, James Madison
Jeffrey Stripling, University of Arkansas, Fayetteville
Linda Walsh, University of Northern Iowa
Jeanette P. Ward, Memphis State University
Margaret White, California State University, Fullerton
Walter Wilczynski, University of Texas at Austin
Dawn Witherspoon, Brock University

My wife and I have prepared a student workbook to accompany this text. A good understanding of the principles of physiological psychology requires active participation in the learning process, and the workbook should provide an excellent framework for guiding the student's study behavior. James W. Moore, Jr. has written an instructor's manual and test bank to accompany the text.

I want to thank the people at Allyn and Bacon. Diane McOscar, my editor, provided assistance, support, and encouragement and helped me gather comments and suggestions from colleagues who have read the book; and Peter Petraitis, my production editor, got things organized and kept them running smoothly. Barbara Gracia, of Woodstock Publishers' Services, demonstrated her masterful skills of organization. Few people realize what a difficult, demanding, and time-consuming job it is to coordinate the production of a project such as this, with hundreds of illustrations, but I do, and I thank her for all she has done. Carol Beal was my copy editor. Her attention to detail uncovered inconsistencies in my terminology, awkwardness in my prose, and disjunctions in my logical discourse and gave me a chance to fix them before anyone else saw them in print. She also organized the file of letters granting permission to use photos and illustrations. Mark Lefkowitz, medical illustrator; Horvath and Cuthbertson, Illustrators; JAK Graphics, Ltd.; and Precision Graphics did a super job on the art, as you can easily see.

I must also thank my family for their assistance. My wife and my daughter Kerstin read drafts of my chapters and helped me clarify my prose. My son Paul ran errands for me and patiently accepted that I was often busily engaged in reading or writing in my study. But even more important than this assistance was the moral support and encouragement that my family provided me.

TO THE READER: USING THIS BOOK

Before you begin reading the first chapter, I want to say a few things about the design of the book that may help you with your studies. I have tried to integrate the text and illustrations as closely as possible. In my experience one of the most annoying aspects of reading some books is not knowing when to look at an illustration. When reading complicated material, I have found that sometimes I look at it too late and realize that I could have made more sense out of the text if I had just looked at the figure sooner. Furthermore, after looking at the illustration, I often find it difficult to return to the place where I stopped reading. Therefore, in this book you will find the figure references in boldface italics (like this: ***Figure 5.6***), which means "stop reading and look at the figure." I have placed these references in the locations I think will be optimal. If you look away from the text then, you will be assured that you will not be interrupting a line of reasoning in a crucial place and will not have to reread several sentences to get going again. You will find sections like this: "Figure 3.1 shows an alligator and a human. This alligator is certainly laid out in a linear fashion; we can draw a straight line that starts between its eyes and continues down the center of its spinal cord. (See ***Figure 3.1.***)" This particular example is a trivial one and will give you no problems no matter when you look at the figure. But in other cases the material is more complex, and you will have less trouble if you know what to look for before you stop reading and examine the illustration.

You will notice that some words in the text are *italicized* and others are printed in **boldface.** Italics mean one of two things: Either the word is being stressed for emphasis and is not a new term, or I am pointing out a new term that I do not think is necessary for you to learn. Most of the boldface terms in the text are part of the vocabulary of the physiological psychologist. Often, they will be used again in a later chapter. As an aid to your studying, I have included a list of them in the margin of the page on which they first occur. Also, the end of the text contains a glossary, which provides definitions for all of the boldfaced terms. In addition, a comprehensive index at the end of the book provides a list of terms and topics, with page references.

The physiology of behavior is a complex subject, and this book contains many concepts and descriptions of experiments that will be new to you. At the end of each major section I have included an *interim summary,* which provides a place for you to stop and think again about what you have just read, in order to make sure that you understand the direction the discussion has gone. The end of the chapter contains a list of key concepts, which summarizes the material covered. Taken together, these sections provide a detailed summary of the information introduced in the chapter. My students tell me that they review the interim summaries just before taking a test.

I hope that in reading this book you will come not only to learn more about the brain but also to appreciate it for the marvelous organ it is. The brain is wonderfully complex, and perhaps the most remarkable thing is that we are able to use it in our attempt to understand it.

While working on this book, I imagined myself talking with students, telling them interesting stories about the findings of clinicians and research scientists. Imagining your presence made the task of writing a little less lonely. I hope that the dialogue will continue. Please write to me and tell me what you like and dislike about the book. My address is: Department of Psychology, Tobin Hall, University of Massachusetts, Amherst, Massachusetts 01003. If you write to me, we can make the conversion a two-way exchange.

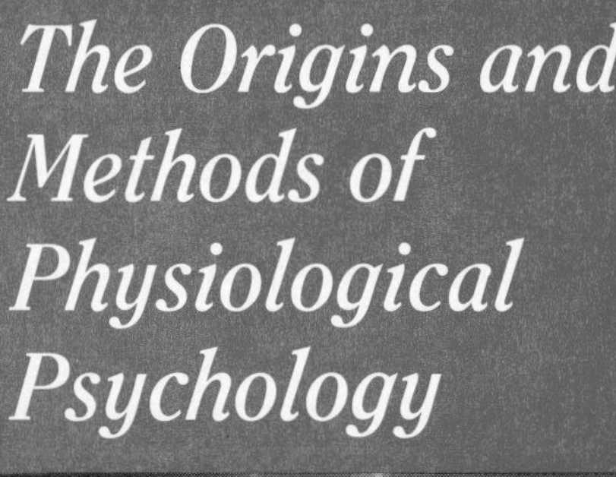

The Origins and Methods of Physiological Psychology

1

CHAPTER OUTLINE

PROLOGUE ►

René, a lonely and intelligent young man of eighteen years, had secluded himself in Saint-Germain, a village to the west of Paris. He had recently suffered a nervous breakdown and chose the retreat to recover. Even before coming to Saint-Germain, he had heard of the fabulous royal gardens built for Henri IV and Marie de Médici, and one sunny day he decided to visit them. The guard stopped him at the gate; but when he identified himself as a student at the King's School at La Flèche, he was permitted to enter. The gardens consisted of a series of six large terraces overlooking the Seine, planted in the symmetrical, orderly fashion so loved by the French. Grottoes were cut into the limestone hillside at the end of each terrace; René entered one of them. He heard eerie music accompanied by the gurgling of water but, at first, could see nothing in the darkness. As his eyes became accustomed to the gloom, he could make out a figure illuminated by a flickering torch. He approached the figure, which he soon recognized as that of a young woman. As he drew closer, he saw that she was actually a bronze statue of Diana, bathing in a pool of water. Suddenly, the Greek goddess fled and hid behind a bronze rose bush. As René pursued her, an imposing statue of Neptune rose in front of him, barring the way with his trident.

René was delighted. He had heard about the hydraulically operated mechanical organs and the moving statues, but he had not expected such realism. As he walked back toward the entrance to the grotto, he saw the plates buried in the ground that controlled the valves operating the machinery. He spent the rest of the afternoon wandering through the grottoes, listening to the music and being entertained by the statues.

During his stay in Saint-Germain René visited the royal gardens again and again. He had been thinking about the relation between the movements of animate and inanimate objects, which had concerned philosophers for some time. He thought he saw in the apparently purposeful, but obviously inanimate, movements of the statues an answer to some important questions about the relation between the mind and the body. Even after he left Saint-Germain, he revisited the grottoes in his memory; and he went so far as to name his daughter Francine after their designers, the Francini brothers of Florence. ▲

The last frontier in this world — and perhaps the greatest one — lies within us. The human nervous system makes possible all that we can do, all that we can know, and all that we can experience. Its complexity is immense, and the task of studying it and understanding it dwarfs all previous explorations our species has undertaken.

One of the most universal of all human characteristics is curiosity. We want to explain what makes things happen. In ancient times people believed that natural phenomena were caused by animating spirits. All moving objects — animals, the wind and tides, the sun, moon, and stars — were assumed to have spirits that caused them to move. For example, stones fell when they were dropped because their animating spirits wanted to be reunited with Mother Earth. As our ancestors became more sophisticated and learned more about nature, they abandoned this approach — which we call *animism* — in favor of physical explanations for inanimate moving objects. But they still used spirits to explain human behavior.

From the earliest historical times people have believed they possess souls. This belief stems from the fact that each of us is aware of his or her own existence. When we think or act, we feel as if something inside us — our mind or our soul — is thinking or deciding to act. But what is the nature of the human mind? We have physical bodies, with muscles that move it and with sensory organs such as eyes and ears that perceive information about the world around us. Within our bodies the nervous system plays a central role, controlling the movements of the muscles and receiving information from the sensory organs. But what role does the mind play? Does it *control* the nervous system? Is it a *part of* the nervous system? Is it physical and tangible, like the rest of the body, or is it a spirit that will always remain hidden?

This puzzle has historically been called the ***mind-body question.*** Philosophers have been trying to answer it for many centuries, and more recently, scientists have taken up the task. Basically, people have followed two different approaches: dualism and monism. **Dualism** is a belief in the dual nature of reality. Mind and body are separate; the body is made of ordinary matter, but the mind is not. **Monism** is a belief that everything in the universe consists of matter and energy and that the mind is a phenomenon produced by the workings of the nervous system.

dualism

monism

Mere speculation about the nature of the mind is futile. If we could answer the mind-body question simply by thinking about it, philosophers would have done so long ago. Physiological psychologists take an empirical, practical, and monistic approach to the study of human nature. We believe that once we understand the workings of the human body — and in particular, the workings of the nervous system — the mind-body problem will have been solved. We will be able to explain how we perceive, how we think, how we remember, and how we act. We will even be able to explain the nature of our own self-awareness. Of course, only time will tell whether this belief is justified.

UNDERSTANDING SELF-AWARENESS: A PHYSIOLOGICAL APPROACH

As you will learn from subsequent chapters, investigators have learned much about the physiology of behavior: of perception, motivation, memory, and control of specific movements. But before I address these problems, I want to show you how physiological psychologists have attempted to understand perhaps the most complex phenomena of all: human self-awareness.

We know that consciousness is altered by changes in the structure or chemistry of the brain; therefore, we may hypothesize that consciousness is a physiological function, just like behavior. We can even speculate about the origins of self-awareness. Consciousness and the ability to communicate seem to go hand in hand. Our species, with its complex social structure and enormous capacity for learning, is well served by our ability to communicate: to express intentions to one another and to make requests of one another. Verbal communication makes cooperation possible and permits us to establish customs and laws of behavior. Perhaps the evolution of this ability is what has given rise to the phenomenon of consciousness. That is, our ability to send and receive messages with other people makes it possible for us to send and receive our own messages — to think and to be aware of our own existence. (See ***Figure 1.1.***)

FIGURE 1.1

A print of a sixteenth-century anatomy woodcut by Andreas Vesalius. (Courtesy National Library of Medicine.)

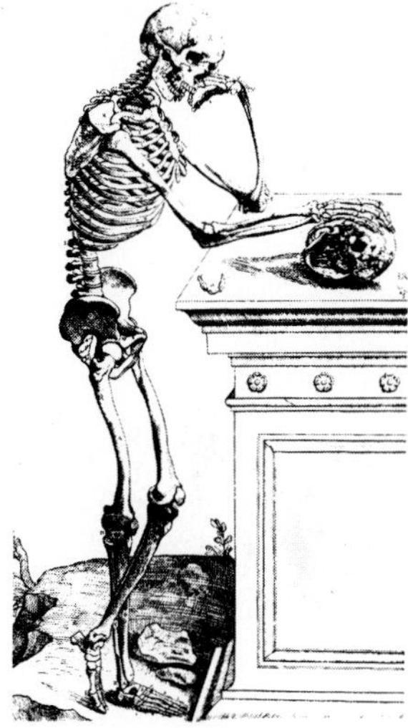

Blindsight

A particularly interesting phenomenon has some implications for our understanding of consciousness. It suggests that the common belief that perceptions must enter consciousness for them to affect our behavior is incorrect. The brain contains not one but several mechanisms involved in vision. To simplify matters somewhat, I will talk about two systems, which evolved at different times. The simpler one, which resembles the visual system of animals such as fish and frogs, evolved first. The more complex one, which is possessed only by mammals, evolved later. This second "mammalian" system seems to be the one that is responsible for our ability to perceive the world around us. The first, the "primitive" visual system, is mainly devoted to controlling eye movements and bringing our attention to sudden movements that occur off to the side of our field of vision.

Neurologists have recognized for a long time that damage to the mammalian visual system on one side of a person's brain produces blindness in the visual field of the opposite side of the body. That is, if the right side of the brain is damaged, the patient will be blind to everything located to the left when he or she looks straight ahead. However, Weiskrantz, Warrington, Sanders, and Marshall (1974) reported a puzzling phenomenon, which they called **blindsight.** If someone places an object in the patient's blind field and asks the patient to reach for it, he or she will be able to do so rather accurately. In fact, if the investigator presents objects of different size, the patient will open his or her hand wider when reaching for large objects than for small ones. The patients are surprised to find their hands repeatedly coming in contact with an object in what appears to them as darkness; they say that they see nothing there.

blindsight

This blindsight phenomenon shows that visual information can control behavior without producing a conscious sensation. Just as rats can learn to turn toward a particular visual stimulus after their mammalian visual system is damaged, humans apparently can use the primitive visual system of their brains to guide hand movements toward an object. The phenomenon of blindsight suggests that *consciousness is not a general property of all parts of the brain;* some parts of the brain, but not others, appear to play a special role in consciousness. Only the mammalian visual system communicates with those parts of the brain responsible for consciousness. The primitive system, which evolved early, before the development of consciousness, does not

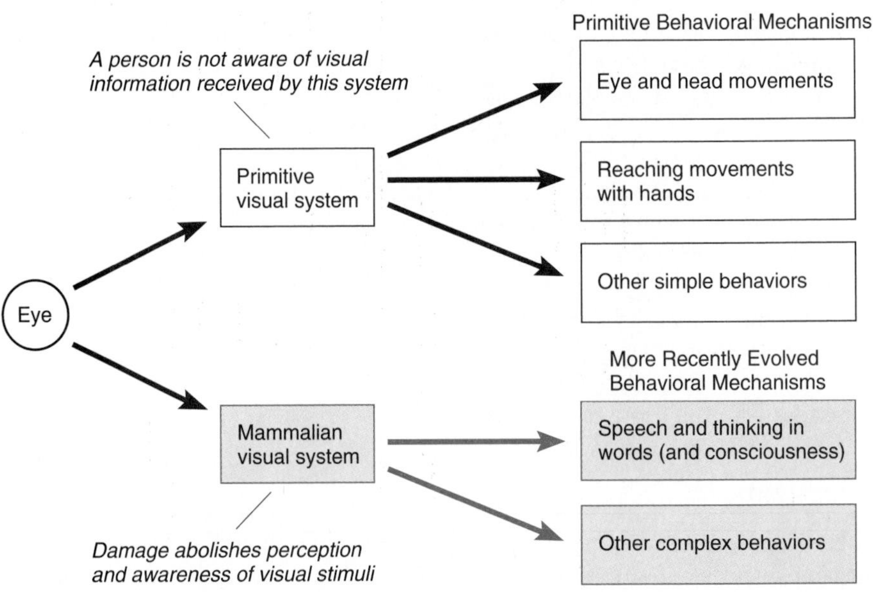

FIGURE 1.2

An explanation of blindsight phenomenon.

have direct connections with these parts of the brain. It *does* have connections with those parts of the brain responsible for controlling hand movements. (See ***Figure 1.2.***)

Split Brains

Studies of humans who have undergone a particular surgical procedure demonstrate dramatically how disconnecting parts of the brain involved with perceptions from parts that are involved with verbal behavior also disconnects them from consciousness. These results suggest that the parts of the brain involved in verbal behavior may be the ones responsible for consciousness.

The surgical procedure is one that has been used for people who have very severe epilepsy that cannot be controlled by drugs. In these people nerve cells in one side of the brain become overactive, and the overactivity is transmitted to the other side of the brain by the corpus callosum. The **corpus callosum** is a large bundle of nerve fibers that connect corresponding parts of one side of the brain with those on the other. Both sides of the brain then engage in wild activity and stimulate each other, causing a generalized epileptic seizure. These seizures can occur many times each day, preventing the patient from leading a normal life. Neurosurgeons discovered that cutting the corpus callosum (the **split-brain operation**) greatly reduced the frequency of the epileptic seizures.

corpus callosum

split-brain operation

Figure 1.3 shows a drawing of the split-brain operation. We see the brain being sliced down the middle, from front to back, dividing it into its two symmetrical halves.

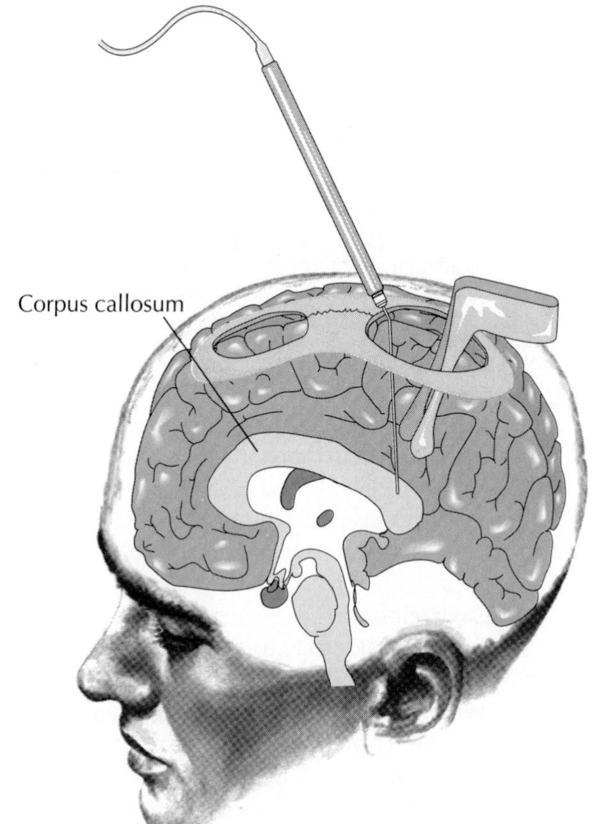

FIGURE 1.3

The split-brain operation. (Adapted from Gazzaniga, M.S. *Fundamentals of Psychology*. New York: Academic Press, 1973.)

The corpus callosum is being cut by the neurosurgeon's special knife. (See ***Figure 1.3.***)

cerebral hemisphere

Sperry (1966) and Gazzaniga and his associates (Gazzaniga, 1970; Gazzaniga and LeDoux, 1978) have studied these patients extensively. The largest part of the brain consists of two symmetrical parts, called the **cerebral hemispheres.** The two cerebral hemispheres receive sensory information from the opposite sides of the body and control movements of the opposite sides, too. The corpus callosum permits the two hemispheres to share information, so that each side knows what the other side is perceiving and doing. After the split-brain operation is performed, the two hemispheres are disconnected and operate independently; their sensory mechanisms, memories, and motor systems can no longer exchange information. The effects of these disconnections are not obvious to the casual observer, for the simple reason that only one hemisphere — in most people, the left — controls speech. The right hemisphere of an epileptic person with a split brain can understand verbal instructions reasonably well but is totally incapable of producing speech.

Because only one side of the brain can talk about what it is experiencing, people speaking with a person with a split brain are communicating with only one hemisphere — the left. The operations of the right hemisphere are more difficult to detect. Even the patient's left hemisphere has to learn about the independent existence of the right hemisphere. One of the first things that these patients say they notice after the operation is that their left hand seems to have a "mind of its own." For example, patients may find themselves putting down a book held in the left hand, even if they have been reading it with great interest. This conflict occurs because the right hemisphere, which controls the left hand, cannot read and therefore finds the book boring. At other times, they surprise themselves by making obscene gestures (with the left hand) when they had not intended to. A psychologist once reported that a man with a split brain attempted to beat his wife with one hand and protect her with the other. Did he *really* want to hurt her? Yes and no, I guess.

One exception to the crossed representation of sensory information is the olfactory system. That is, when a person sniffs a flower through the left nostril, only the left brain receives a sensation of the odor. Thus, if the right nostril of a patient with a split brain is plugged up, leaving the left nostril open, the patient will accurately identify odors verbally. However, if the odor enters the right nostril, the patient will say that he or she smells nothing. But, in fact, the right brain *has* perceived the odor and *can* identify it. To show that this is so, we ask the patient to smell an odor with the right nostril and then reach for some objects that are hidden from view by a partition. If we ask the patient to use the left hand, controlled by the hemisphere that detected the smell, he or she will select the object that corresponds to the odor — a plastic flower for a floral odor, a toy fish for a fishy odor, a model tree for the odor of pine, and so forth. But if we ask the patient to use the right hand, he or she fails the test, because the right hand is connected to the left hemisphere, which did not smell the odor. (See ***Figure 1.4.***)

The effects of cutting the corpus callosum reinforce the conclusion that we become conscious of something only if information about it is able to reach the parts of the brain responsible for verbal communication, which are located in the left hemisphere. If the information does not reach these parts of the brain, then that information does not reach consciousness. Certainly, we still know very little about the physiology of consciousness, but studies of people with brain damage suggest that real progress has been made. I will have more to say about this issue in subsequent chapters.

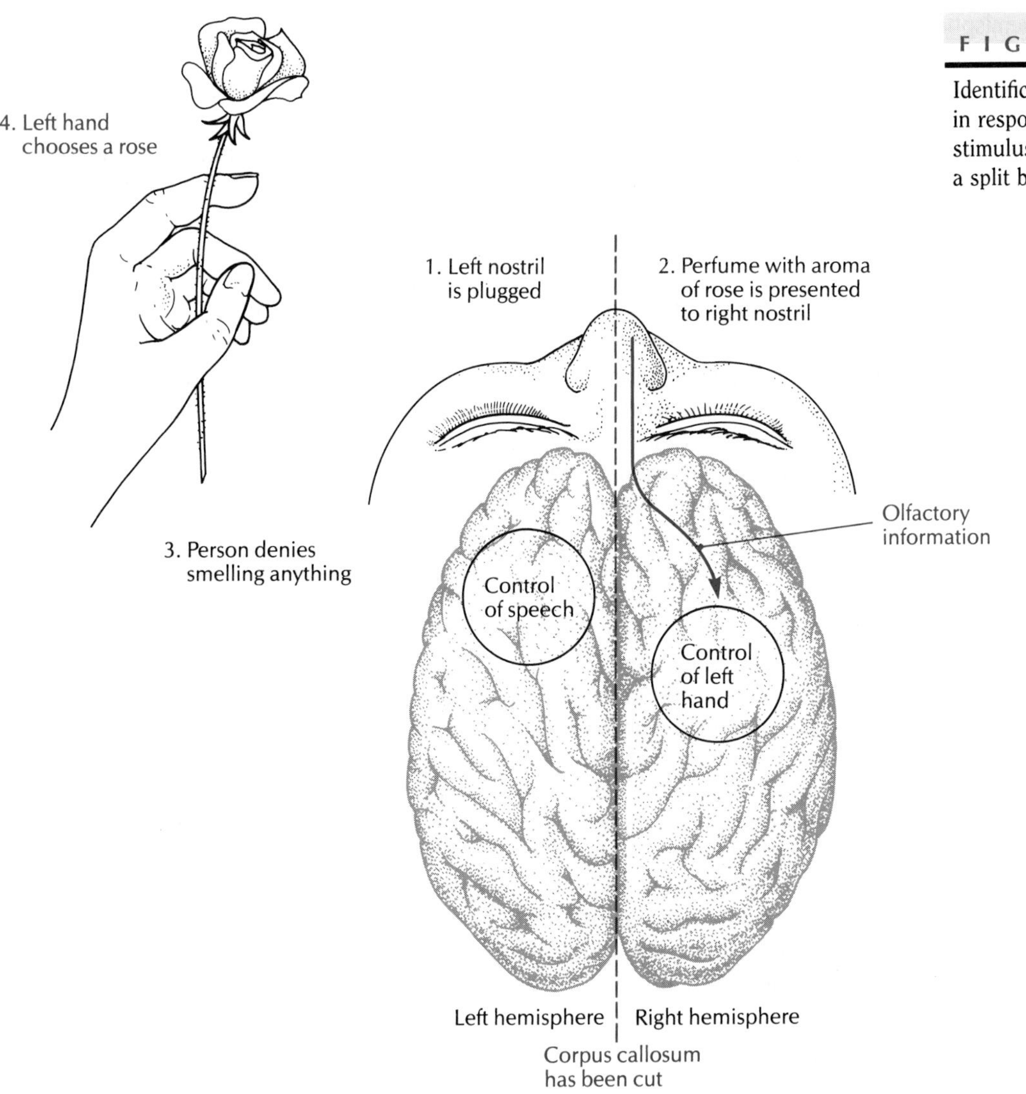
4. Left hand chooses a rose
1. Left nostril is plugged
2. Perfume with aroma of rose is presented to right nostril
3. Person denies smelling anything
Olfactory information
Control of speech
Control of left hand
Left hemisphere
Right hemisphere
Corpus callosum has been cut

FIGURE 1.4

Identification of an object in response to an olfactory stimulus by a person with a split brain.

▶*INTERIM SUMMARY*◀

The mind-body problem has puzzled philosophers for many centuries. Modern science has adopted a monistic position — the belief that the world consists of matter and energy and that nonmaterial entities such as souls are not a part of the universe. Study of the functions of the human nervous system tend to support this position, as two specific examples show. Both phenomena show that brain damage, by damaging conscious brain functions or disconnecting them from the speech mechanisms in the left hemisphere, can reveal the presence of other functions, of which the person is *not* conscious.

Blindsight is a phenomenon seen after partial damage to the "mammalian" visual system on one side of the brain. Although the person is, by the normal meaning of the word, blind to anything presented to part of the visual field, the person can nevertheless reach out and point to objects whose presence he or she is not conscious of. Similarly, when sensory information about a particular object is presented to the

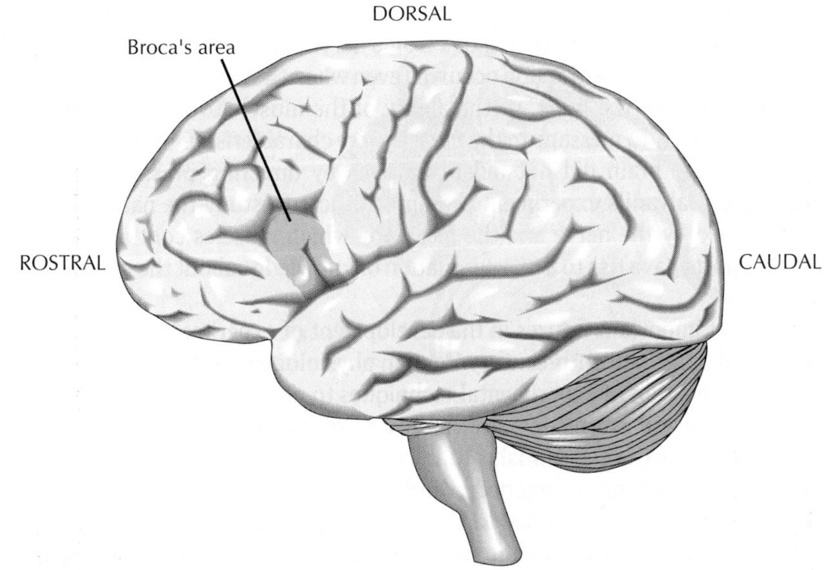

FIGURE 1.7

Broca's area, a region of the brain named for French surgeon Paul Broca. Broca discovered that damage to a part of the left side of the brain disrupted a person's ability to speak.

experimental ablation

Flourens removed various parts of animals' brains and observed their behavior. By seeing what the animal could no longer do, he could infer the function of the missing portion of the brain. This method is called **experimental ablation** (from the Latin *ablatus,* "carried away"). Flourens claimed to have discovered the regions of the brain that control heart rate and breathing, purposeful movements, and visual and auditory reflexes.

Soon after Flourens performed his experiments, Paul Broca, a French surgeon, applied the principle of experimental ablation to the human brain. Of course, he did not intentionally remove parts of human brains to see how they worked. Instead, he observed the behavior of people whose brains had been damaged by strokes. In 1861 he performed an autopsy on the brain of a man who had had a stroke that resulted in the loss of the ability to speak. Broca's observations led him to conclude that a portion of the cerebral cortex on the left side of the brain performs functions necessary for speech. (See ***Figure 1.7.***)

As I mentioned earlier, Luigi Galvani used electricity to demonstrate that muscles contain the source of the energy that powers their contractions. In 1870 German physiologists Gustav Fritsch and Eduard Hitzig used electrical stimulation as a tool for understanding the physiology of the brain. They applied weak electrical current to the exposed surface of a dog's brain and observed the effects of the stimulation. They found that stimulation of different portions of a specific region of the brain caused contraction of specific muscles on the opposite side of the body. We now refer to this region as the *primary motor cortex,* and we know that nerve cells there communicate directly with those that cause muscular contractions. We also know that other regions of the brain communicate with the primary motor cortex and thus control behaviors. For example, the region that Broca found to be necessary for speech communicates with, and controls, the portion of the primary motor cortex that controls the muscles of the lips, tongue, and throat, which we use to speak.

One of the most brilliant contributors to nineteenth-century science was the German physicist and physiologist Hermann von Helmholtz. Helmholtz devised a mathematical formulation of the law of conservation of energy; invented the ophthalmoscope (used to examine the retina of the eye); devised an important and influential theory of color vision and color blindness; and studied audition, music, and many physiological processes. Although Helmholtz had studied under Müller, he opposed Müller's belief that human organs are endowed with a vital nonmaterial force that coordinates their operations. Helmholtz believed that all aspects of physiology are mechanistic, subject to experimental investigation.

Helmholtz was also the first scientist to attempt to measure the speed of conduction through nerves. Scientists had previously believed that such conduction was identical to the conduction that occurs in wires, traveling at approximately the speed of light. But Helmholtz found that neural conduction was much slower — only about 90 feet per second. This measurement proved that neural conduction was more than a simple electrical message, as we will see in the next chapter.

Functionalism: Natural Selection and Evolution

Müller's insistence that biology must be an experimental science provided the starting point for an important tradition. However, other biologists continued to observe, classify, and think about what they saw, and some of them arrived at valuable conclusions. The most important of these biologists was Charles Darwin. (See ***Figure 1.8.***) Darwin formulated the principles of *evolution* and *natural selection,* which revolutionized biology. He noted that across succeeding generations, individual members of a species spontaneously undergo structural changes. If these changes produce favorable effects that permit the individual to reproduce more successfully, some of the individual's offspring will inherit the favorable characteristics and will themselves produce more offspring.

Darwin's theory emphasized that all of an organism's characteristics — its structure, its coloration, its behavior — have functional significance. For example, the strong talons and sharp beaks that eagles possess permit the birds to catch and eat prey. Caterpillars that eat green leaves are themselves green, and their color makes it difficult for birds to see them against their usual background. Mother mice construct nests, which keep their offspring warm and out of harm's way. Obviously, the behavior itself is not inherited — how can it be? What *is* inherited is a brain that causes the

FIGURE 1.8

Charles Darwin (1809–1882). His theory of evolution revolutionized biology and strongly influenced early psychologists. (North Wind Picture Archives.)

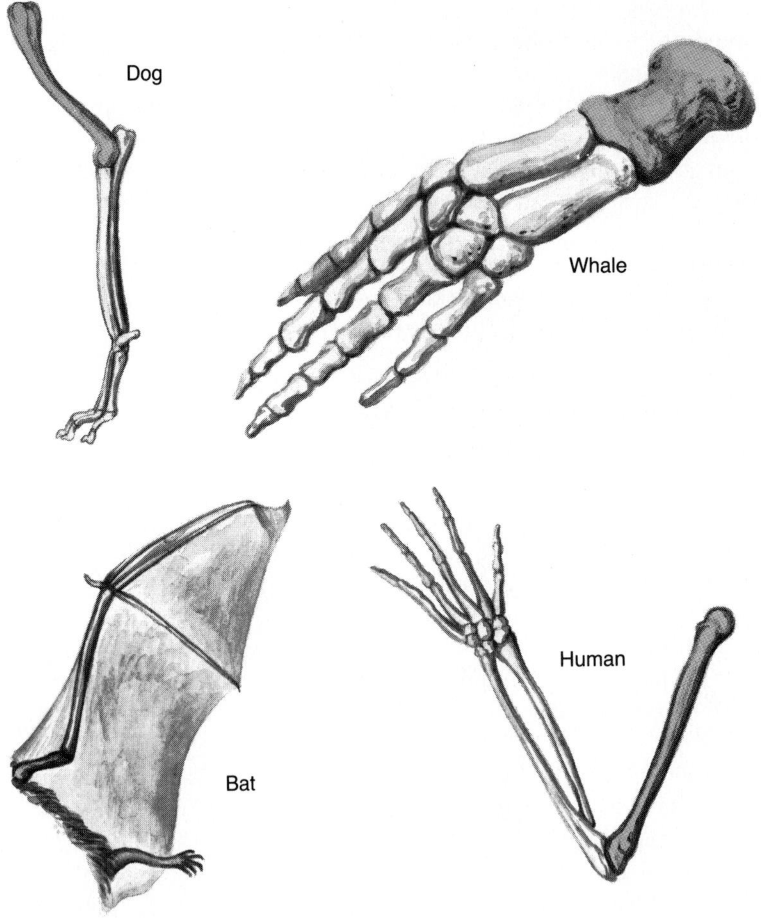

FIGURE 1.9

The humerus bone, shown in color. Through the process of natural selection, this bone has been adapted to suit many different functions. (Adapted from Moore, R. *Evolution*. New York: Life Nature Library, 1964.)

functionalism

behavior to occur. Thus, Darwin's theory gave rise to **functionalism,** a belief that characteristics of living organisms perform useful functions. So to understand the physiological basis of various behaviors, we must first understand what these behaviors accomplish. We must therefore understand something about the natural history of the species being studied so that the behaviors can be seen in context.

To understand the workings of a complex piece of machinery, we should know what its functions are. This principle is just as true for a living organism as it is for a mechanical device. However, an important difference exists between machines and organisms: Machines have inventors who had a purpose when they designed them, whereas organisms are the result of a long series of accidents. Thus, strictly speaking, we cannot say that any physiological mechanisms of living organisms have a *purpose.* But they have *functions,* and these we can try to determine. For example, the forelimbs shown in Figure 1.9 are adapted for different uses in different species of animals. (See ***Figure 1.9.***)

A good example of the functional analysis of an adaptive trait was demonstrated in an experiment by Blest (1957). Certain species of moths and butterflies have spots on their wings that resemble eyes — particularly the eyes of predators such as owls. (See ***Figure 1.10.***) These insects normally rely on camouflage for protection; the back of their wings, when folded, are colored like the bark of a tree. However, when a bird approaches, the insect's wings flip open, which suddenly displays the hidden eyespots.

FIGURE 1.10

The owl butterfly. This butterfly displays its eyespots when approached by a bird. The bird usually will then fly away. (Cosmos/ Photo Researchers Inc.)

The bird then tends to fly away rather than eat the insect. Blest performed an experiment to see whether the eyespots on a moth's or butterfly's wings really disturbed birds who saw them. He placed mealworms on different backgrounds and counted how many worms the birds ate. Indeed, when the worms were placed on a background that contained eyespots, the birds tended to avoid them.

Darwin formulated his theory of evolution in an attempt to explain the means by which species acquired their adaptive characteristics. The cornerstone of his theory is the principle of **natural selection.** Briefly, here is how the process works for sexually reproducing multicellular animals: Every organism consists of a large number of cells, each of which contains chromosomes. Chromosomes are large, complex molecules that contain the recipes for producing the proteins that cells need to grow and to perform their functions. In essence, the chromosomes contain the blueprints for the construction (that is, the embryological development) of a particular member of a particular species. If the plans are altered, a different organism is produced.

natural selection

The plans do get altered; mutations occur from time to time. **Mutations** are accidental changes in the chromosomes of sperms or eggs that join together and develop into new organisms. For example, cosmic radiation might strike a chromosome in a cell of an animal's testis or ovary, thus producing a mutation that affects that animal's offspring. Most mutations are deleterious; the offspring either fails to survive or survives with some sort of deficit. (See ***Figure 1.11.***) However, a small percentage of

mutation

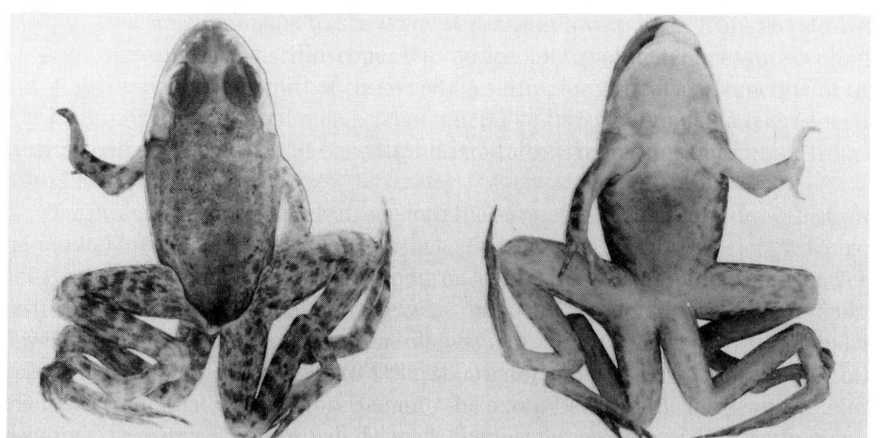

FIGURE 1.11

An example of a maladaptive trait. Most mutations do not produce selective advantages, but those that do are passed on to future generations. (From Volpe, E.P. *Understanding Evolution*, 2nd ed. Dubuque, Ia.: W.C. Brown, 1970. Reprinted with permission.)

selective advantage

mutations are beneficial and confer a **selective advantage** to the organism that possesses them. That is, the animal is more likely than other members of its species to live long enough to reproduce and hence to pass on its chromosomes to its own offspring. Many different kinds of traits can confer a selective advantage: resistance to a particular disease, the ability to digest new kinds of food, more effective weapons for defense or for procurement of prey, and even a more attractive appearance to members of the opposite sex (after all, one must reproduce in order to pass on one's chromosomes).

Naturally, the traits that can be altered by mutations are physical ones; chromosomes make proteins, which affect the structure and chemistry of cells. But the *effects* of these physical alterations can be seen in an animal's behavior. Thus, the process of natural selection can indirectly act upon behavior. For example, if a particular mutation results in changes in the brain that cause an animal to stop moving and freeze when it perceives a novel stimulus, that animal is more likely to escape undetected when a predator passes nearby. This tendency makes the animal more likely to survive to produce offspring and pass on its genes to future generations.

Other mutations are not immediately favorable, but because they do not put their possessors at a disadvantage, they get inherited by at least some members of the species. As a result of thousands of such mutations, the members of a particular species possess a variety of genes and are all at least somewhat different from one another; and variety is a definite advantage for a species. Different environments provide optimal habitats for different kinds of organisms. When the environment changes, species must adapt or run the risk of becoming extinct. If some members of the species possess assortments of genes that provide characteristics permitting them to adapt to the new environment, their offspring will survive, and the species will continue.

An understanding of the principle of natural selection plays some role in the thinking of every person who undertakes research in physiological psychology. Some researchers explicitly consider the genetic mechanisms of various behaviors and the physiological processes upon which these behaviors depend. Others are concerned with comparative aspects of behavior and its physiological basis; they compare the nervous systems of animals from a variety of species in order to make hypotheses about the evolution of brain structure and the behavioral capacities that correspond to this evolutionary development. But even though many researchers are not directly involved with the problem of evolution, the principle of natural selection guides the thinking of all physiological psychologists. We ask ourselves what the selective advantage of a particular trait might be. We think about how nature might have used a physiological mechanism that already existed to perform more complex functions in more complex organisms. When we entertain hypotheses, we ask ourselves whether a particular explanation makes sense in an evolutionary perspective.

The Value of Research with Animals

Most of the research that I describe in this book involves experimentation on living animals.

Any time we use another species of animals for our own purposes, we should be sure that what we are doing is both humane and worthwhile. I believe that a good case can be made that research on the physiology of behavior qualifies on both counts. Humane treatment is a matter of procedure. We know how to maintain laboratory animals in good health in comfortable, sanitary conditions. We know how to administer anesthetics and analgesics so that animals do not suffer during or after surgery, and we know how to prevent infections with proper surgical procedures and the use of antibiotics. Most industrially developed societies have very strict regulations about the care of animals and also require approval of the procedures that will be used in the experiments in which they participate. There is no excuse for mistreating animals in our care. In fact, the vast majority of laboratory animals *are* treated humanely.

Whether an experiment is *worthwhile* is more difficult to say. We use animals for many purposes. We eat their meat and their eggs and drink their milk; we turn their hides into leather; we extract insulin and other hormones from their organs to treat people with diseases; we train them to do useful work on farms or to entertain us. Even having a pet is a form of exploitation; it is we—not they—who decide that they will live in our homes. The fact is, we have been using other animals throughout the history of our species.

Pet owning causes much more suffering among animals than scientific research does. As Miller (1983) notes, pet owners are not required to receive permission from a board of experts including a veterinarian to house their pets, nor are they subject to periodic inspections to be sure that their home is clean and sanitary, that their pets have enough space to exercise properly, that their diets are appropriate; but scientific researchers are. Miller also notes that fifty times more dogs and cats are killed by humane societies each year because they have been abandoned by former pet owners than are used in scientific research.

If a person believes that it is wrong to use another animal in any way, regardless of the benefits to humans, there is nothing I can say to convince him or her of the value of scientific research with animals. For this person the issue is closed from the very beginning. Moral absolutes cannot be settled logically; like religious beliefs, they can be accepted or rejected, but they cannot be proved or disproved. Therefore, I will not try to attack or defend absolute moral positions. My arguments in support of scientific research with animals are based on an evaluation of the benefits the research has to humans. (In addition, we should not lose sight of the fact that research with animals often helps *other animals;* procedures used by veterinarians, as well as those used by physicians, come from such research.)

Before I describe the advantages of research with animals, I want to point out that the use of animals in research and teaching is a special target of animal rights activists. Nicholl and Russell (1990) examined 21 books written by such activists and calculated the number of pages devoted to concern for different uses of animals. Next, they compared the relative concern the authors showed for these uses to the numbers of animals actually involved in each of these categories. The results indicate that the authors showed relatively little concern for animals used for food, hunting, furs, or for those killed in pounds; although only 0.3 percent of the animals are used for research and education, 63.3 percent of the pages are devoted to this use. In terms of pages per million animals used, the authors devoted 0.08 to food, 0.23 to hunting, 1.27 to furs, 1.44 to killing in pounds, and 53.2 to research and education. The authors showed 665 times more concern for research and education compared with food, and 231 times compared with hunting. Even the use of animals for furs (which consumes two-thirds as many animals as research and education) attracted 41.9 times less attention per animal.

The disproportionate amount of concern that animal rights activists show toward the use of animals in research and education is puzzling, particularly because this is the one *indispensable* use of animals. We *can* survive without eating animals, we *can* live without hunting, we *can* do without furs, but without using animals for research and for training future researchers, we *cannot* make progress in understanding and treating diseases. In not too many years, our scientists will probably have developed a vaccine that will prevent the further spread of AIDS. Some animal rights activists believe that preventing the deaths of laboratory animals in the pursuit of such a vaccine is a more worthy goal than preventing the deaths of millions of humans that will occur as a result of the disease if a vaccine is not found. Even diseases we have already conquered would take new victims if drug companies could no longer use animals. If they were deprived of animals, these companies could no longer extract hormones used to treat human diseases, and they could not prepare many of the vaccines we now use to prevent them.

Our species is beset by medical, mental, and behavioral problems, many of which can be solved only through biological research. Let us consider some of the major neurological disorders. Strokes, caused by bleeding or occlusion of a blood vessel within the brain, often leave people partly paralyzed, unable to read or write or communicate verbally with their friends and family. Basic research on the means by which nerve cells communicate with each other has led to important discoveries about the causes of the death of brain cells. This research was not directed toward a specific practical goal; the potential benefits actually came as a surprise to the investigators.

Experiments based on these results have shown that if a blood vessel leading to the brain is blocked for a few minutes, the part of the brain that is nourished by that vessel will die. However, the brain damage can be prevented by first administering a drug that interferes with a particular kind of neural communication. (I will discuss this phenomenon in Chapter 14.) This research is important because it may lead to medical treatments that can help reduce the brain damage caused by strokes. But it involves operating on a laboratory animal such as a rat and pinching off a blood vessel. (The animals are anesthetized, of course.) Some of the animals will sustain brain damage, and all will be killed so that their brains can be examined. However, I think you will agree that research like this is just as legitimate as using animals for food.

As you will learn later in this book, research with laboratory animals has produced important discoveries about the possible causes or potential treatments of neurological and mental disorders, including Parkinson's disease, schizophrenia, manic-depressive illness, anxiety disorders, obsessive-compulsive disorders, anorexia nervosa, obesity, and drug addictions. Although much progress has been made, these problems are still with us and cause much human suffering. Unless we continue our research with laboratory animals, they will not be solved. Some people have suggested that instead of using laboratory animals in our research, we could use tissue cultures or computers. Unfortunately, tissue cultures or computers are not substitutes for living organisms. We have no way to study behavioral problems such as addictions in tissue cultures, nor can we program a computer to simulate the workings of an animal's nervous system. (If we could, that would mean we already had all the answers.)

This book will discuss some of the many important discoveries that have helped reduce human suffering. For example, in Chapter 2 you will learn about the discovery of the cause of myasthenia gravis, a disease that produces muscular weakness than can become so severe that the patient cannot eat or breathe without assistance. Research on this problem involved the use of electric fish and rabbits. The discovery of a vaccine for infantile paralysis, an even more serious disease of the nervous system, involved the use of rhesus monkeys. As you will learn in Chapter 4, Parkinson's disease, an incurable, progressive neurological disorder, has been treated for years with a drug called L-DOPA, discovered through animal research. Now, because of research with rats, mice, rabbits, and monkeys stimulated by the accidental poisoning of several young people with a contaminated batch of synthetic heroin, patients are being treated with a drug that actually slows down the rate of brain degeneration. Researchers have hopes that a drug will be found to prevent the degeneration altogether.

The easiest way to justify research with animals is to point to actual and potential benefits to human health, as I have just done. However, I think that we can also justify this research with a less practical but perhaps equally important argument. One of the things that characterizes our species is a quest for an understanding of our world. For example, astronomers contemplate the universe and try to uncover its mysteries. Even if their discoveries never lead to practical benefits such as better drugs or faster methods of transportation, the fact that they enrich our understanding of the beginning and the fate of our universe justifies their efforts. The pursuit of knowledge is itself a worthwhile endeavor. Surely the attempt to understand the universe within us — our nervous system, which is responsible for all that we are or can be — is also valuable.

▶*INTERIM SUMMARY*◀

All scientists hope to explain natural phenomena. In this context the term *explanation* has two basic meanings: generalization and reduction. Generalization refers to the classification of phenomena according to their essential features so that general laws can be formulated. For example, observing that gravitational attraction is related to the mass of two bodies and to the distance between them helps explain the movement of planets. Reduction refers to the description of phenomena in terms of more basic physical processes. For example, gravitation can be explained in terms of forces and subatomic particles.

Physiological psychologists use both generalization and reduction in explaining behavior. In large part, generalizations use the traditional methods of psychology. Reduction explains behaviors in terms of physiological events within the body — primarily within the nervous system. Thus, physiological psychology builds on the tradition of both experimental psychology and experimental physiology.

A dualist, René Descartes, proposed a model of the brain based on hydraulically actuated statues. His model stimulated observations that produced important discoveries. The results of Galvani's experiments eventually led to an understanding of the nature of the message transmitted by nerves between the brain and the sensory organs and the muscles. Müller's doctrine of specific nerve energies paved the way for study of the functions of specific parts of the brain, through the methods of experimental ablation and electrical stimulation.

Darwin's theory of evolution, which was based on the concept of natural selection, provided an important contribution to modern physiological psychology. The theory asserts that we must understand the functions performed by an organ or body part or by a behavior. Through random mutations, changes in an individual's genetic material cause different proteins to be produced, which results in the alteration of some physical characteristics. If the changes confer a selective advantage to the individual, the new genes will be transmitted to more and more members of the species. Even behaviors can evolve, through the selective advantage of alterations in the structure of the nervous system.

Research on the physiology of behavior necessarily involves the use of laboratory animals. It is incumbent on all scientists using these animals to see that they are housed comfortably and treated humanely, and laws have been enacted to ensure that they are. Such research has already produced many benefits to humankind and promises to continue to do so in the future. ▲

METHODS OF PHYSIOLOGICAL PSYCHOLOGY

In order to build something, we need to use the proper tools. Thus, in constructing a body of knowledge about the physiology of behavior, scientists must have at hand the tools for studying brain functions and behavior. This section discusses some of the most important tools.

Experimental Ablation

As we saw earlier, the method of experimental ablation was first employed by Pierre Flourens. The rationale from this method was subsequently applied to humans who had sustained accidental brain damage. The rationale is simple: The function of a brain-damaged organism is seen in what is *missing* in that organism's behavior. For example, if an animal can no longer see after part of the brain is destroyed, we can conclude that the destroyed area plays some role in vision. However, we must be very careful in interpreting the effects of brain damage. For example, how can we be sure that the brain-damaged animal is blind? Does it bump into objects, or fail to run through a maze toward the light that signals the location of food, or no longer constrict its pupils to light? An animal could bump into objects because of deficits in motor coordination; it could have lost its memory for the maze problem; or it could see quite well but have lost its visual reflexes. The experimenter must be clever enough to ask the right question.

Most of the time, a physiological psychologist is interested in destroying parts of the brain located in its depths. To do so, he or she must use a special device called a stereotaxic apparatus. *Stereotaxis* literally means "solid arrangement"; more specifically, it refers to the ability to locate objects in space. A **stereotaxic apparatus** permits the investigator to operate on brain structures that are hidden from view.

stereotaxic apparatus

A stereotaxic apparatus operates on simple principles. The device includes a head holder, which holds the animal's skull in the proper orientation; an electrode carrier, which holds a wire that is inserted into the brain; and a calibrated mechanism, which moves the electrode carrier in measured distances along the three axes: front-to-back, up-and-down, and side-to-side. Figure 1.12 illustrates a stereotaxic apparatus designed for small animals; various head holders can be used to outfit this device for such species as rats, mice, hamsters, pigeons, and turtles. (See ***Figure 1.12.***)

First, the investigator consults a stereotaxic atlas and looks up the location of the part of the brain he or she is interested in. A **stereotaxic atlas** is a book that contains drawings of slices of an animal's brain, along with numbers that indicate the location of its parts. Once the investigator has the numbers, he or she anesthetizes the animal, places it in the stereotaxic apparatus, and cuts the scalp open, exposing the skull. The investigator dials in the appropriate numbers, which shows where to drill a hole, using a dental drill. Next, the wire (electrode) is lowered into the brain until the dials indicate that its tip is in the proper location. A special device sends a radio frequency electrical current through the wire, which heats the tip and destroys a small region of the brain. The damage is called a **brain lesion** (from the Latin *laesio*, "to injure"). The wire is removed from the brain, the wound is sewed together, and the animal is taken out of the stereotaxic apparatus and allowed to recover from the anesthetic. Later, its behavior is assessed.

stereotaxic atlas

brain lesion

An investigator cannot necessarily assume that the brain damage occurred in the intended place. Brain lesions often miss the mark, and the investigator must verify the precise location of the brain damage after testing the animals behaviorally. After the

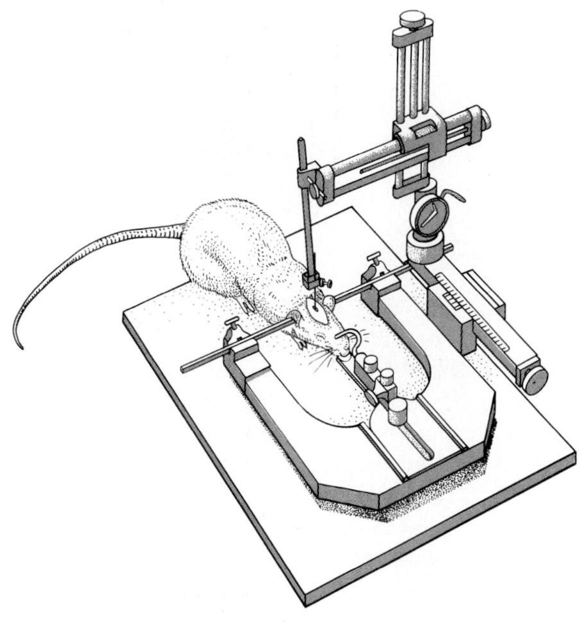

FIGURE 1.12

A stereotaxic apparatus, used to insert an electrode into a specific portion of an animal's brain.

behavioral observations are completed, the investigator cuts the animals' brains into slices and prepares them so that they can be examined under a microscope. (This procedure is described in Chapter 3.) The investigator can then relate the behavioral effects of the lesions to their actual locations.

By the way, there are stereotaxic apparatuses designed for human surgery. Sometimes, a neurosurgeon produces lesions in the depths of the brain. For example, Parkinson's disease produces severe tremors, which can seriously affect a person's ability to control his or her hand movements. Using a stereotaxic atlas, a neurosurgeon can destroy a particular location in the brain and reduce or eliminate the tremors.

Study of the Living Human Brain

A physiological psychologist is able to verify the location of a brain lesion by examining slices of the animal's brain under a microscope. Obviously, a human brain can be studied this way only if a person dies and the family consents to an autopsy. But recently, some methods have been developed that permit an investigator to study the interior of the living human brain without harm to its owner. The first is a technique called **computerized tomography** (CT). This procedure, usually referred to as a *CT scan,* works as follows: The patient's head is placed in a large doughnut-shaped ring. The ring contains an X-ray tube and, directly opposite it (on the other side of the patient's head), an X-ray detector. The X-ray beam passes through the patient's head, and the detector measures the amount of radioactivity that gets through it. The beam scans the head from all angles, and a computer translates the numbers it receives from the detector into pictures of the skull and its contents. (See ***Figures 1.13*** and ***1.14.***)

computerized tomography (CT)

Figure 1.15 shows a series of these CT scans taken through the head of a patient who sustained a stroke. The stroke damaged a part of the brain involved in bodily awareness and perception of space. The patient lost her awareness of the left side of her body and of items located on her left. (Her case will be discussed in the Prologue of

FIGURE 1.13

A CT scanner.

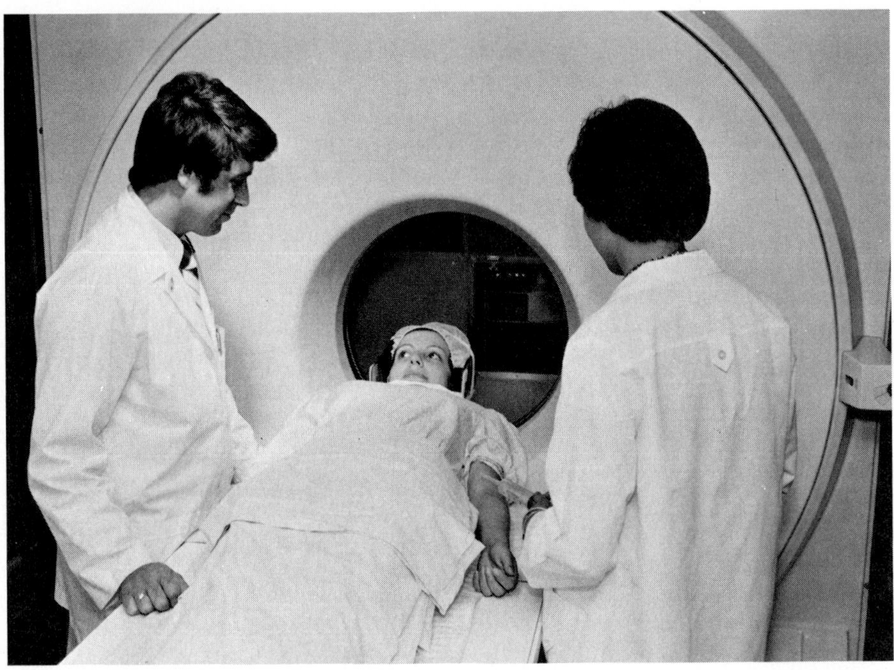

FIGURE 1.14

CT scan. (a) An image from a CT scan. (Courtesy of J. McA. Jones, Good Samaritan Hospital, Portland, Oregon.) (b) A photograph of an actual slice of a brain, cut in approximately the same plane as the scan. (Photograph from *Structure of the Human Brain: A Photographic Atlas*, Second Edition, by Stephen J. DeArmond, Madeline M. Fusco, and Maynard M. Dewey. Copyright © 1976 by Oxford University Press, Inc. Reprinted by permission.)

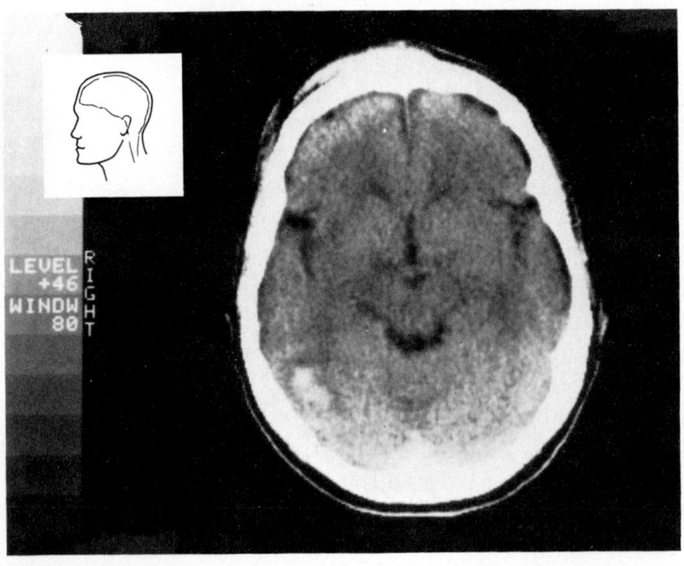

(a)

FRONT

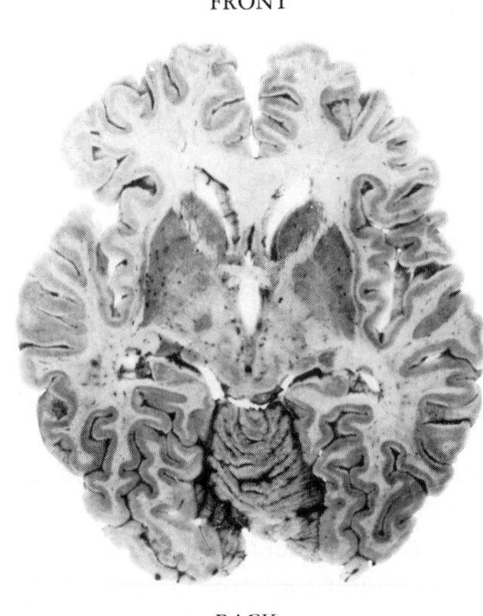

BACK

(b)

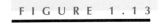

FIGURE 1.15

A series of CT scans from a patient who had a stroke that damaged the right side of the brain (scan 5). The brain damage appears white because it was accompanied by bleeding; blood absorbs more radiation than the surrounding brain tissue. Up is toward the face; down is toward the back of the head; left and right are reversed. Scan 1 shows a section through the eyes and the base of the brain. (Courtesy of J. McA. Jones, Good Samaritan Hospital, Portland, Oregon.)

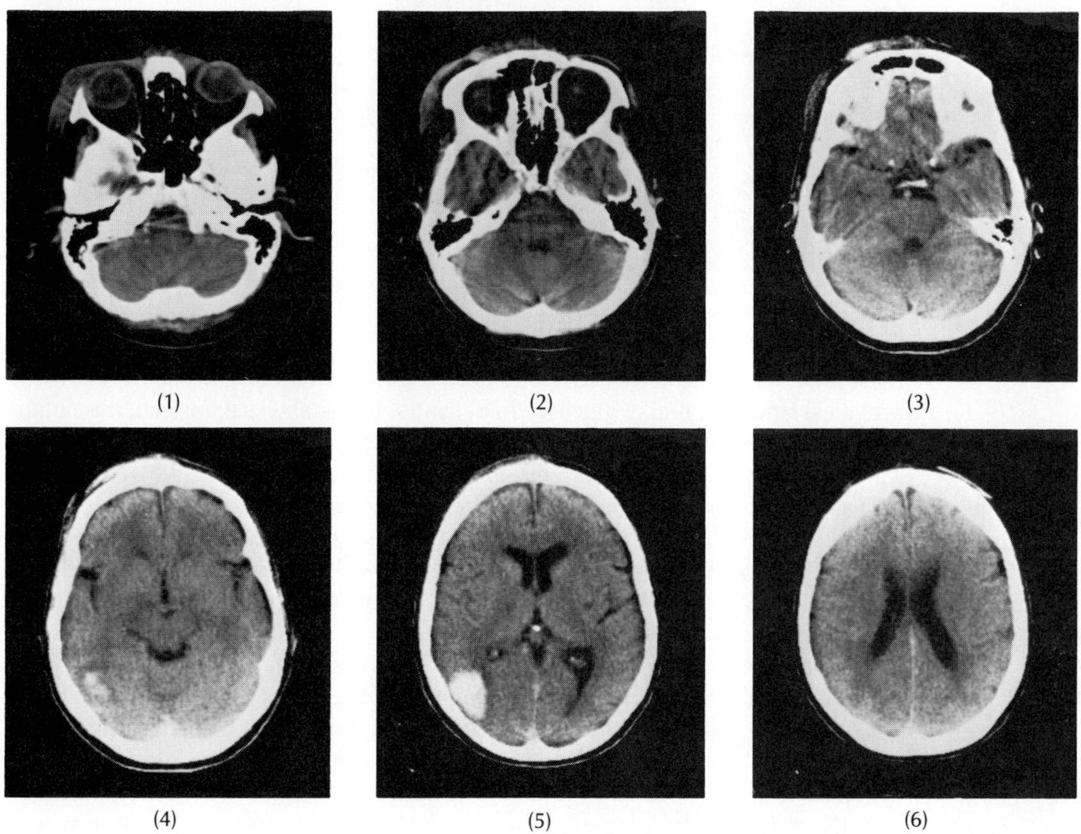

Chapter 3.) You can see the damage as a white spot in the lower left corner of scan 5. (See ***Figure 1.15.***)

Computerized tomography has been used extensively to diagnose various pathological conditions of the brain, including tumors, blood clots, and diseases such as multiple sclerosis. The benefits to the patient are obvious; a CT scan can often tell the physician whether brain surgery is necessary. The technique is also very important to neuropsychologists, who try to discover the functions of the brain by studying the behavioral capacities of people who have sustained brain damage. The CT scan allows them to determine the approximate location of a lesion.

positron emission tomography (PET)

Another technique, **positron emission tomography** (PET), permits investigators to assess the amount of metabolic activity in various parts of the brain. First, the patient receives an injection of radioactive *2-deoxyglucose* (2-DG). Because this chemical resembles glucose (the principal food for the brain), it is taken into cells, especially

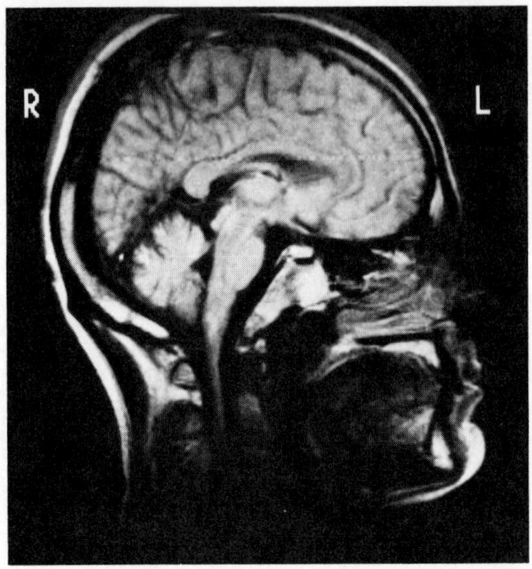

FIGURE 1.16

An MRI scan of a human brain. (Image provided courtesy of Philips Medical Systems, Inc.)

those that are particularly active and need a good supply of glucose to fuel these activities. However, unlike glucose, 2-DG cannot be metabolized; instead, it accumulates within the cells. (Eventually, the chemical is broken down and leaves the cells.) The person's head is placed in a machine similar to a CT scanner. When a beam of X-rays passes through the head, the radioactive molecules of 2-DG emit a subatomic particle called a positron, which is detected by the scanner. The computer determines which regions of the brain have taken up the radioactive substance, and it produces a picture of a slice of the brain, showing different amounts of metabolic activity. (See ***Color Plate 1.1.***)

magnetic resonance imaging (MRI)

The most recently developed tool for seeing what is inside a person's head without opening it is called **magnetic resonance imaging** (MRI). The MRI scanner resembles a CT scanner, but it does not use radiation. Instead, it passes an extremely strong magnetic field through the patient's head. When a person's body is placed in a strong magnetic field, the nuclei of some molecules in the body spin with a particular orientation. If a radio wave is then passed through the body, these nuclei emit radio waves of their own. Different molecules emit energy at different frequencies. The MRI scanner is tuned to detect the radiation from hydrogen molecules. Because these molecules are present in different concentrations in different tissues, the scanner can use the information to prepare pictures of slices of the brain. The pictures provided by the MRI scanner are much clearer and more detailed than those produced by CT scanners. (See ***Figure 1.16.***) Unfortunately, they are much more expensive and presently are found only in research institutions and large medical centers.

Recording the Electrical Activity of the Brain

As we shall see in the next chapter, the signals that are conveyed from one part of the brain to another are electrical. Thus, the activity of nerve cells produces electrical signals, which can be detected by special devices. One such device, the ink-writing oscillograph (often called a *polygraph*) permits an investigator to obtain a continuous record of the electrical activity of various parts of the brain.

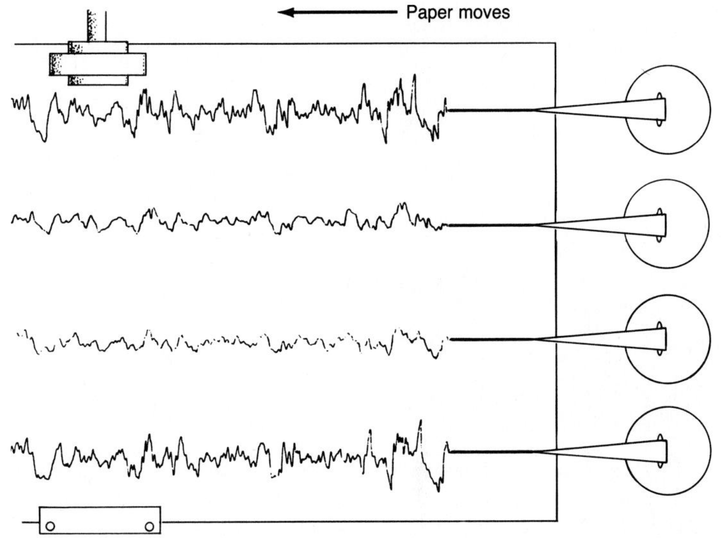

A record from an ink-writing oscillograph of the electrical activity in four locations of a person's scalp.

The investigator applies small silver disks to a person's scalp with a special paste that conducts electricity. The activity of groups of nerve cells within the brain is transmitted through the skull and skin, is picked up by the silver disks, and is carried through wires to an amplifier. The amplifier increases the strength of the electrical signal, much as the amplifier in a stereo system strengthens the signal it receives from the cartridge in a record player. The signal is then fed to the polygraph.

The polygraph contains a device that continuously moves a long sheet of paper at a constant speed. As it moves, pens trace lines on the paper. Essentially, the pens are the pointers of large voltmeters, moving up and down in response to the electrical signals sent to them by the amplifiers. Figure 1.17 shows a polygraph recording the electrical activity from four locations on a person's scalp. The record is called an **electroencephalogram** (EEG). (See ***Figure 1.17.***)

electroencephalogram (EEG)

EEGs are useful in diagnosing epilepsy or brain tumors and in studying stages of sleep and wakefulness, which are associated with particular patterns of electrical activity. For example, an experienced investigator can look at an EEG of a sleeping person and say when that person is dreaming. EEGs can also be taken of laboratory animals. Usually, the records are taken from wires that are placed in the depths of the animals' brain, not from disks pasted to their scalp. Figure 1.18 shows the EEG recorded from a particular location in an animal's brain during sleep and during the performance of various behaviors while it was awake. Note that the pattern of activity changes drastically during different behaviors, which suggests that this part of the brain is involved in some of these behaviors. (See ***Figure 1.18.***)

But how can one record the electrical activity of an animal's brain and still permit the animal to move about? Fine wires can be implanted in the brain with the aid of a stereotaxic apparatus, and an electrical socket attached to the wires can be cemented to the animal's skull by means of an acrylic plastic that is normally used for making dental plates. (See ***Figure 1.19.***) Then after recovery from surgery, the animal can be "plugged in" to the recording system. Using this method, the investigator can discover relations between the activity of regions of the brain and the animal's behavior. Although it may look strange to see rats with small electrical plugs on the top of their heads, the animals are not bothered by them and seem not to be aware of their presence.

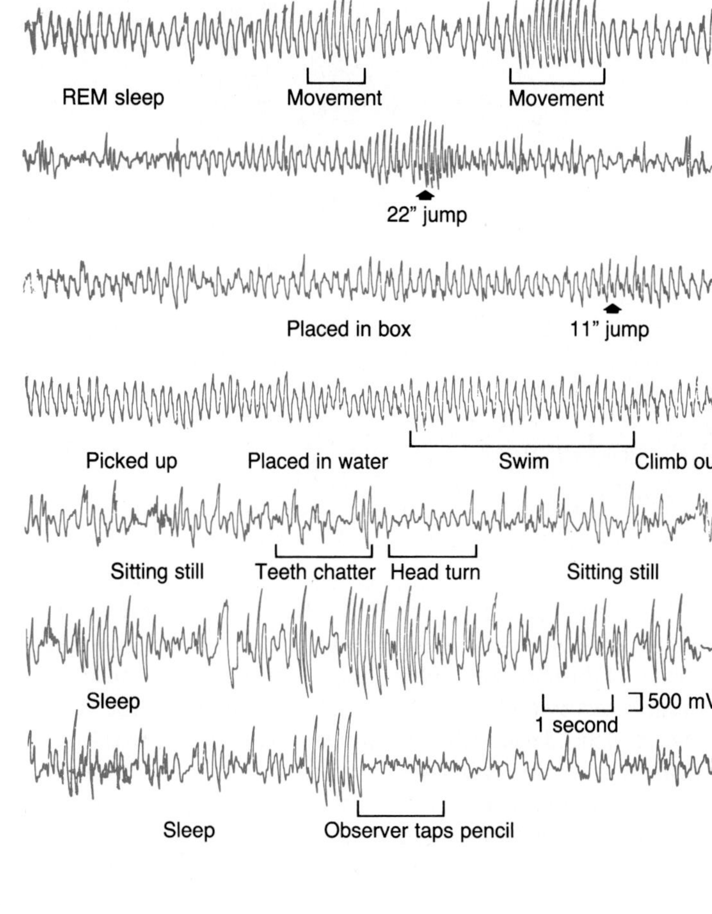

FIGURE 1.18

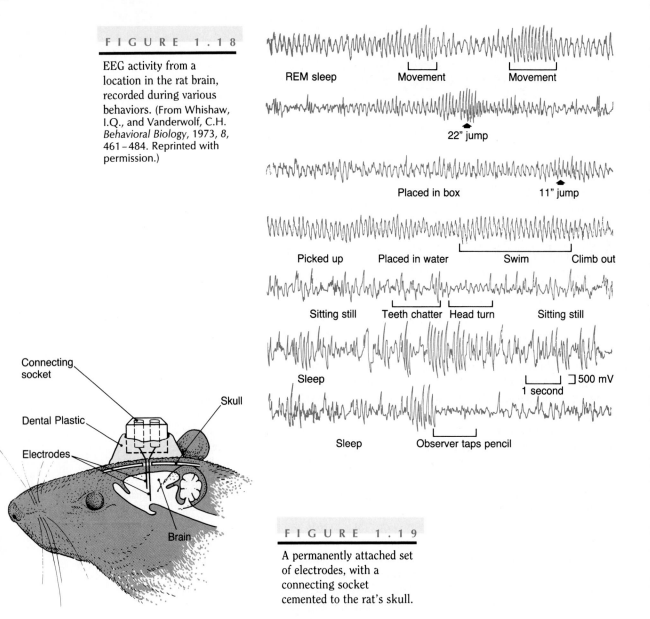

EEG activity from a location in the rat brain, recorded during various behaviors. (From Whishaw, I.Q., and Vanderwolf, C.H. *Behavioral Biology*, 1973, *8*, 461–484. Reprinted with permission.)

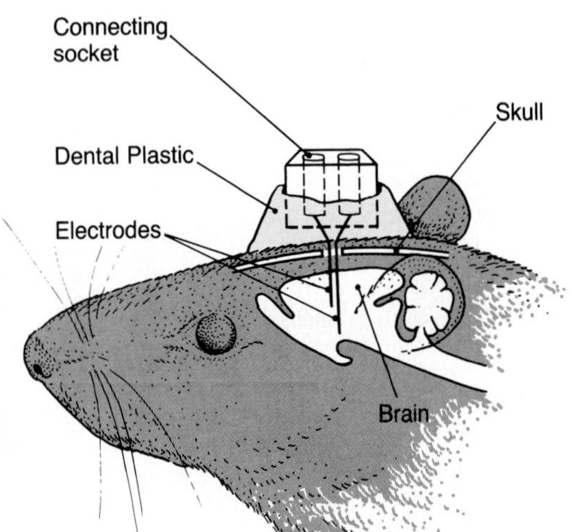

FIGURE 1.19

A permanently attached set of electrodes, with a connecting socket cemented to the rat's skull.

Electrical Stimulation of the Brain

Just as wires can be used to record the electrical activity of specific parts of the brain, they can be used to *induce* such activity. That is, weak electrical current can be sent through wires implanted in a brain, which stimulates the nerve cells close to the wire. Stimulation of an animal's brain often produces behavioral changes. For example, stimulating one part of the brain can elicit behaviors such as feeding, drinking, grooming, attack, or escape, which suggests that this region is involved in their control. Stimulation of another part often halts ongoing behavior, which suggests that this structure is involved in motor inhibition. Brain stimulation can serve as a signal for a learned task or can even reward or punish an animal's behavior. All of these phenomena are discussed in later chapters.

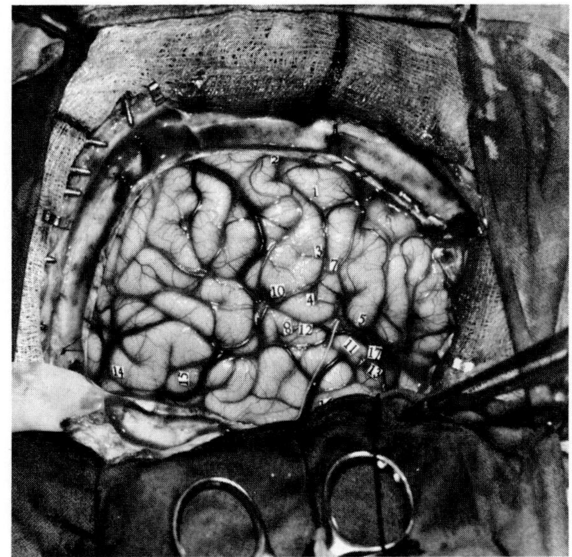

FIGURE 1.20

The appearance of the cortical surface of a conscious patient whose brain has been stimulated. The points of stimulation are indicated by the numbered tags placed there by the surgeon. (From Case M.M., in Wilder Penfield, *The Mystery of the Mind: A Critical Study of Consciousness and the Human Brain,* with Discussions by William Feindel, Charles Hendel, and Charles Symonds. Copyright ©1975 by Princeton University Press. Figure 4, p. 24 reprinted with permission of Princeton University Press.)

One of the more interesting uses of electrical stimulation of the brain was developed by the late Wilder Penfield (Penfield and Jasper, 1954) to treat a particular form of epilepsy. (The procedure is discussed in more detail in Chapter 14.) The surgery requires that a damaged part of the brain be removed. Patients first have their heads shaved, and then, under local anesthesia, the surgeon cuts the scalp and saws through the skull so that a piece of bone can be removed and the brain itself can be exposed. The patient is conscious throughout the entire procedure.

When removing the damaged part of the brain, the surgeon wants to cut away all the abnormal tissue, while sparing healthy neural tissue that performs important functions, such as the comprehension and production of speech. For this reason, Penfield first stimulated parts of the brain to determine which regions he could safely remove. Penfield touched the tip of a metal electrode to various parts of the brain and observed the effects of stimulation on the patient's behavior. For example, stimulation of one part of the brain produced movement, and stimulation of another part produced sensations of sounds. Stimulation of parts of the brain involved in verbal communication stopped the patient's ongoing speech and disrupted the ability to understand what the surgeon and his associates were saying.

Besides giving patients relief from their epileptic attacks, the procedure provided Penfield with interesting data. As he stimulated various parts of the brain, he noted the effect and placed a sterile piece of paper, on which a number was written, on the point stimulated. When various points had been stimulated, Penfield photographed the exposed brain with its numbered locations before removing the slips of paper and proceeding with the surgery. After the operation, he could then compare the recorded notes with the photograph of the patient's brain showing the location of the points of stimulation. (See ***Figure 1.20.***)

Altering or Measuring the Biochemistry of the Brain

Chemicals are important to the brain. Individual nerve cells communicate by means of chemicals, and the physiological processes that take place within nerve cells are controlled by chemicals. (Chapter 4 discusses these processes and the drugs that affect them.) To investigate these functions, neuroscientists have devised ways to alter or

FIGURE 1.21

Infusing chemicals into the brain. A guide tube is permanently attached to the skull, and at a later time a thinner metal tube can be inserted through the guide tube into the brain.

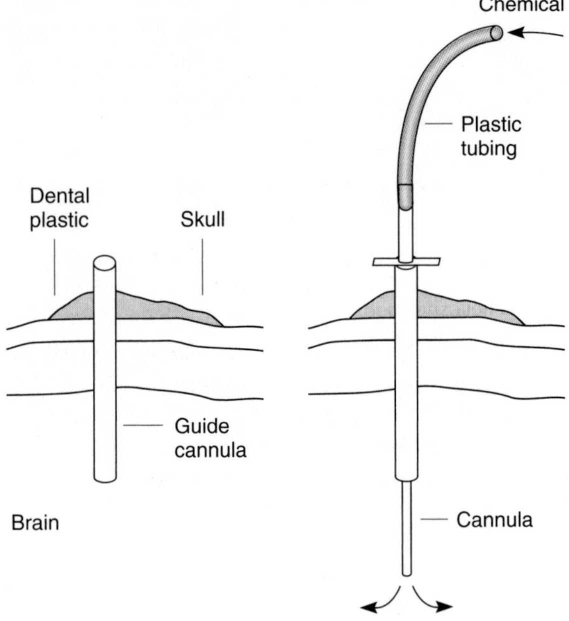

measure them. Drugs that affect the biochemical processes of nerve cells can be given to the animal by injecting them into a vein or a muscle, or they can even be injected directly into the brain, where they will affect only a particular region. To do this, the investigator places a thin metal tube (a guide tube) in an animal's brain and cements the top of it to the skull. At a later date a smaller metal tube of measured length is placed inside the guide tube, and a chemical is injected into the brain while the animal moves about freely. (See ***Figure 1.21.***)

microdialysis

Investigators can also analyze chemicals present in the brain—even in a freely moving animal—through a procedure called **microdialysis.** *Dialysis* is a process in

FIGURE 1.22

Microdialysis. A fluid is slowly infused into the microdialysis tube, where it picks up molecules that diffuse in from the brain. The fluid is then collected in a small vial attached to the animal's head and is analyzed.

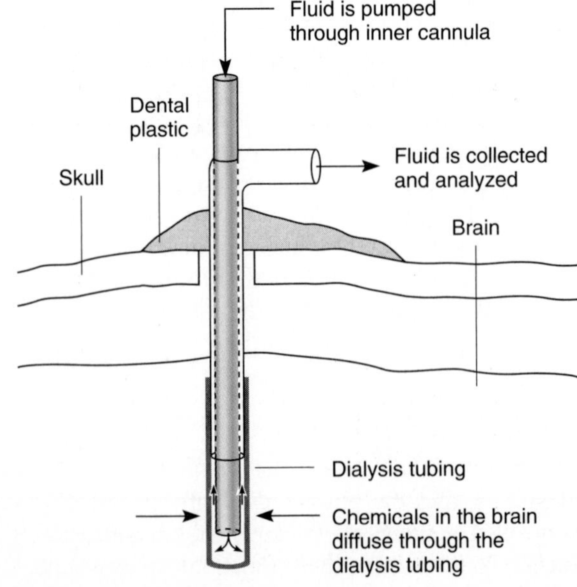

which substances are separated by means of an artificial membrane that lets most chemicals pass through. A microdialysis probe consists of a small metal tube that introduces a solution into a section of dialysis tubing—a piece of artificial membrane shaped in the form of a cylinder. Another small metal tube leads the solution away after it has circulated through the pouch. A drawing of such a probe is shown in ***Figure 1.22.***

The tip of the probe is placed in the animal's brain in the location of interest. A small amount of a solution similar to the fluid normally present in the brain is pumped through one of the small metal tubes into the dialysis tubing. The fluid circulates through the dialysis tubing and passes through the second metal tube, where it is collected in a miniature vial attached to a holder mounted on the animal's head. As the fluid passes through the dialysis tubing, it collects molecules from the fluid of the brain. Every few minutes, the vial is removed so that its contents can be analyzed, and a clean vial is put in its place. As we shall see in Chapter 15, experiments using microdialysis have shown that many addictive drugs, including cocaine, alcohol, marijuana, and nicotine, cause the release of a particular chemical in a particular region of the brain.

▶*INTERIM SUMMARY*◀

Physiological psychologists use many specialized techniques to study the functions of the nervous system. One of the most important is the method of experimental ablation. The stereotaxic apparatus permits investigators to destroy particular parts of an animal's brain in order to study its behavior and see what functions are eliminated by the surgery. In addition, modern investigators also use the same method that Broca used when he studied the behavior of a person with naturally occurring brain damage. But now we have special devices that Broca did not have that permit us to examine the brain of a living person. Computerized tomography (CT scan) and magnetic resonance imaging (MRI) provide excellent pictures of the structure of the human brain, including the location and extent of damage produced by stroke, tumors, infection, or head injury. Positron emission tomography (PET) goes further, giving a picture of the neural activity of various parts of the living brain.

Because information is transmitted from place to place within the nervous system by means of electrical messages, investigators have developed methods that permit these messages to be recorded and analyzed or even to be produced through electrical stimulation. Electrical stimulation has even been used on conscious patients undergoing brain surgery to help locate parts of the brain that the surgeon should be careful not to remove.

Researchers can alter the functions of brain cells by administering drugs into the animal's circulation or directly into a part of the brain. They can also use microdialysis to analyze chemicals being produced in a particular part of the brain while the animal is freely moving and responding normally to events in its environment. ▲

◀ *EPILOGUE: Application*

René Descartes had no way to study the operations of the nervous system. He did, however, understand how the statues in the Royal Gardens at Saint-Germain were powered and controlled, which led him to view the body as a complicated piece of plumbing. Many scientists have followed Descartes's example, using technological devices that were fashionable at the time to explain how the brain worked.

What motivates people to use artificial devices to explain the workings of the brain? The most important reason, I suppose, is that the brain is enormously complicated. Even the most complex human inventions are many times simpler than the brain, and because they have been designed and made by people, people can understand them. If an artificial device can do some of the things that the brain does, then perhaps both the brain and the device accomplish their tasks in the same way.

Most models of brain function that have been developed in the last half of this century have been based on the modern general-purpose digital computer. Actually, they have been based not on the computers themselves but on computer *programs.* Computers can be programmed to store any kind of information that can be coded in numbers or words, can solve any logical problem that can be explicitly described, and can compute any mathematical equations that can be written. Therefore — in principle, at least — they can be programmed to do the things we do: perceive, remember, make deductions, solve problems.

The construction of computer programs that simulate human brain functions can help clarify the nature of these functions. For instance, to construct a program and simulate, say, perception and classification of certain types of patterns, the investigator is forced to specify precisely what is required by the task of pattern perception. If the program fails to recognize the patterns, then the investigator knows that something is wrong with the model or with the way it has been implemented in the program. The investigator revises the model, tries again, and keeps working until it finally works (or until he or she gives up the task as being too ambitious).

Ideally, this task tells the investigator the kinds of processes the brain must perform. However, there is usually more than one way to accomplish a particular goal; critics of computer modeling have pointed out that it is possible to write a program that performs a task that the human brain performs — and comes up with exactly the same results — but does the task in an entirely different way. In fact, some say, given the way that computers work and what we know about the structure of the human brain, the computer program is *guaranteed* to work differently.

When we base a model of brain functions on a physical device with which we are familiar, we enjoy the advantage of being able to think concretely about something that is difficult to observe. However, if the brain does not work like a computer, then our models will not tell us very much about the brain. Such models are *constrained* ("restricted") by the computer metaphor; they will only be able to do things the way that computers can do them. If the brain can actually do some different sorts of things — things that computers cannot do — the models will never contain these features.

In fact, computers and brains are fundamentally different. Modern computers are *serial devices;* they work one step at a time. (*Serial*, from the Latin *serere*, "to join," refers to events that occur in order, one after the other.) Programs consist of a set of instructions stored in the computer's memory. The computer follows these instructions, one at a time. Because each of these steps takes time, a complicated program will take more time to execute. But we do some things extremely quickly that computers take a very long time to do. The best example is visual perception. We can recognize a complex figure about as quickly as a simple one; for example, it takes about the same amount of time to recognize a friend's face as it does to identify a simple triangle. The same is not true at all for a serial computer. A computer must "examine" the scene through an input device something like a television camera. Information about the brightness of each point of the picture must be converted into a number and stored in a memory location. Then the program examines each memory location, one at a time, and does calculations that determine the locations of lines, edges, textures, and shapes; finally, it tries to determine what these shapes represent. Recognizing a face takes *much* longer than recognizing a triangle. In fact, even the best computer programs do a terrible job in recognizing faces.

Unlike the modern computer, the brain is a *parallel processor,* in which many different modules (collections of circuits of neurons) work simultaneously at different tasks. A complex task is broken down into many smaller ones, and separate modules work on each of them. Because the brain consists of many billions of neurons, it can afford to devote different clusters of neurons to different tasks. With so many things happening at the same time, the task gets done quickly.

Very recently, researchers have turned the tables and have begun developing models of *computers* that resemble the *nervous system.* (These models, called *neural networks,* are described in more detail in Chapter 12.) The elements of these computers are based on nerve cells, and the rules that govern the way they interact are based on the rules you will learn about in Chapter 2. Furthermore, instead of programming these models to perform a function, researchers give them information that permits them to learn, just as a real brain does. Some day we may even see organic computers, using materials similar to those found in the body; scientists are developing polymers (special organic compounds) that can take over the functions of the silicon chips used in the integrated circuits that make up present-day computers. ▲

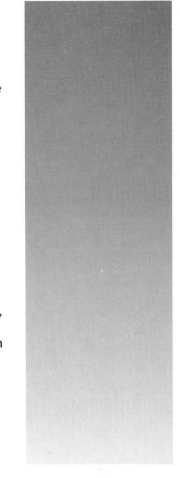

KEY CONCEPTS

Understanding Self-Awareness: A Physiological Approach

- Physiological psychologists follow the monistic approach to the mind-body problem; they believe that the mind is a function performed by the brain.
- Study of human brain functions has helped us gain some insight into the nature of human consciousness, which appears to be related to the language functions of the brain. This chapter described two examples, blindsight and the effects of the split-brain operation.

The Nature of Physiological Psychology

- Scientists attempt to explain natural phenomena by means of generalization and reduction. Because physiological psychologists use the methods of psychology and physiology, they employ both types of explanations.
- Descartes developed the first model to explain how the brain controls movement, based on the animated statues in the royal gardens. Subsequently, investigators tested their ideas with scientific experiments.
- Darwin's theory of evolution, with its emphasis on function, helps physiological psychologists discover the relations between brain mechanisms, behaviors, and an organism's adaptation to its environment.
- Scientific research with animals has taught us most of what we know about the functions of the body, including that of the nervous system. This knowledge is essential in developing ways to prevent and treat neurological and mental disorders.

Methods of Physiological Psychology

- Physiological psychologists employ a variety of research techniques, including experimental ablation, methods of imaging the living brain, electrical recording, electrical stimulation, administration of drugs, and chemical analysis.

SUGGESTED READINGS

Butterfield, H. *The Origins of Modern Science: 1300-1800.* New York: Macmillan, 1959.

Sacks, O. *The Man Who Mistook His Wife for a Hat and Other Clinical Tales.* New York: Harper & Row, 1987.

Schultz, D., and Schultz, S.E. *A History of Modern Psychology,* 4th ed. New York: Academic Press, 1987.

NEW TERMS

blindsight **p. 4**
brain lesion **p. 20**
cerebral hemisphere **p. 6**
computerized tomography (CT) **p. 21**
corpus callosum **p. 5**
doctrine of specific nerve energies **p. 11**
dualism **p. 3**
electroencephalogram (EEG) **p. 25**
experimental ablation **p. 12**
functionalism **p. 14**
generalization **p. 8**
magnetic resonance imaging (MRI) **p. 24**
microdialysis **p. 28**
model **p. 10**
monism **p. 3**
mutation **p. 15**
natural selection **p. 15**
positron emission tomography (PET) **p. 23**
reduction **p. 8**
reflex **p. 10**
selective advantage **p. 16**
split-brain operation **p. 5**
stereotaxic apparatus **p. 20**
stereotaxic atlas **p. 20**

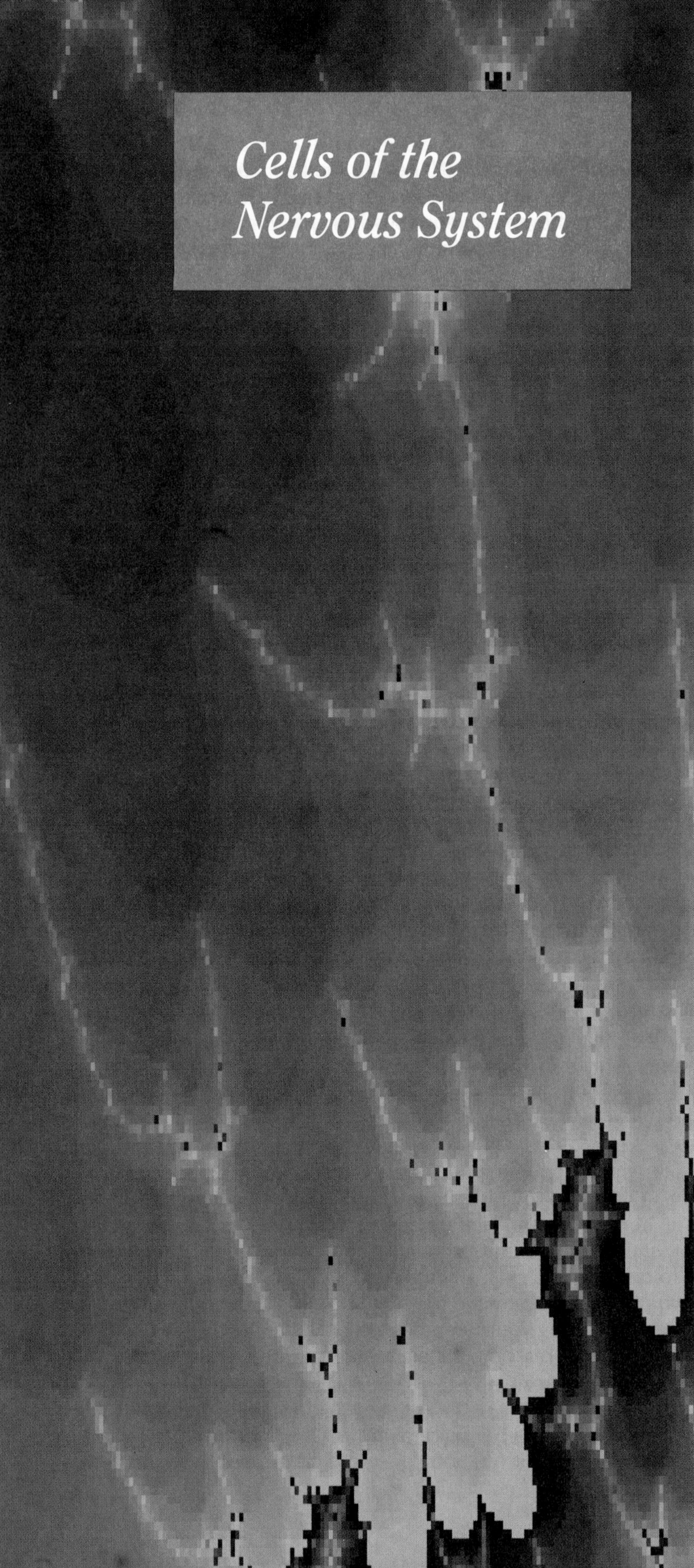

Cells of the Nervous System

2

CHAPTER OUTLINE

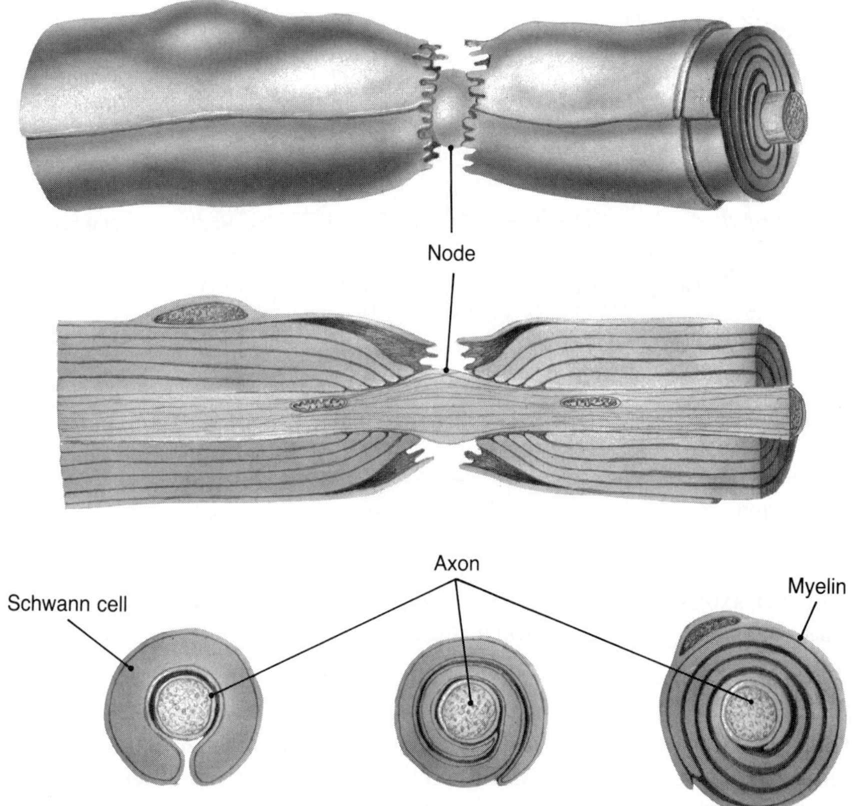

FIGURE 2.8

Schwann cells. During development, Schwann cells tightly wrap themselves many times around an individual axon in the peripheral nervous system and form one segment of the myelin sheath.

lost, and if the nerve was an important one (controlling hand muscles, for example), a piece of nerve of about the same size can be taken from another part of the body. Because many nerves overlap in the area of tissue they innervate, neurosurgeons have no trouble finding a branch of a nerve that the patient can lose without ill effect. The surgeon, using a special microscope and very delicate instruments, grafts this piece of nerve to the damaged one. Of course, the axons in the excised and transplanted piece of nerve die; but if the surgery is successful, the tubes produced by the Schwann cells will guide the sprouts of the damaged nerve and help them find their way back to the muscles.

Unfortunately, the glial cells of the CNS are not as cooperative as the supporting cells of the PNS. If axons in the brain or spinal cord are damaged, new sprouts will form, as in the PNS. However, the budding axons encounter scar tissue produced by the astrocytes, and they cannot penetrate this barrier. Even if they could get through, the axons would not reestablish their original connections without guidance similar to that provided by the Schwann cells of the PNS. During development, axons have two modes of growth. The first mode causes them to elongate so that they reach their target, which could be as far away as the other end of the brain or spinal cord. Schwann cells provide this signal to injured axons. The second mode causes axons to stop elongating and begin sprouting terminal buttons, because they have reached their target. Liuzzi and Lasek (1987) found that even when astrocytes do not produce scar tissue, they appear to produce a chemical signal that instructs regenerating axons to begin the second mode of growth: to stop elongating and start sprouting terminal buttons.

The Blood-Brain Barrier

Long ago, anatomists discovered that when a dye was injected into an animal's bloodstream, all tissues except the brain and spinal cord became stained. This demonstration showed that a barrier exists between the blood and the fluid that surrounds the cells of the brain — the **blood-brain barrier**.

blood-brain barrier

Some substances can cross the blood-brain barrier; others cannot. Thus, it is *selectively permeable* (*per,* "through"; *meare,* "to pass"). In most of the body the cells that line the capillaries do not fit together absolutely tightly. Small gaps are found between them that permit the free exchange of most substances between the blood plasma and the fluid outside the blood vessels that surrounds the cells. In the central nervous system the capillaries lack these gaps, and thus, many substances cannot leave the blood. Substances that can dissolve in lipids pass through the capillaries easily, because they simply dissolve through the membranes of the cells that line the capillaries. Other substances, such as glucose (the primary fuel of the central nervous system) must be actively transported through the capillary walls, carried by special proteins.

The blood-brain barrier is not uniform throughout the nervous system. In several places the barrier is relatively permeable, allowing substances excluded elsewhere to cross freely. For example, the *area postrema* is a part of the brain that controls vomiting. The blood-brain barrier is much weaker there, permitting this region to be more sensitive to toxic substances in the blood. A poison that enters the circulatory system from the stomach can thus stimulate this area to initiate vomiting. If the organism is lucky, the poison can be expelled from the stomach before it causes too much damage.

▶*INTERIM SUMMARY*◀

All cells — including neurons — contain a quantity of clear cytoplasm, enclosed in a membrane. Embedded in the membrane are protein molecules that have special functions, such as the transport of particular substances into and out of the cell. The cytoplasm contains many structures, including the nucleus, which contains the genetic information; microtubules, which compose the internal "skeleton" of the cell and provide the motive power for transporting chemicals from place to place; and the mitochondria, which serve as the location for most of the chemical reactions through which the cell extracts energy from nutrients.

Sensory neurons receive messages directly from the environment (for example, sights, sounds, smells, and tastes), thus providing the information from which perceptions can be formed. Motor neurons control the contractions of muscles, which provide behavior. Communication among neurons, or between neurons and muscles, takes place through synapses, which are junctions between the terminal buttons of one neuron and the dendrites or the soma of another. Terminal buttons are located at the ends of the axons.

Neurons are supported by the glial cells of the central nervous system and the satellite cells of the peripheral nervous system. Within the CNS, astrocytes provide support and also, with microglia, remove debris and form scar tissue in the event of tissue damage. Oligodendroglia form myelin, the substance that insulates axons. Within the PNS, myelin is provided by the Schwann cells.

The blood-brain barrier prevents the cells of the brain from being adversely affected by substances in our blood. The primary reason for its existence is the nature of the cells that line the capillaries of the brain; they lack the gaps found in capillaries of the rest of the body. In a few regions of the brain, such as the area postrema, the blood-brain barrier is weak, which permits cells there to monitor chemicals in the blood. ▲

NEURAL COMMUNICATION

Now that you know about the basic structure of neurons, it is time to explain the ways they can gather sensory information, interact, and initiate behaviors. The discussion begins with an overview of neural communication.

An Overview

Neurons communicate through synapses. The message transmitted by a particular synapse has one of two effects: excitation or inhibition. Excitatory messages increase the likelihood that the neuron receiving them will send a message down *its* axon; inhibitory effects decrease this likelihood. Thus, the rate at which a neuron sends messages down its axons depends on the excitatory and inhibitory messages that it receives from the terminal buttons that form synapses with it.

To illustrate this process, I will describe a specific example. The example is very simple, but more complex ones will be described in following chapters. In Figure 2.9 neuron A can be excited by the terminal buttons of some neurons (gray) and inhibited by the terminal buttons of others (color). The rate at which neuron A sends messages down its axon is determined by the relative activity of the excitatory and inhibitory synapses on the membrane of its soma and dendrites. A high rate of activity in the excitatory synapses will normally increase the rate at which neuron A sends messages down its axon, but this effect can be canceled by a high rate of activity in the inhibitory synapses. (See ***Figure 2.9.***)

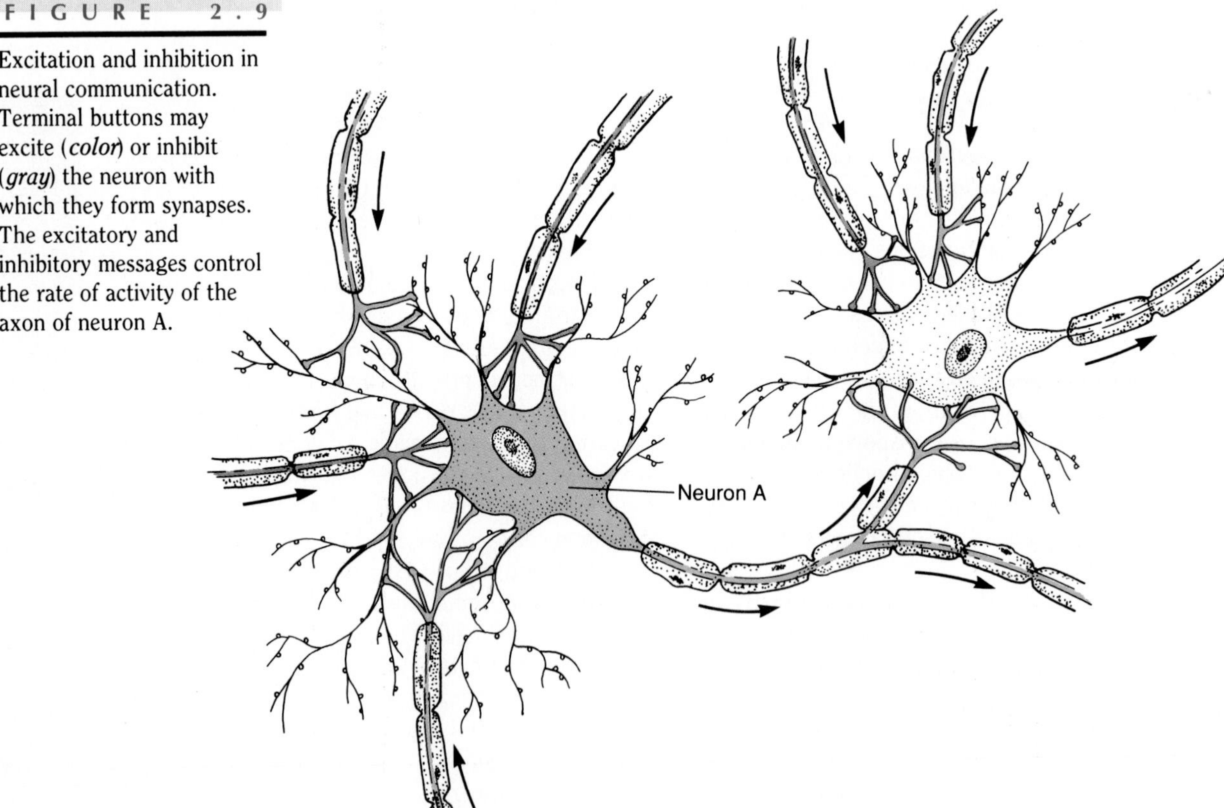

FIGURE 2.9

Excitation and inhibition in neural communication. Terminal buttons may excite (*color*) or inhibit (*gray*) the neuron with which they form synapses. The excitatory and inhibitory messages control the rate of activity of the axon of neuron A.

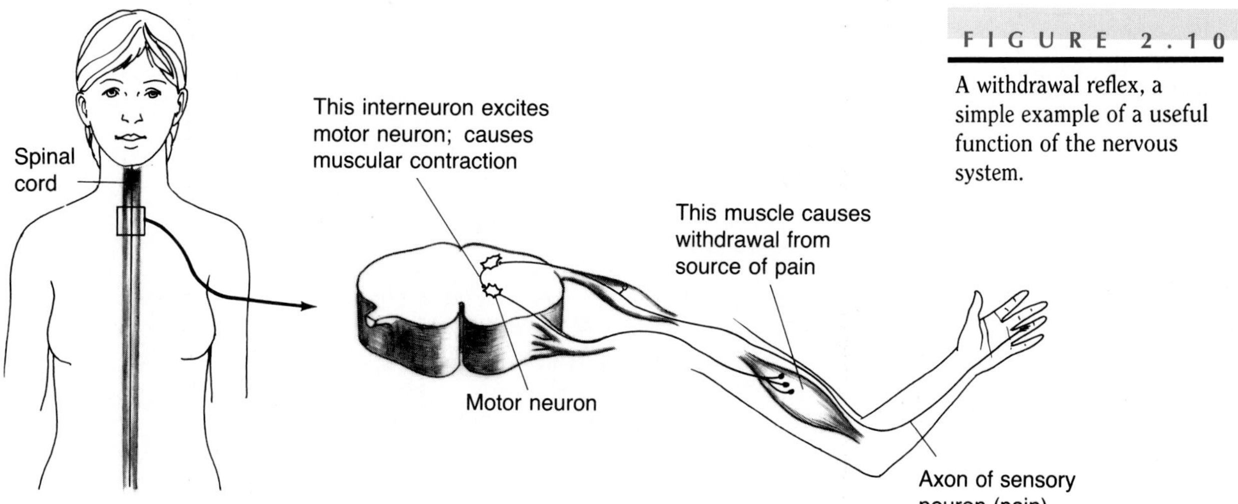
Spinal cord
This interneuron excites motor neuron; causes muscular contraction
This muscle causes withdrawal from source of pain
Motor neuron
Axon of sensory neuron (pain)

FIGURE 2.10

A withdrawal reflex, a simple example of a useful function of the nervous system.

The message that is conducted down the axon, from the cell body to the terminal buttons, is electrical. Normally, there is an electrical charge across the membrane. The activity of excitatory synapses triggers an abrupt electrical change in the electrical charge across the membrane. This abrupt change is conducted down the axon to the terminal buttons. When it reaches the terminal buttons, they release a transmitter substance—a chemical that has either an excitatory or an inhibitory effect on the neurons with which the terminal buttons form synapses. And there the process begins again.

In order to appreciate the operation of this process, consider a simple assembly of three neurons. The first neuron is a sensory receptor that detects painful stimuli. When its dendrites are stimulated by a pinprick, messages are sent down the axon to the terminal buttons, which are located in the spinal cord. (You will recognize this cell as a unipolar neuron; see ***Figure 2.10***.) The terminal buttons of the sensory neuron release a transmitter substance that excites the second neuron (the interneuron), causing it to send messages down its axon. In turn, the terminal buttons of the interneuron release a transmitter substance that excites the third neuron (the motor neuron), which sends messages down its axon. The axon of the motor neuron travels through a nerve to a muscle, where it branches into twigs that end in terminal buttons. These terminal buttons form synapses with the muscle cells. When they release their transmitter substance, the muscle cells contract, causing a part of the body to move. This scheme represents a simplified version of what happens when a pinprick on the end of a finger causes a person to react by reflexively moving his or her arm away from the source of the pain. (See ***Figure 2.10***.)

So far, all of the synaptic effects have been excitatory. Now let us complicate matters a bit to see the effect of inhibitory synapses. Suppose you are carrying a bunch of roses from your garden. As you walk, the thorns begin to prick your fingers. The pain receptors stimulate a withdrawal reflex like the one shown in Figure 2.10, which tends to make you open your hand and let go of the roses. However, because you do not want to drop your flowers, you manage to hold onto them until you have a chance to get a better, less painful grip on them. The message not to drop the roses comes through the axon of a neuron located in the brain. The terminal buttons at the end of this axon form synapses with an inhibitory neuron in the spinal cord. The terminal buttons of the inhibitory neuron release a transmitter substance that inhibits the

FIGURE 2.11

The role of inhibition. Inhibitory signals arising from the brain can prevent the withdrawal reflex from causing the person to drop the rose.

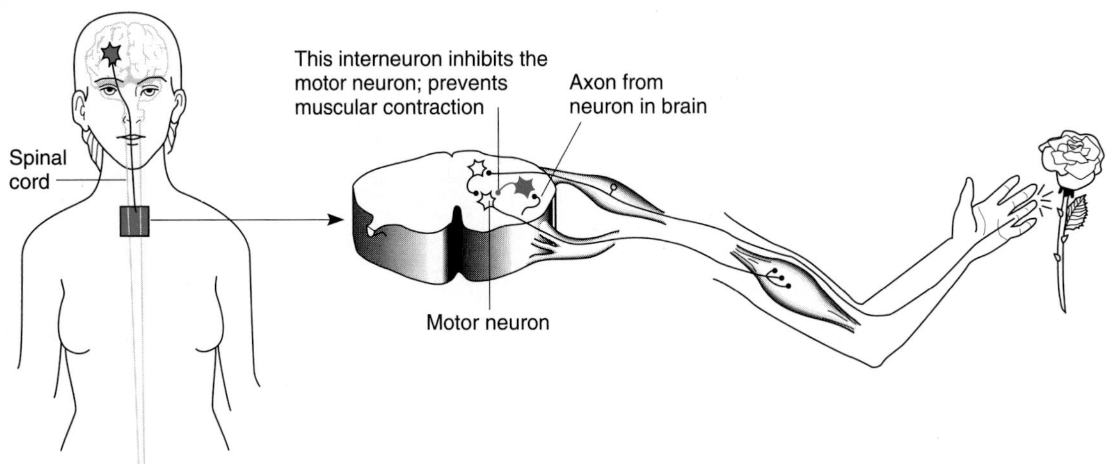
This interneuron inhibits the motor neuron; prevents muscular contraction
Axon from neuron in brain
Spinal cord
Motor neuron

activity of the motor neuron. Thus, messages from the brain prevent the withdrawal reflex from operating. (See ***Figure 2.11***.)

Of course, reflexes are more complicated than this description, and the mechanisms that inhibit them are even more so. In addition, when a person's finger is pricked by a thorn, many hundreds of sensory neurons convey the information to the spinal cord, many hundreds of interneurons are excited, and these interneurons in turn excite many hundreds of motor neurons. The diagram shows only three neurons because they summarize the essential elements of the circuit. Yet even though the model is simplified, it nevertheless demonstrates the importance of excitation and inhibition and provides an overview of the process of neural communication.

I already said that although the message conducted down an axon is electrical, the axon does not carry it the way a wire carries electrical current. As we shall see in the rest of this section, the message is conducted by means of alterations in the membrane of the axon that cause exchanges of various chemicals between the axon and the fluid surrounding it. These exchanges produce electrical currents.

Measuring Electrical Potentials of Axons

Here we will examine the nature of the message that is conducted along the axon. To do so, we obtain an axon that is large enough to work with. Fortunately, nature has provided the neuroscientist with the giant squid axon (the giant axon of a squid, not the axon of a giant squid!). This axon is about 0.5 millimeter in diameter, which is hundreds of times larger than the largest mammalian axon. (This large axon controls an emergency response: sudden contraction of the mantle, which squirts water through a jet and propels the squid away from a source of danger.) We place an isolated giant squid axon in a dish of seawater, in which it can exist for a day or two.

To measure the electrical charges generated by an axon, we will need to use a pair of electrodes. **Electrodes** are electrical conductors that provide a path for electricity to enter or leave a medium. One of the electrodes is a simple wire that we place in the seawater. The other one, which we use to record the message from the axon, has to be

electrode

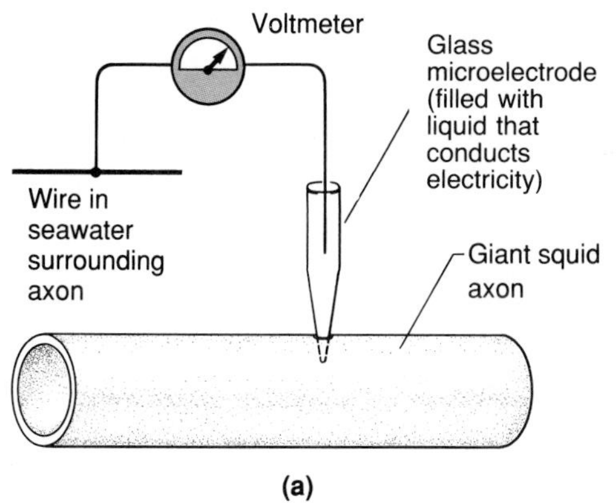

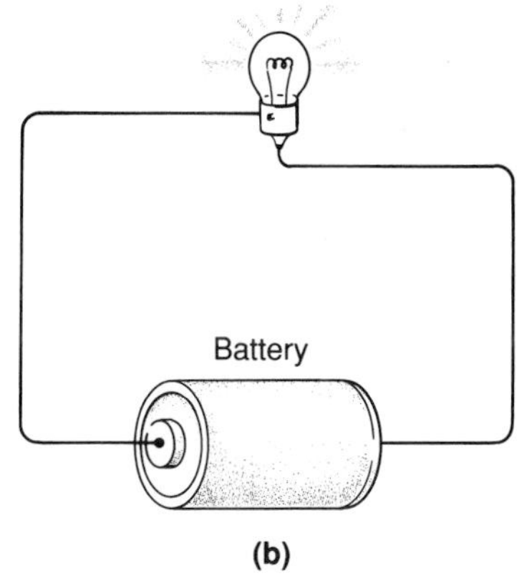

FIGURE 2.12

Measuring electrical charge. (a) A voltmeter detecting the charge across a membrane of an axon. (b) A light bulb detecting the charge across the terminals of a battery.

special. Because even a giant squid axon is rather small, we must use a tiny electrode that will record the membrane potential without damaging the axon. To do so, we use a microelectrode. A **microelectrode** is simply a very small electrode, and it can be made of metal or glass. In this case we will use one made of thin glass tubing, which is heated and drawn down to an exceedingly fine point, less than a thousandth of a millimeter in diameter. Because glass will not conduct electricity, the glass microelectrode is filled with a liquid that conducts electricity, such as a solution of potassium chloride.

microelectrode

We place one electrode outside the membrane and insert the other into the axon. (See ***Figure 2.12.***) As soon as we do so, we discover that the inside of the axon is negatively charged with respect to the outside, the difference in charge being 70 mV (millivolts, or thousandths of a volt). Thus, the inside of the membrane is −70 mV. This electrical charge is called the **membrane potential**. The term *potential* refers to a stored-up source of energy—in this case, electrical energy. For example, a flashlight battery that is not connected to an electrical circuit has a *potential* charge of 1.5 V between its terminals. If we connect a light bulb to the terminals, the potential energy is tapped and converted into radiant energy (light). (See ***Figure 2.12.***) Similarly, if we connect our electrodes—one inside the axon and one outside it—to a very sensitive voltmeter, we will convert the potential energy to movement of the meter's needle. Of course, compared with the potential of a flashlight battery, the potential electrical energy of the axonal membrane is very weak.

membrane potential

As we will see, the message that is conducted down the length of the axon consists of a brief change in the membrane potential. However, this change occurs very rapidly—too rapidly for us to see if we were using a voltmeter. Thus, to study the message, we will use an **oscilloscope**. This device, like a voltmeter, measures voltages, but it also produces a record of these voltages, graphing them as a function of time. These graphs are displayed on a screen, much like the one found in a television. The vertical axis represents voltage, and the horizontal axis represents time, going from left to right.

oscilloscope

Once we insert our microelectrode into the axon, the oscilloscope draws a straight horizontal line at −70 mV, as long as the axon is not disturbed. This electrical charge across the membrane is called, quite appropriately, the **resting potential**. Now let us disturb the resting potential and see what happens. To do so, we will use another device—an electrical stimulator that allows us to alter the membrane potential at a specific location. (See ***Figure 2.13.***) The stimulator can pass current through another microelectrode that we have inserted into the axon. Because the inside of the axon is negative, a positive stimulus will decrease the membrane potential in that region. To

resting potential

FIGURE 2.13

The means by which an axon can be stimulated while its membrane potential is being recorded.

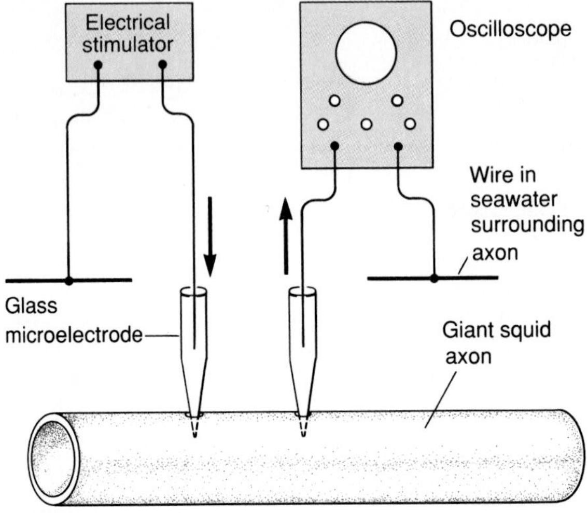

depolarization

put it another way, a positive stimulus applied to the inside of the membrane produces a **depolarization.**

Let us see what happens to an axon when we artificially depolarize the membrane potential at one point. Figure 2.14 shows a graph drawn by an oscilloscope that has been monitoring the effects of brief depolarizing stimuli. The graphs of the effects of these separate stimuli are superimposed on the same drawing so that we can compare them. We deliver a series of depolarizing stimuli, starting with a very weak one and gradually increasing their strength. Each stimulus briefly depolarizes the membrane potential a little more. Finally, after we present stimulus number 4, the membrane

FIGURE 2.14

An action potential. The curves are those that would be seen on an oscilloscope screen if depolarizing stimuli of varying intensities were delivered to the axon shown in Figure 2.13.

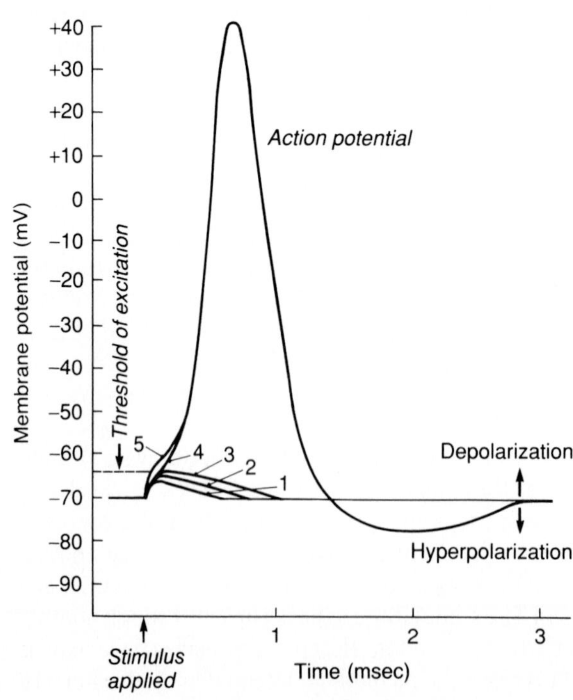

potential suddenly reverses itself, so the inside becomes *positive* (and the outside becomes negative). The membrane potential quickly returns to normal, but first, it overshoots the resting potential, becoming **hyperpolarized**— more polarized— for a short time. The whole process takes about 2 msec (milliseconds). (See ***Figure 2.14.***)

hyperpolarization

This phenomenon, a very rapid reversal of the membrane potential, is called the **action potential.** It is the message that is conducted by the axon from one end to the other. The voltage level that triggers an action potential— which was achieved only by stimulus number 4— is called the **threshold of excitation.**

action potential

threshold of excitation

The Membrane Potential: Dynamic Equilibrium

To understand what causes the action potential to occur, we must first understand the reasons for the existence of the membrane potential. As we will see, this electrical charge is the result of a balance between two opposing forces: diffusion and electrostatic pressure.

THE FORCE OF DIFFUSION

When a spoonful of sugar is carefully poured into a container of water, it settles to the bottom. After a time the sugar dissolves, but it remains close to the bottom of the container. After a much longer time (probably several days), the molecules of sugar distribute themselves evenly throughout the water, even if no one stirs the liquid. The process whereby molecules distribute themselves evenly throughout the medium in which they are dissolved is called **diffusion.**

diffusion

When there are no forces or barriers to prevent diffusion, molecules diffuse from regions of high concentration to regions of low concentration. Molecules are constantly in motion, and their rate of movement is proportional to the temperature. Only at absolute zero [0 K (kelvin) = −273.15°C = −459.7°F] do molecules cease their random movement. At all other temperatures they move about, colliding and veering off in different directions, thus pushing each other away. The result of these collisions in the example of the sugar water is to force sugar molecules upward (and to force water molecules downward), away from the regions in which they are most concentrated. (See ***Figure 2.15.***)

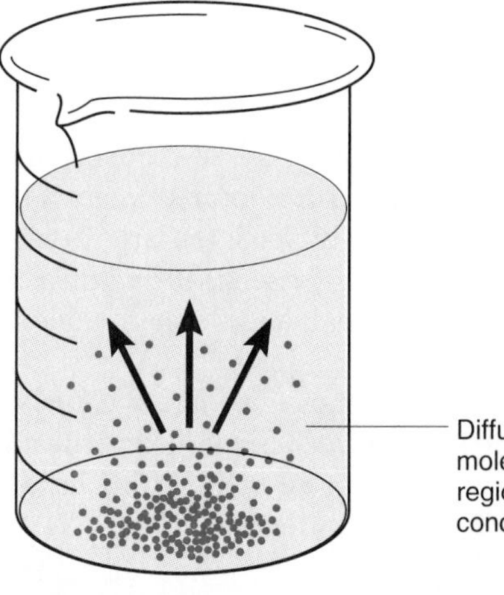
Diffusion forces sugar molecules away from region of highest concentration

FIGURE 2.15

Diffusion. The force of diffusion moves sugar molecules up until they are evenly distributed throughout the liquid in the container.

THE FORCE OF ELECTROSTATIC PRESSURE

electrolyte
ion
cation
anion

When some substances are dissolved in water, they split into two parts, each with an opposing electrical charge. Substances with this property are called **electrolytes;** the charged particles into which they decompose are called **ions.** Ions are of two basic types: **Cations** have a positive charge, and **anions** have a negative charge. For example, when sodium chloride (NaCl, table salt) is dissolved in water, many of the molecules split into sodium cations (Na^+) and chloride anions (Cl^-). (I find that the easiest way to keep the terms *cation* and *anion* straight is to think of the cation's plus sign as a cross, and remember the superstition of a black *cat crossing* your path.)

electrostatic pressure

As you have undoubtedly learned, particles with the same kind of charge repel each other (+ repels +, and − repels −), but particles with different charges are attracted to each other (+ and − attract). Thus, anions repel anions, cations repel cations, but anions and cations attract each other. (See ***Figure 2.16.***) The force exerted by this attraction or repulsion is called **electrostatic pressure.** Just as the force of diffusion moves molecules from regions of high concentration to regions of low concentration, electrostatic pressure moves ions from place to place: Cations are pushed away from regions with an excess of cations, and anions are pushed away from regions with an excess of anions.

IONS IN THE EXTRACELLULAR AND INTRACELLULAR FLUID

intracellular fluid
extracellular fluid

The fluid within cells (**intracellular fluid**) and the fluid surrounding them (**extracellular fluid**) contain different ions. The forces of diffusion and electrostatic pressure contributed by these ions give rise to the membrane potential. Because the membrane potential is produced by a balance between the forces of diffusion and electrostatic pressures, to understand what produces this potential, we must know the concentration of the various ions in the extracellular and intracellular fluids.

FIGURE 2.16

Electrostatic pressure. Particles with the same charge repel each other; particles with different charges attract each other.

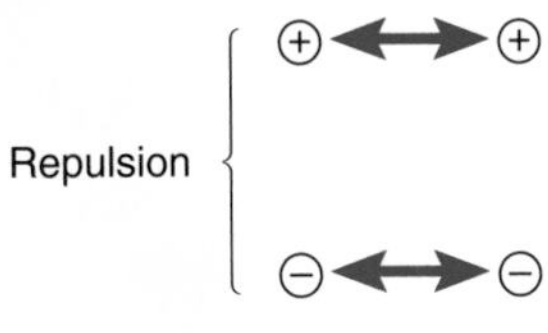

There are several important ions in these fluids. I will discuss four of them here: protein anions (symbolized by A^-), chloride ions (Cl^-), sodium ions (Na^+), and potassium ions (K^+). The Latin words for sodium and potassium are ***natrium*** and ***kalium;*** hence, they are abbreviated *Na* and *K,* respectively. Protein anions (A^-) are found in the intracellular fluid. Although the other three ions are found in both the intracellular and extracellular fluids, K^+ is found predominantly in the intracellular fluid, whereas Na^+ and Cl^- are found predominantly in the extracellular fluid. (See ***Figure 2.17.***) The easiest way to remember which ion is found where is to recall that the fluid that surrounds our cells is similar to seawater, which is predominantly a solution of salt, NaCl. The primitive ancestors of our cells lived in the ocean; thus, the seawater was their extracellular fluid. Our extracellular fluid resembles seawater, produced and maintained by regulatory mechanisms that are described in Chapter 11.

Let us consider the ions in Figure 2.17, examining the forces of diffusion and electrostatic pressure exerted on each and reasoning why each is located where it is. We can quickly dispense with A^-, the protein anion, because this ion is too large to pass through the membrane of the axon. Therefore, although its presence within the cell affects the other ions, it is located where it is because the membrane is impermeable to it.

The potassium ion K^+ is concentrated within the axon; thus, the force of diffusion tends to push it out of the cell. However, the outside of the cell is charged positively with respect to the inside, so electrostatic pressure tends to force the cation inside. Thus, the two opposing forces balance. (See ***Figure 2.17*** at the circled A.)

FIGURE 2.17

The relative concentration of some important ions inside and outside the neuron and the forces acting on them.

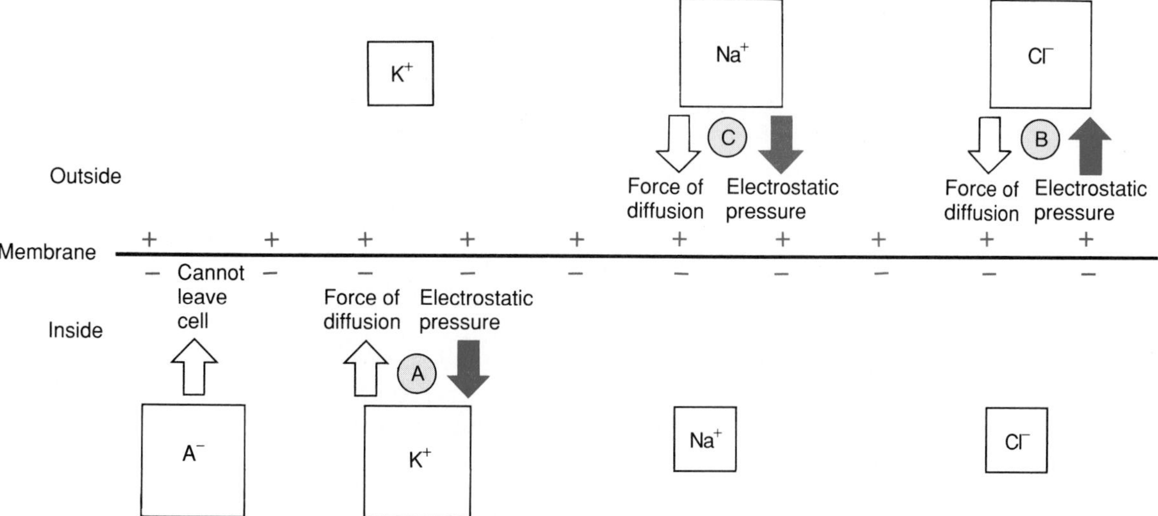

The chloride ion Cl^- is in greatest concentration outside the axon. The force of diffusion pushes it inward. However, because the inside of the axon is negatively charged, electrostatic pressure pushes the anion outward. Again, two opposing forces balance each other. (See ***Figure 2.17*** at the circled B.)

The sodium ion Na^+ is also in greatest concentration outside the axon, so it, like Cl^-, is pushed into the cell by the force of diffusion. But unlike chloride, the sodium ion is *positively* charged. Therefore, electrostatic pressure does *not* prevent Na^+ from entering the cell; indeed, the negative charge inside the axon *attracts* Na^+. (See ***Figure 2.17*** at the circled C.)

How can Na^+ remain in greatest concentration in the extracellular fluid, despite the fact that both forces (diffusion and electrostatic pressure) tend to push it inside? The simplest explanation would be that the membrane is impermeable to Na^+, as it is to A^-, the protein anion. However, experiments have shown that the membrane does allow some Na^+ to leak through. But at the same time another force, provided by the sodium-potassium pump, continuously pumps Na^+ out of the axon. The **sodium-potassium pump** consists of thousands of individual protein molecules situated in the membrane, driven by energy provided by the mitochondria as they metabolize the cell's nutrients. These molecules exchange Na^+ for K^+, pushing three sodium ions out for every two potassium ions they push in. (See ***Figure 2.18***.)

Because the membrane is not very permeable to Na^+, the sodium-potassium pump very effectively keeps the intracellular concentration of Na^+ low. By pumping K^+ into the cell, it also increases the intracellular concentration of K^+ somewhat. The membrane is approximately a hundred times more permeable to K^+ than to Na^+, so the increase is slight; but as we will see when we study the process of neural inhibition later in this chapter, it is very important. The sodium-potassium pump uses considerable energy: Up to 40 percent of the neuron's metabolic resources are used to operate it. And most cells of the body, not just neurons, have a sodium-potassium pump in their membrane.

FIGURE 2.18

The effects of the sodium-potassium pump.

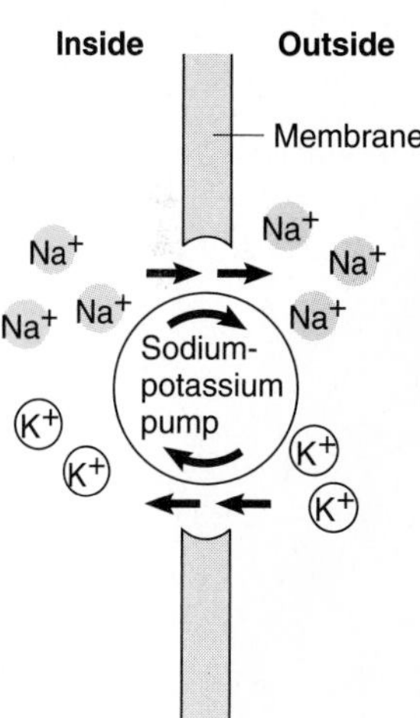

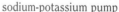

sodium-potassium pump

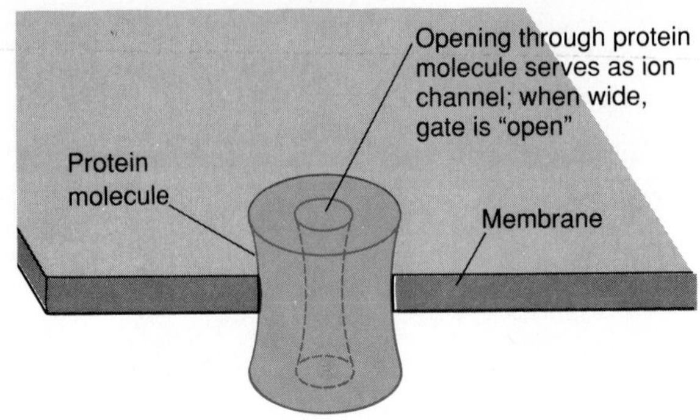
Opening through protein molecule serves as ion channel; when wide, gate is "open"
Protein molecule
Membrane

FIGURE 2.19

An ion channel.

The Action Potential

As we saw, both the forces of diffusion and electrostatic pressure tend to push Na^+ into the cell. However, the membrane is not very permeable to this ion, and the sodium-potassium pump continuously pumps out Na^+, keeping the intracellular level of Na^+ low, even though a little manages to leak in. But imagine what would happen if the membrane suddenly became highly permeable to sodium ions. The forces of diffusion and electrostatic pressure would cause Na^+ to rush into the cell. This sudden influx of positively charged ions would drastically change the membrane potential. Indeed, experiments have shown that this mechanism is precisely what causes the action potential: A brief drop in the membrane resistance to Na^+ (allowing these ions to rush into the cell) is immediately followed by a brief drop in the membrane resistance to K^+ (allowing these ions to rush out of the cell).

ion channel

I said earlier that the membrane consists of a double layer of lipid molecules that contains many different kinds of protein molecules. One class of protein molecules provides a way for ions to enter or leave the cells. These molecules constitute **ion channels**, which contain gates that can open or close. When a gate is open, a particular type of ion can flow through the channel and thus can enter or leave the cell. (See ***Figure 2.19***.) Neural membranes contain many thousands of ion channels. For example, the giant squid axon contains from 100 to 600 sodium channels in each square micrometer of membrane. Thus, the permeability of a membrane to a particular ion is determined by the number of ion channels that are open.

The process of ionic flow occurs in the following sequence (refer to ***Figure 2.20***):

voltage-dependent ion channel

1. As soon as the threshold of excitation is reached, the sodium channels in the membrane open and Na^+ rushes in, propelled by diffusion and electrostatic pressure. The opening of these channels is triggered by the depolarization of the membrane potential; they open at the threshold of excitation. Because these channels are opened by changes in the membrane potential, they are called **voltage-dependent ion channels**. The influx of positively charged sodium ions produces a rapid change in the membrane potential, from -70 to $+50$ mV.
2. At about the time the action potential reaches its peak (in approximately 1 msec) the sodium channels close and the membrane once again becomes resistant to the flow of Na^+. (Why this happens is not yet known.) By now, the voltage-dependent potassium channels in the membrane have opened, letting K^+ ions move freely through the membrane. At the peak of the action potential, the inside of the axon is now *positively* charged, so K^+ is driven out of

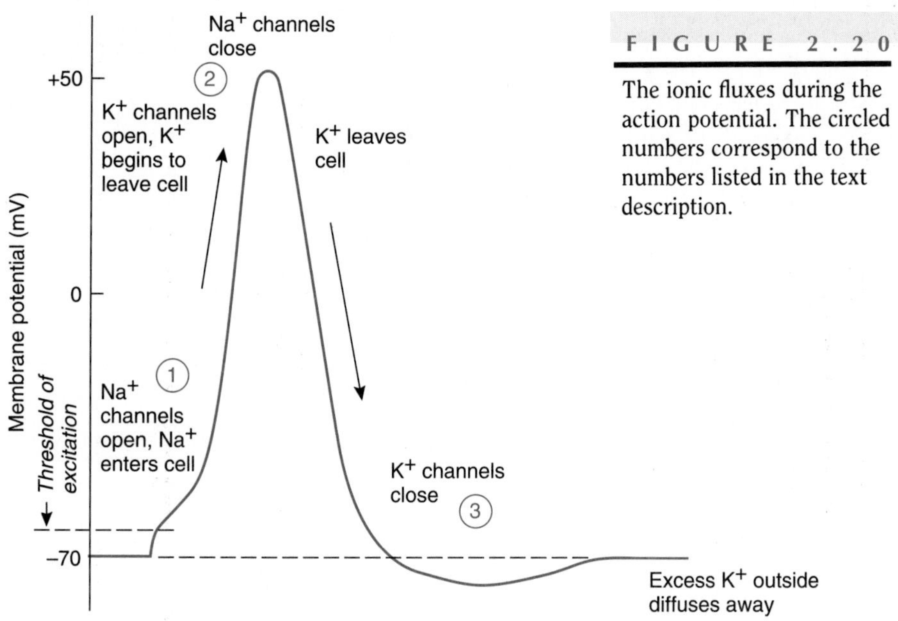

FIGURE 2.20

The ionic fluxes during the action potential. The circled numbers correspond to the numbers listed in the text description.

the cell by diffusion and by electrostatic pressure. This outflow of cations causes the membrane potential to return toward its normal value. As it does so, the potassium channels close again.

3. The membrane potential not only returns to normal but actually overshoots its resting value (−70 mV) and only gradually returns to normal. The accumulation of K^+ ions outside the membrane causes it to become temporarily hyperpolarized. These extra ions soon diffuse away, and the membrane potential returns to −70 mV. Eventually, the sodium-potassium pump removes the Na^+ that leaked in and retrieves the K^+ that leaked out.

How much ionic flow is there? When I say "Na^+ rushes in," I do not mean that the axoplasm becomes flooded with Na^+. Because the sodium and potassium channels open for such a brief time, and because diffusion over any appreciable distance takes time, not too many Na^+ molecules flow in, and not too many K^+ molecules flow out. At the peak of the action potential, a very thin layer of fluid immediately inside the axon becomes full of newly arrived Na^+ ions; this amount is indeed enough to reverse the membrane potential. However, not enough time has elapsed for these ions to fill the entire axon. Before that event would take place, the sodium channels close again, and K^+ starts flowing out. Experiments have shown that an action potential temporarily increases the number of Na^+ ions inside the giant squid axon by 0.0003 percent. Although the concentration just inside the membrane is high, the total number of ions entering the cell is very small relative to the number already there. On a short-term basis, the sodium-potassium pump is not very important. The few Na^+ ions that manage to leak in diffuse into the rest of the axoplasm, and the slight increase in Na^+ concentration is hardly noticeable. However, the sodium-potassium pump is important on a long-term basis, because in many axons action potentials occur at a very high rate. Without the sodium-potassium pump the axoplasm would eventually become full of sodium ions, and the axon would no longer be able to function.

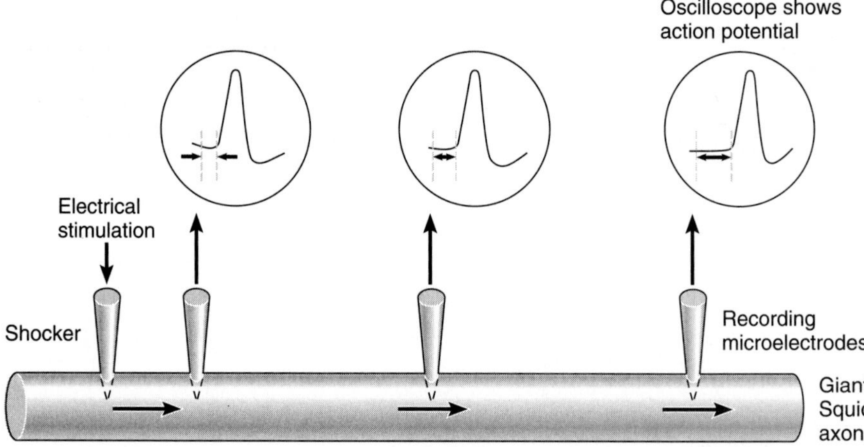

FIGURE 2.21

Conduction of the action potential. When an action potential is triggered, its size remains undiminished as it travels down the axon. The speed of conduction can be calculated from the delay between the stimulus and the action potential.

Conduction of the Action Potential

Now that you have a basic understanding of the resting membrane potential and the production of the action potential, I can describe the movement of the message down the axon, or *conduction of the action potential.* To study this phenomenon, we again make use of the giant squid axon. We attach a stimulating electrode at one end of the axon and place recording electrodes, attached to oscilloscopes, at different distances from the stimulating electrode. Then we apply a depolarizing stimulus to the end of the axon and trigger an action potential. We record the action potential from each of the electrodes, one after the other. Thus, we see that the action potential is conducted down the axon. As it travels, it remains constant in size. (See ***Figure 2.21***.)

all-or-none law

This experiment establishes a basic law of axonal conduction: the **all-or-none law.** This law states that an action potential either occurs or it does not occur; once it has been triggered, it is transmitted down the axon to its end. It always remains the same size, without growing or diminishing. In fact, the axon will transmit an action potential in either direction, or even in both directions, if one is started in the middle of its length. However, because action potentials in living animals always start at the end attached to the soma, axons normally carry one-way traffic.

As you know, the strength of a muscular contraction can vary from very weak to very forceful, and the strength of a stimulus can vary from barely detectable to very intense. We know that the occurrence of action potentials in axons controls the strength of muscular contractions and represents the intensity of a physical stimulus. But if the action potential is an all-or-none event, how can it represent information that can vary in a continuous fashion? The answer is simple: A single action potential is not the basic element of information; rather, variable information is represented by an axon's *rate of firing.* (In this context, *firing* refers to the production of action potentials.) A high rate of firing causes a strong muscular contraction, and a strong stimulus (such as a bright light) causes a high rate of firing in axons that serve the eyes. Thus, the all-or-none law is supplemented by the **rate law.** (See ***Figure 2.22***.)

rate law

Action potentials are not the only kind of electrical signals that occur in neurons. As we shall see in the next section, when a message is sent across a synapse, a small electrical signal is produced in the membrane of the neuron that receives the message. In order to understand this process, and to understand the way that action potentials are conducted in myelinated axons (described below), we must see how such signals

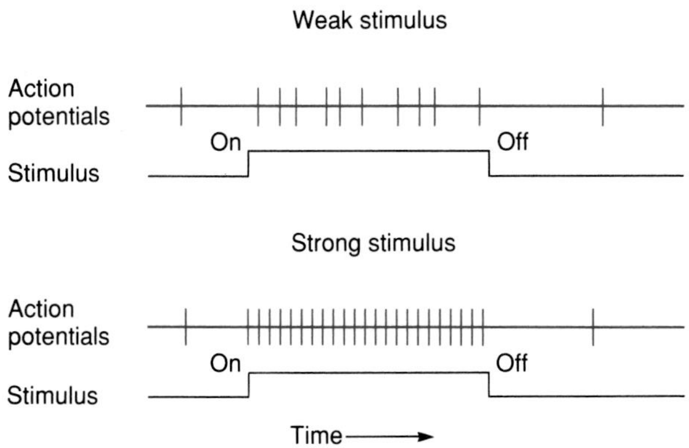

FIGURE 2.22

The rate law. The strength of a stimulus is represented by the rate of firing of an axon. The size of each action potential is always constant.

other than action potentials are conducted. To do so, we produce a below-threshold depolarizing stimulus (too small to produce an action potential) at one end of an axon and record its effects from electrodes placed along the axon. We find that the stimulus produces a disturbance in the membrane potential that becomes smaller as it moves away from the point of stimulation. (See ***Figure 2.23.***)

The transmission of the small, below-threshold depolarization is *passive.* The axon is acting like an electrical cable, carrying along the current started at one end. This property of the axon follows laws discovered in the nineteenth century that describe conduction of electricity through telegraph cables laid along the ocean floor. As a signal passes through a submarine cable, it gets smaller because of the electrical characteristics of the cable, including leakage through the insulator and resistance in the wire. Because the signal decreases in size (decrements), it is referred to as *decremental conduction.* We say that the passive conduction of a small depolarization by the axon follows the laws that describe the **cable properties** of the axon—the same laws that describe the electrical properties of a submarine cable. And because hyperpolarizations never trigger action potentials, these disturbances, like below-threshold depolarizations, are also transmitted by means of the passive cable properties of an axon.

cable properties

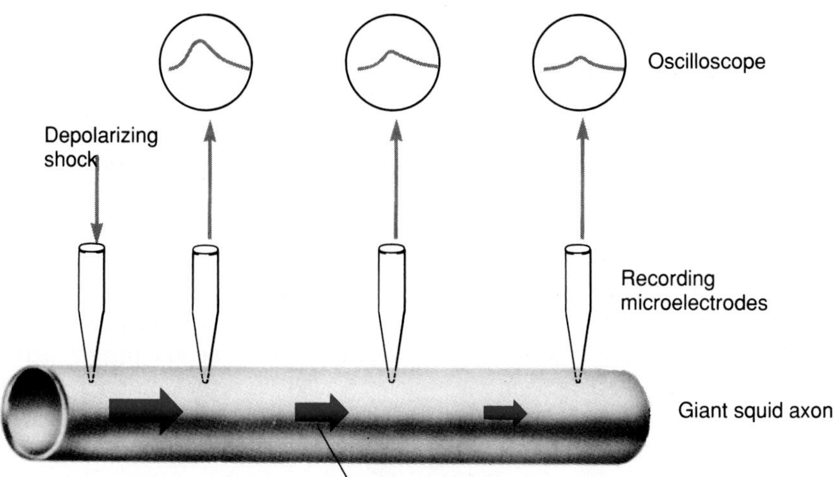

FIGURE 2.23

Decremental conduction. When a below-threshold depolarization is applied, it decreases in size as it travels down the axon.

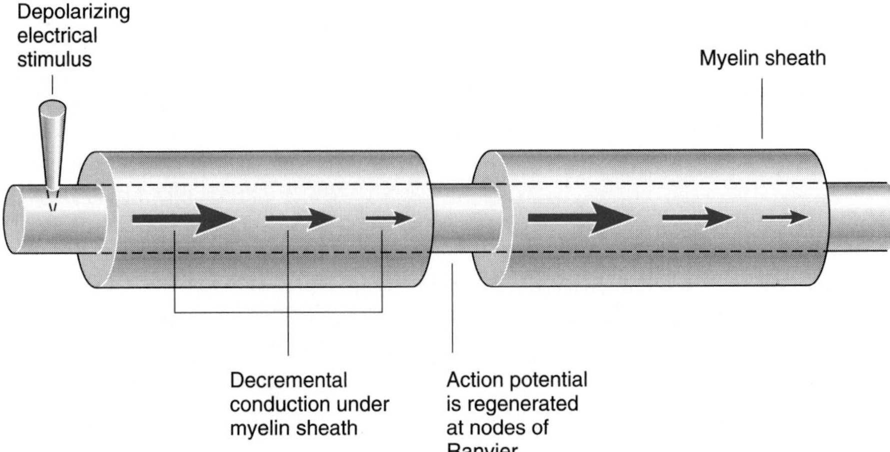

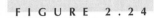

FIGURE 2.24

Saltatory conduction, showing propagation of an action potential down a myelinated axon.

Recall that most axons in mammalian nervous systems are myelinated; segments of them are covered by a myelin sheath produced by the oligodendroglia of the CNS or the Schwann cells of the PNS. These segments are separated by portions of naked axon, the nodes of Ranvier. Conduction of an action potential in a myelinated axon is somewhat different from conduction in an unmyelinated axon, as described next.

Schwann cells (and the oligodendroglia of the CNS) wrap tightly around the axon, leaving no measurable extracellular fluid between them and the axon. The only place where a myelinated axon comes in contact with the extracellular fluid is at a node of Ranvier, where the axon is naked. In the myelinated areas there can be no inward flow of Na^+ when the sodium channels open, because there *is* no extracellular sodium. How, then, does the "action potential" travel along the area of axonal membrane covered by myelin sheath? You guessed it — by cable properties. The axon passively conducts the electrical disturbance from the action potential to the next node of Ranvier. The disturbance gets smaller, but it is still large enough to trigger an action potential at the next node. The action potential gets retriggered, or repeated, at each node of Ranvier and is passed, by means of cable properties of the axon, along the myelinated area to the next node. Its conduction, hopping from node to node, is called **saltatory conduction** (from the Latin *saltare*, "to dance"). (See ***Figure 2.24.***)

saltatory conduction

There are two advantages to saltatory conduction. The most important one is economic. Energy must be expended by the sodium-potassium pump to get rid of the excess Na^+ that leaks into the axon during the action potential. The pump is given work to do all along an unmyelinated axon, because Na^+ leaks in everywhere. But because Na^+ can leak into a myelinated axon only at the nodes of Ranvier, much less gets in; and consequently, much less has to be pumped out again. Therefore, a myelinated axon expends much less energy to maintain its sodium balance.

The second advantage to myelin is speed. Conduction of an action potential is faster in a myelinated axon because the transmission between the nodes, which occurs by means of the axon's cable properties, is very fast. Increased speed makes it possible for an animal to react faster and (undoubtedly) to think faster. One of the ways to increase the speed of conduction is to increase size. Because it is so large, the unmyelinated squid axon, with a diameter of 500 μm (micrometers), achieves a conduction velocity of approximately 35 m/sec (meters per second). However, the same speed is achieved by a myelinated cat axon with a diameter of a mere 6 μm. The fastest myelinated axon, 20 μm in diameter, can conduct action potentials at a speedy 120 m/sec, or 268 mi/h (miles per hour).

▶*INTERIM SUMMARY*◀

Neurons communicate by means of synapses. When a message is sent down an axon, the terminal buttons secrete a chemical that has either an excitatory or an inhibitory effect on the neuron with which it communicates. Ultimately, the effects of these excitatory and inhibitory synapses cause behavior, in the form of muscular contraction.

The message conducted down an axon is called an action potential. The membranes of all cells of the body are electrically charged, but only axons can produce action potentials. The resting membrane potential occurs because various ions are located in different concentrations in the fluid inside and outside the cell. The extracellular fluid (like seawater) is rich in Na^+ and Cl^-, and the intracellular fluid is rich in K^+ and various protein anions, designated as A^-.

The cell membrane is freely permeable to water, but its permeability to various ions—in particular, Na^+ and K^+—is regulated by ion channels. When the membrane potential is at its resting value (−70 mV), the gates of the voltage-dependent sodium and potassium channels are closed. Although some Na^+ continuously leaks into the axon, it is promptly forced out of the cell again by the sodium-potassium pump (which also forces some extra potassium *into* the axon). When an electrical stimulus depolarizes the membrane potential of the axon so that it reaches the threshold of excitation, voltage-dependent sodium channels open, and Na^+ rushes into the cell, driven by the force of diffusion and by electrostatic pressure. The entry of the positively charged ions further reduces the membrane potential and, indeed, causes it to reverse, so the inside becomes positive. The opening of the sodium channels is temporary; they soon close again. The depolarization of the membrane potential caused by the influx of Na^+ opens the gates of voltage-dependent potassium channels, and K^+ leaves the axon, pushed by the force of diffusion. The efflux of K^+ quickly brings the membrane potential back to its resting value.

The action potential normally begins at one end of the axon, where the axon attaches to the soma. It travels continuously down unmyelinated axons, remaining constant in size, until it reaches the terminal buttons. (When the axon divides, the action potential continues down each branch.) In myelinated axons, ions can flow through the membrane only at the nodes of Ranvier, because the axons are covered everywhere else with myelin. Thus, the action potential is conducted from one node of Ranvier to the next by means of passive cable properties. When the electrical message reaches a node, voltage-dependent sodium channels open, and the action potential reaches full strength again. This mechanism saves a considerable amount of energy, because sodium-potassium pumps are not needed along the myelinated portions of the axons; and it is faster. ▲

SYNAPTIC TRANSMISSION

As we just saw, neurons communicate by means of synapses, and the medium used for these one-way conversations is the chemical released by terminal buttons. These chemicals, called transmitter substances, diffuse across the fluid-filled gap between the terminal buttons and the membranes of the neurons with which they form synapses. The transmitter substances cause a brief alteration in the membrane potential of these neurons, which produces either an excitatory or an inhibitory effect on the rate of firing of their axons.

This discussion of synaptic transmission begins with a description of the structure of synapses. The rest of this section describes the nature of neural integration and covers the steps involved in the process of synaptic transmission, from release of the transmitter substance to termination of the postsynaptic potential.

Structure of Synapses

As you have already learned, synapses are junctions between the terminal buttons at the ends of the axonal branches of one neuron and the membrane of another. Because a message is transmitted in only one direction, the membranes on the two sides of the synapse are named in relation to the synapse: The membrane of the terminal button (transmitting neuron) is the **presynaptic membrane**, and that of the receiving neuron is the **postsynaptic membrane**. As Figure 2.25 shows, these membranes are separated by a small gap, which varies in size from synapse to synapse but is usually around 200 Å (angstroms) wide. (An angstrom unit is one ten-millionth of a millimeter.) The space, called the **synaptic cleft**, contains extracellular fluid, through which the transmitter substance diffuses. (See ***Figure 2.25***.)

presynaptic membrane
postsynaptic membrane
synaptic cleft

As you may have noticed in Figure 2.25, two prominent structures are located in the cytoplasm of the terminal button: mitochondria and synaptic vesicles. Many of the biochemical steps in the extraction of energy from glucose take place in the mitochondria; hence their presence near the terminal button suggests that certain processes that occur there require energy. **Synaptic vesicles** are small rounded objects in the shape of spheres or ovoids. They are packages that contain transmitter substance (the term *vesicle* means "little bladder"). They are produced in the soma and are carried down to the terminal buttons along the microtubules that run the length of the axons. This delivery process, which uses the cell's energy resources to fuel it, is called **axoplasmic transport.**

synaptic vesicle
axoplasmic transport

The postsynaptic membrane under the terminal button is somewhat thicker than the membrane elsewhere. As we will see, it contains specialized protein molecules that detect the presence of transmitter substances in the synaptic cleft and initiate the changes in the membrane potential that excite or inhibit the postsynaptic neuron.

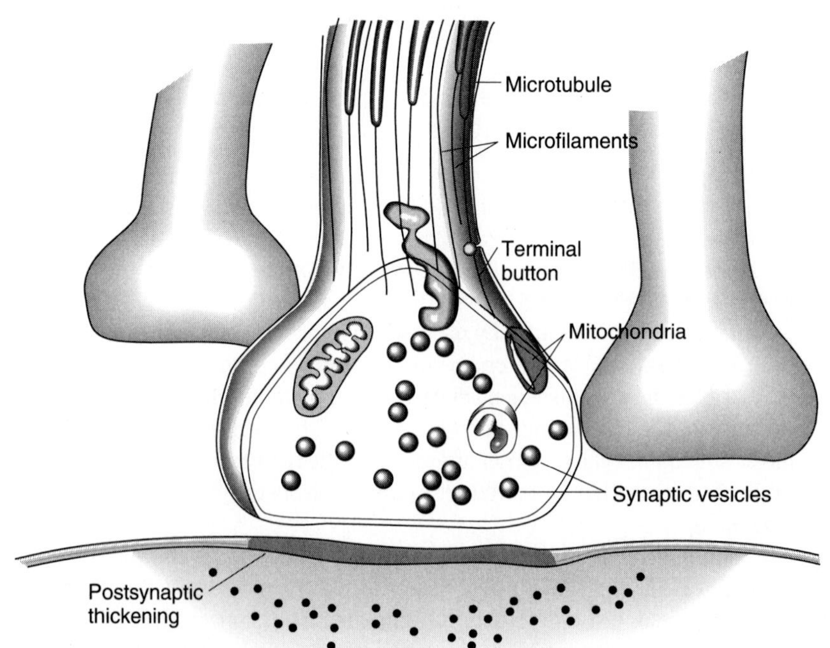

FIGURE 2.25

Details of a synapse.

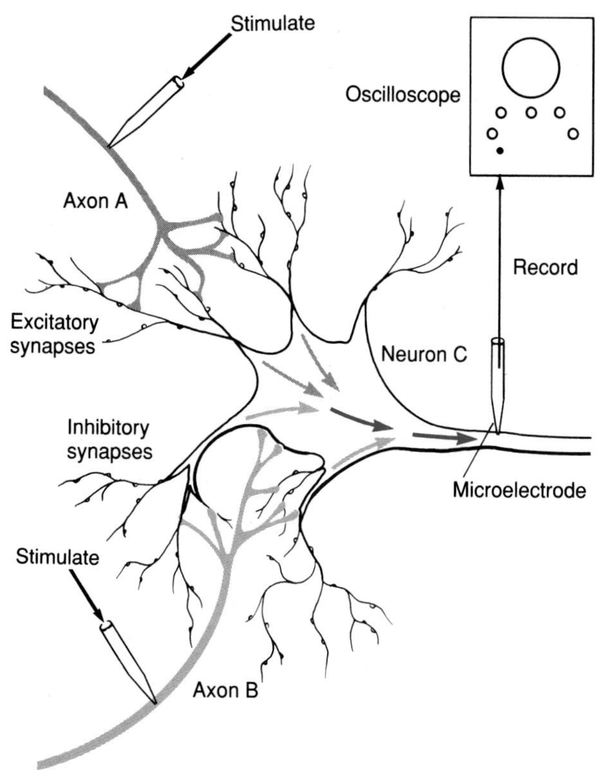

FIGURE 2.26

The means for measuring the effects of the activity of excitatory and inhibitory synapses on the rate of firing of a neuron's axon.

Neural Integration

The interaction of the effects of excitatory and inhibitory synapses on the somatic and dendritic membranes of a neuron determines the rate at which its axon fires. This interaction is called **neural integration** (*integration* here means "to make whole," in the sense of combining two functions). To illustrate this process, we can perform a hypothetical experiment.

neural integration

We anesthetize an animal and place a microelectrode inside the axon of a multipolar neuron in its nervous system (neuron C). We have chosen this hypothetical animal because the neuron receives synaptic inputs from two neurons (A and B), one inhibitory and one excitatory. We attach electrodes from two electrical stimulators to the two axons that communicate with the neuron. (See ***Figure 2.26***.)

First, we stimulate axon A, one of the incoming axons, and record the membrane potential of the axon of neuron C, the postsynaptic neuron. After a brief delay the membrane potential of axon C begins to depolarize, reaches the threshold of excitation, and "fires," transmitting an action potential down its length. (See ***Figure 2.27a***.) Next, we stimulate axon B. This time, we see that the effect is to ***hyperpolarize*** the membrane of axon C. (See ***Figure 2.27b***.) Of course, hyperpolarizations never cause action potentials. Now let us see what happens when we simultaneously stimulate axons A and B. The synapses at the end of axon A cause depolarizations, and those at the end of axon B cause hyperpolarizations. These effects cancel each other; the membrane potential of axon C changes very little, and an action potential is not triggered. (See ***Figure 2.27c***.)

When a synapse becomes active, it causes a brief change in the membrane potential of the cell with which it communicates. This change is called a **postsynaptic potential,**

postsynaptic potential

FIGURE 2.27

Excitatory and inhibitory postsynaptic potentials. (a) Action potential triggered. (b) Hyperpolarization. (c) Canceling effects.

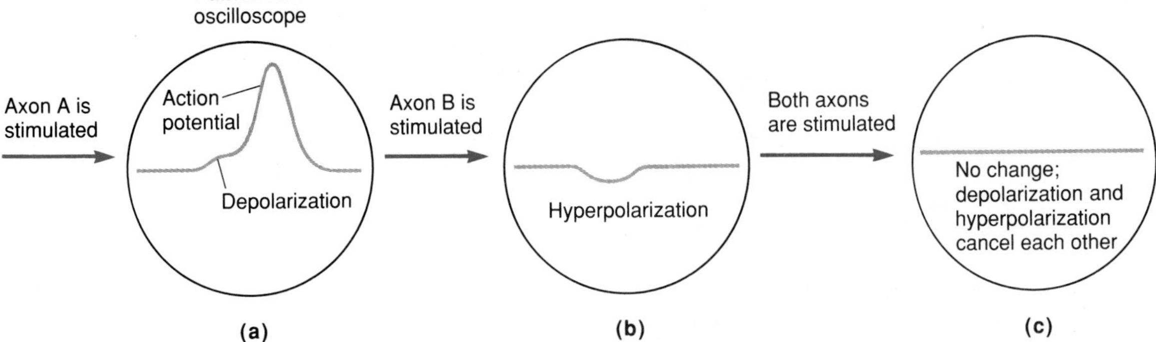

inhibitory postsynaptic potential (IPSP)

excitatory postsynaptic potential (EPSP)

because it occurs in the postsynaptic neuron. Hyperpolarizations *inhibit* the production of action potentials; hence they are called **inhibitory postsynaptic potentials** (IPSPs). Depolarizations *excite* the neuron, making action potentials more likely; hence they are called **excitatory postsynaptic potentials** (EPSPs). An individual neuron may have tens of thousands of synapses on it. Thus, the rate of firing of its axon at a particular time depends on the relative number of EPSPs and IPSPs that are produced on its membrane.

Note that *neural* inhibition (that is, an inhibitory postsynaptic potential) does not always produce *behavioral* inhibition. For example, suppose a group of neurons inhibits a particular movement. If these neurons are inhibited, they will no longer suppress the behavior. Thus, inhibition of the inhibitory neurons makes the behavior more likely to occur. Of course, the same is true for neural excitation. Neural *excitation* of neurons that *inhibit* a behavior suppresses that behavior. For example, when we are dreaming, a particular set of inhibitory neurons in the brain become active and prevent us from getting up and acting out our dreams. (As we will see in Chapter 8, when these neurons are destroyed, people do just that.) Neurons are elements in complex circuits; without knowing the details of these circuits, one cannot predict the effects of the excitation or inhibition of one set of neurons on an organism's behavior.

Release of Transmitter Substance

When action potentials are conducted down an axon (and all of its branches), something happens inside all of the terminal buttons: A number of synaptic vesicles filled with a transmitter substance migrate to the presynaptic membrane, adhere to it, and then rupture, spilling their contents into the synaptic cleft. (See ***Figure 2.28.***)

The evidence for this process comes from several different kinds of experiments. Clark, Hurlbut, and Mauro (1972) removed a muscle from a frog, along with a length of nerve that innervated it. They infused the muscle and terminal buttons with venom of the black widow spider, a drug that causes transmitter substance to be released from the terminal buttons that synapse on the muscle fibers. When they examined the terminal buttons under an electron microscope, they found that the synaptic vesicles were gone.

Heuser and his colleagues (Heuser, 1977; Heuser, et al., 1979) devised a special apparatus that would freeze terminal buttons almost instantaneously. They electrically stimulated the nerve attached to an isolated frog muscle and then dropped the muscle

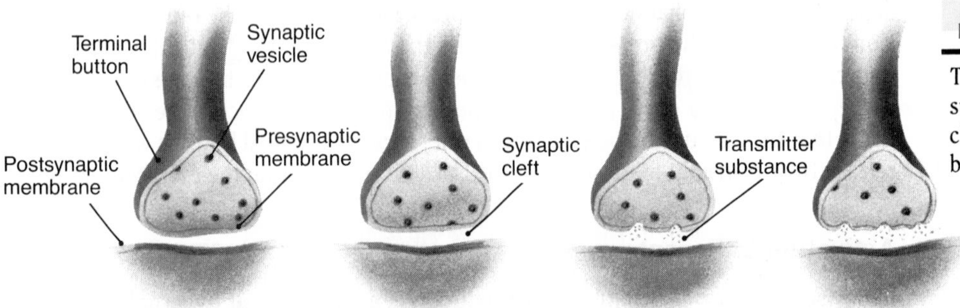

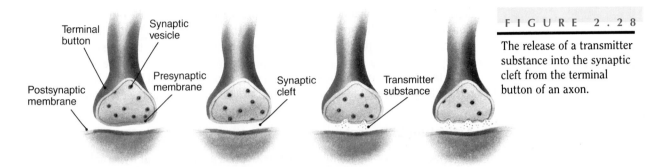

FIGURE 2.28

The release of a transmitter substance into the synaptic cleft from the terminal button of an axon.

against a block of pure copper that had been cooled to 4 K (approximately −453°F). The frozen tissue was then prepared for examination with an electron microscope. Figure 2.29 shows a portion of the synapse in cross section; note that some vesicles appear to be fused with the presynaptic membrane, forming the shape of a Greek letter omega (Ω). (See ***Figure 2.29***.)

The force that moves the synaptic vesicles toward the presynaptic membrane appears to be supplied by a process similar to that of axoplasmic flow. The membrane of synaptic vesicles is coated with a protein. The protein coating of the vesicles interacts with that of the microtubules, causing the microtubules to propel the vesicles to the presynaptic membrane. Once the vesicles reach the presynaptic membrane, their protein coating interacts with a protein coating on the inside of the presynaptic membrane, which is similar to that of the microtubules. This interaction tears open the synaptic vesicles, and the transmitter substance spills into the synaptic cleft.

But how does an action potential, transmitted down to a terminal button, cause the microtubules to propel the synaptic vesicles to the presynaptic membrane? The answer is that the membrane of terminal buttons contains voltage-dependent calcium channels. Calcium ions (Ca^{2+}) are present in the extracellular fluid. When the voltage-

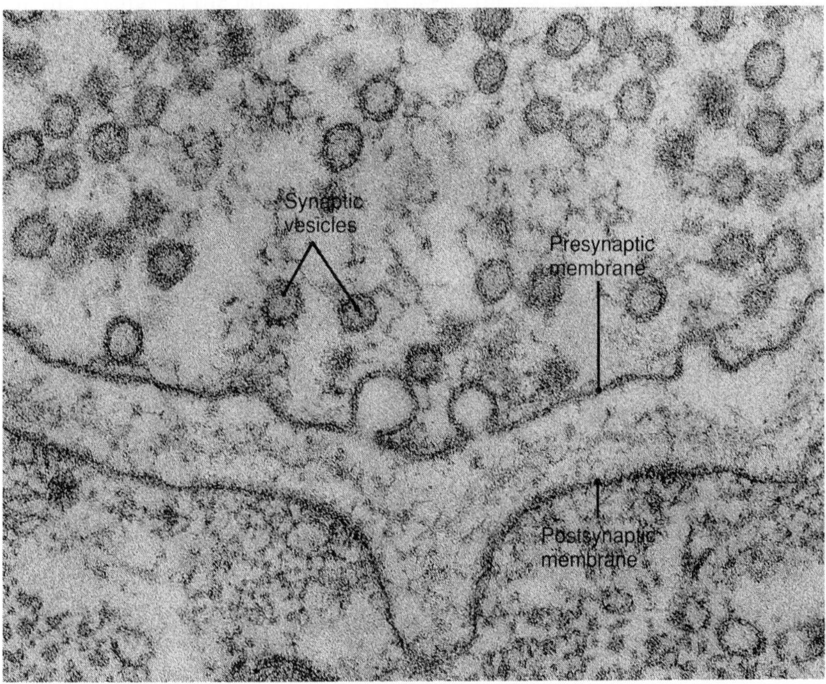

FIGURE 2.29

Photomicrograph of the fusion of synaptic vesicles with the membranes of terminal buttons that form synapses with frog muscle. The synapse is seen in cross section. (From Heuser, J.E., in *Society for Neuroscience Symposia, Vol. II*, edited by W.M. Cowan and J.A. Ferrendelli. Bethesda, Md.: Society for Neuroscience, ©1977. Society for Neuroscience. Photomicrograph produced by Dr. John E. Heuser of Washington University School of Medicine, St. Louis, Mo.)

had just finished eating breakfast. He was sitting in his bed, with a tray in front of him. There was half of a pancake on his plate. 'Are you all done?' I asked. 'Sure,' he said. I turned the plate around so that the uneaten part was on his right. He gave a startled look and said, 'Where the hell did that come from?' " ▲

The goal of neuroscience research is to understand how the brain functions. In order to understand the results of this research, you must be acquainted with the basic structure of the nervous system. I have kept the number of terms introduced in this chapter to a minimum, but as you will see, the minimum is still a rather large number. With the framework you will receive from this chapter, you should have no trouble learning the material presented in subsequent chapters.

NEUROANATOMICAL METHODS

Before beginning a description of the nervous system, I want to discuss the terms used to describe it and some of the methods used to discover its parts and their interconnections. Knowing something about the tools used to study the brain will help you understand the details of its connections.

Basic Nomenclature

The gross anatomy of the brain was described long ago, and everything that could be seen without the aid of a microscope was given a name. Early anatomists named most brain structures according to their similarity to commonplace objects: amygdala, or "almond-shaped object"; hippocampus, or "sea horse"; genu, or "knee"; cortex, or "bark"; pons, or "bridge"; uncus, or "hook," to give a few examples. Throughout this book I will translate the names of anatomical terms as I introduce them, because the translation makes the terms more memorable. For example, knowing that *cortex* means "bark" (like the bark of a tree) will help you remember that the cortex is the outer layer of the brain.

neuraxis

anterior
posterior
rostral
caudal
dorsal
ventral

lateral
medial
ipsilateral

When describing features of a structure as complex as the brain, we need to use terms denoting directions. Directions in the nervous system are normally described relative to the **neuraxis,** an imaginary line drawn through the spinal cord up to the front of the brain. For simplicity's sake, let us consider an animal with a straight neuraxis. Figure 3.1 shows an alligator and a human. This alligator is certainly laid out in a linear fashion; we can draw a straight line that starts between its eyes and continues down the center of its spinal cord. (See ***Figure 3.1.***) The front end is **anterior,** and the tail is **posterior.** The terms **rostral** (toward the beak) and **caudal** (toward the tail) are also employed, especially when referring specifically to the brain. The top of the head and the back are part of the **dorsal** surface, while the **ventral** (front) surface faces the ground. These directions are somewhat more complicated in the human; because we stand upright, our neuraxis bends, so that the top of the head is perpendicular to the back. The frontal views of the alligator and the human illustrate the terms **lateral** and **medial,** toward the side and toward the midline, respectively. (See ***Figure 3.1.***)

Two other useful terms are *ipsilateral* and *contralateral.* **Ipsilateral** refers to a structure on the same side of the body. Thus, if we say that the olfactory bulb sends

FIGURE 3.1

Side and frontal views of an alligator and a human, showing the terms used to denote anatomical directions.

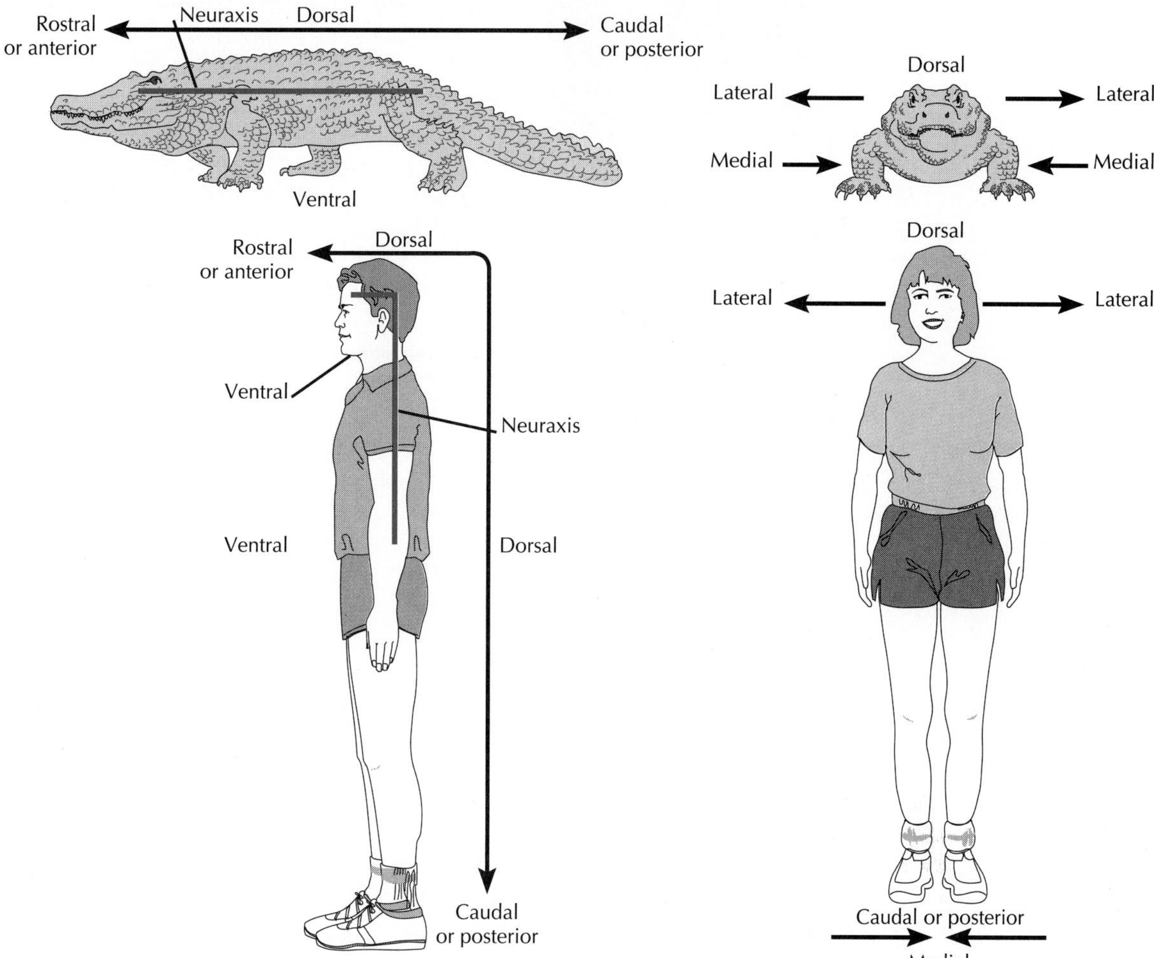

axons to the *ipsilateral* hemisphere, we mean that the left olfactory bulb sends axons to the left hemisphere and the right olfactory bulb sends axons to the right hemisphere. **Contralateral** refers to a structure on the opposite side of the body. If we say that a particular region of the left cortex controls movements of the *contralateral* hand, we mean that the region controls movements of the right hand.

contralateral

To see what is in the nervous system, we have to cut it open; to be able to convey information about what we find, we slice it in a standard way. Figure 3.2 shows a human central nervous system. We can slice the nervous system in three ways:

1. Transversely, like a salami, giving us **cross sections** (also known as **frontal sections,** especially when they concern the brain)
2. Parallel to the ground, giving us **horizontal sections**
3. Perpendicular to the ground and parallel to the neuraxis, giving us **sagittal sections.**

cross section
frontal section
horizontal section
sagittal section

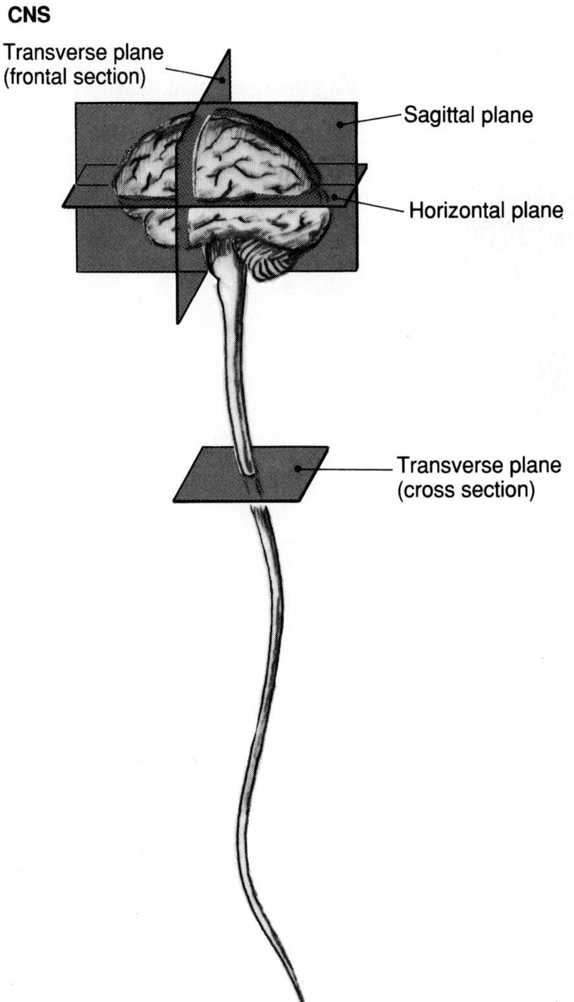

FIGURE 3.2

Planes of section as they pertain to the human central nervous system.

Note that because of our upright posture, cross sections of the spinal cord are actually parallel to the ground. (See ***Figure 3.2.***)

Discovering the Parts and Connections of the Nervous System

Study of the details of the anatomy of the nervous system requires special techniques. These techniques are referred to as *histological* procedures because they deal with the preparation of body tissues. Two basic types of histological procedures are discussed here: (1) fixing, slicing, and staining; (2) tracing neural pathways.

FIXING, SLICING, AND STAINING

If we hope to study the tissue in the form it had at the time of the organism's death, we must destroy the enzymes released when cells die, which would otherwise turn the tissue into shapeless mush. The tissue must also be preserved, to prevent its decomposition by bacteria or molds. To achieve both of these objectives, we place the neural tissue in a *fixative*—a chemical such as formalin. (You probably have already encountered formalin in a biology class, when you examined or dissected preserved speci-

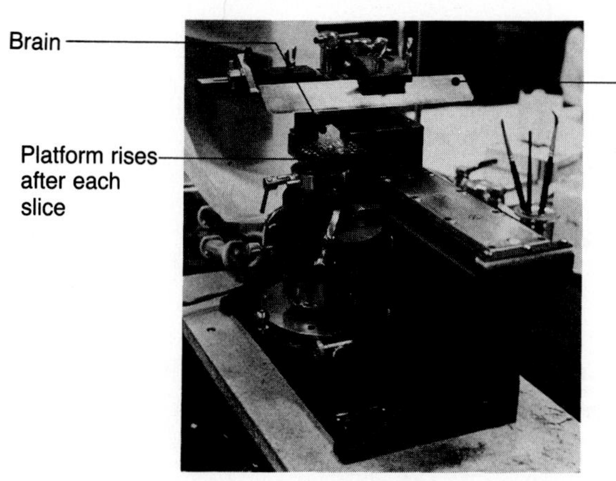

FIGURE 3.3

A microtome, used to slice brains.

mens.) **Formalin** deactivates enzymes, hardens the very soft and fragile brain, and kills any microorganisms that might destroy it.

formalin

In order to slice tissue into very thin sections (approximately 0.01 to 0.08 millimeter thick), the researcher must harden the brain, either by freezing it or by soaking it in warm liquid wax that hardens at room temperature. The brain is then sliced with a **microtome** (literally, "that which slices small"). A microtome contains an extremely sharp blade and a mechanism to advance the brain a small amount after each slice has been taken. (See ***Figure 3.3.***)

microtome

If you looked at an unstained section of brain tissue under a microscope, you would be able to see the outlines of some large masses of cells and some of the more prominent bundles of axons. However, you would not see any fine details. For this reason, the study of microscopic neuroanatomy requires special stains. ***Cell-body stains*** reveal neural and glial cell bodies by coloring particles found in the cytoplasm. ***Myelin stains*** selectively color myelin sheaths.

Color Plates 3.1 and 3.2 show two frontal sections of a cat brain. Color Plate 3.1 has been stained with a cell-body stain. You can see that the brain tissue is not homogeneous; it consists of bundles of axons and groupings of cell bodies. The groupings of cell bodies are called **nuclei,** which is the same term that is used to denote the center of the atom and the part of the cell that contains the chromosomes. Two nuclei are indicated by arrows. (See ***Color Plate 3.1.***) Color Plate 3.2 has been stained with a myelin stain. The dark parts contain bundles of myelinated axons; in fact, much of what is light in Color Plate 3.1 is dark in Color Plate 3.2. (See ***Color Plate 3.2.***)

nucleus

TRACING NEURAL PATHWAYS

The central nervous system contains many billions of neurons, most of which are gathered together in thousands of individual nuclei. These nuclei are interconnected by incredibly complex systems of axons. The problem of the neuroanatomist is to trace these connections and find out which nuclei are connected to which others and what route is taken by the interconnecting fibers. Unfortunately, careful observation of a slice of brain that has been stained with cell-body or myelin stains reveals a tangled mass of neurons. Special techniques must be used to make the connections that are being investigated stand out from all of the others.

Tracing Pathways Originating in a Brain Structure. Suppose an investigator is interested in a particular nucleus (group of neural cell bodies) in the brain and wants to

FIGURE 3.4

The procedure for the use of amino acid autoradiography to reveal the axons leaving a brain region.

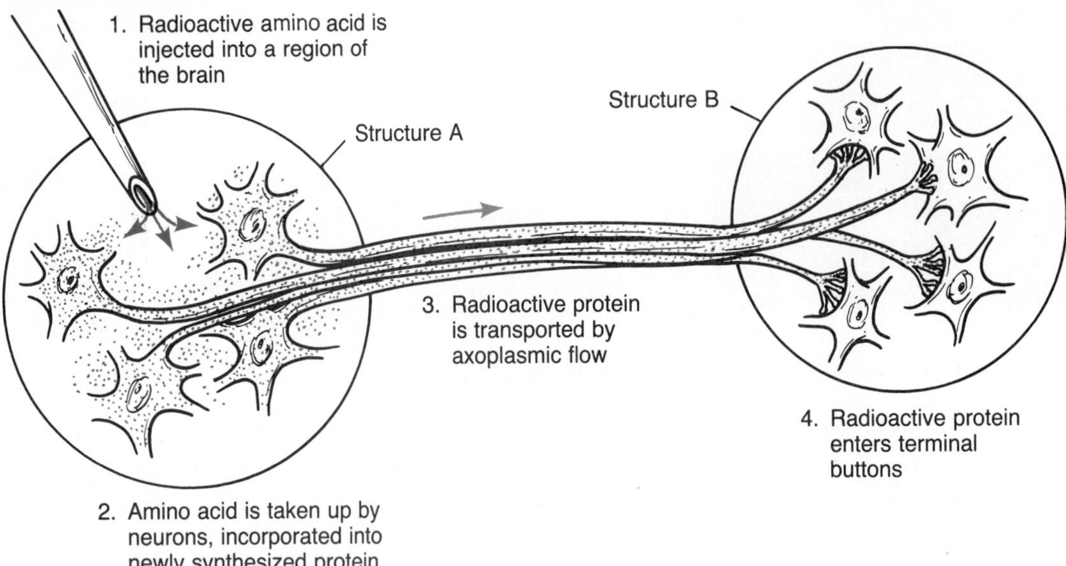
1. Radioactive amino acid is injected into a region of the brain
Structure A
Structure B
3. Radioactive protein is transported by axoplasmic flow
4. Radioactive protein enters terminal buttons
2. Amino acid is taken up by neurons, incorporated into newly synthesized protein

amino acid autoradiography

know what other parts of the brain receive information from the nucleus. The technique of **amino acid autoradiography** will provide the answer. The term *autoradiography* can roughly be translated as "writing with one's own radiation." The investigator injects a radioactive amino acid into the nucleus and then leaves the animal alone for a day or two. During this time the cell bodies take up the radioactive amino acids and incorporate them into proteins. Some of these proteins are transported through the axons to their terminal buttons. (See ***Figure 3.4.***) The animal is then killed, its brain is removed and sliced, and the sections are placed on microscope slides. The slides are taken into a darkroom, where they are coated with a photographic emulsion (the substance found on photographic film). After a wait of several weeks the slides, with their coatings of emulsion, are developed, just like photographic film. The radioactive proteins show themselves as black spots in the developed emulsion because the radioactivity exposes the emulsion, just as X-rays or light will do.

Figure 3.5 illustrates the actual appearance of the grains of exposed silver in the photographic emulsion. A solution containing a radioactive amino acid was injected into one part of a rabbit's brain, where it was taken up by neural cell bodies, incorporated into protein, and transported through axons to their terminal buttons. The two photographs, taken through a microscope, show the part of the brain that contains the terminal buttons. Figure 3.5a was taken with standard illumination. Figure 3.5b was viewed with a special microscope equipped with *dark-field illumination,* which makes the silver grains scatter a beam of light and thus look white. You can clearly see the silver grains in the nucleus labeled Ce (the central nucleus of the amygdala). (See ***Figure 3.5.***)

horseradish peroxidase

Tracing Pathways Leading to a Brain Structure. **Horseradish peroxidase** is a rather unlikely name for a substance that is used in neuroanatomical research. Nevertheless,

FIGURE 3.5

Amino acid autoradiography. A solution of radioactive amino acid was injected into one part of the brain and was carried through axons to the central nucleus of the amygdala (Ce). (a) Photomicrograph taken as a standard exposure. (b) Photomicrograph taken under dark-field illumination, which shows the exposed grains of emulsion as spots of white against a dark background. (Reprinted with permission from Kapp, B.S., Schwaber, J.S., and Driscoll, P.A., *Neuroscience*, 1985, *15*, 327–346. Copyright © 1985, Pergamon Press, plc.)

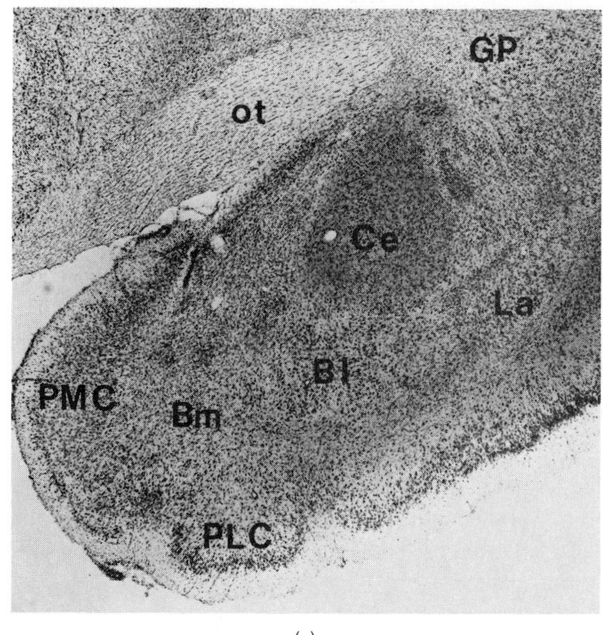

(a)

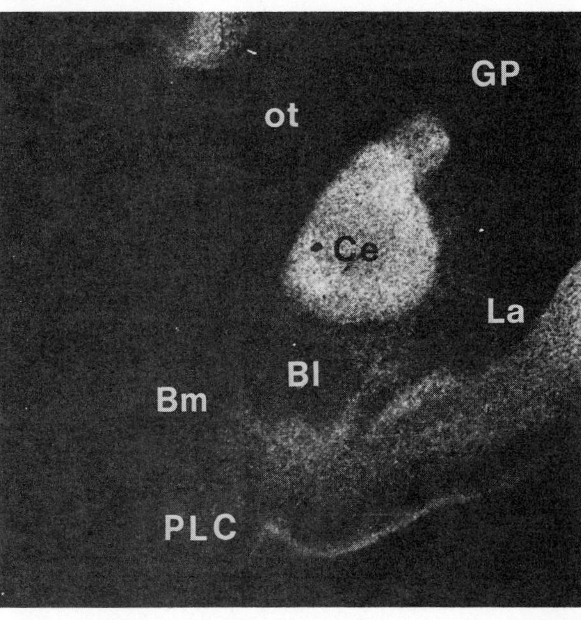

(b)

horseradish peroxidase (usually called HRP) is very useful to neuroanatomists. When HRP is injected into the brain, it is taken up, by means of active transport mechanisms, into terminal buttons. It is subsequently transported *backward* through the axons toward the cell bodies. Thus, when some HRP is injected into a region of the brain, it eventually reaches the cell bodies of neurons whose terminal buttons are located in that region.

The technique works like this: Some HRP is injected into the part of the brain that is under investigation. Axons and terminal buttons in that region take up the chemical and transport it back to the cell bodies. (See ***Figure 3.6.***) After a survival time of a day or two, the animal is killed, the brain is sliced, and the sections are soaked in a sequence of chemical baths that visibly mark the location of the HRP, which has been carried back to the cell bodies. Thus, the HRP technique permits identification of neurons that project axons *to* a particular region.

Figure 3.7 illustrates the appearance of cells that have been labeled with HRP. The chemical was injected into a particular nucleus in the hypothalamus of a rat, where it was taken up by terminal buttons. The HRP was carried back through the axons to cell bodies located in a particular region of the cerebral cortex (the medial prefrontal cortex), shown in the photomicrograph. The results indicate that neurons in the

FIGURE 3.6

The procedure for the use of horseradish peroxidase (HRP) to reveal the location of neurons that send axons to a brain region.

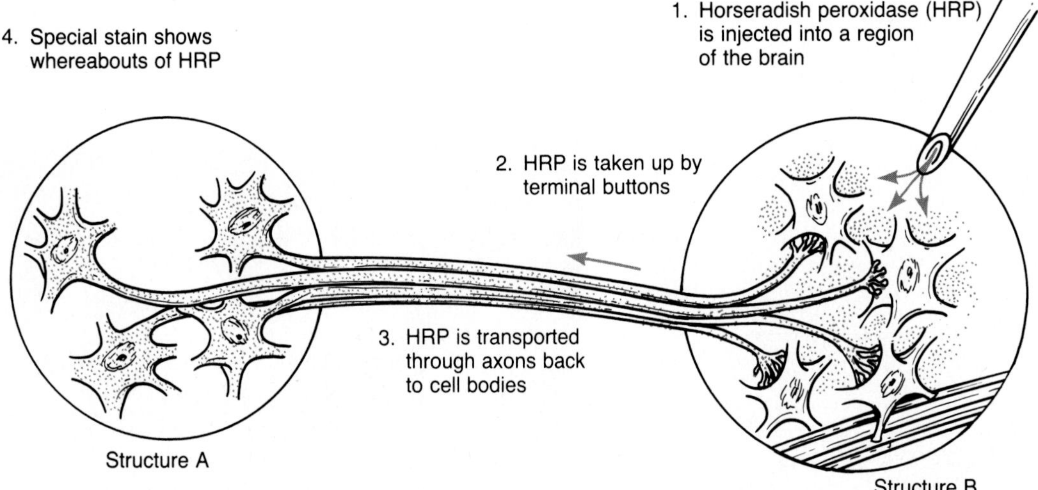
1. Horseradish peroxidase (HRP) is injected into a region of the brain
4. Special stain shows whereabouts of HRP
2. HRP is taken up by terminal buttons
3. HRP is transported through axons back to cell bodies
Structure A
Structure B

hypothalamus receive input from neurons in the medial prefrontal cortex. (See ***Figure 3.7.***)

Together, the HRP technique and the radioactive amino acid technique permit investigators to discover the source of the inputs into a particular part of the brain and the locations to which that region sends axons. Thus, these techniques help to provide us with a "wiring diagram" of the brain.

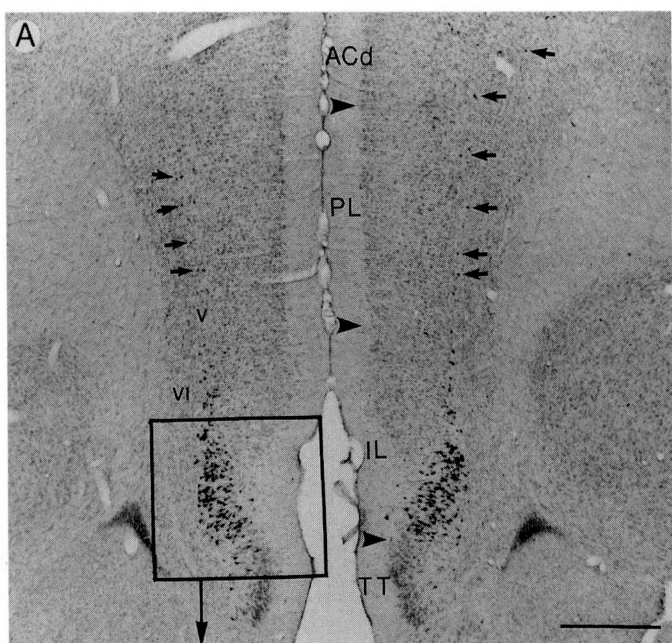
A
ACd
PL
V
VI
IL
TT

FIGURE 3.7

The horseradish peroxidase method. HRP was injected into a region of the hypothalamus where it was taken into terminal buttons and carried back to the cell bodies located in the medial prefrontal cortex. (a) Frontal section through the medial prefrontal cortex. (b) Enlargement of boxed area in (a). The dark spots are the cell bodies. (From Allen, G.V., and Hopkins, D.A. *Journal of Comparative Neurology*, 1989, *286*, 311–336. Copyright © 1989, *Journal of Comparative Neurology*. Reprinted by permission of Wiley-Liss, a division of John Wiley and Sons, Inc.)

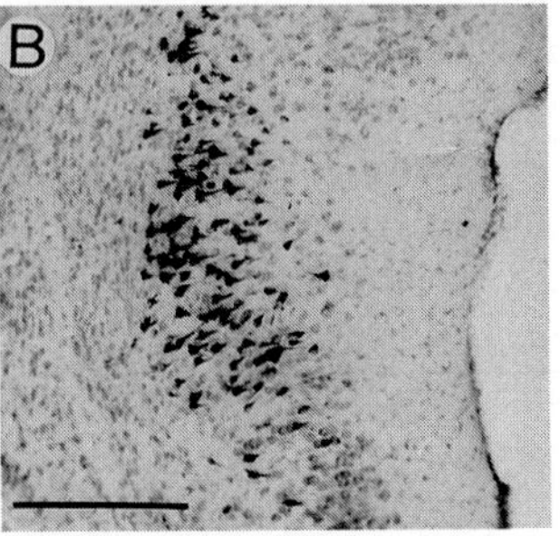
B

▶INTERIM SUMMARY◀

Anatomists have adopted a set of terms to describe the locations of parts of the body. *Anterior* is toward the head, *posterior* is toward the tail, *lateral* is toward the side, *medial* is toward the middle, *dorsal* is toward the back, and *ventral* is toward the front surface of the body. In the special case of the nervous system, *rostral* means toward the beak (or nose) and *caudal* means toward the tail. *Ipsilateral* means on the same side and *contralateral* means on the other side. A cross section (or frontal section) slices the nervous system like a salami, a horizontal section slices it parallel to the ground, and a sagittal section slices it perpendicular to the ground, parallel to the neuraxis.

In order to examine the details of the nervous system, the investigator preserves the tissue in a fixative such as formalin, hardens it by freezing it or soaking it in wax, and then slices it on a microtome. Cell-body stains or myelin stains reveal what their names imply. Tracing pathways involves the use of even more special techniques. Amino acid autoradiography reveals the place *to which* neurons in a particular structure send their axons. Radioactive amino acids, injected into the structure in the living animal, are taken up by the neurons, incorporated into proteins, and carried down the axons to the terminal buttons. Later, the brain is sliced, the sections are mounted on glass slides and coated with a photographic emulsion, and after a period of time the emulsion is developed. The horseradish peroxidase technique reveals the place *from which* inputs to a particular structure come. HRP is injected into the structure, where it is taken up by terminal buttons and carried back to the cell bodies. Later, a special stain shows their whereabouts. ▲

BASIC FEATURES OF THE NERVOUS SYSTEM

The nervous system consists of the brain and spinal cord, which make up the **central nervous system** (CNS), and the cranial nerves, spinal nerves, and peripheral ganglia, which constitute the **peripheral nervous system** (PNS). The CNS is encased in bone: The brain is covered by the skull, and the spinal cord is encased by the vertebral column.

central nervous system (CNS)

peripheral nervous system

Figure 3.8 illustrates the relation of the brain and spinal cord to the head and neck of a human. Do not be concerned now with unfamiliar labels on the figure; these structures will be described later. (See ***Figure 3.8.***) The brain is a large mass of neurons, glia, and other supporting cells. It is the most protected organ of the body, encased in a tough, bony skull and floating in a pool of liquid.

Two fundamental features of the nervous system are the meninges and the ventricular system, which are described in the following subsections.

Meninges

The entire nervous system—brain, spinal cord, cranial and spinal nerves, and autonomic ganglia—is covered by tough connective tissue. The protective sheaths around the brain and spinal cord are referred to as the **meninges** (singular: *meninx*). The meninges consist of three layers, which are shown in Figure 3.9. The outer layer is thick, tough, and flexible but unstretchable; its name, **dura mater,** means "hard mother." The middle layer of the meninges, the **arachnoid membrane,** gets its name from its weblike appearance (*arakhne* means "spider"). The arachnoid membrane is soft and spongy and lies beneath the dura mater. Closely attached to the brain and spinal cord, and following every surface convolution, is the **pia mater** ("pious mother"). The smaller surface blood vessels of the brain and spinal cord are contained

meninges

dura mater

arachnoid membrane

pia mater

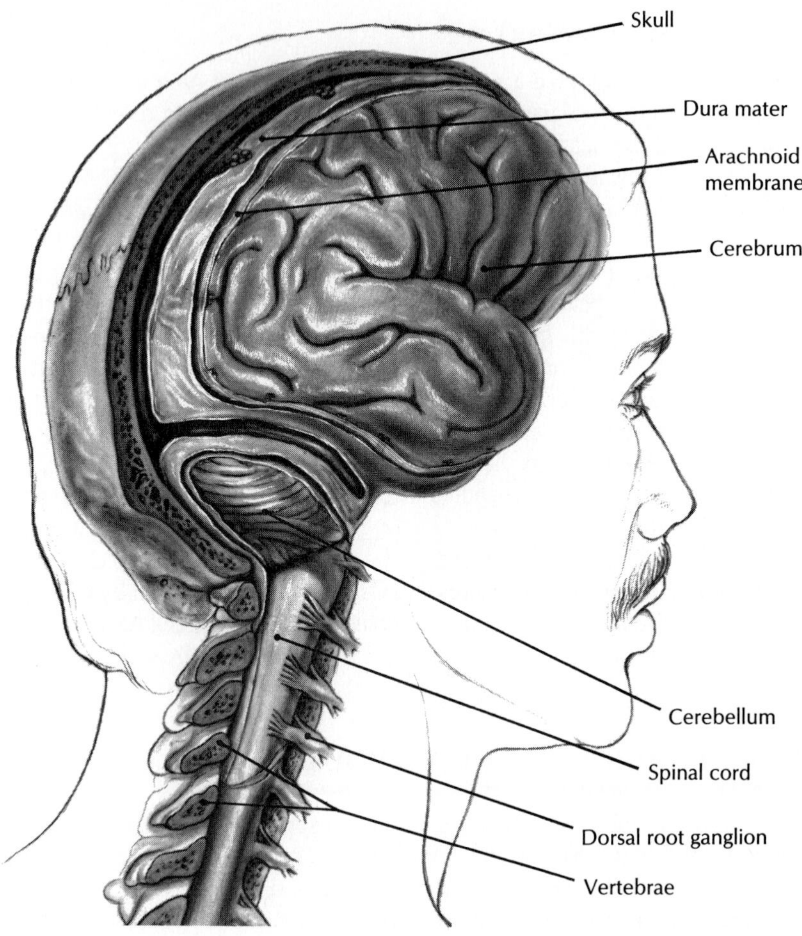

FIGURE 3.8

The relation of the brain and spinal cord to the head and neck.

subarachnoid space
cerebrospinal fluid (CSF)

within this layer. Between the pia mater and arachnoid membrane is a gap called the **subarachnoid space.** This space is filled with a liquid called **cerebrospinal fluid (CSF).** (See ***Figure 3.9.***)

The peripheral nervous system is covered with two layers of meninges. The middle layer (arachnoid membrane), with its associated pool of CSF, covers only the brain and spinal cord. Outside the CNS the outer and inner layers (dura mater and pia mater) fuse and form a sheath that covers the spinal and cranial nerves and the autonomic ganglia.

The Ventricular System

The brain is very soft and jellylike. The considerable weight of a human brain, along with its delicate construction, necessitates that it be protected from shock. A human brain cannot even support its own weight well; it is difficult to remove and handle a fresh brain from a recently deceased human without damaging it.

Fortunately, the intact brain within a living human is well protected. It floats in a bath of cerebrospinal fluid contained within the subarachnoid space. Because the brain is completely immersed in liquid, its net weight is reduced from approximately 1400 g (grams) to approximately 80 g; thus, pressure on the base of the brain is considerably diminished. The CSF surrounding the brain and spinal cord also reduces the shock to the central nervous system that would be caused by sudden head movement.

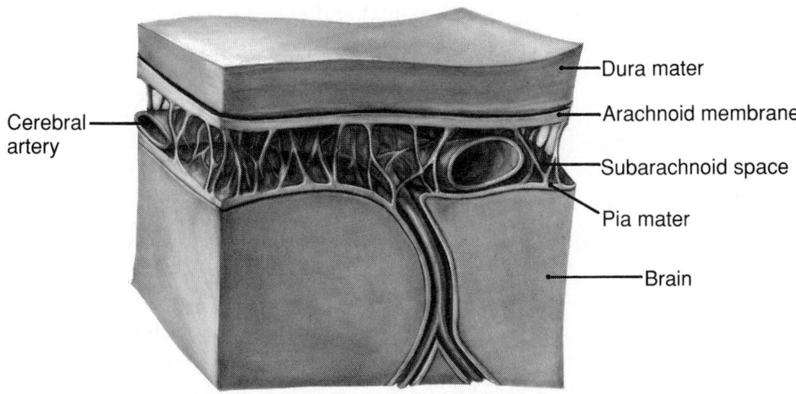

FIGURE 3.9

The meninges: dura mater, arachnoid membrane, and pia mater.

The brain contains a series of hollow, interconnected chambers that are filled with CSF. These chambers, known as **ventricles,** are connected with the subarachnoid space, and they are also continuous with the narrow, tubelike central canal of the spinal cord. (See ***Figure 3.10.***) The largest chamber is the paired set of **lateral ventricles.** The lateral ventricles are connected to the **third ventricle,** which is located in the middle of the brain. The **cerebral aqueduct,** a long tube, connects the third ventricle to

ventricle

lateral ventricle
third ventricle
cerebral aqueduct

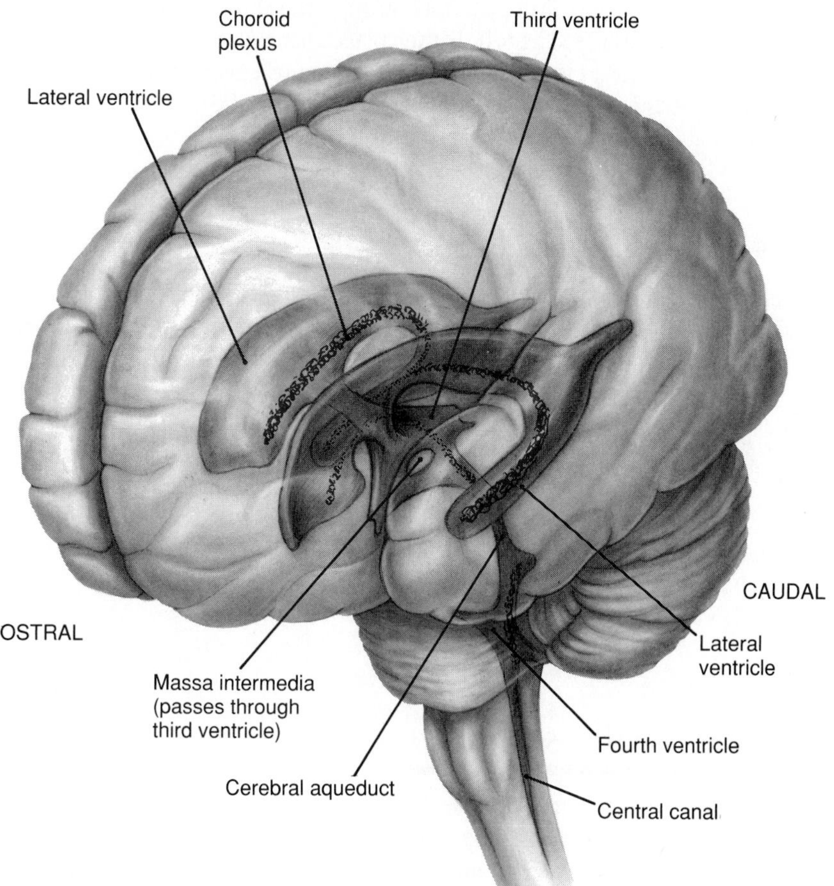

FIGURE 3.10

The ventricular system of the brain.

fourth ventricle

the **fourth ventricle,** which connects at its caudal end with the central canal of the spinal cord. The lateral ventricles constitute the first and second ventricles, but they are never referred to as such. (See ***Figure 3.10.***)

choroid plexus

Cerebrospinal fluid is extracted from the blood and resembles blood plasma in its composition. It is manufactured by a special structure called the **choroid plexus,** which protrudes into all four of the ventricles. (See ***Figure 3.10.***) Circulation of CSF begins in the lateral ventricles, flows into the third ventricle, then flows through the cerebral aqueduct into the fourth ventricle. From there, it flows through a set of openings into the subarachnoid space, which encases the entire central nervous system. Finally, the fluid is reabsorbed into the blood supply.

The total volume of CSF is approximately 125 milliliters (ml), and the half-life (the time it takes for half of the CSF present in the ventricular system to be replaced by fresh fluid) is about 3 hours. Therefore, several times this amount is produced by the choroid plexus each day.

hydrocephalus

Occasionally, the flow of CSF is interrupted at some point in its route of passage. For example, the cerebral aqueduct may be blocked by a tumor. This occlusion causes the pressure within the ventricles to increase, because the choroid plexus continues to produce CSF. The walls of the ventricles then expand and produce a condition known as **hydrocephalus** (literally, "water head"). If the obstruction remains, and if nothing is done to relieve the increased intracerebral pressure, blood vessels will be occluded, and permanent—perhaps fatal—brain damage will occur. Fortunately, a surgeon can usually operate on the person, drilling a hole through the skull and inserting a plastic tube into one of the ventricles. The tube is then placed beneath the skin and connected to a pressure relief valve that is implanted in the abdominal cavity. When the pressure in the ventricles becomes excessive, the valve permits the CSF to escape into the abdomen, where it is eventually reabsorbed into the blood supply.

▶*INTERIM SUMMARY*◀

The central nervous system consists of the brain and spinal cord, and the peripheral nervous system consists of the spinal and cranial nerves and the peripheral ganglia. The CNS is covered with the meninges: dura mater, arachnoid membrane, and pia mater. The space under the arachnoid membrane is filled with cerebrospinal fluid, in which the brain floats. The PNS is covered with only the dura mater and pia mater. Cerebrospinal fluid is produced in the choroid plexus of the lateral, third, and fourth ventricles. It flows from the two lateral ventricles into the third ventricle, through the cerebral aqueduct into the fourth ventricle, then into the subarachnoid space, and finally back into the blood supply. If the flow of CSF is blocked by a tumor or other obstruction, the result is hydrocephalus: enlargement of the ventricles and subsequent brain damage. ▲

THE CENTRAL NERVOUS SYSTEM

Although the brain is exceedingly complicated, an understanding of the basic features of brain development makes it easier to learn and remember the location of the most important structures. With that end in mind, I introduce these features here in the context of development of the central nervous system.

FIGURE 3.11

A cross section through the nervous system early in its development. Radially oriented glial cells help guide the migration of newly formed neurons. (Adapted from Bloom, F.E., and Lazerson, A. *Brain, Mind, and Behavior,* 2nd ed. New York: W.H. Freeman, 1988.)

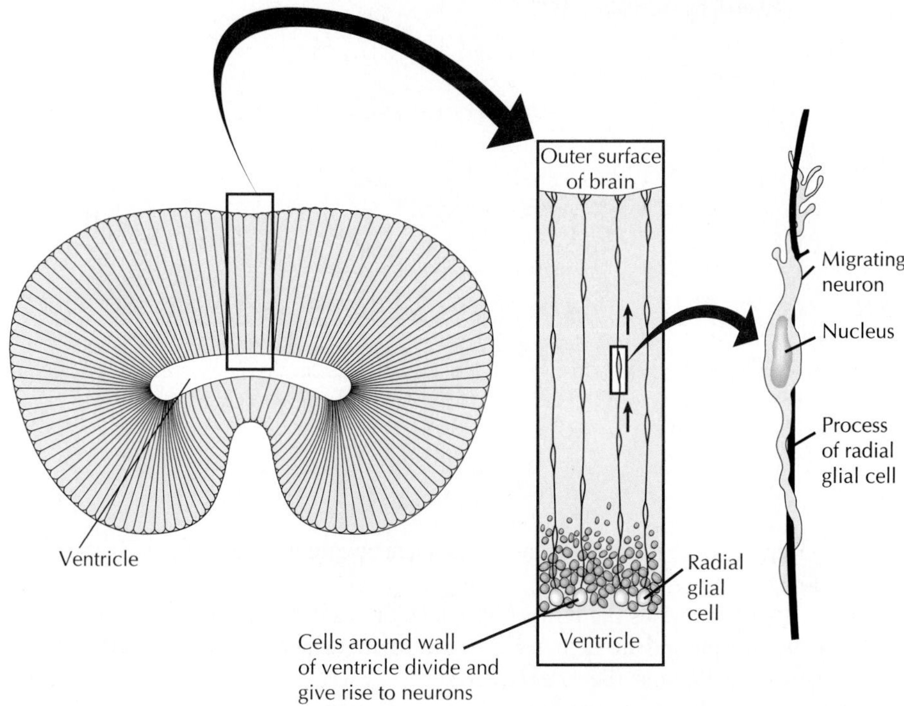

Development of the Central Nervous System

The central nervous system begins its existence early in embryonic life as a hollow tube, and it maintains this basic shape even after it is fully developed. During development, parts of the tube elongate, pockets and folds form, and the tissue around the tube becomes thicker. The cells that give rise to neurons are found on the inner surface of the tube. These cells divide and produce neurons, which then migrate in a radial direction, away from the center. Their final location is guided by both physical and chemical factors. Physical guidance is provided by radially oriented glial cells; the newly born neurons migrate along the processes of these cells. Chemical guidance attracts particular types of neurons to particular locations, where they come to rest. (See ***Figure 3.11.***)

Early in development the central nervous system contains three interconnected chambers. These chambers become ventricles, and the tissue that surround them become the three major parts of the brain: the forebrain, the midbrain, and the hindbrain. (See ***Figure 3.12a.***) Later, the rostral chamber divides into three separate chambers, which become the two lateral ventricles and the third ventricle. The region around the lateral ventricles becomes the telencephalon ("end brain"), and the region around the third ventricle becomes the diencephalon ("interbrain"). (See ***Figure 3.12b.***) In its final form the chamber inside the midbrain (mesencephalon) becomes narrow, forming the cerebral aqueduct, and two structures develop in the hindbrain:

FIGURE 3.12

An outline of brain development, showing its relation to the ventricles. Parts (a) and (b) are horizontal sections through the developing brain; part (c) is a side view. (a) Early development. (b) Mid development. (c) Late development, near time of birth. (Adapted from Gardner, E. *Fundamentals of Neurology,* 6th ed. Philadelphia: Saunders, 1975.)

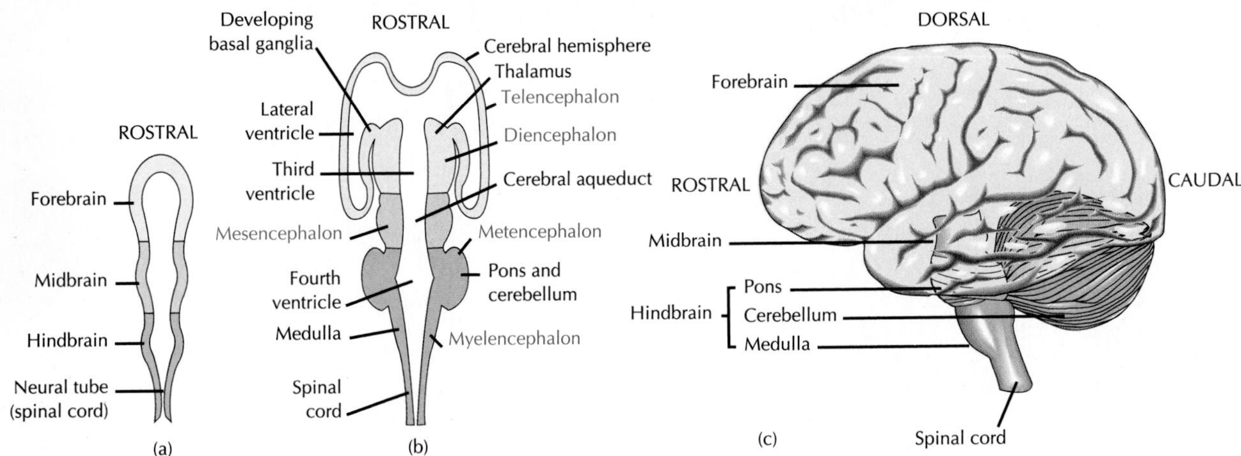

the metencephalon ("afterbrain") and the myelencephalon ("marrowbrain"). (See ***Figure 3.12c.***)

Table 3.1 summarizes the terms I have introduced here and mentions some of the major structures found in each part of the brain, which will be described in the remainder of the chapter. (See ***Table 3.1.***)

Once neurons have migrated to their final locations, they begin forming connections with other cells. They grow dendrites, which receive the terminal buttons from the axons of other neurons, and they grow axons of their own. Like neural migration, axonal growth is guided by physical and chemical factors. Once the growing ends of the axons reach their targets, they form numerous branches. Each of these branches finds a vacant place on the membrane of the appropriate type of postsynaptic cell,

▲ TABLE 3.1 ▲

Anatomical Subdivisions of the Brain

Major Division	*Ventricle*	*Subdivision*	*Principal Structures*
Forebrain	Lateral	Telencephalon	Cerebral cortex Basal ganglia Limbic system
	Third	Diencephalon	Thalamus Hypothalamus
Midbrain	Cerebral aqueduct	Mesencephalon	Tectum Tegmentum
Hindbrain	Fourth	Metencephalon	Cerebellum Pons
		Myelencephalon	Medulla oblongata

grows a terminal button, and establishes a synaptic connection. (Apparently, each type of cell secretes a particular chemical, which attracts a particular type of axon.) Of course, the establishment of a synaptic connection also requires efforts on the part of the postsynaptic cell; this cell must contribute its parts of the synapse, including the postsynaptic receptors. The chemical signals that the cells exchange in order to tell each other to establish these connections are not yet known.

The layer of cells surrounding the neural tube gives rise to many more neurons than are needed. In fact, the neurons that are produced must compete in order to survive. The axons of approximately 50 percent of these neurons do not find vacant postsynaptic cells of the right type to form synaptic connections with — so they die. This phenomenon, too, involves a chemical signal; when a presynaptic neuron establishes synaptic connections, it receives a signal from the postsynaptic cell that permits it to survive. Those that come too late do not find any available space and thus do not receive this life-sustaining signal. This scheme may seem unnecessarily complex, but apparently the evolutionary process found that the safest strategy was to produce too many neurons and let them fight to establish synaptic connections rather than try to produce exactly the right number of each type of neuron.

The subsections that follow describe in detail the three major parts of the brain and the spinal cord.

The Forebrain

As we saw, the **forebrain** surrounds the rostral end of the neural tube. Its two major components are the telencephalon and diencephalon. These features are described in detail below.

forebrain

TELENCEPHALON

The **telencephalon** includes most of the two symmetrical cerebral hemispheres that comprise the cerebrum. The cerebral hemispheres are covered by the cerebral cortex and contain the basal ganglia and the limbic system.

telencephalon

Cerebral Cortex. *Cortex* means "bark," and the **cerebral cortex** surrounds the cerebral hemispheres like the bark of a tree. In humans the cerebral cortex is greatly convoluted. These convolutions — consisting of **sulci** (singular: *sulcus;* small grooves), **fissures** (large grooves), and **gyri** (singular: *gyrus;* bulges between adjacent sulci or fissures) — greatly enlarge the surface area of the cortex, compared with a smooth brain of the same size. In fact, two-thirds of the surface of the cortex is hidden in the grooves; thus, the presence of gyri and sulci triples the area of the cerebral cortex. The total surface area is approximately 2.5 ft^2, and the thickness is approximately 3 mm. The cerebral cortex consists mostly of glia and the cell bodies, dendrites, and interconnecting axons of neurons. Because cells predominate, giving the cerebral cortex a grayish brown appearance, it is referred to as *gray matter.* (See ***Figure 3.13.***) Beneath the cerebral cortex run millions of axons that connect the neurons of the cerebral cortex with those located elsewhere in the brain. The large concentration of myelin gives this tissue an opaque white appearance — hence the term *white matter.*

cerebral cortex

sulcus
fissure
gyrus

The surface of the cerebral hemispheres is divided into four lobes, named after the bones of the skull that overlie them. The **frontal, parietal, temporal,** and **occipital lobes** are visible on the lateral surface and are shown in Figure 3.14. The **central sulcus** divides the frontal lobe from the parietal lobe, and the **lateral fissure** divides the temporal lobe from the overlying frontal and parietal lobes. (See ***Figure 3.14.***)

frontal lobe
temporal lobe
parietal lobe
occipital lobe
central sulcus
lateral fissure

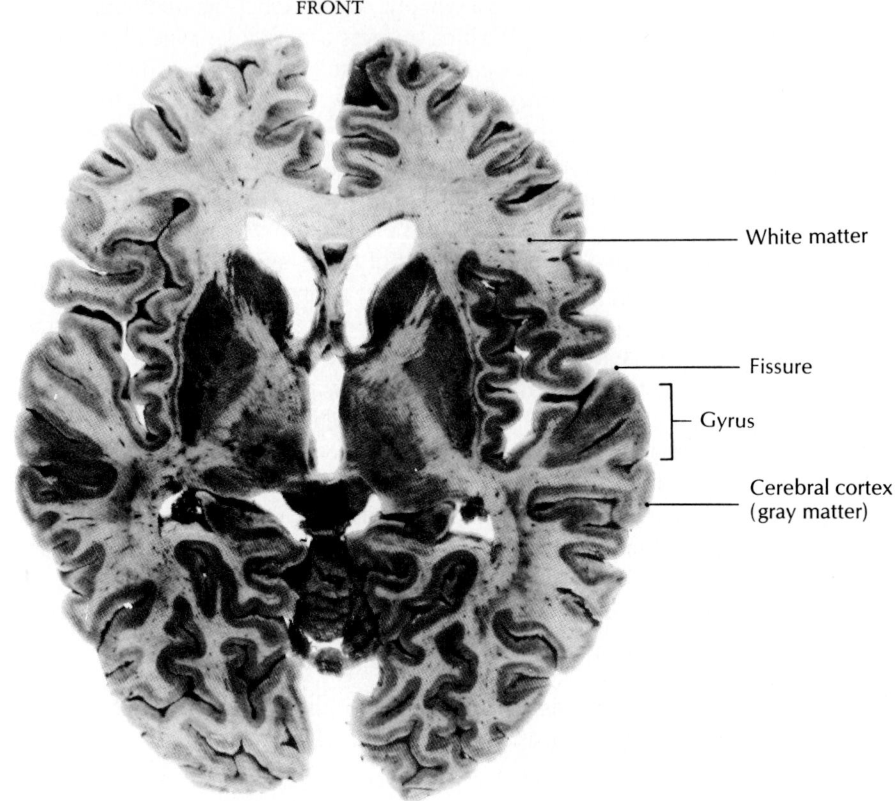

FIGURE 3.13

A photograph of a slice of a human brain showing fissures and gyri and the layer of cerebral cortex that follows these convolutions. (Photograph from *Structure of the Human Brain: A Photographic Atlas,* Second Edition, by Stephen J. DeArmond, Madeline M. Fusco, and Maynard M. Dewey. Copyright © 1976 by Oxford University Press, Inc. Reprinted by permission.)

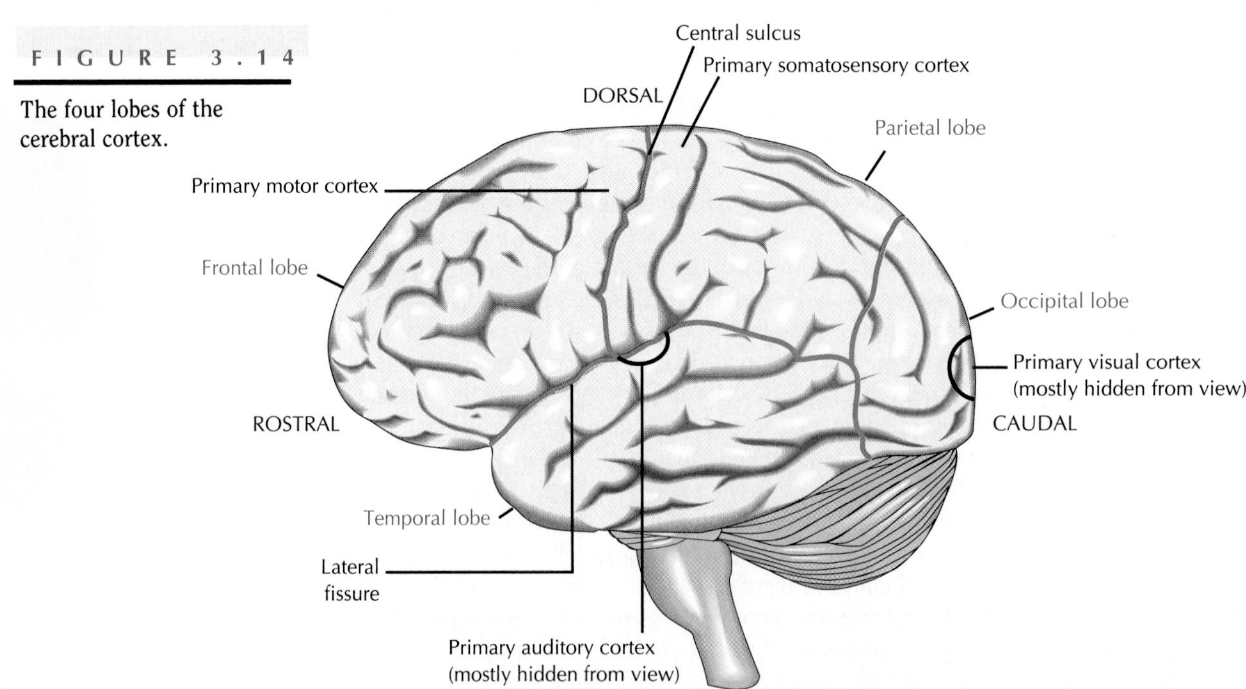

FIGURE 3.14

The four lobes of the cerebral cortex.

FIGURE 3.15

A midsagittal view of the brain and part of the spinal cord.

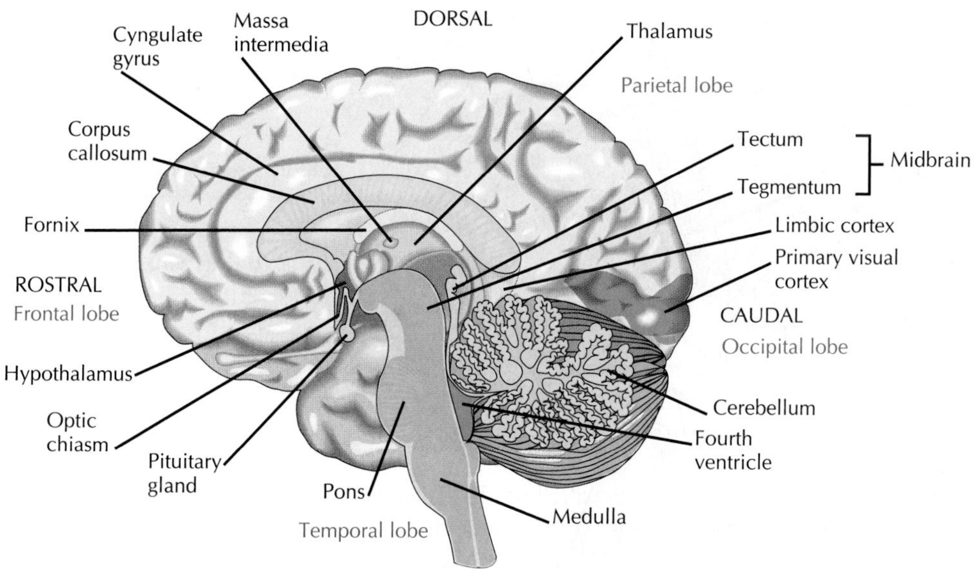

Figure 3.15 shows a *midsagittal* view of the brain. The brain (and part of the spinal cord) has been sliced down the middle, dividing it into its two symmetrical halves. The left half has been removed, so we see the inner surface of the right half. The cerebral cortex that covers most of the surface of the cerebral hemispheres is called the **neocortex** ("new" cortex, because it is of relatively recent evolutionary origin). Another form of cerebral cortex, the **limbic cortex,** is located around the edge of the cerebral hemispheres (*limbus* means "border"). The **cingulate gyrus,** an important region of the limbic cortex, can be seen in this figure. (See ***Figure 3.15.***)

neocortex
limbic cortex
cingulate gyrus

Figure 3.15 also shows the **corpus callosum,** which is the largest **commissure** (cross-hemisphere connection) in the brain. The corpus callosum consists of axons that connect the cortex of the two cerebral hemispheres. The axons unite geographically similar regions of the two sides of the brain. In order to slice the brain into its two symmetrical halves, one must cut through the middle of the corpus callosum. (Recall that I described the split-brain operation in Chapter 1, in which the corpus callosum is severed.) (See ***Figure 3.15.***)

corpus callosum
commissure

The various regions of the cerebral cortex have different functions. The frontal lobes are involved in the planning, execution, and control of movements. The **primary motor cortex,** immediately rostral to the central sulcus, contains neurons that participate in the control of movement. (See ***Figure 3.16.***) If an experimenter places a wire on the surface of the primary motor cortex and stimulates the neurons there with a weak electrical shock, the current will cause movement of a particular part of the body. Moving the wire to a different spot causes a different part of the body to move. Because the cerebral hemispheres are connected with the *opposite* sides of the body, stimulation of the right primary motor cortex moves parts of the left side of the body, and stimulation of the left cortex moves the right side.

primary motor cortex

The posterior lobes of the brain (the parietal, temporal, and occipital lobes) are involved in perception. The **primary somatosensory cortex** lies immediately caudal to the central sulcus, right behind the primary motor cortex. This region of cerebral

primary somatosensory cortex

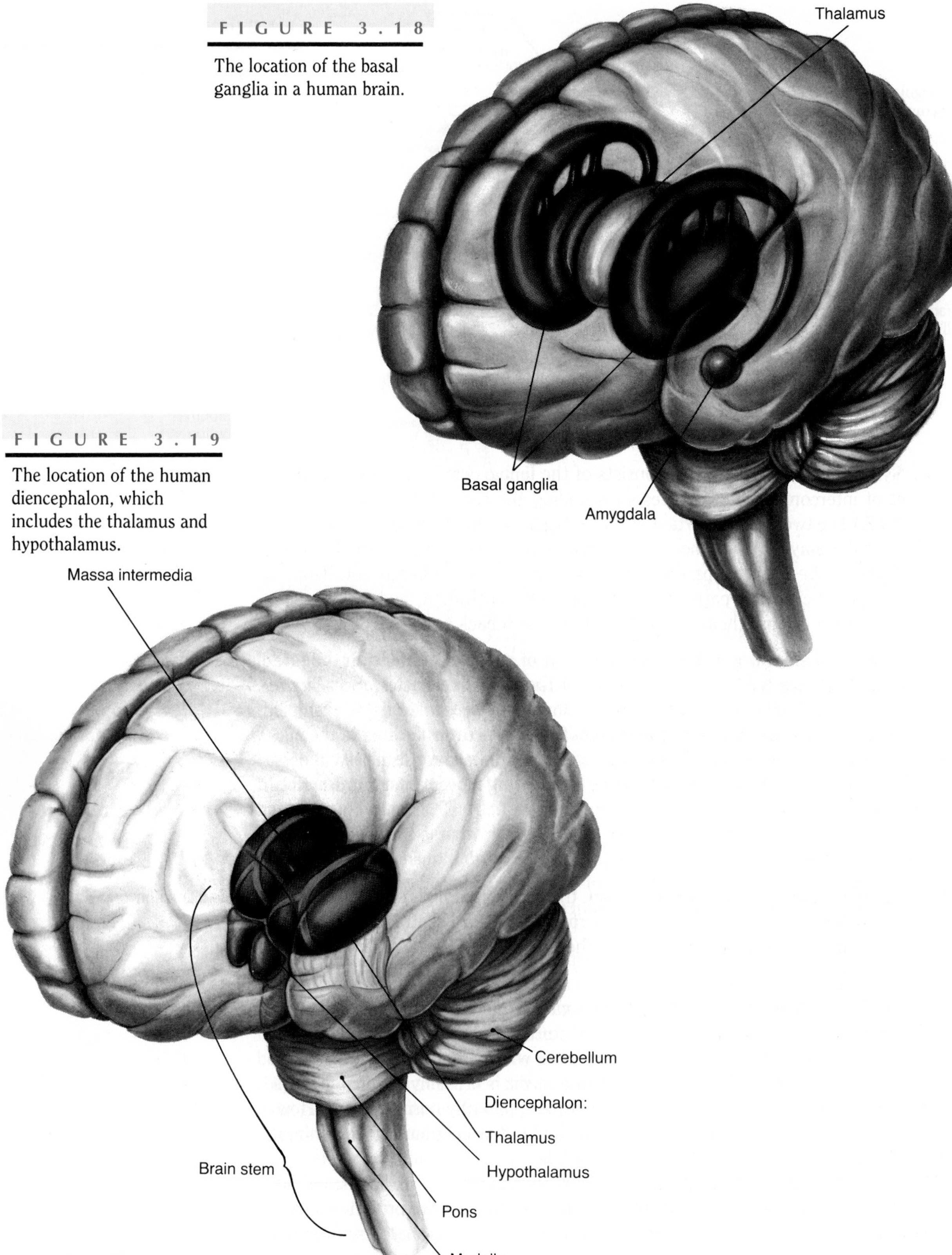

FIGURE 3.18

The location of the basal ganglia in a human brain.

FIGURE 3.19

The location of the human diencephalon, which includes the thalamus and hypothalamus.

bodies located in one region of the brain and synapse on neurons located within another region (that is, they *project to* these regions).

The thalamus is divided into a number of nuclei, some of which receive sensory information that comes from the sensory systems. The neurons in these nuclei then relay the sensory information to specific sensory projection areas of the cerebral cortex. For example, the **lateral geniculate nucleus** projects to the primary visual cortex, and the **medial geniculate nucleus** projects to the primary auditory cortex. Other thalamic nuclei project to specific regions of the cerebral cortex, but they do not relay primary sensory information. For example, the **ventrolateral nucleus** receives information from the cerebellum and projects it to the primary motor cortex.

lateral geniculate nucleus
medial geniculate nucleus
ventrolateral nucleus

Hypothalamus. The **hypothalamus** lies at the base of the brain, under the thalamus. Although it is a relatively small structure, it is an important one. It controls the autonomic nervous system and the endocrine system and organizes behaviors related to survival of the species — the so-called *four Fs:* fighting, feeding, fleeing, and mating.

hypothalamus

The hypothalamus is situated on both sides of the inferior portion of the third ventricle. As its name implies, it is located beneath the thalamus (notice the location of the massa intermedia). (See ***Figure 3.20.***) The hypothalamus is a very complex struc-

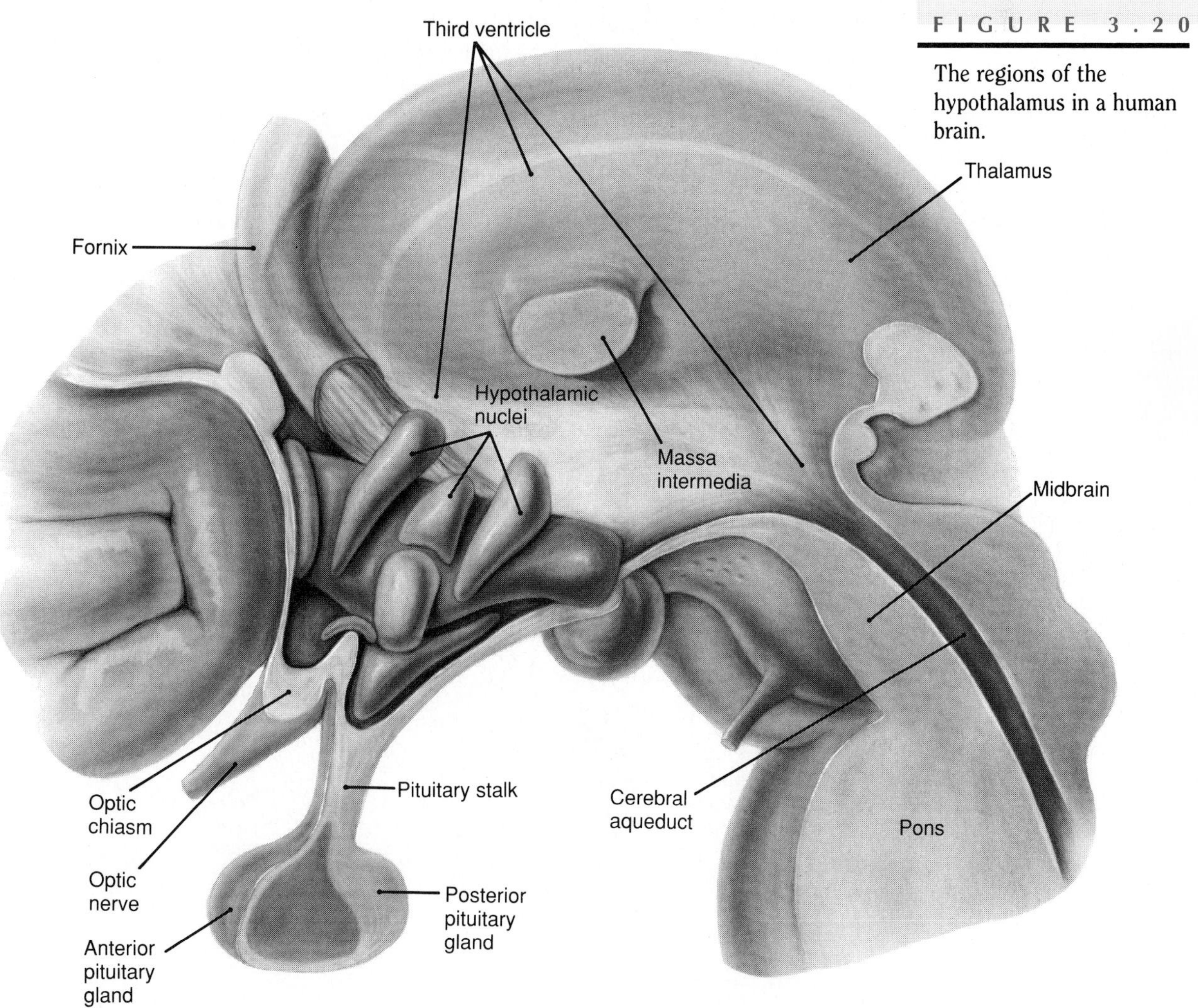

FIGURE 3.20

The regions of the hypothalamus in a human brain.

ture, containing many nuclei and fiber tracts. Note that the pituitary gland is attached to the base of the hypothalamus via the **pituitary stalk.** Just in front of the pituitary stalk is the **optic chiasm,** the place where half of the axons in the optic nerves (from the eyes) cross from one side of the brain to the other. (See ***Figure 3.20.***) The role of the hypothalamus in the control of the four Fs (and other behaviors, such as drinking and sleeping) will be considered in several chapters later in this book.

pituitary stalk
optic chiasm

Much of the endocrine system is controlled by hormones produced by cells in the hypothalamus. A special system of blood vessels directly connects the hypothalamus with the **anterior pituitary gland.** (See ***Figure 3.21.***) The hypothalamic hormones are secreted by specialized neurons called **neurosecretory cells,** located near the base of the pituitary stalk. These hormones stimulate the anterior pituitary gland to secrete its hormones. For example, *gonadotropin-releasing hormone* causes the anterior pituitary gland to secrete the *gonadotropic hormones,* which play a role in reproductive physiology and behavior.

anterior pituitary gland
neurosecretory cell

Most of the hormones secreted by the anterior pituitary gland control other endocrine glands. Because of this function, the anterior pituitary gland has been called the body's "master gland." For example, the gonadotropic hormones stimulate the gonads (ovaries and testes) to release male or female sex hormones. These hormones have effects on cells throughout the body, including some in the brain. Two other anterior pituitary hormones, prolactin and somatotropic hormone (growth hormone), do not control other glands but act as the final messenger. The behavioral effects of some of the anterior pituitary hormones are discussed in later chapters.

posterior pituitary gland

The hypothalamus also produces the hormones of the **posterior pituitary gland** and controls their secretion. These hormones include oxytocin, which stimulates ejection of milk and uterine contractions at the time of childbirth, and vasopressin, which regulates urine output by the kidneys. They are produced by neurons in the

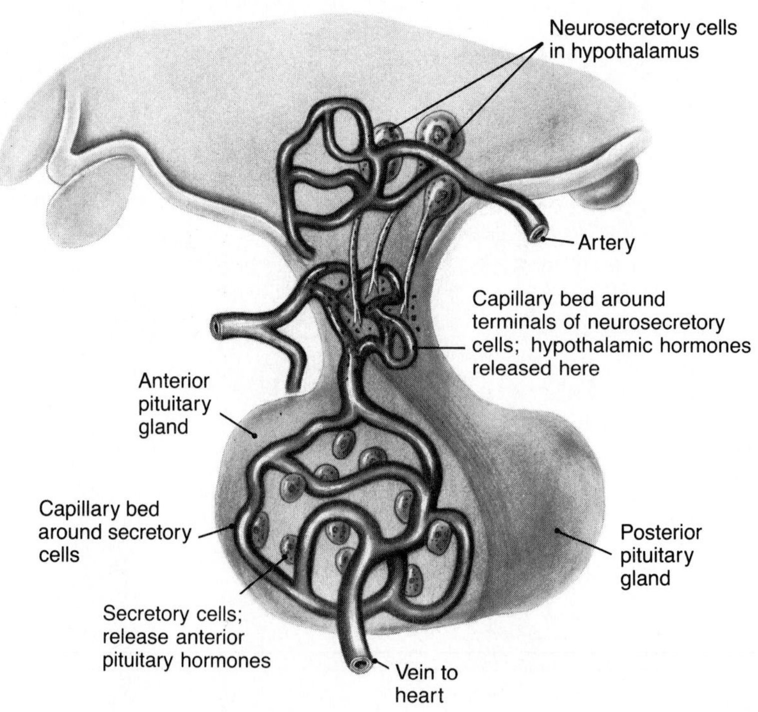

FIGURE 3.21

The pituitary gland. Hormones released by the neurosecretory cells in the hypothalamus enter capillaries and are conveyed to the anterior pituitary gland, where they control its secretion of hormones. The hormones of the posterior pituitary gland are produced in the hypothalamus and transported there in vesicles through axons.

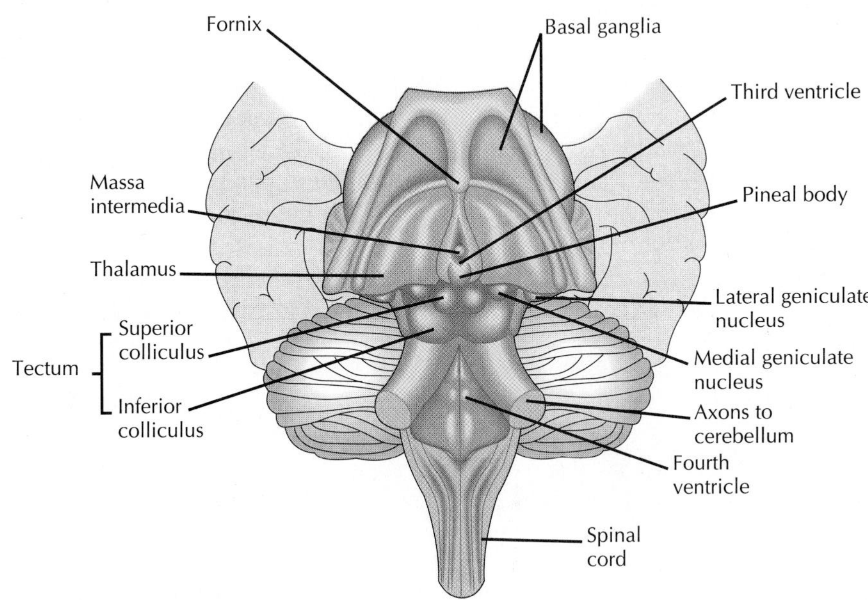

FIGURE 3.22

A dorsal view of the human brain stem.

hypothalamus whose axons travel down the pituitary stalk and terminate in the posterior pituitary gland. The hormones are carried in vesicles through the axoplasm of these neurons and collect in the terminal buttons in the posterior pituitary gland. When these axons fire, the hormone contained within their terminal buttons is released—exactly like a transmitter substance—and enters the circulatory system.

The Midbrain

The **midbrain** (also called the **mesencephalon**) surrounds the cerebral aqueduct and consists of two major parts: the tectum and the tegmentum.

midbrain
mesencephalon

TECTUM

The **tectum** ("roof") is located in the dorsal portion of the mesencephalon. Its principal structures are the **superior colliculi** and **inferior colliculi,** which appear as four bumps on the surface of the **brain stem.** Figure 3.22 illustrates a dorsal view of the brain stem, with the overlying cerebrum and cerebellum removed. (The brain stem includes the diencephalon, midbrain, and hindbrain, and it is so called because it looks just like that.) (See ***Figure 3.22.***) The inferior colliculi are a part of the auditory system. The superior colliculi are part of the visual system. In mammals they are primarily involved in visual reflexes and reactions to moving stimuli.

tectum
superior colliculus
inferior colliculus
brain stem

TEGMENTUM

The **tegmentum** ("covering") consists of the portion of the mesencephalon beneath the tectum. It includes the rostral end of the reticular formation, several nuclei controlling eye movements, the periaqueductal gray matter, the red nucleus, the substantia nigra, and the ventral tegmental area. (See ***Figure 3.23.***)

tegmentum

The **reticular formation** is a large structure consisting of many nuclei (over ninety in all). It is also characterized by a diffuse, interconnected network of neurons with complex dendritic and axonal processes. (Indeed, *reticulum* means "little net"; early

reticular formation

FIGURE 3.23

A cross section through the human tegmentum.

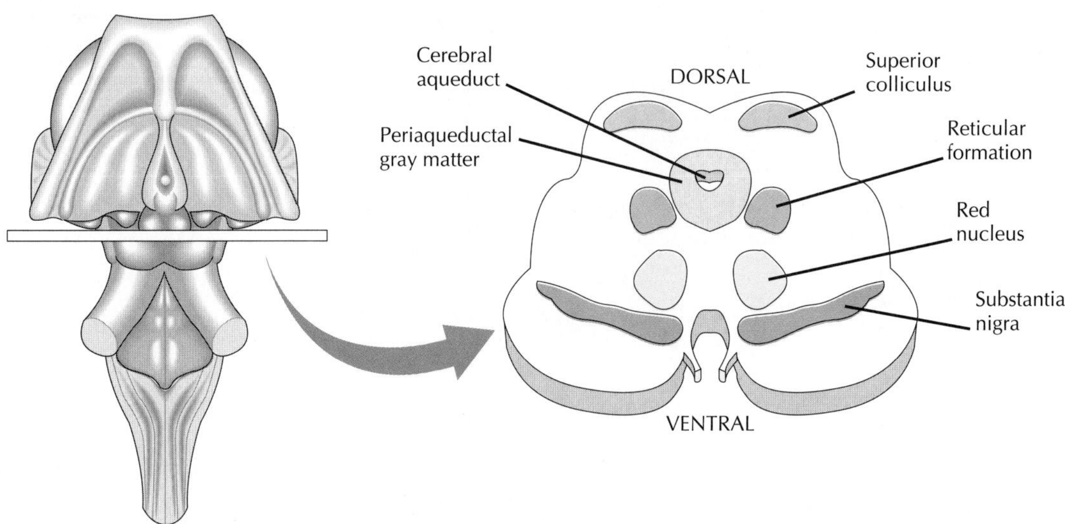

anatomists were struck by the netlike appearance of the reticular formation.) The reticular formation occupies the core of the brain stem, from the lower border of the medulla to the upper border of the midbrain. (See ***Figure 3.23.***) The reticular formation receives sensory information by means of various pathways and projects axons to the cerebral cortex, thalamus, and spinal cord. It plays a role in sleep and arousal, attention, muscle tonus, movement, and various vital reflexes. Some of these functions will be described more fully in later chapters.

periaqueductal gray matter

The **periaqueductal gray matter** is so called because it consists mostly of cell bodies of neurons ("gray matter," as contrasted with the "white matter" of axon bundles) that immediately surround the cerebral aqueduct as it travels from the third to the fourth ventricle. (See ***Figure 3.23.***) The periaqueductal gray matter contains neural circuits that control sequences of movements that constitute species-typical behaviors, such as fighting and mating. As we will see in Chapter 6, opiates such as morphine decrease an organism's sensitivity to pain by stimulating neurons located in this region.

red nucleus
substantia nigra

The **red nucleus** and **substantia nigra** ("black substance") are important components of the motor system. (See ***Figure 3.23.***) A bundle of axons that arises from the red nucleus constitutes one of the two major fiber systems that bring motor information from the brain to the spinal cord. The substantia nigra contains neurons that project to parts of the basal ganglia. Degeneration of these neurons is what causes Parkinson's disease.

The Hindbrain

hindbrain

The **hindbrain,** which surrounds the fourth ventricle, consists of two major divisions: the metencephalon and the myelencephalon. These divisions are described below.

METENCEPHALON

metencephalon

The **metencephalon** ("behind-brain") consists of two structures: the pons and the cerebellum. Each structure is described in detail in the following subsections.

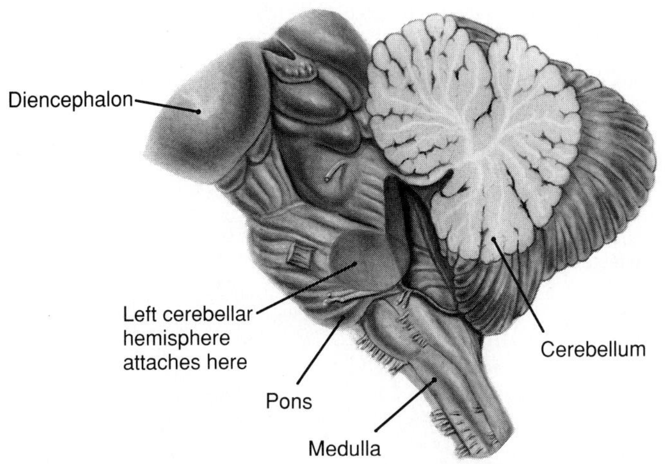

FIGURE 3.24

The attachment of the cerebellum to the human brain stem. Only the right cerebellar hemisphere is shown; the left has been removed to show its site of attachment to the pons.

Cerebellum. The **cerebellum** ("little brain") resembles a miniature version of the cerebrum. It is covered by **cerebellar cortex** and has a set of **deep cerebellar nuclei** that project to its cortex and receive projections from it, just as the thalamic nuclei connect with the cerebral cortex. It attaches to the lateral and dorsal surfaces of the pons. (See ***Figure 3.24.***)

cerebellum
cerebellar cortex
deep cerebellar nuclei

Damage to the cerebellum impairs standing, walking, or performance of coordinated movements. (A virtuoso pianist or other performing musician owes much to his or her cerebellum.) The cerebellum receives visual, auditory, vestibular, and somatosensory information, and it also receives information about individual muscular movements being directed by the brain. The cerebellum integrates this information and modifies the motor outflow, exerting a coordinating and smoothing effect on the movements. Cerebellar damage results in jerky, poorly coordinated, exaggerated movements; extensive cerebellar damage makes it impossible even to stand.

Pons. The **pons,** a large bulge in the brain stem, lies between the mesencephalon and medulla oblongata, immediately ventral to the cerebellum. (*Pons* means "bridge," but it does not really look like one. Refer to ***Figure 3.15.***) The pons contains, in its core, a portion of the reticular formation, including some nuclei that appear to be important in sleep and arousal.

pons

MYELENCEPHALON

myelencephalon

The **myelencephalon** contains one major structure, the **medulla oblongata** ("oblong marrow"), usually just called the *medulla.* This structure constitutes the most caudal portion of the brain stem; its lower border is the rostral end of the spinal cord. (Refer to ***Figure 3.15.***) The medulla contains part of the reticular formation, including nuclei that control vital functions such as regulation of the cardiovascular system, respiration, and skeletal muscle tonus. It also contains nuclei that relay somatosensory information from the spinal cord to the thalamus.

medulla oblongata

Now let us turn to the other major part of the CNS, the spinal cord.

The Spinal Cord

The **spinal cord** is a roughly cylindrical structure, approximately as thick as a person's little finger but considerably longer. The principal function of the spinal cord is to

spinal cord

FIGURE 3.25

The human spinal column, with details showing the anatomy of the vertebrae and the relation between the spinal cord and spinal column.

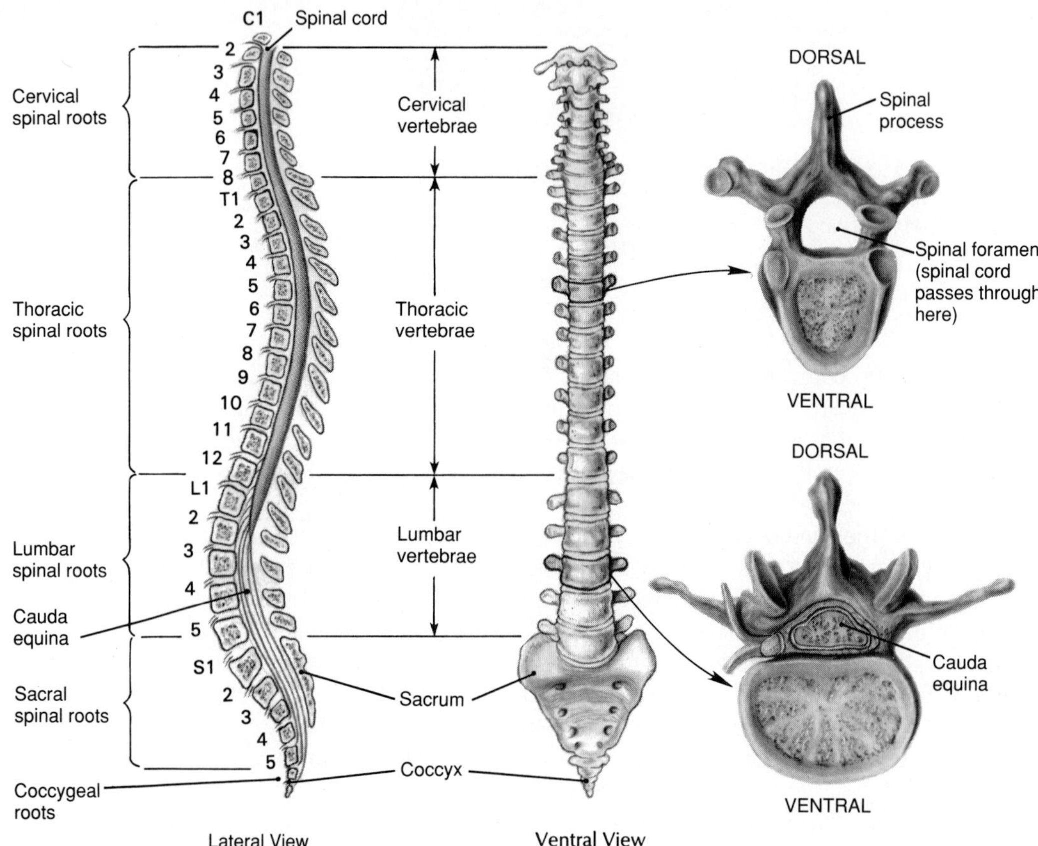

distribute motor fibers to the effector organs of the body (glands and muscles) and to collect somatosensory information to be passed on to the brain. The spinal cord also has a certain degree of autonomy from the brain; various reflexive control circuits are located there.

The spinal cord is protected by the vertebral column, which is composed of twenty-four individual vertebrae of the *cervical* (neck), *thoracic* (chest), and *lumbar* (lower back) regions, and the fused vertebrae making up the *sacral* and *coccygeal* portions of the column. The spinal cord passes through a hole in each of the vertebrae (the *spinal foramens*). Figure 3.25 illustrates the divisions and structures of the spinal cord and vertebral column. Note that the spinal cord is only about two-thirds as long as the vertebral column; the rest of the space is filled by a mass of **spinal roots** composing the **cauda equina** ("mare's tail"). (See ***Figure 3.25.***)

spinal root
cauda equina

Early in embryological development, the vertebral column and spinal cord are of the same length. As development progresses, the vertebral column grows faster than the spinal cord. This differential growth rate causes the spinal roots to be displaced downward; the most caudal roots travel the farthest before they emerge through openings between the vertebrae and thus compose the cauda equina. The *caudal block*

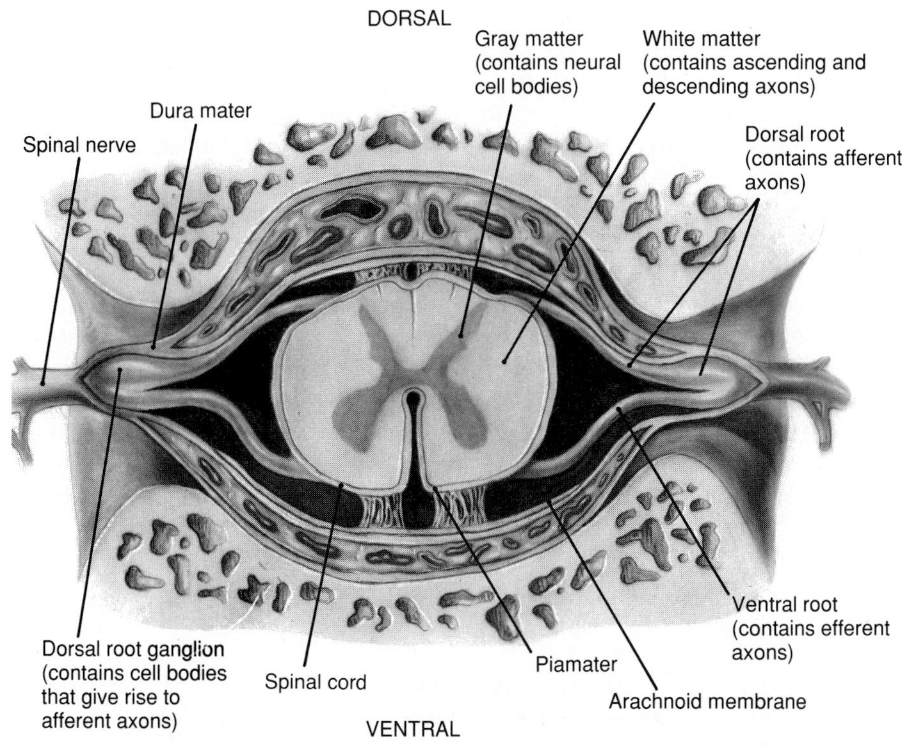

FIGURE 3.26

A cross section through a vertebra, showing the spinal cord, dorsal and ventral roots, and spinal nerves.

sometimes used in pelvic surgery or childbirth is produced by the injection of a local anesthetic into the CSF contained within the sac of dura mater surrounding the cauda equina. The drug blocks conduction in the axons of the cauda equina.

Small bundles of fibers emerge from the sides of the spinal cord, join together, and become the thirty-one paired sets of **dorsal roots** and **ventral roots.** The dorsal and ventral roots join as they leave the spinal foramens and become spinal nerves. Figure 3.26 illustrates a cross section of the spinal column taken between two adjacent vertebrae, showing the junction of the dorsal and ventral roots in the intervertebral foramens. (See ***Figure 3.26.***)

dorsal root
ventral root

The spinal cord, like the brain, consists of white matter and gray matter. Unlike the brain, it has white matter (consisting of ascending and descending bundles of myelinated axons) on the outside; its gray matter (mostly neural cell bodies and short, unmyelinated axons) is on the inside.

▶INTERIM SUMMARY◀

The brain consists of three major divisions, organized around the three chambers of tube that develops early in embryonic life: the forebrain, the midbrain, and the hindbrain. The development of the CNS is illustrated in Figure 3.12, and Table 3.1 outlines the major divisions and subdivisions.

The forebrain, which surrounds the lateral and third ventricles, consists of the telencephalon and diencephalon. The telencephalon contains the cerebral cortex, the limbic system, and the basal ganglia. The cerebral cortex is organized into the frontal, parietal, temporal, and occipital lobes. The central sulcus divides the frontal lobe, which deals specifically with movement and the planning of movement, from the other three lobes, which deal primarily with perceiving and learning. The limbic system, which includes the limbic cortex, the hippocampus, and the amygdala, is involved in emotion, motivation, and learning. The basal ganglia participate in the control of movement. The diencephalon consists of the thalamus, which directs information to and from the cerebral cortex, and the hypothalamus, which controls the endocrine system and modulates species-typical behaviors.

The midbrain, which surrounds the cerebral aqueduct, consists of the tectum and tegmentum. The tectum is involved in audition and the control of visual reflexes and reactions to moving stimuli. The tegmentum contains the reticular formation, which is important in sleep, arousal, and movement; the periaqueductal gray matter, which controls various species-typical behaviors; and the red nucleus and the substantia nigra, both parts of the motor system.

The hindbrain, which surrounds the fourth ventricle, contains the cerebellum, the pons, and the medulla. The cerebellum plays a very important role in integrating movements. The pons contains some nuclei that are important in sleep and arousal. The medulla oblongata is also involved in sleep and arousal; in addition, it plays a role in control of movement and in control of vital functions such as heart rate, breathing, and blood pressure.

The spinal cord distributes motor fibers to the effector organs and receives somatosensory information. The outer part of the spinal cord consists of white matter: axons conveying information up or down. In general, ascending pathways are dorsally located, and descending ones are ventrally located. The central gray matter contains cell bodies. ▲

THE PERIPHERAL NERVOUS SYSTEM

The brain and spinal cord communicate with the rest of the body via the cranial nerves and spinal nerves. These nerves are part of the peripheral nervous system, which conveys sensory information to the central nervous system and conveys messages from the central nervous system to the body's muscles and glands. This section discusses the spinal nerves, the cranial nerves, and the autonomic nervous system, a branch of the PNS involved in control of internal physiological functions.

Spinal Nerves

spinal nerve

The **spinal nerves** begin at the junction of the dorsal and ventral roots of the spinal cord. The nerves leave the vertebral column and travel, branching repeatedly as they go, to the muscles or sensory receptors they innervate. Branches of spinal nerves often follow blood vessels, especially those branches that innervate skeletal muscles. Figure 3.27 is a dorsal view of a human, showing a few branches of the spinal nerves. (See ***Figure 3.27.***)

Now let us consider the pathways by which sensory information enters the spinal cord and motor information leaves it. The cell bodies of all axons that bring sensory information into the brain and spinal cord are located outside the central nervous system. (The sole exception is the visual system; the retina of the eye is considered to be a part of the brain.) These incoming axons are referred to as **afferent axons** because they "bear toward" the CNS, bringing in their sensory information. The cell bodies that give rise to the axons that bring somatosensory information to the spinal cord reside in the **dorsal root ganglia,** rounded swellings of the dorsal root. (Refer to ***Figure 3.26.***) These neurons are of the unipolar type (described in Chapter 2). The axonal stalk divides close to the cell body, sending one limb into the spinal cord and the other limb out to the sensory organ. All of the axons in the dorsal root convey somatosensory information.

afferent axon

dorsal root ganglion

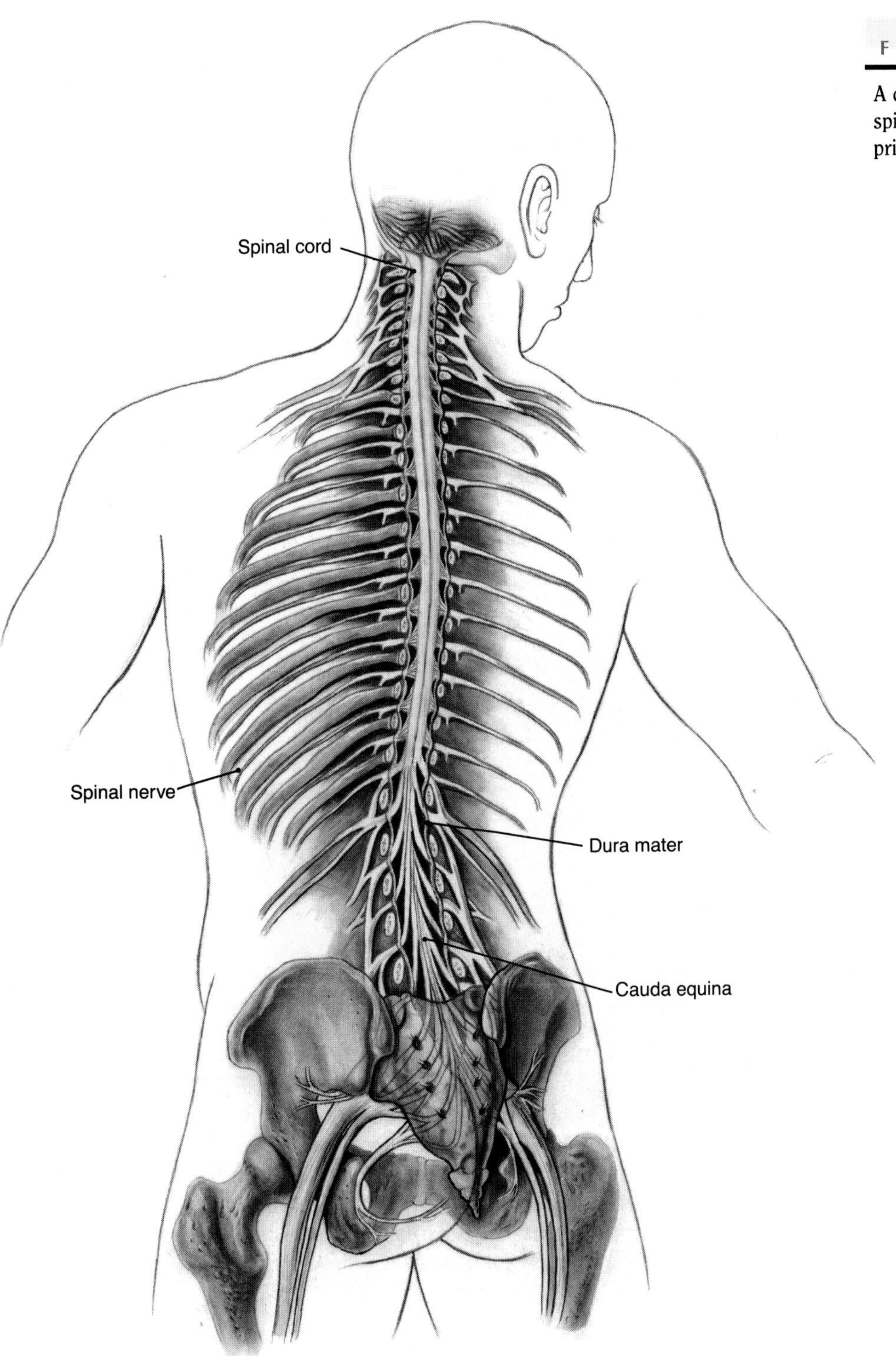

FIGURE 3.27

A dorsal view of the human spinal cord and some of the principal spinal nerves.

SUGGESTED READINGS

Diamond, M.C., Scheibel, A.B., and Elson, L.M. *The Human Brain Coloring Book.* New York: Barnes & Noble, 1985.

Gluhbegovic, N., and Williams, T.H. *The Human Brain: A Photographic Guide.* New York: Harper & Row, 1980.

Netter, F.H. *The Ciba Collection of Medical Illustrations. Vol. 1: Nervous System.* Summit, N.J.: Ciba Pharmaceutical Products Co., 1953.

NEW TERMS

afferent axon **p. 98**
amino acid autoradiography **p. 76**
amygdala **p. 89**
anterior **p. 72**
anterior pituitary gland **p. 92**
arachnoid membrane **p. 79**
association cortex **p. 88**
autonomic nervous system (ANS) **p. 101**
basal ganglia **p. 88**
brain stem **p. 93**
cauda equina **p. 96**
caudal **p. 72**
central nervous system (CNS) **p. 79**
central sulcus **p. 85**
cerebellar cortex **p. 95**
cerebellum **p. 95**
cerebral aqueduct **p. 81**
cerebral cortex **p. 85**
cerebrospinal fluid (CSF) **p. 80**
choroid plexus **p. 82**
cingulate gyrus **p. 87**
commissure **p. 87**
contralateral **p. 73**
corpus callosum **p. 87**
cranial nerve **p. 101**
cross section **p. 73**
deep cerebellar nuclei **p. 95**
diencephalon **p. 89**
dorsal **p. 72**
dorsal root **p. 97**
dorsal root ganglion **p. 98**
dura mater **p. 78**
efferent axon **p. 100**
fissure **p. 85**
forebrain **p. 85**
formalin **p. 75**
fourth ventricle **p. 82**
frontal lobe **p. 85**
frontal section **p. 73**
gyrus **p. 85**
hindbrain **p. 94**
hippocampus **p. 89**
horizontal section **p. 73**
horseradish peroxidase **p. 76**
hydrocephalus **p. 82**
hypothalamus **p. 91**
inferior colliculus **p. 93**
ipsilateral **p. 72**
lateral **p. 72**
lateral fissure **p. 85**
lateral geniculate nucleus **p. 91**
lateral ventricle **p. 81**
limbic cortex **p. 87**
limbic system **p. 89**
medial **p. 72**
medial geniculate nucleus **p. 91**
medulla oblongata **p. 95**
meninges **p. 78**
mesencephalon **p. 93**
metencephalon **p. 94**
microtome **p. 75**
midbrain **p. 93**
myelencephalon **p. 95**
neocortex **p. 87**
neuraxis **p. 72**
neurosecretory cell **p. 92**
nucleus **p. 75**
occipital lobe **p. 85**
olfactory bulb **p. 101**
optic chiasm **p. 92**
parasympathetic division **p. 102**
parietal lobe **p. 85**
periaqueductal gray matter **p. 94**
peripheral nervous system **p. 79**
pia mater **p. 79**
pituitary stalk **p. 92**
pons **p. 95**
posterior **p. 72**
posterior pituitary gland **p. 92**
postganglionic neuron **p. 102**
preganglionic neuron **p. 102**
primary auditory cortex **p. 88**
primary motor cortex **p. 87**
primary somatosensory cortex **p. 87**
primary visual cortex **p. 88**
projection fiber **p. 89**
red nucleus **p. 94**
reticular formation **p. 93**
rostral **p. 72**
sagittal section **p. 73**
somatic nervous system **p. 101**
spinal cord **p. 95**
spinal nerve **p. 98**
spinal root **p. 96**
subarachnoid space **p. 80**
substantia nigra **p. 94**
sulcus **p. 85**
superior colliculus **p. 93**
sympathetic chain **p. 102**
sympathetic division **p. 102**
sympathetic ganglion **p. 102**
tectum **p. 93**
tegmentum **p. 93**
telencephalon **p. 85**
temporal lobe **p. 85**
thalamus **p. 89**
third ventricle **p. 81**
vagus nerve **p. 101**
ventral **p. 72**
ventral root **p. 97**
ventricle **p. 81**
ventrolateral nucleus **p. 91**

4

Biochemistry of Behavior

CHAPTER OUTLINE

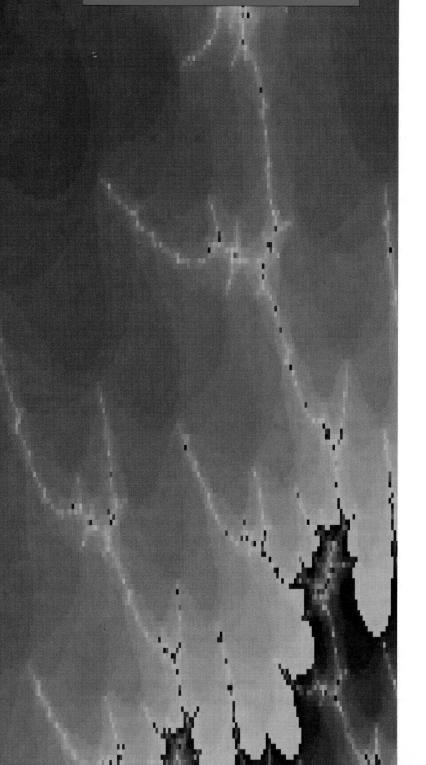

As you learned in Chapter 2, acetylcholine is destroyed by another enzyme, acetylcholinesterase (AChE). The formula for this conversion is shown below.

$$\text{acetylcholine} \xrightarrow{\text{AChE}} \text{choline} + \text{acetate}$$

nicotinic receptor
muscarinic receptor

There are at least two different types of ACh receptors, with different molecular shapes. These receptors were identified when investigators discovered that different drugs activated or inhibited them. One class is stimulated by nicotine (a poison found in tobacco leaves), the other by muscarine (a poison found in a species of mushroom). Consequently, they are referred to as **nicotinic receptors** and **muscarinic receptors,** respectively. Muscle fibers contain only nicotinic receptors, but both kinds of receptors are found in the central nervous system.

The Monoamines

monoamine
catecholamine

Epinephrine, norepinephrine, dopamine, and serotonin are four chemicals that belong to a family of compounds called **monoamines.** Because the molecular structures of these substances are similar, some drugs affect the activity of all of them, to some degree. The first three, epinephrine, norepinephrine, and dopamine, belong to a subclass of monoamines called **catecholamines.** (See ***Table 4.1.***) The subsections that follow describe in detail norepinephrine, dopamine, and serotonin.

NOREPINEPHRINE

norepinephrine
epinephrine

Because **norepinephrine** (NE), like ACh, is found in neurons in the autonomic nervous system, this neurotransmitter has received much experimental attention. I should note that *Adrenalin* and *epinephrine* are synonymous, as are *noradrenalin* and *norepinephrine.* **Epinephrine** is produced by the adrenal medulla, the central core of the adrenal glands, which are small endocrine glands located above the kidneys. It also serves as a transmitter substance in the brain, but it is of minor importance, compared with norepinephrine. *Ad renal* is Latin for "toward kidney." In Greek, one would say *epi nephron* ("upon the kidney")—hence the term *epinephrine.* Pharmacologists use the latter term, probably because the word *Adrenalin* was appropriated by a drug company as a proprietary name; therefore, to be consistent with general usage, I will refer to the transmitter substance as *norepinephrine.* The accepted adjectival form is *noradrenergic;* I suppose that *norepinephrinergic* never caught on because it is too difficult to pronounce.

Noradrenergic neurons in the brain are primarily involved in control of alertness and wakefulness; a small group of neurons located near the pons sends axons to widespread regions of the cerebrum and cerebellum. Noradrenergic synapses in the central nervous system produce inhibitory postsynaptic potentials. By contrast, at the

▲ TABLE 4.1 ▲

Classification of the Monoamine Transmitter Substances

Monoamines	
Catecholamines	**Indolamines**
Norepinephrine	Serotonin (5-HT)
Dopamine	

target organs of the sympathetic nervous system, norepinephrine usually has an excitatory effect.

The synthesis of norepinephrine is somewhat more complicated than that of ACh, but each step is a simple one. The precursor molecule is modified slightly, step by step, until it achieves its final shape. Each step is controlled by a different enzyme, which adds a small part or takes one off. The precursor for both of the catecholamines (dopamine and norepinephrine) is **tyrosine,** an essential amino acid that we obtain from our diet. Tyrosine receives a hydroxyl group (OH, an oxygen atom and a hydrogen atom) and becomes **L-DOPA** (L-3,4-dihydroxyphenylalanine). L-DOPA then loses a carboxyl group (COOH, one carbon atom, two oxygen atoms, and one hydrogen atom) and becomes dopamine. Finally, an enzyme attaches a hydroxyl group to dopamine, which becomes norepinephrine. These reactions are shown in ***Figure 4.3.***

tyrosine

L-DOPA

Most transmitter substances are synthesized in the cell body, packaged in synaptic vesicles, and transported down the axon to the terminal buttons. However, for norepinephrine the final step of synthesis occurs inside the vesicles themselves. The vesicles are filled with dopamine, which is then converted to norepinephrine.

Overproduction of the monoamines is prevented by the presence of an enzyme called **monoamine oxidase** (MAO). This enzyme is found in terminal buttons, where it destroys excess amounts of the neurotransmitter. MAO is also found in the blood, where it deactivates amines that are present in foods such as chocolate, lima beans, and cheese; without such deactivation, these foods could cause dangerous increases in blood pressure.

monoamine oxidase (MAO)

DOPAMINE

The second catecholamine transmitter substance, **dopamine** (DA), can produce either excitatory or inhibitory postsynaptic potentials, depending on the ion channels controlled by the post synaptic receptors. Dopamine is one of the more interesting neurotransmitters because it has been implicated in several important functions, including movement, attention, learning, and addictions; thus, it is discussed in Chapters 7, 12, and 15.

dopamine (DA)

As I mentioned in Chapter 3, degeneration of dopaminergic neurons causes a serious movement disorder called Parkinson's disease, which includes weakness, involuntary trembling, problems with balance, and difficulty in initiating movements. The cell bodies of the dopaminergic neurons are found in the *substantia nigra,* located in the midbrain. This region receives its name from the fact that it is naturally stained black with melanin, the substance that gives color to skin. This compound is produced by the breakdown of dopamine. (The brain damage that causes Parkinson's disease was discovered by pathologists who observed that the substantia nigra of a deceased person who had had this disorder was pale rather than black.) People with Parkinson's disease are given L-DOPA, the precursor to dopamine. Increased levels of L-DOPA in the brain cause more dopamine to be synthesized and released by the remaining dopaminergic neurons, and the patients' symptoms are alleviated.

Dopamine has been implicated as a transmitter substance that might be involved in schizophrenia, a serious mental disorder (psychosis) characterized by hallucinations, delusions, and disruption of normal, logical thought processes. Drugs that block the activity of dopaminergic neurons alleviate these symptoms; hence investigators have speculated that schizophrenia is produced by their overactivity. (Different sets of dopaminergic neurons are involved in Parkinson's disease and schizophrenia.) In fact, symptoms of schizophrenia are an occasional side effect of L-DOPA in patients with Parkinson's disease. Fortunately, these symptoms can usually be eliminated by reducing the dose of the drug. The physiology of schizophrenia is discussed in Chapter 16.

FIGURE 4.3

Biosynthesis of the catecholamines, dopamine and norepinephrine.

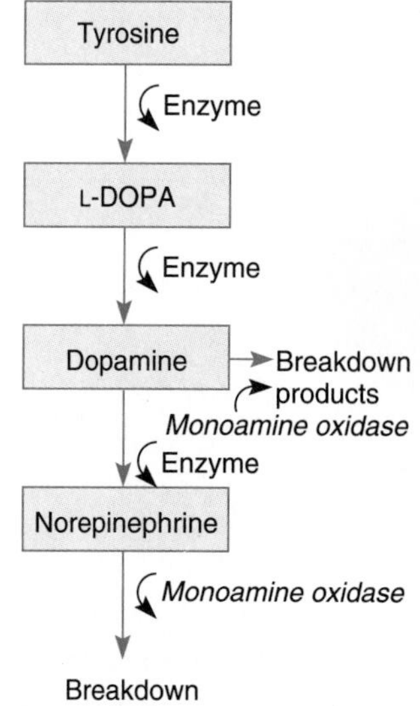

We have already seen the biosynthetic pathway for dopamine in Figure 4.3. This transmitter is the immediate precursor of norepinephrine. As with the other monoamines, excess dopamine in the terminal buttons is destroyed by monoamine oxidase.

SEROTONIN

serotonin (5-HT)

tryptophan

The third monoamine transmitter substance, **serotonin** (also called 5-hydroxytryptamine, or **5-HT**), has also received much experimental attention. Its precursor is the amino acid **tryptophan.** An enzyme adds a hydroxyl group, producing 5-hydroxytryptophan (5-HTP). Another enzyme removes a carboxyl group from 5-HTP, and the result is 5-HT (serotonin). Figure 4.4 illustrates these reactions. (See ***Figure 4.4.***)

FIGURE 4.4

Biosynthesis of serotonin (5-hydroxytryptamine, or 5-HT).

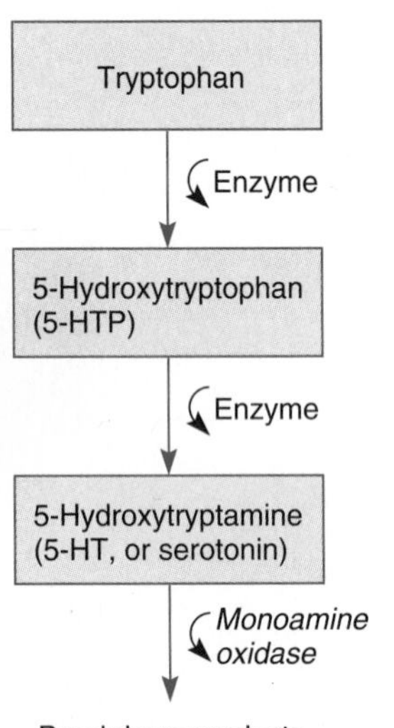

At most synapses, serotonin produces inhibitory postsynaptic potentials. In addition, its behavioral effect is usually inhibitory. Serotonin plays a role in the regulation of mood (producing sedation or relaxation), in the control of eating, sleep, and arousal, and in the regulation of pain. Drugs that excite serotonergic neurons suppress dreaming, whereas drugs that inhibit them (such as LSD) increase dreaming or even cause hallucinations while the person is awake.

Amino Acid Neurotransmitters

So far, all of the transmitter substances I have described are synthesized within neurons: acetylcholine from choline, the catecholamines from the amino acid tyrosine, and serotonin from the amino acid tryptophan. Some neurons secrete simple amino acids as transmitter substances. In fact, investigators believe that at least eight amino acids serve as transmitter substances in the mammalian central nervous system. Three of them are especially important, because they appear to be the most common transmitter substances in the CNS: glutamic acid, gamma-aminobutyric acid (GABA), and glycine. These substances are discussed below.

GLUTAMIC ACID

glutamic acid

Because **glutamic acid** (often called *glutamate*) and gamma-aminobutyric acid (GABA) are found in very simple organisms, many investigators believe that they are the first neurotransmitters to have evolved. Besides their effects on postsynaptic receptors, they have direct excitatory effects (glutamic acid) and inhibitory effects (GABA) on axons; they raise or lower the threshold of excitation, thus affecting the rate at which action potentials occur. These direct effects suggest that these substances had a general modulating role even before the evolutionary development of specific receptor molecules.

Glutamic acid is found throughout the brain. In fact, it appears to be the principal excitatory transmitter substance in the brain. It is produced in abundance by the cells' metabolic processes. Oriental food often contains glutamic acid in the form of monosodium glutamate (MSG), the sodium salt of glutamic acid. Some people are especially sensitive to the effects of MSG and experience mild neurological symptoms, including temporary dizziness and numbness, after eating food that contains large amounts of the chemical. Because MSG does not cross the blood-brain barrier, this chemical presumably produces its effects by acting on the peripheral nervous system.

GABA

gamma-aminobutyric acid (GABA)

Gamma-aminobutyric acid (GABA) is produced from glutamic acid by the action of an enzyme that removes a carboxyl group. GABA is an inhibitory transmitter substance, and it appears to have a widespread distribution throughout the gray matter (cellular areas) of the brain and spinal cord.

GABA has been implicated in a serious hereditary neurological disorder, Huntington's chorea. This disease is characterized by involuntary movements, depression, progressive mental deterioration, and ultimately death. The disease, which apparently results from the degeneration of GABAergic neurons in the basal ganglia, is discussed in Chapter 7.

As you know, neurons in the brain are greatly interconnected. Without the activity of inhibitory synapses these interconnections would make the brain unstable. That is, through excitatory synapses neurons would excite their neighbors, which would then excite *their* neighbors, which would then excite the originally active neurons, and so on, until the whole brain would be firing uncontrollably. In fact, this event does sometimes occur, and we refer to it as a *seizure.* If an inhibitory influence is supplied, the presence of such a large number of GABA-secreting neurons keeps seizures from occurring. Some investigators believe that one of the causes of epilepsy is an abnormality in the biochemistry of GABA-secreting neurons.

GLYCINE

The amino acid **glycine** is an important inhibitory neurotransmitter in the spinal cord and lower portions of the brain. Little is known about how neurons produce glycine. The bacteria that cause tetanus (lockjaw) release a poison called *tetanus toxin* that blocks the activity of glycine synapses. Glycinergic neurons normally inhibit the activity of motor neurons. When their inhibitory effect is eliminated, the muscles they control begin to contract continuously, and the person becomes rigid and unable to move.

glycine

Peptide Neurotransmitters

Recent studies have discovered that a large variety of peptides serve as transmitter substances. As I mentioned earlier, peptides are chains of amino acids. Many different types are released by neurons. Some of them probably serve as transmitter substances, whereas others serve as neuromodulators. Peptides appear to play a role in controlling sensitivity to pain, regulating species-typical defensive behaviors, and regulating eating and drinking. For example, a peptide called angiotensin makes animals thirsty when they lose fluid from their blood. I will have more to say about the behavioral effects of several peptides in later chapters.

Because the synthesis of peptides is complex and must take place in the soma, these chemicals must be delivered to the terminal buttons by axoplasmic flow. Once they are released, they are deactivated by enzymes; they are not returned to the terminal buttons and recycled.

Recently, experimenters have discovered that many peptides are released along with a "classical" neurotransmitter (one of the ones I just described). That is, some terminal buttons contain two different types of synaptic vesicles, each filled with a different substance. Some investigators believe that the peptide serves to regulate the sensitivity of presynaptic or postsynaptic receptors to the neurotransmitter. One example of this interaction has been observed. The terminal buttons of the salivary nerve of the cat (which control the secretion of saliva) release both acetylcholine and a peptide called VIP. When the axons fire at a low rate, only ACh is released, and only a little saliva is secreted. At a higher rate, both ACh and VIP are secreted, and the VIP dramatically increases the sensitivity of the muscarinic receptors in the salivary gland to ACh; thus, much saliva is released.

Biochemically Defined Neural Systems

In this section I have described the major categories of transmitter substances: acetylcholine, the monoamines, the amino acid neurotransmitters, and the peptide neurotransmitters. In some instances I have mentioned the locations of neural circuits containing neurons that release these substances. How do we know where these neurons are found? As we saw in Chapter 3, the parts of the brain and their interconnections have been studied by neuroanatomical methods such as staining of cell bodies or myelin sheaths, amino acid autoradiography, and the use of horseradish peroxidase. Another approach to neuroanatomy has been to identify neural circuits biochemically —by the transmitter substance that the neurons release. A technique discovered by Falck, Hillarp, Thieme, and Torp (1962) provided a method for precisely locating certain kinds of transmitter substances in the brain. These investigators discovered that when brain tissue was exposed to dry formaldehyde gas, noradrenergic neurons would fluoresce a bright yellow when the tissue was examined under ultraviolet light. The technique, which was named the **histofluorescence method,** was refined and applied to the other monoamines. Investigators have drawn "maps" showing the distribution of all three types of monoaminergic neurons in the central nervous system.

histofluorescence method

A noradrenergic map of the rat brain is shown in Figure 4.5. As the figure shows, a small group of neurons located in the *locus coeruleus* ("blue place") sends axons to the cerebellum, to the cerebral cortex, and to some subcortical regions. (See ***Figure 4.5.***) The value of mapping neural circuits whose neurons use a particular transmitter substance is that once the locations of particular types of neurons are known, one can investigate their function. For example, terminal buttons that secrete norepinephrine are widely distributed, and all stem from a small group of neurons. (In humans the total number is probably under a hundred thousand.) A single axon branches many times and contains a vast number of terminal buttons, which suggests that noradrenergic neurons have a general modulating or controlling function and do not convey detailed information.

The release of norepinephrine in the brain seems to increase the sensitivity of neurons to sensory input. After neurons are exposed to norepinephrine, when they receive sensory information from terminal buttons that form synapses with them, they

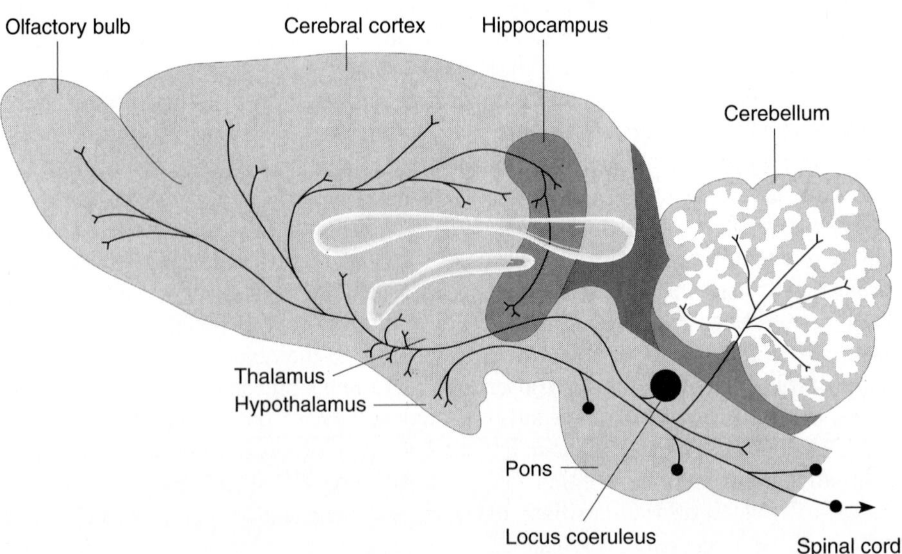

FIGURE 4.5

A map of the regions that receive terminal buttons of noradrenergic neurons.

respond more vigorously. Thus, the release of norepinephrine has an activating effect, making an organism more responsive to changes in its environment.

Researchers have developed other techniques besides the histofluorescence method that enable them to identify biochemically distinct neural circuits. For example, scientists can produce an antibody to a specific peptide, link the antibody to a dye, and soak slices of brain tissue in a solution containing the antibody-dye complex. The antibody binds with the peptide, which means that particular neurons that contain the peptide become stained with the dye, which can be seen under a microscope. Thus, even though peptide-secreting neurons are relatively few in number, techniques are available to localize them precisely. (See ***Color Plate 4.1.***)

Neuroanatomists have also developed a method that identifies the location of receptors for specific neurotransmitters or neuromodulators. In this technique, the brain is exposed to a radioactive ligand for a particular type of receptor. A **ligand** (from *ligare,* "to bind") is a chemical that is capable of binding to a receptor. For example, acetylcholine is the natural ligand for nicotinic ACh receptors, and nicotine is an artificial ligand. Usually, the brain is sliced and sections are mounted on microscope slides. The slides are then soaked in a solution containing the radioactive ligand. After sufficient time has passed to allow the ligand to bind with the receptors, the slides are rinsed and covered with a photographic emulsion, and autoradiograms are prepared. (The process of autoradiography was described in Chapter 3.) The result is a picture of the brain that shows the locations of a particular type of receptor. Figure 4.6 shows an autoradiogram of a horizontal section of a rat brain illustrating the location of opiate receptors. (The functions of these receptors will be discussed later in this chapter.) (See ***Figure 4.6.***)

ligand

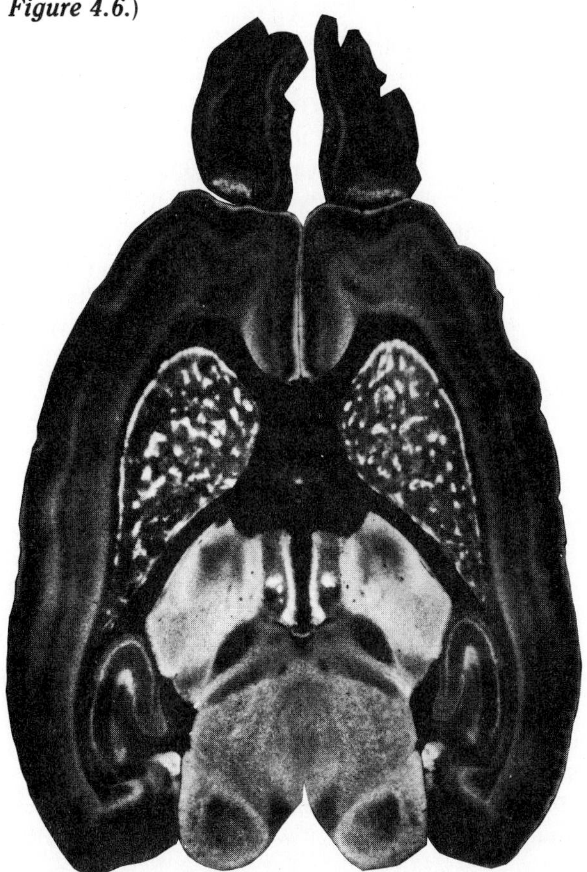

FIGURE 4.6

An autoradiogram of a rat brain (horizontal section, rostral is at top) that has been incubated in a solution containing a radioactive ligand for opiate receptors. The receptors are indicated by white areas. (From Herkenham, M.A., and Pert, C.B. *Journal of Neuroscience,* 1982, *2,* 1129–1149. Reprinted by permission of the *Journal of Neuroscience.*)

▶INTERIM SUMMARY◀

Chemical communication takes place between a cell that secretes a chemical and one that contains receptors for that chemical. The communication can involve neurotransmitters, neuromodulators, hormones, or pheromones; the distance varies from the space that separates the presynaptic and postsynaptic membrane to the space that separates two individual organisms. Peptide hormones are detected by means of receptors in the membrane of the target cells that cause the production of a second messenger, such as cyclic AMP. Steroid hormones enter cells and bind with receptors in the nucleus.

The nervous system contains a variety of transmitter substances, each of which interacts with a specialized receptor. Those that have received the most study are acetylcholine and the monoamines: dopamine, norepinephrine, and 5-hydroxytryptamine (serotonin). The synthesis of these transmitter substances is controlled by enzymes. Several amino acids also serve as transmitter substances, the most important of which are glutamic acid (glutamate), GABA, and glycine. Glutamate serves as an excitatory transmitter substance; the others serve as inhibitory transmitter substances. Peptide transmitter substances consist of chains of amino acids. Like proteins, peptides are synthesized according to instructions contained by the chromosomes.

Many different types of neurons are organized into biochemically defined systems. Special methods have been developed that permit investigators to produce maps of these systems, showing the locations of particular types of neurons in the central nervous system and of the receptors that detect the chemicals they secrete. ▲

PHARMACOLOGY OF SYNAPSES

Investigators have discovered many drugs that act on synapses. Some of these drugs are used to study the functions of the nervous system, and some are used to treat disorders. Some are in common use, and some are found only in research laboratories. Drugs that affect synaptic transmission are classified into two general categories. Those that block or inhibit the postsynaptic effects are called **antagonists;** those that facilitate them are called **agonists.** (The Greek word *agon* means "contest." Thus, an *agonist* is one who takes part in the contest.)

antagonist
agonist

In this section I will describe the basic effects of drugs on synaptic activity and give a few examples. Recall from Chapter 2 that the sequence of synaptic activity goes like this: Transmitter substances are synthesized and stored in synaptic vesicles. When axons fire, the transmitter substances are released into the synaptic cleft, where they activate postsynaptic receptors. So that their effects are brief, they are destroyed by an enzyme or taken back into the terminal button to be recycled. My discussion of the effects of drugs in this section follows the same basic sequence.

Effects on Production of Transmitter Substances

The first step in synaptic activity is the synthesis of the transmitter substance from its precursors. In some cases the rate of synthesis and release of a neurotransmitter is increased when a precursor is administered; in these cases the precursor itself serves as an agonist. As we saw earlier, L-DOPA is given to people with Parkinson's disease, whose symptoms occur when most of their dopaminergic neurons have died. Because L-DOPA causes more dopamine to be synthesized and released by the remaining neurons, it serves as a dopamine agonist. (See step 1 in ***Figure 4.7.***)

The steps in the synthesis of transmitter substances are controlled by enzymes. Therefore, if a drug inactivates one of these enzymes, it will prevent the transmitter

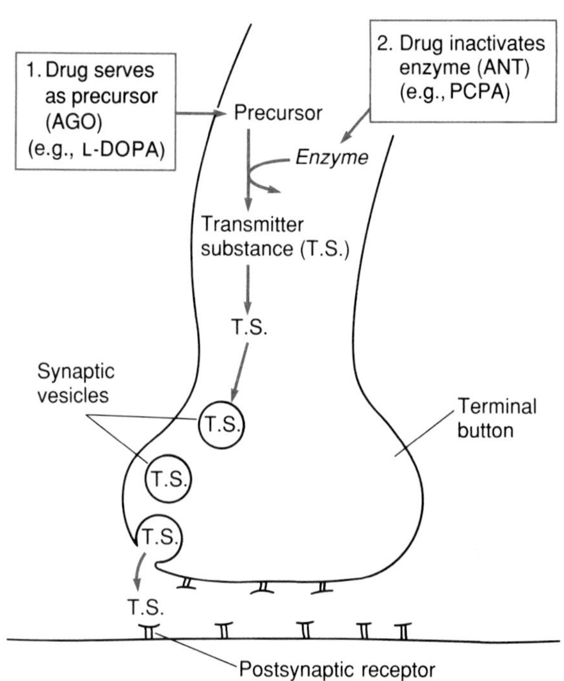

FIGURE 4.7

Effect of drugs on the production of a transmitter substance (AGO = agonist; ANT = antagonist).

substance from being produced. For example, the drug **PCPA** (*para*-chlorophenylalanine) blocks one of the enzymes that are needed for the synthesis of serotonin. Thus, the drug is a serotonin antagonist. (See step 2 in ***Figure 4.7.***) PCPA is sometimes used to block the activity of a tumor composed of cells that secrete serotonin.

PCPA

Effects on Storage and Release of Transmitter Substances

The next two steps in synaptic activity are storage and release. Transmitter substances are stored in synaptic vesicles, which are transported to the presynaptic membrane, where the chemicals are released. One drug, **reserpine,** makes the membrane of monoamine-containing synaptic vesicles become "leaky." The transmitter substances escape into the cytoplasm of the terminal button, where they are destroyed by MAO; hence nothing is released when the vesicles rupture against the presynaptic membrane. Reserpine is thus a monoamine antagonist. (See step 3 in ***Figure 4.8.***) The drug, which comes from the root of a shrub, was discovered over three thousand years ago in India, where it was found to be useful in treating snakebite and seemed to have a calming effect. Pieces of the root are still sold in markets in rural areas of India. In Western medicine reserpine is occasionally used to treat high blood pressure.

reserpine

Some drugs act as antagonists by preventing the release of transmitter substances from the terminal button; for example, **botulinum toxin,** a poison produced by bacteria that can grow in improperly canned food, prevents the release of ACh. Extremely small amounts of this drug can be fatal. Other drugs act as agonists by stimulating the release of a neurotransmitter. As we saw in Chapter 2, the venom of the black widow spider causes acetylcholinergic terminal buttons to release ACh. (See steps 4 and 5 in ***Figure 4.8.***) The effects of black widow spider venom can also be fatal, but the venom is much less toxic. In fact, most healthy adults would have to receive several bites, but infants or frail old people would be more susceptible.

botulinum toxin

surgical shock. Without them most major surgery would be impossible. Even if a person were brave enough to bear the pain, he or she could not withstand the stressful effects of several hours of surgery.

Drugs That Cause Excitation

Several categories of drugs stimulate the central nervous system and thus activate behavior. These drugs include nicotine, amphetamine, and cocaine. Because of the effects some of these drugs have on the brain's reinforcement systems, they tend to be abused. I will describe the behavioral effects of these drugs here, in the subsections that follow, and will leave a more detailed description of their pharmacological effects for Chapter 15, which discusses the physiology of addiction.

NICOTINE

Nicotine is another addictive drug, which, as you already know, serves as an acetylcholine agonist by stimulating nicotinic ACh receptors. Although the dose of nicotine that is received in tobacco smoke or from snuff or chewing tobacco is relatively mild, the other substances in tobacco cause cancer, emphysema, heart attacks, and strokes. Thus, addiction to nicotine exposes people to very serious dangers and costs society billions of dollars each year in lost productivity, medical care of people suffering from tobacco-induced diseases, and insurance and welfare benefits for dependent survivors of those who die from the effects of smoking.

AMPHETAMINE AND COCAINE

Two very popular stimulating drugs, amphetamine and cocaine, have almost identical effects: They inhibit the reuptake of norepinephrine and dopamine and thus serve as agonists at synapses that use these two transmitter substances. The effect of these drugs on noradrenergic synapses causes alertness and hyperactivity. However, their effect on dopaminergic synapses is even more important. As we shall see in Chapter 15, reinforcing stimuli — such as food to a hungry animal, water to a thirsty one, or sexual contact to a sexually aroused one — exert their behavioral effects largely by increasing the activity of a circuit of dopamine-secreting neurons. Thus, amphetamine and cocaine mimic the effects of reinforcing stimuli. In particular, free-base cocaine (crack) has an immediate effect on the reuptake of dopamine and produces such a profound feeling of euphoria and pleasure that the person wants to repeat the experience again and again. Thus, the drug is very addictive.

As I mentioned earlier in this chapter, the dopamine agonist L-DOPA occasionally produces psychotic behaviors in people who are receiving it for treatment of Parkinson's disease. Cocaine and amphetamine, if taken in large enough doses for a sufficient amount of time, will have the same effect. In fact, an experienced clinician cannot distinguish the drug-induced symptoms from those that occur in people with schizophrenia. The hypothesis that schizophrenia is caused by overactivity of dopaminergic synapses will be discussed in more detail in Chapter 16.

Drugs That Modify Perceptions or Produce Hallucinations

Many people enjoy changing their consciousness now and then. Even children enjoy spinning around and making themselves dizzy — presumably for the same reason that people take drugs such as marijuana. Chemicals found in several different plants produce profound changes in consciousness. Behaviorally, these changes are difficult to specify. Large doses of marijuana or LSD tend to make laboratory animals become stuporous, but they give no sign of having their consciousness altered. (But then, how could they?) Only humans can describe the consciousness-altering effects of the drugs.

Undoubtedly, drugs can affect consciousness in several different ways. The only one that we have any understanding of is the effect of serotonin antagonists. Many serotonin antagonists, such as LSD, PCPA, psilocybin, and DMT (dimethyltryptamine) produce hallucinations, which often are interesting and even awe inspiring but which sometimes produce intense fear and anxiety. These drugs presumably produce their effects by disinhibiting neural circuits responsible for dreaming. Normally, we dream only when we are asleep, in a particular stage called *REM sleep* (for the rapid eye movements that occur then). During the rest of the day serotonergic neurons inhibit these mechanisms and prevent them from becoming active. However, when a drug such as LSD suppresses the activity of serotonergic synapses, the dream mechanisms become active, and hallucinations result.

Not all hallucinogens are serotonin antagonists. For example, mescaline, a chemical contained in the peyote plant (a spineless cactus), is a noradrenergic agonist. However, unlike amphetamine and cocaine, which primarily produce auditory hallucinations, mescaline produces visual ones. Thus, the effect of mescaline on noradrenergic synapses is probably not the sole cause of the hallucinations. Two commonly abused drugs, *phencyclidine*(PCP, or angel dust) and THC (tetrahydrocannibinal, the active ingredient of marijuana) stimulate specific receptors. PCP acts as a glutamate agonist; it activates particular binding sites on a special glutamate receptor. (This receptor, the *NMDA receptor,* plays an important role in learning; it is discussed in Chapter 12.)

The THC receptor, which was discovered recently (Matsuda et al., 1990), is located on neurons in the hippocampus, cerebellum, basal ganglia, cerebral cortex, amygdala, and hypothalamus. (See ***Figure 4.13.***) THC produces analgesia and sedation, stimulates appetite, reduces nausea caused by drugs used to treat cancer, relieves asthma attacks, decreases the pressure within the eyes in patients with glaucoma, and reduces the symptoms of certain motor disorders. On the other hand, it makes it difficult to concentrate and remember, alters visual and auditory perception, and distorts perceptions of the passage of time (Howlett, 1990). We can guess the brain regions involved in some of these phenomena: The effects of THC on motor disorders are probably mediated by the receptors on neurons in the basal ganglia and the cerebellum, the effects

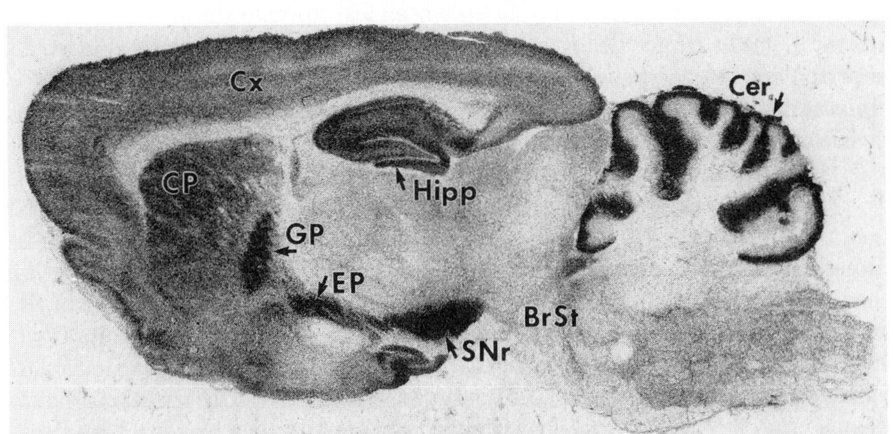

FIGURE 4.13

An autoradiogram of a rat brain (sagittal section, rostral is to the left) that has been incubated in a solution containing a radioactive ligand for THC receptors. The receptors are indicated by dark areas. (Br St = brain stem Cer = cerebellum, Cx = cortex, EP = entopeduncular nucleus, GP = globus pallidus, Hipp = hippocampus, SNr = substantia nigra.) (Autoradiogram courtesy of Miles Herkenham, National Institute of Mental Health, Bethesda, Md.)

on appetite by the receptors in the hypothalamus, and the effects on concentration and memory by the receptors in the hippocampus and cerebral cortex. Now that the THC receptor has been identified, researchers hope to identify the natural ligand that the brain undoubtedly produces. They also hope to find drugs that have the therapeutic effects of THC but not the adverse effects on cognition.

Psychotherapeutic Drugs

The symptoms of schizophrenia and the affective disorders (severe disturbances of mood) can be reduced or even eliminated by two major categories of psychotherapeutic drugs, discussed next.

ANTISCHIZOPHRENIC DRUGS

As we already saw, amphetamine, cocaine, and L-DOPA — drugs that act as dopamine agonists — can intensify the symptoms of schizophrenia or induce them in nonschizophrenic people. In contrast, drugs that block dopamine receptors can be used to reduce or even eliminate these symptoms. The first drug to receive widespread use as an antischizophrenic agent was *chlorpromazine.* Because this drug can relax people without anesthetizing them, it was first used to sedate patients before surgery and was found to have the added benefit of reducing surgical shock. (Indeed, it is still used for this purpose.) Because chlorpromazine was so successful in calming people, it was tried on agitated schizophrenic patients. It calmed them, too, but it did more than that: It reduced or eliminated their hallucinations and delusions and made it possible for them to think more clearly.

Since the discovery of chlorpromazine many other drugs have been discovered that also reduce the symptoms of schizophrenia. All these drugs have one effect in common: They block dopamine receptors and thus act as dopamine antagonists. As I mentioned earlier, Chapter 16 discusses the physiology of schizophrenia in more detail.

ANTIDEPRESSANT DRUGS

The second important category of psychotherapeutic drugs includes the antidepressant medications. As I mentioned earlier in this chapter, the most important of these drugs deactivate monoamine oxidase or inhibit the reuptake of norepinephrine and serotonin. Therefore, both types of drugs act as monoamine agonists. Although these drugs can have serious side effects, including high blood pressure, they have saved many lives that otherwise would have been lost through suicide.

A third type of drug is also used to treat a special category of depression in which the person's mood fluctuates between periods of severe depression and periods of *mania,* a state of excited, unrealistic elation. This drug is a simple inorganic compound called *lithium carbonate.* The biochemical cause of its therapeutic effects is unknown.

Analgesic Drugs

Throughout history, people have tried to find drugs that reduce pain. One quest has led to anesthetics, which I discussed earlier. But some disorders — for example, arthritis, migraine, tumors, and various neurological disorders — lead to chronic pain. Obviously, an anesthetic would not be useful in these cases; the goal is to reduce pain, not to produce unconsciousness. Several substances have been found to be useful in producing **analgesia** — the reduction of pain. (The term comes from the Greek *an-,* "not," and *algos,* "pain.") The oldest category — the opiates — is used primarily to reduce short-

analgesia

term pain caused by injury or pain caused by terminal illnesses, in which the possibility of addiction is not a problem. The second group includes aspirin and related compounds, which produce analgesia by interfering with the production of **prostaglandins,** a special category of hormones that are secreted by many tissues of the body. (They were first found in the prostate gland, which explains how they got their name.) Prostaglandins are involved somehow in mediating pain sensations, and drugs that block the production of some of the prostaglandins thus produce analgesia. Not enough is yet known about the actions of prostaglandins or the physiology of pain sensation to explain precisely how these analgesics work.

prostaglandin

Although the opiates—including such drugs as opium, morphine, heroin, codeine, and methadone—produce analgesia, they produce other effects, too. (After all, no one becomes addicted to aspirin.) These effects are described in Chapters 6 and 15; here I want to address the mechanism by which the drugs affect the brain. Opiates exert their effects by stimulating specialized receptors in the brain. As we have seen in this chapter, several other drugs—including the benzodiazepines, PCP, and THC—also stimulate specialized receptors. We do not yet know why these receptors exist, but we *do* have a pretty good idea about why opiate receptors exist: They exist to detect the presence of the endogenous opioids.

One of the most important neuromodulators produced in the brain is a category of peptides called the **endogenous opioids.** (*Endogenous* means "produced from within"; *opioid* means "like opium.") Several years ago it became clear that opiates reduced pain because they had direct effects on the brain. In particular, investigators found that an injection of a very small amount of morphine into the periaqueductal gray matter of the midbrain produced analgesia. Pert, Snowman, and Snyder (1974) discovered that neurons in this part of the brain contain specialized receptors that respond to opiates. They homogenized the brains of rats (by running pieces of brain tissue through a special blender that broke the cells into small fragments) and used an extraction technique to isolate pieces of cell membranes. They soaked the membranes in a solution that contained a radioactive opiate (morphine), rinsed them, and found that the membranes had become radioactive. This fact indicated that the radioactive morphine had bound with specific opioid receptors, similar in nature to postsynaptic receptors for transmitter substances.

endogenous opioid

Soon after the discovery of the opioid receptor, other neuroscientists discovered the natural ligands—the chemicals that bind with these receptors. Terenius and Wahlström (1975) discovered a chemical in human cerebrospinal fluid that would attach strongly to opiate receptors that they had previously extracted from rat brains. Hughes et al. (1975) performed careful analyses and found two of these chemicals, which they identified as very small peptides, each containing five amino acids. They synthesized these substances and found that the artificial peptides acted as potent opiates, binding with opioid receptors even more effectively than morphine. The authors called them **enkephalins** (from the Greek word *enkephalos,* "in the head").

enkephalin

We now know that the enkephalins are only two members of a family of endogenous opiate peptides, all of which are synthesized from one of three large polypeptides that serve as precursors. The anterior pituitary gland and the adrenal gland also release endogenous opioids, apparently in times of stress.

Several different neural systems are activated when opiate receptors are stimulated. One type produces analgesia, another inhibits species-typical defensive responses such as fleeing and hiding, and another stimulates a system of neurons involved in reinforcement ("reward"). The last effect explains why opiates are often abused. The situations that cause neurons to secrete endogenous opioids are discussed in Chapter 6, and the brain mechanisms of opiate addiction are discussed in Chapter 15.

▶INTERIM SUMMARY◀

Drugs can affect behavior in several ways. The most important effects are sedation, excitation, changes in perceptions, reduction of the symptoms of mental disorders, and analgesia. To review the members of these five categories, refer to ***Table 4.2.***

Barbiturates, alcohol, and benzodiazepines all appear to cause sedation by attaching to various binding sites on the GABA-receptor complex. Stimulant drugs such as cocaine and amphetamine act as dopaminergic agonists, which accounts for their abuse potential. In sufficient doses they also produce the symptoms of a serious psychosis, schizophrenia. Most hallucinogenic drugs exert their effects by acting as serotonin antagonists, thus removing inhibitory control over neural circuits responsible for dreaming; people taking these drugs dream while awake, so to speak. The physiological effects of marijuana are unknown, but the recent discovery of THC receptors promises to aid researchers.

Antischizophrenic drugs block dopamine receptors, and thus, their effects are opposite to those of amphetamine and cocaine. Most antidepressant drugs are monoamine agonists. One class of analgesic drugs inhibits prostaglandins, hormones involved in the detection of painful stimuli. The opiates produce analgesia (and other effects) by binding with opiate receptors. We know that cells in the brain produce endogenous opioids, special neuromodulators that bind with opiate receptors; we suspect that there are also endogenous, natural ligands for THC receptors and for the special binding sites on the GABA-receptor complex. ▲

EPILOGUE: Application ▶

The discovery that MPTP damages the brain and causes the symptoms of Parkinson's disease galvanized researchers interested in the disease. The first step was to find out whether the drug would have the same effect in laboratory animals, so that the details of the process could be studied. It did; Langston, Forno, Rebert, and Irwin (1984) found that injections of MPTP produced parkinsonian symptoms in squirrel monkeys that could be reduced by L-DOPA therapy. And just as the investigators had hoped, examination of the animals' brains showed a selective loss of dopamine-secreting neurons in the substantia nigra.

It turns out that MPTP itself does not cause neural damage; instead, the drug is converted by an enzyme present in glial cells into another substance, MPP^+. *That* chemical is taken up by dopamine-secreting neurons, by means of the reuptake mechanism that normally retrieves dopamine that is released by terminal buttons. MPP^+ accumulates in mitochondria in these cells and blocks their ability to metabolize nutrients, thus killing the cells (Maret et al., 1990). The enzyme that converts MPTP into MPP^+ is none other than monoamine oxidase (MAO), which, as you already know, is responsible for deactivating excess amounts of monoamines present in terminal buttons. Because pharmacologists had already developed MAO inhibitors, Langston and his colleagues decided to see whether one of these drugs (pargyline) would protect squirrel monkeys from the toxic effects of MPTP by preventing its conversion into MPP^+ (Langston et al., 1984). It worked; when MAO was inhibited by pargyline, MPTP injections had no effects.

These results made researchers wonder whether MAO inhibitors might possibly protect against the degeneration of dopamine-secreting neurons in patients with Parkinson's disease. No one thought that Parkinson's disease was caused by MPP^+, but perhaps some other toxins were involved. Epidemiologists have found that Parkinson's disease is more common in highly industrialized countries, which suggests that environmental toxins produced in these societies may be responsible for the brain damage (Tanner, 1989). Fortunately, several MAO inhibitors have been tested and approved for use in humans. One of them, deprenyl, is a specific blocker of the form of MAO responsible for the conversion of MPTP into MPP^+. (It is normally used to treat high blood pressure.) In a controlled, double-blind study of fifty-four patients with Parkinson's disease, Tetrud and Langston (1989) found that deprenyl slowed down the progression of neurological symptoms by up to 83 percent. No adverse side effects were seen.

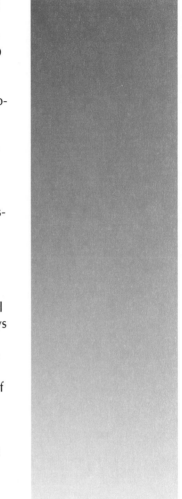

As a result of this study, many neurologists are now treating their Parkinson's patients with deprenyl, as well as with L-DOPA. The benefits of this treatment have probably already paid for all of the research that led to this discovery; in the United States alone each week that patients with Parkinson's disease can continue working saves $10 million dollars in taxes and disability payments (Lewin, 1989).

Deprenyl is the first drug that has been found to retard the progress of a degenerative disease. Many researchers believe that Parkinson's disease is not the only one that will respond to such treatment; other degenerative neurological diseases such as amyotrophic lateral sclerosis may involve an accumulation of toxic chemicals similar in their action to MPP^+. Even normal aging may involve such accumulation; and if so, there is hope of finding ways to slow down the ravages of time on our brains. And the story gets better yet. Knoll, Dallo, and Yen (1989) found that deprenyl increases rats' longevity. Rats that received injections of deprenyl three times a week lived about 45 weeks longer, on the average, than rats that received control injections of saline. (Rats have a normal life span of about 3.5 years, so an increase of 45 weeks is quite substantial.) In addition, unlike the control animals, the deprenyl-treated rats continued to be sexually active in their old age.

We do not yet know why the rats lived longer and, of course, we cannot conclude that similar results will be obtained with humans. Still, I have no doubt that many researchers will find such results sufficiently interesting to follow up on them. Who among us is not hoping that they will succeed? ▲

KEY CONCEPTS

Transmitter Substances

- Cells can use chemicals and receptors to communicate messages within an organism or between them. Depending on the distance these chemicals travel, they are called neurotransmitters, neuromodulators, hormones, or pheromones.
- Neurons use a variety of chemicals as transmitter substances, including acetylcholine, the monoamines (dopamine, norepinephrine, and 5-hydroxytryptamine), the amino acids (glutamic acid, GABA, and glycine), and various peptides.
- The distribution of the various kinds of transmitter substances throughout the brain is not haphazard; to a certain extent, different neural systems, using different transmitter substances, are involved in different functions and behaviors.

Pharmacology of Synapses

- Each of the steps involved in synaptic transmission can be interfered with by drugs, and some can be facilitated. These steps include synthesis of the transmitter substance, storage in synaptic vesicles, release, activation of postsynaptic and presynaptic receptors, and termination of postsynaptic potentials through reuptake or enzymatic deactivation.

Drugs That Affect Behavior

- Drugs can produce sedation, excitation, hallucinations or other changes in perceptions, reduction of the symptoms of mental disorders, and analgesia. Several of these drugs act by stimulating specialized receptors that normally detect the presence of endogenous neuromodulators, most of which remain to be discovered.

SUGGESTED READINGS

Cooper, J.R., Bloom, R.E., and Roth, R.H. *The Biochemical Basis of Neuropharmacology,* 5th ed. New York: Oxford University Press, 1986.

Julien, R.M. *A Primer of Drug Action,* 4th ed. San Francisco: W.H. Freeman, 1985.

NEW TERMS

agonist **p. 118**
amphetamine **p. 123**
analgesia **p. 130**
antagonist **p. 118**
antianxiety drug **p. 125**
apomorphine **p. 122**
atropine **p. 121**
barbiturate **p. 124**
benzodiazepine **p. 125**
binding site **p. 125**
botulinum toxin **p. 119**
CAT (choline acetyltransferase) **p. 111**
catecholamine **p. 112**
cocaine **p. 123**
coenzyme A **p. 111**
curare **p. 121**
dopamine (DA) **p. 113**
endocrine gland **p. 109**
endogenous opioid **p. 131**
enkephalin **p. 131**
epinephrine **p. 112**
gamma-aminobutyric acid (GABA) **p. 114**
glutamic acid **p. 114**
glycine **p. 115**
histofluorescence method **p. 116**
iproniazid **p. 123**
L-DOPA **p. 113**
ligand **p. 117**
monoamine **p. 112**
monoamine oxidase (MAO) **p. 113**
muscarinic receptor **p. 112**
neuromodulator **p. 109**
nicotinic receptor **p. 112**
norepinephrine **p. 112**
PCPA **p. 118**
peptide **p. 109**
pheromone **p. 110**
physostigmine **p. 123**
prostaglandin **p. 131**
receptor blocker **p. 121**
reserpine **p. 119**
serotonin (5-HT) **p. 114**
steroid **p. 109**
supersensitivity, **p. 122**
tryptophan **p. 114**
tyrosine **p. 113**

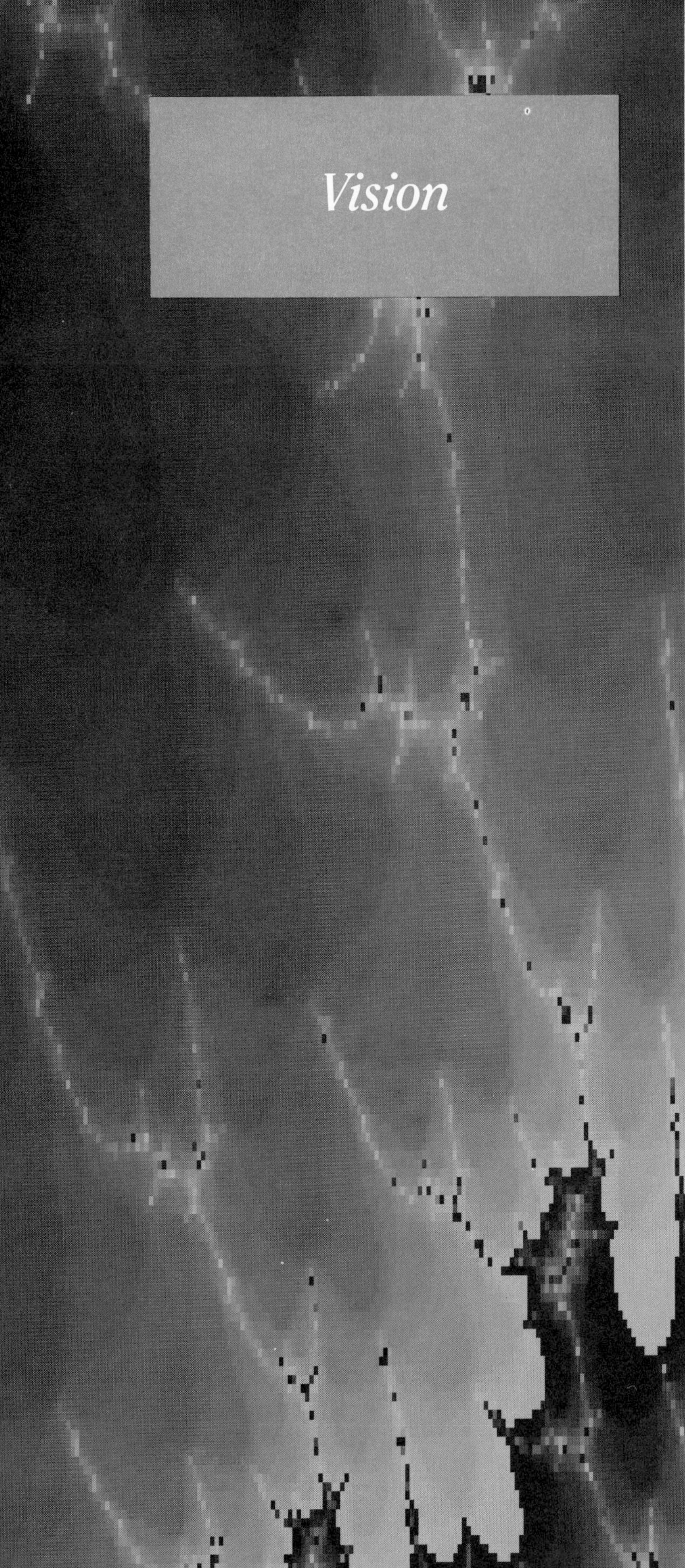

Vision

5

CHAPTER OUTLINE

PROLOGUE ►

One Sunday morning, a colleague called me and asked if I would like to meet him at a nearby hospital to interview a patient with an interesting disorder. I joined him there and met a pleasant man in his midthirties. Mr. M. had sustained brain damage from an inflammatory disease that affected the blood vessels in his brain. His speech appeared to be normal, but he had great difficulty recognizing objects or pictures of them. We went through a book of pictures that is ordinarily used to test children's vocabularies, and we found that he was unable to say what many of them were. However, he sometimes made unintentional gestures when he was studying a picture that gave him enough of a clue to identify it. For example, on one occasion while he was puzzling over a picture of a cow, he held his fists together and started making alternating up-and-down movements with them. Unmistakably, he was acting as if he were milking a cow. He looked at his hands and said, "Oh, a cow!" He laughed. "I live on a farm, you know."

We later learned that his tendency to make movements that helped him "see" things was first discovered by a speech therapist. The brain damage had destroyed his ability to read as well as to recognize objects, and she was trying to help him regain this ability. She wanted to capitalize on the potential of his visual perceptions to trigger automatic hand movements, even though he could not describe those perceptions in words. Therefore, she decided to try to teach him the manual alphabet used by deaf people, in which letters are represented by particular hand and finger movements. (This system is commonly called *finger spelling*.) She showed Mr. M. a letter and asked him to say what it was. He was unable to do so. Then she held his fingers and moved them into the position that "spelled" the letter. Over several sessions she was able to teach him to make the proper movements, which he could do even though he was unable to say what each letter was. Once his fingers moved, he could feel their position and say what the letter must be. He was able to use this ability to read whole words; he looked at individual letters of a word, made the appropriate movements, observed the sequence of letters that he spelled, and recognized the word. The process was slow, but it worked. ▲

We take for granted our ability to tie words and images together and thus express our knowledge of what we see. But as the Prologue suggests, brain damage can interrupt this ability; awareness of our visual perceptions requires that the visual mechanisms of the brain be functioning properly and be able to communicate with the brain's verbal mechanisms.

Vision is the sensory modality that has received the most attention from psychologists, anatomists, and physiologists. Perhaps one reason for this attention is the challenge of understanding the complexity of visual perception; a relatively large proportion of the human brain is devoted to the analysis of visual information. Another reason, I am sure, is that vision is so important to us as individuals. A natural fascination with such a rich source of information about the world leads to curiosity about how this sensory modality works.

My discussion is divided into five parts. The first—the shortest—describes the nature of visual stimuli. The second describes the visual system: the eyes and the brain mechanisms devoted to vision. The third describes the physiology of visual perception, explaining what we know about the functions of the visual system in perception and behavior. The fourth describes color vision, and the fifth describes the effects of brain damage in humans on visual perception.

THE STIMULUS

As we all know, our eyes detect the presence of light. For humans, light is a narrow band of the spectrum of electromagnetic radiation. Electromagnetic radiation with a wavelength of between 380 and 760 nm (a nanometer, nm, is one-billionth of a meter) is visible to us. (See ***Figure 5.1.***) Other animals can detect different ranges of electromagnetic radiation. For example, a rattlesnake can detect its prey by means of infrared radiation; thus, it can locate warm-blooded animals in the dark. Similarly, honeybees can detect differences in ultraviolet radiation reflected by flowers that appear white to

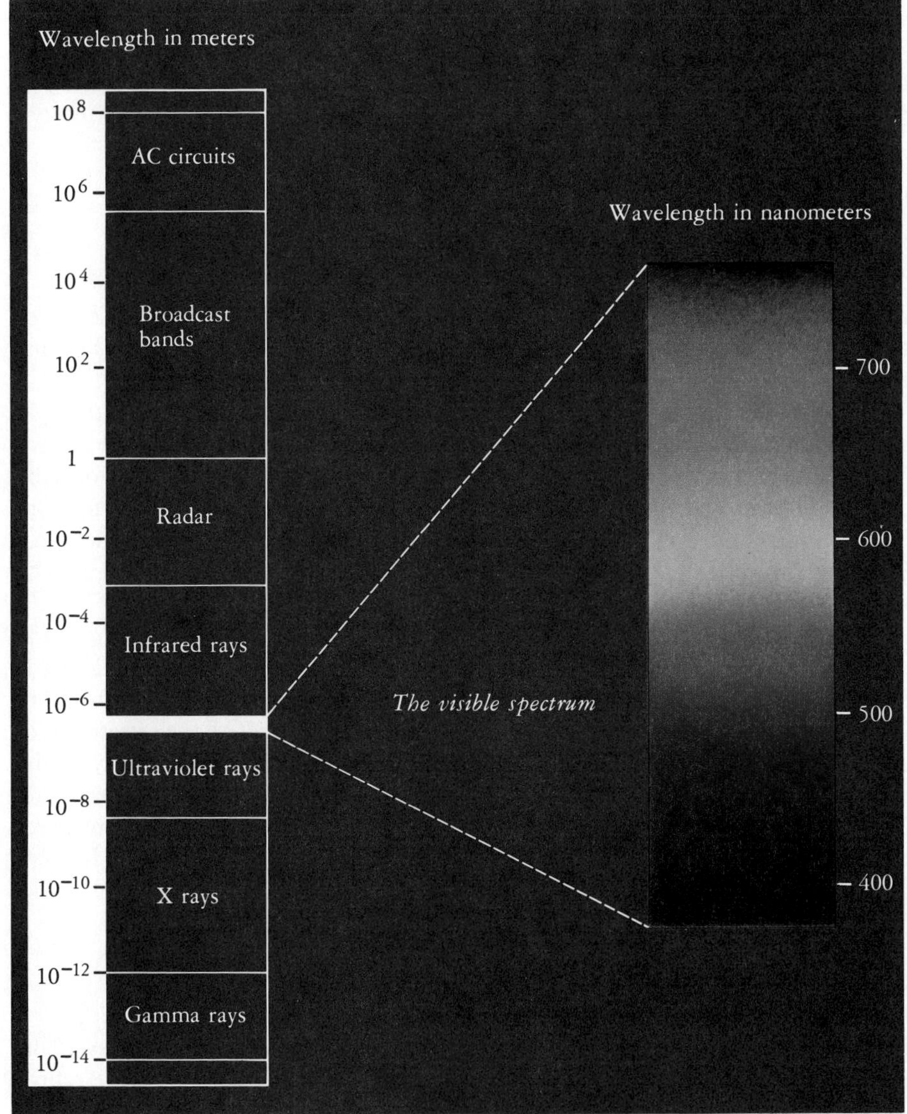

FIGURE 5.1

The spectrum of electromagnetic radiation.

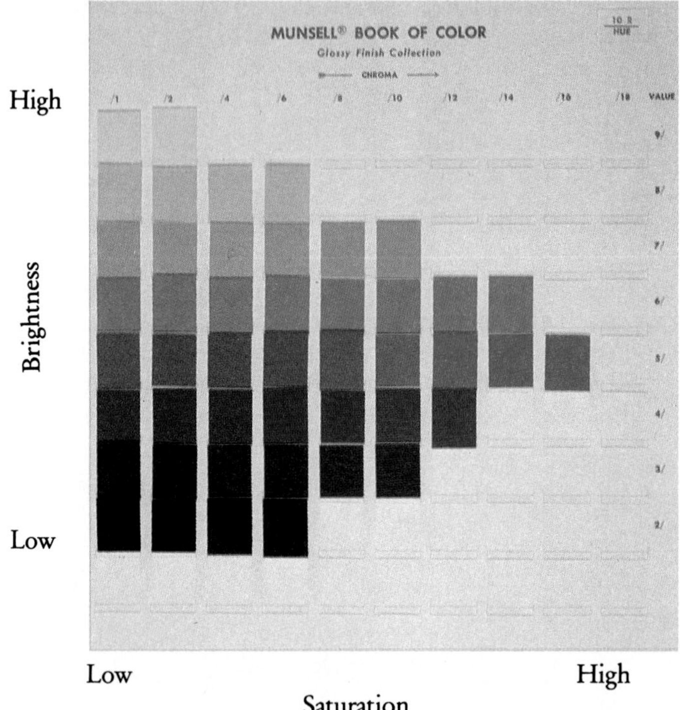

FIGURE 5.2

Examples of colors with the same dominant wavelength (hue) but different saturations and brightnesses. (Courtesy of Munsell Color Corporation.)

us. The range of wavelengths we call *light* is not qualitatively different from the rest of the electromagnetic spectrum; it is simply the part of the continuum that we humans can see.

The perceived color of light is determined by three dimensions: ***hue, saturation,*** and ***brightness.*** Light travels at a constant speed of approximately 300,000 kilometers (186,000 miles) per second. Thus, if the frequency of oscillation of the wave varies, the distance between the peaks of the waves will similarly vary, but in inverse fashion. Slower oscillations lead to longer wavelengths, and faster ones to shorter wavelengths. Wavelength determines the first of the three perceptual dimensions of light: **hue.** The visible spectrum displays the range of hues that our eyes can detect.

hue

Light can also vary in intensity, which corresponds to the second perceptual dimension of light: **brightness.** If the intensity of the electromagnetic radiation is increased, the apparent brightness increases, too. The third dimension, **saturation,** refers to the relative purity of the light that is being perceived. If all the radiation is of one wavelength, the perceived color is pure, or fully saturated. Conversely, if the radiation contains all wavelengths, it produces no sensation of hue—it appears white. Colors with intermediate amounts of saturation consist of different mixtures of wavelengths. Figure 5.2 shows some color samples, all with the same hue but with different levels of brightness and saturation. (See ***Figure 5.2.***)

brightness
saturation

ANATOMY OF THE VISUAL SYSTEM

In order to see, an image must be focused on the retina, the inner lining of the eye. This image causes changes in the electrical activity of millions of neurons in the retina, which results in messages sent through the optic nerves to the rest of the brain. (I said "the rest" because the retina is actually part of the brain; it and the optic nerve are in the central — not peripheral — nervous system.) This section describes the anatomy of the eyes, the photoreceptors in the retina that detect the presence of light, and the connections between the retina and the brain.

The Eyes

The eyes are suspended in the **orbits,** bony pockets in the front of the skull. They are held in place and moved by six extraocular muscles attached to the tough, white outer coat of the eye called the **sclera.** (See ***Figure 5.3.***) Normally, we cannot look behind our eyeballs and see these muscles because their attachments to the eyes are hidden by the **conjunctiva.** These mucous membranes line the eyelid and fold back to attach to the eye (thus preventing a contact lens that has slipped off the cornea from "falling behind the eye"). Figure 5.4 illustrates the external and internal anatomy of the eye. (See ***Figure 5.4.***)

orbit
sclera
conjunctiva

The outer layer of most of the eye, the sclera, is opaque and does not permit entry of light. However, the **cornea,** the outer layer at the front of the eye, is transparent and admits light. The amount of light that enters is regulated by the size of the **pupil,** which is an opening in the **iris,** the pigmented ring of muscles situated behind the cornea. The **lens,** situated immediately behind the iris, consists of a series of transparent, onionlike layers. Its shape can be altered by contraction of the **ciliary muscles.** These changes in shape permit the eye to focus images of near or distant objects on the retina — a process called **accommodation.**

cornea
pupil
iris
lens
ciliary muscle
accommodation

After passing through the lens, light traverses the main part of the eye, which contains the vitreous humor. **Vitreous humor** ("glassy liquid") is a clear, gelatinous substance that gives the eye its bulk. After passing through the vitreous humor, light falls on the **retina,** the interior lining of the back of the eye. In the retina are located the receptor cells, the **rods** and **cones** (named for their shapes), collectively known as **photoreceptors.** The human retina contains approximately 120 million rods and 6 million cones. Although they are greatly outnumbered, cones provide us with most of the information about our environment. In particular, they are responsible for our daytime vision. They provide us with information about small features in the environment and thus are the source of vision of the highest sharpness, or *acuity* (from *acus,*

vitreous humor
retina
rod
cone
photoreceptor

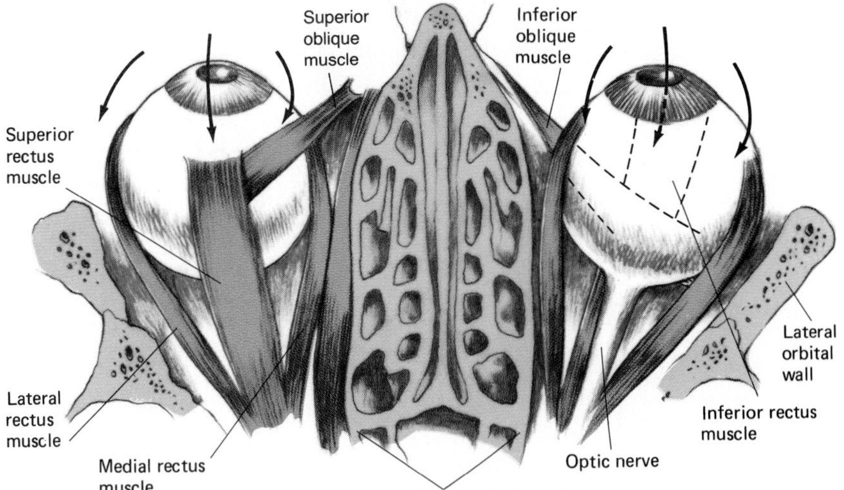

FIGURE 5.3

The extraocular muscles, which move the eyes.

FIGURE 5.4

The human eye.

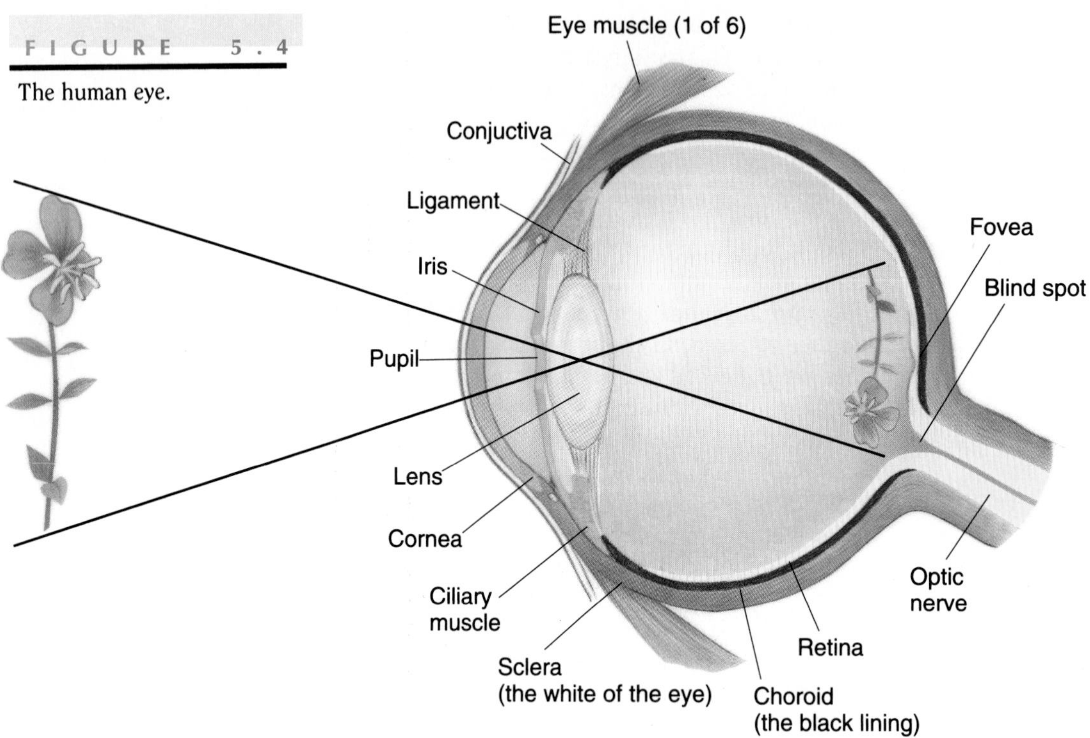

fovea

"needle"). The **fovea,** or central region of the retina, which mediates our most acute vision, contains only cones. Cones are also responsible for color vision — our ability to discriminate light of different wavelengths. Although rods do not detect different colors and provide vision of poor acuity, they are more sensitive to light. In a very dimly lighted environment we use our rod vision; therefore, in dim light we are color-blind and lack foveal vision. You have probably noticed, while out on a dark night, that looking directly at a dim, distant light (that is, placing the image of the light on the fovea) causes it to disappear.

optic disk

Another feature of the retina is the **optic disk,** where the axons conveying visual information gather together and leave the eye through the optic nerve. The optic disk

FIGURE 5.5

A test for the blind spot. With your left eye closed, look at the + with your right eye and move the page nearer and farther from you. When the page is about 20 cm from your face, the color circle disappears, because its image falls on the blind spot of your right eye.

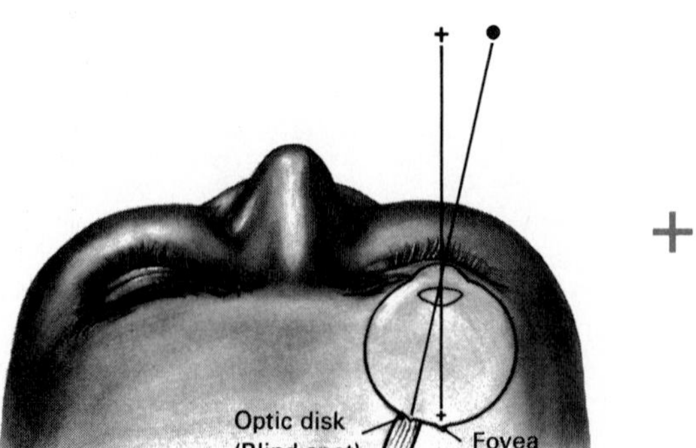

+

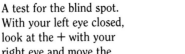

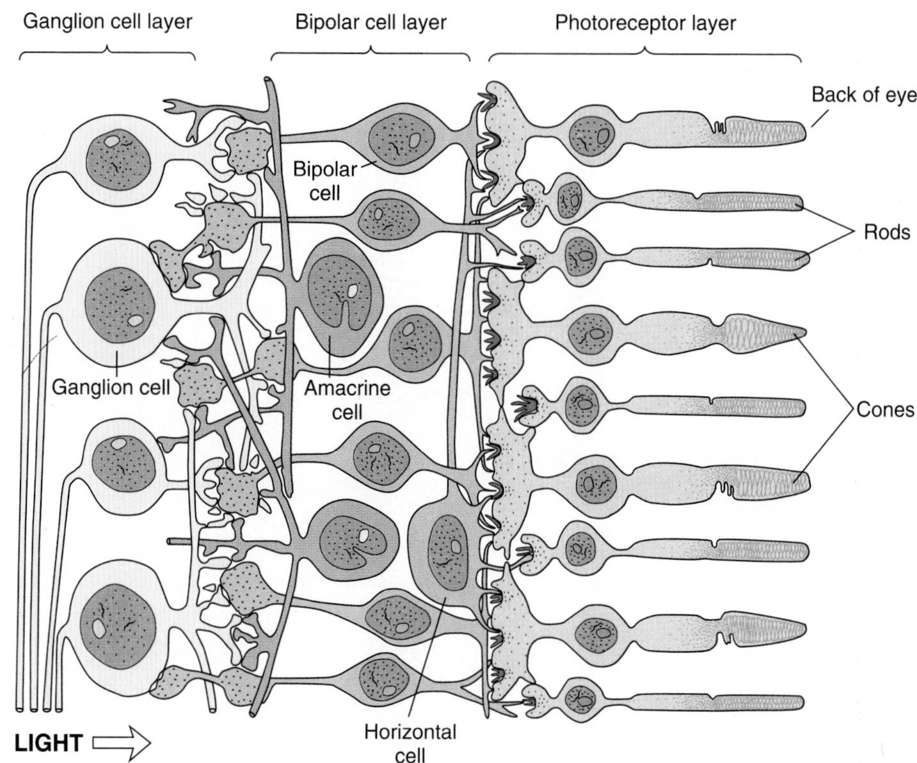

FIGURE 5.6

Details of retinal circuitry. (Adapted from Dowling, J.E., and Boycott, B.B. *Proceedings of the Royal Society of London, B.,* 1966, *166,* 80–111.)

produces a *blind spot,* because no receptors are located there. We do not normally perceive our blind spots, but their presence can be demonstrated. If you have not found yours, you may want to try the exercise described in ***Figure 5.5.***

Close examination of the retina shows that it consists of several layers of neuron cell bodies, their axons and dendrites, and the photoreceptors. Figure 5.6 illustrates a cross section through the primate retina, which is divided into three main layers: the photoreceptive layer, the bipolar cell layer, and the ganglion cell layer. Note that the photoreceptors are at the *back* of the retina; light must pass through the overlying layers to get to them. Fortunately, these layers are transparent. (See ***Figure 5.6.***)

The photoreceptors form synapses with **bipolar cells,** neurons whose two arms connect the shallowest and deepest layers of the retina. In turn, these neurons form synapses with the **ganglion cells,** neurons whose axons travel through the optic nerves (the second cranial nerves) and carry visual information into the brain. In addition, the retina contains **horizontal cells** and **amacrine cells,** both of which transmit information in a direction parallel to the surface of the retina and thus combine messages from adjacent photoreceptors. (See ***Figure 5.6.***)

bipolar cell

ganglion cell

horizontal cell

amacrine cell

Photoreceptors

Figure 5.7 shows a drawing of a rod and a cone. Note that each photoreceptor consists of an outer segment connected by a cilium to the inner segment, which contains the nucleus. (See ***Figure 5.7.***) The outer segment contains several hundred **lamellae,** or thin plates of membrane. (*Lamella* is the diminutive form of *lamina,* "thin layer.")

lamella

The first step in the chain of events that leads to visual perception involves a special chemical called a photopigment. (The steps of this process were discovered by George

FIGURE 5.7

Photoreceptors. (Adapted from Young, R.W., Visual cells. *Scientific American,* 1970.)

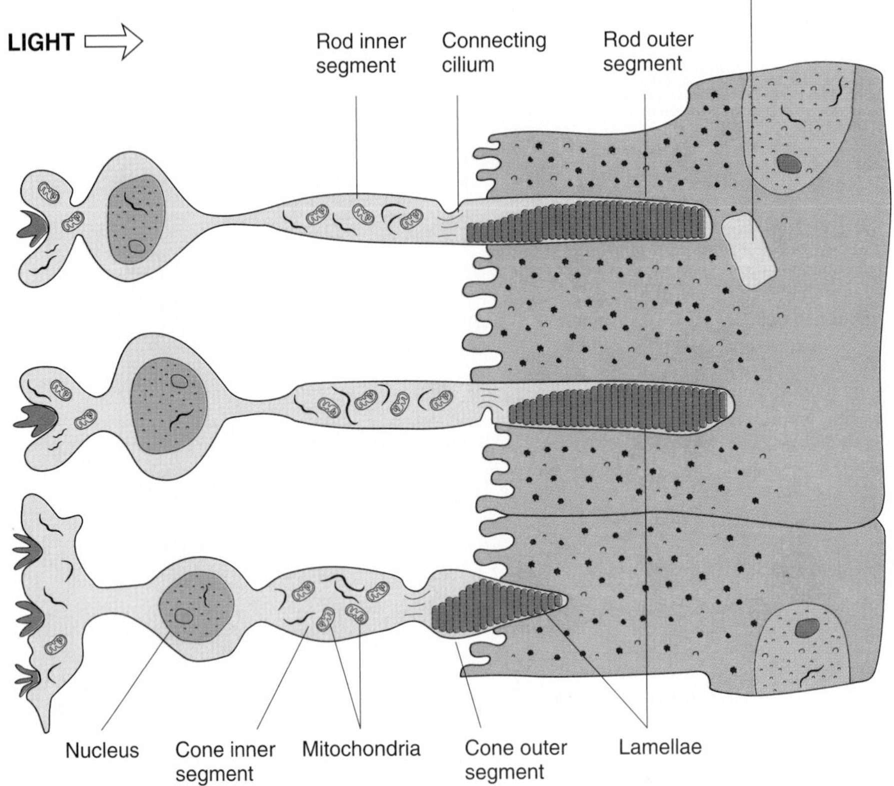

photopigment

opsin

retinal

rhodopsin

receptor potential

Wald, who received a Nobel Prize for his work in 1967.) **Photopigments** are special molecules embedded in the membrane of the lamellae; a single human rod contains approximately 10 million of them. The molecules consist of two parts, an **opsin** (a protein) and **retinal** (a lipid). There are several forms of opsin; for example, the photopigment of human rods, **rhodopsin**, consists of *rod opsin* plus retinal. (*Rhod-* refers to the Greek *rhodon,* "rose," and not to *rod.* Before it is bleached by the action of light, rhodopsin has a pinkish hue.) Retinal is synthesized from vitamin A, which explains why carrots, rich in this vitamin, are said to be good for your eyesight.

When a molecule of rhodopsin is exposed to light, it breaks into its two constituents, rod opsin and retinal. When that happens, the rod opsin changes from its rosy color to a pale yellow; hence, we say that the light *bleaches* the photopigment. The splitting of the photopigment causes a change in the membrane potential of the photoreceptor called the **receptor potential,** which changes the rate at which the photoreceptor releases its transmitter substance. The membrane of photoreceptors is different from that of other neurons — it contains sodium channels that are normally *open.* Thus, the resting membrane potential is less polarized than that of other neurons. Also unlike other neurons, photoreceptors continuously release their neurotransmitter. When light causes a molecule of the photopigment to split, the sodium channels in the outer membrane of the photoreceptor close. The membrane then becomes more polarized, and the transmitter substance is no longer released. (See ***Figure 5.8***.)

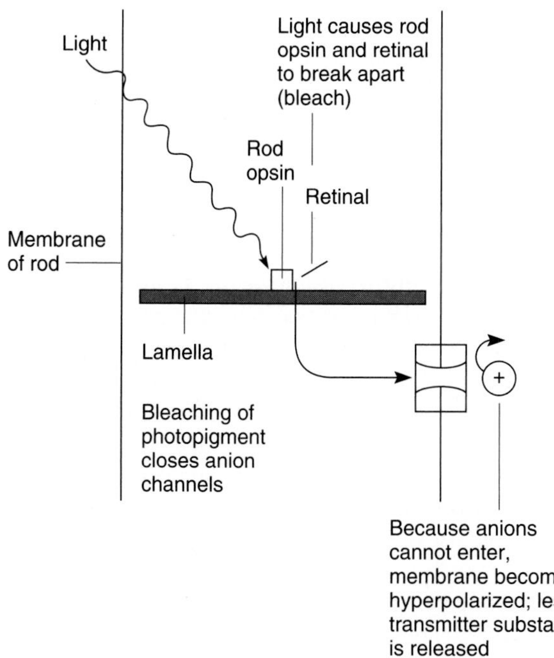

FIGURE 5.8

The process by which light is converted into an electrical signal in a photoreceptor.

In the vertebrate retina photoreceptors provide input to both bipolar cells and horizontal cells. Figure 5.9 shows the neural circuitry from a photoreceptor to a ganglion cell. The circuitry is much simplified and omits the horizontal cells and amacrine cells. The first two types of cells in the circuit—photoreceptors and bipolar cells—do not produce action potentials. Instead, their release of transmitter substance is regulated by the value of their membrane potential; depolarizations increase the release, and hyperpolarizations decrease it. The circles to the left indicate what would be seen on an oscilloscope screen recording changes in the cells' membrane potentials in response to a spot of light shining on the photoreceptor.

The hyperpolarizing effect of light on the membranes of photoreceptors is shown in the top left graph. The hyperpolarization ***reduces*** the release of transmitter substance by the photoreceptor. Because the transmitter substance normally hyperpolarizes the dendrites of the bipolar cell, a ***reduction*** in its release causes the membrane of the

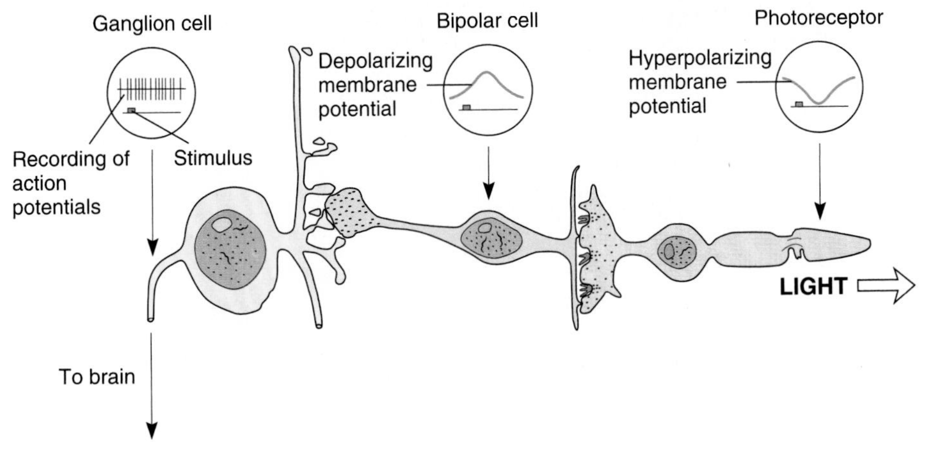

FIGURE 5.9

Neural circuitry in the retina. Light striking a photoreceptor produces a hyperpolarization, so the photoreceptor releases *less* transmitter substance. Because the transmitter substance normally hyperpolarizes the membrane of the bipolar cell, the reduction causes a *depolarization.* The depolarization causes the bipolar cell to release *more* transmitter substance, which excites the ganglion cell. (Adapted from Dowling, J.E., in *The Neurosciences: Fourth Study Program*, edited by F.O. Schmitt and F.G. Worden. Cambridge, Mass.: MIT Press, 1979.)

bipolar cell to *depolarize.* Thus, light hyperpolarizes the photoreceptor and depolarizes the bipolar cell. (See ***Figure 5.9.***) The depolarization causes the bipolar cell to release more transmitter substance, which depolarizes the membrane of the ganglion cell, causing it to increase its rate of firing. Thus, light shining on the photoreceptor causes excitation of the ganglion cell.

Connections Between Eye and Brain

dorsal lateral geniculate nucleus

The axons of the retinal ganglion cells bring information to the rest of the brain. They ascend through the optic nerves and reach the **dorsal lateral geniculate nucleus** of the thalamus. This nucleus receives its name from its resemblance to a bent knee (*genu* means "knee"). It contains six layers of neurons, each of which receives input from only one eye. The neurons in the two inner layers contain larger cell bodies than those in the outer four layers. For this reason, the inner two layers are called the **magnocellular layers** and the outer four layers are called the **parvocellular layers** (*parvo-* refers to the small size of the cells). As we will see later, these two sets of layers belong to different systems, which are responsible for the analysis of different types of visual information. (See ***Figure 5.10.***)

magnocellular layer

parvocellular layer

The neurons in the dorsal lateral geniculate nucleus send their axons via the optic radiations to the primary visual cortex—the region surrounding the **calcarine fissure** (*calcarine* means "spur-shaped"), a horizontal fissure located in the medial and posterior occipital lobe. The primary visual cortex is often called the **striate cortex** because it contains a dark-staining layer *(striation)* of cells. (See ***Figure 5.11.***)

calcarine fissure

striate cortex

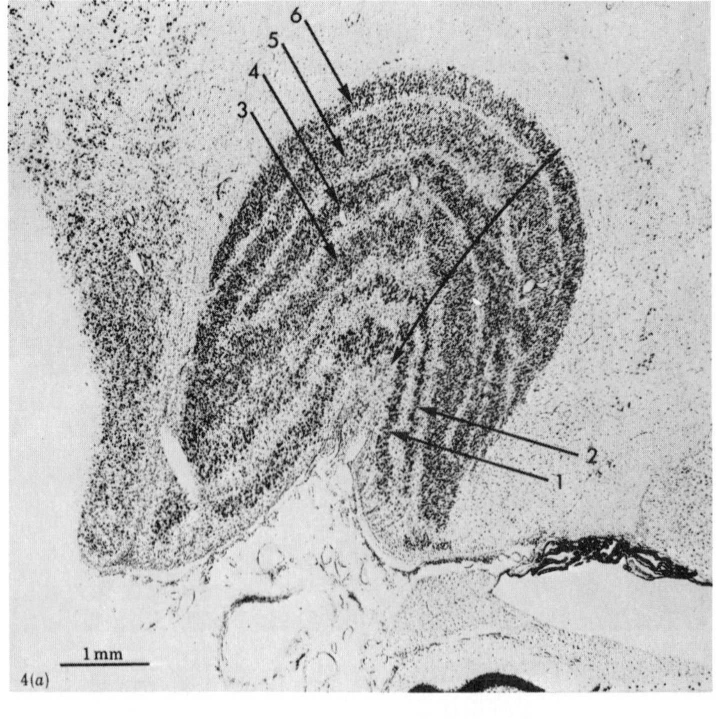

FIGURE 5.10

A photomicrograph of a section through the right lateral geniculate nucleus of a rhesus monkey (cresyl violet stain). Layers 1 and 2 are part of the magnocellular system, and layers 3–6 are part of the parvocellular system. The receptive fields of all six layers are in almost perfect registration; cells located along the line of the unlabeled arrow have receptive fields centered on the same point. (From Hubel, D.H., Wiesel, T.N., and Le Vay, S. *Philosophical Transactions of the Royal Society of London, B.,* 1977, *278,* 131–163. Reprinted with permission.)

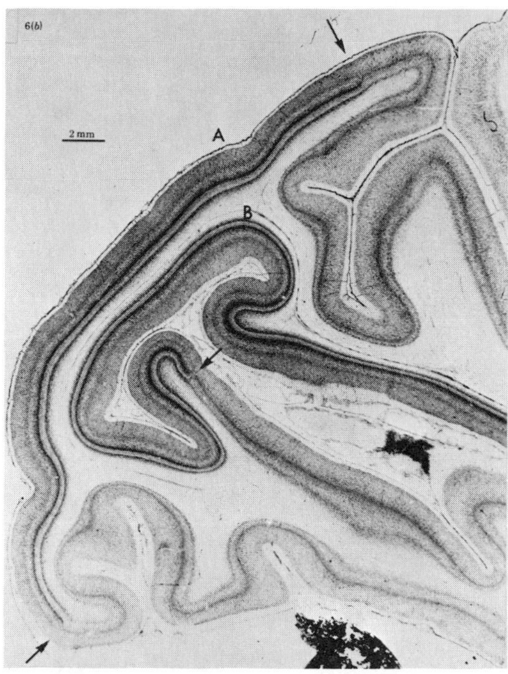

FIGURE 5.11

A photomicrograph of a cross section through the striate cortex of a rhesus macaque monkey. The ends of the striate cortex are shown by arrows. (From Hubel, D.H., and Wiesel, T.N. *Proceedings of the Royal Society of London, B.*, 1977, *198*, 1–59. Reprinted with permission.)

Figure 5.12 shows a diagrammatical view of a horizontal section of the human brain. The optic nerves join together at the base of the brain to form the X-shaped **optic chiasm** (*khiasma* means "cross"). There, axons from ganglion cells serving the inner halves of the retina (the nasal sides) cross through the chiasm and ascend to the dorsal lateral geniculate nucleus of the opposite side of the brain. The axons from the outer halves of the retina (the temporal sides) remain on the same side of the brain. (See ***Figure 5.12.***) The lens inverts the image of the world projected on the retina (and similarly reverses left and right). Therefore, because the axons from the nasal halves of the retinas cross to the other side of the brain, each hemisphere receives information from the contralateral half (opposite side) of the visual scene. That is, if a person looks straight ahead, the right hemisphere receives information from the left half of the visual field, and the left hemisphere receives information from the right. (See ***Figure 5.12.***)

optic chiasm

Figure 5.13 shows the actual appearance of the base of the brain, with neural tissue dissected away so that the optic radiations can be seen. Note the heavy projection to the upper lip of the calcarine fissure. (See ***Figure 5.13.***)

Besides the primary retino-geniculo-cortical pathway, there are several other pathways taken by fibers from the retina. For example, one pathway to the hypothalamus synchronizes an animal's activity cycles to the 24-hour rhythms of day and night. (We will study this system in Chapter 8.) Other pathways, especially those that travel to the tectum, coordinate eye movements, control the muscles of the iris and lens, and help direct our attention to sudden movements in the periphery of our visual field. As we saw in the discussion of blindsight in Chapter 1, damage in the primary retino-geniculo-cortical pathway (the "mammalian visual system") causes blindness, but people can still use the pathway that travels from the retina to the tectum (the "primitive visual system") to control hand movements in reaching for objects.

FIGURE 5.12

The primary visual pathway. (Adapted from Netter, F.H. *The Ciba Collection of Medical Illustrations. Vol. 1, Nervous System.* Summit, N.J.: Ciba Pharmaceutical Products Co., 1953.)

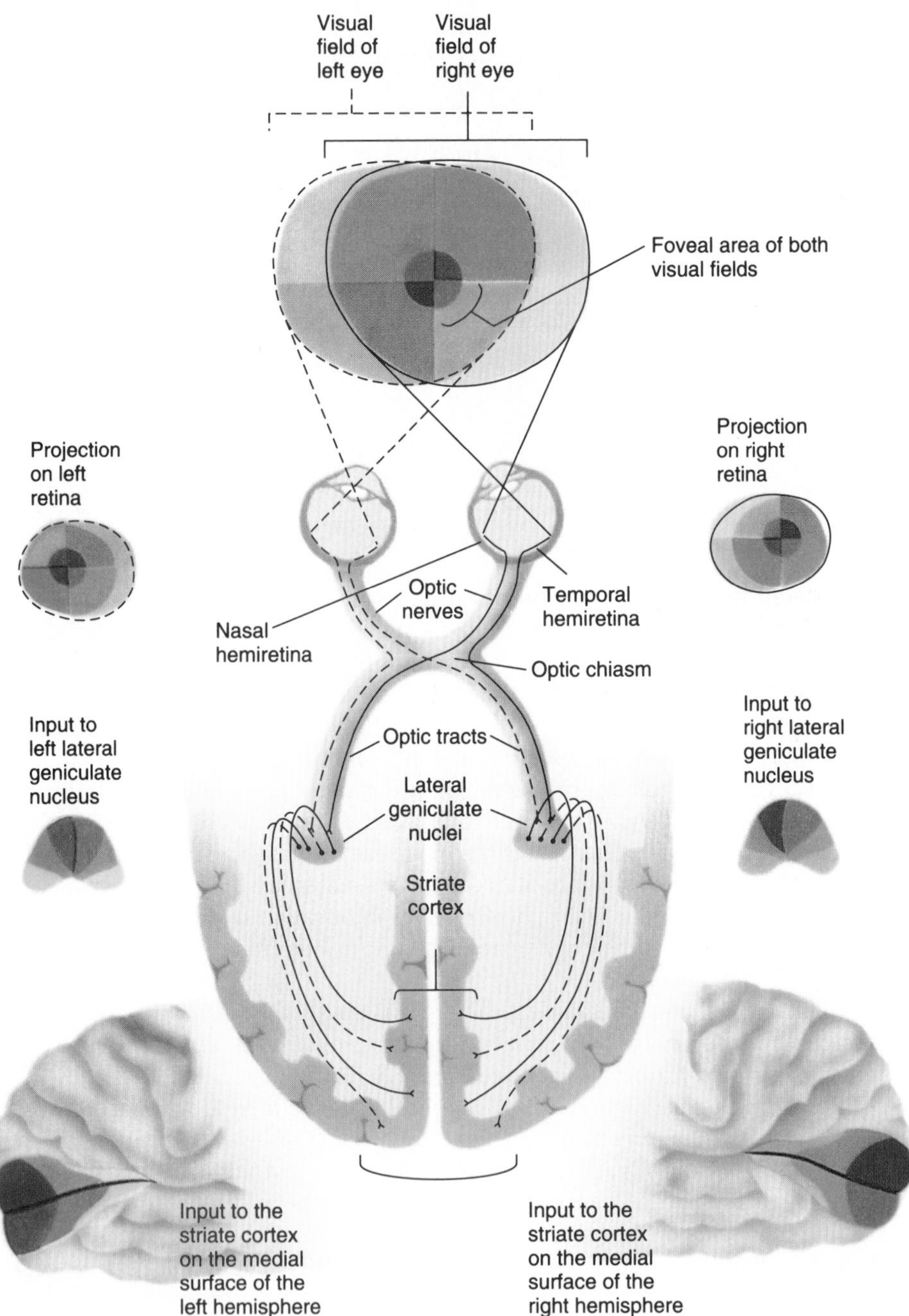

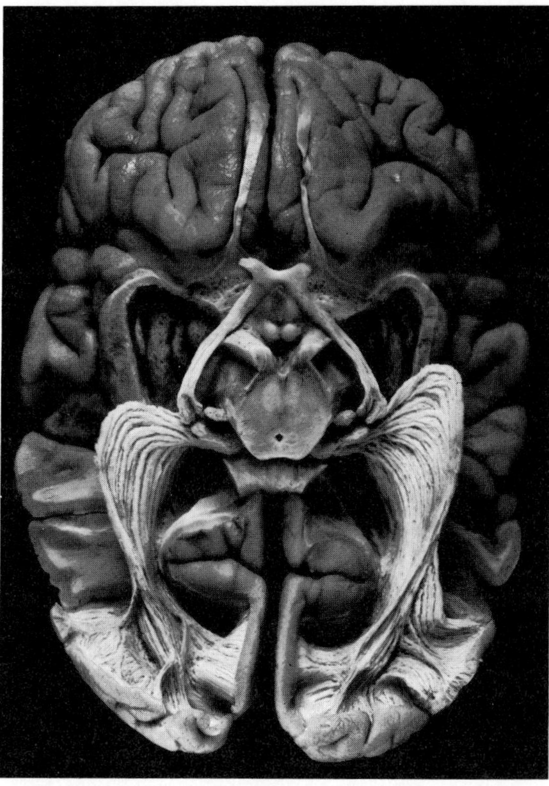

FIGURE 5.13

The base of the brain, with tissue dissected away so that the projections (optic radiations) between the dorsal lateral geniculate nucleus and the striate cortex are visible. (From Gluhbegovic, N., and Williams, T.H. *The Human Brain: A Photographic Atlas.* Hagerstown, Md.: Harper & Row, 1980. Reprinted with permission.)

▶*INTERIM SUMMARY*◀

Light consists of electromagnetic radiation, similar to radio waves but of a different frequency and wavelength. Color can vary in three perceptual dimensions: hue, brightness, and saturation, which correspond to the physical dimensions of wavelength, intensity, and purity.

The photoreceptors in the retina—the rods and the cones—detect light. Muscles move the eyes so that images of the environment fall on the retina. Accommodation is accomplished by the ciliary muscles, which change the shape of the lens. Photoreceptors communicate through synapses with bipolar cells, which communicate through synapses with ganglion cells. In addition, horizontal cells and amacrine cells combine messages from adjacent photoreceptors.

When light strikes a molecule of photopigment in a photoreceptor, the retinal molecule detaches from the opsin molecule. This detachment initiates a series of chemical reactions that closes sodium channels and produces the receptor potential—hyperpolarization of the photoreceptor membrane. As a result, the rate of firing of the ganglion cell changes, signaling the detection of light. Because different types of cones contain different types of opsins, they are most sensitive to light of different wavelengths. This fact provides the basis for color vision.

Visual information from the retina reaches the striate cortex surrounding the calcarine fissure after being relayed through the magnocellular and parvocellular layers of the dorsal lateral geniculate nuclei. Several other regions of the brain, including the hypothalamus and the tectum, also receive visual information. These regions help regulate activity during the day-night cycle, coordinate eye and head movements, control attention to visual stimuli, and regulate the size of the pupils. ▲

ANALYSIS OF VISUAL FORM

This section describes the functions of the visual system, from retinal ganglion cell to the visual association cortex. I will summarize what is known about the nature and response characteristics of the neurons located in each structure and about the nature of the connections between the structures. The discussion begins with a description of the two known visual systems in primates.

Two Visual Systems

Recent research (Livingstone and Hubel, 1987, 1988; Zeki and Shipp, 1988) has shown that the primate visual system consists of two parallel, largely independent systems: the *magnocellular system* and the *parvocellular system,* named after the two types of cell layers in the dorsal lateral geniculate nucleus. The magnocellular system appears to have evolved earlier and is found in all mammals, including primates. The parvocellular system is seen only in primates.

The magnocellular system is involved with the analysis of form, movement, and depth. The parvocellular system is involved with visual functions that only primates possess: color perception and detection of fine details. These additional abilities are very useful for animals that exploit a wide range of habitats and foodstuffs; for example, a monkey can easily discriminate ripe fruit from unripe fruit and from the green leaves of the tree. Specific damage to the parvocellular system causes loss of color vision and the ability to detect fine details but leaves perception of form, movement, and depth intact (Merigan and Eskin, 1986; Merigan, 1989).

Response Characteristics of Neurons in the Retina and Thalamus

One of the most important methods for studying the physiology of the visual system is the use of microelectrodes to record the electrical activity of single neurons. As we just saw, some ganglion cells become excited when light falls on the photoreceptors with which they communicate. The **receptive field** of a neuron in the visual system is the part of the visual field that neuron "sees"—that is, the part in which light must fall for it to be stimulated. Obviously, the location of the receptive field of a particular neuron depends on the location of the photoreceptors that provide it with visual information. If a neuron receives information from photoreceptors located in the fovea, its receptive field will be at the fixation point—the point at which the eye is looking. If it receives information from photoreceptors located in the periphery of the retina, its receptive field will be located off to one side.

receptive field

At the periphery of the retina many individual receptors converge on a single ganglion cell, bringing information from a relatively large area of the retina—and hence a relatively large area of the visual field. However, foveal vision is more direct, with approximately equal numbers of ganglion cells and cones. These receptor-to-axon relationships explain the fact that our foveal (central) vision is very acute, but our peripheral vision is much less precise. (See ***Figure 5.14.***)

Kuffler (1952, 1953), recording from ganglion cells in the retina of the cat, discovered that their receptive field consists of a roughly circular center, surrounded by a ring. Normally, ganglion cells fired continuously, at a moderate rate. When a spot of light was presented to the central field (*center*), the neuron began firing more rapidly. However, when the spot was moved to the surrounding field (*surround*), the cell ceased firing; the light inhibited it. Ganglion cells thus respond in a center-on, surround-off

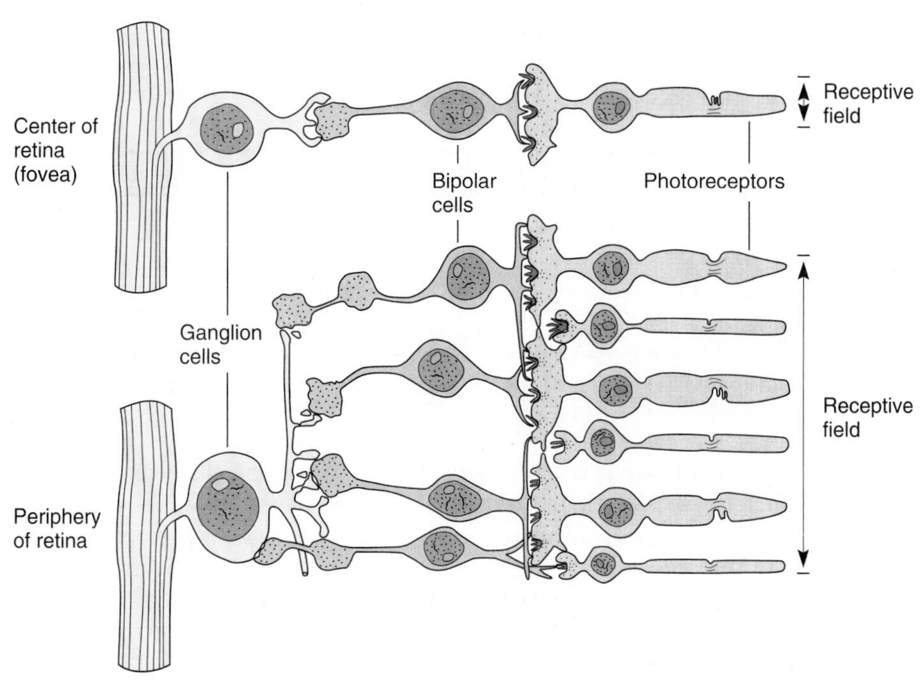

FIGURE 5.14

Central versus peripheral acuity. Ganglion cells in the fovea receive input from a smaller number of photoreceptors than those in the periphery and hence provide more acute visual information.

manner. Kuffler also identified cells that gave the opposite set of responses: center off, surround on. (See ***Figure 5.15.***)

As I mentioned earlier in this chapter, the distinction between the magnocellular and parvocellular system is an important one. The magnocellular layers are found in all mammals, whereas the parvocellular layers are found only in primates. These two types

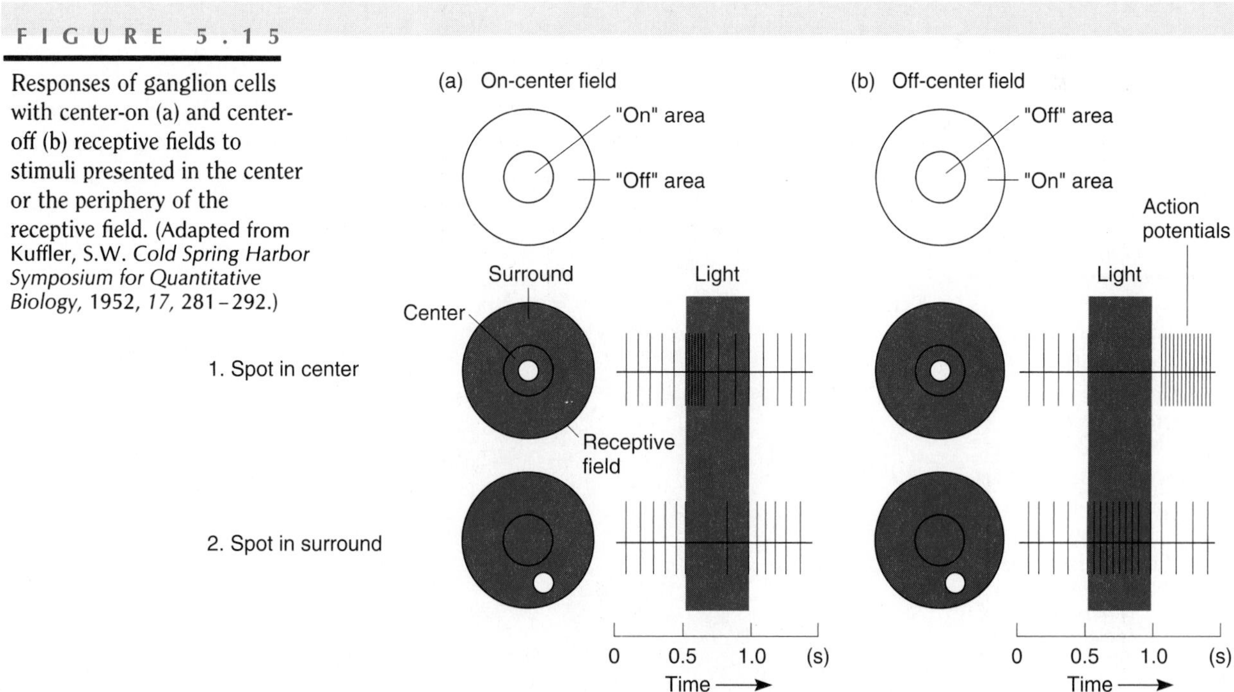

FIGURE 5.15

Responses of ganglion cells with center-on (a) and center-off (b) receptive fields to stimuli presented in the center or the periphery of the receptive field. (Adapted from Kuffler, S.W. *Cold Spring Harbor Symposium for Quantitative Biology*, 1952, *17*, 281–292.)

▲ TABLE 5.1 ▲

Properties of the Magnocellular and Parvocellular Divisions of the Visual System

Property	*Magnocellular Division*	*Parvocellular Division*
Color	No	Yes
Sensitivity to contrast	High	Low
Spatial resolution	Low	High
Temporal resolution	Fast (transient response)	Slow (sustained response)

SOURCE: Adapted from Livingstone, M.S., and Hubel, D.H. *Journal of Neuroscience,* 1987, *7,* 3416–3468.

of layers receive information from different types of ganglion cells, which are connected to different types of bipolar cells and photoreceptors. Indeed, recordings of neurons in the dorsal lateral geniculate nucleus have shown that the parvocellular and magnocellular layers receive very different types of information (Livingstone and Hubel, 1987). Many neurons in the more recent *parvocellular layers* respond to different hues. For example, they might be excited by a red light shone on the center of their receptive field and inhibited by a green light. They also show high spatial resolution and low temporal resolution; that is, they are able to detect very fine details, but their response is slow and prolonged. In contrast, neurons in the older *magnocellular layers* are color-blind, are not able to detect fine details, and respond very briefly to a visual stimulus. And although they appear to be responsible for vision of lower acuity, they are able to detect smaller contrasts between light and dark. They are sensitive to movement and to retinal disparity, a characteristic that I will explain later. (See ***Table 5.1.***)

Response Characteristics of Neurons in the Striate Cortex

The striate cortex consists of six principal layers (and several sublayers), arranged in bands parallel to the surface. These layers contain the nuclei of cell bodies and dendritic trees that show up as bands of light or dark in sections of tissue that have been dyed with a cell-body stain. (See ***Figure 5.16.***)

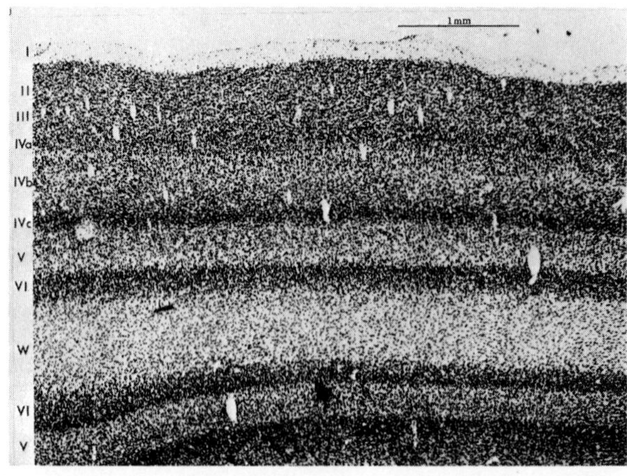

FIGURE 5.16

A photomicrograph of a small section of striate cortex, showing the six principal layers. The letter W refers to the white matter that underlies the visual cortex; beneath the white matter is layer VI of the striate cortex on the opposite side of the gyrus. (From Hubel, D.H., and Wiesel, T.N. *Proceedings of the Royal Society of London, B.,* 1977, *198,* 1–59. Reprinted with permission.)

In primates, information from the dorsal lateral geniculate nucleus enters the middle layer (layer IV_c) of the striate cortex. From there, it is relayed upward and downward, to be analyzed by circuits of neurons in different layers. If we consider the striate cortex as a whole—if we imagine that we remove it and spread it out on a flat surface—we find that it contains a map of the contralateral half of the visual field. (Remember that each side of the brain sees the opposite side of the visual field.) The map is somewhat distorted; approximately 25 percent of the striate cortex is devoted to the analysis of information from the fovea, which represents a small part of the visual field. (The area of the visual field seen by the fovea is approximately the size of a large grape held at arm's length.)

The pioneering studies of David Hubel and Torsten Wiesel at Harvard University during the 1960s began a revolution in the study of the physiology of visual perception (see Hubel and Wiesel, 1977, 1979). Hubel and Wiesel discovered that neurons in the visual cortex did not simply respond to spots of light; they selectively responded to specific *features* of the visual world. The following subsections describe these features: orientation and movement, spatial frequency, and retinal disparity. The analysis of another feature—color—is described in a later section of this chapter.

FIGURE 5.17

Orientation sensitivity. An orientation-sensitive neuron in the striate cortex will become active only when a line of a particular orientation appears within its receptive field. For example, the neuron might respond to the black bar but not to either of the gray bars.

ORIENTATION AND MOVEMENT

Most neurons in the striate cortex are sensitive to *orientation.* That is, if a line is positioned in the cell's receptive field and rotated around its center, the cell will respond only when the line is in a particular position—a particular orientation. (See ***Figure 5.17.***) Some neurons respond best to a vertical line, some to a horizontal line, and some to a line oriented somewhere in between.

Some orientation-sensitive neurons have receptive fields organized in an opponent fashion. Hubel and Wiesel referred to them as **simple cells.** For example, a line of a particular orientation (say, a dark 45-degree line against a white background) might excite the cell if placed in the center of the receptive field but inhibit it if moved away from the center. (See ***Figure 5.18a.***) Another type of neuron, which they referred to as a **complex cell,** also responded best to a line of a particular orientation but did not show an inhibitory surround; that is, it continued to respond while the line was moved within the receptive field. In fact, many complex cells increased their rate of firing when the line was moved perpendicular to its angle of orientation; thus, they also served as movement detectors. In addition, complex cells responded equally well to white lines against black backgrounds and black lines against white backgrounds. (See ***Figure 5.18b.***)

simple cell

complex cell

FIGURE 5.18

Response characteristics of neurons in the striate cortex. (a) Simple cell. (b) Complex cell.

Simple cell is excited

Simple cell is inhibited

(a)

Complex cell is excited by all three stimuli

(b)

FIGURE 5.19

Parallel gratings. (a) Square-wave grating. (b) Sine-wave grating. (Courtesy of R. L. De Valois, University of California, Berkley.)

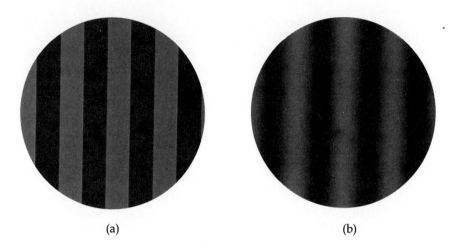

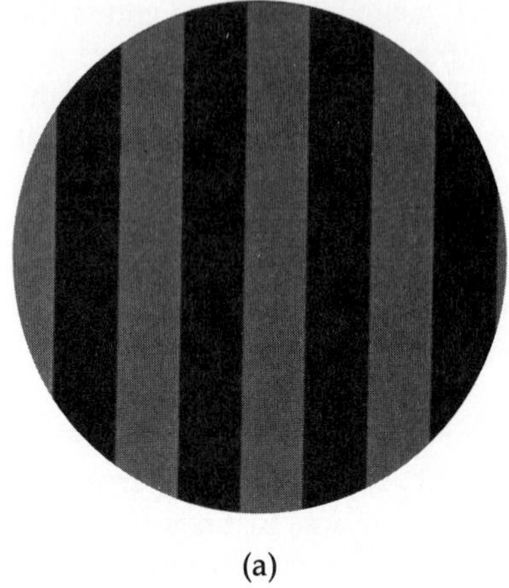

(a)

(b)

SPATIAL FREQUENCY

Although the early studies by Hubel and Wiesel suggested that these neurons detected lines and edges, subsequent research found that they actually responded best to sine-wave gratings (De Valois, Albrecht, and Thorell, 1978). Figure 5.19 compares a sine-wave grating with a more familiar square-wave grating. A square-wave grating consists of a simple set of rectangular bars that vary in brightness; the brightness along the length of a line perpendicular to them would vary in a stepwise (square-wave) fashion. (See ***Figure 5.19a.***) A **sine-wave grating** looks like a series of fuzzy, unfocused parallel bars. Along any line perpendicular to the long axis of the grating, the brightness varies according to a sine-wave function. (See ***Figure 5.19b.***)

sine-wave grating

A sine-wave grating is designated by its spatial frequency. We are accustomed to frequencies (for example, of sound waves or radio waves) being expressed in terms of time or distance (such as cycles per second or cycles per meter). But because the image of a stimulus on the retina varies in size according to how close it is to the eye, the visual angle is generally used instead of the physical distance between adjacent cycles. Thus, the **spatial frequency** of a sine-wave grating is its variation in brightness measured in cycles per degree of visual angle. (See ***Figure 5.20.***)

visual angle
spatial frequency

FIGURE 5.20

The concepts of visual angle and spatial frequency. Angles are drawn between the sine waves, with the apex at the viewer's eye. The *visual angle* between adjacent sine waves is smaller when the waves are closer together.

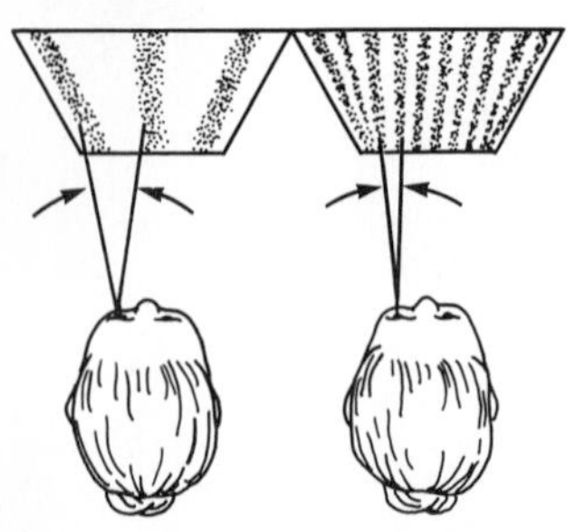

Most neurons in the striate cortex respond best when a sine-wave grating of a particular spatial frequency is placed in the appropriate part of the visual field. For orientation-sensitive neurons the grating must be aligned at the appropriate angle of orientation. Albrecht (1978) mapped the shapes of receptive fields of simple cells by observing their response while moving a very thin flickering line of the appropriate orientation through their receptive fields. He found that many of them had multiple inhibitory and excitatory regions surrounding the center. The profile of the excitatory and inhibitory regions of such neurons looked like a modulated sine wave—precisely what would be needed to detect a few cycles of a sine-wave grating. (See ***Figure 5.21.***) In most cases a neuron's receptive field is large enough to include between 1.5 and 3.5 cycles of the grating (De Valois, Thorell, and Albrecht, 1985).

Before we move on to the next level of the visual association cortex, I should say a few words about the usefulness of spatial frequency. What is the point of having neural circuits that analyze this feature? A complete answer requires some rather complicated mathematics, so I will give a simplified one here. (If you are interested, you can consult De Valois and De Valois, 1988.) Consider the types of information provided by high and low spatial frequencies. Small objects, details within a large object, and large objects

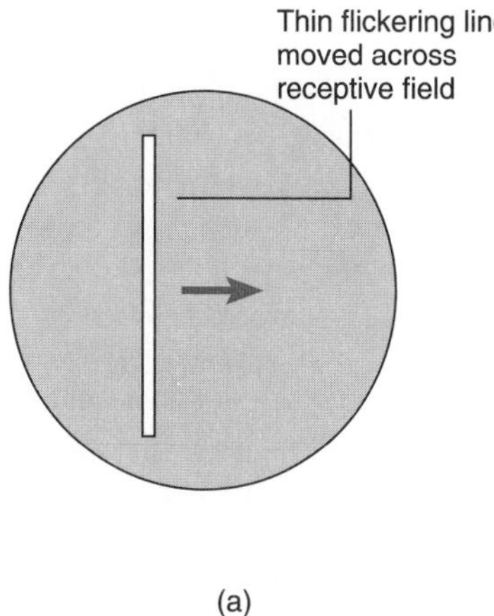

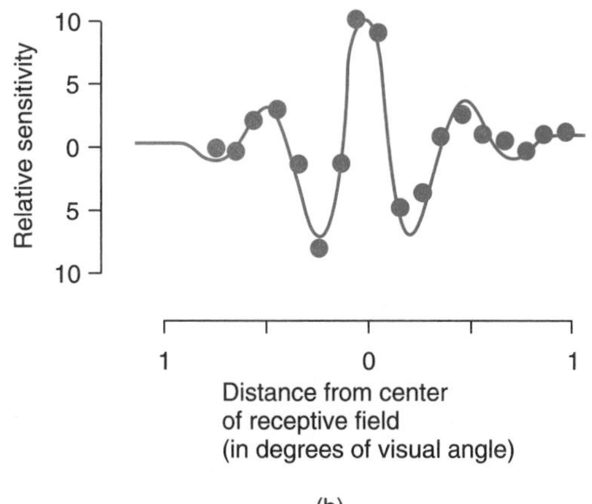

FIGURE 5.21

The experiment by Albrecht, 1978. (a) The stimulus presented to the animal. (b) The response of a simple cell in the striate cortex. (Adapted from De Valois, R.L., and De Valois, K.K. *Spatial Vision.* New York: Oxford University Press, 1988.)

with sharp edges provide a signal rich in high frequencies; whereas large areas of light and dark are represented by low frequencies. An image that is deficient in high-frequency information looks fuzzy and out of focus, like the image seen by a nearsighted person who is not wearing corrective lenses. This image still provides much information about forms and objects in the environment; thus, the most important visual information is that contained in *low spatial frequencies.* When low-frequency information is removed, the shapes of images are very difficult to perceive. (As we saw, the more primitive magnocellular system provides low-frequency information.)

Many experiments have confirmed that the concept of spatial frequency plays a central role in visual perception, and mathematical models have shown that the information present in a scene can be represented very efficiently if it is first encoded in terms of spatial frequency. Thus, the brain probably represents the information in a similar way. Here I will describe just one example to help show the validity of the concept. Look at the two pictures in ***Figure 5.22.*** You can see that the photograph on the bottom looks much more like the face of Abraham Lincoln than the one on the top. And yet both photographs contain the same information. The creators of the photographs, Harmon and Julesz (1973), used a computer to construct the figure on the top, which consists of a series of squares, each representing the average brightness of a portion of a picture of Lincoln. The one on the bottom is simply a transformation of the first one in which high frequencies have been removed. Sharp edges contain high spatial frequencies, so the transformation eliminates them. In the case of the upper picture these frequencies have nothing to do with the information contained in the original picture; thus, they can be seen as visual "noise." The filtration process (accomplished by a computer) removes this noise—and makes the image much clearer to the human visual system. Presumably, the high frequencies produced by the edges of the squares in the upper figure stimulate neurons in the striate cortex that are tuned to high spatial frequencies. When the visual association cortex receives this noisy information, it has difficulty perceiving the underlying form.

If you want to watch the effect of filtering the extraneous high-frequency noise, try the following demonstration. Put the book down and look at the figures from across the room. The distance "erases" the high frequencies, because they exceed the resolving power of the eye, and the two pictures look identical. Now walk toward the book, focusing on the upper figure. As you get closer, the higher frequencies reappear and this face gets harder and harder to recognize. (See ***Figure 5.22.***)

FIGURE 5.22

Spatial filtering. Both pictures contain the same amount of low-frequency information, but extraneous high-frequency information has been filtered from the picture at the bottom. If you look at the pictures from across the room, they look identical. (From Harmon, L.D., and Julesz, B. *Science*, 1973, *180*, 1191–1197. Copyright 1973 by the American Association for the Advancement of Science. Reprinted with permission.)

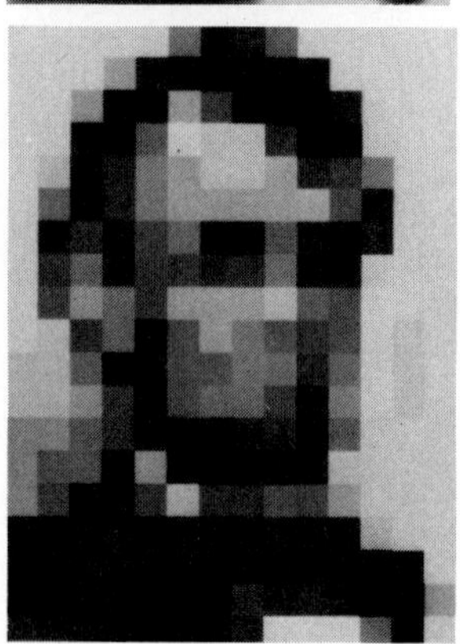

retinal disparity
blob

RETINAL DISPARITY

So far, we have seen that neurons in the primate striate cortex encode information about orientation and spatial frequency, and as we shall see, these two characteristics help us recognize shapes and patterns. Another characteristic helps us perceive depth. We perceive depth by many means, most of which involve cues that can be detected monocularly, by one eye alone. For example, perspective, relative retinal size, loss of detail through the effects of atmospheric haze, and relative apparent movement of retinal images as we move our heads all contribute to depth perception and do not require binocular vision. However, binocular vision provides a vivid perception of depth through the process of stereoscopic vision, or ***stereopsis.*** If you have used a stereoscope (such as a View Master) or have seen a three-dimensional movie, you know what I mean.

Most neurons in the striate cortex are ***binocular***—that is, they respond to visual stimulation of either eye. Many of these binocular cells, especially those found in a layer that receives information from the magnocellular system, have response patterns that appear to contribute to the perception of depth (Poggio and Poggio, 1984). In most cases the cells respond most vigorously when each eye sees a stimulus in a slightly *different* location. That is, the neurons respond to **retinal disparity,** a stimulus that produces images on slightly different parts of the retina of each eye. This is exactly the information that is needed for stereopsis; each eye sees a three-dimensional scene slightly differently, and the presence of retinal disparity indicates differences in the distance of objects from the observer.

To summarize, neurons in the striate cortex respond to several different features of a visual stimulus, including orientation, movement, spatial frequency, and retinal disparity. In addition, as we shall see later in this chapter, some cells respond differentially to color.

Modular Organization of the Striate Cortex

Most investigators believe that the brain is organized in modules, which probably range in size from a hundred thousand to a few million neurons. Each module receives information from other modules, performs some calculations, and then passes the results to other modules. In recent years investigators have been learning the characteristics of the modules that are found in the visual cortex (De Valois and De Valois, 1988; Livingstone and Hubel, 1988).

The striate cortex is divided into approximately 2500 modules, each approximately 0.5 × 0.7 mm (millimeters) and containing approximately 150,000 neurons. The neurons in each module are devoted to the analysis of various features contained in one very small portion of the visual field. Together, these modules receive information from the entire visual field, the individual modules serving like the tiles in a mosaic mural. The modules actually consist of two segments, each centered around a special group of cells known as a **blob.** Blobs were discovered by Wong-Riley (1978), who found that a stain for an enzyme present in mitochondria showed a patchy distribution. Subsequent research with the stain (Horton and Hubel, 1980; Humphrey and Hendrickson, 1980) revealed the presence of a polka-dot pattern of dark columns extending through most of the layers. Blobs are oval in cross section, approximately 150 × 200 μm in diameter, and spaced at 0.5-mm intervals. (A μm, or micrometer, is .001 mm.)

Figure 5.23 shows a photograph of a slice through the visual cortex of a macaque monkey that has been flattened out and stained for the mitochondrial enzyme. You can clearly see the blobs within the striate cortex. Because the curvature of the cortex

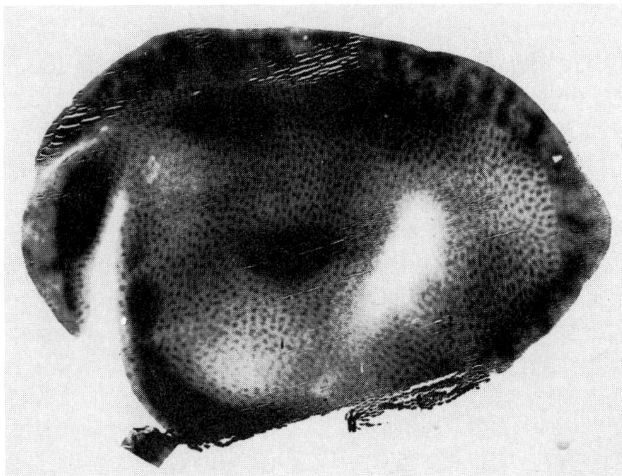

FIGURE 5.23

A photomicrograph of a slice through the striate cortex of a macaque monkey, parallel to the surface, stained for an enzyme found in mitochondria. Blobs are shown as dark spots. (From Hubel, D.H., and Livingstone, M.S. *Journal of Neuroscience,* 1989, *7,* 3378–3415. Reprinted by permission of the *Journal of Neuroscience.*)

prevents it from being perfectly flattened, some of the tissue is missing in the center of the slice. (See ***Figure 5.23.***)

Although the neurons in a given module respond to information from approximately the same part of the visual field, those located within the blobs have a special function: They are sensitive to color but ignore the other features (Livingstone and Hubel, 1982). Outside the blob neurons show sensitivity to orientation, movement, spatial frequency, and binocular disparity—but not to color. Each half of the module receives input from only one eye, but because most neurons in the striate cortex are binocular, the circuitry within the module obviously combines the information from the two eyes. (See ***Figure 5.24.***)

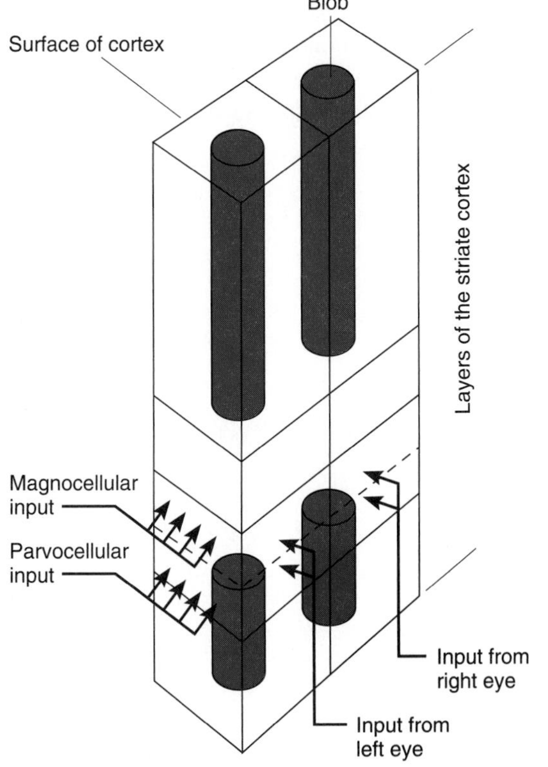

FIGURE 5.24

One of the modules of the striate cortex.

Visual Association Cortex

Perception of objects and of the totality of the visual scene does not take place in the striate cortex. Each module sees only what is happening in one tiny part of the visual field. Thus, in order for us to perceive objects and entire visual scenes, the information from these individual modules must be combined. That combination takes place in the visual association cortex.

Visual information received from the striate cortex is analyzed in two stages. The first stage takes place in the *prestriate cortex.* Further analysis takes place in two other regions—the association cortex of the parietal lobe and the inferior temporal lobe. The inferior temporal cortex recognizes *what* an object is, and the parietal cortex recognizes *where* the object is located. These three regions of the visual association cortex are described in detail below.

PRESTRIATE CORTEX

prestriate cortex

Neurons in the striate cortex send axons to the **prestriate cortex.** *Prestriate* is a misleading term, because it actually comes after striate cortex, rather than before it, in the analysis of visual information. (For this reason some investigators use the term *circumstriate* cortex, because it surrounds the striate cortex.) Zeki and his colleagues (see Zeki and Shipp, 1988) have studied the prestriate cortex in some detail. (See ***Figure 5.25.***)

The primate prestriate cortex consists of at least five subareas, each of which contains one or more independent maps of the visual field. Each subarea is specialized, containing neurons that respond to a particular feature of visual information, such as orientation, movement, spatial frequency, retinal disparity, or color. Possibly, these subareas respond to other features that have not yet been discovered. Zeki (1984) suggests that this system permits interactions among similar kinds of features. For example, placing color-sensitive neurons together in one cortical area provides the basis for phenomena such as color constancy—relatively constant perception of colors even under varying lighting conditions. In addition, placing movement-sensitive

FIGURE 5.25

Areas of visual cortex of the human brain. (a) Lateral view. (b) Midsagittal view.

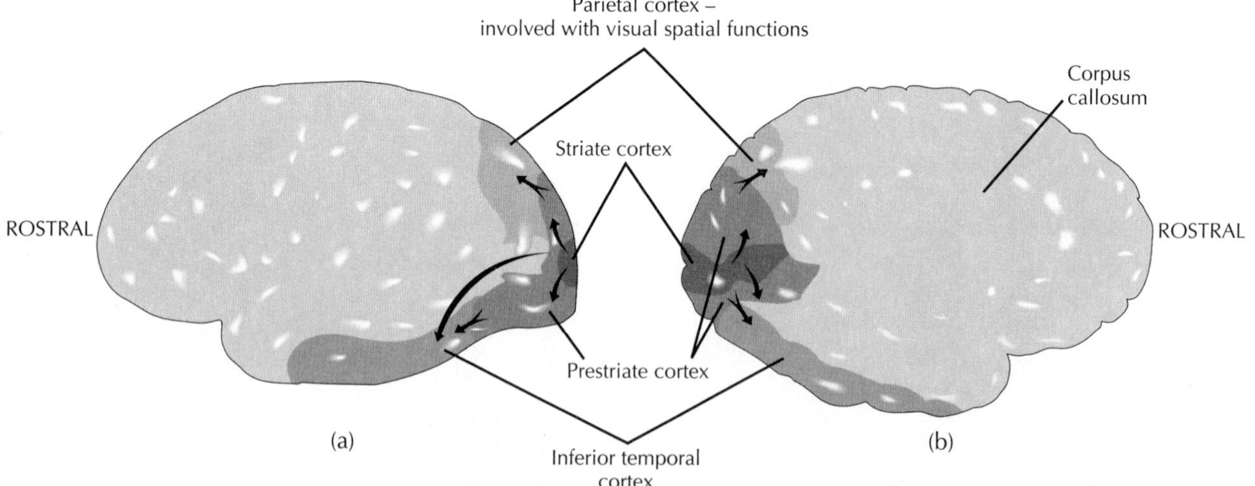

neurons in another cortical area may provide the circuitry that enables the visual system to extract information about form from movement — for example, the ability to perceive elements moving in a particular direction as belonging to the same object. We probably owe our ability to see windblown waves in a field of grain or to recognize someone by the way he or she walks to this region of the prestriate cortex.

INFERIOR TEMPORAL CORTEX

In primates the recognition of visual patterns and identification of particular objects takes place in a region of the brain called the **inferior temporal cortex,** located on the ventral part of the temporal lobe. (See ***Figure 5.25.***) This region of association cortex receives inputs from all subareas of the prestriate cortex. It is here that analyses of form, movement, depth, and color are put together and perceptions of three-dimensional objects and backgrounds are achieved. In many ways it is the most interesting region of all, because neural circuits here "learn" to detect stimuli with particular shapes, regardless of their size or location. For that reason I will discuss this region in more detail in Chapter 12, which deals with the physiology of learning and memory.

inferior temporal cortex

Many studies have investigated the functions of the primate inferior temporal cortex. In general, they respond best to three-dimensional objects (or photographs of them) rather than to simple stimuli such as spots, lines, or sine-wave gratings. For example, some respond best to a photograph of a hand, some to a profile of a monkey's face, and some to the front of a monkey's face. Destruction of the visual association cortex in the temporal lobes of humans results in deficits in visual perception; these deficits will be discussed in the last section of this chapter.

PARIETAL CORTEX

As we just saw, all subareas of the prestriate cortex send information to the inferior temporal cortex, the region in which object perception appears to take place. In addition, three subareas of the prestriate cortex — those involved with color, orientation, and movement — send information to the parietal cortex. The parietal lobe is involved in spatial perception, and it is through these connections that it receives its visual input. Damage to the parietal lobes disrupts performance on a variety of tasks that require perceiving and remembering the locations of objects (Ungerleider and Mishkin, 1982).

A particularly interesting phenomenon called **Balint's syndrome** occurs in humans who have sustained bilateral damage to the parieto-occipital region — the region bordering the parietal lobe and occipital lobe (Balint, 1909; Damasio, 1985). Such damage usually occurs when a person undergoes a period of very low blood pressure, which produces a lack of oxygen in regions of the brain between the areas irrigated by major arteries, where the blood supply is not especially rich. The parieto-occipital region, situated between the areas supplied by the middle and posterior cerebral arteries, is one of these areas. Balint's syndrome consists of three major symptoms: optic ataxia, ocular apraxia, and simultanagnosia. All three symptoms are related to spatial perception.

Balint's syndrome

Optic ataxia is a deficit in reaching for objects under visual guidance (*ataxia* comes from the Greek word for "disorderly"). A person with Balint's syndrome might be able to perceive and recognize a particular object, but when he or she tries to reach for it, the movement is often misdirected. **Ocular apraxia** (literally "without visual action") is a deficit of visual scanning. If a person with Balint's syndrome looks around a room filled

optic ataxia

ocular apraxia

with objects, he or she will see an occasional item and will be able to perceive it normally. However, the patient will not be able to maintain fixation; his or her eyes will begin to wander and another object will come into view for a time. The person is unable to make a systematic scan of the contents of the room and will not be able to perceive the location of the objects he or she sees. If an object moves, or if a light flashes, the person may report seeing something but will not be able to make an eye movement that directs the gaze toward the target.

simultanagnosia

Simultanagnosia is the most interesting of the three symptoms. As I just mentioned, if the gaze of a person with Balint's syndrome happens to fall on an object, he or she will perceive it. But *only one object* will be perceived at a time. For example, if an examiner holds either a comb or a pen in front of a patient's eyes, the patient will recognize the object. But if the examiner holds a pen and a comb together (for example, so that they form the legs of an X), the patient will see either the comb or the pen, but not both. The existence of simultanagnosia means that perception of separate objects takes place at least somewhat independently, even when the outlines of the objects overlap in the visual field.

▶INTERIM SUMMARY◀

Research by Livingstone and Hubel suggests that the primate visual system contains two major components, named after layers of the dorsal lateral geniculate nucleus: the magnocellular system (more primitive; color-blind; sensitive to movement, depth, and small differences in brightness) and the parvocellular system (more recent, color-sensitive, and able to discriminate finer details).

Most retinal ganglion cells respond in an opposing center/surround fashion, becoming excited when light falls in one region and becoming inhibited when it falls in the other. Projections from the parvocellular and magnocellular layers terminate in different layers of the striate cortex. The striate cortex is organized into modules, each surrounding a pair of blobs, which are revealed by a stain for an enzyme found in mitochondria. Each half of a module receives information from one eye; but because information is shared, most of the neurons respond to input to both eyes. The neurons in the blobs are sensitive to color, whereas those between the blobs are sensitive to sine-wave gratings of different spatial frequencies and orientations, and to retinal disparity and movement.

The prestriate cortex receives information from the striate cortex and from the superior colliculus. It is divided into at least five distinct regions where neurons with special functions reside. The prestriate cortex sends information on to two regions of association cortex: the inferior temporal cortex and the parietal cortex. Both lesion studies and electrical-recording studies indicate that object perception takes place in the inferior temporal cortex, whereas the perception of the spatial location of objects takes place in the parietal cortex. Balint's syndrome, which is caused by bilateral damage to the parieto-occipital region, includes the symptoms of optic ataxia, ocular apraxia, and simultanagnosia. ▲

COLOR VISION

Various theories of color vision have been proposed for many years — long before it was possible to disprove or validate them by physiological means. In 1802 Thomas Young, a British physicist and physician, proposed that the eye detected different colors because it contained three types of receptors, each sensitive to a single hue. His theory was referred to as the *trichromatic* (three-color) *theory.* It was suggested by the

FIGURE 5.26

Additive color mixing and paint mixing. When blue, red, and green light of the proper intensity are all shone together, the result is white light. When red, blue, and yellow paints are mixed together, the result is a dark gray. (Photo courtesy of GATF.)

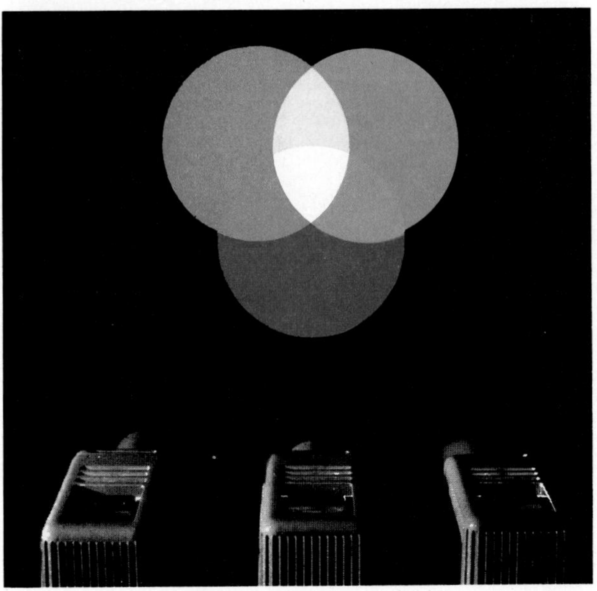

fact that for a human observer any color can be reproduced by mixing various quantities of three colors judiciously selected from different points along the spectrum.

I must emphasize that *color mixing* is different from *pigment mixing.* If we combine yellow and blue pigments (as when we mix paints), the resulting mixture is green. Color mixing refers to the addition of two or more light sources. If we shine a beam of red light and a beam of bluish green light together on a white screen, we will see yellow light. If we mix yellow and blue light, we get white light. When white appears on a color television screen, it actually consists of tiny dots of red, blue, and green light. (See ***Figures 5.26 and 5.27.***)

Another fact of color perception suggested to a German physiologist, Ewald Hering (1905/1965), that hue might be represented in the visual system as *opponent colors.* Humans have long regarded yellow, blue, red, and green as primary colors. (Black and white are primary, too, but we perceive them as colorless.) All other colors can be described as mixtures of these primary colors. The trichromatic system cannot explain why *yellow* is included in this group. In addition, some colors appear to blend, whereas others do not. For example, one can speak of a bluish green or a yellowish green, and orange appears to have both red and yellow qualities. Purple resembles both red and blue. But try to imagine a greenish red or a bluish yellow. It is impossible; these colors seem to be opposite to each other. Again, these facts are not explained by the trichromatic theory. As we shall see in the following section, the visual system uses both trichromatic and opponent-color systems to encode information related to color.

FIGURE 5.27

Color coding. The television screen demonstrates—in reverse—the principle of color coding by the three types of cones in the retina. (a) A small white rectangle shown in the middle of the screen. (b) An enlargement of the same white rectangle. Note that the screen displays only red, blue, and green spots of light. At a distance these colors blend and produce white light.

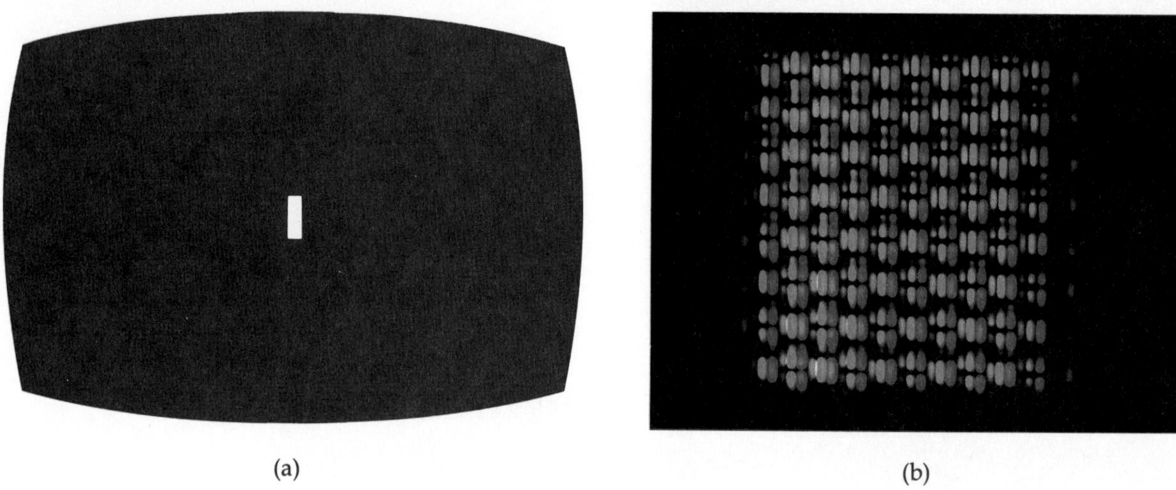

(a) (b)

Color Coding in the Retina

Just as the circuitry of the retina gives rise to the center/surround response characteristics of the ganglion cells, it also gives rise to opponent-color coding. Trichromatic color coding begins with the photoreceptors.

PHOTORECEPTORS

Physiological investigations of retinal photoreceptors in higher primates have found that Young was right: Three different types of photoreceptors (three different types of cones) are responsible for color vision. Investigators have studied the absorption characteristics of individual photoreceptors, determining the amount of light of different wavelengths that is absorbed by the photopigments. These characteristics are controlled by the particular opsin a photoreceptor contains; different opsins absorb particular wavelengths more readily. Figure 5.28 shows the absorption characteristics of the four types of photoreceptors in the human retina: rods and the three types of cones. (See ***Figure 5.28.***)

The peak sensitivities of the three types of cones are approximately 420 nm (blue-violet), 530 nm (green), and 560 nm (yellow-green). The peak sensitivity of the short-wavelength cone is actually 440 nm in the intact eye, because the lens absorbs some short-wavelength light. For convenience, the short-, medium-, and long-wavelength cones are traditionally called "blue," "green," and "red" cones, respectively. The retina contains approximately equal numbers of "red" and "green" cones but a much smaller number of "blue" cones (approximately 8 percent of the total).

Genetic defects in color vision appear to result from anomalies in one or more of the three types of cones (Boynton, 1979; Nathans et al., 1986). The first two kinds of defective color vision described here involve genes on the X chromosome; thus, because males have only one X chromosome, they are much more likely to have this

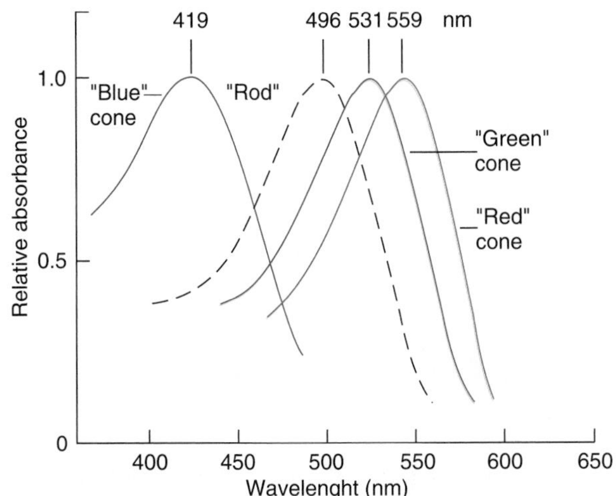

FIGURE 5.28

Relative absorbance of light of various wavelengths by rods and the three types of cones in the human retina. (From Dartnall, H.J.A., Bowmaker, J.K., and Mollon, J.D. Human visual pigments: Microspectrophotometric results from the eyes of seven persons. *Proceedings of the Royal Society of London, B.,* 1983, *220,* 115–130. Reprinted with permission.)

disorder. (Females are likely to have a normal gene on one of their X chromosomes, which compensates for the defective one.) People with **protanopia** ("first-color defect") confuse red and green. They see the world in shades of yellow and blue; both red and green look yellowish to them. Their visual acuity is normal, which suggests that their retinas do not lack "red" or "green" cones. This fact, and their sensitivity to lights of different wavelengths, suggests that their "red" cones are filled with "green" cone opsin. People with **deuteranopia** ("second-color defect") also confuse red and green and also have normal visual acuity. Their "green" cones appear to be filled with "red" cone opsin.

protanopia

deuteranopia

Tritanopia ("third-color defect") is rare, affecting fewer than 1 in 10,000 people. This disorder involves a faulty gene that is not located on an X chromosome; thus, it is equally prevalent in males and females. People with tritanopia have difficulty with hues of short wavelengths and see the world in greens and reds. To them, a clear blue sky is a bright green, and yellow looks pink. Their retinas appear to lack "blue" cones. Because the retina contains so few of these cones, their absence does not noticeably affect visual acuity.

tritanopia

RETINAL GANGLION CELLS

At the level of the retinal ganglion cell, the three-color code gets translated into an opponent-color system. Daw (1968) and Gouras (1968) found that these neurons respond specifically to pairs of primary colors, with red opposing green and blue opposing yellow. Thus, the retina contains two kinds of color-sensitive ganglion cells: *red-green* and *yellow-blue.* Most color-sensitive ganglion cells respond in a center/surround fashion. For example, a cell might be excited by red and inhibited by green in the center of their receptive field, while showing the opposite response in the surrounding ring. Other ganglion cells that receive input from cones do not respond differentially to different wavelengths but simply encode relative brightness in the center and surround.

The response characteristics of retinal ganglion cells to light of different wavelengths are obviously determined by the particular circuits that connect the three types of cones with the two types of ganglion cells. These circuits involve different types of bipolar cells, amacrine cells, and horizontal cells.

FIGURE 5.29

Color coding in the retina. (a) Red light stimulating a "red" cone, which causes excitation of a red-green ganglion cell. (b) Green light stimulating a "green" cone, which causes inhibition of a red-green ganglion cell. (c) Yellow light stimulating "red" and "green" cones equally but not affecting "blue" cones. The stimulation of "red" and "green" cones causes excitation of a yellow-blue ganglion cell. The arrows labeled E and I represent neural circuitry within the retina that translates excitation of a cone into excitation or inhibition of a ganglion cell. For clarity, only some of the circuits are shown.

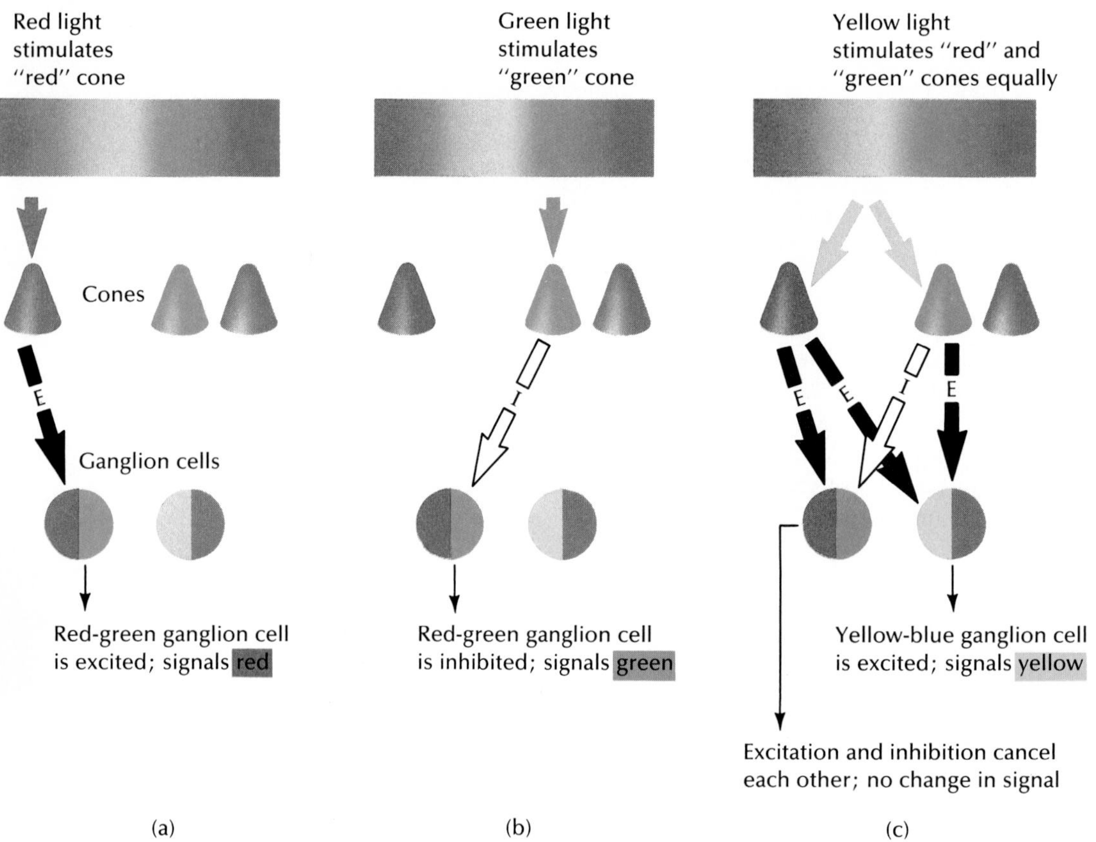

Figure 5.29 helps explain how particular hues are detected by the "red," "green," and "blue" cones and translated into excitation or inhibition of the red-green and yellow-blue ganglion cells. The diagram does not show the actual neural circuitry; the arrows refer merely to the effects of the light falling on the retina. Detection and coding of pure red, green, or blue light is the easiest to understand. For example, red light excites "red" cones, which causes the excitation of red-green ganglion cells. (See ***Figure 5.29a.***) Green light excites "green" cones, which causes the ***inhibition*** of red-green cells. (See ***Figure 5.29b.***) But consider the effect of yellow light. Because the wavelength that produces the sensation of yellow is intermediate between red and green, it will stimulate both "red" and "green" cones about equally. Yellow-blue ganglion cells are excited by both "red" and "green" cones, so their rate of firing increases. However, red-green ganglion cells are excited by red and inhibited by green, so their firing rate does not change. The brain detects an increased firing rate from the axons of yellow-blue ganglion cells, which it interprets as yellow. (See ***Figure 5.29c.***)

The opponent-color system employed by the ganglion cells explains why we can imagine a yellowish red (orange) but not a yellowish blue. The brain perceives yellowish red when the activity of both yellow-blue and red-green ganglion cells increase. But for the brain to perceive a yellowish blue, the activity of yellow-blue ganglion cells would have to increase and decrease at the same time, which they obviously cannot do.

Color Coding in the Cortex

As we saw earlier, neurons within the blobs in the striate cortex respond to colors. Like the ganglion cells in the retina (and the parvocellular neurons in the dorsal lateral geniculate nucleus), they respond in opponent fashion. We saw that in the monkey brain, neurons in the blobs send information about color to a specific subarea of the prestriate cortex. Zeki (1980) found that neurons in this subarea (called *V4*) respond selectively to colors, but their response characteristics are much more complex. Unlike the neurons we have encountered so far, these neurons respond to a *variety* of wavelengths, not just those that correspond to red, green, yellow, and blue. Some neurons respond very selectively to specific hues.

The perceived color of a stimulus is influenced by the surrounding scene (Land, 1974). For example, the appearance of the colors of objects remains much the same whether we observe them under artificial light, under an overcast sky, or at noon on a cloudless day. This phenomenon is known as ***color constancy.*** Our visual system does not simply respond according to the wavelength of the light reflected by objects in each part of the visual field; instead, it compensates for the source of the light. This compensation appears to be made by simultaneously comparing the color composition of each point in the visual field with the mean of all the other points. If the average level of long-wavelength light is high (as it would be if an object were illuminated by the light of a setting sun), then some long-wavelength light is "subtracted out" of the perception of each point in the scene.

Using a procedure devised by Land (1977), Zeki (1980) dramatically demonstrated the role of area V4 in this phenomenon. After locating a neuron in V4 that responded to red light, he placed a special display panel in front of the monkey. The display contained rectangular patches of paper of different colors. (The display is referred to as a ***Mondrian,*** because it resembles the style of paintings made by this artist; see ***Figure 5.30.***) He adjusted the position of the display so that a patch of red paper fell in the

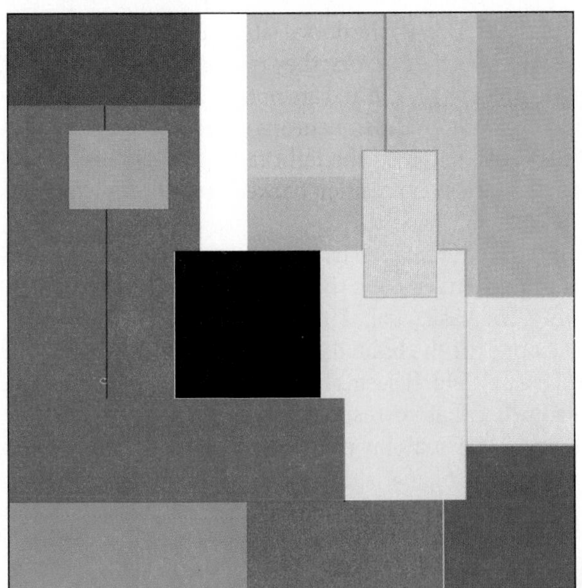

FIGURE 5.30

A Mondrian display used to demonstrate color constancy. (Adapted from Land, E. H. *Scientific American,* 1977, *237,* 108–128.)

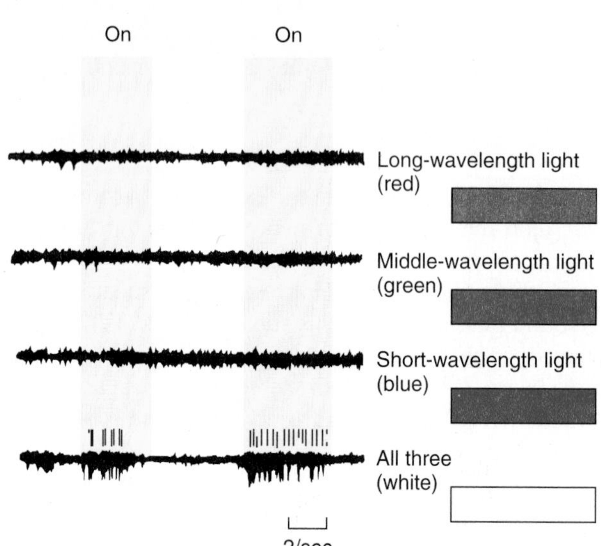

FIGURE 5.31

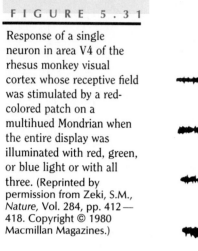

Response of a single neuron in area V4 of the rhesus monkey visual cortex whose receptive field was stimulated by a red-colored patch on a multihued Mondrian when the entire display was illuminated with red, green, or blue light or with all three. (Reprinted by permission from Zeki, S.M., *Nature,* Vol. 284, pp. 412—418. Copyright © 1980 Macmillan Magazines.)

neuron's receptive field. The neuron responded. Then he illuminated the display panel with red light. (Under these conditions the red patch loses its vivid red appearance to a human observer.) Even though its receptive field was flooded with red light, the neuron did *not* respond. Similarly, the neuron failed to respond when he illuminated the display panel with green or blue light. Only when he shone all three lights on the panel (simulating white light) did the neuron respond. This is an important finding, because only when all three lights are used will the red patch appear as a vivid red to an observer. The response of the neuron in V4 thus correlates with the perception of the color red, not simply with the presence of light of a particular wavelength. (See ***Figure 5.31.***)

As Zeki (1984) notes, neurons in the retina, in the dorsal lateral geniculate nucleus, and in the striate cortex act like *wavelength detectors;* they respond according to the wavelength of light that falls on their receptive field and are not affected by light falling on the receptive fields of their neighbors. In contrast, neurons in area V4 act like *color detectors,* showing a response that is adjusted by the light falling on the rest of the visual field. His discovery appears to mark the transition between color *sensation* and color *perception.*

Lesions of a restricted region of the human prestriate cortex can cause complete loss of color vision without disrupting visual acuity; the patients describe their vision as resembling a black-and-white film (Damasio et al., 1980). The condition is known as **achromatopsia** ("vision without color"). If the brain damage is unilateral, people will lose color vision in only half of the visual field. It seems likely that these lesions destroy the part of the human prestriate cortex that corresponds to area V4 of the monkey brain, but not enough is known about the anatomy of the human visual system to be certain.

achromatopsia

▶INTERIM SUMMARY◀

Color vision occurs as a result of information provided by three types of cones, each of which is sensitive to light of a certain wavelength: long, medium, or short. Color-sensitive ganglion cells respond in an opposing center/surround fashion to the pairs of primary colors: red and green, and blue and yellow.

The absorption characteristics of the cones are determined by the particular opsin that their photopigment contains. Most forms of defective color vision appear to be caused by alterations in cone opsins. The "red" cones of people with protanopia are filled with "green" cone opsin, and the "green" cones of people with deuteranopia are filled with "red" cone opsin. The retinas of people with tritanopia appear to lack "blue" cones.

The color-sensitive cells of the dorsal lateral geniculate nucleus respond to red/green or yellow/blue in an opposing center/surround fashion. These neurons send information about color to the blobs in the striate cortex, which send information to area V4 of the prestriate cortex. Neurons in V4 respond selectively to a wide range of wavelengths and are not particularly responsive to spatial features of visual stimuli, such as orientation. Damage to the human prestriate cortex (presumably, damage to area V4) can cause achromatopsia, a loss of color vision. The Mondrian experiment tells us that the responses of neurons in V4 closely correspond to some of the more complex phenomena of color perception. Neurons there encode *color,* not simply *wavelength.* ▲

EFFECTS OF BRAIN DAMAGE ON HUMAN VISUAL PERCEPTION

Damage to portions of the visual system of the human brain have given investigators some insights into the anatomy and physiology of visual perception. In general, the results have been consistent with what has been learned from experiments with other primates. As I mentioned earlier in this chapter, damage to different parts of the prestriate cortex can cause loss of color perception (achromatopsia) or loss of sensitivity to movement. In addition, damage to the visual association cortex can cause a category of deficits known as **visual agnosia.** *Agnosia* ("failure to know") refers to an inability to identify or perceive a stimulus by means of a particular sensory modality, even though its details can be detected by means of that modality and the person retains relatively normal intellectual capacity. *Apperceptive* visual agnosias are failures in high-level perception, whereas *associative* visual agnosias are disconnections between these perceptions and verbal systems. The distinction will be described in more detail in the subsections that follow.

visual agnosia

People with visual agnosia cannot identify or perceive common objects by sight, even though they have relatively normal visual acuity (Warrington and James, 1988). In some cases they can read small print but fail to recognize a common object, such as a wristwatch. However, if they are permitted to hold the object (say, the wristwatch), they can immediately recognize it by touch and say what it is. Thus, they have not lost their memory for the object or forgotten how to say its name. You will note that in the first sentence of this paragraph I said inability to "identify or perceive." Normally, we think of these words as being almost synonymous; it seems that if we can perceive something, we can also identify it. However, we will see that associative visual agnosia involves reasonably normal perception but impaired ability to identify what is perceived.

Apperceptive Visual Agnosia

apperceptive visual agnosia

Apperceptive visual agnosia is a perceptual problem caused by brain damage. Although the person may have normal visual acuity, he or she cannot successfully recognize objects visually by their shape. For example, a brain-damaged patient studied by Benson and Greenberg (1969) was initially believed to be blind but was subsequently observed to navigate his wheelchair around the halls of the hospital. Testing revealed that his visual fields were full (there were no blind spots other than ones we all have) and that he could pick up threads placed on a sheet of white paper. He could discriminate among stimuli that differed in size, brightness, or hue but could not distinguish those that differed only in shape.

prosopagnosia

A common symptom of apperceptive visual agnosia is **prosopagnosia,** an inability to recognize faces (*prosopon* means "face"). Prosopagnosia is a subtle deficit that can occur even when a person has no apparent difficulty recognizing common objects visually. Some investigators have speculated that facial recognition is mediated by special circuits in the brain that are devoted to the specific analysis of facial features. However, several observations suggest that the distinction between prosopagnosia and visual agnosia for common objects is quantitative, not qualitative; that is, visual agnosia for common objects is simply a more severe deficit, caused by more extensive damage to the relevant parts of the visual association cortex. Alexander and Albert (1983) note that although prosopagnosia can occur without visual-object agnosia, all patients with visual-object agnosia also have prosopagnosia.

Damasio, Damasio, and Van Hoesen (1982) describe three patients with prosopagnosia who could recognize common objects but had difficulty discriminating between particular objects of the same class. For example, none of them could recognize their own car, although they could tell a car from other types of motorized vehicles. One of them could find her own car in a parking lot only by reading all the license plates until she found her own. Another patient, a farmer, could no longer recognize his cows (Bornstein, Stroka, and Munitz, 1969). Although it is conceivable that the evolutionary process could have selected for neural mechanisms specialized for the recognition of faces of members of our own species, it is unlikely that it could have done so for the shapes of cars and cows. We can probably conclude that prosopagnosia is simply a relatively mild form of visual agnosia; faces are particularly complex stimuli and even a mild agnosia will make it difficult for a person to recognize them.

From studies of their own patients and from a review of the literature, Damasio, Damasio, and Van Hoesen (1982) conclude that apperceptive visual agnosias are most commonly caused by bilateral damage to the medial portion of the occipital and posterior temporal cortex, which includes regions of prestriate cortex. The syndrome is relatively rare, because bilateral damage to the same relatively small portion of the brain is uncommon. If the lesion is too large, it will invade the optic radiations that lie immediately beneath the cortex and thus produce blindness. From experiments with monkeys we might predict that bilateral lesions of the inferior temporal cortex (on the lateral surface of the brain) would also produce deficits in visual perception.

Associative Visual Agnosia

associative visual agnosia

A person with apperceptive agnosia who cannot recognize common objects also cannot draw them or copy other people's drawings; thus, we properly speak of a deficit in perception. However, people with an **associative visual agnosia** appear to be able to perceive normally but cannot name what they have seen. In fact, they seem to be *unaware* of these perceptions. For example, a patient studied by Ratcliff and

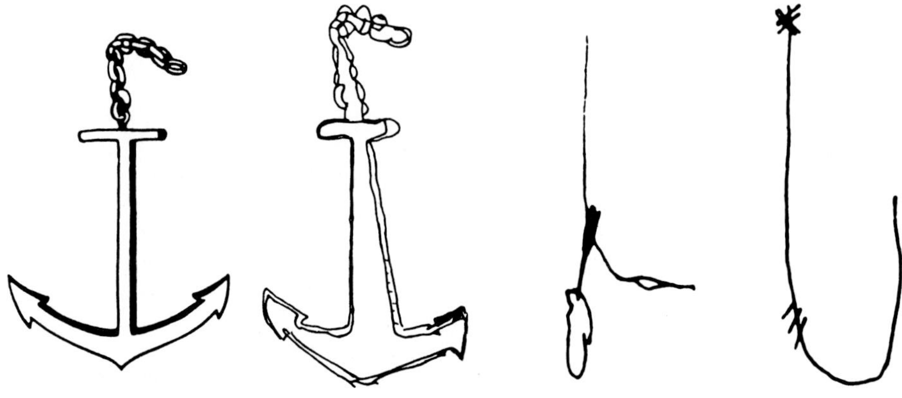

FIGURE 5.32

Associative visual agnosia. The patient successfully copied an anchor (*left*) but failed on two attempts to comply with a request to "draw an anchor" (*right*). (From Ratcliff, G., and Newcombe, F., in *Normality and Pathology in Cognitive Functions,* edited by A.W. Ellis. London: Academic Press, 1982. Reprinted with permission.)

Newcombe (1982) could copy a drawing of an anchor (better than I could have done). Thus, he could perceive the shape of the anchor. However, he could not recognize either the sample or the copy that he had just drawn. When asked on another occasion to draw (not copy) a picture of an anchor, he could not do so; although he could *copy* a real image of an anchor, the word *anchor* failed to produce a mental image of one. (See ***Figure 5.32.***) When asked (on yet another occasion) to define *anchor,* he said "a brake for ships," so we can conclude that he knew what the word meant.

Associative visual agnosia appears to involve a deficit in the ability to transfer information between the visual association cortex and brain mechanisms involved in language. That is, the person perceives the object well enough to draw it, but his or her verbal mechanisms do not receive the necessary information to produce the appropriate word—or to think about what the object is. In the Prologue I described Mr. M., a man who was unable to recognize a picture of a cow until he observed himself making milking movements with his hands. We might speculate that his perceptual mechanisms, in the visual association cortex, were relatively normal, but that connections between these mechanisms and the speech mechanisms of the left hemisphere were

FIGURE 5.33

Associative visual agnosia. A patient was able to identify a picture of a cow by observing himself make milking movements.

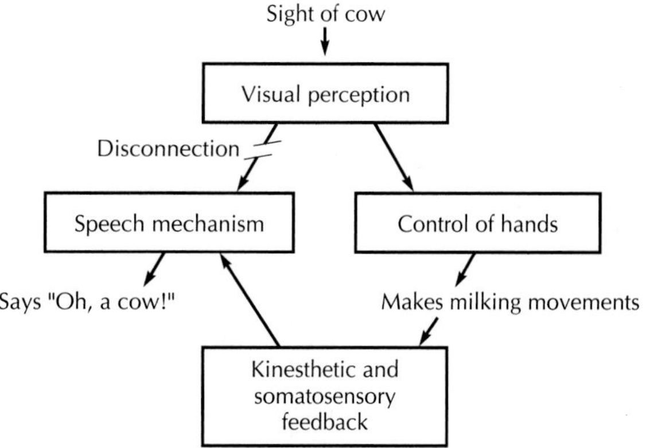

disrupted. However, the connections between the perceptual mechanisms and the motor mechanisms of the frontal lobe were spared, permitting him to make appropriate movements when looking at some pictures. (See ***Figure 5.33.***)

The anatomical basis of associative visual agnosia has not been clearly established. Many investigators believe that the syndrome is caused by damage to white matter underlying the occipital and temporal lobes. The disruption of these axons disconnects regions of the brain that mediate visual perception from those that are needed for verbalization.

▶*INTERIM SUMMARY*◀

Studies with humans who have sustained damage to the visual association cortex have discovered two basic forms of visual agnosia. Apperceptive visual agnosia involves difficulty in perceiving the shapes of objects, even though the fine details can often be detected. Prosopagnosia, failure to recognize faces, has traditionally been regarded as a separate disorder, but it probably represents a mild form of apperceptive visual agnosia. The second basic form of visual agnosia, associative visual agnosia, is characterized by relatively good object perception but the inability to name what has been perceived. This disorder is probably caused by damage to axons that connect the visual association cortex with regions of the brain that are important for verbalization and thinking in words. ▲

EPILOGUE: ▶ *Application*

My discussion of Mr. M. in the prologue raises an issue about research that I'd like to address: the issue of making generalizations from the study of an individual patient. Some researchers have argued that because no two people are alike, we cannot make generalizations from a single individual like Mr. M. They say that valid inferences can only be made from studies that involve *groups* of people, so that individual differences can be accounted for statistically. Is this criticism valid?

The careful, detailed investigation of the abilities and disabilities of a single person is called a *case study.* In my opinion, case studies of people with brain damage can provide very useful information. In the first place, even if we were not able to make firm conclusions from the study of one person, a careful analysis of the pattern of deficits shown by an individual patient might give us some useful ideas for further research—and sources of good ideas for research should not be neglected. But under some circumstances we *can* draw conclusions from a single case.

Before I describe what kinds of inferences we can and cannot make from case studies, let me review what we hope to accomplish by studying the behavior of people with brain damage. The brain seems to be organized in modules. A given module receives information from other modules, performs some kinds of analysis, and sends the results on to other modules with which it communicates. In some cases the wiring of the module may change. That is, synaptic connections may be modified so that in the future the module will respond differently to its inputs. (As we will see in Chapter 12, the ability of modules to modify their synaptic connections serves as the basis for the ability to learn and remember.)

If we want to understand how the brain works, we have to know what the individual modules do. A particular module is not *responsible* for a behavior; instead, it performs one of the many functions that are necessary for a set of behaviors. For example, as I sit here typing this epilogue, I am using modules that perform functions related to posture and balance, to the control of eye movements, to memories related to the topic I am writing about, to memories of English words and their spellings, to control of finger movements, . . . , well, you get the idea. We would rarely try to analyze such a complex task as sitting and writing an epilogue; but we might try to analyze how we spell a familiar English word. Possibly, we use modules that perform functions normally related to hearing: We use these modules to "hear" the word in our head and then use other modules to convert the sounds into the appropriate patterns of letters. Alternatively, we may picture the word we want to spell, which would use modules that perform functions related to vision. I do not want to go into the details of spelling and writing here (I will do that in Chapter 13), but I do want you to see why it is important to try to understand the functions performed by groups of modules located in particular parts of the brain. In practice, this means studying and analyzing the pattern of deficits shown by people with brain damage.

What kinds of conclusions can we make by studying a single individual? We *cannot* conclude that because two behaviors are impaired, the deficit is caused by damage to a set of common modules needed for both behaviors. Instead, it could be that behavior X is impaired by damage to module A, and behavior Y is impaired by damage to module B—and it just happens that modules A and B were both damaged by the brain lesion. However, we *can* conclude that if a brain lesion causes a loss of behavior X but not of behavior Y, then the functions performed by the damaged modules are not required to perform behavior Y. The study of a single patient permits us to make this conclusion.

The conclusion may seem rather modest, but it can advance our understanding of the types of brain functions involved in particular behaviors. For example, Mr. M. could not tell us that a picture he was looking at showed a cow, but he could make hand movements that a person would only make with respect to a cow. Therefore, we can conclude with certainty that brain damage that prevents a person from verbally identifying a particular visual image will not necessarily prevent the person from making hand movements appropriate to that image. Perhaps the brain has two perceptual systems, each with an independent set of modules devoted to analyzing visual images: one perceptual system connected to verbal mechanisms, and the other connected to mechanisms involved with hand movements. Although we cannot rule out this possibility, it seems unlikely that the organization of the brain is so wasteful of resources. (The "primitive" visual system, which I discussed in Chapter 1, is not capable of perceiving complex objects such as cows.) Instead, it seems more likely that a single set of modules is devoted to analyzing visual images, and the information analyzed there is sent to several different parts of the brain. Possibly, then, Mr. M.'s brain lesion disrupted the pathway bringing visual information to modules involved in verbal mechanisms but did not disrupt the pathway bringing it to modules involved in control of hand movements. (If this conclusion were true, we would say that associative visual agnosia is a *disconnection syndrome*—a syndrome caused by a disconnection between particular sets of modules.) Of course, to confirm this hypothesis, we need to make further observations on other patients.

You can see that although case studies do not permit us to make sweeping conclusions, under the right circumstances we can properly draw firm—if modest—conclusions that help us understand the organization of the brain and suggest hypotheses to test with further research. ▲

KEY CONCEPTS

The Stimulus

- Light, a form of electromagnetic radiation, can vary in wavelength, intensity, and purity; it can thus give rise to differences in perceptions of hue, brightness, and saturation.

Anatomy of the Visual System

- The eyes are complex sensory organs that focus an image of the environment on the retina. The retina consists of three layers: the photoreceptor layer (rods and cones), the bipolar cell layer, and the ganglion cell layer.
- When light strikes a molecule of photopigment in a photoreceptor, the molecule splits and initiates a receptor potential.
- Information from the eye is sent to the dorsal lateral geniculate nucleus and then to the primary visual cortex (striate cortex).

Analysis of Visual Form

- Visual information is processed by two parallel systems, the magnocellular system and the parvocellular system.
- Ganglion cells of the retina respond in an opposing center/surround fashion.
- Neurons in the striate cortex are organized in modules, each containing two blobs. Neurons within the blobs respond to color; those outside the blobs respond to orientation, spatial frequency, movement, and retinal disparity.
- Specific regions of the prestriate cortex receive information about specific features of the visual scene from the striate cortex, analyze it, and send their information on to higher levels of association cortex. The association cortex of the inferior temporal gyrus recognizes the shape of objects, whereas the parietal cortex recognizes their location.

Color Vision

- Colors are detected by three types of cones, and the code is changed into an opponent-process system by the time it reaches the retinal ganglion cells.

Effects of Brain Damage on Human Visual Perception

- Damage to the visual association cortex can produce apperceptive or associative visual agnosia in humans.

NEW TERMS

accommodation **p. 139**
achromatopsia **p. 164**
amacrine cell **p. 141**
apperceptive visual agnosia **p. 166**
associative visual agnosia **p. 166**
Balint's syndrome **p. 157**
bipolar cell **p. 141**
blob **p. 154**
brightness **p. 138**
calcarine fissure **p. 144**
ciliary muscle **p. 139**
complex cell **p. 151**
cone **p. 139**
conjunctiva **p. 139**
cornea **p. 139**
deuteranopia **p. 161**
dorsal lateral geniculate nucleus **p. 144**
fovea **p. 140**
ganglion cell **p. 141**
horizontal cell **p. 141**
hue **p. 138**
inferior temporal cortex **p. 157**
iris **p. 139**
lamella **p. 141**
lens **p. 139**
magnocellular layer **p. 144**
ocular apraxia **p. 157**
opsin **p. 142**
optic ataxia **p. 157**
optic chiasm **p. 145**
optic disk **p. 140**
orbit **p. 139**
parvocellular layer **p. 144**
photopigment **p. 142**
photoreceptor **p. 139**
prestriate cortex **p. 156**
prosopagnosia **p. 166**
protanopia **p. 161**
pupil **p. 139**
receptive field **p. 148**
receptor potential **p. 142**
retina **p. 139**
retinal **p. 142**
retinal disparity **p. 154**
rhodopsin **p. 142**
rod **p. 139**
saturation **p. 138**
sclera **p. 139**
simple cell **p. 151**
simultanagnosia **p. 158**
sine-wave grating **p. 152**
spatial frequency **p. 152**
striate cortex **p. 144**
tritanopia **p. 161**
visual agnosia **p. 165**
visual angle **p. 152**
vitreous humor **p. 139**

SUGGESTED READINGS

Bruce, V., and Green, P. *Visual Perception: Physiology, Psychology and Ecology.* London: Lawrence Erlbaum Associates, 1985.

De Valois, R.L., and De Valois, K.K. *Spatial Vision.* New York: Oxford University Press, 1988.

Gregory, R.L. *Eye and Brain.* New York: McGraw-Hill, 1978.

Weale, R.A. *Focus on Vision.* Cambridge, Mass.: Harvard University Press, 1982.

6

CHAPTER OUTLINE

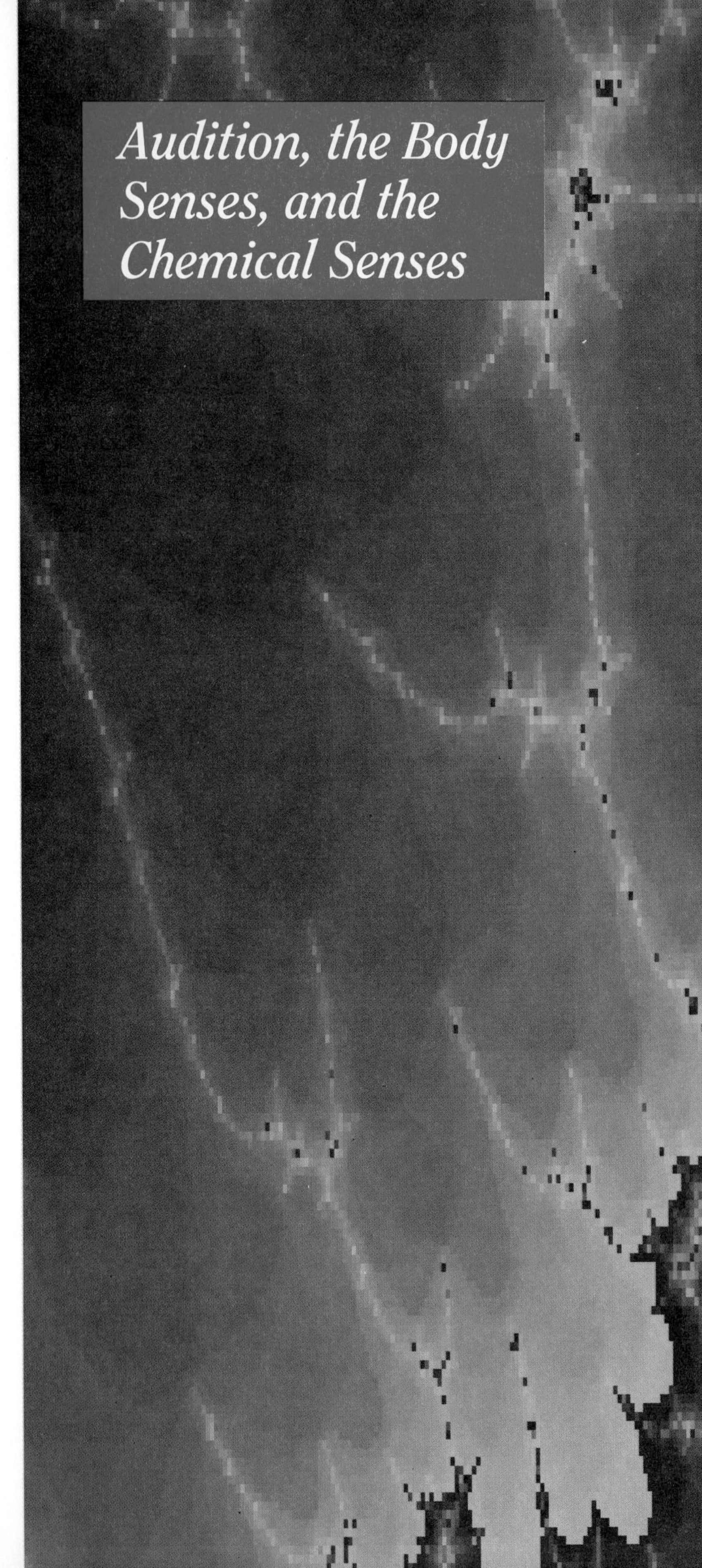

Audition, the Body Senses, and the Chemical Senses

PROLOGUE

Melissa, a junior at the state university, had volunteered to be a subject in an experiment at the dental school. She had been told that she might feel a little pain but that everything was under medical supervision, and no harm would come to her. She didn't particularly like the idea of pain, but she would be well paid; and she saw the experience as an opportunity to live up to her own self-image as being as brave as anyone.

She entered the reception room, where she signed consent forms saying that she agreed to participate in the experiment and knew that a physician would be giving her a drug and that her reaction to pain would be measured. The experimenter greeted her, led her to a room, and asked her to be seated in a dental chair. He inserted a needle attached to a plastic tube into a vein in her right arm so that he could inject drugs.

"First," he said, "we want to find out how sensitive you are to pain." He showed her a device that looked something like an electric toothbrush but that had a metal probe on the end. "This device will stimulate nerves in the pulp of your tooth. Do you have some fillings?" She nodded. "Have you ever bitten on some aluminum foil?" She winced and nodded again. "Good, then you will know what to expect." He adjusted a dial on the stimulator, touched the tip of it to a tooth, and pressed the button. No response. He turned the dial and stimulated the tooth again. Still no response. He turned the dial again, and this time, the stimulation made her gasp and wince. He recorded the voltage setting in his notebook.

"Ok, now we know how sensitive this tooth is to pain. Now I'm going to give you a drug we are testing. It should decrease the pain quite a bit." He injected the drug and after a short while said, "Let's try the tooth again." The drug apparently worked; he had to increase the voltage considerably before she felt any pain.

"Now," he said, "I want to give you some more of the drug to see if we can make you feel even less pain." He gave another injection and, after a little wait, tested her again. But the drug had not further decreased her pain sensitivity; instead, it had *increased* it — she was now as sensitive as she had been before the first injection.

After the experiment was over, the experimenter walked with Melissa into a lounge. "I want to tell you about the experiment you were in, but I'd like to ask you not to talk about it with other people who might also serve as subjects." She nodded her head in agreement.

"Actually, you did not receive a painkiller. The first injection was pure salt water."

"It was? But I thought it made me less sensitive to pain."

"It did. When an innocuous substance such as an injection of salt water or a sugar pill has an effect like that, we call it a placebo effect."

"You mean that it was all in my mind? That I only *thought* that the shock hurt less?"

"No. Well, that is, it was necessary for you to think that you had received a painkiller. But the effect was a physiological one. We know that, because the second injection contained a drug that counteracts the effects of opiates."

"Opiates — you mean like morphine or heroin?"

"Yes." He saw her start to protest, shook his head, and said, "No, I'm sure you don't take drugs. But your brain makes them. For reasons we still do not understand, your believing that you had received a painkiller caused some cells in your brain to release a chemical that acts the way opiates do. The chemical acts on other neurons in your brain and decreases your sensi-

tivity to pain. When I gave you the second injection—the drug that counteracts opiates—your sensitivity to pain came back."

"But then, did my mind or my brain make the placebo effect happen?"

"Well, think about it. Your mind and your brain are not really separate. Experiences can change the way your brain functions, and these changes can alter your experiences. Mind and brain have to be studied together, not separately." ▲

One chapter was devoted to vision, but the rest of the sensory modalities must share a chapter. This unequal allocation of space reflects the relative importance of vision to our species and the relative amount of research that has been devoted to it. People often say that we have five senses: sight, hearing, smell, taste, and touch. Actually, we have more than five. For example, the inner ear supplies information about head orientation and movement as well as providing us with auditory information. And the sense of touch (more accurately, *somatosensation*) detects changes in pressure, warmth, cold, vibration, limb position, and events that damage tissue (that is, produce pain).

This chapter is divided into five major sections, which discuss audition, the vestibular system, the somatosenses, gustation, and olfaction.

AUDITION

For most people audition is the second most important sense. The value of verbal communication makes it even more important than vision in some respects; for example, a blind person can join others in conversation far more easily than a deaf person can. Acoustic stimuli also provide information about things that are hidden from view, and our ears work just as well in the dark. This section describes the nature of the stimulus, the sensory receptors, the brain mechanisms devoted to audition, and some of the details of the physiology of auditory perception.

The Stimulus

We hear sounds, which are produced by objects that vibrate and set the molecules of the air into motion. When an object vibrates, its movements cause the air surrounding it alternately to condense and rarefy (pull apart), producing waves that travel away from the object at approximately 700 miles per hour. If the vibration ranges between approximately 30 and 20,000 times per second, these waves will stimulate receptive cells in our ears and will be perceived as sounds.

In Chapter 5 we saw that light has three perceptual dimensions—hue, brightness, and saturation—which correspond to three physical dimensions. Similarly, sounds vary in their pitch, loudness, and timbre. The perceived **pitch** of an auditory stimulus is determined by the frequency of vibration, which is measured in **hertz (Hz)**, or cycles per second. (The term honors Heinrich Hertz, a nineteenth-century German physicist.) **Loudness** is a function of intensity—the degree to which the condensations and rarefactions of air differ from each other. More vigorous vibrations of an object produce more intense sound waves and, hence, louder ones. **Timbre** provides information about the nature of the particular sound—for example, the sound of an oboe or a train whistle. Most natural acoustic stimuli are complex, consisting of several different frequencies of vibration. The particular mixture determines the sound's timbre. (See ***Figure 6.1.***)

pitch
hertz (Hz)
loudness
timbre

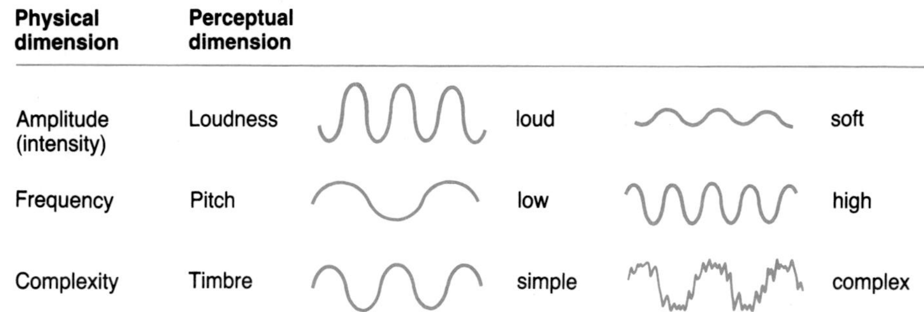

FIGURE 6.1

The physical and perceptual dimensions of sound waves.

The eye is a ***synthetic*** organ (literally, "a putting together"). When two different wavelengths of light are mixed, we perceive a single color. In contrast, the ear is an ***analytical*** organ (from *analuein,* "to undo"). When two different frequencies of sound waves are mixed, we do not perceive an intermediate tone. Instead, we hear both original tones. As we will see, the ability of our auditory system to detect the individual frequencies contained in a complex tone enables us to identify the particular sounds, such as those of different musical instruments.

The Ear

Figure 6.2 shows a section through the ear and auditory canal and illustrates the apparatus of the middle and inner ear. (See ***Figure 6.2.***) Sound travels through to the

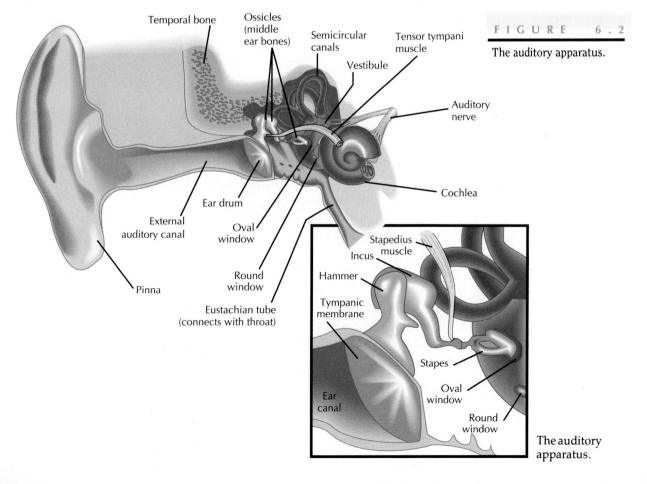

FIGURE 6.2

The auditory apparatus.

The auditory apparatus.

tympanic membrane

ossicle

cochlea

oval window

tympanic membrane (eardrum), which vibrates with the sound. We are not very good at moving our ears; but by orienting our heads, we can modify the sound that finally reaches the receptors.

The **ossicles**, the bones of the middle ear, are set into vibration by the tympanic membrane. The *malleus* (hammer) connects with the tympanic membrane and transmits vibrations through the *incus* (anvil) and *stapes* (stirrup) to the **cochlea**, the inner ear structure that contains the receptors. The baseplate of the stapes presses against the membrane behind the **oval window**, an opening in the bony process surrounding the cochlea. (See ***Figures 6.2 and 6.3.***)

The cochlea is part of the *inner ear.* It is filled with fluid; therefore, sounds transmitted through the air must be transferred into a liquid medium. This process is normally very inefficient—99.9 percent of the energy of airborne sound would be reflected away if the air impinged directly against the oval window of the cochlea. (If you have ever swum underwater, you have probably noted how quiet it is there; most of the sound arising in the air is reflected off the surface of the water.) The chain of ossicles serves as an extremely efficient means of energy transmission. The bones provide a mechanical advantage, with the baseplate of the stapes making smaller but more forceful excursions against the oval window than the tympanic membrane makes against the malleus.

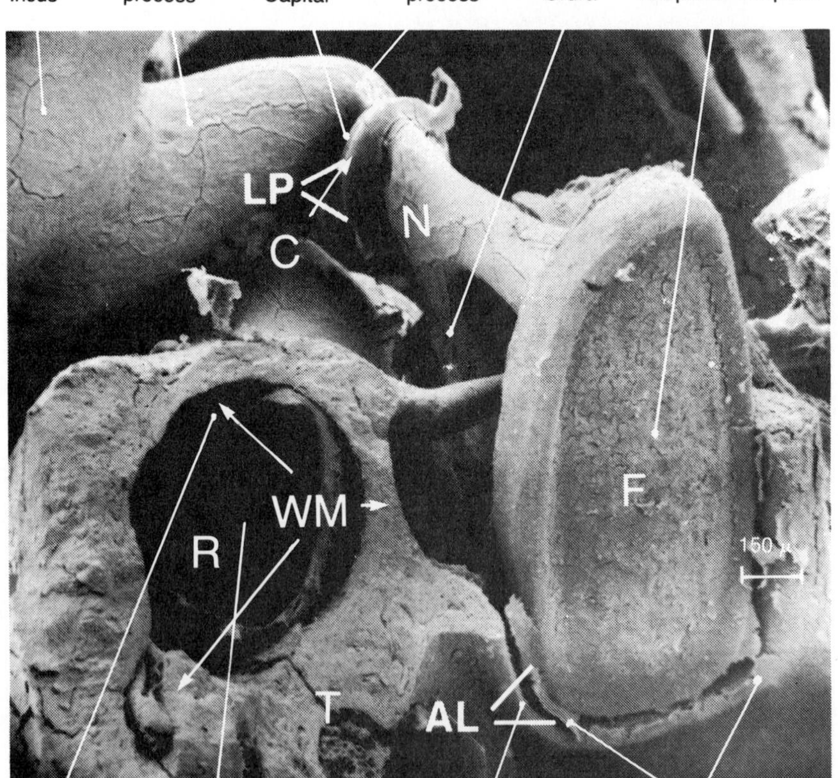

FIGURE 6.3

A scanning electron micrograph of the stapes and the round window. (From *Tissues and Organs: A Text-Atlas of Scanning Electron Microscopy*, by Richard G. Kessel and Randy H. Kardon. Copyright © 1979 by W.H. Freeman and Company. Reprinted with permission.)

FIGURE 6.4

A cross section through the cochlea, showing the organ of Corti.

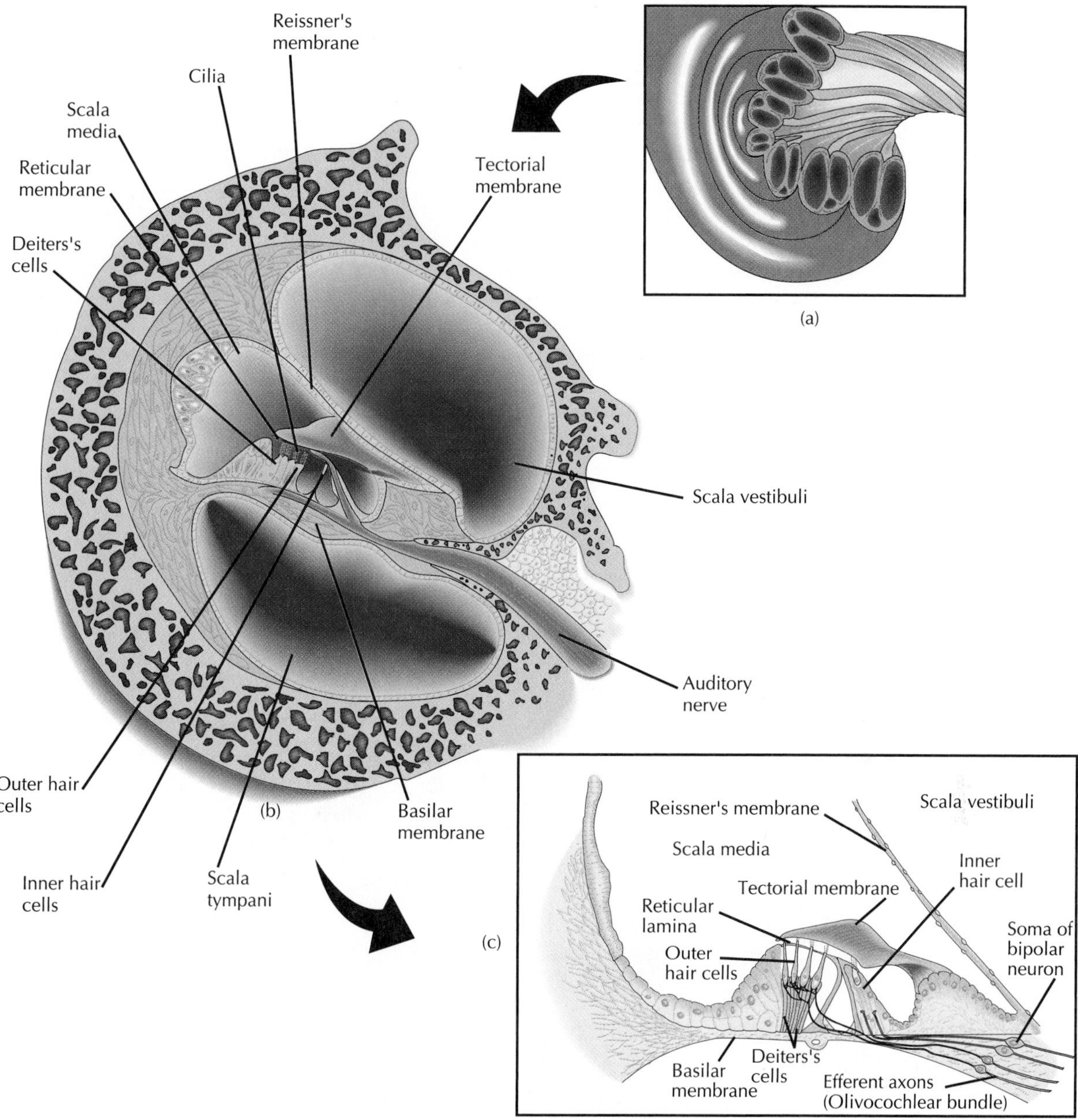

The name *cochlea* comes from the Greek word *kokhlos,* or "land snail." It is indeed snail-shaped, consisting of two and three-quarters turns of a gradually tapering cylinder. The cochlea is divided longitudinally into three sections, as shown in ***Figure 6.4.*** The receptive organ, known as the **organ of Corti**, consists of the *basilar membrane,* the *hair cells,* and the *tectorial membrane.* The auditory receptor cells are called **hair cells,** and they are anchored, via rodlike supporting cells (Deiters's cells), to the **basilar membrane.** The cilia of the hair cells pass through the *reticular membrane,* and the

organ of Corti
hair cell
basilar membrane

tectorial membrane

ends of some of them attach to the fairly rigid **tectorial membrane,** which projects overhead like a shelf. (See ***Figure 6.4.***) Sound waves cause the basilar membrane to move relative to the tectorial membrane, which bends the cilia of the hair cells. This bending produces receptor potentials.

Georg von Békésy—in a lifetime of brilliant studies on the cochleas of various animals, from human cadavers to elephants—found that the vibratory energy exerted on the oval window causes the basilar membrane to bend (von Békésy, 1960). Because of the physical characteristics of the basilar membrane, the portion that bends the most is determined by the frequency of the sound: High-frequency sounds cause the end nearest the oval window to bend.

round window

Figure 6.5 shows this process in a cochlea that has been partially straightened out. If the cochlea were a closed system, no vibration would be transmitted through the oval window, because liquids are essentially incompressible. However, there is a membrane-covered opening, the **round window,** which allows the fluid inside the cochlea to move back and forth. The baseplate of the stapes vibrates against the membrane behind the oval window and introduces sound waves of high or low frequency into the cochlea. The vibrations cause part of the basilar membrane to flex back and forth. Pressure changes in the fluid underneath the basilar membrane are transmitted to the membrane of the round window, which moves in and out in a manner opposite to the movements of the oval window. That is, when the baseplate of the stapes pushes in, the membrane behind the round window bulges out. (See ***Figure 6.5.***)

FIGURE 6.5

Stimulation of the organ of Corti. Sound waves of a particular frequency transmitted through the oval window deform a particular portion of the basilar membrane.

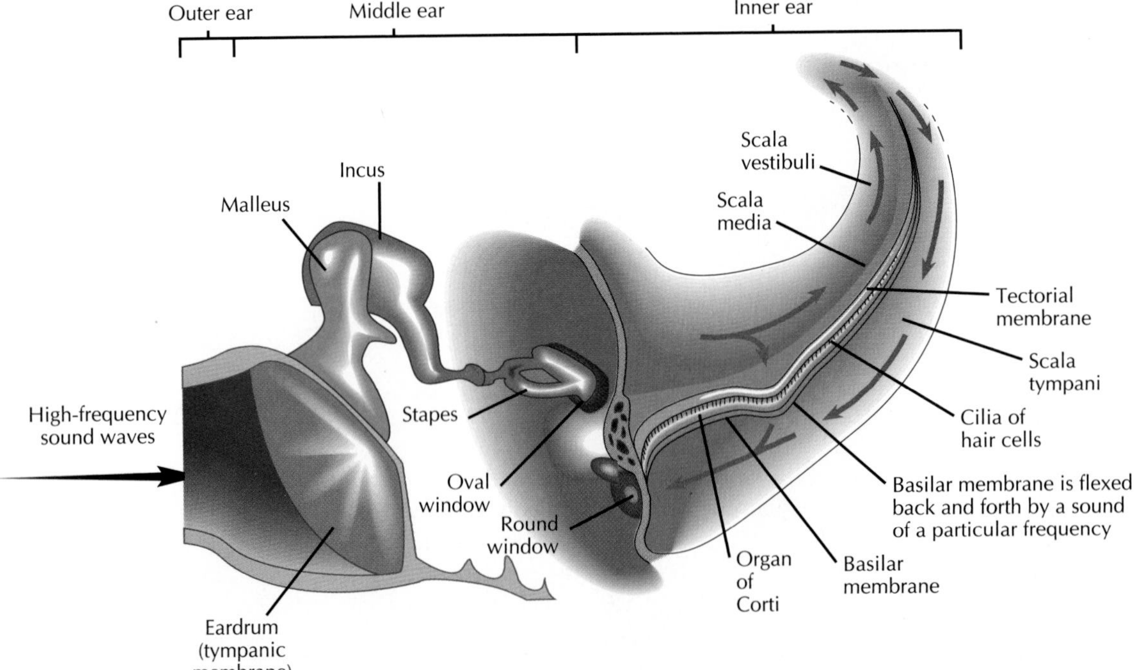

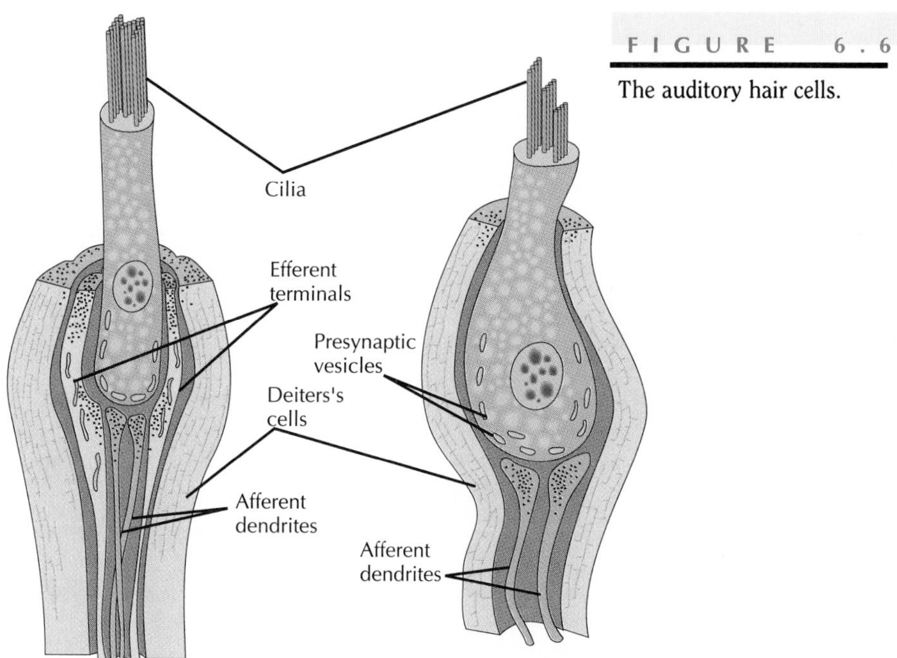

FIGURE 6.6

The auditory hair cells.

Auditory Hair Cells

Two types of auditory receptors, *inner* and *outer* auditory hair cells, lie on the inside and outside of the cochlear coils, respectively. Hair cells contain **cilia** ("eyelashes"), fine hairlike appendages. The human cochlea contains 3400 inner hair cells and 12,000 outer hair cells. Figure 6.6 illustrates these cells and their supporting cells. (See ***Figure 6.6.***) The hair cells form synapses with dendrites of neurons that give rise to the auditory nerve axons. Figure 6.7 shows the actual appearance of the inner and outer hair cells and the reticular membrane in a photograph taken by means of a scanning electron microscope, which shows excellent three-dimensional detail. Note the three rows of outer hair cells on the right and the single row of inner hair cells on the left. (See ***Figure 6.7.***)

cilia

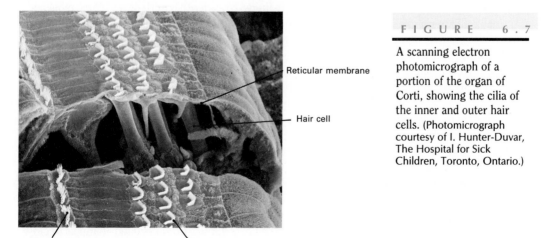

FIGURE 6.7

A scanning electron photomicrograph of a portion of the organ of Corti, showing the cilia of the inner and outer hair cells. (Photomicrograph courtesy of I. Hunter-Duvar, The Hospital for Sick Children, Toronto, Ontario.)

FIGURE 6.8

Cilia of auditory hair cells. (a) Their appearance. (b) Transduction. Movement of the bundle stretches or relaxes tension on the links between the tips of adjacent cilia and changes the rate of firing of the afferent axon. (Adapted from Howard, J., Roberts, W.M., and Hudspeth, A.J. *Annual Review of Biophysics and Biophysical Chemistry*, 1988, *17*, 99–124.)

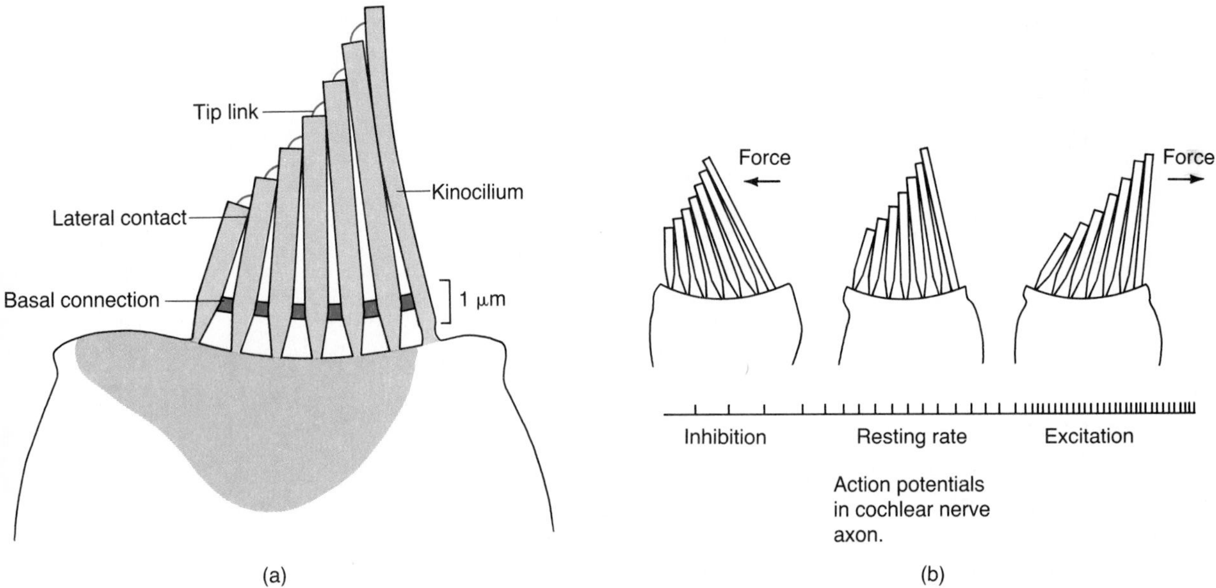

Sound waves cause both the basilar membrane and the tectorial membrane to flex up and down. As they do so, a sideways shearing force is exerted against the bundle of cilia on the auditory hair cells. Cilia contain actin filaments, which make them stiff and rigid (Flock, 1977). Adjacent cilia are linked to each other at their tip. Thus, movement of the bundle of cilia in the direction of the tallest of them stretches the linking fibers, whereas movement in the opposite direction relaxes them. (See ***Figure 6.8a.***)

The bending of the bundle of cilia causes receptor potentials. The resting potential of an auditory hair cell is approximately −60 mV (millivolts). When the bundle of cilia moves toward the tallest one, the flow of K^+ into the cell increases, the membrane depolarizes, and the release of neurotransmitter increases. When the bundle is moved in the opposite direction, the influx of K^+ decreases, the membrane hyperpolarizes, and the release of neurotransmitter decreases. (See ***Figure 6.8b.***) Hudspeth (1982, 1985) showed that the tips of the cilia contain ion channels. Each cilium appears to contain three to seven channels, for a total of approximately one hundred per bundle. When the bundle is straight, approximately 20 percent of the ion channels are open. When the bundle moves toward the tallest one, the increased tension on the connecting fibers pulls more ion channels open and causes depolarization. When the bundle moves in the opposite direction, the relaxation of the fibers allows the opened ion channels to close. (See ***Figure 6.9.***)

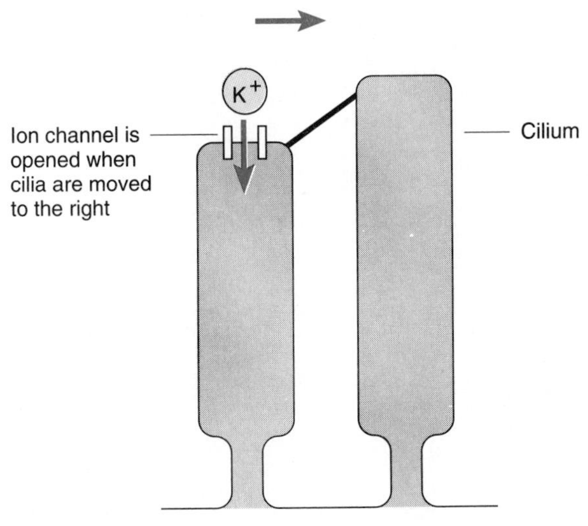
K+
Ion channel is opened when cilia are moved to the right
Cilium

FIGURE 6.9

Transduction. Tension on the links between adjacent cilia opens ion channels, resulting in entry of potassium ions, which depolarizes the membrane potential.

The Auditory Pathway

CONNECTIONS WITH THE COCHLEAR NERVE

The cochlea sends auditory information to the brain by means of the **cochlear nerve**, a branch of the auditory nerve (eighth cranial nerve). The axons of this nerve form synapses with neurons in the medulla.

cochlear nerve

The dendrites of approximately 95 percent of the incoming cochlear nerve axons form synapses with the inner hair cells, on a one-receptor–one-neuron basis (Spoendlin, 1973). The other 5 percent of the sensory fibers form synapses with the much more numerous outer hair cells, on a ten-receptors–one-neuron basis. Thus, although the inner hair cells represent only 22 percent of the total number of receptive cells, they appear to be of primary importance in the transmission of auditory information to the central nervous system. Physiological and behavioral studies indicate that the inner hair cells are necessary for normal hearing. However, no experiments have yet discovered the function of the more numerous outer hair cells.

THE CENTRAL AUDITORY SYSTEM

The anatomy of the auditory system is more complicated than that of the visual system. Rather than give a detailed verbal description of the pathways, I will refer you to ***Figure 6.10.*** Note that axons enter the **cochlear nuclei** of the medulla and synapse there. Most of the neurons in the cochlear nuclei send axons to the **superior olivary complex**, also located in the medulla. Neurons there send axons to the inferior colliculus, located in the dorsal midbrain. Neurons there project to the medial geniculate nucleus, which sends axons to the auditory cortex of the temporal lobe. As you can see, there are many synapses along the way to complicate the story. Each hemisphere receives information from both ears but primarily from the contralateral one. And auditory information is relayed to the cerebellum and reticular formation as well.

cochlear nuclei
superior olivary complex

If we unrolled the basilar membrane into a flat strip and followed afferent axons from adjacent points along its length, we would find that they ultimately convey information to successive points along the surface of the primary auditory cortex. Thus, just as the surface of the primary visual cortex contains a map of the visual field, the primary auditory cortex contains a "map" of sounds of different frequencies.

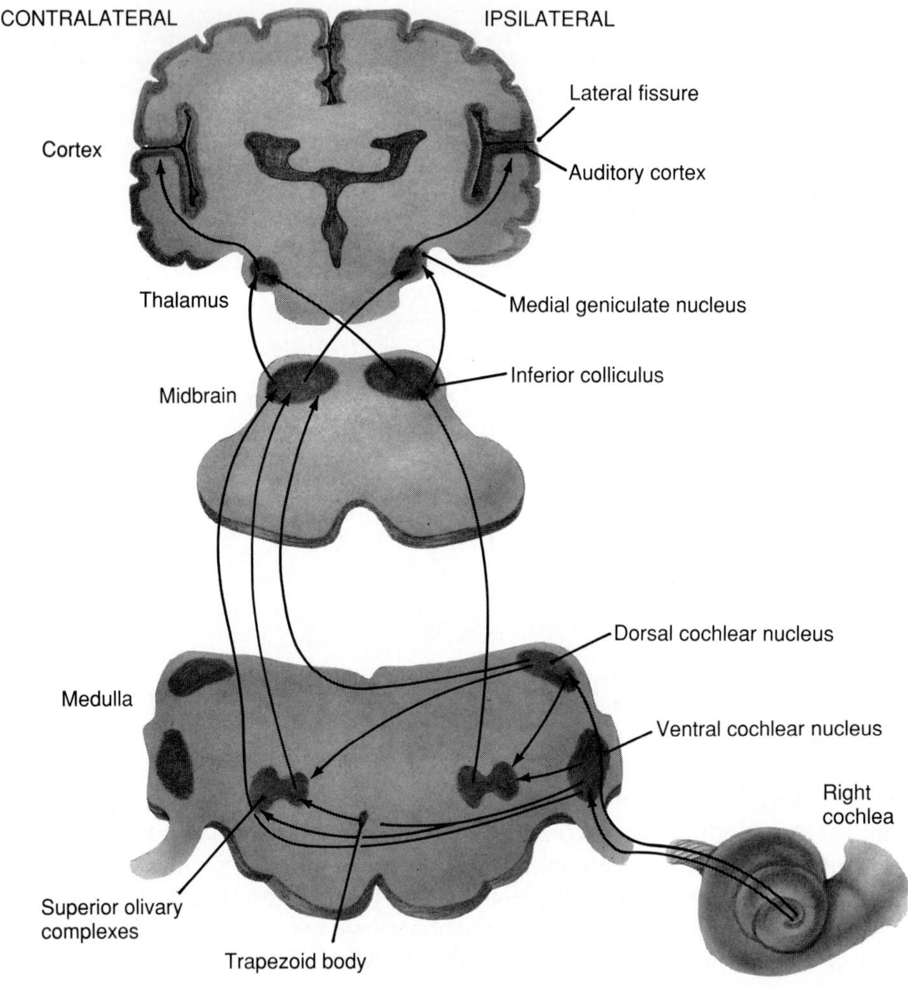

FIGURE 6.10

The pathway of the auditory system.

Neurons in the primary auditory cortex send axons to the auditory association cortex. In Chapter 3 we saw that the primary auditory cortex lies hidden on the inside of the lateral fissure, and that the auditory association cortex lies on the superior part of the temporal lobe.

Detection of Pitch

As we have seen, the perceptual dimension of pitch corresponds to the physical dimension of frequency. The cochlea detects frequency by two means: moderate to high frequencies by place coding and low frequencies by rate coding. These two types of coding are described next.

PLACE CODING

The work of von Békésy has shown us that because of the mechanical construction of the cochlea and basilar membrane, sounds of different frequencies cause different parts of the basilar membrane to flex back and forth. Figure 6.11 illustrates the amount of deformation along the length of the basilar membrane produced by stimula-

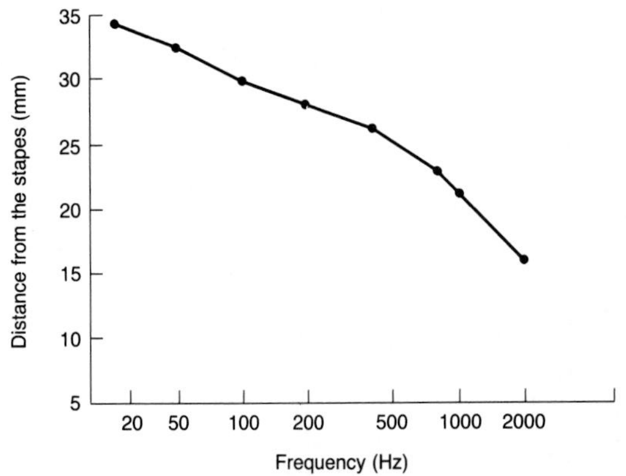

FIGURE 6.11

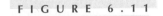

Anatomical coding of pitch. Stimuli of different frequencies maximally deform different regions of the basilar membrane. (From von Békésy, G. *Journal of the Acoustical Society of America,* 1949, *21,* 233–245. Reprinted with permission.)

tion with tones of various frequencies. Note that higher frequencies produce more displacement at the basal end of the membrane (the end closest to the stapes). (See ***Figure 6.11.***)

These results suggest that at least some frequencies of sound waves are detected by means of a **place code**. In this context a code represents a means by which neurons can represent information. Thus, if neurons at one end of the basilar membrane are excited by higher frequencies and those at the other end by lower frequencies, we can say that the frequency of the sound is *coded* by the particular neurons that are active. In turn, the firing of particular axons in the cochlear nerve tells the brain about the presence of particular frequencies of sound.

place code

Other experiments confirm this suggestion. High doses of certain antibiotic drugs produce degeneration of the auditory hair cells. Damage to auditory hair cells begins at the basal end of the cochlea and progresses toward the apical (toward the apex or tip) end; this pattern can be verified by microscopic examination of the auditory hair cells of experimental animals after dosing them with the antibiotic for varying amounts of time. Longer exposures to the drug are associated with increased progress of hair cell damage down the basilar membrane. Stebbins, Miller, Johnsson, and Hawkins (1969) found that the progressive death of hair cells induced by an antibiotic closely parallels a progressive hearing loss: The highest frequencies are the first to go, and the lowest are the last.

RATE CODING

We have seen that the frequency of a sound can be detected by place coding. However, the lowest frequencies do not appear to be accounted for in this manner. Kiang (1965) was unable to find any cells that responded best to frequencies of less than 200 Hz. How, then, can animals distinguish low frequencies? It appears that lower frequencies are detected by neurons that fire in synchrony to the movements of the apical end of the basilar membrane. Thus, lower frequencies are detected by means of **rate coding**.

rate code

Miller and Taylor (1948) provided good evidence that sounds of lower frequencies can be detected by synchronized firing of the auditory hair cells. These investigators presented **white noise** (sound containing all frequencies, similar to the hissing sound you hear between FM radio stations) to human observers. When the investigators rapidly switched the white noise on and off, the observers reported that they heard a tone corresponding to the frequency of pulsation. The white noise, containing all frequencies, stimulated the entire length of the basilar membrane, so the frequency

white noise

that was detected could not be coded for by place. The only frequency-specific information the auditory system could have had was the firing rate of cochlear nerve axons.

Detection of Loudness

The cochlea is an extremely sensitive organ. Wilska (1935) used an ingenious procedure to estimate the smallest vibration needed to produce a perceptible sound. He glued a small wooden rod to a volunteer's tympanic membrane (temporarily, of course) and made the rod vibrate longitudinally by means of an electromagnetic coil that could be energized with alternating current. He could vary the frequency and intensity of the current, which consequently changed the perceived pitch and loudness of the stimulus. He found that subjects could detect a sound even when the eardrum was vibrated over a distance less than the diameter of a hydrogen atom—showing that the auditory system is very sensitive. Thus, in very quiet environments a young, healthy ear is limited in its ability to detect sounds in the air by the masking noise of blood rushing through the cranial blood vessels, rather than by the sensitivity of the auditory system itself. More recent studies using modern instruments (reviewed by Hudspeth, 1983) have essentially confirmed Wilska's measurements. The softest sounds that can be detected appear to move the tip of the hair cells by between 1 and 100 picometers (pm; trillionths of a meter).

The axons of the cochlear nerve appear to inform the brain of the loudness of a stimulus by altering their rate of firing. More intense vibrations produce a more intense shearing force on the cilia of the auditory hair cells, presumably causing them to release more transmitter substance, resulting in a higher rate of firing by the cochlear nerve axons. This explanation seems simple for the axons involved in place coding of pitch; in this case pitch is signaled by which neurons fire, and loudness is signaled by their rate of firing. However, the neurons that signal lower frequencies do so by their rate of firing. If they fire more frequently, they signal a higher pitch. Therefore, most investigators believe that the loudness of low-frequency sounds is signaled by the *number* of axons that are active at a given time.

Detection of Timbre

Although laboratory investigations of the auditory system often employ pure sine waves as stimuli, these waves are seldom encountered outside the laboratory. Instead, we hear sounds with a rich mixture of frequencies—sounds of complex timbre. For example, consider the sound of a clarinet playing a particular note. If we hear it, we can easily say that it is a clarinet and not a flute or a violin. The reason we can do so is that these three instruments produce sounds of different timbre, which our auditory system can distinguish.

fundamental frequency

Figure 6.12 shows the waveform from a clarinet playing a steady note (*top*). The shape of the waveform repeats itself regularly at the **fundamental frequency**, which corresponds to the perceived pitch of the note. Mathematical analyses of the waveform show that it actually consists of a series of sine waves that includes the fundamental frequency and many **overtones**, multiples of the fundamental frequency. Different instruments produce overtones with different intensities. (See ***Figure 6.12.***) Electronic synthesizers simulate the sounds of real instruments by producing a series of overtones of the proper intensities, mixing them, and passing them through a loudspeaker.

overtone

When the basilar membrane is stimulated by the sound of a clarinet, different portions respond to each of the overtones. This response produces a unique pattern of

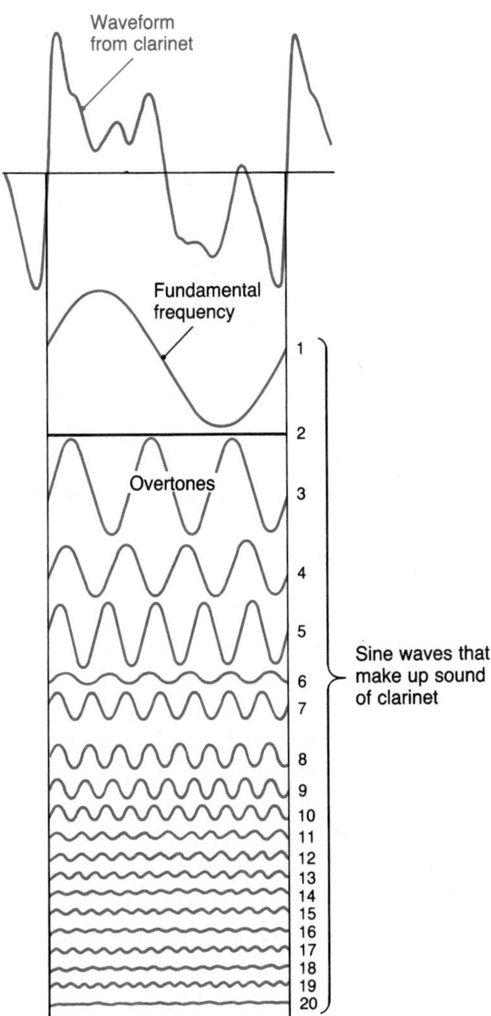

FIGURE 6.12

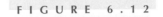

The shape of a sound wave from a clarinet (*top*) and the individual frequencies into which it can be analyzed. (Reprinted from *Stereo Review*, copyright © 1977 by Diamandis Communications Inc.)

activity in the cochlear nerve, which is subsequently identified by the auditory system of the brain. Just how this analysis is done is not known and probably will not be known for many years. When you consider that we can listen to an orchestra and identify several instruments playing simultaneously, you can appreciate the complexity of the analysis performed by the auditory system.

Detection of the Location of Sounds

So far I have discussed the detection of pitch, loudness, and timbre (the last of which is actually a complex frequency analysis). However, the auditory system also responds to other qualities of acoustic stimuli. For example, our ears are very good at determining whether the source of a sound is to the right or left of us. (To discriminate front from back, we merely turn our heads, transforming the discrimination into a left-right decision.) Two separate physiological mechanisms detect the location of sound sources: We use phase differences for low frequencies (less than approximately 3000 Hz) and intensity differences for higher frequencies. Stevens and Newman (1936) found that localization is worst at approximately 3000 Hz, presumably because both mechanisms are rather inefficient at that frequency.

LOCALIZATION BY MEANS OF ARRIVAL TIME AND PHASE DIFFERENCES

If we are blindfolded, we can still determine the location of a stimulus that emits a click with rather good accuracy. We do so because neurons respond selectively to different *arrival times* of the sound waves at the left and right ears. If the source of the click is to the right or left of the midline, the sound pressure wave will reach one ear sooner and initiate action potentials there first. Only if the stimulus is straight ahead will the ears be stimulated simultaneously. Many neurons in the auditory system respond to sounds presented to either ear. Some of these neurons, especially those in the superior olivary complex of the medulla, respond according to the difference in arrival times of sound waves produced by clicks presented *binaurally* (that is, to both ears). Their response rates reflect differences as small as a fraction of a millisecond.

phase difference

Of course, we can hear continuous sounds as well as clicks, and we can also perceive the location of their source. We detect the source of continuous low-pitched sounds by means of phase differences. **Phase differences** refer to the simultaneous arrival, at each ear, of different portions (phases) of the oscillating sound wave. For example, if we assume that sound travels at 700 miles per hour through the air, adjacent cycles of a 1000-Hz tone are 12.3 inches apart. Thus, if the source of the sound is located to one side of the head, one eardrum is pulled out while the other is pushed in. The movement of the eardrums will reverse, or be 180° *out of phase.* If the source were located directly in front of the head, the movements would be perfectly in phase (0° out of phase). (See ***Figure 6.13.***) Because some auditory neurons respond only when the eardrums (and, thus, the bending of the basilar membrane) are at least somewhat out of phase, neurons in the superior olivary complex in the brain are able to use the information they provide to detect the source of a continuous sound.

A possible mechanism to explain the ability of the nervous system to detect very short delays in the arrival times of two signals was first proposed by Jeffress (1948). He suggested that neurons received information from two sets of axons coming from the two ears. Each neuron served as a *coincidence detector;* it responded only if it simultaneously received signals from synapses belonging to both sets of axons. If a signal reached the two ears simultaneously, neurons in the middle of the array would fire. If,

FIGURE 6.13

Phase differences. (a) When a 1000-Hz tone is located to one side of the head, the eardrums vibrate out of phase. (b) When a 1000-Hz tone is located to the front or back of the head, the eardrums vibrate in phase.

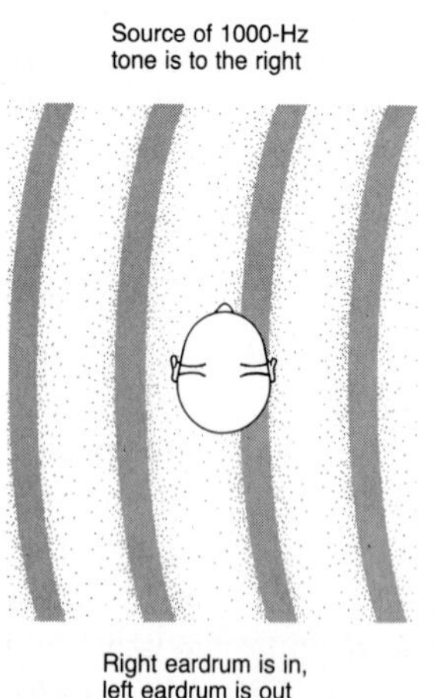

(a)

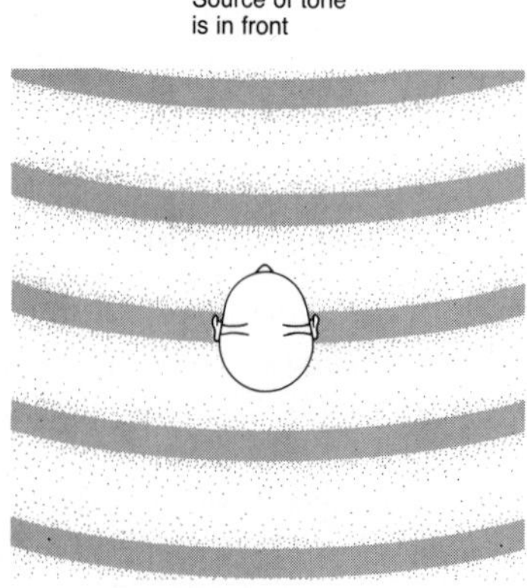

(b)

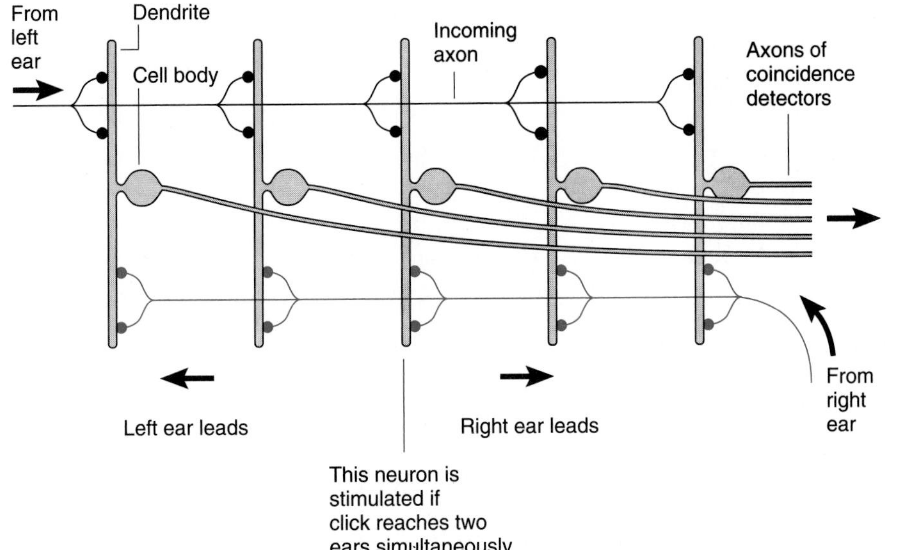

FIGURE 6.14

A model of a coincidence detector that can determine differences in arrival times at each ear of an auditory stimulus.

however, the signal reached one ear before the other, then neurons farther away from the "early" ear would be stimulated. (See ***Figure 6.14.***)

In fact, that is exactly how the mechanism works. Carr and Konishi (1989) obtained anatomical evidence in support of Jeffress's hypothesis from the brain of the barn owl, a nocturnal bird that can very accurately detect the source of a sound (such as that made by an unfortunate mouse). Figure 6.15 shows a drawing of the distribution of the branches of two axons, one from each ear, projecting to the nucleus laminaris, the barn owl analog of the mammalian medial superior olive. As you can see, axons from the ipsilateral and contralateral ears penetrate the nucleus from opposite directions; therefore, dorsally located neurons within the nucleus are stimulated by sounds that first reach the contralateral ear. (Compare ***Figures 6.14 and 6.15.***) Carr and Konishi recorded from single units within the nucleus and found that the response characteristics of the neurons located there were perfectly consistent with these anatomical facts.

LOCALIZATION BY MEANS OF INTENSITY DIFFERENCES

The auditory system cannot readily detect binaural phase differences of high-frequency sounds. The vibrations simply move too rapidly for such small time differences to be detected. However, high-frequency stimuli that occur to the right or left of the midline stimulate the ears unequally. The head absorbs high frequencies, producing a "sonic shadow," so that the ear opposite the source of the sound receives less intense stimulation. Some neurons in the auditory system respond differentially to binaural stimuli of different intensity in each ear.

The neurons that detect binaural differences in loudness are found in the superior olivary complex, near the neurons that detect binaural differences in phase or arrival time. Information from both sets of neurons is sent to other levels of the auditory system, where perception of the source of a sound is ultimately achieved.

Behavioral Functions of the Auditory System

Destruction of the primary visual cortex leads to blindness. In contrast, destruction of the auditory cortex — even in humans — does not impair simple intensity or frequency discriminations.

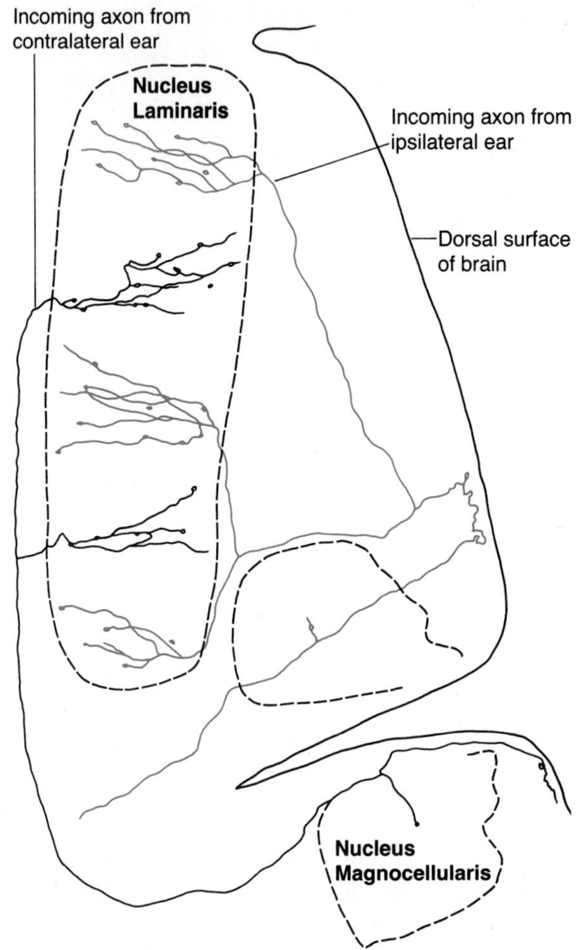

FIGURE 6.15

Evidence for a coincidence detector in the brain of a barn owl. Compare the branches of the axons with those of Figure 6.14. The drawing was prepared from microscopic examination of sections of stained tissue. (Adapted from Carr, C.E., and Konishi, M. *Proceedings of the National Academy of Sciences, USA,* 1989, *85,* 8311–8315.)

Neff (1977) reviewed a large number of studies that he and his colleagues performed with cats and monkeys to investigate the role of various levels of the auditory system in auditory discrimination and localization. (See ***Figure 6.16.***) They found that removing all areas of the auditory cortex on both sides of the brain (both primary

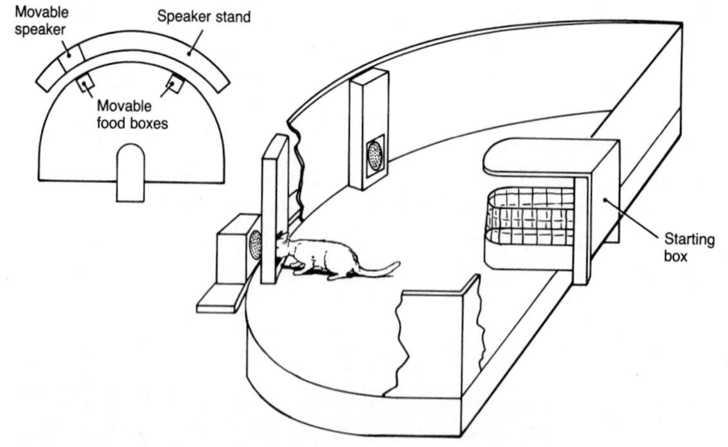

FIGURE 6.16

The experimental apparatus used by Neff and his colleagues to investigate localization of sound sources. (From Neff, W.D. *Annals of Otology, Rhinology and Laryngology,* 1977, *86,* 500–506. Reprinted with permission.)

auditory cortex and auditory association cortex) did not prevent the animals from detecting tones of different frequencies or intensities. However, they could not discriminate between different "tunes" or temporal patterns of acoustic stimuli, they could not detect changes in the duration of tones, they could not localize the source of sounds, they could not detect changes in complex sounds, and they could not determine which ear was stimulated.

The investigators also found that lesions that destroyed all auditory input to the medial geniculate nuclei but left the brain stem structures intact did not affect the animals' ability to detect sounds, but it impaired their ability to detect *differences* in the intensity of sounds and also abolished frequency discrimination. Thus, these two functions must require the thalamus (but not the cortex).

As we saw in the previous chapter, lesions of the visual association cortex in humans can produce visual agnosias. Similarly, lesions of the auditory association cortex can produce auditory agnosias, the inability to comprehend the meaning of sounds. If the lesion occurs in the left hemisphere, the person will sustain a particular form of language disorder. If it occurs in the right hemisphere, the person will be unable to recognize the nature or location of nonspeech sounds. Because of the importance of audition to language, these topics are discussed in much more detail in Chapter 13.

▶*INTERIM SUMMARY*◀

The receptive organ for audition is located on the basilar membrane. When sound strikes the tympanic membrane, it sets the ossicles into motion, and the baseplate of the stapes pushes against the membrane behind the oval window. Pressure changes thus applied to the fluid within the cochlea cause a portion of the basilar membrane to flex, which causes the basilar membrane to move laterally with respect to the tectorial membrane that overhangs it and to exert a shearing force on the cilia. This mechanical force opens ion channels in the hair cells and thus produces receptor potentials.

The hair cells form synapses with the dendrites of the bipolar neurons whose axons give rise to the cochlear branch of the eighth cranial nerve. The central auditory system involves several brain stem nuclei, including the cochlear nuclei, superior olivary complexes, and inferior colliculi. The medial geniculate nucleus relays auditory information to the primary auditory cortex on the medial surface of the temporal lobe.

Pitch is detected by two means: place coding and rate coding. High-frequency sounds cause the base of the basilar membrane (near the oval window) to flex; lower-frequency sounds cause the apex (opposite end) to flex. Thus, different frequencies stimulate different groups of auditory hair cells. The lowest frequencies cause the apex of the basilar membrane to flex back and forth in time with the acoustic vibrations.

The auditory system is analytical in its operation. That is, it can discriminate between sounds with different timbres by detecting the individual overtones that constitute the sounds and producing unique patterns of neural firing in the auditory system.

Left-right localization is performed by analyzing binaural differences in arrival time and in phase relations and binaural differences in intensity. The location of sources of brief sounds (such as clicks) and sounds of frequencies below approximately 3000 Hz is detected by neurons in the superior olivary complex that respond most vigorously when one ear receives the click first, or when the phase of a sine wave received by one ear leads that received by the other. The location of sources of high-frequency sounds is detected by neurons in the superior olivary complex that respond most vigorously when one organ of Corti is stimulated more intensely than the other. Removal of both the primary auditory cortex and the auditory association cortex does not affect the ability to detect differences in fre-

quency or intensity; thus, this analysis must be performed by subcortical components of the auditory system. However, the cortical removal does impair localization of the source of sounds and discrimination between different "tunes," changes in the duration of sounds, and changes in complex sounds. ▲

VESTIBULAR SYSTEM

vestibular sac
semicircular canal

The vestibular system has two components: the vestibular sacs and the semicircular canals. They represent the second and third components of the *bony labyrinths.* (We just studied the first component, the cochlea.) The **vestibular sacs** respond to the force of gravity and inform the brain about the head's orientation. The **semicircular canals** respond to angular acceleration—changes in the rotation of the head—but not to steady rotation. They also respond (but rather weakly) to changes in position or to linear acceleration.

The functions of the vestibular system include balance, maintenance of the head in an upright position, and adjustment of eye movement to compensate for head movements. Vestibular stimulation does not produce any readily definable sensation; certain low-frequency stimulation of the vestibular sacs can produce nausea, and stimulation of the semicircular canals can produce dizziness and rhythmic eye movements (*nystagmus*). However, we are not directly aware of the information received from these organs. This section describes the vestibular system: the vestibular apparatus, the receptor cells, and the vestibular pathway in the brain.

The Vestibular Apparatus

utricle saccule

ampulla crista

cupula

Figure 6.17 shows the bony labyrinths: the cochlea, the semicircular canals, and the two vestibular sacs: the **utricle** ("little pouch") and the **saccule** ("little sack"). (See ***Figure 6.17.***) The semicircular canals lie in the three major planes of the head: sagittal, transverse, and horizontal. Receptors in each canal are activated by changes in rotation in one plane. Figure 6.18 shows cross sections through one semicircular canal. The semicircular canal consists of a membranous canal floating within a bony one. An enlargement in the semicircular canal called the **ampulla** contains the **crista**, the organ in which the sensory receptors reside. The sensory receptors are hair cells similar to those found in the cochlea. Their cilia are embedded in a gelatinous mass called the **cupula**, which blocks part of the ampulla. (See ***Figure 6.18.***)

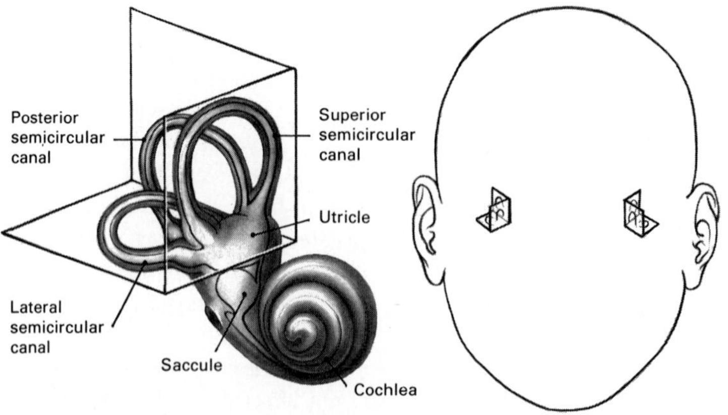

FIGURE 6.17

The bony labyrinths of the inner ear.

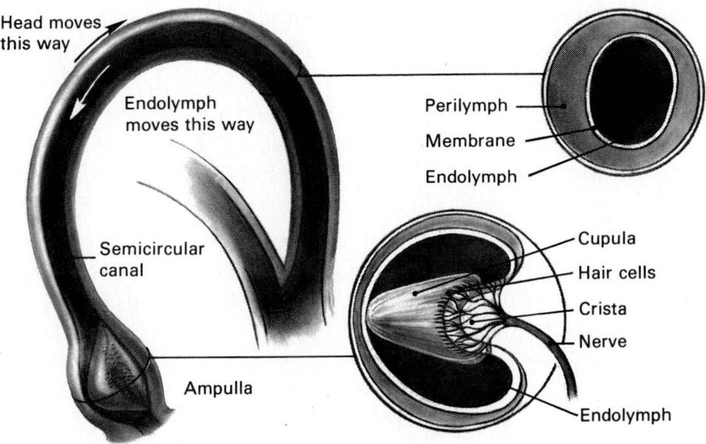

FIGURE 6.18

Cross sections through one semicircular canal.

In order to explain the effects of angular acceleration on the semicircular canals, I will first describe an "experiment." If we place a glass of water on the exact center of a turntable and then start the turntable spinning, the water in the glass will, at first, remain stationary (the glass will move with respect to the water it contains). Eventually, however, the water will begin rotating with the container. If we then stop the turntable, the water will continue spinning for a while, because of its momentum.

The semicircular canals operate on the same principle. The fluid within these canals, like the water in the glass, resists movement when the head begins to rotate. This inertial resistance pushes the fluid against the cupula, causing it to bend, until the fluid begins to move at the same speed as the head. If the head rotation is then stopped,

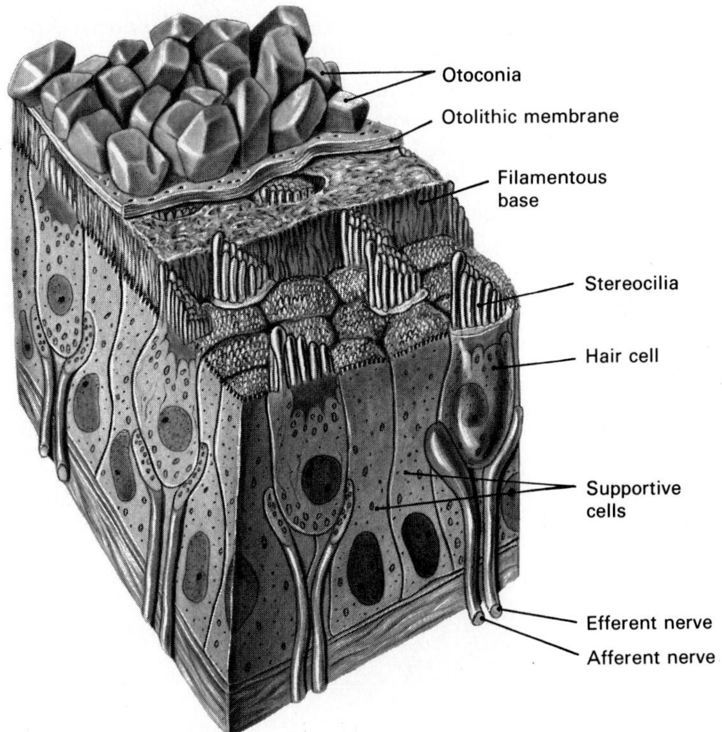

FIGURE 6.19

The receptive tissue of the utricle and saccule.

the fluid, still circulating through the canal, pushes the cupula the other way. Angular acceleration is thus translated into bending of the crista, which exerts a sideways shearing force on the cilia of the hair cells.

The vestibular sacs (the utricle and saccule) work very differently. These organs are roughly circular, and each contains a patch of receptive tissue. The receptive tissue is located on the "floor" of the utricle and on the "wall" of the saccule when the head is in an upright position. The receptive tissue, like that of the semicircular canals and cochlea, contains hair cells. The cilia of these receptors are embedded in an overlying gelatinous mass, which contains something rather unusual: *otoconia,* which are small crystals of calcium carbonate. (See ***Figure 6.19.***) The weight of the crystals causes the gelatinous mass to shift in position as the orientation of the head changes. Thus, movement produces a shearing force on the cilia of the receptive hair cells.

The Receptor Cells

The hair cells of the semicircular canal and vestibular sacs are similar in appearance. Each hair cell contains several cilia, graduated in length from short to long. Figure 6.20a shows a side view of a hair cell of a bullfrog saccule, and Figure 6.20b shows a top view, in which the largest cilium has been pulled away from the rest of the bundle. (See ***Figure 6.20.***)

The Vestibular Pathway

vestibular ganglion

The vestibular and cochlear nerves constitute the two branches of the eighth cranial nerve (auditory nerve). The bipolar cell bodies that give rise to the afferent axons of the vestibular nerve are located in the **vestibular ganglion**, which appears as a nodule on the vestibular nerve.

Most of the axons of the vestibular nerve synapse within the vestibular nuclei in the medulla, but some axons travel directly to the cerebellum. Neurons of the vestibular nuclei send their axons to the cerebellum, spinal cord, medulla, and pons. There also appear to be vestibular projections to the temporal cortex, but the precise pathways have not been determined. Most investigators believe that the cortical projections are responsible for feelings of dizziness; the activity of projections to the lower brain stem can produce the nausea and vomiting that accompany motion sickness. Projections to

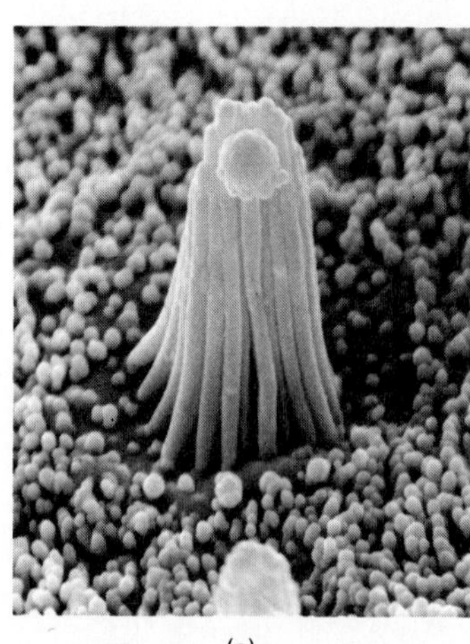

(a)

(b)

FIGURE 6.20

Hair cells. (a) Side view of a normal bundle of vestibular hair cells, with an intact kinocilium. (b) Top view of a bundle of hair cells from which the longest cilium has been detached. (From Hudspeth, A.J., and Jacobs, R. *Proceedings of the National Academy of Sciences, USA,* 1979, *76,* 1506–1509. Reprinted with permission.)

brain stem nuclei controlling neck muscles are clearly involved in maintaining an upright position of the head.

Perhaps the most interesting connections are those to the cranial nerve nuclei (third, fourth, and sixth) that control the eye muscles. As we walk or (especially) run, the head is jarred quite a bit. The vestibular system exerts direct control on eye movement, to compensate for the sudden head movements. This process, called the **vestibulo-ocular reflex**, maintains a fairly steady retinal image. Test this reflex yourself: Look at a distant object and hit yourself (gently) on the side of the head. Note that your image of the world jumps a bit, but not too much. People who have suffered vestibular damage, and who lack the vestibulo-ocular reflex, have difficulty seeing anything while walking or running. Everything becomes a blur of movement.

vestibulo-ocular reflex

▶INTERIM SUMMARY◀

The vestibular system includes the vestibular sacs and the semicircular canals. The semicircular canals are filled with fluid. When the head begins rotating or comes to rest after rotation, inertia causes the fluid to push the cupula to one side or the other. This movement exerts a shearing force on the crista, the organ containing the vestibular hair cells. Within the vestibular sacs is a patch of receptive tissue that contains hair cells whose cilia are embedded in a gelatinous mass. The weight of the otoconia in the gelatinous mass shifts when the head tilts, causing a shearing force on some of the cilia of the hair cells.

The vestibular hair cells form synapses with dendrites of bipolar neurons whose axons travel through the vestibular nerve. Vestibular information is received by the vestibular nuclei in the medulla, which relay it on to the cerebellum, spinal cord, medulla, pons, and temporal cortex. These pathways are responsible for control of posture, head movements, eye movements, and the puzzling phenomenon of motion sickness. ▲

SOMATOSENSES

The somatosenses provide information about what is happening on the surface of our body and inside it. The **cutaneous senses** (skin senses) include several submodalities commonly referred to as *touch.* **Kinesthesia** provides information about body position and movement and arises from receptors in joints, tendons, and muscles. The muscle receptors are discussed in Chapter 7. The **organic senses** arise from receptors in and around the internal organs, providing us with unpleasant stimuli such as stomachaches or gallbladder attacks, or pleasurable ones such as the feeling of a warm drink in our stomach on a cold winter day. Because the cutaneous senses are the most studied of the somatosenses, both perceptually and physiologically, I will devote most of my discussion to them.

cutaneous sense
kinesthesia

organic sense

The Stimuli

The cutaneous senses respond to several different types of stimuli: pressure, vibration, heating, cooling, and events that cause tissue damage (and hence, pain). Feelings of pressure are caused by mechanical deformation of the skin. Vibration is produced in the laboratory or clinic by tuning forks or mechanical devices, but it more commonly occurs when we move our fingers across a rough surface. Thus, we use vibration sensitivity to judge an object's roughness. Obviously, sensations of warmth and coolness are produced by objects that change skin temperature from normal. Sensations of pain can be caused by many different types of stimuli, but it appears that most cause at least some tissue damage.

Kinesthesia is provided by stretch receptors in skeletal muscles that report changes in muscle length to the central nervous system and by stretch receptors in tendons that measure the force being exerted by the muscles. Receptors within joints between adjacent bones respond to the magnitude and direction of limb movement. The muscle length detectors, sensory endings on special muscle fibers called **intrafusal muscle fibers,** do not give rise to conscious sensations; their information is used to control movement. These receptors will be discussed separately in Chapter 7.

intrafusal muscle fiber

Organic sensitivity is provided by receptors in the linings of muscles, outer layers of the gastrointestinal system and other internal organs, and linings of the abdominal and thoracic cavities. Many of these tissues are sensitive only to stretch and do not report sensations when cut, burned, or crushed. In addition, the stomach and esophagus are responsive to heat and cold and to some chemicals.

Anatomy of the Skin and Its Receptive Organs

The skin is a complex and vital organ of the body—one that we tend to take for granted. We cannot survive without it; extensive skin burns are fatal. Our cells, which must be bathed by a warm fluid, are protected from the hostile environment by the skin's outer layers. The skin participates in thermoregulation by producing sweat, thus cooling the body, or by restricting its circulation of blood, thus conserving heat.

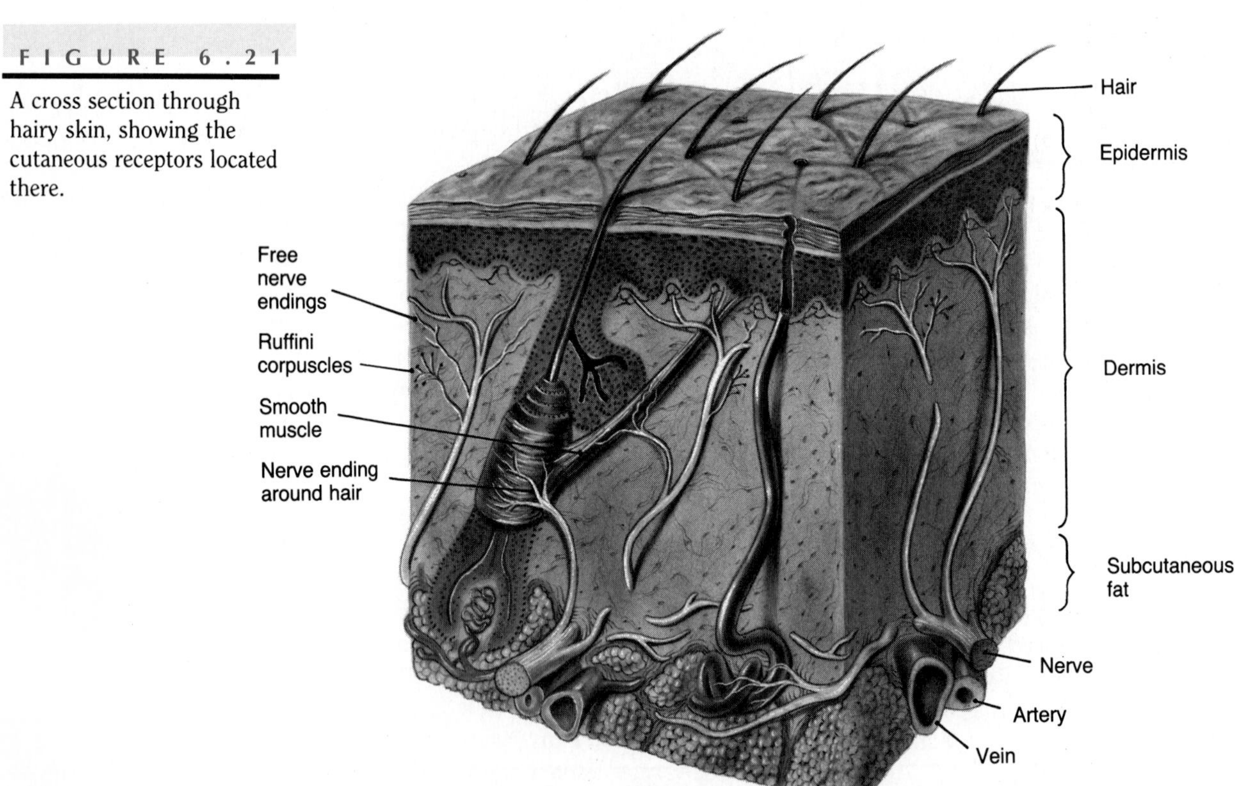

FIGURE 6.21

A cross section through hairy skin, showing the cutaneous receptors located there.

Its appearance varies widely across the body, from mucous membrane to hairy skin to the smooth, hairless skin of the palms and the soles of the feet.

Skin consists of subcutaneous tissue, dermis, and epidermis and contains various receptors scattered throughout these layers. Figures 6.21 and 6.22 show cross sections through hairy and **glabrous skin** (hairless skin, such as we have on our fingertips and palms). Hairy skin contains unencapsulated (free) nerve endings and **Ruffini corpuscles**, which respond to low-frequency vibration. Free nerve endings are found just below the surface of the skin, in a basketwork around the base of hair follicles and around the emergence of hair shafts from the skin. (See ***Figure 6.21.***)

glabrous skin
Ruffini corpuscle

Glabrous skin contains a more complex mixture of free nerve endings and axons that terminate within specialized end organs (Iggo and Andres, 1982). The increased complexity probably reflects the fact that we use the palms of our hands and the inside surfaces of our fingers to explore the environment actively: We use them to hold and touch objects. In contrast, the rest of our body most often contacts the environment passively; that is, other things come in contact with it.

Pacinian corpuscles are the largest sensory end organs in the body. Their size, approximately 0.5 × 1.0 mm, makes them visible to the naked eye. They are found in glabrous skin and in the external genitalia, mammary glands, and various internal organs. These receptors consist of up to seventy onionlike layers wrapped around the terminal button of a single myelinated axon. They are sensitive to touch, particularly to vibration. **Meissner's corpuscles** are found in *papillae* ("nipples"), small elevations of the dermis that project up into the epidermis. These end organs are innervated by between two and six axons. They respond to touch. **Merkel's disks**, which also respond to touch, are found at the base of the epidermis, in the same general locations as Meissner's corpuscles, adjacent to sweat ducts. (See ***Figure 6.22.***)

Pacinian corpuscle
Meissner's corpuscle
Merkel's disk

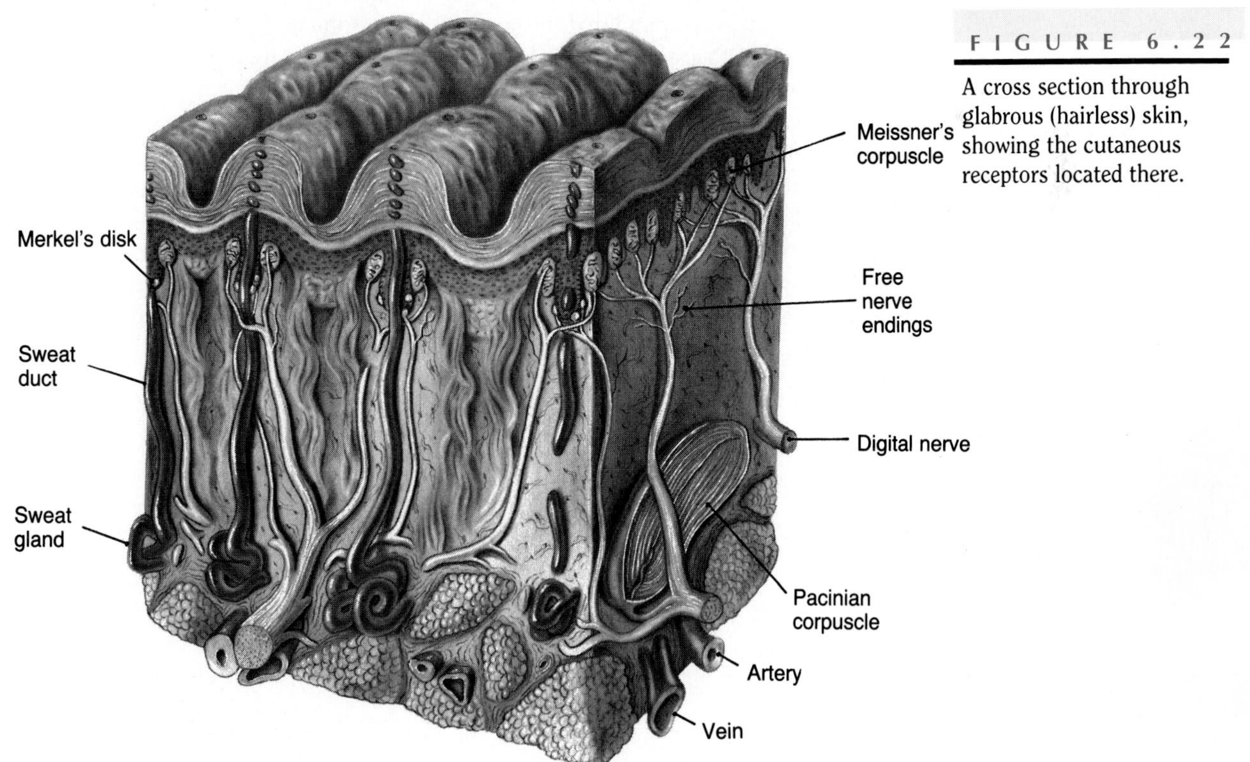

FIGURE 6.22

A cross section through glabrous (hairless) skin, showing the cutaneous receptors located there.

Detection of Cutaneous Stimulation

The three most important qualities of cutaneous stimulation are touch, temperature, and pain. These qualities are described in the section that follows.

TOUCH

Sensitivity to pressure and vibration is caused by movement of the skin. The best-studied receptor is the Pacinian corpuscle, which primarily detects vibration. When the corpuscle is bent relative to the axon, the membrane becomes depolarized. If the threshold of excitation is exceeded, an action potential is produced at the first node of Ranvier. Loewenstein and Mendelson (1965) have shown that the layers of the corpuscle alter the mechanical characteristics of the organ, so the axon responds briefly when the intact organ is bent and again when it is released. Thus, it is sensitive to vibration but not to steady pressure.

The bending of the tip of the nerve ending in a Pacinian corpuscle appears to produce a receptor potential by opening ion channels in the membrane. These channels appear to be anchored to protein filaments beneath the membrane and have long carbohydrate chains attached to them. When a mechanical stimulus changes the shape of the nerve ending, tension is exerted on the carbohydrate chains, which pulls the channel open. (See ***Figure 6.23.***) Most investigators believe that the encapsulated endings serve only to modify the physical stimulus transduced by the axons that enter them.

Adaptation. Investigators have known for a long time that a moderate, constant stimulus applied to the skin fails to produce any sensation after it has been present for a while. We not only ignore the pressure of a wristwatch, but we cannot feel it at all if we keep our arm still (assuming that the band is not painfully tight). Physiological studies have shown that the reason for the lack of sensation is the absence of receptor firing; the receptors adapt to a constant stimulus.

This adaptation is not caused by "fatigue" of physical or chemical processes within the receptor. Instead, it occurs because of the physical construction of the skin and the cutaneous sensory organs. Nafe and Wagoner (1941) recorded the sensations reported by human subjects as a stimulus weight gradually moved downward, deforming the skin. Pressure was reported until the weight finally stopped moving. When the weight was increased, pressure was reported until downward movement stopped again. Pressure sensations were also briefly recorded when the weight was removed, while the

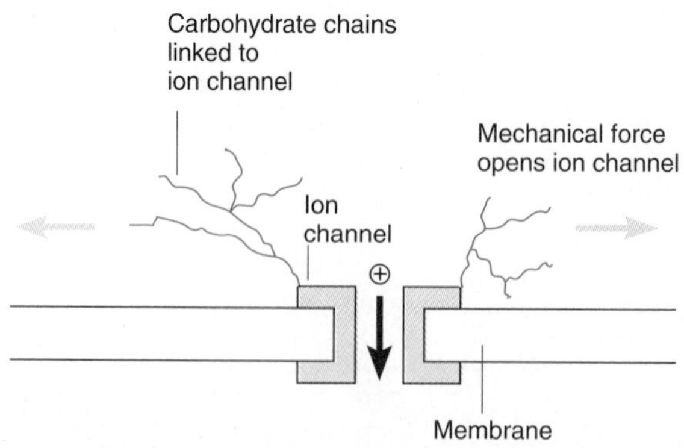

FIGURE 6.23

A hypothetical explanation of transduction of somatosensory information. A mechanical force on the carbohydrate chains linked to ion channels opens the channels, permitting the entry of cations, which depolarizes the membrane potential.

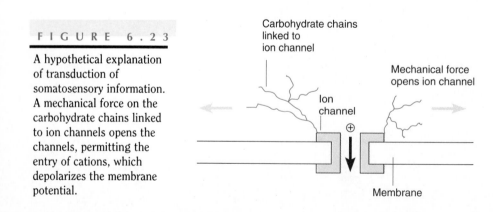

surface of the skin regained its normal shape. (You may have noticed that when you first take your hat off, it feels for a few moments as if you were still wearing it.)

Responsiveness to Moving Stimuli. A moderate, constant, nondamaging stimulus is rarely of any importance to an organism, so this adaptation mechanism is useful. Our cutaneous senses are used much more often to analyze shapes and textures of stimulus objects moving with respect to the surface of the skin. Sometimes, the object itself moves; but more often, we do the moving ourselves.

If I placed an object in your palm and asked you to keep your hand still, you would have a great deal of difficulty recognizing the object by touch alone. If I said you could now move your hand, you would manipulate the object, letting its surface slide across your palm and the pads of your fingers. You would be able to describe its three-dimensional shape, hardness, texture, slipperiness, and so on. Obviously, your motor system must cooperate, and you need kinesthetic sensation from your muscles and joints, besides the cutaneous information. If you squeeze the object and feel a lot of well-localized pressure in return, it is hard. If you feel a less intense, more diffuse pressure in return, it is soft. If it produces vibrations as it moves over the ridges on your fingers, it is rough. If very little effort is needed to move the object while pressing it against your skin, it is slippery. If it does not produce vibrations as it moves across your skin, but moves in a jerky fashion, and if it takes effort to remove your fingers from its surface, it is sticky. Thus, our somatosenses work dynamically with the motor system to provide useful information about the nature of objects that come in contact with our skin.

TEMPERATURE

Feelings of warmth and coolness are relative, not absolute (except at the extremes). There is a temperature level that for a particular region of skin will produce a sensation of temperature neutrality — neither warmth nor coolness. This neutral point is not an absolute value but depends on the prior history of thermal stimulation of that area. If the temperature of a region of skin is raised by a few degrees, the initial feeling of warmth is replaced by one of neutrality. If the skin temperature is lowered to its initial value, it now feels cool. Thus, increases in temperature lower the sensitivity of warmth receptors and raise the sensitivity of cold receptors. The converse holds for decreases in skin temperature. This adaptation to ambient temperature can be easily demonstrated by placing one hand in a bucket of warm water and the other in a bucket of cool water until some adaptation has taken place. If you then simultaneously immerse both hands in water at room temperature, it will feel warm to one hand and cool to the other.

Thermal receptors are difficult to study, because changes in temperature alter the metabolic activity, and also the rate of axonal firing, of a variety of cells. For example, a receptor that responds to pressure might produce varying amounts of activity in response to the same mechanical stimulus, depending upon the temperature. Nevertheless, most investigators agree that changes in temperature are detected by free nerve endings, and that warmth and coolness are detected by different populations of receptors (Sinclair, 1981). The transduction of temperature changes into the rate of axonal firing has not yet been explained.

An ingenious experiment by Bazett, McGlone, Williams, and Lufkin (1932) showed long ago that receptors for warmth and cold lie at different depths in the skin. The investigators lifted the prepuce (foreskin) of uncircumcised males with dull fishhooks. They applied thermal stimuli on one side of the folded skin and recorded the rate at which the temperature changes were transmitted through the skin by placing small temperature sensors on the opposite side. (The prepuce is the only place where such a thin fold of skin is available.) They then correlated these observations with verbal reports of warmth and coolness. The investigators concluded that cold receptors were close to the skin and that warmth receptors were located deeper in the tissue. (This experiment shows the extremities to which scientists will go to obtain information — pun intended.)

PAIN

Most investigators identify pain reception with the networks of free nerve endings in the skin. Pain appears to be produced by a variety of procedures. Intense mechanical stimulation activates a class of high-threshold receptors that produce a sensation of pain. However, most painful stimuli cause tissue damage, which suggested to investigators that pain is caused by the release of a chemical by injured cells (Besson, Guilbaud, Abdelmoumene, and Chaouch, 1982). As we saw in Chapter 4, aspirin, which inhibits the production of a class of hormones known as prostaglandins, produces analgesia. When cells are damaged, they very rapidly synthesize a prostaglandin. This chemical sensitizes free nerve endings to another chemical, histamine, which is also released by damaged cells. The free nerve endings transmit pain messages to the central nervous system. Thus, by inhibiting the release of prostaglandins, aspirin interferes with one of the steps in the transmission of pain information to the brain.

The Somatosensory Pathways

Somatosensory axons from the skin, muscles, or internal organs enter the central nervous system via spinal nerves. Those located in the face and head primarily enter through the trigeminal nerve (fifth cranial nerve). The cell bodies of the unipolar neurons are located in the dorsal root ganglia and cranial nerve ganglia. Axons that convey precisely localized information, such as fine touch, ascend through the white matter of the spinal cord to nuclei in the lower medulla. From there, axons cross the brain and ascend to the ventral posterior nuclei of the thalamus, the relay nuclei for somatosensation. Axons from the thalamus project to the primary somatosensory cortex. In contrast, axons that convey poorly localized information, such as pain or temperature, form synapses with other neurons as soon as they enter the spinal cord. The axons of these neurons cross to the other side of the spinal cord and ascend to the ventral posterior nuclei of the thalamus.

Recall from Chapter 5 that the primary visual cortex contains columns of cells, each of which responds to particular features, such as orientation, ocular dominance, or spatial frequency. Within these columns are blobs that contain cells that respond to particular colors. The somatosensory cortex also has a columnar arrangement; in fact, cortical columns were discovered there by Mountcastle (1957) before they were found in the visual and auditory cortex. Within a column neurons respond to a particular type of stimulus (for example, temperature or pressure) applied to a particular part of the body.

Dykes (1983) has reviewed research indicating that the primary and secondary somatosensory cortical areas are divided into at least five (and perhaps as many as ten) different maps of the body surface. Within each map cells respond to a particular submodality of somatosensory receptors. So far, separate areas have been identified that respond to slowly adapting cutaneous receptors, rapidly adapting cutaneous receptors, receptors that detect changes in muscle length, receptors located in the joints, and Pacinian corpuscles.

As you learned in Chapter 5, the prestriate cortex consists of several subareas, each of which contains an independent representation of the visual field. One area responds specifically to color, another to movement, and two others to orientation. The somatosensory cortex appears to follow a similar scheme: Each cortical map of the body contains neurons that respond to a specific submodality of stimulation. Undoubtedly, further investigations will provide more accurate functional maps of the cortical subareas of both of these sensory systems.

Perception of Pain

Pain is a curious phenomenon. It is more than a mere sensation; it can be defined only by some sort of withdrawal reaction or, in humans, by verbal report. Pain can be modified by opiates, by hypnosis, by the administration of pharmacologically inert sugar pills, by emotions, and even by other forms of stimulation, such as acupuncture. Recent research efforts have made remarkable progress in discovering the physiological bases of these phenomena.

We might reasonably ask *why* we experience pain. In most cases pain serves a constructive role. For example, people who have congenital insensitivity to pain suffer an abnormally large number of injuries, such as cuts and burns. In fact, one woman eventually died as a result of her insensitivity to pain. Because she did not make the shifts in posture that we normally make when our joints start to ache, she suffered damage to the spine that ultimately resulted in her death. Other people have died from ruptured appendixes and ensuing abdominal infections that they did not feel (Sternbach, 1968). I am sure that a person who is passing a kidney stone would not find much comfort in the fact that pain does more good than ill, but it is, nevertheless, very important to our existence.

Some environmental events diminish the perception of pain. For example, Beecher (1959) noted that wounded American soldiers back from the battle at Anzio, Italy, during World War II reported that they felt no pain from their wounds — they did not even want medication. It would appear that their perception of pain was diminished by the relief they felt from surviving such an ordeal. There are other instances in which people still report the perception of pain but are not bothered by it. Some tranquilizers have this effect.

Physiological evidence provides a clear distinction between the perception and tolerance of pain. Mark, Ervin, and Yakovlev (1962) made stereotaxically placed lesions in the thalamus in an attempt to relieve the pain of patients suffering from the advanced stages of cancer. Damage to different parts of the thalamus either abolished cutaneous pain or deep pain or eliminated the emotional component of pain — the patients still felt the pain, but it no longer bothered them.

For many years investigators have known that perception of pain can be modified by environmental stimuli. Recent work, beginning in the 1970s, has revealed the existence of neural circuits whose activity can produce analgesia (decreased sensitivity to pain). A variety of environmental stimuli can activate these analgesia-producing circuits. Most of these stimuli cause the release of the endogenous opiates, which were described in Chapter 4.

Electrical stimulation of particular locations within the brain can cause analgesia, which can even be profound enough to serve as an anesthetic for surgery in rats (Reynolds, 1969). The most effective locations appear to be within the periaqueductal gray matter and in the rostroventral medulla. For example, Mayer and Liebeskind (1974) reported that electrical stimulation of the periaqueductal gray matter produced

FIGURE 6.24

A person who suffers from chronic pain, holding a device that permits him to stimulate the periaqueductal gray matter of his brain through implanted electrodes, thus producing analgesia. (Dan McCoy/Rainbow.)

analgesia in rats equivalent to that produced by at least 10 milligrams (mg) of morphine per kilogram of body weight, which is a large dose. The technique has even found an application in reducing severe, chronic pain in humans: Fine wires are surgically implanted in parts of the central nervous system and attached to a radio-controlled device that permits the patient to administer electrical stimulation when necessary (Kumar, Wyant, and Nath, 1990). (See ***Figure 6.24.***)

Analgesic brain stimulation apparently triggers the neural mechanisms that reduce pain, primarily by causing endogenous opiates to be released. Basbaum and Fields (1978, 1984) summarized their work and that of others and proposed a neural circuit that mediates opiate-induced analgesia. Basically, they proposed the following: Endogenous opiates (released by environmental stimuli or administered as a drug) stimulate opiate receptors on neurons in the periaqueductal gray matter. Because the effect of opiates appears to be inhibitory (Nicoll, Alger, and Nicoll, 1980), Basbaum and Fields propose that the neurons that contain opiate receptors are themselves inhibitory interneurons. Thus, the administration of opiates activates the neurons on which these interneurons synapse. (See ***Figure 6.25.***)

FIGURE 6.25

The neural circuit that mediates opiate-induced analgesia, as hypothesized by Basbaum and Fields (1978).

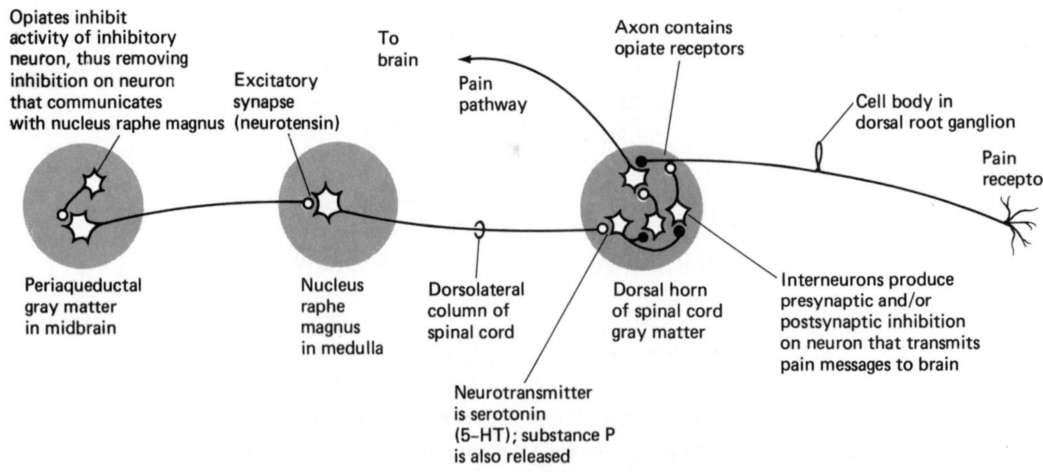

Neurons in the periaqueductal gray matter send axons to the **nucleus raphe magnus**, located in the medulla. The neurons in this nucleus send axons to the dorsal horn of the spinal cord gray matter; destruction of these axons eliminates analgesia induced by an injection of morphine. The inhibitory effects of these neurons apparently involves one or two interneurons in the spinal cord. (See ***Figure 6.25.***)

nucelus raphe magnus

▶*INTERIM SUMMARY*◀

The somatosenses, which tell us what is happening on and within our bodies, include the cutaneous senses, kinesthesia, and organic senses. Cutaneous sensory information is provided by specialized receptors in the skin. Pacinian corpuscles provide information about vibration. Ruffini corpuscles, similar to Pacinian corpuscles but considerably smaller, respond to low-frequency vibration. Meissner's corpuscles and Merkel's disks respond to touch. Painful stimuli are detected primarily by free nerve endings.

Sensory endings in the tendons detect muscular tension, those in the joints detect limb movements, and those in the intrafusal muscle fibers detect changes in muscle length. Free nerve endings and Pacinian corpuscles are found in the fascia covering the muscles and in the tissue lining the joints, and the body of the muscles contains free nerve endings.

Our somatosensory system is most sensitive to changes in mechanical stimuli. Unless the skin is moving, we do not detect nonpainful stimuli, because the receptors adapt to constant mechanical pressure. Temperature receptors also adapt; moderate changes in skin temperature are soon perceived as "neutral," and deviations above or below this temperature are perceived as warmth or coolness.

Somatosensory information reaches the ventral posterior nuclei of the thalamus, which project axons to the primary somatosensory cortex. Neurons there are topographically arranged, according to the part of the body from which they receive sensory information (somatotopic representation). Columns within the somatosensory cortex respond to a particular type of stimulus from a particular region of the body. Recent studies have shown that different types of somatosensory receptors send their information to separate areas of the somatosensory cortex.

Pain perception is not a simple function of stimulation of pain receptors; it is a complex phenomenon that can be modified by experience and the immediate environment. Just as we have mechanisms to perceive pain, we have mechanisms to reduce it—to produce analgesia. Under the appropriate circumstances neurons in the periaqueductal gray matter are stimulated through synaptic connections or by endogenous opiates, released by cells located elsewhere in the brain. Connections from the periaqueductal gray matter to the nucleus raphe magnus of the medulla activate neurons located there. These neurons send axons to the dorsal horn of the spinal cord gray matter, where they inhibit neurons whose axons transmit pain information to the brain. ▲

GUSTATION

The stimuli we have encountered so far produce receptor potentials by imparting physical energy: thermal, photic (involving light), or kinetic. However, the stimuli received by the last two senses to be studied, gustation (taste) and olfaction (smell), interact with their receptors chemically. This section discusses the first of them: gustation.

The Stimuli

For a substance to be tasted, molecules of it must dissolve in the saliva and stimulate the taste receptors on the tongue. Tastes of different substances vary, but much less than we generally realize. There are only four qualities of taste: *bitterness, sourness, sweetness,* and *saltiness.* Flavor, as opposed to taste, is a composite of olfaction and gustation. Much of the flavor of a steak depends on its odor; to an *anosmic* person (lacking the sense of smell) or to a person whose nostrils are stopped up, an onion tastes like an apple, and a steak tastes like salty cardboard.

Most vertebrates possess gustatory systems that respond to all four taste qualities. (An exception is the cat, which does not detect sweetness.) Most investigators believe that sweetness receptors are food detectors. Most sweet-tasting foods, such as fruits and some vegetables, are safe to eat. Saltiness receptors detect the presence of sodium chloride. In some environments inadequate amounts of this mineral are obtained from the usual source of food, so sodium chloride detectors help the animal detect its presence. Injuries that cause bleeding rapidly deplete an organism of its supply of sodium, so the ability to find it quickly can be critical.

Most species of animals will readily ingest substances that taste sweet or somewhat salty. However, they will tend to avoid substances that taste sour or bitter. Because of bacterial activity, many foods become acidic when they spoil. The acidity tastes sour and causes an avoidance reaction. (Of course, we have learned to make highly preferred mixtures of sweet and sour, such as lemonade.) Bitterness is almost universally avoided and cannot easily be improved by adding some sweetness. Many plants produce bitter poisonous alkaloids, which protect them from being eaten by animals. The bitterness receptor undoubtedly serves to warn animals away from these chemicals.

Anatomy of the Taste Buds and Gustatory Cells

The tongue, palate, pharynx, and larynx contain approximately ten thousand taste buds. Most of these receptive organs are arranged around *papillae,* small protuberances of the tongue. Papillae are surrounded by moatlike trenches that serve to trap saliva. The taste buds surround the trenches, and their pores open into them. Figure 6.26 shows the appearance of papillae and a cross section through a trench that contains a taste bud. (See ***Figure 6.26.***)

Taste buds that respond to the different taste qualities have different distributions on the tongue. The tip of the tongue is most sensitive to sweetness and saltiness, the

FIGURE 6.26

The tongue. (a) Papillae on the surface of the tongue. (b) A taste bud.

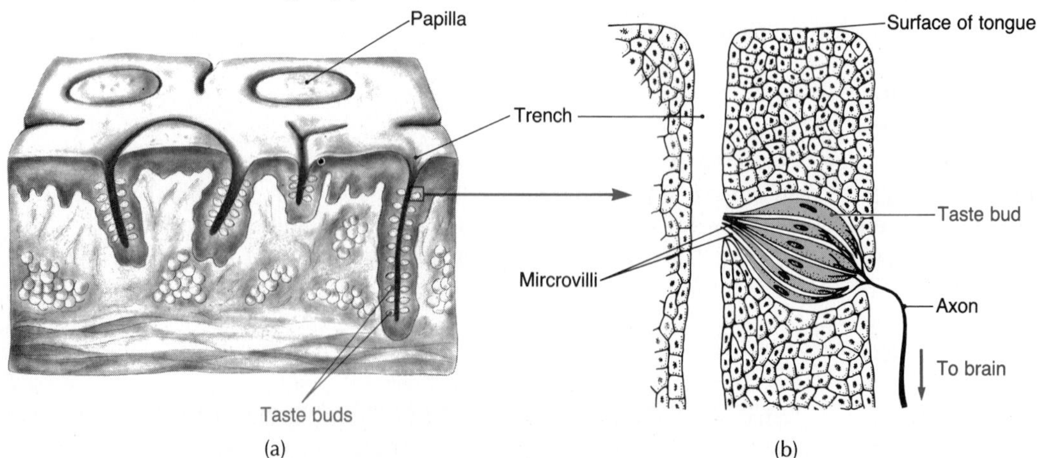

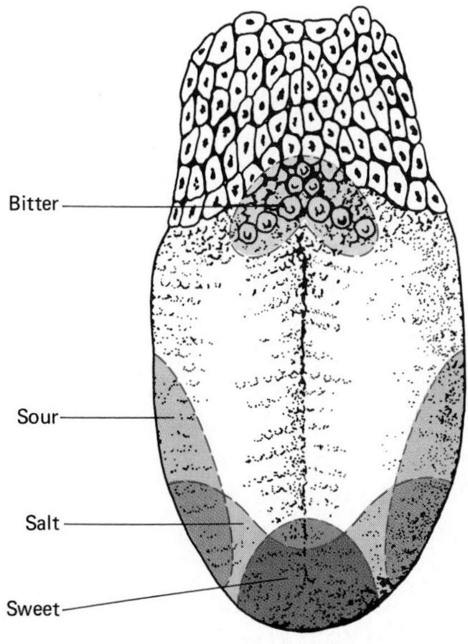

FIGURE 6.27

Different regions of the tongue especially sensitive to different tastes.

sides are most sensitive to sourness, and the back of the tongue, throat, and soft palate are most sensitive to bitterness. (See ***Figure 6.27.***) This distribution explains why saccharin, an artificial sweetener that tastes both sweet and bitter to some people, produces a sensation of sweetness on the front of the tongue when it is first tasted and then a sensation of bitterness in the back of the mouth when it is swallowed.

Taste receptors possess hairlike processes (*microvilli*) that project through the pores of the taste bud into the trench adjacent to the papilla. They form synapses with dendrites of sensory neurons that convey gustatory information to the brain. The receptors have a life span of only ten days. They quickly wear out, being directly exposed to a rather hostile environment. As they degenerate, they are replaced by newly developed cells; the afferent dendrite is passed on to the new cell (Beidler, 1970). The presence of vesicles within the cytoplasm of the receptor cell around the synaptic region suggests that transmission at this synapse is chemical.

Detection of Gustatory Information

It seems most likely that detection of taste is similar to the chemical transmission that takes place at synapses: The tasted molecule binds with the receptor and produces changes in membrane permeability that cause receptor potentials. Different substances bind with different types of receptors, producing different taste sensations.

To taste salty, a substance must ionize. Although the best stimulus for saltiness receptors is sodium chloride (NaCl), a variety of other salts also taste salty. Sourness receptors probably respond to the hydrogen ions present in acidic solutions. Bitter and sweet substances are more difficult to characterize. The typical stimulus for bitterness is a plant alkaloid such as quinine; for sweetness it is a sugar such as fructose. Because some molecules elicit both sensations, bitterness and sweetness receptors must be similar. For example, the Seville orange rind contains a glycoside (complex sugar) that tastes extremely bitter. However, Horowitz and Gentili (1974) discovered that the addition of hydrogen to the molecule makes it intensely sweet. Some amino acids taste sweet. Indeed, the commercial sweetener aspartame consists simply of two amino acids, aspartate and phenylalanine.

The Gustatory Pathway

chorda tympani

Gustatory information is transmitted through three cranial nerves. Information from the anterior part of the tongue travels through the **chorda tympani**, a branch of the seventh cranial nerve (facial nerve). Taste receptors in the posterior part of the tongue send information through the lingual (tongue) branch of the ninth cranial nerve (glossopharyngeal nerve), and the tenth cranial nerve (vagus nerve) carries information from receptors of the palate and epiglottis. The chorda tympani gets its name because it passes through the middle ear just beneath the tympanic membrane. Because of its convenient location, it is accessible to a recording or stimulating electrode. Investigators have even recorded from this nerve during the course of human ear operations.

nucleus of the solitary tract

parabrachial nucleus

thalamic taste area

The first relay station for taste is the **nucleus of the solitary tract**, located in the medulla. The taste-sensitive neurons of this nucleus send their axons a short distance forward, to the **parabrachial nucleus** of the pons (Pfaffmann, Frank, and Norgren, 1979). The pontine neurons then project to a **thalamic taste area**, which in turn relays information to an area of the neocortex located just ventral to the "face" region of the somatosensory cortex. The lateral hypothalamus and parts of the limbic system also receive gustatory information. Many investigators believe that the pathway to the hypothalamus plays a role in mediating the reinforcing effects of sweet and salty tastes.

Neural Coding of Taste

Almost all fibers in the chorda tympani respond to more than one taste quality, and many respond to changes in temperature, as well. However, most show a preference for one of the four qualities (sweet, salty, sour, or bitter). Figure 6.28 shows the average responses of fibers in the rat chorda tympani and glossopharyngeal nerve to sucrose (S), sodium chloride (N), hydrochloric acid (H), quinine (Q), and water (W), as recorded by Nowlis and Frank (1977). These investigators stimulated three different kinds of taste buds and found the same general types of responses from each of them. (See ***Figure 6.28.***)

FIGURE 6.28

Mean number of responses recorded from axons in the chorda tympani and glossopharyngeal nerve during the first 5 seconds after the application of sweet, salty, sour, and bitter stimuli. The response characteristics of the axons are categorized as sweet, salty, sour, or bitter. (From Nowlis, G.H., and Frank, M., in *Olfaction and Taste 6*, edited by J. LeMagnen and P. MacLeod. Washington, D.C.: Information Retrieval, 1977. Reprinted with permission.)

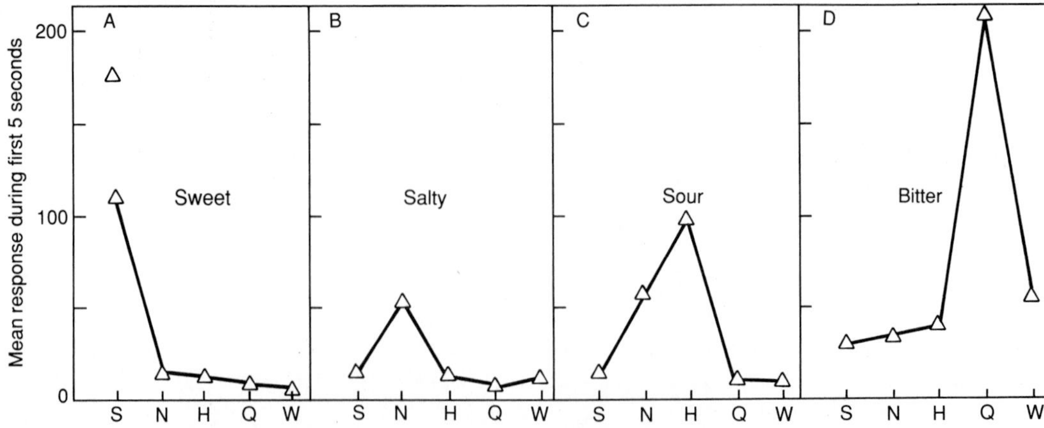

Yamamoto, Yuyama, and Kawamura (1981) attempted to determine whether the taste qualities were represented in different parts of the cortex. In general, they were. When dilute hydrochloric acid and quinine were delivered to the tongue, neurons in adjacent regions at one end of the cortical taste area were activated, but the presence of sucrose activated neurons located at the opposite end. Neurons that were sensitive to sodium chloride were spread throughout the area.

▶*INTERIM SUMMARY*◀

Taste (gustation) receptors detect only four sensory qualities: bitterness, sourness, sweetness, and saltiness. Bitter foods often contain plant alkaloids, many of which are poisonous. Sour foods have usually undergone bacterial fermentation, which can produce toxins. On the other hand, sweet foods (such as fruits) are usually nutritious and safe to eat, and salty foods contain an essential cation, sodium. The fact that people in affluent cultures today tend to ingest excessive amounts of sweet and salty foods suggests that stimulation of these neurons is naturally reinforcing. The means of transduction of gustatory information is not known. Presumably, the mechanism utilizes receptors similar to those that detect hormones and transmitter substances.

Gustatory information from the anterior part of the tongue travels through the chorda tympani, a branch of the facial nerve that passes beneath the eardrum on its way to the brain. The posterior part of the tongue sends gustatory information through the glossopharyngeal nerve, and the palate and epiglottis send gustatory information through the vagus nerve. Gustatory information is received by the nucleus of the solitary tract, located in the medulla, and is relayed to the parabrachial nucleus of the pons, then to the thalamic taste area, and finally to the base of the somatosensory cortex, lateral hypothalamus, and limbic system. ▲

OLFACTION

Olfaction (smell), the second chemical sense, helps us identify food and avoid food that has spoiled and is unfit to eat. It helps the members of many species identify receptive mates. For humans, olfaction is the most enigmatic of all sensory modalities. Odors have a peculiar ability to evoke memories, often vague ones that seem to have occurred in the distant past. Although people can discriminate among many thousands of different odors, we lack a good vocabulary to describe them. It is relatively easy to describe sights we have seen or sounds we have heard, but the description of an odor is difficult. At best, we can say it smells like something else. As we will see, the search for primary odors, like those of taste, vision, and audition, has not yet progressed very far.

The Stimulus

The stimulus for odor consists of volatile substances having a molecular weight in the range of approximately 15 to 300. Almost all odorous compounds are organic. However, many substances that meet these criteria have no odor at all, and we do not yet know why.

Anatomy of the Olfactory Apparatus

olfactory epithelium

Our olfactory receptors reside within two patches of mucous membrane (**olfactory epithelium**), each having an area of about 1 in.^{2}. The olfactory epithelium is located at

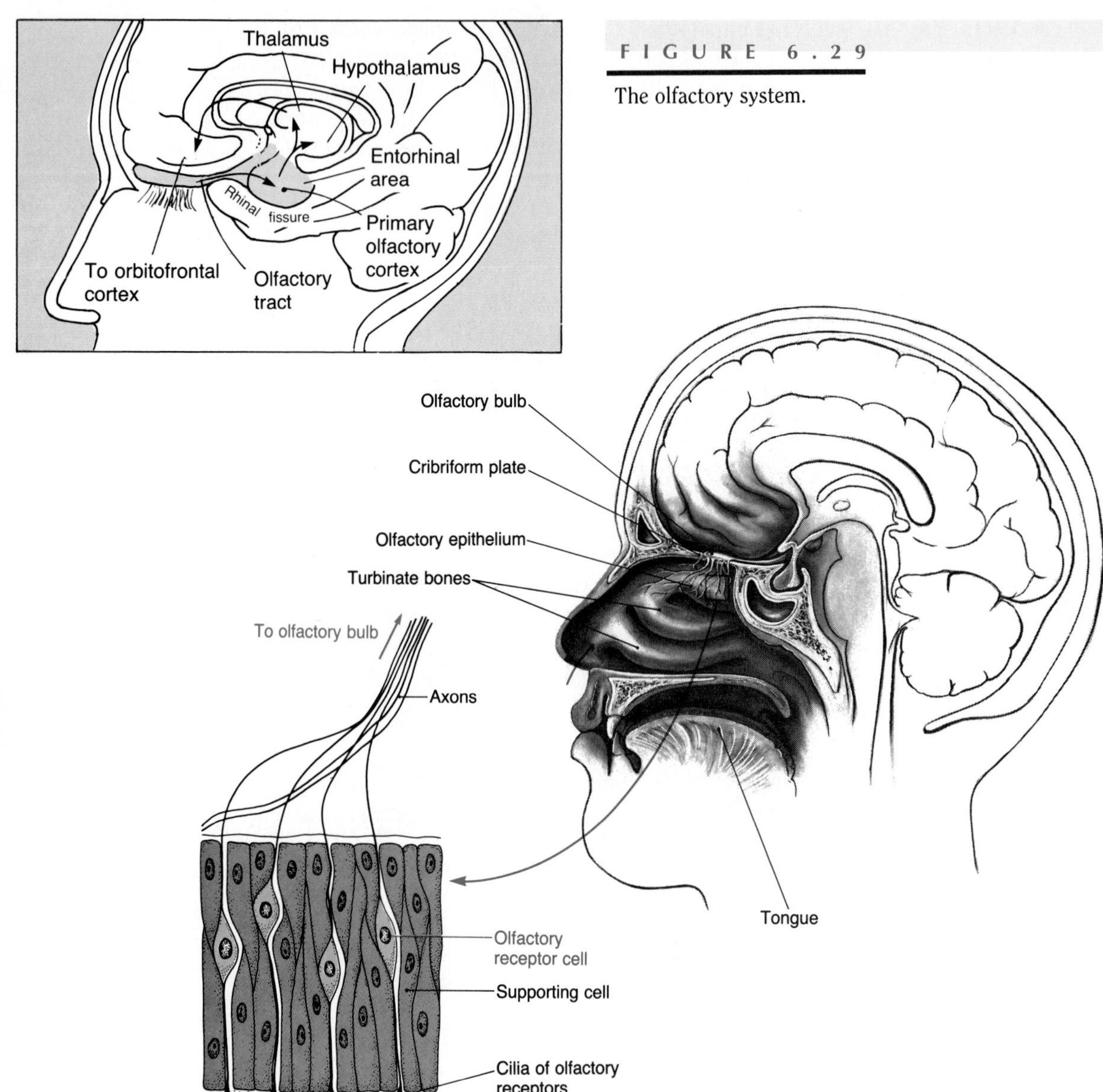

FIGURE 6.29

The olfactory system.

the top of the nasal cavity, as shown in ***Figure 6.29.*** Air that enters the nostrils is swept upward (especially when we sniff) by the action of the ***turbinate bones*** that project into the nasal cavity, until it reaches the olfactory receptors.

cribriform plate

The inset in Figure 6.29 illustrates a group of olfactory receptor cells, along with their supporting cells. (See ***inset, Figure 6.29.***) Olfactory receptors are bipolar neurons whose cell bodies lie within the olfactory mucosa that lines the **cribriform plate,** a bone at the base of the rostral part of the brain. The receptors send one process toward the surface of the mucosa, which divides into several cilia that penetrate the layer of mucus. Presumably, odorous molecules dissolve in the mucus and stimulate receptor molecules on the olfactory cilia. The olfactory receptors possess axons, which enter the skull through small holes in the cribriform (''perforated'') plate. The olfactory mucosa also contains free nerve endings of trigeminal nerve axons; these nerve endings presumably mediate sensations of pain that can be produced by sniffing some irritating chemicals, such as ammonia.

The **olfactory bulbs** lie at the base of the brain on the ends of the stalklike olfactory tracts. Axons of the olfactory receptors terminate in one of the two olfactory bulbs, where they synapse with dendrites of neurons that send axons to the rest of the brain through the olfactory tracts.

olfactory bulb

Olfactory tract axons project directly to the primary olfactory cortex, which is on the pyriform cortex, a part of the limbic lobe. (See ***Figure 6.29***.) The pyriform cortex projects to the hypothalamus and to the dorsomedial thalamus, which projects to the orbitofrontal cortex (Cain, 1988). The orbitofrontal cortex also receives gustatory information; thus, it may be involved in the combining of taste and olfaction into flavor. The hypothalamus also receives a considerable amount of olfactory information, which is probably important for the acceptance or rejection of food and for the olfactory control of reproductive processes seen in many species of mammals.

Most mammals (but probably not adult humans) have another organ that responds to olfactory stimuli: the *vomeronasal organ.* Because it plays an important role in animals' responses to odors that affect sexual physiology and behavior, its structure and function are described in Chapter 9.

Transduction of Olfactory Information

The means by which odor molecules produce receptor potentials are unknown. Investigators assume that olfactory cilia contain receptor molecules (like those found on taste receptors and synaptic membranes) that are stimulated by odor molecules. The resting potential of olfactory neurons is approximately −45 mV, which is relatively weak. Stimulation with odorous molecules opens one or more ion channels, causing the neurons to depolarize slowly and increasing the firing rate of their axons (Lancet, 1984).

Detection of Specific Odors

Although investigators have made many attempts to identify primary odors corresponding to the sweet, sour, bitter, and salty qualities of taste, we still cannot say with any assurance how different odors are detected. For a long time investigators have believed that specific categories or dimensions of odors do exist, primarily because it seems unlikely that the olfactory system contains a myriad of different types of receptors. After all, new chemicals with new odors are synthesized every year, and it would be unreasonable to expect that we have already evolved specific receptors for all of the odors yet to be experienced.

Two other pieces of information suggest that odors may be sorted out according to some classification scheme. First, some people cannot detect certain types of odors. This occurrence would suggest that there are various receptor types and that these people lack one or more kinds of specific receptors. Second, we humans seem to be able to reach some agreements about the similarities of odors. Classifications such as fruity, pinelike, and musky make sense to most of us, and we are willing to say that there is more similarity between the odors of pine oil and cedar oil than between skunk and the smell of limes. However, we certainly know less about the classification of odor qualities than those of colors and sounds.

Recordings of Neural Responses to Olfactory Stimuli

Unfortunately, recordings taken from single olfactory receptors have not helped to identify primary odors. For example, Gesteland (1978) found that no two olfactory receptors responded alike. He reported that although two similar odors might produce similar responses in different cells, a brief search would invariably find another cell that made a sharp distinction between the odors, and the original cells would respond differently to another pair of odors.

Recordings in more central levels of the olfactory system show that neural responses tend to be more finely tuned to particular odors. For example, Tanabe, Iino, Ooshima, and Takagi (1974) and Tanabe, Iino, and Takagi (1975) found that neurons in the olfactory area of the orbitofrontal cortex of monkeys were even more selective than those in the olfactory bulb; most neurons responded to only one or two odors. This fact suggests that cortical neurons respond selectively to particular patterns of activity in neurons in more peripheral parts of the olfactory system. The nature of the coding system is unknown.

Stewart, Kauer, and Shepherd (1979) used a special autoradiographic technique to investigate the responses of neurons in the olfactory bulb. (Autoradiography was described in Chapter 3.) Their results suggest that specific odors may produce responses of neurons in particular regions. They injected rats with radioactive 2-deoxyglucose (2-DG) and exposed them to a particular odor. Then they killed the rats, removed and sliced their olfactory bulbs, and used a photographic emulsion to find the radioactivity. As you learned in Chapter 1, 2-DG is a sugar that cells cannot metabolize; therefore, it accumulates within cells that are most active. The results indicated that different odors increased the metabolic activity (and, presumably, the synaptic activity) of different specific regions of the olfactory bulbs. The distribution of radioactivity in the olfactory bulbs of twenty-seven rats is shown in Figure 6.30. Six were exposed to the odor of camphor (colored areas), and twenty-one were exposed to amyl acetate (unfilled outlines). (See ***Figure 6.30.***)

The results suggest that odor quality is represented spatially by neurons in the olfactory system. Only further research will reveal whether this procedure can be used to identify categories of olfactory qualities.

FIGURE 6.30

Composite drawings prepared from 2-DG autoradiographs of rat olfactory bulbs after the animals were exposed to camphor (*left,* colored areas), amyl acetate (*left,* unfilled outlines), or pure air (*right,* unfilled outlines). LOT = lateral olfactory tract; AOB = accessory olfactory bulb. (From Stewart, W.B., Kauer, J.S., and Shepherd, G.M. *Journal of Comparative Neurology,* 1979, *185,* 715–734. Reprinted with permission.)

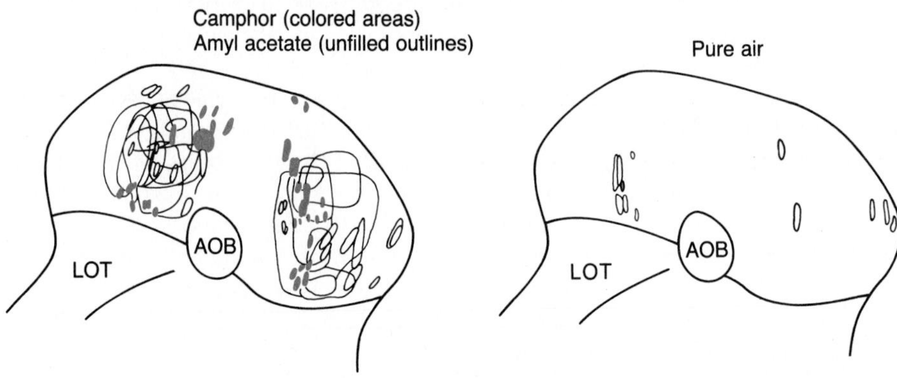

▶*INTERIM SUMMARY*◀

Olfaction (smell) helps us identify good food and avoid food that has spoiled. It also serves reproductive functions in many species, and in humans at least, can evoke memories from the distant past. The olfactory receptors consist of bipolar neurons located in the olfactory epithelium that lines the roof of the nasal sinuses, on the bone that underlies the frontal lobes. The receptors send processes toward the surface of the mucosa, which divide into cilia. The membranes of these cilia appear to contain receptors that detect aromatic molecules dissolved in the air that sweeps past the olfactory mucosa. The axons of the olfactory receptors pass through the perforations of the cribriform plate and form synapses with the dendrites of the mitral cells of the olfactory bulbs. These neurons send axons through the olfactory tracts to the brain, principally to the amygdala, ventral frontal neocortex, and the limbic cortex. Some axons travel to regions that also receive gustatory information; this convergence of olfactory and gustatory information may be responsible for the perception of flavor.

We do not know how aromatic molecules produce membrane potentials. Attempts to analyze primary odors similar to the four primary tastes have met with failure. Studies using 2-DG autoradiography have suggested that different odors excite neurons in particular regions of the olfactory bulbs, but we do not yet understand the significance of these results. ▲

◀ *EPILOGUE: Application*

As we have seen, the brain contains an elaborate system through which certain types of stimuli can produce analgesia—primarily through the release of the endogenous opiates. What functions does this system perform? Most researchers believe that it prevents pain from disrupting animals' behavior in situations in which pain is unavoidable and in which the damaging effect of the painful stimuli are less important than the goals of the animals' behavior. This explanation accounts for several types of situations that produce analgesia, but not all of them; as you will see, some mysteries still remain.

When an animal encounters a noxious stimulus, it usually stops what it is doing and engages in withdrawal or escape behaviors. Obviously, these responses are quite appropriate. However, they are sometimes counterproductive. For example, if an animal sustains a wound that causes chronic pain, a tendency to engage in withdrawal responses will interfere with its performance of everyday activities, such as obtaining food. Thus, the inhibitory effects of chronic, unavoidable pain would best be diminished.

Another useful function of analgesia is the suppression of pain during important behaviors such as fighting or mating. For example, males fighting for access to females during mating season will fail to pass on their genes if pain elicits withdrawal responses that interfere with fighting. As we will see, these conditions (fighting or mating) *do* diminish pain.

Let us consider the effects of unavoidable pain. Several experiments have shown that analgesia can be produced by the application of painful stimuli or even by the presence of nonpainful stimuli that have been paired with painful ones. For example, Maier, Drugan, and Grau (1982) administered inescapable shocks to rats' tails or administered shocks that the animals could learn to escape by making a response. Although both groups of animals received the same amount of shock, only those that received *inescapable* shocks showed analgesia. That is, when their pain sensitivity was tested, it was found to be lower than that of control subjects. The analgesia was abolished by administration of naloxone, which indicates that it was mediated by the release of endogenous opiates. (*Naloxone* is a drug that blocks opiate receptors. The experimenter in the Prologue used this drug when he blocked the analgesic effect of Melissa's own endogenous opiates.) The results make good sense, biologically. If pain is escapable, it serves to motivate the animal to make appropriate responses. If it occurs whatever the animal does, then a reduction in pain sensitivity is in the animal's best interest.

There is evidence that engaging in behaviors that are important to survival also reduces sensitivity to pain. For example, Komisaruk and Larsson (1971) found that genital stimulation produced analgesia. They gently probed the cervix of female rats with a glass rod and found that the procedure diminished the animals' sensitivity to pain. It also increased the activity of neurons in the periaqueductal gray matter and decreased the pain response in the thalamus (Komisaruk and Steinman, 1987). The phenomenon also occurs in humans; Whipple and Komisaruk (1988) found that self-administered vaginal stimulation reduces women's sensitivity to painful stimuli but not to neutral tactile stimuli. Presumably, copulation also triggers analgesic mechanisms. The adaptive significance of this phenomenon is clear: Painful stimuli encountered during the course of copulation are less likely to cause the behavior to be interrupted; thus, the chances of pregnancy are increased. (And as you will recall, passing on one's genes is the ultimate criterion of the adaptive significance of a trait.)

As we saw in the Prologue, pain can also be reduced — at least in some people — by administering a *placebo,* a pharmacologically inert substance. (The term *placebo* comes from *placere*, which means "to please." The physician pleases an anxious patient by giving him or her an innocuous substance.) The pain reduction seems to be mediated by the release of endogenous opiates, because it is blocked by naloxone (Levine, Gordon, and Fields, 1979). Thus, *believing* that pain is going to diminish is a self-fulfilling prophecy. *Why* this particular phenomenon occurs is still a mystery.

Pain can be also reduced by stimulating regions other than those that hurt. For example, people often rub or scratch the area around a wound, in an apparent attempt to diminish the severity of the pain. And as you know, acupuncturists insert needles into various parts of the body in order to reduce pain. The needle is usually then rotated, thus stimulating axons and nerve endings in the vicinity. Often the region that is stimulated is far removed from the region that becomes less sensitive to pain.

Several experimental studies have shown that acupuncture can produce analgesia. Mayer, Price, Rafii, and Barber (1976) reported that the analgesic effects of acupuncture could be blocked by naloxone. However, when pain was reduced by hypnotic suggestion, naloxone had no effect. Thus, acupuncture, but not hypnosis, appears to cause analgesia through the release of endogenous opiates.

The endogenous opiates were first discovered by scientists who were investigating the perception of pain; thus, many of the studies using these peptides have examined their role in mechanisms of analgesia. However, their role in other functions may be even more important. As we will see in subsequent chapters, the endogenous opiates may even be involved in learning, especially in mechanisms of reinforcement. This connection should not come as a surprise; as you know, many people have found injections of opiates like morphine or heroin to be extremely pleasurable. ▲

KEY CONCEPTS

Audition

- The bones of the middle ear transmit sound vibrations from the eardrum to the cochlea, which contains the auditory receptors — the hair cells.
- The hair cells send information through the eighth cranial nerve to nuclei in the brain stem, which is relayed to the medial geniculate nucleus and finally to the primary auditory cortex.
- The ear is analytical; it detects individual frequencies by means of place coding and rate coding. Left-right localization is also accomplished by two means: arrival time (phase differences) and binaural differences in intensity.

Vestibular System

- The vestibular system helps us maintain our balance and makes compensatory eye movements to help us maintain fixation when our head moves. The semicircular canals detect head rotations and the vestibular sacs detect changes in the tilt of the head.

Somatosenses

- Cutaneous receptors in the skin provide information about touch, pressure, vibration, changes in temperature, and stimuli that cause tissue damage.
- Pain perception helps protect us from harmful stimuli. Sensitivity to pain is modulated by the release of the endogenous opiates by cells in the brain.

Gustation

- Taste receptors on the tongue respond to bitterness, sourness, sweetness, and saltiness and, together with olfactory information, provide us with information about complex flavors.

Olfaction

- The olfactory system detects the presence of aromatic molecules, but investigators have not yet discovered whether a system of primary odors exists.

NEW TERMS

ampulla **p. 190**
basilar membrane **p. 177**
chorda tympani **p. 204**
cilia **p. 179**
cochlea **p. 176**
cochlear nerve **p. 181**
cochlear nuclei **p. 181**
cribriform plate **p. 206**
crista **p. 190**
cupula **p. 190**
cutaneous sense **p. 193**
fundamental frequency **p. 184**
glabrous skin **p. 195**
hair cell **p. 177**
hertz (Hz) **p. 174**
intrafusal muscle fiber **p. 194**
kinesthesia **p. 193**
loudness **p. 174**
Meissner's corpuscle **p. 195**
Merkel's disk **p. 195**
nucleus of the solitary tract **p. 204**
nucleus raphe magnus **p. 201**
olfactory bulb **p. 207**
olfactory epithelium **p. 205**
organic sense **p. 193**
organ of Corti **p. 177**
ossicle **p. 176**
oval window **p. 176**
overtone **p. 184**
Pacinian corpuscle **p. 195**
parabrachial nucleus **p. 204**
phase difference **p. 186**
pitch **p. 174**
place code **p. 183**
rate code **p. 183**
round window **p. 178**
Ruffini corpuscle **p. 195**
saccule **p. 190**
semicircular canal **p. 190**
superior olivary complex **p. 181**
tectorial membrane **p. 178**
thalamic taste area **p. 204**
timbre **p. 174**
tympanic membrane **p. 176**
utricle **p. 190**
vestibular ganglion **p. 192**
vestibular sac **p. 190**
vestibulo-ocular reflex **p. 193**
white noise **p. 183**

SUGGESTED READINGS

Audition

Edelman, G.M., Gall, W.E., and Cowan, W.M. *Auditory Functions.* New York: John Wiley & Sons, 1988.

Gulick, W.L., Gescheider, G.A., and Frisina, R.D. *Hearing: Physiological Acoustics, Neural Coding, and Psychoacoustics.* New York: Oxford University Press, 1989.

Howard, J., Roberts, W.M., and Hudspeth, A.J. Mechanoelectrical transduction by hair cells. *Annual Review of Biophysics and Biophysical Chemistry,* 1988, *17,* 99–124.

Somatosenses

Akil, H., Watson, S.J., Young, E., Lewis, M.E., Khachaturian, H., and Walker, J.M. Endogenous opioids: Biology and function. *Annual Review of Neuroscience,* 1984, *7,* 223–256.

Basbaum, A.I., and Fields, H.L. Endogenous pain control systems: Brainstem spinal pathways and endorphin circuitry. *Annual Review of Neuroscience,* 1984, *7,* 309–338.

Darian-Smith, I. Touch in primates. *Annual Review of Psychology,* 1982, *33,* 155–194.

Olfaction and Gustation

Bruch, R.C., Kalinoski, D.L., and Kare, M.R. Biochemistry of vertebrate olfaction and taste. *Annual Review of Nutrition,* 1988, *8,* 21–42.

Lancet, D. Vertebrate olfactory reception. *Annual Review of Neuroscience,* 1986, *9,* 329–355.

Roper, S.D. The cell biology of vertebrate taste receptors. *Annual Review of Neuroscience,* 1989, *12,* 329–354.

7

CHAPTER OUTLINE

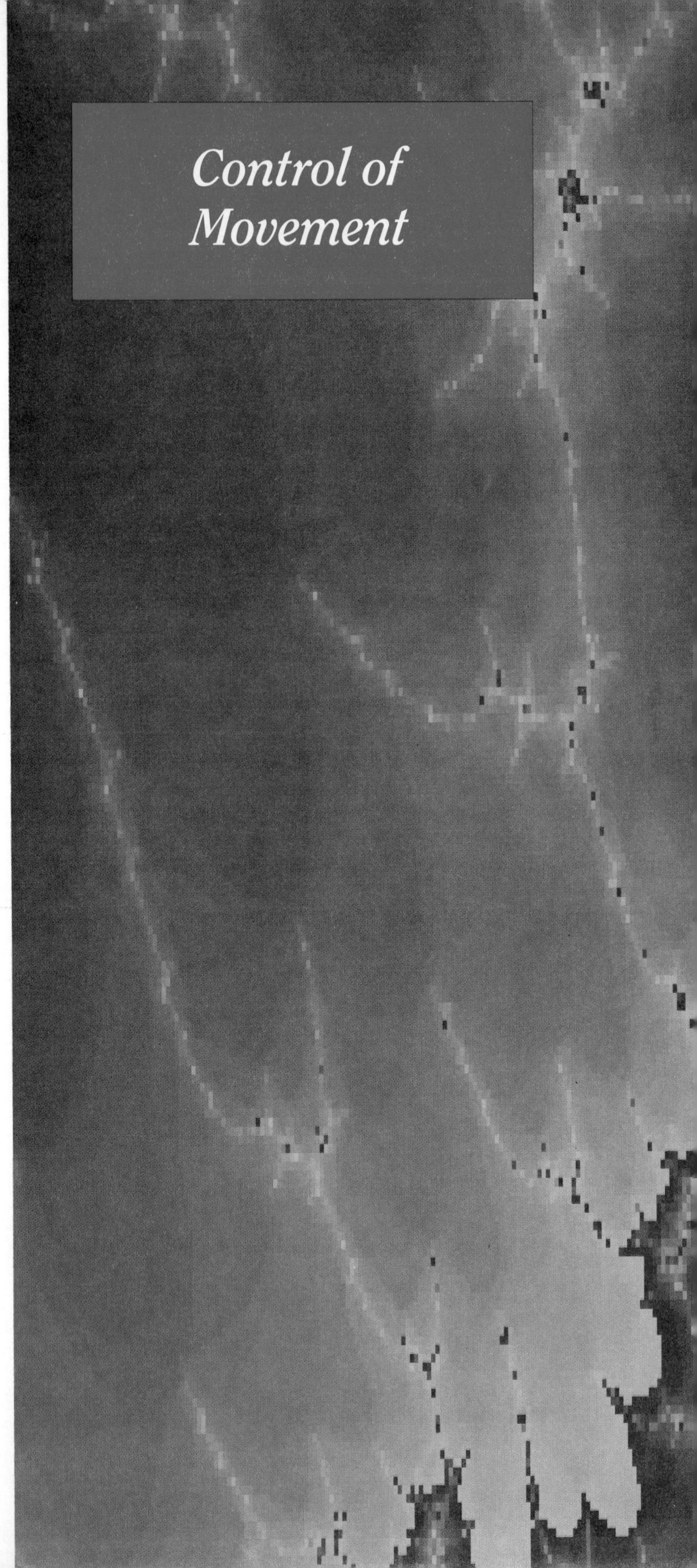

Control of Movement

◀ *PROLOGUE*

Although Mr. J., a 48-year-old photographer, had just had a severe stroke that damaged much of his left parietal lobe, he was still a pleasant, cheerful, and likable man. His neurologist, Dr. R., introduced him to us, and he sat down in a chair in front of the room.

"Mr. J., will you please show us how to wave hello?" asked Dr. R. The patient made a clumsy movement with his right hand and smiled apologetically. "Hold up your index finger, like this," said Dr. R., pointing toward the ceiling. Mr. J. held up his hand, pursed his lips together, and, with a determined look on his face, clenched and unclenched his fist. Clearly, he was trying as hard as he could to point with his index finger, but he just could not move it without also moving his other fingers. "Can you hold your hand like this?" asked Dr. R., who held his hand in front of himself, palm down. Mr. J. watched him and, with obvious effort, copied the movement. "That's good! Now turn your hand over." Mr. J. grunted and began slapping his hand against his thigh. It looked to us as if he were trying to make the requested movement, but the wrong one was coming in its place. Dr. R. took hold of Mr. J.'s hand and, with great effort (Mr. J. was a strong man), managed to turn it over. "Good. Now turn it over again." Mr. J. began slapping his thigh with the back of his hand. Several times, Dr. R. helped him turn his hand over; but despite his efforts, Mr. J. was unable to do so by himself. He appeared to have very poor control of his movements.

Dr. R. addressed the rest of us. "You can see that Mr. J.'s apraxia is severe. But now watch this." He turned to Mr. J. "Will you please take off your glasses?" Mr. J. reached up to his glasses, took hold of the earpieces, and removed them. "Fine. Now put them back on." He did so. Dr. R. then asked, "Do you know what a hammer is?" "Sure," answered Mr. J. "Ok, will you show us how you would use a hammer?" Mr. J. looked at his hand and then began slapping it against his thigh, as he had done before. "Ok, you can stop." Mr. J. continued slapping his thigh, harder and harder. "Stop! That's enough." With great effort Mr. J. finally ceased making the movements. "Now let's try this," said Dr. R., who placed a block of wood on the table in front of Mr. J. and handed him a hammer and a nail. "Can you pound the nail into the wood?" Mr. J. held the nail upright with the fingers of his left hand, grasped the hammer with his right hand, and skillfully drove the nail into the wood.

After Mr. J. had left, Dr. R. said, "Mr. J.'s problem is not that he cannot make skilled movements, but that he cannot make these movements when we ask him to. He can manipulate his glasses and he can use a hammer, but he can't make even the simplest voluntary movements out of context. Did you notice that he waved to you when I introduced him, even though he couldn't do so when I asked him to show us how to wave 'hello'?" We sheepishly admitted that we hadn't been that observant. "The movement was an automatic one that he had learned to make long ago, and it was triggered by the fact that he was meeting other people. The parietal lobe is involved in the control of movements—especially sequences of movements—that are not dictated by the context. Thus, he finds it almost impossible to follow verbal requests to make arbitrary movements." ▲

So far, I have described the nature of neural communication, the basic structure of the nervous system, and the physiology of sensation. Now it is time to consider the ultimate function of the nervous system: control of behavior. The brain is the organ that moves the muscles. It does many other things, but all of them are secondary to making our bodies move. This chapter describes the principles of muscular contraction, some reflex circuitry within the spinal cord, and the means by which the brain initiates behaviors. The rest of the book describes the physiology of particular categories of behaviors and the ways in which our behaviors can be modified by experience.

MUSCLES

Mammals have three types of muscles: skeletal muscle, smooth muscle, and cardiac muscle. Each type is described in detail in the sections that follow.

Skeletal Muscle

skeletal muscle

Skeletal muscles are the ones that move us (our skeletons) around and thus are responsible for our behavior. Most of them are attached to bones at each end and move the bones when they contract. (Exceptions include the eye muscles, the tongue muscles, and some abdominal muscles, which are attached to bone at one end only.) Muscles are fastened to bones via *tendons,* strong bands of connective tissue. Several different classes of movement can be accomplished by the skeletal muscles, but I will refer principally to two of them: flexion and extension. Contraction of a flexor muscle produces *flexion,* the drawing in of a limb. *Extension,* which is the opposite movement, is produced by contraction of extensor muscles. These are the so-called *antigravity muscles*—the ones we use to stand up. When a four-legged animal lifts a paw, the movement is one of flexion. Putting it back down is one of extension. Sometimes, people say they "flex" their muscles, which is an incorrect use of the term. Muscles *contract*; limbs *flex.* Bodybuilders show off their arm muscles by simultaneously contracting the flexor and extensor muscles of that limb.

ANATOMY

extrafusal muscle fiber
alpha motor neuron
muscle spindle
intrafusal muscle fiber
gamma motor neuron

The detailed structure of a skeletal muscle is shown in ***Figure 7.1.*** Contractions of the **extrafusal muscle fibers** provides the muscle's motive force. These fibers are served by axons of the **alpha motor neurons;** thus, it is the activity of the alpha motor neurons that determines the strength of contraction of a muscle. The muscle also has sensory organs known as **muscle spindles.** The central region of the muscle spindles contains sensory endings that are sensitive to stretch. The spindles also contain a muscle fiber: the **intrafusal muscle fiber** (*fusus* means "spindle"). The efferent axon of the **gamma motor neuron** causes the intrafusal muscle fiber to contract; however, this contraction contributes an insubstantial amount of force. As we will see, the function of this contraction is to modify the sensitivity of the fiber's afferent ending to stretch.

motor unit

A single myelinated axon of an alpha motor neuron serves several extrafusal muscle fibers. In primates the number of muscle fibers served by a single axon varies considerably, depending on the precision with which the muscle can be controlled. In muscles that move the fingers or eyes, the ratio can be less than one axon to ten muscle fibers; in muscles that move the leg, it can be one to several hundred. An alpha motor neuron, its axon, and associated extrafusal muscle fibers constitute a **motor unit.**

FIGURE 7.1

Anatomy of skeletal muscle.

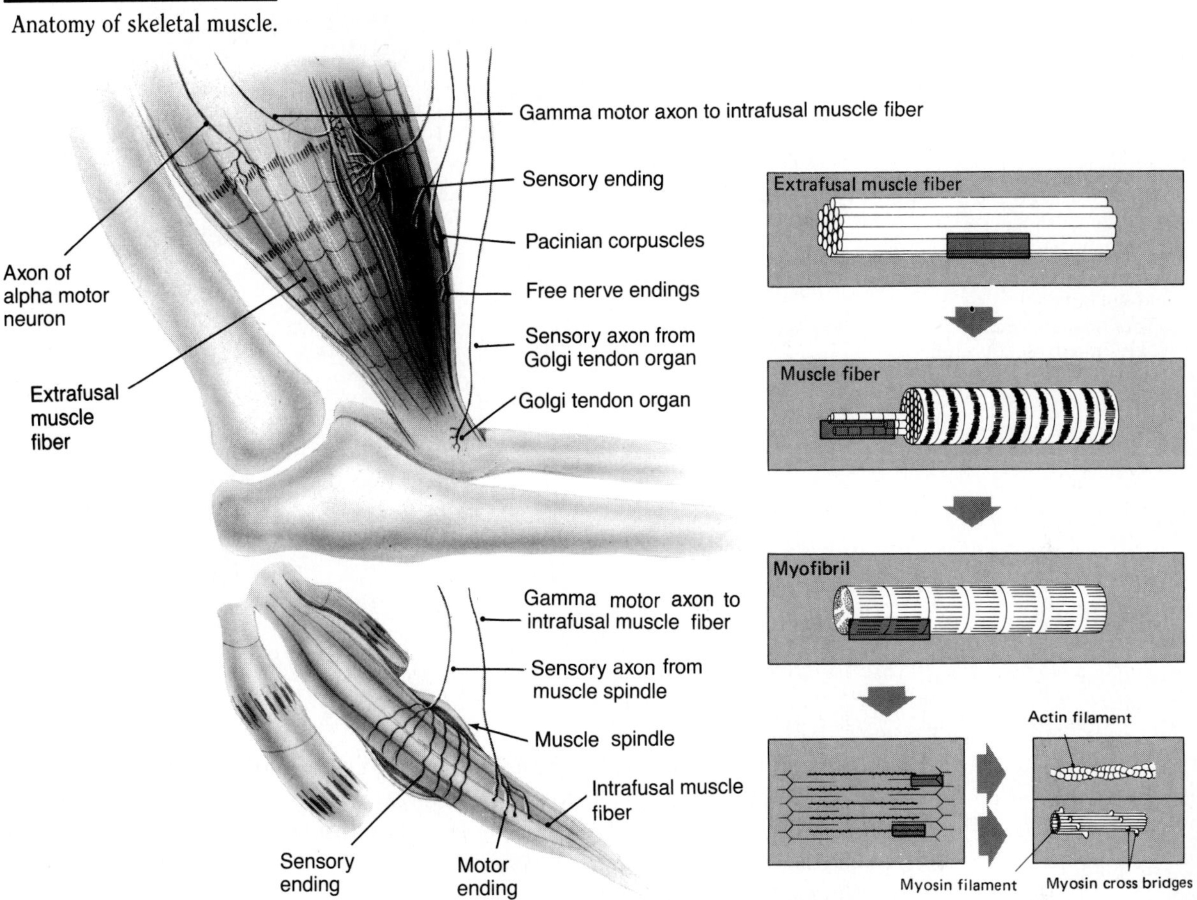

A single muscle fiber consists of a bundle of *myofibrils,* each of which consists of overlapping strands of two kinds of protein, **actin** and **myosin**. Note the small protrusions on the myosin filaments; these structures (*myosin cross bridges*) are the moving elements that interact with the actin filaments and produce muscular contractions. (See ***Figure 7.1.***)

actin

myosin

THE PHYSICAL BASIS OF MUSCULAR CONTRACTION

The synapse between the terminal button of a motor neuron and the membrane of a muscle fiber is called a **neuromuscular junction**. The terminal buttons of the neurons synapse on **motor endplates** — specialized regions of postsynaptic membrane located in grooves along the surface of the muscle fibers. When an axon fires, acetylcholine is released by the terminal buttons and produces a depolarization of the postsynaptic membrane (*endplate potential*). An endplate potential triggers an action potential in the muscle fiber to fire. This action potential induces a contraction, or *twitch,* of the muscle fiber.

neuromuscular junction

motor endplate

The depolarization of a muscle fiber opens the gates of voltage-dependent calcium channels, permitting calcium ions to enter the cytoplasm. This event triggers the contraction. Calcium acts as a cofactor that permits the myofibrils to extract energy

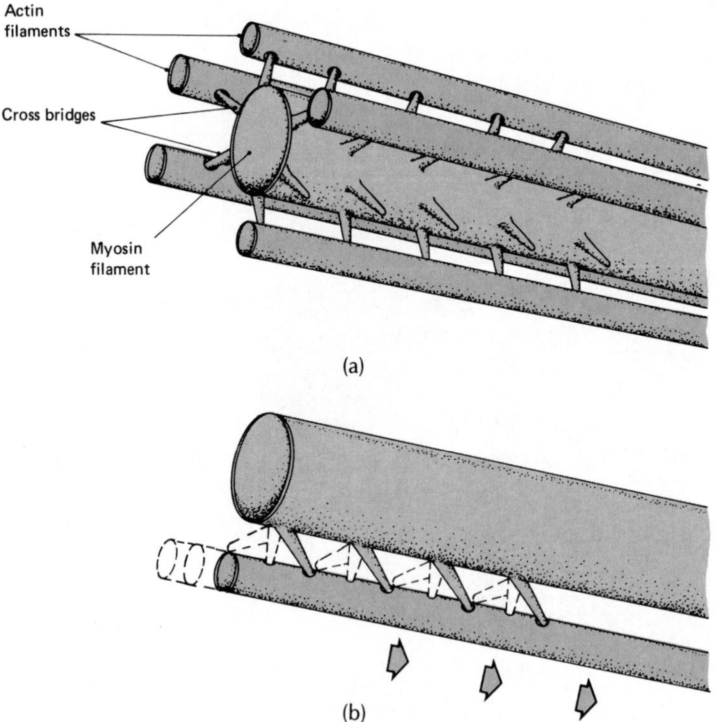

FIGURE 7.2

The mechanism by which muscles contract. (a) Location of the cross-bridges. (b) The myosin cross bridges performing "rowing" movements, which cause the actin and myosin filaments to move relative to each other. (Adapted from Anthony, C.P., and Kolthoff, N.J. *Textbook of Anatomy and Physiology*, 8th ed. St. Louis: C.V. Mosby, 1971.)

provided by the mitochondria. The myosin cross bridges alternately attach to the actin strands, bend in one direction, detach themselves, bend back, reattach to the actin at a point farther down the strand, and so on. Thus, the cross bridges "row" along the actin filaments. Figure 7.2 illustrates this rowing sequence, which shortens the muscle fiber, making it twitch. (See ***Figure 7.2.***)

A single impulse of a motor neuron produces a single twitch of a muscle fiber. The physical effects of the twitch last considerably longer than will the action potential, because of the elasticity of the muscle and the time required to rid the cell of calcium. (Like sodium, calcium is actively extruded by a pump situated in the membrane.) A single motor unit in a leg muscle of a cat can raise a 100-g weight (about four times the weight of a mouse), which attests to the remarkable strength of the contractile mechanism.

As you know from your own experience, muscular contraction is not an all-or-nothing phenomenon, as are the twitches of the constituent muscle fibers. Obviously, the strength of a muscular contraction is determined by the rate of firing of the motor units. If, at a given moment, many units are firing, the contraction will be forceful. If few are firing, the contraction will be weak.

SENSORY FEEDBACK FROM MUSCLES

As we saw, the muscle spindles contain sensory endings that are sensitive to stretch. The intrafusal muscle fibers are arranged in parallel with the extrafusal muscle fibers. Therefore, they are stretched when the muscle lengthens and are relaxed when it shortens. Thus, even though these afferent neurons are ***stretch receptors,*** they actually function as ***muscle length detectors.*** This distinction is important. Another kind of stretch receptor is located within the tendons, in the **Golgi tendon organ.** These receptors detect the total amount of force exerted by the muscle, through its tendons, on the bones to which the muscle is attached. The stretch receptors of the Golgi tendon organ indicate the degree of force by their rate of firing. They respond not to a muscle's length but to how hard it is pulling. You will see the function of these detectors in a later section.

Golgi tendon organ

Smooth Muscle

Our bodies contain two types of **smooth muscle**, both of which are controlled by the autonomic nervous system. ***Multiunit smooth muscles*** are found in large arteries, around hair follicles (where they produce *piloerection*, or fluffing of fur), and in the eye (controlling lens adjustment and pupillary dilation). This type of smooth muscle is normally inactive, but it will contract in response to neural stimulation or to certain hormones. In contrast, ***single-unit smooth muscles*** normally contract in a rhythmical fashion. The efferent nerve supply (and various hormones) can modulate the rhythmical rate, increasing or decreasing it, but the contractions themselves occur independently. Single-unit smooth muscles are found chiefly in the gastrointestinal system and uterus.

smooth muscle

Cardiac Muscle

As its name implies, **cardiac muscle** is found in the heart. This type of muscle looks somewhat like skeletal muscle but acts like single-unit smooth muscle. The heart beats regularly, even if the nerve that connects it to the brain is severed. Neural activity and certain hormones (especially epinephrine and norepinephrine from the adrenal medulla) serve to modulate the heart rate. A group of cells in the *pacemaker* of the heart are rhythmically active and initiate the contractions of cardiac muscle that constitute the heartbeat.

cardiac muscle

▶*INTERIM SUMMARY*◀

Our bodies possess skeletal muscle, smooth muscle, and cardiac muscle. Skeletal muscles contain extrafusal muscle fibers, which provide the force of contraction. The alpha motor neurons form synapses with the extrafusal muscle fibers and control their contraction. Skeletal muscles also contain intrafusal muscle fibers, which detect changes in muscle length. The length of the intrafusal muscle fiber, and hence its sensitivity to increases in muscle length, is controlled by the gamma motor neuron. Besides containing the intrafusal muscle fibers, the muscles contain stretch receptors in the Golgi tendon organs, located at the ends of the muscles.

The force of muscular contraction is provided by long protein molecules called actin and myosin, arranged in overlapping parallel arrays. When an action potential, initiated by the synapse at the motor endplate, causes Ca^{2+} to enter the muscle fiber, the myofibrils extract energy provided by the mitochondria and cause a twitch of the muscle fiber, producing a ratchetlike "rowing" movement of the myosin cross bridges.

Smooth muscle is controlled by the autonomic nervous system through direct neural connections and indirectly through the endocrine system. Multiunit smooth muscles contract only in response to neural or hormonal stimulation. In contrast, single-unit smooth muscles normally contract rhythmically, but their rate is controlled by the autonomic nervous system. Cardiac muscle also contracts spontaneously, and its rate of contraction, too, is influenced by the autonomic nervous system. ▲

REFLEX CONTROL OF MOVEMENT

Although behaviors are controlled by the brain, the spinal cord possesses a certain degree of autonomy. Particular kinds of somatosensory stimuli can elicit rapid responses through neural connections located within the spinal cord. These ***reflexes*** constitute the simplest level of motor integration. This section discusses the simple monosynaptic stretch reflex, its modulation by the gamma motor system, and a polysynaptic reflex that involves inhibition.

The Monosynaptic Stretch Reflex

The activity of the simplest functional neural pathway in the body is easy to demonstrate. Sit on a surface high enough to allow your legs to dangle freely and have someone lightly tap your patellar tendon, just below the kneecap. This stimulus briefly stretches your quadriceps muscle, on the top of your thigh. The stretch causes the muscle to contract, which makes your leg kick forward. (I am sure few of you will bother with this demonstration, because you are already familiar with it; most physical examinations include a test of this reflex.) The time interval between the tendon tap and the start of the leg extension is about 50 milliseconds. That interval is too short for the involvement of the brain; it would take considerably longer for sensory information to be relayed to the brain and for motor information to be relayed back. For example, suppose a person is asked to move his or her leg as quickly as possible after being *touched* on the knee. This response would not be reflexive but would involve sensory and motor mechanisms of the brain. In this case the interval between the stimulus and the start of the response would be several times greater than the time required for the patellar reflex.

Obviously, the patellar reflex as such has no utility; no selective advantage is bestowed upon animals that kick a limb when a tendon is tapped. However, if a more natural stimulus is applied, the utility of this mechanism becomes apparent. Figure 7.3 shows the effects of placing a weight in a person's hand. A piece of the spinal cord, with its roots, is included to show the neural circuit that composes the **monosynaptic stretch reflex**, so-called because it involves only one synapse. First, follow the circuit that makes up this reflex: Starting at the muscle spindle, afferent impulses are conducted to terminal buttons in the gray matter of the spinal cord. These terminal buttons synapse on an alpha motor neuron that innervates the extrafusal muscle fibers of the same muscle. Only one synapse is encountered along the route from receptor to effector — hence the term *monosynaptic.* (See ***Figure 7.3a.***)

monosynaptic stretch reflex

Now consider a useful function this reflex performs. If the weight the person is holding is increased, the forearm begins to move down. This movement lengthens the muscle and increases the firing rate of the muscle spindle afferent neurons, whose terminal buttons then stimulate the alpha motor neurons, increasing their rate of firing. Consequently, the strength of the muscular contraction increases, and the arm pulls the weight up. (See ***Figure 7.3b.***)

The Gamma Motor System

The muscle spindles are very sensitive to changes in muscle length; they will increase their rate of firing when the muscle is lengthened by a very small amount. The interesting thing is that this detection mechanism is adjustable. Remember that the ends of the intrafusal muscle fibers can be contracted by activity of the associated

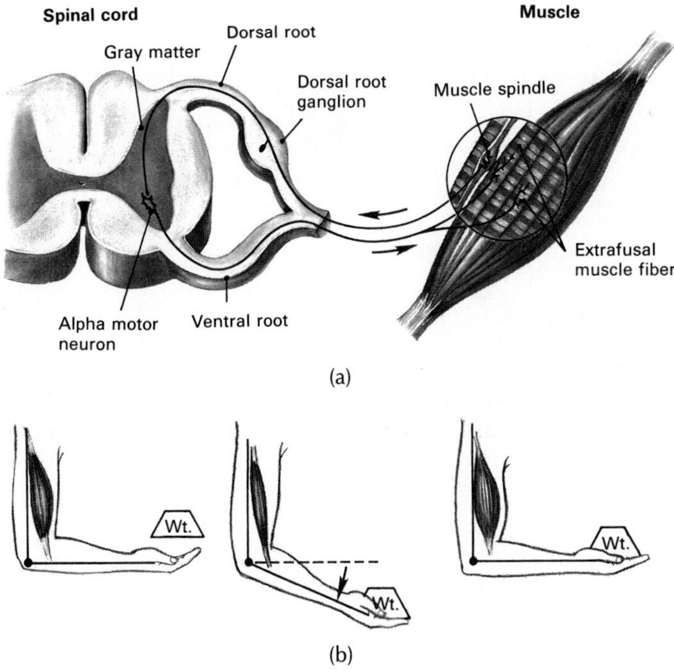

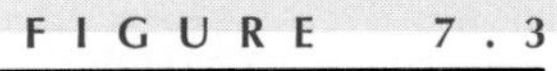

The monosynaptic stretch reflex. (a) Neural circuit. (b) A useful function.

efferent axons of the gamma motor neurons; their rate of firing determines the degree of contraction. When the muscle spindles are relaxed, they are relatively insensitive to stretch. However, when the gamma motor neurons are active, they become shorter and hence become much more sensitive to changes in muscle length. This property of adjustable sensitivity simplifies the role of the brain in controlling movement. The more control that can occur in the spinal cord, the fewer messages must be sent to and from the brain.

We already saw that the afferent axons of the muscle spindle help maintain limb position even when the load carried by the limb is altered. Efferent control of the muscle spindles permits these muscle length detectors to assist in changes in limb position as well. Consider a single muscle spindle. When its efferent axon is completely silent, the spindle is completely relaxed. As the firing rate of the efferent gamma motor axon increases, the spindle gets shorter and shorter. If, simultaneously, the rest of the entire muscle also gets shorter, there will be no stretch on the central region that contains the sensory endings, and the afferent axon will not respond. However, if the muscle spindle contracts faster than does the muscle as a whole, there will be a considerable amount of afferent activity, because the sensory ending within the spindle will be mechanically stretched.

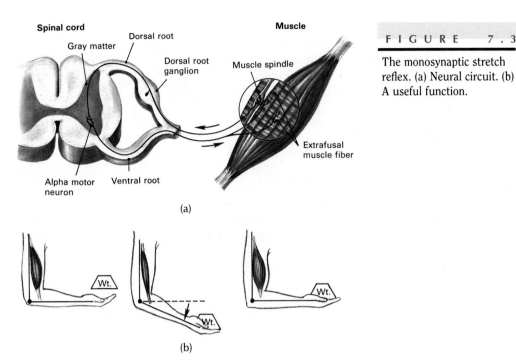

The motor system makes use of this phenomenon in the following way: When commands from the brain are issued to move a limb, both the alpha motor neurons and the gamma motor neurons are activated. The alpha motor neurons start the muscle contracting. If there is little resistance, both the extrafusal and the intrafusal muscle fibers will contract at approximately the same rate, and little activity will be seen from the afferent axons of the muscle spindle. However, if the limb meets with resistance, the intrafusal muscle fibers will shorten more than the extrafusal muscle fibers, and hence sensory axons will begin to fire and cause the monosynaptic stretch reflex to strengthen the contraction. Thus, the brain makes use of the gamma motor system in

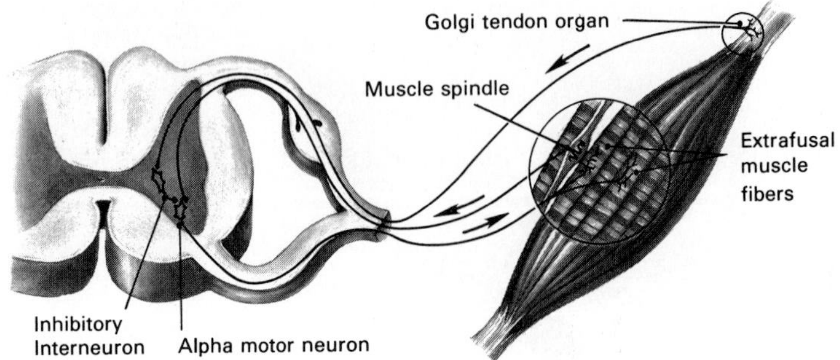

FIGURE 7.4

Polysynaptic reflex. Input from the Golgi tendon organ can cause inhibitory postsynaptic potentials to occur on the alpha motor neuron.

moving the limbs. By establishing a rate of firing in the *gamma motor system,* the brain controls the length of the muscle spindles and, indirectly, the length of the entire muscle.

A Polysynaptic Reflex

The monosynaptic stretch reflex is the only spinal reflex that we know of that involves only one synapse. All others are ***polysynaptic.*** Examples include relatively simple ones, like limb withdrawal in response to pain, and relatively complex ones, like the ejaculation of semen. Spinal reflexes do not exist in isolation; they are normally controlled by the brain. For example, in Chapter 2 I described how inhibition from the brain can prevent a person from dropping a bunch of roses with thorns, even though the painful stimuli received by the fingers serve to cause reflexive extension of the fingers. Here I will describe some general principles by which polysynaptic spinal reflexes operate.

As we previously saw, the afferent axons from the Golgi tendon organ serve to detect the total force that a muscle exerts. Their terminal buttons synapse on spinal cord interneurons, which are located entirely within the gray matter of the spinal cord and serve to interconnect other spinal neurons. These interneurons synapse on the alpha motor neurons serving the same muscle. The terminal buttons liberate glycine and hence produce inhibitory postsynaptic potentials on the motor neurons. (See ***Figure 7.4.***) The function of this polysynaptic reflex pathway is to decrease the strength of muscular contraction when there is danger of damage to the tendons or bones to which the muscles are attached. Weight lifters have been known to have a local anesthetic injected near their Golgi tendon organs, which blocks the messages that they send to their central nervous system. The injections remove the inhibitory influence these organs have on very forceful muscular contractions, thus permitting the weight lifters to lift heavier weights. However, with the control gone, they run the real danger of tearing a tendon from a bone or even breaking the bone.

▶INTERIM SUMMARY◀

Reflexes are simple circuits of sensory neurons, interneurons (usually), and efferent neurons that control simple responses to particular stimuli. In the monosynaptic stretch reflex the terminal buttons of axons that receive sensory information from the intrafusal muscle fibers synapse with alpha motor neurons that innervate the same muscle. Thus, a sudden lengthening of the muscle causes the muscle to contract. By setting the length of the intrafusal muscle fibers, and hence their sensitivity to increases in muscle length, the motor system of the brain can con-

trol limb position. Changes in weight that cause the limb to move will be quickly compensated for by means of the monosynaptic stretch reflex.

Polysynaptic reflexes contain at least one interneuron between the sensory neuron and the motor neuron. For example, when a strong muscular contraction threatens to damage muscles or limbs, the increased rate of firing of the afferent axons of Golgi tendon organs stimulates inhibitory interneurons, which inhibit the alpha motor neurons of those muscles. ▲

CONTROL OF MOVEMENT BY THE BRAIN

Movements can be initiated by several means. For example, rapid stretch of a muscle triggers the monosynaptic stretch reflex; a stumble triggers righting reflexes; and the rapid approach of an object toward the face causes a startle response, a complex reflex consisting of movements of several muscle groups. Other stimuli initiate sequences of movements that we have previously learned. For example, the presence of food may cause eating, and the sight of a loved one may evoke a hug and a kiss. Because there is no single cause of behavior, we cannot find a single starting point in our search for the neural mechanisms that control movement.

The brain and spinal cord include several different motor systems, each of which can simultaneously control particular kinds of movements. For example, a person can walk and talk with a friend simultaneously. While doing so, he or she can make gestures with the hands to emphasize a point, scratch an itch, brush away a fly, wipe sweat off his or her forehead, and so on. Walking, postural adjustments, talking, movement of the arms, and movements of the fingers all involve different specialized motor systems. This section describes the role of the motor cortex in the control of movements and the effects of cortical damage on this control.

Organization of Motor Cortex

The primary motor cortex lies on the precentral gyrus, just rostral to the central sulcus. Stimulation studies (including those in awake humans undergoing brain surgery) have shown that the activity of particular parts of the primary motor cortex causes movements of particular parts of the body. Figure 7.5 shows a *motor homunculus* ("little person") based on the observations of Penfield and Rasmussen (1950). Note that a disproportionate amount of cortical area is devoted to movements of the fingers and muscles used for speech. (See ***Figure 7.5.***)

The principal cortical input to the primary motor cortex is the frontal association cortex, located rostral to it. Lesion studies (some of which I will describe later in this chapter) indicate that the frontal cortex is especially involved in planning complex behaviors. These plans are executed by the primary motor cortex, which directly controls particular movements. In turn, the frontal association cortex receives axons from association areas of the occipital, temporal, and parietal cortex. As we saw, the occipital and temporal lobes contain the visual association cortex, and the temporal lobe also contains the auditory association cortex. In addition, the association cortex of the parietal lobes is responsible for a person's perception of space. Thus, the frontal association cortex receives information about the environment (including memories previously acquired by means of vision, audition, and somatosensation) from the posterior lobes and uses this information to plan movements. Because the parietal lobes are especially involved in spatial perception, the pathway from them to the frontal lobes is important in controlling both locomotion and arm and hand movements. After all, meaningful locomotion requires us to know where we are, and meaningful move-

FIGURE 7.5

A motor homunculus. Stimulation of various regions of the primary motor cortex causes movement in muscles of various parts of the body.

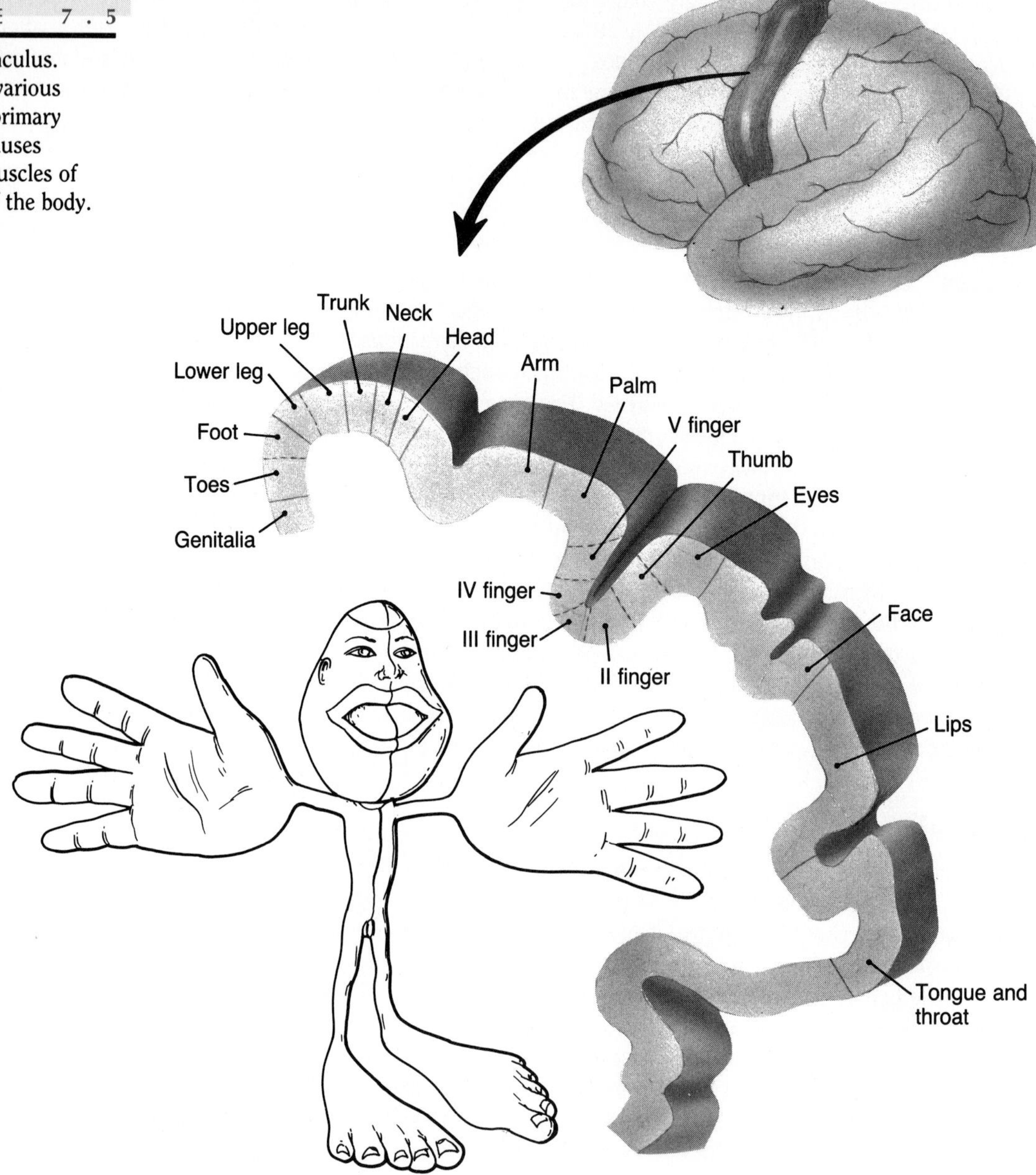

ments of our arms and hands require us to know where objects are located in space. (See ***Figure 7.6.***)

Cortical Control of Movement

Neurons in the primary motor cortex control movements by four different pathways. They directly control the corticospinal and corticobulbar pathways and indirectly control two sets of pathways that originate in the brain stem, which will be described later in this section.

corticospinal pathway

The **corticospinal pathway** consists of axons of cortical neurons that terminate in the gray matter of the spinal cord. The largest concentration of cell bodies of these

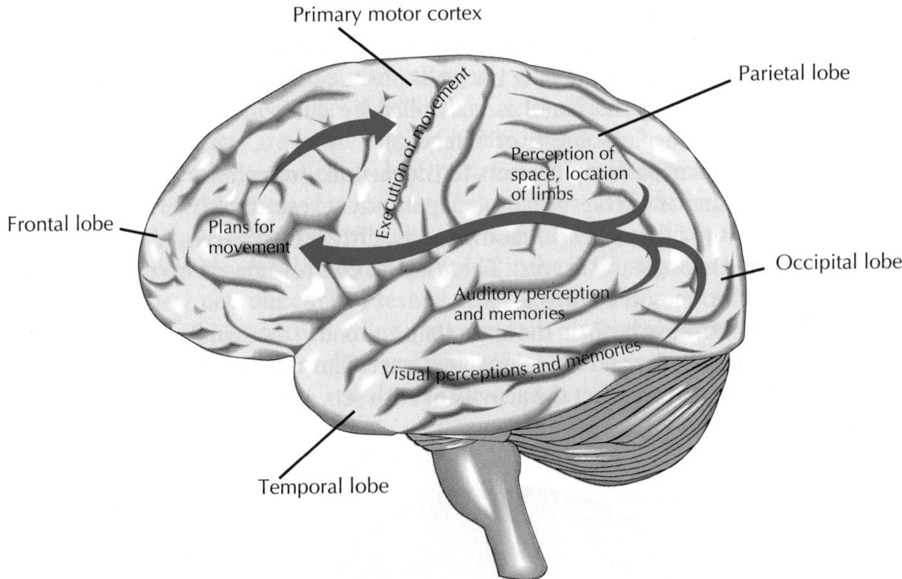

FIGURE 7.6

Cortical inputs. The posterior association cortex is involved with perceptions and memories, and the frontal association cortex is involved with plans for movement.

neurons is located in the primary motor cortex, but the parietal and temporal lobes also send fibers through the corticospinal pathway. The axons leave the cortex through the subcortical white matter and descend to the medulla. There, most of the fibers cross to the other side of the brain and descend through the spinal cord, forming the **lateral corticospinal tract**. The rest of the fibers do not cross to the other side of the brain but descend through the ipsilateral spinal cord, forming the **ventral corticospinal tract**. (See black lines in ***Figure 7.7.***)

lateral corticospinal tract

ventral corticospinal tract

The axons in the lateral corticospinal tract originate in the arm and hand region of the primary motor cortex. They control the motor neurons in the ventral horn of the spinal cord gray matter. These motor neurons control the muscles of the distal limbs, including those that move the arms, hands, and fingers. (See ***Figure 7.7.***)

The axons in the ventral corticospinal tract originate in the trunk region of the primary motor cortex. They descend to the appropriate region of the spinal cord and divide, sending terminal buttons into both sides of the gray matter. They control motor neurons that move the muscles of the trunk. (See ***Figure 7.7.***)

Lawrence and Kuypers (1968a) cut both pyramidal tracts in monkeys in order to assess their motor functions. Within 6 to 10 hours after recovery from the anesthesia, the animals were able to sit upright, but their arms hung loosely from their shoulders. Within a day they could stand, hold the cage bars with their hands, and even climb a little. By six weeks the monkeys could walk and climb rapidly. Thus, posture and locomotion were not disturbed. However, the animals' manual dexterity was poor. They could reach for objects and grasp them, but they used their fingers together as if they were wearing mittens; they could not manipulate their fingers independently to pick up small pieces of food. And once they had grasped food with their hand, they had difficulty releasing their grip. They usually had to use their mouth to pry their hand open. In contrast, they had no difficulty releasing their grip when they were climbing the bars of their cage.

The results confirm what we would predict from the anatomical connections: The corticospinal pathway controls hand and finger movements and is indispensable for moving the fingers independently when reaching and manipulating. Postural adjustments of the trunk and use of the limbs for reaching and locomotion are unaffected;

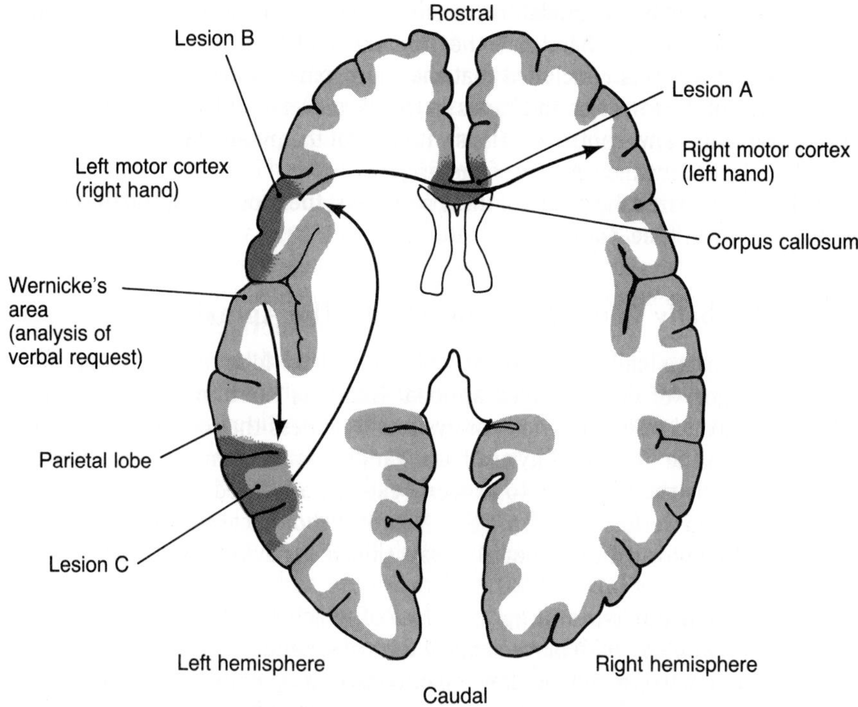

FIGURE 7.9

Apraxias. Lesion A causes callosal apraxia of the left limb, lesion B causes sympathetic apraxia of the right limb, and lesion C causes left parietal apraxia of both limbs.

callosal apraxia

Limb apraxia can be caused by three types of lesions. **Callosal apraxia** is apraxia of the left limb that is caused by damage to the anterior corpus callosum. The explanation for the deficit is as follows: When a person hears a verbal request to perform a movement, the meaning of the speech is analyzed by circuits in the posterior left hemisphere (in *Wernicke's area,* discussed in Chapter 13). A neural command to make the movement is conveyed through a bundle of axons to the prefrontal area. There, the command activates neural circuits that contain the memory of the movements that constitute the behavior. This information is transmitted through the corpus callosum to the right prefrontal cortex and, from there, to the right precentral gyrus. Neurons in this area control the individual movements. Damage to the anterior corpus callosum prevents communication between the left and right premotor areas, regions of the motor association cortex just rostral to the precentral gyrus. Thus, the right arm can perform the requested movement, but the left arm cannot. (See lesion A in ***Figure 7.9.***)

sympathetic apraxia

A similar form of limb apraxia is caused by damage to the anterior left hemisphere, sometimes called **sympathetic apraxia.** The damage causes a primary motor impairment of the right arm and hand: full or partial paralysis. Like anterior callosal lesions, the damage also causes apraxia of the left arm. The term *sympathetic* was originally adopted because the clumsiness of the left hand appeared to be a "sympathetic" response to the paralysis of the right one. (See lesion B in ***Figure 7.9.***)

left parietal apraxia

The third form of limb apraxia is **left parietal apraxia**, caused by lesions of the posterior left hemisphere. These lesions involve both limbs. The posterior parietal lobe contains areas of association cortex that receive information from the surrounding sensory association cortex of the occipital, temporal, and anterior parietal lobes. Mr. J., the patient I described in the Prologue, had left parietal apraxia. (See lesion C in ***Figure 7.9.***)

From the effects of parietal lobe lesions in humans and monkeys, Mountcastle, Lynch, Georgopoulos, Sakata, and Acuna (1975) suggest that this region contains a

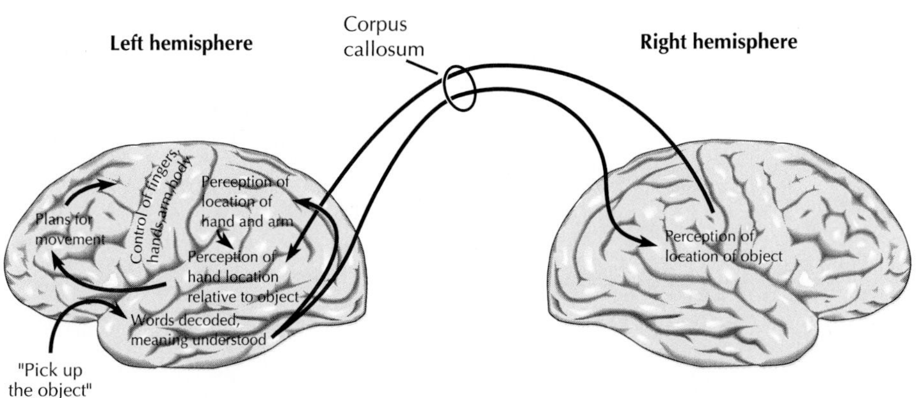

FIGURE 7.10

The "command apparatus" of the left parietal lobe.

sensory representation of the surrounding environment and keeps track of the location of objects in the environment and the location of the organism's body parts in relation to them. Because the right parietal lobe is especially important for perception of three-dimensional space, information about the location of objects external to the person is probably supplied from this region. According to Mountcastle and his colleagues, the left parietal region serves as a "command apparatus for the operation of the limbs, hands, and eyes within immediate extrapersonal space." For example, when a person hears a command to reach for a particular object, the meaning of the request is decoded by the left auditory association cortex and is passed on to the left parietal association cortex. Using information received from the right parietal association cortex about the spatial location of the object, neural circuits in the left parietal association cortex assess the relative location of the person's hand and the object and send information about the starting and ending coordinates to the left premotor cortex. There, the sequence of muscular contractions necessary to perform the movement is organized, and this sequence is executed through the primary motor cortex and its connections with the spinal cord and subcortical motor systems. (See ***Figure 7.10.***)

CONSTRUCTIONAL APRAXIA

constructional apraxia

Constructional apraxia is caused by lesions of the right hemisphere, particularly the right parietal lobe. People with this disorder do not have difficulty making most types of skilled movements with their arms and hands. They have no trouble using objects properly, imitating their use, or pretending to use them. However, they have trouble drawing pictures or assembling objects from elements such as toy building blocks.

The primary deficit in constructional apraxia appears to involve the ability to perceive and imagine geometrical relations. As a result of this deficit, a person cannot draw a picture, say, of a cube, because he or she cannot imagine what the lines and angles of a cube look like, not because he or she cannot control the movements of the arm and hand. (See ***Figure 7.11.***) Besides being unable to draw accurately, a person with constructional apraxia invariably has trouble with other tasks involving spatial perception, such as following a map.

The Basal Ganglia

The basal ganglia constitute an important component of the motor system. We know they are important because their destruction by disease or injury causes severe motor deficits. The motor nuclei of the basal ganglia include the caudate nucleus, putamen,

FIGURE 7.11

Attempt to copy a cube by a patient with constructional apraxia caused by a lesion of the right parietal lobe. (From *Fundamentals of Human Neuropsychology*, 3rd ed., by B. Kolb and I.Q. Whishaw. Copyright © 1990 by W.H. Freeman and Company. Reprinted with permission.)

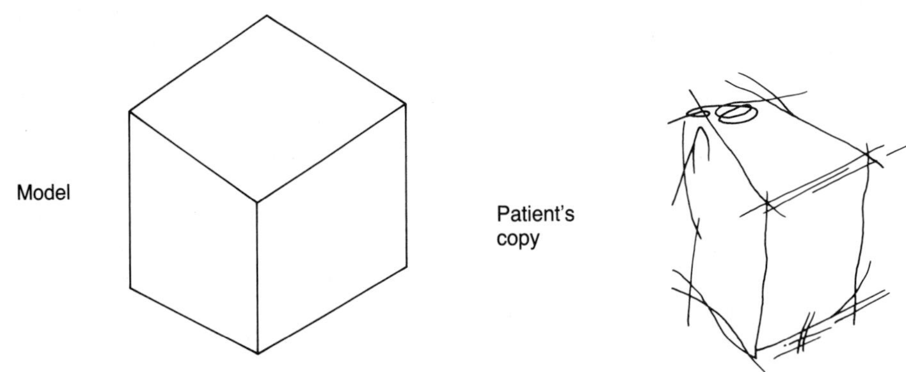

and globus pallidus. The basal ganglia receive inputs from the neocortex and cerebellum. They also communicate with various nuclei located in and beneath the thalamus, the red nucleus, the substantia nigra, and parts of the reticular formation. Through these connections they influence the activity of the corticospinal, rubrospinal, and ventromedial systems. The most important of the connections are shown in ***Figure 7.12.***

We already saw in Chapters 3 and 4 that degeneration of the nigrostriatal bundle, the dopaminergic pathway from the substantia nigra of the midbrain to the caudate nucleus and putamen (the ***neostriatum***), causes Parkinson's disease. The primary disorder is slowness of movement and difficulty in stopping one behavior and starting another. These deficits are seen in all muscle groups—those controlling fingers, hands, arms, and trunk. For example, once a person with Parkinson's disease is seated, she finds it difficult to arise. Once the person begins walking, she has difficulty stopping. Thus, a person with Parkinson's disease cannot easily pace back and forth across a room. Reaching for an object can be accurate, but the movement usually begins only after a considerable delay. Writing is slow and labored; and as it progresses, the letters get smaller and smaller. Postural movements are impaired. If someone bumps into a normal person who is standing, he will quickly move to restore balance—for example, by taking a step in the direction of the impending fall or by reaching out with the arms to grasp onto a piece of furniture. However, a person with Parkinson's disease fails to do so and simply falls. A person with this disorder is even unlikely to put out his arms to break the fall.

Parkinson's disease also produces a resting tremor—vibratory movements of the arms and hands that diminish somewhat when the individual makes purposeful move-

FIGURE 7.12

Some important interconnections of the basal ganglia.

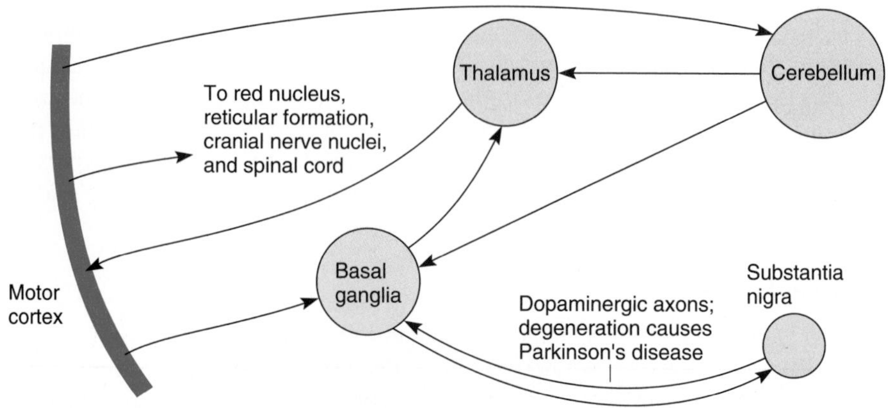

ments. The tremor is accompanied by rigidity; the joints appear stiff. However, the tremor and rigidity are not the cause of the slow movements. Although the slowness appears to be caused by degeneration of the nigrostriatal bundle, the rigidity and tremor probably occur because of damage to neurons in other pathways. Indeed, experimental studies with laboratory animals have found that damage to the substantia nigra produces hypoactivity but not tremors. The tremors probably originate in a feedback circuit consisting of a loop of neurons from the ventral thalamus to the motor cortex and back again. Neurons in the ventral thalamus fire in synchrony with the vibratory movements of the tremor, and stereotaxic lesions of this area can eliminate or reduce the tremor and rigidity (Dray, 1980). However, the lesions do not affect the slowness of movement.

Another basal ganglia disease, **Huntington's chorea**, is caused by degeneration of the caudate nucleus and putamen, especially of GABAergic and acetylcholinergic neurons. (See ***Color Plates 7.1 and 7.2.***) Whereas Parkinson's disease causes a poverty of movements, Huntington's chorea causes uncontrollable ones, especially jerky limb movements. (*Chorea* derives from the Greek *khoros,* meaning "dance.") The movements of Huntington's chorea look like fragments of purposeful movements but occur involuntarily. The disease is progressive and eventually causes death.

Huntington's chorea

A complete description of these two syndromes is much more complicated than my brief outline, but we can easily see that the basal ganglia can either inhibit or facilitate movements. Mainly on the basis of clinical observations of patients with motor disorders, Kornhuber (1974) suggests that the basal ganglia may play a special role in the control of slow, smooth movements. DeLong (1974) obtained some electrophysiological evidence that supports Kornhuber's hypothesis. He found that a majority of the neurons in the putamen fire before and during slow movements but not before and during rapid ones.

Damage to the caudate nucleus or putamen generally causes symptoms of *release*; the patients exhibit rigidity (excessive muscular contraction) or uncontrollable movements of the limbs or facial muscles. Damage to the globus pallidus or ventral thalamus generally causes symptoms of *deficiency,* such as **akinesia** (lack of movement) or mutism (failure to talk). Thus, the caudate nucleus and putamen appear to be inhibitory in function, and the globus pallidus and ventral thalamus appear to be excitatory. In Parkinson's disease the slowness of movement probably occurs because degeneration of the nigrostriatal bundle disrupts an inhibitory input to the caudate nucleus. Loss of inhibition increases the inhibitory function of the caudate nucleus, and movements become slower.

akinesia

The Cerebellum

The cerebellum is an important part of the motor system. When it is damaged, people's movements become jerky, erratic, and uncoordinated. The cerebellum consists of two hemispheres that contain several deep nuclei situated beneath the wrinkled and folded cerebellar cortex. Thus, the cerebellum resembles the cerebrum in miniature. (See ***Figure 7.13.***) The **flocculonodular lobe,** located at the caudal end of the cerebellum, receives input from the vestibular system and projects axons to the vestibular nucleus. You will not be surprised to learn that this system is involved in postural reflexes. (See gray lines, ***Figure 7.14.***) The **vermis** ("worm"), located on the midline, receives cutaneous and kinesthetic information from the spinal cord and sends its outputs to the **fastigial nucleus,** one of the set of deep cerebellar nuclei. Neurons in the fastigial nucleus send axons to the vestibular nucleus and to motor nuclei in the reticular

flocculonodular lobe

vermis

fastigial nucleus

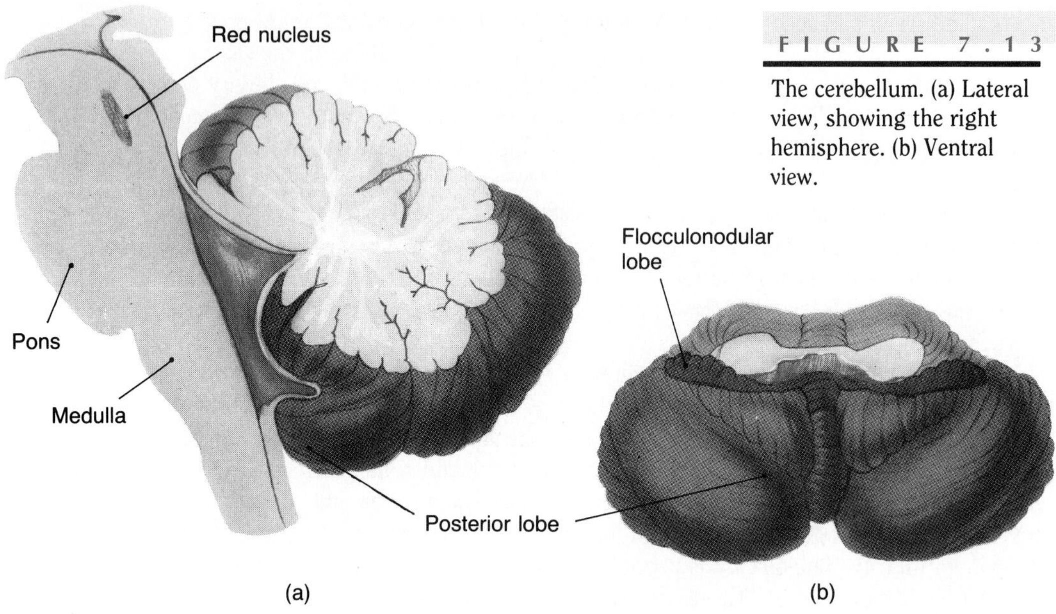

FIGURE 7.13

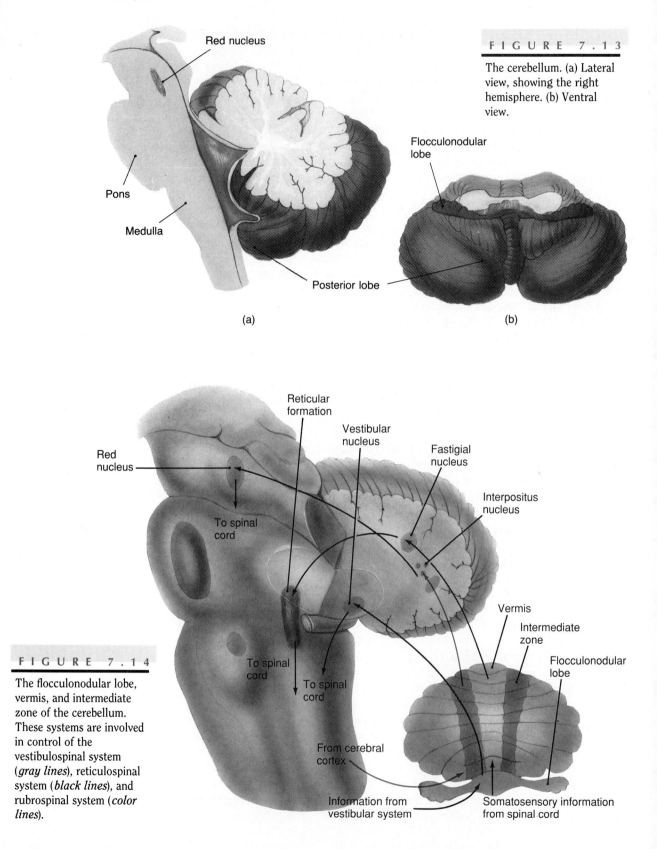

The cerebellum. (a) Lateral view, showing the right hemisphere. (b) Ventral view.

FIGURE 7.14

The flocculonodular lobe, vermis, and intermediate zone of the cerebellum. These systems are involved in control of the vestibulospinal system (*gray lines*), reticulospinal system (*black lines*), and rubrospinal system (*color lines*).

formation. Thus, they influence behavior through the vestibulospinal and reticulospinal tracts, two of the three ventromedial pathways. (See black lines, ***Figure 7.14.***)

The rest of the cerebellar cortex receives inputs (relayed through nuclei in the pons) from the cerebral cortex, including the primary motor cortex and all regions of the association cortex. The intermediate zone of the cerebellar cortex projects to one of the nuclei located deep within the cerebellum, the **interpositus nucleus**, which in turn projects to the red nucleus. Thus, the intermediate zone influences the activity of the rubrospinal system. (See color lines, ***Figure 7.14.***)

interpositus nucleus

The lateral zone of the cerebellum sends axons to another deep cerebellar nucleus, the **dentate nucleus.** From there, some axons travel to the red nucleus; thus, the lateral zone, like the intermediate zone, influences the rubrospinal system. The dentate nucleus also sends axons to the ventrolateral thalamus, which provides the primary source of subcortical projections to the primary motor cortex. Through this projection the lateral zone helps control rapid, skilled movements. Movements are initiated by neurons in the frontal association cortex, which control neurons in the primary motor cortex. Both regions send information about the intended movement to the lateral zone of the cerebellum, via the **pontine nucleus,** the most prominent nucleus in the pons. The cerebellum smooths and integrates the movements through its connections with the primary motor cortex, via the dentate nucleus and ventrolateral thalamus. (See ***Figure 7.15.***)

dentate nucleus

pontine nucleus

In humans, lesions of different regions of the cerebellum produce different symptoms. Damage to the flocculonodular lobe or vermis causes disturbances in posture and balance. Damage to the intermediate zone produces deficits in movements controlled by the rubrospinal system. The principal symptom is limb rigidity. Damage to the lateral zone causes weakness and *decomposition of movement.* For example, if a person attempts to bring the hand to the mouth, he or she will make clumsy, separate movements of the joints of the shoulder, elbow, and wrist instead of performing simultaneous smooth movements.

Lesions of the lateral zone of the cerebellar cortex also appear to impair the timing of rapid *ballistic* movements. Ballistic (literally, "throwing") movements occur too fast to be modified by feedback. So, the sequence of muscular movements must be programmed in advance, and the individual muscles must be activated at the proper times. You might like to try this common neurological test. Have a friend place his or her finger in front of your face, about three-quarters of an arm's length away. While your friend slowly moves his or her finger around to serve as a moving target, alternately touch your nose and your friend's finger as rapidly as you can. If your cerebellum is normal, you can successfully hit your nose and your friend's finger without too much trouble. People with lateral cerebellar damage have great difficulty; they tend to miss the examiner's hand and poke themselves in the eye. (I have often wondered why neurologists do not adopt a less dangerous test.)

When we make rapid, aimed movements, we cannot rely on feedback to stop the movement when we reach the target. By the time we perceive that our finger has reached the proper place, it is too late to stop the movement, and we will overshoot the target if we try to stop it then. Instead of relying on feedback, the movement appears to be timed. We estimate the distance between our hand and the target, and our cerebellum calculates the amount of time that the muscles will have to be turned on. After the proper amount of time the cerebellum briefly turns on antagonistic muscles to stop the movement. In fact, Kornhuber (1974) suggests that one of the primary functions of the cerebellum is timing the duration of rapid movements. Obviously, learning must play a role in controlling such movements.

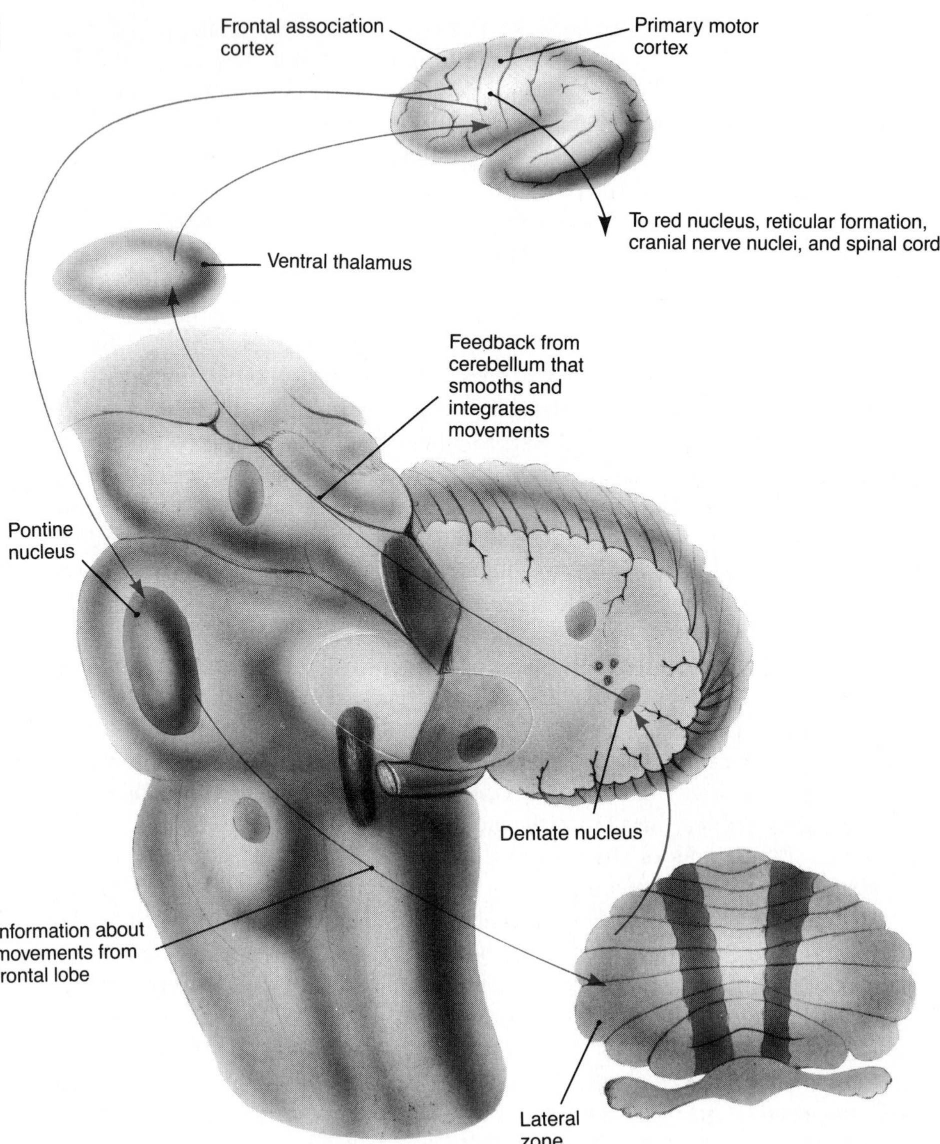

FIGURE 7.15

The lateral zone of the cerebellum. It receives information about impending movements from the frontal lobe, and it helps smooth and integrate the movement through its connections to the primary motor cortex through the dentate nucleus and ventral thalamus.

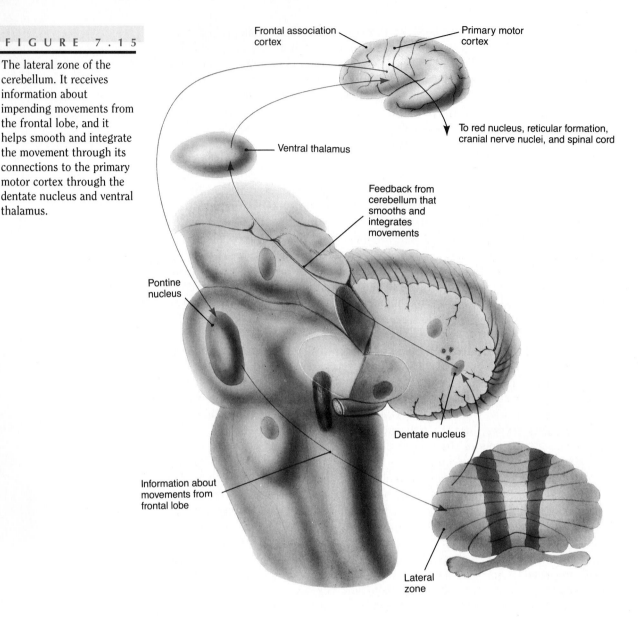

The Reticular Formation

The reticular formation consists of a large number of nuclei located in the core of the medulla, pons, and midbrain. The reticular formation controls the activity of the gamma motor system and hence regulates muscle tonus. In addition, the pons and medulla contain several nuclei with specific motor functions. For example, different locations in the medulla control automatic or semiautomatic responses such as respiration, sneezing, coughing, and vomiting. As we saw, the ventromedial pathways originate in the superior colliculi, vestibular nuclei, and reticular formation. Thus, the reticular formation plays a role in the control of posture.

The reticular formation also plays a role in locomotion. Electrical stimulation of one part, the **mesencephalic locomotor region**, causes a cat to make the pacing movements it normally makes while walking (Shik and Orlovsky, 1976).

mesencephalic locomotor region

Other motor functions of the reticular formation are also being discovered. Siegel and McGinty (1977) recorded from single neurons in the reticular formation of unanesthetized, freely moving cats. Almost all of these neurons responded during ***specific*** movements of the head, tongue, facial muscles, ears, forepaw, or shoulder. The specific nature of the relations suggests that the neurons play some role in controlling the movements. For example, one neuron responded when the tongue moved out and to the left. The function of these neurons and the range of movements they control are not yet known.

▶INTERIM SUMMARY◀

The motor systems of the brain are complex. (Having read this section, you do not need me to tell you that.) A good way to review the systems is through an example. While following my description, you might want to look at Table 7.1 and Figures 7.14 and 7.15 again. Suppose you see, out of the corner of your eye, that something is moving. You quickly turn your head and eyes toward the source of the movement and discover that a vase of flowers on a table someone has just bumped is ready to fall. You quickly reach forward, grab it, and restore it to a stable upright position. (For simplicity's sake I will assume that you are right-handed.)

The rapid movement of your head and eyes is controlled by mechanisms that involve the superior colliculi and nearby nuclei. The head movement and corresponding movement of the trunk are mediated by the tectospinal tract. You perceive the tipping vase because of the activity of neurons in your visual association cortex. Your visual association cortex also contributes information about depth to your right parietal lobe, whose association cortex determines the exact spatial location of the vase. Your left parietal lobe uses the spatial information, together with its own record of the location of your hand, to compute the path your hand must travel to intercept the vase. The information is relayed to your left frontal lobe, where the motor association cortex starts the movement. Because the movement will have to be a ballistic one, the cerebellum controls its timing, on the basis of information it receives from the association cortex of the frontal and parietal lobes. Your hand stops just as it touches the vase, and somatosensory information received from your fingers helps control the movement of your fingers around the vase.

The movement of your hand is controlled through a cooperation between the corticospinal, dorsolateral, and ventromedial pathways. Even before your hand moves, the ventral corticospinal tract and the ventromedial pathways (vestibulospinal and reticulospinal systems, largely under the influence of the basal ganglia) begin adjusting your posture so that you will not fall forward when you suddenly reach in front of you. Depending on how far forward you will have to reach, the reticulospinal tract may even cause one leg to step forward in order to take your weight. The dorsolateral pathway (rubrospinal tract) controls the muscles of your upper arm, and the lateral corticospinal tract controls your finger and hand movements. Perhaps you say, triumphantly, "I got it!" The corticobulbar pathway, under the control of speech mechanisms in the left hemisphere, cause the muscles of your vocal apparatus to say these words.

A person with apraxia will have difficulty making controlled movements of the limb in response to a verbal request. Most cases of apraxia are produced by lesions of the left parietal lobe, which sends information about the requested movement to the left frontal association cortex. This region directly controls movement of the right limb by activating neurons in the left primary motor cortex and indirectly controls movement of the left limb by sending information to the right frontal association cortex. Damage to the left frontal association cortex or its connections with the right hemisphere also produces apraxia. ▲

EPILOGUE: ▶ *Application*

The case of Mr. J.—the patient with damage to the left parietal lobe—illustrates that movements are controlled by more than one brain mechanism. As we saw, Mr. J. spontaneously waved his hand when he met someone, but he could not deliberately make a hand-waving movement when he was requested to do so. Similarly, he could not act out the movements he would make while hammering a nail, but when given a hammer and nail he had no difficulty using them. In many ways his deficit is similar to associative visual agnosia, described in the epilogue of Chapter 5. You will recall that people with associative visual agnosia can make hand movements appropriate to what they are seeing, even though they cannot consciously recognize the object. Obviously, visual perception must be taking place, but the perception remains unconscious. For people like Mr. J. events in the environment can trigger automatic, skilled movements that they cannot make in response to verbal requests. Thus, just as there are both conscious and unconscious perceptions, there are also conscious and unconscious movements.

Although we may like to think that all of our movements are under conscious control, many of them are not. For example, emotional displays such as smiling, laughing, and crying are caused by situations that automatically elicit them. We can *simulate* these responses, of course, but the fact that our language contains phrases such as "fake smile" or "forced laughter" indicates that people can often distinguish simulations from the genuine articles. Try standing in front of a mirror to practice your smile. If you are like me, you will find the attempt so embarrassing that you will have to turn away. A real smile comes unbidden; we feel the corners of our mouth rising without willing the movement. (In fact, sometimes we have to make a real effort *not* to smile if we are trying to spare someone's feelings.) As we shall see in Chapter 10, people with a disorder called pseudobulbar palsy are unable to make voluntary movements of their facial muscles, but they will still smile automatically if something amuses them.

Something else we cannot do is move our eyes slowly. Try to do it; look away from the book and try to shift your gaze in a slow circle. You cannot do so; your eyes are forced to move in small jerky movements (*saccades,* from the old French "to shake"). If you think you really *are* making slow eye movements, ask someone to watch your eyes. Then ask them to try it, and you will see them make a series of small saccades. But under the right conditions we *can* make slow eye movements, which means that our brains possess the mechanisms to control them. Hold your finger in front of you, look at it, and then move your hand around, slowly. You will have no trouble tracking the movement; your eyes will not have to make saccades. Thus, although we are capable of making slow eye movements, we cannot make them under simple voluntary control; there must be a slow-moving object for us to watch.

There are many other examples of movements that are made under automatic guidance. For example, when a skilled pianist plays a difficult etude by Chopin, he or she does not consciously control the details of the arm, hand, and finger movements. These movements must be made so rapidly that they cannot be "thought out." Of course, playing the etude is a conscious, deliberate act—only the details of this act are automatic and unconscious. In this case the cerebellum probably plays an important role, because when it is damaged, rapid and skilled series of movements are very poorly executed. As one patient with a cerebellar lesion put it, "The movements of my left arm are done unconsciously, but I have to think out each movement of the right (affected) arm. I come to a dead stop in turning and have to think before I start again" (Holmes, 1939). Mr. J.'s deficit is just the opposite: He can make automatic skilled movements but cannot consciously control a series of deliberate ones.

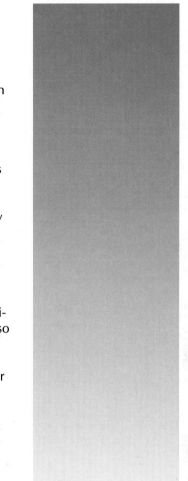

The control of movement is hierarchical. Some types of sequences are done under automatic control of brain mechanisms that evolved long ago. The initiation of these movements is under the control of brain mechanisms that evolved more recently, but the newer mechanisms leave many of the details of the control to the older ones. The newer mechanisms can sometimes make the same movements as the older mechanisms, but they usually make them without the same grace and fluidity. For example, a musician learning a difficult passage may move his or her fingers slowly and deliberately many times until it is learned well enough to be controlled automatically. Undoubtedly, this type of learning involves transferring many of the details of the control to older brain mechanisms that are in charge of automatic movements. I do not know whether Mr. J. ever learned to play a musical instrument, but I suspect that if he did, he can still play it. However, I also suspect that he would not be able to learn to play a new one, because he would not be able to make the conscious, deliberate movements a novice has to make in order to train the brain mechanisms that eventually take over the details of the control and make them become automatic.

I am sure you appreciate that although researchers have learned much about the control of movement, much remains to be discovered. The fact that particular movements can be controlled by more than one mechanism illustrates the complexity that investigators face in trying to disentangle the details of movement control. ▲

KEY CONCEPTS

Muscles

- Skeletal muscles move the body, smooth muscles control various internal organs, and cardiac muscle circulates the blood. Skeletal muscles contain sensory organs: the muscle spindles and the Golgi tendon organs.

Reflex Control of Movement

- Reflexes consist of relatively simple circuits that control stereotyped responses to important stimuli. The monosynaptic stretch reflex helps maintain body posture. The gamma motor system varies the sensitivity of the sensory endings in the muscle spindles.

Control of Movement by the Brain

- Plans for movements are made by neural circuits in the frontal association cortex, based on information received from the posterior cortical association areas. The movements are executed by the primary motor cortex.
- The primary motor cortex controls the hands and fingers through the lateral corticospinal system, the arms and hands through the rubrospinal system, and the rest of the body through the ventromedial system.
- Damage to the left parietal lobe, to the left prefrontal cortex, or to the anterior corpus callosum can cause apraxia; constructional apraxia is caused by damage to the right parietal lobe.
- The deficits caused by Parkinson's disease or Huntington's chorea indicate that the basal ganglia play an important role in the control of movement, but their precise role is not well understood.
- The three major zones of the cerebellum control head and eye movements, help maintain posture, and smooth out movements initiated by the primary motor cortex.

NEW TERMS

actin **p. 215**
akinesia **p. 231**
alpha motor neuron **p. 214**
apraxia **p. 227**
callosal apraxia **p. 228**
cardiac muscle **p. 217**
constructional apraxia **p. 228**
corticobulbar pathway **p. 224**
corticospinal pathway **p. 222**
dentate nucleus **p. 233**
extrafusal muscle fiber **p. 214**
fastigial nucleus **p. 231**
flocculonodular lobe **p. 231**
gamma motor neuron **p. 214**
Golgi tendon organ **p. 217**
Huntington's chorea **p. 231**
interpositus nucleus **p. 233**
intrafusal muscle fiber **p. 214**
lateral corticospinal tract **p. 223**
left parietal apraxia **p. 228**
mesencephalic locomotor region **p. 234**
monosynaptic stretch reflex **p. 218**
motor endplate **p. 215**
motor unit **p. 214**
muscle spindle **p. 214**
myosin **p. 215**
neuromuscular junction **p. 215**
pontine nucleus **p. 233**
reticulospinal tract **p. 225**
rubrospinal tract **p. 226**
skeletal muscle **p. 214**
smooth muscle **p. 217**
sympathetic apraxia **p. 228**
tectospinal tract **p. 225**
ventral corticospinal tract **p. 223**
ventromedial pathway **p. 225**
vermis **p. 231**
vestibulospinal tract **p. 225**

SUGGESTED READINGS

Kandel, E.R., and Schwartz, J.H. *Principles of Neural Science.* Amsterdam: Elsevier/North Holland, 1981.
Rosenbaum, D.A. *Human Motor Control.* San Diego: Academic Press, 1990.

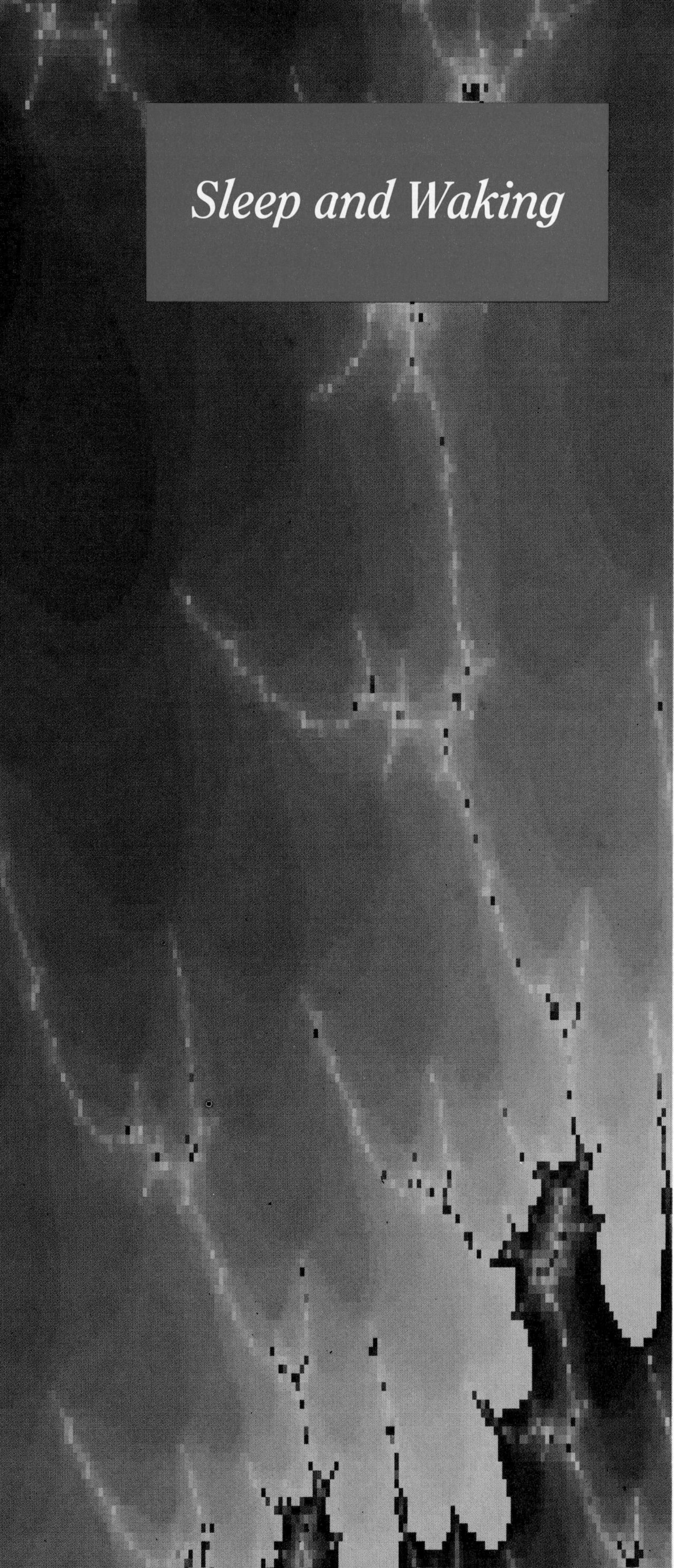

8

Sleep and Waking

CHAPTER OUTLINE

PROLOGUE ►

Lately, Michael almost felt afraid of going to bed, because of the unpleasant experiences he had been having. His dreams seemed to have become more intense, in a rather disturbing way. Several times in the past few months, he felt as if he were paralyzed as he lay in bed, waiting for sleep to come. It was a strange feeling; was he *really* paralyzed, or was he just not trying hard enough to move? He always fell asleep before he was able to decide. A couple of times he woke up just before it was time for his alarm to go off and felt unable to move. Then the alarm would ring, and he would quickly shut it off. That meant that he really wasn't paralyzed, didn't it? Was he going crazy?

Last night brought the worst experience of all. As he was falling asleep, he felt, again, as if he were paralyzed. Then he saw his old roommate enter his bedroom. But that wasn't possible! Since the time he graduated from college, he had lived alone, and he always locked the door. He tried to say something, but he couldn't. His roommate was holding a hammer. He walked up to his bed, stood over him, and suddenly raised the hammer, as if to smash in his forehead. When he awoke in the morning, he shuddered with the remembrance. It seemed so real! It must have been a dream, but he didn't think he was asleep. He was in bed — can a person really dream that he is lying in bed, not yet asleep?

That day at the office he had trouble concentrating on his work. He forced himself to review his notes, because he had to present the details of the new project to the board of directors. This was his big chance; if the project were accepted, he would certainly be chosen to lead it, and that would mean a promotion and a substantial raise. Naturally, with so much at stake, he felt nervous when he entered the boardroom. His boss introduced him and asked him to begin. He glanced at his notes and opened his mouth to talk. Suddenly, he felt his knees buckle. All his strength seemed to slip away. He fell heavily to the floor. He could hear people running over and asking what had happened. He couldn't move anything except his eyes. His boss got down on his knees, looked into his face, and asked, "Michael, are you all right?" Michael looked at his boss and tried to answer, but he couldn't say a thing. A few seconds later, he felt his strength coming back. He opened his mouth and said, "I'm ok." He struggled to his knees and then sat in a chair, feeling weak and frightened.

"You undoubtedly have a condition known as narcolepsy," said the doctor who Michael visited. "It's a problem that concerns the way your brain controls sleep. I'll have you spend a night in the sleep clinic and get some recordings done to confirm my diagnosis, but I'm sure that I'll be proved correct. You told me that lately you've been taking short naps during the day. What were these naps like? Were you suddenly struck by an urge to sleep?" Michael nodded. "I just had to put my head on the desk, even though I was afraid that my boss might see me. But I don't think I slept more than five minutes or so." "Did you still feel sleepy when you woke?" "No," he replied, "I felt fine again." The doctor nodded. "All the symptoms you have reported — the sleep attacks, the paralysis you experienced before sleeping and after waking up, the spell you had today — they all fit together. Fortunately, we can usually control narcolepsy with medication. I'm sure we'll have you back to normal, and there is no reason why you can't continue with your job. If you'd like, I can talk with your boss and reassure him, too." ▲

Why do we sleep? Why do we spend at least one-third of our lives doing something that provides most of us with only a few fleeting memories? I will attempt to answer this question in several ways. In the first part of this chapter I will describe what is known about the phenomenon of sleep: How much do we sleep? What do we do while asleep? What happens if we do not get enough sleep? What factors affect the duration and quality of sleep? How effective are sleeping medications? Does sleep perform a restorative function? What do we know about sleepwalking and other sleep-related disorders? In the second part of the chapter I will discuss the mechanism that controls daily rhythms of sleep and activity. In the third I will describe the search for the chemicals and the neural circuits that control sleep and wakefulness.

A PHYSIOLOGICAL AND BEHAVIORAL DESCRIPTION

Sleep is a behavior. That statement may seem peculiar, because we usually think of behaviors as activities that involve movements, such as walking or talking. Movements do occur during sleep, but except for the rapid eye movements that accompany a particular stage, sleep is not distinguished by movement. What characterizes sleep is that the insistent urge of sleepiness forces us to seek out a quiet, comfortable place, lie down, and remain there for several hours, unresponsive to what goes on around us. Because we remember very little about what happens while we sleep, we tend to think of sleep more as a state of consciousness than as a behavior. The change in consciousness is undeniable, but it should not prevent us from noticing the behavioral changes.

Stages of Sleep

The best research on human sleep is conducted in a sleep laboratory. A sleep laboratory, which is usually located at a university or medical center, consists of one or several small bedrooms adjacent to an observation room, where the experimenter spends the night (trying to stay awake). The experimenter prepares the sleeper for electrophysiological measurements by pasting electrodes to the scalp to monitor the electroencephalogram (EEG) and to the chin to monitor muscle activity, recorded as the **electromyogram** (EMG). Electrodes pasted around the eyes monitor eye movements, recorded as the **electro-oculogram** (EOG). In addition, other electrodes and transducing devices can be used to monitor autonomic measures such as heart rate,

electromyogram
electro-oculogram

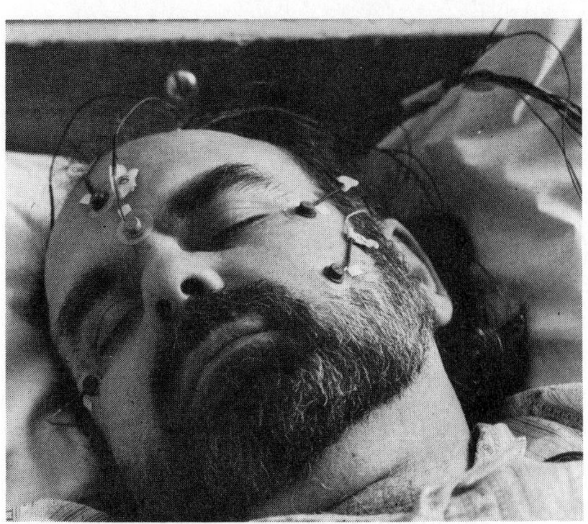

FIGURE 8.1

A subject prepared for a night's sleep in a sleep laboratory. (Woodfin Camp Associates.)

respiration, and skin conductance. Wires from the electrodes are bundled together in a "ponytail," which is then plugged into a junction box at the head of the bed. (See ***Figure 8.1.***)

alpha activity

beta activity

During wakefulness the EEG of a normal person shows two basic patterns of activity: *alpha activity* and *beta activity.* **Alpha activity** consists of regular, medium-frequency waves of 8–12 Hz. The brain produces this activity when a person is resting quietly, not particularly aroused or excited and not engaged in strenuous mental activity (such as problem solving). Although alpha waves sometimes occur when a person's eyes are open, they are much more prevalent when the eyes are closed. The other type of waking EEG pattern, **beta activity,** consists of irregular, mostly low-amplitude waves of 13–30 Hz. This activity occurs when a person is alert and attentive to events in the environment or is thinking actively. (See ***Figure 8.2.***)

Let us follow the progress of a volunteer—a male college student—in a sleep laboratory. The experimenter attaches the electrodes, turns the lights off, and closes the door. Our subject becomes drowsy and soon enters stage 1 sleep, marked by the

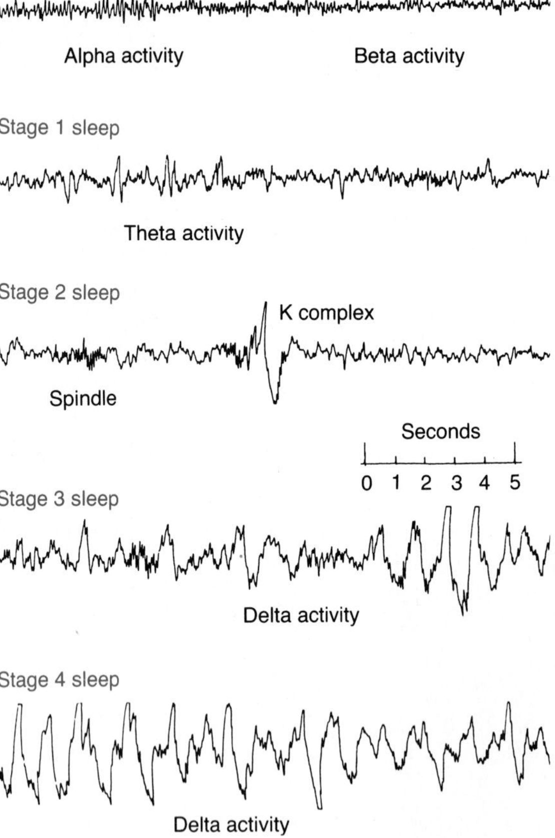

FIGURE 8.2

An EEG recording of the stages of sleep. (From Horne, J.A. *Why We Sleep: The Functions of Sleep in Humans and Other Mammals.* Oxford, England: Oxford University Press, 1988. Copyright 1988 Oxford University Press. By permission of Oxford University Press.)

presence of some **theta activity** (3.5–7.5 Hz). This stage is actually a transition between sleep and wakefulness; if we watch our volunteer's eyelids, we will see that from time to time they slowly open and close, and his eyes roll upward and downward. (See ***Figure 8.2.***) About 10 min later he enters stage 2 sleep. The EEG during this stage is generally irregular but contains periods of theta activity, sleep spindles, and K complexes. *Sleep spindles* are short bursts of waves of 12–14 Hz, which occur between two and five times a minute during stages 1–4 of sleep. Some investigators believe that they represent the activity of a mechanism that decreases the brain's sensitivity to sensory input and thus keeps the person asleep. The sleep of older people contains fewer sleep spindles and is generally accompanied by more awakenings during the night. *K complexes* are sudden, sharp waveforms, which, unlike sleep spindles, are usually found only during stage 2 sleep. They spontaneously occur at the rate of approximately one per minute but can often be triggered by noises. Some investigators believe that they, too, represent mechanisms involved in keeping the person asleep. (See ***Figure 8.2.***)

theta activity

The subject is sleeping soundly now; but if awakened, he might report that he has not been asleep. This phenomenon is often reported by nurses who awaken loudly snoring patients early in the night (probably to give them a sleeping pill) and find that the patients insist they were lying there awake all the time. About 15 min later the subject enters stage 3 sleep, signaled by the occurrence of high-amplitude **delta activity** (less than 3.5 Hz). (See ***Figure 8.2.***) The distinction between stage 3 and stage 4 is not clear-cut; stage 3 contains 20–50 percent delta activity, and stage 4 contains more than 50 percent. (See ***Figure 8.2.***)

delta activity

About 90 min after the beginning of sleep (and about 45 min after the onset of stage 4 sleep), we notice an abrupt change in a number of physiological measures recorded from our subject. The EEG suddenly becomes mostly desynchronized, with a sprinkling of theta waves, very similar to the record obtained during stage 1 sleep. (See ***Figure 8.2.***) We also note that his eyes are rapidly darting back and forth beneath his closed eyelids. We can see this activity in the EOG, recorded from electrodes pasted to the skin around his eyes, or we can observe the eye movements directly. The cornea produces a bulge in the closed eyelids that can be seen to move about. We also see that the EMG becomes silent; there is a profound loss of muscle tonus. (As we shall see later, there is a good reason for this phenomenon.) However, despite the loss of muscle tonus, we do occasionally see brief twitching movements of the hands and feet, and our subject probably has an erection.

This peculiar stage of sleep is quite distinct from the quiet sleep we saw earlier. It is usually referred to as **REM sleep** (for the *r*apid *e*ye *m*ovements that characterize it). It has also been called *paradoxical sleep,* because of the presence of an aroused, "waking" EEG during sleep. The term *paradoxical* merely reflects people's surprise at observing an unexpected phenomenon, but the years since its first discovery (reported by Aserinsky and Kleitman in 1955) have blunted the surprise value.

REM sleep

At this point I should introduce some terminology. Stages 1–4 are usually referred to as **non-REM sleep.** Stages 3 and 4 are referred to as **slow-wave sleep,** because of the presence of delta activity. As we will see, research has focused on the role of REM sleep and of slow-wave sleep; most investigators believe that the other stages of non-REM sleep, stages 1 and 2, are less important than the others. By some criteria stage 4 is the deepest stage of sleep: Only loud noises will cause a person to awaken; and when awakened, the person acts groggy and confused. During REM sleep a person may not react to noises, but he or she is easily aroused by meaningful stimuli, such as the sound of his or her name. Also, when awakened from REM sleep, a person appears alert and attentive.

non-REM sleep
slow-wave sleep

FIGURE 8.3

A typical pattern of the stages of sleep during a single night. (From Hartmann, E. *The Biology of Dreaming*, 1967. Courtesy of Charles C. Thomas, Publisher, Springfield, Illinois.)

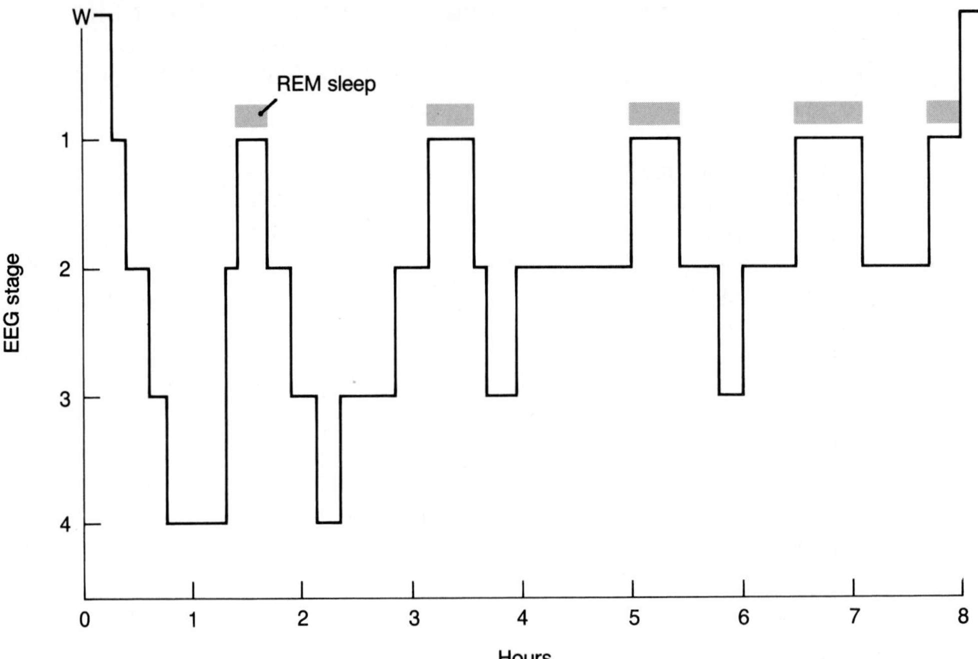

If we arouse our volunteer during REM sleep and ask him what was going on, he will almost certainly report that he had been dreaming. The dreams of REM sleep tend to have a narrative form; there is a storylike progression of events. If we wake him during slow-wave sleep and ask, "Were you dreaming?" he will most likely say, "No." However, if we question him more carefully, he might report the presence of a thought, an image, or some emotion. I will return to this issue later.

During the rest of the night our subject's sleep alternates between periods of REM and slow-wave sleep. Each cycle is approximately 90 min long, containing a 20- to 30-min bout of REM sleep. Thus, an 8-hour sleep will contain four or five periods of REM sleep. Figure 8.3 shows a graph of a typical night's sleep. Note that most slow-wave sleep (stages 3 and 4) occurs during the first half of night. Subsequent bouts of non-REM sleep contain more and more stage 2 sleep, and bouts of REM sleep become more prolonged. (See ***Figure 8.3.***)

The regular 90-min cycles of REM sleep suggest that a brain mechanism alternately causes REM and slow-wave sleep. Normally, a period of slow-wave sleep must precede REM sleep. In addition, there seems to be a refractory period after each occurrence or REM sleep, during which time REM sleep cannot take place again. In fact, the cyclical nature of REM sleep appears to be controlled by a "clock" in the brain that also controls an activity cycle that continues through waking. The first suggestion that a 90-min activity cycle occurs throughout the day came from the observation that infants who are fed on demand show regular feeding patterns (Kleitman, 1961). Later studies found 90-min cycles of rest and activity, including such activities as eating, drinking, smoking, heart rate, oxygen consumption, stomach motility, urine production, and performance on various tasks that make demands upon a person's ability to pay attention. Kleitman termed this phenomenon the **basic rest-activity cycle.** (See Kleitman, 1982, for a review.)

basic rest-activity cycle

During REM sleep we become paralyzed; most of our spinal and cranial motor neurons are strongly inhibited. (Obviously, the ones that control respiration and eye movements are spared.) At the same time, the brain is very active. Cerebral blood flow and oxygen consumption are accelerated. In addition, a male's penis will become at least partially erect, and a female's vaginal secretions will increase. However, Fisher, Gross, and Zuch (1965) found that in males genital changes do not signify that the person is experiencing a dream with sexual content. (Of course, people can have dreams with frank sexual content. In males some of them culminate in ejaculation—the so-called nocturnal emissions, or "wet dreams." Females, too, sometimes experience orgasm during sleep.)

The fact that penile erections occur during REM sleep, independent of sexual arousal, has been used clinically to assess the causes of impotence (Karacan, Salis, and Williams, 1978). A subject sleeps in the laboratory with a device attached to his penis that measures its circumference. If penile enlargement occurs during REM sleep, then his failure to obtain an erection during attempts at intercourse is not caused by physiological problems such as nerve damage or a circulatory disorder. Often, once a man finds out that he is physiologically capable of achieving an erection, the knowledge is therapeutic in itself. (A neurologist told me that there is a less expensive way to gather the same data. The patient obtains a strip of postage stamps, moistens them, and applies them around his penis before going to bed. In the morning he checks to see whether the perforations are broken.)

The important differences between REM and slow-wave sleep are listed in ***Table 8.1.***

▲ TABLE 8.1 ▲

Principal Characteristics of REM and Slow-Wave Sleep

REM Sleep
- EEG desynchrony
- Lack of muscle tonus
- Rapid eye movements
- Penile erection or vaginal secretion
- PGO waves
- Narrative-type dreams

Slow-Wave Sleep
- EEG synchrony
- Moderate muscle tonus
- Slow or absent eye movements
- Lack of genital activity
- Lack of PGO waves
- Static dreams

Mental Activity During Sleep

Although sleep is a period during which we do not respond very much to the environment, it is incorrect to refer to sleep as a state of unconsciousness. During sleep our consciousness is certainly different from consciousness during waking, but we *are* conscious. In the morning we usually forget what we experienced while asleep, and in retrospect we recall a period of "unconsciousness." However, when experimenters wake sleeping subjects, the reports that the subjects give make it clear that they were conscious.

Some people insist that they never dream. They are wrong; everyone dreams. What does happen, however, is that most dreams are subsequently forgotten. Unless a person awakens during or immediately after a dream, the dream will not be remembered. Many people who thought they had not had a dream for years have been startled by the vivid narrations they were able to supply when roused during REM sleep in the laboratory. Even the most vivid experiences can be completely erased from consciousness. I am sure that many of you have had the experience of waking during a particularly vivid dream. You decide to tell your friends about it, and you start to review what you will say. As you do so, the memory just slips away. You can't remember the slightest detail of the dream, which was so vivid and real just a few seconds ago. You may feel that if you could remember just one thing about it, everything would come back. Understanding this phenomenon would probably help us understand the more general issue of learning and forgetting.

FIGURE 8.5

Sleep in a dolphin. The two hemispheres sleep independently, presumably so that the animal remains behaviorally alert. (Adapted from Mukhametov, L.M., in *Sleep Mechanisms,* edited by A.A. Borbély and J.L. Valatx. Munich: Springer-Verlag, 1984.)

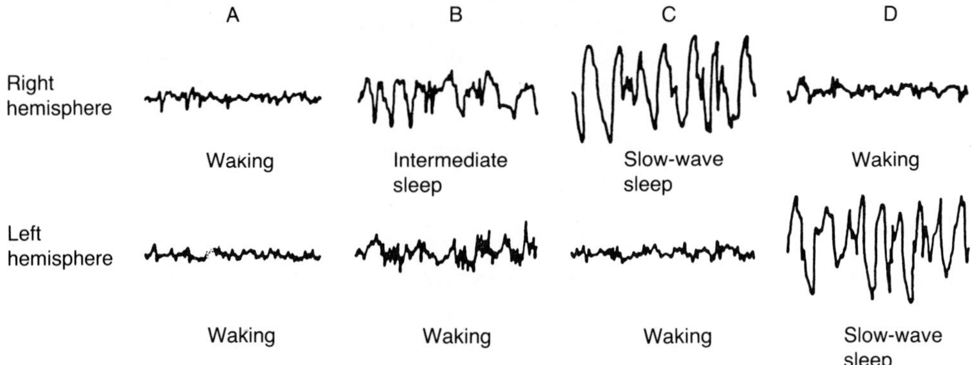

Some other species of marine mammals have developed an extraordinary pattern of sleep: The cerebral hemispheres take turns sleeping, presumably because that strategy always permits at least one hemisphere to be alert. The bottlenose dolphin *(Tursiops truncatus)* and the porpoise *(Phocoena phocoena)* both sleep this way (Mukhametov, 1984). Figure 8.5 shows the EEG records from the two hemispheres; note that slow-wave sleep occurs independently in the left and right hemispheres. (See ***Figure 8.5.***)

Undoubtedly, sleep *does* serve as a useful behavior. The fact that sleeping time varies with environmental factors suggests that sleep is not simply a response to physiological need. But its presence in all species of mammals and birds suggests that at least a certain amount of sleep is physiologically necessary.

Sleep as a Restorative Process

Most investigators believe that sleep accomplishes some sort of restoration from the effects of wear and tear that occur during wakefulness. However, until recently, evidence for this hypothesis was very thin, indeed. In fact, sleep does not seem to be necessary for keeping the body in good condition (at least, in our own species). However, it *does* appear to be needed to keep the brain functioning normally. (For convenience, I will talk about the "body" and the "brain" in the following sections, even though we all know that the brain is a part of the body.)

EFFECTS OF SLEEP DEPRIVATION

When we are forced to miss a night's sleep, we become very sleepy. The fact that sleepiness is so motivating suggests that sleep is a necessity of life. If so, we should be able to deprive people or laboratory animals of sleep and see what capacities are disrupted. We should then be able to infer the role that sleep plays. However, as you will see in the following paragraphs, the results of sleep deprivation studies have not revealed as much as investigators had originally hoped.

Studies with Humans. There is a distinct difference between sleepiness and tiredness. We might want to rest after playing tennis or after having a vigorous swim, but that feeling is quite different from the sleepiness we feel at the end of a day — a sleepiness that occurs even if we have been relatively inactive. What we should do, therefore, to study the role of sleep (as opposed to the restorative function of rest) is to have our subjects rest without sleeping. Unfortunately, that is not possible. When Kleitman first began studying sleep in the early 1920s, he hoped to have subjects undress and lie quietly in bed. They would remain awake so that he could observe the effects of "pure" sleep deprivation. It did not work. People cannot stay awake without engaging in physical activity, no matter how hard they try. So Kleitman had to accept that because his subjects could stay awake only by being active, they were rest-deprived as well as sleep-deprived.

Deprivation studies have not obtained persuasive evidence that sleep is needed to keep the body functioning normally. Horne (1978) reviewed over fifty experiments in which humans had been deprived of sleep. He reported that most of them found that sleep deprivation did not interfere with people's ability to perform physical exercise. In addition, they found no evidence of a physiological stress response to sleep deprivation. If people encounter stressful situations that cause illness or damage to various organ systems, changes can be seen in such physiological measures as blood levels of cortisol and epinephrine. (The physiology of stress is described in more detail in Chapter 10.) Generally, these changes did not occur.

Although sleep deprivation does not seem to damage the body, and sleep does not seem to be necessary for athletic exercise, sleep may be required for normal brain functioning. Most studies have shown that sleep-deprived subjects are able to perform normally on most intellectual tasks, as long as the tasks are short, but have difficulty remaining motivated during prolonged, boring tasks. However, it is difficult to distinguish between motivational changes caused by sleepiness and impairments in brain functions. Several studies suggest that even if motivation is taken into account, people perform more poorly on tasks that require a high level of cortical functioning after two days of sleep deprivation (Horne and Pettitt, 1985).

What happens to sleep-deprived subjects after they are permitted to sleep again? Most of them sleep longer the next night or two, but they never regain all of the sleep they lost. In one remarkable case a seventeen-year-old boy stayed awake for 264 hours so that he could obtain a place in the *Guinness Book of World Records* (Gulevich, Dement, and Johnson, 1966). After his ordeal the boy slept for a little less than 15 hours and awoke feeling fine. He slept slightly more than 10 hours the second night and just under 9 hours the third. Almost 67 hours were never made up. However, percentage of recovery was not equal for all stages of sleep. Only 7 percent of stages 1 and 2 were made up, but 68 percent of stage 4 slow-wave sleep and 53 percent of REM sleep were made up. This finding suggests that stage 4 sleep and REM sleep are more important than the other stages.

As I mentioned earlier, REM sleep will be discussed later. But what do we know about slow-wave sleep? Both cerebral metabolic rate and cerebral blood flow decline during slow-wave sleep, falling to about 75 percent of the waking level during stage 4 sleep (Sakai et al., 1979). In particular, the regions marked by the highest amounts of delta waves decline the most. As we know from behavioral observation, people are unreactive to all but intense stimuli during slow-wave sleep and, if awakened, act groggy and confused—as if their cerebral cortex has been shut down and has not yet resumed its functioning. These observations suggest that during stage 4 sleep the brain is, indeed, resting.

Studies with Laboratory Animals. Until recently, sleep deprivation studies with animals have provided us with little insight into the role of sleep. Because animals cannot

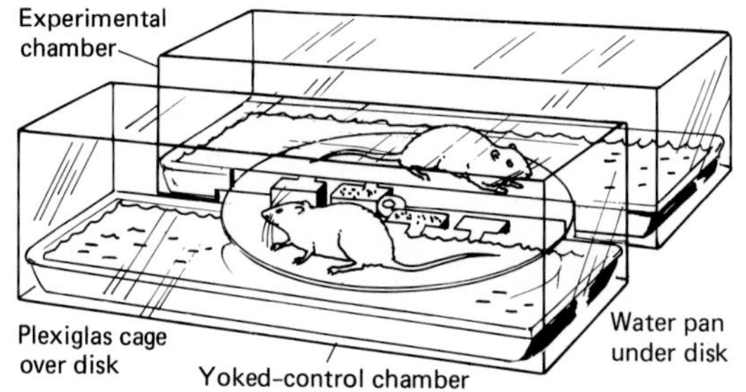

FIGURE 8.6

The apparatus used to deprive rats of sleep. Whenever one of the pair of rats in the experimental chambers fell asleep, the turntable was rotated until the animal was awake for 6 s. (Redrawn from Rechtschaffen, A., Gilliland, M.A., Bergmann, B.M., and Winter, J.B. *Science*, 1983, *221*, 182–184.)

be "persuaded" to stay awake, it is especially difficult to separate the effects of sleep deprivation from those caused by the method used to keep the animals awake. We can ask a human volunteer to try to stay awake and can expect some cooperation. He or she will say, "I'm getting sleepy—help me to stay awake." However, animals are interested only in getting to sleep and must constantly be stimulated—and hence, stressed. Rechtschaffen and his colleagues (Rechtschaffen et al., 1983; 1989) devised a procedure that was designed to control for the effects of forced exercise that are necessary to keep an animal from sleeping. They constructed a circular platform on which two rats lived, each restrained in a plastic cage. When the platform was rotated by an electrical motor, the rats were forced to walk to avoid falling into a pool of water. (See ***Figure 8.6.***)

The investigators employed a ***yoked-control*** procedure to deprive one rat of sleep but force both members of the pair to exercise an equal amount of time. They used a computer to record the EEGs and EMGs of both rats so that they could detect both slow-wave and REM sleep. One rat served as the experimental (sleep-deprived) animal, and the other served as the yoked control. As soon as the EEG record indicated that the experimental animal was falling asleep, the computer turned on the motor that rotated the disk, forcing both animals to exercise. Because the platform rotated whenever the experimental animal started to sleep, the procedure reduced the experimental animal's total sleep time by 87 percent. However, the sleep time of the yoked-control rat was reduced by only 31 percent.

Sleep deprivation had serious effects. The control animals remained in perfect health. However, the experimental animals looked sick and apparently stopped grooming their fur. They became weak and uncoordinated and lost their ability to regulate their body temperature. Although they began eating much more food than normal, their metabolic rate became so high that they lost weight. (The control rats remained in good health.) These results suggest that we must seriously consider the possibility that sleep performs a vital physiological function. However, it could be that the stressful event is forced exercise that occurs immediately after the onset of sleep, not the loss of sleep that this exercise causes. Being forced to begin walking just after falling asleep is undoubtedly more stressful than being forced to walk while awake or after having been asleep for some time.

In any event, the effects of sleep deprivation are less drastic in humans than in rats. Several hypotheses could account for this difference. Perhaps human sleep deprivation studies have just not continued long enough to cause serious harm. Perhaps (as Horne, 1988, suggests) the procedures used to keep humans and rats awake cause different amounts of stress. A human in a sleep deprivation study knows that he or she is being watched carefully by the experimenters and that no serious harm will occur. The subject also knows that even though the experience is somewhat of an ordeal, it will soon be over, and he or she will be able to sleep again. In contrast, the rat knows only that its environment has suddenly become very hostile; it has no way of knowing whether the ordeal will end. In a similar situation perhaps a person would suffer ill effects, also. (In fact, sleep deprivation was an important component of the brainwashing techniques used to persuade captured American servicemen to change their political beliefs during the Korean War.)

EFFECTS OF EXERCISE ON SLEEP

Sleep deprivation studies with humans suggest that the brain may need slow-wave sleep in order to recover from the day's activities but that the rest of the body does not. Another way to determine whether sleep is needed for restoration of physiological functioning is to look at the effects of daytime activity on nighttime sleep. If the function of sleep is to repair the effects of activity during waking hours, then we should expect that sleep and exercise are related. That is, we should sleep more after a day of vigorous exercise than after a day spent quietly at an office desk.

In fact, the relation between sleep and exercise is not very compelling. For example, Ryback and Lewis (1971) found no changes in slow-wave or REM sleep of healthy subjects who spent six weeks resting in bed. If sleep repairs wear and tear, we would expect these people to sleep less. Adey, Bors, and Porter (1968) studied the sleep of *completely* immobile quadriplegics and paraplegics and found only a small decrease in slow-wave sleep as compared with uninjured people.

Horne (1981, 1988) reported that some studies have found that exercise increases slow-wave sleep but others have not. He noted that an important factor seems to be the climate in which the exercise occurs. If the temperature and the humidity are high, the exercise is likely to increase slow-wave sleep. Horne suggested that the important variable might be whether the exercise succeeded in heating the body.

To test this hypothesis, Horne and Moore (1985) had subjects exercise on a treadmill. Some subjects were cooled by electric fans, and their skin was periodically sprayed with water. Their body temperature rose only 1°C. That night, the slow-wave sleep of the "hot exercised" subjects rose by 25 percent, whereas that of the "cool exercised" subjects was unchanged. Horne (1988) now believes that the increased body temperature itself is not the significant factor but that an increase in brain temperature is. Perhaps, he says, an increase in brain temperature raises its metabolic rate and hence its demand for more slow-wave sleep. A preliminary study suggests that this hypothesis may have some merit. Horne and Harley (1988) warmed subjects' heads and faces with a hair dryer, which raised their brain temperature by an estimated 1°C. Four of the six subjects showed an increase in slow-wave sleep the next night. Clearly, further research is needed.

EFFECTS OF MENTAL ACTIVITY ON SLEEP

If slow-wave sleep permits the brain to rest and recover from its daily activity, then we might expect that increased cerebral activity would cause an increase in slow-wave sleep. Indeed, as we just saw, that is precisely the way that Horne interprets the effects of increased body temperature. First of all, tasks that demand alertness and mental activity *do* increase glucose metabolism in the brain, as measured by a PET scanner (Roland, 1984). The most significant increases are seen in the frontal lobes, where delta activity is most intense during slow-wave sleep.

In an ingenious study Horne and Minard (1985) found a way to increase mental activity without affecting physical activity and without causing stress. The investigators told subjects to show up for an experiment in which they were supposed to take some tests designed to test reading skills. In fact, when the subjects turned up, they were told that the plans had been changed. They were invited for a day out, at the expense of the experimenters. (Not surprisingly, the subjects willingly accepted.) They spent the day visiting an art exhibition, a shopping center, a museum, an amusement park, a zoo, and an interesting mansion. After a scenic drive through the countryside they watched a movie in a local theater. They were driven from place to place and certainly did not become overheated by exercise. After the movie they returned to the sleep laboratory. They said they were tired, and they readily fell asleep. Their sleep duration was normal, and they awoke feeling refreshed. However, their slow-wave sleep — particularly stage 4 sleep — was increased.

DOES PHYSICAL RESTORATION OCCUR DURING SLEEP?

The evidence that I have reviewed so far suggests that slow-wave sleep is not necessary for restoration of the body but that it may be necessary for restoration of the brain. I have discussed the effects of sleep deprivation and the effects of physical and mental activity on sleep. One other approach remains: to see whether physiological changes occur during sleep that suggest that restoration and repair takes place at that time.

Investigators who believe that the body repairs itself during sleep point to evidence for restorative processes during sleep. The most important finding is the fact that the secretion of growth hormone occurs during sleep, shortly after the first occurrence of delta activity in slow-wave sleep (Takahashi, 1979). (Growth hormone is, of course, important for stimulating children's growth, but it also has functions in adults.) The sleep-dependent secretion of growth hormone is significant, because this hormone increases the ability of amino acids, the constituents of proteins, to enter cells. Undoubtedly, protein synthesis is an important aspect of restoration of body tissue, because proteins are relatively fragile and must constantly be renewed and replaced.

However, as Horne (1988) points out, growth hormone facilitates protein synthesis only if amino acids are freely available, and that is the case only for about 5 hours after a meal. After that time the amino acids have become incorporated into protein, have been oxidized, or have been converted into fats and stored in the body's adipose tissue. Most people eat several hours before going to bed, so during most of the night the pool of available amino acids is low.

Perhaps for some species, such as the rat, sleep provides the sole opportunity for tissue restoration. When rats are awake, they are actively doing something: foraging for food, seeking sexual partners, grooming, eating, drinking, or otherwise keeping occupied. The only time that they really rest is when they are asleep. However, we humans are able to rest during the day. We are capable of sitting quietly (as I am doing now, and as you will be doing when you read this chapter). In fact, our metabolic rate is only about 9 percent lower during sleep than it is during quiet wakefulness (Reich, Geyer, and Karnovsky, 1972). Thus, we probably do not sleep for physical rest as much as for the opportunity it gives our brain to rest.

THE FUNCTIONS OF REM SLEEP

Clearly, REM sleep is a time of intense physiological activity. The eyes dart about rapidly, the heart rate shows sudden accelerations and decelerations, breathing becomes irregular, and the brain becomes more active. It would be unreasonable to expect that REM sleep has the same functions as slow-wave sleep. An early report on the effects of REM sleep deprivation (Dement, 1960) observed that as the deprivation progressed, subjects had to be awakened from REM sleep more frequently; the "pressure" to enter REM sleep built up. Furthermore, after several days of REM sleep deprivation subjects would show a **rebound phenomenon** when permitted to sleep normally; they spent a much greater-than-normal percentage of the recovery night in REM sleep. This rebound suggests that there is a need for a certain amount of REM sleep—that REM sleep is controlled by a regulatory mechanism. If selective deprivation causes a deficiency in REM sleep, the deficiency is made up later, when uninterrupted sleep is permitted.

rebound phenomenon

How have investigators explained the occurrence of REM sleep? The similarities between REM sleep and waking have led some investigators to suggest that REM sleep permits an animal to become more sensitive to its environment and avoid being surprised by predators (Snyder, 1966). (You will recall that during REM sleep humans are more sensitive to meaningful stimuli, such as the sound of their name.) Others have suggested that REM sleep has a special role in learning. Some investigators suggest that memories of events of the previous day—especially those dealing with emotionally related information—are consolidated and integrated with existing memories (Greenberg and Pearlman, 1974); others have suggested that this time is utilized to accomplish the opposite function—to flush useless information from memory, to prevent the storage of useless clutter (Newman and Evans, 1965; Crick and Mitchison, 1983). Another investigator (Jouvet, 1980) suggests that REM sleep helps integrate learned and instinctive behaviors—it provides a time to modify the neural circuits controlling species-typical behaviors according to the experience gained in the past day. The fact that the sleep of infants consists mainly of REM sleep has suggested to others that this stage is associated with brain development (Roffwarg, Muzio, and Dement, 1966). The association could go either way; brain development could cause REM sleep (perhaps to tidy up after spurts of neural growth), or REM sleep could be setting the stage for brain growth to occur.

As you can see, many hypotheses have been advanced to explain the rather puzzling phenomenon of REM sleep. In the previous paragraph I mentioned four categories: *vigilance, learning* (either consolidation or flushing), *species-typical reprogramming,* and *brain development.* It is probably safe to say that when there are so many hypothetical explanations for a phenomenon, we do not know very much about its causes. So far, none of the hypotheses have been either unambiguously supported or proved wrong. REM sleep deprivation, imposed after a session of training, does impair learning—especially of complicated tasks—but the effect is not very large (McGrath and Cohen, 1978; Smith, 1985). Similarly, a training session does increase REM sleep, especially early in the sleep period. Thus, the learning hypothesis receives a certain amount of support. The vigilance and reprogramming hypotheses have not been developed enough to make specific predictions that can be tested experimentally. The developmental hypothesis is supported by the fact that infant animals born with well-developed brains (such as guinea pigs) spend proportionally less time in REM sleep than infant animals born with less-developed brains (such as rats, cats, or humans). But then, why do adults have REM sleep?

Studies with laboratory animals suggest that REM sleep performs functions that facilitate learning. Experiments have shown that when animals are deprived of REM sleep after participating in a training session, they learn the task more slowly; thus, REM sleep deprivation retards memory formation. In addition, when animals learn a new task, the amount of time they spend in REM sleep increases, as if the learning increases the need for this stage of sleep. For example, Bloch, Hennevin, and Leconte

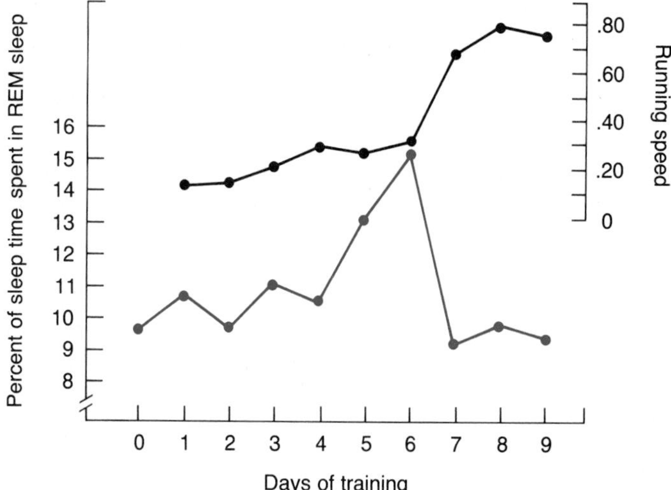

FIGURE 8.7

Percentage of sleep time spent in REM sleep (*lower curve*) as a function of maze-learning performance (*upper curve*). (From Bloch, V., Hennevin, E., and Leconte, P., in *Neurobiology of Sleep and Memory*, edited by R.R. Drucker-Colín and J.L. McGaugh. New York: Academic Press, 1978. Reprinted with permission.)

(1977) gave rats daily training trials in a complex maze. They found that the experience enhanced subsequent REM sleep. Moreover, daily performance was related to subsequent REM sleep. The lower curve in Figure 8.7 shows REM sleep as a percentage of total sleep. The upper curve illustrates the animals' performance in the maze. You can see that the largest increase in running speed (possibly representing the largest increase in learning) was accompanied by the largest amount of REM sleep. Also note that once the task was well learned (after day 6), REM sleep declined back to baseline levels. (See ***Figure 8.7.***)

In contrast to the studies with laboratory animals, studies with human subjects show that REM sleep deprivation has little or no effect on a person's ability to learn or to remember what was previously learned. But a few studies suggest that learning related to emotionally significant material may be affected. Greenberg, Pillard, and Pearlman (1972) had subjects view a film that generally produces anxiety in the observers (a particularly gruesome circumcision rite performed with stone knives by members of a remote South Sea Island tribe). Normally, people who see the film twice show less anxiety during the second viewing. The investigators found that subjects who were permitted to engage in REM sleep between the first and second viewings of the film showed less anxiety the second time than subjects who were deprived of REM sleep. In addition, Breger, Hunter, and Lane (1971) found that the dream content of subjects viewing the film was affected by the anxiety-producing material. Taken together, the studies suggest that REM sleep (and perhaps the dreaming that occurs then) somehow assists people to come to grips with newly learned information that has emotional consequences. As we all know, things generally seem less disturbing after a good night's sleep.

The calming effect of REM sleep appears to be contradicted by a puzzling phenomenon. The symptoms of people with severe, psychotic depression are *reduced* when they are deprived of REM sleep. In addition, treatments that reduce the symptoms of depression, such as antidepressant drugs and electroconvulsive therapy, also suppress REM sleep. (These results will be discussed in more detail in Chapter 16.) If REM sleep helps people assimilate emotionally relevant information, why should REM sleep deprivation relieve the symptoms of people who are suffering from a serious emotional disorder? Unfortunately, we do not have an answer for this question yet.

A particularly interesting case of brain damage suggests that whatever the functions of REM sleep may be, they do not appear to be necessary for survival. Lavie, Pratt, Scharf, Peled, and Brown (1984) reported that a 33-year-old man whose head was injured by shrapnel at age 20 engaged in almost no REM sleep. In the sleep laboratory the man slept an average of 4.5 hours. On 3 of 8 nights he engaged in no REM sleep; the average on the other 5 nights was approximately 6 minutes. The pieces of metal damaged the pons, left temporal lobe, and left thalamus. As we shall see later in this chapter, the pons seems to be the part of the brain that controls REM sleep. The almost complete lack of REM sleep did not appear to cause serious side effects. After receiving his injury, the man completed high school, attended law school, and began practicing law. (I have a feeling that I could work in a lawyer joke here, but I think I'll refrain.)

▶INTERIM SUMMARY◀

The two principal explanations for sleep are that sleep serves as an adaptive response or that it provides a period of restoration. The fact that a species' degree of safety and rate of metabolism are related to the amount of sleep it engages in supports the adaptive hypothesis, but the fact that all vertebrates sleep, including some that would seem to be better off without it, does not.

The effects of several days of sleep deprivation are not devastating to humans; the primary finding is intense sleepiness, difficulty performing tasks that require prolonged concentration, and perceptual distortions and (sometimes) mild hallucinations. These effects suggest that sleep deprivation does impair cerebral functioning. Deep slow-wave sleep appears to be the most important stage, and perhaps its function is to permit the brain (but not necessarily the rest of the body) to recuperate. Animals who are sleep-deprived eventually die, but we cannot be sure that the stress is caused by lack of sleep or by the procedure needed to keep them awake.

Exercise can increase the amount of slow-wave sleep a person receives, but the effect appears to occur only if the brain temperature rises; it can be abolished by cooling the person during exercise or induced by warming the head. Perhaps, then, the fundamental cause is an increase in brain metabolism. Growth hormone normally is secreted only during slow-wave sleep, but the significance of this phenomenon is uncertain, given the fact that the blood level of amino acids during sleep is normally low in humans. In smaller animals such as rats, a meal is normally followed by a bout of sleep.

The function of REM sleep is even less understood than that of slow-wave sleep. It may promote vigilance, learning, species-typical reprogramming, or brain development. So far, the evidence is inconclusive, although several studies have shown a modest relation between REM sleep and learning. ▲

DISORDERS OF SLEEP

Insomnia

Insomnia is a problem that is said to affect at least 20 percent of the population at some time (Raybin and Detre, 1969). At the onset I must emphasize that there is no single definition of insomnia that can apply to all people. The amount of sleep that individuals require is quite variable. A short sleeper may feel fine with 5 hours; a long sleeper may still feel unrefreshed after 10 hours of sleep. Insomnia must be defined in relation to a person's particular sleep needs. Some short sleepers have sought medical assistance because they thought that they were supposed to get more sleep, even though they felt fine. These people should be reassured that whatever amount of sleep seems to be enough *is* enough. Meddis, Pearson, and Langford (1973) reported the case of a seventy-year-old woman who slept approximately 1 hour each day (documented by sessions in a sleep laboratory). She felt fine and was of the opinion that most people "wasted much time" in bed.

Ironically, the most important cause of insomnia seems to be sleeping medication. Insomnia is not a disease that can be corrected with a medicine, in the way that diabetes can be treated with insulin. Insomnia is a symptom. If it is caused by pain or discomfort, the physical ailment that leads to the sleeplessness should be treated. If it is secondary to personal problems or psychological disorders, these problems should be dealt with directly. Patients who receive a sleeping medication develop a tolerance to the drug and suffer rebound symptoms if it is withdrawn (Weitzman, 1981). That is, the drug loses its effectiveness, so the patient requests larger doses from the physician. If the patient attempts to sleep without the accustomed medication or even takes a smaller dose one night, he or she is likely to experience a withdrawal effect: a severe disturbance of sleep. The patient becomes convinced that the insomnia is even worse than before and turns to more medication for relief. This common syndrome is called **drug dependency insomnia.** Kales, Scharf, Kales, and Soldatos (1979) found that withdrawal of some sleeping medications produced a rebound insomnia after the drugs were used for as few as three nights.

drug dependency insomnia

Most patients who receive a prescription for a sleeping medication are given one on the basis of their own description of their symptoms. That is, they tell their physician that they sleep very little at night, and the drug is prescribed on the basis of this testimony. Very few patients are observed during a night's sleep in a sleep laboratory; thus, insomnia is one of the few medical problems that physicians treat without having direct clinical evidence for its existence. But studies on the sleep of people who complain of insomnia show that most of them grossly underestimate the amount of time they actually sleep. The U.S. Institute of Medicine (1979) found that most insomniacs, even without sleeping medication, fall asleep in less than 30 minutes and sleep for at least 6 hours. *With* sleeping medication they obtained less than a 15-minute reduction in falling asleep, and their sleep length was increased by only about 30 minutes. Given the unfortunate side effects, sleeping medication does not seem to be worthwhile.

Some people suffer from an interesting, but unfortunate, form of "pseudoinsomnia": They dream that they are awake. They do not dream that they are running around in some Alice-in-Wonderland fantasy but that they are lying in bed, trying unsuccessfully to fall asleep. In the morning their memories are of a night of insomnia, and they feel as unrefreshed as if they had really been awake.

Another form of insomnia — a true one, not a pseudoinsomnia — is caused by the inability to sleep and breathe at the same time. Patients with this disorder, called **sleep apnea,** fall asleep and then cease to breathe. (Nearly all people have occasional episodes of sleep apnea, especially people who snore, but not to the extent that it interferes with sleep.) During a period of sleep apnea the level of carbon dioxide in the blood stimulates chemoreceptors, and the person wakes up, gasping for air. The oxygen level of the blood returns to normal, the person falls asleep, and the whole cycle begins again. Fortunately, many cases of sleep apnea are caused by an obstruction of the airway that can be corrected surgically.

sleep apnea

Occasionally, infants are found dead in their cribs without any apparent signs of illness, victims of *sudden infant death syndrome* (*SIDS*). Many investigators believe that one of the principal causes for SIDS is sleep apnea; in these cases, however, the infants are *not* awakened by a high level of carbon dioxide in the blood.

Evidence suggests that a susceptibility to SIDS is inherited; parents and siblings of some infants who have died of SIDS do not respond normally to increases in carbon dioxide (Kelly et al, 1980; Schiffman et al., 1980). Often infants who die of SIDS show signs of a low-grade illness, which may increase the tissue need for oxygen while simultaneously depressing respiratory mechanisms. Many infants' lives have been saved by monitoring devices that sound an alarm when a susceptible infant stops breathing during sleep, thus waking the parents in time for them to revive the child.

Problems Associated with REM Sleep

Narcolepsy is a neurological disorder characterized by sleep (or some of its components) at inappropriate times. The symptoms can be described in terms of what we know about the phenomena of sleep. The primary symptom of narcolepsy is the **sleep attack** (*narke* means "numbness," and *lepsis* means "seizure"). The narcoleptic sleep attack is an overwhelming urge to sleep that can happen at any time but occurs most often under monotonous, boring conditions. Sleep (which appears to be entirely normal) usually lasts for 2 to 5 minutes. The person usually wakes up feeling refreshed.

narcolepsy

sleep attack

Another symptom of narcolepsy—in fact, the most striking one—is **cataplexy** (from *kata,* "down," and *plexis,* "stroke"). During a cataplectic attack a person will suddenly wilt and fall like a sack of flour. The person will lie there, *fully conscious,* for a few seconds to several minutes. What apparently happens is that one of the phenomena of REM sleep—muscular paralysis—occurs at an inappropriate time. You will recall that the EMG indicates a loss of muscle tonus during REM sleep. As we will see later, this loss of tonus is caused by massive inhibition of motor neurons. When muscular paralysis occurs during waking, the victim of a cataplectic attack falls as suddenly as if a switch had been thrown.

cataplexy

Cataplexy is quite different from a narcoleptic sleep attack; it is usually precipitated by strong emotion or by sudden physical effort, especially if the patient is caught unawares. Laughter, anger, or trying to catch a suddenly thrown object can trigger a cataplectic attack. Common situations that bring on cataplexy are attempting to discipline one's children or making love (an awkward time to become paralyzed!). Michael, the man in the Prologue, had his first cataplectic attack when he was addressing the board of directors.

REM sleep paralysis sometimes intrudes into waking, but at a time that does not present any physical danger—just before or just after normal sleep, when a person is already lying down. This symptom of narcolepsy is referred to as **sleep paralysis,** an inability to move just before the onset of sleep or upon waking in the morning. A person can be snapped out of sleep paralysis by being touched or by hearing someone call his or her name. Sometimes, the mental components of REM sleep intrude into sleep paralysis; that is, the person dreams while lying awake, paralyzed. These episodes, called **hypnagogic hallucinations,** are often alarming or even terrifying. During his hypnagogic hallucinations Michael thought that his former roommate was trying to kill him. (The term *hypnagogic* comes from the Greek words *hupnos,* "sleep," and *agogos,* "leading.")

sleep paralysis

hypnagogic hallucination

Almost certainly, narcolepsy is produced by a brain abnormality that causes the neural mechanisms responsible for various aspects of REM sleep to become active at inappropriate times. Indeed, Rechtschaffen, Wolpert, Dement, Mitchell, and Fisher (1963) found that narcoleptic patients generally skip the slow-wave sleep that normally begins a night's sleep; instead, they go directly into REM sleep from waking. This finding suggests a deficiency in control over the brain mechanisms that produce REM

FIGURE 8.8

Dogs that have been bred to exhibit the trait of cataplexy and are used for research on this disorder.

(a)

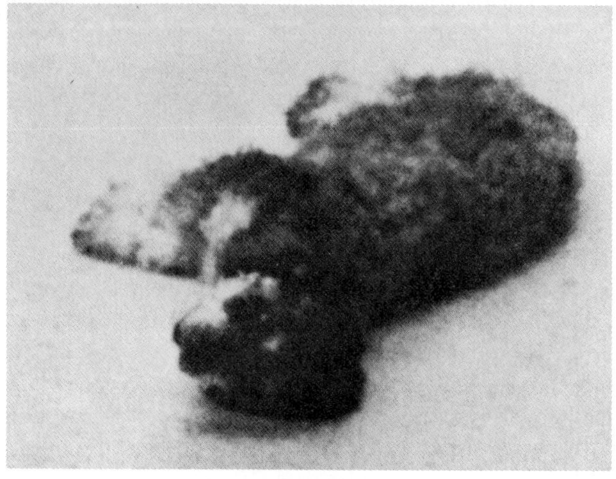

(b)

sleep. Narcolepsy appears to be a genetic disorder. Kessler, Guilleminault, and Dement (1974) found that relatives of narcoleptic patients are sixty times more likely to have this disorder themselves, as compared with people from the general population; and almost all narcoleptics have a particular antigen, called HLA-DR2, in their blood (Juji et al., 1984). Researchers have even successfully bred dogs that are afflicted with narcolepsy. (See ***Figure 8.8.***) The dogs show evidence of biochemical abnormalities in regions of the brain that control REM sleep (Fruhstorfer et al., 1989; Miller et al., 1990). (These regions will be discussed later in this chapter.)

The symptoms of narcolepsy can be successfully treated with drugs, which suggests that the disorder may result from abnormalities in neurotransmitter synthesis, release, or reuptake or receptor sensitivity. Sleep attacks are diminished by stimulants such as amphetamine, a catecholamine agonist; and the REM sleep phenomena (cataplexy, sleep paralysis, and hypnagogic hallucinations) can be alleviated by imipramine, which facilitates both serotonergic and catecholaminergic activity. Most often, the drugs are given together.

REM without atonia

A few years ago, Schenck, Bundlie, Ettinger, and Mahowald (1986) reported the existence of an interesting disorder. The formal name is *REM sleep behavioral disorder,* but a better name is **REM without atonia.** (*Atonia* refers to the lack of muscular activity seen during paralysis.) As you now know, REM sleep is accompanied by paralysis. Despite the fact that the motor cortex and subcortical motor systems are extremely active (McCarley and Hobson, 1979), people are unable to move at this time. The fact that they are dreaming suggests the possibility that but for the paralysis, they would act out their dreams. Indeed, they would. The behavior of people who exhibit REM without atonia corresponds with the contents of their dreams. Consider the following case:

> I was a halfback playing football, and after the quarterback received the ball from the center he lateraled it sideways to me and I'm supposed to go around end and cut

back over tackle and—this is very vivid—as I cut back over tackle there is this big 280-pound tackle waiting, so I, according to football rules, was to give him my shoulder and bounce him out of the way . . . when I came to I was standing in front of our dresser and I had [gotten up out of bed and run and] knocked lamps, mirrors and everything off the dresser, hit my head against the wall and my knee against the dresser. (Schenck, Bundlie, Ettinger, and Mahowald, 1986, p. 294)

As we shall see later in this chapter, the neural circuitry that controls the paralysis that accompanies REM sleep has been discovered in studies with laboratory animals. In humans, REM without atonia seems to be produced by damage to the brain stem—apparently to the same regions (Culebras and Moore, 1989).

Problems Associated with Slow-Wave Sleep

Some maladaptive behaviors occur during slow-wave sleep, especially during its deepest phase, stage 4. These behaviors include bedwetting *(nocturnal enuresis),* sleepwalking *(somnambulism),* and night terrors *(pavor nocturnus).* All three events occur most frequently in children. Bedwetting can often be cured by training methods, such as having a bell ring when the first few drops of urine are detected in the bed sheet by a special electronic circuit (a few drops usually precede the ensuing flood). Night terrors consist of anguished screams, trembling, a rapid pulse, and usually no memory for what caused the terror. Night terrors and somnambulism usually cure themselves as the child gets older. Neither of these phenomena is related to REM sleep; a sleepwalking person is *not* acting out a dream. Most authorities firmly advise that the best treatment for these two disorders is no treatment at all. There is no evidence that they are associated (at least in childhood) with mental disorders or personality variables.

▶*INTERIM SUMMARY*◀

Although many people believe that they have insomnia—that they do not obtain as much sleep as they would like—insomnia is not a disease. Insomnia can be caused by depression, pain, illness, or even excited anticipation of a pleasurable event. Far too many people receive sleeping medications, which often lead to a condition called drug dependency insomnia. Sometimes, insomnia is caused by sleep apnea, which can often be corrected surgically. When sleep apnea occurs in infants, it can lead to sudden infant death; hence the respiration rate of susceptible infants should be monitored electronically until they are old enough to be past danger.

Narcolepsy is characterized by four symptoms. *Sleep attacks* consist of overwhelming urges to sleep for a few minutes. *Cataplexy* is sudden paralysis, during which the person remains conscious. *Sleep paralysis* is similar to cataplexy, but it occurs just before sleep or upon waking. *Hypnagogic hallucinations* are dreams that occur during periods of sleep paralysis, just before a night's sleep. Sleep attacks are treated with stimulants such as amphetamine, and the other symptoms are treated with drugs such as imipramine. Studies with narcoleptic dogs suggest that the disorder may involve biochemical abnormalities in the brain. Another disorder associated with REM sleep, REM without atonia, occurs because of damage to brain stem mechanisms that produce paralysis during REM sleep.

During slow-wave sleep, especially during stage 4, some people are afflicted by bedwetting (nocturnal enuresis), sleepwalking (somnambulism), or night terrors (pavor nocturnus). These problems are most common in children, who usually outgrow them. Only if they occur in adults do they suggest the existence of a physical or psychological disorder. ▲

BIOLOGICAL CLOCKS

Much of our behavior follows regular rhythms. For example, we saw that the stages of sleep are organized around a 90-minute cycle of REM and slow-wave sleep. The same rhythm continues during the day as the basic rest-activity cycle (BRAC). And, of course, our daily pattern of sleep and waking follows a 24-hour cycle. In recent years investigators have learned much about the neural mechanisms responsible for these rhythms, as we shall see in this section.

Circadian Rhythms and Zeitgebers

circadian rhythm

Daily rhythms in behavior and physiological processes are found throughout the plant and animal world. These cycles are generally called **circadian rhythms.** (*Circa* means "about," and *dies* means "day"; therefore, a circadian rhythm is one that varies on a 24-hour cycle.) Some circadian rhythms, such as the rate of plant growth, are a direct consequence of variations in the level of illumination and have no relevance to the study of sleep. However, other rhythms are controlled by mechanisms within the organism. For example, Figure 8.9 shows the activity of a rat during various conditions of illumination. Each horizontal line represents 24 hours. Vertical tick marks represent the animal's activity in a running wheel. The upper portion of the figure shows the activity of the rat during a normal day-night cycle, with alternating 12-hour periods of light and dark. Notice that the animal is active during the night, which is normal for a rat. (See ***Figure 8.9.***)

Next, the day was moved forward by 6 hours; the animal's activity cycle quickly followed the change. (See ***Figure 8.9.***) Finally, dim lights were left on continuously. The cyclical pattern in the rat's activity remained. Because there were no cycles in the rat's environment, the source of rhythmicity must be located within the animal; that is, the animal must contain an internal, biological clock. You can see that the rat's clock was not set precisely to 24 hours; when the illumination was held constant, the clock ran a bit slow. The animal began its bout of activity about 1 hour later each day. (See ***Figure 8.9.***)

FIGURE 8.9

Wheel-running activity of a rat. Note that the animal's activity occurs at "night" (that is, during the 12 hours the light is off) and that the active period is reset when the light period is changed. When the animal is maintained in constant dim illumination, it displays a free-running activity cycle of approximately 25 hours. (From Groblewski, T.A., Nuñez, A., and Gold, R.M. Paper presented at the meeting of the Eastern Psychological Association, April 1980. Reprinted with permission.)

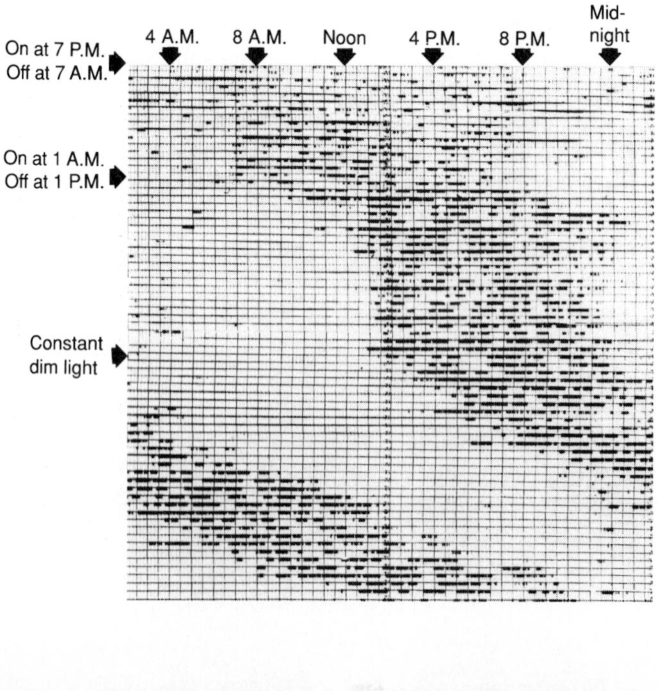

The phenomenon illustrated in Figure 8.9 is typical of the circadian rhythms shown by many species. A free-running clock, with a cycle a little longer than 24 hours, controls some biological functions — in this case, motor activity. Regular daily variation in the level of illumination (that is, sunlight and darkness) normally keeps the clock adjusted to 24 hours. In the parlance of scientists who study circadian rhythms, light serves as a **zeitgeber** (German for "time giver"); it synchronizes the endogenous rhythm. Studies with many species of animals have shown that if they are maintained in constant darkness, a brief flash of light will reset their internal clock, advancing or retarding it, depending upon when the light flash occurs (Aschoff, 1979). In the absence of light cycles other environmental stimuli (such as fluctuations in temperature) can serve as zeitgebers, synchronizing the animal's rhythms.

zeitgeber

Like other animals, humans exhibit circadian rhythms. Our normal period of inactivity begins several hours after the start of the dark portion of the day-night cycle and persists for a variable amount of time into the light portion. Without the benefits of modern civilization we would probably go to sleep earlier and get up earlier than we do; we use artificial lights to delay our bedtime and window shades to extend our time for sleep. Under constant illumination our biological clocks will run free, gaining or losing time like a not-too-accurate watch. Different people have different cycle lengths, but most people in that situation will begin to live a "day" that is approximately 25 hours long.

Discovery of the Suprachiasmatic Nucleus

Researchers working independently in two laboratories (Moore and Eichler, 1972; Stephan and Zucker, 1972) discovered that the primary biological clock of the rat is located in the **suprachiasmatic nucleus** (SCN) of the hypothalamus; they found that lesions disrupted circadian rhythms of wheel running, drinking, and hormonal secretion. The SCN also provides the primary control over the timing of sleep cycles. Rats are nocturnal animals; they sleep during the day and forage and feed at night. Lesions of the SCN abolish this pattern; sleep occurs in bouts randomly dispersed throughout both day and night (Ibuka and Kawamura, 1975; Stephan and Nuñez, 1977). However, rats with SCN lesions still obtain the same amount of sleep that normal animals do. The lesions disrupt the circadian pattern but do not affect the total amount of sleep.

suprachiasmatic nucleus

Figure 8.10 shows the suprachiasmatic nuclei in a transverse section through the hypothalamus of a mouse; they appear as two clusters of dark-staining neurons at the

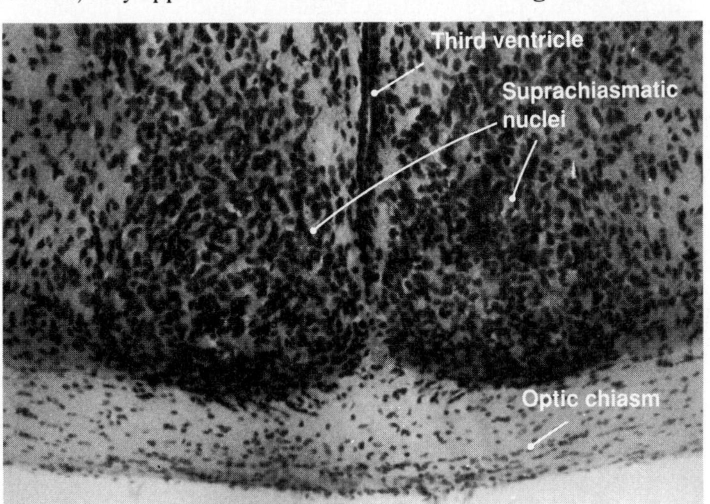

FIGURE 8.10

A transverse section through a mouse brain, showing the location and appearance of the suprachiasmatic nuclei. Cresyl violet stain.

base of the brain, just above the optic chiasm. (See ***Figure 8.10.***) Because light is the primary zeitgeber for most mammals' activity cycles, one would expect that the SCN receives fibers from the visual system. Indeed, it does; it receives input directly from the retina. If you look carefully at Figure 8.10, you can see small dark spots within the optic chiasm, just ventral and medial to the base of the SCN; these are cell bodies of oligodendroglia that serve axons that enter the SCN and provide information from the retina. (See ***Figure 8.10.***)

As we saw earlier, pulses of light reset an animal's circadian rhythms. So do pulses of electrical stimulation delivered directly to the SCN, or injections of an excitatory amino acid (Rusak and Groos, 1982; Meijer, van der Zee, and Dietz, 1988). Thus, the effects of a zeitgeber do take place in this nucleus.

How does the SCN control drinking, eating, sleep cycles, and hormone secretion? Neurons of the SCN project caudally to the midbrain and to other hypothalamic nuclei, dorsally to other diencephalic regions, and rostrally to other hypothalamic nuclei and to the septum. If all of these connections are severed by large semicircular knife cuts around most of the SCN, circadian rhythms are disrupted (Meijer and Rietveld, 1989).

Evidence also suggests that some of the control of the SCN over the rest of the brain may be mediated by the secretion of neuromodulators. Lehman et al. (1987) destroyed the SCN and then transplanted a new set of suprachiasmatic nuclei in their place, obtained from donor animals. The grafts succeeded in reestablishing circadian rhythms, even though very few efferent connections were observed. Ralph, Foster, Davis, and Menaker (1990) found that such transplants could establish circadian rhythms within six or seven days. Thus, either the SCN needs very few connections with the rest of the brain to exert its control, or that control is mediated through the secretion of neuromodulators.

EVIDENCE THAT CIRCADIAN RHYTHMS ORIGINATE IN THE SCN

Obviously, the SCN is the crucial element in the generation of circadian rhythms. And yet the evidence presented so far does not prove that the cycles *originate* there; it is conceivable that they could originate elsewhere, be passed on to the SCN, and from there be distributed to the rest of the brain. But as it turns out, the SCN *is* the source of the rhythms.

A study by Schwartz and Gainer (1977) nicely demonstrated day-night fluctuations in the activity of the SCN. These investigators injected rats with radioactive 2-deoxyglucose (2-DG). As you will recall, this chemical is structurally similar to ordinary glucose; thus, it is taken up by cells that are metabolically active. However, it cannot be utilized, nor can it leave the cell. Therefore, metabolically active cells will accumulate radioactivity.

The investigators injected some rats with radioactive 2-DG during the day and injected others at night. The animals were then killed, and autoradiographs of cross sections through the brain were prepared. Figure 8.11 shows photographs of two of these cross sections. Note the evidence of radioactivity (and hence a high metabolic rate) in the SCN of the brain that was injected during the day (*left*). (See ***Figure 8.11.***)

Schwartz and his colleagues (Schwartz, Reppert, Eagan, and Moore-Ede, 1983) found a similar pattern of activity in the SCN of squirrel monkeys, which are diurnal animals (active during the day). That is, the metabolic activity of the SCN was high during the day and low during the night. These results suggest that differences in the SCN are not what determine whether an animal is nocturnal or diurnal. The SCN keeps track of day and night, but it is up to mechanisms located elsewhere in the brain to determine when the animal will be active.

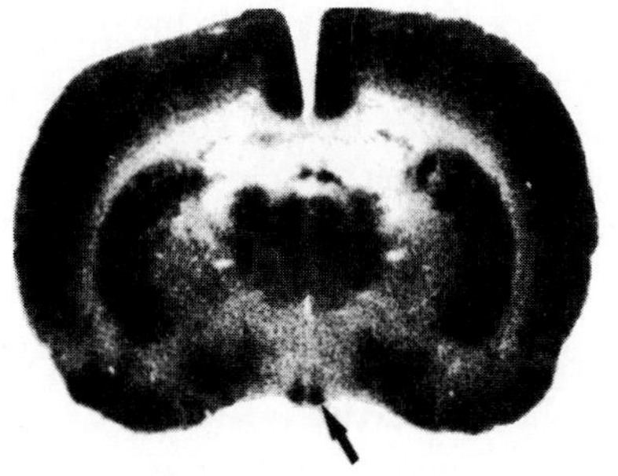
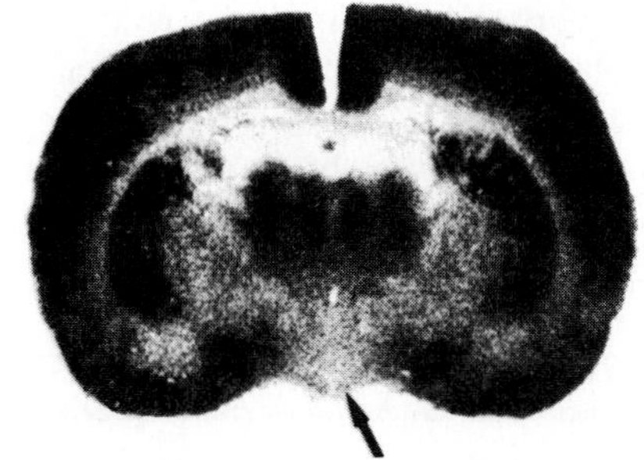

FIGURE 8.11

Autoradiographs of transverse sections through the brains of rats that had been injected with carbon 14-labeled 2-deoxyglucose during the day (*left*) and the night (*right*). The dark region at the base of the brain (*arrows*) indicates increased metabolic activity of the suprachiasmatic nuclei. (From Schwartz, W.J., and Gainer, H. *Science*, 1977, *197*, 1089-1091. Copyright 1977 by the American Association for the Advancement of Science.)

THE NATURE OF THE CLOCK

All clocks must have a time base. Mechanical clocks use flywheels or pendulums; electronic clocks use quartz crystals. The SCN, too, must contain a physiological mechanism that parses time into units. So far, we do not know what this mechanism is.

The "ticking" of the biological clock within the SCN could involve interactions of circuits of neurons, or it could be intrinsic to individual neurons themselves. Evidence suggests the latter—that each neuron contains a clock. Schwartz, Gross, and Morton (1987) continuously infused TTX (tetrodotoxin) into the SCN. This drug prevents action potentials by blocking voltage-dependent sodium channels and thus prevents neurons from communicating with each other. The drug abolished circadian rhythms. However, it did not appear to stop the "ticking" of the individual cells; when the infusions were stopped, the animals' circadian rhythms continued as if the clock had been running the whole time. That is, the clock was still keeping the correct time of day.

EVIDENCE FOR OTHER BIOLOGICAL CLOCKS

The SCN is not the only biological clock in the mammalian nervous system. For example, the basic rest-activity cycle (which controls the occurrence of REM sleep) is considerably shorter than 24 hours; in humans, it has a 90-minute period.

Although the SCN has an intrinsic rhythm of approximately 24 hours, it plays a role in much longer rhythms. Male hamsters show annual rhythms of testosterone secretion, which appear to be based upon the amount of light that occurs each day. Their breeding season begins as the day length increases and ends when it decreases. Lesions of the SCN abolish these annual breeding cycles; the animals' testes then secrete testosterone all year (Rusak and Morin, 1976). Possibly, the lesions disrupt these annual cycles because they destroy the 24-hour clock against which the daily light period is measured to determine the season. That is, if the light period is considerably shorter than 12 hours, the season is winter; if it is considerably longer than 12 hours, the season is summer.

▶*INTERIM SUMMARY*◀

Our daily lives are characterized by cycles in physical activity, sleep, body temperature, secretion of hormones, and many other physiological changes. Circadian rhythms, those with a period of approximately one day, are controlled by biological clocks in the brain. The principal biological clock appears to be located in the suprachiasmatic nuclei of the hypothalamus; lesions of these nuclei disrupt most circadian rhythms, and the activity of neurons located there correlates

with the day-night cycle. Light serves as a zeitgeber for most circadian rhythms. That is, the biological clocks tend to run a bit slow, with a period of approximately 25 hours. The sight of sunlight in the morning is conveyed from the retina to the SCN, resetting the clock to the start of a new cycle. We do not know how biological clocks keep time, although we do know that individual neurons, rather than circuits of neurons, are responsible for the "ticks." ▲

PHYSIOLOGICAL MECHANISMS OF SLEEP AND WAKING

So far, I have discussed the nature of sleep, its functions, problems associated with it, and the control of biological rhythms. Now it is time to examine what researchers have discovered about the physiological mechanisms that are responsible for the behavior of sleep. But before I do so, I must emphasize that sleep does not occur simply because neurons get tired and begin to fire more slowly. Like other behaviors, sleep occurs when certain neural circuits become *active.*

Chemical Control of Sleep

As we have seen, sleep is *regulated;* that is, if an organism is deprived of slow-wave sleep or REM sleep, the organism will make up at least part of the missed sleep when permitted to do so. In addition, the amount of slow-wave sleep that a person obtains during a daytime nap is deducted from the amount of slow-wave sleep he or she obtains the next night (Karacan, Williams, Finley, and Hursch, 1970). These facts suggest that some physiological mechanism monitors the amount of sleep that an organism receives. What might this mechanism be?

The most obvious explanation would be that the body produces either *sleep-promoting substances* during wakefulness or *wakefulness-promoting* substances during sleep. For example, a sleep-promoting substance might accumulate in the blood during wakefulness and be destroyed during sleep. The longer someone is awake, the longer he or she has to sleep in order to deactivate this substance. Obviously, because slow-wave sleep and REM sleep are mostly independent of each other, there would have to be two substances, one for each stage of sleep. Alternatively, sleep could be regulated by a *wakefulness-promoting* substance. This substance would be used up during wakefulness and be manufactured only during sleep. A *decline* in the blood level of this substance would cause sleepiness.

Evidence suggests that these hypotheses are false. De Andres, Gutierrez-Rivas, Nava, and Reinoso-Suarez (1976) attached a second head to a dog and found that the two brains slept independently. If sleep and wakefulness were controlled by factors present in the blood, one would expect that the sleep cycles of the two brains would be synchronized. (Of course, the second head was neurally isolated from the rest of the body and had no control of the animal's behavior.) But perhaps the strongest evidence against a hypothetical blood-borne sleep-promoting (or wakefulness-promoting) substance comes from the sleep of dolphins and porpoises. As we saw earlier, the cerebral hemispheres of these animals sleep at different times (Mukhametov, 1984). If their sleep were controlled by *blood-borne* chemicals, the hemispheres should sleep at the same time.

These observations suggest that if sleep is controlled by chemicals, these chemicals are produced within the brain and remain there. As we saw, evidence seems to support the hypothesis that slow-wave sleep serves as a period of rest and recuperation for the cerebral hemispheres. Perhaps chemicals produced by the brain serve as neuromodulators, activating neural circuits responsible for sleep (or deactivating circuits necessary for wakefulness).

In a fifty-two-page article that cites over four hundred papers, Borbély and Tobler (1989) report that the search for sleep-promoting substances within the brain has not yet yielded unambiguous results. But we should not conclude that because a sleep-promoting (or wakefulness-promoting) substance has not yet been unambiguously identified means that there is none to be found; after all, there are undoubtedly many thousands of chemicals present in the fluid that bathes the cells of the brain. The fact that sleep is regulated means that *something* has to keep track of the sleep debt, and I find it difficult to imagine what that something would be if it were not a chemical. Perhaps it is a chemical that accumulates *inside* individual neurons in the brain; if so, it will probably take some time before investigators succeed in identifying it.

Neural Control of Arousal

As we have seen, sleep is not a unitary condition but consists of several different stages with very different characteristics. Wakefulness, too, is nonuniform; sometimes, we are alert and attentive, and sometimes, we fail to notice much about what is happening around us. Of course, sleepiness has an effect on wakefulness; if we are fighting to stay awake, the struggle might impair our ability to concentrate on other things. But everyday observations suggest that even when we are not sleepy, our alertness can vary. For example, when we observe something very interesting (or frightening, or simply surprising), we feel ourselves become more activated and aware of our surroundings.

THE RETICULAR FORMATION

Experimental evidence suggests that the brain stem contains circuits of neurons that can increase an animal's level of alertness and activation—what is commonly referred to as *arousal.* In 1949 Moruzzi and Magoun found that electrical stimulation of the brain stem reticular formation produced arousal. The reticular formation, which occupies the central core of the brain stem, receives collateral axons from ascending sensory pathways. Presumably, sensory input, the event that normally produces arousal, activates the reticular formation by means of these collateral axons. The activated reticular formation then arouses the cerebral cortex by means of direct axonal connections and by connections relayed through various nuclei of the thalamus. (See ***Figures 8.12 and 8.13.***)

Recording studies soon provided evidence that supported the effects of electrical stimulation. Multiple-unit activity (the action potentials of a large population of neurons located near the tip of the recording electrode) showed a relation between arousal and the firing rate of neurons in the reticular formation.

The reticular formation is an extensive and complex brain structure, and once its role in arousal was well accepted, investigators attempted to find out the specific location of the arousal mechanisms. They began to study *single-unit* activity in freely moving cats, which allows for maximum specificity. However, careful study of the activity patterns of individual neurons failed to support the hypothesis that the reticular formation performs a general arousal function. Investigators found, instead, that the activity of individual neurons was closely related to specific movements of the eyes, ears, face, head, body, and limbs (Siegel, 1979, 1983). Their response rate was not related to general levels of arousal or to sleep-waking cycles.

FIGURE 8.12

A midsagittal view of a cat brain, showing the reticular formation and its hypothesized role in arousal.

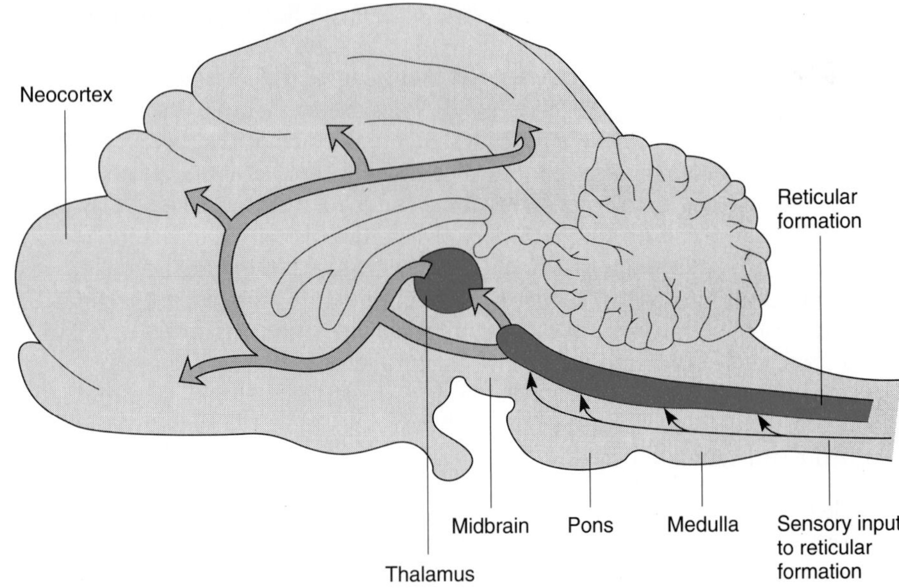

Siegel (1979, 1983) suggests two reasons for the discrepancy between his results and those of previous studies. First, many of the earlier studies employed animals who were anesthetized or restrained; obviously, it is impossible to observe a relation between movements and single-unit activity in animals that cannot move. Second, the earlier studies that employed freely moving animals obtained multiple-unit records, which average the activity of many neurons. If different groups of neurons are active during different types of movements, then the population *as a whole* may respond nonspecifically, which may lead the investigator to conclude erroneously that *all* of them are responding nonspecifically. For example, suppose that an investigator finds that multiple-unit activity increases when a cat anticipates receiving a painful foot shock or receiving some food. Because both events can be thought of as "arousing," the investigator may conclude that the units mediate nonspecific arousal. However, the results could actually have been produced by two different groups of neurons: one

FIGURE 8.13

The human brain stem, showing the location of the locus coeruleus and the reticular formation.

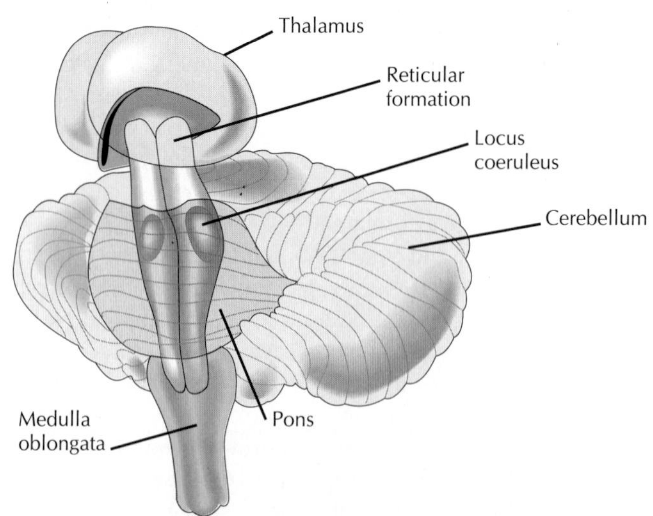

group that fires during ear flattening (a response that cats commonly make when they are fearful) and another group that fires during the postural adjustments the cat makes in anticipation of obtaining food.

THE NORADRENERGIC SYSTEM OF THE LOCUS COERULEUS

Although the reticular formation as a whole appears to be primarily involved in the control of movement rather than arousal, a small nucleus found there does appear to have a profound effect on arousal. Investigators have long known that catecholamine agonists such as amphetamine produce arousal and sleeplessness. These effects appear to be mediated by the noradrenergic system of the **locus coeruleus,** located in the dorsal pons. Neurons of the locus coeruleus send axons that branch widely, terminating in the neocortex, hippocampus, thalamus, cerebellar cortex, pons, and medulla; thus, they potentially affect widespread and important regions of the brain. (See ***Figure 8.13.***)

locus coeruleus

Aston-Jones and Bloom (1981a) recorded from noradrenergic neurons of the locus coeruleus across the sleep-waking cycle in unrestrained rats. As Figure 8.14 shows, these neurons exhibited an excellent relation to behavioral arousal. Note the decline in firing rate before and during sleep and the abrupt increase when the animal wakes. The rate of firing of neurons in the locus coeruleus falls almost to zero during REM sleep and increases dramatically when the animal wakes. As we shall see later in this chapter, these facts suggest that these neurons play a role in controlling REM sleep. (See ***Figure 8.14.***)

Aston-Jones and Bloom (1981a, 1981b) found that when they aroused the animals by sudden environmental stimuli during sleep or quiet wakefulness, the noradrenergic neurons suddenly increased their activity. Thus, these neurons may well be involved in arousal. However, the firing rate of these neurons was very low while the animals were grooming or drinking sweetened water—activities that are accompanied by a high level of arousal. The authors suggested that the activity of noradrenergic neurons showed a better correlation with *vigilance* than with arousal. That is, at times when the animals were sensitive to external stimuli, the neurons were found to be firing at a high rate. While an animal is grooming or drinking, it is certainly aroused and busy, but it is not paying much attention to external stimuli.

Aston-Jones, Ennis, Pieribone, Nickell, and Shipley (1986) used neuroanatomical methods to study the afferent connections of the locus coeruleus, and to their surprise,

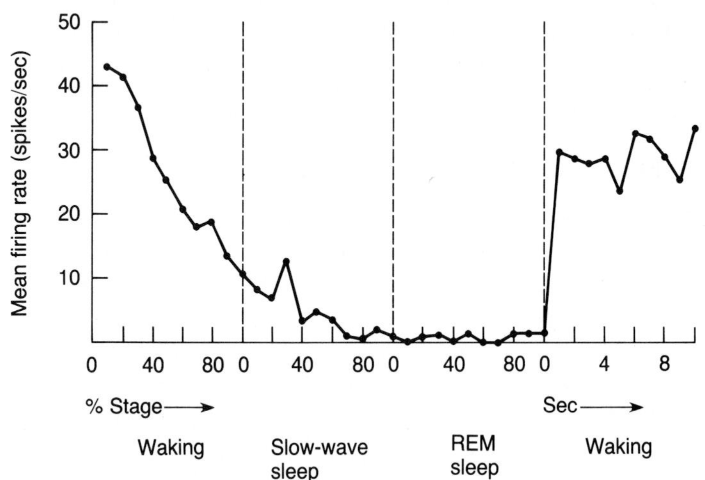

FIGURE 8.14

Activity of noradrenergic neurons in the locus coeruleus of freely moving cats during various stages of sleep and waking. (From Aston-Jones, G., and Bloom, F.E. *The Journal of Neuroscience,* 1981, *1,* 876–886. Copyright 1981, The Society for Neuroscience.)

they found only two significant inputs: a nucleus in the ventrolateral medulla and another in the dorsomedial medulla. Ennis and Aston-Jones (1986, 1988) found that one input excited neurons in the locus coeruleus, while the other inhibited them. Obviously, the next step will be to investigate the sources of input to *these* regions.

Neural Control of Slow-Wave Sleep

Although researchers have made considerable progress in identifying the neural circuits responsible for REM sleep (discussed in the final section of this chapter), relatively little is known about the neural control of slow-wave sleep.

basal forebrain region

Some evidence suggests that the brain stem may play a role in the control of slow-wave sleep, but the most important circuits appears to be located in the **basal forebrain region,** just rostral to the hypothalamus. Nauta (1946) found that destruction of this area produced total insomnia in rats. The animals subsequently fell into a coma and died; the average survival time was only three days. McGinty and Sterman (1968) found that cats reacted somewhat differently; the animals did not become sleepless until several days after the lesion was made. Two of the cats, whose sleep was totally suppressed, died within ten days. Infusions of kainic acid, which destroys cell bodies without damaging axons passing through the region, also suppresses sleep; thus, the neurons of the basal forebrain appear to be important for sleep (Szymusiak and McGinty, 1986b.)

The effects of the lesion experiments are corroborated by the effects of electrical stimulation of the basal forebrain region. Sterman and Clemente (1962a, 1962b) found that electrical stimulation of this region produced signs of drowsiness in the behavior and the EEG of unanesthetized, freely moving cats. The average latency period between the stimulation and the changes in the EEG was 30 seconds; often the effect was immediate. The animals often subsequently fell asleep. In addition, a recording study by Szymusiak and McGinty (1986a) found that many neurons in the basal forebrain changed their rate of firing when the animals fell asleep.

One part of the basal forebrain, the preoptic area, contains neurons that are involved in temperature regulation. Some of these neurons are directly sensitive to changes in brain temperature, and some receive information from thermosensors located in the skin. Warming of the preoptic area, like electrical stimulation, produces drowsiness and EEG synchrony (Roberts and Robinson, 1969; Benedek, Obal, Lelkes, and Obal, 1982). Thus, a more "natural" stimulation mimics the effects of electrical stimulation. The excessive sleepiness that accompanies a fever may be produced by this mechanism. And perhaps the connections between the preoptic area and thermosensors in the skin account for the drowsiness and lassitude we feel on a hot day.

Neural Control of REM Sleep

PGO wave

As we saw earlier in this chapter, REM sleep consists of desynchronized EEG activity, muscular paralysis, rapid eye movements, and (in humans, at least) increased genital activity. In laboratory animals REM sleep also includes *PGO waves.* **PGO waves** (for *p*ons, *g*eniculate, and *o*ccipital) are the first manifestation of REM sleep. They consist of brief, phasic bursts of electrical activity that originate in the pons and are propagated to the lateral geniculate nuclei and then to the primary visual (occipital) cortex. They can only be seen when electrodes are placed directly into the brain, so they have not been recorded in humans. It seems likely, however, that they occur in our species, too. Figure 8.15 shows the typical onset of REM sleep, recorded in a cat. The first sign of an

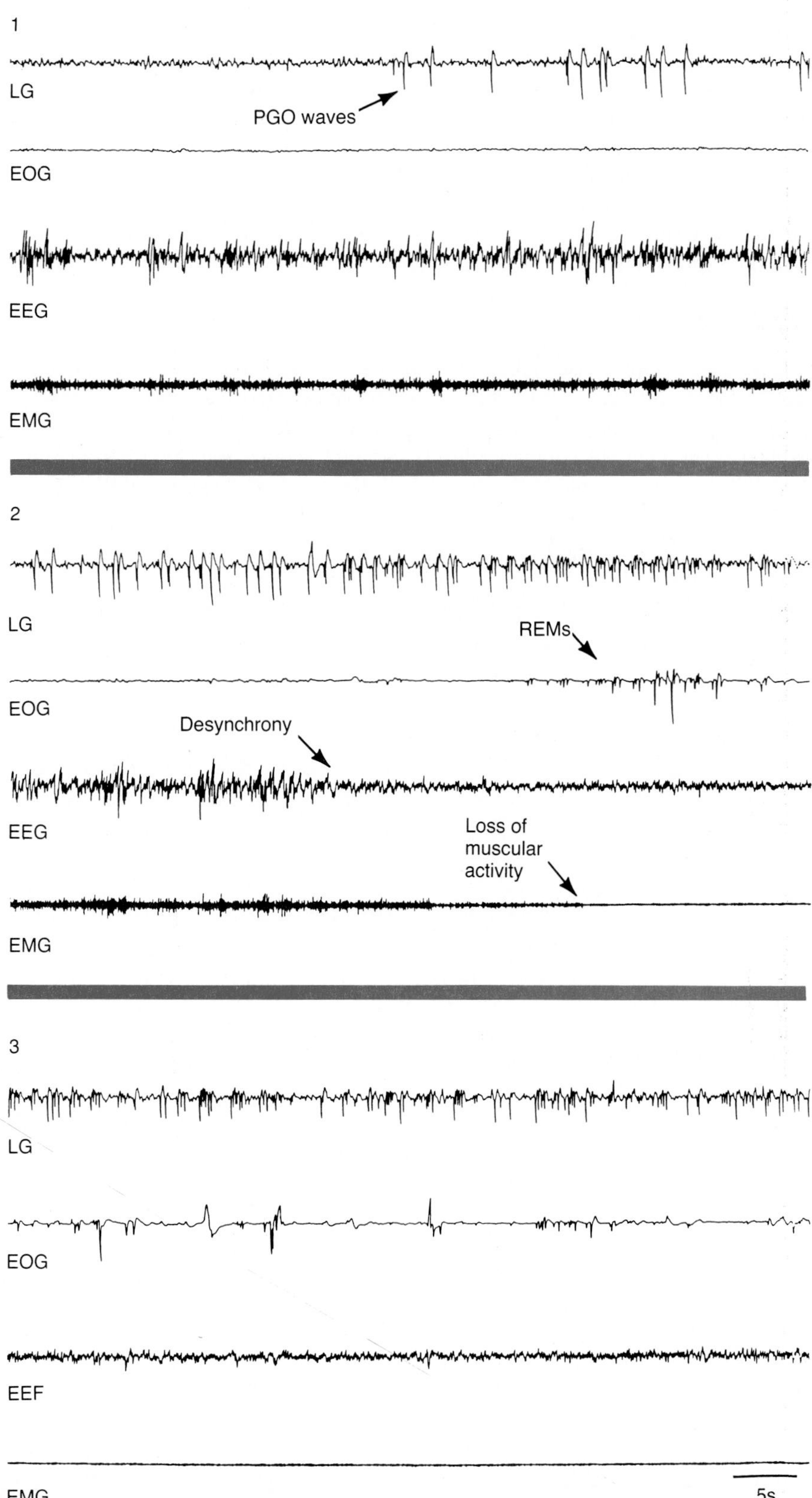

FIGURE 8.15

Onset of REM sleep in a cat. The arrows indicate the onset of PGO waves, EEG desynchrony, loss of muscular activity, and rapid eye movements. LG = lateral geniculate nucleus; EOG = electro-oculogram (eye movements). (Adapted from Steriade, M., Paré, D., Bouhassira, D., Deschênes, M., and Oakson, G. *Journal of Neuroscience,* 1989, *9,* 2215–2229. Reprinted by permission of the Journal of Neuroscience.)

impending bout of REM sleep is the presence of PGO waves—in this case, recorded from electrodes implanted in the lateral geniculate nucleus. Next, the EEG becomes desynchronized, and then muscular activity ceases and rapid eye movements commence. (See ***Figure 8.15.***)

As we shall see, REM sleep is controlled by mechanisms located within the brain stem, primarily within the pons. The executive mechanism (that is, the one whose activity turns on the various components of REM sleep) consists of neurons that secrete acetylcholine. This mechanism is normally inhibited by the serotonergic neurons of the raphe nuclei and the noradrenergic neurons of the locus coeruleus.

ACETYLCHOLINE

Drugs that excite acetylcholinergic synapses facilitate REM sleep. Stoyva and Metcalf (1968) found that people who have been exposed to organophosphate insecticides, which act as acetylcholine agonists, spend an increased time in REM sleep. In a controlled experiment with human subjects, Sitaram, Moore, and Gillin (1978) found that an ACh agonist (arecoline) shortened the interval between periods of REM sleep, and a cholinergic antagonist (scopolamine) lengthened it.

Jasper and Tessier (1969) analyzed the levels of acetylcholine that had been released by terminal buttons in the cat cerebral cortex. The levels were highest during waking and REM sleep and were lowest during slow-wave sleep. This finding suggests

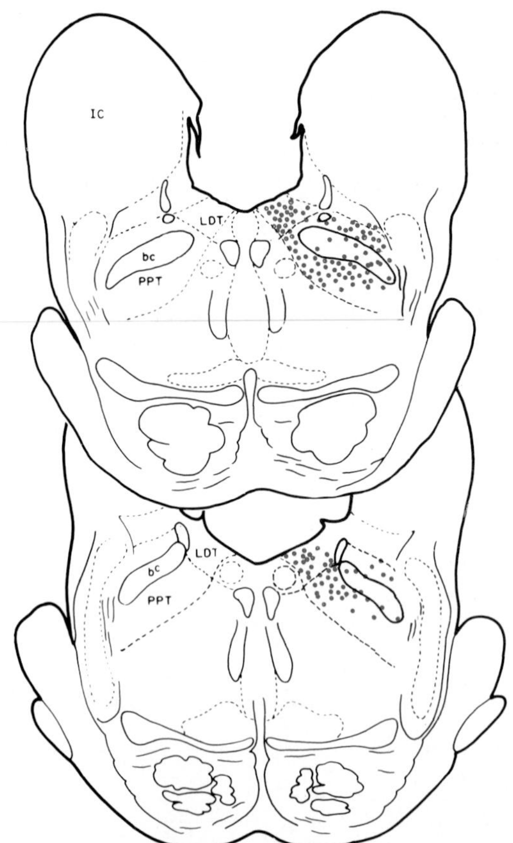

FIGURE 8.16

Acetylcholinergic neurons in the brain stem of the cat (colored circles) as revealed by a stain for choline acetyltransferase. LDT = lateral tegmental nucleus; PPT = pedunculopontine tegmental nucleus; bc = brachium conjunctivum, IC = inferior colliculus. (Adapted from Jones, B.E., and Beaudet, A. *Journal of Comparative Neurology,* 1987, *261,* 15–32. Reprinted by permission of the *Journal of Neuroscience.*)

that acetylcholinergic neurons are responsible for the desynchronized electrical activity seen during waking and REM sleep.

The brain contains several acetylcholinergic pathways. The one that plays a role in REM sleep is found in the dorsolateral pons, primarily in the ***pedunculopontine tegmental nucleus*** (PPT) and ***laterodorsal tegmental nucleus*** (LDT) (Jones and Beaudet, 1987). These neurons project to several regions of the forebrain, including the thalamus, hippocampus, hypothalamus, and cingulate cortex.

If a small amount of an acetylcholinergic agonist is infused into the dorsolateral pons, the animal will exhibit PGO waves alone, muscular paralysis alone, or all the signs of REM sleep, depending on the location of the infusion (Katayama et al., 1986; Callaway et al., 1987). Figure 8.16 shows two drawings through the brain stem of a cat, prepared by Jones and Beaudet (1987). The location of acetylcholinergic cell bodies is shown by colored circles. As you can see by comparing the labels on the left side with the filled circles on the right, most of these neurons are found in the LDT and the PPT. (See ***Figure 8.16.***)

Destruction of the region of the pons that contains these acetylcholinergic neurons drastically reduces REM sleep. Webster and Jones (1988) made lesions by infusing kainic acid into this region. They found that the amount of REM sleep that remained was directly related to the number of cholinergic neurons that were spared. Figure 8.17 contains a photomicrograph through the pons of a normal cat (a) and a cat with a kainic acid lesion (b). Acetylcholinergic neurons show up as black granules. As you can see, very few of them remain in the cat with the lesion. (See ***Figure 8.17.***)

If the acetylcholinergic neurons in the dorsolateral pons are responsible for the onset of REM sleep, how do they control each of its components, PGO waves, rapid eye

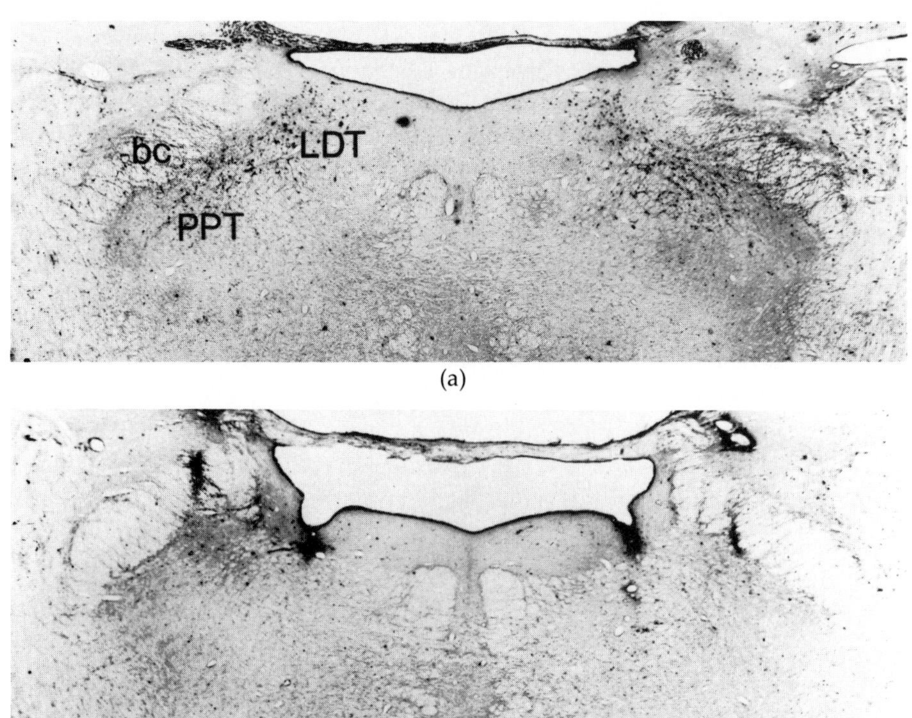

FIGURE 8.17

Destruction of acetylcholine-secreting neurons in the pons. (a) A section through the pons of an intact brain. (b) A section through the pons after infusions of kainic acid. Acetylcholine-secreting neurons show up as black spots in (a). LDT = lateral tegmental nucleus; PPT = pedunculopontine tegmental nucleus; bc = brachium conjunctivum. (From Jones, B.E., and Webster, H.H. *Brain Research,* 1988, *451,* 13–32. Reprinted with permission.)

movements, cortical desynchrony, and muscular paralysis? Sakai and Jouvet (1980) found that PGO waves appear to be controlled by connections between the pons and the lateral geniculate nucleus. Webster and Jones (1988) suggest that the control of rapid eye movements may be achieved by projections from the dorsolateral pons to the tectum, and the control of cortical desynchrony by projections to several thalamic nuclei that have widespread projections to the cerebral cortex.

The muscular paralysis that accompanies REM sleep is a particularly interesting phenomenon. As we saw earlier, some patients with lesions in the brain stem fail to become paralyzed during REM sleep and thus act out their dreams. (As you will recall, the phenomenon is called *REM without atonia.*) The same thing happens—that is, assuming that cats dream—when a lesion is placed just caudal to the acetylcholinergic neurons of the dorsolateral pons. Jouvet (1972) described this phenomenon.

> To a naive observer, the cat, which is standing, looks awake since it may attack unknown enemies, play with an absent mouse, or display flight behavior. There are orienting movements of the head or eyes toward imaginary stimuli, although the animal does not respond to visual or auditory stimuli. These extraordinary episodes . . . are a good argument that "dreaming" occurs during [REM sleep] in the cat. (Jouvet, 1972, pp. 236–237)

magnocellular nucleus

Jouvet's lesions destroyed the axons of neurons responsible for the muscular paralysis that occurs during REM sleep. These axons belong to acetylcholinergic neurons in the dorsolateral pons that travel caudally to the **magnocellular nucleus,** located in the medial medulla (Sakai, 1980). Neurons in the magnocellular nucleus send axons to the spinal cord, where they form inhibitory synapses with motor neurons (Morales, Boxer, and Chase, 1987).

The evidence for this pathway is strong. Kanamori, Sakai, and Jouvet (1980) recorded from single neurons in the magnocellular nucleus in unrestrained cats and found that they became active during REM sleep. Sakai (1980) found that electrical stimulation of this nucleus caused paralysis in awake cats, and Schenkel and Siegel (1989) found that lesions produced REM without atonia.

The fact that our brains contain an elaborate mechanism whose sole function is to keep us paralyzed while we dream—that is, to prevent us from acting out our dreams—suggests that the motor components of dreams are as important as the sensory components. Perhaps the practice our motor system gets during REM sleep helps us improve our performance of behaviors we have learned that day. The inhibition of the motor neurons in the spinal cord prevents the movements being practiced from actually occurring, with the exception of a few harmless twitches of the hands and feet.

SEROTONIN AND NOREPINEPHRINE

As you will recall from the earlier discussion of narcolepsy, serotonergic and noradrenergic agonists have inhibitory effects on REM sleep. Thus, it appears that

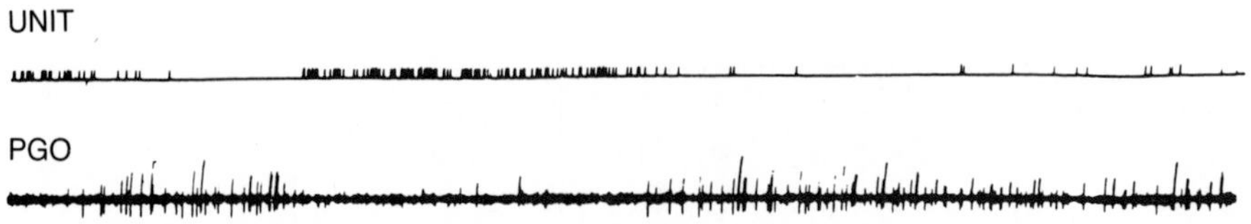

FIGURE 8.18

Activity of a single unit in the dorsal raphe nucleus. Note that the activity is *inversely* related to the occurrence of PGO waves, the first sign of REM sleep. (Adapted from Lydic, R., McCarley, R.W., and Hobson, J.A. *Brain Research,* 1983, *274,* 365–370.)

UNIT

PGO

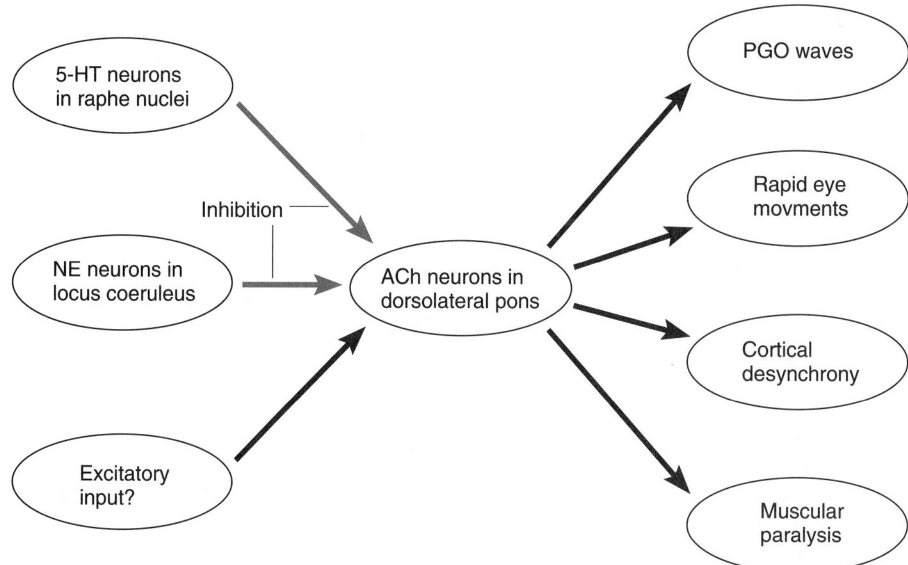

FIGURE 8.19

Interactions between serotonergic, noradrenergic, and acetylcholinergic neurons in the control of REM sleep.

noradrenergic and serotonergic neurons play an inhibitory role in REM sleep. Evidence for this inhibitory role is shown in Figure 8.18, which illustrates the very close linkage between the activity of a single serotonergic neuron in the dorsal raphe nucleus and the occurrence of PGO waves, the first manifestation of REM sleep (Lydic, McCarley, and Hobson, 1983). Note that the PGO waves occur only when the serotonergic neuron is silent. (See ***Figure 8.18.***)

So far, we have seen that REM sleep occurs when acetylcholinergic neurons in the dorsolateral pons become active. That event occurs when serotonergic and noradrenergic neurons in the raphe nuclei and the locus coeruleus become silent. In fact, acetylcholinergic neurons receive inhibitory inputs from both noradrenergic and serotonergic neurons. (See ***Figure 8.19.***) But what makes the noradrenergic and serotonergic neurons become silent when it is time to engage in REM sleep? And is there an excitatory input to the dorsolateral pons as well as the inhibitory ones, which *increases* at the beginning of REM sleep? Where is the pacemaker that controls the cycles of REM and slow-wave sleep, and how is this connected to the neurons in the dorsolateral pons? Research efforts will probably answer these questions in the next few years.

▶*INTERIM SUMMARY*◀

The fact that the amount of sleep is regulated suggests that sleep-promoting substances (produced during wakefulness) or wakefulness-promoting substances (produced during sleep) may exist. The sleeping pattern of the dolphin brain and studies with artificial or natural Siamese twins suggest that such substances do not accumulate in the blood. They may accumulate in the brain, but so far, attempts to find them have not been successful.

Contrary to earlier beliefs, the reticular formation is involved in movement, not in generalized arousal. However, the noradrenergic neurons of the locus coeruleus do seem to be involved in controlling vigilance. This nucleus has only two inputs, one inhibitory and one excitatory, so we can anticipate that research will discover the mechanisms that control its activity.

Slow-wave sleep is promoted by the basal forebrain region, but so far, no one has been able to discover a more comprehensive set of neural circuits that explain just what role this region plays. REM sleep occurs when the activity of acetylcholinergic neurons in the dorsolateral pons increases; some of these neurons control PGO waves, some initiate cortical arousal, and others produce rapid eye movements. Atonia (muscular paralysis that prevents our acting out our dreams) is produced by a group of acetylcholinergic neurons located near the locus coeruleus that activates neurons in the magnocellular nucleus of the medulla, which in turn produce inhibition of motor neurons in the spinal cord.

The noradrenergic neurons of the locus coeruleus and the serotonergic neurons of the raphe nuclei have inhibitory effects on the acetylcholinergic neurons of the pons that are responsible for REM sleep. Bouts of REM sleep begin only after the activity of the noradrenergic and serotonergic neurons ceases; whether this is the only event that triggers REM sleep or whether direct excitation of acetylcholinergic neurons also occurs is not yet known. ▲

EPILOGUE: Application ►

Even though we are still not sure why REM sleep occurs, the elaborate neural circuitry involved with its control indicates that it must be important. Nature would probably not invent this circuitry if it did not do something useful. Michael's attacks of sleep paralysis, hypnagogic hallucinations, and cataplexy, described in the Prologue, occurred when two of the aspects of REM sleep (paralysis and dreaming) occurred at inappropriate times. Normally, the brain mechanisms responsible for these phenomena are inhibited during waking; perhaps this inhibition is too weak in Michael's case.

As we saw, researchers have proposed four categories of hypothetical explanations for REM sleep: vigilance, learning, species-typical reprogramming, and brain development. Each of these explanations has some support, and possibly, REM sleep performs more than one function. But what about the subjective aspect of REM sleep — dreaming? Is there some special purpose served by those vivid, storylike hallucinations we have while we sleep, or are dreams just irrelevant side effects of more important things going on in the brain?

Since ancient times, people have regarded dreams as important, using them to prophesy the future, decide whether to go to war, or determine the guilt or innocence of a person accused of a crime. In this century Sigmund Freud proposed a very influential theory about dreaming. He said that dreams arise out of inner conflicts between unconscious desires (primarily sexual ones) and prohibitions against acting out these desires, which we learn from society. According to Freud, although all dreams represent unfulfilled wishes, their contents are disguised. The *latent content* of the dream (from the Latin word for "hidden") is transformed into the *manifest content* (the actual story line or plot). Taken at face value, the manifest content is innocuous, but a knowledgeable psychoanalyst can recognize unconscious desires disguised as symbols in the dream. For example, climbing a set of stairs might represent sexual intercourse. The problem with Freud's theory is that it is not disprovable; even if it is wrong, a psychoanalyst can always provide a plausible interpretation of a dream that reveals hidden conflicts, disguised in obscure symbols.

Many sleep researchers — especially those interested in the biological aspects of dreaming — disagree with Freud and suggest alternative explanations. For example, Hobson (1988) suggests that the brain activation that occurs during REM sleep leads to hallucinations that we try to make sense of by creating a more or less plausible story. As you learned in this chapter,

REM sleep occurs when a circuit of acetylcholinergic neurons in the dorsolateral pons becomes active, stimulating rapid eye movements and cortical arousal. The visual system is especially active. So is the motor system—in fact, we have a mechanism that paralyzes us to prevent the activity of the motor system from causing us to get out of bed and do something that might harm us. (As we saw, people who suffer from REM without atonia actually *do* act out their dreams and sometimes injure themselves. On occasion, they have even attacked their spouses while dreaming they were fighting with someone.)

Research indicates that the two systems of the brain that are most active—the visual system and the motor system—account for most of the sensations that occur during dreams. Many dreams are silent, but almost all are full of visual images. In addition, many dreams contains sensations of movements, which are probably caused by feedback from the activity of the motor system. Very few dreamers report tactile sensations, smells, or tastes. Hobson, a wine lover, reported that although he has drunk wine in his dreams, he has never experienced any taste or smell. (He reported this fact rather wistfully; I suspect that he would have appreciated the opportunity to taste a fine wine without having to open one of his own bottles.) Why are these sensations absent? Is it because our "hidden desires" involve only sight and movement, or is it because the neural activation that occurs during REM sleep simply does not involve other systems to a very great extent? Hobson suggests the latter, and I agree with him.

Several experiments have found that the particular eye movements that a person makes during a dream correspond reasonably well with the content of a dream; that is, the eye movements are those that one would expect a person to make if the imaginary events were really occurring (Dement, 1974). Similarly, we know from reports of people who suffer from REM without atonia that the activity in their brain's motor systems corresponds to the imaginary movements they make while dreaming. A plausible explanation for dreaming, then, is that periodic arousal of the REM sleep mechanism (for reasons that we still do not completely understand) activates the visual system and produces both eye movements and images. The particular images often incorporate memories of episodes that have occurred recently or of things that a person has been thinking about lately; presumably, the circuits responsible for these memories are more excitable because they have recently been active. At the same time, the motor system is activated in ways that correspond to the visual images. This idea is not a new one; Vold (1896) suggested that during dreaming "the nervous signals produced by the motor states go not only to the motor cortex but also to the visual centers to produce an image."

Hobson suggests that although the activation of these brain mechanisms produces fragmentary images, our brains try to tie these images together and make sense of them. As he puts it, the brain seems to obey the following rule: "Integrate all signals received into the most meaningful story possible; however farcical the result, believe it; and then forget it" (Hobson, 1988, p. 214). In fact, although dreams are often bizarre—they may contain sudden jumps in place or time and characters who can change their identity or appear or disappear without explanation—we invariably accept these impossible or illogical events at face value. Rarely does a dreamer say, "No, this

can't be; I must be dreaming." And then, as soon as the dream is over, we forget it. Most sleep researchers believe that the dreams we do manage to remember are those that we awakened from. As Hobson suggests, the activity of noradrenergic and serotonergic neurons may be necessary for stamping-in the memories of dreams — and these neurons are silent while we are dreaming.

We still do not know whether the particular topics we dream about are somehow related to the functions that dreams serve, or whether the purposes of REM sleep are fulfilled regardless of the plots of our dreams. Given that we do not really know why we dream at all, this uncertainty is not surprising. But the rapid progress being made in most fields of neuroscience suggests that we will have some answers in the not-too-distant future. ▲

KEY CONCEPTS

A Physiological and Behavioral Description

- Sleep consists of slow-wave sleep, divided into four stages, and REM sleep. Dreaming occurs during REM sleep.

Why Do We Sleep?

- Sleep may occur because it was an adaptive behavior in the history of our species or because it permits the body to repair itself after a day of wear and tear. Evidence suggests that slow-wave sleep permits the cerebral cortex to rest and that REM sleep may be involved somehow in learning.

Disorders of Sleep

- People sometimes suffer from such sleep disorders as insomnia, sleep apnea, narcolepsy, REM without atonia, bedwetting, sleepwalking, or night terrors. The symptoms of narcolepsy (cataplexy, sleep paralysis, and hypnagogic hallucinations) can be understood as components of REM sleep occurring at inappropriate times.

Biological Clocks

- Circadian rhythms are largely under the control of a mechanism located in the suprachiasmatic nucleus. They are synchronized by the day-night light cycle.

Physiological Mechanisms of Sleep and Waking

- The brain stem contains an arousal mechanism, previously thought to be the reticular formation, but probably largely confined to the noradrenergic system originating in the locus coeruleus. The basal forebrain region contains a mechanism that appears to be necessary for sleep.
- REM sleep is produced by the activity of acetylcholinergic neurons in the dorsolateral pons, which are normally inhibited by both noradrenergic and serotonergic synapses. The circuit responsible for the muscular paralysis that accompanies REM sleep has been located, and damage to it is responsible for REM without atonia.

NEW TERMS

alpha activity **p. 242**
basal forebrain region **p. 268**
basic rest-activity cycle **p. 245**
beta activity **p. 242**
cataplexy **p. 257**
circadian rhythm **p. 260**
delta activity **p. 243**
drug dependency insomnia **p. 256**
electromyogram **p. 241**
electro-oculogram **p. 241**
hypnagogic hallucination **p. 257**
locus coeruleus **p. 267**
magnocellular nucleus **p. 272**
narcolepsy **p. 257**
non-REM sleep **p. 243**
PGO wave **p. 268**
rebound phenomenon **p. 253**
REM sleep **p. 243**
REM without atonia **p. 258**
sleep apnea **p. 256**
sleep attack **p. 257**
sleep paralysis **p. 257**
slow-wave sleep **p. 243**
suprachiasmatic nucleus **p. 261**
theta activity **p. 243**
zeitgeber **p. 261**

SUGGESTED READINGS

Cohen, D.B. *Sleep and Dreaming: Origins, Nature and Functions.* Oxford, England: Pergamon Press, 1979.

Horne, J. *Why We Sleep: The Functions of Sleep in Humans and Other Mammals.* Oxford, England: Oxford University Press, 1988.

Kryger, M.H., Roth, T., and Dement, W.C. *Principles and Practices of Sleep Disorders in Medicine.* New York: Saunders, 1989.

Moore-Ede, M.C., Sulzman, F.M., and Fuller, C.A. *The Clocks That Time Us.* Cambridge, Mass.: Harvard University Press, 1982.

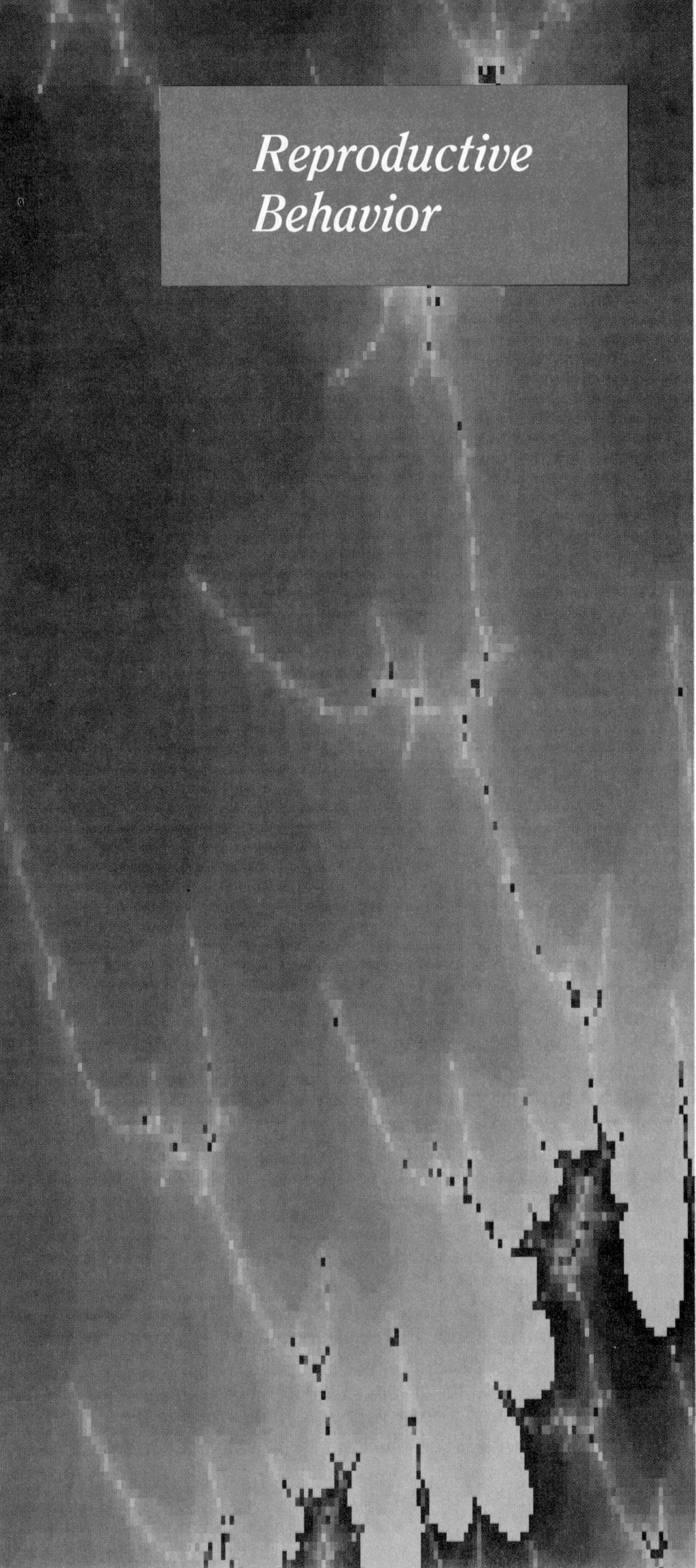

9 Reproductive Behavior

CHAPTER OUTLINE

enlarged breasts and widened hips or a beard and deep voice, do not appear until puberty. Without seeing genitals, we must guess the sex of a prepubescent child from his or her haircut and clothing; the bodies of young boys and girls are rather similar. However, at puberty the gonads are stimulated to produce their hormones, and these hormones cause the person to mature sexually. The onset of puberty occurs when cells in the hypothalamus secrete a hormone that stimulates the anterior pituitary gland to secrete two **gonadotropic hormones.** The gonadotropic ("gonad-changing") hormones stimulate the gonads to produce *their* hormones, which are ultimately responsible for sexual maturation.

gonadotropic hormone

The two gonadotropic hormones are **follicle-stimulating hormone** (FSH), and **luteinizing hormone** (LH), named for the effects they produce in the female (production of a *follicle* and its subsequent *luteinization,* to be described in the next section of this chapter). However, the same hormones are produced in the male, where they stimulate the testes to produce sperms and to secrete testosterone. If male and female pituitary glands are exchanged in rats, the ovaries and testes respond perfectly to the hormones secreted by the new glands (Harris and Jacobsohn, 1951–1952).

follicle-stimulating hormone
luteinizing hormone

In response to the gonadotropic hormones (usually called *gonadotropins*), the gonads secrete sex steroid hormones. At puberty young men's testes begin to secrete **testosterone**; this hormone causes their muscles to develop, their facial hair to grow, and their voices to deepen. Young women's ovaries secrete estradiol, which is the most important **estrogen,** or female sex hormone. **Estradiol** causes women's breasts to grow and their pelvises to widen, and it produces changes in the layer of fat beneath the skin and in the texture of the skin itself.

testosterone

estrogen estradiol

This last change explains why older women, whose ovaries no longer secrete hormones, often use skin creams that contain estrogens. In one rather bizarre case a six-year-old girl who had begun to show signs of premature puberty was found to have been eating her grandmother's skin cream. The cream contained enough estrogen to stimulate the changes that normally occur several years later.

Table 9.1 lists the categories of sex hormones, along with their principal effects on reproductive physiology. (See ***Table 9.1.***)

▲ TABLE 9.1 ▲

Classification of Sex Steroid Hormones

Class	*Principal Hormone in Humans (Where Produced)*	*Examples of Effects*
Androgens	Testosterone (testes)	Maturation of male genitalia; production of sperms, growth of facial, pubic, and axillary hair; muscular development; enlargement of larynx; inhibition of bone growth
	Androstenedione (adrenal glands)	In females, growth of pubic and axillary hair; less important than testosterone in males
Estrogens	Estradiol (ovaries)	Maturation of female genitalia; growth of breasts; alterations in fat deposits; growth of uterine lining; inhibition of bone growth
Gestagens	Progesterone (ovaries)	Maintenance of uterine lining

▶*INTERIM SUMMARY*◀

Gender is determined by the sex chromosomes: XX produces a female, and XY produces a male. Males are produced by the action of a gene on the Y chromosome that causes the primordial gonads to become testes. The testes secrete two kinds hormones that cause a male to develop. Androgens stimulate the development of the Wolffian system (masculinization), and Müllerian-inhibiting substance suppresses the development of the Müllerian system (defeminization). Without these hormones, the Müllerian system develops into the female internal sex organs. The external genitalia, too, develop the female form in the absence of sex hormones; androgens cause them to develop the male form. Thus, by default, the body is female ("Nature's impulse . . ."); only by the actions of testicular hormones does it become male. Masculinization and defeminization are referred to as *organizational* effects of hormones; *activational* effects occur after development is complete. A person with Turner's syndrome (X0) fails to develop gonads but nevertheless develops female internal sex organs and external genitalia.

Sexual maturity occurs when the hypothalamus stimulates the anterior pituitary gland to secrete follicle-stimulating hormone and luteinizing hormone. These hormones stimulate the gonads to secrete *their* hormones, which cause the genitals to mature and cause the body to develop the appropriate secondary sex characteristics (activational effects). ▲

HORMONAL CONTROL OF SEXUAL BEHAVIOR

We have seen that hormones are responsible for sexual dimorphism in the structure of the body and its organs. Hormones have organizational and activational effects on the internal sex organs, genitals, and secondary sex characteristics. Naturally, all of these effects influence a person's behavior. Simply having the physique and genitals of a man or a woman exerts a powerful effect. But hormones do more than give us masculine or feminine bodies; they also affect behavior by interacting directly with the nervous system. Androgens present during prenatal development affect the development of the nervous system. In addition, sex hormones have activational effects on the adult nervous system, influencing physiological processes and behavior. This section considers some of these hormonal effects.

Hormonal Control of Female Reproductive Cycles

The reproductive cycle of female primates is called a **menstrual cycle** (from *mensis,* meaning "month"). Females of other species of mammals also have reproductive cycles, called **estrous cycles.** *Estrus* means "gadfly"; when a female rat is in estrus, her hormonal condition goads her to act differently than she does at other times. (For that matter, it goads male rats to act differently, too.) The primary feature that distinguishes menstrual cycles from estrous cycles is the monthly growth and loss of the lining of the uterus. The other features are approximately the same.

menstrual cycle

estrous cycle

Menstrual cycles and estrous cycles consist of a sequence of events that are controlled by hormonal secretions of the pituitary gland and ovaries. These glands interact, the secretions of one affecting those of the other. A cycle begins with the secretion of gonadotropins by the anterior pituitary gland. These hormones (especially FSH) stimulate the growth of **ovarian follicles,** small spheres of epithelial cells surrounding each ovum. Women normally produce one ovarian follicle each month; if two are produced and fertilized, dizygotic (fraternal) twins will develop. As ovarian follicles mature, they secrete estradiol, which causes the growth of the lining of the uterus in preparation for implantation of the ovum, should it be fertilized by a sperm.

ovarian follicle

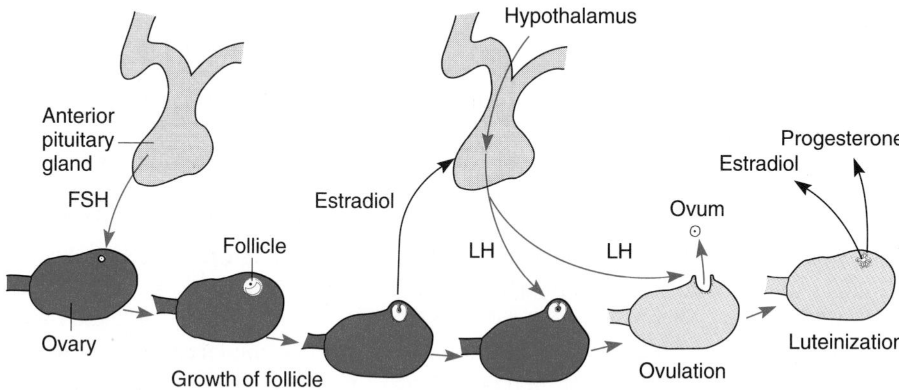

FIGURE 9.5

Neuroendocrine control of the menstrual cycle.

Feedback from the increasing level of estradiol eventually triggers the release of a surge of LH by the anterior pituitary gland. (See ***Figure 9.5.***)

corpus luteum
progesterone

The LH surge causes *ovulation:* The ovarian follicle ruptures, releasing the ovum. Under the continued influence of LH the ruptured ovarian follicle becomes a **corpus luteum** ("yellow body"), which produces estradiol and **progesterone.** (See ***Figure 9.5.***) The latter hormone promotes pregnancy *(gestation).* It maintains the lining of the uterus, and it inhibits the ovaries from producing another follicle. Meanwhile, the ovum enters one of the Fallopian tubes and begins its progress toward the uterus. If it meets sperm cells during its travel down the Fallopian tube and becomes fertilized, it begins to divide, and several days later it attaches itself to the uterine wall.

If the ovum is not fertilized, or if it is fertilized too late for it to develop sufficiently by the time it gets to the uterus, the corpus luteum will stop producing estradiol and progesterone, and then the lining of the walls of the uterus will slough off. At this point menstruation will commence.

Hormonal Control of Sexual Behavior of Laboratory Animals

The interactions between sex hormones and development of the human brain are difficult to study. We must turn to two sources of information: experiments with animals and various developmental disorders in humans, which serve as nature's own "experiments." Let us first consider the evidence gathered from research with laboratory animals.

MALES

Male sexual behavior is quite varied, although the essential features of *intromission* (entry of the penis into the female's vagina), *pelvic thrusting* (rhythmic movement of the hindquarters, causing genital friction), and *ejaculation* (discharge of semen) are characteristic of all male mammals. Humans, of course, have invented all kinds of copulatory and noncopulatory sexual behavior. For example, the pelvic movements leading to ejaculation may be performed by the woman, and sex play can lead to orgasm without intromission.

The male rat (along with many other male mammals) is most responsive to females who are in estrus ("in heat"). Males will ignore a female whose ovaries have been removed, but an injection of estradiol will restore her sex appeal (and also change her behavior toward the male). The stimuli that arouse a male rat's sexual interest include her odor and her behavior. In some species visible changes, such as the swollen skin in the genital region of a female monkey, also affect sex appeal.

Sexual behavior of male rodents depends on testosterone, a fact that has long been recognized (Bermant and Davidson, 1974). If a male rat is castrated (that is, if his testes are removed), his sexual activity eventually ceases. However, the behavior can be reinstated by injections of testosterone. I will describe the brain mechanisms involved in this activational effect later in this chapter.

FEMALES

The mammalian female is generally described as being the passive participant in copulation. It is true that in many species the female's role during mounting and intromission is merely to assume a posture that exposes her genitals to the male. This behavior is called the **lordosis** response (from the Greek ***lordos,*** meaning "bent backward"). The female will also move her tail away (if she has one) and stand rigidly enough to support the weight of the male.

lordosis

The behavior of a female laboratory animal in initiating copulation is often very active, however. Certainly, if copulation with a nonestrous rodent is attempted, she will either actively flee or rebuff the male. But when she is in a receptive state, she will often approach the male, nuzzle him, sniff his genitals, and show behaviors characteristic of her species. For example, a female rat will exhibit quick, short, hopping movements and rapid ear wiggling, which male rats find irresistible (McClintock and Adler, 1978).

Sexual behavior of female rodents depends on the gonadal hormones present during estrus: estradiol and progesterone. In rats estradiol increases about 40 hours before the female becomes receptive; and just before receptivity occurs, the corpus luteum begins secreting large quantities of progesterone (Feder, 1981). Although sexual receptivity can be produced in ovariectomized rodents by administering large doses of estradiol alone, the most effective treatment duplicates the normal sequence of hormones: a small amount of estradiol, followed by progesterone. Progesterone alone is ineffective; thus, the estradiol "primes" its effectiveness. Priming with estradiol takes about 16–24 hours, after which an injection of progesterone produces receptive behaviors within an hour (Lisk, 1978).

ORGANIZATIONAL EFFECTS OF ANDROGENS ON BEHAVIOR: MASCULINIZATION AND DEFEMINIZATION

The dictum "Nature's impulse is to create a female" applies to sexual behavior as well as to sex organs. That is, if a rodent brain is *not* exposed to androgens during a critical period of development, the animal will engage in female sexual behavior as an adult (if it is given estradiol and progesterone then). Fortunately for experimenters, this critical time comes shortly after birth for rats and for several other species of rodents, who are born in a rather immature condition. Thus, if a male rat is castrated immediately after birth, permitted to grow to adulthood, and then given injections of estradiol and progesterone, it will respond to the presence of another male by arching its back and presenting its hindquarters. It will act as if it were a female (Blaustein and Olster, 1989).

In contrast, if a rodent brain is exposed to androgens during development, two phenomena occur: behavioral defeminization and behavioral masculinization. *Behavioral defeminization* refers to the organizational effect of androgens that prevents the animal from displaying female sexual behavior in adulthood. As we shall see later, this effect is accomplished by suppressing the development of neural circuits controlling female sexual behavior. For example, if a female rodent is ovariectomized and given an injection of testosterone immediately after birth, she will *not* respond to a male rat when, as an adult, she is given injections of estradiol and progesterone. *Behavioral*

FIGURE 9.6

Organizational effects of testosterone. Around the time of birth, testosterone masculinizes and defeminizes rodents' sexual behavior.

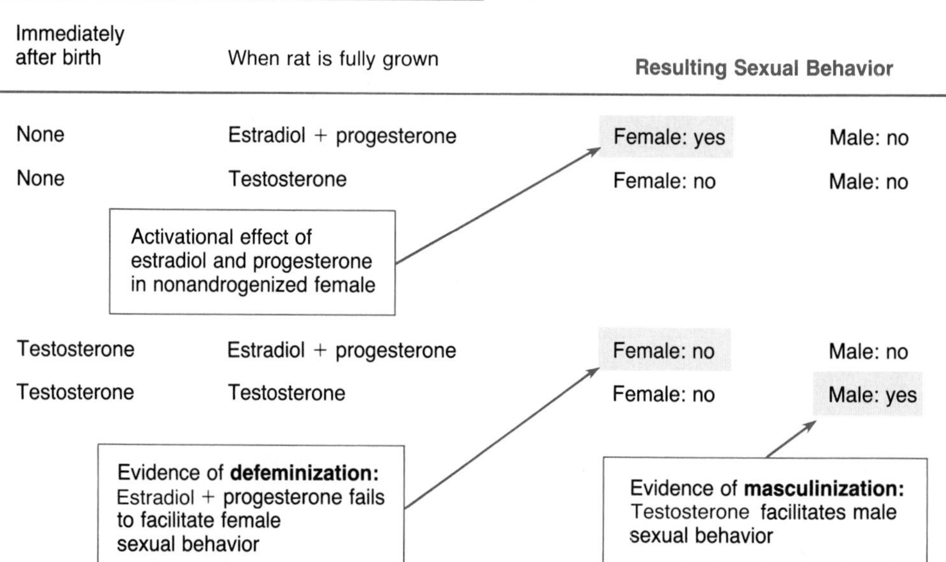

masculinization refers to the organizational effect of androgens that enables animals to engage in male sexual behavior in adulthood. This effect is accomplished by stimulating the development of neural circuits controlling male sexual behavior. For example, if the female rodent in my previous example is given testosterone in adulthood, rather than estradiol and progesterone, she will mount and attempt to copulate with a receptive female. (See Feder, 1984, for references to specific studies.) (See ***Figure 9.6.***)

Effects of Pheromones

pheromone

Hormones transmit messages from one part of the body (the secreting gland) to another (the target tissue). Another class of chemicals, called **pheromones,** carries messages from one animal to another. These chemicals, like hormones, affect reproductive behavior. Karlson and Luscher (1959) coined the term, from the Greek *pherein,* "to carry," and *horman,* "to excite." Pheromones are released by one animal and directly affect the physiology or behavior of another. Most pheromones are detected by means of olfaction, but some are ingested or absorbed through the skin.

Lee-Boot effect

Whitten effect

Vandenbergh effect

Pheromones can affect reproductive physiology or behavior. First, let us consider the effects on reproductive physiology. When groups of female mice are housed together, their estrous cycles slow down and eventually stop. This phenomenon is known as the **Lee-Boot effect** (van der Lee and Boot, 1955). If groups of females are exposed to the odor of a male (or of his urine), they begin cycling again, and their cycles tend to be synchronized. This phenomenon is known as the **Whitten effect** (Whitten, 1959). The **Vandenbergh effect** (Vandenbergh, Whitsett, and Lombardi, 1975) is the acceleration of the onset of puberty in a female rodent caused by the odor of a male. Both the Whitten effect and the Vandenbergh effect are caused by a pheromone present only in the urine of intact adult males; the urine of a juvenile or castrated male has no effect. Thus, the production of the pheromone requires the presence of testosterone.

The **Bruce effect** (Bruce, 1960a, 1960b) is a particularly interesting phenomenon: When a recently impregnated female mouse encounters a normal male mouse other than the one with which she mated, the pregnancy is very likely to fail. This effect, too, is caused by a substance secreted in the urine of intact adult males—but not of males that have been castrated. Thus, a male mouse is able to kill the genetic material of another male and subsequently impregnate the female himself.

Bruce effect

As you learned in Chapter 6, detection of odors is accomplished by the olfactory bulbs, which constitute the primary olfactory system. However, the four effects that pheromones have on reproductive cycles appear to be mediated by another organ—the **vomeronasal organ**—which consists of a small group of sensory receptors arranged around a pouch connected by a duct to the nasal passage. The vomeronasal organ, which is present in all orders of mammals except for cetaceans (whales and dolphins), projects to the **accessory olfactory bulb,** located immediately behind the olfactory bulb (Wysocki, 1979). This organ is found in human fetuses but disappears later; thus, it cannot be important in our species. (See ***Figure 9.7.***) The vomeronasal organ probably does not detect airborne molecules, as the olfactory bulbs do, but instead is sensitive to nonvolatile compounds found in urine or other substances. In fact, stimulation of a nerve that serves the nasal region causes fluid to be pumped into the vomeronasal organ, which exposes the receptors to any substances that may be present (Meredith and O'Connell, 1979).

vomeronasal organ

accessory olfactory bulb

Removal of the accessory olfactory bulb disrupts the Lee-Boot effect, the Whitten effect, the Vandenbergh effect, and the Bruce effect; thus, this organ is essential for these phenomena (Halpern, 1987). The accessory olfactory bulb sends axons to the **medial nucleus of the amygdala,** which in turn projects to the preoptic area and anterior hypothalamus and to the ventromedial nucleus of the hypothalamus. (As you learned in Chapter 6, so does the main olfactory bulb.) Thus, the neural circuit responsible for the effects of these pheromones appears to involve these regions. As we shall see, both the preoptic area and the ventromedial nucleus of the hypothalamus play critical roles in reproductive behavior. (Refer to ***Figure 9.16.***)

medial nucleus of the amygdala

The Bruce effect involves learning; the female obviously learns to recognize the odor of the male with which she mates, because his odor will not cause her to abort if

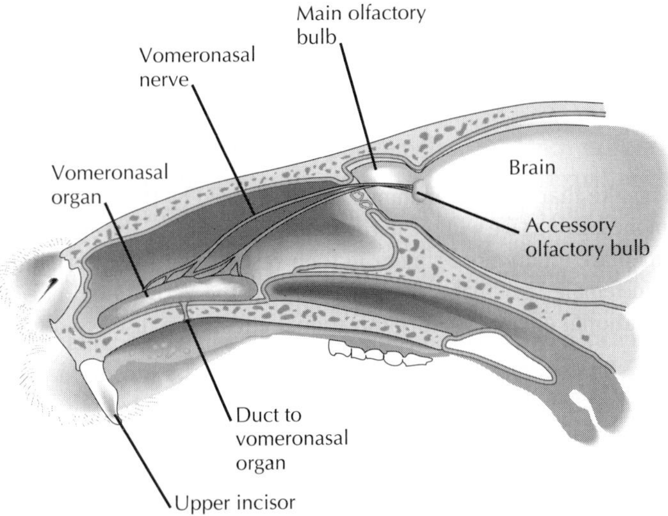

FIGURE 9.7

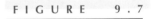

The rodent accessory olfactory system. (Adapted from Wysocki, C.J. *Neuroscience & Biobehavioral Reviews,* 1979, *3,* 301–341.)

Money, Schwartz, and Lewis (1984) studied thirty young women with a history of adrenogenital syndrome. They had all been born with enlarged clitorises and partly fused labia, which led to the diagnosis. (A few mild cases were not diagnosed for several years.) Once the diagnosis was made, they were medically treated and, if necessary, genital surgery was performed. Money and his colleagues asked the young women to describe their sexual orientation. Eleven of the women (37 percent of the total) described themselves as bisexual or homosexual, twelve (40 percent) said they were exclusively heterosexual, and seven (23 percent) refused to talk about their sex lives. If the noncommittal women are excluded from the sample, the percentage of homo- or bisexuality rises to 48 percent.

The Kinsey report on sexuality in women (Kinsey et al., 1953) reported that approximately 10 percent of American women had had some sexual contact with another woman by the age of twenty; in the sample of androgenized women the percentage was at least four times as high. The results therefore suggest that the exposure of a female fetus to an abnormally high level of androgens does affect sexual orientation. A plausible explanation is that the effect takes place in the brain, but we must remember that the androgens also affect the genitals; possibly, the changes in the genitals played a role in shaping the development of the girls' sexual orientation. If the differences seen in sexual orientation *were* caused by effects of the prenatal androgens on brain development, then we could reasonably conclude that androgens have this effect in males, too. That is, these results support the hypothesis that male sexual orientation is at least partly determined by masculinizing (and defeminizing) effects of androgens on the human brain.

Because controlled experiments cannot be performed on humans, some investigators have turned to our close relatives to see whether prenatal androgenization has enduring behavioral effects. Goy, Bercovitch, and McBrair (1988) administered injections of testosterone to pregnant monkeys. The testosterone entered the blood supply of the fetuses and masculinized them. Female infants that had been androgenized early during fetal development were born with masculinized genitals; the genitals of those that had been androgenized later were normal. *Both* groups showed differences in their sociosexual interactions with peers, displaying a higher proportion of malelike behavior than normal females did. For example, even as young adults, the group with normal genitals continued to mount their peers significantly more than normal females did. The results suggest that genital changes cannot account for all the behavioral effects of prenatal androgenization in primates. Whether *human* primates share these characteristics is, of course, another question.

Failure of Androgenization. Nature has performed the equivalent of a prenatal castration experiment in humans (Money and Ehrhardt, 1972). Some people are insensitive to androgens; they have **androgen insensitivity syndrome,** one of the more aptly named disorders. The cause of androgen insensitivity syndrome is a genetic mutation that prevents the formation of functioning androgen receptors. The primordial gonads of a genetic male with androgen insensitivity syndrome become testes and secrete Müllerian-inhibiting substance and androgens. However, only the Müllerian-inhibiting substance has an effect on development. Because the cells of the body cannot respond to the androgens, the person develops female external genitalia. The Müllerian-inhibiting substance prevents the female internal sex organs from developing, though; the uterus fails to develop and the vagina is shallow.

androgen insensitivity syndrome

If an individual with this syndrome is raised as a girl, all is well. Normally, the testes are removed because they often become cancerous; but if they are not, the body will become feminized at the time of puberty by the small amounts of estradiol produced by the testes. (If the testes are removed, the person will be given estradiol.) At adulthood the individual will function sexually as a woman, although surgical lengthening of the vagina may be necessary. Women with this syndrome report average sex drives, including normal frequency of orgasm in intercourse. Most marry and lead normal sex lives. Of course, lacking a uterus and ovaries, they cannot have children. (See ***Figure 9.8.***)

FIGURE 9.8

An XY female displaying androgen insensitivity syndrome. The absence of pubic hair can be explained by the person's insensitivity to androgens, which are responsible for the growth of pubic hair in both men and women. (From Money, J., and Ehrhardt, A.A. *Man & Woman, Boy & Girl.* Copyright 1973 by The Johns Hopkins University Press, Baltimore, Maryland. By permission.)

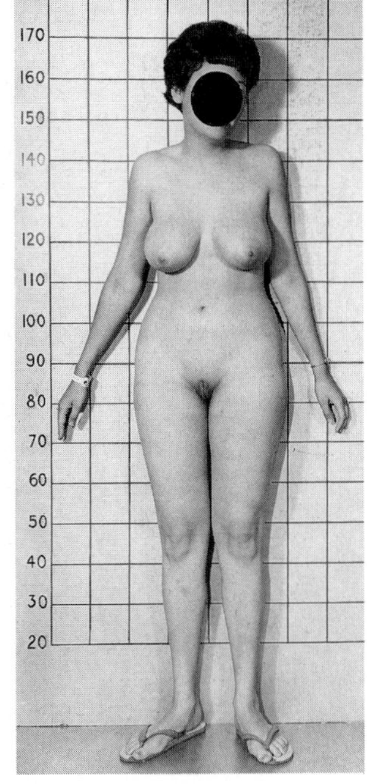

ACTIVATIONAL EFFECTS OF SEX HORMONES ON WOMEN'S SEXUAL BEHAVIOR

As we saw, the sexual behavior of female mammals other than higher primates is controlled by estradiol and progesterone. However, this is not the case for women. Although these hormones may influence sexual activity, they do not *control* it. As we saw, a female rat will copulate only during estrus, when her estradiol and progesterone levels are high. However, women can become sexually aroused at any time of their menstrual cycle. Fluctuations in the level of the ovarian hormones may have an effect on women's sexual interest, but these effects are usually not very strong (Adams, Gold, and Burt, 1978; Morris et al., 1987).

Another difference between women and animals with estrous cycles is indicated by their contrasting reactions to androgens. Persky et al. (1978) studied the sexual activity and blood levels of various hormones in married couples over a period of three menstrual cycles. They found that the frequency of intercourse over the entire cycle was correlated with the wife's peak testosterone level during ovulation. In addition, the wives reported more sexual gratification when their testosterone levels were high.

Although experiments with humans are not possible, research on the effects of hormones on female sexual behavior has been performed with rhesus macaques, a common species of laboratory monkey. In general, results have confirmed a role for androgens in the sexual behavior of this species. Everitt, Herbert, and Hamer (1972) found that removal of the adrenal glands (which secrete some androgens) decreased the sexual interest of female rhesus macaques who had previously been ovariectomized. The effect was seen most strikingly in the animals' soliciting behavior—what researchers have called *proceptivity*. Removal of the adrenal glands had a much smaller effect on *receptivity*—the animal's willingness to engage in sexual activity with a male who initiates the behavior. Administration of testosterone reinstituted these behaviors to normal levels.

ACTIVATIONAL EFFECTS OF SEX HORMONES IN MEN

Although women and female rodents are very different in their behavioral responsiveness to sex hormones, men and male rodents (and other mammals, for that matter) resemble each other in their behavioral responsiveness to testosterone. With normal levels they can be potent and fertile; without testosterone sperm production ceases, and sooner or later, so does sexual activity. Some investigators have said that the sexual activity of humans is "emancipated" from the effects of hormones. In one sense this is true. Men who have been castrated for medical reasons do report a continuing interest in sexual activity with their wives. Even if sexual activity no longer takes the form of intercourse, other types of sexual contact can occur.

Davidson, Camargo, and Smith (1979) performed a double-blind study that demonstrates the activational effects of testosterone on men's sexual activity. Their subjects were married men with ***hypogonadal syndrome,*** whose testes failed to produce adequate amounts of testosterone. The investigators gave the men injections of testosterone or a placebo and asked the subjects to keep a written log of their sexual activities. They found that the testosterone significantly increased the frequency of these activities.

Testosterone not only affects sexual activity but also is affected by it — or even by thinking about it. A scientist stationed on a remote island (Anonymous, 1970) removed his beard with an electrical shaver each day and weighed the clippings. Just before he left for visits to the mainland (and to female company), his beard began growing faster. Because rate of beard growth is related to androgen levels, the effect indicates that his anticipation of sexual activity stimulated testosterone production. Confirming these results, Hellhammer, Hubert, and Schurmeyer (1985) found that watching an erotic film increased men's testosterone level.

SEXUAL ORIENTATION

What controls a person's sexual orientation, or gender of the preferred sex partner? Some people are exclusively homosexual, being attracted only to partners of the same sex; some are bisexual, being attracted to members of both sexes; and some are heterosexual, being attracted only to partners of the other sex. Many humans (especially males) who are essentially heterosexual engage in homosexual episodes sometime during their lives. Although many animals occasionally engage in sexual activity with a member of the same sex, *exclusive* homosexuality appears to occur only in humans (Ehrhardt and Meyer-Bahlburg, 1981).

Some investigators believe that homosexuality is a result of childhood experiences, especially interactions between the child and parents. A large-scale study of several hundred male and female homosexuals reported by Bell, Weinberg, and Hammersmith (1981) attempted to assess the effects of these factors. The researchers found no evidence that homosexuals had been raised by domineering mothers or submissive fathers, as some clinicians had suggested. The best predictor of adult homosexuality was a self-report of homosexual feelings, which usually preceded homosexual activity by three years. The investigators concluded that their data did not support social explanations for homosexuality but were consistent with the possibility that homosexuality is at least partly biologically determined.

If homosexuality does have a physiological cause, a likely possibility is a subtle difference in brain structure caused by the presence or absence of prenatal androgenization. As we saw, men and women do not differ from one another so much in their sexual *behavior* as in the gender of their sex partners. The same comparison is true for heterosexual and homosexual people; the gender of their partner, not the kind of sexual activity they engage in, distinguishes them. Therefore, if prenatal androgenization influences human brain development, the effects are likely to be seen in a person's choice of sex partner, not in the form of his or her sexual behavior. Perhaps, then, the brains of male homosexuals are neither masculinized nor defeminized, those of female homosexuals are masculinized and defeminized, and those of bisexuals are masculinized but not defeminized. Of course, these are *speculations* that so far cannot be supported by human data; they are not *conclusions.* They should be regarded as suggestions to guide future research.

A study performed with laboratory animals suggests that prenatal stress can alter adult sexual behavior. Ward (1972) subjected pregnant rats to periods of stress by confining them and exposing them to a bright light, which suppresses androgen production in male fetuses. The male rats born to the stressed mothers were less likely than control subjects to display male sexual behavior and were more likely to display female sexual behavior when they were given injections of estradiol and progesterone. Other studies have shown that besides having behavioral effects, prenatal stress reduces the size of a part of the forebrain that is normally larger in males than in females (Anderson, Fleming, Rhees, and Kinghorn, 1986). Although we cannot assume that prenatal stress in humans has similar effects on the brain and behavior, the results of these studies are consistent with the hypothesis that male homosexuality may be related to events that reduce prenatal androgenization.

For some people homosexuality is immoral; others regard it as a mental disorder. However, both of these characterizations have been denounced by professional mental health organizations. It is clear that homosexuals can be as happy and as well adjusted as heterosexuals (Bell and Weinberg, 1978). If the hypotheses I have outlined here are correct, then homosexuals are no more responsible for their sexual orientation than heterosexuals are. The question "Why does someone become homosexual?" will probably be answered when we find out why someone becomes *heterosexual.*

▶INTERIM SUMMARY◀

Sexual behaviors are controlled by the organizational and activational effects of hormones. The female reproductive cycle (menstrual cycle or estrous cycle) begins with the maturation of one or more ovarian follicles, which occurs in response to the secretion of FSH by the anterior pituitary gland. As the ovarian follicle matures, it secretes estradiol, which causes the lining of the uterus to develop. When estradiol reaches a critical level, it causes the pituitary gland to secrete a surge of LH, triggering ovulation. The empty ovarian follicle becomes a corpus luteum, under the continued influence of LH, and secretes estradiol and progesterone. If pregnancy does not occur, the corpus luteum dies and stops producing hormones, and menstruation begins.

In most mammals female sexual behavior is the norm, just as the female body and female sex organs are the norm. That is, unless prenatal androgens masculinize and defeminize the animal's brain, its sexual behavior will be feminine. Behavioral masculinization refers to the androgen-stimulated development of neural circuits that respond to testosterone in adulthood, producing male sexual behavior. Behavioral defeminization refers to the inhibitory effects of androgens on the development of neural circuits that respond to estradiol and progesterone in adulthood, producing female sexual behavior.

The sexual behavior of males of all mammalian species appears to depend on the presence of androgens. Female mammals other than primates depend primarily on estradiol and progesterone and will copulate only during the period of estrus, when the levels of these hormones are high. In particular, estradiol has a priming effect on the subsequent appearance of progesterone.

Pheromones can affect sexual physiology and behavior. Odorants present in the urine of female mice affect their estrous cycles, lengthening and eventually stopping them (Lee-Boot effect). Odorants present in the urine of male mice abolish these effects and cause the females' cycles to become synchronized (Whitten effect). They can also accelerate the onset of puberty in females (Vandenbergh effect). In addition, the odor of the urine from a male other than the one that impregnated the female mouse will cause her to abort (Bruce effect). The Bruce effect involves learning the odor of the male that impregnates the female, and the activity of a noradrenergic input to the olfactory bulb is involved in this learning.

In the hamster the attractiveness of an estrous female to the male derives in part from chemicals present in her vaginal secretions, detected by the olfactory epithelium and vomeronasal organ. Connections between the olfactory system and the amygdala appear to be important in stimulating male sexual behavior. The search for sex attractant pheromones in humans has so far been fruitless, although we may well recognize our sex partners by their odors.

The behavioral effects of prenatal androgenization in humans, if any, are not well under-

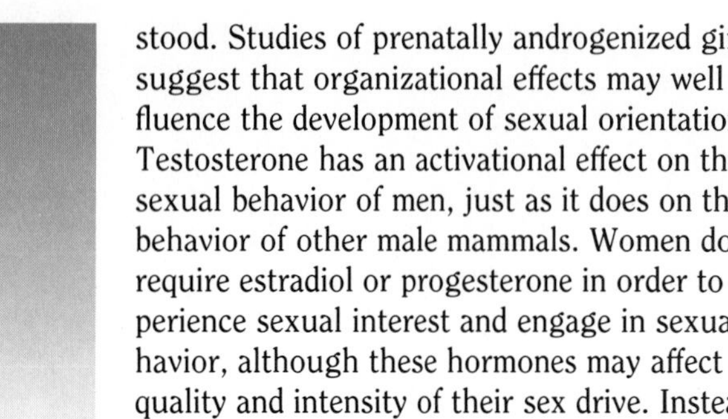

stood. Studies of prenatally androgenized girls suggest that organizational effects may well influence the development of sexual orientation. Testosterone has an activational effect on the sexual behavior of men, just as it does on the behavior of other male mammals. Women do not require estradiol or progesterone in order to experience sexual interest and engage in sexual behavior, although these hormones may affect the quality and intensity of their sex drive. Instead, the most important activational effect on women's sex drives seems to be provided by androgens.

Sexual orientation (that is, heterosexuality or homosexuality) may be influenced by prenatal androgenization, but conclusive evidence is lacking. Studies with rats have shown that events that cause stress during pregnancy can interfere with defeminization of the sexual behavior of the male offspring. ▲

NEURAL CONTROL OF SEXUAL BEHAVIOR

The control of sexual behavior—at least in laboratory animals—involves different brain mechanisms in males and females. This section describes these mechanisms.

Males

medial preoptic area (MPA)

The **medial preoptic area** (MPA), located just rostral to the hypothalamus, is the forebrain region most critical for male sexual behavior. (As we will see later in this chapter, it is also critical for other sexually dimorphic behavior, including maternal behavior and territorial aggression.) Electrical stimulation of this region elicits male

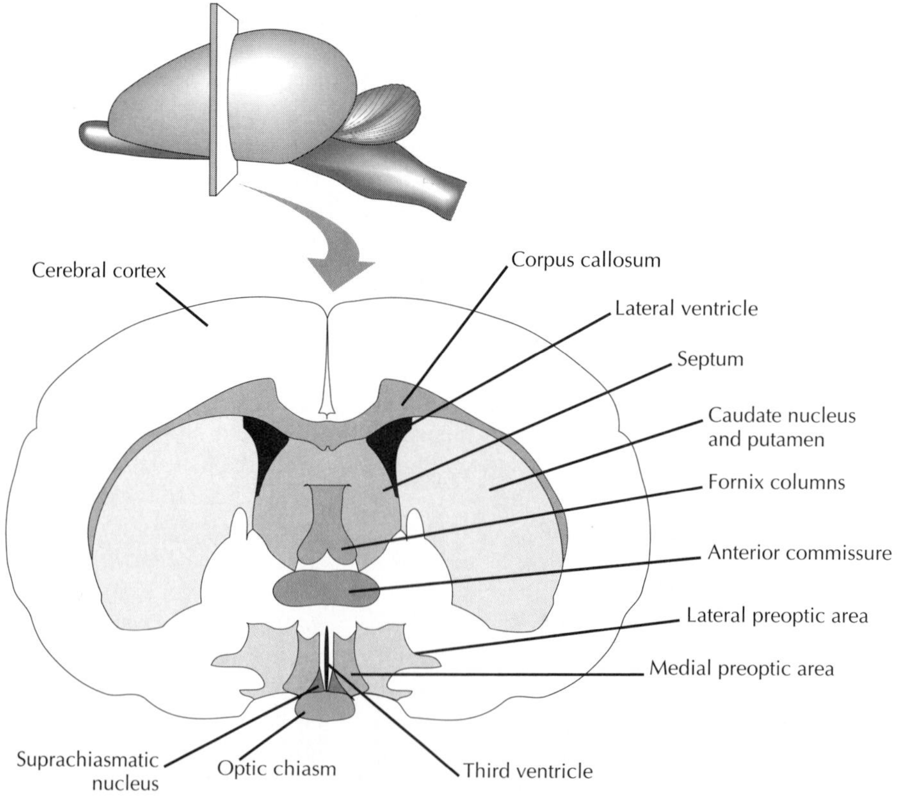

FIGURE 9.9

A cross section through the rat brain showing the location of the medial preoptic area. (Adapted from Paxinos, G., and Watson, C. *The Brain in Stereotaxic Coordinates.* Sydney: Academic Press, 1982. Redrawn with permission.)

copulatory behavior (Malsbury, 1971), and the act of copulation increases the metabolic activity of the MPA (Oaknin et al., 1989). Destruction of the MPA permanently abolishes male sexual behavior (Heimer and Larsson, 1966/1967). (See ***Figure 9.9.***)

Androgens exert their activational effects on neurons in the medial preoptic area. If a male rat is castrated in adulthood, its sexual behavior will cease. However, the behavior can be reinstated by implanting a small amount of testosterone directly into the medial preoptic area (Davidson, 1980). This region has been shown to contain a high concentration of androgen receptors in the male rat brain—more than five times as many as are found in females (Roselli, Handa, and Resko, 1989).

The difference in the concentration of androgen receptors in males and females is a result of an organizational effect of androgens. Gorski, Gordon, Shryne, and Southam (1978) discovered a nucleus within the MPA of the rat that is three to seven times larger in males than in females. This area is called (appropriately enough) the **sexually dimorphic nucleus** (SDN) of the preoptic area. The size of this nucleus is controlled by the amount of androgens present during fetal development. (See ***Figure 9.10.***)

sexually dimorphic nucleus

In the section on sexual orientation I mentioned that Anderson, Fleming, Rhees, and Kinghorn (1986) found that the size of the SDN in male rats was reduced by prenatal stress. They also found that volume of the SDN in an individual male rat was directly related to the animal's level of sexual activity. In addition, De Jonge et al. (1989) found that lesions of the SDN decrease masculine sexual behavior. Thus, the SDN appears to play an important role in male sexual behavior.

Neurons in the medial preoptic area send axons to the lateral tegmental field of the midbrain (just dorsal and medial to the substantia nigra), and destruction of these axons disrupt male sexual behavior (Brackett and Edwards, 1984). These results suggest that the medial preoptic area exerts its effect by controlling motor mechanisms in the midbrain; however, little is known about these mechanisms.

The medial preoptic area of the human brain is sexually dimorphic, too (Swaab and Fliers, 1985; Allen, Hines, Shryne, and Gorski, 1989). Swaab and Hofman (1988) measured the size of this nucleus in the brains of deceased fetuses, children, and adults. They found that although the SDN could be distinguished in the brain of a fetus at

FIGURE 9.10

Photomicrographs of sections through the preoptic area of the rat brain. (a) Normal male. (b) Normal female. (c) Androgenized female. SDN-POA = sexually dimorphic nucleus of the preoptic area; OC = optic chiasm; V = third ventricle; SCN = suprachiasmatic nucleus; AC = anterior commissure. (From Gorski, R.A., in *Neuroendocrine Perspectives,* Vol. 2, edited by E.E. Müller and R.M. MacLeod. Amsterdam: Elsevier-North Holland, 1983. Reprinted with permission.)

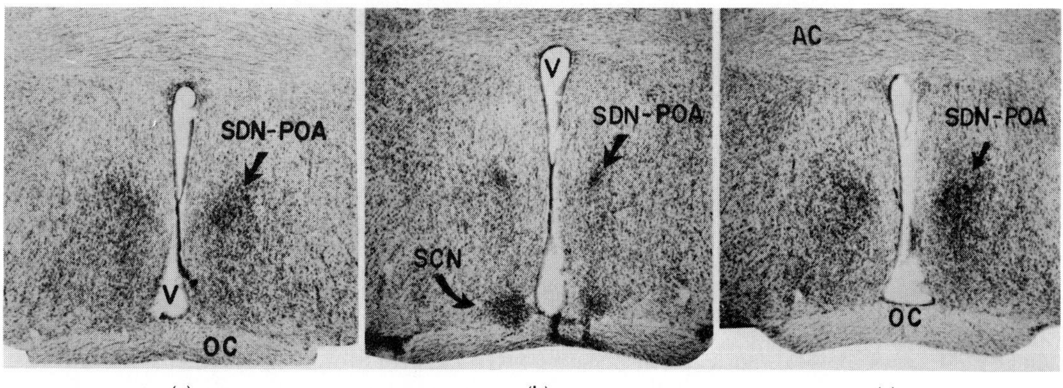

midpregnancy, no sex differences were shown until about four years of age, at which time the SDN of females showed a decline in size. Incidentally, they studied the brains of nine homosexual men and found no evidence that their sexually dimorphic nuclei were any smaller than those of other men.

Other parts of the brain play a role in sexual behavior, too. In humans temporal lobe dysfunctions are often correlated with decreased sex drives. For example, seizures that originate from localized, irritative lesions of the temporal lobes are sometimes associated with lack of interest in sexual activity (Blumer, 1975; Blumer and Walker, 1975). Usually, if the seizures are successfully treated by medication or by surgical removal of the affected tissue, the person attains normal sexual interest.

Females

ventromedial nucleus of the hypothalamus (VMH)

The one part of the brain that is most critical for performance of female sexual behavior is the **ventromedial nucleus of the hypothalamus** (VMH). Female rats with bilateral lesions of the ventromedial nuclei will not display lordosis, even if they are treated with estradiol and progesterone. In fact, when trapped in a corner by a male rat, they will attack him (Pfaff and Sakuma, 1979). Conversely, electrical stimulation of the ventromedial nucleus facilitates female sexual behavior (Pfaff and Sakuma, 1979). The critical region appears to be the anterior third of the VMH (Richmond and Clemens, 1988). (See ***Figure 9.11.***)

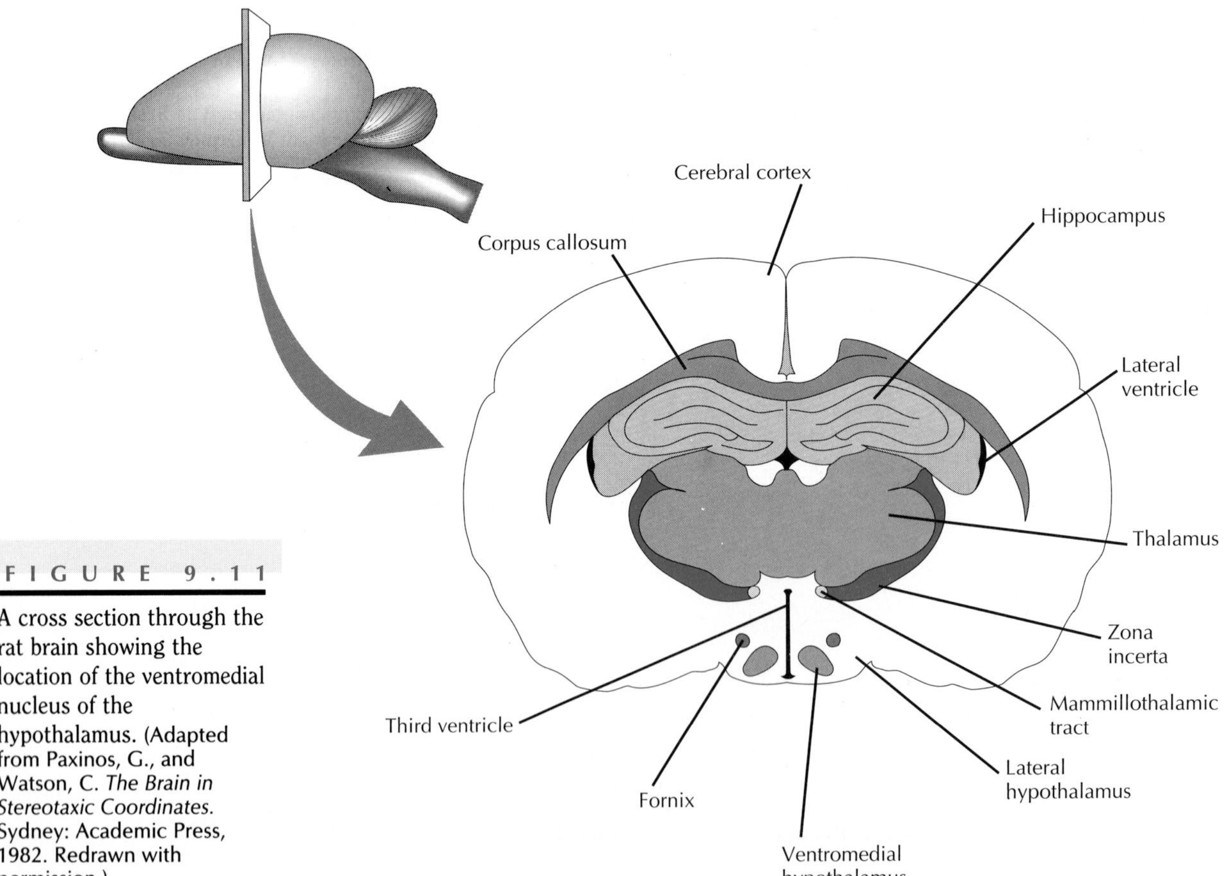

FIGURE 9.11

A cross section through the rat brain showing the location of the ventromedial nucleus of the hypothalamus. (Adapted from Paxinos, G., and Watson, C. *The Brain in Stereotaxic Coordinates.* Sydney: Academic Press, 1982. Redrawn with permission.)

As we saw earlier, sexual behavior of female rats is activated by a priming dose of estradiol, followed by progesterone. Injections of these hormones directly into the VMH will stimulate sexual behavior even in females whose ovaries have been removed (Rubin and Barfield, 1980; Pleim and Barfield, 1988). Thus, these hormones exert their effects on behavior by activating neurons in this nucleus.

The neurons of the ventromedial nucleus send axons to the **periaqueductal gray matter** (PAG) of the midbrain, surrounding the cerebral aqueduct. This region, too, has been implicated in female sexual behavior; Sakuma and Pfaff (1979a, 1979b) found that electrical stimulation of the PAG facilitates lordosis in female rats and that lesions there disrupt it. In addition, Hennessey, Camak, Gordon, and Edwards (1990) found that lesions that disconnect the VMH from the PAG abolish female sexual behavior. Finally, Sakuma and Pfaff (1980a, 1980b) found that estradiol treatment or electrical stimulation of the ventromedial nuclei increased the firing rate of neurons in the PAG.

periaqueductal gray matter

The neurons of the periaqueductal gray matter send axons to the reticular formation of the medulla, and cells there send axons to the spinal cord. It seems likely that this pathway is the final link between the hormone-sensitive neurons in the ventromedial nucleus of the hypothalamus and the muscles that are responsible for female sexual behavior.

▶INTERIM SUMMARY◀

In laboratory animals, different brain mechanisms control male and female sexual behavior. The medial preoptic area is the forebrain region most critical for male sexual behavior. Stimulation of this area produces copulatory behavior; lesioning permanently abolishes it. Neurons in the MPA contain testosterone receptors. Copulatory activity causes an increase in the metabolic activity of this region. Implantation of testosterone directly into the MPA reinstates copulatory behavior that was previously abolished by castration in adulthood.

The sexually dimorphic nucleus, located in the medial preoptic area, develops only if an animal is exposed to androgens early in life. This nucleus is found in humans, as well. The size of the SDN (part of the MPA) is reduced by prenatal stress and correlates with an animal's level of sexual behavior. The temporal lobes, too, appear to play a role in sexual interest, particularly in humans.

The most important forebrain region for female sexual behavior is the ventromedial nucleus of the hypothalamus. Its destruction abolishes copulatory behavior, and its stimulation facilitates the behavior. Both estradiol and progesterone exert their facilitating effects on female sexual behavior in this region, and studies have confirmed the existence of progesterone and estrogen receptors there. The estradiol-sensitive neurons of the VMH send axons to the periaqueductal gray matter of the midbrain; presumably, neurons in the midbrain, through their connections with the medullary reticular formation, control the particular responses that constitute female sexual behavior. ▲

MATERNAL BEHAVIOR

In most mammalian species reproductive behavior takes place after the offspring are born as well as at the time they are conceived. This section examines the role of hormones in the initiation and maintenance of maternal behavior and the role of the neural circuits that are responsible for their expression. Most of the research has involved rodents; less is known about the neural and endocrine bases of maternal behavior in primates.

In focusing on maternal behavior, I do not deny the existence of paternal behavior, but male parental behavior is most prominent in higher primates such as humans—and we know little about the neurological basis of human parental behavior. Most male rodents do not show parental behavior except under special circumstances. There are, of course, other classes of animals (for example, many species of fish) in which the male takes care of the young, and in many species of birds the task of caring for the offspring is shared equally. However, neural mechanisms of parental behavior have not received much study in these species.

This section describes nurturing behaviors; defensive behaviors, directed by a female against other animals that might threaten her offspring, are described later in this chapter. We begin the discussion by examining rodent maternal behavior.

Maternal Behavior in Rodents

The final test of the fitness of an animal's genes is the number of offspring that survive to a reproductive age. Just as the process of natural selection favors reproductively competent animals, it favors those that care adequately for their young (if their young in fact require any care). Rat and mouse pups certainly do require care; they cannot survive without a mother who attends to their needs.

At birth rats and mice resemble fetuses. The infants are blind (their eyes are still shut), and they can only helplessly wriggle. They are poikilothermous ("cold-blooded"); their brain is not yet developed enough to regulate body temperature. They even lack the ability to release their own urine and feces spontaneously and must be

FIGURE 9.12

A mouse's brood nest. Beside it is a length of the kind of rope the mouse used to construct it.

helped to do so by their mother. As we will see shortly, this phenomenon actually serves a useful function.

During gestation female rats and mice build nests. The form this structure takes depends on the material available for its construction. In the laboratory the animals are usually given strips of paper or lengths of rope or twine. A good *brood nest,* as it is called, is shown in Figure 9.12. This nest is made of hemp rope; a piece of the rope is shown below the nest. The mouse laboriously shredded the rope and then wove an enclosed nest, with a small hole for access to the interior. (See ***Figure 9.12.***)

At the time of *parturition* (delivery of offspring) the female begins to groom and lick the area around the vagina. As a pup begins to emerge, she assists the uterine contractions by pulling the pup out with her teeth. She then eats the placenta and umbilical cord and cleans off the fetal membranes—a quite delicate operation. (A newborn pup looks like it is sealed in very thin plastic wrap.) After all the pups are born and cleaned up, the mother will probably nurse them. Milk is usually present very near the time of birth.

Periodically, the mother licks the pups' anogenital region, stimulating reflexive urination and defecation. Friedman and Bruno (1976) have shown the utility of this mechanism. They noted that a lactating female rat produces approximately 48 grams (g) of milk on the tenth day of lactation. This milk contains approximately 35 milliliters (ml) of water. The experimenters injected some of the pups with tritiated (radioactive) water and later found radioactivity in the mother and in the littermates. They calculated that a lactating rat normally consumes 21 ml of water in the urine of her young, thus recycling approximately two-thirds of the water she gives to the pups in the form of milk. The water, traded back and forth between mother and young, serves as a vehicle for the nutrients—fats, protein, and sugar—contained in milk. Because each day the milk production of a lactating rat is approximately 14 percent of her body weight (for a woman weighing 120 lb, that would be around 2 gal), the recycling is extremely useful, especially when the availability of water is a problem.

Besides cleaning, nursing, and purging her offspring, a female rodent will retrieve pups if they leave or are removed from the nest. The mother will even construct another nest in a new location and move her litter there, should the conditions at the old site become unfavorable (for example, when an inconsiderate experimenter puts a heat lamp over it). The way a female rodent picks up her pup is quite consistent: She gingerly grasps the animal by the back, managing not to injure it with her very sharp teeth. (I can personally attest to the ease with which these teeth can penetrate skin.) She then carries the pup with a characteristic prancing walk, her head held high. (See ***Figure 9.13.***) The pup is brought back to the nest and is left there. The female then leaves the nest again to search for another pup. She continues to retrieve pups until she finds no more; she does not count her pups and stop retrieving when they are all back. A mouse or rat will usually accept all the pups she is offered, if they are young enough. I once observed two lactating female mice with nests in corners of the same cage, diagonally opposite each other. I disturbed their nests, which triggered a long bout of retrieving, during which each mother stole youngsters from the other's nest. The mothers kept up their exchange for a long time, passing each other in the middle of the cage.

Maternal behavior begins to wane as the pups become more active and begin to look more like adults. At around sixteen to eighteen days of age they are able to get about easily by themselves, and they begin to obtain their own food. The mother ceases to retrieve them when they leave the nest and will eventually run away from them if they attempt to nurse.

FIGURE 9.13

A female mouse carrying one of her pups.

Another hormone present during lactation — prolactin — may also have stimulating effects on maternal behavior; and its effects, like those of estradiol, may be exerted in the medial preoptic area. Bridges et al. (1990) infused minute quantities of prolactin into the lateral ventricles or directly into the MPA of virgin female rats. They found that the animals quickly began taking care of pups. The effect occurred only if the animals were first given a series of injections of progesterone and estradiol; thus, the maternal behavior of normal females may depend on an interaction between several hormones.

Neural Control of Maternal Behavior

The most critical brain region responsible for maternal behavior appears to be the medial preoptic area, located in the forebrain. Numan (1974) found that lesions of the MPA disrupted both nest building and pup care. The mothers simply ignored their offspring. However, female sexual behavior was unaffected by these lesions. You will recall that male sexual behavior, but not female sexual behavior, is also disrupted by lesions of the MPA.

As you learned earlier, in the discussion of the neural basis of male sexual behavior, the MPA sends axons to the midbrain. Numan and his colleagues found that the pathway critical for maternal behavior runs from the MPA to the **ventral tegmental area** (VTA) of the midbrain. Numan and Smith (1984) found that lesions that interrupted this pathway disrupted maternal behavior.

ventral tegmental area (VTA)

The medial preoptic area appears to be the place where estradiol affects maternal behavior. The MPA contains estrogen receptors (Pfaff and Keiner, 1973), and Giordano et al. (1986) found that the concentration of estrogen receptors in the MPA increases during pregnancy. Direct implants of estradiol in the MPA facilitate maternal behavior (Numan, Rosenblatt, and Komisaruk, 1977), whereas injection of an antiestrogen chemical in the MPA blocks it (Adieh, Mayer, and Rosenblatt, 1987).

As we just saw, zinc sulfate treatment (which abolishes olfactory sensitivity), lesions of the medial amygdala, or lesions of the stria terminalis (which connects the

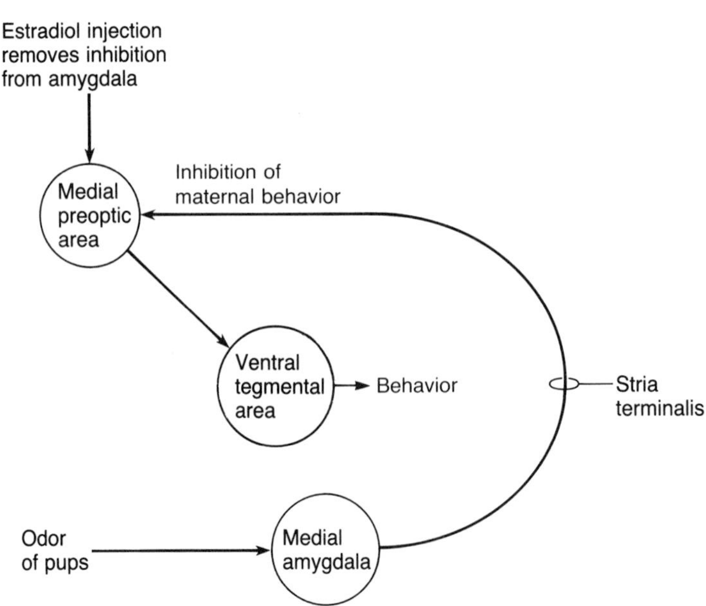

FIGURE 9.15

A possible explanation of the facilitating effects of estradiol on maternal behavior.

medial amygdala with the medial preoptic area) all facilitate maternal behavior in virgin female rats by eliminating the inhibitory effects caused by the odor of pups. Perhaps the stimulating effect of estradiol on the medial preoptic area works in a similar fashion, removing the inhibitory influence of the amygdala. (See ***Figure 9.15.***)

▶*INTERIM SUMMARY*◀

Many species must care for their offspring. Among rodents, this duty falls to the mother, who must build a nest, deliver her own pups, clean them, keep them warm, nurse them, and retrieve them if they are moved out of the nest. They must even induce their pups' urination and defecation, and their ingestion of the urine recycles water, which is often a scarce commodity.

Exposure to young pups stimulates maternal behavior within a few days. Apparently, the odor of pups elicits handling and licking, whereas the sound of their distress calls elicits nest building. Unsensitized virgin female rats appear to be repelled by the odor of pups, but deafferentation of the olfactory system with zinc sulfate abolishes this aversion and causes the animals to begin caring for pups more quickly. The inhibitory effect of the odor of pups may be mediated by the accessory olfactory system; cutting the vomeronasal nerve facilitates maternal behavior. Both components of the olfactory system project to the medial amygdala. Lesions of the medial amygdala or the stria terminalis also facilitate maternal responsiveness. Therefore, the inhibitory effects of olfaction on maternal behavior may be mediated by the pathway from the olfactory system to the medial amygdala to the medial preoptic area, via the stria terminalis.

Nest building appears to be facilitated by progesterone during pregnancy and by prolactin during the lactation period. The sequence of progesterone + estradiol facilitates maternal behavior, and so does injection of prolactin directly in to the brain.

The medial preoptic area is the most important forebrain structure for maternal behavior, and the ventral tegmental area of the midbrain is the most important brain stem structure. Neurons in the medial preoptic area send axons caudally to the ventral tegmental area; if these connections are interrupted bilaterally, rats cease providing maternal care of offspring. ▲

AGGRESSIVE BEHAVIOR

Almost all species of animals engage in aggressive behaviors, which involve threatening gestures or actual attack directed toward another animal. Aggressive behaviors are species-typical; that is, the patterns of movements (for example, posturing, biting, striking, and hissing) are organized by neural circuits whose development is largely programmed by an animal's genes. Most aggressive behaviors are related to reproduction. For example, aggressive behaviors that gain access to mates, defend territory needed to attract mates or to provide a site for building a nest, or defend offspring against intruders can all be regarded as reproductive behaviors. Because the reproductive roles of males and females differ, their aggressive behaviors differ also.

Although aggressive behaviors can be regarded as sexually dimorphic, the behaviors themselves are identical in males and females. What differs is the situations in which these behaviors occur and, in some cases, the hormones that arouse or inhibit these behaviors. Thus, we would not expect to see sex differences in the neural circuits responsible for the execution of aggressive behaviors, but we *would* expect to find differences in the brain mechanisms that, in response to hormonal conditions and environmental stimuli, excite or inhibit these circuits.

Aggressive behavior can take different forms and can be provoked by different situations. In this section I will first describe aggressive behaviors and their neural organization. Then I will discuss the situations that provoke these behaviors and the role that hormones play in regulating their occurrence.

Nature and Functions of Aggressive Behavior

offensive behavior
defensive behavior
threat behavior
submissive behavior

In cats and rodents (the species most often studied in the laboratory), aggressive behavior takes three basic forms: *offense, defense,* and *predation* (Adams, 1986). **Offensive behaviors** consist of physical assaults of one animal on another. When threatened or attacked, an animal often exhibits **defensive behaviors.** Defensive behaviors can consist of actual attacks, or they may simply involve **threat behaviors,** which consist of postures or gestures that warn the adversary to leave or it will become the target of an attack. The threatened animal might show **submissive behaviors,** which indicate that it will not challenge the other animal.

predation

In the natural environment most animals display far more threats than actual attacks. Threat behaviors are useful in reinforcing social hierarchies in organized groups of animals or in warning intruders away from an animal's territory. They have the advantage of not involving actual fighting, which can harm one or both of the combatants. **Predation** is the attack of a member of one species on that of another, usually because the latter serves as food for the former.

Neural Control of Aggressive Behavior

As we shall see in this section, the three major types of aggressive behavior — offense, defense, and predation — are controlled by different brain mechanisms, which implies that the behaviors are at least somewhat independent. The neural control of aggressive behavior is hierarchical. That is, the particular muscular movements an animal makes in attacking or defending itself are programmed by neural circuits in the midbrain. These circuits are controlled by neurons located in the forebrain. Whether an animal attacks depends on many factors, including the nature of the eliciting stimuli in the environment and the animal's previous experience. The activity of the midbrain circuits appears to be controlled by the hypothalamus and the limbic system (especially the amygdala), which also influence many other species-typical behaviors. And, of course, the activity of the limbic system is controlled by perceptual systems that detect the status of the environment, including the presence of other animals.

Two parts of the midbrain, the periaqueductal gray matter and the ventral tegmental area, are involved in the organization of aggressive behaviors. Offensive behavior appears to be controlled by neurons in the ventral tegmental area, and defensive behavior and predation appear to be controlled by neurons in the periaqueductal gray matter. One study suggests that neurons controlling defensive behavior are located dorsal to those that control predatory behavior.

First, let us consider offensive behavior. The best evidence that the ventral tegmental area (VTA) of the midbrain is involved in these behaviors comes from a study by Adams (1986), who made lesions in the VTA of rats and tested the animals offensive, defensive, and predatory behavior. The lesions disrupted only offensive attack; predation and defensive behavior were unaffected.

The other aggressive behaviors are controlled by neurons in the periaqueductal gray matter (PAG). Stimulation of different parts of the PAG with electricity or excitatory amino acids produce defensive behavior, predatory behavior, flight, or immobility

(Bandler and Carrive, 1988; Shaikh and Siegel, 1989; Zhang, Bandler, and Carrive, 1990). Flight and immobility are not aggressive behaviors, but they are clearly related to aggression, because they often occur in response to threat gestures from another animal.

The hypothalamus and the amygdala clearly play a role in aggressive behaviors, because stimulation or lesions of various parts of both regions can elicit or inhibit one or more of these behaviors. The amygdaloid complex is located in the rostromedial temporal lobe in humans and in analogous locations in other mammals. It contains several nuclei, divided into two principal groups: the *corticomedial nuclei* (phylogenetically older) and the *basolateral nuclei* (evolved more recently). Neurons in the corticomedial nuclei send axons through the stria terminalis to the hypothalamus and other forebrain structures; neurons in the basolateral nuclei send axons through the more diffuse *ventral amygdalofugal pathway* (*amygdalofugal* means "amygdala fleeing"). The ventral amygdalofugal pathway reaches the hypothalamus, preoptic region, and septal nuclei, and it also sends fibers to the midbrain tegmentum and periaqueductal gray matter. The anatomy of the amygdala thus provides a basis for its role in modulating hypothalamic-midbrain mechanisms in aggressive and defensive behavior. (See ***Figure 9.16.***)

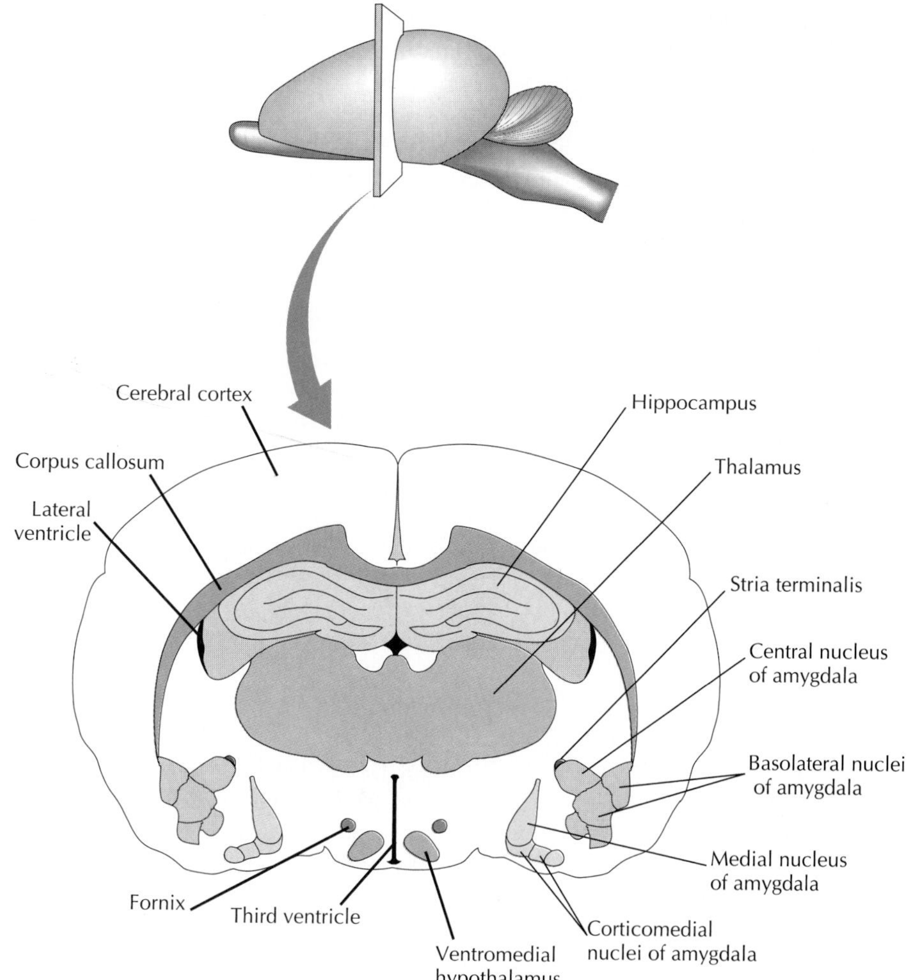

FIGURE 9.16

A cross section through the rat brain showing the location of the amygdala. (Adapted from Paxinos, G., and Watson, C. *The Brain in Stereotaxic Coordinates.* Sydney: Academic Press, 1982. Redrawn with permission.)

As we saw earlier in this chapter, the amygdala contains estrogen and androgen receptors and receives input from the primary and accessory olfactory systems. Lesions of the amygdala reduce a male hamster's attraction to the odor of the urine of receptive females and remove the inhibitory effects of the odor of rat pups on the behavior of virgin female rats. As we will see in Chapter 10, the amygdala plays a role in controlling emotional reactions to harmful stimuli. The fact that lesions or electrical stimulation of the amygdala can arouse or inhibit aggressive behaviors is certainly consistent with these general functions. Future studies will have to focus on specific nuclei, which have specific inputs and outputs and, undoubtedly, have specific roles.

Hormonal Control of Aggressive Behavior

With the exception of self-defense and predatory aggression, most instances of aggressive behavior are in some way related to reproduction. For example, males of some species establish territories that attract females during the breeding season. To do so, they must defend them against the intrusion of other males. Even in species in which breeding does not depend on the establishment of a territory, males may compete for access to females, which also involves aggressive behavior. Females, too, often compete with other females for space in which to build nests or dens in which to rear their offspring, and they will defend their offspring against the intrusion of other animals. As you learned earlier in this chapter, most reproductive behaviors are controlled by the organizational and activational effects of hormones; thus, we should not be surprised that most forms of aggressive behavior, like mating, are affected by hormones.

The five subsections that follow discuss aggression among males, aggression among females, maternal aggression, infanticide, and the possible role of androgens in human aggression.

INTERMALE AGGRESSION

Adult males of many species fight for territory or access to females. In laboratory rodents androgen secretion occurs prenatally, decreases, and then increases again at the time of puberty. Intermale aggressiveness also begins around the time of puberty, which suggests that the behavior is controlled by neural circuits that are stimulated by androgens. Indeed, many years ago Beeman (1947) found that castration reduced aggressiveness and that injections of testosterone reinstated it.

We saw that early androgenization has an *organizational effect.* The secretion of androgens early in development modifies the developing brain, making neural circuits that control male sexual behavior become more responsive to testosterone. Similarly, early androgenization has an organizational effect that stimulates the development of testosterone-sensitive neural circuits that facilitate intermale aggression. (See ***Figure 9.17.***)

As you learned earlier in this chapter, when a pregnant female is subjected to stress, her male offspring show less male sexual behavior, presumably because the stress interferes with the prenatal secretion of androgens. Kinsley and Svare (1986) found that prenatal stress also reduces intermale aggression. They subjected pregnant female mice to stress by restraining them several times in a plastic tube that was placed under bright lights. The male offspring were tested as adults for intermale aggression by placing them in a cage with an unfamiliar male. The prenatally stressed animals were much less likely than the control animals to attack the intruder. Thus, a treatment that interferes with prenatal masculinization of sexual behavior also interferes with the masculinization of aggressive behavior.

FIGURE 9.17

Organizational and activational effects of testosterone on social aggression.

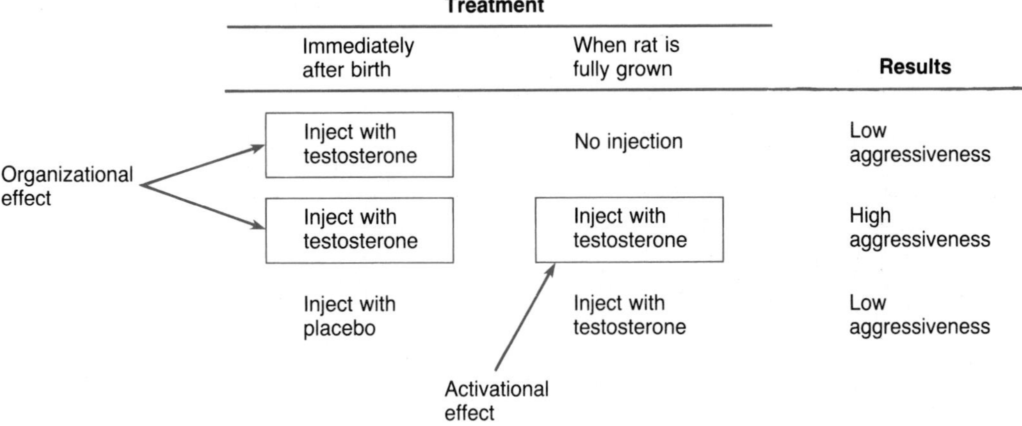

Treatment
Immediately after birth
When rat is fully grown
Results
Organizational effect
Inject with testosterone
No injection
Low aggressiveness
Inject with testosterone
Inject with testosterone
High aggressiveness
Inject with placebo
Inject with testosterone
Low aggressiveness
Activational effect

We saw earlier in this chapter that androgens stimulate male sexual behavior by interacting with androgen receptors in neurons located in the medial preoptic area (MPA). This region also appears to be important in mediating the effects of androgens on intermale aggression. Bean and Conner (1978) found that implanting testosterone in the MPA reinstated intermale aggression in castrated male rats. Presumably, the testosterone directly activated the behavior by stimulating the androgen-sensitive neurons located there.

The medial preoptic area, then, appears to be involved in several behaviors related to reproduction: male sexual behavior, maternal behavior, and intermale aggression. As we saw earlier, both male sexual behavior and maternal behavior appear to involve projections from the MPA to the region of the ventral tegmental area (VTA) of the midbrain. We also saw that the lesions of the VTA abolish offensive behavior (but not defensive behavior or predation). I suspect that the connections between the MPA and the VTA are important for the effects of androgens on intermale aggression, although there is not yet, to my knowledge, any experimental evidence to support this hypothesis.

Males readily attack other males but usually do not attack females. Their ability to discriminate the sex of the intruder appears to be based on odor. Bean (1982) found that intermale aggression was abolished in mice by cutting the vomeronasal nerve. Rinsing the olfactory epithelium with zinc sulfate (which deafferents the primary olfactory system) had no effect. (See ***Figure 9.18.***) Thus, intermale aggression of mice (and probably of other species of rodents) depends on a pheromonal stimulus. Undoubtedly, the medial amygdala plays a role in modulating this effect, as it does in all other phenomena controlled by pheromones.

INTERFEMALE AGGRESSION

Many researchers have concluded that in most species females are less aggressive than males. Indeed, when two adult female rodents meet in a neutral territory, they are unlikely to fight, whereas adult males are very likely to do so. Interfemale aggression, like intermale aggression, appears to be dependent on testosterone. Van de Poll, Taminiau, Endert, and Louwerse (1988) ovariectomized female rats and then gave them daily injections of testosterone, estradiol, or a placebo for fourteen days. The

FIGURE 9.18

Effects of transection of the vomeronasal nerve and lack of olfactory sensitivity produced by zinc sulfate treatment on intermale aggression in mice. (Adapted from Bean, N.J. *Physiology and Behavior,* 1982, *29,* 433–437.)

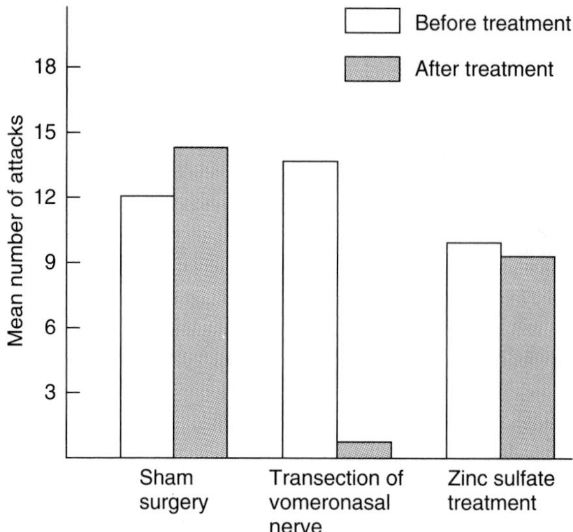

animals were then placed in a test cage and an unfamiliar female was introduced. As Figure 9.19 shows, testosterone increased aggressiveness, whereas estradiol decreased it. (See ***Figure 9.19.***)

As we saw earlier, females will become as aggressive as males if they are given testosterone immediately after birth. Apparently, a certain amount of prenatal androgenization occurs naturally. Most rodent fetuses share their mother's uterus with brothers and sisters, arranged in a row like peas in a pod. A female mouse may have zero, one, or two brothers adjacent to her. Researchers refer to these females as 0M, 1M, or 2M, respectively. (See ***Figure 9.20.***) Being next to a male fetus has an effect on a female's blood levels of androgens prenatally. Vom Saal and Bronson (1980b) found that females located between two males had significantly higher levels of testosterone in their blood than females located between two females (or between a female and the end of the uterus). When they are tested as adults, 2M females are more likely to exhibit interfemale aggressiveness.

Females of some primate species (for example, rhesus monkeys and baboons) are more likely to engage in fights around the time of ovulation (Carpenter, 1942; Saayman, 1971). This phenomenon is probably caused by their increased sexual interest and consequent proximity to males. As Carpenter noted, "She actively approaches

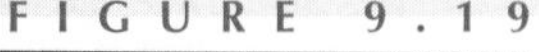

FIGURE 9.19

Effects of estradiol and testosterone on interfemale aggression in rats. (Adapted from van de Poll, N.E., Taminiau, M.S., Endert, E., and Louwerse, A.L. *International Journal of Neuroscience,* 1988, *41,* 271–286.)

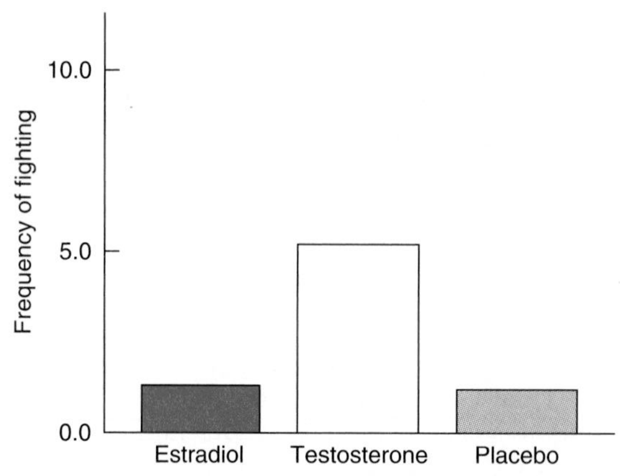

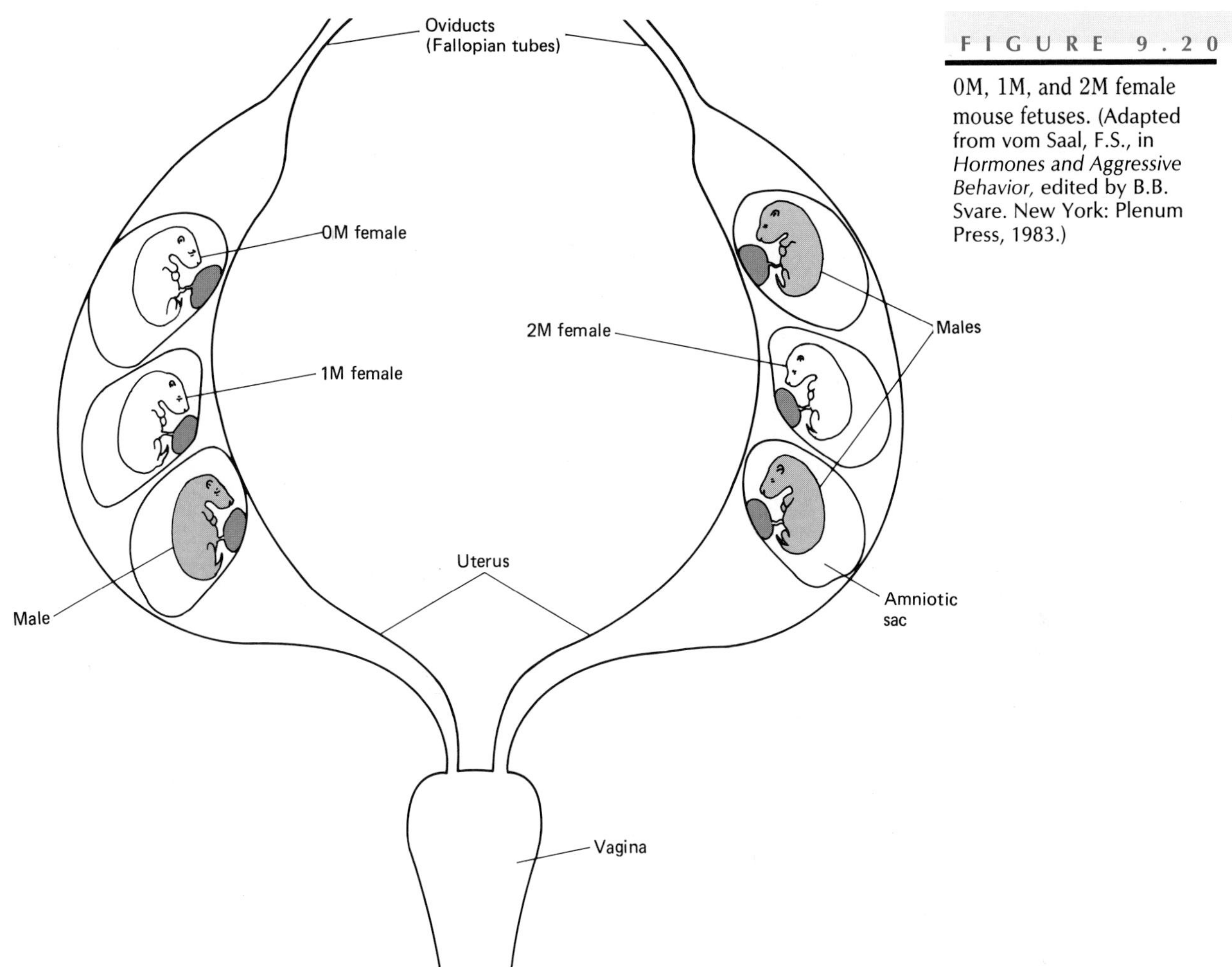

FIGURE 9.20

0M, 1M, and 2M female mouse fetuses. (Adapted from vom Saal, F.S., in *Hormones and Aggressive Behavior,* edited by B.B. Svare. New York: Plenum Press, 1983.)

males and must overcome their usual resistance to close association, hence she becomes an object of attacks by them" (p. 136). Another period of fighting occurs just before menstruation (Sassenrath, Powell, and Hendrickx, 1973; Mallow, 1979). During this time females tend to attack other females.

Researchers have studied the possibility that irritability and aggressiveness may increase in women just before the time of menstruation, as it does in some other primate species. Floody (1983) reviewed the literature on the so-called *premenstrual syndrome* (PMS). Almost all studies that observed actual aggressiveness, primarily of women in institutions, found decreases around the time of ovulation and increases just before menstruation. Clearly, the changes in irritability are not universal; some women experience little or no mood shift before menstruation. And even if changes in mood occur, most women do not actually become aggressive. Although women with a history of criminal behavior (such as those in prison) may indeed exhibit premenstrual aggressiveness, emotionally stable women may fail to show even a small increase in aggressiveness (Persky, 1974). Depending on their history and temperament, different people respond differently to similar physiological changes.

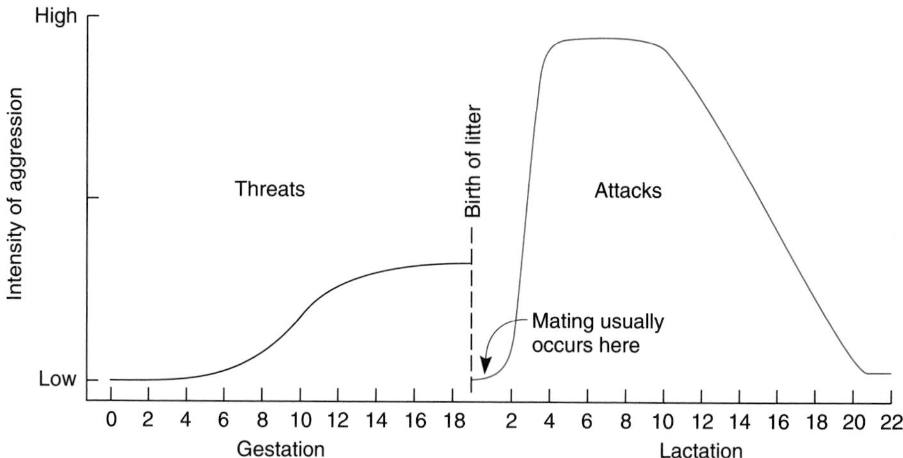

FIGURE 9.21

Level of aggressiveness of pregnant and lactating female mice. (Adapted from Svare, B. in *Mammalian Parenting: Biochemical, Neurobiological, and Behavioral Determinants,* edited by N.A. Krasnegor and R.S. Bridges. New York: Oxford University Press, 1990.)

MATERNAL AGGRESSION

Most parents who actively raise their offspring will vigorously defend them against intruders. In laboratory rodents the responsible parent is the female, so the most commonly studied form of parental defense is maternal aggression. Female mice very effectively defend their young, driving away intruding adults of either sex. Counterattacks by the intruder are rare (Svare, Betteridge, Katz, and Samuels, 1981). Whereas strange males who encounter each other engage in mutual investigation for a minute or two before fighting begins, the attack of a lactating female on an intruder is immediate (Svare, 1983).

Immediately after giving birth, for a period of approximately 48 hours, female mice become completely docile; they do not attack intruders (Ghiraldi and Svare, 1989). As Svare (1989) notes, it is at this time that female mice typically mate again; thus, the fact that they do not attack a male is biologically significant. (See ***Figure 9.21.***) This phenomenon is probably caused by the high level of estradiol that is present at that time. Ghiraldi and Svare found that ovariectomy just before parturition shortened the period of docility by 24 hours, and administration of estradiol restored it.

The tendency for a lactating female mouse to attack a stranger is not a direct effect of ovarian or pituitary hormones; it is induced by tactile stimuli provided by her offspring. If the newborn mice are removed, the mother fails to become aggressive. Normally, maternal aggressiveness begins after the mother has suckled her young for 48 hours. If the mother's nipples are surgically removed, she does not become aggressive, even if pups are present, as Svare and Gandelman (1976) and Gandelman and Simon (1980) found. These two studies also showed that although virgin female mice will begin exhibiting maternal behavior when they are housed with pups, they fail to show maternal aggression unless they are given daily injections of estrogen and progesterone, which causes their nipples to develop.

INFANTICIDE

Although the evolutionary process has selected parents who nurture and defend their young, adults — both male and female — sometimes kill infants, including their own. Although this behavior may appear to be aberrant and maladaptive, under some circumstances it has survival value for the species.

Hrdy (1977), in a report of infanticide among langurs (a primate species), suggested that the killing of infants by a male who was not the father "is a reproductive strategy whereby the usurping male increases his own reproductive success at the expense of the former leader (presumably the father of the infant killed)" (p. 48). Because lactation suppresses a female's fertility, she is unlikely to become pregnant by the new male. However, when the male kills her offspring, she soon becomes fertile and thus capable of becoming pregnant by him. (The male tends *not* to kill his own offspring.)

Vom Saal (1985) discovered that the tendency of male mice to kill infants is regulated by copulation. He found that after male mice successfully copulated and ejaculated, the likelihood of infanticide increased within a few days but then decreased nineteen days later, around the time that the pups would be born. In fact, the males not only did not kill pups but actually cared for them, just as their mothers do. This docility and solicitude lasted until about fifty days after the time of copulation, which is about the time that the pups would be weaned. Thus, the act of ejaculation initiates a series of events that increases the likelihood that a would-be father mouse will kill the infants of other males but not his own. (A male mouse cannot tell which pups are his own.)

The timing of these behavioral changes is remarkable. What internal mechanism keeps track of the nineteen-day gestation period of the female? Perrigo, Bryant, and vom Saal (1990) found that however this mechanism works, it does so by counting days, not hours. They permitted male mice to copulate and then divided them into two groups, which they put in rooms with light-dark cycles of different lengths: 22 or 27 hours. They found that the reduction in the likelihood of infanticide occurred after approximately eighteen "days," whether the days were short or long. It will be interesting to discover the mechanism that permits the mouse brain to count to eighteen.

Female rodents sometimes kill their own pups. Obviously, infanticide by males and females must occur for different reasons. Indeed, female infanticide appears to achieve at least two advantages: It decreases crowding, and it helps attain an optimal litter size. The first hypothetical advantage was supported by Calhoun (1962), who reported that severe crowding greatly increased the incidence of female infanticide in rats. Presumably, this behavior helped prevent the crowding from increasing still further. Gandelman and Simon (1978) obtained data that supported the second hypothetical advantage. They adjusted the size of litters of newborn mice to either twelve or sixteen pups by adding foster pups or removing them. In both groups the mean number of surviving offspring was nine. The mothers with sixteen pups tended to kill more than those with twelve pups. The smallest pups were most likely to be killed. Because these pups were probably the least fit, the behavior tends to select for an optimally sized litter that consists of the healthiest pups. (Mice have ten nipples, which suggests that the optimal size is ten or fewer.)

EFFECTS OF ANDROGENS ON HUMAN AGGRESSIVE BEHAVIOR

Boys are generally more aggressive than girls. Clearly, Western society tolerates assertiveness and aggressive behavior from boys more than girls. Without doubt, the way we treat boys and girls and the models we expose them to play important roles in sex differences in aggressiveness in our species. The question is not whether socialization has an effect but whether biological influences (primarily, exposure to androgens) has an effect, too.

I have already reviewed some of the evidence concerning intermale aggression in laboratory animals, and we saw that androgens have strong organizational and activational effects. Prenatal androgenization increases aggressive behavior in all species that have been studied, including primates. Therefore, if androgens did not affect aggressive behavior in humans, our species would be exceptional. Boys' testosterone levels begin to increase during the early teens, at which time aggressive behavior and intermale fighting also increase (Mazur, 1983). Of course, boys' social status changes during puberty, and their testosterone affects their muscles as well as their brains; so we cannot be sure that the effect is hormonally produced, or if it is, that it is mediated by the brain.

Males of many species can be gentled by castration. In the past, authorities have attempted to suppress sex-related aggression by castrating convicted male sex offenders. Investigators have reported that both heterosexual and homosexual aggressive attacks disappear, along with the offender's sex drive (Hawke, 1951; Sturup, 1961; Laschet, 1973). However, the studies typically lack appropriate control groups and do not always measure aggressive behavior directly. Because the studies with castrated males were not performed with the appropriate double-blind controls, we cannot conclude that testosterone was the responsible agent for the increase in aggressive behavior.

Some cases of aggressiveness — especially sexual assault — have been treated with drugs that block androgen receptors and thus prevent androgens from exerting their normal effects. The rationale is based on animal research that indicates that androgens promote male sexual behavior and intermale aggression. Clearly, treatment with drugs is preferable to castration, because the effects are not irreversible. However, the efficacy of treatment with antiandrogens has yet to be established conclusively (Bain, 1987).

Another way to determine whether androgens affect aggressiveness in humans is to examine the testosterone levels of people who exhibit varying levels of aggressive behavior. However, even though this approach poses fewer ethical problems, it presents methodological ones. First, let me review some evidence. Dabbs, Frady, Carr, and Besch (1987) measured the testosterone levels of male prison inmates and found a significant correlation with several measures of violence, including the nature of the crime for which they were convicted, infractions of prison rules, and ratings of "toughness" by their peers. These relations are seen in female prison inmates too; Dabbs et al. (1988) found that women prisoners who showed unprovoked violence and had several prior convictions also showed higher levels of testosterone. (As we saw earlier, testosterone increases interfemale aggression in laboratory animals as well.)

But we must remember that *correlation* does not necessarily indicate *causation.* A person's environment can affect his or her testosterone level. For example, losing a tennis match or a wrestling competition causes a fall in blood levels of testosterone (Mazur and Lamb, 1980; Elias, 1981). In a very elaborate study Jeffcoate, Lincoln, Selby, and Herbert (1986) found that the blood levels of a group of five men confined on a boat for fourteen days changed as they established a dominance-aggression ranking among themselves: The higher the rank, the higher the testosterone level was. Thus, we cannot be sure in any correlational study that high testosterone levels *cause* people to become dominant or violent; perhaps their success in establishing a position of dominance increases their testosterone levels relative to those of the people they dominate.

A few studies have looked at the behavioral effects of administering androgens. Because of ethical concerns, people cannot be given androgen supplements merely to see whether they become more aggressive. First, excessive amounts of androgens have deleterious effects on a person's health. Second, it would be wrong to subject innocent people to possible harm from the aggressive behavior of someone who receives androgens while participating in an experiment. Thus, the only evidence we have comes from

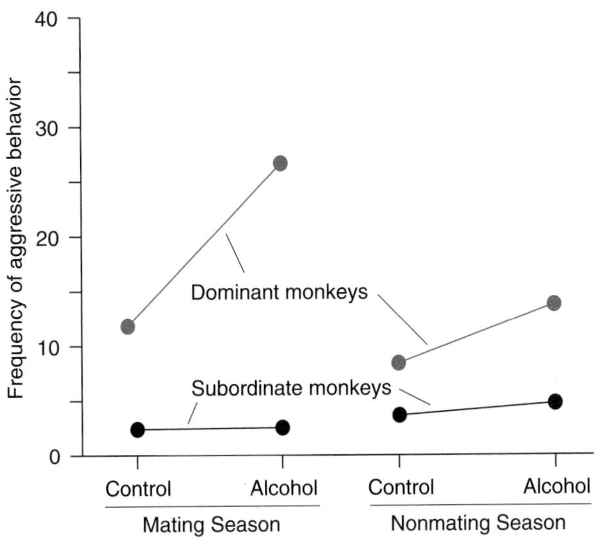

FIGURE 9.22

Effect of alcohol intake on frequency of aggressive behavior of dominant and subordinate male squirrel monkeys during the mating season and the nonmating season. (Based on data from Winslow, J.T., and Miczek, J.A. *Psychopharmacologia,* 1988, *95,* 92–98.)

case studies in which a person with abnormally low levels of testosterone is given the hormone to replace what would normally be present. For example, O'Carroll and Bancroft (1985) reported the case of an institutionalized, mentally retarded man who had lost his testes when he was seven years old. When he received an injection of testosterone, he became violent.

An interesting set of experiments with another species of primates may have some relevance to human aggression. As you undoubtedly know, alcohol intake is often associated with aggression in humans. Alcohol increases intermale aggression in dominant male squirrel monkeys, but only during the mating season, when their blood level of testosterone is two to three times higher than during the nonmating season (Winslow and Miczek, 1985, 1988). Alcohol does *not* increase the aggressive behavior of subordinate monkeys at any time of the year. These studies suggest that the effects of alcohol interact with both social status and with testosterone. (See ***Figure 9.22.***) This suggestion was confirmed by Winslow, Ellingoe, and Miczek (1988), who tested monkeys during the nonmating season. They found that alcohol increased the aggressive behavior of dominant monkeys if they were also given injections of testosterone. However, these treatments were ineffective in subordinate monkeys, who had presumably learned not to be aggressive. The next step will be to find the neural mechanisms that are responsible for these interactions.

▶*INTERIM SUMMARY*◀

Aggressive behaviors are species-typical and serve useful functions most of the time. Their primary forms are offense, defense, and predation. In addition, animals may exhibit threat or submissive behaviors, which may avoid an actual fight.

The ventral tegmental area of the midbrain appears to be involved in the control of offensive behavior; lesions there abolish this behavior without affecting defense or predation. The periaqueductal gray matter appears to be involved in defensive behavior and predation and also in flight behavior and immobility, which are possible responses to attack by another animal. The midbrain mechanisms are modulated by the hypothalamus and amygdala.

Because many aggressive behaviors are related to reproduction, they are influenced by hormones, especially sex steroid hormones. Androgens primarily affect offensive attack; they are not necessary for defensive behaviors, which are shown by females as well as males. In males androgens have organizational and activational effects on offensive attack, just as they have on male sexual behavior. Prenatal stress reduces the incidence of intermale aggression.

The effects of androgens on intermale aggression appear to be mediated by the medial preoptic area. Recognition of the odor of a male is necessary for stimulating an attack; cutting of the vomeronasal nerve abolishes intermale aggression. The medial amygdala undoubtedly is involved in the effects of odors on aggression.

Female aggressiveness is more common than was previously believed. Females who have been slightly androgenized (2M females) are more likely to attack other females. Female primates are most likely to fight around the time of ovulation, perhaps because their increased sexual interest brings them closer to males. Although some women report irritability just before menstruation, the phenomenon is not universal.

Maternal aggression is a very swift and effective behavior. It is stimulated by the tactile feedback from suckling. Infanticide by male mice is regulated by copulation. After ejaculating, the males become more likely to kill infants; but around the time that their pups would be born, this tendency is suppressed. Female infanticide appears to promote optimal litter size and tends to weed out less healthy offspring.

Androgens apparently promote aggressive behavior in humans, but this topic is more difficult to study in our species than in laboratory animals. Differences in testosterone levels have been observed in criminals with a history of violence, but we cannot be sure whether higher androgen levels promote violence or whether successful aggression increases androgen levels. Studies with monkeys suggest that testosterone and alcohol have synergistic effects, particularly in dominant animals. (*Synergy,* from a Greek word meaning "working together," refers to combinations of factors that are more effective than the sum of their individual actions.) Perhaps these effects are related to our observations that some men with a history of violent behavior become more aggressive when they drink. ▲

EPILOGUE: ▶ Application

In the Prologue I described a perfume maker's fantasy—discovering a sex attractant pheromone that works for humans. An exclusive patent on such a chemical would certainly bring fabulous wealth. Think of how much money people spend on perfumes, makeup, shampoos, styling mousse, acne cream, and other beauty aids. Think of how much more money people would be willing to spend on a chemical that would go right from the nose to the brain and arouse romantic ardor.

Unfortunately for perfume makers, there is no evidence that human sex attractant pheromones exist. For a while researchers believed that they had discovered one in monkeys—which provided at least some hope for finding them in humans—but subsequent studies found that the effect was produced by something altogether different. In the original studies the experimenters found that extracts obtained from the vaginal fluid of female monkeys during the middle of her menstrual cycle (when she is most attractive to males) served as a sex attractant pheromone. If this chemical were swabbed on the vagina of another female during an early or late part of her cycle, a male would find her more attractive. It turned out, however, that something other than pheromones was responsible for the phenomenon. In some cases the treatment simply provided a novel odor, which made the male notice the female. In other cases the smell apparently reminded the male of the odor of one of his favorite partners.

Odors of a particular person—a loved one, for example—can affect sexual arousal, just as the sight of that person or the sound of his or her voice can do. We are not generally conscious of the fact, but we can learn to recognize other people by their odor. For example, a study by Russell (1976) found that people were able to distinguish by odor between T-shirts that they had worn and those previously worn by other people. They could also tell whether the unknown owner of a T-shirt was male or female. Thus, it is likely that men and women can *learn* to be attracted by their partners' characteristic odors. However, this phenomenon is different from the responses produced by pheromones, which apparently need not be learned.

Learning to recognize sex partners (primarily by their odor) is important for species in which a male controls a herd of females and impregnates all of them. In many species of mammals, if a male is presented with a single female, he will copulate with her several times but will eventually appear to be exhausted. However, if the male is presented with a new female, he will begin to respond again. If he is introduced to a series of new females, his performance will continue for prolonged periods of time. If one of the original females is reintroduced, the male will *not* respond.

In one of the most unusual studies I have read about, Beamer, Bermant, and Clegg (1969) tested the ability of a ram (male sheep) to recognize ewes with which he had mated. If a ram is given a new ewe each time, it will quickly begin copulating and will ejaculate within two minutes. (In one study a ram kept up this performance with twelve ewes. The experimenters finally got tired of shuffling sheep around; the ram was still ready to go.) Beamer and his colleagues tried to fool rams by putting trench coats and Halloween face masks on females with which they had mated. (No, I'm not making this up.) The males were not fooled by the disguise; they apparently recognized their former partners by their odor, and they were no longer interested in them.

The rejuvenating effect of a new female, also seen in roosters, is usually called the *Coolidge effect.* The following story is reputed to be true, but I cannot vouch for that fact. (If it is not true, it ought to be.) The late former U.S. president Calvin Coolidge and his wife were touring a farm, when Mrs. Coolidge pointedly asked the farmer whether the continuous and vigorous sexual activity among the flock of hens was the work of just one rooster. The reply was yes. She smiled and said, "You might point that out to Mr. Coolidge." The president looked thoughtfully at the birds and then asked the farmer whether a different hen was involved each time. The answer, again, was yes. "You might point *that* out to Mrs. Coolidge," he said, dryly. ▲

KEY CONCEPTS

Sexual Development

- Gender is determined by the sex chromosomes, which control development of the gonads. Two hormones secreted by the testes, testosterone and Müllerian-inhibiting substance, cause masculinization and defeminization; otherwise, the organism will be female.
- Sexual maturation occurs when the anterior pituitary gland secretes gonadotropic hormones, which instruct the gonads to secrete sex steroid hormones.

Hormonal Control of Sexual Behavior

- Female reproductive cycles are caused by interactions between the ovaries and the anterior pituitary gland.
- Androgens cause behavioral masculinization and defeminization by affecting brain development.
- In mammals other than primates estradiol and progesterone activate female sexual behavior. Testosterone activates male sexual behavior in all mammalian species.
- Pheromones permit animals to affect the reproductive status

or sexual interest o
mere presence.

- In humans the org
exist) may manifest
gens appear to hav
for both men and w

Neural Control of Se

- In laboratory anima
medial preoptic are
the ventromedial nu
female sexual behav
behavioral effects o

Maternal Behavior

- Maternal behavior i
tradiol and prolacti
vided by the female

NEW TERMS

accessory olfactory bu
activational effect **p. 28**
adrenogenital syndrom
androgen **p. 282**
androgen insensitivity
Bruce effect **p. 289**
corpus luteum **p. 286**
defeminizing effect **p. 2**
defensive behavior **p. 3**
estradiol **p. 284**
estrogen **p. 284**
estrous cycle **p. 285**
follicle-stimulating hor
gamete **p. 279**
gonad **p. 280**
gonadotropic hormone
Lee-Boot effect **p. 288**

SUGGESTED REAI

Sexual Behavior

Halpern, M. The organiza
Annual Review of Ne
Kelley, D.B. Sexually din
science, 1988, *11,* 22
Knobil, E., and Neill, J.
Raven Press, 1988.
Martini, L., and Ganong,
10. New York: Raven
Rosen, R.C., and Beck, J
Guilford Press, 1988.

Maternal Behavior

Krasnegor, N.A., and Bri

Recent anatomical studies have shown that the central nucleus of the amygdala projects to other parts of the brain that are involved in reactions to aversive stimuli, including two regions in the lower brain stem that are involved in control of the autonomic nervous system and a nucleus of the hypothalamus that is involved in the secretion of stress-related hormones (Cassell and Gray, 1989; Danielsen, Magnuson, and Gray, 1989; Gray, Carney, and Magnuson, 1989). It seems likely that these connections, too, are involved in the expression of specific aspects of conditioned emotional responses.

Although most of the experiments investigating the role of the central nucleus of the amygdala in conditioned emotional responses have used auditory stimuli, results from studies using stimuli of other sensory modalities are consistent with the ones I have reviewed. For example, lesions of the central nucleus disrupt conditioned responses evoked by visual or olfactory stimuli that have been paired with a foot shock, and they make an animal act less timid in a strange environment (Hitchcock and Davis, 1986; Sananes and Campbell, 1989; Grijalva et al., 1990). Timidity in a strange environment is a useful trait; animals that enter an unfamiliar place boldly and heedlessly may find something waiting for them that will end their opportunity to contribute to the gene pool.

Stimulation of the central nucleus of the amygdala produces emotional responses; Iwata, Chida, and LeDoux (1987) found that an injection of an excitatory amino acid into this region caused increases in heart rate and blood pressure. In fact, long-term stimulation of the central amygdala produces gastric ulcers (Henke, 1982), and its destruction helps *prevent* the development of ulcers in a stressful situation (Ray, Henke, and Sullivan, 1987). These observations suggest that the autonomic responses controlled by the central nucleus are among those responsible for the harmful effects of long-term stress, which are discussed in the final section of this chapter.

Electrical-recording studies have obtained results consistent with those obtained from lesion studies and stimulation studies. Researchers in several different laboratories have shown that single neurons in various nuclei of the amygdala become active when emotionally relevant stimuli are presented. For example, these neurons are excited by such stimuli as the sight of a device that has been used to squirt either a bad-tasting or a sweet solution into the animal's mouth, the sound of another animal's vocalization, the sound of the opening of the laboratory door, the smell of smoke, or the sight of another animal's face (O'Keefe and Bouma, 1969; Jacobs and McGinty, 1972; Rolls, 1981; Leonard, Rolls, Wilson, and Baylis, 1985).

Perception of Stimuli with Emotional Significance

The amygdala plays a critical role in several kinds of emotional behaviors. At the very least, it plays a role in anger (aggression), fear (defensive responses), and disgust (conditioned flavor aversions — to be described in Chapter 11). The fact that it receives input from the olfactory bulbs and from the vomeronasal organ and influences sexual behavior and maternal behavior indicates that it may also play a role in some positive emotions. What we know about the amygdala so far suggests that it organizes patterns of behavioral, autonomic, and hormonal responses that constitute emotions by activating the appropriate neural circuits, which are mostly located in the hypothalamus and brain stem. The next question to ask is, "What causes the amygdala to act?" or, more precisely, is, "What neural mechanisms are responsible for deciding that the present situation demands an emotional response?" There are several kinds of stimuli, from the very simple to the very complex, that can produce emotional reactions. Thus, several different neural mechanisms are undoubtedly involved in producing these reactions. We will look at three neural mechanisms involved in emotional reactions in the following section: the thalamus, the sensory association cortex, and the orbitofrontal cortex.

SIMPLE STIMULI: THE THALAMUS

Most emotional reactions—especially those associated with defensive or aggressive behaviors—are rather primitive. That is, they emerged early in the evolutionary process and thus involve some of the older parts of the brain. The perception of a simple stimulus can be accomplished by subcortical structures and does not require the presence of the cerebral cortex. In fact, lesions of the primary auditory cortex do not disrupt the learning of a conditioned emotional response to a simple auditory stimulus, but thalamic lesions do (LeDoux, Sakaguchi, and Reis, 1984). The critical part of the thalamus appears to be the **medial division of the medial geniculate nucleus** (MGM). (See ***Figure 10.3.***) As you will recall from Chapters 3 and 6, the medial geniculate nucleus of the thalamus relays auditory information to the primary auditory cortex. However, the MGM projects only to other subcortical structures, including the amygdala. Destruction of the MGM or the connections between the MGM and the amygdala

medial division of the medial geniculate nucleus

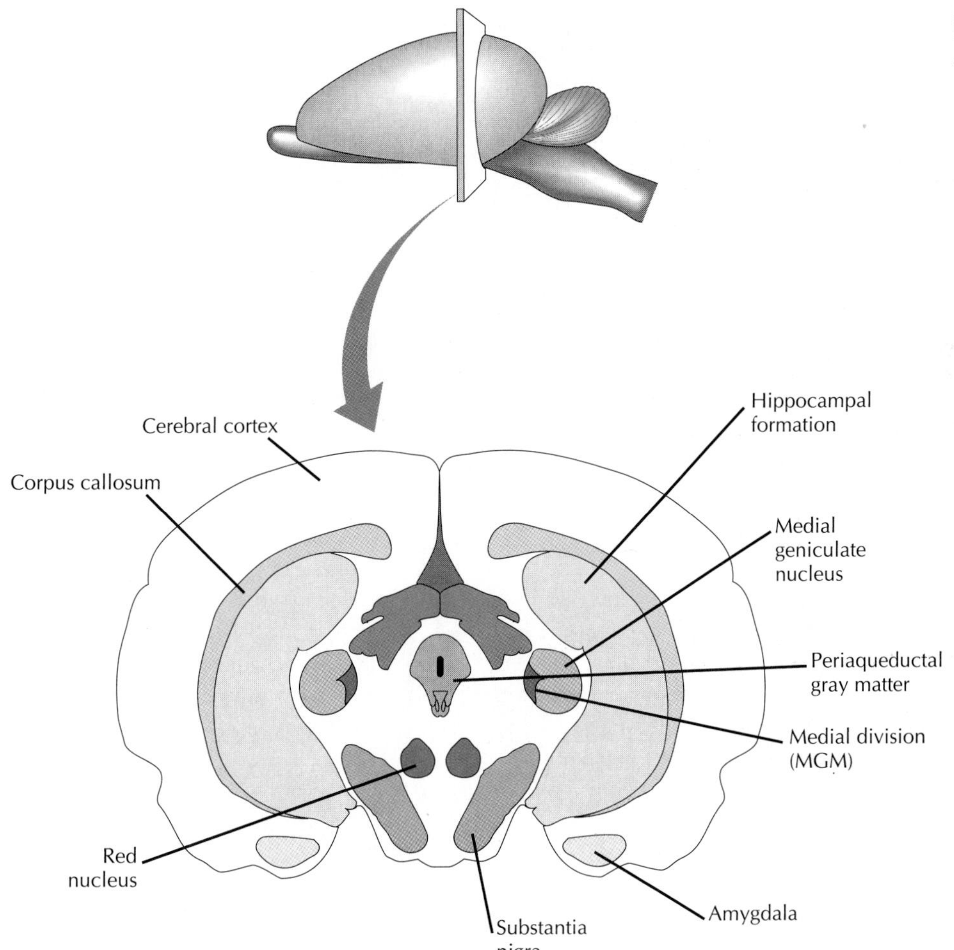

FIGURE 10.3

The medial division of the medial geniculate nucleus, a part of the thalamus that receives information from the auditory system and projects to subcortical regions, including the amygdala. (Adapted from Paxinos, G., and Watson, C. *The Rat Brain in Stereotaxic Coordinates.* Sydney: Academic Press, 1982. Redrawn with permission.)

prevent rats from learning a conditioned emotional responses (Iwata et al., 1986; LeDoux et al., 1986). The lesions have no effect on defensive learning cued by a visual stimulus, so the effect appears to be specific to the auditory system.

COMPLEX STIMULI: SENSORY ASSOCIATION CORTEX

Although a few emotional reactions seen in humans are produced by simple stimuli (such as the buzzing sound of a wasp), most of them involve more complex stimuli, such as the sight of a particular person with whom we have had unpleasant encounters. For these reactions to occur, we must first recognize the individual, and such recognition involves the visual association cortex. Similarly, recognition of a particular person's voice involves the auditory association cortex; and comprehension of the meaning of his or her words requires even more of the brain's resources.

The amygdala receives information from the inferior temporal cortex and the cortex at the very end of the temporal lobe — the *temporal pole.* These regions receive information from the visual, auditory, and somatosensory association cortex; thus, the amygdala is informed about all that is happening around the individual. As I mentioned earlier in this chapter, several studies have shown that individual neurons in the amygdala become active when an animal perceives complex stimuli with emotional significance. The information concerning these stimuli is received through the inputs from the temporal cortex.

A study by Downer (1962) showed the importance of these connections. Downer operated on a monkey, destroying the amygdala on the left side of the brain and cutting the corpus callosum, anterior commissure, and the optic chiasm. Cutting the corpus callosum and the anterior commissure prevented visual information received by one side of the brain from reaching the other. (The anterior commissure is a bundle of axons

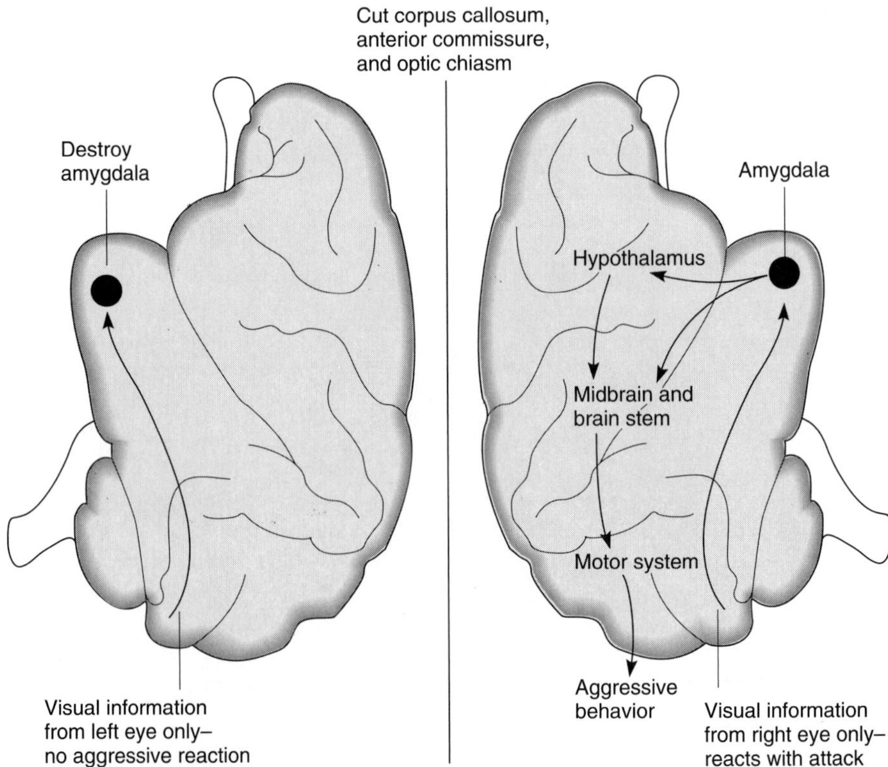

FIGURE 10.4

The experiment by Downer (1962). Visual information did not provoke an aggressive response unless it reached the intact amygdala on the right side of the monkey's brain.

that interconnects the right and left temporal lobes.) Cutting the optic chiasm meant that visual information received by the left eye went only to the left hemisphere, and information received by the right eye went only to the right hemisphere.

The monkey was an aggressive and emotional animal. Before the surgery, it would become enraged when it saw a human and would try to attack. Afterward, it was still aggressive and emotional, but only under certain conditions. If it was touched anywhere, it would react violently and try to attack. If it saw a person with its right eye, it would do the same. However, if its right eye were covered, it remained calm and passive. It would even approach the experimenter and take raisins from his hand. Its left eye was not blind; the monkey could still perceive visual stimuli when only this eye was open. However, these stimuli just did not evoke an emotional response. (See ***Figure 10.4.***).

SOCIAL SITUATIONS: THE ORBITOFRONTAL CORTEX

We humans are capable of reacting emotionally to very complex situations, especially those involving other people. Perceiving the meaning of social situations is obviously more complex than perceiving individual stimuli. The analysis of social situations involves much more than sensory analysis; it involves experiences and memories, inferences, and judgments. In fact, the skills involved include some of the most complex ones we possess. These skills are not localized in any one part of the cerebral cortex, although research does suggest that the right hemisphere is more important than the left. But one region of the brain — the orbitofrontal cortex — plays a special role.

orbitofrontal cortex

The **orbitofrontal cortex** is located at the base of the frontal lobes. It covers the part of the brain just above the *orbits*— the bones that form the eye sockets — hence the term *orbitofrontal.* (See ***Figure 10.5.***) The orbitofrontal cortex receives direct inputs from the dorsomedial thalamus, from the temporal cortex, and from the ventral tegmental area. It also receives indirect inputs from the amygdala and from the olfactory system. Its outputs go to several brain regions, including the cingulate cortex, hippocampal system, temporal cortex, lateral hypothalamus, and amygdala. Finally, it communicates with other parts of the frontal lobes. Thus, its inputs provide it with information about what is happening in the environment and what plans are being made by the rest of the frontal lobes, and its outputs permit it to affect a variety of

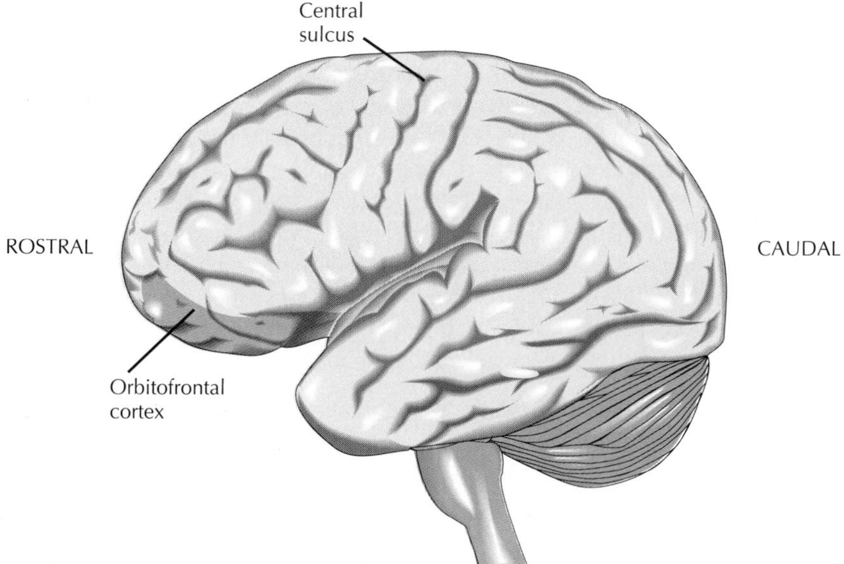

FIGURE 10.5

The orbitofrontal cortex.

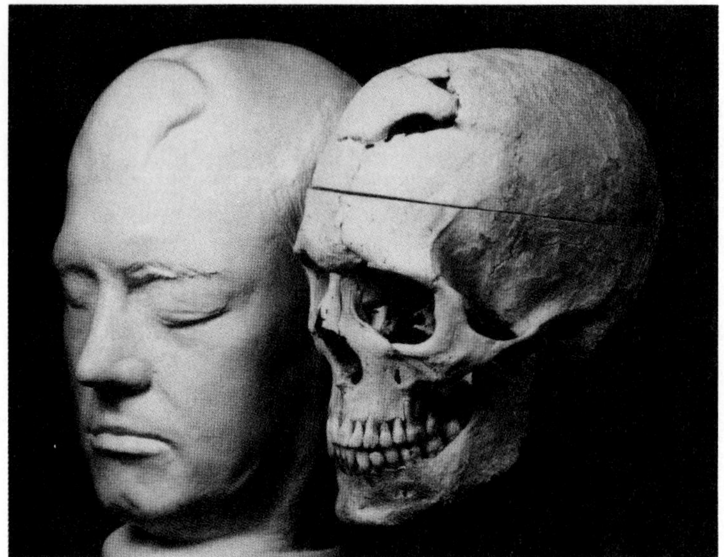

FIGURE 10.6

A bust and skull of Phineas Gage. The steel rod entered his left cheek and exited through his left forehead. (From Blakemore, C. *Mechanics of the Mind.* Cambridge, England: Cambridge University Press, 1977. Reprinted with permission.)

behaviors and physiological responses, including emotional responses organized by the amygdala.

The fact that the orbitofrontal cortex plays an important role in emotional behavior is shown by the effects of damage to this region. The first—and most famous—case comes from the mid-1800s. Phineas Gage, a dynamite worker, was using a steel rod to ram a charge of dynamite into a hole drilled in solid rock. Suddenly, the charge exploded and sent the rod into his cheek, through his brain, and out the top of his head. (See ***Figure 10.6.***) He survived, but he was a different man. Before his injury he was serious, industrious, and energetic. Afterward, he became childish, irresponsible, and thoughtless of others. He was unable to make or carry out plans, and his actions appeared to be capricious and whimsical. His accident largely destroyed the orbitofrontal cortex.

Over the succeeding years physicians reported several cases similar to that of Phineas Gage. In general, damage to the orbitofrontal cortex reduced people's inhibitions and self-concern; they became indifferent to the consequences of their actions. In addition, although they remained sensitive to noxious stimuli, the pain no longer bothered them—it no longer produced an emotional reaction. Then in 1935 the report of an experiment with a chimpanzee triggered events whose repercussions are still felt today. Jacobsen, Wolf, and Jackson (1935) tested various species of nonhuman primates on a ***delayed-response test.*** While the animal watches, the experimenter hides a piece of food in one of two locations and then lowers an opaque screen in front of the animal. After a delay the opaque screen is raised, and the animal is given one chance to find the food. If it chooses the wrong location, it gets nothing and has to wait until the next trial. Obviously, this task requires the animal to remember where the food is hidden during the delay period. Jacobsen and his colleagues described the case of one chimpanzee, Becky, who displayed a violent emotional reaction to this task.

> In the normal phase, this animal was extremely eager to work and apparently well motivated; but this subject was highly emotional and profoundly upset whenever she made an error. Violent temper tantrums after a mistake were not infrequent occurrences. She observed closely loading of the cup with food, and often whimpered softly as the cup was placed over the food. [When] the experimenter lowered . . . the opaque door to exclude the animal's view of the cups, she immediately

> flew into a temper tantrum, rolled on the floor, defecated and urinated. After a few such reactions during the training period, the animal would make no further responses. . . . [After a bilateral lesion of the frontal lobes was performed,] a profound change occurred. The chimpanzee offered its usual friendly greeting, and eagerly ran from its living quarters to the transfer cage, and in turn went properly to the experimental cage. The usual procedure of baiting the cup and lowering the opaque screen was followed. But the chimpanzee did not show any excitement and sat quietly before the door or walked around the cage. . . If the animal made a mistake, it showed no evidence of emotional disturbance but quietly awaited the loading of the cups for the next trial. (Jacobsen, Wolf, and Jackson, 1935, pp. 9–10)

These findings were reported at a scientific meeting in 1935, which was attended by Egas Moniz, a Portuguese neuropsychiatrist. Another report presented at that meeting indicated that radical removal of the frontal lobes in a human patient (performed because of a tumor) did not appear to produce intellectual impairment (Brickner, 1936). These two reports suggested that frontal lobotomy might reduce pathological emotional reactions and that the operation might not have serious consequences for the patient's intellect. One of Jacobson's colleagues, John Fulton, reported that after Jacobsen had described the results of Becky's surgery, "Dr. Moniz arose and asked if frontal-lobe removal . . . eliminates frustrational behavior, why would it not be feasible to relieve anxiety states in man by surgical means?" (Fulton, 1949, pp. 63–64). In fact, Moniz did persuade a neurosurgeon to do so, and approximately one hundred operations were eventually performed under his supervision. (In 1949 Moniz received the Nobel Prize for the development of this procedure.)

A few paragraphs ago I said that the repercussions of the 1935 meeting are still felt today. Since that time tens of thousands of people have received prefrontal lobotomies, primarily to reduce symptoms of emotional distress, and many of these people are still alive. At first the procedure was welcomed by the medical community because it provided their patients with relief from emotional anguish. Only after many years were careful studies performed on the side effects of the procedure. These studies showed that although patients did perform well on standard tests of intellectual ability, they showed serious changes in personality, becoming irresponsible and childish. They also lost the ability to carry out plans and most were unemployable. And although pathological emotional reactions were eliminated, so were normal ones. Because of these findings, and because of the discovery of drugs and therapeutic methods that relieve the patients' symptoms without producing such drastic side effects, neurosurgeons eventually abandoned the prefrontal lobotomy procedure (Valenstein, 1986).

I should point out that the prefrontal lobotomies performed under Moniz's supervision, and by the neurosurgeons who followed, were not as drastic as the surgery performed by Jacobsen and his colleagues on Becky, the chimpanzee. In fact, no brain tissue was removed. Instead, the surgeons introduced various kinds of cutting devices into the frontal lobes and severed white matter — bundles of axons. One rather gruesome procedure did not even require an operating room; it could be performed in a physician's office. A *transorbital leucotome,* shaped like an ice pick, was introduced into the brain by passing it beneath the upper eyelid until the point reached the orbital bone above the eye. The instrument was hit with a mallet, driving it through the bone into the brain. The end was then swept back and forth so that it cut through the white matter. The patient often left the office within an hour. (See ***Figure 10.7.***)

Many physicians objected to the "ice pick" procedure because it was done blind (that is, the surgeon could not see just where the blade of the leucotome was located)

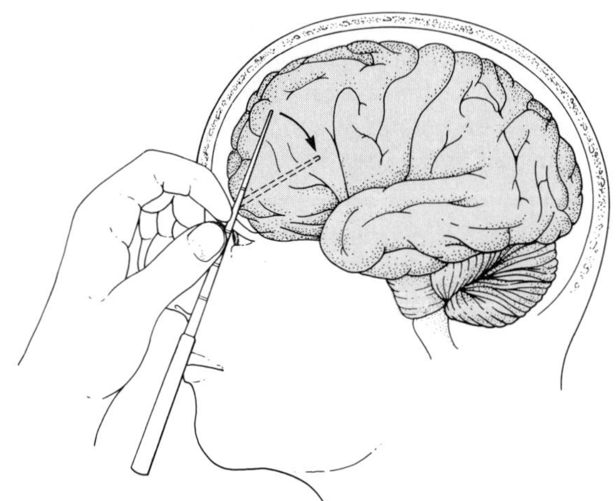

FIGURE 10.7

"Ice pick" prefrontal lobotomy. The sharp metal rod is inserted under the eyelid and just above the eye, so that it pierces the skull and enters the base of the frontal lobe. (Adapted from Freeman, W. *Proceedings of the Royal Society of Medicine,* 1949, *42(suppl.),* 8–12.)

and because it produced more damage than was necessary. Also, the fact that it was so easy and left no external signs other than a pair of black eyes may have tempted its practitioners to perform it too casually. In fact, at least twenty-five hundred patients received this form of surgery (Valenstein, 1986).

What we know today about the effects of prefrontal lobotomy—whether done transorbitally or by more conventional means—tells us that such radical surgery should never have been performed. For too long the harmful side effects were ignored. (As we will see later in this chapter, neurosurgeons eventually developed a much restricted version of this surgery, which reduces the symptoms without producing the harmful side effects.) But the fact remains that the surgery *did* reduce people's emotional suffering, or it would never have become so popular. Primarily, the surgery reduced anxiety, obsessions, and compulsions. People's groundless fears disappeared and they no longer felt compelled to perform rituals to ward off some (imaginary) disastrous events. Before the surgery the world was a threatening place, and their emotional responses and behavior caused them anguish and made shambles of their lives. After surgery their cares disappeared and they could function more normally.

In one extraordinary case a patient performed his own psychosurgery. Solyom, Turnbull, and Wilensky (1987) reported the case of a young man with a serious obsessive compulsive disorder whose ritual hand washing and other behaviors made it impossible for him to continue his schooling or lead a normal life. (This disorder is described in more detail in Chapter 16.) Finding that his life was no longer worthwhile, he decided to end it. He placed the muzzle of a .22-caliber rifle in his mouth and pulled the trigger. The bullet entered the base of the brain and damaged the frontal lobes. He survived, and he was amazed to find that his compulsions were gone. Fortunately, the damage did not disrupt his ability to make or execute plans; he went back to school and completed his education and now has a job. His IQ was unchanged. Ordinary surgery would have been less hazardous and messy, but it could hardly have been more successful.

All types of prefrontal lobotomies disrupted the functions of the frontal lobes (primarily the orbitofrontal cortex) by severing connections between this area and the rest of the brain. Some procedures approached the frontal lobes from the base of the brain, primarily cutting their connections with the diencephalon and temporal lobes. Other procedures approached the frontal lobes from above and disconnected the orbitofrontal cortex from the cingulate gyrus. In either case the patients' emotional distress was usually reduced.

What, exactly, does the orbitofrontal cortex do? One possibility is that it is involved in assessing the personal consequences of what is presently happening. However, this analysis does not appear to be correct. People whose orbitofrontal cortex has been damaged by disease or accident are still able to accurately assess the significance of particular situations, but only in a *theoretical* sense. For example, Eslinger and Damasio (1985) found that a patient with bilateral damage of the orbitofrontal cortex (produced by a benign tumor, which was successfully removed) displayed excellent social judgment. When he was given hypothetical situations that required him to make decisions about what the people involved should do — situations involving moral, ethical, or practical dilemmas — he always gave sensible answers and justified them with carefully reasoned logic. However, his own life was a different matter. He frittered away his life savings on investments that his family and friends pointed out were bound to fail. He lost one job after another because of his irresponsibility. He became unable to distinguish between trivial decisions and important ones, spending hours trying to decide where to have dinner but failing to use good judgment in situations that concerned his occupation and family life. (His wife finally left him and sued for divorce.) As the authors noted, "He had learned and used normal patterns of social behavior before his brain lesion, and although he could recall such patterns when he was questioned about their applicability, *real-life situations failed to evoke them*" (p. 1737). Thus, it appears that the orbitofrontal cortex is not directly involved in making judgments and conclusions about events (these occur elsewhere in the brain) but in translating these judgments into appropriate feelings and behaviors.

As I mentioned earlier, in performing prefrontal lobotomies, neurosurgeons have made two different approaches toward the frontal lobes. The ventral connections with the diencephalon and temporal lobes presumably bring environmental information to the orbitofrontal cortex, tell it about emotionally relevant activity of the amygdala, and permit it to influence the amygdala, in turn. The dorsal connections with the cingulate gyrus presumably provide a way for the orbitofrontal cortex to influence both behavior and the autonomic nervous system.

The cingulate gyrus deserves some discussion. The cortex that covers this gyrus is an important part of the limbic system. A neuroanatomist, Papez (1937), suggested that the cingulate cortex, entorhinal cortex, hippocampus, and parts of the hypothalamus and thalamus formed a circuit whose primary function was motivation and emotion. A physiologist, MacLean (1949), expanded the system to include other structures, such as the amygdala, and coined the term *limbic system.* (See ***Figure 10.8.***) He noted that the evolution of this system, which includes the first and simplest form of cerebral cortex, appears to have coincided with the development of emotional responses. As you will see in Chapter 12, we now know that parts of the limbic system (notably, the hippocampal formation and the region of limbic cortex that surrounds it) are involved in learning and memory rather than emotional behavior. However, the rest of the limbic system does seem to do what Papez and MacLean hypothesized.

The cingulate gyrus appears to provide an interface between the decision-making processes of the frontal cortex, the emotional functions of the limbic system, and the brain mechanisms controlling movement. It communicates (in both directions) with the rest of the limbic system, as well as with other regions of the frontal cortex. Electrical stimulation of the cingulate gyrus in humans can produce feelings of either positive or negative emotions (Talairach et al., 1973). Damage to this region leads to **akinetic mutism,** a syndrome accurately described by its name — the patient stops talking and moving (Amyes and Nielsen, 1955). If the damage is severe, the patient dies. Thus, the cingulate gyrus plays an excitatory role in emotions and in motivated behavior in general.

akinetic mutism

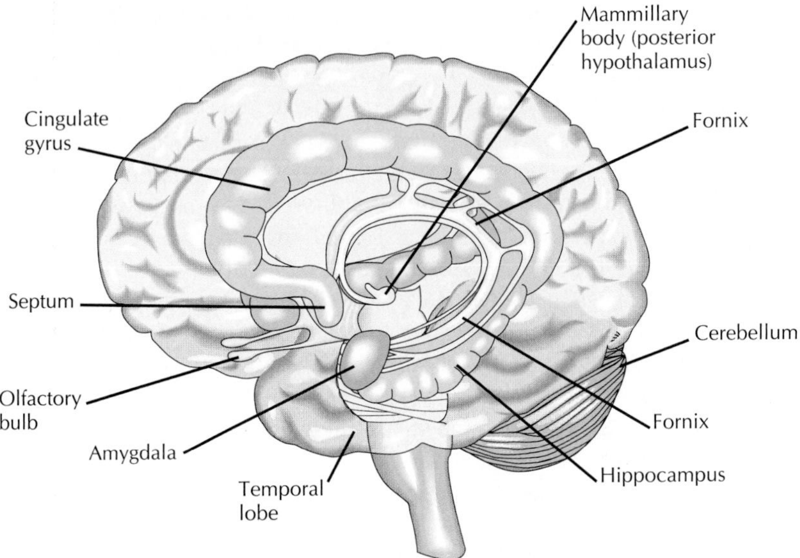

FIGURE 10.8

The limbic system.

▶INTERIM SUMMARY◀

The word *emotion* refers to behaviors, physiological responses, and feelings. This section has discussed emotional response patterns, which consist of behaviors that deal with particular situations and physiological responses (both autonomic and hormonal) that support the behaviors. The amygdala organizes behavioral, autonomic, and hormonal responses to a variety of situations, including those that produce fear, anger, or disgust. In addition, it is involved in the effects of odors and pheromones on sexual and maternal behavior. It receives inputs from the olfactory system, the association cortex of the temporal lobe, the frontal cortex, and the rest of the limbic system. Its outputs go to the frontal cortex, hypothalamus, hippocampal formation, and brain stem nuclei that control autonomic functions and some species-typical behaviors. Damage to specific brain regions that receive these outputs will abolish particular components of emotional response patterns. Stimulation of the amygdala leads to emotional responses, and its destruction disrupts them. Electrical recordings of single neurons in the amygdala indicate that some of them respond when the animal perceives particular stimuli with emotional significance.

Emotional reactions to simple stimuli can be accomplished by subcortical mechanisms. For example, conditioned emotional responses to auditory stimuli occur when the central nucleus of the amygdala receives auditory information from the medial division of the medial geniculate nucleus; input from the auditory cortex is unnecessary. Emotional reactions to more complex situations require input from the neocortex. For visual stimuli this input is provided by the inferotemporal cortex and the temporal pole.

The orbitofrontal cortex plays an important role in emotional reactions. People with orbitofrontal lesions are able to explain the implications of complex social situations but are unable to respond appropriately when these situations concern *them.* Thus, this region does not appear to be necessary for making judgments about the personal significance of social situations, but it does appear to be necessary for translating these judgments into actions and emotional responses. The orbitofrontal cortex receives information from other regions of the frontal lobes, from the temporal pole, and from the amygdala and other parts of the limbic system via the mediodorsal nucleus of the thalamus. It produces emotional reactions through its connections with the amygdala and the cingulate gyrus.

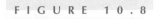

The cingulate gyrus is involved in the activation of behavior—what we might refer to as motivation. Damage to the cingulate gyrus produces akinetic mutism and, if the damage is severe, causes death. Electrical stimulation produces feelings of both positive and negative emotions. Its outputs include the rest of the limbic system and most of the frontal cortex.

Between the late 1930s and the late 1950s many people received prefrontal lobotomies, which involved cutting the white matter in the ventromedial frontal lobes. Although the operations affected many parts of the frontal lobes, the most important region was probably the orbitofrontal cortex. The surgery did often relieve emotional anguish and the suffering caused by pain, but it also made people become largely indifferent to the social consequences of their own behavior and to the feelings of others, and it interfered with their ability to make and execute plans. Prefrontal lobotomies are no longer performed; neurosurgeons have developed a procedure in which they cut just the cingulum bundle. The procedure provides most of the benefits of prefrontal lobotomy without the adverse side effects. ▲

EXPRESSION AND RECOGNITION OF EMOTIONS

The previous section described emotions as organized responses (behavioral, autonomic, and hormonal) that deal with the existing situation in the environment, such as events that pose a threat to the organism. For our earliest premammalian ancestors that is undoubtedly all there was to emotions. But over time other responses, with new functions, evolved. Many species of animals (including our own) communicate their emotions to others by means of postural changes and facial expressions. These expressions serve useful social functions; they tell other individuals how we feel and—more to the point—what we are likely to do. For example, they warn a rival that we are angry or tell friends that we are sad and would like some comfort and reassurance. This section examines the expression and communication of emotions.

Facial Expression of Emotions: Innate Responses

Charles Darwin (1872/1965) suggested that human expressions of emotion have evolved from similar expressions in other animals. He said that emotional expressions are innate, unlearned responses consisting of a complex set of movements, principally of the facial muscles. Thus, a man's sneer and a wolf's snarl are biologically determined response patterns, both controlled by innate brain mechanisms, just as coughing and sneezing are. (Of course, men can sneer and wolves can snarl for quite different reasons.) Some of these movements resemble the behaviors themselves and may have evolved from them. For example, a snarl shows one's teeth and can be seen as an anticipation of biting.

Darwin obtained evidence for his conclusion that emotional expressions were innate by observing his own children and by corresponding with people living in various isolated cultures around the world. He reasoned that if people all over the world, no matter how isolated, show the same facial expressions of emotion, then these expressions must be inherited instead of learned. The logical argument goes like this: When groups of people are isolated for many years, they develop different languages. Thus, we can say that the words people use are arbitrary; there is no biological basis for using particular words to represent particular concepts. However, if facial expressions are inherited, then they should take approximately the same form in people from all cultures, despite their isolation from one another. And Darwin did, indeed, find that people in different cultures used the same patterns of movement of facial muscles to express a particular emotional state.

In 1967 and 1968 Ekman and Friesen carried out some interesting cross-cultural observations that validated those of Darwin (Ekman, 1980). They visited an isolated tribe in a remote area of New Guinea—the South Fore tribe. This group of 319 adults and children had never been exposed to Western culture. They had never seen a movie, lived in a Western town, or worked for someone from outside their culture. Therefore, if they were able to identify accurately the emotional expressions of Westerners as well as they could identify those of members of their own tribe, and if their own facial expressions were the same as those of Westerners, then the researchers could conclude that these expressions were not culturally determined.

Because translations of single words from one language to another are not always accurate, Ekman and Friesen told little stories to describe an emotion instead of presenting a single word. They told the story to a subject, presented three photographs of Westerners depicting three different emotions, and asked the subject to choose the appropriate one. Here are three examples of the stories:

> *Fear*—She is sitting in her house all alone and there is no one else in the village; and there is no knife, ax, or bow and arrow in the house. A wild pig is standing in the door of the house and the woman is looking at the pig and is very afraid of it. The pig has been standing in the doorway for a few minutes and the person is looking at it very afraid and the pig won't move away from the door and she is afraid the pig will bite her.
>
> *Happy*—Her friends have come and she is happy.
>
> *Anger*—She is angry and is about to fight. (Ekman, 1980, p. 130)

Now look at ***Figure 10.9*** to see whether you would have any trouble matching each of these stories with one of the photographs shown there.

FIGURE 10.9

Emotional expressions. South Fore tribespeople were asked to match each story with the appropriate photograph. (From Ekman, P. *The Face of Man: Expressions of Universal Emotions in a New Guinea Village*. New York: Garland STPM Press, 1980. By permission of Silvan Tompkins. Photo by Ed Gallob.)

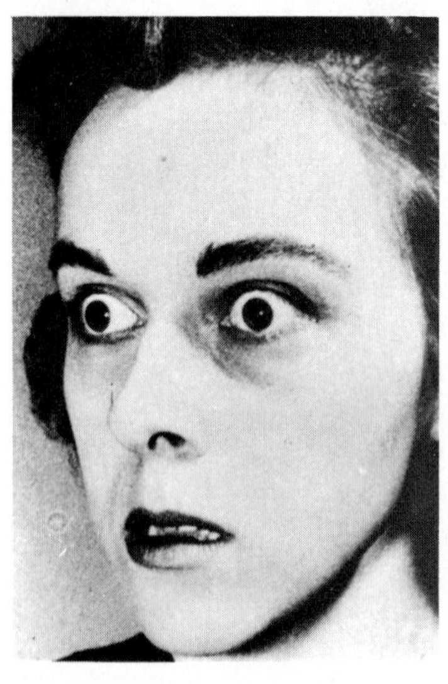

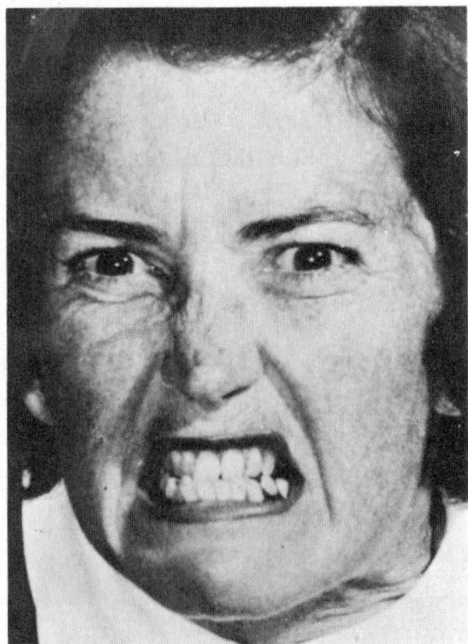

FIGURE 10.10

A member of an isolated New Guinea tribe, studied by Ekman and Friesen, making faces when told stories. (a) "Your friend has come and you are happy." (b) "Your child had died." (c) "You are angry and about to fight." (d) "You see a dead pig that has been lying there a long time." (From Ekman, P. *The Face of Man: Expressions of Universal Emotions in a New Guinea Village.* New York: Garland STPM Press, 1980. Reprinted with permission.)

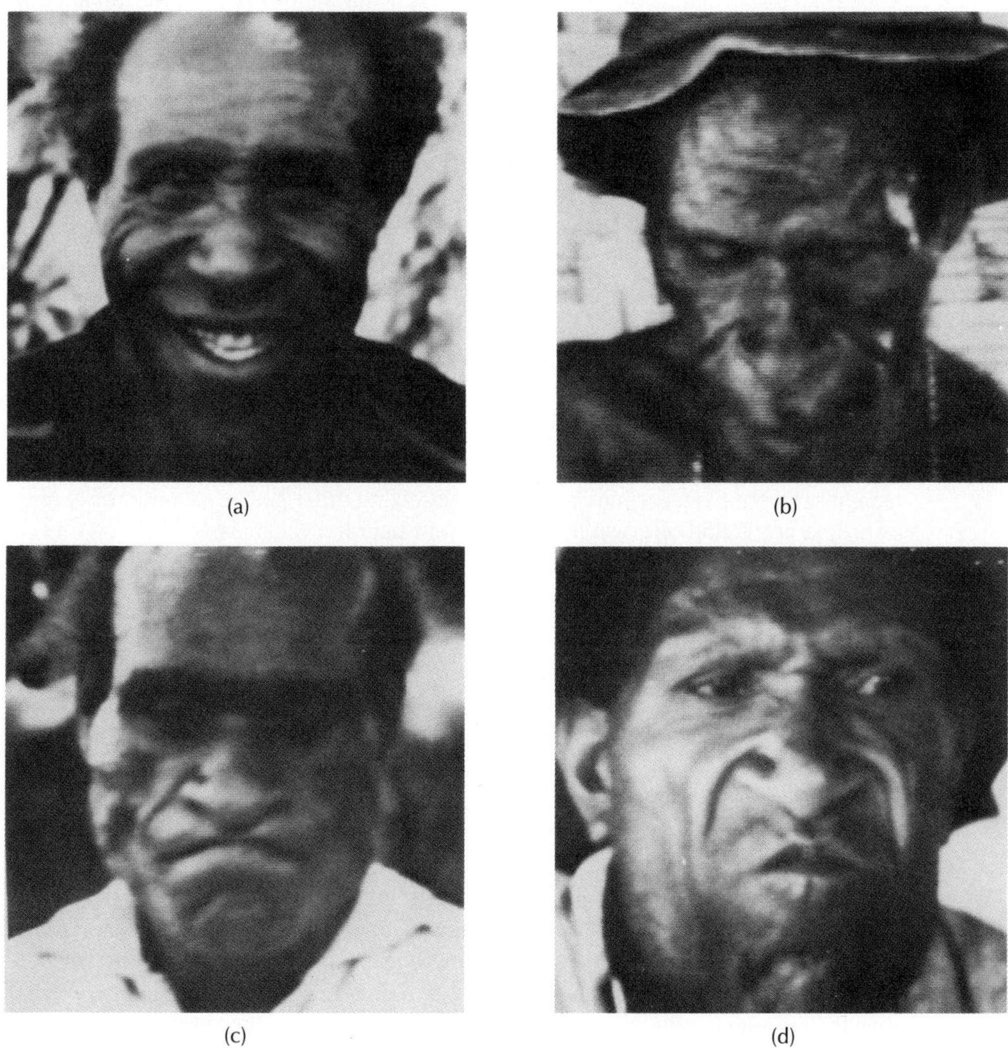

(a) (b) (c) (d)

I am sure that you did not have any trouble—and neither did the members of the Fore tribe. In a second study Ekman and Friesen asked Fore tribespeople to imagine how they would feel in situations that would produce various emotions and videotaped their facial expressions. They showed photographs of the videotapes to American college students, who had no trouble identifying the emotions. Four of them are shown in Figure 10.10. The caption describes the story that was used to elicit the expression. (See ***Figure 10.10.***)

Other researchers have compared the facial expressions of blind and normally sighted children. They reasoned that if the facial expressions of both groups are similar, then the expressions are natural for our species and do not require learning by imitation. (Studies of blind adults would not be conclusive, because adults would have heard enough descriptions of facial expressions to be able to pose them.)

In fact, the facial expressions of young blind and sighted children are very similar. However, as blind children grow older, their facial gestures tend to become somewhat less expressive (Woodworth and Schlosberg, 1954; Izard, 1971). This finding suggests that social reinforcement is important in maintaining our displays of emotion. However, the evidence clearly shows that we do not have to learn to smile, frown, or show other feelings with our facial gestures. Both the cross-cultural studies and the investigations with blind children confirm the naturalness of these expressions.

The results of cross-cultural studies and studies with blind people suggest strongly that situations expected to have motivational relevance produce consistent patterns of contraction in the facial muscles. Thus, the patterns of movement are apparently inherited—wired into the brain, so to speak. The consistency of facial movements suggests an underlying consistency of emotional feeling throughout our species.

Neural Basis of Communication of Emotions: Studies with Normal Subjects

Effective communication is a two-way process. That is, the ability to display one's emotional state by changes in expression is useful only if other people are able to recognize them. Evidence indicates that recognizing other people's emotional expressions and producing our own involve different neural mechanisms.

RECOGNITION OF OTHER PEOPLE'S EMOTIONS

We recognize other people's feelings by means of vision and audition—seeing their facial expressions and hearing their tone of voice and choice of words. Several studies by Bryden, Ley, and colleagues have found that the right hemisphere plays a more important role than the left hemisphere in comprehension of emotion. The rationale for these studies is that each hemisphere directly receives information from the contralateral part of the environment. For example, when a person looks directly ahead, visual stimuli to the left of the fixation point (seen with *both* eyes) are transmitted to the right hemisphere, and stimuli to the right are transmitted to the left hemisphere. Of course, the hemispheres exchange information by means of the corpus callosum, but it appears that this transcommissural information is not as precise and detailed as information that is directly received. Similarly, although each hemisphere receives auditory information from both ears, the contralateral projections are richer than the ipsilateral ones. Thus, when stimuli are presented to the left visual field or left ear, the right hemisphere receives more specific information than the left hemisphere does.

In studies of hemispherical differences in visual recognition, stimuli are usually presented with a *tachistoscope* (literally, "seen most swiftly"), which flashes an image in a specific part of the visual field so fast that the subject does not have time to move his or her eyes. Many studies (reviewed by Bryden and Ley, 1983) have shown that the left hemisphere is better than the right at recognizing words or letter strings. Knowing what you do about the verbal functions of the left hemisphere, this finding will come as no surprise to you. However, when a person is required to discriminate among different faces or detect differences in the tilt of lines presented to one side of the visual field, the right hemisphere performs better than the left.

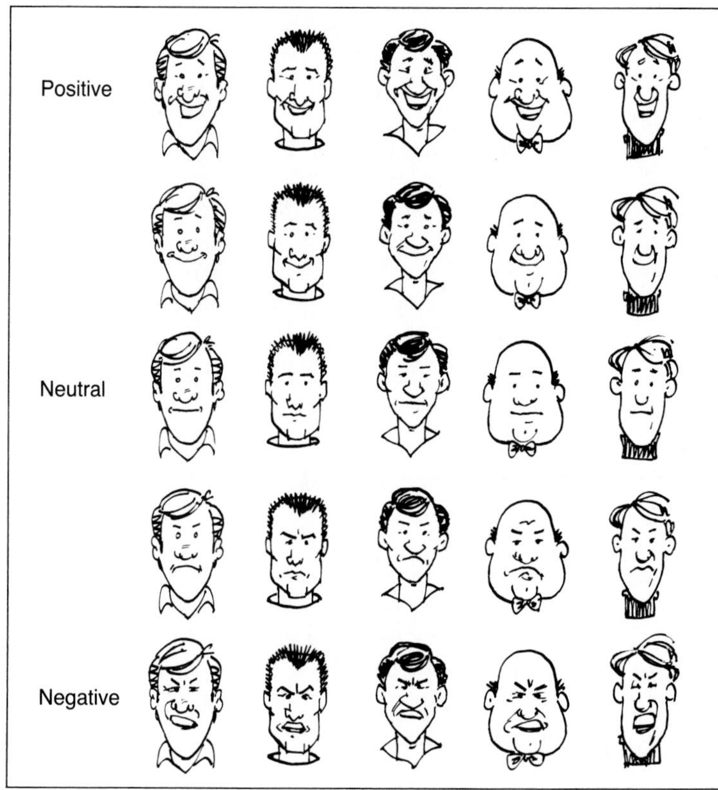

FIGURE 10.11

The faces and expressions used as stimuli in the study by Ley and Bryden. (From Ley, R.G., and Bryden, M.P. *Brain and Language*, 1979, *7*, 127–138. Reprinted with permission.)

Ley and Bryden (1979) prepared cartoon drawings of five different people, each displaying one of five facial expressions, ranging from negative to neutral to positive. (See ***Figure 10.11.***) Using a tachistoscope, they showed these drawings briefly in the right or left visual field, one at a time. After each presentation they showed the same face or a different one in the center of the visual field (to both hemispheres) and asked the subjects to say whether the same emotion was presented. When the experimenters showed the subjects neutral or mild expressions, the hemispheres performed approximately the same. However, when the experimenters showed the subjects strong expressions, the right hemisphere judged them more accurately.

Ley and Bryden (1982) also investigated perception of tone of voice. They simultaneously presented different verbal messages with a different (happy, neutral, or sad) tone of voice to each ear and asked the subjects to attend to the message presented to one ear and report on its verbal content and emotion. Most of the subjects more accurately detected the verbal content of the message when it was presented to the left hemisphere and more accurately detected the emotional tone of the voice when it was presented to the right hemisphere. The results suggested that when a message is heard, the right hemisphere assesses the emotional expression of the voice, while the left hemisphere assesses the meaning of the words.

EXPRESSION OF EMOTION

When people show emotions with their facial muscles, the left side of the face usually makes a more intense expression. For example, Sackheim and Gur (1978) cut photographs of people who were posing emotions into right and left halves, prepared

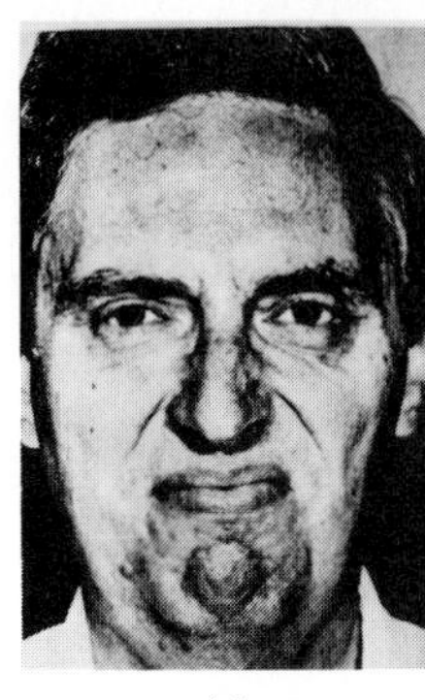
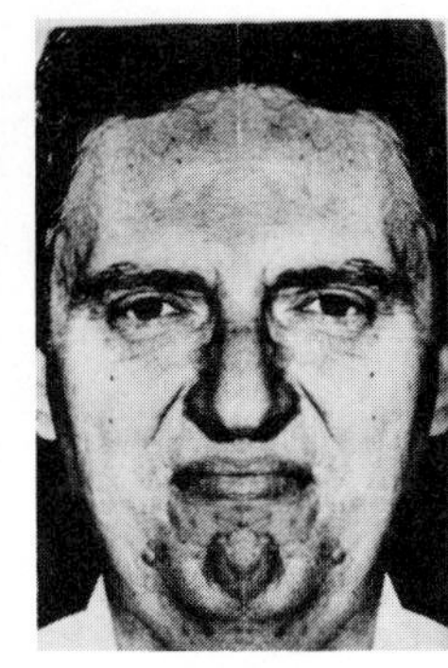
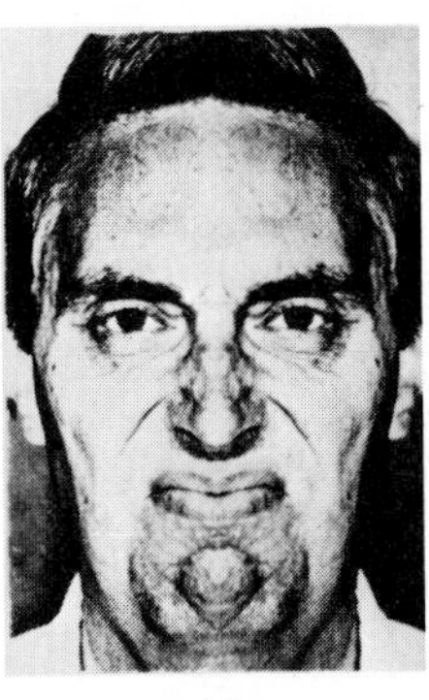

(a) (b) (c)

FIGURE 10.12

An example of a stimulus used by Sackheim and Gur (1978). (a) Original photo. (b) Composite of the right side of the man's face. (c) Composite of the left side of the man's face. (Reprinted with permission from *Neuropsychologia, 16,* H.A. Sackheim and R.C. Gur. Lateral asymmetry in intensity of emotional expression. Copyright 1978, Pergamon Journals, Ltd.)

mirror images of each of them, and pasted them together. They found that the left halves were more expressive than the right ones. (See ***Figure 10.12.***) Because motor control is contralateral, the results suggest that the right hemisphere is more expressive than the left.

Moscovitch and Olds (1982) made more natural observations of people in restaurants and parks and found that the left side of their faces appeared to make stronger expressions of emotions. They confirmed these results in the laboratory by analyzing videotapes of people telling sad or humorous stories.

Neural Basis of Communication of Emotions: Studies of People with Brain Damage

pseudobulbar palsy

The control of facial expressions appears to be organized in the brain stem but controlled by the frontal lobes. The best evidence for this proposition comes from a syndrome known as *pseudobulbar palsy.* Damage to the medulla (also known as the *bulb*) can cause a paralysis of the facial region known as *bulbar palsy.* **Pseudobulbar palsy** resembles this disorder but is caused by damage to the pathway between the motor cortex and the cranial nerve nuclei of the lower pons and medulla that control the facial muscles. People with pseudobulbar palsy cannot make voluntary movements of the facial muscles, but they can still show *automatic* movements such as yawning, coughing, and clearing the throat. More to the point, they can still smile, frown, laugh, and cry. In fact, seemingly trivial events can trigger a prolonged bout of uncontrollable laughing or crying, which the patient is helpless to stop. Apparently, once the brain stem mechanisms are deprived of their normal control by the frontal lobe, they are more easily aroused by the excitatory inputs from subcortical mechanisms of emotion.

RECOGNITION OF OTHER PEOPLE'S EMOTIONS

Observations of people with brain damage suggest that the right hemisphere plays a special role in both recognition and expression of emotion. Damage to the right hemisphere (especially to the caudal part) appears to impair the recognition of emotions being expressed by other people. For example, Heilman, Scholes, and Watson (1975) presented patients who had unilateral lesions of the temporal-parietal region with sentences with neutral content (such as *The boy went to the store*), said in a happy, sad, angry, or indifferent tone of voice. Patients with right-hemisphere damage judged the emotion being expressed less accurately. Heilman, Watson, and Bowers (1983) recorded an interesting case of a man with a disorder called *pure word deafness* (described in Chapter 13). The man could not comprehend the meaning of speech but had no difficulty identifying the emotion being expressed by its intonation. This case demonstrates that comprehension of words and recognition of tone of voice are independent functions.

Visual recognition of emotions, as well as auditory recognition, also appears to be a right-hemisphere function more than a left-hemisphere function. DeKosky, Heilman, Bowers, and Valenstein (1980) found that right-hemisphere damage, more than left-hemisphere damage, disrupted patients' ability to discriminate among different facial expressions of emotion. In addition, Bowers and Heilman (1981) reported the case of a patient with a large tumor of the posterior right hemisphere who could accurately distinguish among faces of different people but not among different emotional expressions. In contrast, he had no trouble recognizing the emotional content of voices. Thus, although recognition of different faces and recognition of different expressions are both primarily right-hemisphere tasks, their anatomical basis differs.

Hemispheric differences in the recognition of emotions are seen in children as well as adults. Voeller, Hanson, and Wendt (1988) showed pictures of the faces of children expressing happiness, sadness, anger, or fright to children (mean age = 8 years, 3 months) with damage to the right or left hemisphere. The children with the right-hemisphere damage had much more difficulty identifying the expressions. The authors pointed out that misidentifying the emotions of other children could potentially cause serious problems with their socialization.

EXPRESSION OF EMOTION

Left-hemisphere lesions do not usually impair vocal expressions of emotion. For example, a person with Wernicke's aphasia (described in Chapter 13) usually modulates his or her voice according to mood, even though the words he or she says make no sense. However, right-hemisphere lesions do impair expression of emotion, both facially and by tone of voice.

Buck and Duffy (1980) showed slides that were designed to elicit expressions of emotions to patients with damage to the right or left hemisphere. For example, they showed a picture of a starving child and a crying woman. The investigators found that people with right-hemisphere damage showed fewer facial expressions of emotion. Heilman, Watson, and Bowers (1983) asked patients with unilateral brain lesions to *pose* expressions of emotions and found no differences between patients with right- or left-hemisphere lesions. However, they suggest a plausible explanation for this failure. People with damage to the left frontal lobe often exhibit an oral and facial apraxia, having difficulty making particular facial movements on command. Thus, they have difficulty responding to the suggestion to smile but nevertheless smile spontaneously when they are told a joke.

▶*INTERIM SUMMARY*◀

We (and members of other species) communicate our emotions primarily through facial gestures. Darwin believed that such expressions of emotion were innate — that these muscular movements were inherited behavioral patterns. Ekman and his colleagues performed cross-cultural studies with members of the Fore tribe. Their results, and other investigators' observations of blind children, supported Darwin's hypothesis.

Facial expression of emotions (and other stereotyped behaviors such as laughing and crying) are controlled by neural circuits in the brain stem. The best evidence for this conclusion comes from pseudobulbar palsy, caused by

damage to the outputs of the motor cortex. People with this disorder cannot make voluntary movements of their facial muscles, but events in the environment (often trivial ones) can still elicit laughing and crying and facial gestures of emotion.

Expression and comprehension of emotions involve the right hemisphere more than the left. Studies with normal people have shown that people can judge facial expressions or tone of voice better when the information is presented to the right hemisphere than when it is presented to the left hemisphere. In addition, the left halves of people's faces tend to be more expressive than the right halves.

Damage to the right hemisphere is more likely to produce deficits in expression and comprehension of emotions conveyed by tone of voice or by facial expression than is damage to the left hemisphere. In fact, people with right-hemisphere lesions sometimes do not even react emotionally to their own neurological deficits. ▲

FEELINGS OF EMOTIONS

So far, we have examined two aspects of emotions: the organization of patterns of responses that deal with the situation that provokes the emotion, and the communication of emotional states with other members of the species. The final aspect of emotion to be examined in this chapter is the subjective component—feelings of emotion.

The James-Lange Theory

James-Lange theory

William James (1842–1910), an American psychologist, and Carl Lange (1834–1900), a Danish physiologist, independently suggested similar explanations for emotion, which most people refer to collectively as the **James-Lange theory** (James, 1884; Lange, 1887). Basically, the theory states that emotion-producing situations elicit an appropriate set of physiological responses, such as trembling, sweating, and increased heart rate. The situations also elicit behaviors, such as clenching of the fists or fighting. The brain receives sensory feedback from the muscles and from the organs that produce these responses, and it is this feedback that constitutes our feelings emotion. As James put it:

> *The bodily changes follow directly the perception of the exciting fact, and . . . our feelings of the same changes as they occur is the emotion.* Common sense says we lose our fortune, are sorry, and weep; we meet a bear, are frightened, and run; we are insulted by a rival, are angry, and strike. The hypothesis here to be defended says that this order of sequence is incorrect, that the one mental state is not immediately induced by the other and that the bodily manifestations must first be interposed between. The more rational statement is that we feel sorry because we cry, angry because we strike, afraid because we tremble, and not that we cry, strike, or tremble because we are sorry, angry or fearful, as the case may be. (James, 1890, p. 449)

James says that our own emotional feelings are based on what we find ourselves doing and on the sensory feedback we receive from the activity of our muscles and internal organs. Thus, when we find ourselves trembling and feel queasy, we experience fear. Where feelings of emotions are concerned, we are self-observers. Thus, the two aspects of emotions reported in the first two sections of this chapter (patterns of

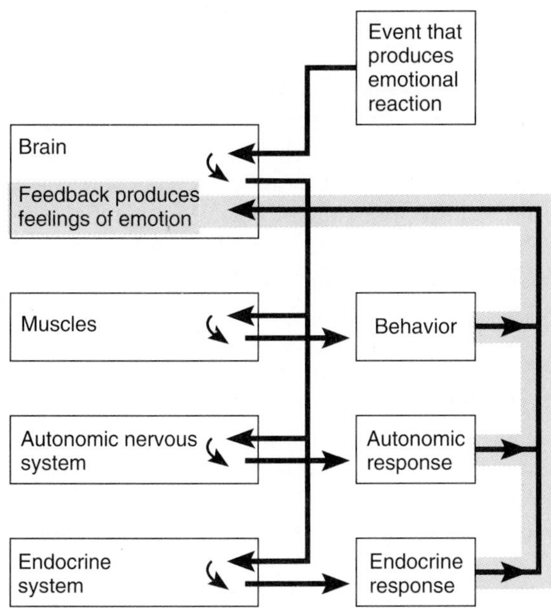

FIGURE 10.13

A diagrammatic representation of the James-Lange theory of emotion. An event in the environment triggers behavioral, autonomic, and endocrine responses. Feedback from these responses produces feelings of emotions.

emotional responses and expressions of emotions) give rise to the third—feelings. (See ***Figure 10.13.***)

James's description of the process of emotion might strike you as being at odds with your own experience. Many people feel that they experience emotions directly, internally. They consider the outward manifestations of emotions to be secondary events. But have you ever found yourself in an unpleasant confrontation with someone else and discovered that you were trembling, even though you did not think that you were so bothered by the encounter? Or did you ever find yourself blushing in response to some public remark that was made about you? Or did you ever find tears coming to your eyes while watching a film that you did not think was affecting you? What would you conclude about your emotional states in situations like these? Would you ignore the evidence from your own physiological reactions?

A famous physiologist, Walter Cannon, criticized James's theory. For example, he said that the internal organs were relatively insensitive and that they could not respond very quickly, so feedback from them could not account for our feelings of emotions. In addition, he observed that cutting the nerves that provide feedback from the internal organs to the brain did not alter emotional behavior (Cannon, 1927). However, subsequent research indicated that Cannon's criticisms are not relevant. For example, although the viscera are not sensitive to some kinds of stimuli, such as cutting and burning, they provide much better feedback than Cannon suspected. Moreover, many changes in the viscera can occur rapidly enough so that they *could* be the causes of feelings of emotion.

Cannon cited the fact that cutting the sensory nerves between the internal organs and the central nervous system does not abolish emotional behavior in animals. However, this observation misses the point. It does not prove that *feelings* of emotion survive this surgical disruption. We do not know how the animals feel; we know only that they will snarl and attempt to bite if threatened. In any case, James did not attribute all feelings of emotion to the internal organs; he also said that feedback from muscles was important. The threat might make the animal snarl and bite, and the feedback from the facial and neck muscles might constitute a "feeling" of anger, even if feedback from the internal organs was cut off.

The suggestion that we experience our emotions indirectly, through feedback from emotional behaviors and autonomic reactions, receives some support from neuroanatomy. As we saw earlier in this chapter, the limbic system seems to play the most important role in controlling emotional reactions. There are few direct connections between the limbic system and the parts of the brain that are involved in language. As we will see in Chapter 13, the brain's verbal mechanisms appear to be responsible for our self-awareness; thus, indirect feedback through the sensory cortex may provide the richest source of information about our own emotional responses.

Hohman (1966) collected data from humans that directly tested James's hypothesis. He questioned people who had suffered damage to the spinal cord about how intense their emotional feelings were. If feedback is important, one would expect that emotional feelings would be less intense if the injury were high (that is, close to the brain) than if it were low, because a high spinal cord injury would make the person become insensitive to a larger part of the body. In fact, this result is precisely what Hohman found: The higher the injury, the less intense the feeling was. (See ***Figure 10.14.***)

The comments of patients with high spinal cord injuries suggest that the severely diminished feedback does change their feelings but not necessarily their behavior.

> I sit around and build things up in my mind, and I worry a lot, but it's not much but the power of thought. I was at home alone in bed one day and dropped a cigarette where I couldn't reach it. I finally managed to scrounge around and put it out. I could have burned up right there, but the funny thing is, I didn't get all shook up about it. I just didn't feel afraid at all, like you would suppose.

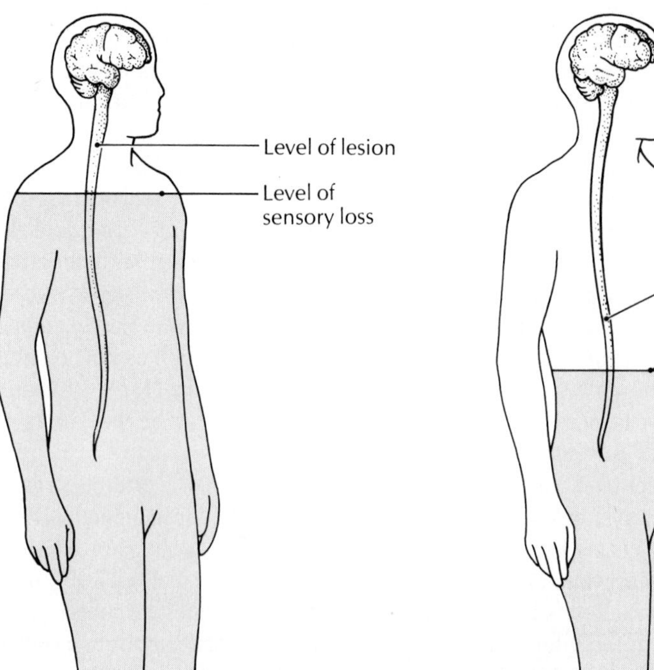

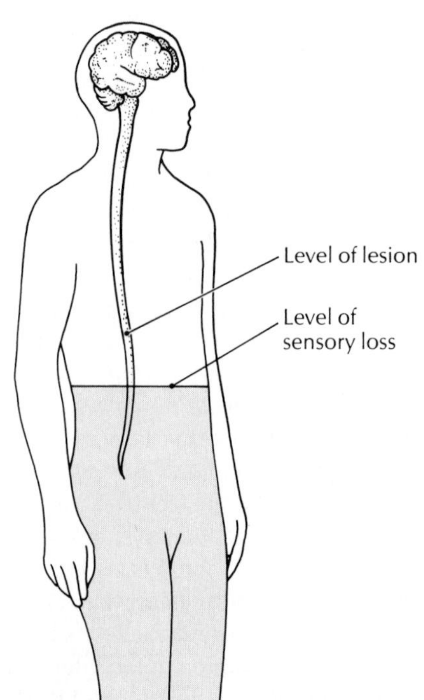

FIGURE 10.14

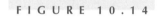

The rationale for Hohman's investigation of the intensity of feelings of emotion in people with spinal cord damage.

> Now, I don't get a feeling of physical animation, it's sort of cold anger. Sometimes I act angry when I see some injustice. I yell and cuss and raise hell, because if you don't do it sometimes, I've learned people will take advantage of you, but it doesn't have the heat to it that it used to. It's a mental kind of anger. (Hohman, 1966, pp. 150–151)

These comments suggest that people do not necessarily engage in emotional behavior *because of* their feelings; lacking these feelings, people still engage in the same behaviors for "rational" reasons.

Feedback from Simulated Emotions

James stressed the importance of two aspects of emotional responses, emotional behaviors and autonomic responses. As we saw earlier in this chapter, a particular set of muscles—those of the face—helps us communicate our emotional state to other people. Several experiments suggest that feedback from the contraction of facial muscles can affect people's moods and even alter the activity of the autonomic nervous system.

Ekman and his colleagues (Ekman, Levenson, and Friesen, 1983; Levenson, Ekman, and Friesen, 1990) asked subjects to move particular facial muscles to simulate the emotional expressions of fear, anger, surprise, disgust, sadness, and happiness. They did not tell the subjects what emotion they were trying to make them produce but only what movements they should make. For example, to simulate fear, they told the subjects to "Raise your brows. While holding them raised pull your brows together. Now raise your upper eyelids and tighten the lower eyelids. Now stretch your lips horizontally." (You can see this expression if you examine the left photograph in Figure 10.9.) While the subjects made the expressions, the investigators monitored several physiological responses controlled by the autonomic nervous system.

The simulated expressions *did* alter the activity of the autonomic nervous system. In fact, different facial expressions produced somewhat different patterns of activity. For example, anger increased heart rate and skin temperature, fear increased heart rate but decreased skin temperature, and happiness decreased heart rate without affecting skin temperature.

Why should a particular pattern of movements of the facial muscles cause changes in mood or in the activity of the autonomic nervous system? Perhaps the connection is a result of experience; in other words, perhaps the occurrence of particular facial movements along with changes in the autonomic nervous system leads to classical conditioning, so that feedback from the facial movements becomes capable of eliciting the autonomic response—and a change in perceived emotion. Or perhaps the connection is innate. As we saw earlier, the adaptive value of emotional expressions is that they communicate feelings and intentions to others. One of the ways we communicate feelings may be through imitation.

When people see someone expressing an emotion, they tend to imitate the expression. This tendency to imitate appears to be innate. Field, Woodson, Greenberg, and Cohen (1982) had adults make facial expressions in front of infants. The infants' own facial expressions were videotaped and were subsequently rated by people who did not know what expressions were being displayed by the adults. Field and her colleagues found that even newborn babies (with an average age of thirty-six hours) tended to imitate the expressions they saw. Clearly, the effect occurs too early in life to be a result of learning. Figure 10.15 shows three photographs of the adult expressions and the

FIGURE 10.15

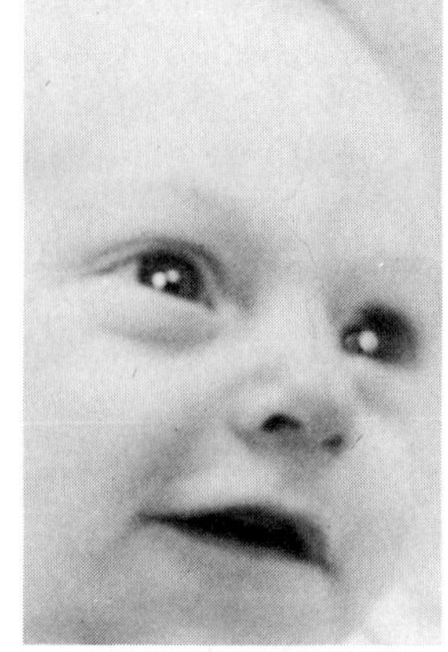

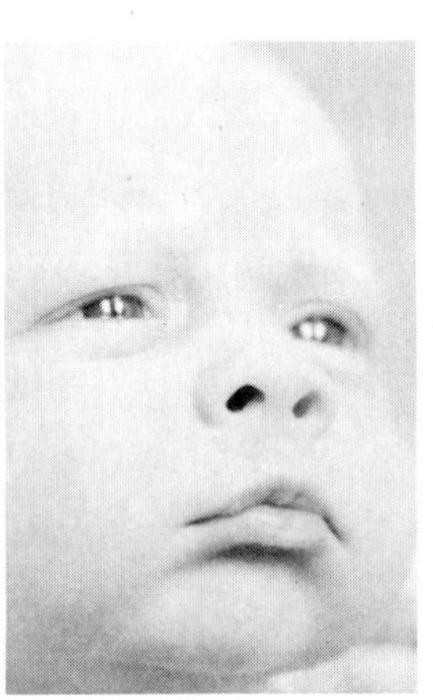
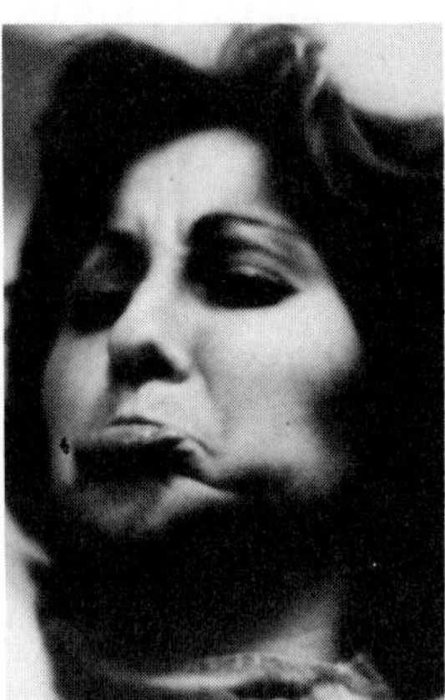
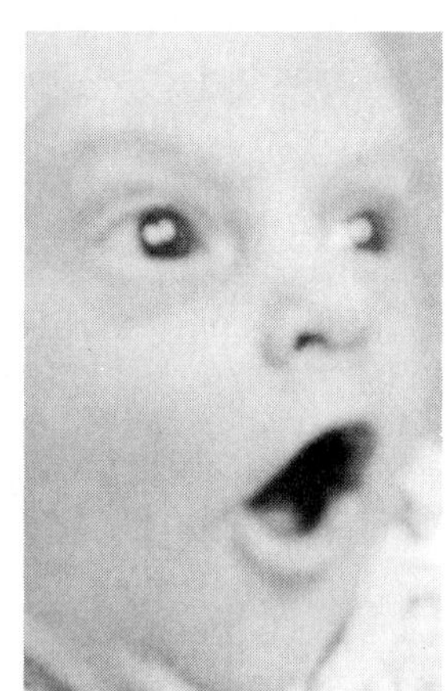
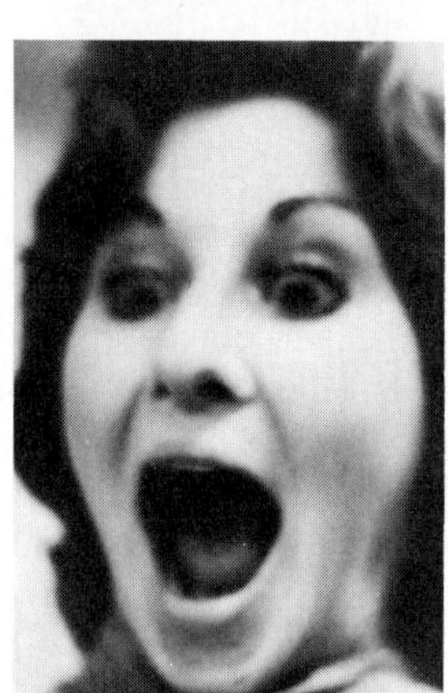

Photographs of happy, sad, and surprised faces posed by an adult, and the responses made by the infant. (From Field, T., in *Development of Nonverbal Behavior in Children,* edited by R.S. Feldman. New York: Springer-Verlag, 1982. Reprinted with permission.)

expressions they elicited in a baby. Can you look at them yourself without changing your own expression, at least a little? (See ***Figure 10.15***.)

Perhaps imitation provides one of the channels by which organisms communicate their emotions. For example, if we see someone looking sad, we tend to assume a sad expression ourselves. The feedback from our own expression helps put us in the other person's place and makes us more likely to respond with solace or assistance. And perhaps one of the reasons we derive pleasure from making someone else smile is that their smile makes *us* smile and feel happy.

▶*INTERIM SUMMARY*◀

From the earliest times people recognized that emotions were accompanied by feelings that seemed to come from inside the body, which probably provided the impetus for developing physiological theories of emotion. James and Lange suggested that the physiological and behavioral reactions to emotion-producing situations were perceived by people as states of emotion, and that emotional states were not the *causes* of these reactions. Cannon criticized this theory, but many of the physiological data on which his criticisms were based were later shown to be incorrect. Hohman's study of people with spinal cord damage supported the James-Lange theory; people who could no longer feel the reactions from most of their body reported that they no longer experienced intense emotional states. However, the loss of feelings did not necessarily affect their behavior; thus, emotional feelings and behaviors may be at least somewhat independent.

Ekman and his colleagues have shown that even simulating an emotional expression causes changes in the activity of the autonomic nervous system. Perhaps feedback from these changes explains why an emotion can be "contagious": We see someone smile with pleasure, we ourselves imitate their smile, and the internal feedback makes us feel at least somewhat happier. ▲

STRESS

Aversive stimuli can produce more than negative emotional responses; they can also harm people's health. Many of these harmful effects are produced not by the stimuli themselves but by our reactions to them. Thus, the expression of negative emotions can have adverse effects on ourselves as well as the people with whom we interact. Walter Cannon, the physiologist who criticized the James-Lange theory, introduced the term **stress** to refer to the physiological reaction caused by the perception of aversive or threatening situations. This section discusses the stress response and its effects on health.

stress

Stress and Health

Stress definitely can be hazardous to one's health. Some disease conditions, such as peptic ulcers, are often caused by the physiological responses that accompany negative emotions. Other disorders, such as heart attacks, strokes, asthma, menstrual problems, headaches, and skin rashes, can occur in the absence of stress but are aggravated by it. As we saw in the first section of this chapter, emotional responses evolved because they are useful and adaptive. Why, then, can they harm our health?

The answer to this question appears to be that our emotional responses are designed primarily to cope with short-term events. The physiological responses that accompany the negative emotions prepare us to threaten rivals or fight them, or to run away from dangerous situations. Walter Cannon introduced the phrase **fight or flight response,** which refers to the physiological reactions that prepare us for the strenuous efforts required by fighting or running away. Normally, once we have bluffed or fought with an adversary or run away from a dangerous situation, the threat is over and our physiological condition can return to normal. The fact that the physiological responses may have adverse long-term effects on our health is unimportant as long as the responses are brief. But sometimes, the threatening situations are continuous rather than episodic, producing a more or less continuous stress response.

fight or flight response

There is no doubt about the deleterious effects of stress on health. For example, survivors of concentration camps, who were obviously subjected to long-term stress, have generally poorer health later in life compared with other people of the same age (Cohen, 1953). Air traffic controllers—especially those who work at busy airports where the danger of collisions is greatest—show a greater incidence of high blood pressure, which gets worse as the people grow older (Cobb and Rose, 1973). (See ***Figure 10.16.***) They also are more likely to suffer from ulcers or diabetes.

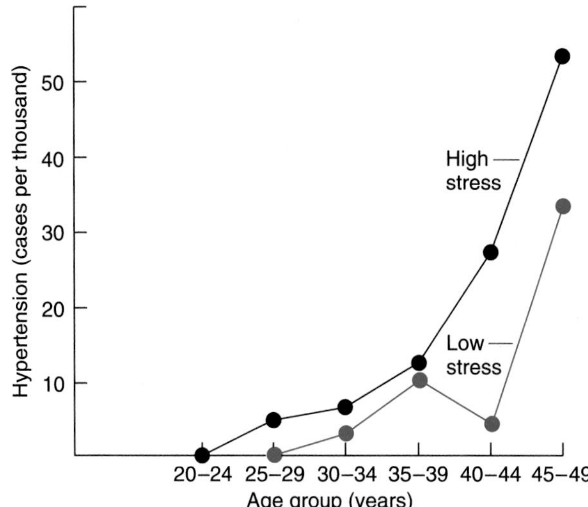

FIGURE 10.16

Incidence of hypertension in various age groups of air traffic controllers at high-stress and low-stress airports. (Based on data from Cobb and Rose, 1973.)

Physiology of Stress

As we saw earlier in this chapter, emotions consist of behavioral, autonomic, and endocrine (hormonal) responses. The latter two components—the autonomic and endocrine responses—are the ones that can have adverse effects on health. (Well, I guess the behavioral components can, too, if a person rashly gets into a fight with someone much bigger and stronger.) Because threatening situations generally call for vigorous activity, the autonomic and endocrine responses that accompany them are catabolic in nature; that is, they help mobilize the body's energy resources. The sympathetic branch of the autonomic nervous system is active, and the adrenal glands secrete epinephrine, norepinephrine, and steroid stress hormones. Because the effects of sympathetic activity are similar to those of the adrenal hormones, I will limit my discussion to the hormonal responses.

Epinephrine affects glucose metabolism, causing muscle glycogen to become available to provide energy for strenuous exercise. Along with norepinephrine, the hormone also increases blood flow to the muscles by increasing the output of the heart. In doing so, they also increase blood pressure, which, over the long term, contributes to cardiovascular disease. The other stress-related hormone is *cortisol,* a steroid secreted by the adrenal cortex. Cortisol is called a **glucocorticoid** because it has profound effects on glucose metabolism. (Aldosterone, the other steroid secreted by the adrenal cortex, is called a *mineralocorticoid* because of its effects on sodium metabolism.) In addition, glucocorticoids help break down protein and convert it to glucose, help make fats available for energy, increase blood flow, and stimulate behavioral responsiveness, presumably by affecting the brain. They have other physiological effects, too, some of which are only poorly understood. Almost every cell in the body contains glucocorticoid receptors, which means that few of them are unaffected by these hormones. (See ***Figure 10.17.***)

glucocorticoid

The secretion of glucocorticoids does more than help an animal react to a stressful situation—it helps it survive. If a rat's adrenal glands are removed, it becomes much more susceptible to the effects of stress. In fact, a stressful situation that a normal rat would take in its stride may kill one whose adrenal glands have been removed. And physicians know that if an adrenalectomized human is subjected to stress, he or she must be given additional amounts of glucocorticoid (Tyrell and Baxter, 1981).

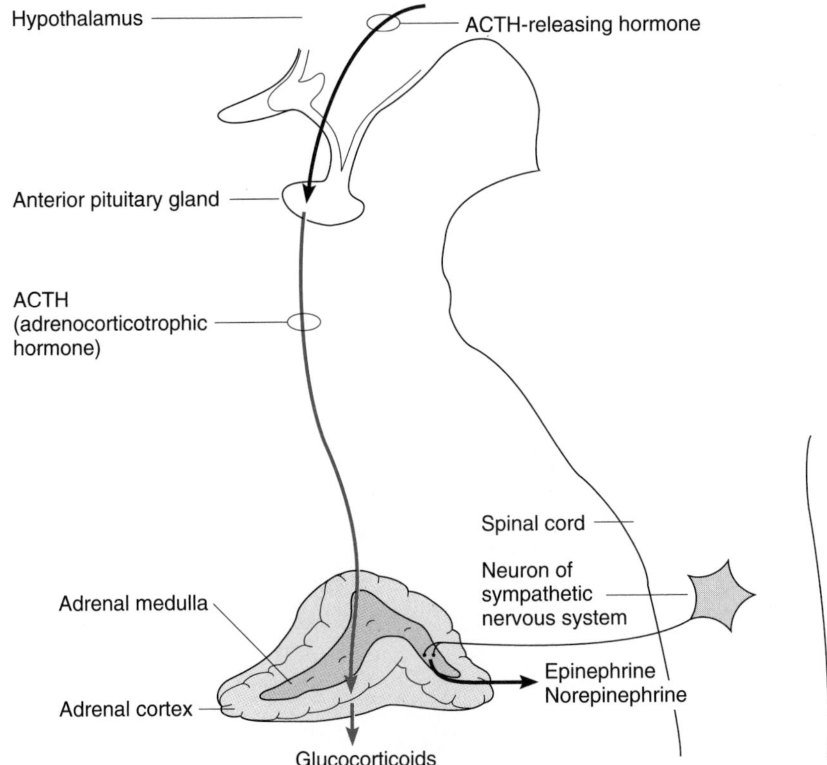

FIGURE 10.17

Control of the secretion of glucocorticoids by the adrenal cortex and catecholamines by the adrenal medulla.

A pioneer in the study of stress, Hans Selye, suggested that most of the harmful effects of stress were produced by the prolonged secretion of glucocorticoids (Selye, 1976). Although the short-term effects of glucocorticoids are essential, the long-term effects are damaging. These effects include increased blood pressure, damage to muscle tissue, steroid diabetes, infertility, inhibition of growth, inhibition of the inflammatory responses, and suppression of the immune system. High blood pressure can lead to heart attacks and stroke. Inhibition of growth in children subjected to prolonged stress prevents them from attaining their full height. Inhibition of the inflammatory response makes it more difficult for the body to heal itself after an injury, and suppression of the immune system makes an individual vulnerable to infections and (perhaps) cancer.

Several lines of research suggest that stress is related to aging in at least two ways. First, older organisms, even when they are perfectly healthy, do not tolerate stress as well as younger ones (Shock, 1977). Second, stress may accelerate the aging process (Selye and Tuchweber, 1976). Sapolsky and his colleagues have investigated one rather serious long-term effect of stress: brain damage. As you will learn in Chapter 12, the hippocampal formation plays a crucial role in learning and memory, and evidence suggests that one of the causes of memory loss that occurs with aging is degeneration of this brain structure. Research with animals has shown that long-term exposure to glucocorticoids destroys neurons located in a particular zone of the hippocampal formation. The hormone appears to destroy the neurons by making them more susceptible to potentially harmful events, such as decreased blood flow, which often occurs as a result of the aging process. The primary effect of the hormone is to lower the ability of the neurons in the hippocampus to utilize glucose, so that when the blood flow

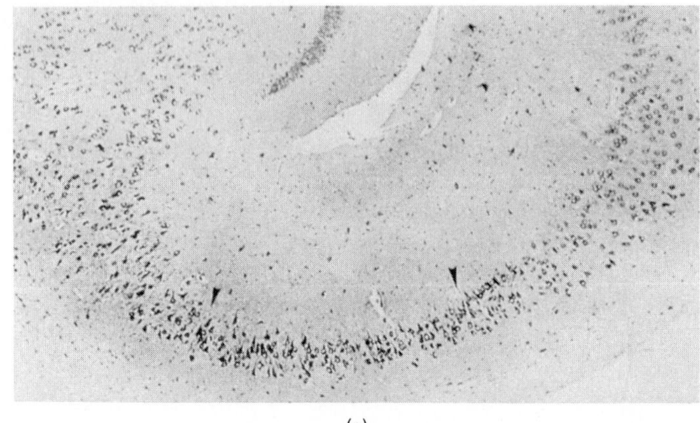

(a)

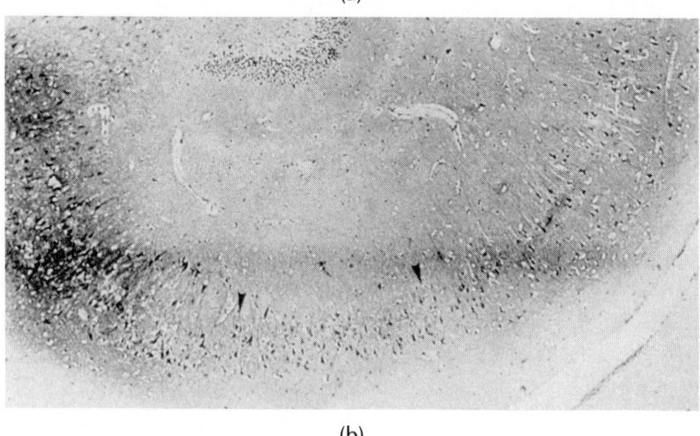

(b)

FIGURE 10.18

Photomicrographs showing brain damage caused by stress. (a) Section through the hippocampus of a normal monkey. (b) Section through the hippocampus of a monkey of low social status subjected to stress. Compare the regions between the arrowheads, normally filled with large pyramidal cells. (From Uno, H., Tarara, R., Else, J.G., Suleman, M.A., and Sapolsky, R.M. *The Journal of Neuroscience,* 1989, *9,* 1706–1711. Reprinted by permission of the *Journal of Neuroscience.*)

decreases, their metabolism falls and they begin to die (Sapolsky, 1986; Sapolsky, Krey, and McEwen, 1986). Perhaps, then, the stress to which people are subjected throughout their lives increases the likelihood of memory problems later in life.

Uno et al. (1989) found that if stress is intense enough, it can even cause brain damage in young primates. The investigators studied a colony of vervet monkeys housed in a primate center in Kenya. They found that some monkeys died, apparently from stress. Vervet monkeys have a hierarchical society, and monkeys near the bottom of the hierarchy are picked on by the others; thus, they are almost continuously subjected to stress. (Ours is not the only species with social structures that cause stress in some of its members.) The deceased monkeys had gastric ulcers and enlarged adrenal glands, which are signs of chronic stress. And as Figure 10.18 shows, neurons in a particular region of their hippocampal formation were completely destroyed. (See ***Figure 10.18.***) Severe stress appears to cause brain damage in humans as well; Jensen, Genefke, and Hyldebrandt (1982) found evidence of brain degeneration in CT scans of people who had been subjected to torture.

Coping with Stress

As we have seen, many of the harmful effects of long-term stress are caused by our own reactions — primarily the secretion of stress hormones. Some events that cause stress, such as prolonged exertion or extreme cold, cause damage directly. These stressors will affect everyone; their severity will depend on each person's physical capacity. The effects of other stressors, such as situations that cause fear or anxiety, depend on people's perceptions and emotional reactivity. That is, because of individual differences in temperament or experience with a particular situation, some people may find a situation stressful and others may not. In these cases it is the perception that counts.

One of the most important variables that determines whether an aversive stimulus will cause a stress reaction is the degree to which the situation can be controlled. As I mentioned earlier in this chapter, when an animal can learn a coping response that avoids contact with an aversive stimulus, its emotional response will disappear. Weiss (1968) found that rats who learned to minimize (but not completely avoid) shocks by making a response whenever they heard a warning tone developed fewer stomach ulcers than rats who had no control over the shocks. The effect was not caused by the pain itself, because both groups of animals received exactly the same number of shocks. Thus, being able to exert some control over an aversive situation reduces an animal's stress response. Humans react similarly. Situations that permit some control are less likely to produce signs of stress than those in which other people (or machines) control the situation (Gatchel, Baum, and Krantz, 1989). Perhaps this phenomenon explains why some people like to have a magic charm or other "security blanket" with them in stressful situations. Perhaps even the *illusion* of control can be reassuring.

Personality variables also affect people's reactions to stress. Some people are simply not bothered by situations that others perceive to be stressful. Because of this fact, researchers have tried to identify the nature of these individual differences. Knowing how such people differ might provide practical benefits—it might even be possible to change their reactions through training.

One of the most important attempts to relate personality differences to the ability to cope with stress was made by Friedman and Rosenman (1959), who identified a behavior pattern that appeared to predict susceptibility to cardiovascular disease. They characterized the disease-prone **type A pattern** as one of excessive competitive drive, impatience, hostility, fast movements, and rapid speech. People with the **type B pattern** were less competitive, less hostile, more patient, and more easygoing and tolerant, and they moved and talked more slowly; they were also less likely to suffer from cardiovascular disease. Friedman and Rosenman developed a questionnaire that distinguished these two types of people. And indeed, several studies found that type A people were more likely than type B people to have heart attacks (Review Panel, 1981).

type A pattern
type B pattern

Subsequent research has provided many conflicting results. For one thing, investigators have developed many different tests that supposedly distinguish between the type A and type B personalities, and unfortunately, these tests do not all appear to measure the same variables. Thus, it is difficult to compare the results of experiments using different tests. One large study found that although people classified as type A were more likely to have a heart attack, the long-term survival rate was higher for type A patients than for type B patients (Ragland and Brand, 1988). In this case it would seem better to be type A, at least after having a nonfatal heart attack. Many investigators believe that personality variables *are* involved in susceptibility to heart attack but that we need a better definition of just what these variables are.

An interesting study with monkeys showed that interactions between personality differences and diet can affect heart disease. Manuck et al. (1983, 1986) fed a high-cholesterol diet to a group of monkeys. They identified individual differences in reactivity to stress by threatening to capture the animals. (Monkeys avoid contact with humans, and they perceive being captured as a stressful situation.) Those animals who showed the strongest negative reactions eventually developed the highest rates of coronary artery disease. Presumably, these animals reacted more strongly to all types of stress, and their reactions had detrimental effects on their health.

Psychoneuroimmunology

As we have seen, long-term stress can be harmful to one's health and can even result in brain damage. The most important cause of these effects is elevated levels of glucocorticoids, but the high blood pressure caused by epinephrine and norepinephrine also plays a contributing role. In addition, stress can impair the functions of the immune system, which protects us against assault from viruses, microbes, fungi, and other types of parasites. Study of the interactions between the immune system and behavior (mediated by the nervous system, of course) is called **psychoneuroimmunology.** This new field is described in the following section.

psychoneuroimmunology

THE IMMUNE SYSTEM

The immune system is one of the most complex systems of the body. Its function is to protect us from infection; and because infectious organisms have developed devious tricks through the process of evolution, our immune system has evolved devious tricks of its own. The description I provide here is abbreviated and simplified, but it presents some of the important elements of the system.

The immune system derives from white blood cells that develop in the bone marrow and in the thymus gland. Some of the cells roam through the blood or lymphatic system; others reside permanently in one place. The immune reaction occurs when the body is invaded by foreign organisms, including bacteria, fungi, and viruses. Two types of reactions occur, *nonspecific* and *specific.* One nonspecific reaction, called the *inflammatory reaction,* occurs early, in response to tissue damage produced by an invading organism. The damaged tissue secretes substances that increase the local blood circulation and make capillaries leak fluids, which causes the region to become inflamed. The secretions also attract phagocytic white blood cells that destroy both the invading cells and the debris produced by the breakdown of the body's own cells. Another nonspecific reaction occurs when a virus infects a cell. The infection causes the cell to release a peptide called *interferon,* which suppresses the ability of viruses to reproduce. In addition, **natural killer cells** continuously prowl through tissue; when they encounter a cell that has been infected by a virus or that has become transformed into a cancer cell, they engulf and destroy it. Thus, natural killer cells constitute our first defense against the development of malignant tumors.

natural killer cell

Two types of specific immune reactions occur: *chemically mediated* and *cell-mediated.* Chemically mediated immune reactions involves antibodies. All bacteria have unique proteins on their surfaces, called **antigens.** These proteins serve as the invaders' calling cards, identifying them to the immune system. Through exposure to the bacteria, the immune system learns to recognize these proteins. (I will not try to explain the mechanism by which this learning takes place.) The result of this learning is the development of special lines of cells that produce specific **antibodies**—proteins that recognize antigens and help kill the invading microorganism. One type of antibody is released into the circulation by **B-lymphocytes,** which receive their name from the fact that they develop in bone marrow. These antibodies, called **immunoglobulins,** are chains of protein. Each type of immunoglobulin (there are five of them) is identical except for one end, which contains a unique receptor. A particular receptor binds with a particular antigen, just as a molecule of a hormone or neurotransmitter binds with its receptor. When the appropriate line of B-lymphocytes detects the presence of an invading bacterium, the cells release their antibodies, which bind with the bacterial

antigen

antibody

B-lymphocyte

immunoglobulin

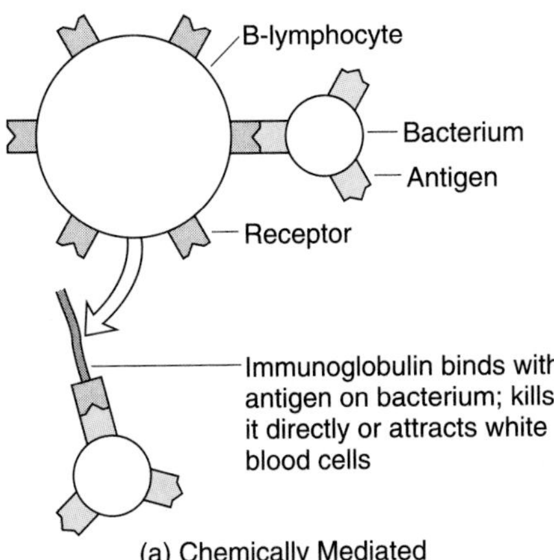

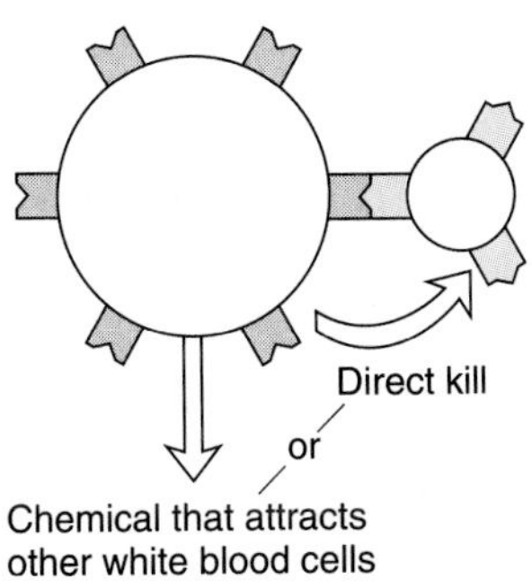

FIGURE 10.19

Immune reactions. (a) Chemically mediated reaction. B-lymphocyte detects antigen on bacterium, releases specific immunoglobulin. (b) Cell-mediated reaction. T-lymphocyte detects antigen on bacterium; kills it directly or releases chemical that attracts other white blood cells.

antigens. The antigens either kill the invaders directly or attract other white blood cells, which then destroy them. (See ***Figure 10.19a.***)

The other type of defense by the immune system—cell-mediated immune reactions—are produced by **T-lymphocytes,** which originally develop in the thymus gland. These cells also produce antibodies, but the antibodies remain attached to the outside of their membrane. T-lymphocytes primarily defend the body against fungi, viruses, and multicellular parasites. When antigens bind with their surface antibodies, the cells either directly kill the invaders or signal other white blood cells to come and kill them. (See ***Figure 10.19b.***)

T-lymphocyte

Although the immune system normally protects us, it can cause us harm, too. Allergic reactions occur when an antigen causes cells of the immune system to overreact, releasing a particular immunoglobulin that produces a localized inflammatory response. The chemicals released during this reaction can enter the general circulation and cause life-threatening complications. Obviously, allergic responses are harmful, and why they occur is unknown. The immune system can do something else that harms the body—it can attack its cells. **Autoimmune diseases** occur when the immune system becomes sensitized to a protein present in the body and attacks the tissue that contains this protein. Exactly what causes the protein to be so targeted is not known. What is known is that autoimmune diseases often follow viral or bacterial infections. Presumably, in learning to recognize antigens that belong to the infectious agent, the immune system develops a line of cells that treat one of the body's own proteins as foreign. Some common autoimmune diseases include rheumatoid arthritis, diabetes mellitus, lupus, and multiple sclerosis. As we shall see in Chapter 16, some researchers even believe that schizophrenia is caused by an autoimmune dysfunction.

autoimmune disease

INTERACTIONS BETWEEN THE IMMUNE SYSTEM AND BEHAVIOR

Often when a married person dies, his or her spouse dies soon afterward, frequently of an infection. In fact, a wide variety of stress-producing events in a person's life can increase the susceptibility to illness (Holmes and Rahe, 1967). These events appear to increase the risk or severity of illness by suppressing the activity of the immune system.

Several studies have demonstrated increases in infectious illnesses during times of stress. For example, Glaser et al. (1987) found that medical students were more likely to contract acute infections—and to show evidence of suppression of the immune system—during the time that final examinations were given. In addition, autoimmune diseases often get worse when a person is subjected to stress, as Feigenbaum, Masi, and Kaplan (1979) found for rheumatoid arthritis. In a laboratory study Rogers et al. (1980) found that when rats were stressed by handling them or exposing them to a cat, they developed a more severe case of an artificially induced autoimmune disease.

Several studies have suggested that cancer may be related to stress. Some investigators have even claimed to have found a "cancer-prone personality" that increases the likelihood of the disease. However, malignancies can have physiological effects that alter people's emotions and personality, which can occur even before the cancer is detected. Thus, what may look like a *cause* of the disease can actually be an *effect* (Borysenko, 1982). In addition, many studies that have found a higher incidence of cancer in stressed or depressed people have not controlled for other factors related to personality, such as diet, alcohol intake, and smoking (Dorian and Garfinkel, 1987).

In any event, most investigators believe that if stress (and personality variables related to people's ability to tolerate stress) plays a role in cancer, it affects the *growth* of tumors, not their formation. Most of the research with animals investigating the effects of stress on cancer has involved tumors induced by viruses, and viruses do not appear to play a significant role in human tumors (Justice, 1987). Thus, this research may not be directly relevant to cancer in humans.

One careful study did find that psychotherapy directed at fear and anxiety reduction appears to have increased the survival rate of cancer patients. In an experiment originally designed to see whether psychotherapy could help people cope with their disease, Spiegel, Bloom, and Yalom (1982) randomly selected two groups of women with advanced breast cancer; one received psychotherapy and the other did not. All patients received standard medical treatment, including surgery, radiation, and chemotherapy. The psychotherapy did indeed help them cope with their cancer; they became less anxious and depressed, and through self-hypnosis they learned to reduce their pain. Thirteen years later, Spiegel and his colleagues decided to examine the medical records of the 86 subjects to see whether the psychotherapy had affected the course of their disease (Spiegel, Bloom, Kraemer, and Gottheil, 1989). They expected to find that it had not. But it had; those who received a year of therapy lived an average of 37 months, compared with 19 months for the control subjects. Three women were still alive, all of whom had received the psychotherapy.

According to Spiegel, we cannot necessarily conclude that the psychotherapy prolonged the patients' survival time because it reduced stress. Instead, the psychotherapy could have encouraged them to comply better with their physicians' orders concerning medication and diet, and the reduction in pain may have made it possible for them to get more exercise. But clearly, these findings are important; identifying the factors that helped retard the course of the illness could lead to the development of even more effective therapies.

Although Spiegel's report is encouraging, advocating and publicizing the belief that thinking negatively causes illnesses and thinking positively cures them has some harmful side effects. Even if the belief is true, variables such as heredity and exposure to carcinogens are by far the most important risk factors in tumor formation, and standard medical treatments provide by far the most effective forms of therapy. Some people may be tempted to forgo medical treatment, hoping that they can make their tumors wither away by thinking positively. Because early treatment is important, any delays in receiving such treatment may reduce the likelihood of a cure. In addition, a belief in the power of positive thinking can too easily turn into a game of "blame the

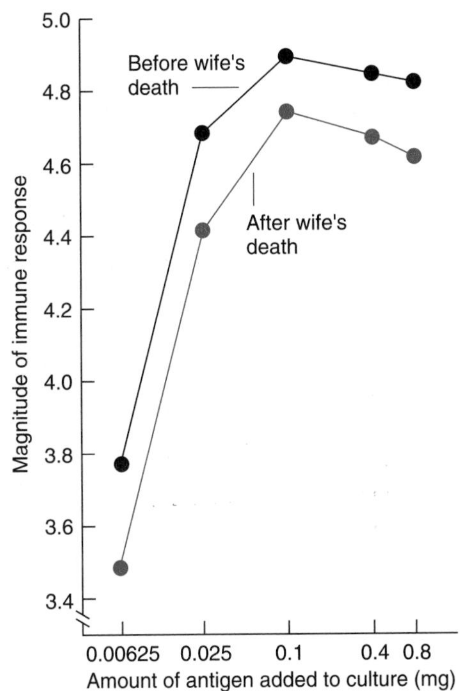

FIGURE 10.20

Stimulation of white blood cell (lymphocyte) production by an antigen in blood of husbands before and after their wives' death. (Adapted from Schleifer, S.J., Keller, S.E., Camerino, M., Thornton, J.C., and Stein, M. *Journal of the American Medical Association,* 1983, *250,* 374–377.)

victim." If someone tries to beat his or her cancer and fails to do so, then the implication is that he or she simply did not try hard enough or had the wrong attitude. People dying of cancer should certainly not be led to believe that they are responsible for their condition; they do not need to be given an additional burden of guilt.

The studies I have described so far have examined the effects of stress on disease and thus provide indirect evidence that stress can suppress the immune system. Several studies have examined the immune system itself and have obtained direct evidence for such an interaction. For example, Kiecolt-Glaser et al. (1987) found that caregivers of family members with Alzheimer's disease, who undoubtedly underwent considerable stress, showed weaker immune systems, based on several different laboratory tests. Bereavement also suppresses the immune system. Schleifer et al. (1983) tested the husbands of women with breast cancer and found that their lymphocyte-mediated immune response was lower after their wives died. (See ***Figure 10.20.***)

MECHANISMS OF STRESS-RELATED IMMUNOSUPPRESSION

As we have seen, stress can suppress the immune system, resulting in a greater likelihood of infectious diseases, and it can also aggravate autoimmune diseases. It may even affect the growth of cancers. What is the physiological explanation for these effects? One answer, and probably the most important one, is that (as you know) stress increases the secretion of glucocorticoids, and these hormones directly suppress the activity of the immune system. All types of white blood cells have glucocorticoid receptors, and immunosuppression is presumably mediated by these receptors (Solomon, 1987).

Because the secretion of glucocorticoids is controlled by the brain (through its secretion of ACTH releasing hormone), the brain is obviously responsible for immuno-

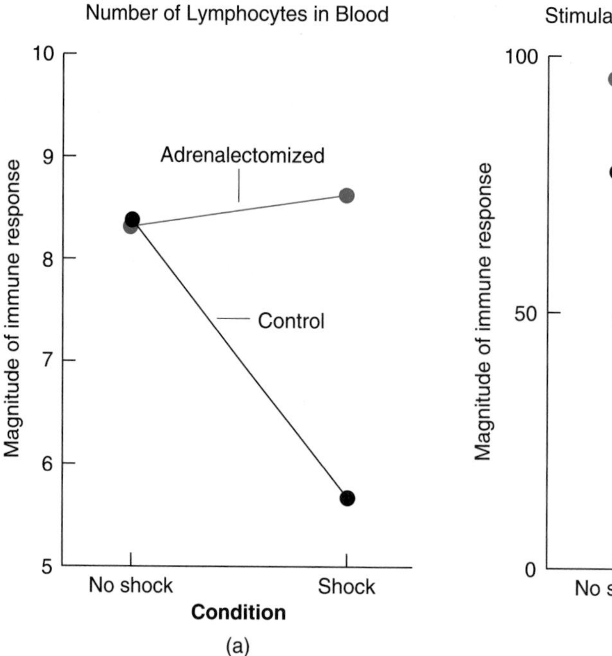

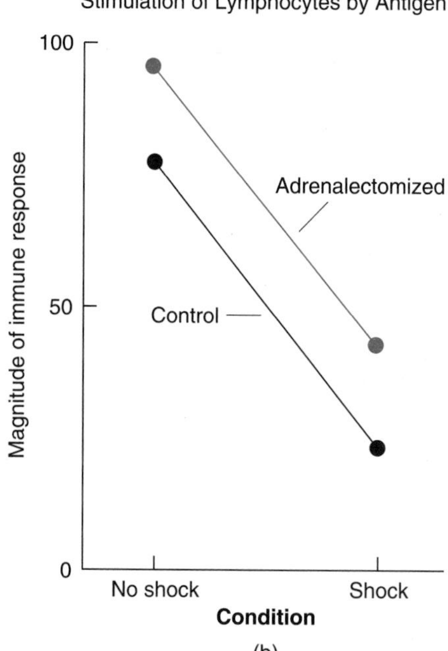

FIGURE 10.21

Effects of adrenalectomy on immunosuppression in rats produced by inescapable shocks. (a) Number of white blood cells (lymphocytes) found in the blood. (b) Stimulation of lymphocyte production after exposure to an antigen. (Based on data from Keller, Weiss, Schleifer, Miller, and Stein, 1983.)

suppression produced by these hormones. For example, in a study with rats Keller et al. (1983) found that the stress of inescapable shock decreased the number of lymphocytes (B-cells, T-cells, and natural killer cells) found in the blood. This effect was abolished by adrenalectomy; thus, it appears to have been caused by the release of glucocorticoids triggered by the stress. (See ***Figure 10.21a.***) However, the same authors found that adrenalectomy did not abolish the effects of stress on another type of immune response: stimulation of lymphocytes by an antigen. (See ***Figure 10.21b.***) Thus, not all the effects of stress on the immune system are mediated by glucocorticoids; there must be other mechanisms as well.

The bone marrow, the thymus gland, and the lymph nodes all receive neural input. Although researchers have not yet obtained direct proof that this input modulates immune function, it would be surprising if it did not. In addition, the immune system appears to be sensitive to neuropeptides. The best evidence comes from studies with the endogenous opioids. Shavit et al. (1984) found that inescapable intermittent shock produced both pain reduction and suppression of the production of natural killer cells. These effects both seem to have been mediated by endogenous opioids because both effects were abolished by naloxone, a drug that blocks opiate receptors. Shavit et al. (1986) found that natural killer cell activity could be suppressed by injecting morphine directly into the lateral ventricles; thus, the effect of the opiates appears to take place in the brain. The mechanism by which the brain affects the natural killer cells is not yet known.

▶INTERIM SUMMARY◀

People's emotional reactions to aversive stimuli can harm their health. The stress response, which Cannon called the fight or flight response, is useful as a short-term response to threatening stimuli but is harmful in the long term. This response includes increased activity of the sympathetic branch of the autonomic nervous system and increased secretion of hormones by the adrenal gland: epinephrine, norepinephrine, and glucocorticoids.

Although increased levels of epinephrine and norepinephrine can raise blood pressure, most of the harm to health comes from glucocorticoids. Prolonged exposure to high levels of these hormones can increase blood pressure, damage muscle tissue, lead to infertility, inhibit growth, inhibit the inflammatory response, and suppress the immune system. It can also damage the hippocampus, and some investigators believe glucocorticoids accelerate the aging process.

Because the harm of most forms of stress comes from our own response to it, individual differences in personality variables can alter the effects of stressful situations. Research on the type A behavior pattern suggests that some of these variables can predict the likelihood of cardiovascular disease and provides the hope that people can be taught behavior patterns that will reduce the incidence of the disease.

Psychoneuroimmunology is a new field of study that investigates interactions between behavior and the immune system, mediated by the nervous system. The immune system consists of several types of white blood cells that produce both nonspecific and specific responses to invading microorganisms. The nonspecific responses include the inflammatory response, the antiviral effect of interferon, and the action of natural killer cells against viruses and cancer cells. The specific responses include chemically mediated and cell-mediated responses. Chemically mediated responses are carried out by B-lymphocytes, which release antibodies that bind with the antigens on microorganisms and kill them directly or target them for attack by other white blood cells. Cell-mediated responses are carried out by T-lymphocytes, whose antibodies remain attached to their membranes. The immune system can produce harm when it triggers an allergic reaction or when it attacks the body's own tissues, in so-called autoimmune diseases.

A wide variety of stressful situations have been shown to increase people's susceptibility to infectious diseases. Animal research suggests that stress can even encourage the growth of malignant tumors, and allergies and autoimmune diseases can be exacerbated by stress. A study on the effects of psychotherapy suggest that learning to cope with the pain and stress of cancer can increase survival rate. The most important mechanism by which stress impairs immune function is the increased blood levels of glucocorticoids. In addition, the neural input to the bone marrow, lymph nodes, and thymus gland may also play a role, and the endogenous opioids appear to suppress the activity of natural killer cells. ▲

◀ *EPILOGUE: Application*

After our visit to Mr. V. (described in the Prologue), we were discussing the case; and Lisa, the student, asked why Mr. V. talked about continuing his walking schedule when he obviously knew that he couldn't walk. Did he think that he would recover soon?

"No, that's not it," said Dr. W. "He *knows* what his problem is, but he doesn't really *understand* it. The people at the rehab center are having trouble with him because he keeps trying to go outside for a walk. The first time, he managed to wheel his chair to the top of the stairs, but someone caught him just in time. Now they have a chain across the doorframe of his room so that he can't get into the hall without an attendant.

"Mr. V.'s problem is not that he can't verbally recognize what's going on; it's that he just can't grasp its significance. The right hemisphere is specialized in seeing many things at once: in seeing all the parts of a geometric shape and grasping its form, or in seeing all the elements of a situation and understanding what they mean. That's what's wrong. He can tell you about his paralyzed leg, about the fact that he is in a wheelchair, and so on, but he doesn't put these facts together and realize that his days of walking are over.

"As you could see, Mr. V. can still express emotions." We all smiled at the thought of the contemptuous look on Mr. V.'s face. "But the right hemisphere is especially important in assessing the significance of a situation and making conclusions that lead to our being happy or sad or whatever. People with certain right-hemisphere lesions are not bothered at all by their conditions. They can *tell* you about their problems, so I guess they verbally understand it, but their problems just don't affect them emotionally."

He turned to me. "Neil, do you remember Mr. P.?" I nodded. "Mr. P. had a left-hemisphere lesion. He had a severe aphasia and could hardly say a word. We showed him a picture of some objects and asked him to try to name them. He looked at them and started crying. Although he couldn't talk, he knew that he had a serious problem and that things would never be the same for him. His right hemisphere was still working. It could assess the situation and give rise to feelings of sadness and despair."

Dr. W. suggested that the right hemisphere's special role in emotional processes is related to its ability to deal with perception and evaluation of patterns of stimuli that occur simultaneously. His suggestion is plausible, but we still do not know enough about hemispheric differences to be sure that it is correct. In any event, many studies have shown that the right hemisphere does play a special role in evaluating the emotional significance of a situation. I described some of these studies in the chapter, but let's look at a few more examples. Bear and Fedio (1977) reported that people with seizures that primarily involve the left hemisphere tend to have thought disorders, whereas those with right-hemisphere seizures tend to have emotional disorders. Mesulam (1985) reported that people with damage to the right temporal lobe (but not the left temporal lobe) are likely to lose their sensitivity to social cues. Obviously, this observation is only meaningful for patients who were sensitive to social cues prior to the brain damage; if someone is socially insensitive *before* having a stroke, we can hardly blame the behavior on brain damage. In particular, people with right-temporal lobe lesions tend to show bad manners. They talk when they feel like it and do not yield the floor to someone else who has something to say; they simply ignore the social cues that polite people observe and follow. They also adopt a familiar conversational style with people to whom they would normally be deferential (usually, the physician who is treating them and writes up a report of their behavior).

Perhaps my favorite example of possible hemispheric specialization is hypnosis. Sackheim (1982) reported that when people are hypnotized, the left side of their body is more responsive to hypnotic suggestion than the right side. Because the left side of the body is controlled by the right hemisphere, this observation indicates that the right hemisphere may be more susceptible to hypnotic suggestion. In addition, Sackheim, Paulus, and Weiman (1979) found that students who are easily hypnotized tend to sit on the right side of the classroom. In this position they see most of the front of the room (including the teacher) with their right hemispheres, so perhaps their choice represents a preference for right-hemisphere involvement in watching another person.

One of the reasons I enjoy writing these epilogues is that I can permit myself to be more speculative than I am in the text of the chapter itself. Why might the right hemisphere be more involved in hypnosis? One explanation of hypnosis, which I find appealing, is that it derives from our ability to get emotionally involved in a story—to get wrapped up in what is happening to the characters in a film or a novel (Barber, 1975). When we become involved in a story, we experience genuine feelings of emotion: happiness, sadness, fear, or anger. We laugh, cry, and show the same sorts of physiological changes that we would if the story were really happening to us. Similarly, according to Barber, we become involved in the "story" that the hypnotist is creating for us, and we suspend our belief and act it out. According to this explanation, hypnosis is related to our susceptibility to social situations and to our ability to empathize with others. In fact, people with the ability to produce vivid mental images, a high capacity for becoming involved in imaginative activities, and a rich, vivid imagination are those most likely to be susceptible to hypnosis (Kihlstrom, 1985).

As we saw in this chapter, the right hemisphere appears to play a special role in assessing social situations and appreciating their emotional significance. If Barber's explanation of hypnosis is correct, then we can see why the right hemisphere might play a special role in hypnosis, too. Perhaps researchers interested in hypnosis will begin studying patients with right- or left-hemisphere damage, and neuropsychologists already studying these people will start investigating hypnosis and its possible relation to social and emotional variables—and either confirm or disprove these speculations. ▲

KEY CONCEPTS

Emotions as Response Patterns

- Emotional responses consist of three components: behavioral, autonomic, and hormonal.
- The amygdala plays a focal role in coordinating all three components in response to threatening or aversive stimuli. In particular, the central nucleus is involved in conditioned emotional responses.
- Perception of simple threatening stimuli is accomplished by subcortical mechanisms, but more complex stimuli require the sensory association cortex.
- The orbitofrontal cortex plays a special role in control of emotional responses to social situations. Connections with the cingulate gyrus may be involved in motivational aspects of emotional responses.
- Prefrontal lobotomy—surgery that disrupts the connections of the orbitofrontal cortex with the limbic system or cingulate gyrus—can reduce severe abnormal emotional reactions, but because of adverse side effects, the procedure has been abandoned.

Expression and Recognition of Emotions

- Facial expressions of emotions appear to be species-typical responses, even in humans.
- Expression and recognition of emotions is largely accomplished by neural mechanisms located in the right hemisphere.

Feelings of Emotion

- The James-Lange theory suggests that we experience our own emotions through feedback from the expression of the physiological and behavioral components. Evidence from people with spinal cord injuries supports this theory.
- Simulated expressions of emotions produce characteristic physiological responses, which suggests a possible basis for the phenomenon of empathy.

Stress

- The stress responses consists of the physiological components of an emotional response to threatening stimuli. The long-term effects of these responses—particularly of the secretion of the glucocorticoids—can damage a person's health.
- The way people cope with stress can affect their physiological reaction and, thus, their health.
- Stress can suppress the immune system—primarily but not solely through the secretion of glucocorticoids—and therefore can make a person more susceptible to infections and (possibly) to cancer.

NEW TERMS

akinetic mutism **p. 331**
antibody **p. 350**
antigen **p. 350**
autoimmune disease **p. 351**
B-lymphocyte **p. 350**
central nucleus **p. 323**
conditioned emotional response **p. 322**
coping response **p. 322**
fight or flight response **p. 345**
glucocorticoid **p. 346**
immunoglobulin **p. 350**
James-Lange theory **p. 340**
medial division of the medial geniculate nucleus (MGM) **p. 325**
natural killer cell **p. 350**
orbitofrontal cortex **p. 327**
pseudobulbar palsy **p. 338**
psychoneuroimmunology **p. 350**
stress **p. 345**
T-lymphocyte **p. 351**
type A pattern **p. 349**
type B pattern **p. 349**

SUGGESTED READINGS

Ader, R., Felten, D.L., and Cohen, N. (eds.). *Psychoneuroimmunology,* 2nd ed. San Diego: Academic Press, 1990.

Brown, M.R., Koob, G.F., and Rivier, C. (eds.) *Stress: Neurobiology and Neuroendocrinology.* New York: Dekker, 1990.

Gatchel, R.J., Baum, A., and Krantz, D.S. *An Introduction to Health Psychology,* 2nd ed. New York: Newbery Award Records, 1989.

Heilman, K.M., and Satz, P. *Neuropsychology of Human Emotion.* New York: The Guilford Press, 1983.

McNaughton, Neil. *Biology and Emotion.* Cambridge, England: Cambridge University Press, 1989.

Stein, N.L., Leventhal, B., and Trabasso, T. (eds.) *Psychological and Biological Approaches to Emotion.* Hillsdale, N.J.: Lawrence Erlbaum Associates, 1990.

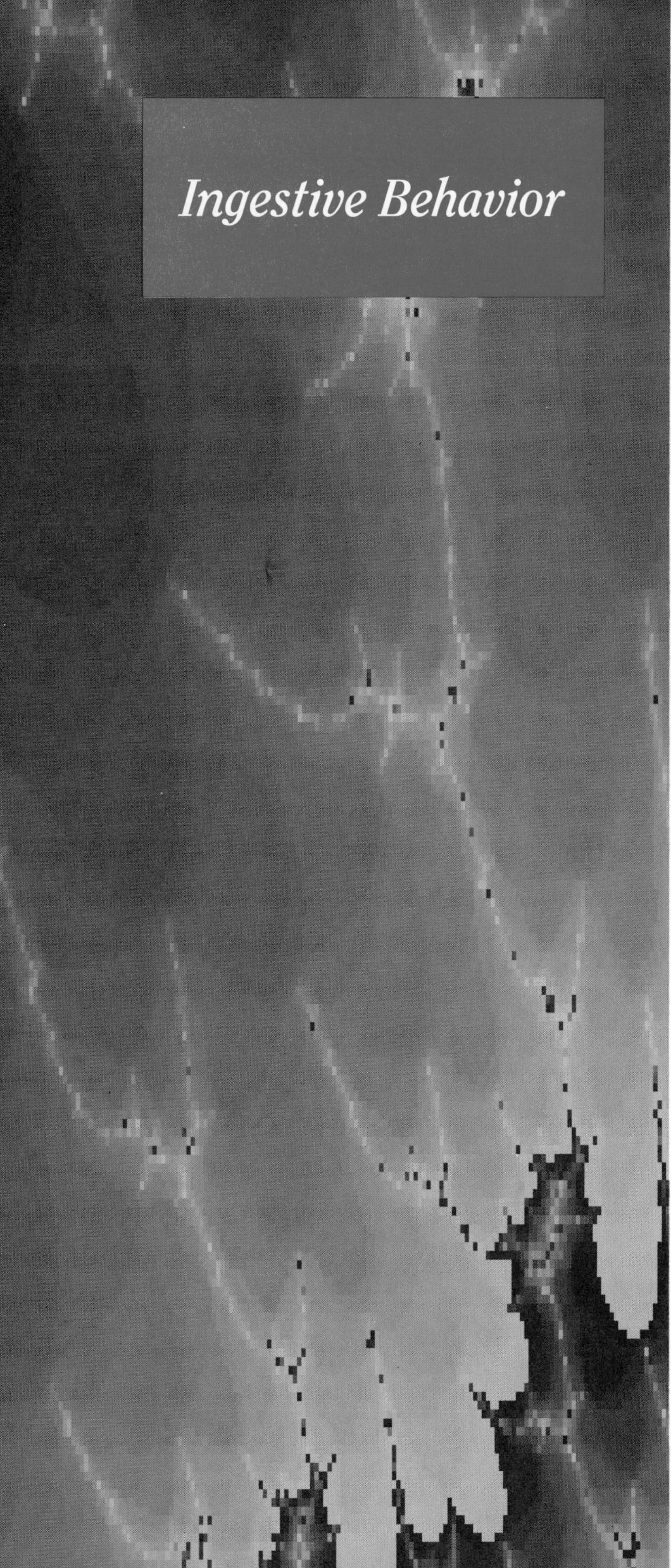

Ingestive Behavior

11

CHAPTER OUTLINE

PROLOGUE ▶

Emily and her younger brother, Jonathan, prided themselves on their lack of racial and religious prejudice. Jonathan was a self-proclaimed "feminist" and enjoyed telling his friends how well his sister was doing in her engineering courses at a famous and prestigious university. He and his sister shared a contempt for intolerance and chauvinism and felt that if other people were more like themselves, the world would be a better place in which to live. The few times that acquaintances had told jokes in their presence that stereotyped other cultures or racial groups, they immediately pounced on them and chided them for their bigotry.

Just before the end of Emily's first year of college, she saw a notice asking for students to provide living accommodations for foreign students who could not afford to return home during summer vacation. She called her parents, and they readily agreed to put someone up at their house. The whole family felt that they would enjoy getting to get to know a foreign student really well and looked forward to showing how nice a North American family could be.

When Emily met her guest at a party that was held to introduce the students to their hosts, she was dismayed. The girl, Norella, was fat! Well, not grossly obese, but certainly far heavier than she should be. Her face was pretty, and she was intelligent and witty; why didn't she pay attention to her diet?

Emily and her brother exchanged a significant glance when she introduced Norella to her family. However, within a few days Norella fit right into the family routine, and they almost forget that she was fat. She helped prepare the meals and do the dishes afterward; she charmed the whole family with her stories of her own country and delighted them with her astute observations of life in their country.

Three weeks after Norella had come to live with them, Emily and Jonathan began talking about a topic they previously had studiously ignored. "You know," Jonathan said, "I just realized this evening that Norella eats less than you do."

Emily looked startled, then said, "You're right! I hadn't thought about that! How can that be?"

"I don't know," he said. "Does she eat between meals?"

"No," answered Emily, "I don't think I've ever seen her do that." She paused, looking pensive, then shook her head. "No. I'm positive that I've never seen her eat between meals. When we've gone out shopping together, I always buy something to eat, but Norella never does. I've offered her some of mine, but she's always said, 'No.'"

Emily and Jonathan sat together in silence. "You know," Jonathan said, "I've never really liked fat people, because it seems like they don't have enough self-respect to keep from overeating. I've always thought that they ate like pigs. But Norella doesn't even eat as much as you do, and she's fat! Maybe it's not her fault." ▲

As the French physiologist Claude Bernard (1813–1878) said, "The constancy of the internal milieu is a necessary condition for a free life." This famous quotation succinctly says what organisms must do to be able to exist in environments hostile to the living cells that compose them (that is, to live a "free life"): They must regulate the nature of the internal fluid that bathes their cells.

The physiological characteristics of the cells that constitute our bodies evolved long ago, when these cells floated freely in the ocean. In essence, what the evolutionary process has accomplished is the ability to make our own seawater for bathing our cells, to add to this seawater the oxygen and nutrients that our cells need, and to remove from it waste products that would otherwise poison them. To perform these functions, we have digestive, respiratory, circulatory, and excretory systems. We also have the behaviors necessary for finding and ingesting food and water.

Regulation of the fluid that bathes our cells is part of a process called **homeostasis** ("similar standing"). This chapter discusses the means by which we mammals achieve homeostatic control of the vital characteristics of our extracellular fluid through our **ingestive behavior:** intake of food, water, and minerals such as sodium. First, we will examine the general nature of regulatory mechanisms; then we will consider our drinking and eating behavior. Next, we will examine the neural mechanisms involved, and finally, we will look at some research on the eating disorders.

homeostasis

ingestive behavior

PHYSIOLOGICAL REGULATORY SYSTEMS

A physiological regulatory system is one that maintains the constancy of some internal characteristic of the organism in the face of external variability — for example, maintenance of a constant body temperature despite changes in the ambient temperature. A regulatory system contains four essential features: the **system variable** (the characteristic to be regulated), a **set point** (the optimal value of the system variable), a **detector** that monitors the value of the system variable, and a **correctional mechanism** that restores the system variable to the set point.

system variable
set point
detector
correctional mechanism

An example of a regulatory system is a room whose temperature is regulated by a thermostatically controlled heater. The system variable is the air temperature of the room, and the detector for this variable is a thermostat. This device can be adjusted so that contacts of a switch will be closed when the temperature falls below a preset value (the set point). Closure of the contacts turns on the correctional mechanism — the coils of the heater. (See ***Figure 11.1.***)

If the room cools below the set point of the thermostat, the thermostat turns the heater on, which warms the room. The rise in room temperature causes the thermostat to turn the heater off. Because the activity of the correctional mechanism (heat production) feeds back to the thermostat and causes it to turn the heater off, this process is

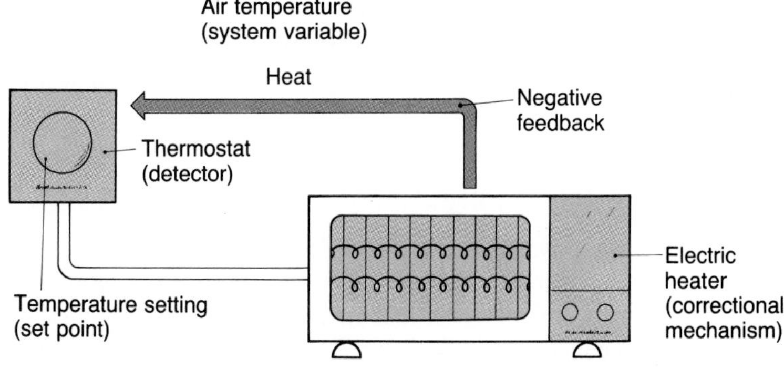

FIGURE 11.1

An example of a regulatory system.

FIGURE 11.2

An outline of the system that controls drinking.

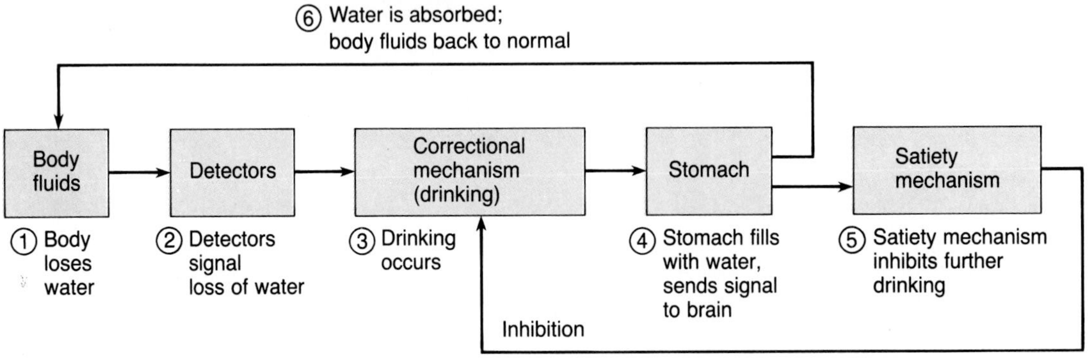

negative feedback

called **negative feedback.** Negative feedback is an essential characteristic of all regulatory systems.

satiety mechanism

This chapter considers regulatory systems that involve ingestive behaviors: drinking and eating. These behaviors are correctional mechanisms that replenish the body's depleted stores of water or nutrients. Because of the delay between ingestion and replenishment of the depleted stores, ingestive behaviors are controlled by **satiety mechanisms** as well as by detectors that monitor the system variables. Satiety mechanisms are required because of the physiology of our digestive system. For example, suppose you exercise in a hot, dry environment and lose body water. The loss of water causes internal detectors to initiate the correctional mechanism—drinking. You quickly drink a glass or two of water and then stop. What stops your ingestive behavior? The water is still in your digestive system, not yet in the fluid surrounding your cells, where it is needed. Therefore, although drinking was initiated by detectors that measure your body's need for water, *it was stopped by other means.* There must be a satiety mechanism that says, in effect, "Stop—this water, when absorbed by the digestive system into the blood, will eventually replenish the body's need." Satiety mechanisms monitor the activity of the correctional mechanism (in this case, drinking), not the system variables themselves. When a sufficient amount of drinking occurs, the satiety mechanisms stop further drinking *in anticipation* of the replenishment that will occur later. (See ***Figure 11.2.***)

DRINKING

In order to maintain our "internal milieu" at its optimal state, we have to drink some water from time to time. This section describes the control of this form of ingestive behavior.

Some Facts About Fluid Balance

Before you can understand the physiological control of drinking, you must know something about the fluid compartments of the body and their relations with each other. The body contains four major fluid compartments: one compartment of intracellular fluid and three compartments of extracellular fluid. Approximately two-thirds of

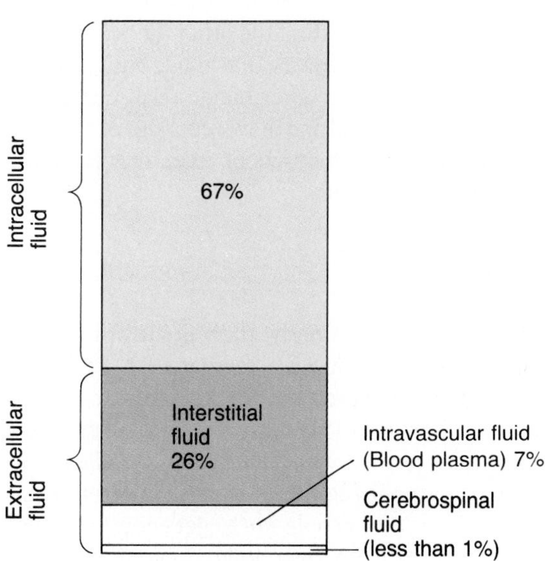

FIGURE 11.3

The relative size of the body's fluid compartments.

the body's water is contained in the **intracellular fluid**—the fluid portion of the cytoplasm of cells. The rest is **extracellular fluid,** which includes the **intravascular fluid** (the blood plasma), the cerebrospinal fluid, and the **interstitial fluid.** *Interstitial* means "standing between"; indeed, the interstitial fluid stands between our cells—it is the "seawater" that bathes them. For the purposes of this chapter I will ignore the cerebrospinal fluid and concentrate on the other three compartments. (See ***Figure 11.3.***)

intracellular fluid
extracellular fluid
intravascular fluid
interstitial fluid

Two of the fluid compartments of the body must be kept within precise limits—the intracellular fluid and the intravascular fluid. The intracellular fluid is controlled by the concentration of solutes in the interstitial fluid. (*Solutes* are the substances dissolved in a solution.) Normally, the interstitial fluid is **isotonic** (from *isos,* "same," and *tonos,* "tension") with the intracellular fluid. That is, the concentration of solutes in the cells and in the interstitial fluid that bathes them is balanced, so that water does not tend to move into or out of the cells. If the interstitial fluid loses water (becomes more concentrated, or **hypertonic**), water will then move out of the cells, through osmosis. On the other hand, if the interstitial fluid gains water (becomes more dilute, or **hypotonic**), water will move into the cells. Either condition endangers cells; a loss of water deprives them of the ability to perform many chemical reactions, and a gain of water can cause their membranes to rupture. Thus, the concentration of the interstitial fluid must be closely regulated.

isotonic

hypertonic
hypotonic

The volume of the blood plasma must be closely regulated because of the mechanics of the operation of the heart. If the blood volume falls too low, the heart can no longer pump the blood effectively; if the volume is not restored, heart failure will result. This condition is called **hypovolemia,** literally, "low volume of the blood" (*-emia* comes from the Greek *haima,* "blood"). The vascular system of the body can make some adjustments for loss of blood volume by contracting the muscles in smaller veins and arteries, thereby presenting a smaller space for the blood to fill, but this correctional mechanism has definite limits.

hypovolemia

As we shall see, the two important characteristics of the body fluids—the tonicity of the intracellular fluid and the volume of the blood—are monitored by two different sets of receptors. A single set of receptors would not work, because it is possible for one of these fluid compartments to be changed without affecting the other. For example, a loss of blood obviously reduces the volume of the intravascular fluid, but it has no effect on the volume of the intracellular fluid. On the other hand, a salty meal will increase the solute concentration of the interstitial fluid and draw water out of the cells without causing hypovolemia. Thus, the body needs two sets of receptors, one measuring blood volume and another measuring cell volume.

Two Types of Thirst

As we just saw, in order for our bodies to function properly, the volume of two fluid compartments—intracellular and intravascular—must be regulated. Most of the time, we ingest more water and sodium than we need, and the kidneys excrete the excess. However, if the levels of water or sodium fall too low, correctional mechanisms—drinking of water or ingestion of sodium—are activated. Everyone is familiar with the sensation of thirst, which occurs when we need to ingest water. However, a salt appetite is much more rare, because it is difficult for people *not* to get enough sodium in their diet, even if they do not put extra salt on their food. Nevertheless, the mechanisms to increase sodium intake exist, even though they are seldom called upon in members of our species.

Because loss of water from either the intracellular or intravascular fluid compartments stimulates drinking, researchers have adopted the terms *osmometric thirst* and *volumetric thirst* to describe them. The term *volumetric* is clear—it refers to the metering (measuring) of the volume of the blood plasma. The term *osmometric* requires more explanation, which I will provide in the next section. The term *thirst* means different things in different circumstances. Its original definition referred to a sensation that people say they have when they are dehydrated. Here I use it in a descriptive sense. Because we do not know how other animals feel, *thirst* simply means a tendency to seek water and to ingest it.

Our bodies lose water continuously, primarily through evaporation. Each breath exposes the moist inner surfaces of the respiratory system to the air; thus, each breath causes the loss of a small amount of water. In addition, our skin is not completely waterproof; some water finds its way through the layers of the skin and evaporates from the surface. The moisture lost through evaporation is, of course, pure distilled water. (Sweating loses water, too; but because it loses salt along with the water, it produces a sodium need as well.) Figure 11.4 illustrates how the loss of water through evaporation depletes both the intracellular and intravascular fluid compartments. For the sake of simplicity, only a few cells are shown, and the volume of the interstitial fluid is greatly exaggerated. Water is lost directly from the interstitial fluid, which becomes slightly more concentrated than either the intracellular or the intravascular fluid. Thus, water is drawn from both the cells and the blood plasma. Eventually, the loss of water from the cells and the blood plasma will be great enough that both osmometric and volumetric thirst will be produced. (See ***Figure 11.4.***)

OSMOMETRIC THIRST

osmometric thirst

Osmometric thirst occurs when the tonicity (solute concentration) of the interstitial fluid increases. This event draws water out of the cells, and they shrink in volume. The term *osmometric* refers to the fact that the detectors are actually responding to (metering) differences in concentration of the intracellular fluid and the interstitial fluid that surrounds them.

FIGURE 11.4

The loss of water through evaporation.

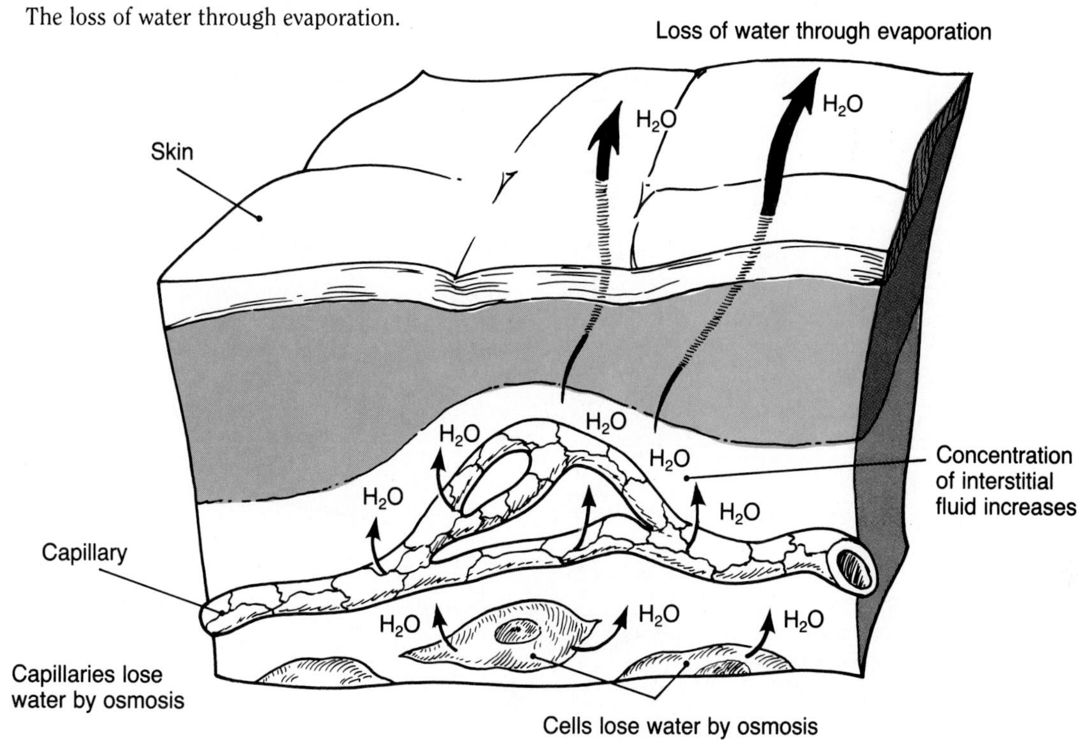

The existence of neurons that respond to changes in the solute concentration of the interstitial fluid was first hypothesized by Verney (1947). Verney suggested that these detectors, which he called **osmoreceptors,** were neurons whose firing rate was affected by their level of hydration. That is, if the interstitial fluid surrounding them became more concentrated, they would lose water through osmosis. The shrinkage would cause them to alter their firing rate, which would send signals to other parts of the brain. (See ***Figure 11.5.***)

osmoreceptor

When we eat a salty meal, we incur a pure osmometric thirst. The salt is absorbed from the digestive system into the blood plasma; hence the blood plasma becomes hypertonic. This condition draws water from the interstitial fluid, which makes this compartment become hypertonic, too, and thus causes water to leave the cells. As the blood plasma increases in volume, the kidneys begin excreting large amounts of both

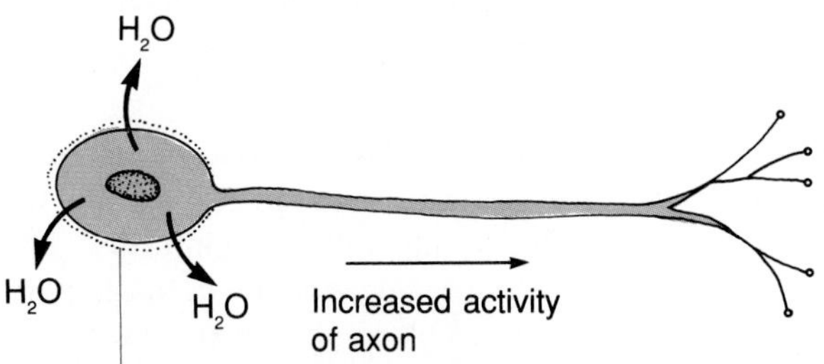

FIGURE 11.5

A hypothetical explanation of the workings of an osmoreceptor.

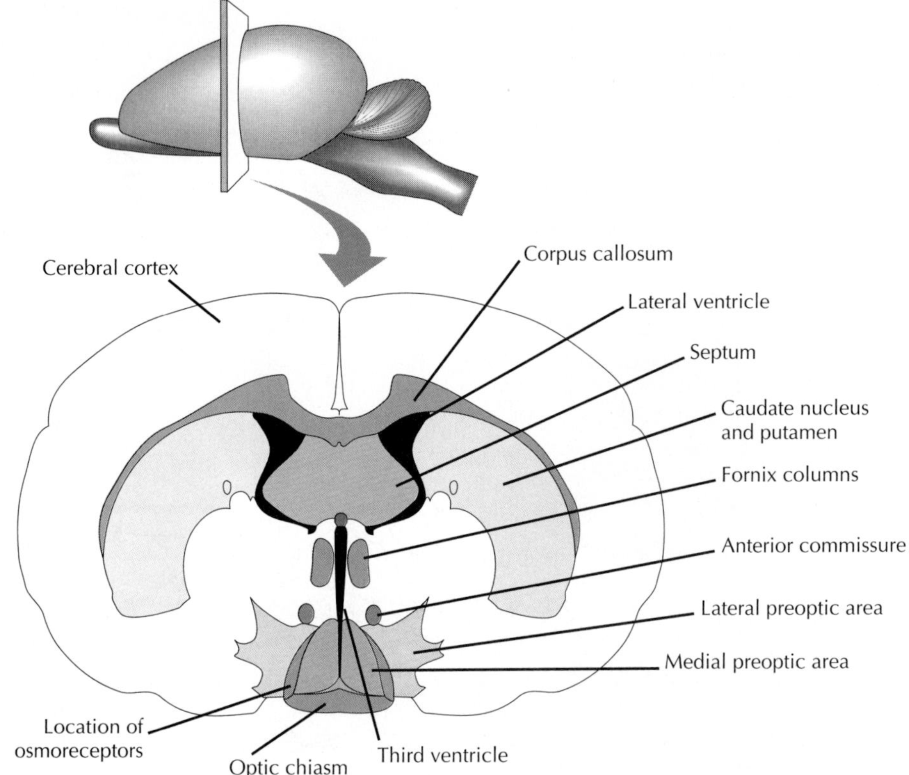

FIGURE 11.6

The location of the osmoreceptors in the preoptic areas, area and anterior hypothalamus. (Adapted from Paxinos, G., and Watson, C. *The Rat Brain in Stereotaxic Coordinates*. Sydney: Academic Press, 1982. Redrawn with permission.)

sodium and water. Eventually, the excess sodium is excreted, along with the water that was taken from the interstitial and intracellular fluid. The net result is a loss of water from the cells. ***At no time does the volume of the blood plasma fall.***

Peck and Blass (1975) injected hypertonic sucrose in many parts of the brain to see if they could find the location of the osmoreceptors that are responsible for thirst. They found that injections in the preoptic area and the anterior hypothalamus produced drinking; thus, the osmoreceptors appeared to be located there. (See ***Figure 11.6.***) Presumably, the hypertonic solution turned on the signal for thirst at the detectors. (This manipulation is similar to what would happen if we cooled the thermostat in a warm room; we would "fool" the thermostat and cause it to turn on the heat.)

Many electrophysiological studies have found evidence of neurons whose firing rate is altered by infusions of hypertonic solutions. For example, Arnauld, Dufy, and Vincent (1975) and Blank and Wayner (1975) found that water deprivation or injections of hypertonic saline produce responses of neurons in the preoptic area.

VOLUMETRIC THIRST

volumetric thirst

Volumetric thirst occurs when the volume of the blood plasma — the intravascular volume — decreases. As we saw earlier, when we lose water through evaporation, we lose it from all three fluid compartments, intracellular, interstitial, and intravascular. Thus, evaporation produces both volumetric thirst and osmometric thirst. In addition, loss of blood, vomiting, and diarrhea all cause loss of blood volume (hypovolemia) without depleting the intracellular fluid.

Loss of blood is the most obvious cause of pure volumetric thirst. From the earliest recorded history, reports of battles note that the wounded survivors called out for water. Volumetric thirst provides a second line of defense against a loss of water should damage occur to the osmometric system, and it provides the means for the loss of isotonic fluid to instigate drinking. In addition, because hypovolemia involves a loss of sodium as well as water (that is, the sodium that was contained in the isotonic fluid that was lost), volumetric thirst leads to a salt appetite.

What detectors are responsible for initiating volumetric thirst and a salt appetite? There are two sets of receptors that accomplish this dual function: one set in the kidneys, which controls the secretion of angiotensin, and one set in the heart and large blood vessels (atrial baroreceptors).

The Role of Angiotensin. The kidneys contain cells that are able to detect decreases in the flow of blood to the kidneys. The usual cause of a reduced flow of blood is a loss of blood volume; thus, these cells detect the presence of hypovolemia. When the flow of blood to the kidneys decreases, these cells secrete an enzyme called **renin.** Renin enters the blood, where it catalyzes the conversion of a protein called **angiotensinogen** into a hormone called **angiotensin.**

renin
angiotensinogen
angiotensin

Angiotensin has several physiological effects: It stimulates the secretion of hormones by the posterior pituitary gland and the adrenal cortex that cause the kidneys to conserve water and sodium, and it increases blood pressure by causing muscles in the small arteries to contract. In addition, it has two behavioral effects: It initiates both drinking and a salt appetite. Therefore, a reduction in the flow of blood to the kidneys causes water and sodium to be retained by the body, helps compensate for their loss by reducing the size of the blood vessels, and encourages the animal to find and ingest both water and salt. (See ***Figure 11.7.***)

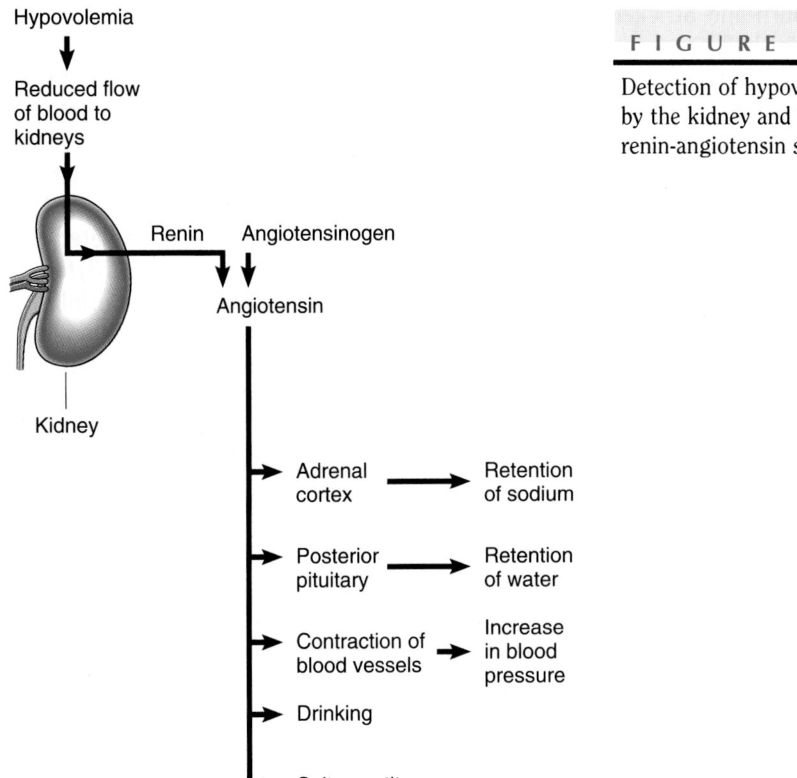

FIGURE 11.7

Detection of hypovolemia by the kidney and the renin-angiotensin system.

Several kinds of evidence support this conclusion. Simpson, Epstein, and Camardo (1978) found that very low doses of angiotensin injected directly into the SFO caused drinking. They also found that when they destroyed the SFO or injected a drug that blocks angiotensin receptors, an injection of angiotensin no longer caused the animals to drink. In addition, Phillips and Felix (1976) found that injections of extremely small amounts of angiotensin into the SFO increased the firing rate of single neurons located there. Finally, Lind, Thunhorst, and Johnson (1984) reported that lesions of the ventral stalk of the SFO, which destroys its efferent connections with the rest of the brain, abolished the drinking response that is produced by an injection of angiotensin.

The Atrial Stretch Receptor System. You will recall that the secretion of renin (and its conversion to angiotensin) is only one of the two ways that hypovolemia produces thirst. The other way is through activation of stretch receptors located in the atria of the heart. Little is known about the neural pathways that connect these receptors to brain mechanisms that control the behavior of drinking. One study suggests that part of this pathway may lie in the basal forebrain. Thornton, de Beaurepaire, and Nicolaïdis (1984) recorded the activity of single neurons in the medial anterior hypothalamus, just in front of the anteroventral third ventricle, in rats. They found that the neurons were sensitive to changes in blood pressure that occurred spontaneously or were experimentally induced. Possibly, these neurons receive information from stretch receptors located in the atria of the heart, and they may be part of a neural circuit responsible for volumetric thirst.

▶*INTERIM SUMMARY*◀

A regulatory system contains four features: a system variable (the variable that is regulated), a set point (the optimal value of the system variable), a detector to measure the system variable, and a correctional mechanism to change it. Physiological regulatory systems, such as control of body fluids and nutrients, require a satiety mechanism to anticipate the effects of the correctional mechanism, because the changes brought about by eating and drinking occur only after a considerable period of time.

The body contains three major fluid compartments: the intracellular fluid, the interstitial fluid, and the intravascular fluid. Sodium and water can easily pass between the intravascular fluid and the interstitial fluid, but sodium cannot penetrate the cell membrane. The solute concentration of the interstitial fluid must be closely regulated. If it becomes hypertonic, cells lose water; if it becomes hypotonic, they gain water. The volume of the intravascular fluid (blood plasma) must also be kept within bounds.

Osmometric thirst occurs when the interstitial fluid becomes hypertonic, drawing water out of cells. This event, which can be caused by evaporation of water from the body or by ingestion of a salty meal, is detected by specialized neurons in the preoptic area and anterior hypothalamus.

Volumetric thirst occurs when a fall in blood flow to the kidneys stimulates the secretion of renin, which converts plasma angiotensinogen to angiotensin. Angiotensin inhibits the excretion of water and sodium by the kidneys, increases blood pressure, and causes drinking and a sodium appetite. Volumetric drinking can be stimulated independently of angiotensin by a set of baroreceptors in the atria of the heart that sends messages to the brain.

The osmoreceptors in the anterior basal forebrain send axons to the zona incerta. Electrical stimulation of the zona incerta causes drinking. The zona incerta sends axons to many parts of the brain involved in motor control.

Angiotensin produces volumetric thirst by stimulating receptors on neurons in the subfornical organ. The atrial stretch receptor system may stimulate thirst through connections with the neurons in the medial hypothalamus, just in front of the anteroventral third ventricle. ▲

EATING AND METABOLISM

Clearly, eating is one of the most important things we do — and it can also be one of the most pleasurable. Much of what an animal learns to do is motivated by the constant struggle to obtain food; thus, the need to ingest undoubtedly shaped the evolutionary development of our own species. After having read the first part of this chapter, in which you saw that the signals that cause thirst are well understood, you may be surprised to learn that we still are not sure just what the system variables for hunger are. Control of eating is even more complicated than the control of drinking and sodium intake. We can achieve water balance by the intake of two ingredients: water and sodium chloride. When we eat, we must obtain adequate amounts of carbohydrates, fats, amino acids, vitamins, and minerals other than sodium. Thus, our food-ingestive behaviors are more complex, and so are the physiological mechanisms that control them.

This section describes research on the control of eating: metabolism, regulation of body weight, the environmental and physiological factors that begin and stop a meal, and the neural mechanisms that monitor the nutritional state of our bodies and control our ingestive behavior.

Absorption, Fasting, and the Two Nutrient Reservoirs

As you saw earlier in this chapter, you must know something about the fluid compartments of the body in order to understand the physiology of drinking. Thus, you will not be surprised that this section on eating begins with a discussion of metabolism.

When we eat, we incorporate into our own bodies molecules that were once part of other living organisms, plant and animal. We ingest these molecules for two reasons: to construct and maintain our own organs and to obtain energy for muscular movements and for keeping our bodies warm. In other words, we need both building blocks and fuel. Although food used for building blocks is essential, I will discuss only the food used for fuel, because most of the molecules we eat get "burned" to provide energy for movement and heating.

In order to stay alive, our cells must be supplied with fuel and oxygen. Obviously, fuel comes from the digestive tract, and its presence there is a result of eating. But the digestive tract is sometimes empty; in fact, most of us wake up in the morning in that condition. So there has to be a reservoir that stores nutrients to keep the cells of the body nourished when the gut is empty. Indeed, there are two reservoirs — one short-term and the other long-term. The short-term reservoir stores carbohydrates, and the long-term reservoir stores fats.

The short-term reservoir is located in the cells of the liver and the muscles, and it is filled with a complex, insoluble carbohydrate called **glycogen.** I will consider only the most important of these locations — the liver. Cells in the liver convert glucose (a simple, soluble carbohydrate) into glycogen and store the glycogen. They are stimulated to do so by the presence of **insulin,** a peptide hormone produced by the pancreas. Thus, when glucose and insulin are present in the blood, some of the glucose is used as a fuel, and some of it is stored as glycogen. Later, when all of the food has been absorbed from the digestive tract, the level of glucose in the blood begins to fall.

glucagon

insulin

The fall in glucose is detected by cells in the brain, which cause an increase in the activity of sympathetic axons that innervate the pancreas. This activity inhibits the secretion of insulin and causes another set of cells of the pancreas to begin secreting a different peptide hormone, **glucagon.** The effect of glucagon is opposite that of insulin;

glycogen

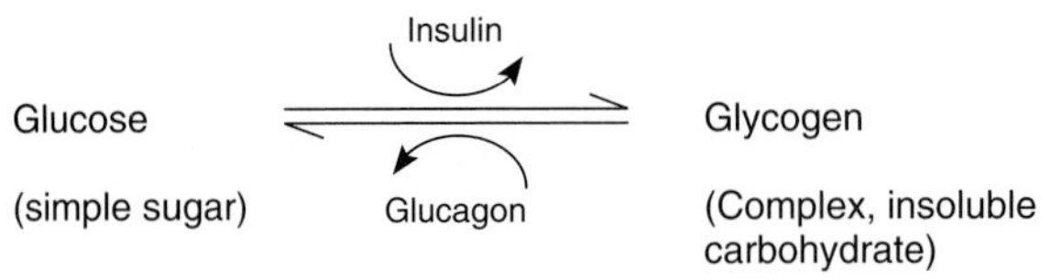

FIGURE 11.9

Effects of insulin and glucagon on glucose and glycogen.

Glucose (simple sugar) ⇄ Glycogen (Complex, insoluble carbohydrate)

Insulin (→); Glucagon (←)

it converts glycogen into glucose. (Unfortunately, the terms *glucose, glycogen,* and *glucagon* are similar enough that it is easy to confuse them. Even worse, you will soon encounter another one, *glycerol.*) (See ***Figure 11.9.***) Thus, the liver soaks up excess glucose and stores it as glycogen when plenty of glucose is available, and it releases glucose from its reservoir when the digestive tract becomes empty and the level of glucose in the blood begins to fall.

The carbohydrate reservoir in the liver is primarily reserved for the central nervous system (CNS). When you wake in the morning, your brain is being fed by your liver, which is in the process of converting glycogen to glucose and releasing it into the blood. The glucose reaches the CNS, where it is absorbed and metabolized by the neurons and the glia. This process can continue for a few hours, until all of the carbohydrate reservoir in the liver is used up. (The average liver holds approximately 300 calories of carbohydrate.) Usually, we eat some food before this reservoir gets depleted, which permits us to refill it. But if we do not eat, the CNS has to start living on the products of the long-term reservoir.

triglyceride
glycerol
fatty acid

Our long-term reservoir consists of adipose tissue (fat tissue). This reservoir is filled with fats, or, more precisely, with **triglycerides.** Triglycerides are complex molecules that contain **glycerol** (a soluble carbohydrate, also called *glycerine*) combined with three **fatty acids** (stearic acid, oleic acid, and palmitic acid). Adipose tissue is found beneath the skin and in various locations in the abdominal cavity. It consists of cells capable of absorbing nutrients from the blood, converting them to triglycerides, and storing them. They can expand in size enormously; in fact, the primary physical difference between an obese person and a person of normal weight is the size of their fat cells, which is determined by the amount of triglycerides that these cells contain.

The long-term fat reservoir is obviously what keeps us alive during a prolonged fast. Once our short-term carbohydrate reservoir is depleted, fat cells start converting triglycerides into fuels that the cells can use and releasing these fuels into the bloodstream. But the fat reservoir is used on a short-term basis, as well. As I said earlier, when we wake in the morning with an empty digestive tract, our brain (in fact, all of the central nervous system) is living on glucose released by the liver. But what about the other cells of the body? They are living on fatty acids, sparing the glucose for the brain. As you will recall from Chapter 3, the sympathetic nervous system is primarily involved in the breakdown and utilization of stored nutrients. When the digestive system is empty, there is an increase in the activity of the sympathetic axons that innervate adipose tissue, the pancreas, and the adrenal medulla. All three effects (direct neural stimulation, secretion of glucagon, and secretion of catecholamines) cause triglycerides in the long-term fat reservoir to be broken down into glycerol and fatty acids. The fatty acids can be directly metabolized by cells in all of the body *except the brain,* which needs glucose. That leaves glycerol. The liver takes up glycerol and converts it to glucose. That glucose, too, is available to the brain.

You may be asking *why* the cells of the rest of the body treat the brain so kindly, letting it consume almost all the glucose that the liver releases from its carbohydrate reservoir and constructs from glycerol. The answer, fortunately, is simple: Insulin has several other functions besides causing glucose to be converted to glycogen. One of these functions is the control of the entry of glucose into cells. Glucose easily dissolves in water, but it will not dissolve in fats. Cell membranes are made of lipids (fatlike substances); thus, glucose cannot directly pass through them. In order for glucose to be taken into a cell, it must be transported there by an active mechanism in the membrane, similar in principle to the sodium-potassium pump and to the mechanisms responsible for the reuptake of transmitter substances. This glucose transport mechanism is controlled by insulin receptors in the membrane; only when insulin is present can glucose be pumped into the cell. But the cells of the nervous system are an exception to this rule; *they can absorb glucose even when insulin is not present.*

Figure 11.10 reviews what I have said so far about the metabolism that takes place while the digestive tract is empty, which physiologists refer to as the **fasting phase** of metabolism. A fall in the blood glucose level causes the pancreas to stop secreting insulin and to start secreting glucagon. The absence of insulin means that most of the cells of the body can no longer use glucose; thus, all the glucose present in the blood is reserved for the central nervous system. The presence of glucagon instructs the liver to start drawing on the short-term carbohydrate reservoir — to start converting its glycogen into glucose. The presence of glucagon, along with increased activity of the sympathetic nervous system, instructs fat cells to start drawing on the long-term fat reservoir — to start breaking down triglycerides into fatty acids and glycerol. Most of the body lives on the fatty acids, and the glycerol, which is converted into glucose by the liver, gets used by the brain. (See the black lines in ***Figure 11.10.***)

fasting phase

The phase of metabolism that occurs when food is present in the digestive tract is called the **absorptive phase.** Now that you understand the fasting phase, this one is simple. Suppose that we eat a balanced meal of carbohydrates, proteins, and fats. The carbohydrates are broken down into glucose and the proteins are broken down into amino acids. The fats basically remain as fats. Let us consider each of these three nutrients.

absorptive phase

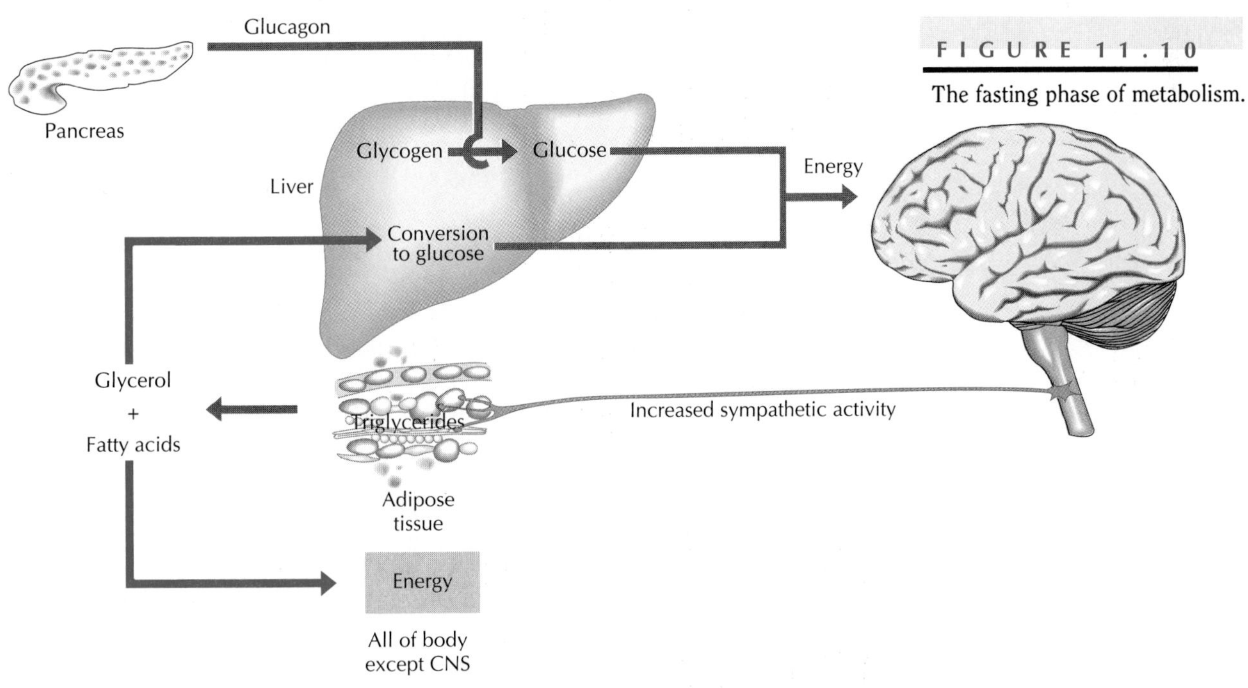

FIGURE 11.10

The fasting phase of metabolism.

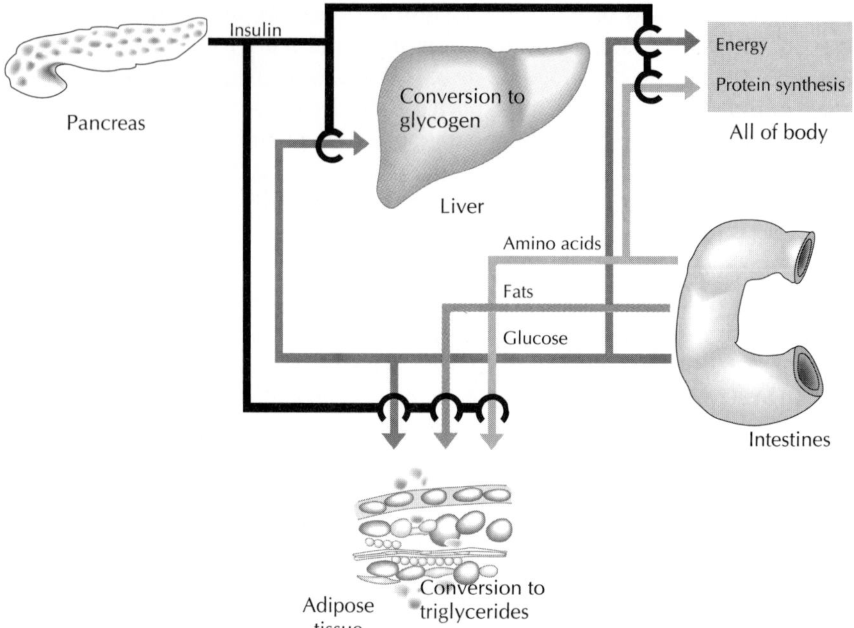

FIGURE 11.11

The absorptive phase of metabolism. The black lines indicate the effects of insulin.

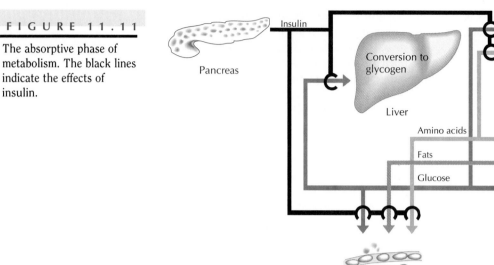

1. As we start absorbing the nutrients, the level of glucose in the blood rises. This rise is detected by cells in the brain, which causes the activity of the sympathetic nervous system to decrease and the activity of the parasympathetic nervous system to increase. This change tells the pancreas to stop secreting glucagon and to begin secreting insulin. The insulin permits all the cells of the body to use glucose as a fuel. Extra glucose is converted into glycogen, which fills the short-term carbohydrate reservoir. If some glucose is left over, fat cells absorb it and convert it to triglycerides.
2. A small proportion of the amino acids received from the digestive tract are used as building blocks to construct proteins and polypeptides; the rest are converted to fats and stored in adipose tissue.
3. Fats are not used at this time; they are simply stored in adipose tissue. (See ***Figure 11.11.***)

Is Body Weight Regulated?

No one questions the fact that body fluids are regulated, but some people have suggested that body weight might not be. The reason for this suggestion is easy to see: Many people are obese, and some of those who are not say that they have to make a real effort to remain thin. If body weight is truly regulated, then we might expect that people should get hungry only when they need to eat and should stop eating when they have eaten enough. But obviously, we sometimes eat when we are not really hungry, and we continue to eat even when we have had enough.

There are several reasons to explain the apparent failure of the body to regulate weight. First, as we shall see, some of the eating habits imposed on us by our society interfere with regulatory mechanisms that evolved in different types of environments. Second, regulation is not as bad as it may seem. The fact that many people show visible fat in their abdomens or in their hips and thighs does not mean that their body weights are not regulated; it may only mean that the amount of fat that is normal for them is higher than what we find esthetically pleasing nowadays. Consider the purpose of fat — to provide a reservoir that can be drawn upon in time of need. In the past (and in the present, in some parts of the world), the supply of food was (is) unreliable. When certain plants were in season, when the fish were running in the river, or when migratory animals were passing through the region, there was plenty to eat. At other times people ate very little and made up the difference by living off their fat. If they had *not* stored some fat during the good seasons, they would have died during times when food was harder to find.

As we will see in the section on eating disorders near the end of this chapter, heredity plays an important role in determining a person's body size and shape. Primarily because of genetic differences, some people are just naturally fatter than others. In other words, people's "set points" can vary. The reasons for these differences and their implications for control of body weight will be discussed later.

The best evidence that body weight is regulated comes from studies that indicate that changes in diet cause compensatory changes in behavior or in metabolism. For example, if animals are given a diet with fewer calories, they soon eat more of it; whereas if they are given a richer diet, they begin to eat less. In addition, if the animal's energy balance is altered, its food intake will follow suit. For example, if a rat is put into a cold environment, where it must expend more energy to keep warm, its food intake will increase and its body weight will remain stable. If it is put into a warmer environment, it will compensate by eating less. People respond this way too; Foltin et al. (1990) found that when they varied the number of calories in people's lunches (by changing either the carbohydrate or the fat content), the subjects altered the amount of food they ate the rest of the day, keeping the intake of calories relatively constant.

What, exactly, is the system variable that permits the body weight of most organisms to remain relatively stable? It seems highly unlikely that body *weight* itself is regulated — this variable would have to be measured by detectors in the soles of our feet or (for those of us who are more sedentary) in the skin of our buttocks. What is more likely is that some variable related to body fat is regulated. The basic difference between obese and nonobese people is the amount of fat stored in their adipose tissue. Perhaps fat tissue provides a signal to the brain that indicates how much of it there is. If so, the signal is almost certainly some sort of chemical, because cutting the nerves that serve the fat tissue in an animal's body do not affect its body weight.

As you might expect, several investigators have tried to identify a chemical signal that is produced by adipose tissue. For example, Cook et al. (1987) found that fat tissue produces a protein that they named ***adipsin,*** and Knoll (1982) isolated an appetite-suppressing glycoprotein from human blood that he named ***satietin.*** In a more recent attempt Harris, Bruch, and Martin (1989) removed fat tissue from rats that they had overfed by 200 percent for 6 – 12 days. They were able to extract a substance, probably a protein, that inhibits growth of fat cells. Further studies will have to be performed to determine whether one or more of these substances actually do tell the brain how much fat the body possesses.

▶INTERIM SUMMARY◀

Metabolism consists of two phases. During the absorptive phase we receive glucose, amino acids, and fats from the intestines. The blood level of insulin is high, which permits all cells to metabolize glucose. In addition, the liver and the muscles convert glucose to glycogen, which replenishes the short-term reservoir. Excess carbohydrates and amino acids are converted to fats, and fats are placed into the long-term reservoir in the adipose tissue.

During the fasting phase the activity of the parasympathetic nervous system falls and the activity of the sympathetic nervous system increases. In response, the level of insulin falls, and the level of glucagon and the adrenal catecholamines rises. These events cause liver glycogen to be converted to glucose and triglycerides to be broken down into glycerol and fatty acids. In the absence of insulin only the central nervous system can use the glucose available in the blood; the rest of the body lives on fatty acids. Glycerol is converted to glucose by the liver, which is used by the central nervous system.

Body weight (or, more likely, quantity of adipose tissue) is regulated, although the amount of fat people's bodies contain can vary widely. Both people and laboratory animals will eat less of a rich diet and more of a diet low in calories, and they will change their food intake if their metabolic requirements change. Three different chemicals have been extracted from blood and from fat tissue; one or more of them may convey a signal telling the brain how much fat the body contains. ▲

WHAT STARTS A MEAL?

The heading to this section is a very simple question, but the answer is complex. The short answer, I suppose, is that we still are not sure, but that will not stop me from writing the rest of this section. In fact, many factors start a meal, including the presence of appetizing food, the company of people who are eating, or the words "It's time to eat!" More fundamentally, there must be some sort of signal that tells the brain that the supply of nutrients has gotten low and that it is time to begin looking for, and ingesting, some food. This section considers all of these factors.

Before I begin, I will point out that the physiological signals that cause a meal to begin need not be the ones that cause it to end. As I said in the discussion of regulatory systems at the beginning of this chapter, there is a considerable delay between the act of eating (the correctional mechanism) and a change in the system variable. We may start eating because the supply of nutrients has fallen below a certain level, but we certainly do not stop eating because the level of those nutrients has been restored to normal. In fact, we stop eating long before that happens, because digestion takes several hours. Thus, the signals for hunger and satiety are sure to be different.

Social and Environmental Factors

Most people, if they were asked why they eat, would say that they do so because they get hungry. By that they probably mean that something happens inside their body that provides a sensation that makes them want to eat. In other words, we tend to think of eating as something provoked by physiological factors. But often, we eat because of habit or because of some stimuli present in our environment. These stimuli include a clock indicating that it is time to eat, the sight of a plate of food, the smell of food cooking in the kitchen, or the presence of other people.

One of the most important appetite stimulators is the taste of food. As we saw in Chapter 6, sweetness detectors on our tongue are probably there because they helped our ancestors identify food that was safe to eat. Even when we are not particularly hungry, we tend to find a sweet taste pleasant, and eating something sweet tends to increase our appetite. For example, Brala and Hagen (1983) had college students drink a milk shake. Half of the subjects first rinsed their mouths with gymnemic acid, a chemical that blocks the perception of sweetness; to them, the milk shake did not taste sweet. Ninety minutes later, the subjects were offered a platter containing a variety of snack food. The subjects who had experienced a sweet taste from the milk shake reported feeling hungrier and, in fact, ate more than those who did not. Thus, a sweet taste can increase subsequent food intake.

Another factor that strongly affects our eating behavior is the presence of other people. De Castro and de Castro (1989) asked people to keep diaries that listed all the food they ate during a seven-day period and the number of other people who were present while they were eating. The investigators found that the amount of food eaten was directly related to the number of other people who were present — the more people present, the more the subjects ate. In addition, the correlation that is normally seen between the time since the previous meal and the size of the present meal was observed only when the subjects ate alone; when other people were present, the correlation was abolished.

Dietary Selection: Responding to the Consequences

Animals need to obtain a variety of different nutrients: carbohydrates, fats, essential amino acids, minerals, and various chemicals that the body cannot make, which we call vitamins. Some animals can get along well eating only one type of food. For example, the physiology of a koala is perfectly suited to a diet of eucalyptus leaves, and that of a giant panda to bamboo shoots. Predators can count on their prey to get a balanced diet and, by eating them, obtain all the nutrients, vitamins, and minerals they need. But animals that eat only one type of food will be limited by the distribution of their food; you will not find koalas where there are not eucalyptus trees, nor giant pandas where there are not bamboo forests. Similarly, predators are utterly dependent on their prey.

It is probably not a coincidence that two of the most successful species on earth, humans and rats, are omnivores. (Please excuse the comparison.) Omnivores ("all-devouring creatures") are liberated from dependency on a particular type of food. However, as always, with freedom comes responsibility. The metabolism of omnivores is such that no single food will provide all essential nutrients. Thus, it is advantageous to eat many different kinds of foods. As we shall see, we tend to do that, naturally. But in some situations, when the foods available at a particular time and place lack an essential nutrient, such as a vitamin or mineral, the animal must make special efforts to find a food that supplies what is needed. In addition, omnivores are exposed to foods that may contain toxic substances. All plants produce chemicals designed by the evolutionary process to poison animals (primarily insects) that might eat them. Most of these poisons are harmless to mammals, but some are not. In addition, food that has been infected with various types of bacteria or molds can become toxic. Thus, omnivores must learn to avoid foods that might cause harm.

Let us consider the tendency to obtain a varied diet. Most of us find a meal that consists of moderate quantities of several different foods to be more interesting than a huge platter of only one food. If we eat a single food, we soon become tired of it, a phenomenon that has been labeled **sensory-specific satiety.** Le Magnen (1956) demonstrated this phenomenon elegantly. He fed rats a diet to which he could add a flavoring. He let the rats eat one flavor for 30 minutes. By that time they had pretty much stopped eating. He replaced the dish with a second flavor, and the rats began eating again. He presented a total of four different flavors (of the same basic food, remember) and found that the rats would eat a meal that was two to three times larger than a 2-hour meal consisting of a single course. Rolls et al. (1981) observed the same phenomenon in humans; they found that people would eat a larger meal when they were offered four types of sandwich fillings or four different flavors of yogurt. Obviously, the phenomenon of sensory-specific satiety encourages the consumption of a varied diet.

sensory-specific satiety

As we saw in Chapter 6, most mammals come provided with specialized receptors that detect substances that are possibly poisonous. Our tongue contains receptors that detect alkaloids and acids (the bitterness and sourness detectors), many of which are poisonous. Thus, we tend to reject bitter or sour tastes. (As we shall see, this tendency is controlled by mechanisms in the brain stem; thus, it is undoubtedly a very primitive reaction.) But taste tells us about the nature of food only when it is in the mouth, so taste provides us with a limited range of information. Much more information is provided by the olfactory system. For example, the odor of rotten meat warns us not to eat it.

conditioned flavor aversion

If an animal encounters a particular food, eats it, becomes sick, and survives, the animal will avoid eating that food afterward. That is, the animal will have formed a **conditioned flavor aversion.** The phenomenon was first experimentally demonstrated by Garcia and Koelling (1966). The investigators let rats taste some saccharin and then injected them with lithium chloride, which produces nausea. (Rats cannot vomit, but their behavior indicates that lithium chloride makes them feel ill.) Afterward, the rats refused to drink saccharin. Other studies have shown that conditioned aversions can readily be formed to the complex flavors of particular foods, which are the composites of odors and tastes.

If a rat encounters a new and potentially interesting food, it only takes a small nibble of the food. If the food contained something toxic, and if it survives its subsequent illness, it will never eat that food again. But if it does *not* get ill, it will take a larger meal the next time; it acts as if it has learned that the food is safe. Humans, too, can form conditioned flavor aversions, which can sometimes occur by chance. A friend of mine often took trips on airplanes with her parents when she was a child. Unfortunately, she usually got airsick. Just before takeoff, her mother would give her some spearmint-flavored chewing gum to help relieve the pressure on her eardrums that would occur when the plane ascended. Yes, she developed a conditioned flavor aversion to spearmint gum. In fact, the odor of the gum still makes her feel nauseated. A more serious problem is encountered by patients undergoing chemotherapy for cancer. The drugs they are given often cause nausea, and the patients can form an aversion to the foods they eat during the course of therapy (Bernstein, 1978).

Thus, we omnivores are endowed with some innate tendencies and with the ability to learn from our experience with particular foods. These tendencies and abilities permit us to obtain the nutrients we need from an enormous variety of foodstuffs, while avoiding foods that could be dangerous to us. Later in this chapter, I will discuss the physiology of sensory-specific satiety and conditioned flavor aversions.

Depletion of Nutrients

Even though environmental factors play a role in starting and controlling a meal, especially in our own species, physiological factors also play an important role. For example, we saw in the previous section that many species of animals (including our own, if clocks and dinner bells are not present) eat soon after a small meal but wait longer after a large one. This fact suggests that hunger is inversely related to the amount of nutrients left over from the previous meal.

Most investigators believe that the physiological signal that initiates a meal is a fall in the level of available nutrients in the blood. As you learned earlier in this chapter, during the absorptive phase of metabolism we live on food that is being absorbed from the digestive tract. After that, we start drawing on our two nutrient reservoirs: The brain lives on glucose provided by the carbohydrate reservoir, and the rest of the body lives on fatty acids provided by the fat reservoir. Although the needs of the cells of the body are being met, the level of nutrients in the blood falls slightly. And later, when the carbohydrate reservoir of the liver is depleted and all the body must live on the fat reservoir, the level decreases slightly again. Surely, then, these decreases in the nutrient content of the blood provide the physiological stimulus for hunger. This section describes research on the role that nutrient depletion plays in starting a meal.

THE GLUCOSTATIC HYPOTHESIS

But what nutrient is measured, and *how* is it measured? For several reasons the most obvious candidate is glucose. To begin with, glucose is the primary fuel during the absorptive phase of metabolism; thus, when it is plentiful, the animal does not need to eat. In addition, a drop in the level of blood glucose is the event that inhibits the secretion of insulin and stimulates sympathetic activity, thus triggering the fasting phase of metabolism. If a fall in glucose is responsible for the fasting phase of metabolism, perhaps it is responsible for hunger, too. Finally, because the brain controls eating, it seems reasonable that hunger might be triggered by a decrease in the brain's primary fuel.

The hypothesis that the signal for hunger is a fall in blood glucose is called the **glucostatic hypothesis** (Mayer, 1955). A *glucostat* is assumed to be a neuron that measures blood glucose the way a thermostat measures temperature. The glucostatic hypothesis suggests that the firing rate of glucostats is related to the level of glucose in the interstitial fluid. A fall in the level of glucose produces a signal in these neurons that stimulates food seeking and eating.

glucostatic hypothesis

Louis-Sylvestre and Le Magnen (1980) devised a procedure that permitted them to continuously analyze the level of glucose in a rat's blood. They withdrew 15 microliters of blood each minute from a catheter implanted in a rat's jugular vein and replaced it with an equal amount of blood from a donor rat; thus, the subject's blood volume was not reduced. They found that the blood glucose level fell by 6–8 percent approximately 6 or 7 minutes before each meal. Several minutes after the start of the meal, the blood glucose level rose, and another meal was not taken until the blood glucose level fell again. (See ***Figure 11.12.***)

Evidence suggests that the fall in blood glucose just before a spontaneous meal is not just *related* to the onset of a meal, it is the *cause* of it. Campfield, Brandon, and Smith (1985) continuously monitored the blood glucose level of rats. If they injected a very small amount of glucose into their veins when they detected a decline in the blood glucose level, the predicted meal was postponed. It was as if the injection removed the hunger signal.

As you know, insulin is necessary for the utilization of glucose; if it is not present, the mechanism that transports glucose into cells cannot function. Thus, hunger is related to the level of insulin in the blood as well as to the level of glucose. Continuous

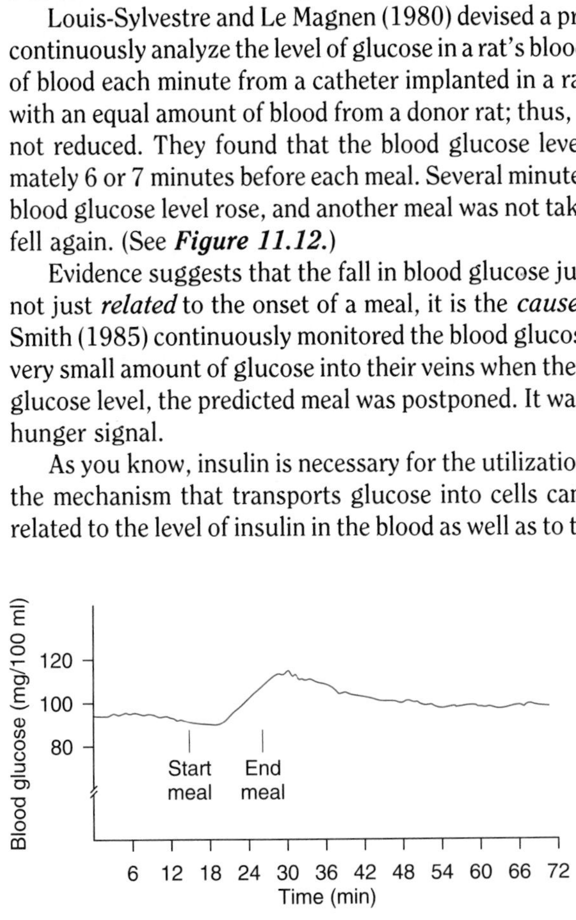

Blood glucose (mg/100 ml)
120
100
80
Start meal
End meal
6 12 18 24 30 36 42 48 54 60 66 72
Time (min)

FIGURE 11.12

Blood glucose level before, during, and after a spontaneous meal of a rat. (Adapted from Le Magnen, J. *Hunger.* Cambridge, England: Cambridge University Press, 1985.)

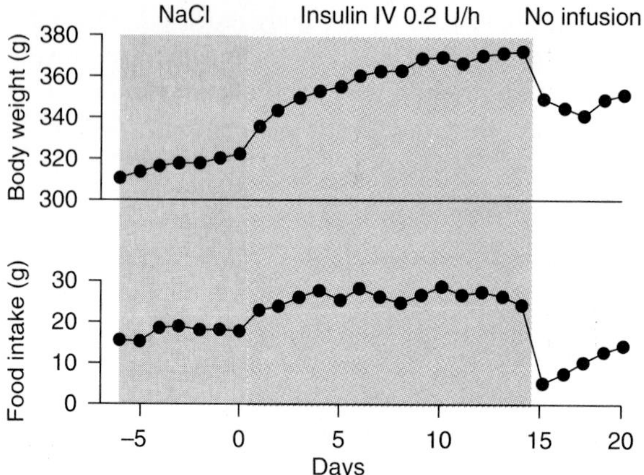

FIGURE 11.13

Effects of continuous intravenous infusion of insulin on the body weight and food intake of rats. (Adapted from Larue-Achagiotis, C., and Le Magnen, J. *Appetite*, 1985, 6, 319–329.)

infusion of insulin makes animals overeat and become obese, because the hormone causes most of the glucose to be stored in fat tissue and prevents it from being released again; hence the animals must eat more frequently in order to keep up their blood glucose level. Figure 11.13 shows the effects of a continuous infusion of insulin on food intake and body weight in rats. Note that after the infusion is stopped, the animals eat very little food until they lose most of the weight they gained. This recovery provides further evidence that body fat is regulated. (See ***Figure 11.13.***)

cephalic phase

In the previous section I noted that the sight, smell, and taste of food can stimulate appetite. One of the reasons for this phenomenon is the so-called **cephalic phase** ("head" phase) of food intake (Powley, 1977). When we eat, or even when we encounter stimuli normally associated with eating, many changes occur in our body. These changes (which include the phenomena that Pavlov was studying when he discovered classical conditioning) prepare our digestive system and related organs for the ingestion of a meal. The changes include salivation, secretion of gastric acid, and secretion of insulin. One of these responses — the secretion of insulin — has an important effect on appetite. The secretion of insulin, triggered by the stimuli associated with eating, switches the body from the fasting phase to the absorptive phase of metabolism. Fat tissue stops releasing fatty acids, and all cells start using the glucose present in the blood. Of course, this process soon causes a further fall in the blood glucose level, which causes an increase in hunger.

I think you can see why a snack has an appetizing effect. The taste — especially if it is sweet – initiates the cephalic phase. The increased secretion of insulin causes a fall in the blood sugar level, and the person (or the animal) becomes hungrier.

BEYOND THE GLUCOSTATIC HYPOTHESIS

More recent evidence suggests that although a fall in the level of glucose may be the most important physiological signal for hunger, it is not the only one. After all, our cells can use other nutrients besides glucose. If animals eat a meal low in carbohydrates but high in proteins and fats, they still manage to eat a relatively constant amount of calories, even though their blood glucose level is reduced slightly. If their eating were solely controlled by the level of glucose in their blood, they would be expected to overeat and get fat.

An experiment by Friedman, Tordoff, and Ramirez (1986) suggests that fatty acid metabolism, as well as glucose metabolism, plays a role in hunger. They used two drugs that interfere with glucose or fatty acid metabolism. One of them you are already

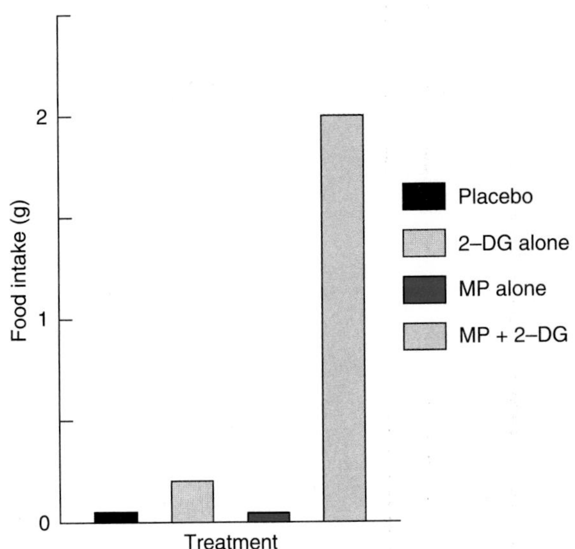

FIGURE 11.14

Effects of methyl palmoxirate (MP) and 2-deoxyglucose (2-DG) on food intake of rats. Intake is significantly stimulated only when both fatty acid and carbohydrate metabolism are impaired. (Adapted from Friedman, M.I., Tordoff, M.G., and Ramirez, I. *Brain Research Bulletin,* 1986, *17,* 855–859.)

familiar with, 2-deoxyglucose (2-DG), because I have described several experiments that used radioactive 2-DG in conjunction with PET scanners or autoradiography to study the metabolic rate of different parts of the brain. When (nonradioactive) 2-DG is given in large doses, it interferes with glucose metabolism by competing with glucose for access to the mechanism that transports glucose through the cell membrane and for access to the enzymes that metabolize glucose. Another chemical, *methyl palmoxirate* (MP), interferes with the metabolism of fatty acids by interfering with their transport into mitochondria, where they are normally metabolized.

Friedman and his colleagues found that a moderate dose of 2-DG or a moderate dose of MP had little effect on food intake when they were given alone. However, when the chemicals were given together, food intake increased significantly. (See ***Figure 11.14.***) Presumably, when the metabolism of only one fuel was reduced, the animal simply relied more heavily on the other type of fuel. The investigators also found that if rats were fed a diet high in fats but low in carbohydrates, treatment with MP alone caused food intake to increase. With no carbohydrates for the animals to fall back on, a treatment that interferes with fatty acid metabolism is enough to stimulate eating.

This experiment raises the following question: Are the availabilities of carbohydrates and fatty acids monitored by the same receptors or by different ones? Possibly, the information is provided by a single set of receptors, which may accomplish the task by simply varying their rate of firing according to how much fuel (of any kind) is available to them. Alternatively, the information could be gathered by two types of receptors: glucose detectors and fatty acid detectors. Although we cannot be sure which alternative is correct, Ritter and Taylor (1989) obtained some evidence that supports the two-receptor hypothesis. They administered capsaicin, a neurotoxin found in red peppers, to rats. The drug destroyed fine-diameter unmyelinated axons of the peripheral nervous system, many of which convey sensory information from the internal organs to the brain. After this treatment the rats increased their food intake when they were given injections of 2-DG but not when they were given MA (a drug similar to MP); nor were injections of both substances more effective than injections of 2-DG alone. Thus, the capsaicin blocked the response to a lowering of fatty acid availability. (See ***Figure 11.15.***)

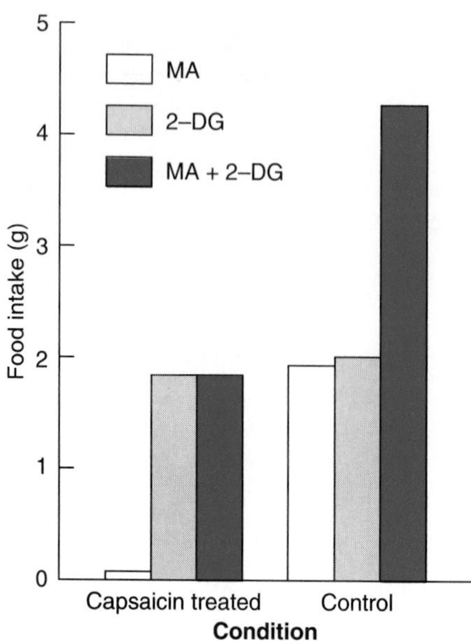

FIGURE 11.15

Effects of capsaicin-induced damage to peripheral axons on hunger produced by interference with fatty acid metabolism (MA) or glucose metabolism (2-DG). (Based on data from Ritter, S., and Taylor, J.S. *American Journal of Physiology,* 1989, *256,* R1232–R1239.)

▶*INTERIM SUMMARY*◀

Many stimuli, environmental and physiological, can initiate a meal. Stimuli associated with eating —such as clocks pointing to lunchtime or dinnertime, the smell or sight of food, or (especially) the taste of food—increase appetite. The presence of other people tends to increase the amount we eat and removes the controlling effect of the previous meal.

Omnivores are naturally attracted to sweet tastes and avoid sour or bitter ones. In addition, they can learn to avoid (form an aversion to) the flavors of foods that make them ill. Sensory-specific satiety encourages the consumption of a varied diet.

The primary physiological signal for hunger appears to be a fall in the level of nutrients in the blood. A few minutes before each meal, the blood level of glucose falls, and the meal can be postponed by infusing a small amount of glucose into the blood. The cephalic phase of a meal, stimulated by the presence of food, includes the secretion of insulin. This hormone stimulates appetite by causing the blood glucose level to fall.

Although the level of glucose available in the blood is probably the most important hunger signal, it is not the only one. Studies with inhibitors of the metabolism of glucose and fatty acids indicate that both of these nutrients are involved. In fact, a study using a neurotoxin that destroys very fine unmyelinated axons in the peripheral nervous system suggests that signals may be provided by two types of receptors: glucose detectors and fatty acid detectors. ▲

WHAT STOPS A MEAL?

The search for the signals that stop a meal follows the pathway traveled by ingested food: the eyes, nose, and mouth; the stomach; the small intestine; and the liver. Each of these locations provides a signal to the brain that indicates that food has been ingested and is progressing on the way toward absorption. To discover the nature of the detectors in these locations and their effects on behavior, experimenters "trick" the organism by taking food out of the digestive system, placing food there, or surgically disconnecting receptors along the digestive tract from the brain.

Head Factors

The term *head factors* refers to several sets of receptors located in the head: the eyes, the nose, the tongue, and the throat. Information about the appearance, odor, taste, texture, and temperature of food has some automatic effects on food intake, but most of the effects involve learning. Satiety can be produced by head factors alone, but this effect is weak and short-lived. (I refer to satiety for an entire meal, not sensory-specific satiety, which was discussed earlier.)

Undoubtedly, the most important role of head factors in satiety is the fact that taste and odor of food can serve as stimuli that permit animals to learn about the caloric contents of different foods. Thus, animals can learn to adjust their intake according to the caloric value of what they are eating. Mather, Nicolaïdis, and Booth (1978) found that rats learned to eat less of a food with a particular flavor when the eating of that food was accompanied by intravenous infusions of glucose, which supplied extra calories.

Gastric Factors

Although most people associate feelings of hunger with "hunger pangs" in the stomach and feelings of satiety with an impression of gastric fullness, the stomach is not necessary for feelings of hunger. Humans whose stomachs have been removed because of cancer or the presence of large ulcers still periodically get hungry (Ingelfinger, 1944). However, although the stomach may not be especially important in producing hunger, it does appear to play an important role in satiety.

Investigators have known for a long time that a hungry animal will eat less if nutrients are injected directly into its stomach just before it is given access to food (Berkun, Kessen, and Miller, 1952). What is the nature of this signal? One possibility is that stretch detectors in the walls of the stomach simply respond to the pressure of food. However, Young and Deutsch (1980) found that when a hungry rat ate all the food it wanted, the pressure within the stomach remained remarkably constant; it did *not* show an increase at the end of the meal that would be expected if pressure were providing a satiety signal.

In fact, the stomach appears to contain receptors that can detect the presence of nutrients, not merely bulk. Deutsch and Gonzalez (1980) operated on rats and attached an inflatable cuff around the pylorus — something that looked like a miniature blood pressure cuff. The cuff could be inflated by remote control, which would cause it to compress the pylorus, preventing the stomach from emptying. With their device Deutsch and Gonzalez could confine food to the stomach, eliminating the possible influence of receptors in the intestine or liver. After observations were made, the cuff could be deflated so that the stomach would empty normally.

Each day, the investigators inflated the pyloric cuff and gave the rats a 30-minute opportunity to drink a commercial high-calorie liquid diet. Because the rats had not eaten for 15 hours, they readily consumed the liquid diet. After the meal the investigators removed 5 milliliters of the stomach's contents through an implanted tube. On some days they replaced the contents with a saline solution. The rats adjusted their food intake perfectly, compensating for the calories that were removed but ignoring the added nonnutritive saline solution. The results indicate that animals can monitor the total amount of nutrients received by the stomach. They do not do so simply by measuring the volume of the food there, because they are not fooled by the infusion of a saline solution. And the detection takes place in the stomach, not the intestine, because the pyloric cuff keeps all the food in the stomach.

How are the signals transmitted from the stomach to the brain? The most likely route would be the gastric branch of the vagus nerve. Indeed, Gonzalez and Deutsch (1981) found that the vagus nerve does carry emergency signals from stretch receptors in the walls of the stomach. The activation of these receptors prevents us from eating too much and damaging our stomachs. However, the signal from the nutrient receptors in the stomach appears to be conveyed to the brain by means of a chemical released into the blood by cells located in the wall of the stomach. The nature of this signal is not yet known.

Intestinal Factors

cholecystokinin (CCK)

After food reaches the stomach, it is mixed with hydrochloric acid and pepsin, an enzyme that breaks proteins into their constituent amino acids. As digestion proceeds, food is gradually introduced into the first portion of the small intestine, the ***duodenum.*** There, the food is mixed with bile and pancreatic enzymes, which continue the digestive process. The duodenum controls the rate of stomach emptying by secreting a peptide hormone called **cholecystokinin** (CCK). This hormone receives its name from the fact that it causes the gallbladder (cholecyst) to contract, injecting bile into the duodenum. (Bile breaks down fats into small particles so that they can be absorbed from the intestines.) CCK is secreted in response to the presence of fats, which are detected by receptors in the walls of the duodenum. In addition to stimulating contraction of the gallbladder, CCK causes the pylorus to contract and inhibits gastric contractions, thus keeping the stomach from giving it more food.

Obviously, the blood level of CCK must be related to the amount of nutrients (particularly fats) that the duodenum receives from the stomach. Thus, this hormone could potentially provide a satiety signal to the brain, telling it that the duodenum was receiving food from the stomach. In fact, many studies have indeed found that injections of CCK suppress eating (Gibbs, Young, and Smith, 1973; Smith, Gibbs, and Kulkosky, 1982). Because CCK cannot cross the blood-brain barrier, its site of action must be either outside the central nervous system or in one of several small organs located around the edge of the ventricular system. (The subfornical organ, which detects the presence of angiotensin in the blood, is one such organ.)

In fact, CCK seems to act peripherally, on receptors located outside the brain. Smith, Gibbs, and Kulkosky (1982) reported that the inhibitory effect of CCK on food intake was abolished by cutting the gastric branch of the vagus nerve, which disconnects the stomach from the brain. In another study, Wolkowitz et al. (1990) gave people injections of a drug that blocks CCK receptors in the peripheral nervous system (but not those in the brain) and found that the subjects felt more hungry and less full after eating a meal than did subjects who received injections of a placebo.

Evidence suggests that the pylorus, a region rich in CCK receptors, may be an important site of action. Moran, Shnayder, Hostetler, and McHugh (1989) removed rats' pyloruses, attaching the stomach directly to the cut end of the duodenum. After the surgery the suppressive effect of CCK on the animals' eating was significantly decreased. However, by 2–3 months after the surgery the junction between the stomach and the duodenum had grown new CCK receptors, and the hormone again suppressed food intake. (See ***Figure 11.16.***)

The suppressive effect of CCK on eating is well established. However, several investigators have questioned whether the suppression is caused by *aversion* or by *satiety.* That is, CCK might simply make the animals feel nauseated, so they stop

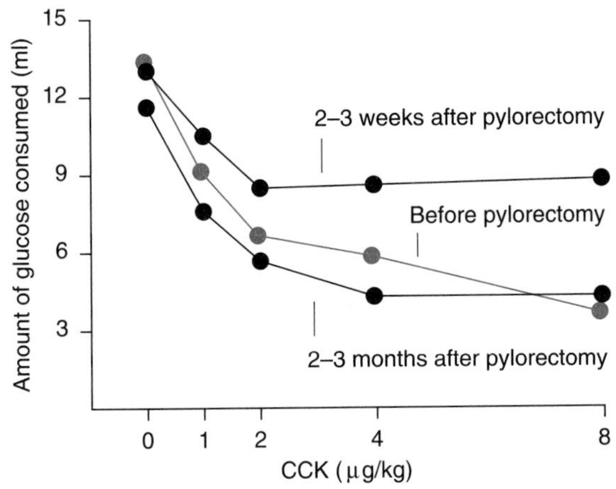

FIGURE 11.16

Effects of cholecystokinin (CCK) on the amount of glucose consumed by rats before and after removal of the pyloric region. (Based on data from Moran, Shnayder, Hostetler, and McHugh, 1989.)

eating. Moore and Deutsch (1985) found that an injection of an *antiemetic* drug (one that suppresses nausea and vomiting) diminished the inhibitory effect of CCK on eating. The fact that CCK can produce an aversion is clear; whether it can also produce true satiety is still uncertain.

Several studies have shown that the brain contains CCK, that it is synthesized there, and that some neurons contain CCK receptors (Rehfeld, 1978; Zarbin et al., 1983). Thus, CCK apparently serves as a neurotransmitter or neuromodulator in the brain. We do not yet know what it does there. Some experiments have shown that infusion of CCK into the cerebral ventricles suppresses feeding, but others have not (Griesbacher et al., 1989). Thus, the CCK story is unfinished. The CCK found in the brain obviously does something, and once we find out what it does, we will know more about brain functions.

Liver Factors

Satiety produced by head factors and gastric factors is anticipatory; that is, these factors predict that the food in the digestive system will, when absorbed, eventually restore the system variables that cause hunger. Food in the mouth or stomach does not restore the body's store of nutrients. Not until nutrients are absorbed from the intestines are the internal system variables that cause hunger returned to normal. The last stage of satiety appears to occur in the liver, which is the first organ to learn that food is finally being received from the intestines.

Evidence for the role of the liver in satiety comes from several sources. For example, Tordoff and Friedman (1988) infused small amounts of two nutrients, glucose and fructose, into the **hepatic portal vein** of freely moving rats. This vein connects the small intestine with the liver, bringing it nutrient-rich blood when the digestive system contains food. (See ***Figure 11.17.***) The infusions "fooled" the liver; both nutrients reduced the amount of food that the rats ate. Fructose cannot cross the blood-brain barrier and is metabolized very poorly by cells in the rest of the body; however, it can be readily metabolized by the liver. Therefore, the results strongly suggest that when the liver receives nutrients from the intestines, it sends a signal to the brain that produces satiety. (More accurately, the signal *continues* the satiety that was already started by head factors and gastric factors.)

hepatic portal vein

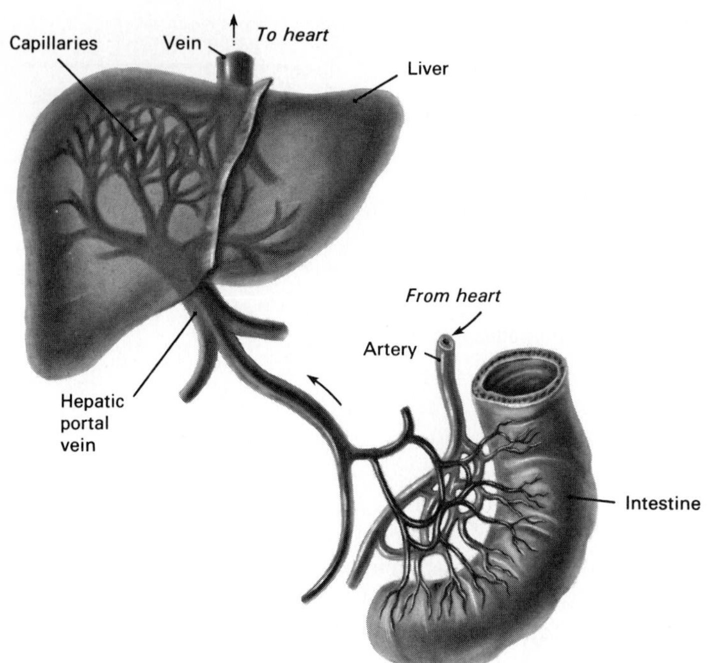

FIGURE 11.17

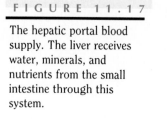

The hepatic portal blood supply. The liver receives water, minerals, and nutrients from the small intestine through this system.

▶INTERIM SUMMARY◀

Because of the long delay between swallowing food and digesting it, the regulation of food intake requires a satiety mechanism; without it, we would overeat and damage our stomachs. The feedback produced by tasting, smelling, and swallowing food provides the first satiety signal, but unless this signal is followed by feedback from the stomach indicating that food has arrived there, the animal will eat again. The stomach contains nutrient detectors that tell the brain how much food has been received. If some food is removed from the stomach, the animal eats enough to replace it, even if the experimenter tries to fool the animal by injecting an equal volume of a saline solution. Although an emergency signal from stretch receptors in the walls of the stomach is carried to the brain by the vagus nerve, the information about the nutrient content seems to be conveyed by means of a hormone.

Several investigators have suggested that cholecystokinin, released by the duodenum when it receives fat-rich food from the stomach, provides a satiety signal. The inhibitory effect of CCK on eating appears to be mediated by receptors in the pylorus. However, studies have shown that CCK has an aversive effect. CCK and CCK receptors are present in the brain; what they do is not yet known.

The final satiety signal comes from the liver, which detects that nutrients are being received from the intestines. ▲

NEURAL MECHANISMS

Neural mechanisms in the brain stem and in the hypothalamus play important roles in the control of food intake. Research on these two regions is described in this section.

Brain Stem

Ingestive behaviors are phylogenetically ancient; obviously, all our ancestors ate and drank or died. Thus, we should expect that the basic ingestive behaviors of chewing and swallowing are programmed by phylogenetically ancient brain circuits. Indeed, studies have shown that these behaviors can be performed by *decerebrate* rats, animals whose brains were transected between the diencephalon and the midbrain (Norgren and Grill, 1982). Of course, they cannot approach and eat food; the experimenters must place food, in liquid form, into their mouths. Decerebrate animals can distinguish between different tastes; they drink and swallow sweet or slightly salty liquids and spit out bitter ones. They even respond to hunger and satiety cues. They drink more sucrose after having been deprived of food for 24 hours, and they drink less of it if some sucrose is injected directly into their stomachs.

As you learned in Chapter 6, gustatory information reaches the brain through three cranial nerves (the seventh, ninth, and tenth). The axons in these nerves form synapses with neurons in the nucleus of the solitary tract, which is situated in the dorsal medulla. This nucleus also receives information from the internal organs, including the stomach and the liver; thus, it is in a position to monitor hunger and satiety signals. The caudal brain stem also appears to contain nutrient-sensitive receptors. Ritter, Slusser, and Stone (1981) injected cold cream into the cerebral aqueduct, which blocked communication between the third and fourth ventricles. Next, they injected a drug called 5-TG (which, like 2-DG, inhibits glucose metabolism) into either the third ventricle or the fourth ventricle. Injections into the fourth ventricle stimulated eating, but injections into the third ventricle (located in the middle of the hypothalamus) had no effect. Thus, it appears that the brain stem contains the circuitry necessary for integrating hunger and satiety signals and controlling the acceptance or rejection of food.

Scott and his colleagues have performed a series of experiments that indicate that in rats the coding of gustatory information in the brain stem is changed by the physiological condition of the animal and by its prior experience with particular foods. For example, Jacobs, Mark, and Scott (1988) examined the pattern of the response of neurons in the nucleus of the solitary tract to various types of gustatory stimuli. They found that when they induced a sodium deficiency, the response pattern to sodium chloride changed so that it resembled the pattern seen when they presented sucrose. Thus, to a rat with a sodium appetite, "salty" tastes "sweet" (or, as the authors suggest, it simply tastes "good"). In addition, Chang and Scott (1984) found that after animals had developed a conditioned aversion to saccharin from its pairing with injections of lithium chloride, the response pattern for saccharin changed. Normally, the pattern resembled that of sucrose; after the aversion was established, it resembled that of quinine. What was coded as "good" now came to be coded as "bad."

Although coding of "good" and "bad" tastes occurs in the brain stem, conditioned flavor aversions are abolished by lesions of the basolateral amygdala (Kemble and Nagel, 1973; Nachman and Ashe, 1974). Thus, one might expect that the learning takes place in the amygdala, and the changes in the response patterns recorded in the nucleus of the solitary tract simply reflect these changes. However, Mark and Scott (1988) found that pairing saccharin with an injection of lithium chloride changed the response patterns of these neurons in decerebrate rats, even though the animals did not show a conditioned flavor aversion. Thus, we can conclude that although the changes take place in the brain stem, the amygdala is necessary for *expressing* an aversion. The learning takes place in one part of the brain, but another part is required for the learning to affect behavior.

Hypothalamus

Discoveries made in the 1940s and 1950s focused the attention of researchers interested in ingestive behavior on two regions of the hypothalamus: the lateral area and the ventromedial nucleus. For many years investigators believed that these two regions controlled hunger and satiety, respectively; one was the accelerator, and the other was the brake. The basic findings were these: After the lateral hypothalamus was destroyed, animals stopped eating or drinking (Anand and Brobeck, 1951; Teitelbaum and Stellar, 1954). Electrical stimulation of the same region would produce eating, drinking, or both behaviors. Conversely, lesions of the ventromedial nucleus of the hypothalamus produced overeating that led to gross obesity, whereas electrical stimulation suppressed eating (Hetherington and Ranson, 1942). The story was too simple, of course. Although the lateral hypothalamus appears to play a role in the control of food intake, we are not certain that the ventromedial nucleus plays a role in satiety. The following subsections give the details.

VENTROMEDIAL HYPOTHALAMUS/PARAVENTRICULAR NUCLEUS

One of the most striking effects of a localized brain lesion is the overeating and obesity that is produced by a lesion of the ventromedial hypothalamus (VMH). The

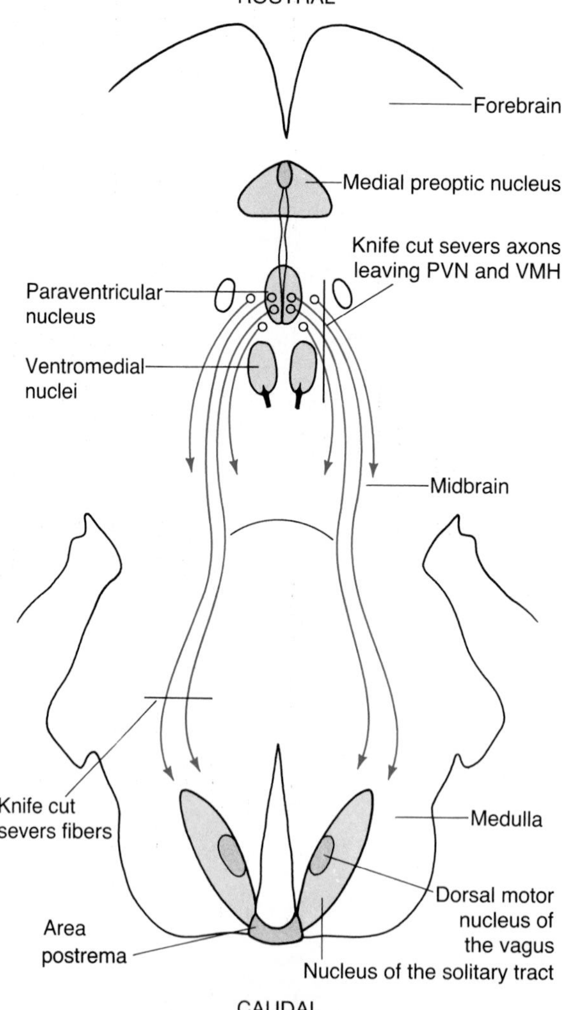

FIGURE 11.18

An outline of the connections between the paraventricular nucleus, ventromedial nucleus, and the medulla that may be involved in the effects of ventromedial lesions on food intake. (Adapted with permission from Kirchgessner, A.L., and Sclafani, A. *Physiology and Behavior, 42,* 517–528, copyright 1988, Pergamon Press plc.)

most plausible explanation for a lesion causing an increase in eating is that it damages satiety mechanisms in the brain, and this explanation was accepted for many years. However, the *VMH syndrome* (the set of behaviors that accompanies these lesions) turns out to be much more complex than a loss of inhibitory control of eating. Animals with VMH lesions are "finicky"; they will not overeat if some quinine is added to their diet (Ferguson and Keesey, 1975). If given a choice of different diets, animals with VMH lesions will primarily overeat carbohydrates (Sclafani and Aravich, 1983). In addition to affecting behavior, VMH lesions disrupt the control of the autonomic nervous system. In particular, they cause an increase in parasympathetic activity of the vagus nerve, which stimulates the secretion of insulin and inhibits the secretion of glucagon and adrenal catecholamines (Weingarten, Chang, and McDonald, 1985). Thus, the liver and adipose tissue of an animal with a VMH lesion are unable to release their nutrients during the fasting phase of metabolism; consequently, the animal *has* to eat to keep up the supply of nutrients in its blood.

The VMH syndrome is complex anatomically as well as behaviorally. In fact, VMH lesions destroy axons that connect the paraventricular nucleus of the hypothalamus (PVN) with structures in the brain stem. Kirchgessner and Sclafani (1988) found that the destination of the axons from the VMH and the PVN seems to be the nucleus of the solitary tract and the dorsal motor nucleus of the vagus. (See ***Figure 11.18.***) The

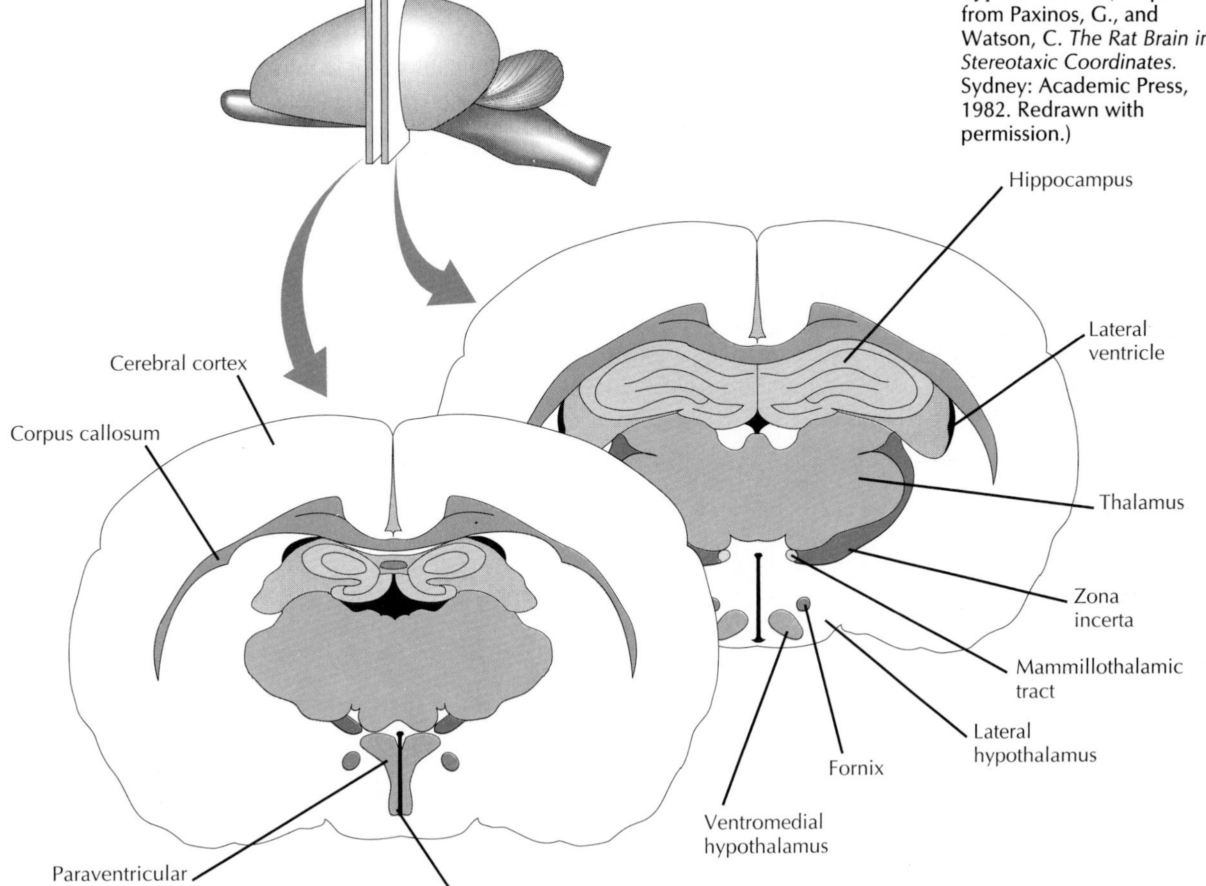

FIGURE 11.19

Cross sections through the rat brain, showing the location of the paraventricular nucleus, zona incerta, and the ventromedial nuclei of the hypothalamus. (Adapted from Paxinos, G., and Watson, C. *The Rat Brain in Stereotaxic Coordinates.* Sydney: Academic Press, 1982. Redrawn with permission.)

nucleus of the solitary tract receives nutrient-related information from the tongue, liver, and stomach; thus, changes in its activity could affect an animal's intake of food. The dorsal motor nucleus of the vagus nerve controls the activity of the parasympathetic axons that stimulate insulin secretion; thus, the increased insulin secretion produced by VMH lesions may be caused by disruption of this pathway.

Most of the research interest in the VMH syndrome in recent years has focused on the role of the paraventricular nucleus, located in the medial hypothalamus. (See ***Figure 11.19.***) The PVN appears to play an important role in carbohydrate intake. Rats, being nocturnal animals, generally sleep and fast during the day; then when night comes, they take their first big meal. This meal tends to be high in carbohydrates, which are the most easily digested and metabolized nutrients; later meals are higher in fats and protein (Leibowitz, Weiss, and Shor-Posner, 1988). This carbohydrate appetite appears to be under the control of neurons in the paraventricular nucleus.

Two neurotransmitters present in the medial hypothalamus play an important role in appetite for carbohydrates. Norepinephrine (NE) stimulates carbohydrate intake, and serotonin (5-HT) inhibits it. Leibowitz, Weiss, Yee, and Tretter (1985) found that microinfusion of NE into the PVN stimulates eating, especially of carbohydrates. (See ***Figure 11.20.***) It is not clear whether the effects of NE stimulate eating directly or indirectly, by increasing the secretion of insulin by the pancreas.

Stanley, Schwartz, Hernandez, Hoebel, and Leibowitz (1989) placed a microdialysis probe in the paraventricular nucleus of rats and recorded the level of extracellular NE across the sleep-waking cycle. (Microdialysis was described in Chapter 1.) The investigators found that the level of NE showed a sharp rise just after the onset of the dark phase of the light cycle, at about the time when the animals ate their first meal. (See ***Figure 11.21.***)

So far, little is known about the control of NE secretion in the PVN. As we saw in Chapter 8, the locus coeruleus, the primary source of the noradrenergic axons to the PVN, is itself controlled by two regions of the medulla. Perhaps the activity of the noradrenergic neurons is regulated by signals from nutrient receptors in the brain stem and liver, by taste signals from the tongue, and by information from the suprachiasmatic nucleus that the active period of the light-dark cycle has begun.

The release of 5-HT has an effect opposite that of NE: It *inhibits* the eating of carbohydrates. In fact, a 5-HT agonist, *fenfluramine,* is commonly used to suppress appetite in obese people. Leibowitz, Weiss, Walsh, and Viswanath (1989) found that an

FIGURE 11.20

Effects of infusion of norepinephrine into the paraventricular nucleus on intake of carbohydrate, protein, and fat. (Reprinted with permission from Leibowitz, S.F., Weiss, G.F., Yee, F., and Tretter, J.B. *Brain Research Bulletin, 14,* 561–567, copyright 1985, Pergamon Press plc.)

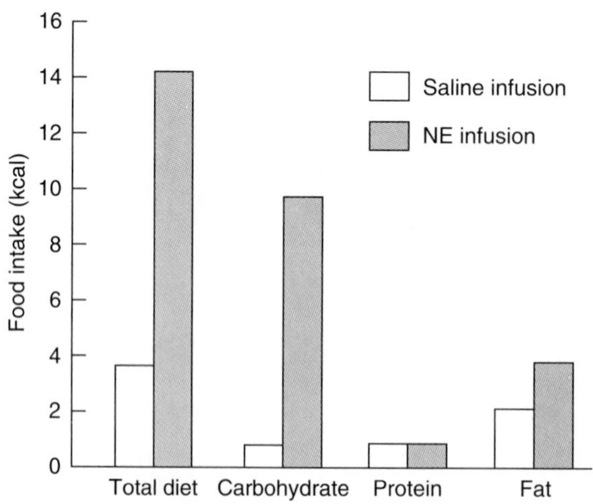

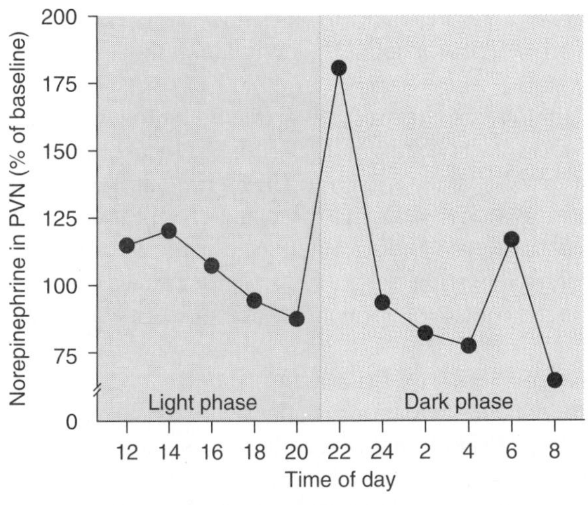

FIGURE 11.21

Extracellular norepinephrine levels in the paraventricular nucleus during the light and dark phases of the day-night cycle, as measured by microdialysis. (Adapted with permission from Stanley, B.G., Schwartz, D.H., Hernandez, L., Hoebel, B.G., and Leibowitz, S.F. *Life Sciences, 45,* 275–282, copyright 1989, Pergamon Press plc.)

infusion of 5-HT into the PVN reduces the amount of carbohydrates that rats eat but has little effect on the intake of fats and proteins.

Experiments using the microdialysis procedure suggest that 5-HT is released throughout the hypothalamus when a rat eats its first meal during the active portion of the light-dark cycle (Schwartz, McClane, Hernandez, and Hoebel, 1989; Stanley et al., 1989). Presumably, this 5-HT release reflects the activation of a satiety mechanism.

LATERAL HYPOTHALAMUS

For approximately two decades after the discovery that lesions of the lateral hypothalamus abolished eating behavior, most investigators subscribed to the hypothesis that this region was a "feeding center." (Refer to ***Figure 11.19.***) During the 1970s researchers finally began to pay attention to the fact that rats with these lesions have other types of behavioral impairments. In fact, they hardly move at all and pay little attention to stimuli around them. Stricker and Zigmond (1976) reviewed the existing evidence and concluded that the behavioral effects of lateral hypothalamic lesions, including the suppression of eating, were produced by damage to dopaminergic axons of the nigrostriatal bundle that pass through this region, which are known to play a role in the control of movement. However, subsequent research showed that neurotoxic lesions made with ibotenic acid, which kills cells while sparing axons passing through the region, produce a long-lasting decrease in food intake and body weight (Winn, Tarbuck, and Dunnett, 1984; Dunnett, Lane, and Winn, 1985). The lesions did not affect dopamine levels in the forebrain. Thus, the neurons of the lateral hypothalamus, as well as the axons passing through this region, appear to play a role in the control of ingestive behavior.

Another piece of evidence indicating that the lateral hypothalamus plays a role in ingestive behavior is the fact that a neurotransmitter (or neuromodulator) called **neuropeptide Y** is an extremely potent stimulator of food intake (Levine and Morley, 1984). An infusion of this substance into the mid-lateral hypothalamus causes frantic, ravenous eating (Stanley, Magdalin, and Leibowitz, 1989). Sahu, Kalra, and Kalra (1988) found that hypothalamic levels of neuropeptide Y are increased by food deprivation and lowered by eating. Beyond that fact, little is known about the physiological conditions that cause the release of neuropeptide Y or of the neural circuitry responsible for carrying out its effects. Whatever its specific role in the control of appetite,

neuropeptide Y

neuropeptide Y appears to be part of a phylogenetically ancient system; Morris and Crews (1990) found that injections of neuropeptide Y stimulate eating in garter snakes.

Many neurons in the hypothalamus act as glucoreceptors; that is, they change their firing rate when glucose is infused in their vicinity. Most of these glucose-sensitive neurons are located in the lateral hypothalamus (Oomura, 1976). Himmi, Boyer, and Orsini (1988) found that many neurons in the lateral hypothalamus change their firing rate in response to spontaneous fluctuations in the level of glucose in the blood supply to the brain or in fluctuations produced by glucose infusions. These neurons may be involved in the control of eating, in the control of hormones that regulate metabolism, or both.

Rolls and his colleagues (see Rolls, 1986) have studied the response characteristics of single neurons in the lateral hypothalamus and nearby regions of the basal forebrain in monkeys. Burton, Rolls, and Mora (1976) found that some neurons located there respond to either the sight or taste of food, but do so *only if the animal is hungry.* These neurons may be involved in the motivational aspects of eating. In support of this suggestion Rolls et al. (1986) found that the firing rate of these neurons was related to sensory-specific satiety. For example, one neuron showed a high rate of firing when the monkey was shown a peanut, a banana, an orange, or a syringe that was used to squirt a glucose solution into its mouth. The animal was then given repeated drinks of the glucose solution. At first, it drank the solution enthusiastically, but after a while, acceptance turned to rejection. At the same time, the neuron responded less and less when the monkey was shown the syringe. However, the neuron still responded to the sight of a peanut, an orange, or a banana. The monkey was then allowed to eat all the banana it wanted. The neuron stopped responding to the sight of the banana, but it still responded to the sight of the peanut. It pretty much stopped responding to the sight of an orange, too, but perhaps after drinking 440 milliliters of a glucose solution and eating all the banana one wants, an orange provides less of a flavor contrast than a peanut does. (See ***Figure 11.22.***)

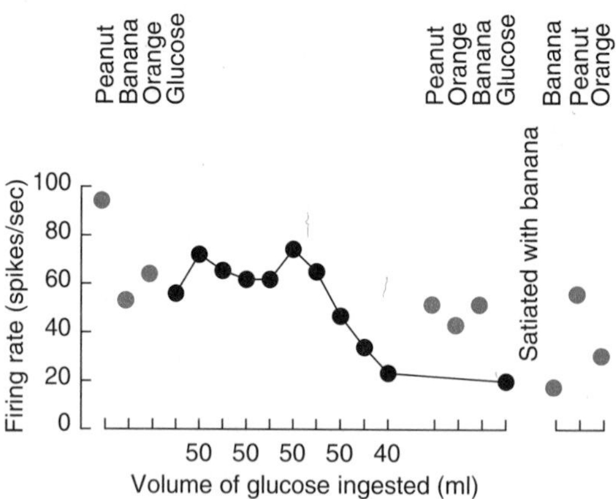

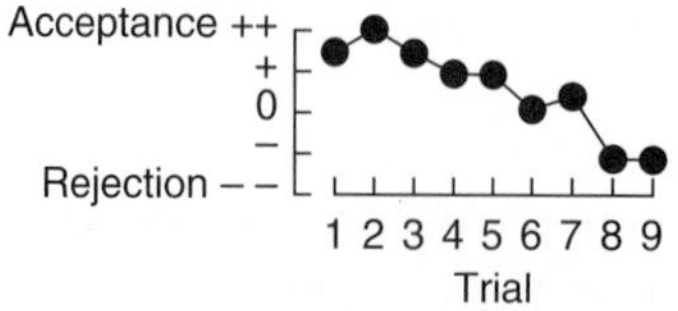

FIGURE 11.22

Sensory-specific satiety. The graph plots the firing rate of a single neuron in a monkey's lateral hypothalamus when the animal is shown various foods. The smaller graph at the bottom indicates ratings of the monkey's acceptance or rejection of the glucose solution, presented nine times. (Adapted from Rolls, E.T., Murzi, E., Yaxley, S., Thorpe, S.J., and Simpson, S.J. *Brain Research,* 1986, *368,* 79–86.)

▶*INTERIM SUMMARY*◀

Neural mechanisms that control ingestive behavior are found in the brain stem and the hypothalamus. The brain stem contains neural circuits that are able to control acceptance or rejection of sweet or bitter foods and can even be modulated by satiation or physiological hunger signals, such as a decrease in glucose metabolism. Neurons in the nucleus of the solitary tract appear to encode "good" and "bad" tastes; they change their response from "saltiness" to "good" when the animal is sodium-deficient, and they change their response from "sweet" to "bad" when saccharin is paired with an injection of lithium chloride. These changes can take place in a decerebrate rat, even though the basolateral amygdala is necessary for the expression of a conditioned flavor aversion.

Lesions of the ventromedial hypothalamus produce overeating and obesity, and electrical stimulation of this area inhibits eating. However, this region is not a simple "satiety center." The lesions make an animal finicky and increase the secretion of insulin (thus forcing the animal to eat more). Some (perhaps most) of the VMH syndrome is caused by damage to fibers from the PVN to the nucleus of the solitary tract and the dorsal motor nucleus of the vagus.

The first meal of the active portion of the dark-light cycle tends to be high in carbohydrates. It is preceded by a large increase in norepinephrine in the PVN. In addition, when NE is infused into the PVN, the animal eats—especially carbohydrates. The response may be a result of changes in the activity of the autonomic nervous system, direct stimulation of circuits that control eating, or both.

The presence of another transmitter substance in the PVN, 5-HT, has an inhibitory effect on eating. This hormone is secreted during mealtime, which suggests that it may play a role in satiety. The most common appetite suppressant, fenfluramine, is a 5-HT agonist.

Lesions of the lateral hypothalamus abolish eating (along with many other behaviors). Although many of the behavioral effects of these lesions are caused by damage to dopamine-secreting axons that pass through this region, experiments with neurotoxic lesions indicate that the lateral hypothalamus, by itself, plays an excitatory role in eating. When infused into the mid-lateral hypothalamus, neuropeptide Y stimulates vigorous eating. The lateral hypothalamus contains glucose receptors and neurons whose firing rate increases when food-related stimuli are presented and the animal is hungry. Studies with sensory-specific satiety show that the activity of these neurons is closely tied to food-related motivation. ▲

EATING DISORDERS

Unfortunately, some people are susceptible to eating disorders. Some people grow obese, even though they know that our society regards this condition as unattractive and that obese people tend to have more health problems—and to die sooner—than people of normal weight. Other people (especially young women) can become obsessed with losing weight, eating little and increasing their activity level until their body weight becomes extremely low—often fatally so. Has what we have learned about the physiology of appetite helped us understand these conditions? The following subsections address this question.

Obesity

There are undoubtedly many causes of obesity, including learning and innate or acquired differences in metabolism. The behavior of eating, like most other behaviors, is subject to modification through learning. Unfortunately, many aspects of modern, industrialized societies tend to weaken physiological controls over eating. For example, as children we learn to eat what is put on our plates; indeed, many children are praised for eating all that they have been given and punished for failing to do so. As

Birch et al. (1987) showed, the effect of this kind of training can be to make children less sensitive to the nutrient content of their diet. As we get older, our metabolic requirements decrease; and if we continue to eat as we did when we were younger, we tend to accumulate fat. The inhibitory signals associated with food consumption are certainly not absolute; they can be overridden by habit or by the simple pleasure of ingesting good-tasting food. In fact, the typical arrangement of meals into courses followed by a dessert inhibits the development of sensory-specific satiety and encourages increased food intake. An earlier section in this chapter, "Social and Environmental Factors," discussed some other environmental variables that can encourage overeating.

Obesity is extremely difficult to treat; the enormous financial success of diet books, fat farms, and weight reduction programs attests to the trouble people have losing weight. Kramer, Jeffery, Forster, and Snell (1989) reported that four to five years after participating in a fifteen-week behavioral weight loss program, fewer than 3 percent of the participants managed to maintain the weight loss they had achieved during the program. Even drastic means such as gastric and intestinal surgery (designed to limit the amount of food that the stomach can hold or to prevent food from being fully digested before it is eliminated) are not the answer. These procedures have risks of their own, often produce unpleasant side effects, and have a failure rate of at least 40 percent (Kral, 1989).

Many psychological variables have been suggested as causes of obesity, including lack of impulse control, poor ability to delay gratification, and maladaptive eating styles (primarily eating too fast). However, in a review of the literature Rodin, Schank, and Striegel-Moore (1989) found that none of these suggestions has received empirical support. Rodin and her colleagues also found that unhappiness and depression seem to be the *effects* of obesity, not its causes, and that dieting behavior seems to make the problem worse. (As we shall see later in this section, repeated bouts of weight loss and gain make subsequent weight loss more difficult to achieve.)

Almost all excess body weight is carried in the form of fat. Normally, we carry a certain amount of fat in our long-term nutrient reservoir, making deposits and withdrawals each day during the absorptive and fasting phases of metabolism but keeping the total amount stable. Obesity occurs when deposits exceed withdrawals. We expend energy in two basic ways: through exercise (muscular activity) and through the production of heat.

One reason that many people have so much difficulty losing weight is that metabolic factors appear to play an important role in obesity. Just as cars differ in their fuel efficiency, so do people. Rose and Williams (1961) studied pairs of people who were matched for weight, height, age, and activity. Some of these matched pairs differed by a factor of two in the number of calories they ate each day. People with an efficient metabolism have calories left over to deposit in the long-term nutrient reservoir; thus, they have difficulty keeping this reservoir from growing. In contrast, people with an inefficient metabolism can eat large meals without getting fat.

Differences in metabolism appear to have a hereditary basis. Stunkard et al. (1986) found that the body weight of a sample of people who had been adopted as infants was highly correlated with their *biological* parents but not with their *adoptive* parents. Thus, people inherit genes that predispose them to obesity; they do not simply learn bad eating habits by the example their parents set. A similar study comparing adopted people with their full and half siblings (with whom they had not been raised) also obtained evidence for genetic factors in obesity (Sørensen, Price, Stunkard, and Schulsinger, 1989).

Why are there genetic differences in metabolic efficiency? James and Trayhurn (1981) suggest that under some environmental conditions metabolic efficiency is advantageous. That is, in times and places where food is only intermittently available in sufficient quantities, being able to stay alive on small amounts of food and to store up extra nutrients in the form of fat when food becomes available for a while is a highly adaptive trait. Therefore, people's metabolic rates may reflect the nature of the environment experienced by their ancestors. For example, physically active lactating women in Gambia manage to maintain their weight on only 1500 calories per day (Whitehead et al., 1978). This efficiency allows people to survive in environments in which food is scarce. However, in a society that produces an abundance of food, an inefficient metabolism is a definite advantage.

Another factor—this one nonhereditary—can influence people's metabolism. Many obese people diet and then relapse, thus undergoing large changes in body weight. Some investigators have suggested that starvation causes the body's metabolism to become more efficient. For example, Brownell, Greenwood, Stellar, and Shrager (1986) fed rats a diet that made them become obese and then restricted their food intake until their body weights returned to normal. Then they made the rats fat again and reduced their food intake again. The first time, the rats became fat within 46 days and returned to normal within 21 days. The second time, they became fat in only 14 days but required 46 days to lose the excess weight. Clearly, the experience of gaining and losing large amounts of body weight altered the animals' metabolic efficiency.

Steen, Oppliger, and Brownell (1988) obtained evidence that the same phenomenon (which we can call the "yo-yo" effect) takes place in humans. They measured the resting metabolic rate in two groups of high school wrestlers: those who fasted just before a meet and binged afterwards, and those who did not. (The motive for fasting just before a match is to qualify for a lower-weight group, where the competition is presumably less challenging.) The investigators found that wrestlers who fasted and binged had a resting metabolic rate 14 percent lower than those who did not. Possibly, these people will have difficulty maintaining a normal body weight as they get older.

In normal animals overeating causes a rise in metabolic rate, which partly compensates for the increased intake of calories. Rothwell and Stock (1979) fed rats a very palatable diet consisting of supermarket "junk" foods such as potato chips and cookies, which caused them to increase their daily caloric intake greatly. Despite an average caloric increase of 80 percent, weight gain was only 27 percent higher than that of control animals. For this effect to occur, the animals would have had to increase their energy expenditure by approximately 100 percent. Indeed, their resting oxygen consumption was consistently higher than that of control animals. However, the increase was probably not caused by an increase in physical activity, because the animals were housed in pairs in small cages, and they would have had to walk 6 kilometers per day to expend this much energy. Therefore, their metabolic rates must have risen.

This phenomenon occurs in humans, as well. Welle, Nair, and Campbell (1989) had human subjects overeat by 1600 calories per day for ten days. At the end of that time their metabolic rate had increased by 22 percent. Even a single meal—or stimuli associated with eating—can cause a rise in metabolic rate. LeBlanc and Cabanac (1989) placed human subjects in a chamber so that they could continuously monitor their oxygen consumption and, thereby, calculate their metabolic rate. They found that eating a sugar pie or tasting it, chewing it, and spitting it out again caused an increase in metabolic rate. Even when the subjects simply went through the motions

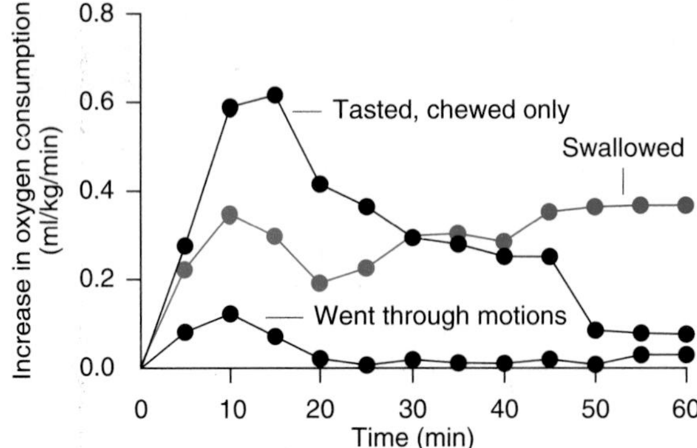

FIGURE 11.23

Effects of eating a sugar pie, tasting and chewing it only, or simply going through the motions on metabolic rate of human subjects, as measured by oxygen consumption. (Adapted with permission from LeBlanc, J., and Cabanac, M. *Physiology and Behavior, 46,* 479–482, copyright 1989, Pergamon Press plc.)

of eating—moving their hands to their mouths and making chewing and swallowing motions—their metabolic rates increased slightly. (See ***Figure 11.23.***)

What are the physiological differences between people with efficient and inefficient metabolisms? So far, no one knows for sure. Research with laboratory animals has focused on specialized adipose cells that convert calories of food directly into heat. These cells are especially important for hibernating animals, who must warm up before they can wake in the spring. Heat production by this tissue is called **nonshivering thermogenesis** (*thermo,* "heat"; *genesis,* "creation"). These specialized fat cells are rich in mitochondria, which serve as sites of fuel breakdown and heat production (Nichols, 1979). The mitochondria give the fat a brown appearance, which gives this tissue the name **brown adipose tissue.** (The fat tissue that comprises the body's long-term nutrient reservoir is called *white* adipose tissue.)

nonshivering thermogenesis

brown adipose tissue

In rats, feeding-induced thermogenesis appears to be mediated primarily by the activity of the brown adipose tissue. For example, Glick, Teague, and Bray (1981) found that a single meal increased the metabolism of brown adipose tissue by up to 200 percent. Studies have shown that the brown adipose tissue of an obese strain of rats does not respond to a meal (Triandafillou and Himms-Hagen, 1983); thus, at least one form of genetic obesity is accompanied by deficient meal-induced thermogenesis.

The excitatory effect of a meal on the metabolic activity of brown adipose tissue is controlled by the medial hypothalamus. After the medial hypothalamus has been surgically destroyed, a meal no longer produces a rise in the temperature of the brown adipose tissue (Hogan, Himms-Hagen, and Coscina, 1985). The PVN appears to be the most critical region. Freeman and Wellman (1987) found that electrical stimulation of the PVN increased the temperature of brown adipose tissue, and Amir (1990) confirmed these findings by using an infusion of glutamate, which stimulates neurons but not axons passing through the area.

What about human obesity? Although humans do possess some brown adipose tissue, investigators disagree about its role in meal-induced thermogenesis and obesity (Himms-Hagen, 1980; Blaza, 1983). Clearly, metabolic differences are an important cause of human obesity, but the sources of these differences are not yet known.

Anorexia Nervosa/Bulimia Nervosa

Most people, if they have an eating problem, tend to overeat. However, some people, especially young adolescent women, have the opposite problem: They eat too little, even to the point of starvation. This disorder is called **anorexia nervosa.** The literal meaning of the word *anorexia* suggests a loss of appetite, but people with this disorder

anorexia nervosa

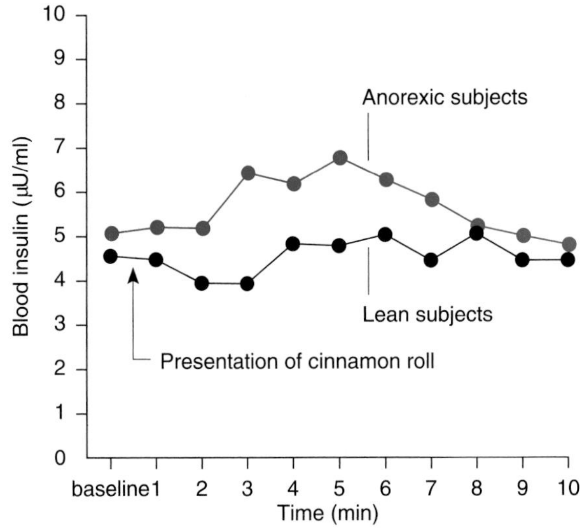

FIGURE 11.24

Effects of the sight and smell of a warm cinnamon roll on insulin secretion in anorexic women and thin, nonanorexic women. (Adapted with permission from Broberg, D.J., and Bernstein, I.L. *Physiology and Behavior, 45,* 871–874, copyright 1989, Pergamon Press, plc.)

are usually interested in — even preoccupied with — food. They may enjoy preparing meals for others to consume, collect recipes, and even hoard food that they do not eat. Broberg and Bernstein (1989) presented anorexic and lean (but nonanorexic) young women with a warm, appetizing cinnamon roll. They cut the roll and said that the subjects could eat it if they wanted. For the next 10 minutes the experimenters withdrew blood samples and analyzed the insulin content. They found that both groups of subjects showed an increase in insulin level; surprisingly, the increase was even higher in the anorexic subjects. Thus, we cannot conclude that anorexics are simply unresponsive to food. (See ***Figure 11.24.***) Incidentally, as you might expect, the normal subjects ate the roll, but the anorexics did not, saying that they "were not hungry."

Although anorexics may not be oblivious to the effects of food, they express an intense fear of becoming obese, which continues even if they become dangerously thin. Many exercise by cycling, running, or almost constant walking and pacing. Sometimes, their control of food intake fails, and they gorge themselves with food, a phenomenon known as **bulimia** (from *bous,* "ox," and *limos,* "hunger"). These binges are usually followed by self-induced vomiting or use of laxatives, along with feelings of depression and guilt (Mawson, 1974; Halmi, 1978). Sometimes, bulimia occurs by itself, without anorexia, in which case it is referred to as *bulimia nervosa.*

bulimia

The fact that anorexia nervosa is seen primarily in young women has prompted both biological and social explanations. Most psychologists favor the latter, concluding that the emphasis our society places on slimness — especially in women — is responsible for this disorder. However, the success of psychotherapy is not especially encouraging (Patton, 1989). About one patient in thirty dies of the disorder. Many anorexics suffer from osteoporosis, and bone fractures are common. When the weight loss becomes severe enough, they cease menstruating. Two disturbing reports (Artmann, et al., 1985; Lankenau, et al., 1985) indicate that CT scans of anorexic patients show enlarged ventricles and widened sulci, which indicates loss of brain tissue. The widened sulci, but not the enlarged ventricles, apparently return to normal after recovery.

As you might suspect, many investigators have suggested that anorexia and bulimia may be caused by biochemical or structural abnormalities in the brain mechanisms

In order to avoid the necessity of surgery, some therapists have tried putting balloons in people's stomachs and then inflating them to reduce the amount of food they will hold. The results have not been entirely successful; as Kral (1989) noted, "After a brief period of extraordinary financial success for the gastroenterologists placing the balloons, the 'Gastric Bubble' has been taken off the market in the United States, largely because of proven lack of efficacy and the realization that chronic balloon placement is not tolerated by the gastric mucosa" (p. 254).

The variety of methods — surgical, mechanical, behavioral, and pharmacological — that therapists and surgeons have developed to treat obesity attests to the tenacity of the problem. The basic difficulty, beyond that caused by having an efficient metabolism, is that eating is pleasurable and satiety signals are easy to ignore or override. Despite the fact that relatively little success has been seen until now, I am personally optimistic about what the future may hold. I think that if we learn more about the physiology of hunger signals, satiety signals, and the reinforcement provided by eating, we will be able to develop drugs that attenuate the signals that encourage us to eat and strengthen those that encourage us to stop eating. ▲

KEY CONCEPTS

Physiological Regulatory Systems

- Regulatory systems include four essential features: a system variable, a set point, a detector, and a correctional mechanism. Because of the time it takes for substances to be absorbed from the digestive system, eating and drinking behaviors are also controlled by satiety mechanisms.

Drinking

- The body's water is located in the intracellular and extracellular compartments; the latter consists of the interstitial fluid and the blood plasma.
- Normal loss of water depletes both major compartments and produces both osmometric and volumetric thirst.
- Osmometric thirst is detected by neurons in the preoptic region; volumetric thirst is detected by the kidney, which secretes an enzyme that produces angiotensin, and baroreceptors in the atria of the heart, which communicate directly with the brain.

Eating and Metabolism

- The body has two nutrient reservoirs, one containing glycogen (a carbohydrate) and one containing fats.
- Metabolism is divided into the absorptive and fasting phases, controlled primarily by the hormones insulin and glucagon.

What Starts A Meal?

- Hunger is affected by social and environmental factors, such as time of day, the presence of other people, and experience with particular foods.
- The most important physiological signal for hunger occurs when receptors signal a low availability of nutrients.

What Stops A Meal?

- Satiety is controlled by receptors in several locations. Nutrient receptors in the stomach communicate with the brain chemically. The release of CCK by the duodenum may decrease food intake by its effects on neurons serving the pyloric region. Receptors in the liver detect the presence of nutrients coming from the small intestine.

Neural Mechanisms

- Neural mechanisms in the brain stem are able to control acceptance or rejection of food, even when they are isolated from the forebrain.
- The hypothalamus plays some role in control of eating, but the dual-centers hypothesis has been shown to be too simple. Noradrenergic input to the paraventricular nucleus stimulates carbohydrate intake, and serotonergic input inhibits it. Damage to the lateral hypothalamus decreases food intake and release of neuropeptide Y in this region causes ravenous eating.

Easting Disorders

- An important cause of obesity is an efficient metabolism, which may have a genetic basis or may be a response of the body to periods of starvation.
- Some investigators believe that physiological mechanisms such as misregulation of the release of NE, 5-HT, or neuropeptide Y in the hypothalamus may play a role in anorexia nervosa, but evidence is lacking so far.

NEW TERMS

absorptive phase **p. 373**
angiotensin **p. 367**
angiotensinogen **p. 367**
anorexia nervosa **p. 396**
brown adipose tissue **p. 396**
bulimia **p. 397**
cephalic phase **p. 380**
cholecystokinin (CCK) **p. 384**
conditioned flavor aversion **p. 378**
correctional mechanism **p. 361**
detector **p. 361**
extracellular fluid **p. 363**
fasting phase **p. 373**
fatty acid **p. 372**
glucagon **p. 371**
glucostatic hypothesis **p. 379**
glycerol **p. 372**
glycogen **p. 371**
hepatic portal vein **p. 385**
homeostasis **p. 361**
hypertonic **p. 363**
hypotonic **p. 363**
hypovolemia **p. 363**
ingestive behavior **p. 361**
insulin **p. 371**
interstitial fluid **p. 363**
intracellular fluid **p. 363**
intravascular fluid **p. 363**
isotonic **p. 363**
negative feedback **p. 362**
neuropeptide Y **p. 391**
nonshivering thermogenesis **p. 396**
osmometric thirst **p. 364**
osmoreceptor **p. 365**
renin **p. 367**
satiety mechanism **p. 362**
sensory-specific satiety **p. 377**
set point **p. 361**
subfornical organ (SFO) **p. 369**
system variable **p. 361**
triglyceride **p. 372**
volumetric thirst **p. 366**
zona incerta **p. 368**

SUGGESTED READINGS

De Caro, G., Epstein, A.N., and Massi, M. *The Physiology of Thirst and Sodium Appetite.* New York: Plenum Press, 1986.

Gross, P. *Circumventricular Organs and Body Fluids. Vol. III.* Boca Raton, Fla.: CRC Press, 1987.

Le Magnen, J. *Hunger.* Cambridge, England: Cambridge University Press, 1985.

Stricker, E.M. *Handbook of Behavioral Neurobiology. Vol. 10. Neurobiology of Food and Fluid Intake.* New York: Plenum Press, 1990.

Walsh, B.T. *Eating Disorders.* Washington, D.C.: American Psychiatric Press, 1988.

Winick, M. *Control of Appetite.* New York: John Wiley & Sons, 1988.

12

Learning and Memory

CHAPTER OUTLINE

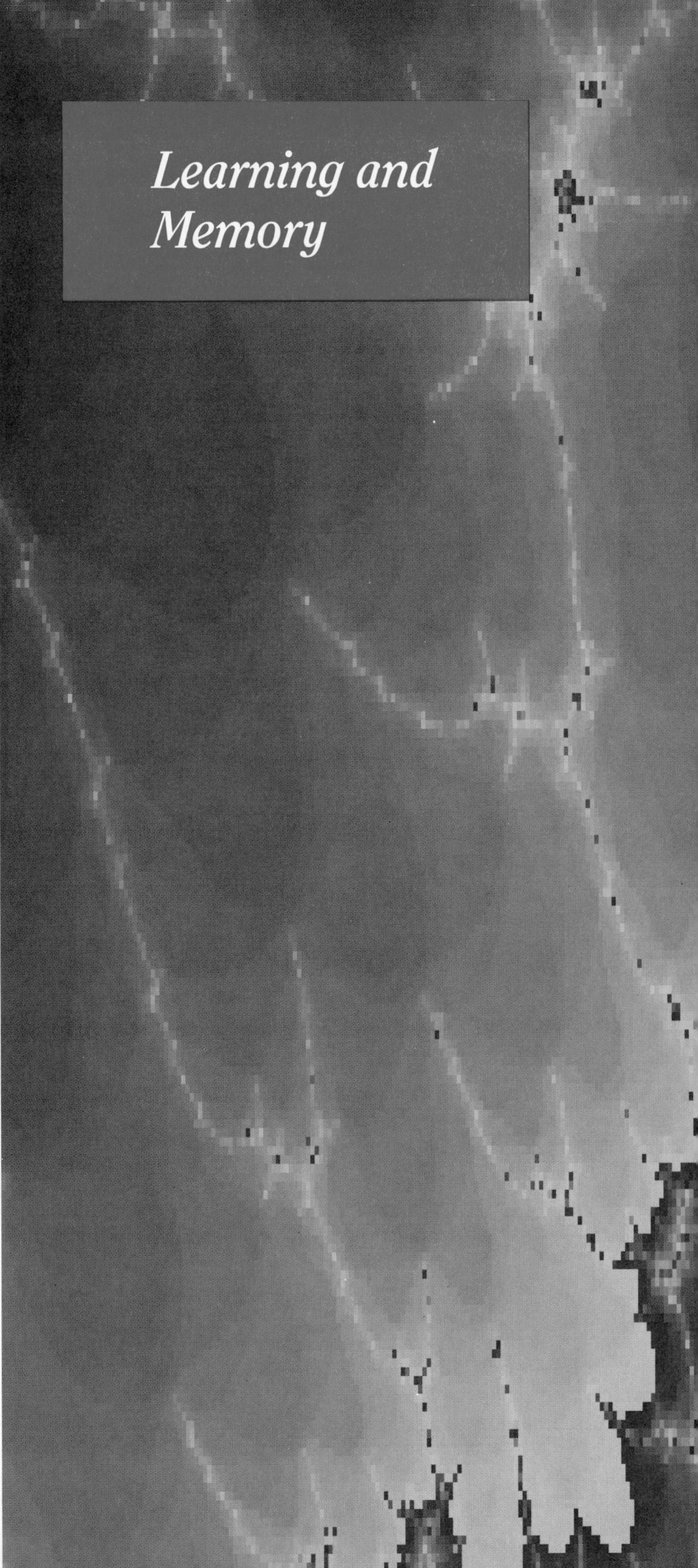

PROLOGUE

Several years ago, I accompanied Fred, my graduate student, to the Veteran's Administration Hospital in a nearby town, where he had been studying several patients. We met Mr. P. in the lounge. Fred asked Mr. P. if he had met me.

"No, I don't believe I have. How do you do, sir?" he said, as Fred introduced us. We walked to the room where he had set up his equipment. Fred and Mr. P. sat down in a pair of chairs facing a white projection screen; I sat in a third chair near the back of the room.

"How long have you been here?" Fred asked the man.

"Oh, about a week."

"Uh-huh. What brought you here?"

"I'm having some work done on my teeth. I'll be going back home in a couple of days. I have to help my father on the farm."

I knew that Mr. P. had actually been in the hospital for eleven years. He had been an alcoholic for a long time before that, and he was brought to the hospital in a severely malnourished condition. His father had died several years ago. Fred pointed to a slide projector and the screen and asked Mr. P. whether he had seen them before. He looked at them and said, "No, I don't think so." Fred turned in his chair, looked at me, and said, "Say, have you met Dr. Carlson?" Mr. P. turned around and saw me, stood up, and extended his hand. "No, I don't believe I have. How do you do, sir?" he said. We shook hands, and I greeted him in return.

Fred and Mr. P. sat down again. "Mr. P., a few days ago you saw some pictures here," said Fred. Mr. P. looked doubtful but said politely, "Well, if you say so." Fred dimmed the lights and showed him the first slide. Two pictures of two different automobiles were projected on the screen, side by side.

"Which one did you see before," Fred asked.

"Neither of them."

"Well," Fred persisted, "point to the one you *might* have seen." Mr. P. looked nonplused but pointed to the one on the right. Fred made a notation in his notebook and then showed the next slide, which showed views of two different trees.

"Which one?" he asked.

"I'm just guessing, you know. I didn't see either of them," said Mr. P.

"That's ok," said Fred. "Just point."

Silently, Mr. P. pointed to the one on the left. After showing eighteen pairs of slides, Fred said, "That's it; thanks for helping me. By the way, have you met Dr. Carlson?" Mr. P. looked at Fred, then followed his gaze and turned around and saw me. He stood up, and we shook hands and introduced ourselves.

As we left the hospital I asked Fred how Mr. P. had done. "He got seventeen correct!" he exulted. ▲

As many investigators have said, an understanding of the physiology of memory is the ultimate challenge to neuroscience research. The brain is complex, and so is learning and remembering. Although the individual changes that occur within the cells of the brain may be relatively simple, the brain consists of many billions of neurons. Therefore, isolating and identifying the particular changes that are responsible for a particular memory is exceedingly difficult. Similarly, although the elements of a particular learning task may be simple, its implications for an organism may be complex. The behavior that the investigator observes and measures may be only one of many that change as a result of an experience. However, despite the difficulties, the long years of work finally seem to be paying off. New approaches and new methods have evolved from old ones, and real progress has been made in understanding the anatomy and physiology of learning and remembering.

THE NATURE OF MEMORY

Although it is convenient to describe memories as if they were notes placed in filing cabinets, this is certainly not the way experiences are reflected within the brain. Experiences are not "stored"; they change the way we perceive, perform, think, and plan. They do so by physically changing the structure of the nervous system, altering neural circuits that participate in perceiving, performing, thinking, and planning.

The primary function of the ability to learn is to develop behaviors that are adapted to an ever-changing environment. The ability to learn permits us to find food when we are hungry, warmth when we are cold, companions when we are lonely. It also permits us to avoid objects or situations that might harm us. However, the fact that the ultimate function of learning is a useful change in behavior does not mean that learning takes place only in the parts of the brain that control movement. Learning can take at least four basic forms: perceptual learning, stimulus-response learning, motor learning, and relational learning.

Perceptual learning is the ability to learn to recognize stimuli that have been seen before. The primary function of this type of learning is the ability to identify and categorize objects (including other members of our own species) and situations. Unless we have learned to recognize something, we cannot learn how we should behave with respect to it—we will not profit from our experiences with it, and profiting from experience is what learning is all about.

Each of our sensory systems is capable of perceptual learning. We can learn to recognize objects by their visual appearance, the sounds they make, how they feel, or how they smell. We can recognize people by the shape of their faces, the movements they make when they walk, or the sound of their voices. When we hear people talk, we can recognize the words they are saying and, perhaps, their emotional state. As we shall see, perceptual learning appears to be accomplished primarily by changes in the sensory association cortex. That is, learning to recognize complex visual stimuli involves changes in the visual association cortex, learning to recognize complex auditory stimuli involves changes in the auditory association cortex, and so on. (Very simple stimuli, such as changes in brightness, do not require the neocortex; learning that involves these stimuli can be accomplished by subcortical components of the sensory systems.)

Stimulus-response learning is the ability to learn to perform a particular behavior when a particular stimulus is present. Thus, it involves the establishment of connections between circuits involved in perception with those involved in movement. The behavior could be an automatic response such as a defensive reflex, or it could be a complicated sequence of movements that was learned previously. Stimulus-response learning includes two major categories of learning that have been studied by psychologists: *classical conditioning* and *instrumental conditioning.*

Classical conditioning is a form of learning in which an unimportant stimulus acquires the properties of an important one. It involves an ***association between two stimuli.*** A stimulus that previously had little effect on behavior becomes able to evoke a reflexive, species-typical behavior. For example, we flinch when we see a balloon being overinflated near our face. The flinch is a species-typical defensive reaction that serves to protect our eyes. Normally, this reaction occurs when we hear a loud noise, when something rapidly approaches our face, or when our eyes or the skin around them is touched; we do not have to learn to make this response. We respond this way when we see an overinflated balloon because of our prior experience with bursting balloons. Sometime in the past, probably when we were children, an overinflated balloon burst near our face, and the blast of air elicited a defensive flinch. Through classical conditioning the stimulus that preceded the blast of air—the sight of an overinflated balloon—became an elicitor of flinching.

classical conditioning

The names that have been assigned to the stimuli and responses that constitute classical conditioning are shown in Figure 12.1. I will use these terms again in this chapter, so it is worth your while learning them now, if they are not already familiar to you. The blast of air, the original eliciting stimulus, is called the **unconditional stimulus** (US): It unconditionally elicits the species-typical response. The response of flinching is itself called the **unconditional response** (UR). After a few experiences with bursting balloons, the sight of the inflated balloon—the **conditional stimulus** (CS)—comes to elicit flinching, which is now called the **conditional response** (CR): The response is conditional on the pairing of the conditional and unconditional stimuli. (See ***Figure 12.1.***)

unconditional stimulus (US)

unconditional response (UR)

conditional stimulus (CS)

conditional response (CR)

FIGURE 12.1

The process of classical conditioning.

The child watches the balloon grow large (neutral stimulus) until it bursts (US), which causes a defensive startle reaction (UR).

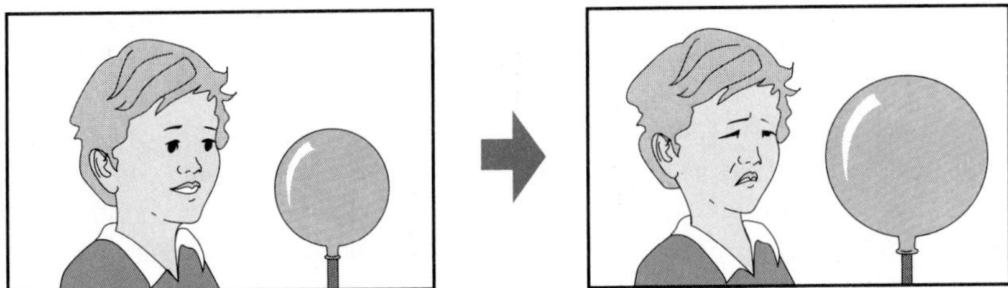

After the child's first experience with a bursting balloon, the mere sight of an inflating balloon (CS) elicits a defensive reaction (CR).

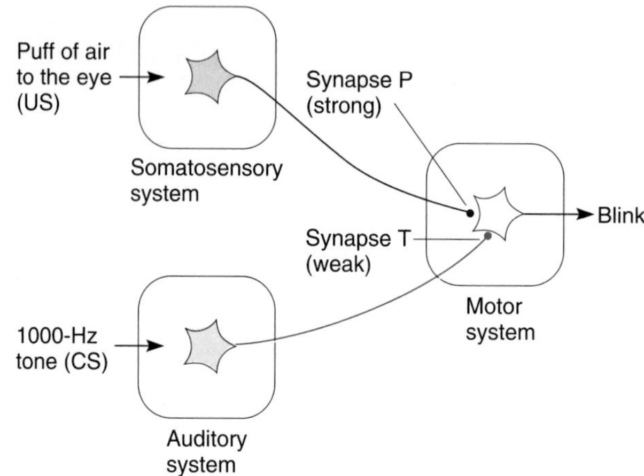

FIGURE 12.2

A simple neural model of classical conditioning. When the 1000-Hz tone is presented just before the puff of air to the eye, synapse T is strengthened.

Classical conditioning occurs when a neutral stimulus is followed by one that automatically elicits a response. It enables organisms to learn to make species-typical responses under new conditions. Thus, classical conditioning serves to prepare an organism for a forthcoming event. For example, a warning signal can permit the organism to defend itself against harm; stimuli associated with a potential mate can cause it to make a response that serves as a sexual display; and stimuli associated with food can cause secretion of saliva, digestive juices, and insulin.

How does classical conditioning work? Figure 12.2 shows a simplified neural circuit that could account for this type of learning. I will use an example that I will discuss in more detail later in this chapter, a defensive eyeblink response of a rabbit. A small puff of air aimed at the eye can trigger this reflex; thus, a puff of air serves as a US. The CS is a 1000-Hz tone. For the sake of simplicity, we will assume that the US is detected by a single neuron in the somatosensory system, and the CS is detected by a single neuron in the auditory system. We will also assume that the response—the eyeblink—is controlled by a single neuron in the motor system. (See ***Figure 12.2.***)

Now let us see how the circuits works. If we present a 1000-Hz tone, we find that the animal makes no reaction, because the synapse connecting the tone-sensitive neuron with the neuron in the motor system is weak. However, if we present a puff of air to the eye, the eye blinks. This reaction occurs because nature has provided the animal with a strong synapse between the somatosensory neuron and the motor neuron that causes a blink (synapse P, for "puff"). To establish classical conditioning, we first present the 1000-Hz tone and then almost immediately follow it with a puff of air. After we repeat these pairs of stimuli several times, we find that we can dispense with the air puff; the 1000-Hz tone produces the blink all by itself.

Over forty years ago, Hebb proposed a rule that might explain how neurons are changed by experience in a way that would cause changes in behavior (Hebb, 1949). The **Hebb rule** says that if a synapse repeatedly becomes active at about the same time that the postsynaptic neuron fires, changes will take place in the structure or chemistry of the synapse that will strengthen it. How would the Hebb rule apply to our circuit? If the 1000-Hz tone is presented first, then weak synapse T (for "tone") becomes active. If the puff is presented immediately afterward, then strong synapse P becomes active and makes the motor neuron fire. The act of firing then strengthens any synapse with the motor neuron *that has just been active.* Of course, this means synapse T. After

Hebb rule

several pairings of the two stimuli, and several increments of strengthening, synapse T becomes strong enough to cause the motor neuron to fire by itself. Learning has occurred. (See ***Figure 12.2.***)

When Hebb formulated his rule, he was unable to determine whether it was true or false. Now, finally, enough progress has been made in laboratory techniques that the strength of individual synapses can be determined, and investigators are studying the physiological bases of learning. We will see the results of some of these approaches in this chapter.

The second major class of stimulus-response learning is **instrumental conditioning** (also called *operant conditioning*). Whereas classical conditioning involves automatic, species-typical responses, instrumental conditioning involves behaviors that have been learned. And whereas classical conditioning involves an association between two stimuli, instrumental conditioning involves an *association between a response and a stimulus.* Instrumental conditioning is a more flexible form of learning. It permits an organism to adjust its behavior according to the consequences of that behavior. That is, when a behavior is followed by favorable consequences, the behavior tends to occur more frequently; when it is followed by unfavorable consequences, it tends to occur less frequently. Collectively, "favorable consequences" are referred to as **reinforcing stimuli**, and "unfavorable consequences" are referred to as **punishing stimuli.** For example, a response that enables a hungry organism to find food will be reinforced, and a response that causes pain will be punished. I will discuss instrumental conditioning in more detail in Chapter 15, which deals with reinforcement and addictive behaviors.

instrumental conditioning

reinforcing stimuli
punishing stimuli

The third major category of learning, *motor learning,* is actually a special form of stimulus-response learning; for that reason I will not discuss it separately in this chapter. For simplicity's sake, we can think of perceptual learning as the establishment of changes within the sensory systems of the brain, stimulus-response learning as the establishment of connections between sensory systems and motor systems, and motor learning as the establishment of changes within motor systems. But, in fact, motor learning cannot occur without sensory guidance from the environment. Thus, it is actually a special form of stimulus-response learning. For example, most skilled movements involve interactions with objects: bicycles, pinball machines, knitting needles, and so on. Even skilled movements we make by ourselves, such as solitary dance steps, involve feedback from the joints, muscles, vestibular apparatus, eyes, and contact between the feet and the floor. Motor learning differs from other forms of learning primarily in the degree to which new forms of behavior are learned; the more novel the behavior, the more the neural circuits in the motor systems of the brain must be modified. (See ***Figure 12.3.***)

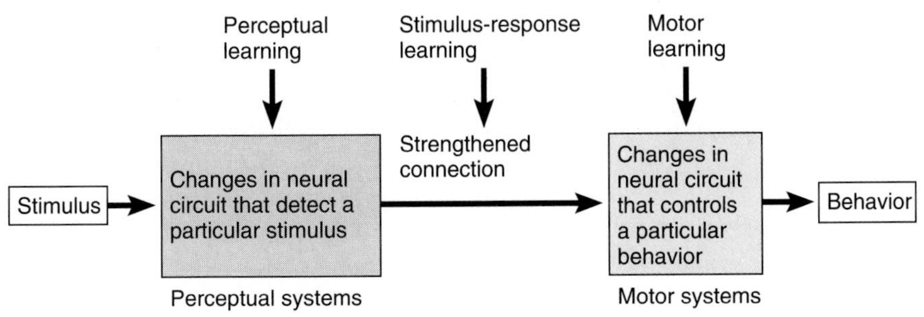

FIGURE 12.3

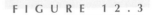

An overview of perceptual, stimulus-response, and motor learning.

The three forms of learning I have described so far consist primarily of changes in one sensory system, between one sensory system and the motor system, or in the motor system. But obviously, learning is usually more complex than that. The fourth form of learning involves learning the *relations* among individual stimuli. For example, a somewhat more complex form of perceptual learning involves connections between different areas of the association cortex. When we hear the sound of a cat meowing in the dark, we can imagine what a cat looks like and what it would feel like if we stroked its fur. Thus, the neural circuits in the auditory association cortex that recognize the meow are somehow connected to the appropriate circuits in the visual association cortex and the somatosensory association cortex. These interconnections, too, are accomplished as a result of learning.

Perception of spatial location — *spatial learning*— also involves learning about the relations among many stimuli. For example, consider what we must learn in order to become familiar with the contents of a room. First, we must learn to recognize each of the objects. But then, in addition, we must learn the relative locations of the objects with respect to each other. As a result, when we find ourselves located in a particular place in the room, our perceptions of these objects and their locations relative to us tell us exactly where we are.

Other types of relational learning are even more complex. *Episodic learning*— remembering sequences of events (episodes) that we witness — requires that we keep track not only of individual stimuli but also of the order in which they occur. *Observational learning*— learning by watching and imitating other people — requires that we remember what someone else does, the situation in which the behavior is performed, and the relation between the other person's movements and our own. As we will see later in this chapter, a special system that involves the hippocampus and associated structures appears to perform coordinating functions that are necessary for many types of learning that go beyond single regions of the cerebral cortex.

▶INTERIM SUMMARY◀

Learning produces memories, which are changes in the way we perceive, act, think, and feel. It does so by producing changes in the nervous system in the circuits responsible for perception, in those responsible for the control of movement, and in connections between the two.

Perceptual learning consists primarily of changes in perceptual systems that allow us to recognize stimuli so that we can respond to them appropriately. Stimulus-response learning consists of connections between perceptual and motor systems. The most important forms are classical and instrumental conditioning. Classical conditioning occurs when a neutral stimulus is followed by an unconditional stimulus (US) that naturally elicits an unconditional response (UR). After this pairing the neutral stimulus becomes a conditional stimulus (CS); it now elicits the conditional response (CR) by itself.

Instrumental conditioning occurs when a response is followed by a reinforcing stimulus, such as a drink of water for a thirsty animal. The reinforcing stimulus increases the likelihood that the other stimuli present when the response was made will evoke the response. Both forms of stimulus-response learning may occur as a result of strengthened synaptic connections, as described by the Hebb rule.

Motor learning, although it may primarily involve changes within neural circuits that control movement, is guided by sensory stimuli; thus, it is actually a form of stimulus-response learning. Relational learning is the most complex form of all. It includes the ability to recognize objects through more than one sensory modality, to recognize the relative locations of objects in the environment, to learn through observation of other people's behavior, and to remember the sequence in which events occurred during particular episodes. ▲

PERCEPTUAL LEARNING

Perceptual learning involves changes in neural circuits in the sensory association cortex. Because visual learning has received more attention than any other form of perceptual learning, I will concentrate on this sensory modality. In primates, perception of complex objects takes place in the neocortex of the inferior temporal lobe. As we saw in Chapter 5, individual modules of neurons within the primary visual cortex (striate cortex) analyze information from restricted regions of the visual scene that pertain to movement, orientation, color, binocular disparity, and spatial frequency. Information about each of these attributes is collected in subregions of the prestriate cortex, which surrounds the striate cortex. For example, one area is devoted to the analysis of orientation, another to the analysis of color, and another to the analysis of movement.

After analyzing particular attributes of the visual scene, the subregions of the prestriate cortex send the results of their analysis to the inferior temporal cortex, where the information is combined, producing neural activity that corresponds to the perception of particular three-dimensional objects. It is here that visual learning takes place. (See ***Figure 12.4***.)

Lesion Studies

Over fifty years ago, Klüver and Bucy (1939) discovered that monkeys with bilateral lesions of the temporal lobes had difficulty perceiving visual stimuli. They referred to the phenomenon as "psychic blindness." The animals could move around in their environment and could see well enough to pick up small objects. However, they had great difficulty *recognizing* what they saw. They would pick up items from a tray containing small edible and inedible objects, bring them to their mouth, and then eat the pieces of food and drop the pieces of hardware. They also showed no signs of fear to visual stimuli that normal monkeys avoid, such as snakes.

In subsequent years studies have shown that the critical region for psychic blindness is the inferior temporal cortex. For example, Mishkin (1966) showed that when

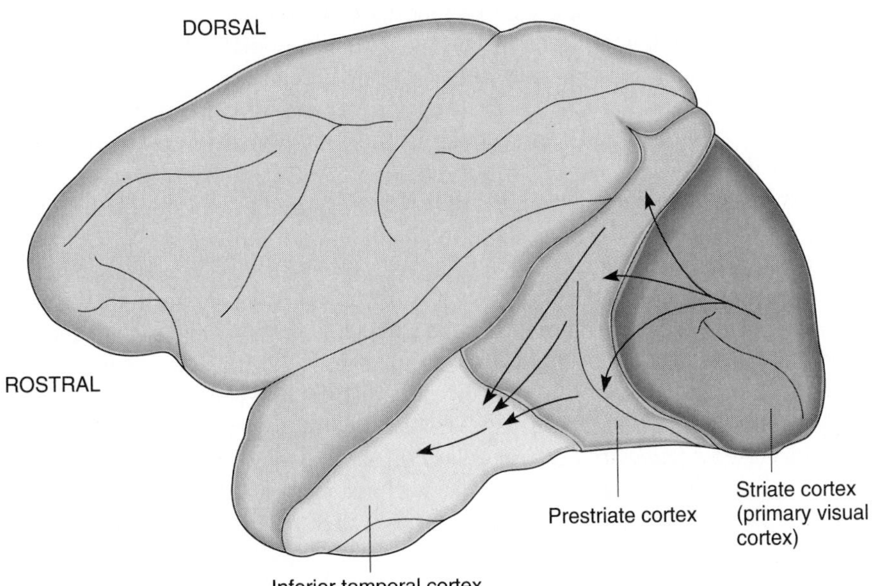

FIGURE 12.4

The major divisions of the visual cortex of the rhesus monkey. The arrows indicate the primary direction of the flow of information.

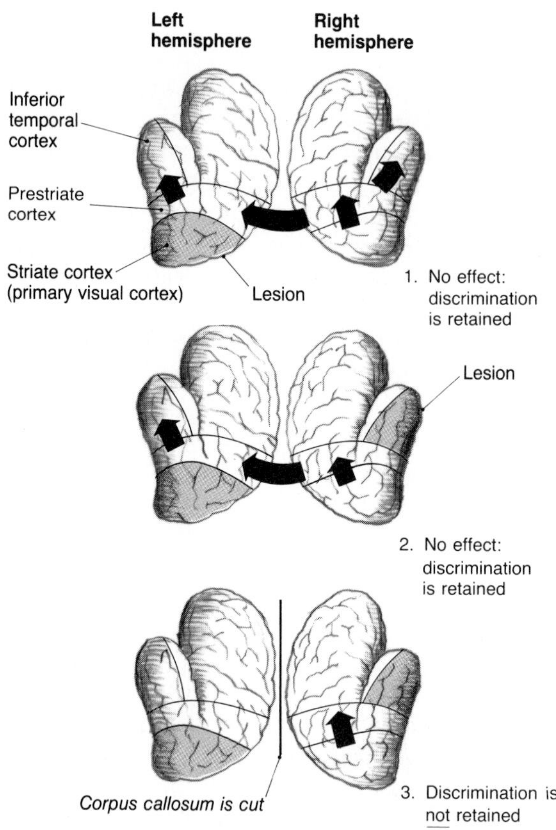

FIGURE 12.5

The procedure used by Mishkin (1966). Not all of the control groups used in the experiment are shown here. (Adapted from Mishkin, M., in *Frontiers in Physiological Psychology,* edited by R.W. Russell. New York: Academic Press, 1966.)

visual information was prevented from reaching this region, monkeys lost the ability to distinguish between different visual patterns. First, he removed the striate cortex on one side of the brain and tested the animals' ability to discriminate between visual patterns. They performed well. Next, he removed the contralateral inferior temporal cortex; again, no deficit. Finally, he cut the corpus callosum, which isolated the remaining inferior temporal cortex from the remaining primary visual cortex. This time, the animals could no longer perform the visual discrimination task. Therefore, we can conclude that the inferior temporal cortex is necessary for visual pattern discrimination and that it must receive information from the primary visual cortex. (See ***Figure 12.5.***)

Subsequent studies have shown that the two major regions of the inferior temporal cortex perform different functions. The region bordering the prestriate cortex is necessary for perception of simple shapes; its destruction impairs monkeys' ability to discriminate among different two-dimensional patterns (Blake, Jarvis, and Mishkin, 1977). In contrast, destruction of the region closer to the rostral end of the temporal lobe area impairs monkeys' ability to discriminate among different *three-dimensional* objects. Mishkin and his colleagues (reported by Mishkin, 1982) trained monkeys on a *delayed nonmatching-to-sample task.* They showed monkeys a small three-dimensional object (the *sample*) from a large collection of "junk objects" assembled for that purpose. The monkeys moved the object aside to uncover and eat a peanut placed in a small well underneath. After a 10-second delay the experimenters showed the monkeys two objects: the one they had just seen and a new one. If the monkeys moved the *new* object, they found another peanut; but none was to be found under the old one. A

FIGURE 12.6

The delayed nonmatching-to-sample procedure used by Mishkin and his colleagues (reported by Mishkin, 1982).

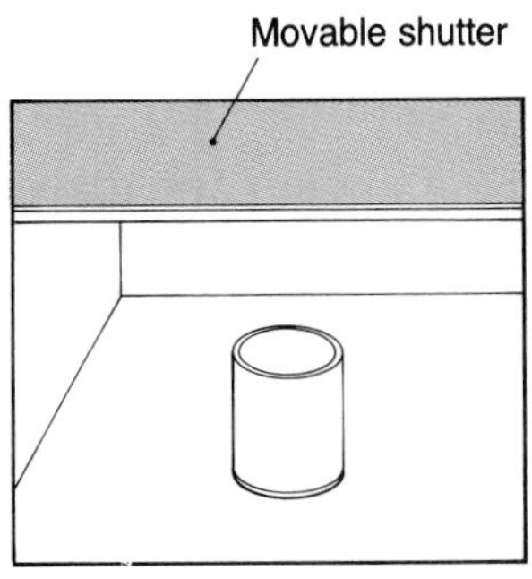

Sample interval
Shutter is opened, monkey obtains food from well underneath by moving object aside

Delay interval
Shutter is closed

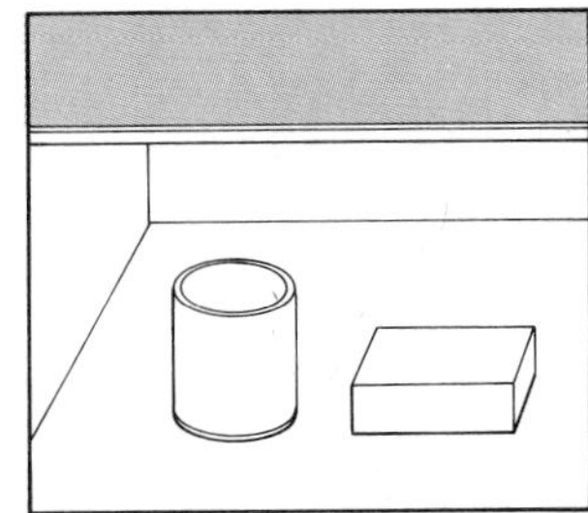

Choice interval
Shutter is opened, food is hidden under novel object

different stimulus was used on each trial. This task is easy for monkeys to perform; they learn it within a few days. (See ***Figure 12.6.***)

After the preliminary training Mishkin and his colleagues destroyed the inferior temporal cortex bilaterally. After surgery the animals required 1500 trials to relearn the task; and even then they did not quite attain the criterion of 90 percent correct. After administering these retraining trials, the experimenters tested the monkeys with delays longer than 10 seconds. The monkeys with lesions of the inferior temporal cortex performed poorly when the delay was lengthened. Thus, the inferior temporal cortex plays an important role in a monkey's ability to remember a particular three-dimensional object.

Recording Studies

The conclusions from the lesion studies are supported by an electrophysiological study by Fuster and Jervey (1981), who obtained evidence that neurons in the inferior temporal cortex retain information about a just-perceived stimulus. They turned on a colored light (yellow, green, red, or blue) behind a translucent disk (the sample stimulus), turned it off, and, after a delay interval, turned on yellow, green, red, and blue lights behind four other disks (the matching stimuli). (See ***Figure 12.7.***) If the monkey

FIGURE 12.7

The delayed matching-to-sample procedure used by Fuster and Jervey (1981).

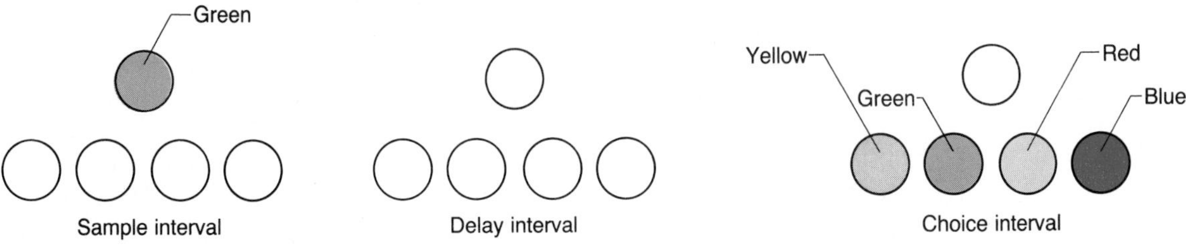

pressed the disk whose color matched the one it had just seen, it received a piece of food.

While the monkeys were performing this task, the experimenters recorded the activity of single neurons in the inferior temporal cortex. Some neurons responded selectively to color, maintaining a high response rate during the delay interval. For example, Figure 12.8 shows data from a neuron that responded to red light, but not to green light, during a 16-second delay interval. The horizontal lines above each graph represent individual trials; vertical tick marks represent action potentials. The graphs beneath the horizontal lines are sums of the individual trials, showing the total responses during successive intervals. As you can see, when the sample stimulus consisted of a red light, the neuron became active and remained active even after the sample stimulus went off. (See ***Figure 12.8.***) Under normal conditions a stimulus causes a

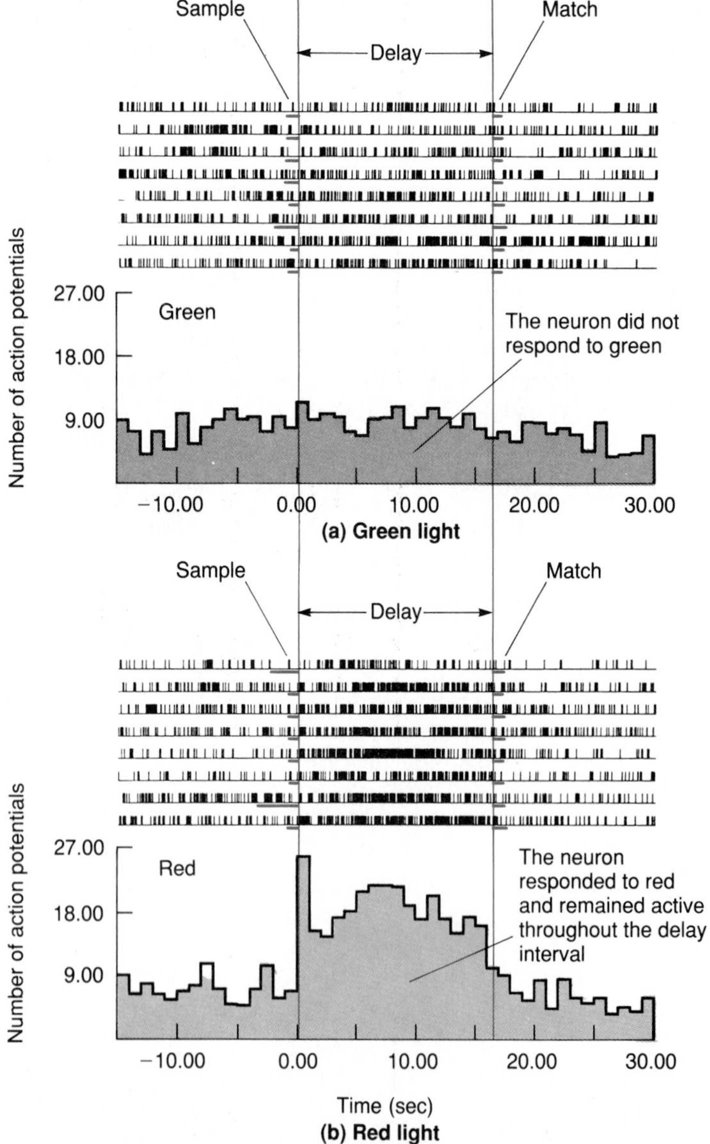

FIGURE 12.8

Responses of a single unit during the presentation of the sample stimulus, the delay interval, and the presentation of matching stimuli in the experiment outlined in Figure 12.7. (From Fuster, J.M., in *Conditioning: Representation of Involved Neural Functions,* edited by C.D. Woody. New York: Plenum Press, 1982. Reprinted with permission.)

FIGURE 12.9

Responses of a single neuron in the inferior temporal cortex to photographs of a monkey's face, oriented at different angles to the viewer. Each stimulus was presented for 2.5 seconds, as indicated by the color bars. The height of the vertical black bars indicates the number of the times the neuron fired during each interval of time. (From Desimone, R., Albright, T.D., Gross, C.G., and Bruce, D. *Journal of Neuroscience,* 1984, *4,* 2051–2062. Reprinted by permission of the *Journal of Neuroscience.*)

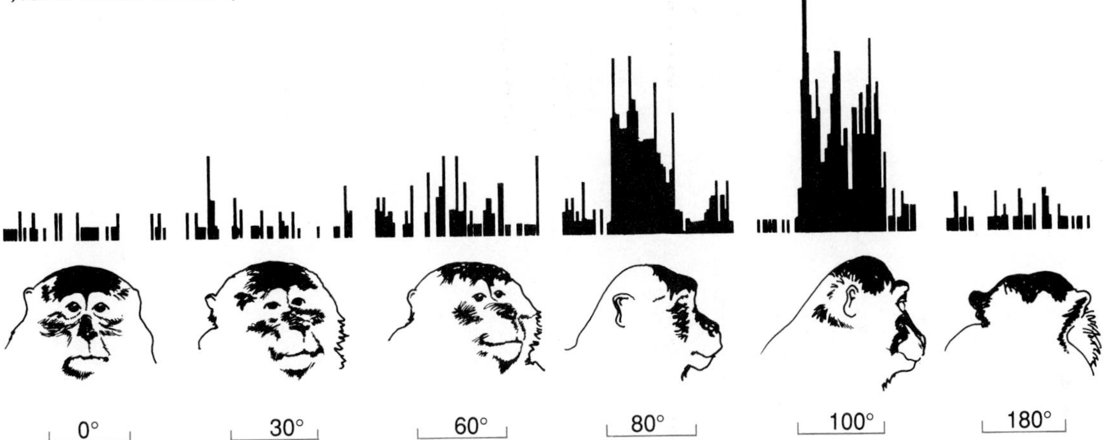

neuron to respond briefly. Thus, the sustained response that occurs during the delay interval suggests that the neuron is part of a circuit responsible for remembering a just-perceived stimulus.

Some neurons in the inferior temporal cortex show remarkable specificity in their response characteristics, which suggests that they are part of circuits that detect the presence of specific stimuli. For example, Desimone, Albright, Gross, and Bruce (1984) found neurons in this region that responded to such stimuli as hands and faces. Figure 12.9 shows the response of a neuron that responded best to a profile view of another monkey's face. Other neurons responded best to full face views. (See ***Figure 12.9.***)

Rolls and his colleagues (reported in Rolls, 1989) have studied the responses of neurons in the inferior temporal cortex of monkeys to the sight of monkey's faces. Neurons that specifically respond to the sight of faces are not scattered throughout the visual association cortex; instead, they are localized in a particular region, which suggests that face recognition may be a specialty of that region.

The responses of many neurons that respond to the sight of faces remain constant even if the picture is blurred or changed in color, size, or distance (Rolls and Baylis, 1986). (See ***Figure 12.10.***) Baylis, Rolls, and Leonard (1985) found that most of these neurons are sensitive to differences between faces, which suggests that the circuits of which they are a part are responsible for a monkey's ability to recognize particular individuals.

Rolls, Baylis, Hasselmo, and Nalwa (1989) found that as monkeys became familiar with particular faces, the response characteristics of some face-sensitive neurons in the inferior temporal cortex changed. They presented monkeys with pictures of human and monkey faces on the screen of a video monitor. They found that many cells showed changes in their response characteristics when new faces were shown to the monkey. For example, in one experiment they showed the same set of five faces, one at a time, for several trials. Most neurons showed rather stable responses. Then the experimenters

FIGURE 12.10

Examples of photographs of faces that produced similar responses in face-sensitive neurons in the inferior temporal cortex. (a) Faces of different sizes. (b) Faces of reduced and reversed contrast. (From Rolls, E.T., and Baylis, G.C. *Experimental Brain Research*, 1986, *65*, 38–48. Reprinted with permission.)

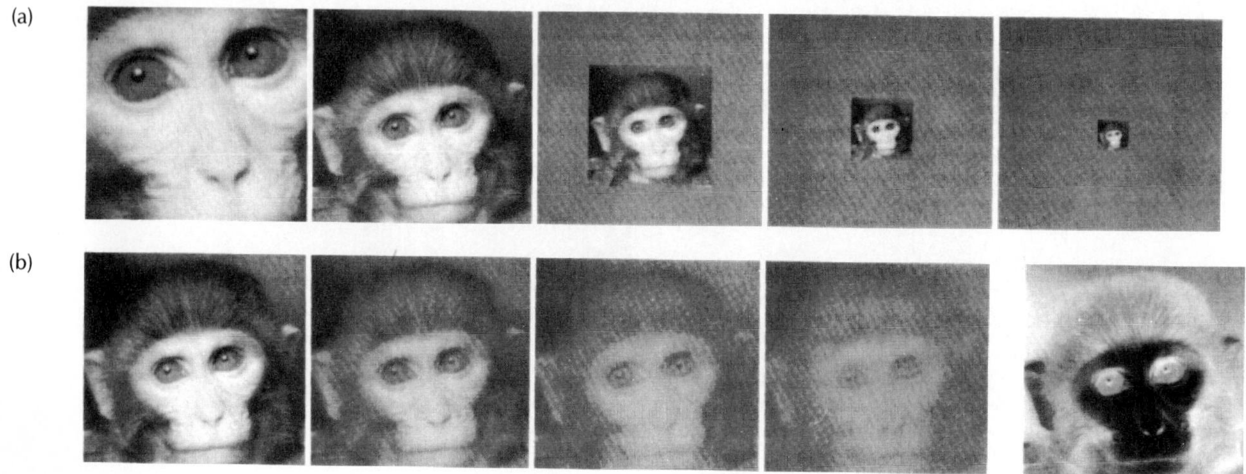

introduced a new face into the series. After one or two presentations the response pattern to the familiar faces changed. This finding suggests that learning caused a "rewiring" of the neural circuits.

Modeling the Brain's Ability to Learn: Neural Networks

The results of the electrical-recording study by Rolls and his colleagues strongly suggest that the inferior temporal cortex is an important site of visual perceptual learning, and that perception is not simply a result of analysis by prewired circuits. That is, experience changes the wiring, and these wiring changes represent what is learned. But what is the nature of these changes?

neural network

A possible answer comes from a recent approach to modeling the function of neural circuits, called **neural networks.** Investigators have discovered that when they construct a network of simple elements, interconnected in certain ways, the network does some surprising things. (The authors of neural networks use computers to model them; they do not construct actual networks with electrical components.) The elements are given properties like those of neurons. They are connected to each other through junctions similar to synapses. Like synapses, these junctions can have either excitatory or inhibitory effects. When an element receives a critical amount of excitation, it sends a message to the elements with which it communicates, and so on. Some of the elements of a network have input lines that can receive signals from the "outside," which could represent a sensory organ or the information received from another network. Other elements have output lines, which communicate with other networks or control muscles, producing behavior. Thus, particular patterns of input can represent particular stimuli, and particular patterns of output can represent responses. (See ***Figure 12.11.***)

Neural networks can be taught to recognize particular stimuli. For example, an author of a neural network can specify that the connections between elements are strengthened by an unconditional stimulus or by a reinforcement system. Or they can

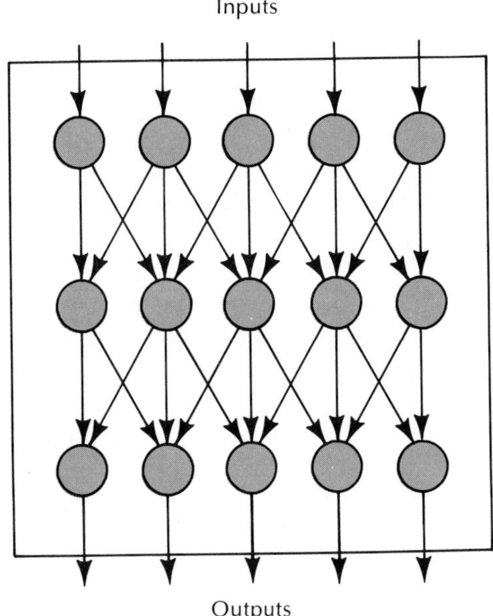

FIGURE 12.11

A very simple neural network, used as a model of brain function. The connections (arrows) can be excitatory or inhibitory, depending on the particular model.

use other techniques to teach a network to recognize a particular stimulus. In this case the networks receive only one input pattern (there is no "reinforcing stimulus"), but inhibitory elements within the circuit refine the response the network makes to a particular input. Networks such as these are "shown" a particular stimulus by being presented with a particular pattern of activity on the input lines, and their output is monitored. The first time a particular stimulus is presented, the output elements respond weakly and nonspecifically; but after it is presented several times, a strong and reliable output pattern emerges. The network can be shown more and more stimuli, producing unique output patterns for each of them.

The characteristics of neural networks are similar to many of those exhibited by real nervous systems, which is what makes them exciting to scientists interested in the neural basis of learning. Obviously, because the brain is made of networks of neurons, learning occurs in neural networks. The question is whether the neural networks that scientists construct work the same way that the brain does, and the only way to find that out is to learn the detailed anatomy of real neural circuits and the physiological characteristics of individual neurons and synaptic connections. As more is learned about these subjects, more realistic models of neural networks can be constructed. The reason that neural networks have captured the imagination of neuroscientists is that even though investigators have been working with them for only a few years, and thus the state of the art is still relatively primitive, the resemblance of these model networks to the workings of the nervous system is uncanny. In just a few years investigators have constructed many models, including those that recognize patterns, learn names of objects, control the finger movements used by a typist, read words, and learn the past tenses of English verbs (Rumelhart et al., 1986). Of course, with only a few years of experience with this new approach, we cannot be sure that it will live up to its promise. In my decision to describe the approach to you, I am obviously betting that it will; I expect to be writing about neural networks for some years to come.

Investigators studying the properties of neural networks emphasize that their models deal with the *microstructure* of the brain. The brain contains a large number of networks — probably many thousands of them — each devoted to performing individual functions. The networks probably exist in a sort of hierarchy, with some controlling the functions of others and regulating the exchanges of information between them. Thus, understanding the operations of individual neural networks will never reveal all we need to know about the functions of the brain. We will also need to know the organization of the brain — the relations between the individual networks of which it is constructed. We will need to know the *macrostructure* of the brain as well as its microstructure.

So what about the face-sensitive neurons in the inferior temporal cortex? Rolls (1989) suggests that the findings he and his colleagues have obtained are exactly what would be predicted if they were recording from neurons that were elements in a neural network devoted to learning to recognize particular faces. Somehow, other neural networks in the prestriate cortex do a rough sorting, sending information about stimuli that resemble faces to the face-sensitive region of the inferior temporal cortex. Because of the type of input they receive, and because of the details of their circuitry, the neural networks in this region learn to discriminate among different faces and continue to recognize them (that is, demonstrate generalization) even when the face is near or far, clear or blurry. The output of this region is sent to other parts of the brain, where learning about the significance of these faces takes place. For example, some faces might belong to aggressive monkeys that should be avoided, some might belong to friendly sex partners, and so on.

▶INTERIM SUMMARY◀

Perceptual learning occurs as a result of changes in synaptic connections within the sensory association cortex. Damage to a monkey's inferior temporal cortex — the highest level of the visual association cortex — disrupts the animal's ability to perceive three-dimensional objects, as tested by a delayed non-matching-to-sample test. Electrical-recording studies have shown that some neurons in the inferior temporal cortex encode the information presented during the sample period of a delayed matching-to-sample task and continue to fire during the delay interval. Other recording studies have shown that some neurons respond preferentially to particular complex stimuli, including faces. When new stimuli are presented, the response patterns of some neurons in the inferior temporal cortex change, which indicates that "rewiring" may be taking place.

Recently, investigators have begun to construct models of neural networks, in which interconnected elements that have some of the known properties of neurons are presented with "stimuli" encoded by particular patterns of inputs to the network. Although these networks are very simple, they have been found to be capable of simulating many characteristics of the brain, including perceptual and stimulus-response learning. ▲

STIMULUS-RESPONSE LEARNING

Most learning occurs as a result of the establishment of new connections between perceptual systems and motor mechanisms; thus, most learning comes under the heading of stimulus-response learning. Although instrumental conditioning is probably the most important form of stimulus-response learning in the daily lives of most species of mammals, this topic is discussed in Chapter 15, which deals with reinforcement and addiction. In any case, more progress has been made in the understanding of the neurobiology of classical conditioning. The first two parts of this section describe study of the circuitry of simple classically conditioned responses: one in a mammal and the other in a marine invertebrate. The third part describes some of the progress that has been made in understanding the ways that learning can alter the strength of synaptic connections.

Conditioned Nictitating Membrane Response

In recent years several laboratories have been investigating the neural circuitry responsible for a classically conditioned defensive response in the rabbit: the nictitating membrane response. The advantage of this response is that the neural circuitry is simple; in fact, more is known about it than any other learned response in mammals. The work is important because it raises the possibility that studies in the near future will be able to identify the biochemical and structural changes in neurons that are responsible for memory. When the pathways necessary for a particular form of learning are understood, investigators know where to look for changes. The synaptic changes that are responsible for the classically conditioned nictitating membrane response are not yet known, but what has been discovered so far tends to support the Hebb rule.

The experiments cited in this section use a procedure developed by Gormezano (1972). The **nictitating membrane** (from *nictare,* "to wink") is a tough inner eyelid possessed by many mammals, birds, and fish. When a stimulus threatens the animal's eye, the nictitating membrane sweeps across the eye, covering it. Unconditional responses of the nictitating membrane are elicited by presenting a somatosensory stimulus to the eye, such as a puff of air. The conditional stimulus is usually a tone. In most cases the experimenter turns on the tone (CS) and then 250 milliseconds later turns on the unconditional stimulus (US). The CS and the US are then terminated simultaneously. At first, the animal makes only unconditional responses; but then it begins to move its nictitating membrane when it hears the CS, in anticipation of the puff of air.

nictitating membrane

Movement of the rabbit's nictitating membrane is controlled by neurons that lie in the **accessory abducens nucleus,** just adjacent to the abducens nucleus in the caudal pons (Powell, Berthier, and Moore, 1979). Therefore, the pathways by which conditional or unconditional nictitating membrane responses are produced must terminate in this region. The circuit responsible for the unconditional response is simple. Somatosensory information concerning the unconditional stimulus (such as a puff of air) is transmitted through the fifth cranial nerve (trigeminal nerve) to a particular region of the *sensory trigeminal nucleus* (Berthier and Moore, 1983). Neurons in this nucleus send axons to the accessory abducens nucleus; activation of the neurons in this nucleus produce the unconditional response. (See the dotted black line in ***Figure 12.12.***)

accessory abducens nucleus

For classical conditioning to take place, there must be a convergence of information concerning the CS and the US in the same location. That convergence takes place in the cerebellum. Two laboratories independently discovered that lesions in either of two places within the cerebellum—a particular region of the cerebellar cortex or the **interpositus nucleus**—abolished conditional nictitating membrane responses but not unconditional ones. That is, although the rabbits would continue to make unconditional nictitating membrane responses when a puff of air was directed to their eye, they no longer made conditional (learned) responses to a tone that had been paired with the puff of air (McCormick and Thompson, 1984; Yeo, Hardiman, and Glickstein, 1984).

interpositus nucleus

Figure 12.12 shows the circuit that is hypothesized to be responsible for the conditional (learned) response, as proposed by Thompson (1989). *Granule cells* in the cerebellar cortex receive information about the CS (tone) from a pathway that includes

FIGURE 12.12

The proposed neural pathway responsible for a classically conditioned nictitating membrane response. The pathway for the unconditional response is shown as a dotted black line; the pathway for the conditional response is shown as a color line.

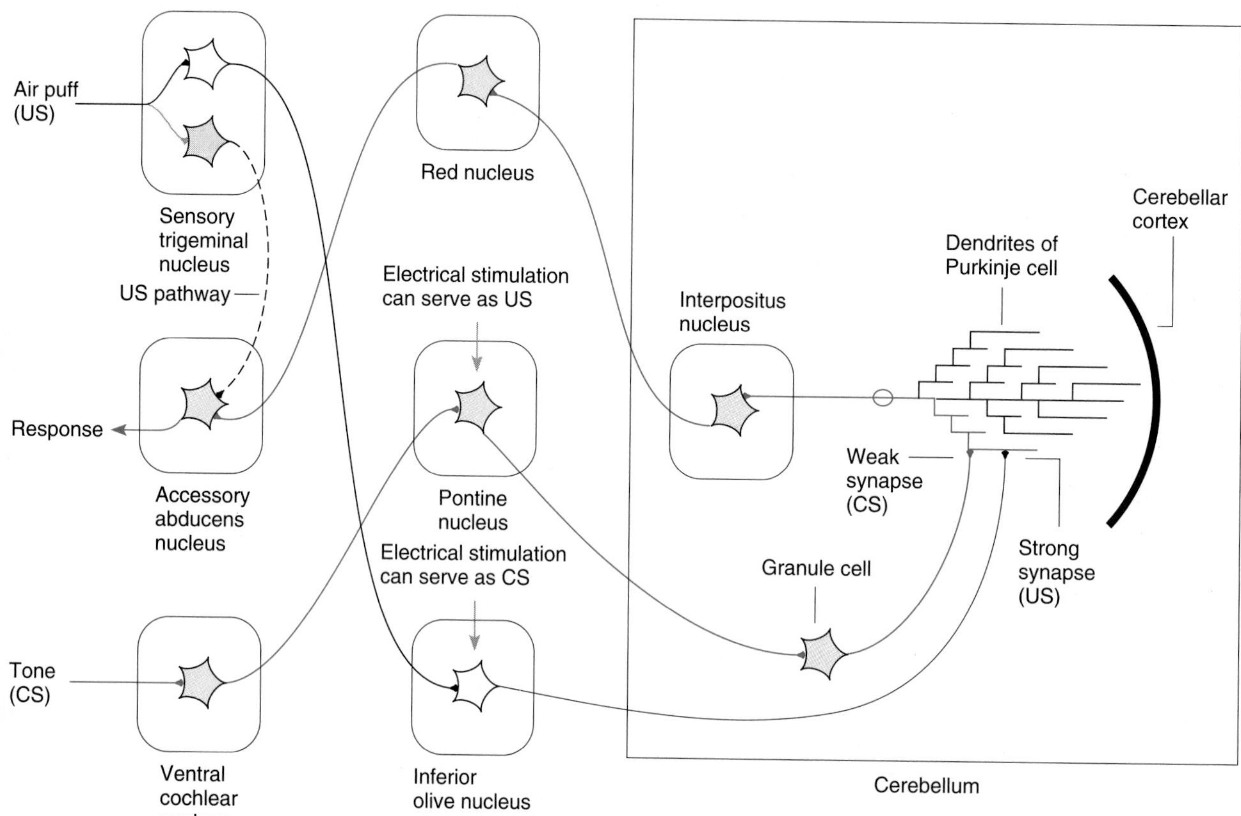

the *cochlear nucleus* and the *pontine nucleus.* This information is then transmitted to the dendrites of the *Purkinje cells,* which provide the output of the cerebellar cortex. Information about the US (air puff) is transmitted from the sensory trigeminal nucleus to the *inferior olive,* and from there to another region on the dendrites of the Purkinje cells. Presumably, the joint activity of the two sets of synapses with the dendrites of the Purkinje cells strengthens the one transmitting auditory information (the CS). The axons of the Purkinje cells transmit information to the interpositus nucleus. From there, information is transmitted to the *red nucleus* of the pons, then to the accessory abducens nucleus. (See ***Figure 12.12.***)

The circuitry I have just described has been discovered through the efforts of many investigators. For example, the importance of the inferior olive was originally discovered by McCormick, Steinmetz, and Thompson (1985); that of the red nucleus by Rosenfield and Moore (1983); and that of the pontine nucleus by Steinmetz et al. (1987). Mauk, Steinmetz, and Thompson (1986) found that electrical stimulation of different locations in the inferior olive produced various movements, such as head turning, eyelid closure, or leg movements. This finding indicates that the synapses of the olivary neurons on the dendrites of the Purkinje cells are "strong." When the experimenters paired this stimulation with an auditory CS (presenting the CS first, of course), the behavioral response, whatever it was, became conditioned to the CS. In fact, researchers can even establish a classically conditioned response entirely through artificial stimulation. Steinmetz, Lavond, and Thompson (1989) paired stimulation of the pontine nucleus (CS) with stimulation of the inferior olive (US). They found that whatever unconditional response was produced by the olivary stimulation became classically conditioned to the pontine stimulation. (See ***Figure 12.12.***)

The goals of many neuroscientists are not only to find the neural circuits responsible for learning but also to discover the structural and biochemical changes that take place within the neurons in these circuits. The recent research on the neuroanatomy of simple classical conditioning is especially important, because it appears to have identified structures involved in a particular form of stimulus-response learning. With the hundreds of millions of neurons in even the smallest mammalian brain, discovering the structural basis of learning is even more difficult than finding the proverbial needle in a haystack. However, the research described in this section has helped divide the haystack into much smaller and more manageable pieces. Perhaps in the next few years investigators will begin to discover what kinds of changes occur in neurons in the cerebellum during classical conditioning.

Learning in a Simple Nervous System

One way to avoid the difficulties in trying to find learning-induced changes in the mammalian nervous system is to study animals with simple nervous systems. For several years researchers have been studying *Aplysia californica* (the sea hare), a shell-less marine mollusk. They have discovered much about the physiological basis of classical conditioning.

Behavioral studies of *Aplysia* have focused on the external organs of the mantle cavity: the gill, mantle shelf, and siphon. The gill exchanges gases with seawater, thus obtaining oxygen and releasing carbon dioxide. The mantle shelf is a protective sheet that forms a funnellike siphon at its posterior end. Normally, movements of the mantle cause water to be pumped into and out of the mantle cavity. (See ***Figure 12.13.***)

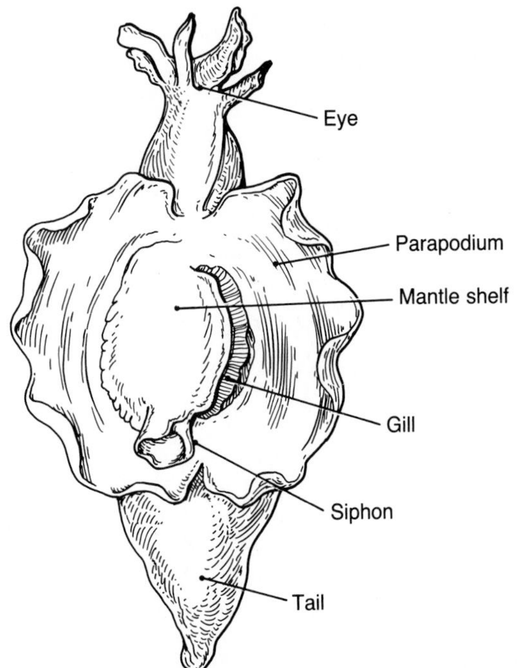

FIGURE 12.13

Aplysia californica.

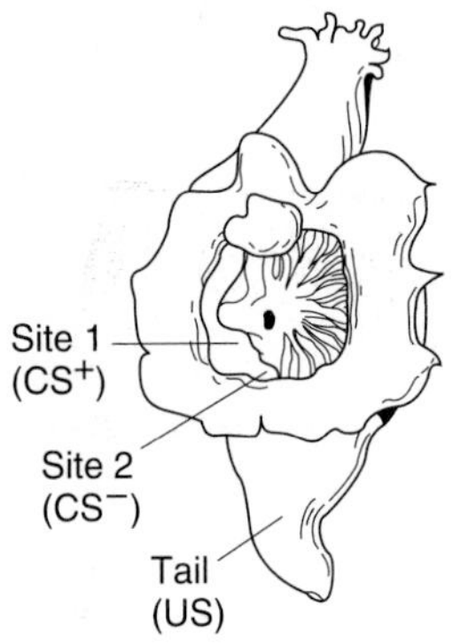

FIGURE 12.14

Differential classical conditioning of the siphon withdrawal reflex. CS^+ and CS^- are tactile stimuli applied to different portions of the siphon and mantle.

When the siphon or mantle shelf is touched, all three external organs retract into the mantle cavity. This defensive response presumably serves to protect these appendages from harm. Withdrawal of the siphon and gill can be classically conditioned by presenting a light touch to the siphon or mantle (CS) and then presenting a strong electrical shock to the tail (US). Carew, Hawkins, and Kandel (1983) applied gentle tactile stimuli to two different places, the siphon and mantle, but followed only one of these stimuli (CS^+) with a strong shock to the tail; the other stimulus (CS^-) was never followed by shock. (See ***Figure 12.14.***) After fifteen training trials the CS^+ produced a strong withdrawal reaction, but the CS^- did not.

The location of the synaptic change responsible for classical conditioning of the retraction response has been found (Hawkins, Abrams, Carew, and Kandel, 1983). Classical conditioning is produced by serotonin-secreting facilitatory interneurons that form axoaxonic synapses with sensory neurons. Initially, the synapse between the terminal button of the sensory neuron and the motor neuron is weak; but if the sensory neuron and the serotonergic interneuron are active at the same time, the weak synapse is strengthened. After classical conditioning has taken place, this previously weak terminal button will release more of its transmitter substance when it fires. Thus, the next time the siphon skin is stimulated, a gill withdrawal will be produced. (See ***Figure 12.15.***)

The increase in the release of transmitter substance is caused by an increase in the amount of calcium that enters the terminal button. You will recall from Chapter 2 that the release of a transmitter substance is triggered by the entry of calcium ions (Ca^{2+}) into the terminal button, which activates protein molecules that propel the synaptic vesicles to the presynaptic membrane. Thus, an increased influx of Ca^{2+} causes more transmitter substance to be released.

FIGURE 12.15

A hypothetical circuit responsible for differential classical conditioning of the siphon withdrawal response. (Adapted from Byrne, J.H., and Gingrich, K.J., in *Neural Models of Plasticity: Experimental and Theoretical Approaches,* edited by J.H. Byrne and W.O. Berry. San Diego: Academic Press, 1989.)

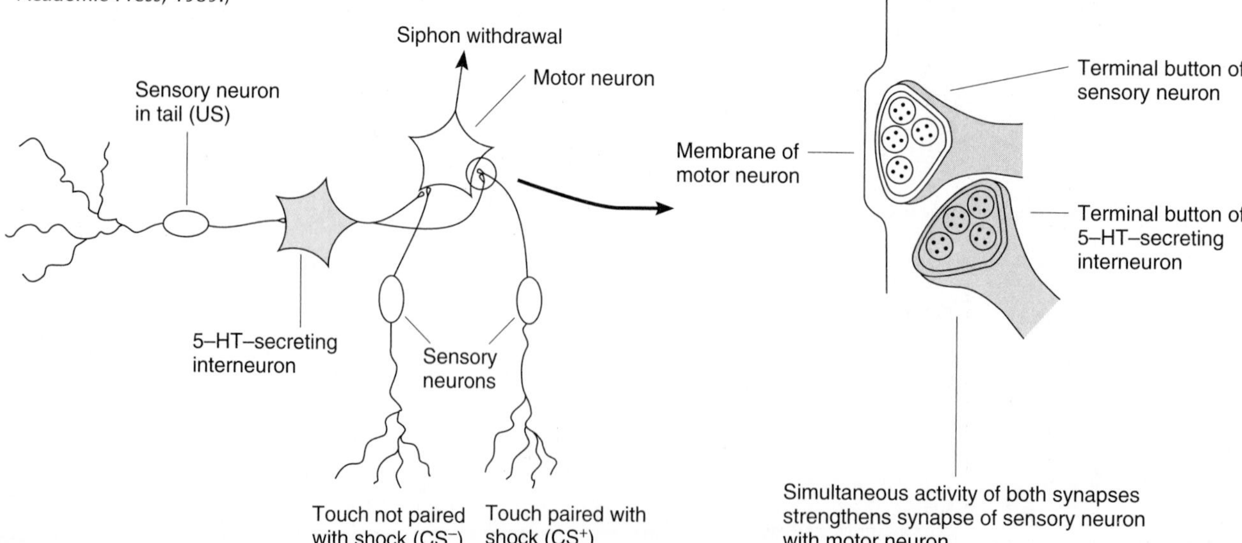

Most investigators believe that long-term classical conditioning in *Aplysia* involves some structural changes in the terminal buttons that cause more calcium to enter when an action potential arrives. For example, Montarolo et al. (1986) produced long-term synaptic strengthening by directly applying serotonin to the synapses of sensory neurons. When they also applied drugs that interfere with protein synthesis, this strengthening did not occur. Thus, it seems likely that the serotonin stimulates the synthesis of proteins that play some role in producing structural changes. Now that classical conditioning in *Aplysia* has been pinned down to a particular location, investigators should soon be able to discover the steps involved in the changes that occur there.

Long-Term Potentiation

Recently, many investigators have begun studying the effects of electrical stimulation on structural changes in synaptic connections in the mammalian nervous system, based on the conviction that all long-term memories must be initiated by neural activity. This approach has proved to be extremely useful; electrical stimulation of circuits within the hippocampal formation can lead to long-term physiological changes that may very well be among those responsible for learning. But before I can describe the phenomenon, we must review some anatomy.

ANATOMY OF THE HIPPOCAMPAL FORMATION

The **hippocampal formation** is a specialized region of the limbic cortex located in the temporal lobe. (Its location in a human brain is shown in Figure 3.17.) Because the hippocampal formation is folded in one dimension and then curved in another, it has a complex, three-dimensional shape. Thus, it is difficult to show what it looks like with a diagram on a two-dimensional sheet of paper. Fortunately, the structure of the hippocampal formation is orderly; a slice taken anywhere contains the same set of circuits. Figure 12.16 shows a photomicrograph of a horizontal section through the hippocampal formation of a rat brain and an accompanying drawing that shows the most important internal connections. (The circuitry within the human hippocampus is similar.) The hippocampus is also called "Ammon's horn," or, in Latin, *cornu ammonis* — from which come the names of its two major divisions, **CA1** and **CA3**. (CA2 and CA4 exist, too, but we will not need to talk about them.)

hippocampal formation

CA1 CA3

The major connections of the hippocampal formation with the neocortex are funneled through the **entorhinal cortex,** an adjacent region of limbic cortex. Neurons in the entorhinal cortex relay incoming information through a bundle of axons called the **perforant path** to neurons in the **dentate gyrus,** a subregion of the hippocampal formation. These neurons then send axons to field CA3, where they form synapses with *pyramidal cells,* named for their shape. These cells send axons to the adjacent field CA1, where they synapse with another set of pyramidal cells. CA1 pyramidal cells send axons to the *subicular complex* (also part of the hippocampal formation), which, finally, sends axons back to the entorhinal cortex, where the circuit started. (See ***Figure 12.16.***)

entorhinal cortex

perforant path

dentate gyrus

Figure 12.17 shows the connections of the hippocampal system with the neocortex. This figure illustrates a monkey brain, because the neocortex of this animal is much more developed and differentiated than that of a rat; the connections of the human brain are undoubtedly similar. As you can see, all association areas of the brain send information to, and receive information from, the hippocampal formation, funneled through the entorhinal cortex. Thus, the hippocampal formation is in a position

FIGURE 12.25

Long-term potentiation produced by four pulses of stimulation presented 170 msec after a priming pulse. (a) Pattern of the electrical stimulation. (b) Population EPSP. (Adapted from Diamond, D.M., Dunwiddie, T.V., and Rose, G.M. *Journal of Neuroscience*, 1988, *8*, 4079–4088. Reprinted by permission of the Journal of Neuroscience.)

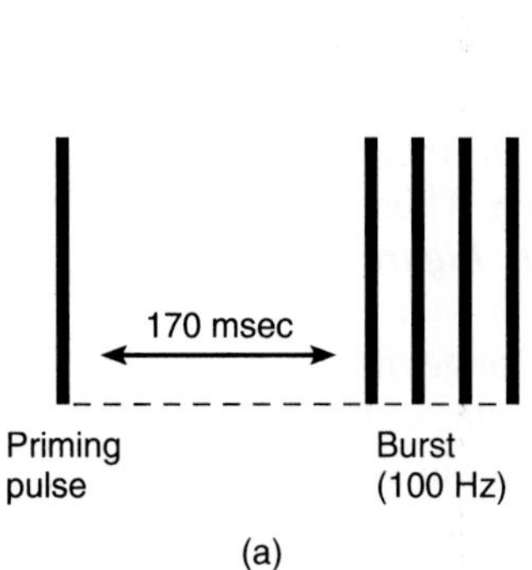

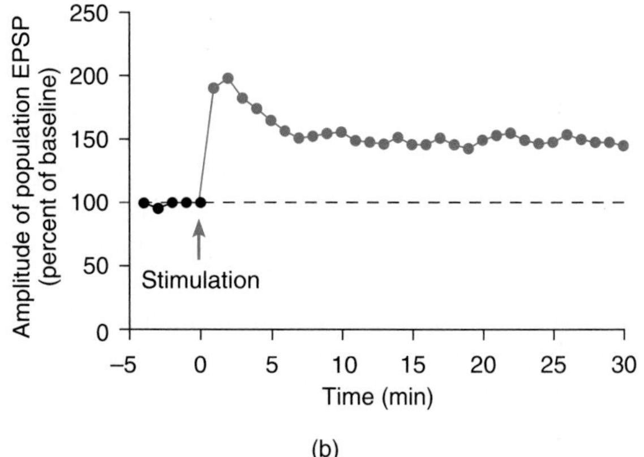

Experiments have clearly shown that the priming effect consists of a depolarization of the postsynaptic membrane; the depolarization caused by one pulse primes the synapse for the next one. In *associative* long-term potentiation the depolarization caused by the activity of a strong synapse primes the weak synapse so that it can be strengthened. In other words, long-term potentiation requires two events: activation of a synapse while the membrane of the dendritic spine is already depolarized.

A special receptor is responsible for long-term potentiation. One of the most important excitatory neurotransmitters in the brain is glutamic acid (usually referred to as *glutamate*). As you have already learned, many neurotransmitters are detected by more than one type of receptor. For example, there are two types of acetylcholine receptors—nicotinic and muscarinic, named for the agonists that best stimulate them. Similarly, there are several different types of glutamate receptors, also named for their agonists. One of them, the NMDA receptor (short for *N*-methyl-D-aspartate), plays a critical role in long-term potentiation.

NMDA receptor

The **NMDA receptor** has some unusual properties (see Cotman, Monaghan, and Ganong, 1988, for a review). It is found in the hippocampal formation, especially in field CA1. It controls a calcium ion channel. However, this channel is normally blocked by magnesium ions (Mg^{2+}), which prevent calcium ions from entering the cell, even when the receptor is stimulated by glutamate. Thus, glutamate is ineffective by itself. But if the postsynaptic membrane is first depolarized (say, by the activity of nearby synapses), the Mg^{2+} is ejected from the ion channel; then the presence of glutamate will open the channel and Ca^{2+} ions will enter the spine. Thus, the calcium channels controlled by NMDA receptors allow Ca^{2+} to enter the dendritic spine only when two things happen: when glutamate is present *and* when the postsynaptic membrane is depolarized. As we just saw, once calcium enters the dendritic spine it initiates the physical changes responsible for long-term potentiation. (See ***Figure 12.26.***)

The strongest evidence implicating NMDA receptors in long-term potentiation comes from research with drugs that block NMDA receptors, such as AP5 (2-amino-5-phosphonopentanoate). AP5 prevents long-term potentiation from taking place in field CA1 and the dentate gyrus. However, it has no effect on long-term potentiation that has already been established (Brown et al., 1989).

If molecule of glutamate stimulates NMDA receptor, calcium channel cannot open, because magnesium ion blocks channel

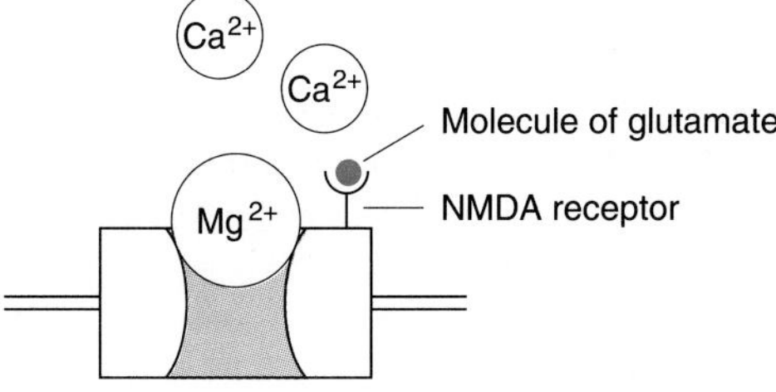

(a)

Priming
EPSP arrives from nearby synapses; depolarization evicts magnesium ion

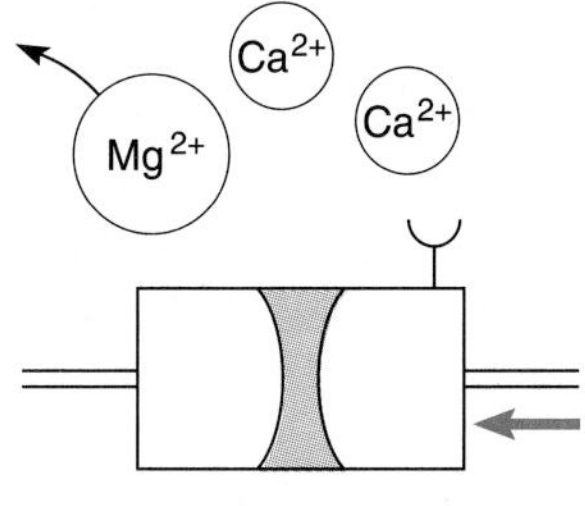

(b)

Potentiation
Molecule of glutamate stimulates NMDA receptor, opens calcium channel

Because membrane is still depolarized, magnesium ion is still gone; calcium enters, activates calpain, initiates changes in dendritic spine

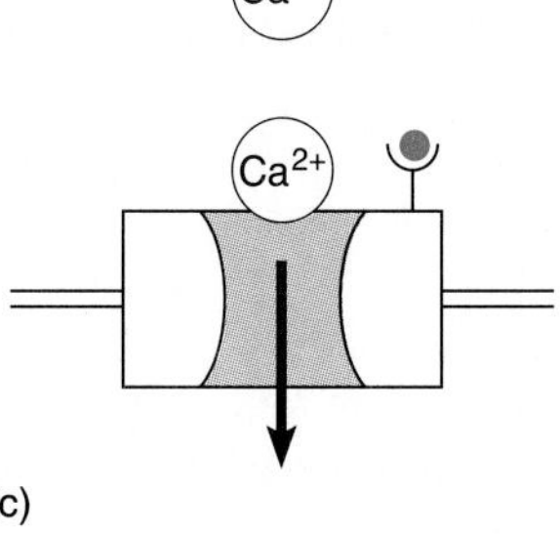

(c)

FIGURE 12.26

The mechanism through which NMDA receptors are believed to be responsible for long-term potentiation. (a) Glutamate alone, which does not open calcium channel. (b) Priming. Depolarization from nearby synapse evicts Mg^{2+} ion. (c) Potentiation.

Let me put all these facts together and explain how associative long-term potentiation works. If weak synapses are active by themselves, nothing happens, because the calcium channels are blocked by magnesium ions. However, if strong synapses on the same dendrite are active at the same time, then the postsynaptic membrane will be depolarized and the magnesium ions will be evicted; the glutamate released by the weak synapses will allow calcium to enter the dendritic spines. Thus, the special properties of NMDA receptors account not only for the existence of long-term potentiation but also for its associative nature.

RELATION TO LEARNING

I have discussed the physiology of long-term potentiation in some detail because understanding this phenomenon will probably help us understand how learning takes place. Several experiments have found that long-term potentiation is more than a laboratory curiosity; it is directly related to learning in the intact animal.

As we will see later, the pyramidal cells of the hippocampal formation are stimulated as an animal explores its environment. The sensory information reaches the dentate gyrus from the entorhinal cortex by means of the perforant path. If learning about complex environments produces changes in the hippocampal formation similar to those caused by electrical stimulation, then the exploration of a new environment should alter the excitability of the neurons in the dentate gyrus. In fact, it does. Sharp, McNaughton, and Barnes (1983) placed rats in a novel environment filled with boxes, ramps, and other objects; they found that this experience increased the extracellular population spike by 48 percent. Thus, an animal's experience can affect synaptic strength in the hippocampal formation.

If the kinds of neural changes seen in long-term potentiation are really those that take place during learning, then treatments that interfere with long-term potentiation should also interfere with the learning of tasks in which the hippocampus is involved. As we shall see in the final section of this chapter, the hippocampal formation is necessary for learning spatially guided tasks. Morris, Anderson, Lynch, and Baudry (1986) trained rats in such a task (the Morris "milk maze," to be described later). They infused a drug called AP5 into the animals' lateral ventricles. This drug, which blocks NMDA receptors, prevented the animals from learning the task. Thus, at least one form of learning in which the hippocampus is involved is disrupted by preventing long-term potentiation.

In recent years the phenomenon of long-term potentiation has received a considerable amount of attention from scientists interested in the cellular basis of learning, and their interest appears to be justified. The fact that long-term potentiation can be produced in the cerebral cortex as well as in the hippocampal formation suggests that the mechanisms that underlie this phenomenon may be widespread in the brain. The discovery of the functions of the NMDA receptor provides solid evidence for a mechanism that produces the type of synapse that Hebb predicted over forty years ago.

▶*INTERIM SUMMARY*◀

Investigators are beginning to understand the circuitry responsible for some forms of stimulus-response learning and are even discovering some of the ways that synapses can be modified by learning. In the past few years much progress has been made in tracing the neural circuits that are responsible for a rabbit's ability to learn a classically conditioned nictitating membrane response. A puff of air directed to the eye causes the unconditional response by means of the following circuit: The trigeminal nerve conveys the somatosensory information to the sensory trigeminal nucleus. Neurons there send axons to the accessory abducens nucleus, which controls the nictitating membrane response.

The conditional response involves the participation of neurons in the cerebellum. Information about the unconditional stimulus (air puff) reaches the dendrites of Purkinje cells in the cerebellar cortex through the inferior olive of the medulla. Information about the conditional stimulus (tone) is passed through the cochlear nucleus and the pontine nucleus to granule cells in the cerebellar cortex. These cells pass the information on to the dendrites of the Purkinje cells. If the auditory input (weak synapses) to the Purkinje cells is immediately followed by the somatosensory input (strong synapses), the former get strengthened, resulting in classical conditioning. Knowing the circuitry responsible for a learned response will help investigators discover the nature of the synaptic changes that are responsible for learning.

Some researchers have investigated the cellular mechanisms of learning in organisms with simple nervous systems in the hope that what they discover will help others understand such mechanisms in more complex organisms. Classical conditioning of the retraction response in *Aplysia* appears to be caused by serotonergic facilitatory interneurons that form synapses with the terminal buttons of sensory neurons. The release of 5-HT by these interneurons increases the amount of calcium that enters the terminal button, which increases the amount of the transmitter substance that is released. In addition, studies with drugs that inhibit protein synthesis indicate that long-term synaptic strengthening occurs only when protein synthesis can take place.

The study of long-term potentiation in the hippocampal formation has suggested a mechanism that might be responsible for at least some forms of long-term memory. A circuit of neurons passes through the hippocampal formation, from the entorhinal cortex to the dentate gyrus to field CA3 to field CA1 to the subiculum and back to the entorhinal cortex. High-frequency stimulation of the axons in this circuit strengthens synapses; it leads to an increase in the size of the EPSPs in the dendritic spines of the postsynaptic neurons. Associative long-term potentiation can also occur, in which weak synapses are strengthened by the action of strong ones. In fact, the only requirement for long-term potentiation is that the postsynaptic membrane be depolarized at the same time the synapses are active.

Long-term potentiation, like classical conditioning in *Aplysia,* is initiated by the entry of calcium into the postsynaptic neuron. The calcium appears to activate an enzyme (calpain) that causes changes in the structure of the dendritic spine by breaking apart a protein called spectrin. These changes decrease the electrical resistance between the spine and the rest of the dendrite, thus increasing the effect of EPSPs on the dendritic membrane potential.

In field CA1 and in the dentate gyrus, NMDA receptors play a special role in long-term potentiation. These receptors, sensitive to glutamate, control calcium channels but can open them only if the membrane is already depolarized. Thus, the combination of membrane depolarization (from a priming pulse or from the activity of a strong synapse nearby) and activation of a NMDA receptor causes the entry of calcium ions, producing long-term potentiation.

Long-term potentiation appears to be related to learning. When rats are exposed to novel, complex environments, the extracellular population spike in the dentate gyrus increases, just as it does when the entorhinal cortex is subjected to high-frequency stimulation. In addition, when AP5, a drug that blocks NMDA receptors, is chronically infused into the lateral ventricles, rats cannot learn a spatially guided task — one that is also disrupted by damage to the hippocampus. ▲

RELATIONAL LEARNING

So far, I have been discussing relatively simple forms of learning, which can be understood as changes in neural networks that detect the presence of particular stimuli, or as strengthened connections between neurons that convey sensory information and those that produce responses. But most forms of learning are more complex; most memories of real objects and events are related to other memories. Seeing a photograph of an old friend may remind you of the sound of the person's name and of the movements you have to make to pronounce it. You may also be reminded of things you have done with your friend: places you have visited, conversations you have had, experiences you have shared. Each of these memories can contain a series of events, complete with sights and sounds, which you will be able to recall in the proper sequence. Obviously, the neural circuits in the inferotemporal cortex that recognize your friend's face are connected to circuits in many other parts of the brain, and these circuits are connected to many others.

One of the most dramatic and intriguing phenomena caused by brain damage is *anterograde amnesia,* which, at first glance, appears to be the inability to learn new information. However, when we examine the phenomenon more carefully, we find that the basic abilities of perceptual learning, stimulus-response learning, and motor learning are intact, but that complex relational learning, of the type I just described, is gone. This section discusses the nature of anterograde amnesia in humans, its anatomical basis, and related research in laboratory animals.

FIGURE 12.27

A schematic definition of retrograde amnesia and anterograde amnesia.

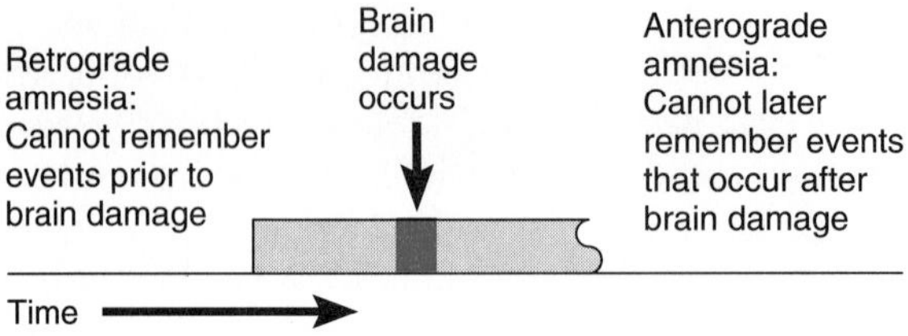

Human Anterograde Amnesia

anterograde amnesia

retrograde amnesia

The term **anterograde amnesia** refers to difficulty in learning new information. A person with pure anterograde amnesia can remember events that occurred in the past, during the time before the brain damage occurred, but cannot retain information he or she encountered *after* the damage. In contrast, **retrograde amnesia** refers to inability to remember events that happened *before* the brain damage occurred. (See ***Figure 12.27.***) As we shall see, pure anterograde amnesia is rare; usually, there is also a retrograde amnesia for events that occurred for a period of time before the brain damage occurred.

Korsakaoff's syndrome

In 1889 Sergei Korsakoff, a Russian physician, first described a severe memory impairment caused by brain damage, and the disorder was given his name. The most profound symptom of **Korsakoff's syndrome** is a severe anterograde amnesia: The patients appear to be unable to form new memories, although they can still remember old ones. They can converse normally and can remember events that happened long before their brain damage occurred, but they cannot remember events that occur afterward.

Korsakoff's syndrome is usually a result of chronic alcoholism. The disorder actually results from a thiamine (vitamin B_1) deficiency caused by the alcoholism (Adams, 1969; Haas, 1988). Because alcoholics receive a substantial number of calories from the alcohol they ingest, they usually eat a poor diet, so their vitamin intake is consequently low. Furthermore, alcohol appears to interfere with intestinal absorption of thiamine and the ensuing deficiency produces brain damage.

The location of the brain damage that causes Korsakoff's syndrome is still uncertain. In a thorough review of the literature Markowitsch (1988) concluded that because all cases of Korsakoff's syndrome are accompanied by damage to many structures in the brain, the available evidence does not permit us to conclude that a single structure is uniquely responsible for producing this phenomenon. We will probably have to turn to studies with animals, where precisely localized brain damage can be produced.

Anterograde amnesia can also be caused by damage to the temporal lobes. Scoville and Milner (1957) reported that bilateral removal of the medial temporal lobe produced a memory impairment in humans that was apparently identical to that seen in Korsakoff's syndrome. Thirty operations had been performed on psychotic patients in an attempt to alleviate their mental disorder, but it was not until this operation was performed on patient H.M. that the anterograde amnesia was discovered. The psychotic patients' behaviors were already so disturbed that amnesia was not detected. However, patient H.M. was reasonably intelligent and was not psychotic; therefore, his postoperative deficit was discovered immediately. He received the surgery in an attempt to treat his very severe epilepsy, which could not be controlled even by high doses of anticonvulsant medication.

The surgery successfully treated H.M.'s seizure disorder, but it became apparent that he suffered a serious memory impairment. Subsequently, Scoville and Milner

(1957) examined eight of the psychotic patients who were able to cooperate with them. Careful testing revealed that some of these patients also had anterograde amnesia; the deficit appeared to occur only when the hippocampus was removed. Thus, they concluded that the hippocampus was the critical structure destroyed by the surgery.

BASIC DESCRIPTION

In order for you to understand more fully the nature of anterograde amnesia, I will discuss the case of patient H.M. in more detail (Milner, Corkin, and Teuber, 1968; Milner, 1970; Corkin, Sullivan, Twitchell, and Grove, 1981). Patient H.M. has been extensively studied because his amnesia is relatively pure. His intellectual ability and his immediate verbal memory appear to be normal. He can repeat seven numbers forward and five numbers backward; and he can carry on conversations, rephrase sentences, and perform mental arithmetic. He has a retrograde amnesia for events that occurred during several years preceding the operation, but he can recall older memories very well. He showed no personality change after the operation, and he appears to be polite and well mannered.

However, since the operation, H.M. has been unable to learn anything new. He cannot identify by name people he has met since the operation (performed in 1953, when he was twenty-seven years old), nor can he find his way back home if he leaves his house. (His family moved to a new house after his operation, and he has been unable to learn how to get around in the new neighborhood.) He is aware of his disorder and often says something like this:

> Every day is alone in itself, whatever enjoyment I've had, and whatever sorrow I've had. . . . Right now, I'm wondering. Have I done or said anything amiss? You see, at this moment everything looks clear to me, but what happened just before? That's what worries me. It's like waking from a dream; I just don't remember. (Milner, 1970, p. 37)

H.M. is capable of remembering a small amount of verbal information as long as he is not distracted; constant rehearsal can keep information in his immediate memory for a long time. However, rehearsal does not appear to have any long-term effects; if he is distracted for a moment, he will completely forget whatever he had been rehearsing. He works very well at repetitive tasks. Indeed, because he so quickly forgets what previously happened, he does not become bored easily. He can endlessly reread the same magazine or laugh at the same jokes, finding them fresh and new each time. His time is typically spent solving crossword puzzles and watching television.

From these findings Milner and her colleagues made the following conclusions:

1. *The hippocampus is not the location of long-term memories; nor is it necessary for the retrieval of long-term memories.* If it were, H.M. would not have been able to remember events from early in his life, he would not know how to talk, he would not know how to dress himself, and so on.
2. *The hippocampus is not the location of immediate (short-term) memories.* If it were, H.M. would not be able to carry on a conversation, because he would not remember what the other person said long enough to think of a reply.
3. *The hippocampus is involved in converting immediate (short-term) memories into long-term memories.* This conclusion is based on a particular hypothesis of memory function: that our immediate memory of an event is retained by neural activity, and that long-term memories consist of relatively

permanent biochemical or structural changes in neurons. The conclusion seems a reasonable explanation for the fact that when presented with new information, H.M. seems to understand it and remember it as long as he thinks about it, but that a permanent record of the information is just never made.

The first two conclusions have stood the test of time; most investigators agree that they are correct. However, the third conclusion is too simple. Subsequent research on patients with anterograde amnesia indicates that the facts are more complicated — and more interesting — than they first appeared to be.

FIGURE 12.28

Examples of broken drawings. (Reprinted with permission of author and publisher from Gollin, E.S. Developmental studies of visual recognition of incomplete objects. *Perceptual and Motor Skills*, 1960, *11*, 289–298.)

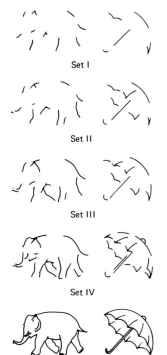

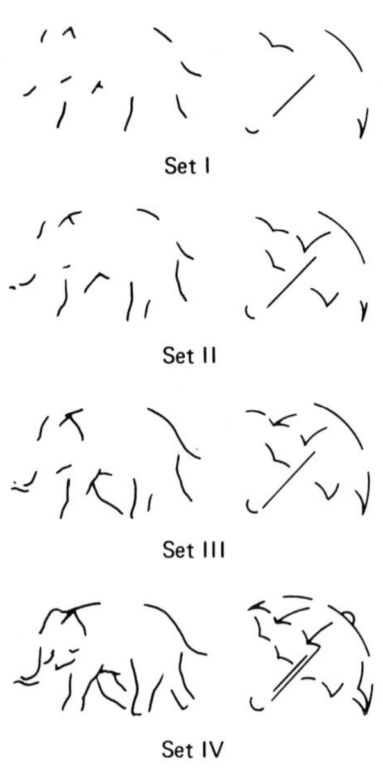

SPARED LEARNING ABILITIES

H.M.'s memory deficit is striking and dramatic. However, when he and other patients with anterograde amnesia are more carefully studied, it becomes apparent that the amnesia does not represent a total failure in learning ability. When the patients are appropriately trained and tested, we find that they are capable of perceptual learning, sensory-response learning, and motor learning.

First, let us consider perceptual learning. Figure 12.28 shows two sample items from a test of the ability to recognize broken drawings; note how the drawings are successively more complete. (See ***Figure 12.28.***) Subjects are first shown the least complete version (version I) of each of twenty different drawings. If they do not recognize a figure (and most people do not recognize version I), they are shown more complete versions until they identify it. One hour later, the subjects are tested again for retention, starting with version I. H.M. was given this test and, when retested an hour later, showed considerable improvement (Milner, 1970). When he was retested four months later, he *still* showed this improvement. His performance was not as good as that of normal control subjects, but he showed unmistakable evidence of long-term perceptual learning.

Investigators have succeeded in teaching amnesic subjects a wide variety of simple stimulus-response tasks. For example, Weiskrantz and Warrington (1979) found that amnesic subjects could acquire a classically conditioned eyeblink response. Sidman, Stoddard, and Mohr (1968) successfully trained patient H.M. on a visual discrimination task in which pennies were given for correct responses. Johnson, Kim, and Risse (1985) played unfamiliar melodies from Korean songs to amnesic patients and found that when they were tested later, they preferred these melodies to ones they had not heard before. The experimenters also presented photographs of two men along with stories of their lives: One man was dishonest, mean, and vicious, and the other was nice enough to invite home to dinner. Twenty days later, the amnesic patients said they liked the picture of the "nice" man better than the "nasty" one.

Although the patients can learn simple stimulus-response tasks like these, *they do not remember anything about having learned them.* They do not remember the experimenters, the room in which the training took place, the apparatus that was used, or any events that occurred during the training. Thus, although the amnesic patients in the study by Johnson, Kim, and Risse liked some melodies better, they did not recognize that they had heard them before; nor did they remember having seen the pictures of the two young men. Similarly, in the experiment by Sidman, Stoddard, and Mohr, although H.M. learned to make the correct response (press a panel with a picture of a circle on it), he was unable to recall having done so. In fact, once H.M. had learned the task, the experimenters interrupted him, had him count his pennies (to distract him for a little while), and then asked him to say what he was supposed to do. He had absolutely

▲ TABLE 12.1 ▲

Terms That Have Been Used to Describe Two Types of Memory (Not All Are Synonymous)

Names		*Authors*
Knowing how	Knowing that	Ryle (1949)
Procedural memory	Declarative memory	Winograd (1975)
Taxon	Locale	O'Keefe and Nadel (1978)
Reference memory	Working memory	Olton, Becker, and Handelmann (1979)
Automatic recollection	Conscious recollection	Baddeley (1982)
Semantic memory	Cognitive mediation	Warrington and Weiskrantz (1982)
Habit	Memory	Mishkin, Malamut, and Bachevalier (1984)
Dispositional memory	Representational memory	Thomas (1984)
Implicit memory	Explicit memory	Graf and Schacter (1985)
Nondeclarative memory	Declarative memory	Benzing and Squire (1989)

Source: Adapted from Squire, L.R. *Memory and Brain.* New York: Oxford University Press, 1987.

no idea. But when they turned on the stimuli again, he immediately made the correct response.

ANALYSIS OF ANTEROGRADE AMNESIA

The distinction between what people with anterograde amnesia can and cannot learn is obviously important, because it reflects the basic organization of the learning process. Investigators have proposed many different hypotheses to account for the pattern of deficits seen in anterograde amnesia. Some of the terms they have employed are shown in ***Table 12.1.***

Many of the hypothetical explanations about the nature of anterograde amnesia focus on the distinction between verbal and nonverbal behavior. For example, Squire and his colleagues (Squire, Shimamura, and Amaral, 1989) suggest that patients with anterograde amnesia are unable to form **declarative memories,** which they define as memories "explicitly available to conscious recollection as facts, events, or specific stimuli" (p. 218). The term *declarative* obviously comes from *declare,* which means "to proclaim; to announce." The term reflects the fact that patients with anterograde amnesia cannot talk about experiences that they have had since the time of their brain damage. In their definition Squire and his colleagues do not use the word *verbal,* but the term *consciousness* implies verbal awareness; if we are aware of something, then we are able to talk about it.

declarative memory

Clearly, verbal learning is disrupted in anterograde amnesia. Gabrieli, Cohen, and Corkin (1988) found that patient H.M. does not seem to have learned any words that have been introduced into the English language since his surgery. For example, he defined *biodegradable* as "two grades," *flower child* as "a young person who grows flowers," and *soul food* as "forgiveness." As the authors noted, for H.M. modern-day English is partly a foreign language.

But if the learning deficit of people with anterograde amnesia were simply a verbal deficit, then we would predict that similar damage to the brains of members of other species would not affect their ability to learn. After all, they cannot talk. But as we shall see later in this chapter, nonverbal animals can have anterograde amnesia, too. Therefore, we must look beyond a verbal-nonverbal distinction to understand what functions have been disrupted. As the title for this major section ("Relational Learning") suggests, the deficit might be a loss of the ability to learn complex relations. For example, consider the fact that patient H.M. can successfully learn several different kinds of perceptual or stimulus-response tasks. He can learn to recognize a particular stimulus or to make a particular response whenever a particular stimulus appears. However, if we ask him later whether he remembers the room where the testing took place, he will say no. He has no memory for the many other stimuli that were also present at the time: the experimenter, the room, the apparatus, the words that were spoken, and so on.

What is the difference between learning to perform a particular response when a particular stimulus is present and being able to remember that an experience occurred? In the first case learning would seem to consist of strengthened connections between neurons that perceive a stimulus and neurons that control a behavior. This basic capacity is not damaged in people with anterograde amnesia. But to be able to talk about an event later, a person must have learned much more. The person must have learned the *relation* between the stimuli that were present at the time and the sequence of events that occurred during the episode. When the person is asked about the episode later, he or she is able to picture the scene and describe it. Anterograde amnesia appears to be a loss of the ability to learn about complex relations between many stimuli, including the order of their occurrence in time.

ANATOMY OF ANTEROGRADE AMNESIA

The phenomenon of anterograde amnesia — and its implications for the nature of relational learning — has led investigators to study the phenomenon in laboratory animals. But before I review behavioral research with laboratory animals (which has provided some very interesting results), we should examine the brain damage that

FIGURE 12.29

Damage to field CA1 caused by anoxia. (a) Section through a normal hippocampus. (b) Section through the hippocampus of patient R.B. The pyramidal cells of field CA1 (between the two arrowheads) have degenerated. (DG = dentate gyrus, PrS = presubiculum, S = subiculum, F = fornix) (From Squire, L.R., in *Molecules to Models: Advances in Neurosciences,* edited by K.L. Kelner and D.E. Koshland. Washington, D.C.: American Association for the Advancement of Science, 1989. Reprinted with permission.)

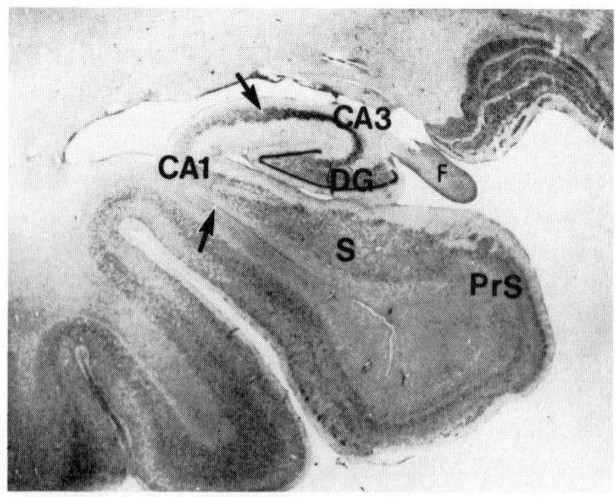

(a)

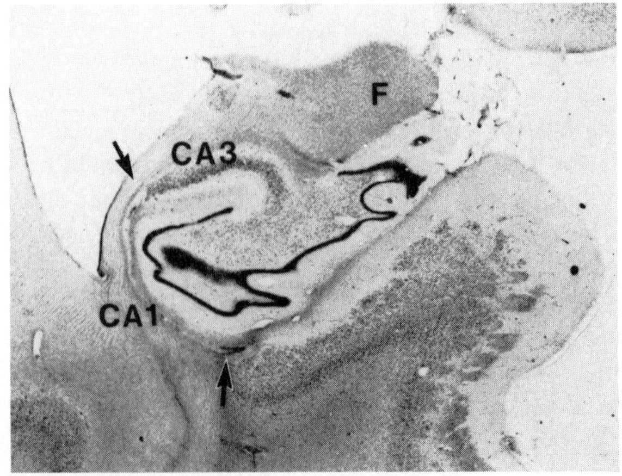

(b)

produces anterograde amnesia. One fact is certain: Damage to the hippocampus, or to regions that supply its inputs and receive its outputs, causes anterograde amnesia.

The clearest evidence that damage to the hippocampal formation produces anterograde amnesia comes from a case studied by Zola-Morgan, Squire, and Amaral (1986). Patient R.B., a 52-year-old man with a history of heart trouble, sustained a cardiac arrest. Although his heart was successfully restarted, the period of anoxia caused by the temporary halt in blood flow caused brain damage. The primary symptom of this brain damage was a permanent anterograde amnesia, which Zola-Morgan and his colleagues carefully documented. Five years after the onset of the amnesia, R.B. died of heart failure. His family gave permission for histological examination of his brain.

The investigators discovered that field CA1 of the hippocampal formation was gone; its neurons had completely degenerated. Figure 12.29 shows two photomicrographs, one of a section through a normal hippocampus and one of a section through that of patient R.B. Although the sections were taken at slightly different angles, you will have no difficulty seeing the difference in the appearance of field CA1 in the two brains. (See ***Figure 12.29.***)

Studies of the Hippocampal Formation in Laboratory Animals

The discovery that hippocampal lesions produced anterograde amnesia in humans stimulated interest in the exact role that this structure plays in the learning process. To pursue this interest, many investigators turned to studies with laboratory animals, which are described in the rest of this section.

SPATIAL PERCEPTION AND LEARNING

When experimenters began making lesions of the hippocampus in animals and testing their learning ability, they quickly found that the animals remained capable of learning most tasks. At the time they were surprised, and some even thought that the hippocampus had different functions in humans than it had in other animals. We now realize that most of the learning tasks that the animals were given tested simple sensory-response learning, which even humans with anterograde amnesia can do well. But from the beginning consistent deficits were seen in tasks that required the animals to learn to navigate through space. In particular, hippocampal lesions impaired animals' ability to learn complex mazes.

Remembering Places Visited. Olton and Samuelson (1976) devised a task that requires rats to remember where they have just been and discovered that hippocampal lesions impaired performance on this task even more than they do on a standard maze task. The investigators placed the rats on a circular platform located at the junction of eight arms, which radiated away from the center like the spokes of a wheel. (See ***Figure 12.30.***) The entire maze was elevated high enough above the ground so that the rats would not jump to the floor. Before placing the rats on the platform in the center, the experimenters put a piece of food at the end of each of the arms. The rats (who were hungry, of course) were permitted to explore the maze and eat the food. The animals soon learned to retrieve the food efficiently, entering each arm once. After twenty trials most animals did not enter an arm from which they had already obtained food during that session. A later study (Olton, Collison, and Werz, 1977) showed that rats could perform well even when they were prevented from following a fixed sequence of visits to the arms; thus, they had to remember where they had been, not simply follow the same pattern of responses each time. Control procedures in several studies ruled out

FIGURE 12.30

An eight-arm radial maze.

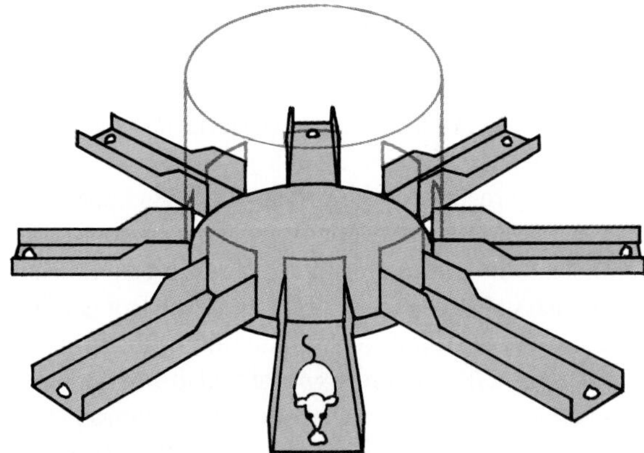

the possibility that rats simply smelled their own odor in the arms they had previously visited.

The radial-arm-maze task uses a behavioral capacity that is well developed in rats. Rats are scavengers and often find food in different locations each day. Thus, they must be able to find their way around the environment efficiently, not getting lost and not revisiting too soon a place where they previously found food. Of course, they must also learn which places in the environment are likely to contain food and visit them occasionally. Olton and his colleagues (reviewed by Olton, 1983) found that lesions of the hippocampus, fimbria/fornix, or entorhinal cortex severely disrupted the ability of rats to visit the arms of a radial maze efficiently. In fact, their postoperative performance reached chance levels; they acted as if they had no memory of which arms they had previously entered. They eventually obtained all the food, but only after entering many of the arms repeatedly.

On the basis of such results, Olton (1983) has suggested that lesions of the hippocampus or its connections impair working memory but leave reference memory relatively intact. **Working memory** consists of information about things that have just happened, which are useful in the immediate future but which change from day to day. Thus, it is "erasable" memory that is replaced on a regular basis. **Reference memory** is more permanent memory, produced by consistent conditions. For example, my remembering where I parked my car in the parking lot *today* is working memory. Tomorrow I will park in a new place and remember that. However, my remembering that when I come to work I park in lot number 40 is reference memory, which is unchanging.

working memory

reference memory

Whether or not the deficit caused by lesions of the hippocampal formation is one of working memory, the hippocampal formation does play a special role in spatial perception. Morris, Garrud, Rawlins, and O'Keefe (1982) trained rats to perform a task that required them to find a particular location in space solely by means of visual cues external to the apparatus. The "maze" consisted of a circular pool, 1.3 meters in diameter, filled with a mixture of water and milk. The milk hid the location of a small platform, situated just beneath the surface of the liquid. (I mentioned this maze earlier in this chapter, in the section on long-term potentiation.) The experimenters put the rats into the milky water and let them swim until they encountered the hidden platform and climbed onto it. They released the rats from a new position on each trial. After a few trials normal rats learned to swim directly to the hidden platform from wherever they were released.

Because the maze was circular and provided no cues as to spatial location, the animals had to determine where they were from the relative positions of objects in the room outside the maze. Rats with hippocampal lesions did *not* learn the location of the platform; they swam in what appeared to be an aimless fashion until they encountered it by chance. Figure 12.31 shows the performance of three rats: a normal rat, one with a neocortical lesion (to control for the fact that removal of the hippocampus entails damage to the overlying neocortex), and one with a hippocampal lesion. The difference in the animals' performance is easy to see. (See ***Figure 12.31.***)

Many different types of studies have confirmed the importance of the hippocampus in spatial learning. For example, Bingman and Mench (1990) found that hippocampal lesions disrupted navigation in homing pigeons. In fact, Rehkämper, Haase, and Frahm (1988) found that homing pigeons have larger hippocampal formations than breeds of pigeons who do not have such good navigational ability. Sherry, Vaccarino, Buckenham, and Herz (1989) found that the hippocampal complex of species of birds who normally store seeds in thousands of hidden caches and later retrieve them (and who have excellent memories for spatial locations) are larger than those of birds without this ability.

Recording Studies: Neurons That Respond to Particular Places. One of the most intriguing discoveries about the hippocampal formation was made by O'Keefe and Dostrovsky (1971), who recorded the activity of individual neurons in the hippocampus as an animal moved around the environment. The experimenters found that some neurons fired at a high rate only when the rat was in a particular location. Different neurons had different *spatial receptive fields;* that is, they responded in different locations. For example, one neuron might fire when the rat is in the northeast corner of its cage, another when it stands near the metal drinking spout, and yet another when it stands in the middle of the cage. For obvious reasons these neurons were named **place cells.**

place cell

Muller and Kubie (1987) examined the spatial receptive fields of hippocampal place cells in different environments. They found that if environments differed only in size, the receptive fields would be found in the same relative locations. However, if the environments differed in shape, the locations of the receptive fields would change in unpredictable ways. If they placed a barrier in the middle of a neuron's receptive field, the shape of the field would change; but if the barrier was outside the field, no change would occur.

FIGURE 12.31

Effects of hippocampal lesions and neocortical control lesions on performance in the circular "milk maze." The small circle marks the location of the submerged platform. (Reprinted by permission from Morris, R.G.M., Garrud, P., Rawlins, J.N.P., and O'Keefe, J. *Nature,* Vol. 297, pp. 681–683. Copyright © 1982, Macmillan Magazines LTD.)

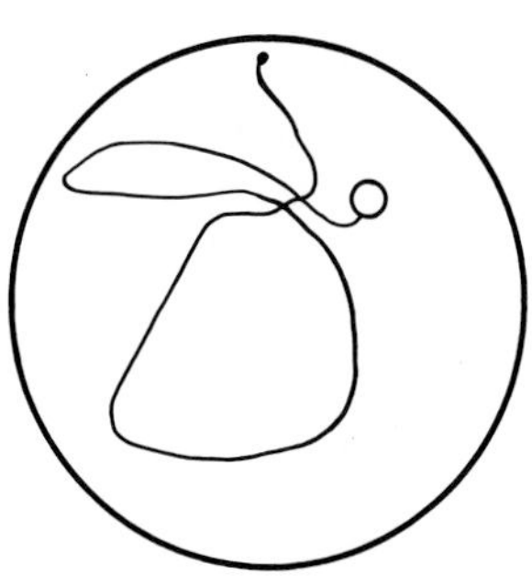

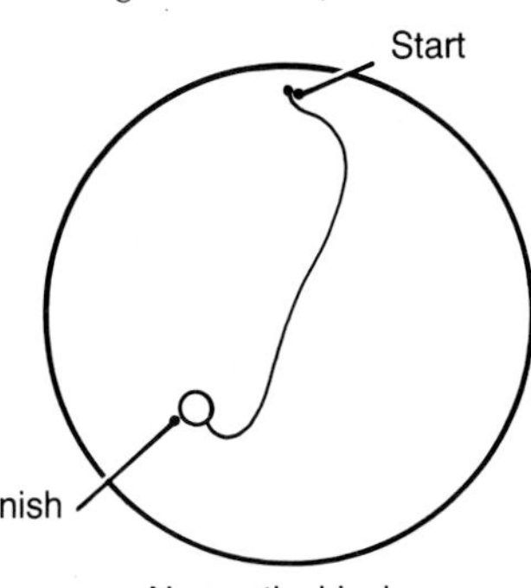

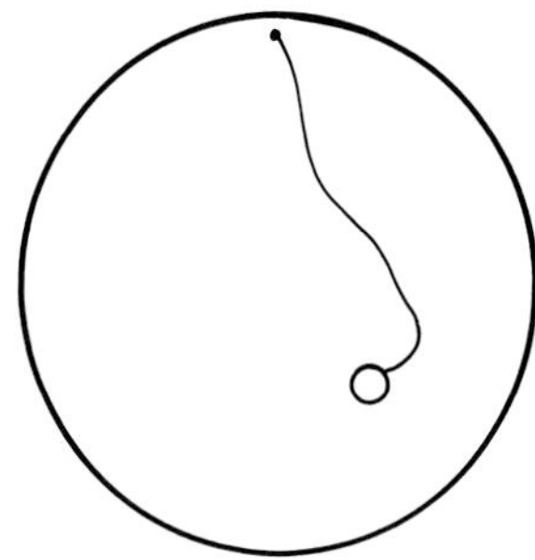

Hippocampal place cells are obviously guided by visual stimuli, because their receptive fields change when objects in the animal's environment are moved. They also receive internally generated stimuli, from the parietal cortex. (As we saw in Chapter 5, the association cortex of the parietal lobes is involved with spatial perception.) Hill and Best (1981) blindfolded rats and found that the spatial receptive fields of most of their place cells remained constant — even when they rotated the maze. At first, the experimenters were surprised and puzzled by the results, but then it occurred to them that the animals may have been keeping track of where they were by feedback from their own movements. The rats may have been keeping track of their starting point, left and right turns, and so on, which kept resetting their "mental map." To test this hypothesis, Hill and Best wrapped their blindfolded rats in a towel, spun them around, and then placed them in the maze. (If you have ever played blindman's buff or pin-the-tail-on-the-donkey, you will understand how disorienting this treatment is.) The experimenter's hypothesis was correct; after the rats had been spun, the receptive fields of their place cells were disrupted.

The fact that neurons in the hippocampal formation have spatial receptive fields does not mean that each neuron encodes a particular location. Instead, information about an animal's location is undoubtedly represented by particular *patterns* of activity in neural networks within the hippocampal formation. An individual neuron is only a single element of a particular network.

THE ROLE OF THE HIPPOCAMPUS IN RELATIONAL LEARNING

As we saw earlier, people with anterograde amnesia can learn to recognize new stimuli, can learn new responses, and can learn to make a particular response when a particular stimulus is presented. What they cannot do is to talk about what they have learned or learn nonverbal tasks that depend on their remembering relations among stimuli. Anterograde amnesia appears to be a loss of the ability to learn about relations among stimuli, including the order in which the events of a particular episode take place. How does research with laboratory animals help us understand this process?

Many investigators have come to the conclusion that the deficit in spatial learning produced by hippocampal lesions is caused by a failure to learn complex relations. For example, according to Wiener, Paul, and Eichenbaum (1989), "An emerging consensus . . . has indicated that the hippocampus is critical to learning and memory over a large range of information modalities that share a common demand for representing relationships among multiple independent percepts, but not for acquiring independent stimulus-reinforcement associations" (p. 2761). Sutherland and Rudy (1989) present a "configurational association theory," which suggests that the hippocampal system "combines the representations of elementary stimulus events to construct unique representations and allows for the formation of associations between these configural representations and other elementary representations" (p. 129).

I think it is likely that the original function of the hippocampus was to help the animal learn to navigate in the environment. In other words, spatial learning came first, and then other forms of relational learning were added through the evolutionary process. Let us consider how this spatial localization might be accomplished. Suppose you are standing in an environment similar to the circular "milk maze" I described earlier: a large field covered with grass, surrounded by distinctive objects, such as trees and buildings. You are familiar with the environment, having walked across it and played games on it many times. If someone blindfolds you and then picks you up and sets you down somewhere on the field, you will recognize your location as soon as you remove the blindfold. Your location is defined by the *configuration* of objects you see — the *relation* they have with respect to each other. You will get a different view of these objects from each position on the field. Of course, if there are distinctive objects present on the field itself (trees, garbage cans, drinking fountains), the task will be even easier, because you can judge your position relative to nearby objects as well as distant ones.

Many experiments have shown that hippocampal lesions disrupt the performance of tasks that require the animal to remember relations among stimuli, rather than individual stimuli. For example, Rudy and Sutherland (1989) trained rats on a *conditional discrimination task.* A conditional discrimination is one in which a response to a particular stimulus is reinforced under one condition but not under another. Thus, a response depends on the *relation* between stimuli. They trained rats to press a lever when a light was present *or* when a tone was present, but not when both were present at the same time. This task cannot be learned simply by establishing connections between the visual system and the motor system, and between the auditory system and the motor system. As you have undoubtedly guessed, Rudy and Sutherland found that rats with hippocampal lesions were unable to learn this task. That is, they readily learned to respond when either the light or the tone was present, but they failed to learn *not to respond* when they were present at the same time.

In the experiment by Rudy and Sutherland the contextual stimulus was the joint presence of a light and a tone. Another contextual stimulus is *time.* Several experiments have shown that the hippocampal formation is involved in an animal's ability to distinguish between situations that differ only in terms of time (Aggleton, Hunt, and Rawlins, 1986; Rafaele and Olton, 1988).

How do all these facts about the hippocampal complex fit together and explain its role in relational learning? As I mentioned earlier in this chapter, the hippocampal complex receives information from all regions of the sensory association cortex and from the motor association cortex of the frontal lobe. It also receives information from the amygdala concerning odors, dangerous stimuli, and information about the animal's emotional state: whether it is hungry, sexually aroused, frightened, and so on. Thus, the hippocampal complex knows what is going on in the environment, where the animal is located, and how it feels. When something happens, the hippocampal system has all the information necessary to put that event into the proper context.

Let us try to explain anterograde amnesia in humans with the contextual hypothesis. Consider a normal person learning to press a panel with a picture of a circle on it, as patient H.M. did in an experiment by Sidman, Stoddard, and Mohr (1968). While the person is seated in front of the apparatus, his or her hippocampal formation receives information about the context in which the learning is taking place: the room, the other people present, the person's mood, and so on. These pieces of information are collected together and are somehow "attached" to the patterns of activity in many different parts of the brain. Later, when the person is asked about the task, the question reactivates the pattern of activity in the hippocampus, which causes the retrieval of the memory of that particular episode, pieces of which are stored all over the brain. Patient H.M., lacking a functioning hippocampal system, has nothing that can put together the individual pieces of information, so he is unable to remember the episode.

Of course, this hypothetical explanation is vague about many parts of the process. For example, how does asking someone a question reactivate the pattern of activity in the hippocampus? And how, exactly, are pieces of information collected together and attached to sets of neural circuits? Obviously, we need to think about these questions, design clever experiments to obtain useful information, think about the questions in light of the new information, design more clever experiments . . . .

▶INTERIM SUMMARY◀

Considerable progress has been made in understanding the role of the hippocampal formation in relational learning. Brain damage can produce anterograde amnesia, which consists of the inability to remember events that happen after the damage occurs, even though immediate memory (such as that needed to carry on a conversation) is largely intact. The patients also have a retrograde amnesia of several years' duration but can remember information from the distant past. Simple perceptual and stimulus-response learning does not appear to be impaired; people can learn to recognize new stimuli, they are capable of instrumental and classical conditioning, and they can acquire conditioned emotional responses. However, they are not capable of *declarative learning*—of remembering and describing events that happen to them. They are also unable to learn the meanings of words they did not know before the brain damage took place.

Although other structures may be involved, researchers are now confident that the primary cause of anterograde amnesia is damage to the hippocampal formation or to its inputs and outputs. Studies with laboratory animals indicate that damage to the hippocampal formation disrupts the ability to learn spatial relations and to distinguish events that have just occurred from those that have occurred at another time. The basic deficit appears to an inability to distinguish among different contexts, which includes positions in space and in time. Although the animals can learn simple discrimination tasks, they cannot learn conditional discrimination tasks, in which a stimulus has different meanings in different contexts.

The hippocampal formation contains neurons that respond when the animal is in a particular location, which implies that the hippocampus contains neural networks that keep track of the relations among stimuli in the environment that define the animal's location. Much of this information is received from the parietal cortex.

The original role of the hippocampal formation may well have been to provide animals with the ability to orient in space, keeping track of the multiple stimuli that define spatial location; but it is clear that its role has expanded to learning relations among nonspatial stimuli and situations, as well. Presumably, people with anterograde amnesia can no longer learn new episodes because their inability to distinguish one context from another prevents the elements that make up an episode from being tied together. ▲

EPILOGUE: ▶ Application

As my graduate student Fred (see the Prologue) learned from his study of patients with Korsakoff's syndrome (and as many other investigators have shown), anterograde amnesia abolishes declarative (relational) learning while leaving perceptual, stimulus-response, and motor learning relatively intact. The obvious conclusion from this observation is that normal people, too, have unconscious memories as well as conscious ones.

Most cognitive psychologists use the terms *explicit memory* and *implicit memory* to distinguish between conscious and unconscious memories. Explicit memories are declarative ones that we can talk about. Implicit memories operate automatically. Acquiring implicit memories does not require deliberate attempts on the part of the learner to memorize something.

A good example of an implicit memory is learning to ride a bicycle. Of course, we do so quite consciously and develop episodic, declarative memories about our attempts: who helped us learn, where we rode, how we felt, the times we fell, and so on. But we also *learn to ride.* We learn to make automatic adjustments with our hands and bodies that keep our center of gravity above the wheels. Most of us cannot describe the rules that govern our behavior. For example, what do you think you must do if you start falling to the right while riding a bicycle? Many cyclists would say that they compensate by leaning to the left. But they are wrong; what they really do is turn the handlebars to the right. Leaning to the left would actually make them fall faster, because it would force the bicycle even farther to the right. The point is that although they have learned to make the appropriate movements, they cannot necessarily describe in words what these movements are.

Special procedures must be used to demonstrate implicit memories in normal people because of the presence of explicit memories, which tend to obscure the implicit ones. When people try to answer a test of memory, they almost always base their decisions on conscious deliberations; implicit memories, being unconscious, are ignored. A good example of implicit learning in normal subjects was provided in an experiment by Graf and Mandler (1984). These investigators showed subjects a list of six-letter words and had some of them engage in a task that involved thoughts that would lead to explicit, declarative memories associated with each word: to think about each word and decide how much they liked it. Other subjects were given a task that discouraged them from thinking about the words themselves and what they meant; they were asked to look at the words and simply decide whether they contained particular letters. Later, the subjects' explicit and implicit memories for the words were assessed. In both cases the basic task was the same, but the instructions to the subjects were different. The subjects were shown the first three letters of each word. For example, if one of the words had been DEFINE, they would have been shown a card on which DEF was printed. Many different six-letter words besides *define* begin with the letters DEF, such as *deface, defame, defeat, defect, defend, defied,* and *deform,* so there are several possible responses. The experimenters assessed *explicit memory* by asking the subjects to try to remember the words they had previously seen, using the first three letters as hints. They assessed *implicit memory* by asking the subjects to say the first word that came to mind that started with the three letters on the card.

The way the subjects had thought about the words when they first looked at them had a striking effect on the explicit memory task but not on the implicit memory task. When subjects used the three letters as cues for deliberate retrieval, they were much more successful if they had thought about whether they liked the word than if they had only looked for the occurrence of particular letters. Thus, thinking about the words and what they meant helped establish explicit memories. However, when subjects simply said the first word that came to mind, the way they had studied the words had no effect; merely looking at the words was as effective in establishing implicit memories as studying them and thinking about their meaning. In a follow-up study Graf, Squire, and Mandler (1984) found that although subjects with anterograde amnesia did poorly on a test of explicit memory, they performed as well as normal subjects on the implicit memory test.

Implicit memories are obviously important in learning to recognize stimuli, and they also control behaviors—not only skills, such as riding a bicycle, but also emotional responses that contribute to our attitudes and preferences. For example, you may recall that Johnson, Kim, and Risse (1985) found that amnesic patients preferred Korean songs they had heard before to those they had not heard. The same is true for normal subjects—and it is true even if the subjects cannot remember having heard the songs and deny that they sound familiar to them. Until recent years, psychologists focused most of their attention on explicit memories, which explains why it took so

long for researchers to discover the memory functions that are *not* destroyed in people with anterograde amnesia. Now that implicit memories are receiving more attention from researchers, we will learn more about the roles played by unconscious memories as well as conscious ones in our daily lives. ▲

KEY CONCEPTS

The Nature of Memory

- Learning takes many forms. The most important categories appear to be perceptual learning, stimulus-response learning, motor learning, and relational learning.
- The Hebb rule describes the synaptic change that appears to be responsible for stimulus-response learning: If an initially weak synapse repeatedly fires at the same time that the postsynaptic neuron fires, the synapse will become strengthened.

Perceptual Learning

- Learning to recognize complex stimuli involves changes in the association cortex of the appropriate sensory modality; simple perceptual learning can take place in subcortical regions.
- Perceptual learning appears to involve changes in the synaptic connections in neural networks. Models of neural networks are able to "learn" surprisingly well.

Stimulus-Response Learning

- Researchers have discovered the neural circuit responsible for a particular form of classical conditioning in the rabbit brain and in a marine invertebrate, *Aplysia californica.*
- Long-term potentiation occurs when axons in the hippocampal formation are repeatedly stimulated.
- Associative long-term potentiation appears to follow the Hebb rule and understanding it may help us understand the physiological basis of learning.
- The special properties of NMDA receptor account for associative long-term potentiation.

Relational Learning

- Damage to the hippocampal complex causes a syndrome of anterograde amnesia, in which people can learn to perform some simple stimulus-response tasks but cannot describe what they have learned.
- Studies with laboratory animals suggest that the hippocampal formation, which may originally have developed as part of a mechanism for spatial learning, now also is responsible for all forms of relational learning, recognizing contexts and coordinating learning taking place in many parts of the brain.

NEW TERMS

accessory abducens nucleus **p. 417**
anterograde amnesia **p. 432**
associative long-term potentiation **p. 424**
CA1 **p. 421**
CA3 **p. 421**
calpain **p. 426**
classical conditioning **p. 405**
conditional response (CR) **p. 405**
conditional stimulus (CS) **p. 405**
declarative memory **p. 435**
dentate gyrus **p. 421**
entorhinal cortex **p. 421**
Hebb rule **p. 406**
hippocampal formation **p. 421**
instrumental conditioning **p. 407**
interpositus nucleus **p. 417**
Korsakoff's syndrome **p. 432**
leupeptin **p. 427**
long-term potentiation **p. 422**
neural network **p. 414**
nictitating membrane **p. 417**
NMDA receptor **p. 428**
perforant path **p. 421**
place cell **p. 439**
population EPSP **p. 422**
punishing stimulus **p. 407**
reference memory **p. 438**
reinforcing stimulus **p. 407**
retrograde amnesia **p. 432**
spectrin **p. 426**
unconditional response (UR) **p. 405**
unconditional stimulus (US) **p. 405**
working memory **p. 438**

SUGGESTED READINGS

Byrne, J.H., and Berry, W.O. *Neural Models of Plasticity: Experimental and Theoretical Approaches.* San Diego: Academic Press, 1989.

Changeux, J.-P., and Konishi, M. *The Neural and Molecular Bases of Learning.* Chichester, England: John Wiley & Sons, 1987.

Cotman, C.W., Monaghan, D.T., and Ganong, A.H. Excitatory amino acid neurotransmission: NMDA receptors and Hebb-type synaptic plasticity. *Annual Review of Neuroscience,* 1988, *11,* 61–80.

Landfield, P.W., and Deadwyler, S. *Long-term Potentiation: From Biophysics to Behavior.* New York: A.R. Liss, 1988.

Matthies, H. Neurobiological aspects of learning and memory. *Annual Review of Psychology,* 1989, *40,* 381–404.

Olton, D.S., and Kesner, R.P. *Neurobiology of Comparative Cognition.* Hillsdale, N.J.: Lawrence Erlbaum Associates, 1989.

Squire, L.R. *Memory and Brain.* New York: Oxford University Press, 1987.

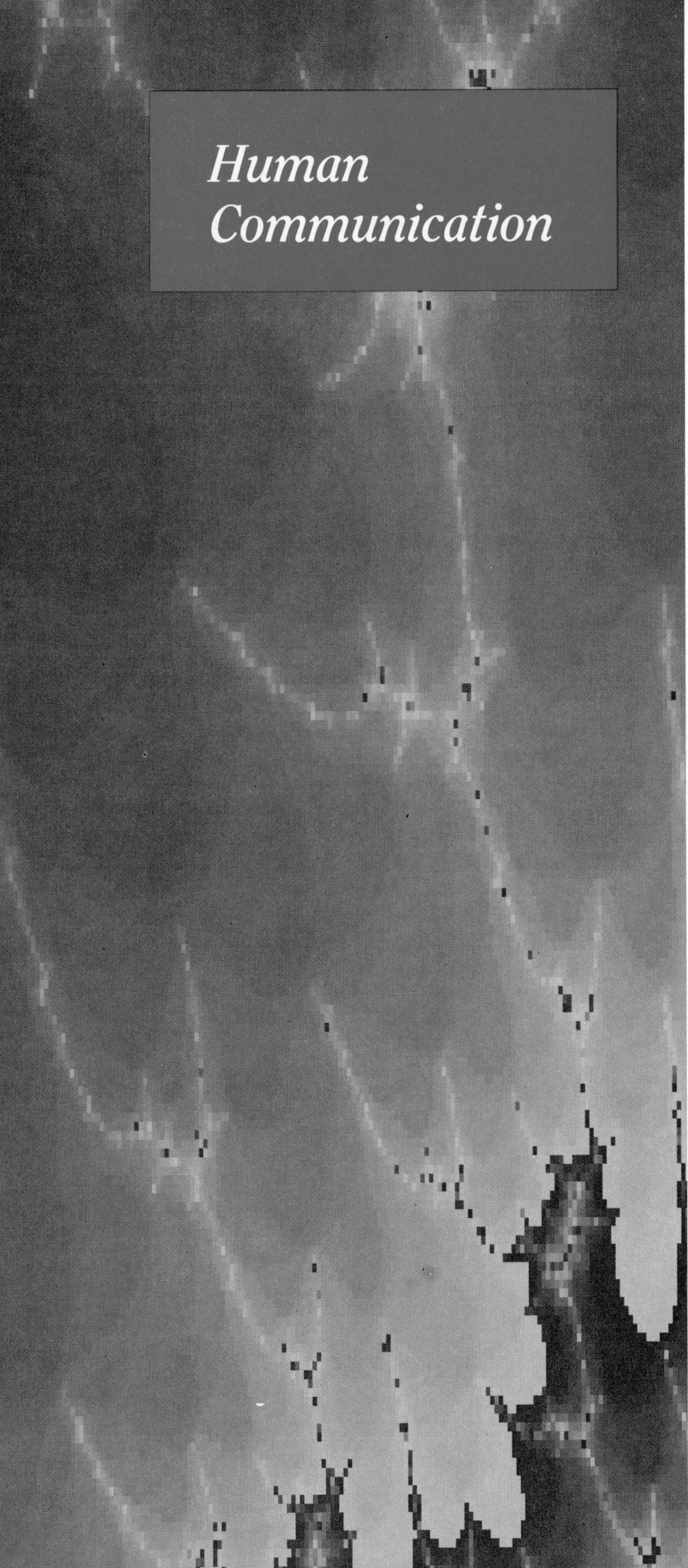

13

CHAPTER OUTLINE

PROLOGUE ►

Dr. D. presented the case. "Mr. S. had two strokes about ten years ago, which damaged both temporal lobes. His hearing, tested by an audiologist, is in the normal range. But as you will see, his speech comprehension is deficient."

Actually, as we soon saw, it was nonexistent. Mr. S. was ushered into the conference room and shown an empty chair at the head of the table, where we could all see and hear him. He looked calm and unworried; in fact, he seemed to be enjoying himself, and it occurred to me that this was probably not the first time he had been the center of attention. I had read about the syndrome I was about to see, and I knew that it was very rare.

"Mr. S., will you tell us how you are feeling?" asked Dr. D.

The patient turned his head at the sound of his voice and said, "Sorry, I can't understand you."

"*How are you feeling?*" he asked in a loud voice.

"Oh, I can hear you all right, I just can't understand you. Here," he said, handing him a pencil and a small pad of paper.

Dr. D. took the pencil and paper and wrote something. He handed them back to Mr. S., who looked at it and said, "Fine. I'm just fine."

"Will you tell us about what you have been doing lately?" asked Dr. D. Mr. S. smiled, shook his head, and handed him the paper and pencil again.

"Oh sure," he said after reading the new question, and he proceeded to tell us about his garden and his other hobbies. "I don't get much from television unless there are a lot of close-ups, where I can read their lips. I like to listen to music on the radio, but, of course, the lyrics don't mean too much to me!" He laughed at his own joke, which had probably already seen some mileage.

"You mean that you can read lips?" someone asked.

Mr. S. immediately turned toward the sound of the voice and said, "What did you say? Say it slow, so I can try to read your lips." We all laughed, and Mr. S. joined us when the question was repeated slowly enough for him to decode. Another person tried to ask him a question, but apparently his Spanish accent made it impossible for Mr. S. to read his lips.

Suddenly, the phone rang. We all—including Mr. S.—looked up at the wall where it was hanging. "Someone else had better get that," he said. "I'm not much good on the phone."

After Mr. S. had left the room, someone observed that although Mr. S.'s speech was easy to understand, it seemed a bit strange. "Yes," said a speech therapist, "he almost sounds like a deaf person who has learned to talk but doesn't get the pronunciation of the words just right."

Dr. D. nodded and played a tape for us. "This recording was made a few months after his strokes, ten years ago." We heard the same voice, but this time it sounded absolutely normal.

"Oh," said the speech therapist. "He has lost the ability to monitor his own speech, and over the years he has forgotten some of the details of how various words are pronounced."

"Exactly," said Dr. D. "The change has been a gradual one." ▲

Verbal behaviors constitute one of the most important classes of human social behavior. Our cultural evolution has been possible because we can talk and listen, write and read. Language enables our discoveries to be cumulative; knowledge gained by one generation can be passed on to the next.

The basic function of verbal communication is seen in its effects on other people. When we talk to someone, we almost always expect our speech to induce the person to engage in some sort of behavior. Sometimes, the behavior is of obvious advantage to us, as when we ask for an object or for help performing a task. At other times, we are simply asking for a social exchange: some attention and perhaps some conversation. Even "idle" conversation is not idle, because it causes another person to look at us and say something in return.

This chapter discusses the neural basis of verbal behavior: talking, understanding speech, reading, and writing.

SPEECH PRODUCTION AND COMPREHENSION: BRAIN MECHANISMS

Our knowledge of the physiology of language has been obtained primarily by observing the effects of brain lesions on people's verbal behavior. Although investigators have studied people who have undergone brain surgery or who have sustained head injuries, brain tumors, or infections, most of the observations have been made on people who have suffered strokes, or **cerebrovascular accidents.** The most common type of cerebrovascular accident is caused by obstruction of a blood vessel. The interruption in blood flow deprives a region of the brain of its blood supply, which causes cells in that region to die. Figure 13.1 shows two CT scans from a person with a stroke that caused Broca's aphasia (described later). The lesion is the dark region indicated by the arrows. (See ***Figure 13.1.***)

cerebrovascular accident

FIGURE 13.1

Two CT scans from a patient with Broca's aphasia. The lesion, located in the left frontal lobe, is indicated by the arrows. (Scans courtesy of Brian Chiango and Jean Dempster, Brigham and Women's Hospital, Boston, Massachusetts.)

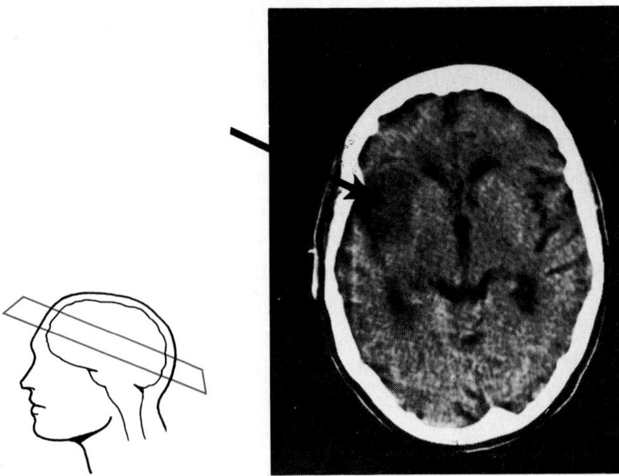

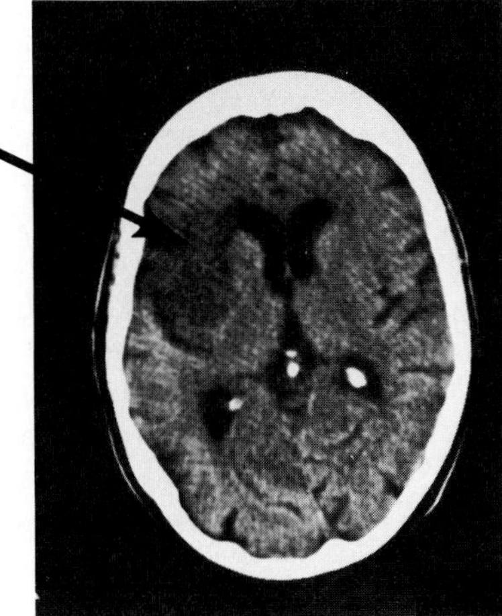

aphasia

The most important category of speech disorders is **aphasia,** a primary disturbance in the comprehension or production of speech, caused by brain damage. Not all speech disturbances are aphasias; a patient must have difficulty comprehending, repeating, or producing meaningful speech, and this difficulty must not be caused by simple sensory or motor deficits or by lack of motivation. For example, inability to speak caused by deafness or paralysis of the speech muscles is not considered to be aphasia. In addition, the deficit must be relatively isolated; that is, the patient must appear to be aware of what is happening in his or her environment and to comprehend that others are attempting to communicate.

Lateralization

Verbal behavior is a *lateralized* function; most language disturbances occur after damage to the left side of the brain. The best way to determine which side of the brain is dominant for speech is to perform a *Wada test* (named after its inventor). A patient who is about to undergo surgery that might encroach on a speech area receives a short-acting anesthetic in one carotid artery and then, when the effects have worn off, in the other. This procedure anesthetizes first one cerebral hemisphere and then the other; thus, in a few minutes the involvement of each hemisphere in speech functions can be assessed. In over 95 percent of right-handed people the left hemisphere is dominant for speech. That is, when the left hemisphere is anesthetized, the person loses the ability to speak. However, when the right hemisphere is anesthetized, the person can still talk and carry on a conversation. The figure is somewhat lower in left-handed people: approximately 70 percent. Therefore, unless I say otherwise, you can assume that the brain damage described in the first part of this chapter is located in the left (speech-dominant) hemisphere.

Why is one hemisphere specialized for speech? The perceptual functions of the left hemisphere are more specialized for the analysis of sequences of stimuli, occurring one after the other. The perceptual functions of the right hemisphere are more specialized for the analysis of space and geometrical shapes and forms, the elements of which are all present at the same time. Speech is certainly sequential; it consists of sequences of words, which are composed of sequences of sounds. Thus, it makes sense for the left hemisphere to have become specialized at perceiving speech. In addition, as we saw in Chapter 7, the left hemisphere is involved in the control of sequences of voluntary movements. Perhaps this fact accounts for the localization of neural circuits involved in speech production, as well as speech perception, in the left hemisphere.

Although the circuits *primarily* involved in speech comprehension and production are located in the left hemisphere, it would be a mistake to conclude that the right hemisphere plays no role in speech. Speech is not simply a matter of talking — it is also having something to say. Similarly, listening is not simply hearing and recognizing words — it is understanding the meaning of what has been said. When we hear and understand words, and when we talk about or think about our own perceptions or memories, we are using neural circuits besides those directly involved in speech. Thus, these circuits, too, play a role in verbal behavior. For example, damage to the right hemisphere makes it difficult for a person to read maps, perceive spatial relations, and recognize complex geometrical forms. People with such damage will also have trouble talking about things like maps and complex geometrical forms or understanding what other people have to say about them. And as we saw in Chapter 10, the right hemisphere is involved in the expression and recognition of emotion in the tone of voice.

Therefore, both hemispheres of the brain have a contribution to make to our language abilities.

Speech Production

Being able to talk—that is, to produce meaningful speech—requires several abilities. First, the person must have something to talk about. Let us consider what this means. We can talk about something that is presently happening or something that happened in the past. In the first case we are talking about our perceptions: of things we are seeing, hearing, feeling, smelling, and so on. In the second case we are talking about our memories of what happened in the past. Both perceptions of current events and memories of events that occurred in the past involve brain mechanisms in the posterior part of the cerebral hemispheres (the occipital, temporal, and parietal lobes). Thus, this region is largely responsible for having something to say.

Of course, we can also talk about something that *did not* happen. That is, we can use our imagination to make up a story (or to tell a lie). We know very little about the neural mechanisms responsible for imagination, but it seems likely that they involve the mechanisms responsible for perceptions and memories; after all, when we make up a story, we must base it on knowledge that we originally acquired through perception and have retained in our memory.

Given that a person has something to say, actually doing so requires some additional brain functions. As we shall see in this section, the conversion of perceptions, memories, and thoughts into speech makes use of neural mechanisms located in the frontal lobes.

Damage to a region of the inferior left frontal lobe (Broca's area) disrupts the ability to speak: It causes **Broca's aphasia.** This disorder is characterized by slow, laborious, and nonfluent speech. When trying to talk with patients who have Broca's aphasia, most people find it hard to resist supplying the words they are obviously groping for. But although they often mispronounce words, the ones they manage to come out with are meaningful. The posterior part of the cerebral hemispheres has something to say, but the damage to the frontal lobe makes it difficult for the patients to express these thoughts.

Broca's aphasia

People with Broca's aphasia find it easier to say some types of words than others. They have great difficulty saying the little words with grammatical meaning, such as *a, the, some, in,* or *about.* These words are called **function words,** because they have important grammatical functions. The words that they do manage to say consist almost entirely of **content words**—words that convey meaning, including nouns, verbs, adjectives, and adverbs, such as *apple, house, throw,* or *heavy.* Here is a sample of speech from a man with Broca's aphasia, who is telling the examiner why he has come to the hospital. As you will see, his words are meaningful, but what he says is certainly not grammatical. The dots indicate long pauses.

function word

content word

> Ah . . . Monday . . . ah Dad and Paul [patient's name] . . . and Dad . . . hospital. Two . . . ah doctors . . . , and ah . . . thirty minutes . . . and yes . . . ah . . . hospital. And, er Wednesday . . . nine o'clock. And er Thursday, ten o' clock . . . doctors. Two doctors . . . and ah . . . teeth. Yeah, . . . , fine. (Goodglass, 1976, p. 278)

People with Broca's aphasia can comprehend speech much better than they can produce it. In fact, some observers have said that their comprehension is unimpaired,

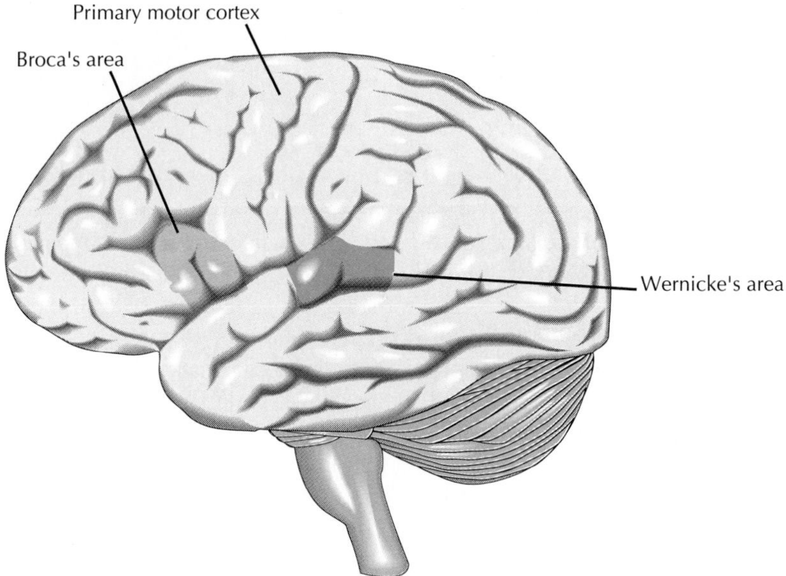

FIGURE 13.2

The location of the primary speech areas of the brain. (Wernicke's area will be described later.)

but as we will see, this is not quite true. Broca (1861) suggested that this form of aphasia is produced by a lesion of the frontal association cortex, just anterior to the face region of the primary motor cortex. Subsequent research proved him to be essentially correct, and we now call the region **Broca's area.** (See ***Figure 13.2.***)

Broca's area

Lesions that produce Broca's aphasia are certainly centered in the vicinity of Broca's area. However, although Broca's aphasia has been studied for many years, the anatomical basis of this disorder is still unsettled. For example, damage to the primary motor cortex or to the subcortical white matter of the frontal lobe, as well as to Broca's area itself, may contribute to this disorder. In any event, the frontal cortex and its connections with other parts of the brain are important in converting thoughts into speech.

Wernicke (1874) suggested (and many modern investigators concur) that Broca's area contains motor memories — in particular, *memories of the sequences of muscular movements that are needed to articulate words.* Talking involves rapid movements of the tongue, lips, and jaw, and these movements must be coordinated with each other and with those of the vocal cords; thus, talking requires some very sophisticated motor control mechanisms. Obviously, circuits of neurons somewhere in our brain will, when properly activated, cause these sequences of movements to be executed. Because damage to the inferior caudal left frontal lobe (including Broca's area) disrupts the ability to articulate words, this region is the most likely candidate for the location of these "programs." The fact that this region is located just in front of the part of the primary motor cortex that controls the muscles used for speech certainly supports this conclusion.

But the speech functions of the left frontal lobe include more than programming the movements used to speak. In general, three major speech deficits are produced by lesions in and around Broca's area: *agrammatism, anomia,* and *articulation difficulties.* Although most patients with Broca's aphasia will have all of these deficits to some degree, their severity can vary considerably from person to person.

agrammatism

Agrammatism refers to a patient's difficulty in using grammatical constructions. This disorder can appear all by itself, without any difficulty in pronouncing words (Nadeau, 1988). As we saw, people with Broca's aphasia rarely use function words. In addition, they rarely use grammatical markers such as *-ed* or auxiliaries such as *have* (as in *I have gone*). For some reason, they *do* often use *-ing,* perhaps because this ending converts a verb into a noun. A study by Saffran, Schwartz, and Marin (1980) illustrates this difficulty. The following quotations are from agrammatic patients attempting to describe pictures:

> *Picture of a boy being hit in the head by a baseball*
> The boy is catch . . . the boy is hitch . . . the boy is hit the ball. (Saffran, Schwartz, and Marin, 1980, p. 229)
>
> *Picture of a girl giving flowers to her teacher*
> Girl . . . wants to . . . flowers . . . flowers and wants to . . . . The woman . . . wants to . . . . The girl wants to . . . the flowers and the woman. (Saffran, Schwartz, and Marin, 1980, p. 234)

The second major speech deficit seen in Broca's aphasia is **anomia** ("without name"). Anomia refers to a word-finding difficulty; and because all aphasics omit words or use inappropriate ones, anomia is actually a primary symptom of *all* forms of aphasia. However, because the speech of Broca's aphasics lacks fluency, their anomia is especially apparent; their facial expression and frequent use of sounds like "uh" make it obvious that they are groping for the correct words.

anomia

The third major characteristic of Broca's aphasia is *difficulty with articulation.* Patients mispronounce words, often altering the sequence of sounds. For example, *lipstick* might be pronounced "likstip." People with Broca's aphasia recognize that their pronunciation is erroneous, and they usually try to correct it.

As I said, these three deficits are seen in various combinations in different patients, depending on the exact location of the lesion and, to a certain extent, on their stage of recovery. Although the anatomical correlates are not yet worked out, we can characterize these deficits hierarchically. On the lowest, most elementary level is control of the sequence of movements of the muscles of speech; damage to this ability leads to articulation difficulties. The next higher level is selection of the particular "programs" for individual words; damage to this ability leads to anomia. Finally, the highest level is selection of grammatical structure, including word order, use of function words, and word endings; damage to this ability leads to agrammatism. Presumably, the control of articulation involves the face area of the primary motor cortex and portions of the basal ganglia; the selection of words, word order, and grammatical markers involves Broca's area and adjacent regions of the frontal association cortex.

So far, I have described Broca's aphasia as a disorder in speech *production.* In an ordinary conversation Broca's aphasics seem to understand everything that is said to them. They appear to be irritated and annoyed by their inability to express their thoughts well, and they often make gestures to supplement their scanty speech. The striking disparity between their speech and their comprehension often leads people to assume that their comprehension is normal. But it is not. Schwartz, Saffran, and Marin (1980) showed Broca's aphasics pairs of pictures in which agents and objects of the action were reversed: for example, a horse kicking a cow and a cow kicking a horse, a truck pulling a car and a car pulling a truck, and a dancer applauding a clown and a clown applauding a dancer. As they showed each pair of pictures, they read the subject a sentence, for example, *The horse kicks the cow.* The subjects' task was to point to the appropriate picture, indicating whether they understood the grammatical construction of the sentence. (See ***Figure 13.3.***) They performed very poorly.

FIGURE 13.3

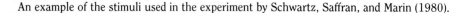

An example of the stimuli used in the experiment by Schwartz, Saffran, and Marin (1980).

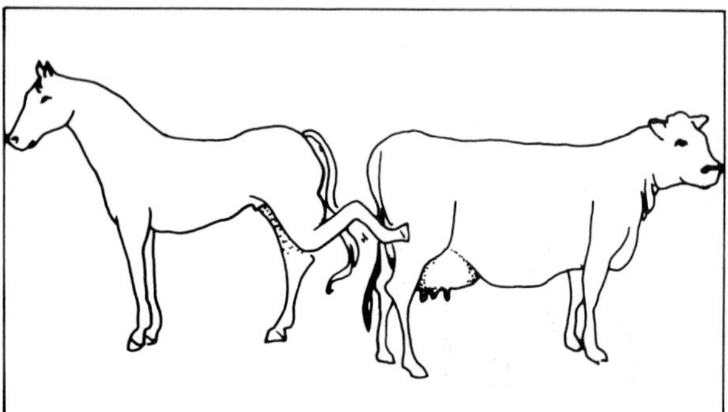

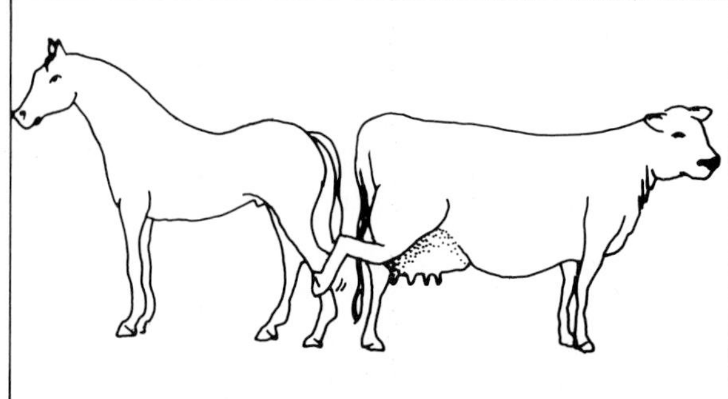

The correct picture in the study by Schwartz and her colleagues was specified by a particular aspect of grammar: word order. The agrammatism that accompanies Broca's aphasia appears to disrupt patients' ability to use grammatical information, including word order, to decode the meaning of a sentence. Thus, their deficit in comprehension parallels their deficit in production. If they heard a sentence such as *The man swats the mosquito,* they would understand that it concerns a man and a mosquito and the action of swatting. Obviously, they would have no trouble figuring out who is doing what to whom. But a sentence such as *The horse kicks the cow* does not provide any extra cues; if the grammar is not understood, neither is the meaning of the sentence.

Other experiments have shown that people with Broca's aphasia have difficulty carrying out a sequence of commands such as "Pick up the red circle and touch the green square with it" (Boller and Dennis, 1979). This finding, along with the other symptoms I have described in this section, suggests that an important function of the left frontal lobe is sequencing—of movements of the muscles of speech (producing words) and of words (comprehending and producing grammatical speech).

Speech Comprehension

Wernicke's area

Comprehension of speech obviously begins in the auditory system, which is needed to detect and analyze sounds. But *recognizing* words is one thing; *comprehending* them is another. Recognizing a spoken word is a complex perceptual task that relies on memories of sequences of sounds. This task appears to be accomplished by neural circuits in the middle and posterior portion of the superior temporal gyrus of the left hemisphere—a region that has come to be known as **Wernicke's area.** (Refer to *Figure 13.2.*)

WERNICKE'S APHASIA: DESCRIPTION

Wernicke's aphasia

The primary characteristics of **Wernicke's aphasia** are poor speech comprehension and production of meaningless speech. Unlike Broca's aphasia, Wernicke's aphasia is fluent and unlabored; the person does not strain to articulate words and does not appear to be searching for them. The patient maintains a melodic line, with the voice rising and falling normally. When you listen to the speech of a person with Wernicke's aphasia, it appears to be grammatical. That is, the person uses function words such as *the* and *but* and employs complex verb tenses and subordinate clauses. However, the person uses few content words, and the words that he or she strings together just do not make sense. In the extreme, speech deteriorates into a meaningless jumble, illustrated by the following quotation:

> *Examiner:* What kind of work did you do before you came into the hospital?
> *Patient:* Never, now mista oyge I wanna tell you this happened when happened when he rent. His — his kell come down here and is — he got ren something. It happened. In thesse ropiers were with him for hi — is friend — like was. And it just happened so I don't know, he did not bring around anything. And he did not pay it. And he roden all o these arranjen from the pedis on from iss pescid. In these floors now and so. He hadn't had em round here. (Kertesz, 1981, p. 73)

Because of the speech deficit of people with Wernicke's aphasia, when we try to assess their ability to comprehend speech, we must ask them to use nonverbal responses. That is, we cannot assume that they do not understand what other people say to them just because they do not give the proper answer. A commonly used test of comprehension assesses their ability to understand questions by pointing to objects on a table in front of them. For example, they are asked to "Point to the one with ink." If they point to an object other than the pen, they have not understood the request. When tested this way, people with severe Wernicke's aphasia do indeed show poor comprehension.

A remarkable fact about people with Wernicke's aphasia is that they often seem unaware of their deficit. That is, they do not appear to recognize that their speech is faulty, nor do they recognize that they cannot understand the speech of others. They do not look puzzled when someone tells them something, even though they obviously cannot understand what they hear. Perhaps their comprehension deficit prevents them from realizing that what they say and hear makes no sense. They still follow social conventions, taking turns in conversation with the examiner, even though they do not understand what the examiner says — and what they say in return makes little sense. They remain sensitive to the other person's facial expression and tone of voice and begin talking when he or she asks a question and pauses for an answer. One patient with Wernicke's aphasia made the following responses when asked to name ten common objects:

> *toothbrush* ⟶ "stoktery," *cigarette* ⟶ "cigarette," *pen* ⟶ "tankt," *knife* ⟶ "nike," *fork* ⟶ "fahk," *quarter* ⟶ "minkt," *pen* ⟶ "spentee," *matches* ⟶ "senktr," *key* ⟶ "seek," *comb* ⟶ "sahk."

He acted sure of himself and gave no indication that he recognized that most of his responses were meaningless. The responses he made were not simply new words that he had invented; he was asked several times to name the objects and gave different responses each time (except for *cigarette,* which he always named correctly).

Even when patients recognize that something is wrong, they appear unsure of what the problem is. The following quotation illustrates this puzzlement.

> *Examiner:* Can you tell me a little bit about why you're here?
> *Patient:* I don't know whata wasa down here for me, I just don't know why I wasn't with up here, at all you, it was neva, had it been walked me today ta died.
> *Examiner:* Uh huh. Okay.
> *Patient:* Sine just don't know why, what is really wrong, I don't know, cause I can eaten treffren eatly an everythin like that I'm all right at home. (Kertesz, 1980)

The patient appears to recognize that she has a problem of some kind, but she is also saying (I think) that at home she can prepare her own meals and otherwise take care of herself.

WERNICKE'S APHASIA: ANALYSIS

Because the superior temporal gyrus is a region of auditory association cortex, and because a comprehension deficit is so prominent in Wernicke's aphasia, this disorder has been characterized as a *receptive* aphasia. Some investigators have suggested Wernicke's area is the location of *memories of the sequences of sounds that constitute words.* Thus, the auditory association cortex of the superior temporal gyrus recognizes the sounds of words, just as the visual association cortex of the inferior temporal gyrus recognizes the sight of objects.

Evidence obtained from studies of patients using CT and MRI scans suggests that this conclusion is correct (Kertesz, 1979; Damasio, 1981). But why should damage to an area responsible for the ability to recognize spoken words disrupt people's ability to speak? In fact, it does not; Wernicke's aphasia—like Broca's aphasia—actually appears to consist of several deficits. The abilities that are disrupted include *recognition of spoken words, comprehension of the meaning of words,* and the *ability to convert thoughts into words.* Let us consider each of these abilities in turn.

Recognition: Pure Word Deafness. As I said in the introduction to this section, *recognizing* a word is not the same as *comprehending* it. If you hear a foreign word several times, you will learn to recognize it; but unless someone tells you what it means, you will not comprehend it. Recognition is a perceptual task; comprehension involves retrieval of additional information from memory.

pure word deafness

Damage to the left temporal lobe can produce a disorder of auditory word recognition, uncontaminated by other problems. This syndrome, called **pure word deafness,** was described in the Prologue. Although people with pure word deafness are not deaf, they cannot understand speech. As one patient put it, "I can hear you talking, I just can't understand what you're saying." Another said, "It's as if there were a bypass somewhere, and my ears were not connected to my voice" (Saffran, Marin, and Yeni-Komshian, 1976, p. 211). These patients can recognize nonspeech sounds such as the barking of a dog, the sound of a doorbell, the chirping of a bird, and so on. More significantly, their own speech is excellent. They can often understand what other people are saying by reading their lips. They can also read and write, and sometimes they ask people to communicate with them in writing. Clearly, pure word deafness is not an inability to comprehend the meaning of words; if it were, people with this disorder would not be able to read people's lips or read words written on paper.

Apparently, two types of brain injury can cause this disorder: disruption of auditory input to Wernicke's area or damage to Wernicke's area itself. Disruption of auditory input can be produced by bilateral damage to the primary auditory cortex, or it can be caused by damage to the white matter in the left temporal lobes that cuts axons bringing auditory information from the primary auditory cortex to Wernicke's area. (See ***Figure 13.4.***) Either type of damage—disruption of auditory input or damage to Wernicke's area—disrupts the analysis of the sounds of words and, hence, prevents people from recognizing other people's speech.

Comprehension: Transcortical Sensory Aphasia. The other symptoms of Wernicke's aphasia—failure to comprehend the meaning of words and inability to express thoughts in meaningful speech—appear to be produced by damage that extends

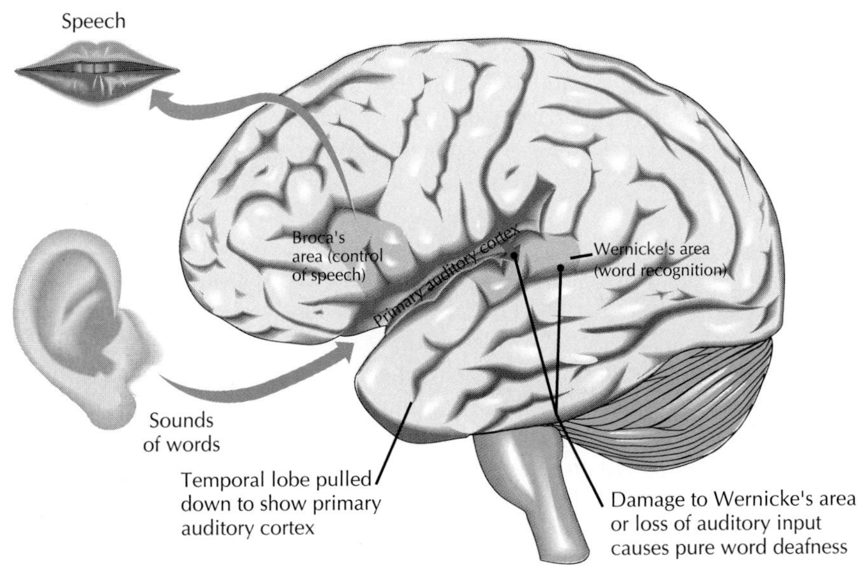

FIGURE 13.4

The brain damage that causes pure word deafness.

beyond Wernicke's area into the region just caudal to Wernicke's area, near the junction of the temporal, occipital, and parietal lobes. For want of a better term, I will refer to this region as the *posterior language area.* (See ***Figure 13.5.***) The posterior language area appears to serve as a place for interchanging information between the auditory representation of words and the meanings of these words, stored as memories in the rest of the sensory association cortex.

Damage to the posterior language area produces a disorder known as **transcortical sensory aphasia.** (See ***Figure 13.5.***) The difference between transcortical sensory aphasia and Wernicke's aphasia is that patients with this disorder *can repeat what*

transcortical sensory aphasia

FIGURE 13.5

The location of the posterior language area and an explanation of transcortical sensory aphasia.

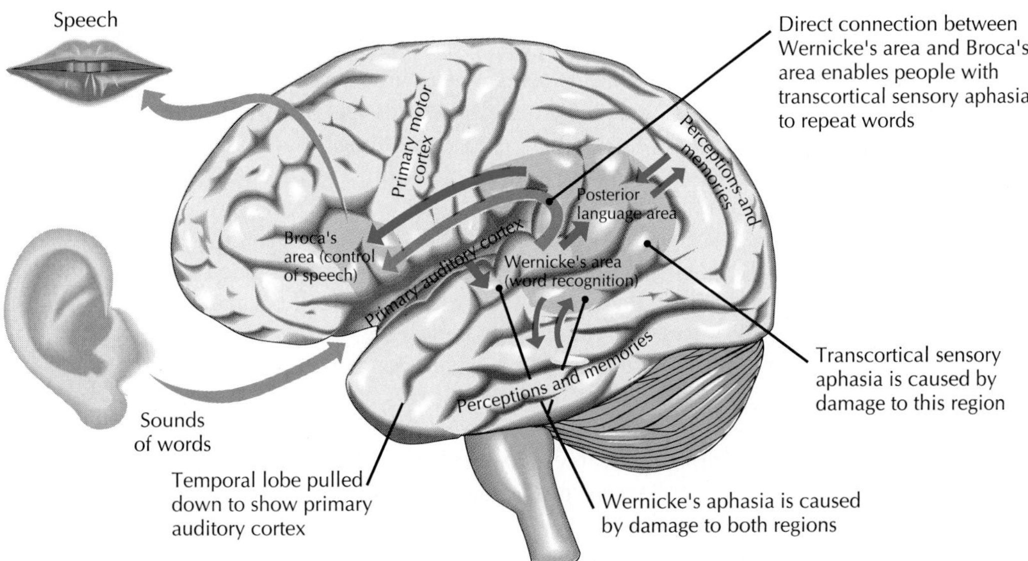

other people say to them; thus, they can recognize words. However, *they cannot comprehend the meaning of what they hear and repeat; nor can they produce meaningful speech of their own.* How can these people repeat what they hear? Because the posterior language area is damaged, repetition does not involve this part of the brain. Obviously, there must be a direct connection between Wernicke's area and Broca's area. (See ***Figure 13.5.***)

The fact that recognition and comprehension of speech require separate brain functions is illustrated dramatically by a case reported by Geschwind, Quadfasel, and Segarra (1968). The patient sustained extensive brain damage from carbon monoxide produced by a faulty water heater. (The damage included considerably more brain tissue than occurs in most cases of transcortical sensory aphasia, but it illustrates the distinction between the recognition and comprehension of speech.) The patient spent several years in the hospital before she died, without ever saying anything meaningful on her own. She did not follow verbal commands or otherwise give signs of understanding them. However, she often repeated what was said to her. The repetition was not parrotlike; she did not imitate accents different from her own, and if someone made a grammatical error while saying something to her, she sometimes repeated correctly, without the error. She could also recite poems if someone started them. For example, when an examiner said "Roses are red, violets are blue," she continued with "Sugar is sweet and so are you." She could sing and would do so when someone started singing a song she knew. She even learned new songs from the radio while in the hospital. Remember, though, that she gave *no signs of understanding anything she heard or said.* This disorder, along with pure word deafness, clearly confirm the conclusion that *recognizing* spoken words and *comprehending* them involve different brain mechanisms.

What Is Meaning? As we have seen, Wernicke's area is involved in the analysis of speech sounds and, thus, in the recognition of words. Damage to the posterior language area does not disrupt people's ability to recognize words, but it does disrupt their ability to understand them or to produce meaningful speech of their own. But what, exactly, do we mean by the word *meaning?* And what types of brain mechanisms are involved?

Words refer to objects, actions, or relations in the world. Thus, the meaning of a word is defined by particular memories associated with it. For example, knowing the meaning of the word *tree* means being able to imagine the physical characteristics of trees: what they look like, what the wind sounds like blowing through their leaves, what the bark feels like, and so on. It also means knowing facts about trees: about their roots, buds, flowers, nuts, wood, and the chlorophyll in their leaves. These memories are not stored in the primary speech areas but in other parts of the brain, especially regions of the association cortex. Different categories of memories may be stored in particular regions of the brain, but they are somehow tied together, so that hearing the word *tree* activates all of them. (As we saw in Chapter 12, the hippocampal formation is involved in this process of tying related memories together.)

In thinking of the brain's verbal mechanisms involved in recognizing words and comprehending their meaning, I find that the concept of a dictionary serves as a useful analogy. Dictionaries contain entries (the words) and definitions (the meanings of the words). In the brain we have at least two types of entries: auditory and visual. That is, we can look up a word according to how it sounds or looks (in writing). Let us just consider just one type of entry: the sound of a word. (I will discuss reading and writing later in this chapter.) We hear a familiar word and understand its meaning. How do we do so?

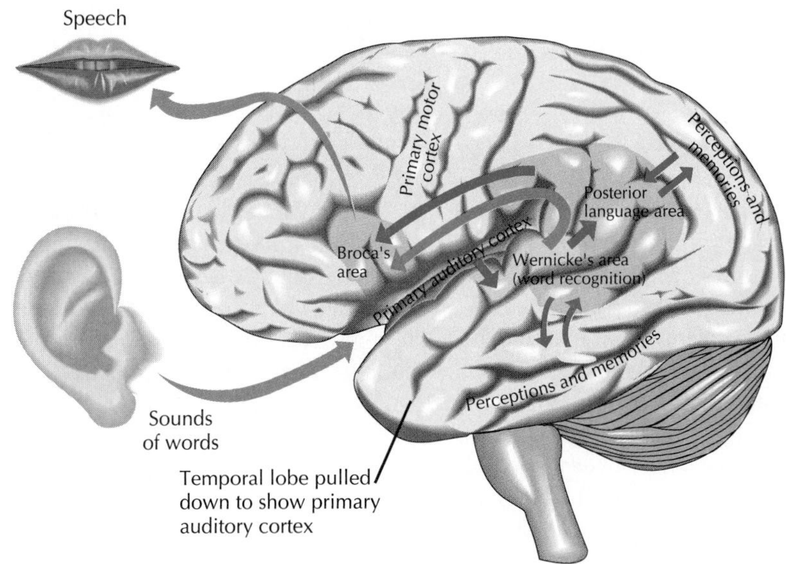

FIGURE 13.6

The "dictionary" in the brain. Wernicke's area contains the auditory entries of words; the meanings are contained as memories in the sensory association areas.

First, we must recognize the sequence of sounds that constitute the word—we find the auditory entry for the word in our "dictionary." As we saw, this entry appears in Wernicke's area. Next, the memories that constitute the meaning of the word must be activated. Presumably, Wernicke's area is connected—through the posterior language area—with the neural circuits that contain these memories. (See ***Figure 13.6.***)

The process works in reverse when we describe our thoughts or perceptions in words. Suppose we want to tell someone about a tree that we just planted in our lawn. Thoughts about the tree (for example, a visual image of it) occur in our association cortex—the visual association cortex, in this example. Information about the activity of these circuits is sent first to the posterior language area and then to Broca's area, which causes the words to be set into a grammatical sentence and pronounced. (See ***Figure 13.6.***)

What evidence do we have that meanings of words are represented by neural circuits in various regions of association cortex? The best evidence comes from the fact that damage to particular regions of the sensory association cortex can damage particular kinds of information and thus abolish particular kinds of meanings. For example, I met a patient who had recently had a stroke that damaged a part of her right parietal lobe that played a role in spatial perception. She was alert and intelligent and showed no signs of aphasia. However, she was confused about directions and other spatial relations. When asked to, she could point to the ceiling and the floor, but she could not say which was *over* the other. Her perception of other people appeared to be normal, but she could not say whether a person's head was at the *top* or *bottom* of the body.

I wrote a set of multiple-choice questions to test her ability to use words denoting spatial relations. The results of the test indicated that she did not know the meaning of words such as *up, down,* or *under* when they referred to spatial relations, but she could use these words normally when they referred to nonspatial relations. For example, here are some of her incorrect responses when the words referred to spatial relations:

A tree's branches are *under* its roots.
The sky is *down.*
The ceiling is *under* the floor.

She made only ten correct responses on the sixteen-item test. In contrast, she got all eight items correct when the words referred to nonspatial relations like the following:

After exchanging pleasantries, they got *down* to business.
He got sick and threw *up*.

Damage to part of the association cortex of the *left* parietal lobe can produce an inability to name the body parts. (The disorder is called *autotopagnosia,* or "poor knowledge of one's own topography." A better name would have been *autotopanomia,* "poor naming of one's own topography.") People who can otherwise converse normally cannot reliably point to their elbow, knee, or cheek when asked to do so and cannot name body parts when the examiner points to them. However, they have no difficulty understanding the meaning of other words.

Other investigators have reported verbal deficits that include disruption of particular categories of meaning. For example, McCarthy and Warrington (1988) reported the case of a man with left temporal lobe damage (patient T.B.) who was unable to explain the meaning of words that denoted living things. For example, when he was asked to define the word *rhinoceros,* he said, "Animal, can't give you any functions." However, when he was shown a *picture* of a rhinoceros, he said, "Enormous, weighs over one ton, lives in Africa." Similarly, when asked what a *dolphin* was, he said, "A fish or a bird"; but he responded to a *picture* of a dolphin by saying "Dolphin lives in water . . . they are trained to jump up and come out . . . In America during the war years they started to get this particular animal to go through to look into ships." When patient T.B. was asked to define the meanings of words that denoted inanimate objects such as lighthouses or wheelbarrows, he had no trouble at all.

The case of patient T.B. raises some interesting issues. His brain damage appears not to have destroyed his knowledge of living things, because once the circuits concerning the information are activated by showing him a picture, he can describe that information very well. But the damage does appear to have disconnected the neural circuits that analyze the sounds of words from the neural circuits that contain that information. Are the connections *from* speech areas *to* the circuits containing the information different from connections going in the opposite direction? And is information about living and nonliving things contained in different parts of the brain? We will need much more information to answer these questions.

Repetition: Conduction Aphasia. As we saw earlier in this section, the fact that people with transcortical sensory aphasia can repeat what they hear suggests that there is a direct connection between Wernicke's area and Broca's area—and there is, the **arcuate fasciculus** ("arch-shaped bundle"). This bundle of axons conveys information about the *sounds* of words but not their *meanings.* The best evidence for this conclusion comes from a syndrome known as conduction aphasia, which is produced by damage to the inferior parietal lobe that extends into the subcortical white matter and damages the arcuate fasciculus (Damasio and Damasio, 1980).

arcuate fasciculus

Conduction aphasia is characterized by meaningful, fluent speech; relatively good comprehension; but very poor repetition. For example, the spontaneous speech of patient L.B. (observed by Margolin and Walker, 1981) was excellent; he made very few errors and had no difficulty naming objects. But let us see how patient L.B. performed when he was asked to repeat words.

conduction aphasia

Examiner: bicycle
Patient: bicycle

Examiner: hippopotamus
Patient: hippopotamus
Examiner: blaynge
Patient: I didn't get it.
Examiner: Okay, some of these won't be real words, they'll just be sounds. Blaynge.
Patient: I'm not . . .
Examiner: blanch
Patient: blanch
Examiner: north
Patient: north
Examiner: rilld
Patient: Nope, I can't say.

You will notice that the patient can repeat individual words (all nouns, in this case) but utterly fails to repeat nonwords. People with conduction aphasia can repeat speech sounds they hear *only if these sounds have meaning.*

Sometimes, when a person with conduction aphasia is asked to repeat a word, he or she says a word with the same meaning — or at least, one that is related. For example, if the examiner says *house,* the patient may say "home." If the examiner says *chair,* the patient may say "sit." One patient made the following response when asked to repeat an entire sentence:

Examiner: The auto's leaking gas tank soiled the roadway.
Patient: The car's tank leaked and made a mess on the street.

The symptoms seen in transcortical sensory aphasia and conduction aphasia lead to the conclusion that there are pathways that connect the speech mechanisms of the temporal lobe with those of the frontal lobe. The direct pathway through the arcuate fasciculus simply conveys speech sounds to the frontal lobes. We use this pathway to repeat unfamiliar words — for example, when we are learning a foreign language or trying to repeat a nonword such as *blaynge.* The second pathway is indirect and is based on the *meaning* of words, not the sounds they make. When patients with conduction aphasia hear a word or a sentence, the meaning of what they hear evokes some sort of image related to that meaning. (For example, the patient in the second example presumably "saw" an automobile leaking fuel onto the pavement.) They are then able to describe that image, just as they would put their own thoughts into words. Of course, the words they choose may not be the same ones that were used by the person who spoke to them. (See ***Figure 13.7.***)

MEMORY OF WORDS: ANOMIC APHASIA

As I already noted, anomia, in one form or other, is a hallmark of aphasia. However, one category of aphasia consists of almost pure anomia, the other symptoms being inconsequential. Speech of patients with anomic aphasia is fluent and grammatical, and their comprehension is excellent, but they have difficulty finding the appropriate words. They often employ **circumlocutions** (literally, "to speak in a roundabout way") to get around missing words. For example, the following quotation is from a patient that some colleagues and I studied (Margolin, Marcel, and Carlson, 1985). We asked her to describe the picture shown in ***Figure 13.8.*** Her pauses, which are marked with three dots, indicate word-finding difficulties. In some cases, when she could not find a word, she supplied a definition instead or went off on a new track. I have added the words in brackets that I think she intended to use.

circumlocution

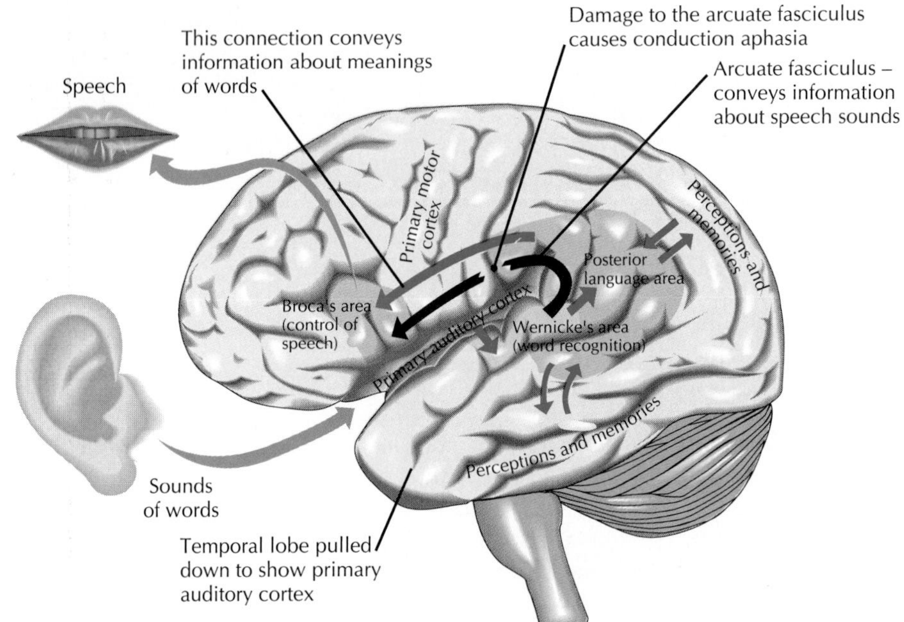

FIGURE 13.7

A hypothetical explanation of conduction aphasia. A lesion that damages the arcuate fasciculus disrupts transmission of auditory information, but not information related to meaning, to the frontal lobe. The color arrows represent the flow of information as a patient hears a sentence, understands it, and then says it back, in his or her own words.

Examiner: Tell us about that picture.

Patient: It's a woman who has two children, a son and a daughter, and her son is to get into the . . . cupboard in the kitchen to get out [*take*] some . . . cookies out of the [*cookie jar*] . . . that she possibly had made, and consequently he's slipping [*falling*] . . . the wrong direction [*backward*] . . . on the . . . what he's standing on [*stool*], heading to the . . . the cupboard [*floor*] and if he falls backwards he could have some problems [*get hurt*], because that [*the stool*] is off balance.

The patient's anomia was most obvious when we asked her to name pictures of common objects. When a person talks spontaneously, he or she has more flexibility in choosing words. If the person has difficulty finding a word to express a particular

FIGURE 13.8

The drawing of the kitchen story, part of the Boston Diagnostic Aphasia Test. (From Goodglass, H., and Kaplan, E. *The Assessment of Aphasia and Related Disorders.* Philadelphia: Lea & Febiger, 1972. Reprinted with permission.)

thought, he or she can either find a circumlocution or change the subject. But when confronted with a picture, the person must find a particular word, and failure to do so is obvious. On one occasion she correctly named only fourteen of a list of fifty of them. Here is her attempt to name a picture of a carpenter's saw. Note that she tried to remember the word by starting sentences that would use it. She almost, but not quite, got the word. Clearly, she knows what the object is, so her deficit is not one of perception or comprehension.

> *Patient:* I know what it is. I can't tell you — maybe I can. If I was to carry the wood and cut it in half with that . . . you know, if I had to cut the wood down and bring it in . . .
>
> *Examiner:* You'd use one of these?
>
> *Patient:* It's called a . . . I have 'em in the garage. They are your . . . You cut the wood with them . . . it . . . sah! . . . ah . . . Ss . . . sahbing . . . sah . . . I can't say it. I know what it is and I can cut the wood with it and it's in my garage. . . .

Anomia has been characterized as a partial amnesia for words. It can be produced by lesions in either the anterior or posterior regions of the brain (that is, lesions that include Broca's area or Wernicke's area), but only posterior lesions produce a *fluent* anomia. Little is known about the precise location of lesions that produce anomia without the other symptoms of aphasia, such as comprehension deficits, agrammatism, or difficulties in articulation, except that they generally occur in the left temporal or parietal lobe, usually sparing Wernicke's area. In the case of the woman described above, the damage included the middle and inferior temporal gyri, which includes an important region of the visual association cortex. Because her right hemisphere was undamaged, she did not have visual agnosia (a deficit of visual perception described in Chapter 5). Obviously, when we learn more about the anatomy of pure anomia, we will know more about the anatomy of verbal memories.

The picture I have drawn so far suggests that comprehension of speech includes a flow of information from Wernicke's area to the posterior language area to the sensory association cortex. Production of spontaneous speech involves the flow of information concerning perceptions and memories to the posterior language area to Broca's area. This model is certainly an oversimplification, but it is a useful starting point in conceptualizing basic mental processes. For example, thinking in words probably involves two-way communication between the speech areas and surrounding association cortex (and subcortical regions such as the hippocampus, of course).

Prosody: Rhythm, Tone, and Emphasis in Speech

When we speak, we do not merely utter words. Our speech has a regular rhythm and cadence; we give some words stress (that is, pronounce them louder), and we vary the pitch of our voice to indicate phrasing and to distinguish between assertions and questions. In addition, we can impart information about our emotional state through the rhythm, emphasis, and tone of our speech. These rhythmic, emphatic, and melodic aspects of speech are referred to as **prosody.** The importance of these aspects of speech is illustrated by our use of punctuation symbols to indicate some elements of prosody when we write. For example, a comma indicates a short pause; a period indicates a longer one with an accompanying fall in the pitch of the voice; a question mark indicates a pause and a rise in the pitch of the voice; an exclamation mark indicates that the words are articulated with special emphasis; and so on.

prosody

The prosody of people with fluent aphasias, caused by posterior lesions, sounds normal. Their speech is rhythmical, pausing after phrases and sentences, and has a melodic line. Even when the speech of a person with severe Wernicke's aphasia makes no sense, the prosody sounds normal. As Goodglass and Kaplan (1972) note, a person with Wernicke's aphasia may "sound like a normal speaker at a distance, because of his fluency and normal melodic contour of his speech." (Up close, of course, we hear the speech clearly enough to realize that it is meaningless.) In contrast, just as the lesions that produce Broca's aphasia destroy grammar, they also severely disrupt prosody. In patients with Broca's aphasia articulation is so labored and words are uttered so slowly that there is little opportunity for the patient to demonstrate any rhythmic elements; and because of the relative lack of function words, there is little variation in stress or pitch of voice.

Evidence from studies of normal people and patients with brain lesions suggests that prosody is a special function of the right hemisphere. This function is undoubtedly related to the more general role of this hemisphere in musical skills and the expression and recognition of emotions; production of prosody is rather like singing, and prosody often serves as a vehicle for conveying emotion.

Weintraub, Mesulam, and Kramer (1981) tested the ability of patients with right-hemisphere damage to recognize and express prosodic elements of speech. In one experiment they showed their subjects two pictures, named one of them, and asked them to point to the appropriate one. For example, they showed them a picture of a greenhouse and a house that was painted green. In speech we distinguish between *greenhouse* and *green house* by stress: *GREEN house* means the former and *GREEN HOUSE* (syllables equally stressed) means the latter. In a second experiment Weintraub and her colleagues tested the subjects' ability simply to detect differences in prosody. They presented pairs of sentences and asked the subjects whether they were the same or different. The pairs of sentences either were identical or differed in terms of intonation (for example, *Margo plays the piano?* and *Margo plays the piano*) or location of stress (for example, *STEVE drives the car* and *Steve drives the CAR*). The patients with right-hemisphere lesions (but not control subjects) performed poorly on both of these tasks. Thus, they showed a deficit in prosodic comprehension.

To test production, the investigators presented two written sentences and asked a question about them. For example, they presented the following pair:

> The man walked to the grocery store.
> The woman rode to the shoe store.

The subjects were instructed to answer questions by reading one of the sentences. Try this one yourself. Read the question below and then read aloud the sentence (above) that answers it.

> Who walked to the grocery store, the man or the woman?

The question asserts that someone walked to the grocery store but asks who that person was. When answering a question like this, people normally stress the requested item of information—in this case they say, "The *man* walked to the grocery store." However, Weintraub and her colleagues found that although patients with right-hemisphere brain damage chose the correct sentence, they either failed to stress a word or stressed the wrong one. Thus, the right hemisphere plays a role in production as well as perception of prosody.

▶INTERIM SUMMARY◀

Two regions of the brain are especially important in understanding and producing speech. Wernicke's area, in the posterior superior temporal lobe, is involved with speech perception. The region just adjacent to Wernicke's area, which I have called the posterior language area, is necessary for speech comprehension and the translation of thoughts into words. Broca's area, in the frontal lobe just rostral to the region of the primary motor cortex that controls the muscles of speech, is involved with speech production. This region contains memories of the sequences of muscular movements that produce words, each of which is connected with its auditory counterpart in the posterior part of the brain. Presumably, Wernicke's area contains memories of the sounds of words, each of which is connected through the posterior speech area with memories about the properties of the things the words denote. The fact that people with transcortical sensory aphasia can repeat words they cannot understand suggests that there is a direct connection between Wernicke's area and Broca's area. Indeed, there is — the arcuate fasciculus — and damage to this bundle of axons produces conduction aphasia.

The meanings of words are our memories of objects, actions, and other concepts associated with them. These meanings are memories and are stored in the association cortex, not in the speech areas themselves. Damage to specific regions of the association cortex effectively "erases" some categories of the meanings of words.

Prosody includes changes in intonation, rhythm, and stress that add meaning, to the sentences that we speak. The neural mechanisms that control the prosodic elements of speech appear to be in the right hemisphere.

Because so many terms and symptoms were described in this section, I have provided a table that summarizes them. (See ***Table 13.1.***) ▲

▲ TABLE 13.1 ▲

Disorder	*Area of Lesion*	*Spontaneous Speech*	*Speech Comprehension*	*Repetition*	*Naming*	*Reading Comprehension*	*Writing*
Wernicke's aphasia	Posterior portion of superior temporal gyrus (Wernicke's area) plus region posterior to it	Fluent	Poor	Poor	Poor	Poor	Poor
Pure word deafness	Wernicke's area or axons supplying auditory input	Fluent	Poor	Poor	Good	Good	Good
Broca's aphasia	Frontal cortex rostral to base of primary motor cortex (Broca's area)	Nonfluent	Good	Poor	Poor	Good	Poor
Conduction aphasia	Axons connecting Wernicke's area with Broca's area	Fluent	Good	Poor	Good	Good to poor	Good
Anomic aphasia	Various parts of parietal or temporal lobes	Fluent	Good	Good	Poor	Good to poor	Good to poor
Transcortical sensory aphasia	Region posterior to Wernicke's area	Nonfluent or even absent	Poor	Good	Poor	Poor	Poor

You will recall from Chapter 5 that visual agnosia is a perceptual deficit in which people with bilateral damage to the visual association cortex cannot recognize objects by sight. Patients with pure alexia do *not* have visual agnosia; they can recognize objects and supply their names. Similarly, people with visual agnosia can still read. Thus, the perceptual analysis of objects and words requires different mechanisms. I find this fact both interesting and puzzling. Certainly, the ability to read cannot have had an effect on the evolution of the human brain, because the invention of writing is only a few thousand years old, and until very recently, the vast majority of the world's population was illiterate. Thus, reading and object recognition use brain mechanisms that undoubtedly existed even before the invention of writing. What is the nature of these mechanisms? What features of the world around us require analysis similar to the analysis we use to recognize objects versus words?

Toward an Understanding of Reading

Most investigators believe that reading involves at least two different processes: direct recognition of the word as a whole, and sounding it out letter by letter. When we see a familiar word, we normally recognize it by its shape and pronounce it—a process known as **whole-word reading.** (With very long words we might instead perceive segments of several letters each.) The second method, which we use for unfamiliar words, requires recognition of individual letters and knowledge of the sounds they make. This process is known as **phonetic reading.** (See ***Figure 13.11.***)

whole-word reading

phonetic reading

Evidence for our ability to sound out words is easy to obtain. In fact, you can prove to yourself that phonetic reading exists by trying to read the following words:

glab trisk chint

Well, as you could see, they are not really words, but I doubt that you had trouble pronouncing them. Obviously, you did not *recognize* them, because you probably never saw them before. Therefore, you had to use what you know about the sounds that are represented by particular letters (or groups of letters, such as *ch*) to figure out how to pronounce the words.

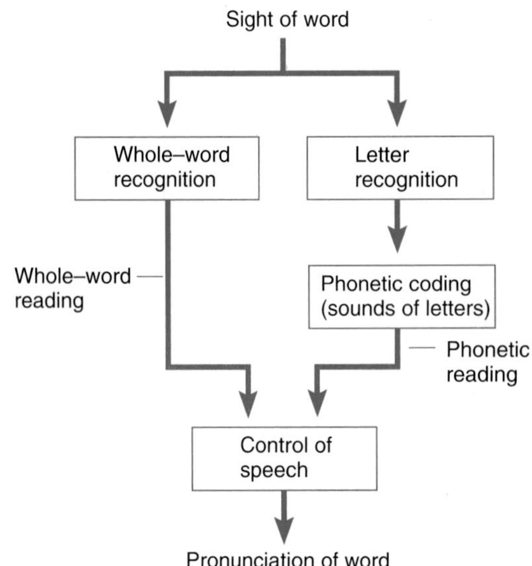

FIGURE 13.11

A simplified model of the reading process, showing whole-word and phonetic reading. Whole-word reading is used for most familiar words; phonetic reading is used for unfamiliar words and for nonwords such as *glab, trisk,* or *chint.*

The best evidence that proves that people can read words without sounding them out, using the whole-word method, comes from studies of patients with dyslexias. (*Dyslexia* means "faulty reading." *Acquired* dyslexias are those caused by damage to the brains of people who already know how to read. In contrast, *developmental* dyslexias refer to reading difficulties that become apparent when children are learning to read. Developmental dyslexias may involve anomalies in brain circuitry, and they are discussed in a later section.)

Although investigators have reported several types of acquired dyslexias, I will mention only three of them here. **Word-form dyslexia** is a fairly common disorder (Warrington and Shallice, 1980). Although patients with word-form dyslexia cannot immediately recognize words, they can read them if they are permitted to name the individual letters. Thus, they read slowly, taking more time with longer words. As you might expect, they can identify words that someone else spells aloud, just as they can recognize their own oral spelling.

word-form dyslexia

Warrington and Shallice suggested the term *word-form* dyslexia because they concluded that these patients have a type of perceptual deficit: They are unable to recognize words as a whole. In fact, sometimes the deficit is so severe that patients have difficulty identifying individual letters, in which case they make mistakes in spelling that prevent them from reading test words. For example, a patient studied by Patterson and Kay (1980) was shown the word *men* and said, "h, e, n, hen."

Patients with **phonological dyslexia** can read most familiar words but have great difficulty reading nonwords such as the ones I recently asked you to try to pronounce (Beauvois and Dérouesné, 1979; Dérouesné and Beauvois, 1979). (*Phonology*—loosely translated as "laws of sound"—refers to the relation between letters and the sounds they represent.) Phonological dyslexia provides further evidence that whole-word reading and phonological reading involve different brain mechanisms. Phonological reading, which is the only way we can read nonwords or words we have not yet learned, entails some sort of letter-to-sound decoding. Obviously, phonological reading of English requires more than decoding of the sounds produced by single letters, because, for example, some sounds are transcribed as two-letter sequences (such as *th* or *sh*) and the addition of the letter *e* to the end of a word lengthens an internal vowel (*can* becomes *cane*). People with phonological dyslexia have lost the ability to read phonetically. (See ***Figure 13.11.***)

phonological dyslexia

The Japanese language provides a particularly interesting distinction between phonetic and whole-word reading. The Japanese language makes use of two kinds of written symbols. *Kanji* symbols are pictographs, adopted from the Chinese language (although they are pronounced as Japanese words). Thus, they represent concepts by means of visual symbols but do not provide a guide to their pronunciation. Reading words expressed in kanji symbols is analogous, then, to whole-word reading. *Kana* symbols are phonetic representations of syllables; thus, they encode acoustical information. Reading words expressed in kana symbols is obviously phonetic.

Studies of Japanese people with localized brain damage have shown that the reading of kana and kanji symbols involves different brain mechanisms (Iwata, 1984). In general, damage to the posterior parietal lobe produces dyslexia for kanji symbols, and damage to the posterior temporal lobe produces dyslexia for kana symbols.

As we saw earlier in this chapter, recognizing a spoken word is different from understanding it; patients with transcortical sensory aphasia can repeat what is said to them but show no signs of understanding what they hear or say. The same is true for reading. **Direct dyslexia** resembles transcortical sensory aphasia, except that the words in question are written, not spoken (Schwartz, Marin, and Saffran, 1979; Lytton

direct dyslexia

and Brust, 1989). Patients with direct dyslexia are able to read aloud *even though they cannot understand the words they are saying.* After sustaining a stroke that damaged his left frontal and temporal lobes, Lytton and Brust's patient lost the ability to communicate verbally; his speech was meaningless and he was unable to comprehend what other people said to him. However, he could read words with which he was already familiar. He could *not* read pronounceable nonwords; thus, he had lost the ability to read phonetically. His comprehension deficit seemed complete; when the investigators presented him with a word and several pictures, one of which corresponded to the word, he read the word correctly but had no idea what picture went with it.

Toward an Understanding of Writing

Writing depends on knowledge of the words that are to be used, along with the proper grammatical structure of the sentences they are to form. Thus, if a patient is unable to express himself or herself by speech, we should not be surprised to see a writing disturbance as well.

One type of writing disorder involves difficulties in motor control — in directing the movements of a pen or pencil to form letters and words. Such a disorder may have much to tell us about the organization of the motor system, but it will not help us understand the organization of language. For this reason I will restrict my discussion to writing disorders that impair people's abilities to *spell* words, not simply to make accurate movements with their fingers.

When children acquire language skills, they first learn the sounds of words, then learn to say them, then learn to read, and then learn to write. Undoubtedly, reading and writing depend heavily on the skills that are learned earlier. For example, in order to write most words, we must be able to "sound them out in our heads," that is, to hear them and to articulate them subvocally. If you want to demonstrate this to yourself, try to write a long word such as *antidisestablishmentarianism* from memory and see whether you can do it without saying the word to yourself. If you recite a poem or sing a song to yourself under your breath at the same time, you will see that the writing comes to a halt.

A second way of writing involves transcribing an image of what a particular word looks like — copying a visual mental image. Have you ever looked off into the distance to picture a word so that you can remember how to spell it? Some people are not very good at phonological spelling, and have to write some words down to see whether they look correct. This method obviously involves visual memories, not acoustical ones.

phonological dysgraphia

Neurological evidence supports these speculations. Brain damage can sometimes impair people's ability to write phonetically, a deficit called **phonological dysgraphia** (Shallice, 1981). (*Dysgraphia* refers to a writing deficit just as *dyslexia* refers to a reading deficit.) People with this disorder are unable to sound out words and write them phonetically. Thus, they cannot write nonsense words, such as the ones I presented in the section on reading. They can, however, imagine words visually and then write them.

orthographic dysgraphia

Orthographic dysgraphia is just the opposite — a disorder of visually based writing. People with orthographic dysgraphia can *only* sound words out; thus, they can spell regular words such as *care* or *tree* and they can write nonsense words. However, they have difficulty spelling irregular words such as *half* or *choir* (Beauvois and Dérouesné, 1981). In general, phonological dysgraphia (impaired phonological writing) is caused by damage to the superior temporal lobe, whereas orthographic dysgraphia (impaired visual, whole-word writing) is caused by damage to the inferior parietal lobe (Benson and Geschwind, 1985).

FIGURE 13.12

The writing of a Japanese patient with damage to the middle part of the corpus callosum. He could write both kanji and kana characters with his right hand, but he could not write kanji characters with his left hand (color). He could, however, *copy* kanji characters with his left hand if he was given a model to look at. (From Kawamura, M., Hirayama, K., and Yamamoto, H. *Brain,* 1989, *112,* 1011–1018. Reprinted with permission.)

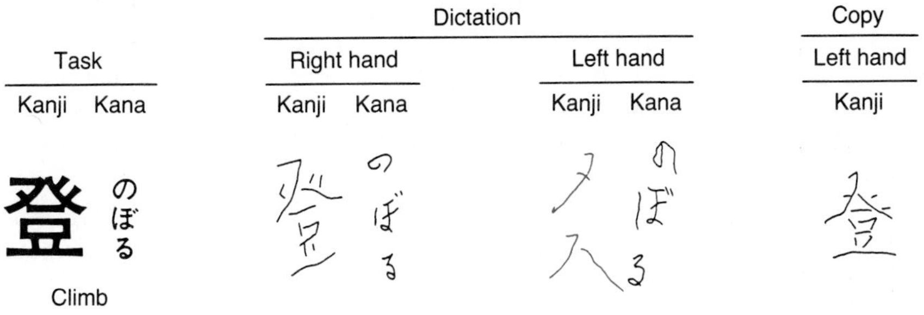

Task		Dictation				Copy
		Right hand		Left hand		Left hand
Kanji	Kana	Kanji	Kana	Kanji	Kana	Kanji
登	のぼる					
Climb						

Japanese patients show writing deficits similar to those of patients whose languages use the Roman alphabet; some patients have difficulty writing kana symbols, whereas others have difficulty with kanji symbols (Iwata, 1984). Kawamura, Hirayama, and Yamamoto (1989) reported a case of a man with damage to the middle part of the corpus callosum who could write kana symbols with both hands and could write kanji symbols with the right hand but not the left. He could *copy* kanji symbols with his left hand; he just could not write them down when the investigators dictated them to him. (See ***Figure 13.12.***) These results have interesting implications. Writing appears to be organized in the left hemisphere; that is, the information needed to specify the shape of the symbols is provided by circuits in this hemisphere. When a person uses his or her left hand to write these symbols, the information must be sent across the corpus callosum to the motor cortex of the right hemisphere, which controls the left hand. Apparently, information about the two forms of Japanese symbols is transmitted through different parts of the corpus callosum; the man's brain damage disrupted one of these pathways but not the other. (See ***Figure 13.13.***)

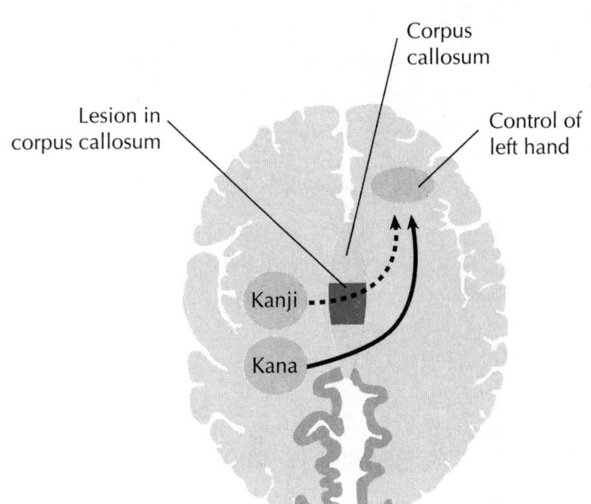

FIGURE 13.13

The role of the corpus callosum in Japanese writing. Information about kana and kanji characters apparently crosses different parts of the corpus callosum.

Developmental Dyslexias

Some children have great difficulty learning to read and never become fluent readers, even though they are otherwise intelligent. Specific language learning disorders, called **developmental dyslexias**, tend to occur in families, which suggests a genetic (and hence biological) component.

developmental dyslexia

Several studies (Galaburda and Kemper, 1979; Galaburda et al., 1985; Galaburda, 1988) have found evidence that brain abnormalities may be responsible for at least some cases of developmental dyslexia. The investigators obtained the brains of deceased people with histories of developmental dyslexia. In all cases they found abnormalities in the **planum temporale,** a part of Wernicke's area. Figure 13.14 shows a section through the left planum temporale of a normal person (a) and of a dyslexic accident victim (b). Notice the regular columnar arrangement of cells in the normal brain but not in the brain of the dyslexic accident victim. (See ***Figure 13.14.***) Galaburda and Kemper (1979) observed that certain cells apparently failed to migrate during development and were left in the location they occupied during an earlier fetal stage. Cortical neurons develop in the central core of the brain before the twentieth week of gestation and then migrate to the position they are to occupy in the mature brain (Rakic, 1972). In this case something apparently prevented normal migration of these cells.

planum temporale

Geschwind and Behan (1984) noted that investigators have long recognized that a disproportionate number of people with developmental dyslexias are also left-handed. Furthermore, clinical observations suggested a relation between left-handedness and various immune disorders. Therefore, Geschwind and Behan studied a group of left-handed and right-handed people to see whether the relations were statistically significant. They found that they were: The left-handed subjects were ten times more likely to

FIGURE 13.14

Photomicrographs of the left planum temporale (a portion of Wernicke's area). (a) Of a normal person. (b) Of a person with developmental dyslexia. Nissl stain. (Photographs courtesy of A. Galaburda.)

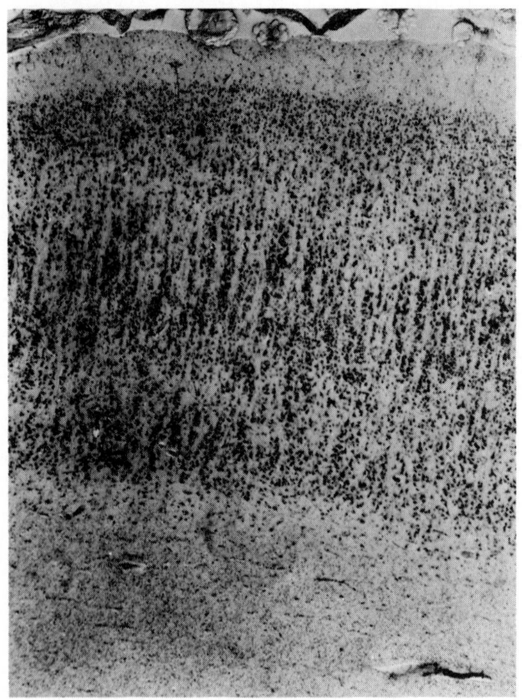

(a)

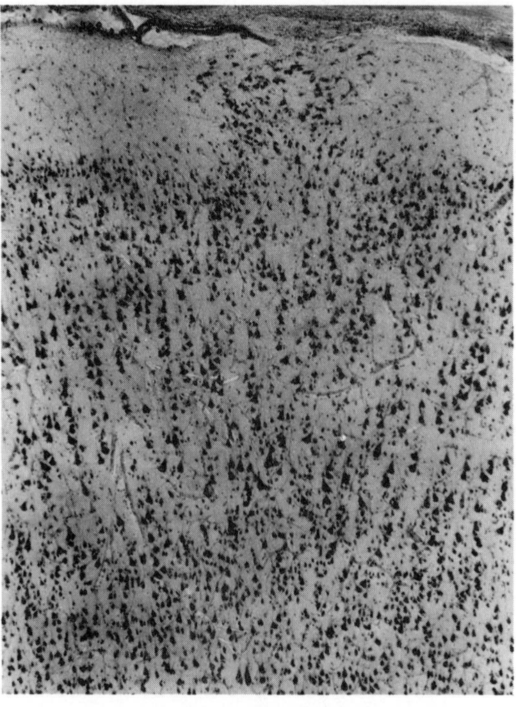

(b)

have specific learning disorders (10 percent versus 1 percent) and two and one-half times more likely to have immune disorders (8 percent versus 3 percent). The immune disorders included various thyroid and bowel diseases, diabetes, and rheumatoid arthritis. Of course, although the relation was statistically significant, it was not perfect. After all, most left-handed people are healthy and are good readers.

Geschwind and Behan suggested that left-handedness, developmental dyslexia, and immune disorders are causally related. They noted that although the superior temporal gyrus develops one to two weeks earlier on the right, the left superior temporal gyrus ultimately becomes larger (Chi, Dooling, and Gilles, 1977). In fact, slowing the rate of development may be the mechanism that causes the left language area to become larger than the corresponding region of the right hemisphere; by growing more slowly, it ultimately achieves a larger size. Perhaps dyslexia occurs when the development of the left hemisphere is suppressed so much that it fails to develop normally. The hypothesis is interesting, but much research has yet to be done to test it experimentally.

▶INTERIM SUMMARY◀

Brain damage can produce reading and writing disorders. All cases of aphasia are accompanied by writing deficits that parallel the speech production deficits and by reading deficits that parallel the speech comprehension deficits. The reading and writing abilities of a person with pure word deafness are generally good. The first reading and writing disorders to be identified that were not accompanied by aphasia were pure alexia and alexia with agraphia. Pure alexia is caused by lesions that produce blindness in the right visual field and that destroy fibers of the posterior corpus callosum. Alexia with agraphia is usually caused by lesions of the left angular gyrus.

Research in the past few decades has discovered that acquired reading disorders (dyslexias) can fall into one of several categories, and the study of these disorders has provided neuropsychologists and cognitive psychologists with thought-provoking information that has helped them understand how normal people read. Phonological dyslexia is the inability to read phonetically. Word-form dyslexia is a visual impairment that prevents recognition of whole words, although patients can read slowly by pronouncing the individual letters to themselves. Direct dyslexia is analogous to transcortical sensory aphasia; the patients can read words aloud but cannot understand what they are reading.

At least two different types of dysgraphia—phonological and orthographic—have been observed, which indicates that several different brain mechanisms are involved in the process of writing. Developmental dyslexia appears to involve abnormal development of parts of the brain that play a role in language. A better understanding of the components of reading and writing may help us develop effective teaching methods that will permit people with dyslexia to take advantage of the abilities that they do have. ▲

◀ EPILOGUE: Application

Mr. S., the man described in the Prologue, had pure word deafness. As you learned in this chapter, pure word deafness is a perceptual deficit that does not affect people's general language abilities; nor does it affect their ability to recognize nonspeech sounds.

As we saw in this chapter, pure word deafness is caused by lesions that damage Wernicke's area or prevent it from receiving auditory input. Thus, Wernicke's area appears to contain the neural network responsible for analyzing speech sounds. The auditory association cortex of the right hemisphere is apparently involved in perception of nonspeech sounds and of the prosodic elements of speech. Many patients with pure word deafness can recognize the emotion expressed by the intonation of speech even though they cannot understand what is being said. In addition, perception of the melodic and harmonic structure of music is accomplished by the right hemisphere; damage to this hemisphere can result in *amusia,* or loss of musical ability.

Hemispheric specialization in auditory function is not limited to the human brain. Heffner and Heffner (1990) reviewed a series of experiments from their laboratory indicating that the auditory system of the left hemisphere in monkeys plays a special role in recognizing vocal communications. Although Japanese macaques obviously cannot talk, they do have a repertoire of vocal calls that they use to communicate with each other. Heffner and Heffner found that lesions of the left auditory cortex produce a much more severe impairment than right-hemisphere lesions.

Exactly what do we mean when we say that the auditory system of the left hemisphere is specialized for the analysis of speech sounds? First, the specialization is only for the discrimination of the sounds that distinguish one word from another, not the sounds related to the prosodic aspects of speech. In general, the sounds that distinguish between words are very brief, whereas those that convey prosody are of longer duration. Perhaps the auditory system of the left hemisphere is simply specialized for the recognition of acoustical events of short duration.

In a review of the literature Phillips and Farmer (1990) suggest precisely this hypothesis. They note that careful studies of patients with pure word deafness have shown that the patients can distinguish between different vowels but not between different consonants—especially between different stop consonants, such as /t/, /d/, /k/, or /p/. (Linguists represent speech sounds by putting letters or special phonetic symbols between pairs of slashes.) Patients with pure word deafness *can* generally recognize consonants with a long duration, such as /s/, /z/, or /f/. (Say these consonants to yourself and you will see how different they sound.)

Phillips and Farmer note that the important acoustical events in speech sounds fall within a time range of a few milliseconds to a few tens of milliseconds. Speech sounds are made by rapidly moving lips, tongue, and soft palate, which can produce acoustical events that can be distinguished only by a fine-grained analysis. In contrast, most environmental sounds do not contain such a fine temporal structure. The authors also note that "pure" word deafness is not absolutely pure. That is, when people with this disorder are tested carefully with recordings of a variety of environmental sounds, they have difficulty recognizing at least some of them. Although *most* environmental sounds do not contain a fine temporal structure, some do—and patients have difficulty recognizing them.

Several studies have found deficits in auditory perception that support Phillips and Farmer's "temporal grain" hypothesis of pure word deafness. For example, normal subjects can perceive a series of clicks as being separate events when they are separated by only 1–3 msec; in contrast, patients with pure word deafness require a separation of 15–30 msec. In addition, although normal subjects can count clicks that are presented at a rate of up to 9–11 per second, patients with pure word deafness cannot count clicks presented faster than 2 per second. This perceptual difficulty shows up in recognition of nonspeech sounds in which the timing of brief events is important; one study reported that a patient with pure word deafness could no longer understand messages in Morse code, although he could still *send* messages that way. Thus, his deficit was perceptual, not motor.

Although more research needs to be done on hemispheric differences in the functions of the auditory system, the temporal grain hypothesis appears to be quite reasonable and has considerable support. Most investigators have focused on the linguistic aspects of language deficits produced by brain damage; it is clear that study of the brain mechanisms involved in the perceptual aspects of speech deserves attention, too. ▲

KEY CONCEPTS

Speech Production and Comprehension: Brain Mechanisms

- Broca's area, located in the left frontal lobe, is important in articulating words and producing and understanding grammatical constructions.
- Wernicke's area, located in the auditory association cortex of the left hemisphere, is important in recognizing the sounds of words.
- Comprehension of speech involves connections between Wernicke's area and memories that define words. These memories are located in the sensory association cortex, and the connections are made via the posterior language area.
- Conduction aphasia occurs when Wernicke's area and Broca's area can no longer communicate directly.

Reading and Writing Disorders

- Brain damage can produce a variety of reading and writing disorders. Study of these disorders is helping investigators discover the brain functions necessary for these behaviors.
- Reading takes two forms: whole-word and phonetic. Writing can be based on memories of the sounds the words make or their visual shape.
- Developmental dyslexia may be caused by abnormal development of the brain regions involved in language abilities.

NEW TERMS

agrammatism **p. 450**
alexia with agraphia **p. 464**
angular gyrus **p. 464**
anomia **p. 450**
aphasia **p. 448**
arcuate fasciculus **p. 458**
Broca's aphasia **p. 459**
Broca's area **p. 450**
cerebrovascular accident **p. 447**
circumlocution **p. 459**
conduction aphasia **p. 458**
content word **p. 449**
developmental dyslexia **p. 470**
direct dyslexia **p. 467**
function word **p. 449**
orthographic dysgraphia **p. 468**
phonetic reading **p. 466**
phonological dysgraphia **p. 468**
phonological dyslexia **p. 467**
planum temporale **p. 470**
prosody **p. 461**
pure alexia **p. 465**
pure word deafness **p. 454**
transcortical sensory aphasia **p. 455**
Wernicke's aphasia **p. 452**
Wernicke's area **p. 452**
whole-word reading **p. 466**
word-form dyslexia **p. 467**

SUGGESTED READINGS

Caplan, D. *Neurolinguistics and Linguistic Aphasiology.* Cambridge, England: Cambridge University Press, 1987.

Coltheart, M., Patterson, K., and Marshall, J.C. *Deep Dyslexia,* 2nd ed. London: Routledge and Kegan Paul, 1987.

Kertesz, A. *Localization in Neuropsychology.* New York: Academic Press, 1983.

Kolb, B., and Whishaw, I.Q. *Fundamentals of Human Neuropsychology,* 3rd ed. New York: W.H. Freeman, 1990.

Mesulam, M.-M. *Principles of Behavioral Neurology.* Philadelphia: F.A. Davis, 1985.

Plum, F. *Language, Communication, and the Brain.* New York: Raven Press, 1988.

14

CHAPTER OUTLINE

Neurological Disorders

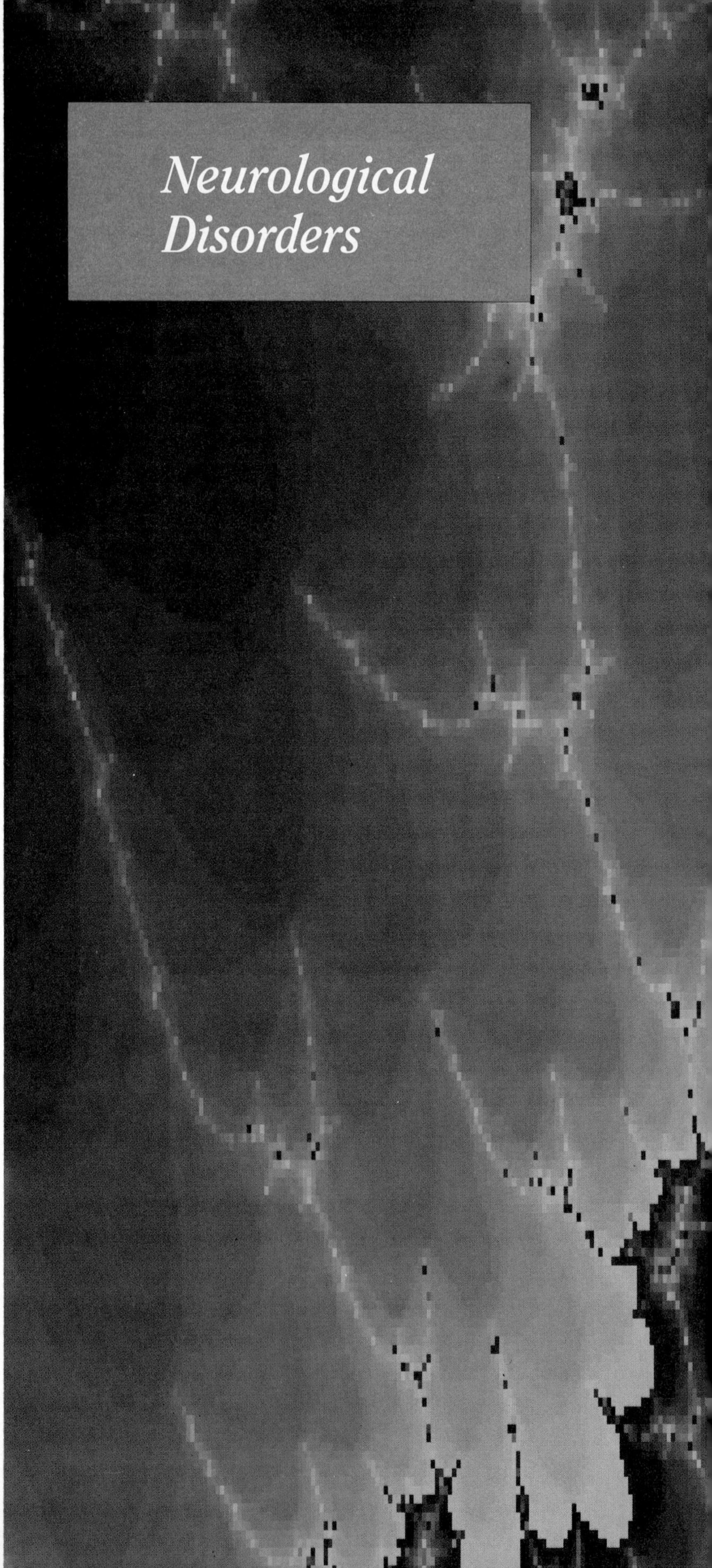

◀ PROLOGUE

Mrs. R., a divorced, fifty-year-old, elementary school teacher, was sitting in her car, waiting for the traffic light to change. Suddenly, her right foot began to shake. Afraid that she would inadvertently press the accelerator and lurch forward into the intersection, she quickly grabbed the shift lever and switched the transmission into neutral. Now her lower leg was shaking; then her upper leg, as well. With horrified fascination she felt her body, then her arm, begin to shake in rhythm with her leg. The shaking slowed and finally stopped. By this time the light had changed to green, and the cars behind her began honking at her. She missed that green light, but by the time the light changed again, she had recovered enough to put the car in gear and drive home.

Mrs. R. was frightened by her experience and tried in vain to think what she might have done to cause it. The next evening, some close friends visited her apartment for dinner. She found it hard to concentrate on their conversation and thought of telling them about her spell, but she finally decided not to bring the matter up. After dinner, while she was clearing the dishes off the table, her right foot began shaking again. This time she was standing up, and the contractions—much more violent than before—caused her to fall. Her friends, seated in the living room, heard the noise and came running to see what had happened. They saw Mrs. R. lying on the floor, her legs and arms held out stiffly before her, vibrating uncontrollably. Her head was thrown back and she seemed not to hear their anxious questions. The convulsion soon ceased; and less than a minute later, Mrs. R. regained consciousness but seemed dazed and confused.

Mrs. R. was brought by ambulance to a hospital; and after learning about her first spell and hearing her friends describe the convulsion, the emergency room physician immediately called a neurologist, who ordered a CT scan. The scan showed a small, circular white spot right where the neurologist expected it, between the frontal lobes, above the corpus callosum. Two days later, a neurosurgeon removed a small benign tumor, and Mrs. R. made an uneventful recovery.

When my colleagues and I met Mrs. R., we saw a pleasant, intelligent woman, much relieved to know that her type of brain tumor rarely produces brain damage if it is removed in time. Indeed, although we tested her carefully, we found no signs of intellectual impairment. ▲

Although the brain is the most protected organ, many pathological processes can damage it or disrupt its functioning. Because much of what we have learned about the functions of the human brain has been gained by studying people with brain damage, you have already encountered many neurological disorders in this book: movement disorders such as Parkinson's disease and apraxia; perceptual disorders such as visual agnosia and blindness caused by damage to the visual system; language disorders such as aphasia, alexia, and agraphia; and memory disorders such as Korsakoff's syndrome. This chapter describes the major categories of the neuropathological conditions that the brain can sustain—tumors, seizure disorders, cerebrovascular accidents, disorders of development, degenerative disorders, and disorders caused by infectious diseases—and discusses the behavioral effects of these conditions and their treatments.

TUMORS

malignant benign

A tumor is a mass of cells whose growth is uncontrolled and which serves no useful function. Some are **malignant**, or cancerous, and others are **benign** ("harmless"). The major distinction between malignancy and benignancy is whether the tumor is *encapsulated*: whether there is a distinct border between the mass of tumor cells and the surrounding tissue. If there is such a border, the tumor is benign; the surgeon can cut it out, and it will not regrow. If, however, the tumor grows by *infiltrating* the surrounding tissue, there will be no clear-cut border between the tumor and normal tissue. If the surgeon removes the tumor, some cells may be missed, and these cells will produce a new tumor. In addition, malignant tumors often give rise to **metastases**. A metastasizing tumor will shed cells, which then travel through the bloodstream, lodge in capillaries, and serve as seeds for the growth of new tumors in different locations of the body.

metastasis

Tumors damage brain tissue by two means: compression and infiltration. Obviously, *any* tumor growing in the brain, malignant or benign, can produce neurological symptoms and threaten the patient's life. Even a benign tumor occupies space and thus pushes against the brain. The compression can directly destroy brain tissue or can do so indirectly, by blocking the flow of cerebrospinal fluid and causing hydrocephalus. Even worse are malignant tumors, which cause both compression and infiltration. As a malignant tumor grows, it invades the surrounding region and destroys cells in its path. Figure 14.1 illustrates the compressive effect of a large nonmalignant tumor. As you can see, the tumor has displaced the lateral and third ventricles. (See ***Figure 14.1.***)

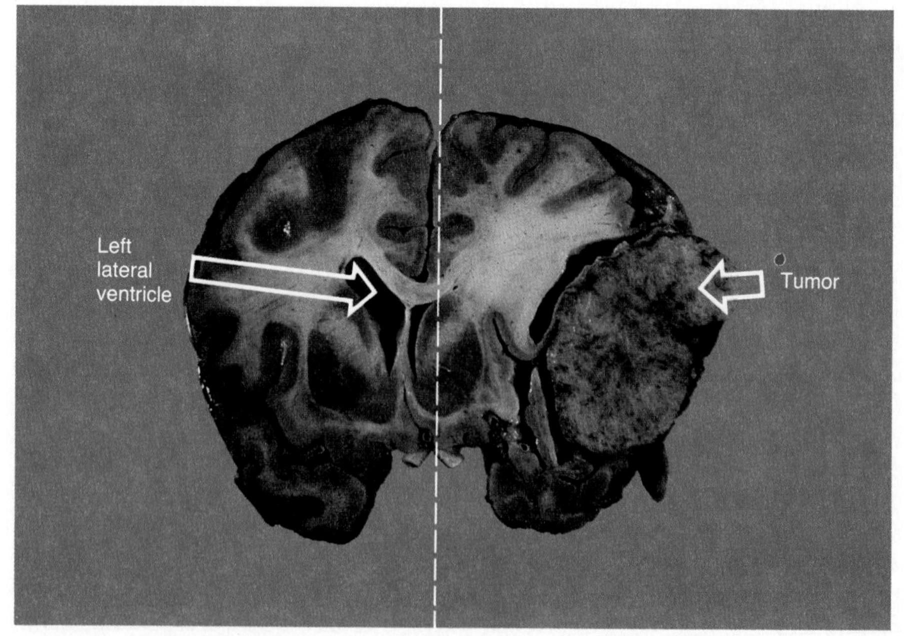

FIGURE 14.1

A slice of a human brain, showing how a large nonmalignant tumor (a meningioma) has displaced the right side of the brain toward the left. (The dotted line indicates the location of the midline.) The right lateral ventricle is almost completely occluded. (Courtesy of A. D'Agostino, Good Samaritan Hospital, Portland, Oregon.)

▲ TABLE 14.1 ▲

Types of Brain Tumors

Gliomas

Glioblastoma multiformae (poorly differentiated glial cells)

Astrocytoma (astrocytes)

Ependymoma (ependymal cells that line ventricles)

Medulloblastoma (cells in roof of the fourth ventricle)

Oligodendrocytoma (oliogodendroglial cells)

Meningioma (cells of the meninges)

Pituitary adenoma (hormone-secreting cells of the pituitary gland)

Neurinoma (Schwann cells or cells of connective tissue covering cranial nerves)

Metastatic carcinoma (depends on nature of primary tumor)

Angioma (cells of blood vessels)

Pinealoma (cells of pineal gland)

Tumors do not arise from nerve cells, which are not capable of dividing. Instead, they arise from other cells found in the brain or from metastases originating elsewhere in the body. The most common types are listed in Table 14.1. (See ***Table 14.1.***) The most serious types of tumors are metastases and the **gliomas** (derived from various types of glial cells), which are usually very malignant and fast growing. Figures 14.2 and 14.3 show gliomas located in the basal ganglia and the pons, respectively. (See ***Figures 14.2 and 14.3.***) Figure 14.4 shows an ependymoma in the lateral ventricles. (See ***Figure 14.4.***) Some tumors are sensitive to radiation and can be destroyed by a beam of radiation focused on them. Usually, a neurosurgeon first removes as much of the tumor as possible, and then the remaining cells are targeted by the radiation.

glioma

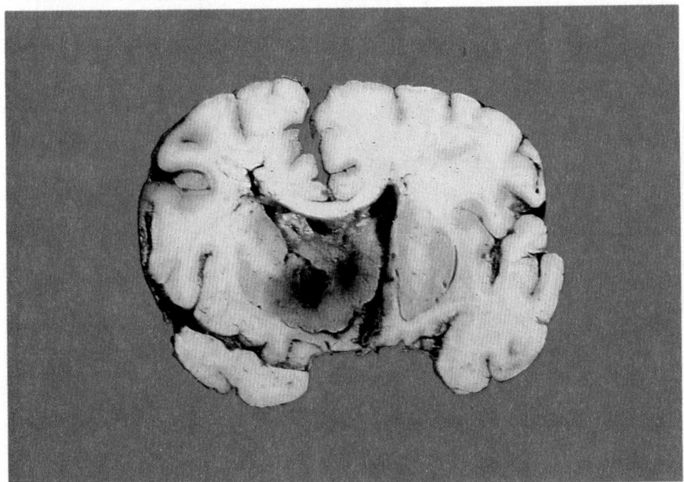

FIGURE 14.2

A slice of a human brain, showing a large glioma located in the basal ganglia, which has invaded both the left and right lateral ventricles. (Courtesy of A. D'Agostino, Good Samaritan Hospital, Portland, Oregon.)

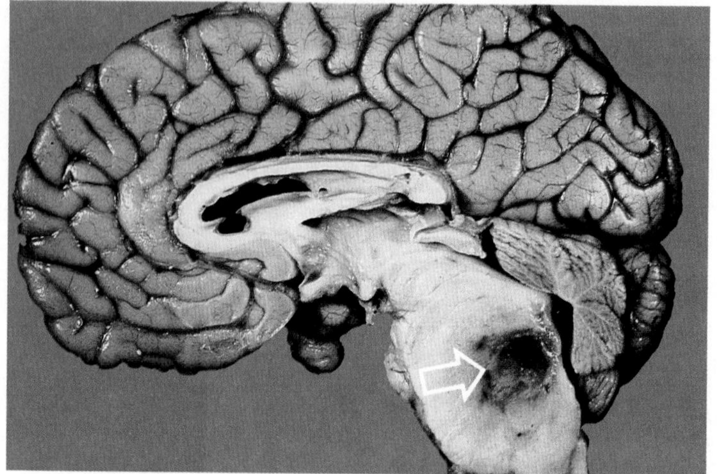

FIGURE 14.3

A midsagittal view of a human brain, showing a glioma located in the dorsal pons (*arrowhead*). (Courtesy of A. D'Agostino, Good Samaritan Hospital, Portland, Oregon.)

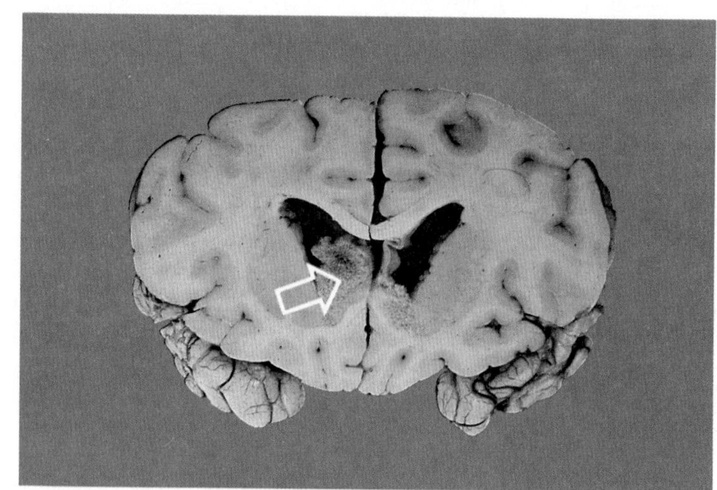

FIGURE 14.4

A slice of a human brain, showing an ependymoma of the left lateral ventricle (*arrowhead*). (Courtesy of A. D'Agostino, Good Samaritan Hospital, Portland, Oregon.)

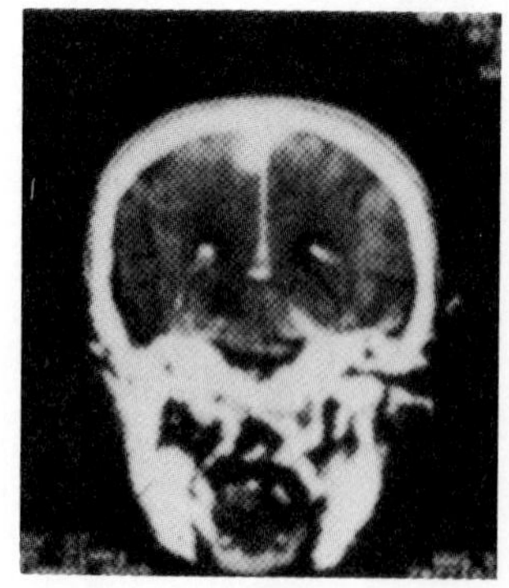

FIGURE 14.5

A CT scan of a brain, showing the presence of a meningioma (round white spot). (Courtesy of J.McA. Jones, Good Samaritan Hospital, Portland, Oregon.)

In the Prologue I described a woman whose sudden onset of seizures suggested the presence of a tumor near the top of the primary motor cortex. Indeed, she had a **meningioma**, an encapsulated, benign tumor consisting of cells that constitute the dura mater or arachnoid membrane. Such tumors tend to originate in the part of the dura mater that is found between the two cerebral hemispheres, or along the tentorium, the sheet of dura mater that lies between the occipital lobes and the cerebellum. (See ***Figure 14.5***.)

meningioma

SEIZURE DISORDERS

Because of negative connotations that were acquired in the past, most physicians prefer not to use the term *epilepsy*. Instead, they use the phrase **seizure disorder** to refer to a condition that has many causes. Seizure disorders constitute the second most important category of neurological disorders, following stroke. A *seizure* is a period of sudden, excessive activity of cerebral neurons. Sometimes—if neurons that comprise the motor system are involved—a seizure can cause a **convulsion**, which is wild, uncontrollable activity of the muscles. But not all seizures cause convulsions; in fact, most do not.

seizure disorder

convulsion

Table 14.2 presents a summary of the most important categories of seizure disorders. Two distinctions are important: *partial* versus *generalized* seizures, and *simple* versus *complex* ones. **Partial seizures** have a definite *focus*, or source of irritation: typically, a scarred region caused by an old injury. The neurons that become involved in the seizure are restricted to a small part of the brain. **Generalized seizures** are widespread, involving most of the brain. In many cases they grow from a focus, but in some cases their origin is not discovered. Simple and complex seizures are two categories of partial seizures. **Simple partial seizures** often cause *changes* in consciousness but do

partial seizure

generalized seizure

simple partial seizure

▲ TABLE 14.2 ▲

The Classification of Seizure Disorders

I. Generalized seizures (with no apparent local onset)
   A. Tonic-clonic (grand mal)
   B. Absence (petit mal)
   C. Atonic (loss of muscle tone; temporary paryalysis)
II. Partial seizures (starting from a focus)
   A. Simple (no major change in consciousness)
      1. Localized motor seizure
      2. Motor seizure, with progression of movements as seizure spreads along the primary motor cortex
      3. Sensory (somatosensory, visual, auditory, olfactory, vestibular)
      4. Psychic (forced thinking, fear, anger, etc.)
      5. Autonomic (e.g., sweating, salivating, etc.)
   B. Complex (with altered consciousness)
      Includes 1–5, as above
III. Partial seizures (simple or complex) evolving to generalized cortical seizure: Starts as IIA or IIB, then becomes a grand mal seizure

not cause *loss* of consciousness. In contrast, because of their particular location and severity, **complex partial seizures** lead to loss of consciousness. (See ***Table 14.2***.)

complex partial seizure

grand mal

The most severe form of seizure is often referred to as **grand mal**. This seizure is generalized; and because it includes the motor systems of the brain, it is accompanied by convulsions. Often before having a grand mal seizure, a person has warning symptoms, such as changes in mood or perhaps a few sudden jerks of muscular activity upon awakening. (Almost everyone sometimes experiences these jolts occasionally while falling asleep.) A few seconds before the seizure occurs, the person often experiences an **aura**, which is presumably caused by excitation of neurons surrounding a seizure focus. This excitation has effects similar to those that would be produced by electrical stimulation of the region. Obviously, the nature of an aura varies according to the location of the focus. For example, because structures in the temporal lobe are involved in the control of emotional behaviors, seizures that originate from a focus located there often begin with feelings of fear and dread or, occasionally, euphoria.

aura

tonic phase

The beginning of a grand mal seizure is called the **tonic phase**. All the patient's muscles contract forcefully. The arms are rigidly outstretched, and he or she may make an involuntary cry as the tense muscles force air out of the lungs. (At this point the patient is completely unconscious.) The patient holds a rigid posture for about 15 seconds, and then the **clonic phase** begins. (*Clonic* means "agitated.") The muscles begin trembling, then start jerking convulsively — quickly at first, then more and more slowly. Meanwhile, the eyes roll, the patient's face is contorted with violent grimaces, and the tongue may be bitten. Intense activity of the autonomic nervous system manifests itself in sweating and salivation. After about 30 seconds the patient's muscles relax, and only then does breathing begin again. The patient falls into a stuporous, unresponsive sleep, which lasts for about 15 minutes. After that the patient may awaken briefly but usually falls back into an exhausted sleep that may last for a few hours.

clonic phase

Recordings made during grand mal seizures from electrodes implanted into patients' brains show that neural firing first begins in the focus at the time of the aura, and it then spreads to other regions of the brain (Adams and Victor, 1981). The activity spreads to regions surrounding the focus and then to the contralateral cortex (through the corpus callosum), the basal ganglia, the thalamus, and various nuclei of the brain stem reticular formation. At this point the symptoms begin. The excited subcortical regions feed back more excitation to the cortex, amplifying the activity there. Neurons in the motor cortex begin firing continuously, producing the tonic phase. Next, diencephalic structures begin quenching the seizure by sending inhibitory messages to the cortex. At first, the inhibition comes in brief bursts, which causes the jerking movements of the clonic phase, as the muscles repeatedly relax and then contract again. Then the bursts of inhibition become more and more prolonged, and the jerks occur more and more slowly. Finally, the inhibition wins, and the patient's muscles relax.

Other types of seizures are far less dramatic. Partial seizures involve relatively small portions of the brain. The symptoms can include sensory changes, motor activity, or both. For example, a simple partial seizure that begins in or near the motor cortex can involve jerking movements that begin in one place and spread throughout the body as the excitation spreads along the precentral gyrus. In the Prologue I described such a progression, caused by a seizure triggered by a meningioma. The tumor was pressing against the "foot" region of the left primary motor cortex. When a seizure began, it involved the foot; and as it spread, it began involving the other parts of the body. (See ***Figure 14.6***.) Mrs. R.'s first spell was a simple partial seizure, but her second one —

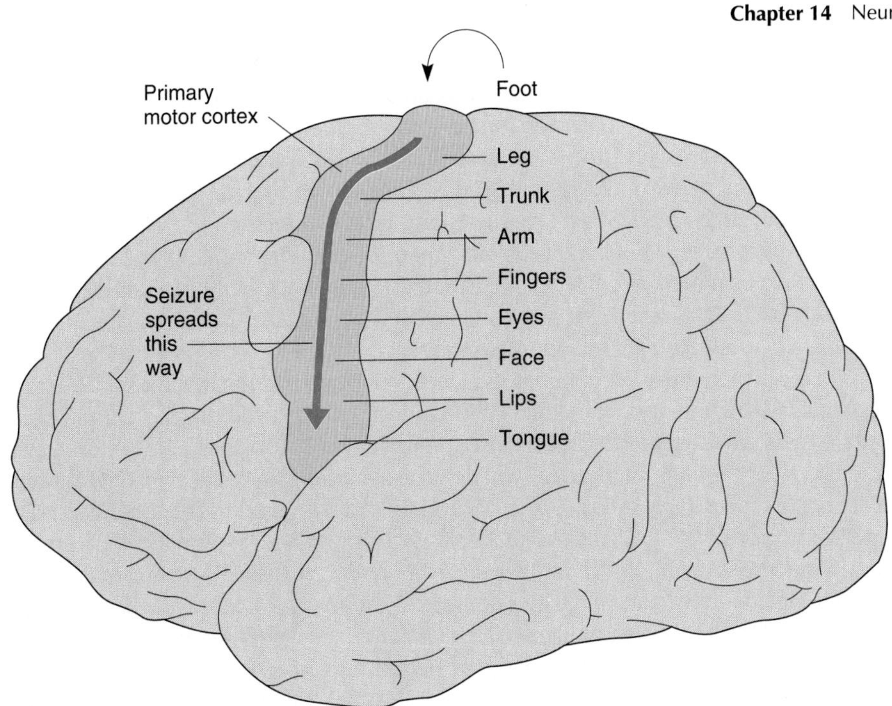

FIGURE 14.6

Primary motor cortex and seizures. Mrs. R.'s seizure began in the foot region of the primary motor cortex, and as the seizure spread, more and more parts of her body became involved.

much more severe—would be classed as a complex partial seizure, because she lost consciousness. A seizure beginning in the occipital lobe may produce visual symptoms such as spots of color, flashes of light, or temporary blindness; and one originating in the parietal lobe can evoke somatosensations, such as feelings of pins and needles or heat and cold. Seizures in the temporal lobes may cause hallucinations that include old memories; presumably, neural circuits involved in these memories are activated by the spreading excitation. Depending on the location and extent of the seizure, the patient may or may not lose consciousness.

Children are especially susceptible to seizure disorders. Many of them do not have grand mal episodes but, instead, have very brief seizures referred to as spells of **absence**. In an absence seizure they stop what they are doing and stare off into the distance for a few seconds, often blinking their eyes repeatedly. (These spells are also sometimes referred to as *petit mal* seizures.) During this time they are unresponsive and usually do not notice their attacks. Because absence seizures can occur up to several hundred times each day, they can disrupt a child's performance in school. Unfortunately, many of these children are considered to be inattentive and unmotivated unless the disorder is diagnosed.

absence

Seizures have many causes. As I have already noted, the most common cause is scarring, which may be produced by an injury, a stroke, or the irritating effect of a growing tumor. For injuries the development of seizures may take a considerable amount of time. Often a person who receives a head injury from an automobile accident will start having seizures several months later.

Various drugs and infections that cause a high fever can also produce seizures. In addition, seizures are commonly seen in alcohol or barbiturate addicts who suddenly stop taking the drug; the sudden release from the inhibiting effects of the alcohol or barbiturate leaves the brain in a hyperexcitable condition. In fact, this condition is a medical emergency, because it can be fatal.

Evidence suggests that NMDA receptors may be involved in the seizures caused by alcohol withdrawal. As we saw in Chapter 12, NMDA receptors are specialized glutamate receptors that control calcium channels. These channels open only when glutamate binds with the receptor *and* the membrane is depolarized. This double contingency is what seems to be responsible for at least one kind of synaptic modification involved in learning. Several studies have shown that alcohol blocks NMDA receptors (Gonzales, 1990). Perhaps, then, long-term suppression of NMDA receptors caused by chronic alcohol intake results in supersensitivity or "up regulation," a compensatory mechanism described in Chapter 4. When an alcoholic suddenly stops drinking, the NMDA receptors, which have been suppressed for so long, suddenly rebound. The increased activity causes seizures.

Two recent experiments obtained evidence that supports this hypothesis. Valverius, Crabbe, Hoffman, and Tabakoff (1990) studied two strains of mice that had been bred for their sensitivity to the effects of alcohol withdrawal (Crabbe, Merrill, Kim, and Belknap, 1990). Like humans, mice will develop seizures if they are given large doses of alcohol for several days and are then abruptly withdrawn from the drug. Under these conditions animals from the *withdrawal seizure-prone* (WSP) strain are much more likely than those from the *withdrawal seizure-resistant* (WSR) strain to develop seizures. (Incidentally, the WSP mice do not voluntarily drink more alcohol than the WSR mice; thus, the neural mechanisms of seizure susceptibility are different from those of alcohol preference. The genetics of alcohol addiction are discussed in Chapter 15.) Valverius and his colleagues found that the WSP mice had a greater number of NMDA receptors in the hippocampus than the WSR mice. Confirming these results, Liljequist (1991) found that seizures caused by alcohol withdrawal could be prevented by giving mice a drug that blocks NMDA receptors. These observations strongly suggest that NMDA receptors are responsible for seizures produced by alcohol withdrawal.

Seizure disorders are treated with anticonvulsant drugs, many of which work by increasing the effectiveness of inhibitory synapses. Most disorders respond well enough that the patient can lead a normal life. In a few instances drugs provide little or no help. Sometimes, seizure foci remain so irritable that despite drug treatment, brain surgery is required. The surgeon removes the region of the brain surrounding the focus (almost always, the medial temporal lobe), and most patients recover well, with their seizures eliminated or greatly reduced in frequency. Mrs. R.'s treatment was a different matter; in her case the removal of a meningioma eliminated the source of the irritation and ended her seizures. No brain tissue was removed.

The development of computers capable of calculating and presenting detailed color graphics displays has allowed researchers to combine images obtained by different techniques in ways that greatly assist the neurosurgeon. Figure 14.7 shows a side view of the head of a seven-year-old girl who had almost continuous seizures. The seizure focus was near the part of the motor cortex that controls the muscles responsible for speech and respiration, and consequently, she was unable to talk and had great difficulty breathing. The seizures could not be controlled by medication, so removal of the abnormal brain tissue was the only recourse. Because this abnormal tissue was so close to Broca's area, it was important that the neurosurgeon be able to identify its location precisely so that a minimum of brain tissue could be removed. The image shown in the photograph was derived from a series of PET and MRI scans, presented in three dimensions; it revealed the location of the seizure focus, which showed up as an area of abnormal metabolic activity. Next to it is a photograph of the same area made during the operation. As you can see, the neurosurgeon knew what to expect even before the skull was opened. (See ***Figure 14.7.***) The operation was successful; the seizures stopped, and the girl was able to breathe without assistance.

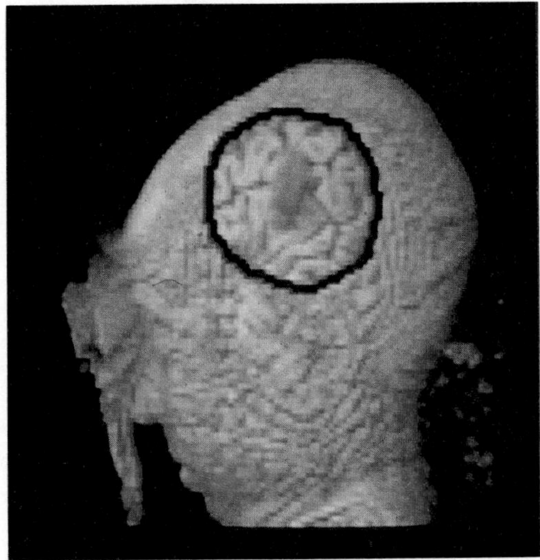

(a)

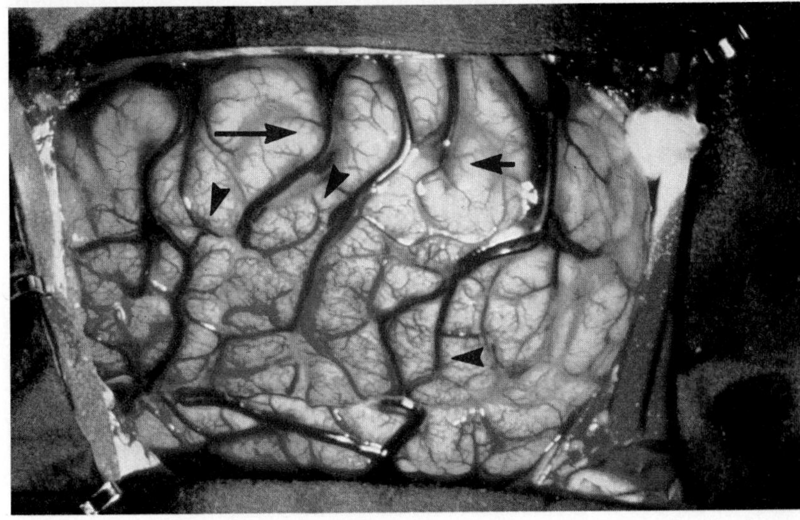

(b)

FIGURE 14.7

Seizure focus. (a) A computer display of a composite scan of the head of a seven-year-old girl, made from a series of PET and MRI scans. The purple spot shows the seizure focus, whose metabolic activity is higher than that of the rest of the brain. (b) A photograph of the surface of the skull made during surgery. Long arrows point to the primary motor cortex; short arrows point to the primary somatosensory cortex; arrowheads point to the seizure focus. You can see that the large blood vessels are smaller in this region but that the small blood vessels contained within the pia mater are dilated. (From Levin, D.N., Hu, X., Tan, K.K., Galhotra, S., Pelizzari, C.A., Chen, G.T.Y., Beck, R.N., Chen, C.-T., Cooper, M.D., Mullan, J.F., Hekmatpanah, J., and Spire, J.-P. *Radiology,* 1989, *172,* 783–789. Reprinted with permission.)

CEREBROVASCULAR ACCIDENTS

You have already learned about the *effects* of cerebrovascular accidents, or *strokes,* in earlier chapters. In this section I will describe only their causes and treatments. The two major types are hemorrhagic strokes and obstructive strokes. **Hemorrhagic strokes** are caused by bleeding within the brain, usually from a malformed blood vessel or from one weakened by high blood pressure. The blood that seeps out of the defective blood vessel accumulates within the brain, putting pressure on the surrounding brain tissue and damaging it. **Obstructive strokes**—those that plug up a blood vessel and prevent the flow of blood—can be caused by thrombi or emboli. A **thrombus** is a blood clot that forms in blood vessels, especially in places where their walls are already damaged. Sometimes, thrombi become so large that blood cannot flow through the vessel, causing a stroke. People susceptible to the formation of thrombi usually take a drug such as aspirin, which helps prevent clot formation. An **embolus** is a piece of

hemorrhagic stroke

obstructive stroke

thrombus

embolus

material that forms in one part of the vascular system, breaks off, and is carried through the bloodstream until it reaches an artery too small to pass through. It lodges there, damming the flow of blood through the rest of the vascular tree (the "branches" and "twigs" arising from the artery). Emboli can consist of a variety of materials, including bacterial debris from an infection in the lining of the heart or pieces broken off from a blood clot. As we will see in a later section, emboli can introduce a bacterial infection into the brain.

Strokes produce permanent brain damage, but the amount of damage can vary from negligible to massive. If a hemorrhagic stroke is caused by high blood pressure, medication is given to reduce it. If one is caused by weak and malformed blood vessels, brain surgery may be used to seal off the faulty vessels to prevent another hemorrhage. If a thrombus was responsible for the stroke, anticoagulant drugs will be given to make the blood less likely to clot. If an embolus broke away from a bacterial infection, antibiotics will be given to suppress the infection.

What, exactly, causes the death of neurons when the blood supply to a region of the brain is interrupted? One might expect that the neurons simply starve to death because they lose their supply of glucose and oxygen to metabolize it. However, research indicates that the immediate cause of neuron death is overstimulation. Disturbances of various kinds, including seizures, anoxia, or hypoglycemia, cause glutamergic terminal buttons to release abnormally high levels of glutamate. Within a few minutes the high concentration of glutamate excites neurons so strongly that they begin to die. The actual cause of death appears to be an excessive accumulation of intracellular calcium ions. In other words, the brain damage produced by occlusion (obstruction) of a blood vessel is actually an excitotoxic lesion—just like the lesions produced in laboratory animals by the injection of a chemical such as kainic acid. (See Rothman and Olney, 1987, for a review.)

Evidence suggests that NMDA receptors are at least partly responsible for this effect. These receptors are present in highest concentrations in field CA1 of the hippocampus, but they are also found in many other parts of the brain. Researchers have found that even short periods of anoxia, produced by temporarily occluding a blood vessel, will produce brain damage in laboratory animals. If, however, the animal is first treated with a drug that blocks NMDA receptors, the period of anoxia is much less likely to produce brain damage. These results provide hope that such drugs may help minimize the damage to the human brain caused by strokes.

Depending on the location of the brain damage, people who have strokes will receive physical therapy, and perhaps speech therapy, to help them recover from their disability. In addition, the patient—and often the family as well—should receive counseling from an experienced clinical neuropsychologist who can help them cope with the effects of the brain damage and make realistic plans for the future.

▶*INTERIM SUMMARY*◀

Neurological disorders have many causes. Because we have learned much about the functions of the human brain from studying the behavior of people with various neurological disorders, you have already learned about many of them in previous chapters of this book. Brain tumors are caused by the uncontrolled growth of various types of cells *other than neurons.* They can be benign or malignant. Benign tumors are encapsulated and thus have a distinct border; when one is surgically removed, the surgeon has a good chance of getting all of it. Tumors produce brain damage by compression and, in the case of malignant tumors, infiltration.

Seizures are periodic episodes of abnormal electrical activity of the brain. Partial seizures are localized, beginning with a focus—usually, some scar tissue caused by previous damage or a tumor. When they begin, they often produce an aura, consisting of particular sensations or changes in mood. Simple partial seizures do not produce profound changes in consciousness; complex partial seizures do. Generalized seizures may or may not originate at a single focus, but they involve most of the brain. Some seizures involve motor activity; the most serious are the grand mal convulsions that accompany generalized seizures. The convulsions are caused by involvement of the motor cortex; the patient first shows a tonic phase, consisting of a few seconds of rigidity, and then a clonic phase, consisting of rhythmic jerking. Absence seizures, also called petit mal seizures, are common in children. They are characterized by periods of inattention and temporary loss of awareness. Seizures produced by abstinence after prolonged heavy intake of alcohol appear to be produced by supersensitivity (up regulation) of NMDA receptors.

Cerebrovascular accidents damage parts of the brain through rupture of a blood vessel or occlusion (obstruction) of a blood vessel by a thrombus or embolus. A thrombus is a blood clot that forms within a blood vessel. An embolus is a piece of debris that is carried through the bloodstream and lodges in an artery. Emboli can arise from infections within the chambers of the heart or can consist of pieces of thrombi. The lack of blood flow appears to damage neurons through overstimulation of NMDA receptors and subsequent entry of excessive amounts of calcium, caused by a massive release of glutamate. ▲

DISORDERS OF DEVELOPMENT

As we will see in this section, brain development can be affected adversely by the presence of toxic chemicals during pregnancy and by genetic abnormalities, both hereditary and nonhereditary. In some instances the result is mental retardation.

Toxic Chemicals

A common cause of mental retardation is the presence of toxins that impair fetal development during pregnancy. For example, if a woman contracts rubella (German measles) early in pregnancy, the toxic chemicals released by the virus interfere with the chemical signals that control normal development of the brain. Therefore, most women who receive good health care will be immunized for rubella to prevent them from contracting it during pregnancy.

In addition to the toxins produced by viruses, various drugs can adversely affect fetal development. For example, mental retardation can be caused by the ingestion of alcohol during pregnancy. Babies born to alcoholic women are typically smaller than average and develop more slowly. Many of them exhibit **fetal alcohol syndrome**, which is characterized by abnormal facial development and deficient brain development. Figure 14.8 shows photographs of the face of a child with fetal alcohol syndrome, of a rat fetus whose mother was fed alcohol during pregnancy, and of a normal rat fetus. As you can see, alcohol produces similar abnormalities in the offspring of both species. (See ***Figure 14.8***.) A woman need not be an alcoholic to impair the development of her offspring; some investigators believe that fetal alcohol syndrome can be caused by a single alcoholic "binge" during a critical period of fetal development. Now that we recognize the dangers of this syndrome, pregnant women are advised to abstain from alcohol (and from other drugs not specifically prescribed by their physician) while their bodies are engaged in the task of sustaining the development of another human being.

fetal alcohol syndrome

FIGURE 14.8

A child with fetal alcohol syndrome, along with magnified views of a rat fetus. (a) Fetus whose mother received alcohol during pregnancy. (b) Normal rat fetus. (Photograph courtesy of Katherine K. Sulik.)

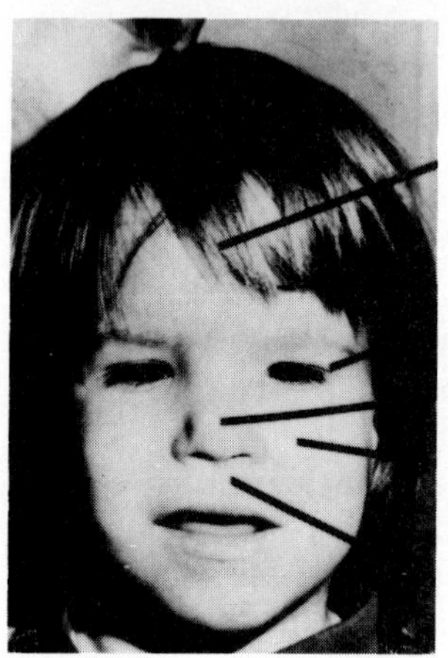

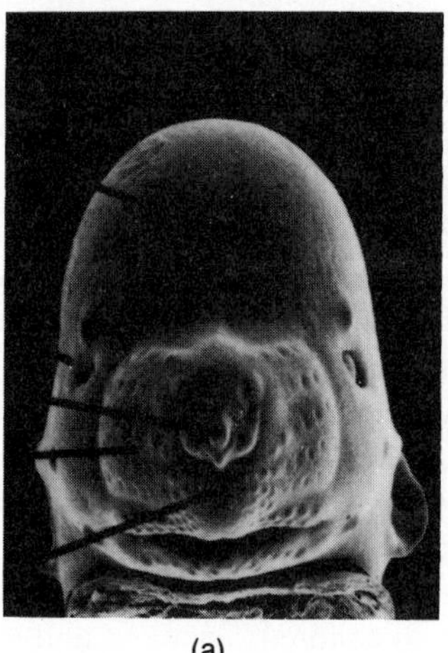
(a)

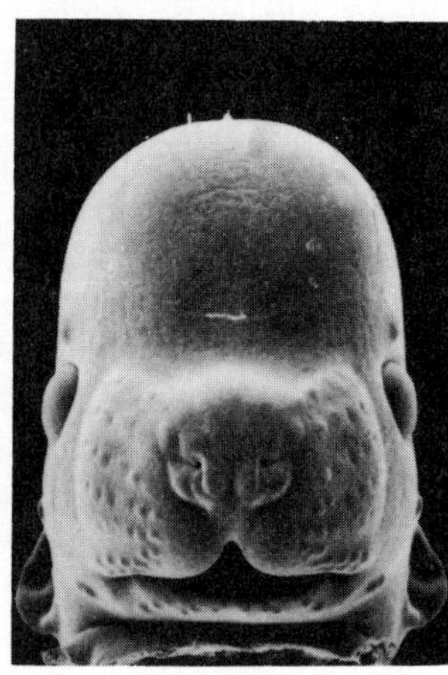
(b)

Inherited Metabolic Disorders

Several inherited "errors of metabolism" can cause brain damage or impair brain development. Normal functioning of cells requires intricate interactions among countless biochemical systems. As you know, these systems depend on enzymes, which are responsible for constructing or breaking down particular chemical compounds. Enzymes are proteins and thus are produced by mechanisms involving the chromosomes, which contain the recipes for their synthesis. "Errors of metabolism" refer to genetic abnormalities in which the recipe for a particular enzyme is in error, so the enzyme cannot be synthesized. If the enzyme is a critical one, the results can be very serious.

phenylketonuria

There are at least a hundred different inherited metabolic disorders that can affect the development of the brain. The most common and best-known is called **phenylketonuria** (PKU). This disease is caused by an inherited lack of an enzyme that converts phenylalanine (an amino acid) into tyrosine (another amino acid). Excessive amounts of phenylalanine in the blood interfere with the myelinization of neurons in the central nervous system. Much of the myelinization of the cerebral hemispheres takes place after birth. Thus, when an infant born with PKU receives foods containing phenylalanine, the amino acid accumulates and the brain fails to develop normally. The result is a severe mental retardation, with an average IQ of approximately 20 by six years of age.

Fortunately, PKU can be treated by putting the infant on a low-phenylalanine diet. The diet keeps the blood level of phenylalanine low, and myelinization of the central nervous system takes place normally. Once myelinization is complete, the dietary restraints can be relaxed, because a high level of phenylalanine no longer threatens brain development. During prenatal development a fetus is protected by its mother's normal metabolism, which removes the phenylalanine from its circulation. However, if the *mother* has PKU, she must follow a strict diet during pregnancy or her infant will be born with brain damage. If she eats a normal diet, rich in phenylalanine, the high blood level of this compound will not damage her brain, but it will damage that of her fetus.

Diagnosing PKU immediately after birth is imperative so that the infant's brain is never exposed to high levels of phenylalanine. Consequently, many governments have passed laws that mandate a PKU test for all newborn babies. The test is inexpensive and accurate, and it has prevented many cases of mental retardation.

Other genetic errors of metabolism can be treated in similar fashion. For example, untreated **pyridoxine dependency** results in damage to cerebral white matter, to the thalamus, and to the cerebellum. It is treated by large doses of vitamin B_6. Another error of metabolism, **galactosemia**, is an inability to metabolize galactose, a sugar found in milk. If it is not treated, it, too, causes damage to cerebral white matter and to the cerebellum. The treatment is use of a milk substitute that does not contain galactose.

pyridoxine dependency

galactosemia

Some other inherited metabolic disorders cannot yet be treated successfully. For example, **Tay-Sachs disease**, which occurs mainly in children of Eastern European Jewish descent, causes the brain to swell and damage itself against the inside of the skull and against the folds of the dura mater that encase it. The neurological symptoms begin by four months of age and include an exaggerated startle response to sounds, listlessness, irritability, spasticity, seizures, dementia, and finally, death.

Tay-Sachs disease

Tay-Sachs disease is one of several metabolic "storage" disorders. All cells contain sacs of material encased in membrane, called **lysosomes** ("dissolving bodies"). These sacs constitute the cell's rubbish removal system; they contain enzymes that break down waste substances that cells produce in the course of their normal activities. The broken-down waste products are then recycled (used by the cells again) or excreted. Metabolic storage disorders are genetic errors of metabolism in which one or more vital enzymes are missing. Particular kinds of waste products cannot be destroyed by the lysosomes, so they accumulate. The lysosomes get larger and larger, the cells get larger and larger, and eventually, the brain begins to swell and become damaged.

lysosome

Researchers investigating hereditary errors of metabolism hope to prevent or treat these disorders in several ways. Some will be treated like PKU or galactosemia, by avoiding a constituent of the diet that cannot be tolerated. Others, such as pyridoxine dependency, will be treated by administering a substance that the body requires. Still others may be cured someday by the techniques of genetic engineering. Viruses infect cells by inserting their own genetic material into them and thus taking over the cells' genetic machinery, using it to reproduce themselves. Perhaps one day, researchers will develop special viruses that will "infect" an infant's cells with genetic information that is needed to produce the enzymes that the cells lack, leaving the rest of the cells' functions intact. Such viruses have already yielded useful results, such as the development of bacteria that produce human insulin. Someday, they may cure human genetic disorders as well.

Down Syndrome

Down syndrome is a congenital disorder that results in abnormal development of the brain, producing mental retardation in varying degrees. *Congenital* does not necessarily mean *hereditary*; it simply refers to a disorder that one is born with. Down syndrome is not caused by the inheritance of a faulty gene but by the possession of an extra twenty-first chromosome. The syndrome is closely associated with the mother's age; in most cases something goes wrong with some of her ova, resulting in the presence of two, rather than one, twenty-first chromosomes. When fertilization occurs, the addition of the father's twenty-first chromosome makes three, rather than two. The extra chromosome presumably causes biochemical changes that impair normal brain development. The development of *amniocentesis*—a procedure whereby some fluid is withdrawn from a pregnant woman's uterus through a hypodermic syringe—has

Down syndrome

allowed physicians to identify fetal cells with chromosomal abnormalities and thus determine whether the fetus carries Down syndrome.

Down syndrome, described in 1866 by John Langdon Down, occurs in approximately 1 out of 700 births. People with this disorder can be recognized by an experienced observer; they have round heads, thick, protruding tongues that tend to keep the mouth open much of the time, stubby hands, short stature, low-set ears, and somewhat slanting eyelids. They are slow to learn to talk, but most do talk by age five. The brain of a person with Down syndrome is approximately 10 percent lighter than that of a normal person, the convolutions (gyri and sulci) are simpler and smaller, the frontal lobes are small, and the superior temporal gyrus (the location of Wernicke's area) is thin. After age thirty, the brain develops abnormal microscopic structures called ***neurofibrillary tangles*** and begins to degenerate. Because this degeneration resembles that of Alzheimer's disease, it will be discussed in the next section.

Although the occurrence of any form of mental retardation is a tragedy, people with Down syndrome are often only moderately retarded. Given proper training, many of them can function well with only minimal supervision.

▶*INTERIM SUMMARY*◀

Developmental disorders can result in brain damage serious enough to cause mental retardation. During pregnancy the fetus is especially sensitive to toxins, such as alcohol or chemicals produced by some viruses. Several inherited metabolic disorders can also impair brain development. For example, phenylketonuria is caused by the lack of an enzyme that converts phenylalanine into tyrosine. Brain damage can be averted by feeding the baby a diet low in phenylalanine, so early diagnosis is essential. Other inherited metabolic disorders include pyridoxine dependency, which can be treated by vitamin B_6, and galactosemia, which can be treated with a diet that does not contain milk sugar. Storage disorders, such as Tay-Sachs disease, are caused by the inability of cells to destroy waste products within the lysosomes, which causes the cells to swell and, eventually, die. So far, these disorders cannot be treated. Down syndrome is produced by the presence of an extra twenty-first chromosome. The brain development of people with Down syndrome is abnormal, and after age thirty, their brains develop features similar to those of people with Alzheimer's disease. ▲

DEGENERATIVE DISORDERS

Many disease processes — in particular, Parkinson's disease, Alzheimer's disease, and multiple sclerosis — can cause degeneration of the cells of the brain. Some of these conditions injure particular kinds of cells, which provides the hope that research will uncover the causes of the damage and find a way to halt it and prevent it from occurring in other people.

Parkinson's Disease

One of the most common degenerative disorders, Parkinson's disease, has already been discussed in previous chapters, so I will not say more about its symptoms here. As you have learned, the cause of Parkinson's disease is degeneration of dopamine-secreting neurons of the substantia nigra that send axons to the basal ganglia. Recent research has suggested that Parkinson's disease may be caused by toxins — present in the environment, caused by faulty metabolism, or produced by unrecognized infectious disorders.

As we saw in the Prologue and Epilogue of Chapter 4, the experience of several young people who took a contaminated drug led to research that found that various toxins can cause the degeneration of dopaminergic neurons. This research suggests that Parkinson's disease may be caused by toxins present in the environment. Fortunately, it also led to the discovery that an MAO inhibitor, deprenyl, can retard the progress of the neural degeneration.

Alzheimer's Disease

Several neurological disorders result in **dementia**, a deterioration of intellectual abilities resulting from an organic brain disorder. A common form of dementia is called **Alzheimer's disease**, which occurs in approximately 5 percent of the population above the age of sixty-five. It is characterized by progressive loss of memory and other mental functions. At first, the person may have difficulty remembering appointments and sometimes fails to think of words or people's names. As time passes, he or she shows increasing confusion and increasing difficulty with tasks such as balancing a checkbook. The memory deficit most critically involves recent events, and it thus resembles the anterograde amnesia of Korsakoff's syndrome. If the person ventures outside alone, he or she is likely to get lost. Eventually, the person becomes bedridden, completely helpless, and finally, succumbs (Terry and Davies, 1980).

dementia

Alzheimer's disease

Alzheimer's disease produces severe degeneration of the hippocampus and neocortex, especially the association cortex of the frontal and temporal lobes. Figures 14.9 and 14.10 show photographs of the brain of a patient with Alzheimer's disease and of a normal brain. You can see how much wider the sulci are, especially in the frontal and temporal lobes, indicating substantial loss of cortical tissue. (See ***Figures 14.9*** and ***14.10.***)

Earlier, I mentioned that the brains of patients with Down syndrome usually develop abnormal microscopic structures called neurofibrillary tangles that are also seen in patients with Alzheimer's disease. These structures appear to be caused by the secretion of a protein called **amyloid**; thus, the production of amyloid may be one of the factors that causes the brain damage. (See ***Figure 14.11.***)

amyloid

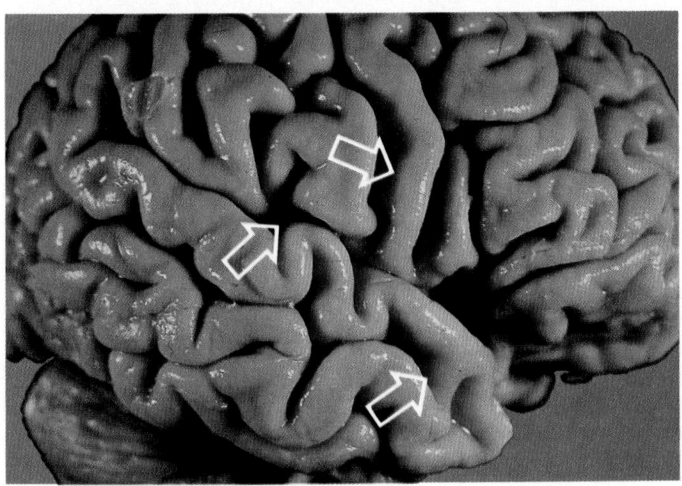

FIGURE 14.9

A lateral view of the right side of the brain of a person who had Alzheimer's disease. (Rostral is to the right; dorsal is up.) Note that the sulci of the temporal lobe and parietal lobe are especially wide, indicating degeneration of the neocortex (*arrowheads*). Compare this photograph with Figure 14.10. (Courtesy of J.McA. Jones, Good Samaritan Hospital, Portland, Oregon.)

FIGURE 14.10

A lateral view of the right side of a normal brain. (© Dan McCoy/Rainbow.)

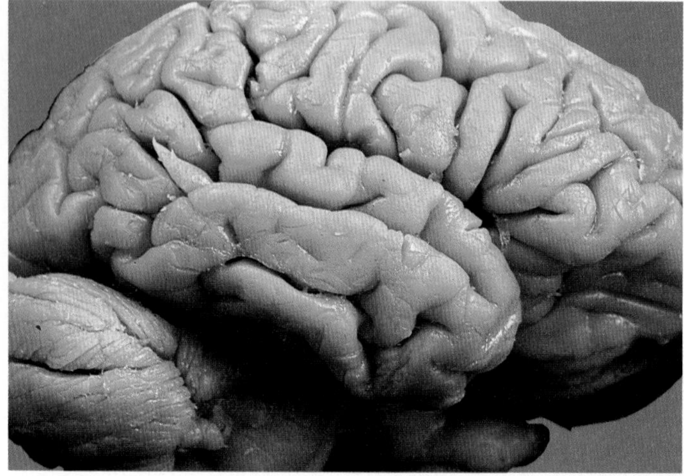

Research has shown that at least some forms of Alzheimer's disease appear to run in families and, thus, appear to be hereditary. Because the brains of people with Down syndrome (caused by an extra twenty-first chromosome) also contain deposits of amyloid, some investigators hypothesized that the twenty-first chromosome may be involved in the production of amyloid and in Alzheimer's disease, as well. In fact, St. George-Hyslop et al. (1987) found that this chromosome *does* contains a gene that produces amyloid. Presumably, the presence of an extra twenty-first chromosome causes amyloid to be produced in the brains of people with Down syndrome, and the presence of a faulty gene (perhaps one that regulates its production) causes it to occur in the brains of people with Alzheimer's disease. If research shows that amyloid formation is the primary cause of brain degeneration in disease, perhaps its formation can be suppressed with drugs.

FIGURE 14.11

Damaged cells in the cerebral cortex, showing an accumulation of amyloid protein (*arrow*). (From Coyle, J.T., Price, D.L., and DeLong, M.R. *Science*, 1983, *219*, 1184–1190. Copyright 1983 by the American Association for the Advancement of Science.)

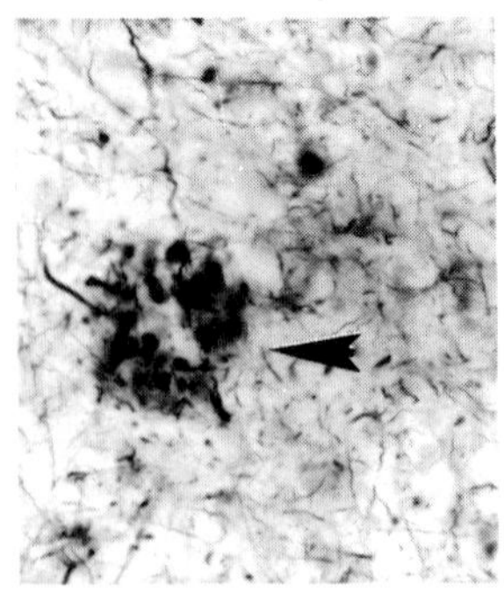

As we have already seen, Parkinson's disease is caused by the death of a specific class of neurons—the dopamine-secreting neurons of the nigrostriatal bundle. Investigators have analyzed the brains of deceased patients who had Alzheimer's disease with the hopes of finding specific degeneration in them, as well. Although Alzheimer's disease eventually involves death of many different types of neurons, studies (reviewed by Price, 1986) have found that acetylcholinergic neurons are among the first to degenerate, and their death is probably responsible for the earliest symptoms of the disease: memory impairments. The loss of acetylcholine is undoubtedly not the only cause of the memory deficit; Hyman et al. (1984) found that the neurons that give rise to the perforant path (from the entorhinal cortex to the dentate gyrus) degenerate in Alzheimer's disease. As we saw in Chapter 12, the hippocampal complex (which includes these neurons) plays an important role in memory.

The cell bodies of ACh-secreting neurons reside in subcortical areas and send their axons throughout the cerebral cortex and hippocampus, where they terminate on many millions of neurons. The primary location of these cell bodies is in the basal forebrain, near the preoptic area. Whitehouse et al. (1982) examined slices of the basal forebrain of deceased patients with Alzheimer's disease. They found that the number of neurons in this nucleus was decreased by 79 percent in the brains of these patients, compared with age-matched normal controls. Figure 14.12 shows the microscopic appearance of tissue from normal and diseased brains. (See ***Figure 14.12***.)

Several studies have shown that memory impairments can be produced in humans and laboratory animals by administering drugs that block muscarinic ACh receptors. For example, Sitaram, Weingartner, and Gillin (1978) had normal subjects learn lists of words. Subjects who received an injection of a drug that blocks muscarinic receptors took more time to learn the words than those who received a placebo. In contrast, subjects who received an injection of a drug that *stimulates* muscarinic receptors learned the list faster. Thus, the level of ACh activity does indeed affect people's learning ability.

As you have learned, the precursor of dopamine, L-DOPA, has been successfully used to treat the symptoms of Parkinson's disease, which is caused by degeneration of dopaminergic neurons. Thus, because Alzheimer's disease includes degeneration of ACh-secreting neurons, it occurred to investigators to try to improve patients' cognitive performance with choline, the precursor of acetylcholine, or with *its* precursor, lecithin. These treatments have not been very successful in either healthy elderly people or patients with Alzheimer's disease (Bartus, Dean, Beer, and Lippa, 1982). However, because a few studies reported some promising results with infusion of a cholinergic agonist directly into the cerebral ventricles, a collaborative double-blind study was established at several medical centers to see whether this procedure would help people with Alzheimer's disease (Harbaugh et al., 1989). Unfortunately, it did not. As the authors concluded, "the degree of improvement was not sufficient to justify further treatment of Alzheimer's disease patients by intracerebroventricular infusion of benthanechol chloride" (p. 481). Given what we know about the damage of noncholinergic neurons in the brains of Alzheimer's patients, these results are disappointing but hardly surprising.

FIGURE 14.12

Photomicrographs from the basal forebrain. (a) Age-matched normal person. (b) Person with Alzheimer's disease. (From Whitehouse, P.J., Price, D.L., Struble, R.G., Clark, A.W., Coyle, J.T., and DeLong, M.R. *Science*, 1982, *215*, 1237-1239. Copyright 1982 by the American Association for the Advancement of Science.)

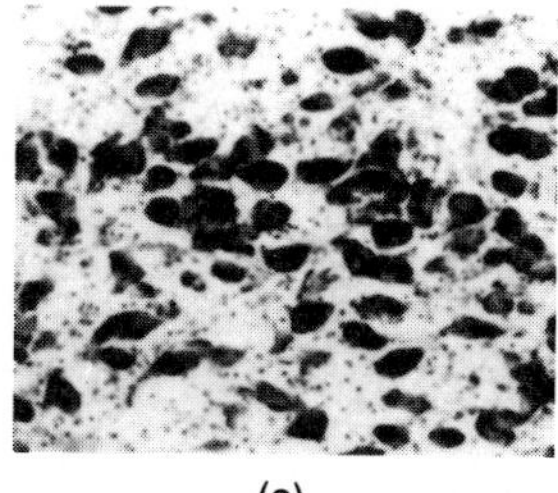

(a)

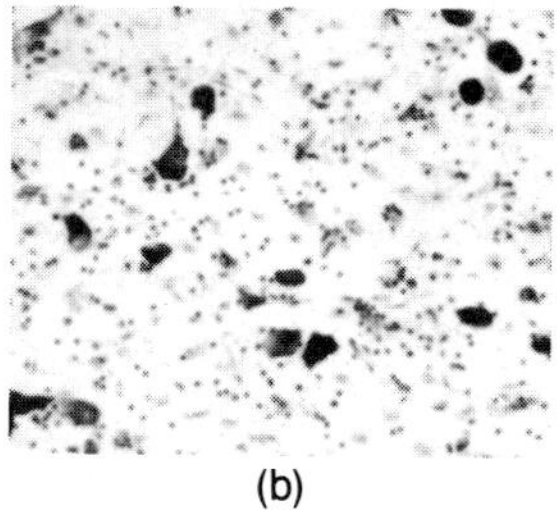

(b)

Multiple Sclerosis

Multiple sclerosis is an autoimmune demyelinating disease; at scattered locations within the central nervous system, myelin sheaths are attacked by the person's immune system, leaving behind hard patches of debris called *sclerotic plaques.* (See ***Figure 14.13.***) The normal transmission of neural messages through the demyelinated axons is interrupted. Because the damage occurs in white matter located throughout the brain and spinal cord, a wide variety of neurological disorders is seen.

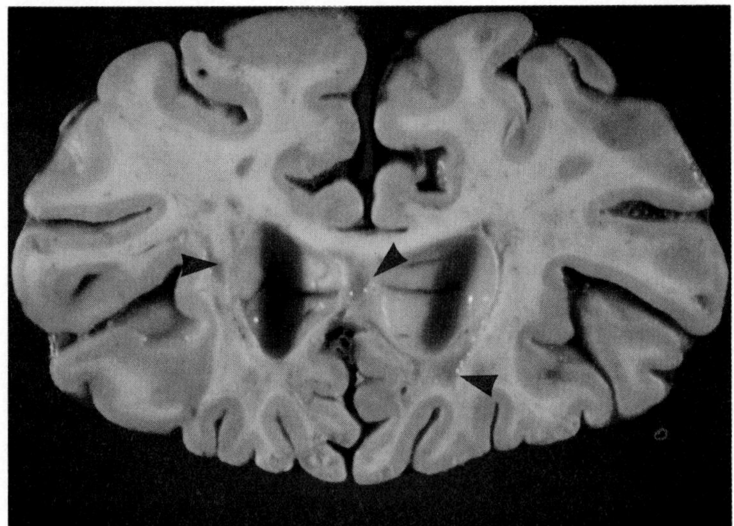

FIGURE 14.13

A slice of a human brain of a person who had multiple sclerosis. The arrowheads point to sclerotic plaques in the white matter. (Courtesy of A. D'Agostino, Good Samaritan Hospital, Portland, Oregon.)

Multiple sclerosis afflicts women somewhat more frequently than men, and the disorder usually occurs in people in their late twenties or thirties. People who spend their childhood in places far from the equator are more likely to come down with the disease than those who live close to it. In addition, people born during the late winter and early spring are also at higher risk. Hence, it is likely that some disease contracted during a childhood spent in a region in which the virus is prevalent causes the person's immune system to attack his or her own myelin. Perhaps a virus weakens the blood-brain barrier, allowing myelin protein into the general circulation and sensitizing the immune system to it, or perhaps the virus attaches itself to myelin. In any event the process is a long-lived one, lasting for many decades.

Unfortunately, there is presently no specific treatment for multiple sclerosis. Because the symptoms of the disease are usually episodic — new or worsening symptoms followed by partial recovery — patients and their families often attribute the changes in the symptoms to whatever has happened recently. For example, if the patient has taken a new medication or gone on a new diet and the symptoms get worse, they will blame the symptoms on the medication or diet. Conversely, if the patient gets better, they will credit the medication or diet.

▶*INTERIM SUMMARY*◀

Parkinson's disease is caused by degeneration of dopamine-secreting neurons of the substantia nigra that send axons to the basal ganglia. Recent evidence suggests that the disease may be caused by toxic substances present in the environment. Alzheimer's disease, another degenerative disorder, is much more widespread, eventually destroying most of the hippocampus and cortical gray matter. The first cells to be destroyed are acetylcholinergic neurons of the basal forebrain, which may account for the memory deficits that are seen early in the course of the disease. However, the hippocampal complex is damaged, too, so the memory impairment is not caused only by the loss of the acetylcholinergic neurons. Multiple sclerosis, a demyelinating disease, is characterized by periodic attacks of neurological symptoms, usually with partial remission between attacks. The damage appears to be caused by the body's immune system, which attacks the protein contained in myelin. ▲

DISORDERS CAUSED BY INFECTIOUS DISEASES

Several neurological disorders can be caused by infectious diseases, transmitted by bacteria, fungi or other parasites, or viruses. The most common are encephalitis and meningitis. **Encephalitis** is an infection that invades the entire brain. The most common cause of encephalitis is a virus that is transmitted by mosquitoes, who pick up the infectious agent from horses, birds, or rodents. The symptoms of acute encephalitis include fever, irritability, and nausea, often followed by convulsions, delirium, and signs of brain damage, such as aphasia or paralysis. Unfortunately, there is no specific treatment besides supportive care, and between 5 and 20 percent of the cases are fatal; 20 percent of the survivors show some residual neurological symptoms.

encephalitis

Encephalitis can also be caused by the **herpes simplex virus**, which is the cause of cold sores (or "fever blisters") that most people develop in and around their mouth

herpes simplex virus

from time to time. Normally, the viruses live quietly in the *trigeminal nerve ganglia* — nodules on the fifth cranial nerve that contain the cell bodies of somatosensory neurons that serve the face. The viruses proliferate periodically, traveling down to the ends of nerve fibers, where they cause sores to develop in mucous membrane. Unfortunately, they occasionally (but rarely) go the other way — into the brain. Herpes encephalitis is a serious disease; the virus attacks the frontal and temporal lobes in particular and can severely damage them.

Two other forms of viral encephalitis are probably already familiar to you — polio and rabies. **Acute anterior poliomyelitis** ("polio") is fortunately very rare in developed countries since the development of vaccines that immunize people against the disease. The virus causes specific damage to motor neurons of the brain and spinal cord: neurons in the primary motor cortex, in the motor nuclei of the thalamus, hypothalamus, and brain stem, in the cerebellum, and in the ventral horns of the gray matter of the spinal cord. Undoubtedly, these motor neurons contain some chemical substance that attracts the virus or in some way makes the virus become lethal to them.

acute anterior poliomyelitis

Rabies is caused by a virus that is passed from the saliva of an infected mammal directly into a person's flesh by means of a bite wound. The virus travels through peripheral nerves to the central nervous system and there causes severe damage. The symptoms include a short period of fever and headache, followed by anxiety, excessive movement and talking, difficulty in swallowing, movement disorders, difficulty in speaking, seizures, confusion, and finally, death within two to seven days of the onset of the symptoms. The virus has a special affinity for cells in the cerebellum and hippocampus, and damage to the hippocampus probably accounts for the emotional changes that are seen in the early symptoms.

rabies

Fortunately, the incubation period for rabies lasts up to several months, while the virus climbs through the peripheral nerves. (If the bite is received in the face or neck, the incubation time will be much shorter because the virus has a smaller distance to travel before it reaches the brain.) During the incubation period a person can receive a vaccine that will confer an immunity to the disease; the person's own immune system will destroy the virus before it reaches the brain.

Several infectious diseases cause brain damage even though they are not primarily diseases of the central nervous system. One such disease is acquired immune deficiency syndrome (AIDS). Records of autopsies have revealed that at least 75 percent of people who died of AIDS show evidence of brain damage (Levy and Bredesen, 1989). The brain damage often results in a syndrome called *AIDS dementia complex,* which is characterized by a loss of cognitive and motor functions. At first, the patients may become forgetful, they may think and reason more slowly, and they may have word-finding difficulties (anomia). Eventually, they may become almost mute. Motor deficits may begin with tremor and difficulty in making complex movement but then may progress so much that the patient becomes bedridden (Maj, 1990).

A recent study suggests that the cause of AIDS dementia complex may be the entry of excessive amounts of calcium into neurons. For several years researchers have been puzzled by the fact that although AIDS certainly causes neural damage, neurons appear not to be directly infected by the HIV virus (the organism responsible for the disease). Lipton, Dreyer, Kaiser, and Offermann (1990) found that the protein molecule that coats the virus appears to affect the calcium channels found in the neural membrane; when they applied a solution of this molecule to rat neurons isolated in a tissue culture, the amount of Ca^{2+} in the cells increased to 33 times the normal level. As a result of this increase, the neurons died. (As we saw earlier, the death of neurons caused by anoxia also involves the entry of excessive amounts of Ca^{2+}.) The investigators found that a drug that blocks calcium channels prevented the influx of calcium ions. Perhaps, they speculate, the damage can be minimized in AIDS patients by use of such a drug.

meningitis

Another category of infectious diseases of the brain actually involves inflammation of the meninges, the layers of connective tissue that surround the central nervous system. **Meningitis** can be caused by viruses or bacteria. The symptoms of all forms include headache, a stiff neck, and, depending on the severity of the disorder, convulsions, confusion or loss of consciousness, and sometimes death. The stiff neck is one of the most important symptoms. Neck movements cause the meninges to stretch; because they are inflamed, the stretch causes severe pain. Thus, the patient resists having his or her neck moved.

The most common form of viral meningitis usually does not cause significant brain damage. However, various forms of bacterial meningitis do. The usual causes are spread of a middle-ear infection into the brain, introduction of an infection into the brain from a head injury, or the presence of emboli that have dislodged from a bacterial infection present in the chambers of the heart. Such an infection is often caused by unclean hypodermic needles; thus, drug addicts are at particular risk for meningitis (as well as many other diseases). The inflammation of the meninges can damage the brain by interfering with circulation of blood or by blocking the flow of cerebrospinal fluid through the subarachnoid space, causing hydrocephalus. In addition, the cranial nerves are susceptible to damage. Fortunately, bacterial meningitis can usually be treated effectively with antibiotics. Of course, early diagnosis and prompt treatment are essential, because neither antibiotics nor any other known treatment can repair a damaged brain.

▶INTERIM SUMMARY◀

Infectious diseases can damage the brain. Encephalitis, usually caused by a virus, affects the entire brain. One form is caused by the herpes simplex virus, which infects the trigeminal nerve ganglia of most of the population. This virus tends to attack the frontal and temporal lobes. The polio virus attacks motor neurons in the brain and spinal cord, resulting in motor deficits or even paralysis. The rabies virus, acquired by an animal bite, travels through peripheral nerves and attacks the brain, particularly the cerebellum and hippocampus. An AIDS infection also produces brain damage, perhaps by opening calcium channels that permit a lethal dose of the ion to enter the cells of the brain. Meningitis is an infection of the meninges, caused by viruses or bacteria. The bacterial form, which is usually more serious, is generally caused by an ear infection, a head injury, or an embolus from a heart infection. ▲

EPILOGUE: ▶ *Application*

Mrs. R.'s surgery was performed to remove a noncancerous brain tumor that, incidentally, produced seizures. As I mentioned in this chapter, neurosurgeons occasionally perform surgery specifically to remove brain tissue that contains a seizure focus. Such an operation, called *seizure surgery,* is performed only when drug therapy is unsuccessful.

Because seizure surgery often involves the removal of a substantial amount of brain tissue (usually, from one of the temporal lobes), we might expect it to cause behavioral deficits. But in most cases the reverse is true;

people's performance on tests of neuropsychological functioning usually *increases.* How can the removal of brain tissue improve a person's performance?

The answer is provided by looking at what happens in the brain not *during* seizures but *between* them. The seizure focus — usually, a region of scar tissue — irritates the brain tissue surrounding it, causing increased neural activity that tends to spread to adjacent regions. Between seizures, this increased excitatory activity is held in check by a compensatory increase in inhibitory activity. That is, inhibitory neurons in the region surrounding the seizure focus become more active. (This phenomenon is known as *interictal inhibition; ictus* means "stroke" in Latin.) A seizure occurs when the excitation overcomes the inhibition.

The problem is that the compensatory inhibition does more than hold the excitation in check; it also suppresses the normal functions of a rather large region of brain tissue surrounding the seizure focus. Thus, even though the focus may be small, its effects are felt over a much larger area — even between seizures. Removing the seizure focus and some surrounding brain tissue eliminates the source of the irritation and makes the compensatory inhibition unnecessary. Freed from interictal inhibition, the brain tissue located near the site of the former seizure focus can now function normally, and the patient's neuropsychological abilities will show an improvement.

As I mentioned in this chapter, seizures often occur after a head injury, but only after a delay of several months. The cause of the delay is related to some properties of neurons that make learning possible. Goddard (1967) implanted electrodes in the brains of rats and administered a brief, weak electrical stimulus once a day. At first, the stimulation produced no effects, but after several days the stimulation began to trigger small, short seizures. As days went by, the seizures became larger and longer until the animal was finally having full-blown clonic-tonic convulsions. Goddard called the phenomenon *kindling,* because it resembled the way a small fire can be kindled to start a larger one.

Kindling appears to be analogous to learning, and it presumably involves changes in synaptic strength like those seen in long-term potentiation. It can most easily be induced in the temporal lobe, which is the place where seizure foci are most likely to occur. The probable reason for the delayed occurrence of seizures after a head injury is that it takes time for kindling to occur. The irritation produced by the brain injury eventually causes increased synaptic strength in excitatory synapses located nearby.

Kindling has become an animal model of focal-seizure disorders, and it has proved useful in research on the causes and treatment of these disorders. For example, Silver, Shin, and McNamara (1991) produced seizure foci in rats through kindling and compared the effects of some commonly used medications on both seizures (the electrical events within the brain) and convulsions (the motor manifestations of the seizures). They found that one of the drugs they tested prevented the convulsions but left seizures intact, whereas another prevented both seizures and convulsions. Because each seizure is capable of producing some brain damage through overstimulation of neurons (especially those in the hippocampal formation, which become especially active during a seizure), the goal of medical treatment should be the elimination of seizures, not simply the convulsions that accompany them. Research with the animal model of kindling will undoubtedly contribute to the effective treatment of focal-seizure disorders. ▲

KEY CONCEPTS

Tumors

- Brain tumors are uncontrolled growths of cells other than neurons within the skull that damage normal tissue by compression or infiltration.

Seizure Disorders

- Seizures are periodic episodes of abnormal neural firing, which can produce a variety of symptoms. They usually originate from a focus, but some have no apparent source of localized irritation.

Cerebrovascular Accidents

- Cerebrovascular accidents, hemorrhagic or obstructive in nature, produce localized brain damage. The two most common sources of obstructive strokes are emboli and thrombi.

Disorders of Development

- Developmental disorders can be caused by drugs or disease-produced toxins or by chromosomal or genetic abnormalities.

Degenerative Disorders

- Several degenerative disorders of the nervous system, including Parkinson's disease, Alzheimer's disease, and multiple sclerosis, have received much attention from scientists in recent years.

Disorders Caused by Infectious Diseases

- Infectious diseases, either viral or bacterial, can damage the brain. The two most important infections of the central nervous system are encephalitis and meningitis, but with the rise of the AIDS epidemic, AIDS dementia complex is becoming more common.

NEW TERMS

absence **p. 481**
acute anterior poliomyelitis **p. 493**
Alzheimer's disease **p. 489**
amyloid **p. 489**
aura **p. 480**
benign **p. 476**
clonic phase **p. 480**
complex partial seizure **p. 480**
convulsion **p. 479**
dementia **p. 489**
Down syndrome **p. 487**
embolus **p. 483**
encephalitis **p. 492**
fetal alcohol syndrome **p. 485**
galactosemia **p. 487**
generalized seizure **p. 479**
glioma **p. 477**
grand mal **p. 480**
hemorrhagic stroke **p. 483**
herpes simplex virus **p. 492**
lysosome **p. 487**
malignant **p. 476**
meningioma **p. 479**
meningitis **p. 494**
metastasis **p. 476**
obstructive stroke **p. 483**
partial seizure **p. 479**
phenylketonuria **p. 486**
pyridoxine dependency **p. 487**
rabies **p. 493**
seizure disorder **p. 479**
simple partial seizure **p. 479**
Tay-Sachs disease **p. 487**
thrombus **p. 483**
tonic phase **p. 480**

SUGGESTED READINGS

Adams, R.D., and Victor, M. *Principles of Neurology,* 2nd ed. New York: McGraw-Hill, 1981.

Mesulam, M.-M. *Principles of Behavioral Neurology.* Philadelphia: F.A. Davis, 1985.

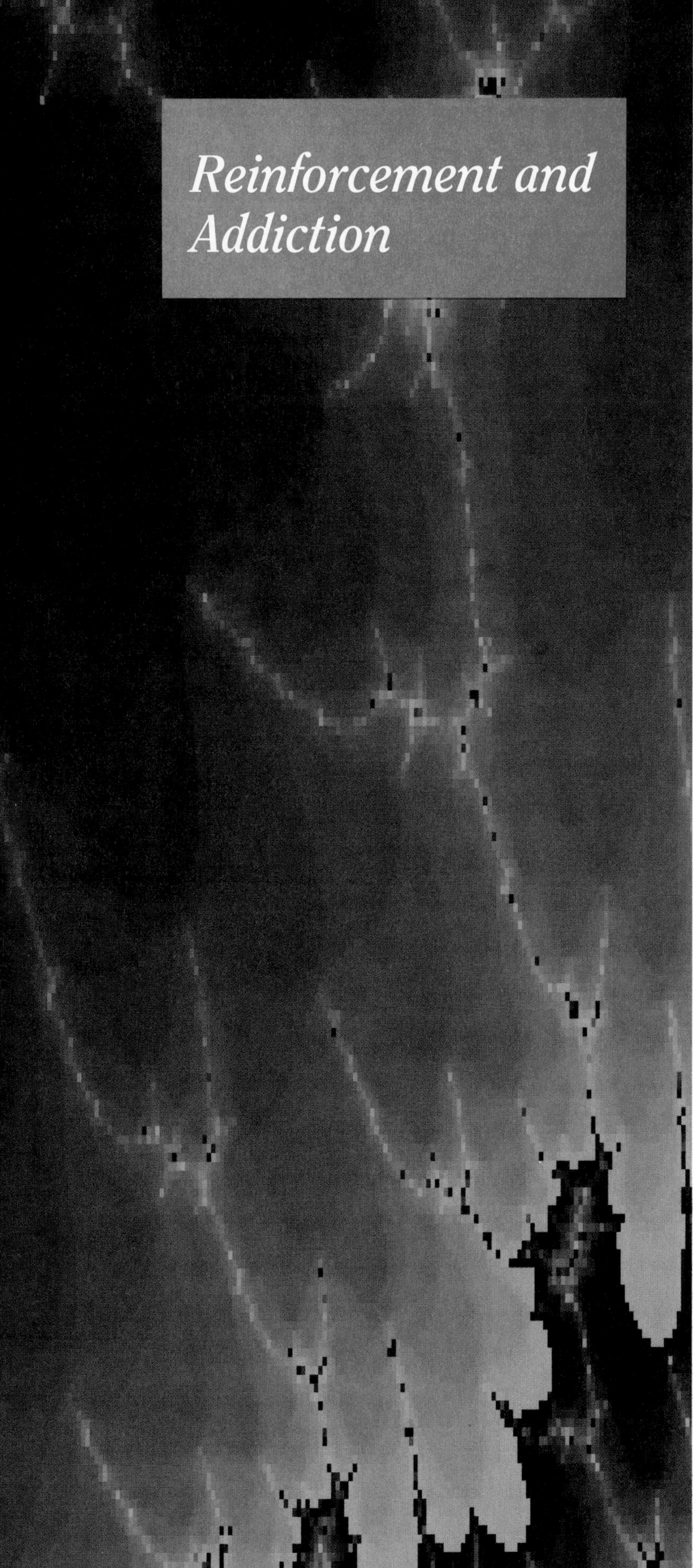

Reinforcement and Addiction

15

CHAPTER OUTLINE

PROLOGUE ►

John was beginning to feel that perhaps he would be able to get his life back together. It looked like his drug habit was going to be licked. He had started taking drugs several years ago. At first, he had used them only on special occasions — mostly, on weekends with his friends — but heroin proved to be his undoing. One of his acquaintances had introduced him to the needle, and he had found the rush so blissful that he couldn't wait a whole week for his next fix. Soon he was shooting up daily. Shortly after that, he lost his job and, to support his habit, began earning money through car theft and small-time drug dealing. As time went on, he needed more and more heroin at shorter and shorter intervals, which necessitated even more money. Eventually, he was arrested and convicted of selling heroin to an undercover agent.

The judge gave John the choice of prison or a drug rehabilitation program, and he chose the latter. Soon after starting the program, he realized that he was relieved to have been caught. Now that he was clean and could reflect on his life, he realized what would have become of him had he continued to take drugs. Withdrawal from heroin was not an experience he would want to live through again, but it turned out not to be as bad as he had feared. The counselors in his program told him to avoid his old neighborhood and to break contact with his old acquaintances, and he followed their advice. He had been clean for eight weeks, he had a job, and he had met a woman who really seemed sympathetic. He knew that he hadn't completely kicked his habit, because every now and then, despite his best intentions, he found himself thinking about the wonderful glow that heroin provided him. But things were definitely looking up.

Then one day, while walking home from work, he turned a corner and saw a new poster plastered on the wall of a building. The poster, produced by an anti-drug agency, showed all sorts of drug paraphernalia in full color: glassine envelopes with white powder spilling out of them, syringes, needles, a spoon and candle used to heat and dissolve the drug. He was seized with a sudden, intense compulsion to take some heroin. He closed his eyes, trying to will the feeling away, but all he could feel was his churning stomach and his trembling limbs and all he could think about was getting a fix. He hopped on a bus and went back to his old neighborhood. ▲

The process of reinforcement enables us to profit from experience by shaping our behaviors according to their consequences. Reinforcing stimuli, and stimuli that are associated with them, motivate us. As we saw in Chapter 12, instrumental conditioning involves the establishment of connections between perceptual mechanisms and motor mechanisms, under the control of a reinforcement system. This chapter discusses the nature of that system.

Although the ideal function of the reinforcement system is to determine when responses have favorable outcomes, our species has discovered substances that stimulate this system artificially. Thus, taking these substances produces a reinforcing effect, often to our detriment. The topic of the second part of this chapter is addiction to substances that stimulate the reinforcement system.

REINFORCEMENT

The discovery of reinforcing brain stimulation, one of the most fascinating discoveries in the history of neuroscience, was made by accident. This discovery captured the imagination of many writers, who warned of a future in which a totalitarian state would put electrodes in the brains of its subjects so that rewards could be given for correct behaviors — or even for correct thoughts. People no longer worry about this prospect of mass neurosurgery, but it is still fascinating to contemplate the fact that the reinforcing effects of things that give us pleasure seem to act on specific circuits in the brain.

Discovery of Reinforcing Brain Stimulation

In 1954 James Olds was trying to determine whether electrical stimulation of the reticular formation might increase arousal and thus facilitate learning. He was assisted in this project by Peter Milner, who was a graduate student at the time. Olds had heard a talk by Neal Miller that described the aversive effects of electrical stimulation of the brain. Therefore, he decided to make sure that stimulation of the reticular formation was not aversive — if it were, the effects of this stimulation on the speed of learning would be difficult to assess. Fortunately for the investigators, one of the electrodes missed its target; the tip wound up some millimeters away, probably in the hypothalamus. (Unfortunately, the brain of the animal was lost, so histological verification could not be obtained.) If all of the electrodes had reached their intended target, Olds and Milner would not have discovered what they did.

Here is Olds's description of what happened when he tested this animal to see whether the brain stimulation was aversive:

> I applied a brief train of 60-cycle sine-wave electrical current whenever the animal entered one corner of the enclosure. The animal did not stay away from the corner, but rather came back quickly after a brief sortie which followed the first stimulation and came back even more quickly after a briefer sortie which followed the second stimulation. By the time the third electrical stimulus had been applied the animal seemed indubitably to be "coming back for more." (Olds, 1973, p. 81)

Olds and Milner were intrigued and excited by this result. They implanted electrodes in the brains of a group of rats and allowed the animals to administer their own stimulation by pressing a lever-operated switch in an operant chamber. (See ***Figure 15.1.***) The animals readily pressed the lever; in their initial study Olds and Milner (1954) reported response rates of over seven hundred per hour. (The self-administration of electrical brain stimulation is usually referred to as **self-stimulation.**) In subsequent studies rates of many thousands of responses per hour have been obtained. Clearly, electrical stimulation of the brain can be a very potent reinforcer.

self-stimulation

The anatomy of reinforcement will be discussed a little later in this chapter. Here I will note only that electrical stimulation of many parts of the brain can reinforce behavior. In general, stimulation of parts of the limbic system and motor system are effective, but the best and most reliable location is the **medial forebrain bundle** (MFB), a bundle of axons that travel in a rostral-caudal axis from the midbrain to the rostral basal forebrain. The MFB passes through the lateral hypothalamus, and it is in this region that most investigators place the tips of their electrodes. The MFB contains long ascending and descending axons that interconnect forebrain and midbrain structures,

medial forebrain bundle

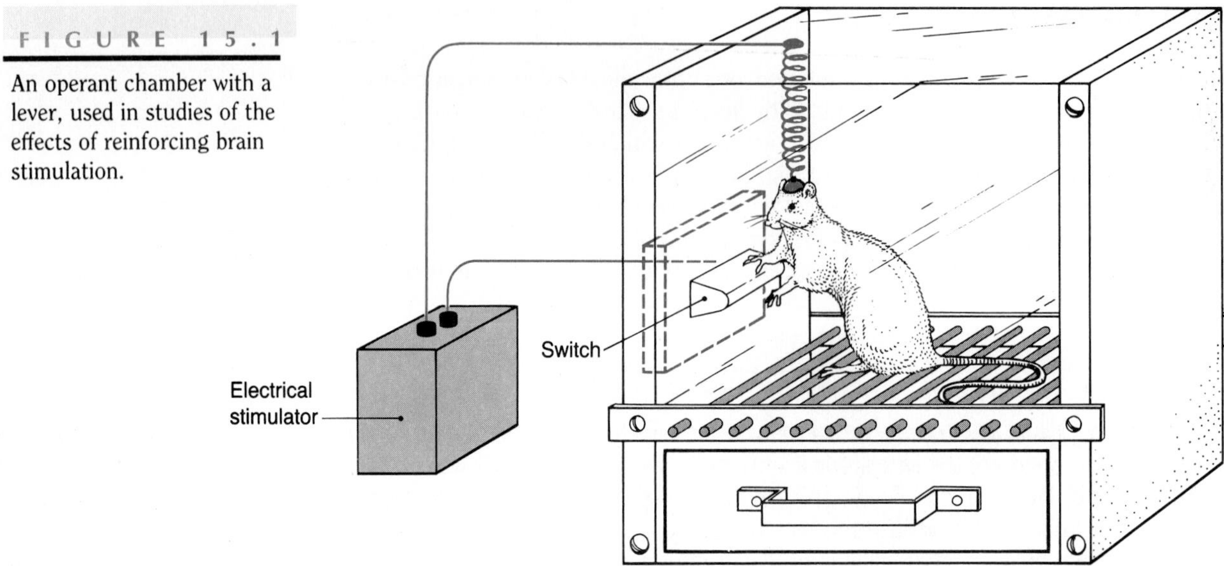

FIGURE 15.1

An operant chamber with a lever, used in studies of the effects of reinforcing brain stimulation.

and short axons that connect adjacent regions. It also contains ascending dopaminergic, noradrenergic, and serotonergic axons on their way from the brain stem to their diencephalic and telencephalic projection areas. As we will see later in this chapter, recent studies suggest that a particular subset of these fibers is responsible for the reinforcing effects of stimulation of the MFB.

How Brain Stimulation Reinforces Behavior

Almost all investigators believe that the electrical stimulation of the medial forebrain bundle is reinforcing because it activates the same system that is activated by natural reinforcers, such as food, water, or sexual contact. The reinforcement system must perform two functions: detect the presence of a reinforcing stimulus, and strengthen the connections between the neurons that detect the discriminative stimulus (such as the sight of a lever) and the neurons that produce the instrumental response (a lever press). (See ***Figure 15.2.***)

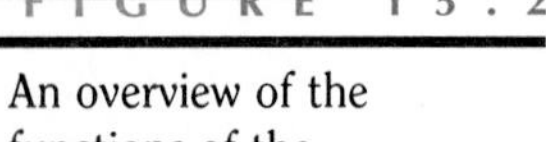

FIGURE 15.2

An overview of the functions of the reinforcement system.

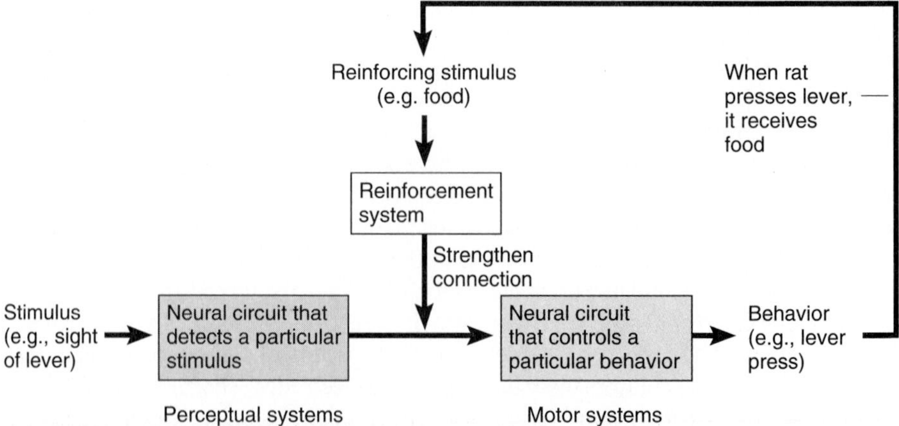

Detection of a reinforcing event is not a simple matter; a stimulus that serves as a reinforcer on one occasion may fail to do so on another. For example, the presence of food will reinforce the behavior of a hungry organism but not one that has just eaten. Thus, the reinforcement system does not simply detect particular stimuli; it must also monitor the state of the organism to determine whether a given stimulus should serve as a reinforcer.

There is a less complicated possibility. Many psychologists prefer to define reinforcers as stimuli that provide an opportunity to perform a behavior rather than as pleasurable stimuli (Premack, 1965). In this view *eating*—and not the presence of food—is the reinforcing event. Eating occurs only when the organism is hungry; therefore, the presence of food will not reinforce the behavior of a satiated organism, because the organism does not eat. In fact, it is a general principle that *reinforcing stimuli are elicitors of behavior* (Donahoe, Crowley, Millard, and Stickney, 1982). If this characterization is correct, then the reinforcement system does not have to detect environmental stimuli and compare them with the animal's motivational condition; instead, it only has to monitor the animal's behavior. The reinforcement system is activated by feedback from making an appetitive response such as eating, drinking, or mating; and this system strengthens the link between the discriminative stimulus and the instrumental response.

If this model of the reinforcement system is correct, then we might expect that reinforcing brain stimulation would be related to the elicitation of responses. In fact, it is; reinforcing brain stimulation almost always elicits appetitive responses. For example, if the tip of an electrode is placed in a rat's MFB and the experimenter turns on the stimulator, the animal will engage in species-typical behaviors such as eating, drinking, fighting, copulation, gnawing on wooden blocks, carrying of objects, or shredding of nesting material. Which of these behaviors the animal performs depends on the location of the electrode and the objects that are present in its environment. If no objects are present, the rat will engage in sniffing and frantic exploratory behavior. If the rat is given the opportunity to turn on the stimulator itself by pressing a lever, it will eagerly do so. Thus, activation of neural circuits that produce appetitive behaviors is reinforcing.

Electrical stimulation of some parts of the brain causes aversive effects, not reinforcing ones. If an animal presses a lever that delivers aversive electrical stimulation, it will avoid pressing it again—in other words, the lever pressing is punished. It will also learn to make a response that turns off such stimulation or prevents it from happening. In general, aversive brain stimulation, like reinforcing brain stimulation, elicits species-typical behaviors; but these behaviors tend to be negative ones, such as defense, attack, or attempts to escape. Thus, activation of neural circuits that produce escape or avoidance behaviors is punishing.

Anatomy of Reinforcement

An animal's behavior can be reinforced by electrical stimulation of many parts of the brain, including the olfactory bulb, prefrontal cortex, nucleus accumbens, caudate nucleus, putamen, various thalamic nuclei, reticular formation, amygdala, ventral tegmental area, substantia nigra, locus coeruleus, and, of course, the MFB (Olds and Fobes, 1981). The finding that stimulation of so many structures is reinforcing suggests that more than one system is involved in reinforcement.

In the past several years investigators have made considerable progress in identifying the neural systems that mediate reinforcement. We now know that dopaminergic neurons play a critical role, and that the axons that are activated by stimulation of the MFB descend to brain stem structures, including a nucleus that contains dopaminergic neurons. In addition, the endogenous opiates have been shown to play a role in reinforcement, perhaps by modulating the effectiveness or activity of dopamine-secreting neurons. It is likely that other systems of neurons, which do not contain dopaminergic axons, mediate reinforcing effects, too, but I shall restrict my discussion to the dopaminergic system, because this is the one that has also been implicated in drug addiction.

ANATOMY OF DOPAMINERGIC PATHWAYS

As we saw in Chapter 4, the development of special staining methods has permitted investigators to trace the pathways of neurons that secrete particular transmitter substances. Investigators soon discovered that the distribution of reinforcing electrode sites nicely coincided with the distribution of catecholaminergic neurons — those that secrete norepinephrine and dopamine. That is, brain stimulation through electrodes whose tips were placed in fiber bundles that contained catecholaminergic axons or in structures that received catecholaminergic projections generally had reinforcing effects. This finding suggested that perhaps one or both of the catecholamines were involved in reinforcement. In fact, one of them is: dopamine.

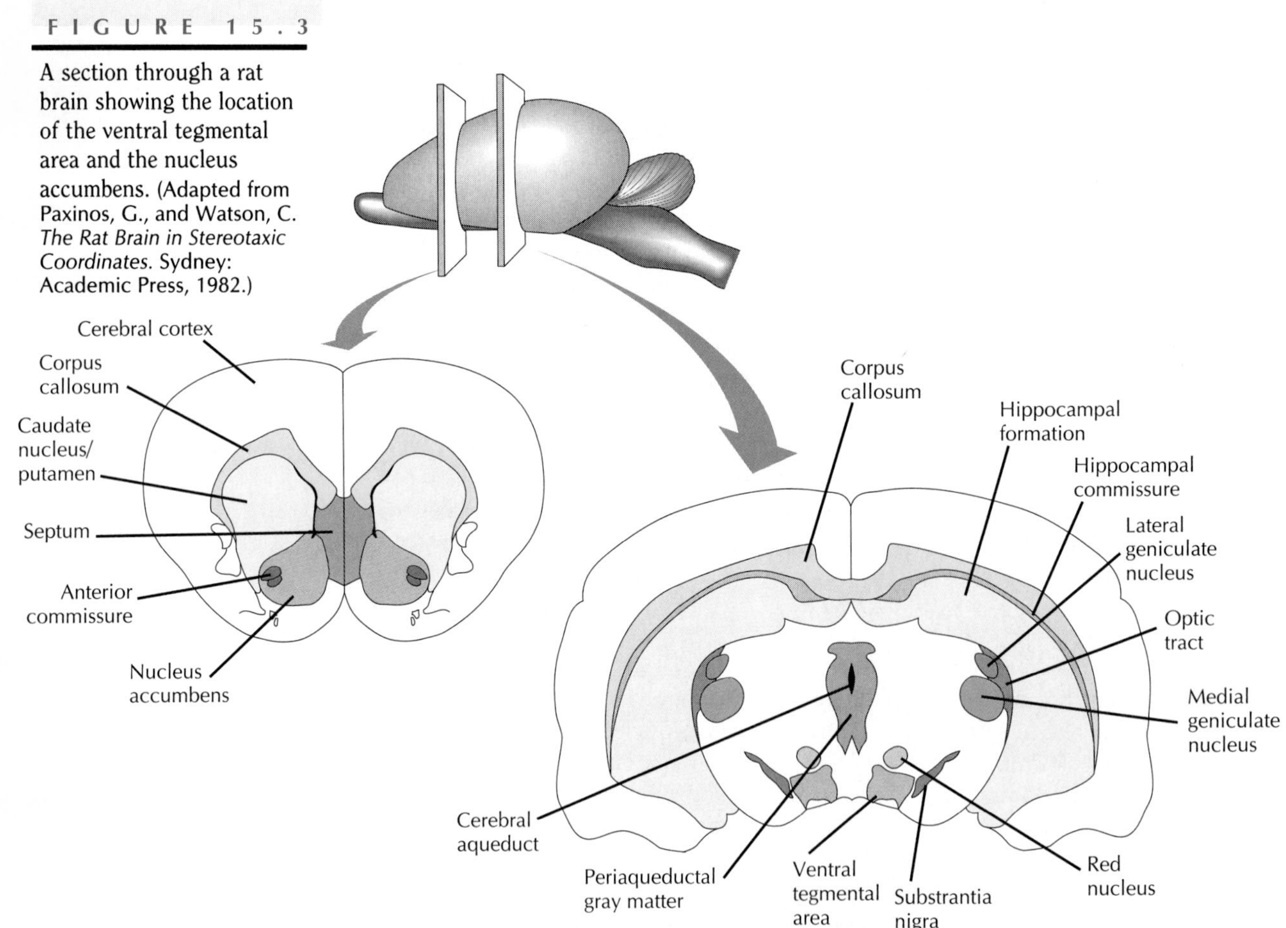

FIGURE 15.3

A section through a rat brain showing the location of the ventral tegmental area and the nucleus accumbens. (Adapted from Paxinos, G., and Watson, C. *The Rat Brain in Stereotaxic Coordinates.* Sydney: Academic Press, 1982.)

There are several systems of neurons whose terminal buttons secrete dopamine. The major pathways begin in the substantia nigra and the ventral tegmental area (Lindvall, 1979; Fallon, 1988). The *nigrostriatal system* starts in the *pars compacta* of the substantia nigra and projects to the *neostriatum*—the caudate nucleus and putamen. As we saw in Chapters 4 and 7, this system is important in the control of movement; its degeneration results in Parkinson's disease. The **tegmentostriatal system** begins in the ventral tegmental area and projects through the medial forebrain bundle to the **nucleus accumbens,** a region of the *paleostriatum,* located in the basal forebrain rostral to the preoptic area and immediately adjacent to the septum. (See ***Figure 15.3.***) As we will see, this system appears to play the most important role in reinforcement.

tegmentostriatal system

nucleus accumbens

The prefrontal cortex also receives dopaminergic projections from the ventral tegmental area. Given the importance of the prefrontal cortex in planning, it seems likely that this system, too, is involved in reinforcement, but so far conclusive evidence is lacking.

EFFECTS OF SYSTEMIC ADMINISTRATION OF DOPAMINE ANTAGONISTS

Studies using drugs that block dopamine receptors clearly indicate that dopamine is involved in reinforcement—provided not only by electrical stimulation of the brain but also by natural reinforcing stimuli. The discovery of the antipsychotic drugs, which exert their therapeutic effects by blocking dopamine receptors, gave researchers a tool to investigate the role of dopaminergic activity in reinforcement. (The role of these synapses in schizophrenia will be discussed in Chapter 16.)

Many studies have shown that drugs that block dopamine receptors also block the process of reinforcement. For example, Rolls et al. (1974) trained rats to press a lever for several different types of reinforcement (including brain stimulation, food, and water) and then administered a drug that blocks dopamine receptors (spiroperidol). They found that the drug suppressed the animals' instrumental responding. However, we cannot determine from studies such as this one whether the animals stopped responding because the food, water, or electrical stimulation was no longer reinforcing, or whether they stopped because the drug interfered with motor systems that controlled their behavior. The drug could have simply made it difficult for the animal to move.

Subsequent studies have shown that the drugs do block reinforcement and do not simply produce side effects that interfere with movement. For example, if an animal receives food (or another reinforcer) in a particular location, it will return to that location later. In other words, reinforcement in a particular place produces a **conditioned place preference.** Spyraki, Fibiger, and Phillips (1982a) trained two groups of hungry rats in a conditioned place preference task. On alternate days the rats were placed in each of two chambers. They received food in one chamber but not the other. After eight days of training the animals were permitted to choose between the two chambers. Rats in the control group, which received an injection of saline just before each day's training, chose the chamber where they had received food. Rats in the experimental group, which received an injection of haloperidol, a drug that blocks dopamine receptors, showed no preference. Thus, interfering with dopaminergic synapses does, indeed, prevent the establishment of a conditioned place preference.

conditioned place preference

Spyraki and her colleagues noted that when food was present in the chamber, the rats in the experimental group *did* eat. Thus, haloperidol did not simply block the response normally elicited by the reinforcing stimulus; it blocked the *reinforcing consequences* of this response. Because all animals were tested in a drug-free condition, the effects were obviously not caused by changes in motor performance.

Drugs that block dopamine receptors interfere with excitatory effects of appetitive stimuli, as well as their reinforcing effects. For example, Falk (1972) discovered that when a very hungry rat receives small pieces of food at infrequent intervals — say, every 2 minutes — the animal becomes very active, engaging in a variety of species-typical behaviors. If water is present, the animal will drink copiously, sometimes consuming an amount equal to 30 percent of its body weight during a 3-hour session. The behaviors are not limited to ingestive ones: If a block of wood is present, the rat will gnaw on it; if another male is present, the rat will attack it; and so on. Behaviors elicited by these means are called **adjunctive behaviors,** because they occur as an adjunct (auxiliary feature) of intermittent reinforcement. Salamone (1988) found that an injection of haloperidol blocked these excitatory effects of reinforcing stimuli; the drug abolished adjunctive activity when rats were given small pieces of food every 30 to 360 seconds. The drug did *not* interfere with eating; the animals simply stayed next to the food dish and ate the food when it was delivered. These excitatory effects, then, appear to be caused by the activity of dopaminergic neurons.

adjunctive behavior

SYSTEMIC ADMINISTRATION OF DOPAMINE AGONISTS

If dopamine antagonists interfere with the effects of reinforcing stimuli, then we might expect that dopamine agonists would enhance them. Indeed, they do — and when these drugs are given by themselves, they produce their own reinforcing effect. For example, Gallistel and Karras (1984) found that injections of amphetamine, a dopaminergic agonist, increase the rate at which a rat will press a lever to obtain reinforcing brain stimulation. Spyraki, Fibiger, and Phillips (1982b) found that rats would learn a conditioned place preference if they were given an injection of amphetamine just before being put in a particular chamber. (They did not receive any food — only the drug.)

Probably the most dramatic effect of dopamine agonists is seen in experiments in which animals administer the drugs themselves. In such **self-administration** studies, animals are able to press a lever that turns on a pump that injects the drug directly into their veins, by means of a flexible plastic tube. Members of a variety of species, including rats, monkeys, and humans, will eagerly and vigorously inject themselves with dopamine agonists such as amphetamine and cocaine (Koob and Bloom, 1988). (I am sure you realize that the evidence concerning humans did not require laboratory experiments.)

self-administration

INTRACRANIAL ADMINISTRATION OF DRUGS

A large body of experimental evidence indicates that the tegmentostriatal pathway, which begins in the ventral tegmental area and terminates in the nucleus accumbens, is the pathway responsible for the reinforcing effects of electrical stimulation of the medial forebrain bundle, for the reinforcing effects of injections of amphetamine and cocaine, and for the reinforcing effects of many natural appetitive stimuli. Any treatment that stimulates dopamine receptors in the nucleus accumbens will reinforce behaviors; thus, animals will press a lever that causes electrical stimulation of the ventral tegmental area, medial forebrain bundle, or nucleus accumbens itself (Routtenberg and Malsbury, 1969; Crow, 1972; Olds and Fobes, 1981). They will also press a lever that delivers direct injections of very small amounts of dopamine or amphetamine directly into the nucleus accumbens (Hoebel et al., 1983; Guerin, Goeders, Dworkin, and Smith, 1984).

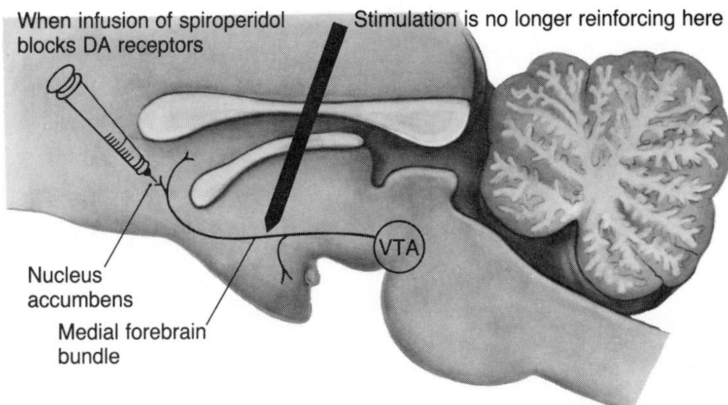

FIGURE 15.4

An explanation of the experiment by Stellar, Kelley, and Corbett (1983).

If the activation of dopamine receptors in the nucleus accumbens is responsible for reinforcement, then we would expect that the injection of drugs that block these receptors would interfere with reinforcement. And it does. Stellar, Kelley, and Corbett (1983) trained rats to travel through a runway in order to receive electrical stimulation of the medial forebrain bundle. They found that when they injected a dopamine receptor blocker into the nucleus accumbens, they had to turn up the current level of the stimulator in order to get the animals to run. That is, the drug reduced the reinforcing value of the electrical brain stimulation. (See ***Figure 15.4.***)

Dopaminergic neurons can be selectively killed by the drug 6-HD (6-hydroxydopamine). When injected into the brain, the drug is taken up by the cell bodies, axons, or terminals of these cells, collects inside them, and kills them. (The drug will also kill noradrenergic neurons; but if it is administered along with imipramine, a drug that blocks the reuptake mechanism in these cells, they will be spared.) You will probably not be surprised to learn that 6-HD lesions of the ventral tegmental area, medial forebrain bundle, or nucleus accumbens disrupt the reinforcing effects of electrical stimulation of the brain (Fibiger, Le Piane, Jakubovic, and Phillips, 1987).

Several types of studies indicate that both cocaine and amphetamine exert their reinforcing effects in the nucleus accumbens, which contains the terminal buttons of the neurons of the tegmentostriatal pathway. An interesting approach employs the **drug discrimination procedure.** This procedure uses the physiological effects of drugs as discriminative stimuli in order to learn something about the nature of these effects (Schuster and Balster, 1977). An animal is given a drug and then is trained to press one of two levers to receive food. The next day, it receives an injection of saline and is trained to press the other lever. Each day thereafter, it receives either the drug or the saline, and it receives food only if it presses the appropriate lever. Obviously, the presence or absence of feedback from the effects of the drug tells the animal which lever to press. Then on test days the animal is given another drug. If the animal presses the "drug" lever, we can conclude that the feedback feels similar to the first drug; if it presses the "saline" lever, we can conclude that it does not.

drug discrimination procedure

Wood and Emmett-Oglesby (1989) trained rats to discriminate between the effects of injections of cocaine and saline and then administered cocaine directly into the brain on test days. During test days they injected the drug into three locations where dopaminergic terminal buttons are found: the nucleus accumbens, the caudate nucleus, and the prefrontal cortex. They found that the rats pressed the "cocaine" lever only when they had received the drug in the nucleus accumbens; when they received the drug in the caudate nucleus or prefrontal cortex, they pressed the "saline" lever. Thus, to the rats, the effects of an injection of cocaine in the nucleus accumbens felt like the effects of a injection into a vein.

MICRODIALYSIS STUDIES

Chapter 1 described a research technique called ***microdialysis*** that is being adopted by an increasing number of laboratories. As we saw in Chapter 1, microdialysis has been used to measure the relation between hunger and satiety and the release of norepinephrine and serotonin in the hypothalamus. Researchers using this method have shown that reinforcing electrical stimulation of the medial forebrain bundle or the administration of cocaine or amphetamine cause the release of dopamine in the nucleus accumbens (Moghaddam and Bunney, 1989; Nakahara et al., 1989). Even more importantly, natural reinforcers stimulate this release: drinking, induced by dehydration or by an injection of angiotensin; salt intake, induced by sodium depletion; or eating, induced by food deprivation (Blander et al., 1988; Chang et al., 1988; Hernandez and Hoebel, 1988).

Sexual behavior, too, causes the release of dopamine in the nucleus accumbens (Pfaus et al., 1990; Pleim et al., 1990). Figure 15.5 shows the effects of sexual contact on the level of dopamine in the nucleus accumbens of a male rat. When the rat was placed in the test chamber (where he had copulated before), the dopamine level increased. Next, a female rat was introduced behind a wire screen; the dopamine level increased further. Finally, the screen was removed and the rats were permitted to copulate; the dopamine level increased still further. After copulation, the female was removed and the dopamine level declined. (See ***Figure 15.5.***)

As I mentioned earlier in this chapter, whether a particular stimulus is reinforcing depends on the physiological condition of the animal. For example, food will reinforce the behavior of a hungry animal but not a satiated one. Another way to change the reinforcing value of a stimulus is to pair it with another one. As we saw in Chapter 11, a conditioned flavor aversion can be established by pairing a particular flavor with treatments that produce illness, such as an injection of lithium chloride. Mark, Blander, Hernandez, and Hoebel (1989) found that although the taste of saccharin normally caused an increase in dopamine release in the nucleus accumbens of naive

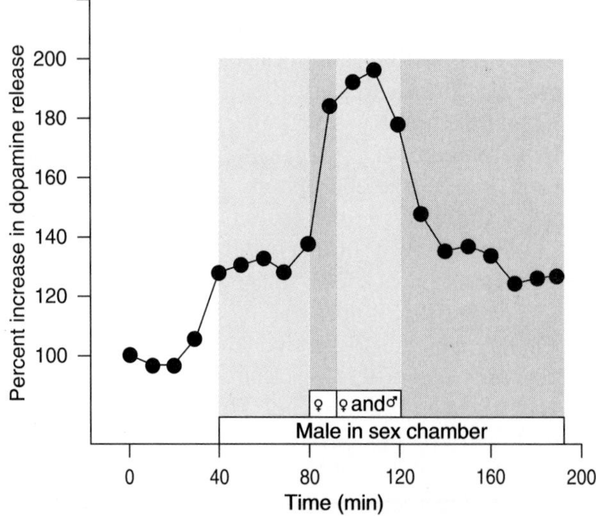

FIGURE 15.5

Levels of extracellular dopamine in the nucleus accumbens of a male rat before, during, and after engaging in sexual behavior, measured by microdialysis. ♀ = female, ♂ = male. (Adapted with permission from Pfaus, J.G., Damsma, G., Nomikos, G.G., Wenkstern, D.G., Blaha, C.D., Phillips, A.G., and Fibiger, H.C. *Brain Research,* 1990, *530,* 345–348.)

animals, it caused a *decrease* in dopamine release if the flavor of saccharin had previously been paired with an injection of lithium chloride. Thus, the same stimulus had very different effects on the activity of neurons involved with reinforcement, depending on the animal's prior experience with this stimulus.

DOPAMINE AND NEURAL PLASTICITY

The fact that the release of dopamine reinforces behavior does not prove that dopamine itself is responsible for synaptic changes affecting learning; possibly, these changes are controlled farther "downstream," by neurons that receive dopaminergic input or even by neurons that *these* neurons communicate with. In any case, some interesting studies summarized by Stein and Belluzzi (1988) indicate that dopamine does appear to be capable of changing the response characteristics of single neurons.

Stein and Belluzzi prepared hippocampal slices according to the method described in Chapter 12. They recorded from single pyramidal neurons in field CA1, which are known to contain dopamine receptors. They attempted to reinforce bursts of neural activity by infusing dopamine or dopamine agonists onto the neuron through a micropipette. Whenever the neuron spontaneously produced a burst of action potentials lasting at least 0.5 second, they applied the dopamine. Figure 15.6 shows the results of administering dopamine, cocaine, or saline. *Baseline* refers to periods during which they simply recorded the number of bursts of action potentials. During *reinforcement* periods they followed each burst with the infusion. During *noncontingent* periods they administered infusions that were not paired with the bursts. As you can see, both dopamine and cocaine increased the rate of the bursts, but only when they were applied contingently. (See ***Figure 15.6.***)

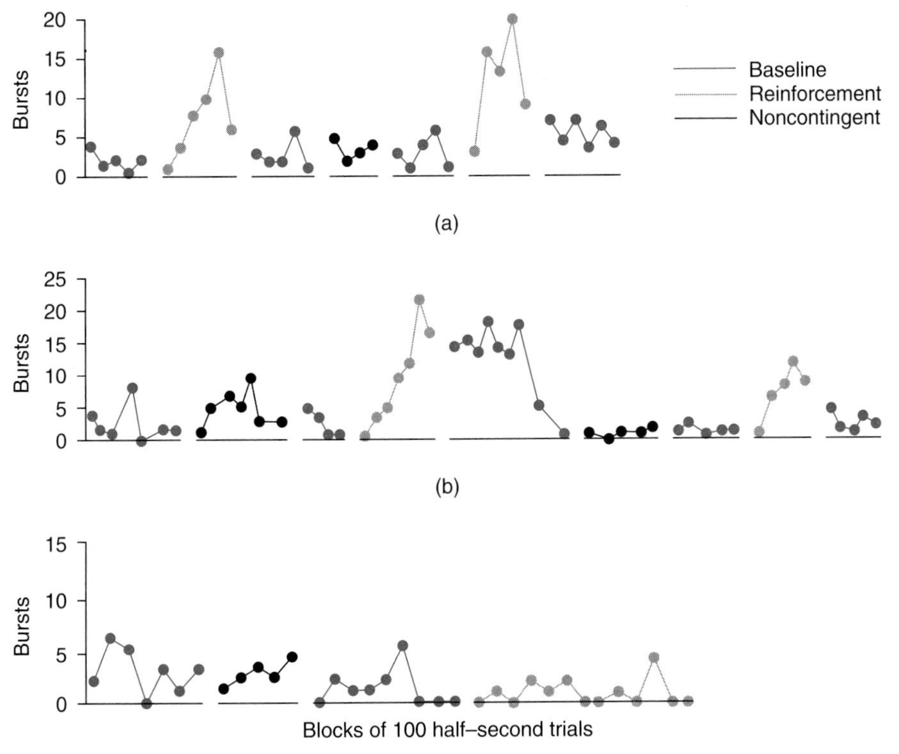

FIGURE 15.6

Instrumental conditioning of single neurons in the CA1 field of the hippocampal formation. (a) Dopamine infusion. (b) Cocaine infusion. (c) Saline infusion. (Adapted from Stein, L., and Belluzzi, J.D., in *Brain Reward Systems and Abuse,* edited by J. Engel and L. Oreland. New York: Raven Press, 1987.)

These findings indicate that if dopamine is administered at the time that cells are already firing, their firing rate will increase. We do not know the mechanism responsible for this phenomenon. If it involves the strengthening of synaptic connections with other neurons in the slice, then it could imply that dopamine itself can reinforce weak connections between neurons. Obviously, more research needs to be done.

RELATION OF SELF-STIMULATION TO NATURAL REINFORCEMENT

The experiments with self-stimulation tell us that behaviors can be reinforced by the activation of neurons located in the basal forebrain that send axons to the ventral tegmental area, where they activate dopaminergic neurons whose axons travel to the nucleus accumbens. We also know that the reinforcing effects of natural appetitive stimuli are abolished by dopamine antagonists and that natural reinforcers increase the release of dopamine in the nucleus accumbens. So this circuit probably is not simply a curiosity for neuroscientists; it plays an important role in reinforcement in the world outside the laboratory. The obvious questions are, then, "When natural reinforcers occur, what neural circuits are responsible for stimulating these neurons in the basal forebrain?" and "How does the release of dopamine in the nucleus accumbens reinforce behaviors?"

A tentative answer to the first question comes from studies described in Chapter 11. As we saw, evidence gathered by Rolls and his colleagues indicates that neurons in the lateral hypothalamus of the monkey become active when an animal sees food, but only when it is hungry. These neurons even show sensory-specific satiety. That is, once a monkey has had all it wants of a particular food, the neurons stop responding to the sight of that food but continue to respond to the sight of foods that the animal is still willing to eat. Thus, the activity of these neurons is clearly related to motivation.

As we saw earlier in this chapter, many psychologists believe that the signal for reinforcement is produced by feedback from certain categories of appetitive species-typical responses. Thus, the lateral hypothalamic neurons whose activity was observed by Rolls and his colleagues may produce two effects: stimulation of motivated behavior by means of connections with brain stem motor systems, and stimulation of reinforcement by means of connections with the ventral tegmental area. Of course, it remains to be established that these lateral hypothalamic neurons have these connections.

Not much progress has yet been made on providing an answer to the second question, "How does the release of dopamine in the nucleus accumbens reinforce behaviors?" Obviously, since the activity of the dopaminergic neurons of the tegmentostriatal system reinforces behaviors, there must be some outputs from the nucleus accumbens that are responsible for this effect. In fact, its outputs reach motor circuits in the midbrain, especially those that control locomotion (Swanson, Mogenson, Gerfen, and Robinson, 1984). It remains to be seen whether these connections are responsible for the reinforcing effects described in this chapter.

▶*INTERIM SUMMARY*◀

When our actions have favorable consequences we tend to repeat them. The process responsible for this fact — reinforcement — is what enables us to profit from experience. Olds and Milner discovered that rats would perform a response that caused electrical current to be delivered through an electrode placed in their brain; thus, the stimulation was reinforcing. Subsequent studies found that stimulation of many locations had reinforcing effects but that the medial forebrain bundle produced the strongest and most reliable ones.

Reinforcing brain stimulation appears also to elicit behaviors, or at least to increase the ability of environmental stimuli to elicit behaviors. These effects suggest that the stimulation mimics the feedback from having made an appetitive response, which is the normal condition for reinforcement. This artificial feedback strengthens the connection between neurons that detect stimuli and neurons whose activity produces behaviors. For example, if an animal receives MFB stimulation when it presses a lever, the sight of the lever becomes an eliciting stimulus that produces pressing.

For several years investigators have believed that the catecholamines — norepinephrine and dopamine — play a role in reinforcement. The most important neurons appear to be dopaminergic cells located in the ventral tegmental area that send their axons to the nucleus accumbens. Systemic injections of dopamine agonists are reinforcing, and systemic injections of dopamine antagonists will block the reinforcing effects of natural stimuli or electrical stimulation of the medial forebrain bundle. Infusions of dopamine antagonists directly into the nucleus accumbens have the same effects as systemic injections. Microdialysis studies have also shown that natural and artificial reinforcers stimulate the release of dopamine in the nucleus accumbens. An increase in the spontaneous response rate of neurons in hippocampal slices can even be increased by contingent infusions of dopamine; thus, single neurons can be instrumentally conditioned.

The neurons that activate the dopaminergic neurons in the tegmentostriatal system are probably located in the lateral hypothalamus and preoptic area. These neurons fire in response to food-related stimuli capable of reinforcing an animal's behavior. On their way to motor circuits in the brain stem, the axons of these neurons may activate dopaminergic neurons in the ventral tegmental area, producing reinforcement. ▲

ADDICTION

Drug addiction is one of the most serious problems that our species presently faces. Consider the disastrous effects caused by the abuse of humankind's oldest drug, alcohol: automobile accidents, fetal alcohol syndrome, cirrhosis of the liver, Korsakoff's syndrome, increased rate of heart disease, and increased rate of intracerebral hemorrhage. Smoking (nicotine addiction) greatly increases the chances of dying of lung cancer, heart attack, and stroke; and women who smoke give birth to smaller, less healthy babies. Cocaine addiction often causes psychosis, brain damage, and death from overdose; it produces babies born with severe brain damage and consequent psychological problems; and competition for lucrative markets terrorizes neighborhoods, subverts political and judicial systems, and causes many deaths. The use of "designer drugs" exposes users to unknown dangers of untested and often contaminated products, as several young people discovered when they acquired Parkinson's disease. Addicts who take their drug intravenously run a serious risk of contracting AIDS. Why do people use these drugs and subject themselves to these dangers?

The answer, as you may have predicted from what you have read in this chapter so far, is that all of these substances stimulate the release of dopamine in the nucleus accumbens; thus, they reinforce the behaviors responsible for their delivery to the body: swallowing, smoking, sniffing, or injecting. The immediate consequences of these drugs are more powerful than the realization that in the long term bad things will happen.

Physiological Effects of Addictive Substances

Most substances to which people can become addicted produce an excitatory effect, although some, like opiates and alcohol, produce both excitation and inhibition. Most investigators believe that the excitatory effects are the most important in producing addiction. Table 15.1 lists some of the most important addictive drugs, along with their relative potential for abuse. (See ***Table 15.1.***) The subsections that follow describe these drugs and their effects.

▲ TABLE 15.1 ▲

Toxic Effects and Addiction Risk of the Major Psychoactive Drugs

Drug Category	*Acute Toxicity*	*Chronic Toxicity*	*Relative Risk of Addiction*
Alcohol	Psychomotor impairment, impaired thinking and judgment, reckless or violent behavior. Lowering of body temperature, respiratory depression.	Hypertension, stroke, hepatitis, cirrhosis, gastritis, pancreatitis. Organic brain damage, cognitive deficits. Fetal alcohol syndrome. Withdrawal effects: shakes, seizures, delirium tremens.	3
Cocaine, amphetamine	Sympathetic overactivity: hypertension, cardiac arrhythmias, hyperthermia. Acute toxic psychosis: delusions, hallucinations, paranoia, violence. Anorexia.	Unpleasant tactile sensations. Stereotyped movements. Seizures, withdrawal depression. Chronic rhinitis, perforation of nasal septum.	1
Caffeine	Cardiac arrhythmias. Insomnia, restlessness, excitement. Muscle tension, jitteriness. Gastric discomfort.	Hypertension. Anxiety, depression. Withdrawal headaches.	5
Cannabis (marijuana, hashish)	Psychomotor impairment. Additive effect with alcohol and sedatives.	Apathy and mental slowing, impaired memory and learning (brain damage?). Impaired immune response?	4
Nicotine	Nausea, tremor, tachycardia. High doses: hypertension, bradycardia, diarrhea, muscle twitching, respiratory paralysis.	Coronary, cerebral, and peripheral vascular disease, gangrene. Gastric acidity, peptic ulcer. Withdrawal irritability, impaired attention and concentration. Retarded fetal growth, spontaneous abortion. Other substances in tobacco smoke: bronchitis, emphysema, lung cancer.	2
Opiates	Sedation, analgesia, emotional blunting, dream state. Nausea, vomiting, spasm of ureter and bile duct. Respiratory depression, coma, additive effects with alcohol and sedatives. Impaired thermoregulation. Suppression of sex hormones.	Disorders of hypothalamic and pituitary hormone secretion. Constipation. Withdrawal cramps, diarrhea, vomiting, gooseflesh, lacrimation.	2
Hallucinogen (LSD, PCP)	Sympathetic overactivity. Visual and auditory illusions, hallucinations, depersonalization. PCP: muscle rigidity, elevated body temperature, staggering gait, agitation, violence, stereotyped movements, convulsions.	Flashbacks. Depression, prolonged psychotic episodes.	5

Source: Goldstein, A., and Kalant, H. Drug policy: Striking the right balance. *Science,* 1990, *249,* 1513–1521.

Listed here are effects due to the drugs themselves. The effects are dose-related and subject to individual variation in sensitivity, so not all are expected to be seen in every user. Approximate rankings for relative risk of addiction are on a 5-point scale, where 1 is most severe.

OPIATES

Opium, derived from a sticky resin produced by the opium poppy, has been eaten and smoked for centuries. Morphine, one of the naturally occurring ingredients of opium, is sometimes used as a painkiller but has largely been supplanted by synthetic opiates. Heroin, a compound produced from morphine, is the most commonly abused opiate.

Opiate addiction has several high personal and social costs. First, because heroin is an illegal drug, an addict becomes, by definition, a criminal. Second, the behavioral response to opiates declines with continued use, which means that a person must take increasing amounts of the drug to achieve a "high." The habit thus becomes more and more expensive, and the person often turns to crime to obtain enough money to support his or her habit. (If the addict is a pregnant woman, her infant will also become dependent on the drug, which easily crosses the placental barrier. The infant must be given opiates right after being born and then be given gradually decreasing doses.) Third, an opiate addict often uses unsanitary needles; at present, a substantial percentage of people who inject illicit drugs have been exposed in this way to the AIDS virus. Fourth, the uncertainty about the strength of a given batch of heroin makes it possible for a user to receive an unusually large dose of the drug, with possibly fatal consequences. In addition, dealers typically dilute pure heroin with various adulterants such as milk sugar, quinine, or talcum powder; and dealers are not known for taking scrupulous care with the quality and sterility of the substances they use. Some heroin-induced deaths have actually been reactions to the adulterants mixed with the drugs.

Tolerance and Withdrawal Symptoms. Many people—including many health care professionals—think of heroin as the prototype for addiction. People who habitually take heroin (or other opiates) become physically dependent on the drug. Eddy, Halbach, Isbell, and Seevers (1965) define *physical dependence* as "an adaptive state that manifests itself by intense physical disturbances when the administration of a drug is suspended" (p. 723). In contrast, they define *psychic dependence* as a condition in which a drug produces "a feeling of satisfaction and a psychic drive that requires periodic or continuous administration of the drug to produce pleasure or to avoid discomfort" (p. 723). In fact, as we shall see, the distinction between "physical" and "psychic" dependence reflects a misunderstanding of the process of addiction.

Tolerance is the decreased sensitivity to a drug that comes from its continued use; the drug user must take larger and larger amounts of the drug in order for it to be effective. Once a person has taken an opiate regularly enough to develop tolerance, that person will suffer **withdrawal symptoms** if he or she stops taking the drug. Withdrawal symptoms are primarily the opposite of the effects of the drug itself. That is, heroin produces euphoria; withdrawal from it produces *dysphoria*—a feeling of anxious misery. (*Euphoria* and *dysphoria* mean "easy to bear" and "hard to bear," respectively.) Heroin produces constipation; withdrawal from it produces nausea, cramping, and diarrhea. Heroin produces relaxation; withdrawal from it produces agitation.

tolerance

withdrawal symptom

Most investigators believe that the withdrawal symptoms are produced by the body's attempt to compensate for the unusual condition of heroin intoxication. That is, most systems of the body, including those controlled by the brain, are regulated so that they stay at an optimal value. When a drug artificially changes these systems for a prolonged time, homeostatic mechanisms begin to produce the opposite reaction, thus partially compensating for the disturbance from the optimal value. These compensatory mechanisms account for the fact that more and more heroin must be taken in order to achieve the effects that were produced when the person first started taking the drug (tolerance). They also account for the symptoms of withdrawal: When the person stops taking the drug, the compensatory mechanisms make themselves felt, unopposed by the action of the drug.

Heroin addiction has provided such a striking example of drug dependence that some authorities have concluded that "real" addiction does not occur unless a drug causes tolerance and withdrawal. Without doubt, withdrawal symptoms make it difficult for a person to stop taking heroin — they keep the person hooked, so to speak. However, withdrawal symptoms do not explain why a person *becomes* a heroin addict, nor do they explain why people continue taking the drug. Certainly, people do not start taking heroin so that they will become physically dependent on it and feel miserable when they go without it. In fact, when the cost of the habit gets too high, some addicts stop taking heroin "cold turkey." Doing so is not as painful as most people believe; withdrawal symptoms have been described as similar to a bad case of the flu. After a week or two, when their nervous system adapts to the absence of the drug, they recommence their habit. If their only reason for taking the drug was to avoid unpleasant withdrawal symptoms, they would never be capable of following this strategy. The reason that people take — and continue to take — drugs such as heroin is that the drugs give them a pleasurable "rush"; in other words, the drugs have a reinforcing effect on their behavior.

There are two kinds of evidence that contradict the belief that drug addition is caused by physical dependence. First, some very potent drugs — including cocaine — do not produce physical dependence. That is, people who take the drug do not show tolerance, and if they stop, they do not show any withdrawal symptoms. And yet the people show just as strong an addiction as heroin addicts. Second, some drugs produce physical dependence (tolerance and withdrawal symptoms) but are not abused (Jaffe, 1985). The reason they are not abused is that they do not have reinforcing effects on behavior.

Effects on Dopaminergic Neurons. As you learned in Chapter 4, opiates act by stimulating specialized receptors on the membranes of neurons located in various parts of the nervous system. When an opiate is administered systemically, it stimulates all of these receptors and produces a variety of effects, including analgesia, hypothermia (lowering of body temperature), sedation, and reinforcement. Opiate receptors in the periaqueductal gray matter are responsible for the analgesia, those in the preoptic area are responsible for the hypothermia, those in the mesencephalic reticular formation are responsible for the sedation, and those in the ventral tegmental area and the nucleus accumbens are responsible for the reinforcement. In addition, opiate receptors in the periaqueductal gray matter appear to be responsible for the withdrawal effects seen in animals with heroin dependency (Wise, 1989). (See ***Table 15.2.***)

Laboratory animals, like humans, will self-administer opiates. They will work for them to be injected into two regions of the brain known to be involved in the effects of dopamine on reinforcement: the ventral tegmental area and the nucleus accumbens (Bozarth and Wise, 1984; Goeders, Lane, and Smith, 1984). In addition, if a drug that blocks opiate receptors is injected into either the ventral tegmental area or the nucleus accumbens, the reinforcing effect of intravenous heroin is decreased (Britt and Wise, 1983; Vaccarino, Bloom, and Koob, 1985). Bozarth and Wise (1984) found that repeated injections of morphine into the ventral tegmental area do not seem to produce signs of withdrawal when the injections stop; however, repeated injections into the periaqueductal gray matter *do* lead to withdrawal symptoms, *even though the*

▲ TABLE 15.2 ▲

Locations of Opiate Receptors and their Functions

Location	*Physiological Effect*
Periaqueductal gray matter	Analgesia, withdrawal effects
Preoptic area	Hypothermia
Mesencephalic reticular formation	Sedation
Ventral tegmental area and nucleus accumbens	Reinforcement

injections are not reinforcing. Thus, receptors in different parts of the brain are responsible for the reinforcing effects of opiates and the aversive effects produced by opiate withdrawal.

Several different kinds of experimental evidence indicate that opiates exert their reinforcing effects in the ventral tegmental area by activating dopaminergic neurons. For example, an injection of morphine into the ventral tegmental area increases the activity of dopaminergic neurons located there (Matthews and German, 1984). In addition, after the dopaminergic neurons of the tegmentostriatal system have been destroyed with 6-HD, rats will not press a lever that administers intravenous heroin (Bozarth and Wise, 1986).

As we saw earlier in this chapter, microdialysis studies have shown that reinforcing brain stimulation and many natural stimuli that reinforce behaviors cause dopamine to be released in the nucleus accumbens. Di Chiara and Imperato (1987) constructed special microdialysis tubes that they inserted into the brain so they passed through the nucleus accumbens or the caudate nucleus. (See ***Figure 15.7.***) They found that injections of opiates caused the release of dopamine, especially in the nucleus accumbens.

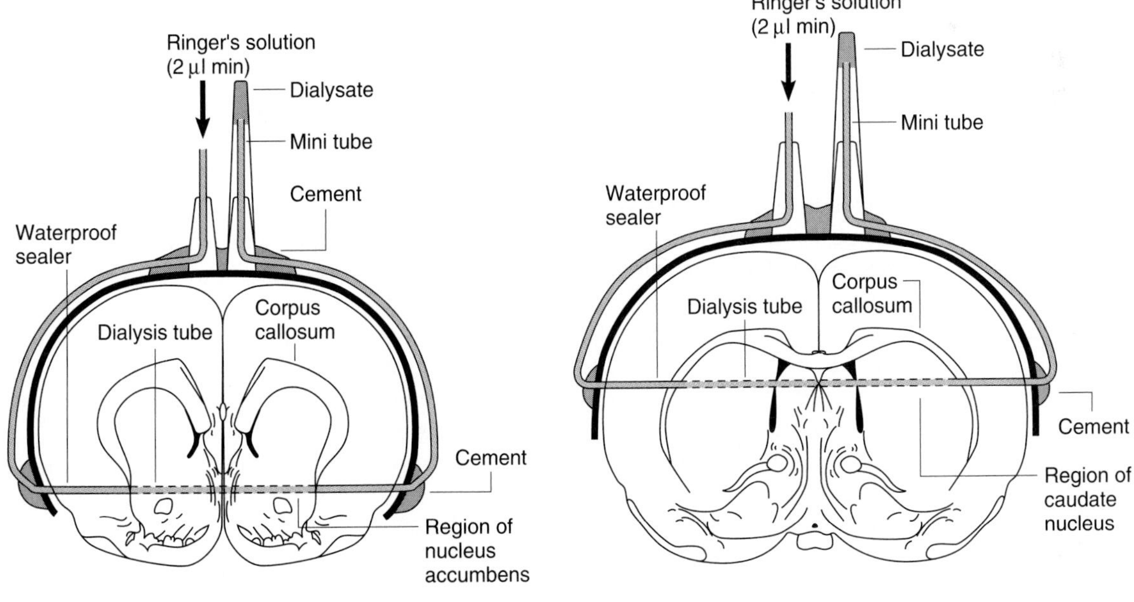

FIGURE 15.7

The microdialysis procedure used by Di Chiara and Imperato (1987) to measure the release of dopamine. Ringer's solution resembles the interstitial fluid that surrounds cells. (a) Nucleus accumbens. (b) Caudate nucleus. (Adapted with permission from Carboni, E., Imperato, A., Perezzani, L., and Di Chiara, G. *Neuroscience, 28,* 653–661, copyright 1989, Pergamon Press plc.)

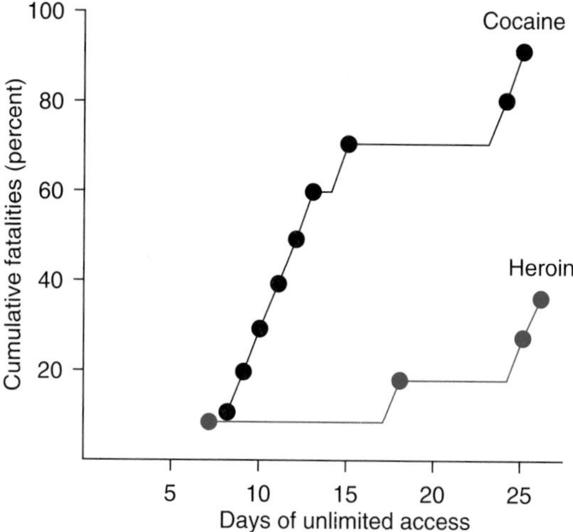

FIGURE 15.8

Cumulative fatalities in groups of rats self-administering cocaine or heroin. (From Bozarth, M.A., and Wise, R.A. *Journal of the American Medical Association,* 1985, *254,* 81–83. Copyright 1985, American Medical Association.)

COCAINE AND AMPHETAMINE

Cocaine and amphetamine have similar behavioral effects, because both act as dopamine agonists by blocking its reuptake after it is released by the terminal buttons. In addition, amphetamine directly stimulates the release of dopamine. "Crack," a particularly potent form of cocaine, is smoked and thus enters the blood supply of the lungs and reaches the brain very quickly. Because its effects are so potent and so rapid, it is probably the most effective reinforcer of all available drugs.

When people take cocaine, they become euphoric, active, and talkative. They say that they feel powerful and alert. Some of them become addicted to the drug, and obtaining it becomes an obsession to which they devote more and more time and money. Laboratory animals, who will quickly learn to self-administer cocaine intravenously, also act excited and show intense exploratory activity. After receiving the drug for a day or two, rats start showing stereotyped movements, such as grooming, head bobbing, and persistent locomotion (Geary, 1987). If rats or monkeys are given continuous access to a lever that permits them to self-administer cocaine, they often self-inject so much cocaine that they die. In fact, Bozarth and Wise (1985) found that rats that self-administered cocaine were almost three times more likely to die than rats that self-administered heroin. (See ***Figure 15.8.***)

One of the alarming effects of cocaine and amphetamine seen in people who abuse these drugs regularly is psychotic behavior: hallucinations, delusions of persecution, mood disturbances, and repetitive behaviors. These symptoms so closely resemble those of paranoid schizophrenia that even a trained mental health professional cannot distinguish them unless he or she knows about the person's history of drug abuse. The fact that these symptoms are provoked by dopamine agonists and reduced by drugs that block dopamine receptors suggests that overactivity of dopaminergic synapses is one of the causes of schizophrenia. I will say more about this subject in Chapter 16, which is devoted to the biology of mental disorders.

Usually, a psychotic reaction caused by use of cocaine or amphetamine will subside once the person stops taking the drug. However, the exposure to the drug appears to produce long-term changes in the brain that make the person more likely to display psychotic symptoms if he or she takes the drug later—even months or years later (Sato, Chen, Akiyama, and Otsuki, 1983; Sato, 1986). A study with rats suggests that this effect is produced by long-term changes in the nucleus accumbens. Robinson,

FIGURE 15.9

Sensitization to the effects of amphetamine in rats that had been pretreated for five weeks with amphetamine or saline. (a) Effects of amphetamine on the release of dopamine in the nucleus accumbens. (b) and (c) Effects of amphetamine on stereotyped behaviors. (Adapted from Robinson, T.E., Jurson, P.A., Bennett, J.A., and Bentgen, K.M. *Brain Research,* 1988, *462,* 211–222.)

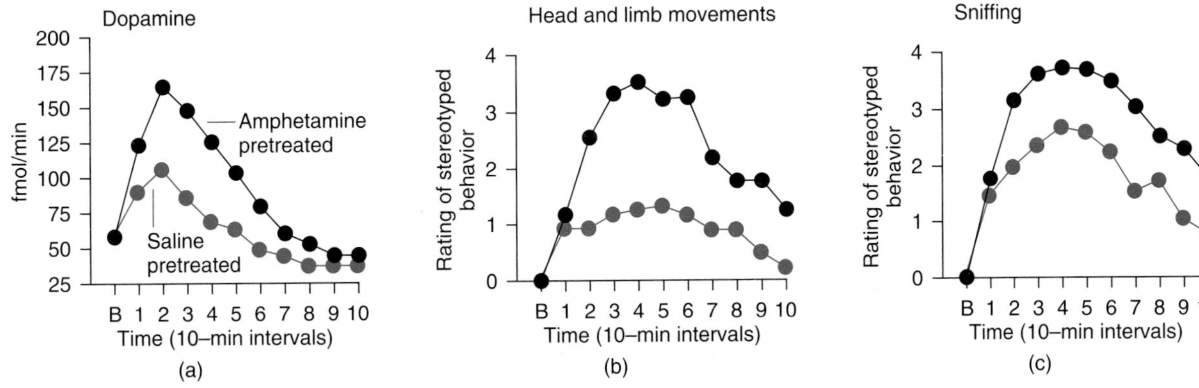

Jurson, Bennett, and Bentgen (1988) administered escalating daily doses of amphetamine to rats over a period of five weeks, in a pattern designed to mimic that of people who abuse the drug and become psychotic. Two to three weeks later, the investigators administered a single dose of amphetamine and observed the animals' behavior and measured the release of dopamine in the nucleus accumbens by means of microdialysis. As Figure 15.9 shows, the rates of head and limb movements, sniffing, and dopamine release were much higher in animals that had previously received the amphetamine. (See ***Figure 15.9.***)

NICOTINE AND CAFFEINE

Stimulant drugs such as nicotine and caffeine may seem rather tame after a discussion of opiates, cocaine, and amphetamine. Nevertheless, these drugs, too, have addictive potential. Fortunately, caffeine is relatively innocuous; most people do not take enough to impair their health or produce serious behavioral effects. Nicotine is a different story. The combination of nicotine and other substances in tobacco smoke is carcinogenic and leads to cancer of the lungs, mouth, throat, and esophagus. Also, if the smoker is a pregnant woman, the development of her fetus is likely to be adversely affected. Although nicotine is less potent than the "hard" drugs, many more people who try it go on to become addicts. The addictive potential of nicotine should not be underestimated; many people continue to smoke even when doing so causes serious health problems. For example, Sigmund Freud, whose theory of psychoanalysis stressed the importance of insight in changing one's behavior, was unable to stop smoking even after most of his jaw had been removed because of the cancer that this habit had caused (Brecher, 1972). His cancer finally killed him.

As we saw in Chapter 4, many transmitter substances exert their effects on the postsynaptic membrane through the production of a second messenger, such as cyclic AMP. Caffeine prevents the destruction of the second messenger by inactivating an enzyme that normally destroys it; thus, caffeine acts as an agonist at many synapses. Cyclic AMP and related substances have many other functions as well, so the effects of caffeine are not at all specific. Nevertheless, there is some evidence that caffeine activates dopaminergic neurons (Wise, 1988).

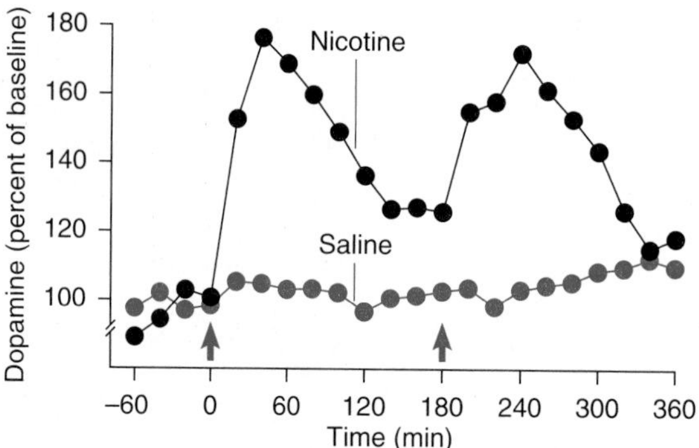

FIGURE 15.10

Release of dopamine in the nucleus accumbens caused by injections of nicotine or saline. The arrows indicate the time of the injections. (From Damsma, G., Day, J., and Fibiger, H.C. *European Journal of Pharmacology,* 1989, *168,* 363–368. Reprinted with permission.)

Ours is not the only species willing to self-administer nicotine; so will laboratory animals (Henningfield and Goldberg, 1983). As you learned in Chapter 4, nicotine stimulates acetylcholine receptors. It also increases the activity level of dopaminergic neurons, which contain these receptors (Svensson, Grenhoff, and Aston-Jones, 1986), and causes dopamine to be released in the nucleus accumbens (Damsma, Day, and Fibiger, 1989). Figure 15.10 shows the effects of two injections of nicotine or saline on the extracellular dopamine level of the nucleus accumbens, measured by microdialysis probes. You can see that the injections of nicotine caused dopamine to be released, but the injections of saline had no effect. (See ***Figure 15.10.***)

Wise (1988) notes that because nicotine stimulates the tegmentostriatal dopaminergic system, smoking could potentially make it more difficult for a cocaine or heroin addict to stop taking the drug. As several studies with laboratory animals have shown, if self-administration of cocaine or heroin is extinguished through nonreinforcement, an injection of drugs that stimulate dopaminergic neurons can reinstate the responding. A similar "cross-priming" effect from cigarette smoking could potentially contribute to a relapse in people who are trying to abstain. (As we shall see, alcohol also stimulates dopaminergic neurons, so drinking could present the same problem.)

MARIJUANA

Another drug that people regularly self-administer—almost exclusively by smoking—is THC, the active ingredient in marijuana. As you learned in Chapter 4, THC receptors have been discovered, and their distribution in the brain has been mapped. However, we still do not know what types of neurons contain these receptors, and we still do not know the physiological effects of THC. The fact that the brain contains THC receptors implies that the brain produces an endogenous ligand for them. What this chemical is and what functions it serves are yet to be discovered.

One thing we do now know about THC is that it, like other drugs with abuse potential, has an effect on dopaminergic neurons. Chen et al. (1990) injected rats with low doses of THC and measured the release of dopamine in the nucleus accumbens by means of microdialysis. Sure enough, they found that the injections caused the release of dopamine. (See ***Figure 15.11.***) As we saw in Chapter 4, the hippocampus contains a large concentration of THC receptors. Given the fact that the hippocampus is involved in learning, perhaps it is ultimately responsible for stimulating the release of dopamine in the nucleus accumbens. Marijuana is known to affect people's short-term memory; specifically, it impairs their ability to keep track of a particular topic—they frequently lose the thread of a conversation. Perhaps the drug does so by disrupting the normal functions of the hippocampus.

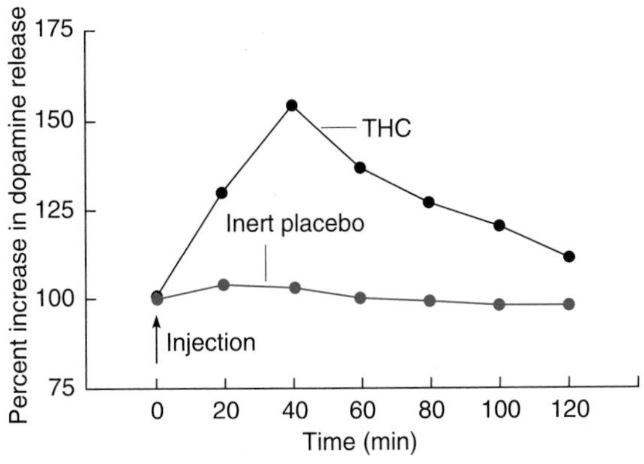

FIGURE 15.11

Release of dopamine in the nucleus accumbens caused by injections of THC or an inert placebo. (From Chen, J., Paredes, W., Li, J., Smith, D., Lowinson, J., and Gardner, E.L. *Psychopharmacology,* 1990, *102,* 156–162. Reprinted with permission.)

ALCOHOL AND BARBITURATES

Alcohol costs society more than any other drug. A large percentage of deaths and injuries caused by motor vehicle accidents are related to alcohol use, and alcohol contributes to violence and aggression. Chronic alcoholics often lose their jobs, their homes, and their families; and many die of cirrhosis of the liver, exposure, or diseases caused by poor living conditions and abuse of their body. Women who drink during pregnancy run the risk of giving birth to babies with fetal alcohol syndrome, which includes malformation of the head and the brain. In fact, the leading cause of mental retardation in the Western world today is alcohol consumption by pregnant women (Abel and Sokol, 1986). Thus, understanding the physiological and behavioral effects of this drug is an important issue.

At low doses alcohol produces mild euphoria and has an *anxiolytic* effect—that is, it reduces the discomfort of anxiety. At higher doses it produces incoordination and sedation. In studies with laboratory animals the anxiolytic effects manifest themselves as a release from the punishing effects of aversive stimuli. For example, if an animal is given electric shocks whenever it makes a particular response (say, one that obtains food or water), it will stop doing so. However, if it is then given some alcohol, it will begin making the response again (Koob et al., 1984). This phenomenon explains why people often do things they normally would not when they have had too much to drink; the alcohol removes the inhibitory effect of social controls on their behavior.

Alcohol probably produces both positive and negative reinforcement. *Positive* reinforcement is reinforcement caused by the presence of an appetitive stimulus, which, as we have seen, is related to the release of dopamine by neurons of the tegmentostriatal system. *Negative* reinforcement is reinforcement caused by the termination of an aversive stimulus. For example, an animal can be trained to press a lever if doing so turns off a loud noise. Similarly, if we find a medication that makes a painful headache go away, we will quickly turn to that medication the next time we have a headache. Negative reinforcement is provided by the anxiolytic effect of alcohol. If a person feels anxious and uncomfortable, then a drug that relieves this discomfort provides at least a temporary escape from an unpleasant situation.

The negative reinforcement provided by the anxiolytic effect of alcohol is probably not enough to explain the drug's addictive potential. Other drugs, such as the benzodiazepines (tranquilizers such as Valium), are even more potent anxiolytics than alcohol, and yet such drugs are rarely abused. It is probably the unique combination of stimulating and anxiolytic effects—of positive and negative reinforcement—that makes alcohol so difficult for some people to resist.

In low doses alcohol appears to produce its anxiolytic effect and produce drunkenness by stimulating the GABA-benzodiazepine receptor complex. As we saw in Chapter 4, Suzdak et al. (1986) found that alcohol makes GABA receptors become more sensitive. In fact, they discovered a drug (Ro15-4513) that reverses alcohol intoxication, presumably by blocking one of the receptor sites on the GABA-benzodiazepine receptor complex.

The site (or sites) of action of alcohol in the brain is not yet known. However, the positive reinforcement produced by the drug apparently involves the release of dopamine. Alcohol increases the firing of dopaminergic neurons in the ventral tegmental area (Gessa et al., 1985). It also causes the release of dopamine in the nucleus accumbens, as measured by microdialysis (Imperato and Di Chiara, 1986). It remains to be seen just how alcohol activates dopaminergic neurons and causes this dopamine release.

Barbiturates have behavioral effects very similar to those of alcohol. In fact, both drugs may act on the GABA-benzodiazepine receptor complex (Maksay and Ticku, 1985). However, if they do so, they act at different sites in the complex; Ro15-4513, the alcohol antagonist, does not reverse the intoxicating effects of barbiturates (Suzdak et al., 1986). The effects of alcohol and barbiturates are additive; if a person takes a moderate dose of alcohol and a moderate dose of a barbiturate, the effect can be fatal. Barbiturates do *not* appear to affect dopaminergic neurons (Wood, 1982).

Although the effects of heroin withdrawal have been exaggerated, those produced by barbiturate or alcohol withdrawal are serious and can even be fatal (Julien, 1981). Convulsions caused by alcohol withdrawal are considered to be a medical emergency and are usually treated with benzodiazepines or barbiturates. As we saw in Chapter 14, NMDA receptors appear to be involved in seizures produced by alcohol withdrawal.

Genetics of Addiction

Not everyone is equally likely to become addicted to a drug. Many people manage to drink alcohol moderately, and even many users of potent drugs such as cocaine and heroin use them "recreationally," without becoming dependent on them. There are only two possible sources of individual differences in any characteristic: heredity and environment. Because this book considers the *physiology* of behavior, I will not discuss the role that environment plays in a person's susceptibility to the addicting effects of drugs. Obviously, environmental effects are important; people raised in a squalid environment without any real hope for a better life are more likely than other people to turn to drugs for some temporary euphoria and removal from the unpleasant world that surrounds them. But even in a given environment, poor or privileged, some people become addicts and some do not — and some of these behavioral differences are a result of genetic differences, as we will see in the following subsections.

RESEARCH ON HUMAN HEREDITY

Most of the research on the effects of heredity on addiction have been devoted to alcoholism. One of the most important reasons for this focus — aside from the importance of the problems caused by alcohol — is that almost everyone is exposed to alcohol. Most people drink alcohol sometime in their lives and thus receive firsthand experience with its reinforcing effects. The same is not true for cocaine, heroin, and other drugs that have even more potent effects. In most countries alcohol is freely and legally available in local shops, whereas cocaine and heroin must often be purchased in dangerous neighborhoods from unsavory dealers. From what we now know about the effects of addictive drugs on the nervous system, it seems likely that the results of studies on the heredity of alcoholism will apply to other types of drug addiction as well.

Alcohol consumption is not distributed equally across the population; in the United States 10 percent of the people drink 50 percent of the alcohol (Heckler, 1983). The best evidence for an effect of heredity on susceptibility to alcoholism comes from two main sources: twin studies and cross-fostering studies. As you know, there are two types of twins. Monozygotic twins come from a single fertilized ovum, which splits apart early in development, becoming two independent individuals with identical heredity. Dizygotic twins come from two different ova, fertilized by two different sperms. Thus, they share (on the average) 50 percent of their chromosomes, just like any two siblings. If a trait is influenced by heredity, then we would expect that, with respect to this trait, monozygotic twins would resemble each other more than dizygotic twins. Monozygotic twins (identical twins) have the same body shape, facial characteristics, and hair and eye color, because these traits certainly are influenced by heredity. Many of their personality characteristics are also similar, which tells us that these traits, too, are influenced by heredity. Alcoholism is one of those traits; monozygotic twins are more likely to resemble each other with respect to alcohol abuse than dizygotic twins (Goodwin, 1979).

The second type of heritability study uses children who were adopted by nonrelatives when they were young. A study like this permits the investigator to estimate the effects of family environment as well as genetics. That is, one can examine the effects of being raised by an alcoholic parent, or having a biological parent who is an alcoholic, or both, on the probability of becoming alcoholic. Such a study was carried out in Sweden by Cloninger, Bohmann, Sigvardsson, and von Knorring (1985). Briefly, the study found that heredity was much more important than family environment. But the story is not quite that simple.

In a review of the literature on alcohol abuse Cloninger (1987) notes that many investigators have concluded that there are two principal types of alcoholics: those who cannot abstain but drink consistently, and those who are able to go without drinking for long periods of time but are unable to control themselves once they start. (For convenience, I will refer to these two groups as "steady drinkers" and "bingers.") (See ***Table 15.3.***) Steady drinking is associated with antisocial personality disorder, which includes a lifelong history of impulsiveness, fighting, lying, and lack of remorse

▲ TABLE 15.3 ▲

Characteristic Features of Two Types of Alcoholism

	Type of Alcoholism	
Feature	*Steady*	*Binge*
Usual age of onset (years)	Before 25	After 25
Spontaneous alcohol seeking (inability to abstain)	Frequent	Infrequent
Fighting and arrests when drinking	Frequent	Infrequent
Psychological dependence (loss of control)	Infrequent	Frequent
Guilt and fear about alcohol dependence	Infrequent	Frequent
Novelty seeking	High	Low
Harm avoidance	Low	High
Reward dependence	Low	High

Source: From Cloninger, C.R. *Science*, 1987, *236*, 410–416. Reprinted with permission.

for antisocial acts. Binge drinking is associated with emotional dependence, behavioral rigidity, perfectionism, introversion, and guilt feelings about one's drinking behavior. Steady drinkers usually begin their alcohol consumption early in life, whereas binge drinkers begin much later. (See ***Table 15.3.***)

Steady drinking is strongly influenced by heredity. The Swedish adoption study (Cloninger et al., 1985) found that men with fathers who were steady drinkers were almost seven times more likely to become steady drinkers themselves than men whose fathers did not abuse alcohol. Family environment had no measurable effect; the boys began drinking whether or not the members of their adoptive family drank heavily. Very few women become steady drinkers; the daughters of steady-drinking fathers instead tend to develop *somatization disorder.* People with this disorder chronically complain of symptoms for which no physiological cause can be found, leading them to seek medical care almost continuously. Thus, the genes that predispose a man to become a steady-drinking alcoholic (antisocial type) predispose a woman to develop somatization disorder. The reason for this interaction with gender is not known.

Binge drinking is influenced both by heredity and by environment and is seen in both males and females. The Swedish adoption study found that having a biological parent who was a binge drinker had little effect on the development of binge drinking unless the child was exposed to a family environment in which there was heavy drinking.

POSSIBLE MECHANISMS

When we find an effect of heredity on behavior, we have good reason to suspect the existence of a biological difference. That is, genes affect behavior only by affecting the body. A susceptibility to alcoholism could conceivably be caused by differences in the ability to digest or metabolize alcohol or by differences in the structure or biochemistry of the brain. Most investigators believe that differences in brain physiology are more likely to play a role. Cloninger (1987) notes that many studies have shown that people with antisocial tendencies, which includes the group of steady drinkers, show a strong tendency to seek novelty and excitement, are disorderly and distractible (many have a history of hyperactivity), and show little restraint in their behavior. They tend not to fear dangerous situations or social disapproval. They are easily bored. They tend to have low levels of 5-HT and dopamine metabolites in their cerebrospinal fluid, which suggests that serotonergic and dopaminergic neurons may be less active than those of other people (Linnoila et al., 1983; Cloninger, 1986). On the other hand, binge drinkers tend to be anxious, emotionally dependent, sentimental, sensitive to social cues, cautious and apprehensive, fearful of novelty or change, rigid, and attentive to details. Their EEGs show little slow alpha activity, which is characteristic of a relaxed state (Propping, Kruger, and Mark, 1981). When they take alcohol, they report a pleasant relief of tension (Propping, Kruger, and Janah, 1980). Perhaps, as Cloninger suggests, these personality differences are a result of differences in the sensitivity of neural mechanisms involved in reinforcement, exploration, and punishment.

For example, steady drinkers may have an undersensitive punishment mechanism, which makes them unresponsive to danger and to social disapproval. They may also have an undersensitive reinforcement system, which leads them to seek more intense thrills (including those provided by alcohol) in order to experience pleasurable sensations. Thus, they seek the excitatory (dopamine-stimulating) effect of alcohol. Binge drinkers may have oversensitive punishment systems. Normally, they avoid drinking because of the guilt they experience afterward; but once they begin, and once the sedative effect begins, the alcohol-induced suppression of the punishment system makes it impossible for them to stop.

Recently, investigators have focused on the possibility that susceptibility to addiction may involve differences in dopaminergic mechanisms — for reasons you will understand, having read this chapter. Blum et al. (1990) reported that severe alcoholism was related to differences in the gene responsible for the production of the D_2 dopamine receptor, which is found on chromosome 11. The idea that susceptibility to addiction is related to genetic differences in receptors known to be involved in the physiology of reinforcement is an intriguing one, and the report of the research was greeted with considerable interest from clinicians and other researchers. However, a subsequent study (Bolos et al., 1990) failed to find such a difference. Although Blum and his colleagues may be right — their research studied the brains of people who had died as a result of alcoholism and thus may have had a more severe form of the disease than the patients studied by Bolos and her colleagues — more research is clearly needed.

Another approach to study of the physiology of addiction is through the use of animal models. At least two different strains of alcohol-preferring rats have been developed through selective breeding, and studies have shown that these animals differ in interesting ways. Alcohol-preferring rats do just what their name implies: If given a drinking tube containing a solution of alcohol along with their water and food, they become heavy drinkers. The alcohol-nonpreferring rats abstain. Fadda et al. (1990) found that alcohol appeared to produce a larger release of dopamine in the brains of alcohol-preferring rats than in the brains of alcohol-nonpreferring rats. The investigators measure of dopamine release was indirect; it will be interesting to see whether the results are confirmed by means of microdialysis.

All of the hypotheses concerning the physiology of addiction are speculative; we should view them as suggestions for further research rather than explanations. Even if these particular hypotheses are wrong, they do give us hope that research with humans and laboratory animals may some day help us understand the causes of addictive behaviors.

▶*INTERIM SUMMARY*◀

Research on the physiology of reinforcement has led to considerable progress in understanding the physiology of drug addiction, which is one of the most serious problems our society faces today. Apparently, all substances that produce addiction have an excitatory effect, although several addictive drugs, such as alcohol and the opiates, produce an inhibitory effect as well. The excitatory effect, correlated with reinforcement, appears to involve the release of dopamine in the nucleus accumbens, as microdialysis studies and studies with dopamine antagonists have shown.

Opiates produce tolerance and withdrawal symptoms, which make the habit become expensive and makes quitting more difficult; but the primary reason for addiction is the reinforcing effect, not the unpleasant symptoms produced when an addict tries to quit. Tolerance appears to be produced by homeostatic mechanisms that counteract the effects of the drug. Both the ventral tegmental area and the nucleus accumbens contain opiate receptors that are involved in the reinforcing effects of opiates. Withdrawal symptoms appear to involve opiate receptors on neurons in the periaqueductal gray matter.

Cocaine and amphetamine are potent dopamine agonists and thus serve as potent reinforcers — and substances with a high addictive potential. Nicotine, caffeine, and the active ingredient in marijuana also increase the release of dopamine in the nucleus accumbens.

Alcohol has both excitatory and antianxiety effects and thus is able to produce both positive and negative reinforcement. Its sedative effects are initiated by stimulation of a receptor associated with the GABA-benzodiazepine complex. Its reinforcing effects involve the release of dopamine in the nucleus accumbens, but how this process is accomplished is not known.

16

CHAPTER OUTLINE

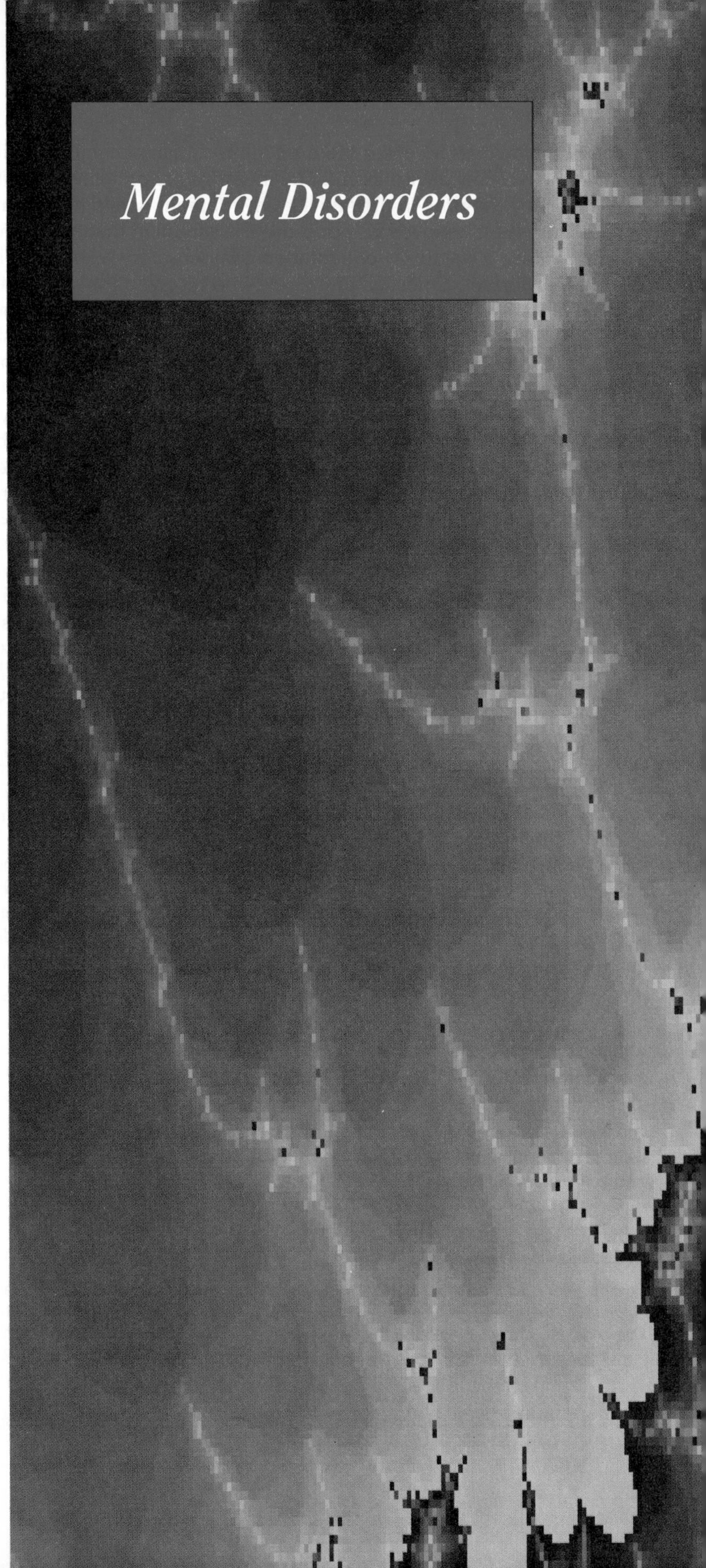

Mental Disorders

◀ PROLOGUE

Larry had become a permanent resident of the state hospital. His parents had originally hoped that treatment would help him enough so that he could live in a halfway house with a small group of other young men, but his condition was so serious that he required constant supervision. Larry had severe schizophrenia. The medication he was taking helped, but he still exhibited severe psychotic symptoms. In addition, he had begun showing signs of a neurological disorder that seemed to be getting worse.

Larry had always been a difficult child, shy and socially awkward. He had no real friends. During adolescence he became even more withdrawn and insisted that his parents and older sister keep out of his room. He stopped taking meals with the family, and he even bought a small refrigerator for his room so that he could keep his own food, which he said he preferred to that "pesticide-contaminated" food his parents ate. His grades in school, which were never outstanding, got progressively worse; and when he was seventeen years old, he dropped out of high school.

Larry's parents recognized that something was seriously wrong with him. Their family physician suggested that he see a psychiatrist and gave them the name of a colleague that he respected, but Larry flatly refused to go. Within a year after he had quit high school, he became frankly psychotic. He heard voices talking to him, and sometimes, his parents could hear him shouting for the voices to go away. He was convinced that his parents were trying to poison him, and he would only eat factory-sealed food that he had opened himself. Although he kept his body clean—sometimes he would stand in the shower for an hour "purifying" himself—his room became frightfully messy. He insisted on keeping old tins and food packages because, he said, he needed to compare them with items his parents brought from the store to be sure they were not counterfeit.

One day, while Larry was in the shower purifying himself, his mother cleaned his room. She filled several large plastic garbage bags with the tins and packages and put them out for the trash collector. As she re-entered the house, she heard a howling noise from upstairs. Larry had emerged from the shower and discovered that his room had been cleaned. When he saw his mother coming up the stairs, he screamed at her, cursed her savagely, and rushed down the stairs toward her. He hit her so hard that she flew through the air, landing heavily on the floor below. He wheeled around, ran up the stairs, and went into his room, slamming the door behind him.

An hour later, Larry's father discovered his wife unconscious at the foot of the stairs. She soon recovered from the mild concussion she had sustained, but Larry's parents realized that it was time for him to be put in custody. Because he had attacked his mother, a judge ordered that he be temporarily detained and, as a result of a psychiatric evaluation, had him committed to the state hospital. The diagnosis was "schizophrenia, paranoid type."

In the state hospital Larry was given Thorazine (chlorpromazine), which helped considerably. The first few weeks he showed some symptoms commonly seen in Parkinson's disease—tremors, rigidity, a shuffling gait, and lack of facial expression—but these symptoms cleared up spontaneously, as his physician had predicted. The voices still talked to him occasionally, but less often than before, and even then he could ignore them most of the time.

His suspiciousness decreased, and he was willing to eat with the other residents in the dining room. But he still obviously had paranoid delusions, and the psychiatric staff was unwilling to let him leave the hospital. For one thing, he refused to take his medication voluntarily. Once, after he had suffered a serious relapse, the staff discovered that he had only been pretending to swallow his pills and was later throwing them away. After that, they made sure that he swallowed them.

After ten years Larry began developing more serious neurological symptoms. He began pursing his lips and making puffing sounds, and later, he started grimacing, sticking his tongue out, and turning his head sharply to the left. The symptoms became so severe that they interfered with his ability to eat. His physician prescribed an additional drug, which reduced the symptoms considerably but did not eliminate them. As he explained to Larry's parents, "His neurological problems are caused by the medication that we are using to help with his psychiatric symptoms. These problems usually do not develop until a patient has taken the medication for many years, but Larry appears to be one of the unfortunate exceptions. If we take him off the medication the neurological symptoms will get even worse. We could reduce the symptoms by giving him a higher dose of the medication, but then the problem would come back later, and it would be even worse. All we can do is try to treat the symptoms with another drug, as we have been doing. We really need a medication that helps treat schizophrenia without producing these tragic side effects." ▲

Most of the discussion in this book has concentrated on the physiology of normal, adaptive behavior. This chapter summarizes research on the nature and physiology of mental disorders — of syndromes characterized by maladaptive behavior. The symptoms of mental disorders include deficient or inappropriate social behaviors; illogical, incoherent, or obsessional thoughts; inappropriate emotional responses, including depression, mania, or anxiety; and delusions and hallucinations. Research in recent years indicates that many of these symptoms are caused by abnormalities in the brain, both structural and biochemical.

psychosis

The most serious mental disorders are called **psychoses.** This chapter discusses the two most important psychoses, schizophrenia and the major affective disorders, which can disrupt people's behavior so severely that they cannot survive without the care of others. Their thoughts seem so different from those of other people that past generations concluded that patients with these disorders were possessed by inhuman devils. Most **neuroses** are less severe. People with neuroses are often unhappy, but most of them can reason logically and do not have hallucinations or delusions. They often have good insight into their problems and can articulate them well. In some cases, however, even neurotic disorders can seriously interfere with people's lives. This chapter discusses two of the most serious neuroses, also called anxiety disorders: panic disorder and obsessive compulsive disorder.

neurosis

SCHIZOPHRENIA

When people imagine someone being "crazy," they most likely have in mind a mental disorder with the symptoms of schizophrenia.

Description

Schizophrenia is the most common psychosis, afflicting approximately 1 percent of the world's population. Descriptions of symptoms in ancient writings indicate that the disorder has been around for thousands of years (Jeste et al., 1985). *Schizophrenia* is probably the most misused psychological term in existence. The word literally means "split mind," but it does *not* imply a split or multiple personality. People often say that they "feel schizophrenic" about an issue when they really mean that they have mixed feelings about it. A person who sometimes wants to build a cabin in Alaska and live off the land and at other times wants to take over the family insurance business may be undecided, but he or she is not schizophrenic. The man who invented the term, Eugen Bleuler, intended it to refer to a break with reality, caused by disorganization of the various functions of the mind, so that thoughts and feelings no longer worked together normally.

schizophrenia

Schizophrenia is characterized by two categories of symptoms, positive and negative. **Positive symptoms** are those that make themselves known by their presence. These symptoms include thought disorders, hallucinations, and delusions. A **thought disorder**—disorganized, irrational thinking—is probably the most important symptom of schizophrenia. Schizophrenics have great difficulty arranging their thoughts logically and sorting out plausible conclusions from absurd ones. In conversation they jump from one topic to another, as new associations come up. Sometimes, they utter meaningless words or choose words for their rhyme rather than for their meaning. **Delusions** are beliefs that are obviously contrary to fact. Delusions of *persecution* are false beliefs that others are plotting and conspiring against oneself. Delusions of *grandeur* are false beliefs in one's power and importance, such as a conviction that one has godlike powers or has special knowledge that no one else possesses. Delusions of *control* are related to delusions of persecution; the person believes (for example) that he or she is being controlled by others through such means as radar or tiny radio receivers implanted in his or her brain.

positive symptom
thought disorder
delusion

The third positive symptom of schizophrenia is **hallucinations,** which are perceptions of stimuli that are not actually present. The most common schizophrenic hallucinations are auditory, but they can also involve any of the other senses. The typical schizophrenic hallucination consists of voices talking to the person. Sometimes, they order the person to do something; sometimes, they scold the person for his or her unworthiness; sometimes, they just utter meaningless phrases. Olfactory hallucinations are also fairly common; often they contribute to the delusion that others are trying to kill the person with poison gas.

hallucination

In contrast to the positive symptoms, the **negative symptoms** of schizophrenia are known by the absence of normal behaviors: flattened emotional response, poverty of speech, lack of initiative and persistence, inability to experience pleasure, and social withdrawal (Crow, 1980; Andreasen and Olsen, 1982). Negative symptoms are not specific to schizophrenia; they are seen in many neurological disorders that involve brain damage, especially to the frontal lobes. As we will see later in this chapter, evidence suggests that these two sets of symptoms result from different physiological disorders: Positive symptoms appear to involve excessive activity in some neural

negative symptom

circuits that include dopamine as a neurotransmitter, and negative symptoms appear to be caused by brain damage. Many researchers suspect that these two sets of symptoms involve a common set of underlying causes, but these causes have yet to be discovered.

Heritability

One of the strongest pieces of evidence that schizophrenia is a biological disorder is that it appears to be heritable. Two approaches have established a linkage between schizophrenia and genes: adoption studies and twin studies.

Kety, Rosenthal, Wender, and Schulsinger (1968) performed one of the earliest and best-known adoption studies. Kety and his colleagues identified a group of schizophrenic people who had been adopted when they were children. They found that the incidence of schizophrenia in the adopted families of the patients was exactly what would be expected in the general population. Thus, it did not appear that the patients became schizophrenic because they were raised in a family of schizophrenics. However, the investigators did find an unusually high incidence of schizophrenia in the patients' *biological* relatives (parents and siblings), even though they were not raised by and with them — and probably, in most cases, did not even know them. The results clearly favor the conclusion that a tendency to develop schizophrenia is heritable.

Twin studies have produced similar results. These studies take advantage of the fact that monozygotic twins have identical genotypes, whereas the genetic similarity between dizygotic twins is, on the average, 50 percent. Investigators study records to identify pairs of twins in which at least one member has received a diagnosis of schizophrenia or perhaps of a related but milder condition, such as schizotypal personality disorder. If both twins have been diagnosed as having schizophrenia, then they are said to be *concordant.* If only one has received this diagnosis, the twins are said to be *discordant.* Thus, if a disorder has a genetic basis, the percentage of monozygotic twins concordant for the diagnosis will be higher than that for dizygotic twins. As many studies have shown, this is exactly what occurs (Gottesman and Shields, 1976). One of the more recent studies found that the concordance rate for monozygotic twins was over five times higher than the concordance rate for dizygotic twins (Farmer, McGuffin, and Gottesman, 1987).

If schizophrenia were a simple trait produced by a single gene, we would expect to see this disorder in at least 75 percent of the children of two schizophrenic parents if the gene were dominant. If it were recessive, *all* children of two schizophrenic parents should become schizophrenic. However, the actual incidence is less than 75 percent, which means either that several genes are involved or that having a "schizophrenia gene" imparts a *susceptibility* to develop schizophrenia, the disease itself being triggered by other factors. Perhaps in certain kinds of environments the susceptible individual develops schizophrenia or at least a schizotypal personality disorder. As we will see, evidence suggests that one of the inherited traits may include susceptibility to a virally triggered autoimmune disorder that disrupts the functioning of the brain and eventually causes brain damage.

If the susceptibility hypothesis is true, then we would expect that some people carry a "schizophrenia gene" but do not express it; that is, their environment is such that schizophrenia is never triggered. One such person would be the nonschizophrenic member of a pair of monozygotic twins discordant for schizophrenia. The logical way to test this hypothesis is to examine the children of both members of discordant pairs. Gottesman and Bertelsen (1989) found that the percentage of schizophrenic children was nearly identical for both members of such pairs: 16.8% for the schizophrenic

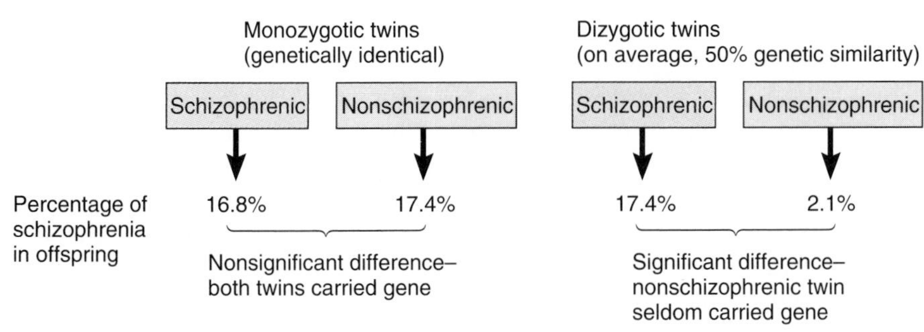

FIGURE 16.1

An explanation for evidence that people can have an unexpressed "schizophrenia gene."

parents and 17.4% for the nonschizophrenic parents. For the dizygotic twins the percentages were 17.4% and 2.1%, respectively. These results provide strong evidence for the heritability of schizophrenia and also support the conclusion that carrying a "schizophrenia gene" does not mean that a person will necessarily become schizophrenic. (See ***Figure 16.1.***)

Evidence suggests that schizophrenia can sometimes be caused by nongenetic factors. Schwarzkopf et al. (1989) found that if a schizophrenic person does not have relatives with a schizophrenic disorder, he or she is more likely to have had a history of complications at or around the time of childbirth. Thus, brain damage not related to heredity may also be a cause of schizophrenia.

Some investigators have attempted to find other traits that correlate with schizophrenia, traits that may allow us to detect the presence of even an unexpressed "schizophrenia gene" (that is, a "schizophrenia gene" in a person without the disorder). For example, many studies have found that difficulty in tracking a smoothly moving object with the eyes is highly correlated with schizophrenia. Up to 85 percent of all schizophrenics show abnormal eye tracking, as compared with under 10 percent in nonschizophrenics. Approximately half of the first-degree relatives (children, parents, and siblings) of schizophrenic people show this abnormality, even if they themselves are not schizophrenic (Holzman et al., 1974; Rea et al., 1989). Allen and Sarich (1988) conclude that the data suggest that a single gene is responsible for both schizophrenia and abnormal eye tracking. Presumably, a brain abnormality is responsible for the two conditions. Two locations have been suggested for the "schizophrenia gene": chromosome 5 and a special region at the end of the X chromosome (Bassett et al., 1988; Crow, DeLisi, and Johnstone, 1989).

Pharmacology: The Dopamine Hypothesis

Pharmacological evidence suggests that the positive symptoms of schizophrenia are caused by a biochemical disorder. The explanation that has accrued the most evidence is the *dopamine hypothesis,* which suggests that schizophrenia is caused by overactivity of the mesolimbic and mesocortical dopaminergic neurons, projecting from the ventral tegmental area to the basal forebrain, limbic cortex, and neocortex. (These circuits were described in Chapter 15.) The following subsections discuss the role of dopamine in schizophrenia.

EFFECTS OF DOPAMINE AGONISTS AND ANTAGONISTS

The treatments for most physiological disorders are developed after we understand their causes. For example, once it was discovered that diabetes was caused by the lack of a hormone produced by the pancreas, researchers were able to extract a substance from pancreatic tissue (insulin) that would alleviate the symptoms of this disease. However, in some cases treatments are discovered before the causes of the disease. For example, natives of tropical regions discovered that tea made from the bark of the cinchona tree would prevent death from malaria many years before scientists discovered that this disease is caused by microscopic parasites that are transmitted in the saliva of a certain species of mosquito. (The bark of the cinchona tree contains quinine, now used to treat malaria.)

In the case of schizophrenia a treatment was discovered before its causes were understood. (In fact, its causes are *still* not completely understood.) The discovery was accidental (Snyder, 1974). Antihistamine drugs were discovered in the early 1940s and were found to be useful in the treatment of allergic reactions. Because one of the effects of histamine release is a lowering of blood pressure, a French surgeon named Henri Laborit began to study the effects of antihistamine drugs on the sometimes-fatal low blood pressure that can be produced by surgical shock. He found that one of the drugs, promethazine, had an interesting effect: It reduced anxiety in his presurgical patients without causing mental confusion.

chlorpromazine

Laborit's findings spurred drug companies to examine other antihistamine drugs for sedative effects. Paul Charpentier, a chemist with a French drug company, developed **chlorpromazine,** which appeared to be promising from tests with animals. Laborit tried the drug in humans and found that it had profound calming effects but did not seem to decrease the patient's alertness. This drug produced "not any loss in consciousness, nor any change in the patients' mentality but a slight tendency to sleep and above all 'disinterest' for all that goes on around him" (Laborit, 1950, quoted by Snyder, 1974). Chlorpromazine was tried on patients with a variety of mental disorders: mania, depression, anxiety, neuroses, and schizophrenia (Delay and Deniker, 1952a, 1952b). The drug was not very effective in treating neuroses or affective psychoses, but it had dramatic effects on schizophrenia.

The discovery of the antipsychotic effects of chlorpromazine profoundly altered the way physicians treated schizophrenic patients and made prolonged hospital stays unnecessary for many of them (the patients, that is). The efficacy of antipsychotic drugs has been established in many double-blind studies (Baldessarini, 1977). They actually eliminate, or at least diminish, the patients' symptoms; they do not simply mask them by tranquilizing the patients. Although some antipsychotic drugs do have tranquilizing effects, these effects are not related to the amount of relief the patients receive from their psychotic symptoms. Moreover, antipsychotic drugs can have either activating or calming effects, depending upon the patient's symptoms. An immobile patient becomes more active, whereas a furiously active patient who is suffering from frightening hallucinations becomes more calm and placid. The results are not just a change in the patient's attitudes; the hallucinations and delusions go away, or at least become less severe.

Since the discovery of chlorpromazine, many other drugs have been discovered that relieve the positive symptoms of schizophrenia. All of these drugs have one property in common: They block dopamine receptors. In fact, the better a drug blocks D_2 dopamine receptors, the more effectively it reduces the symptoms of schizophrenia (Creese, Burt, and Snyder, 1976). (See ***Figure 16.2.***) Other drugs that interfere with dopaminergic transmission, such as reserpine (which prevents the storage of monoamines in synaptic vesicles), α-methyl *p*-tyrosine (which blocks the synthesis of dopamine), and apomorphine (which stimulates dopamine autoreceptors and hence inhibits

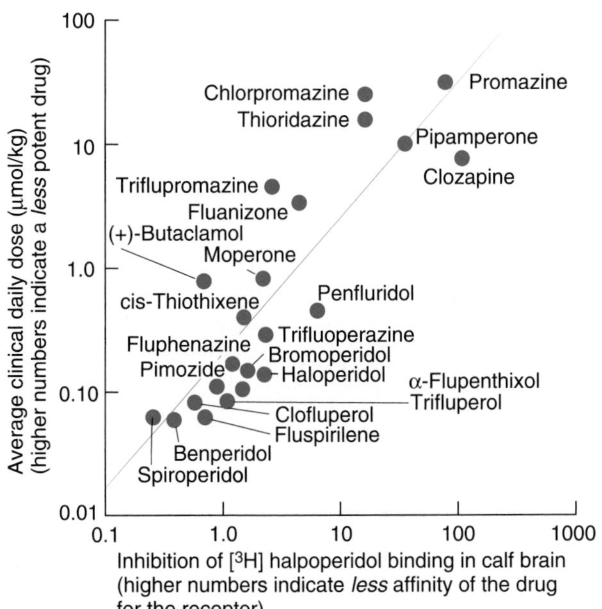

FIGURE 16.2

The relation between the ability of an antischizophrenic drug to bind with dopamine receptors on cell membranes extracted from calf caudate nucleus and the dose of the drug needed to achieve a therapeutic response. (From Snyder, S.H. *Journal of Continuing Education in Psychiatry*, 1978, *39*, 21–31. Reprinted with permission.)

the release of dopamine), either facilitate the antipsychotic action of drugs such as chlorpromazine or themselves exert antipsychotic effects (Tamminga et al., 1988).

Another category of drugs has the opposite effect, namely, the ***production*** of the positive symptoms of schizophrenia. The drugs that can produce these symptoms have one known pharmacological effect in common: They act as dopamine agonists. These drugs include amphetamine, cocaine, and methylphenidate (which all block the reuptake of dopamine) and L-DOPA (which stimulates the synthesis of dopamine). The symptoms that these drugs produce can be alleviated with antipsychotic drugs, which further strengthens the argument that these drugs exert their therapeutic effects by blocking dopamine receptors.

An example of the psychosis-inducing effect of amphetamine was demonstrated by Griffith, Cavanaugh, Held, and Oates (1972). The investigators recruited a group of people who had a history of amphetamine use and gave them large doses (10 mg) of dextroamphetamine every hour for up to five days. (Experimentally, it would have been better to study nonusers. Ethically, it was better not to introduce this drug to people who did not normally use it.) None of the subjects had prior histories of psychotic behavior. All seven volunteers became psychotic within two to five days. They became suspicious and began to believe that the experimenters were trying to poison them. One developed a delusion that an electric dynamo was controlling his thoughts. Most had auditory hallucinations. Similar symptoms—the classic positive symptoms of schizophrenia—are seen today in many people who abuse cocaine.

The fact that dopamine antagonists relieve the positive symptoms of schizophrenia and dopamine agonists produce them suggests that schizophrenia may be caused by abnormal activity in dopaminergic pathways. However, even if this suggestion is true, it is possible that nothing is wrong with dopaminergic neurons themselves; the abnormality could lie elsewhere. For example, neurons that stimulate dopaminergic neurons could be overactive, or neurons that *inhibit* them could be *underactive* (Freed, 1989; Reynolds, 1989). So far, there is little evidence in favor of either of these hypotheses.

THE SEARCH FOR ABNORMALITIES IN DOPAMINE TRANSMISSION IN THE BRAINS OF SCHIZOPHRENIC PATIENTS

The dopamine hypothesis suggests that schizophrenia is caused by the overactivity of dopaminergic synapses. There are basically two ways that this overactivity could occur: (1) Dopaminergic neurons could be more active, releasing more dopamine than they do in the normal brain, or (2) the postsynaptic dopamine receptors could be more sensitive in the brains of people with schizophrenia.

There is little evidence to suggest that the production and release of dopamine in the brains of schizophrenic patients is abnormal. Several studies have measured the amount of the principal breakdown product of dopamine (homovanillic acid) in the cerebrospinal fluid (CSF). The rationale is as follows: If a greater-than-normal amount of dopamine were being released, then more of the metabolite should be found in the CSF, because not all of the dopamine is recycled; some escapes from the synaptic clefts and is broken down by enzymes. These studies have *not* found an abnormally high level of the metabolite (Wyatt, Kirch, and DeLisi, 1988).

Several laboratories have studied the possibility that too many dopamine receptors are present on the postsynaptic membrane at dopaminergic synapses. This overabundance of dopamine receptors would increase the size of the postsynaptic potentials at dopaminergic synapses and thus exaggerate the effects of dopamine release. Two types of analyses have been made: postmortem measurements in the brains of deceased schizophrenic patients and PET scans after treatment with radioactive ligands for dopamine receptors.

Postmortem measurements of dopamine receptors are performed by removing the regions of the brain that contain dopaminergic terminals, homogenizing the tissue, extracting the cell membranes, and incubating them with a radioactive ligand of dopamine receptors. The degree of radioactivity of the tissue reveals the relative number of dopamine receptors. Jaskiw and Kleinman (1988) reviewed twelve such studies published between 1978 and 1987 and found that ten of them observed an increase in the number of D_2 dopamine receptors present in the neostriatum (caudate nucleus and putamen). For example, Crow, Johnstone, Longden, and Owen (1978) found that the binding of radioactive spiroperidol (a ligand for D_2 receptors) was twice as high in the brain tissue of schizophrenic patients compared with that of control subjects. (See ***Figure 16.3.***)

FIGURE 16.3

Amount of binding of radioactive spiroperidol in the cortex and caudate nucleus of brains of deceased schizophrenics and nonschizophrenic controls. (Reprinted with permission from Crow, T.J., Johnstone, E.C., Longden, A.J., and Owen, F. *Life Sciences,* 1978, *23,* 563–568. Copyright 1978, Pergamon Press, Ltd.)

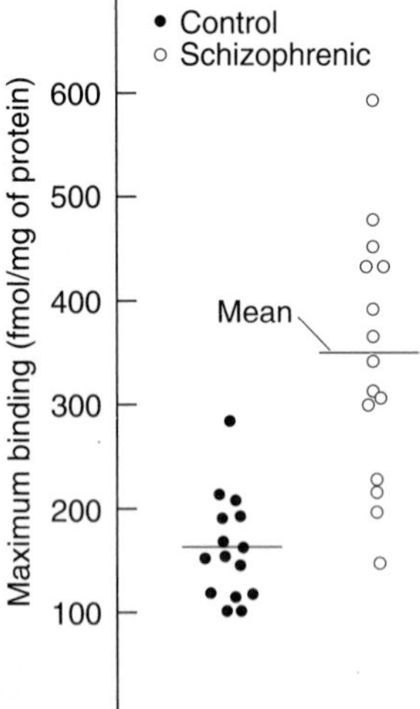

Measurements of levels of D_2 receptors in the brains of living schizophrenic patients have yielded mixed results. Wong et al. (1986) administered a radioactive ligand for D_2 receptors and used a PET scanner to measure the radioactivity in the caudate nucleus. Their results suggested that the number of D_2 receptors was 30 to 100 percent higher in the brains of schizophrenic patients. However, Farde et al. (1990) and Martinot et al. (1990), using even more specific ligands for D_2 receptors, found no differences in the level of these receptors in schizophrenic and normal brains.

The failure to obtain solid, unambiguous evidence that dopaminergic synapses are hyperactive in schizophrenic patients does not mean that the dopamine hypothesis should be abandoned. For one thing, investigators may have been looking in the wrong part of the brain. The neostriatum contains many dopamine receptors, which makes this region the easiest one in which to study their concentration. If schizophrenia were caused by a genetic defect that created an overproduction of dopamine receptors, then we would expect to find more of the receptors in the neostriatum. But what we know about the functions of the dopaminergic pathways in the brain would not make us suspect that the neostriatum would be involved in schizophrenia. The neostriatum is involved in motor control. A deficiency in the release of dopamine in the neostriatum causes Parkinson's disease; thus, we would expect that excessive dopaminergic activity there would cause excessive movement, not schizophrenia.

The nucleus accumbens and the prefrontal cortex, which also receive input from dopaminergic neurons, seem to be much better candidates than the neostriatum. As we saw in Chapter 15, the activity of dopaminergic terminal buttons in the nucleus accumbens appears to be a vital link in the process of reinforcement. In addition, the prefrontal cortex plays an important role in making plans and shifting strategies in order to adapt one's behavior to changes in environmental contingencies. Overactivity of either or both of these systems could conceivably produce the positive symptoms of schizophrenia.

Let us consider the dopaminergic neurons involved in reinforcement. As we saw, drugs that strongly reinforce behaviors (such as cocaine and amphetamine) also produce the positive symptoms of schizophrenia. Perhaps the two effects of the drugs are related. If reinforcement mechanisms were activated at inappropriate times, then inappropriate behaviors — including delusional thoughts — might be reinforced. At one time or another, all of us have had some irrational thoughts, which we normally brush aside and forget. But if neural mechanisms of reinforcement became active while these thoughts were occurring, we would tend to take them more seriously. In time, full-fledged delusions might develop.

Schizophrenia as a Neurological Disorder

So far, I have been discussing the physiology of the positive symptoms of schizophrenia — principally, hallucinations, delusions, and thought disorders. These symptoms are plausibly related to one of the known functions of dopaminergic neurons: reinforcement. But the negative symptoms of schizophrenia — social withdrawal, flattened emotional reaction, and poverty of thought and speech — are very different. Whereas the positive symptoms are unique to schizophrenia (and to amphetamine or cocaine psychosis), the negative symptoms are similar to those produced by brain damage caused by several different means. Many pieces of evidence suggest that the negative symptoms of schizophrenia are a result of brain damage, as we will see in the subsections that follow.

EVIDENCE FOR BRAIN DAMAGE IN SCHIZOPHRENIA

Although schizophrenia has been traditionally labeled as a psychiatric disorder, most patients with schizophrenia exhibit neurological symptoms that suggest the presence of brain damage. These symptoms include catatonia; abnormal facial movements; unusually high or low rates of blinking; staring and avoidance of eye contact; absent blink reflex in response to a tap on the forehead; episodes of deviation of the eyes (especially to the right), accompanied by speech arrest; bursts of jerky eye movements; poor visual pursuit of a smoothly moving object; inability to move the eyes without moving the head; poor pupillary light reactions; and continuous elevation of the brows, causing characteristic horizontal creasing of the forehead (Stevens, 1982). Although these symptoms can be caused by a variety of neuropathological conditions and are hence not unique to schizophrenia, their presence suggests that schizophrenia may be associated with brain damage of some kind.

Several studies have found evidence of brain damage in CT and MRI scans of schizophrenic patients. For example, Weinberger and Wyatt (1982) obtained CT scans of eighty chronic schizophrenics and sixty-six normal controls of the same mean age

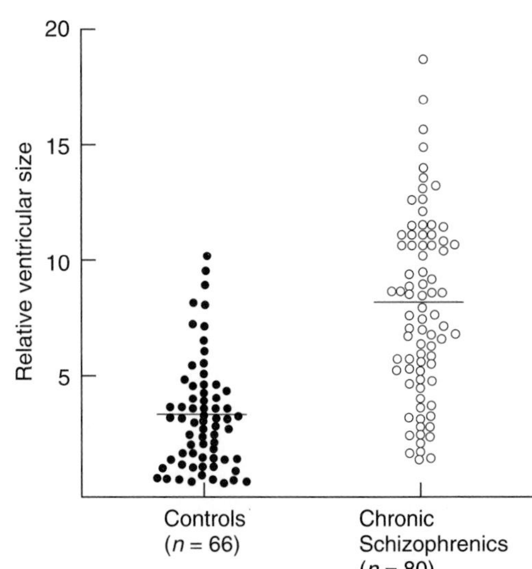

FIGURE 16.4

Relative ventricular size in chronic schizophrenics and controls. (From *Schizophrenia as a Brain Disease,* edited by Fritz A. Henn and Henry A. Nasrallah. Copyright © 1982 by: Oxford University Press, Inc. Reprinted by permission.)

FIGURE 16.5

MRI scans of the brains of twins discordant for schizophrenia. (a) Normal twin. (b) Twin with schizophrenia. (Courtesy of D.R. Weinberger, National Institute of Mental Health, Saint Elizabeth's Hospital, Washington D.C.)

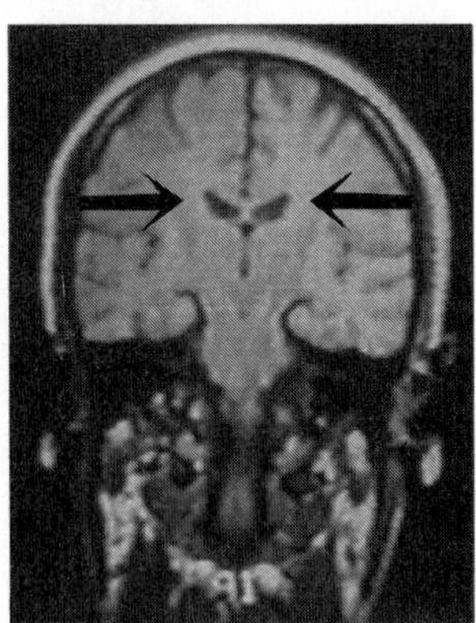

(a)

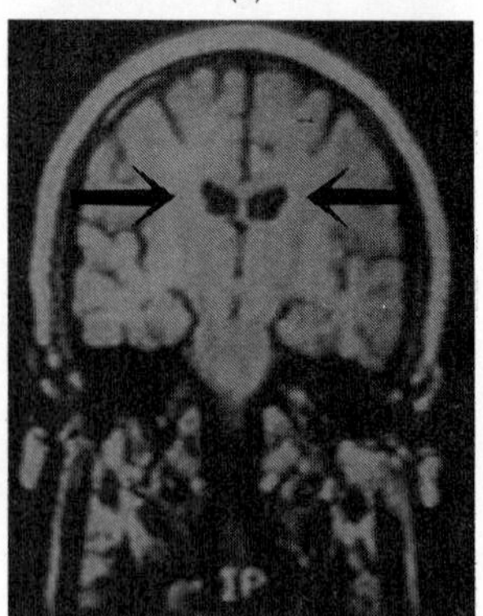

(b)

(twenty-nine years). Without knowledge of the patients' diagnoses, they measured the area of the lateral ventricles in the scan that cut through them at their largest extent, and they expressed this area relative to the area of brain tissue in the same scan. The relative ventricle size of the schizophrenic patients was more than twice as great as that of normal control subjects. (See ***Figure 16.4.***) The most likely cause of the enlarged ventricles is therefore loss of brain tissue; thus, the CT scans provide evidence that chronic schizophrenia is associated with brain damage.

Bogerts (1989) compared CT scans of fifty-four schizophrenic patients and age-matched controls, making careful measurements of all the ventricles and major fissures and sulci. He found evidence for a loss of tissue in the frontal lobes, anterior temporal lobes, and hypothalamus. There was no relation between any of his measurements and the duration of the illness, which suggests that the changes in the brain occur early in life. Andreasen (1988) notes that the brains of many schizophrenic patients show abnormalities in the shape of the corpus callosum and hippocampus, which are embryologically related. This result suggests that the abnormalities may occur during brain development.

A study by Suddath et al. (1990) provided further evidence for the conclusion that the brain damage associated with schizophrenia is not caused directly by the patient's genes, but that heredity predisposes some people for the damaging effects of some environmental factors, such as a virus. The investigators examined MRI scans of monozygotic twins discordant for schizophrenia and found that in almost every case the twin with schizophrenia had larger lateral and third ventricles. In addition, the anterior hippocampus was smaller in the schizophrenic twins, and the total volume of the gray matter in the left temporal lobe was reduced. Figure 16.5 shows a set of MRI scans from a pair of twins; as you can see, the lateral ventricles are larger in the brain of the twin with schizophrenia. (See ***Figure 16.5.)***

CAUSES OF THE BRAIN DAMAGE

As we saw earlier, schizophrenia is a heritable disease, but its heritability is less than perfect. Why do fewer than half the children of parents with chronic schizophrenia become schizophrenic? A possible answer is that what is inherited is a susceptibility to the damaging effects of a viral disease. If a child with schizophrenic parents contracts the disease, he or she is likely to develop brain damage. If a person without a family history of schizophrenia contracts the same disease, brain damage is unlikely.

No direct evidence for virally induced schizophrenia exists, but evidence reveals similarities between schizophrenia and known viral disorders. There is no doubt that viruses can cause brain damage. As we saw in Chapter 14, the herpes simplex virus, which normally hides in the trigeminal nerve ganglion, can, in rare instances, enter the brain and damage neurons in the frontal and temporal lobes. In addition, the virus that caused the 1918 influenza epidemic caused brain damage in many patients and produced illnesses that resembled schizophrenia (Menninger, 1926).

Stevens (1988) notes some interesting similarities between schizophrenia and a known neuropathological condition, multiple sclerosis. As we saw in Chapter 14, multiple sclerosis appears to be an autoimmune disease—triggered by a virus—in which the patient's own immune system attacks myelin. The natural histories of multiple sclerosis and schizophrenia are similar in several ways. Both diseases are more prevalent and more malignant in people who spent their childhood in latitudes far from the equator. Both diseases are more common in people with low socioeconomic status, who live in crowded, deprived conditions. Both diseases are characterized by one of three general courses: (1) attacks followed by remissions, many of which produce no residual deficits; (2) recurrent attacks with only partial remissions, causing an increasingly major deficit; or (3) an insidious onset with a steady and relentless progression, leading to permanent and severe deficits. These similarities suggest that schizophrenia, like multiple sclerosis, could be a virally induced autoimmune disease.

A second possible cause of schizophrenia is interference with normal prenatal brain development. Several studies show that people born during the winter months are more likely to develop schizophrenia later in life. Torrey, Torrey, and Peterson (1977) suggest that the causal factor could be seasonal variations in nutritional factors or—more likely—variations in toxins or infectious agents in air, water, or food. The fact that known viruses such as measles, German measles, and chicken pox show similar seasonality suggests that the causal factor might be a virus. The "seasonality effect" is seen more strongly in poor, urban locations, where people are at greater risk for viral infections (Machon, Mednick, and Schulsinger, 1983).

A seasonally related virus could affect either a pregnant woman or her newborn infant. Two pieces of evidence suggest that the damage is done prenatally. First, brain development is more susceptible to disruption prenatally than postnatally. Second, a study of the offspring of women who were pregnant during an epidemic of type A2 influenza in Finland during 1957 showed an elevated incidence of schizophrenia (Mednick, Machon, and Huttunen, 1990). The increased incidence was seen only in the children of women who were in the second trimester of their pregnancy when the epidemic occurred. (See ***Figure 16.6.***) Presumably, the viral infection produced toxins that interfered with the brain development of some of the fetuses, resulting in the development of schizophrenia later in life.

As we saw earlier in this chapter, nonhereditary schizophrenia could also be caused by brain damage produced by obstetrical problems. I mentioned that some monozygotic twins are discordant for schizophrenia; that is, one of them develops schizophrenic and the other does not. In these cases the schizophrenic twin is more likely to have been involved in a difficult delivery (Gottesman and Bertelsen, 1989).

In the interest of clarity and brevity, I have been selective in my review of research on schizophrenia. This puzzling and serious disorder has stimulated many ingenious hypotheses and much research. Some hypotheses have been proved wrong; others

FIGURE 16.6

Incidence of schizophrenia in the offspring of women who were pregnant during the 1957 influenza epidemic in Finland. (Based on data of Mednick, S.A., Machon, R.A., and Huttunen, M.O. *Archives of General Psychiatry,* 1990, *47,* 292.)

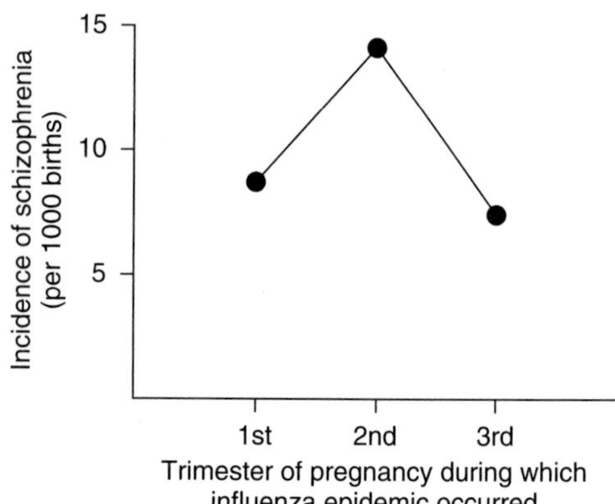

have not yet been adequately tested. Possibly, future research will find that all of these hypotheses (including the ones I have discussed) are incorrect, or one that I have not mentioned is correct. However, I am impressed with recent research, and I believe that we have real hope of finding the causes of schizophrenia in the near future. With the discovery of the causes we can hope for the discovery of methods of prevention.

▶*INTERIM SUMMARY*◀

Researchers have made considerable progress in the past few years in their study of the physiology of mental disorders, but many puzzles still remain. Schizophrenia consists of positive and negative symptoms, the former involving the presence of an unusual behavior and the latter involving the absence of a normal behavior. Because schizophrenia is at least somewhat heritable, it appears to have a biological basis. But evidence indicates that not all cases are caused by heredity, and some people who appear to carry a "schizophrenia gene" do not become schizophrenic. The location of this gene (if, indeed, a single gene exists) may be chromosome 5 or the end of the X chromosome.

The dopamine hypothesis—inspired by the findings that dopamine antagonists alleviate the positive symptoms of schizophrenia and that dopamine agonists increase or even produce them—is still dominant. This hypothesis states that the positive symptoms of schizophrenia are caused by hyperactivity of dopaminergic synapses. There is no evidence that an abnormally large amount of dopamine is released. Some studies suggest that the brains of schizophrenic patients contain increased numbers of D_2 dopamine receptors in the neostriatum, but the evidence is mixed. The involvement of dopamine in reinforcement could explain the positive effects of schizophrenia.

CT and MRI scans indicate that brain damage is associated with the negative symptoms of schizophrenia. Studies of the epidemiology of schizophrenia suggest that, as in multiple sclerosis, one of the causes may be an autoimmune process produced by an infection in people who are genetically vulnerable. In addition, the disorder may be caused by toxins (such as those produced by viral infections) present during pregnancy, or by brain damage sustained during a difficult delivery. ▲

MAJOR AFFECTIVE DISORDERS

major affective disorder

Affect, as a noun, refers to feelings or emotions. Just as schizophrenia is characterized by disordered thoughts, the **major affective disorders** (also called *mood disorders*) are characterized by disordered feelings.

Description

Feelings and emotions are essential parts of human existence; they represent our evaluation of the events in our lives. In a very real sense, feelings and emotions are what human life is all about. The emotional state of most of us reflects what is happening to us: Our feelings are tied to events in the real world, and they are usually the result of reasonable assessments of the importance these events have for our lives. But for some people affect becomes divorced from reality. These people have feelings of extreme elation (*mania*) or despair (*depression*) that are not justified by events in their lives. For example, depression that accompanies the loss of a loved one is normal, but depression that becomes a way of life, and will not respond to the sympathetic effort of friends and relatives or even to psychotherapy, is pathological.

Almost everyone experiences some depression from time to time, mostly caused by events that sadden us. This form of depression is called **reactive depression** because it occurs as a reaction to events in the world. The form of depression seen in the major affective disorders is quite different. It seems to be an intrinsic characteristic of the person rather than a reaction to the environment; thus, it is referred to as **endogenous depression.**

reactive depression

endogenous depression

There are two principal types of major affective disorders. The first type is characterized by alternating periods of mania and depression — a condition called **bipolar disorder.** This disorder afflicts men and women in approximately equal numbers. Episodes of mania can last a few days or several months, but they usually take a few weeks to run their course. The episodes of depression that follow generally last three times as long as the mania. The second type is **unipolar depression,** or depression without mania. This depression may be continuous and unremitting or, more typically, may come in episodes. Unipolar depression strikes women two to three times more often than men. Mania without periods of depression sometimes occurs, but it is rare.

bipolar disorder

unipolar depression

Severely depressed people usually feel extremely unworthy and have strong feelings of guilt. The affective disorders are dangerous; a person who suffers from endogenous depression runs a considerable risk of death by suicide. Depressed people have very little energy, and they move and talk slowly, sometimes becoming almost torpid. At other times they may pace around restlessly and aimlessly. They may cry a lot. They are unable to experience pleasure; they lose their appetite for food and sex. Their sleep is disturbed; they usually fall asleep readily but awaken early and find it difficult to get to sleep again. (In contrast, people with reactive depression usually have trouble falling asleep and do not awaken early.) Even their body functions become depressed; they often become constipated, and secretion of saliva decreases.

Episodes of mania are characterized by a sense of euphoria that does not seem to be justified by circumstances. The diagnosis of mania is partly a matter of degree — one would not call exuberance and a zest for life pathological. People with mania usually exhibit nonstop speech and motor activity. They flit from topic to topic and often have delusions, but they lack the severe disorganization that is seen in schizophrenia. They are usually full of their own importance and often become angry or defensive if they are contradicted. Frequently, they go for long periods without sleep, working furiously on projects that are often unrealistic. (Sometimes, their work is fruitful; George Frederic Handel wrote *The Messiah,* one of the masterpieces of choral music, during one of his periods of mania.)

Heritability

The tendency to develop an affective disorder appears to be heritable. For example, Rosenthal (1971) found that close relatives of people who suffer from affective psychoses are ten times more likely to develop these disorders than people without afflicted relatives. Of course, this study does not prove that genetic mechanisms are operating; relatives have similar environments as well as similar genes. However, Gershon et al. (1976) found that if one member of a set of monozygotic twins was afflicted with an affective disorder, the likelihood that the other twin was similarly afflicted was 69 percent. In contrast, the concordance rate for dizygotic twins was only 13 percent. Furthermore, the concordance rate for monozygotic twins appears to be the same whether the twins were raised together or apart (Price, 1968). The heritability of the affective disorders implies that they have a physiological basis.

For a while it looked as if the locus of a gene responsible for bipolar disorder had been found. Egeland et al. (1987) studied a large Amish family in which several members had bipolar disorder. They correlated the presence or absence of the disorder with the presence or absence of various proteins in the blood that are controlled by genes with known locations. They concluded that the gene appeared to be located at the tip of the short arm of chromosome 11. However, several studies failed to confirm their results in other families (Byerley et al., 1989); and finally, after having found more family members and reanalyzing the data, Kelsoe et al. (1990) concluded that the earlier study was mistaken.

Physiological Treatments

There are four effective biological treatments for endogenous depression: monoamine oxidase (MAO) inhibitors, the tricyclic antidepressant drugs, electroconvulsive therapy (ECT), and sleep deprivation. Bipolar disorder is effectively treated by lithium salts. The response of these disorders to medical treatment provides additional evidence that they have a physiological basis. Furthermore, the fact that lithium is very effective in treating bipolar affective disorders but not unipolar depression suggests that there is a fundamental difference between these two illnesses.

Prior to the 1950s there was no effective drug treatment for depression. In the late 1940s clinicians noticed that some drugs used for treating tuberculosis seemed to elevate the patient's mood. Researchers subsequently found that a derivative of these drugs, iproniazid, reduced symptoms of psychotic depression (Crane, 1957). Iproniazid inhibits the activity of MAO, which destroys excess monoamine transmitter substances within terminal buttons. Thus, the drug increases the release of dopamine, norepinephrine, and serotonin. Other MAO inhibitors were soon discovered. Unfortunately, MAO inhibitors can have harmful side effects. The most common problem is the *cheese effect.* Many foods (for example, cheese, yogurt, wine, yeast breads, chocolate, and various fruits and nuts) contain *pressor amines*— substances similar to catecholamines. Normally, these amines are deactivated by MAO, which is present in the blood and in other tissues of the body. But a person who is being treated with an MAO inhibitor may suffer a serious sympathetic reaction after eating food containing pressor amines. The pressor amines simulate the effects of increased activity of the sympathetic nervous system, increasing blood pressure and heart rate. The reaction can raise blood pressure enough to produce intracranial bleeding or cardiovascular collapse.

tricyclic antidepressant

Fortunately, another class of antidepressant drugs was soon discovered that did not produce a cheese effect: the **tricyclic antidepressants.** These drugs were found to inhibit the reuptake of 5-HT and norepinephrine by terminal buttons. By retarding reuptake, the drugs keep the neurotransmitter in contact with the postsynaptic receptors, thus prolonging the postsynaptic potentials. Therefore, both the MAO inhibitors and the tricyclic antidepressant drugs are monoaminergic agonists.

The third biological treatment for depression has an interesting history. Earlier in this century, a physician named von Meduna noted that psychotic patients who were also subject to epileptic seizures showed improvement immediately after each attack. He reasoned that the violent storm of neural activity in the brain that constitutes an epileptic seizure somehow improved the patients' mental condition. He developed a way to produce seizures by administering a drug, but the procedure was dangerous to the patient. In 1937 Ugo Cerletti, an Italian psychiatrist, developed a less dangerous method for producing seizures. He had previously learned that the local slaughterhouse applied a jolt of electricity to animals' heads to stun them before killing them. The electricity appeared to produce a seizure that resembled an epileptic attack. He decided to attempt to use electricity to induce a seizure more safely.

Cerletti tried the procedure on dogs and found that an electrical shock to the skull did produce a seizure and that the animals recovered with no apparent ill effects. He then used the procedure on humans and found it to be safer than the chemical treatment previously used. As a result, **electroconvulsive therapy** (ECT) became a common treatment for mental illness. Although it was originally used for a variety of disorders, including schizophrenia, we now know that its usefulness is limited to depression. (See ***Figure 16.7.***)

electroconvulsive therapy (ECT)

A depressed patient does not respond immediately to treatment with MAO inhibitors or to one of the tricyclic antidepressant drugs; improvement in symptoms is not usually seen before two to three weeks of drug treatment. In contrast, the effects of ECT are more rapid. A few seizures induced by ECT can often snap a person out of a deep depression within a few days. Although prolonged and excessive use of ECT causes brain damage, resulting in long-lasting impairments in memory (Squire, 1974), the judicious use of ECT during the interim period before antidepressant drugs become effective has undoubtedly saved the lives of some suicidal patients (Baldessarini, 1977). In addition, some severely depressed people are not helped by drug therapy; for them, occasional ECT is the only effective treatment.

The therapeutic effect of **lithium**, the drug used to treat bipolar affective disorders, is very rapid. This drug, which is administered in the form of lithium carbonate, is most effective in treating the manic phase of a bipolar affective disorder; once the mania is eliminated, depression usually does not follow (Gerbino, Oleshansky, and Gershon,

lithium

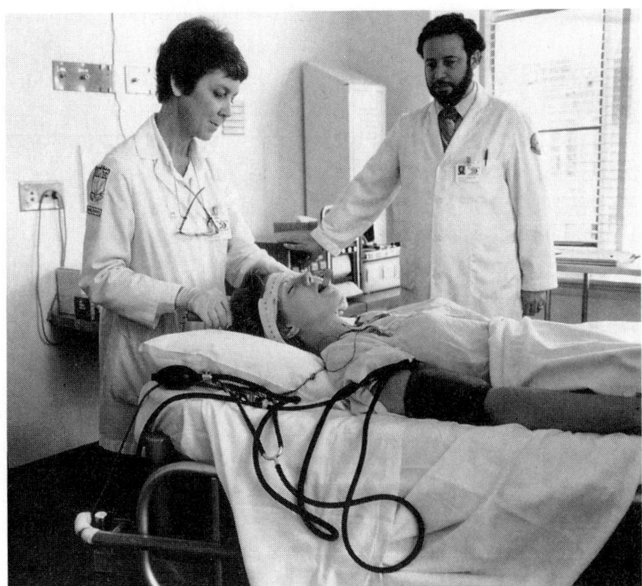

FIGURE 16.7

A patient being prepared for ECT. (Will McIntyre/Photo Researchers, Inc.)

1978). Many clinicians and investigators have referred to lithium as psychiatry's wonder drug: It does not suppress normal feelings of emotions, but it leaves patients able to feel and express joy and sadness to events in their lives. Similarly, it does not impair intellectual processes; many patients have received the drug continuously for years without any apparent ill effects (Fieve, 1979). Reifman and Wyatt (1980) calculated that during a ten-year period in the United States lithium treatment saved at least $4 billion in treatment costs and lost productivity.

Investigators have not yet discovered the pharmacological effects of lithium that are responsible for its ability to eliminate mania. Some suggest that the drug stabilizes the population of certain classes of neurotransmitter receptors in the brain, thus preventing wide shifts in neural sensitivity.

The Monoamine Hypothesis

The fact that depression can be treated effectively with tricyclic antidepressants and MAO inhibitors, both of which are monoamine agonists, suggested the **monoamine hypothesis:** Depression is caused by insufficient activity of monoaminergic neurons. Because the symptoms of depression do not respond to potent dopamine agonists such as amphetamine or cocaine, most investigators have focused their research efforts on the other two monoamines: norepinephrine and serotonin.

As we saw, the dopamine hypothesis of schizophrenia receives support from the fact that dopamine agonists can produce the symptoms of schizophrenia. Similarly, the monoamine hypothesis of depression receives support from the fact that depression can be caused by monoamine antagonists. Many hundreds of years ago, an alkaloid extract from *Rauwolfia serpentina,* a shrub of Southeast Asia, was found to be useful for treating snakebite, circulatory disorders, and insanity. Modern research has confirmed that the alkaloid, now called reserpine, has both an antipsychotic effect and a hypotensive effect (that is, it lowers blood pressure). The effect on blood pressure rules out its use in treating schizophrenia, but the drug is still occasionally used to treat patients with high blood pressure.

Reserpine has a serious side effect: It can cause depression. In fact, in the early years of its use as a hypotensive agent, up to 15 percent of the people who received it became depressed (Sachar and Baron, 1979). Reserpine prevents the monoamines from being stored in synaptic vesicles in the terminal buttons of monoaminergic neurons, preventing these neurotransmitters from being released. Thus, the drug serves as a potent norepinephrine, dopamine, and serotonin antagonist. The pharmacological and behavioral effects of reserpine complement the pharmacological and behavioral effects of the drugs used to treat depression — MAO inhibitors and most of the tricyclic antidepressants. That is, a monoamine antagonist produces depression, whereas monoamine agonists alleviate it.

5-HIAA

Several studies have found that suicidal depression is related to decreased CSF levels of **5-HIAA** (5-hydroxyindoleacetic acid), a chemical produced when serotonin is broken down. A decreased level of 5-HIAA implies that less 5-HT (serotonin) is being produced and released in the brain. Träskmann, Åsberg, Bertilsson, and Sjöstrand (1981) found that CSF levels of 5-HIAA in people who had attempted suicide were significantly lower than those of controls. In a follow-up study of depressed and potentially suicidal patients, 20 percent of those with levels of 5-HIAA below the median subsequently killed themselves, whereas none of those with levels above the median committed suicide. More recent studies have confirmed these results (Roy, De Jong, and Linnoila, 1989).

Sedvall et al. (1980) analyzed the CSF of healthy, nondepressed volunteers. The families of subjects with unusually low levels of 5-HIAA were more likely to include people with depression. The results suggest that serotonin metabolism or release is genetically controlled and that it is linked to depression. Thus, these findings clearly support the monoamine hypothesis.

As you learned in Chapter 15, reinforcement involves the release of dopamine in the nucleus accumbens. Because inability to experience pleasure is one of the most important symptoms of depression, we might expect to find some involvement of dopaminergic neurons in this disorder. However, cocaine, a potent dopamine agonist, does not relieve depression—it simply makes depressed people become agitated and anxious. Therefore, of the three monoamines, only serotonin and norepinephrine have been shown to play a role in depression.

Role of Circadian Rhythms

One of the most prominent symptoms of depression is disordered sleep. The sleep of people with endogenous depression tends to be shallow; slow-wave delta sleep (stages 3 and 4) is reduced and stage 1 is increased. Sleep is fragmented; people tend to waken frequently, especially toward the morning. In addition, REM sleep occurs earlier, the first half of the night contains a higher proportion of REM periods, and REM sleep contains an increased number of rapid eye movements (Kupfer, 1976; Vogel, Vogel, McAbee, and Thurmond, 1980). (See ***Figure 16.8.***) As we will see in this section, some investigators believe that understanding the link between circadian rhythms and depression will help us understand the biological causes of the disorder.

FIGURE 16.8

Patterns of the stages of sleep of a normal subject and a patient with endogenous depression. Note the reduced sleep latency, reduced REM latency, reduction in slow-wave sleep (stages 3 and 4), and general fragmentation of sleep (*arrows*) in the depressed patient. (From Gillin, J.C., and Borbély, A.A. *Trends in Neurosciences,* 1985, *8,* 537–542. Reprinted with permission.)

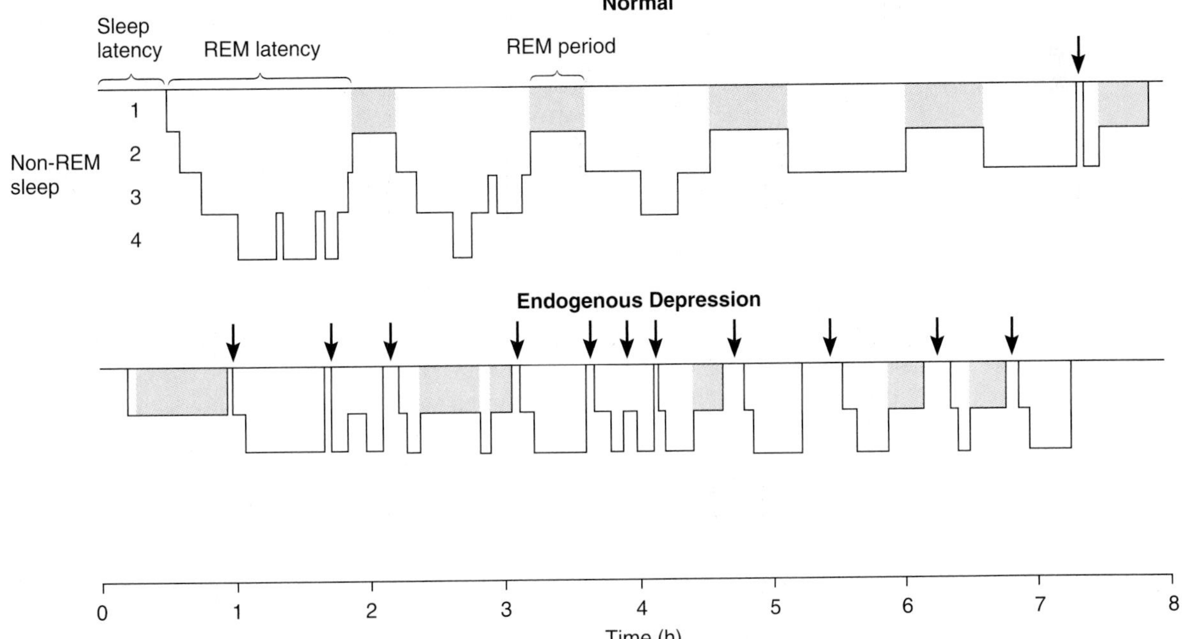

REM SLEEP DEPRIVATION

One of the most effective antidepressant treatments is sleep deprivation, either total or selective. Selective deprivation of REM sleep, accomplished by monitoring people's EEG and awakening them whenever they show signs of REM sleep, alleviates depression (Vogel et al., 1975; Vogel, Buffenstein, Minter, and Hennessey, 1990). The therapeutic effect, like that of the antidepressant medications, occurs slowly, over the course of several weeks. Some patients show long-term improvement even after the deprivation is discontinued; thus, it is a practical as well as an effective treatment. In addition, regardless of their specific pharmacological effects, other treatments for depression suppress REM sleep, delaying its onset and decreasing its duration. These facts suggest that REM sleep and mood might somehow be causally related.

Scherschlicht, Polc, Schneeberger, Steiner, and Haefely (1982) examined the effects of twenty antidepressant drugs on the sleep cycles of cats and found that all of them profoundly reduced REM sleep and most of them increased slow-wave sleep. In an extensive review of the literature Vogel, Buffenstein, Minter, and Hennessey (1990) found that all drugs that suppressed REM sleep (and produced a rebound effect when their administration was discontinued) acted as antidepressants. These results suggest that the primary effect of antidepressant medication may be to suppress REM sleep, and the changes in mood may be a result of this suppression. However, some drugs that relieve the symptoms of depression (such as iprindole and trimipramine) do not suppress REM sleep. Thus, suppression of REM sleep cannot be the *only* way that antidepressant drugs work.

Studies of families with a history of endogenous depression also suggest a link between this disorder and abnormalities in REM sleep. For example, Giles, Roffwarg, and Rush (1987) found that first-degree relatives of people with depression are likely to show a short REM sleep latency, even if they have not yet had an episode of depression. Giles, Biggs, Rush, and Roffwarg (1988) found that the members of these families who had the lowest REM latency had the highest risk of subsequently becoming depressed. Abnormalities in REM sleep are seen early in life; Coble et al. (1988) found that newborn infants of mothers with a history of endogenous depression showed patterns of REM sleep that were different from those of the infants of mothers without such a history.

Vogel, Neill, Hagler, and Kors (1990) have developed what they believe to be an animal model of depression, which may be useful in studying the physiological basis of this disorder. Twice a day, they gave young rats, between the ages of eight days and twenty-one days, injections of an antidepressant drug that blocks the reuptake of 5-HT. This early treatment appears to have affected the development of the brain, because when the rats reached maturity, they showed many of the symptoms of endogenous depression: decreased sexual behavior, increased irritability, and decreased pleasure-seeking behavior (specifically, decreased willingness to work for reinforcing brain stimulation or for a taste of sucrose). The animals' sleep was also altered; the latency to the first bout of REM sleep was shorter, and the proportion of REM sleep was higher. The animals even responded to antidepressant treatment; imipramine and REM sleep deprivation both increased sexual behavior. It will be interesting to see whether this model provides us with useful information about the physiology of depression.

TOTAL SLEEP DEPRIVATION

Total sleep deprivation also has an antidepressant effect. Unlike specific deprivation of REM sleep, which takes several weeks to reduce depression, total sleep depriva-

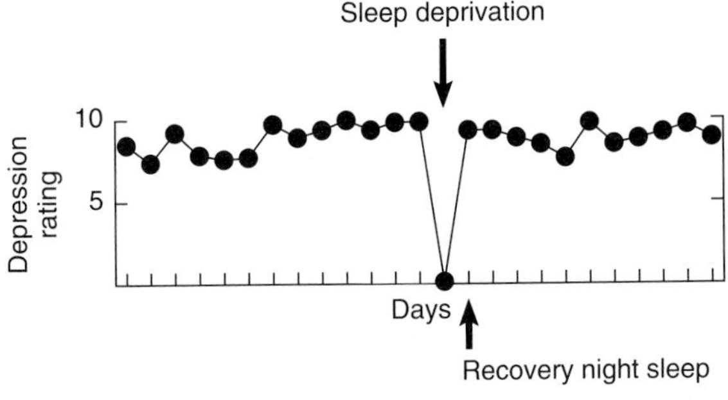

FIGURE 16.9

Changes in the depression rating of a depressed patient produced by a single night's total sleep deprivation. (From Wu, J.C., and Bunney, W.E. *American Journal of Psychiatry,* 1990, *147,* 14–21. Copyright 1990, the American Psychiatric Association. Reprinted by permission.)

tion produces immediate effects (Wu and Bunney, 1990). Figure 16.9 shows the mood rating of a patient who stayed awake one night; as you can see, the depression was lifted by the sleep deprivation but returned the next day, after a normal night's sleep. (See ***Figure 16.9.***)

Wu and Bunney suggest that during sleep a substance is produced that has a *depressogenic* effect. That is, the substance produces depression in a susceptible person. Presumably, this substance is produced in the brain and acts as a neuromodulator. During waking this substance is gradually metabolized and hence inactivated. Some of the evidence for this hypothesis is presented in Figure 16.10. The data are taken from eight different studies (cited by Wu and Bunney, 1990) and show self-ratings of depression of people who did and did not respond to sleep deprivation. (Total sleep deprivation improves the mood of patients with endogenous depression approximately two-thirds of the time.) People who responded to the sleep depression started the day depressed, but their mood gradually improved. This improvement continued through the sleepless night and during the following day. The next night they were permitted to sleep normally, and their depression was back the next morning. The data are consistent with the hypothesis that sleep produces a substance with a depressogenic effect. (See ***Figure 16.10.***)

Why do some depressed people profit from total sleep deprivation while others do not? Although we cannot yet answer this question, an interesting study by Reinink et al. (1990) found that one can *predict* a person's responsiveness from his or her circadian pattern of mood. Most people feel better at a particular time of day—

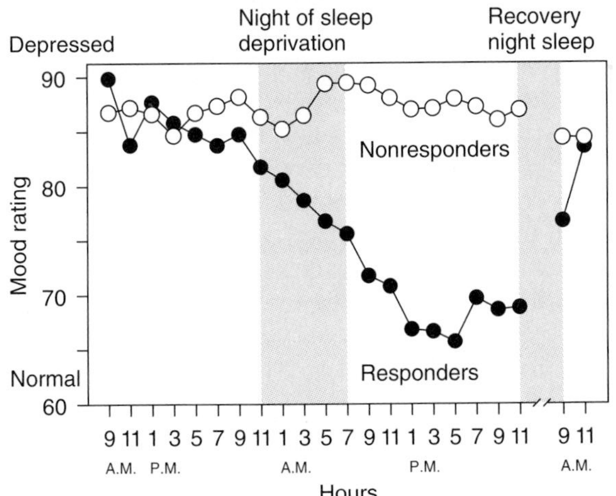

FIGURE 16.10

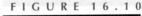

Mean mood rating of responding and nonresponding patients deprived of one night's sleep as a function of the time of day. (From Wu, J.C., and Bunney, W.E. *American Journal of Psychiatry,* 1990, *147,* 14–21. Reprinted with permission.)

generally, either the morning or the evening. Depressed people, too, show these fluctuations in mood. Reinink and his colleagues found that the depressed people who were most likely to show an improvement in mood after a night of total sleep deprivation were those who felt worst in the morning and best in the evening. Perhaps these people are most sensitive to the hypothetical depressogenic substance produced during sleep. This substance makes them feel worst in the morning, and as the day progresses, the chemical is metabolized and they start feeling better. A night without sleep simply prolongs this improvement in mood.

An alternative interpretation of the mood-elevating effects of total sleep deprivation is that waking might produce a substance with *antidepressant* effects, which is destroyed during sleep. However, Wu and Bunney point out that several studies have found that for some subjects a short nap reinstates the depression that had been reduced by sleep deprivation. In some cases a nap as short as 90 seconds (timed by EEG monitoring) can eliminate the beneficial effects of sleep deprivation. They conclude that the simplest hypothesis is that a nap produces a sudden secretion of a substance that causes depression. It seems less likely that a nap could be responsible for the sudden *destruction* of a substance with an antidepressant effect.

The relation between the antidepressant effects of REM sleep deprivation and that of total sleep deprivation are unclear. They may very well be produced by different means, because one is slow and long-lasting, whereas the other is fast and short-lived. At the present time total sleep deprivation does not provide a practical way of reducing people's depression, but biochemical comparisons made in people before and after sleep deprivation may help researchers discover whether an endogenous depressogenic substance does exist.

ROLE OF ZEITGEBERS

Yet another phenomenon relates depression to sleep and waking—or, more specifically, to the phenomena responsible for circadian rhythms. Some people become depressed during the winter season, when days are short and nights are long. The symptoms of this form of depression, called **seasonal affective disorder,** are somewhat different from those of major depression; both forms include lethargy and sleep disturbances, but seasonal depression includes a craving for carbohydrate and an accompanying weight gain. (As you will recall, people with major depression tend to lose their appetite.)

seasonal affective disorder

Many people are sensitive to seasonal changes in the hours of sunlight and darkness. Ninety-two percent of the respondents to a survey by Kasper et al. (1989a) said that they noticed seasonal changes in their mood, 27 percent reported that these changes caused problems, and 4 percent reported problems severe enough to qualify as a seasonal affective disorder. Kasper et al. (1989b) recruited people with "winter blahs" through newspaper advertisements. They excluded people with evidence of a true seasonal affective disorder and exposed the others to bright light each day. They found that the exposure to bright light improved the mood of the subjects with the "blahs," whereas the mood of normal subjects was not changed. Of course, a placebo effect may have affected the results, but it is difficult to imagine how one could design a double-blind study in which subjects would spend a few hours each day under a bright light without noticing it. In any case, the study suggests that we should consider increasing the level of illumination in the home or workplace. The only negative aspect of the change would seem to be a higher electric bill.

Studies have shown that true seasonal affective disorder can also be treated by exposing people to bright light for several hours a day (Rosenthal et al., 1985). As you will recall, circadian rhythms of sleep and wakefulness are controlled by the activity of the suprachiasmatic nucleus of the hypothalamus. Light serves as a *zeitgeber;* that is, it synchronizes the activity of the biological clock to the day-night cycle. Possibly, people with seasonal affective disorder require a stronger-than-normal zeitgeber to synchronize their biological clock with the day-night cycle.

Several investigators have noticed that the symptoms of seasonal affective disorder resemble the behavioral characteristics of hibernation: carbohydrate craving, overeating and weight gain, oversleeping, and lethargy (Rosenthal et al., 1986). Animals who hibernate do so during the winter, and the behavior is triggered by a combination of short day length and cooler temperature. Thus, some of the brain mechanisms involved in hibernation may also be responsible for the mood changes associated with the time of year. This hypothesis has some support; Zvolsky et al. (1981) found that imipramine, a tricyclic antidepressant drug, suppressed hibernation in hamsters.

Another possibility is that all the phenomena discussed in this section — unipolar depression, bipolar disorder, and seasonal affective disorder — are related in a fundamental way. Goodwin, Wirz-Justice, and Wehr (1982) have suggested that all affective disorders are caused by a disturbance in circadian rhythms. Several hormonal and biochemical systems vary with the day-night cycle. In a depressed person some of these systems may become uncoupled from the normal control mechanisms, so that specific components of interrelated systems occur at the wrong time of day. One of the consequences of this uncoupling could be the production of a depressogenic substance during sleep.

▶*INTERIM SUMMARY*◀

The major affective disorders include bipolar affective disorder, with its cyclical episodes of mania and depression, and unipolar depression. Heritability studies suggest that genetic anomalies are at least partly responsible for these disorders. Endogenous depression can be successfully treated by MAO inhibitors, tricyclic antidepressant drugs (which block the reuptake of norepinephrine and serotonin), electroconvulsive therapy, and sleep deprivation. Bipolar disorder can be successfully treated by lithium salts.

Several lines of evidence suggest that depression is caused by abnormalities in monoamine metabolism, release, or transmission. Indeed, low levels of 5-HIAA (a serotonin metabolite) in the cerebrospinal fluid correlate with attempts at suicide.

Sleep disturbances are characteristic of affective disorders. In fact, total sleep deprivation rapidly (but temporarily) reduces depression in many people, and selective deprivation of REM sleep does so slowly (but more lastingly). In addition, almost all effective antidepressant treatments suppress REM sleep. An animal model of depression has been developed in which rats are exposed to an antidepressant early in life. As a result of this treatment, they show changes in REM sleep similar to those seen in depressed patients, and antidepressant treatment reduces their symptoms. Also, a specific form of depression, seasonal affective disorder, can be treated by exposure to bright light, the zeitgeber that synchronizes the biological clock with the day-night cycle. Clearly, the affective disorders are somehow linked to biological rhythms, perhaps through their regulatory effects on neuromodulators that affect mood. ▲

ANXIETY DISORDERS

As we have just seen, the affective disorders are characterized by unrealistic extremes of emotion: depression or elation (mania). The **anxiety disorders** are characterized by unrealistic, unfounded fear and anxiety. This section will describe two of the anxiety

anxiety disorder

disorders that appear to have biological causes: panic disorder and obsessive compulsive disorder.

Panic Disorder

DESCRIPTION

panic disorder

People with **panic disorder** suffer from episodic attacks of acute anxiety — periods of acute and unremitting terror that grip them for variable lengths of time, from a few seconds to a few hours. The estimated incidence of panic disorder is between 1 and 2 percent of the population (Robbins et al., 1984). Women are approximately twice as likely as men to suffer from panic disorder. The disorder usually has its onset in young adulthood; it rarely begins after age thirty-five (Woodruff, Guze, and Clayton, 1972).

Panic attacks include many physical symptoms, such as shortness of breath, clammy sweat, irregularities in heartbeat, dizziness, faintness, and feelings of unreality. The victim of a panic attack often feels that he or she is going to die. Anxiety is a normal reaction to many stresses of life, and none of us is completely free from it. In fact, anxiety is undoubtedly useful in causing us to be more alert and to take important things seriously. However, the anxiety we all feel from time to time is obviously different from the intense fear and terror experienced by a person gripped by a panic attack.

anticipatory anxiety

agoraphobia

Between panic attacks many people with panic disorder suffer from **anticipatory anxiety** — the fear that another panic attack will strike them. This anticipatory anxiety often leads to the development of a serious phobic disorder: **agoraphobia** (*agora* means "open space"). According to the American Psychiatric Association's official *Diagnostic and Statistical Manual III-R,* agoraphobia associated with panic attacks is a fear of "being in places or situations from which escape might be difficult (or embarrassing) or in which help might not be available in the event of a panic attack. . . . As a result of this fear, the person either restricts travel or needs a companion when away from home." Agoraphobia can be severely disabling; some people with this disorder have stayed inside their houses or apartments for years, afraid to venture outside.

POSSIBLE CAUSES

Because the physical symptoms of panic attacks are so overwhelming, many patients reject the suggestion that they have a mental disorder, insisting that their problem is medical. In fact, they may be correct: A considerable amount of evidence suggests that panic disorder may have biological origins. First, the disorder appears to be hereditary; there is a higher concordance rate for the disorder between monozygotic twins than between dizygotic twins (Slater and Shields, 1969), and almost 30 percent of the first-degree relatives of a person with panic disorder also have panic disorder (Crowe et al., 1983). Second, the pattern of panic disorder within a family tree suggests that the disorder is caused by a single, dominant gene (Crowe et al., 1987).

Panic attacks can be triggered in people with a history of panic disorder by giving them injections of lactic acid (a by-product of muscular activity) or by having them breathe air containing an elevated amount of carbon dioxide (Woods, Charney, Goodman, and Heninger, 1988; Cowley and Arana, 1990). Susceptibility to lactate-induced panic attacks appears to be at least partly heritable. Balon, Jordan, Pohl, and Yeragani (1989) injected forty-five normal subjects with sodium lactate and found that ten of them had panic attacks. The investigators obtained the family history of their subjects, using an interviewer who did not know which subjects had had panic attacks. They found that over 24 percent of the relatives of the subjects with the panic attacks themselves had a history of anxiety disorders, compared with less than 8 percent in the nonresponders.

Several studies have measured cerebral blood flow by means of PET scans during panic attacks triggered by an injection of lactate. Reiman et al. (1987) found that the activity of the parahippocampal gyrus rose just before the panic attack occurred, and that the activity of the anterior ends of the temporal lobes was elevated during the attack itself. Reiman, Fusselman, Fox, and Raichle (1989) produced anticipatory anxiety in normal subjects by leading them to believe that they were about to receive an intensely painful electric shock. (The subjects received a mild shock at the beginning of the experiment to make them believe what the experimenters said, but they did not actually receive a strong shock.) The PET scan showed that in normal subjects, too, anxiety produces increased activity of the temporal poles. (See ***Color Plate 16.1.***)

Reiman and his colleagues note that studies with laboratory animals also suggest that the temporal poles are involved in anxiety reactions. For example, stimulation of this region in monkeys produces autonomic responses and facial expressions indicating fear, and humans with epilepsy caused by a focus in the anterior temporal lobes often report feelings of anxiety and fear just before their seizures occur. As we saw in Chapter 10, the temporal poles are an important source of sensory input to the amygdala, which is involved in aversive emotional reactions.

Anxiety disorders are usually treated by a combination of behavior therapy and a benzodiazepine. As we saw in Chapter 4, benzodiazepines have strong antianxiety effects. The brain possesses benzodiazepine receptors, which are part of the GABA-receptor complex. When a benzodiazepine agonist binds with its receptor, it increases the sensitivity of the GABA binding site and produces antianxiety effects. On the other hand, some drugs that bind to these receptors have the opposite effect: They reduce the sensitivity of the GABA binding site and *increase* anxiety. Anxiety disorders, then, might be caused by a diminished number of benzodiazepine receptors or by the secretion of a neuromodulator that has an effect opposite to that of benzodiazepines.

As we saw earlier in this chapter, rats who receive daily doses of an antidepressant medication early in life later develop the symptoms of depression, which can be reduced by an antidepressant drug or by REM sleep deprivation. This animal model may help us understand the physiology of depression. Marczynski and Urbancic (1988) developed a similar animal model for the anxiety disorders. They gave pregnant cats injections of diazepam (Valium), which exposed their fetuses to the drug. When the offspring of these cats were one year old, the investigators tested their emotional reactions. They found that the animals showed restlessness and anxiety when they were placed in novel situations. This fearfulness could be reduced with an injection of diazepam. Later, they measured the level of benzodiazepine receptors in the animals' brains and found a decrease in several regions. Thus, fearfulness appears to be associated with a decreased number of benzodiazepine receptors and, presumably, lower sensitivity to a neuromodulator that serves as a benzodiazepine agonist—assuming that such a substance exists.

Obsessive Compulsive Disorder

DESCRIPTION

As the name implies, people with an **obsessive compulsive disorder** suffer from **obsessions**—thoughts that will not leave them—and **compulsions**—behaviors that

obsessive compulsive disorder
obsession compulsion

they cannot keep from performing. Obsessions are seen in a variety of mental disorders, including schizophrenia. However, unlike schizophrenics, people with obsessive compulsive disorder recognize that their thoughts and behaviors are senseless and desperately wish that they would go away. They hate being compelled to do what they do, but they are unable to stop. Compulsions often become more and more demanding, until they interfere with people's careers and daily lives.

The incidence of obsessive compulsive disorder is approximately 2 percent. Like panic disorder, obsessive compulsive disorder most commonly begins in young adulthood (Robbins et al., 1984). People with this disorder are unlikely to marry, perhaps because of the common obsessional fear of dirt and contamination or because of the shame associated with the rituals they are compelled to perform, which causes them to avoid social contacts (Turner, Beidel, and Nathan, 1985).

▲ TABLE 16.1 ▲

Reported Obsessions and Compulsions of Child and Adolescent Patients

Major Presenting Symptom	*Percent Reporting Symptom at Initial Interview*
Obsession	
Concern or disgust with bodily wastes or secretions (urine, stool, saliva), dirt, germs, environmental toxins, and so on	43
Fear something terrible might happen (fire, death/illness of loved one, self, or others)	24
Concern or need for symmetry, order, or exactness	17
Scrupulosity (excessive praying or religious concerns out of keeping with patient's background)	13
Lucky/unlucky numbers	18
Forbidden or perverse sexual thoughts, images, or impulses	14
Intrusive nonsense sounds, words, or music	11
Compulsion	
Excessive or ritualized hand washing, showering, bathing, toothbrushing, or grooming	85
Repeating rituals (going in/out of door, up/down from chair, and so on)	51
Checking doors, locks, stove, appliances, car brakes, and the like	46
Cleaning and other rituals to remove contact with contaminants	23
Touching	20
Ordering/arranging	17
Measures to prevent harm to self or others (hanging clothes a certain way)	16
Counting	18
Hoarding/collecting	11
Miscellaneous rituals (licking, spitting, special dress pattern)	26

Source: From Rapoport, J.L. *Journal of the American Medical Association,* 1988, *260,* 2888–2890. Reprinted with permission.

Most compulsions fall into one of four categories: *counting, checking, cleaning,* and *avoidance.* For example, people might repeatedly check burners on the stove to see that they are off and windows and locks to be sure that they are locked. Some people wash their hands hundreds of times a day, even when they become covered with painful sores. Others meticulously clean their apartment or endlessly wash, dry, and fold their clothes. Some become afraid to leave home because they fear contamination and refuse to touch other members of their family. If they do accidentally become "contaminated," they usually have lengthy purification rituals. (See ***Table 16.1.***)

Some investigators believe that the compulsive behaviors seen in obsessive compulsive disorder are forms of species-typical behaviors—for example, grooming, cleaning, and attention toward sources of potential danger—that are released from normal control mechanisms by a brain dysfunction (Wise and Rapoport, 1988).

POSSIBLE CAUSES

Evidence is beginning to accumulate suggesting that obsessive compulsive disorder may have a genetic origin. Family studies have found that this disorder is associated with a neurological disorder called Tourette's syndrome, which appears during childhood (Pauls et al., 1986). That is, families of people with obsessive compulsive disorder will also contain people with Tourette's syndrome. **Tourette's syndrome** is characterized by muscular and vocal tics: facial grimaces, squatting, pacing, twirling, barking, sniffing, coughing, grunting, or repeating specific words (especially vulgarities). Pauls and his colleagues believe that the two disorders are produced by the same single, dominant gene. It is not clear why some people with the faulty gene develop Tourette's syndrome early in childhood and others develop obsessive compulsive disorder later in life.

Tourette's syndrome

Not all cases of obsessive compulsive disorder have a genetic origin; the disorder sometimes occurs after brain damage caused by various means, such as birth trauma, encephalitis, and head trauma (Hollander et al., 1990). As we saw in the first part of this chapter, schizophrenia, too, appears to have both hereditary and nonhereditary causes.

Several studies using PET scans have found evidence of increased glucose metabolism in the frontal lobes, caudate nucleus, and cingulate gyrus (Baxter et al., 1987, 1989; Swedo et al., 1989). These three structures are closely interconnected, and as we saw in Chapter 10, there is good evidence that they are involved in emotional reactions. In fact, some patients with severe obsessive compulsive disorder have been successfully treated with cingulectomies—surgical destruction of axons connecting the orbitofrontal cortex with the cingulate gyrus (Ballantine, Bouckoms, Thomas, and Giriunas, 1987). These operations are *much* less drastic than the prefrontal lobotomies that were performed in the 1940s and 1950s, and they do not produce the personality changes and deficits in planning that occur after the more radical surgery. But obviously, because a brain lesion cannot be undone, these operations are performed only in severe cases, after behavior therapy and drug therapy have been found to be ineffective.

By far, the most effective treatment of obsessive compulsive disorder is drug therapy. So far, three effective drugs have been found: clomipramine, fluoxetine, and fluvoxamine. Although these drugs are also effective antidepressants, their antidepressant action does not seem to be related to their ability to relieve the symptoms of obsessive compulsive disorder. For example, Leonard et al. (1989) compared the effects of clomipramine and desipramine (an antidepressant drug) on the symptoms of children and adolescents with severe obsessive compulsive disorder. For three weeks all patients received a placebo. Then for five weeks half of them received clomipramine

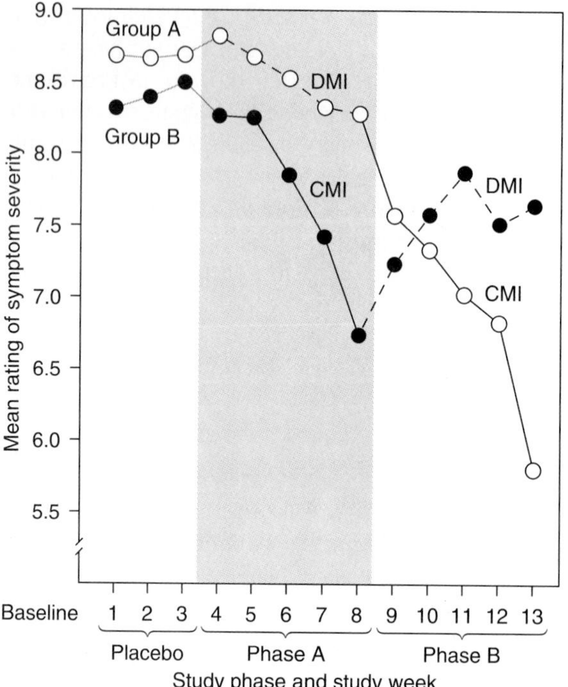

FIGURE 16.11

Mean rating of symptom severity of patients with obsessive compulsive disorder treated with desipramine (DMI) or clomipramine (CMI). (From Leonard, H.L., Swedo, S.E., Rapoport, J.L., Koby, E.V., Lenane, M.C., Cheslow, D.L., and Hamburger, S.D. *Archives of General Psychiatry,* 1989, *46,* 1088–1092. Copyright 1989, American Medical Association.)

(CMI) and the other half received desipramine (DMI), on a double-blind basis. At the end of that time the drugs were switched. As Figure 16.11 shows, CMI was a much more effective drug; in fact, when the patients were switched from CMI to DMI, their symptoms got worse. (See ***Figure 16.11.***)

All of the effective antiobsessional drugs are specific blockers of 5-HT reuptake; thus, they are specific serotonergic agonists. In general, serotonin has an inhibitory effect on species-typical behaviors, which has tempted several investigators to speculate that these drugs alleviate the symptoms of obsessive compulsive disorder by reducing the strength of the grooming, cleaning, and danger avoidance behaviors that may underlie this disorder.

▶INTERIM SUMMARY◀

The anxiety disorders severely disrupt some people's lives. People with panic disorder periodically have panic attacks, during which they experience intense symptoms of autonomic activity and often feel as if they are going to die. Frequently, panic attacks lead to the development of agoraphobia, an avoidance of being away from a safe place, such as home. Panic disorder is at least partly heritable, which suggests that it has biological causes.

Panic attacks can be triggered in many susceptible people by inhalation of air containing an elevated amount of carbon dioxide or by giving them an injection of lactic acid. During a panic attack people show increased activity of the anterior ends of the temporal lobes.

Panic attacks can be alleviated by the administration of a benzodiazepine, which suggests that the disorder may involve decreased numbers of benzodiazepine receptors or an inadequate secretion of an endogenous benzodiazepine agonist. Cats given a benzodiazepine prenatally will become especially fearful when they reach adulthood, and the treatment decreases the number of benzodiazepine receptors in parts of their brain.

Obsessive compulsive disorder is characterized by obsessions — unwanted thoughts — and compulsions — uncontrollable behaviors, especially those involving cleanliness and attention to danger. Some investigators believe that these behaviors represent overactivity of species-typical behavioral tendencies.

Obsessive compulsive disorder has a heritable basis and is related to a neurological disorder characterized by tics and strange vocalizations, called Tourette's syndrome. It can also be caused by brain damage at birth, encephalitis, and head injuries. PET scans indicate that people with obsessive compulsive disorder tend to show increased glucose metabolism in the frontal lobes, caudate nucleus, and cingulate gyrus, structures that are probably involved in emotional reactions. The destruction of the cingulum bundle, which links the orbitofrontal cortex with the cingulate gyrus, reduces the symptoms, as do drugs such as clomipramine, which specifically block the reuptake of serotonin. Some investigators believe that clomipramine and related drugs alleviate the symptoms of obsessive compulsive disorder by increasing the activity of serotonergic pathways that play an inhibitory role on species-typical behaviors. ▲

CONCLUDING REMARKS

Schizophrenia, the major affective disorders, and the anxiety disorders are serious problems. Early in this century most psychiatrists believed that the psychoses, at least, were caused by brain abnormalities, but with the ascendancy of psychotherapy, this belief fell into disrepute. More recently, with the discovery of the hereditary basis of these disorders and the efficacy of drug treatment, most researchers and clinicians again believe that the serious mental disorders reflect abnormalities in brain structure or biochemistry. We have seen some of the more important hypotheses being investigated by researchers today, and some of the progress that has been made in understanding and treating the disorders. The future offers hope to people who suffer from the major mental disorders, and to their families and friends.

A personal note: You are now at the end of the book (as you well know), and you have spent a considerable amount of time reading my words. While working on this book, I have tried to imagine myself talking to someone who is interested in learning something about the physiology of behavior. As I mentioned in the preface, writing is often a lonely activity, and the imaginary audience helped keep me company. If you would like to turn this communication into a two-way conversation, write to me—my address is given at the end of the preface.

◀ *EPILOGUE: Application*

As a result of taking an antipsychotic medication, Larry, the schizophrenic man described in the Prologue, developed a neurological disorder called *tardive dyskinesia. Tardus* means "slow" and *dyskinesia* means "faulty movement"; thus, tardive dyskinesia is a late-developing movement disorder. (In Larry's case it actually came rather early.)

Tardive dyskinesia appears to be the opposite of Parkinson's disease. Whereas patients with Parkinson's disease have difficulty moving, patients with tardive dyskinesia are unable to stop moving. Indeed, dyskinesia commonly occurs when patients with Parkinson's disease receive too much L-DOPA. In schizophrenic patients tardive dyskinesia is made *worse* by discontinuing the antipsychotic drug and is improved by increasing the dose. The symptoms are also intensified by dopamine agonists such as L-DOPA or amphetamine. Therefore, the disorder appears to be produced by an overstimulation of dopamine receptors. But if it is, why should it be originally caused by antipsychotic drugs, which are dopamine *antagonists?*

The answer seems to be provided by a phenomenon described in Chapter 4, called *supersensitivity*. Supersensitivity is a compensatory mechanism in which some types of receptors become more sensitive if they are inhibited for a period of time by a drug that blocks them. For tardive dyskinesia the relevant dopamine receptors are in the caudate nucleus, an important component of the motor system. (You will recall that Parkinson's disease is caused by degeneration of dopamine-secreting neurons that connect the substantia nigra with the caudate nucleus.) When these receptors are chronically blocked by an antipsychotic drug, they become supersensitive. In some cases, the supersensitivity becomes so great that it overcompensates for the effects of the drug, causing the neurological symptoms to occur.

Fortunately, the wish expressed by Larry's physician has come true. Researchers *have* discovered a medication that treats the symptoms of schizophrenia without producing neurological side effects, and early indications suggest that tardive dyskinesia may become a thing of the past. Better yet, the new drug, called *clozapine,* reduces the psychotic symptoms of many patients who are not significantly helped by the older antipsychotic drugs.

As you have learned in this chapter, most investigators believe that the therapeutic effects of antipsychotic drugs occur because the drugs block dopamine receptors in the nucleus accumbens and the prefrontal cortex. The fact that the drugs also block dopamine receptors in the caudate nucleus is unrelated to its therapeutic effects and, as we have seen, can produce neurological side effects. Thus, the ideal antipsychotic drug would inhibit dopaminergic transmission in the nucleus accumbens and prefrontal cortex but not in the caudate nucleus. And that, apparently, is just what clozapine does. Several studies using laboratory animals have shown that clozapine profoundly affects activity of the mesolimbic dopamine system without affecting the nigrostriatal dopamine system. For example, Chen, Paredes, and Gardner (1991) found that chronic daily treatment with clozapine reduced the release of dopamine (measured by means of microdialysis) in the nucleus accumbens but not in the caudate nucleus.

Clozapine does not appear to produce neurological side effects in human patients (Bruhwyler, Chleide, and Mercier, 1990). Although not enough time has elapsed to be sure what the drug's long-term effects will be, researchers hope that the drug will not produce tardive dyskinesia either. In addition, clozapine appears to be even more effective than other antipsychotic drugs in helping hard-to-treat patients. In a double-blind study Kane et al. (1988) compared the effectiveness of clozapine and chlorpromazine (Thorazine—the drug Larry was taking) on 268 patients with severe schizophrenia and a proven history of poor response to antipsychotic medication. The study found that in six weeks of treatment 30 percent of the clozapine-treated patients improved, compared with only 4 percent of the chlorpromazine-treated patients.

Clozapine is not yet routinely administered to all schizophrenic patients. For one thing, researchers discovered during early clinical trials that a small percentage of individuals taking the drug develop *agranulocytosis,* a life-threatening suppression of the production of white blood cells. Other antipsychotic drugs can cause agranulocytosis, but apparently the incidence of this disease is higher with clozapine. For this reason the white blood cell count of patients who receive the drug is carefully monitored.

Undoubtedly, the story is not over yet. The biochemical action of clozapine is different from that of other antipsychotic drugs, and researchers are working on the development of similar drugs that may prove to be even more effective in treating schizophrenia, produce no neurological side effects, and avoid the problem of agranulocytosis altogether. ▲

KEY CONCEPTS

Schizophrenia

- Because a tendency to develop schizophrenia is heritable, biological factors may be important.
- The effects of dopamine agonists and antagonists on the positive symptoms of schizophrenia gives support to the dopamine hypothesis.
- Because evidence of brain damage is found in people who display the negative symptoms of schizophrenia, some researchers believe that a pathological process, perhaps triggered by a virus, is responsible for schizophrenia.

Major Affective Disorders

- The major affective disorders include major depression and bipolar disorder. Evidence suggests that both types are heritable.
- The monoamine hypothesis was suggested by the findings that dopamine agonists and antagonists affect the symptoms of the affective disorders and that depressed people tend to have a low level of a serotonin metabolite in their CSF.
- An animal model of depression has been developed, which may help researchers in their work with human patients.
- The affective disorders are related to sleep disturbances and can be relieved by REM sleep deprivation or total sleep deprivation. In addition, some people suffer from seasonal affective disorders. Thus, affective disorders may be caused by malfunctions of the neural systems that regulate circadian rhythms.

Anxiety Disorders

- The two most serious anxiety disorders are panic disorder and obsessive compulsive disorder. Both disorders appear to have a strong hereditary component.
- Panic disorder is treated with benzodiazepines and may involve abnormalities in these receptors. An animal model of this disorder has also been developed.
- Obsessive compulsive disorder may be related to the species-typical behaviors of grooming, cleaning, and attention to danger. It is treated with clomipramine, a serotonin agonist, which has inhibitory effects on these behaviors in laboratory animals.

NEW TERMS

agoraphobia **p. 546**
anticipatory anxiety **p. 546**
anxiety disorder **p. 545**
bipolar disorder **p. 537**
chlorpromazine **p. 530**
compulsion **p. 547**
delusion **p. 527**
electroconvulsive therapy (ECT) **p. 539**
endogenous depression **p. 537**
hallucination **p. 527**
5-HIAA **p. 540**
lithium **p. 539**
major affective disorder **p. 536**
monoamine hypothesis **p. 546**
negative symptom **p. 527**
neurosis **p. 526**
obsession **p. 547**
obsessive compulsive disorder **p. 547**
panic disorder **p. 546**
positive symptom **p. 527**
psychosis **p. 526**
reactive depression **p. 537**
schizophrenia **p. 527**
seasonal affective disorder **p. 544**
thought disorder **p. 527**
Tourette's syndrome **p. 549**
tricyclic antidepressant **p. 538**
unipolar depression **p. 537**

SUGGESTED READINGS

Goodwin, D.W., and Guze, S.B. *Psychiatric Diagnosis,* 3rd ed. New York: Oxford University Press, 1984.

Kaplan, H.I., and Sadock, B.J. *Comprehensive Textbook of Psychiatry,* 5th ed. Baltimore: Williams and Wilkins, 1988.

Nasrallah, H.A., and Weinberger, D.R. *Handbook of Schizophrenia. Vol. 1. The Neurology of Schizophrenia.* Amsterdam: Elsevier Science Publishers, 1986.

Schulz, S.C., and Tamminga, C.A. *Schizophrenia: A Scientific Focus.* New York: Oxford University Press, 1988.

Glossary

Absence. A type of seizure disorder often seen in children; characterized by periods of inattention, which are not subsequently remembered; also called *petit mal* seizures.

Absorptive phase. The phase of metabolism during which nutrients are absorbed from the digestive system. Glucose and amino acids constitute the principal sources of energy for cells during this phase. Stores of glycogen are increased, and excess nutrients are stored in adipose tissue in the form of triglycerides.

Accessory abducens nucleus. A nucleus in the medulla of the rabbit located next to the abducens (cranial nerve) nucleus; contains motor neurons responsible for the nictitating membrane response.

Accessory olfactory bulb. A neural structure located in the main olfactory bulb; receives information from the vomeronasal organ.

Accommodation. Changes in the thickness of the lens of the eye, accomplished by the ciliary muscles, that focus images of near or distant objects on the retina.

Acetylcholine (ACh). A neurotransmitter found in the brain, spinal cord, and ganglia of the autonomic nervous system and the postganglionic terminal buttons of the parasympathetic division of the autonomic nervous system.

Acetylcholinesterase (AChE). The enzyme that destroys acetylcholine soon after it is liberated by the terminal buttons, thus terminating the postsynaptic potential.

Achromatopsia. The inability to discriminate among different hues; caused by damage to the visual association cortex.

Actin. Actin and myosin are the proteins that provide the physical basis for muscular contraction. See Figures 7.1 and 7.2.

Action potential. The brief electrical impulse that provides the basis for conduction of information along an axon. The action potential results from brief changes in membrane permeability to sodium and potassium ions. See Figure 2.20.

Activational effect. See under *hormone.*

Acute anterior poliomyelitis. A viral disease that destroys motor neurons of the brain and spinal cord.

Adjunctive behavior. A species-typical behavior such as drinking that occurs when a very hungry animal receives small pieces of food intermittently.

Adrenal gland. An endocrine gland located atop the kidney. The *adrenal cortex* produces steroid hormones such as corticosterone, androstenedione, and aldosterone. The *adrenal medulla,* controlled by sympathetic nerve fibers, secretes epinephrine and norepinephrine.

Adrenocorticotropic hormone (ACTH). A hormone produced and liberated by the anterior pituitary gland in response to corticotropin-releasing hormone, produced by the hypothalamus. ACTH stimulates the adrenal cortex to produce various steroid hormones.

Adrenogenital syndrome. A condition characterized by hypersecretion of androgens by the adrenal cortex. The result, in females, is masculinization of the external genitalia.

Afferent axon. An axon directed toward a structure; all neurons afferent to the central nervous system convey sensory information.

Agonist. Literally, a contestant, or one who takes part in the contest. An agonistic drug facilitates the effects of a particular neurotransmitter on the postsynaptic cell. An agonistic muscle produces or facilitates a particular movement. Antonym: *antagonist.*

Agoraphobia. A mental disorder; fear of and avoidance of being alone in public places; often accompanied by panic attacks.

Agrammatism. One of the usual symptoms of Broca's aphasia; difficulty in comprehending or properly employing grammatical devices, such as verb endings and word order.

Akinesia. A motor disorder characterized by a relative lack of movement; unlike paralysis, movement is possible if the patient is adequately stimulated.

Akinetic mutism. A motor disorder characterized by a relative lack of movement and lack of speech.

Alexia with agraphia. A loss of the ability to read or write caused by brain damage.

All-or-none law. States that once an action potential is triggered in an axon, it is propagated, without decrement, to the end of the fiber.

Alpha activity. A smooth electrical activity of 8 to 12 Hz recorded from the brain. Alpha activity is generally associated with a state of relaxation.

Alpha motor neuron. A neuron whose cell body is located in the ventral horn of the spinal cord or in one of the motor nuclei of the cranial nerves. Stimulation of an alpha motor neuron results in contraction of the extrafusal muscle fibers upon which its terminal buttons synapse.

Alzheimer's disease. A degenerative brain disorder of unknown origin; causes progressive memory loss, motor deficits, and eventual death. Acetylcholine-secreting neurons are the first to be affected.

Amacrine cell. A neuron in the retina that interconnects adjacent ganglion cells and the inner arborizations of the bipolar cells.

Amino acid. A molecule that contains both an amino group and a carboxyl group. Amino acids are linked by peptide bonds and serve as the constituents of proteins.

Amino acid autoradiography. A neuroanatomical technique that permits the tracing of efferent pathways from a region of the brain. A radioactive amino acid such as proline is injected into a region, where it is taken up by neurons and incorporated into proteins. These radioactive proteins are carried by axoplasmic transport to the terminal buttons. The location of the terminal buttons is determined by means of autoradiography.

Amphetamine. A catecholamine agonist: facilitates neurotransmitter release, stimulates postsynaptic receptors (slightly), and retards reuptake by the terminal buttons.

Ampulla. An enlargement in a semicircular canal; contains the cupula and the crista.

Amygdala. The term commonly used for the *amygdaloid complex,* a set of nuclei located in the base of the temporal lobe, just rostral to the hippocampus. The amygdala is a part of the limbic system and is involved in species-typical behaviors, especially predatory, defensive, and sexual behaviors.

Amyloid. A protein found in excessive amounts in degenerating neurons in the brains of patients with Alzheimer's disease.

Analgesia. A lack of sensitivity to pain.

Androgen. A male sex steroid hormone. Testosterone is the principal mammalian androgen.

Androgen insensitivity syndrome. A condition, also called *testicular feminization,* caused by a congenital lack of functioning androgen receptors. Because androgens cannot exert their effects, a person with XY sex chromosomes develops as a female, with female external genitalia. Because the fetal testes produce Müllerian-inhibiting substance, neither the Wolffian nor the Müllerian systems develop into internal sex organs.

Androgenization. The process initiated by exposure of the cells of a developing animal to androgens. Exposure to androgens causes embryonic sex organs to develop as male and produces certain changes in the brain. See also *hormone.*

Angiotensin. See under *renin.*

Angiotensinogen. See under *renin.*

Angular gyrus. A gyrus in the parietal lobe; the left angular gyrus is important for verbal functions, especially reading.

Anion. See under *ion.*

Anomia. A difficulty in finding (remembering) the appropriate word to describe an object, action, or attribute; one of the symptoms of aphasia.

Anorexia nervosa. A disorder that most frequently afflicts young women; exaggerated concern with overweight that leads to excessive dieting and often compulsive exercising; can lead to starvation.

ANS. See *autonomic nervous system (ANS).*

Antagonist. An antagonistic muscle produces a movement contrary or opposite to the one being described. An antagonistic drug opposes or inhibits the effects of a particular neurotransmitter on the postsynaptic cell. Antonym: *agonist.*

Anterior. See Figure 3.1.

Anterior pituitary gland. See under *pituitary gland.*

Anterograde amnesia. An amnesia for events that occur after some disturbance to the brain, such as head injury, electroconvulsive shock, or certain degenerative brain diseases.

Antianxiety drug. A drug that reduces anxiety; also called tranquilizing drug.

Antibody. A protein produced by a cell of the immune system that recognizes antigens present on invading microorganisms.

Anticipatory anxiety. A fear of having a panic attack; may lead to the development of agoraphobia.

Antigen. A protein present on a microorganism that permits the immune system to recognize it as an invader.

Anxiety disorder. A psychological disorder characterized by tension, overactivity of the autonomic nervous system, expectation of an impending disaster, and continuous vigilance for danger.

Aphasia. A difficulty in producing or comprehending speech not produced by deafness or a simple motor deficit, caused by brain damage.

Apomorphine. A drug that blocks dopamine autoreceptors when administered at low doses; at higher doses it blocks postsynaptic receptors as well.

Apperceptive visual agnosia. See under *visual agnosia.*

Apraxia. A difficulty in carrying out purposeful movements, in the absence of paralysis or muscular weakness.

Arachnoid membrane. The middle layer of the meninges, between the outer dura mater and inner pia mater. The subarachnoid space beneath the arachnoid membrane is filled with cerebrospinal fluid, which cushions the brain.

Arcuate fasciculus. A bundle of axons that connects Wernicke's area with Broca's area; damage causes conduction aphasia.

Association cortex. Those regions of cortex that receive information from the sensory areas (sensory association cortex) or that project to the primary motor cortex (motor association cortex); plays an important role in perception, learning, and planning.

Associative long-term potentiation. A long-term potentiation in which concurrent stimulation of weak and strong synapses to a given neuron strengthens the weak ones.

Associative visual agnosia. See under *visual agnosia.*

Astrocyte (astroglia). A glial cell that provides support for neurons of the central nervous system. Astrocytes also participate in the formation of scar tissue after injury to the brain or spinal cord.

Atropine. A drug that blocks muscarinic acetylcholine receptors.

Aura. A sensation that precedes a seizure; its exact nature depends on the location of the seizure focus.

Auditory nerve. The auditory nerve has two principal branches. The *cochlear nerve* transmits auditory information, and the *vestibular nerve* transmits information related to balance.

Autoimmune disease. A disease in which the immune system attacks and damages some of the body's own tissue. Examples include multiple sclerosis, diabetes mellitus, and rheumatoid arthritis.

Autonomic ganglia. See under *ganglion.*

Autonomic nervous system (ANS). The portion of the peripheral nervous system that controls the body's vegetative function. The *sympathetic division* mediates functions that accompany arousal; the *parasympathetic division* mediates functions that occur during a relaxed state. See also *somatic nervous system.*

Autoradiography. A procedure that locates radioactive substances in body tissue, usually in the brain or spinal cord. The tissue is sliced, mounted on a microscope slide, and covered with a photographic emulsion or piece of film. The radiation exposes the emulsion, which is subsequently developed.

Autoreceptor. A receptor molecule located on a neuron that responds to the neurotransmitter or neuromodulator that the neuron itself secretes. Some autoreceptors are located on the presynaptic membrane; they participate in the regulation of the amount of neurotransmitter that is synthesized and released.

Axon. A thin, elongated process of a neuron that can transmit action potentials toward its terminal buttons, which synapse upon other neurons, gland cells, or muscle cells.

Axoplasmic transport. An active mechanism involving proteins similar to actin and myosin that propel substances down the axons from the soma to the terminal buttons. A slower form of axoplasmic transport carries substances in the opposite direction.

Balint's syndrome. A syndrome caused by bilateral damage to the parieto-occipital region; includes *optic ataxia* (difficulty in reaching for objects under visual guidance), *ocular apraxia* (difficulty in visual scanning), and *simultanagnosia* (difficulty in perceiving more than one object at a time).

Barbiturate. A drug that causes sedation; one of several derivatives of barbituric acid.

Basal forebrain region. The region at the base of the forebrain rostral to the hypothalamus.

Basal ganglia. The caudate nucleus, globus pallidus, putamen, and amygdala. The first three are important parts of the motor system, located just rostral to the thalamus. See also *ganglion.*

Basic rest-activity cycle (BRAC). A 90-minute cycle (in humans) of waxing and waning alertness, controlled by a biological clock in the caudal brain stem; during sleep it controls cycles of REM sleep and slow-wave sleep.

Basilar membrane. A membrane in the cochlea of the inner ear; contains the organ of Corti, the receptor organ for hearing.

Benign. Harmless. A benign tumor is not cancerous (malignant) because it has a distinct border and does not metastasize.

Benzodiazepine. A class of drug with anxiolytic ("tranquilizing") effects; works by activating benzodiazepine receptors coupled to GABA receptors on neurons, making the latter more sensitive to the neurotransmitter.

Beta activity. An irregular electrical activity of 13 to 30 Hz recorded from the brain. Beta activity is generally associated with a state of arousal.

Bilateral. On both sides of the midline of the body.

Binding site. The location on a receptor protein to which a ligand binds. For example, acetylcholine binds to the binding site of a nicotinic receptor and opens the associated neurotransmitter-dependent ion channel.

Bipolar cell. See under *bipolar neuron.*

Bipolar disorder. A psychosis characterized by cyclical periods of mania and depression; effectively treated with lithium carbonate.

Bipolar neuron. A neuron with only two processes — a dendritic process at one end and an axonal process at the other end. (See Figure 2.5.) *Bipolar cells* constitute the middle layer of the retina, conveying information from the receptor cells to the ganglion cells, whose axons give rise to the optic nerves.

Blindsight. The ability of a person to reach for objects located in his or her "blind" field; occurs after damage restricted to the primary visual cortex.

Blob. The central region of a module of the primary visual cortex, revealed by a stain for cytochrome oxidase; contains wavelength-sensitive neurons; part of the parvocellular system.

Blood-brain barrier. A barrier produced by the astrocytes and cells in the walls of the capillaries in the brain; this barrier permits passage of only certain substances.

B-lymphocyte. A white blood cell that originates in the bone marrow; part of the immune system.

Botulinum toxin. An acetylcholine antagonist: prevents release by terminal buttons.

Brain lesion. A damage to part of the brain.

Brain stem. The "stem" of the brain, from the medulla to the midbrain, excluding the cerebellum.

Brightness. A perceptual dimension of color, most closely related to the intensity or degree of radiant energy emitted by a visual stimulus.

Broca's area. A region of frontal cortex, located just rostral to the base of the left primary motor cortex, that is necessary for normal speech production. Damage to this region results in *Broca's aphasia,* characterized by extreme difficulty in speech articulation.

Brown adipose tissue. Fat cells densely packed with mitochondria, which can generate heat; important in hibernating animals and thought to play an important role in converting excessive calories of nutrients into heat rather than increased size of fat deposits.

Bruce effect. The termination of pregnancy caused by the odor of a pheromone in the urine of a male other than the one that impregnated the female; first identified in mice.

Bulimia. Bouts of excessive hunger and eating; often seen in people with anorexia nervosa.

CA1, CA3. See under *hippocampal formation.*

Cable properties. The passive conduction of electrical current, in a decremental fashion, down the length of an axon, similar to the way electrical current traverses a submarine cable.

Calcarine fissure. A horizontal fissure on the inner surface of the posterior cerebral cortex; the location of the primary visual cortex.

Callosal apraxia. An apraxia of the left hand caused by damage to the anterior corpus callosum.

Calpain. A proteolytic (protein-dissolving) enzyme that may play a role in long-term potentiation. See also *spectrin.*

Cardiac muscle. The muscle responsible for the contraction of the heart.

Cataplexy. A symptom of narcolepsy; complete paralysis that occurs during waking; thought to be related to REM sleep mechanisms.

Catecholamine. A class of biologically active amines that includes the neurotransmitters dopamine, norepinephrine, and epinephrine.

Cation. See under *ion.*

Cauda equina. A bundle of spinal roots located caudal to the end of the spinal cord.

Caudal. See Figure 3.1.

CCK. See *cholecystokinin (CCK).*

Central canal. The narrow tube, filled with cerebrospinal fluid, that runs through the length of the spinal cord.

Central nervous system (CNS). The brain and spinal cord.

Central nucleus. A nucleus of the amygdala that is involved in organizing the behavioral, autonomic, and endocrine components of conditioned emotional responses.

Central sulcus. The sulcus that separates the frontal lobe from the parietal lobe.

Cephalic phase. The set of autonomic and endocrine responses initiated by stimuli associated with the onset of a meal; includes salivation, secretion of gastric juices, and the secretion of insulin.

Cerebellar cortex. The cortex that covers the cerebellar hemispheres.

Cerebellum. A major part of the brain, situated dorsal to the pons, containing the two cerebellar hemispheres, covered with the cerebellar cortex; an important component of the motor system, involved in integrating, sequencing, and smoothing movements.

Cerebral aqueduct. A narrow tube interconnecting the third and fourth ventricles of the brain.

Cerebral cortex. The outermost layer of gray matter of the cerebral hemispheres.

Cerebral hemisphere. The two major portions of the forebrain, covered by the cerebral cortex.

Cerebrospinal fluid (CSF). A clear fluid, similar to blood plasma, that fills the ventricular system of the brain and the subarachnoid space surrounding the brain and spinal cord.

Cerebrovascular accident. A "stroke"; brain damage caused by occlusion or rupture of a blood vessel in the brain.

Chlorpromazine. A dopamine antagonist: blocks postsynaptic receptors. It is the most commonly prescribed antischizophrenic drug.

Cholecystokinin (CCK). A hormone secreted by the duodenum that regulates gastric motility and causes the gallbladder (cholecyst) to contract, expelling bile into the digestive system; also found in neurons in the brain, where it may serve as a neurotransmitter or neuromodulator.

Choline acetyltransferase (CAT). The enzyme that transfers the acetate ion from acetyl coenzyme A to choline, producing the neurotransmitter acetylcholine.

Chorda tympani. A branch of the facial nerve (seventh cranial nerve) that passes beneath the eardrum; conveys taste information from the anterior part of the tongue and controls the secretion of some salivary glands.

Choroid plexus. A highly vascular tissue that protrudes into the ventricles and produces cerebrospinal fluid.

Chromosome. A strand of DNA, with associated proteins, found in the nucleus; carries genetic information.

Ciliary muscles. Muscles arranged around the lens of the eye; control the shape of the eye to focus images of near or distant objects on the retina.

Cilium. A hairlike appendage of a cell; involved in movement or in transducing sensory information. Cilia are found on the receptors in the auditory and vestibular system.

Cingulate gyrus. A strip of limbic cortex lying along the lateral walls of the groove separating the cerebral hemispheres, just above the corpus callosum.

Circadian rhythm. A daily rhythmical change in behavior or physiological process.

Circumlocution. A strategy by which a person with anomia finds alternate ways to say something when he or she is unable to think of the most appropriate word.

Classical conditioning. A learning procedure. When a stimulus that initially produces no more than an orienting response is followed several times by an *unconditional stimulus* that produces a defensive or appetitive response (the *unconditional response*), the first stimulus (now called a *conditional stimulus*) itself evokes the response (now called a *conditional response*).

Clonic phase. The phase of a grand mal seizure in which the patient shows rhythmic jerking movements.

CNS. See *central nervous system (CNS).*

Cocaine. A drug that retards the reuptake of the catecholamines, especially dopamine; a potent dopamine agonist.

Cochlea. The snail-shaped structure of the inner ear that contains the auditory transducing mechanisms.

Cochlear nerve. See under *auditory nerve.*

Cochlear nuclei. A group of nuclei in the medulla that receive auditory information from the cochlea.

Coenzyme A. A chemical that facilitates the action of an enzyme in a chemical reaction.

Commissure. A fiber bundle that interconnects corresponding regions on each side of the brain.

Complex cell. A neuron in the visual cortex that responds to the presence of a line segment with a particular orientation located within its receptive field, especially when the line moves perpendicularly to its orientation; distinguished from *simple* *cells* by their larger receptive fields and their response to movement.

Complex partial seizure. A partial seizure, starting from a focus and remaining localized, that produces loss of consciousness.

Compulsion. The feeling that one is obliged to perform a behavior, even if one prefers not to do so.

Computerized axial tomography. See *CT scanner.*

Conditional response (CR). See under *classical conditioning.*

Conditional stimulus (CS). See under *classical conditioning.*

Conditioned emotional response. A classically conditioned response that occurs when a neutral stimulus is followed by an aversive stimulus; usually includes autonomic, behavioral, and endocrine components such as changes in heart rate, freezing, and secretion of stress-related hormones.

Conditioned flavor aversion. The avoidance of a relatively unfamiliar flavor that previously caused (or was followed by) illness.

Conditioned place preference. The learned preference for a location in which an organism encountered a reinforcing stimulus, such as food or a reinforcing drug.

Conduction aphasia. The damage to the connections between Wernicke's area and Broca's area; results in the inability to repeat words that are heard, although they can usually be understood and responded to appropriately.

Cone. See under *photoreceptor.*

Conjunctiva. A transparent membrane that lines the inside of the eyelids and attaches to the area near the edge of the cornea.

Constructional apraxia. A difficulty in drawing pictures or diagrams or in making geometrical constructions of elements such as building blocks or sticks; caused by brain damage, especially to the right parietal lobe.

Content word. A noun, verb, adjective, or adverb that conveys meaning. See also *function word.*

Contralateral. Residing in the side of the body opposite to the reference point.

Convulsion. A violent sequence of uncontrollable muscular movements caused by a seizure.

Coolidge effect. The restorative effect of introducing a new female sex partner to a male that has apparently become "exhausted" by sexual activity.

Coping response. A response through which an organism can avoid, escape from, or minimize an aversive stimulus. The opportunity to make a coping response minimizes the stressful effects of an aversive stimulus.

Cornea. The transparent outer surface of the eye, in front of the iris and pupil.

Corpus callosum. The largest commissure of the brain, interconnecting the areas of neocortex on each side of the brain.

Corpus luteum. The mass of tissue that develops from the ovarian follicle after ovulation; secretes estradiol and progesterone.

Correctional mechanism. In a regulatory process, the mechanism that is capable of changing the value of the system variable.

Corticobulbar pathway. A bundle of axons from the neocortex (principally the primary motor cortex) to the nuclei of the fifth, seventh, and twelfth cranial nerves in the medulla, which control movements of the face and tongue.

Corticospinal pathway. The system of axons that originates in the cortex (especially the primary motor cortex) and terminates in the ventral gray matter of the spinal cord. Axons of the *lateral corticospinal tract* cross the midline in the pyramids of the medulla and synapse on spinal motor neurons and interneurons that control the arms and hands. Axons of the *ventral corticospinal tract* cross the midline near their site of termination in the spinal cord and primarily control movements of the trunk muscles.

CR. Conditional response. See under *classical conditioning.*

Cranial nerve. One of a set of twelve pairs of nerves that exit from the base of the brain.

Cranial nerve ganglion. See under *ganglion.*

Cribriform plate. A part of the bone at the base of the skull below the frontal lobes. Axons of the olfactory receptors pass through small holes in this bone on their way to the olfactory bulbs.

Crista. The sensory organ of the semicircular canals; found in the ampulla.

Cross section. See Figure 3.2.

CS. Conditional stimulus. See under *classical conditioning.*

CSF. See *cerebrospinal fluid (CSF).*

CT scanner. A device that uses a computer to analyze data obtained by a scanning beam of X-rays to produce a two-dimensional picture of a "slice" through the body.

Cupula. A gelatinous mass found in the ampulla of the semicircular canals; moves in response to the flow of the fluid in the canals.

Curare. A drug that blocks nicotinic acetylcholine receptors.

Cutaneous sense. One of the somatosenses; includes sensitivity to stimuli that involve the skin.

Cyclic adenosine monophosphate (cyclic AMP). The intermediate messenger in the production of postsynaptic potentials by some neurotransmitters and in the mediation of the effects of peptide hormones.

Cyclic nucleotide. A compound such as cyclic AMP, important in mediating the intracellular effects of many neurotransmitters and peptide hormones.

Cytoplasm. The viscous, semiliquid substance contained in the interior of a cell.

DA. See *dopamine (DA).*

Declarative memory. Memory that can be verbally expressed, such as memory for events in a person's past. The ability to form new declarative memories is disrupted by lesions of the hippocampal formation or related structures.

Deep cerebellar nuclei. A group of nuclei within the cerebellum that convey information to and from the cerebellar cortex.

Defeminizing effect. The effect of a hormone present early in development; reduces or prevents the later development of anatomical or behavioral characteristics typical of females. See also *masculinizing effect.*

Defensive behavior. A species-typical behavior by which an animal defends itself against the threat of another animal.

Delta activity. A regular, synchronous electrical activity of approximately 1 to 4 Hz recorded from the brain. Delta activity is generally associated with slow-wave sleep.

Delusion. A belief that is clearly in contradiction to reality.

Dementia. A loss of cognitive abilities such as memory, perception, verbal ability, and judgment; common causes are multiple strokes or Alzheimer's disease.

Dendrite. A treelike process attached to the soma of a neuron, which receives messages from the terminal buttons of other neurons.

Dendritic spine. The small buds on the surface of a dendrite, upon which terminal buttons from other neurons synapse.

Dentate gyrus. A part of the hippocampal formation; receives inputs from the entorhinal cortex via the perforant path and projects to the hippocampus.

Dentate nucleus. A deep cerebellar nucleus; involved in the control of rapid, skilled movements by the corticospinal and rubrospinal systems.

2-Deoxyglucose (2-DG). A sugar that interferes with the metabolism of glucose.

Deoxyribonucleic acid (DNA). A long, complex macromolecule consisting of two interconnected helical strands. Strands of DNA, along with their associated proteins, constitute the chromosomes, which contain the genetic information of the animal.

Depolarization. A reduction (toward zero) of the membrane potential of a cell from its normal resting potential of approximately −70 mV.

Detector. In a regulatory process, a mechanism that signals when the system variable deviates from its set point.

Deuteranopia. An inherited form of defective color vision in which red and green hues are confused. "Green" cones appear to be filled with "red" cone opsin.

Developmental dyslexia. Reading difficulty in a person of normal intelligence and perceptual ability; of genetic origin or caused by prenatal or perinatal factors.

2-DG. See *2-deoxyglucose (2-DG).*

Diabetes mellitus. A disease that results from insufficient production of insulin, thus causing, in an untreated state, a high level of blood glucose.

Diencephalon. See Table 3.1.

Diffusion. A movement of molecules from regions of high concentration to regions of low concentration.

Direct dyslexia. A language disorder caused by brain damage in which the person can read words aloud without understanding them.

DNA. See *deoxyribonucleic acid (DNA).*

Doctrine of specific nerve energies. Müller's observation that different nerve fibers convey different information, but that the basic nature of the message (later found to be the action potential) is the same.

Dopamine (DA). A neurotransmitter; one of the catecholamines.

Dorsal. See Figure 3.1.

Dorsal lateral geniculate nucleus. See under *lateral geniculate nucleus.*

Dorsal root. See under *spinal root.*

Dorsal root ganglion. See under *ganglion.*

Down syndrome. A disorder caused by the presence of an extra twenty-first chromosome, characterized by moderate to severe mental retardation and often by physical abnormalities; previously called *mongolism.*

Drug dependency insomnia. An insomnia caused by the side effects of ever-increasing doses of sleeping medications.

Drug discrimination procedure. An experimental procedure in which an animal shows, through instrumental conditioning, whether the perceived effects of two drugs are similar.

Dualism. The philosophical position that the universe is divided into two realms: the physical and the nonphysical (spiritual). Thus, people have physical bodies and nonphysical minds or souls.

Duodenum. The portion of the small intestine immediately adjacent to the stomach.

Dura mater. The outermost layer of the three meninges.

Dynorphin. See under *endogenous opiate.*

Dyslexia. A term that refers to a variety of reading disorders.

EEG. See *electroencephalogram (EEG).*

Efferent axon. An axon that is directed away from a structure. Efferent axons of the central nervous system control the muscles and glands.

Electroconvulsive therapy (ECT). The administration of a brief electrical shock, applied to the head, that results in a seizure. It is used therapeutically to alleviate severe depression.

Electrode. A conductive medium (generally made of metal) that can be used to apply electrical stimulation or to record electrical potentials.

Electroencephalogram (EEG). Electrical brain potentials recorded by placing electrodes on or in the scalp or on the surface of the brain.

Electrolyte. An aqueous solution of a material that ionizes—namely, a soluble acid, base, or salt.

Electromyogram (EMG). Electrical potentials recorded from an electrode placed on or in a muscle.

Electro-oculogram (EOG). Electrical potentials from the eyes, recorded by means of electrodes placed on the skin around them; detects eye movements.

Electrostatic pressure. The attractive force between atomic particles charged with opposite signs, or the repulsive force between atomic particles charged with the same sign.

Embolus. A piece of matter (such as a blood clot, fat, or bacterial debris) that dislodges from its site of origin and occludes an artery. In the brain an embolus can lead to a stroke.

Encephalitis. An inflammation of the brain; caused by bacteria, viruses, or toxic chemicals.

Endocrine gland. A gland that liberates its secretions into the extracellular fluid around capillaries and hence into the bloodstream.

Endogenous depression. A depression that appears to have no environmental cause and is thus apparently of biological origin.

Endogenous opiate. A class of peptides secreted by the brain or pituitary gland that act as opiates; includes the *endorphins, dynorphins,* and *enkephalins.*

Endorphin. See under *endogenous opiate.*

Enkephalin. See under *endogenous opiate.*

Entorhinal cortex. A region of the limbic cortex that provides the major source of input to the hippocampal formation.

Enzymatic deactivation. The destruction of a transmitter substance by an enzyme after its release. The destruction of acetylcholine by acetylcholinesterase is the most common example.

Enzyme. A protein that facilitates a biochemical reaction without itself becoming part of the end product.

EOG. See *electro-oculogram (EOG).*

Epinephrine. A hormone, secreted by the adrenal medulla, that produces physiological effects characteristic of the sympathetic division of the autonomic nervous system.

EPSP. See under *postsynaptic potential.*

Estradiol. The principal estrogen of many mammals, including humans.

Estrogen. A class of sex hormones that cause maturation of the female genitalia, growth of breast tissue, and development of other physical features characteristic of females. Estrogens are also necessary for normal sexual behavior of most mammals other than primates.

Estrous cycle. A cyclic change in the hormonal level and sexual receptivity of subprimate mammals.

Estrus. That portion of the estrous cycle during which a female is sexually receptive.

Excitatory postsynaptic potential (EPSP). See under *postsynaptic potential.*

Experimental ablation. The intentional damage to a part of the brain for the purposes of discovering the function of that part.

Extracellular fluid. All body fluids outside cells: interstitial fluid, blood plasma, and cerebrospinal fluid.

Extrafusal muscle fiber. One of the muscle fibers that are responsible for the force exerted by a muscular contraction.

Fastigial nucleus. A deep cerebellar nucleus; involved in the control of movement by the reticulospinal and vestibulospinal tracts.

Fasting phase. The phase of metabolism during which nutrients are not available from the digestive system. Glucose, amino acids, fatty acids, and ketones are derived from glycogen, protein, and adipose tissue during this phase.

Fatty acid. A substance of importance to metabolism during the fasting phase. Fats can be broken down to fatty acids and glycerol. Fatty acids can be metabolized by most cells of the body. Their basic structure is an alkyl group (CH) attached to a carboxyl group (COOH).

Fetal alcohol syndrome. A birth defect caused by ingestion of alcohol by a pregnant woman; includes characteristic facial anomalies and brain damage.

Fight or flight response. A species-typical response preparatory to fighting or fleeing; thought to be responsible for some of the deleterious effects of stressful situations on health.

Flocculonodular lobe. A region of the cerebellum; involved in control of postural reflexes.

Follicle-stimulating hormone (FSH). The hormone of the anterior pituitary gland that causes development of an ovarian follicle and the maturation of its oocyte into an ovum.

Forebrain. See Table 3.1.

Formalin. The aqueous solution of formaldehyde gas; the most commonly used tissue fixative.

Fourth ventricle. See under *ventricle.*

Fovea. The region of the retina that mediates the most acute vision of birds and higher mammals. Color-sensitive cones constitute the only type of photoreceptor found in the fovea.

Frontal lobe. The front portion of the cerebral cortex, including Broca's speech area and the motor cortex. Damage to the frontal lobe impairs movement, planning, and flexibility in behavioral strategies.

Frontal section. See Figure 3.2.

FSH. See *follicle-stimulating hormone (FSH).*

Functionalism. The strategy of understanding a species' structural or behavioral features by attempting to establish their usefulness with respect to survival or reproductive success.

Function word. A preposition, article, or other word that conveys little of the meaning of a sentence but is important in specifying its grammatical structure. See also *content word.*

Fundamental frequency. The lowest, and usually most intense, frequency of a complex sound; most often perceived as the sound's basic pitch.

GABA. See *gamma-aminobutyric acid (GABA).*

Galactosemia. An inherited metabolic disorder in which galactose (milk sugar) cannot easily be metabolized.

Gamete. A mature reproductive cell; a sperm or ovum.

Gamma-aminobutyric acid (GABA). An important inhibitory transmitter substance.

Gamma motor neuron. A lower motor neuron whose terminal buttons synapse upon intrafusal muscle fibers.

Ganglion. A collection of neural cell bodies, covered with connective tissue, located outside the central nervous system. *Autonomic ganglia* contain the cell bodies of postganglionic neurons of the sympathetic and parasympathetic branches of the autonomic nervous system. *Dorsal root ganglia* contain cell bodies of afferent spinal nerve neurons. *Cranial nerve ganglia* contain cell bodies of afferent cranial nerve neurons. The *basal ganglia* are actually nuclei of the brain that are involved in the control of movement.

Ganglion cells. Neurons located in the retina; receive visual information from bipolar cells. Their axons give rise to the optic nerve.

Gene. The functional unit of the chromosome, which directs synthesis of one or more proteins.

Generalization. Along with reduction, one of the forms of explanation in science; describing a phenomenon in general terms that permits one to explain similar phenomena.

Generalized seizure. A seizure that involves most of the brain, as contrasted with a partial seizure, which remains localized.

Glabrous skin. Skin that does not contain hair; found on the palms and soles of the feet.

Glia (glial cells). The supportive cells of the central nervous system—the astroglia, oligodendroglia, and microglia.

Glioma. A cancerous brain tumor composed of one of several types of glial cells.

Globus pallidus. One of the basal ganglia; an excitatory structure of the extrapyramidal motor system.

Glucagon. A pancreatic hormone that promotes the conversion of liver glycogen into glucose.

Glucocorticoid. One of a group of hormones of the adrenal cortex that are important in protein and carbohydrate metabolism, secreted especially in times of stress.

Glucose. A simple sugar, of great importance in metabolism. Glucose and ketones constitute the major sources of energy for the brain.

Glucostatic hypothesis. States that the level or availability of glucose in the interstitial fluid determines whether an organism is hungry or satiated.

Glutamic acid (glutamate). An amino acid; an important excitatory transmitter substance.

Glycerol (glycerin). A trihydric alcohol; the breakdown of triglycerides (fats stored in adipose tissue) yields fatty acids and glycerol; can be converted by the liver into glucose.

Glycine. An amino acid; an important inhibitory transmitter substance.

Glycogen. A polysaccharide often referred to as *animal starch.* The hormone glucagon causes conversion of liver glycogen into glucose.

Golgi apparatus. A complex of parallel membranes in the cytoplasm that wraps the products of a secretory cell.

Golgi tendon organ. The receptor organ at the junction of the tendon and muscle that is sensitive to stretch.

Gonad. The ovaries or testes.

Gonadotropic hormone. A hormone of the anterior pituitary gland that has a stimulating effect on cells of the gonads. See also *follicle-stimulating hormone (FSH)* and *luteinizing hormone (LH).*

Grand mal. A generalized seizure, which results in a convulsion.

Gyrus. A convolution of the cortex of the cerebral hemispheres, separated by sulci or fissures.

Hair cell. The receptive cell of the auditory or vestibular apparatus.

Hallucination. The perception of objects or events that have no basis in reality.

Hebb rule. The hypothesis proposed by David Hebb that the cellular basis of learning involves strengthening of a synapse that is repeatedly active at the time when the postsynaptic neuron fires.

Hemorrhagic stroke. A cerebrovascular accident that involves rupture of a cerebral blood vessel.

Hepatic portal vein. The vein leading from the small intestine to the liver.

Herpes simplex virus. A virus that normally causes cold sores near the lips, but that can also cause brain damage.

Hertz (Hz). Cycles per second; a measure of frequency of vibration.

5-HIAA. See *5-hydroxyindoleacetic acid (5-HIAA).*

Hindbrain. See Table 3.1.

Hippocampal formation. A forebrain structure of the temporal lobe, constituting an important part of the limbic system. Includes fields CA1 and CA3 of the hippocampus proper (Ammon's horn), dentate gyrus, and subiculum.

Hippocampus. See under *hippocampal formation.*

Histofluorescence method. A histological method that reveals the location of monoaminergic-containing neurons.

Homeostasis. The process by which the body's substances and characteristics (such as temperature and glucose level) are maintained at their optimal level.

Horizontal cell. A neuron in the retina that interconnects adjacent photoreceptors and the outer arborizations of the bipolar cells.

Horizontal section. See Figure 3.2.

Hormone. A chemical substance liberated by an endocrine gland that has effects on target cells in other organs. *Organizational effects* of a hormone affect tissue differentiation and development; for example, androgens cause prenatal development of male genitalia. *Activational effects* of a hormone are those that occur in the fully developed organism; many of them depend upon the organism's prior exposure to the organizational effects of hormones.

Horseradish peroxidase (HRP). An enzyme extracted from the horseradish root; can be made visible by special histological techniques. Because it is taken up by terminal buttons or by severed axons and is carried by axoplasmic transport, it is useful in anatomical studies.

Hue. A perceptual dimension of color, most closely related to the wavelength of a pure light. The effect of a particular hue is caused by the mixture of lights of various wavelengths.

Huntington's chorea. An inherited disorder that causes degeneration of the basal ganglia; characterized by progressively more severe uncontrollable jerking movements, writhing movements, dementia, and finally, death.

Hydrocephalus. A condition in which all or some of the brain's ventricles are enlarged. *Obstructive hydrocephalus* occurs when the normal flow of cerebrospinal fluid is impeded, increasing the intraventricular pressure. *Hydrocephalus ex vacuo* occurs when brain tissue degenerates and the ventricles expand to take up the space the tissue formerly occupied.

6-Hydroxydopamine (6-HD). A chemical that is selectively taken up by axons and terminal buttons of noradrenergic or dopaminergic neurons and that acts as a poison, damaging or killing them.

5-Hydroxyindoleacetic acid (5-HIAA). A breakdown product of the neurotransmitter serotonin.

5-Hydroxytryptamine (5-HT). An indolamine transmitter substance; also called *serotonin.*

Hyperpolarization. An increase in the membrane potential of a cell relative to the normal resting potential. Inhibitory postsynaptic potentials (IPSPs) are hyperpolarizations.

Hypertonic. The characteristic of a solution that contains enough solute that it will draw water out of a cell placed in it, through the process of osmosis.

Hypnagogic hallucinations. A symptom of narcolepsy; vivid dreams that occur just before a person falls asleep; accompanied by sleep paralysis.

Hypothalamus. The part of the diencephalon situated beneath the thalamus; involved in regulation of the autonomic nervous system, control of the anterior and posterior pituitary glands, and integration of species-typical behaviors.

Hypotonic. The characteristic of a solution that contains so little solute that a cell placed in it will lose water, through the process of osmosis.

Hypovolemia. Blood volume lower than normal. See also *volumetric thirst.*

Hz. See *hertz (Hz).*

Immune system. The system by which the body protects itself from foreign proteins. In response to an infection the white blood cells produce antibodies that attack and destroy the foreign antigen.

Immunoglobulin. An antibody released by B-lymphocytes that bind with antigens and help destroy invading microorganisms.

Incus. One of the bones of the middle ear, shaped somewhat like an anvil. See Figure 6.2.

Inferior. See Figure 3.1.

Inferior colliculi. Protrusions on top of the midbrain that relay auditory information to the medial geniculate nucleus.

Inferior temporal cortex. In monkeys, the highest level of visual association cortex, located on the inferior surface of the temporal lobe.

Ingestive behavior. Eating or drinking.

Inhibitory postsynaptic potential (IPSP). See under *postsynaptic potential.*

Instrumental conditioning. A learning procedure whereby the effects of a particular behavior in a particular situation increase (reinforce) or decrease (punish) the probability of the behavior; also called *operant conditioning.*

Insulin. A pancreatic hormone that facilitates entry of glucose and amino acids into the cell, facilitates conversion of glucose into glycogen, and facilitates transport of fats into adipose tissue.

Interpositus nucleus. A deep cerebellar nucleus; involved in the control of the rubrospinal system.

Interstitial fluid. The fluid that bathes the cells of the body, filling the space between the cells of the body (the "interstices").

Intracellular fluid. The fluid contained within cells.

Intrafusal muscle fiber. A muscle fiber that functions as a stretch receptor, arranged parallel to the extrafusal muscle fibers, thus detecting muscle length; also called *muscle spindle.*

Intraperitoneal (IP). Pertaining to the peritoneal cavity, the space surrounding the abdominal organs.

Intravascular fluid. The fluid portion of the blood.

Ion. A charged molecule. *Cations* are positively charged, and *anions* are negatively charged.

Ion channel. A specialized protein molecule that permits specific ions to enter or leave cells. *Voltage-dependent ion channels* open or close according to the value of the membrane potential. *Neurotransmitter-dependent ion channels* open when they detect molecules of the appropriate neurotransmitter or molecules of a cyclic nucleotide that serves as a second messenger.

IP. See *intraperitoneal (IP).*

Iproniazid. A monoamine agonist: deactivates monoamine oxidase and thus prevents destruction of extravesicular monoamines in the terminal buttons.

Ipsilateral. Located on the same side of the body as the point of reference.

IPSP. See under *postsynaptic potential.*

Iris. The pigmented muscle of the eye that controls the size of the pupil.

Isotonic. Equal in osmotic pressure to the contents of a cell. A cell placed in an isotonic solution neither gains nor loses water.

James-Lange theory. A theory of emotion that suggests that behaviors and physiological responses are directly elicited by situations, and that feelings of emotions are produced by feedback from these behaviors and responses.

Kinesthesia. Perception of the body's own movements.

Korsakoff's syndrome. A permanent anterograde amnesia (inability to learn new information) caused by brain damage resulting from chronic alcoholism or malnutrition.

Lamella. A layer of membrane containing photopigments; found in rods and cones of the retina.

Lateral. See Figure 3.1.

Lateral corticospinal tract. See under *corticospinal pathway.*

Lateral fissure. The fissure that separates the temporal lobe from the overlying frontal and parietal lobes.

Lateral geniculate nucleus. A group of cell bodies within the lateral geniculate body of the thalamus. The *dorsal lateral geniculate nucleus* receives fibers from the retina and projects fibers to the primary visual cortex.

Lateral ventricle. See under *ventricle.*

L-DOPA. The levorotatory (L) form of dihydroxyphenylalanine; the precursor of the catecholamines dopamine, norepinephrine, and epinephrine; often used to treat Parkinson's disease because of its effect as a dopamine agonist.

Lee-Boot effect. The increased incidence of false pregnancies seen in female animals that are housed together; caused by a pheromone in the animals' urine; first observed in mice.

Left parietal apraxia. An apraxia caused by damage to the left parietal lobe; characterized by difficulty in producing sequences of movements by verbal request or in imitation of movements made by someone else.

Lens. The transparent organ situated behind the iris of the eye; helps focus an image on the retina.

Leupeptin. A drug that inactivates calpain, an enzyme that cleaves fodrin, which is a protein present just inside the neural membrane.

LH. See *luteinizing hormone (LH).*

Ligand. A chemical that binds with the binding site of a receptor.

Limbic cortex. The phylogenetically old cortex, located at the edge ("limbus") of the cerebral hemispheres; part of the limbic system.

Limbic system. A group of brain regions including the anterior thalamic nuclei, amygdala, hippocampus, limbic cortex, and parts of the hypothalamus, as well as their interconnecting fiber bundles.

Lithium. An element. Lithium carbonate is used to treat bipolar disorder.

Locus coeruleus. A dark-colored group of noradrenergic cell bodies located in the pons near the rostral end of the floor of the fourth ventricle.

Long-term potentiation. An increase in the excitability of neurons in the trisynaptic circuit of the entorhinal cortex and hippocampal formation, caused by repeated electrical stimulation; thought to be related to learning.

Lordosis. A spinal sexual reflex seen in many four-legged female mammals; arching of the back in response to approach of a male or to touching of the flanks, which elevates the hindquarters.

Loudness. A perceptual dimension of sound, most closely associated with intensity (amplitude).

Luteinizing hormone (LH). A hormone of the anterior pituitary gland that causes ovulation and development of the ovarian follicle into a corpus luteum.

Lysosome. An organelle surrounded by membrane; contains enzymes that break down waste products.

Magnetic resonance imaging (MRI). A technique whereby the interior of the living body (particularly the brain) can be accurately imaged; involves the interaction between radio waves and a strong magnetic field.

Magnocellular layer. See under *magnocellular system.*

Magnocellular nucleus. A nucleus in the medulla; involved in the atonia (muscular paralysis) that accompanies REM sleep.

Magnocellular system. The phylogenetically older portion of the visual system, named after the magnocellular layers of the lateral geniculate nucleus; responsible for perception of form, movement, depth, and small differences in brightness.

Major affective disorder. A serious mood disorder; includes unipolar depression and bipolar disorder.

Malignant. Harm-producing. A malignant tumor is cancerous; it lacks a distinct border and may metastasize.

Malleus. One of the bones of the middle ear, shaped somewhat like a hammer. See Figure 6.2.

Mammillary body. A protrusion of the bottom of the brain at the posterior end of the hypothalamus, containing the medial and lateral mammillary nuclei.

MAO. See *monoamine oxidase (MAO).*

Masculinizing effect. The effect of a hormone present early in development; promotes the later development of anatomical or behavioral characteristics typical of males. See also *defeminizing effect.*

Medial. See Figure 3.1.

Medial division of the medial geniculate nucleus (MGM). A part of the medial geniculate nucleus, involved in audition, that projects information to subcortical structures such as the amygdala rather than the cerebral cortex.

Medial forebrain bundle (MFB). A fiber bundle that runs in a rostral-caudal direction through the basal forebrain and lateral hypothalamus.

Medial geniculate nucleus. A group of cell bodies within the medial geniculate body of the thalamus; part of the auditory system.

Medial nucleus of the amygdala. A nucleus that receives olfactory information from the olfactory bulb and accessory olfactory bulb. It is involved in the effects of odors and pheromones on reproductive behavior.

Medial preoptic area. An area of cell bodies located just rostral to the hypothalamus. It is involved in maternal behavior and male sexual behavior.

Medulla oblongata (usually medulla). The most caudal portion of the brain, immediately rostral to the spinal cord.

Meissner's corpuscle. The touch-sensitive end organs located in the papillae, small elevations of the dermis that project up into the epidermis.

Membrane. A structure consisting principally of lipid molecules that defines the outer boundaries of a cell and also constitutes many of the cell organelles, such as the Golgi apparatus.

Membrane potential. The electrical charge across a cell membrane; the difference in electrical potential inside and outside the cell; expressed as inside voltage relative to outside voltage (for example, −70 mV signifies that the inside is 70 millivolts negative with respect to the outside).

Meninges (singular: **meninx**). The three layers of tissue that encase the central nervous system: the dura mater, arachnoid membrane, and pia mater.

Meningioma. A benign brain tumor composed of the cells that constitute the meninges.

Meningitis. An inflammation of the meninges; can be caused by viruses or bacteria.

Menstrual cycle. The twenty-eight-day reproductive cycle of female primates; consists of a buildup of the lining of the uterus, ovulation, and sloughing off of the uterine lining.

Merkel's disk. The touch-sensitive end organs found at the base of the epidermis, adjacent to sweat ducts.

Mesencephalic locomotor region. A region of the reticular formation of the midbrain; stimulation causes alternating movements of the limbs normally seen during locomotion.

Mesencephalon. See Table 3.1.

Messenger ribonucleic acid (mRNA). See under *ribonucleic acid.*

Metastasis. The process by which cells break off of a tumor, travel through the vascular system, and grow elsewhere in the body.

Metencephalon. See Table 3.1.

MFB. See *medial forebrain bundle (MFB).*

Microdialysis. A procedure for analyzing chemicals present in the interstitial fluid. A small piece of tubing made of a semipermeable membrane is implanted in the brain, and fluid circulating within it receives substances from the brain through the process of diffusion.

Microelectrode. A very fine electrode, generally used to record activity of individual neurons.

Microglia. The small glial cells that serve as phagocytes.

Micrometer (μm). A unit of measurement; one-millionth of a meter, or one-thousandth of a millimeter.

Microtome. An instrument that produces very thin slices of body tissues.

Microtubule. An organelle consisting of long protein filaments; involved in maintaining the structure of a cell and in transporting substances from place to place within the cell.

Midbrain. See Table 3.1.

Mitochondrion. A cell organelle in which many of the chemical reactions necessary for metabolism take place.

Model. A mathematical or physical analogy for a physiological process; for example, computers have been used as models for various functions of the brain.

Monism. The philosophical position that all aspects of the universe are subject to physical laws, and that nothing exists besides matter and energy; thus, the mind is part of the body.

Monoamine. A class of amines that includes indolamines (e.g., serotonin) and catecholamines (e.g., dopamine and norepinephrine).

Monoamine hypothesis. The hypothesis that depression is caused by a low level of one or more of the monoamines in the brain; could involve underactivity of monoaminergic neurons or underresponsiveness of postsynaptic monoaminergic receptors.

Monoamine oxidase (MAO). A class of enzymes that destroy the monoamines: dopamine, norepinephrine, and serotonin.

Monosynaptic stretch reflex. A reflex consisting of the afferent axon of the intrafusal muscle fiber synapsing upon an alpha motor neuron, and the efferent axon of the alpha motor neuron synapsing on the extrafusal muscle fibers in the same muscle. When a muscle is quickly stretched, the monosynaptic stretch reflex causes it to contract.

Motor endplate. The region of the membrane of a muscle fiber upon which the terminal buttons of the efferent axon synapse.

Motor neuron (motoneuron). A neuron whose stimulation results in contractions of muscle fibers.

Motor unit. A motor neuron and its associated muscle fibers.

mRNA. See under *ribonucleic acid (RNA).*

Müllerian-inhibiting substance. A peptide secreted by the fetal testes that inhibits the development of the Müllerian system, which would otherwise become the female internal sex organs.

Müllerian system. The embryonic precursors of the female internal sex organs.

Multipolar neuron. A neuron with a single axon and numerous dendritic processes originating from the somatic membrane.

Muscarinic receptor. One of the two major types of acetylcholine (ACh) receptors; stimulated by muscarine and blocked by atropine.

Muscle spindle. See *intrafusal muscle fiber.*

Mutation. A change in the genetic information contained by the chromosomes of gametes, which can be passed on to an organism's offspring.

Myelencephalon. See Table 3.1.

Myelin sheath. A sheath of complex fatlike substance produced by the oligodendroglia in the central nervous system and by the Schwann cells in the peripheral nervous system, which surrounds and insulates myelinated axons.

Myosin. A protein. Actin and myosin are the proteins that provide the physical basis for muscular contraction. See Figures 7.1 and 7.2.

Narcolepsy. A sleep disorder characterized by periods of irresistible sleep, attacks of cataplexy, sleep paralysis, and hypnagogic hallucinations.

Natural killer cell. A white blood cell that destroys cells infected by viruses.

Natural selection. The process by which the characteristics of organisms that produce more offspring come to be more dominant in future generations of the species.

NE. See *norepinephrine (NE).*

Negative feedback. A process whereby the effect produced by an action serves to diminish or terminate that action. Regulatory systems are characterized by negative feedback loops.

Negative symptom. A symptom of schizophrenia characterized by the absence of behaviors that are normally present; examples are social withdrawal, lack of affect, and reduced motivation.

Neocortex. The phylogenetically newest cortex, including primary sensory cortex, primary motor cortex, and association cortex.

Neural integration. The process by which inhibitory and excitatory postsynaptic potentials summate and control the rate of firing of a neuron.

Neural network. A model of the nervous system based on interconnected networks of elements that have some of the properties of neurons.

Neuraxis. An imaginary line drawn through the center of the length of the central nervous system, from the bottom of the spinal cord to the front of the forebrain.

Neuroglia. The formal name for *glia.*

Neuromodulator. A naturally secreted substance that acts like a neurotransmitter except that it is not restricted to the synaptic cleft but diffuses through the interstitial fluid. Presumably, it activates receptors on neurons that are not located at synapses.

Neuromuscular junction. The synapse between the terminal buttons of an axon and a muscle fiber.

Neuron. A cell of the nervous system that communicates with other neurons, muscle cells, or secretory cells by means of synapses or gap junctions. Most neurons have axons, which are capable of producing action potentials, and secrete a transmitter substance.

Neuropeptide Y. A biologically active peptide secreted by a neuron or a neurosecretory cell.

Neurosecretory cell. A neuron that secretes a hormone or hormonelike substance into the interstitial fluid.

Neurosis. A mental disorder of less severity than a psychosis. The term is not used in the *Diagnostic and Statistical Manual III* of the American Psychiatric Association.

Neurotransmitter. See under *transmitter substance.*

Neurotransmitter-dependent ion channel. See under *ion channel.*

Nicotinic receptor. One of the two major types of acetylcholine (ACh) receptors; stimulated by nicotine and blocked by curare; found on skeletal muscle fibers and in the central nervous system.

Nictitating membrane. The inner "third eyelid" of several species of mammals, birds, amphibians, and reptiles.

Nigrostriatal bundle. A bundle of axons originating in the substantia nigra and terminating in the neostriatum (caudate nucleus and putamen).

NMDA receptor. A specialized glutamate receptor that controls a calcium channel that is normally blocked by Mg^{2+} ions; involved in long-term potentiation, seizures, brain damage produced by anoxia, and learning.

Node of Ranvier. A naked portion of a myelinated axon, between adjacent oligodendroglia or Schwann cells.

Non-REM sleep. All stages of sleep except REM sleep.

Nonshivering thermogenesis. Heat production by means of cell metabolism that does not involve muscular movement.

Norepinephrine (NE). A neurotransmitter found in the brain and in the terminal buttons of postganglionic fibers of the sympathetic division of the autonomic nervous system.

Nucleus. **1.** The central portion of an atom. **2.** A spherical structure, enclosed by a membrane, located in the cytoplasm of most cells and containing the chromosomes. **3.** A histologically identifiable group of neural cell bodies in the central nervous system.

Nucleus accumbens. A nucleus of the basal forebrain near the septum; receives dopamine-secreting terminal buttons from neurons of the ventral tegmental area; thought to be involved in reinforcement and attention.

Nucleus basalis. A nucleus of the basal forebrain that contains most of the acetylcholine-secreting neurons that send axons to the neocortex; degenerates in patients with Alzheimer's disease.

Nucleus of the solitary tract. A nucleus of the medulla that receives information from visceral organs and from the gustatory system; appears to play a role in sleep.

Nucleus raphe magnus. One of the nuclei of the raphe; contains serotonin-secreting neurons that project to the dorsal gray matter of the spinal cord via the dorsolateral columns; involved in analgesia produced by opiates.

Obsession. Recurrent, persistent thoughts and ideas.

Obsessive compulsive disorder. A neurotic disorder characterized by obsessions and compulsions.

Obstructive stroke. A cerebrovascular accident caused by occlusion of a blood vessel.

Occipital lobe. The rearmost portion of the cerebral cortex; contains the primary visual cortex.

Ocular apraxia. See under *Balint's syndrome.*

Offensive behavior. A species-typical behavior in which an animal approaches another animal and threatens or attacks it.

Olfactory bulb. The protrusion at the end of the olfactory nerve; receives input from the olfactory receptors.

Olfactory epithelium. The epithelial tissue of the nasal sinus that covers the cribriform plate; contains the cilia of the olfactory receptors.

Oligodendroglia. A type of glial cell in the central nervous system that forms myelin sheaths.

Opsin. A class of protein that, together with retinal, constitutes the photopigments that are responsible for the transduction of visual information in the eye.

Optic ataxia. See under *Balint's syndrome.*

Optic chiasm. A cross-shaped connection between the optic nerves, located below the base of the brain, just anterior to the pituitary gland.

Optic disk. See under *optic nerve.*

Optic nerve. The second cranial nerve, carrying visual information from the retina to the brain. The *optic disk* is formed at the exit point from the retina of the fibers of the ganglion cells that form the optic nerve.

Optic radiation. The band of axons that project from the dorsal lateral geniculate nuclei of the thalamus to the primary visual cortex.

Orbit. The bony socket in the skull that accommodates the eye.

Orbitofrontal cortex. The region of the prefrontal cortex at the base of the anterior frontal lobes.

Organic sense. A sense modality that arises from receptors located within the inner organs of the body.

Organizational effect. See under *hormone.*

Falk, J.L. The nature and determinants of adjunctive behavior. In *Schedule Effects: Drugs, Drinking, and Aggression,* edited by R.M. Gilbert and J.D. Keehn. Toronto: University of Toronto Press, 1972.

Fallon, J.H. Topographic organization of ascending dopaminergic projections. *Annals of the New York Academy of Sciences,* 1988, *537,* 1–9.

Farde, L., Wiesel, F.-A., Stone-Elander, S., Halldin, C., Nördstrom, A.-L., Hall, H., and Sedvall, G. D_2 dopamine receptors in neuroleptic-naive schizophrenic patients: A positron emission tomography study with [^{11}C]raclopride. *Archives of General Psychiatry,* 1990, *47,* 213–219.

Farmer, A., McGuffin, P., and Gottesman, I. Twin concordance in DSM-III schizophrenia. *Archives of General Psychiatry,* 1987, *44,* 634–641.

Fava, M., Copeland, P.M., Schweiger, U., and Herzog, M.D. Neurochemical abnormalities of anorexia nervosa and bulimia nervosa. *American Journal of Psychiatry,* 1989, *146,* 963–971.

Feder, H.H. Estrous cyclicity in mammals. In *Neuroendocrinology of Reproduction,* edited by N.T. Adler. New York: Plenum Press, 1981.

Feder, H.H. Hormones and sexual behavior. *Annual Review of Psychology,* 1984, *35,* 165–200.

Feigenbaum, S.L., Masi, A.T., and Kaplan, S.B. Prognosis in rheumatoid arthritis: A longitudinal study of newly diagnosed younger adult patients. *American Journal of Medicine,* 1979, *66,* 377–384.

Ferguson, N.B.L., and Keesey, R.E. Effect of a quinine-adulterated diet upon body weight maintenance in male rats with ventromedial hypothalamic lesions. *Journal of Comparative and Physiological Psychology,* 1975, *89,* 478–488.

Fibiger, H.C., Le Piane, F.G., Jakubovic, A., and Phillips, A.G. The role of dopamine in intracranial self-stimulation of the ventral tegmental area. *Journal of Neuroscience,* 1987, *7,* 3888–3896.

Field, T., Woodson, R., Greenberg, R., and Cohen, D. Discrimination and imitation of facial expressions in neonates. *Science,* 1982, *218,* 179–181.

Fieve, R.R. The clinical effects of lithium treatment. *Trends in Neurosciences,* 1979, *2,* 66–68.

Fisher, C., Gross, J., and Zuch, J. Cycle of penile erection synchronous with dreaming (REM) sleep: Preliminary report. *Archives of General Psychiatry,* 1965, *12,* 29–45.

Fitzsimons, J.T., and Moore-Gillon, M.J. Drinking and antidiuresis in response to reductions in venous return in the dog: Neural and endocrine mechanisms. *Journal of Physiology (London),* 1980, *308,* 403–416.

Fleming, A., Cheung, U., Myhal, N., and Kessler, Z. Effects of maternal hormones on "timidity" and attraction to pup-related odors in female rats. *Physiology and Behavior,* 1989, *46,* 449–453.

Fleming, A., and Rosenblatt, J.S. Olfactory regulation of maternal behavior in rats. II. Effects of peripherally induced anosmia and lesions of the lateral olfactory tract in pup-induced virgins. *Journal of Comparative and Physiological Psychology,* 1974, *86,* 233–246.

Fleming, A., Vaccarino, F., and Luebke, C. Amygdaloid inhibition of maternal behavior in the nulliparous female rat. *Physiology and Behavior,* 1980, *25,* 731–745.

Fleming, A., Vaccarino, F., Tambosso, L., and Chee, P. Vomeronasal and olfactory system modulation of maternal behavior in the rat. *Science,* 1979, *203,* 372–374.

Flock, A. Physiological properties of sensory hairs in the ear. In *Psychophysics and Physiology of Hearing,* edited by E.F. Evans and J.P. Wilson. London: Academic Press, 1977.

Floody, O.R. Hormones and aggression in female mammals. In *Hormones and Aggressive Behavior,* edited by B.B. Svare. New York: Plenum Press, 1983.

Foltin, R.W., Fischman, M.W., Moran, T.H., Rolls, B.J., and Kelly, T.H. Caloric compensation for lunches varying in fat and carbohydrate content by humans in a residential laboratory. *American Journal of Clinical Nutrition,* 1990, *52,* 969–980.

Freed, W.J. An hypothesis regarding the antipsychotic effect of neuroleptic drugs. *Pharmacology, Biochemistry and Behavior,* 1989, *32,* 337–345.

Freeman, P.H., and Wellman, P.J. Brown adipose tissue thermogenesis induced by low level electrical stimulation of hypothalamus in rats. *Brain Research Bulletin,* 1987, *18,* 7–11.

Friedman, M., and Rosenman, R.H. *Type A Behavior and Your Heart.* New York: Knopf, 1974.

Friedman, M.I., and Bruno, J.P. Exchange of water during lactation. *Science,* 1976, *191,* 409–410.

Friedman, M.I., Tordoff, M.G., and Ramirez, I. Integrated metabolic control of food intake. *Brain Research Bulletin,* 1986, *17,* 855–859.

Fruhstorfer, B., Mignot, E., Bowersox, S., Nishino, S., Dement, W.C., and Guilleminault, C. Canine narcolepsy is associated with an elevated number of α_2-receptors in the locus coeruleus. *Brain Research,* 1989, *500,* 209–214.

Fulton, J.F. *Functional Localization in Relation to Frontal Lobotomy.* New York: Oxford University Press, 1949.

Fuster, J.M., and Jervey, J.P. Inferotemporal neurons distinguish and retain behaviorally relevant features of visual stimuli. *Science,* 1981, *212,* 952–955.

Gabrieli, J.D.E., Cohen, N.J., and Corkin, S. The impaired learning of semantic knowledge following bilateral medial temporal-lobe resection. *Brain and Cognition,* 1988, *7,* 157–177.

Galaburda, A., and Kemper, T.L. Observations cited by Geschwind, N. Specializations of the human brain. *Scientific American,* 1979, *241,* 180–199.

Galaburda, A.M. The pathogenesis of childhood dyslexia. In *Language, Communication, and the Brain,* edited by F. Plum. New York: Raven Press, 1988.

Galaburda, A.M., Sherman, G.F., Rosen, G.D., Aboitiz, F., and Geschwind, N. Developmental dyslexia: Four consecutive patients with cortical anomalies. *Annals of Neurology,* 1985, *18,* 222–233.

Gallistel, C.R., and Karras, D. Pimozide and amphetamine have opposing effects on the reward summation function. *Pharmacology, Biochemistry, and Behavior,* 1984, *20,* 73–77.

Gandelman, R., and Simon, N.G. Spontaneous pup-killing by mice in response to large litters. *Developmental Psychobiology,* 1978, *11,* 235–241.

Gandelman, R., and Simon, N.G. Postpartum fighting in the rat: Nipple development and the presence of young. *Behavioral and Neural Biology,* 1980, *28,* 350–360.

Garcia, J., and Koelling, R.A. Relation of cue to consequence in avoidance learning. *Psychonomic Science,* 1966, *4,* 123–124.

Gatchel, R.J., Baum, A., and Krantz, D.S. *An Introduction to Health Psychology,* 2nd ed. New York: Newbery Award Records, 1989.

Gazzaniga, M.S. *The Bisected Brain.* New York: Appleton-Century-Crofts, 1970.

Gazzaniga, M.S., and LeDoux, J.E. *The Integrated Mind.* New York: Plenum Press, 1978.

Geary, N. Cocaine: Animal research studies. In *Cocaine Abuse: New*

Directions in Treatment and Research, edited by H.I. Spitz and J.S. Rosecan. New York: Brunner/Mazel, 1987.

Gerbino, L., Oleshansky, M., and Gershon, S. Clinical use and mode of action of lithium. In *Psychopharmacology: A Generation of Progress,* edited by M.A. Lipton, A. DiMascio, and K.F. Killam. New York: Raven Press, 1978.

Gershon, E.S., Bunney, W.E., Leckman, J., Van Eerdewegh, M., and DeBauche, B. The inheritance of affective disorders: A review of data and hypotheses. *Behavior Genetics,* 1976, *6,* 227–261.

Geschwind, N., Quadfasel, F.A., and Segarra, J.M. Isolation of the speech area. *Neuropsychologia,* 1968, *6,* 327–340.

Geschwind, N.A., and Behan, P.O. Laterality, hormones, and immunity. In *Cerebral Dominance: The Biological Foundations,* edited by N. Geschwind and A.M. Galaburda. Cambridge, Mass.: Harvard University Press, 1984.

Gessa, G.L., Muntoni, F., Collu, M., Vargiu L., and Mereu, G. Low doses of ethanol activate dopaminergic neurons in the ventral tegmental area. *Brain Research,* 1985, *348,* 201–204.

Gesteland, R.C. The neural code: Integrative neural mechanisms. In *Handbook of Perception. Vol. VIA. Tasting and Smelling,* edited by E.C. Carterette and M.P. Friedman. New York: Academic Press, 1978.

Ghiraldi, L., and Svare, B. Unpublished observations cited in Svare, B. Recent advances in the study of female aggressive behavior in mice. In *House Mouse Aggression: A Model for Understanding the Evolution of Social Behavior,* edited by S. Parmigiani, D. Mainardi, and P. Brain. London: Gordon and Breach, 1989.

Gibbs, J., Young, R.C., and Smith, G.P. Cholecystokinin decreases food intake in rats. *Journal of Comparative and Physiological Psychology,* 1973, *84,* 488–495.

Giles, D.E., Biggs, M.M., Rush, A.J., and Roffwarg, H.P. Risk factors in families of unipolar depression. I: Psychiatric illness and reduced REM latency. *Journal of Affective Disorders,* 1988, *14,* 51–59.

Giles, D.E., Roffwarg, H.P., and Rush, A.J. REM latency concordance in depressed family members. *Biological Psychiatry,* 1987, *22,* 910–924.

Giordano, A.L., Ahdieh, H.B., Mayer, A.D., Siegel, H.I., and Rosenblatt, J.S. Cytosol and nuclear estrogen receptor binding in the preoptic area and hypothalamus of female rats during pregnancy and ovariectomized, nulliparous rats after steroid priming: Correlation with maternal behavior. *Hormones and Behavior,* 1990, *24,* 232–255.

Glaser, R., Rice, J., Sheridan, J., Post, A., Fertel, R., Stout, J., Speicher, C.E., Kotur, M., and Kiecolt-Glaser, J.K. Stress-related immune suppression: Health implications. *Brain, Behavior, and Immunity,* 1987, *1,* 7–20.

Glick, Z., Teague, R.J., and Bray, G.A. Brown adipose tissue: Thermic response increased by a single low protein, high carbohydrate meal. *Science,* 1981, *213,* 1125–1127.

Goddard, G.V. Development of epileptic seizures through brain stimulation at low intensity. *Nature,* 1967, *214,* 1020–1021.

Goeders, N.E., Lane, J.D., and Smith, J.E. Self-administration of methionine enkephalin into the nucleus accumbens. *Pharmacology, Biochemistry, and Behavior,* 1984, *20,* 451–455.

Gonzales, R.A. NMDA receptors excite alcohol research. *Trends in Pharmacological Science,* 1990, *11,* 137–139.

Gonzalez, M.F., and Deutsch, J.A. Vagotomy abolishes cues of satiety produced by gastric distension. *Science,* 1981, *212,* 1283–1284.

Goodglass, H. Agrammatism. In *Studies of Neurolinguistics,* edited by H. Whitaker and H.A. Whitaker. New York: Academic Press, 1976.

Goodglass, H., and Kaplan, E. *Assessment of Aphasia and Related Disorders.* Philadelphia: Lea & Febiger, 1972.

Goodwin, D.W. Alcoholism and heredity: A review and hypothesis. *Archives of General Psychiatry,* 1979, *36,* 57–61.

Goodwin, F.K., Wirz-Justice, A., and Wehr, T.A. Evidence that the pathophysiology of depression and the mechanisms of action of antidepressant drugs both involve alterations in circadian rhythms. In *Typical and Atypical Antidepressants: Clinical Practice,* edited by E. Costa and G. Racagni. New York: Raven Press, 1982.

Gormezano, I. Classical conditioning: Investigations of defense and reward conditioning in the rabbit. In *Classical Conditioning II,* edited by A.H. Black and W.R. Prokasy. New York: Appleton-Century-Crofts, 1972.

Gorski, R.A., Gordon, J.H., Shryne, J.E., and Southam, A.M. Evidence for a morphological sex difference within the medial preoptic area of the rat brain. *Brain Research,* 1978, *148,* 333–346.

Gottesman, I.I., and Bertelsen, A. Confirming unexpressed genotypes for schizophrenia. *Archives of General Psychiatry,* 1989, *46,* 867–872.

Gottesman, I.I., and Shields, J. A critical review of recent adoption, twin, and family studies of schizophrenia: Behavioral genetics perspectives. *Schizophrenia Bulletin,* 1976, *2,* 360–401.

Gouras, P. Identification of cone mechanisms in monkey ganglion cells. *Journal of Physiology (London),* 1968, *199,* 533–538.

Goy, R.W., Bercovitch, F.B., and McBrair, M.C. Behavioral masculinization is independent of genital masculinization in prenatally androgenized female rhesus macaques. *Hormones and Behavior,* 1988, *22,* 552–571.

Graf, P., and Mandler, G. Activation makes words more accessible, but not necessarily more retrievable. *Journal of Verbal Learning and Verbal Behavior,* 1984, *23,* 553–568.

Graf, P., Squire, L.R., and Mandler, G. The information that amnesic patients do not forget. Raffaele, K.C., and Olton, D.S. Hippocampal and amygdala involvement in working memory for nonspatial stimuli. *Behavioral Neuroscience,* 1988, *102,* 349–355.

Gray, T.S., Carney, M.E., and Magnuson, D.J. Direct projections from the central amygdaloid nucleus to the hypothalamic paraventricular nucleus: Possible role in stress-induced adrenocorticotropin release. *Neuroendocrinology,* 1989, *50,* 433–446.

Greenberg, R., and Pearlman, C.A. Cutting the REM nerve: An approach to the adaptive role of REM sleep. *Perspectives in Biology and Medicine,* 1974, *17,* 513–521.

Greenberg, R., Pillard, R., and Pearlman, C. The effect of dream (stage REM) deprivation on adaptation to stress. *Psychosomatic Medicine,* 1972, *34,* 257–262.

Griesbacher, T., Leighton, G.E., Hill, R.G., and Hughes, J. Reduction of food intake by central administration of cholecystokinin octapeptide in the rat is dependent upon inhibition of brain peptidases. *British Journal of Pharmacology,* 1989, *96,* 236–242.

Griffith, J.D., Cavanaugh, J., Held, N.N., and Oates, J.A. Dextroamphetamine: Evaluation of psychotomimetic properties in man. *Archives of General Psychiatry,* 1972, *26,* 97–100.

Grijalva, C.V., Levin, E.D., Morgan, M., Roland, B., and Martin, F.C. Contrasting effects of centromedial and basolateral amygdaloid lesions on stress-related responses in the rat. *Physiology and Behavior,* 1990, *48,* 495–500.

Guerin, G.F., Goeders, N.E., Dworkin, S.I., and Smith, J.E. Intracranial self-administration of dopamine into the nucleus accumbens. *Society for Neuroscience Abstracts,* 1984, *10,* 1072.

Gulevich, G., Dement, W.C., and Johnson, L. Psychiatric and EEG observations on a case of prolonged (264 hours) wakefulness. *Archives of General Psychiatry,* 1966, *15,* 29–35.

Haas, R.H. Thiamin and the brain. *Annual Review of Nutrition,* 1988, *8,* 483–515.

Halmi, K.A. Anorexia nervosa: Recent investigations. *Annual Review of Medicine,* 1978, *29,* 137–148.

Halpern, M. The organization and function of the vomeronasal system. *Annual Review of Neuroscience,* 1987, *10,* 325–362.

Harbaugh, R.E., Reeder, T.M., Senter, H.J., Knopman, D.S., Baskin, D.S., Pirozzolo, F., Chui, H.C., Shetter, A.G., Bakay, R.A.E., Leblanc, R., Watson, R.T., DeKosky, S.T., Schmitt, F.A., Read, S.L., and Johnston, J.T. Intracerebroventricular bethanechol chloride infusion in Alzheimer's disease. *Journal of Neurosurgery,* 1989, *71,* 481–486.

Harmon, L.D., and Julesz, B. Masking in visual recognition: Effects of two-dimensional filtered noise. *Science,* 1973, *180,* 1194–1197.

Harris, G.W., and Jacobsohn, D. Functional grafts of the anterior pituitary gland. *Proceedings of the Royal Society of London, B.,* 1951–1952, *139,* 263–267.

Harris, R.B.S., Bruch, R.C., and Martin, R.J. In vitro evidence for an inhibitor of lipogenesis in serum from overfed obese rats. *American Journal of Physiology,* 1989, *257,* R326–R336.

Hawke, C. Castration and sex crimes. *American Journal of Mental Deficiency,* 1951, *55,* 220–226.

Hawkins, R.D., Abrams, T.W., Carew, T.J., and Kandel, E.R. A cellular mechanism of classical conditioning in *Aplysia*: Activity-dependent amplification of presynaptic facilitation. *Science,* 1983, *219,* 400–405.

Hebb, D.O. *The Organization of Behaviour.* New York: Wiley-Interscience, 1949.

Heckler, M.M. *Fifth Special Report to the U.S. Congress on Alcohol and Health.* Washington, D.C.: U.S. Government Printing Office, 1983.

Heffner, H.E., and Heffner, R.S. Role of primate auditory cortex in hearing. In *Comparative Perception. Vol. II: Complex Signals,* edited by W.C. Stebbins and M.A. Berkley. New York: John Wiley & Sons, 1990.

Heilman, K.M., Rothi, L., and Kertesz, A. Localization of apraxia-producing lesions. In *Localization in Neuropsychology,* edited by A. Kertesz. New York: Academic Press, 1983.

Heilman, K.M., Scholes, R., and Watson, R.T. Auditory affective agnosia: Disturbed comprehension of affective speech. *Journal of Neurology, Neurosurgery, and Psychiatry,* 1975, *38,* 69–72.

Heilman, K.M., Watson, R.T., and Bowers, D. Affective disorders associated with hemispheric disease. In *Neuropsychology of Human Emotion,* edited by K.M. Heilman and P. Satz. New York: Guilford Press, 1983.

Heimer, L., and Larsson, K. Impairment of mating behavior in male rats following lesions in the preoptic-anterior hypothalamic continuum. *Brain Research,* 1966/1967, *3,* 248–263.

Hellhammer, D.H., Hubert, W., and Schurmeyer, T. Changes in saliva testosterone after psychological stimulation in men. *Psychoneuroendocrinology,* 1985, *10,* 77–81.

Henke, P.G. The telencephalic limbic system and experimental gastric pathology: A review. *Neuroscience and Biobehavioral Reviews,* 1982, *6,* 381–390.

Hennessey, A.C., Camak, L., Gordon, F., and Edwards, D.A. Connections between the pontine central gray and the ventromedial hypothalamus are essential for lordosis in female rats. *Behavioral Neuroscience,* 1990, *104,* 477–488.

Henningfield, J.E., and Goldberg, S.R. Nicotine as a reinforcer in human subjects and laboratory animals. *Pharmacology, Biochemistry, and Behavior,* 1983, *19,* 989–992.

Hering, E. *Outlines of a Theory of the Light Sense,* 1905. Translated by L.M. Hurvich and D. Jameson. Cambridge, Mass.: Harvard University Press, 1965.

Hernandez, L., and Hoebel, B.G. Food reward and cocaine increase extracellular dopamine in the nucleus accumbens as measured by microdialysis. *Life Sciences,* 1988, *42,* 1705–1712.

Hetherington, A.W., and Ranson, S.W. Hypothalamic lesions and adiposity in the rat. *Anatomical Record,* 1942, *78,* 149–172.

Heuser, J.E. Synaptic vesicle exocytosis revealed in quick-frozen frog neuromuscular junctions treated with 4-aminopyridine and given a single electrical shock. In *Society for Neuroscience Symposia, Vol. II,* edited by W.M. Cowan and J.A. Ferrendelli. Bethesda, Md.: Society for Neuroscience, 1977.

Heuser, J.E., Reese, T.S., Dennis, M.J., Jan, Y., Jan, L., and Evans, L. Synaptic vesicle exocytosis captured by quick freezing and correlated with quantal transmitter release. *Journal of Cell Biology,* 1979, *81,* 275–300.

Hill, A.J., and Best, P.J. Effects of deafness and blindness on the spatial correlates of hippocampal unit activity in the rat. *Experimental Neurology,* 1981, *74,* 204–217.

Himmi, T., Boyer, A., and Orsini, J.C. Changes in lateral hypothalamic neuronal activity accompanying hyper- and hypoglycemias. *Physiology and Behavior,* 1988, *44,* 347–354.

Himms-Hagen, J. Current status of nonshivering thermogenesis. In *Assessment of Energy Metabolism in Health and Disease,* edited by J.W. Kinney. Columbus, Ohio: Ross Laboratories, 1980.

Hitchcock, J., and Davis, M. Lesions of the amygdala, but not of the cerebellum or red nucleus, block conditioned fear as measured with the potentiated startle paradigm. *Behavioral Neuroscience,* 1986, *100,* 11–22.

Hobson, J.A. *The Dreaming Brain.* New York: Basic Books, 1988.

Hoebel, B.G., Monaco, A.P., Hernandez, L., Aulisi, E.F., Stanley, B.G., and Lenard, L. Self-injection of amphetamine directly into the brain. *Psychopharmacology,* 1983, *81,* 158–163.

Hogan, S., Himms-Hagen, J., and Coscina, D.V. Lack of diet-induced thermogenesis in brown adipose tissue of obese medial hypothalamic-lesioned rats. *Physiology and Behavior,* 1985, *35,* 287–294.

Hohman, G.W. Some effects of spinal cord lesions on experienced emotional feelings. *Psychophysiology,* 1966, *3,* 143–156.

Hollander, E., Schiffman, E., Cohen, B., Rivera-Stein, M.A., Rosen, W., Gorman, J.M., Fyer, A.J., Papp, L., and Liebowitz, M.R. Signs of central nervous system dysfunction in obsessive-compulsive disorder. *Archives of General Psychiatry,* 1990, *47,* 27–32.

Holmes, G. The cerebellum of man. *Brain,* 1939, *62,* 21–30.

Holmes, T., and Rahe, R. The social readjustment rating scale. *Journal of Psychosomatic Research,* 1967, *11,* 213–218.

Holzman, P.S., Proctor, L.R., Levy, D.L., Yasillo, N.J., Meltzer, H.Y., and Hurt, S.W. Eye tracking dysfunction in schizophrenic patients and their relatives. *Archives of General Psychiatry,* 1974, *31,* 143–151.

Horne, J.A. A review of the biological effects of total sleep deprivation in man. *Biological Psychology,* 1978, *7,* 55–102.

Horne, J.A. The effects of exercise on sleep. *Biological Psychology,* 1981, *12,* 241–291.

Horne, J.A. *Why We Sleep: The Functions of Sleep in Humans and Other Mammals.* Oxford, England: Oxford University Press, 1988.

Horne, J.A., and Harley, L.J. Human SWS following selective head heating during wakefulness. In *Sleep '88*, edited by J. Horne. New York: Gustav Fischer Verlag, 1989.

Horne, J.A., and Minard, A. Sleep and sleepiness following a behaviourally "active" day. *Ergonomics*, 1985, *28*, 567-575.

Horne, J.A., and Moore, V.J. Sleep effects of exercise with and without additional body cooling. *Electroencephalography and Clinical Neurophysiology*, 1985, *60*, 347-353.

Horne, J.A., and Pettitt, A.N. High incentive effects on vigilance performance during 72 hours of total sleep deprivation. *Acta Physiologica*, 1985, *58*, 123-139.

Horowitz, R.M., and Gentili, B. Dihydrochalcone sweeteners. In *Symposium: Sweeteners*, edited by G.E. Inglett. Westport, Conn.: Avi Publishing, 1974.

Horton, J.C., and Hubel, D.H. Cytochrome oxidase stain preferentially labels intersection of ocular dominance and vertical orientation columns in macaque striate cortex. *Society for Neuroscience Abstracts*, 1980, *6*, 315.

Howlett, A.C. Reverse pharmacology applied to the cannabinoid receptor. *Trends in Pharmacological Sciences*, 1990, *11*, 395-397.

Hrdy, S.B. Infanticide as a primate reproductive strategy. *American Scientist*, 1977, *65*, 38-47.

Huang, Y.H., and Mogenson, G.J. Neural pathways mediating drinking and feeding in rats. *Experimental Neurology*, 1972, *37*, 269-286.

Hubel, D.H., and Wiesel, T.N. Functional architecture of macaque monkey visual cortex. *Proceedings of the Royal Society of London*, 1977, *198*, 1-59.

Hubel, D.H., and Wiesel, T.N. Brain mechanisms of vision. *Scientific American*, 1979, *241*, 150-162.

Hudspeth, A.J. Extracellular current flow and the site of transduction by hair cells. *Journal of Neuroscience*, 1982, *2*, 1-10.

Hudspeth, A.J. The cellular basis of hearing: The biophysics of hair cells. *Science*, 1985, *230*, 745-752.

Hudspeth, A.J., and Jacobs, R. Stereocilia mediate transduction in vertebrate hair cells. *Proceedings of the National Academy of Sciences, USA*, 1979, *76*, 1506-1509.

Hughes, J., Smith, T.W., Kosterlitz, H.W., Fothergill, L.A., Morgan, B.A., and Morris, H.R. Identification of two related pentapeptides from the brain with potent opiate agonist activity. *Nature*, 1975, *258*, 577-579.

Humphrey, A.L., and Hendrickson, A.E. Radial zones of high metabolic activity in squirrel monkey striate cortex. *Society for Neuroscience Abstracts*, 1980, *6*, 315.

Hyman, B.T., Van Hoesen, G.W., Damasio, A.R., and Barnes, C.L. Alzheimer's disease: Cell-specific pathology isolates the hippocampal formation. *Science*, 1984, *225*, 1168-1170.

Ibuka, N., and Kawamura, H. Loss of circadian rhythm in sleep-wakefulness cycle in the rat by suprachiasmatic nucleus lesions. *Brain Research*, 1975, *96*, 76-81.

Iggo, A., and Andres, K.H. Morphology of cutaneous receptors. *Annual Review of Neuroscience*, 1982, *5*, 1-32.

Imperato, A., and Di Chiara, G. Preferential stimulation of dopamine-release in the accumbens of freely moving rats by ethanol. *Journal of Pharmacology and Experimental Therapeutics*, 1986, *239*, 219-228.

Ingelfinger, F.J. The late effects of total and subtotal gastrectomy. *New England Journal of Medicine*, 1944, *231*, 321-327.

Institute of Medicine. *Sleeping Pills, Insomnia, and Medical Practice.* Washington, D.C.: National Academy of Sciences, 1979.

Iwata, J., Chida, K., and LeDoux, J.E. Cardiovascular responses elicited by stimulation of neurons in the central amygdaloid nucleus in awake but not anesthetized rats resemble conditioned emotional responses. *Brain Research*, 1987, *418*, 183-188.

Iwata, J., LeDoux, J.E., Meeley, M.P., Arneric, S., and Reis, D.J. Intrinsic neurons in the amygdaloid field projected to by the medial geniculate body mediate emotional responses conditioned to acoustic stimuli. *Brain Research*, 1986, *383*, 195-214.

Iwata, M. Kanji versus Kana: Neuropsychological correlates of the Japanese writing system. *Trends in Neurosciences*, 1984, *7*, 290-293.

Izard, C.E. *The Face of Emotion.* New York: Appleton-Century-Crofts, 1971.

Jacobs, B.L., and McGinty, D.J. Participation of the amygdala in complex stimulus recognition and behavioral inhibition: Evidence from unit studies. *Brain Research*, 1972, *36*, 431-436.

Jacobs, K.M., Mark, G.P., and Scott, T.R. Taste responses in the nucleus tractus solitarius of sodium-deprived rats. *Journal of Physiology (London)*, 1988, *406*, 393-410.

Jacobsen, C.F., Wolfe, J.B., and Jackson, T.A. An experimental analysis of the functions of the frontal association areas in primates. *Journal of Nervous and Mental Disorders*, 1935, *82*, 1-14.

Jaffe, J.H. Drug addiction and drug abuse. In *The Pharmacological Basis of Therapeutics, Vol. 7*, edited by L.S. Goodman and A. Gilman. New York: Macmillan, 1985.

James, W. What is an emotion? *Mind*, 1884, *9*, 188-205.

James, W. *Principles of Psychology.* New York: Henry Holt, 1890.

James, W.P.T., and Trayhurn, P. Thermogenesis and obesity. *British Medical Bulletin*, 1981, *27*, 43-48.

Jaskiw, G., and Kleinman, J. Postmortem neurochemistry studies in schizophrenia. In *Schizophrenia: A Scientific Focus*, edited by S.C. Schulz and C.A. Tamminga. New York: Oxford University Press, 1988.

Jasper, J.H., and Tessier, J. Acetylcholine liberation from cerebral cortex during paradoxical (REM) sleep. *Science*, 1969, *172*, 601-602.

Jaynes, J. The problem of animate motion in the seventeenth century. *Journal of the History of Ideas*, 1970, *6*, 219-234.

Jeffcoate, W.J., Lincoln, N.B., Selby, C., and Herbert, M. Correlations between anxiety and serum prolactin in humans. *Journal of Psychosomatic Research*, 1986, *30*, 217-222.

Jeffress, L.A. A place theory of sound localization. *Journal of Comparative and Physiological Psychology*, 1948, *41*, 35-39.

Jensen, T., Genefke, I., and Hyldebrandt, N. Cerebral atrophy in young torture victims. *New England Journal of Medicine*, 1982, *307*, 1341.

Jeste, D.V., Del Carmen, R., Lohr, J.B., and Wyatt, R.J. Did schizophrenia exist before the eighteenth century? *Comprehensive Psychiatry*, 1985, *26*, 493-503.

Johnson, M.K., Kim, J.K., and Risse, G. Do alcoholic Korsakoff's syndrome patients acquire affective reactions? *Journal of Experimental Psychology: Learning, Memory, and Cognition*, 1985, *11*, 22-36.

Jones, B.E., and Beaudet, A. Distribution of acetylcholine and catecholamine neurons in the cat brain stem studied by choline acetyltransferase and tyrosine hydroxylase immunohistochemistry. *Journal of Comparative Neurology*, 1987, *261*, 15-32.

Jouvet, M. The role of monoamines and acetylcholine-containing neurons in the regulation of the sleep-waking cycle. *Ergebnisse der Physiologie*, 1972, *64*, 166-307.

Jouvet, M. Paradoxical sleep and the nature-nurture controversy. *Progress in Brain Research*, 1980, *53*, 331-346.

Juji, T.M., Satake, Y., Honda, Y., and Doi, Y. HLA antigens in Japanese patients with narcolepsy: All the patients were CR2 positive. *Tissue Antigens*, 1984, *24*, 316-319.

Julien, R.M. *A Primer of Drug Action.* San Francisco: W.H. Freeman, 1981.

Justice, A. Review of the effects of stress on cancer in laboratory animals: Importance of time of stress application and type of tumor. *Psychological Bulletin,* 1985, *98,* 108–138.

Kales, A., Scharf, M.B., Kales, J.D., and Soldatos, C.R. Rebound insomnia: A potential hazard following withdrawal of certain benzodiazepines. *Journal of the American Medical Association,* 1979, *241,* 1692–1695.

Kanamori, N., Sakai, K., and Jouvet, M. Neuronal activity specific to paradoxical sleep in the ventromedial medullary reticular formation of unrestrained cats. *Brain Research,* 1980, *189,* 251–255.

Kane, J., Honigfeld, G., Singer, J., Meltzer, H., and the Clozaril Collaborative Study Group. Clozapine for the treatment-resistant schizophrenic: A double-blind comparison with chlorpromazine. *Archives of General Psychiatry,* 1988, *45,* 789–796.

Karacan, I., Salis, P.J., and Williams, R.L. The role of the sleep laboratory in diagnosis and treatment of impotence. In *Sleep Disorders: Diagnosis and Treatment,* edited by R.J. Williams and I. Karacan. New York: John Wiley & Sons, 1978.

Karacan, I., Williams, R.L., Finley, W.W., and Hursch, C.J. The effects of naps on nocturnal sleep: Influence on the need for stage-1 REM and stage 4 sleep. *Biological Psychiatry,* 1970, *2,* 391–399.

Karlson, P., and Luscher, M. "Pheromones": A new term for a class of biologically active substances. *Nature,* 1959, *183,* 55–56.

Kasper, S., Rogers, S.L.B., Yancey, A., Schulz, P.M., Skwerer, R.G., and Rosenthal, N.E. Phototherapy in individuals with and without subsyndromal seasonal affective disorder. *Archives of General Psychiatry,* 1989a, *46,* 837–844.

Kasper, S., Wehr, T.A., Bartko, J.J., Gaist, P.A., and Rosenthal, N.E. Epidemiological findings of seasonal changes in mood and behavior: A telephone survey of Montgomery County, Maryland. *Archives of General Psychiatry,* 1989b, *46,* 823–833.

Katayama, Y., DeWitt, D.S., Becker, D.P., and Hayes, R.L. Behavioral evidence for cholinoceptive pontine inhibitory area: Descending control of spinal motor output and sensory input. *Brain Research,* 1986, *296,* 241–262.

Kawamura, M., Hirayama, K., and Yamamoto, H. Different interhemispheric transfer of kanji and kana writing evidenced by a case with left unilateral agraphia without apraxia. *Brain,* 1989, *112,* 1011–1018.

Keller, S.E., Weiss, J.M., Schleifer, S.J., Miller, N.E., and Stein, M. Stress-induced suppression of immunity in adrenalectomized rats. *Science,* 1983, *221,* 1301–1304.

Kelly, D.H., Walker, A.M., Cahen, L.A., and Shannon, D.C. Periodic breathing in siblings of SIDS victims. *Pediatric Research,* 1980, *14,* 645–650.

Kelso, S.R., and Brown, T.H. Differential conditioning of associative synaptic enhancement in hippocampal brain slices. *Science,* 1986, *232,* 85–87.

Kelsoe, J.R., Ginns, E.I., Egeland, J.A., Gerhard, D.S., Goldstein, A.M., Bale, S.J., Pauls, D.L., Long, R.T., Kidd, K.K., Conte, G., Housman, D.E., and Paul, S.M. Re-evaluation of the linkage relationship between chromosome 11p loci and the gene for bipolar affective disorder in the Old Order Amish. *Nature,* 1989, *342,* 238–243.

Kemble, E.D., and Nagel, J.A. Failure to form a learned taste aversion in rats with amygdaloid lesions. *Bulletin of the Psychonomic Society,* 1973, *2,* 155–156.

Kertesz, A. *Aphasia and Associated Disorders: Taxonomy, Localization, and Recovery.* New York: Grune & Stratton, 1979.

Kertesz, A. Personal communication, 1980.

Kertesz, A. Anatomy of jargon. In *Jargonaphasia,* edited by J. Brown. New York: Academic Press, 1981.

Kessler, S., Guilleminault, C., and Dement, W.C. A family study of 50 REM narcoleptics. *Acta Neurologica Scandinavica,* 1974, *50,* 503–512.

Kety, S.S., Rosenthal, D., Wender, P.H., and Schulsinger, K.F. The types and prevalence of mental illness in the biological and adoptive families of adopted schizophrenics. In *The Transmission of Schizophrenia,* edited by D. Rosenthal and S.S. Kety. New York: Pergamon Press, 1968.

Keverne, E.G., and de la Riva, C. Pheromones in mice: Reciprocal interactions between the nose and brain. *Nature,* 1982, *296,* 148–150.

Kiang, N.Y.-S. *Discharge Patterns of Single Fibers in the Cat's Auditory Nerve.* Cambridge, Mass.: MIT Press, 1965.

Kiecolt-Glaser, J.K., Glaser, R., Shuttleworth, E.C., Dyer, C.S., Ogrocki, P., and Speicher, C.E. Chronic stress and immunity in family caregivers of Alzheimer's disease victims. *Psychosomatic Medicine,* 1987, *49,* 523–535.

Kihlstrom, J.F. Hypnosis. *Annual Review of Psychology,* 1985, *36,* 385–418.

Kinsey, A.C., Pomeroy, W.B., Martin, C.E., and Gebhard, P.H. *Sexual Behavior in the Human Female.* Philadelphia: Saunders, 1943.

Kinsley, C., and Svare, B. Prenatal stress reduces intermale aggression in mice. *Physiology and Behavior,* 1986, *36,* 783–785.

Kirchgessner, A.L., and Sclafani, A. PVN-hindbrain pathway involved in the hypothalamic hyperphagia-obesity syndrome. *Physiology and Behavior,* 1988, *42,* 517–528.

Kleitman, N. The nature of dreaming. In *The Nature of Sleep,* edited by G.E.W. Wolstenholme and M. O'Connor. London: J.&A. Churchill, 1961.

Kleitman, N. Basic rest-activity cycle—22 years later. *Sleep,* 1982, *4,* 311–317.

Klüver, H., and Bucy, P.C. Preliminary analysis of functions of the temporal lobes in monkeys. *Archives of Neurology and Psychiatry (Chicago),* 1939, *42,* 979–1000.

Knoll, J. Satietin: A centrally acting potent anorectic substance with a long-lasting effect in human and mammalian blood. *Polish Journal of Pharmacology and Pharmacy,* 1982, *34,* 3–16.

Knoll, J., Dallo, J., and Yen, T.T. Striatal dopamine, sexual activity and lifespan. Longevity of rats treated with (-)deprenyl. *Life Sciences,* 1989, *45,* 525–531.

Komisaruk, B.R., and Larsson, K. Suppression of a spinal and a cranial nerve reflex by vaginal or rectal probing in rats. *Brain Research,* 1971, *35,* 231–235.

Komisaruk, B.R., and Steinman, J.L. Genital stimulation as a trigger for neuroendocrine and behavioral control of reproduction. *Annals of the New York Academy of Sciences,* 1987, *474,* 64–75.

Koob, G.F., and Bloom, F.E. Cellular and molecular mechanisms of drug dependence. *Science,* 1988, *242,* 715–723.

Koob, G.F., Thatcher-Britton, K., Britton, D., Roberts, D.C.S., and Bloom, F.E. Destruction of the locus coeruleus or the dorsal NE bundle does not alter the release of punished responding by ethanol and chlordiazepoxide. *Physiology and Behavior,* 1984, *33,* 479–485.

Koopman, P., Münsterberg, A., Capel, B., Vivian, N., and Lovell-Badge, R. Expression of a candidate sex-determining gene during mouse testis differentiation. *Nature,* 1990, *348,* 450–452.

Kornhuber, H.H. Cerebral cortex, cerebellum, and basal ganglia: An introduction to their motor functions. In *The Neurosciences: Third*

Study Program, edited by F.O. Schmitt and F.G. Worden. Cambridge, Mass.: MIT Press, 1974.

Kral, J.G. Surgical treatment of obesity. *Medical Clinics of North America,* 1989, *73,* 251-264.

Kramer, F.M., Jeffery, R.W., Forster, J.L., and Snell, M.K. Long-term follow-up of behavioral treatment for obesity: Patterns of weight regain among men and women. *International Journal of Obesity,* 1989, *13,* 123-136.

Kuffler, S.W. Neurons in the retina: Organization, inhibition and excitation problems. *Cold Spring Harbor Symposium on Quantitative Biology,* 1952, *17,* 281-292.

Kuffler, S.W. Discharge patterns and functional organization of mammalian retina. *Journal of Neurophysiology,* 1953, *16,* 37-68.

Kumar, K., Wyant, G.M., and Nath, R. Deep brain stimulation for control of intractable pain in humans, present and future: A ten-year follow-up. *Neurosurgery,* 1990, *26,* 774-782.

Kupfer, D.J. REM latency: A psychobiologic marker for primary depressive disease. *Biological Psychiatry,* 1976, *11,* 159-174.

Laborit, H. La thérapeutique neuro-végétate du choc et de la maladie post-traumatique. *Presse Medicale,* 1950, *58,* 138-140. Cited by Snyder, 1974.

Lancet, D. Vertebrate olfactory reception. *Annual Review of Neuroscience,* 1986, *9,* 329-355.

Land, E.H. The retinex theory of colour vision. *Proceedings of the Royal Institute of Great Britain,* 1974, *47,* 23-57.

Land, E.H. The retinex theory of color vision. *Scientific American,* 1977, *237,* 108-128.

Lange, C.G. *Über Gemüthsbewegungen.* Leipzig: T. Thomas, 1987.

Langston, J.W., and Ballard, P. Parkinsonism induced by 1-methyl-4-phenyl-1,2,3,6-tetrahydropyridine (MPTP): Implications for treatment and the pathogenesis of Parkinson's disease. *Canadian Journal of Neurological Science,* 1984, *11,* 160-165.

Langston, J.W., Ballard, P., Tetrud, J., and Irwin, I. Chronic parkinsonism in humans due to a product of meperidine-analog synthesis. *Science,* 1983, *219,* 979-980.

Langston, J.W., Forno, L.S., Rebert, C.S., and Irwin, I. Selective nigral toxicity after systemic administration of 1-methyl-4-phenyl-1,2,3,6-tetrahydropyridine (MPTP) in the squirrel monkey. *Brain Research,* 1984, *292,* 390-394.

Lankenau, H., Swigar, M.E., Bhimani, S., Luchins, S., and Quinlon, D.M. Cranial CT scans in eating disorder patients and controls. *Comprehensive Psychiatry,* 1985, *26,* 136-147.

Laschet, U. Antiandrogen in the treatment of sex offenders: Mode of action and therapeutic outcome. In *Contemporary Sexual Behavior: Critical Issues in the 1970's,* edited by J. Zubin and J. Money. Baltimore: Johns Hopkins University Press, 1973.

Lavie, P., Pratt, H., Scharf, B., Peled, R., and Brown, J. Localized pontine lesion: Nearly total absence of REM sleep. *Neurology,* 1984, *34,* 1118-1120.

Lawrence, D.G., and Kuypers, G.J.M. The functional organization of the motor system in the monkey. I. The effects of bilateral pyramidal lesions. *Brain,* 1968a, *91,* 1-14.

Lawrence, D.G., and Kuypers, G.J.M. The functional organization of the motor system in the monkey. II. The effects of lesions of the descending brain-stem pathways. *Brain,* 1968b, *91,* 15-36.

LeBlanc, J., and Cabanac, M. Cephalic postprandial thermogenesis in human subjects. *Physiology and Behavior,* 1989, *46,* 479-482.

LeDoux, J.E. Emotion. In *Handbook of Physiology: Nervous System V,* edited by F. Plum. Washington, D.C.: American Physiological Society, 1987.

LeDoux, J.E., Iwata, J., Cicchetti, P., and Reis, D.J. Different projections of the central amygdaloid nucleus mediate autonomic and behavioral correlates of conditioned fear. *Journal of Neuroscience,* 1988, *8,* 2517-2529.

LeDoux, J.E., Iwata, J., Pearl, D., and Reis, D.J. Disruption of auditory but not visual learning by destruction of intrinsic neurons in the rat medial geniculate body. *Brain Research,* 1986, *371,* 395-399.

LeDoux, J.E., Sakaguchi, A., and Reis, D.J. Subcortical efferent projections of the medial geniculate nucleus mediate emotional responses conditioned to acoustic stimuli. *Journal of Neuroscience,* 1984, *4,* 683-698.

Lehman, M.N., Silver, R., Gladstone, W.R., Kahn, R.M., Gibson, M., and Bittman, E.L. Circadian rhythmicity restored by neural transplant: Immunocytochemical characterization with the host brain. *Journal of Neuroscience,* 1987, *7,* 1626-1638.

Lehman, M.N., and Winans, S.S. Vomeronasal and olfactory pathways to the amygdala controlling male hamster sexual behavior: Autoradiographic and behavioral analyses. *Brain Research,* 1982, *240,* 27-41.

Leibowitz, S.F., Weiss, G.F., and Shor-Posner, G. Hypothalamic serotonin: Pharmacological, biochemical and behavioral analyses of its feeding-suppressive action. *Clinical Neuropharmacology,* 1988, *11,* 551-571.

Leibowitz, S.F., Weiss, G.F., Walsh, U.A., and Viswanath, D. Medial hypothalamic serotonin: Role in circadian patterns of feeding and macronutrient selection. *Brain Research,* 1989, *503,* 132-140.

Leibowitz, S.F., Weiss, G.F., Yee, F., and Tretter, J.B. Noradrenergic innervation of the paraventricular nucleus: Specific role in control of carbohydrate ingestions. *Brain Research Bulletin,* 1985, *14,* 561-567.

Le Magnen, J. Hyperphagie provoquée chez le rat blanc par l'altération du méchanisme de satiéte périphérique. *Comptes Rendus de la Société de Biologie,* 1956, *147,* 1753-1757.

Leonard, C.M., Rolls, E.T., Wilson, F.A.W., and Baylis, G.C. Neurons in the amygdala of the monkey with responses selective for faces. *Behavioral Brain Research,* 1985, *15,* 159-176.

Leonard, H.L., Swedo, S.E., Rapoport, J.L., Koby, E.V., Lenane, M.C., Cheslow, D.L., and Hamburger, S.D. Treatment of obsessive-compulsive disorder with clomipramine and desipramine in children and adolescents: A double-blind crossover comparison. *Archives of General Psychiatry,* 1989, *46,* 1088-1092.

Levenson, R.W., Ekman, P., and Friesen, W.V. Voluntary facial action generates emotion-specific autonomic nervous system activity. *Psychophysiology,* 1990, *27,* 363-384.

Levine, A.S., and Morley, J.E. Neuropeptide Y: A potent inducer of consummatory behavior in rats. *Peptides,* 1984, *5,* 1025-1029.

Levine, J.D., Gordon, N.C., and Fields, H.L. The role of endorphins in placebo analgesia. In *Advances in Pain Research and Therapy, Vol. 3,* edited by J.J. Bonica, J.C. Liebeskind, and D. Albe-Fessard. New York: Raven Press, 1979.

Levy, R.M., and Bredesen, D.E. Controversies in HIV-related central nervous system disease: Neuropsychological aspects of HIV-1 infection. In *AIDS Clinical Review 1989,* edited by P. Volberding, and M.A. Jacobson. New York: Marcel Dekker, 1989.

Lewin, R. Big first scored with nerve diseases. *Science,* 1989, *245,* 467-468.

Ley, R.G., and Bryden, M.P. Hemispheric differences in recognizing faces and emotions. *Brain and Language,* 1979, *7,* 127-138.

Ley, R.G., and Bryden, M.P. A dissociation of right and left hemispheric effects for recognizing emotional tone and verbal content. *Brain and Cognition,* 1982, *1,* 3–9.

Liljequist, S. The competitive NMDA receptor antagonist, CGP 39551, inhibits ethanol withdrawal seizures. *European Journal of Pharmacology,* 1991, *192,* 197–198.

Lind, R.W., Thunhorst, R.L., and Johnson, A.K. The subfornical organ and the integration of multiple factors in thirst. *Physiology and Behavior,* 1984, *32,* 69–74.

Lindvall, O. Dopamine pathways in the rat brain. In *The Neurobiology of Dopamine,* edited by A.S. Horn, J. Korb, and B.H.C. Westerink. New York: Academic Press, 1979.

Linnoila, M., Virkkunen, M., Scheinin, M., Nuutila, A., Rimon, R., and Goodwin, F.K. Low cerebrospinal fluid 5-hydroxyindoleacetic acid concentration differentiates impulsive from nonimpulsive violent behavior. *Life Sciences,* 1983, *33,* 2609–2614.

Lipton, S.A., Dreyer, E.B., Kaiser, P.K., and Offermann, J.T. HIV-1 coat protein neurotoxicity prevented by calcium channel antagonists. *Science,* 1990, *248,* 364–367.

Lisk, R.D. The regulation of sexual "heat." In *Biological Determinants of Sexual Behaviour,* edited by J.B. Hutchison. New York: John Wiley & Sons, 1978.

Lisk, R.D., Pretlow, R.A., and Friedman, S. Hormonal stimulation necessary for elicitation of maternal nest-building in the mouse (*Mus musculus*). *Animal Behaviour,* 1969, *17,* 730–737.

Liuzzi, F.J., and Lasek, R.J. Astrocytes block axonal regeneration in mammals by activating the physiological stop pathway. *Science,* 1987, *237,* 642–645.

Livingstone, M.S., and Hubel, D. Segregation of form, color, movement, and depth: Anatomy, physiology, and perception. *Science,* 1988, *240,* 740–749.

Livingstone, M.S., and Hubel, D.H. Thalamic inputs to cytochrome oxidase-rich regions in monkey visual cortex. *Proceedings of the National Academy of Sciences, USA,* 1982, *79,* 6098–6101.

Livingstone, M.S., and Hubel, D.H. Psychophysical evidence for separate channels for the perception of form, color, movement, and depth. *Journal of Neuroscience,* 1987, *7,* 3416–3468.

Loewenstein, W.R., and Mendelson, M. Components of receptor adaptation in a Pacinian corpuscle. *Journal of Physiology (London),* 1965, *177,* 377–397.

Lømo, T. Frequency potentiation of excitatory synaptic activity in the dentate area of the hippocampal formation. *Acta Physiologica Scandinavica,* 1966, *68* (Suppl. 227), 128.

Louis-Sylvestre, J., and Le Magnen, J. A fall in blood glucose level precedes meal onset in free-feeding rats. *Neuroscience and Biobehavioral Reviews,* 1980, *4,* 13–16.

Lynch, G., Muller, D., Seubert, P., and Larson, J. Long-term potentiation: Persisting problems and recent results. *Brain Research Bulletin,* 1988, *21,* 363–372.

Lytton, W.W., and Brust, J.C.M. Direct dyslexia: Preserved oral reading of real words in Wernicke's aphasia. *Brain,* 1989, *112,* 583–594.

Machon, R.A., Mednick, S.A., and Schulsinger, F. The interaction of seasonality, place of birth, genetic risk and subsequent schizophrenia in a high risk sample. *British Journal of Psychiatry,* 1983, *143,* 383–388.

MacLean, P.D. Psychosomatic disease and the "visceral brain": Recent developments bearing on the Papez theory of emotion. *Psychosomatic Medicine,* 1949, *11,* 338–353.

Maier, S.F., Drugan, R.C., and Grau, J.W. Controllability, coping behavior, and stress-induced analgesia in the rat. *Pain,* 1982, *12,* 47–56.

Maj, M. Organic mental disorders in HIV-1 infection. *AIDS,* 1990, *4,* 831–840.

Maksay, G., and Ticku, M.K. Dissociation of [^{35}S]t-butylbicyclophosphorothionate binding differentiates convulsant and depressant drugs that modulate GABAergic transmission. *Journal of Neurochemistry,* 1985, *44,* 480–486.

Mallow, G.K. The relationship between aggression and cycle stage in adult female rhesus monkeys (*Macaca mulatta*). *Dissertation Abstracts,* 1979, *39,* 3194.

Malsbury, C.W. Facilitation of male rat copulatory behavior by electrical stimulation of the medial preoptic area. *Physiology and Behavior,* 1971, *7,* 797–805.

Manuck, S.B., Kaplan, J.R., and Clarkson, T.B. Behaviorally-induced heart rate reactivity and atherosclerosis in cynomolgous monkeys. *Psychosomatic Medicine,* 1983, *45,* 95–108.

Manuck, S.B., Kaplan, J.R., and Matthews, K.A. Behavioral antecedents of coronary heart disease and atherosclerosis. *Arteriosclerosis,* 1986, *6,* 1–14.

Marczynski, T.J., and Urbancic, M. Animal models of chronic anxiety and "fearlessness." *Brain Research Bulletin,* 1988, *21,* 483–490.

Maret, G., Testa, B., Jenner, P., El Tayar, N., and Carrupt, P.-A. The MPTP story: MAO activates tetrahydropyridine derivatives to toxins causing parkinsonism. *Drug Metabolism Reviews,* 1990, *22,* 221–232.

Margolin, D.I., Marcel, A.J., and Carlson, N.R. Common mechanisms in dysnomia and post-semantic surface dyslexia: Processing deficits and selective attention. In *Surface Dyslexia: Neuropsychological and Cognitive Studies of Phonological Reading,* edited by M. Coltheart. London: Lawrence Erlbaum Associates, 1985.

Margolin, D.I., and Walker, J.A. Personal communication, 1981.

Mark, G.P., Blander, D.S., Hernandez, L., and Hoebel, B.G. Effects of salt intake, rehydration and conditioned taste aversion (CTA) development on dopamine output in the rat nucleus accumbens. *Appetite,* 1989, *12,* 224.

Mark, G.P., and Scott, T.R. Conditioned taste aversions affect gustatory activity in the NTS of chronic decerebrate rats. *Neuroscience Abstracts,* 1988, *14,* 1185.

Mark, V.H., Ervin, F.R., and Yakovlev, P.I. The treatment of pain by stereotaxic methods. *Confina Neurologica,* 1962, *22,* 238–245.

Markowitsch, H.J. Diencephalic amnesia: A reorientation towards tracts. *Brain Research Reviews,* 1988, *13,* 351–370.

Martinot, J.-L., Peron-Magnan, P., Huret, J.-D., Mazoyer, B., Baron, J.-C., Boulenger, J.P., Loc'h, C., Maziere, B., Caillard, V., Loo, H., and Syrota, A. Striatal D_2 dopaminergic receptors assessed with positron emission tomography and [^{76}Br]bromospiperone in untreated schizophrenic patients. *American Journal of Psychiatry,* 1990, *147,* 44–50.

Mather, P., Nicolaïdis, S., and Booth, D.A. Compensatory and conditioned feeding responses to scheduled glucose infusions in the rat. *Nature,* 1978, *273,* 461–463.

Matsuda, L.A., Lolait, S.J., Brownstein, M.J., Young, A.C., and Bonner, T.I. Structure of a cannabinoid receptor and functional expression of the cloned cDNA. *Nature,* 1990, *346,* 561–564.

Matthews, R.T., and German, D.C. Electrophysiological evidence for excitation of rat ventral tegmental area dopaminergic neurons by morphine. *Neuroscience,* 1984, *11,* 617–626.

Mauk, M.D., Steinmetz, J.E., and Thompson, R.F. Classical conditioning using stimulation of the inferior olive as the unconditioned stimulus. *Proceedings of the National Academy of Sciences, USA,* 1986, *83,* 5349–5353.

Mawson, A.R. Anorexia nervosa and the regulation of intake: A review. *Psychological Medicine,* 1974, *4,* 289–308.

Mayer, D.J., and Liebeskind, J.C. Pain reduction by focal electrical stimulation of the brain: An anatomical and behavioral analysis. *Brain Research,* 1974, *68,* 73–93.

Mayer, D.J., Price, D.D., Rafii, A., and Barber, J. Acupuncture hypalgesia: Evidence for activation of a central control system as a mechanism of action. In *Advances in Pain Research and Therapy, Vol. 1,* edited by J.J. Bonica, and D. Albe-Fessard. New York: Raven Press, 1976.

Mayer, J. Regulation of energy intake and the body weight: The glucostatic theory and the lipostatic hypothesis. *Annals of the New York Academy of Sciences,* 1955, *63,* 15–43.

Mazur, A., and Lamb, T. Testosterone, status, and mood in human males. *Hormones and Behavior,* 1980, *14,* 236–246.

McCarley, R.W., and Hobson, J.A. The form of dreams and the biology of sleep. In *Handbook of Dreams: Research, Theory, and Applications,* edited by B. Wolman. New York: Van Nostrand Reinhold, 1979.

McCarthy, R.A., and Warrington, E.K. Evidence for modality-specific meaning systems in the brain. *Nature,* 1988, *334,* 428–435.

McClintock, M.K. Menstrual synchrony and suppression. *Nature,* 1971, *229,* 244–245.

McClintock, M.K., and Adler, N.T. The role of the female during copulation in wild and domestic Norway rats (*Rattus norvegicus*). *Behaviour,* 1978, *67,* 67–96.

McCormick, D.A., Steinmetz, J.E., and Thompson, R.F. Lesions of the inferior olivary complex cause extinction of the classically conditioned eyeblink response. *Brain Research,* 1985, *359,* 120–130.

McCormick, D.A., and Thompson, R.F. Cerebellum: Essential involvement in the classically conditioned eyelid response. *Science,* 1984, *223,* 296–299.

McGinty, D.J., and Sterman, M.B. Sleep suppression after basal forebrain lesions in the cat. *Science,* 1968, *160,* 1253–1255.

McGrath, M.J., and Cohen, D.B. REM sleep facilitation of adaptive waking behavior: A review of the literature. *Psychological Bulletin,* 1978, *85,* 24–57.

Meddis, R., Pearson, A., and Langford, G. An extreme case of healthy insomnia. *Electroencephalography and Clinical Neurophysiology,* 1973, *35,* 213–214.

Mednick, S.A., Machon, R.A., and Huttunen, M.O. An update on the Helsinki influenza project. *Archives of General Psychiatry,* 1990, *47,* 292.

Meijer, J.H., and Rietveld, W.J. Neurophysiology of the suprachiasmatic circadian pacemaker in rodents. *Physiological Reviews,* 1989, *69,* 671–707.

Meijer, J.H., van der Zee, E.A., and Dietz, M. Glutamate phase shifts circadian activity rhythms in hamsters. *Neuroscience Letters,* 1988, *86,* 177–183.

Mendelsohn, F.A.O., Quirion, R., Saavedra, J.M., Aguilera, G., and Catt, K.J. Autoradiographic localization of angiotensin II receptors in rat brain. *Proceedings of the National Academy of Sciences, USA,* 1984, *81,* 1575–1579.

Menninger, K.A. Influenza and schizophrenia. An analysis of post-influenzal "dementia praecox" as of 1918 and five years later. *American Journal of Psychiatry,* 1926, *5,* 469–529.

Meredith, M., and O'Connell, R.J. Efferent control of stimulus access to the hamster vomeronasal organ. *Journal of Physiology,* 1979, *286,* 301–316.

Merigan, W.H. Chromatic and achromatic vision of macaques: Role of the P pathway. *Journal of Neuroscience,* 1989, *9,* 776–783.

Merigan, W.H., and Eskin, T.A. Spatio-temporal vision of macaques with severe loss of Pb retinal ganglion cells. *Vision Research,* 1986, *26,* 1751–1761.

Mesulam, M.-M. Patterns in behavioral neuroanatomy: Association areas, the limbic system, and hemispheric specialization. In *Principles of Behavioral Neurology,* edited by M.-M. Mesulam. Philadelphia: F.A. Davis, 1985.

Miller, G.A., and Taylor, W.G. The perception of repeated bursts of noise. *Journal of the Acoustical Society of America,* 1948, *20,* 171–182.

Miller, J.D., Faull, K.F., Bowersox, F.S., and Dement, W.C. CNS monoamines and their metabolites in canine narcolepsy: A replication study. *Brain Research,* 1990, *509,* 169–171.

Miller, N.E. Understanding the use of animals in behavioral research: Some critical issues. *Annals of the New York Academy of Sciences,* 1983, *406,* 113–118.

Milner, B. Memory and the temporal regions of the brain. In *Biology of Memory,* edited by K.H. Pribram and D.E. Broadbent. New York: Academic Press, 1970.

Milner, B., Corkin, S., and Teuber, H.-L. Further analysis of the hippocampal amnesic syndrome: 14-year follow-up study of H.M. *Neuropsychologia,* 1968, *6,* 317–338.

Mishkin, M. Visual mechanisms beyond the striate cortex. In *Frontiers in Physiological Psychology,* edited by R.W. Russell. New York: Academic Press, 1966.

Mishkin, M. A memory system in the monkey. *Philosophical Transactions of the Royal Society of London,* 1982, *298,* 85–95.

Mishkin, M., Malamut, B., and Bachevalier, J. Memories and habits: Two neural systems. In *Neurobiology of Learning and Memory,* edited by G. Lynch, J.L. McGaugh, and N.M. Weinberger. New York: Guilford Press, 1984.

Moghaddam, B., and Bunney, B.S. Differential effect of cocaine on extracellular dopamine levels in rat medial prefrontal cortex and nucleus accumbens: Comparison to amphetamine. *Synapse,* 1989, *4,* 156–161.

Mok, D., and Mogenson, G.J. Contribution of zona incerta to osmotically induced drinking in rats. *American Journal of Physiology,* 1986, *251,* R823–R832.

Moltz, H., Lubin, M., Leon, M., and Numan, M. Hormonal induction of maternal behavior in the ovariectomized nulliparous rat. *Physiology and Behavior,* 1970, *5,* 1373–1377.

Money, J., and Ehrhardt, A. *Man & Woman, Boy & Girl.* Baltimore: Johns Hopkins University Press, 1972.

Money, J., Schwartz, M., and Lewis, V.G. Adult erotosexual status and fetal hormonal masculinization and demasculinization: 46,XX congenital virilizing adrenal hyperplasia and 46,XY androgen-insensitivity syndrome compared. *Psychoneuroendocrinology,* 1984, *9,* 405–414.

Montarolo, P.G., Goelet, P., Castellucci, V.F., Morgan, J., Kandel, E.R., and Schacher, S. A critical time period for macromolecular synthesis in long-term heterosynaptic facilitation in *Aplysia. Science,* 1986, *234,* 1249–1254.

Moore, B.O., and Deutsch, J.A. An antiemetic is antidotal to the satiety effects of cholecystokinin. *Nature,* 1985, *315,* 321–322.

Moore, R.Y., and Eichler, V.B. Loss of a circadian adrenal corticosterone rhythm following suprachiasmatic lesions in the rat. *Brain Research,* 1972, *42,* 201–206.

Morales, F.R., Boxer, P.A., and Chase, M.H. Behavioral state-specific inhibitory postsynaptic potentials impinge on cat lumbar motoneurons during active sleep. *Experimental Neurology,* 1987, *98,* 418–435.

Moran, T.H., Shnayder, L., Hostetler, A.M., and McHugh, P.R. Pylorectomy reduces the satiety action of cholecystokinin. *American Journal of Physiology,* 1989, *255,* R1059–R1063.

Mori, E., Yamadori, A., and Furumoto, M. Left precentral gyrus and Broca's aphasia: A clinicopathologic study. *Neurology,* 1989, *39,* 51–54.

Morris, N.M., Udry, J.R., Khan-Dawood, F., and Dawood, M.Y. Marital sex frequency and midcycle female testosterone. *Archives of Sexual Behavior,* 1987, *16,* 27–37.

Morris, R.G.M., Anderson, E., Lynch, G., and Baudry, M. Selective impairment of learning and blockade of long-term potentiation by an N-methyl-D-aspartate receptor antagonist, AP5. *Nature,* 1986, *319,* 774–776.

Morris, R.G.M., Garrud, P., Rawlins, J.N.P., and O'Keefe, J. Place navigation impaired in rats with hippocampal lesions. *Nature,* 1982, *297,* 681–683.

Morris, Y.A., and Crews, D. The effects of exogenous neuropeptide Y on feeding and sexual behavior in the red-sided garter snake *(Thamnophis sirtalis parietalis). Brain Research,* 1990, *530,* 339–341.

Moscovitch, M., and Olds, J. Asymmetries in emotional facial expressions and their possible relation to hemispheric specialization. *Neuropsychologia,* 1982, *20,* 71–81.

Mountcastle, V.B. Modality and topographic properties of single neurons of cat's somatic sensory cortex. *Journal of Neurophysiology,* 1957, *20,* 408–434.

Mountcastle, V.B., Lynch, J.C., Georgopoulos, A., Sakata, H., and Acuna, C. Posterior parietal association cortex: Command functions for operations within extra-personal space. *Journal of Neurophysiology,* 1975, *38,* 871–908.

Mukhametov, L.M. Sleep in marine mammals. In *Sleep Mechanisms,* edited by A.A. Borbély and J.L. Valatx. Munich: Springer-Verlag, 1984.

Muller, R.U., and Kubie, J.L. The effects of changes in the environment on the spatial firing of hippocampal complex-spike cells. *Journal of Neuroscience,* 1987, *7,* 1935–1950.

Munro, J.F., Stewart, I.C., Seidelin, P.H., Mackenzie, H.S., and Dewhusrt, N.E. Mechanical treatment for obesity. *Annals of the New York Academy of Science,* 1987, *499,* 305–312.

Nachman, M., and Ashe, J.H. Effects of basolateral amygdala lesions on neophobia, learned taste aversions, and sodium appetite in rats. *Journal of Comparative and Physiological Psychology,* 1974, *87,* 622–643.

Nadeau, S.E. Impaired grammar with normal fluency and phonology. *Brain,* 1988, *111,* 1111–1137.

Nafe, J.P., and Wagoner, K.S. The nature of pressure adaptation. *Journal of General Psychology,* 1941, *25,* 323–351.

Nakahara, D., Ozaki, N., Miura, Y., Miura, H., and Nagatsu, T. Increased dopamine and serotonin metabolism in rat nucleus accumbens produced by intracranial self-stimulation of medial forebrain bundle as measured by in vivo microdialysis. *Brain Research,* 1989, *495,* 178–181.

Nathans, J., Piantanida, T.P., Eddy, R.L., Shows, T.B., and Hogness, D.S. Molecular genetics of inherited variation in human color vision. *Science,* 1986, *232,* 203–210.

Nauta, W.J.H. Hypothalamic regulation of sleep in rats: Experimental study. *Journal of Neurophysiology,* 1946, *9,* 285–316.

Neff, W.D. The brain and hearing: Auditory discriminations affected by brain lesions. *Annals of Otology, Rhinology and Laryngology,* 1977, *86,* 500–506.

Newman, E.A., and Evans, C.R. Human dream processes as analogous to computer programme clearance. *Nature,* 1965, *206,* 54.

Nicholl, C.S., and Russell, R.M. Analysis of animal rights literature reveals the underlying motives of the movement: Ammunition for counter offensive by scientists. *Endocrinology,* 1990, *127,* 985–989.

Nichols, D.G. Brown adipose tissue mitochondria. *Biochimica et Biophysica Acta,* 1979, *549,* 1–29.

Nicoll, R.A., Alger, B.E., and Nicoll, R.A. Enkephalin blocks inhibitory pathways in the vertebrate CNS. *Nature,* 1980, *287,* 22–25.

Noirot, E. Selective priming of maternal responses by auditory and olfactory cues from mouse pups. *Developmental Psychobiology,* 1972, *5,* 371–387.

Norgren, R., and Grill, H. Brain-stem control of ingestive behavior. In *The Physiological Mechanisms of Motivation,* edited by D.W. Pfaff. New York: Springer-Verlag, 1982.

Nowlis, G.H., and Frank, M. Qualities in hamster taste: Behavioral and neural evidence. In *Olfaction and Taste, Vol. 6,* edited by J. LeMagnen and P. MacLeod. Washington, D.C.: Information Retrieval, 1977.

Numan, M. Medial preoptic area and maternal behavior in the female rat. *Journal of Comparative and Physiological Psychology,* 1974, *87,* 746–759.

Numan, M., Rosenblatt, J.S., and Komisaruk, B.R. Medial preoptic area and onset of maternal behavior in the rat. *Journal of Comparative and Physiological Psychology,* 1977, *91,* 146–164.

Numan, M., and Smith, H.G. Maternal behavior in rats: Evidence for the involvement of preoptic projections to the ventral tegmental area. *Behavioral Neuroscience,* 1984, *98,* 712–727.

Oaknin, S., Rodriguez del Castillo, A., Guerra, M., Battaner, E., and Mas, M. Change in forebrain Na,K-ATPase activity and serum hormone levels during sexual behavior in male rats. *Physiology and Behavior,* 1989, *45,* 407–410.

O'Carroll, R.E., and Bancroft, J. Androgens and aggression in man: A controlled case study. *Aggressive Behavior,* 1985, *11,* 1–7.

O'Keefe, J., and Bouma, H. Complex sensory properties of certain amygdala units in the freely moving cat. *Experimental Neurology,* 1969, *23,* 384–398.

O'Keefe, J., and Dostrovsky, T. The hippocampus as a spatial map: Preliminary evidence from unit activity in the freely moving rat. *Brain Research,* 1971, *34,* 171–175.

Olds, J. Commentary. In *Brain Stimulation and Motivation,* edited by E.S. Valenstein. Glenview, Ill.: Scott, Foresman, 1973.

Olds, M.E., and Fobes, J.L. The central basis of motivation: Intracranial self-stimulation studies. *Annual Review of Psychology,* 1981, *32,* 523–574.

Olton, D.S. Memory functions and the hippocampus. In *Neurobiology of the Hippocampus,* edited by W. Siefert. New York: Academic Press, 1983.

Olton, D.S., Collison, C., and Werz, M.A. Spatial memory and radial arm maze performance in rats. *Learning and Motivation,* 1977, *8,* 289–314.

Olton, D.S., and Samuelson, R.J. Remembrance of places past: Spatial memory in rats. *Journal of Experimental Psychology: Animal Behavior Processes,* 1976, *2,* 97–116.

Oomura, Y. Significance of glucose, insulin and free fatty acid on the hypothalamic feeding and satiety neurons. In *Hunger: Basic Mecha-*

nisms and Clinical Implications, edited by D. Novin, W. Wyrwicka, and G. Bray. New York: Raven Press, 1976.

Papez, J.W. A proposed mechanism of emotion. *Archives of Neurology and Psychiatry,* 1937, *38,* 725–744.

Patterson, K., and Kay, J.A. How word-form dyslexics form words. Paper presented at the meeting of the British Psychological Society Conference on Reading, Exeter, England, 1980.

Patton, G. The course of anorexia nervosa. *British Medical Journal,* 1989, *299,* 139–140.

Pauls, D.L., Towbin, K.E., Leckman, J.F., Zahner, G.E.P., and Cohen, D.J. Gilles de la Tourette's syndrome and obsessive-compulsive disorder. *Archives of General Psychiatry,* 1986, *43,* 1180–1182.

Peck, J., and Novin, D. Evidence that osmoreceptors mediating drinking in rabbits are in the lateral preoptic area. *Journal of Comparative and Physiological Psychology,* 1971, *74,* 134–147.

Peck, J.W., and Blass, E.M. Localization of thirst and antidiuretic osmoreceptors by intracranial injections in rats. *American Journal of Physiology,* 1975, *5,* 1501–1509.

Penfield, W., and Jasper, H. *Epilepsy and the Functional Anatomy of the Human Brain.* Boston: Little, Brown & Co., 1954.

Penfield, W., and Rasmussen, T. *The Cerebral Cortex of Man: A Clinical Study of Localization.* Boston: Little, Brown & Co., 1950.

Perkins, A.T., and Teyler, T.J. A critical period for long-term potentiation in the developing rat visual cortex. *Brain Research,* 1988, *439,* 25–47.

Perlmutter, L.S., Siman, R., Gall, C., Seubert, P., Baudry, M., and Lynch, G. The ultrastructural localization of calcium-activated protease "calpain" in rat brain. *Synapse,* 1988, *2,* 79–88.

Perrigo, G., Bryant, W.C., and vom Saal, F.S. A unique neural timing system prevents male mice from harming their own offspring. *Animal Behaviour,* 1990, *39,* 535–539.

Persky, H. Reproductive hormones, moods, and the menstrual cycle. In *Sex Differences in Behavior,* edited by R.C. Friedman, R.M. Richart, and R.L. Vande Wiele. New York: John Wiley & Sons, 1974.

Persky, H., Lief, H.I., Strauss, D., Miller, W.R., and O'Brien, C.P. Plasma testosterone level and sexual behavior of couples. *Archives of Sexual Behavior,* 1978, *7,* 157–173.

Pert, C.B, Snowman, A.M., and Snyder, S.H. Localization of opiate receptor binding in presynaptic membranes of rat brain. *Brain Research,* 1974, *70,* 184–188.

Pfaff, D.W., and Keiner, M. Atlas of estradiol-concentrating cells in the central nervous system of the female rat. *Journal of Comparative Neurology,* 1973, *151,* 121–158.

Pfaff, D.W., and Sakuma, Y. Deficit in the lordosis reflex of female rats caused by lesions in the ventromedial nucleus of the hypothalamus. *Journal of Physiology,* 1979, *288,* 203–210.

Pfaffman, C., Frank, M., and Norgren, R. Neural mechanisms and behavioral aspects of taste. *Annual Review of Psychology,* 1979, *31,* 283–325.

Pfaus, J.G., Damsma, G., Nomikos, G.G., Wenkstern, D.G., Blaha, C.D., Phillips, A.G., and Fibiger, H.C. Sexual behavior enhances central dopamine transmission in the male rat. *Brain Research,* 1990, *530,* 345–348.

Phillips, D.P., and Farmer, M.E. Acquired word deafness, and the temporal grain of sound representation in the primary auditory cortex. *Behavioural Brain Research,* 1990, *40,* 85–94.

Phillips, M.I., and Felix, D. Specific angiotensin II receptive neurons in the cat subfornical organ. *Brain Research,* 1976, *109,* 531–540.

Pilleri, G. The blind Indus dolphin, *Platanista indi. Endeavours,* 1979, *3,* 48–56.

Pleim, E.T., and Barfield, R.J. Progesterone versus estrogen facilitation of female sexual behavior by intracranial administration to female rats. *Hormones and Behavior,* 1988, *22,* 150–159.

Pleim, E.T., Matochik, J.A., Barfield, R.J., and Auerbach, S.B. Correlation of dopamine release in the nucleus accumbens with masculine sexual behavior in rats. *Brain Research,* 1990, *524,* 160–163.

Poggio, G.F., and Poggio, T. The analysis of stereopsis. *Annual Review of Neuroscience,* 1984, *7,* 379–412.

Powell, G.M., Berthier, N.E., and Moore, J.W. Efferent neuronal control of the nictitating membrane response in the rabbit (*Oryctolagus cuniculus*): A reexamination. *Physiology and Behavior,* 1979, *23,* 299–308.

Powers, J.B., and Winans, S.S. Vomeronasal organ: Critical role in mediating sexual behavior of the male hamster. *Science,* 1975, *187,* 961–963.

Powley, T.L. The ventromedial hypothalamic syndrome, satiety, and a cephalic phase hypothesis. *Psychological Review,* 1977, *84,* 89–126.

Premack, D. Reinforcement theory. In *Nebraska Symposium on Motivation,* edited by D. Levine. Lincoln: University of Nebraska Press, 1965.

Price, J. The genetics of depressive behavior. *British Journal of Psychiatry,* 1968, *2,* 37–45.

Propping, P., Kruger, J., and Janah, A. Effect of alcohol on genetically determined variants of the normal electroencephalogram. *Psychiatry Research,* 1980, *2,* 85–98.

Propping, P., Kruger, J., and Mark, N. Genetic disposition to alcoholism: An EEG study in alcoholics and their relatives. *Human Genetics,* 1981, *59,* 51–59.

Raffaele, K.C., and Olton, D.S. Hippocampal and amygdala involvement in working memory for nonspatial stimuli. *Behavioral Neuroscience,* 1988, *102,* 349–355.

Ragland, D.R., and Brand, R.J. Type A behavior and mortality from coronary heart disease. *New England Journal of Medicine,* 1988, *318,* 65–69.

Rakic, P. Mode of cell migration to the superficial layers of fetal monkey neocortex. *Journal of Comparative Neurology,* 1972, *145,* 61–83.

Ralph, M.R., Foster, R.G., Davis, F.C., and Menaker, M. Transplanted suprachiasmatic nucleus determines circadian period. *Science,* 1990, *247,* 975–978.

Ratcliff, G., and Newcombe, F. Object recognition: Some deductions from the clinical evidence. In *Normality and Pathology in Cognitive Functions,* edited by A.W. Ellis. London: Academic Press, 1982.

Ray, A., Henke, P.G., and Sullivan, R. The central amygdala and immobilization stress-induced gastric pathology in rats: Neurotensin and dopamine. *Brain Research,* 1987, *409,* 398–402.

Raybin, J.B., and Detre, T.P. Sleep disorder and symptomatology among medical and nursing students. *Comprehensive Psychiatry,* 1969, *10,* 452–467.

Rea, M.M., Sweeney, J.A., Solomon, C.M., Walsh, V., and Frances, A. Changes in eye tracking during clinical stabilization in schizophrenia. *Psychiatry Research,* 1989, *28,* 31–39.

Rechtschaffen, A., Bergmann, B.M., Everson, C.A., Kushida, C.A., and Gilliland, M.A. Sleep deprivation in the rat: X. Integration and discussion of the findings. *Sleep,* 1989, *12,* 68–87.

Rechtschaffen, A., Gilliland, M.A., Bergmann, B.M., and Winter, J.B.

Physiological correlates of prolonged sleep deprivation in rats. *Science,* 1983, *221,* 182–184.

Rechtschaffen, A., Wolpert, E.A., Dement, W.C., Mitchell, S.A., and Fisher, C. Nocturnal sleep of narcoleptics. *Electroencephalography and Clinical Neurophysiology,* 1963, *15,* 599–609.

Rehfeld, J.F. Immunochemical studies on cholecystokinin. II. Distribution and molecular heterogeneity in the central nervous system of man and hog. *Journal of Biological Chemistry,* 1978, *253,* 4022–4030.

Rehkämper, G., Haase, E., and Frahm, H.D. Allometric comparison of brain weight and brain structure volumes in different breeds of the domestic pigeon, *Columbia livia f.d.* (fantails, homing pigeons, strassers). *Brain, Behavior and Evolution,* 1988, *31,* 141–149.

Reich, P., Geyer, S.J., and Karnovsky, M.L. Metabolism of brain during sleep and wakefulness. *Journal of Neurochemistry,* 1972, *19,* 487–497.

Reifman, A., and Wyatt, R.J. Lithium: A brake in the rising cost of mental illness. *Archives of General Psychiatry,* 1980, *37,* 385–388.

Reiman, E.M., Fusselman, M.J., Fox, P.T., and Raichle, M.E. Neuroanatomical correlates of anticipatory anxiety. *Science,* 1989, *243,* 1071–1074.

Reiman, E.M., Raichle, M., Robins, E., Butler, F.K., Herscovitch, P., Fox, P., and Perlmutter, J. The application of positron emission tomography to the study of panic disorder. *American Journal of Psychiatry,* 1986, *143,* 469–477.

Reinink, E., Bouhuys, N., Wirz-Justice, A., and van den Hoofdakker, R. Prediction of the antidepressant response to total sleep deprivation by diurnal variation of mood. *Psychiatry Research,* 1990, *32,* 113–124.

Review Panel. Coronary-prone behavior and coronary heart disease: A critical review. *Circulation,* 1981, *673,* 1199–1215.

Reynolds, D.V. Surgery in the rat during electrical analgesia induced by focal brain stimulation. *Science,* 1969, *164,* 444–445.

Reynolds, G.P. Beyond the dopamine hypothesis: The neurochemical pathology of schizophrenia. *British Journal of Psychiatry,* 1989, *155,* 315–316.

Ricardo, J.A. Efferent connections of the subthalamic region in the rat. II. The zona incerta. *Brain Research,* 1981, *214,* 43–60.

Richmond, G., and Clemens, L. Ventromedial hypothalamic lesions and cholinergic control of female sexual behavior. *Physiology and Behavior,* 1988, *42,* 179–182.

Ritter, R.C., Slusser, P.G., and Stone, S. Glucoreceptors controlling feeding and blood glucose: Location in the hindbrain. *Science,* 1981, *213,* 451–453.

Ritter, S., and Taylor, J.S. Capsaicin abolishes lipoprivic but not glucoprivic feeding in rats. *American Journal of Physiology,* 1989, *256,* R1232–R1239.

Robbins, L.N., Helzer, J.E., Weissman, M.M., Orvaschel, H., Gruenberg, E., Burke, J.D., and Regier, D.A. Lifetime prevalence of specific psychiatric disorders in three sites. *Archives of General Psychiatry,* 1984, *41,* 949–958.

Roberts, W.W., and Robinson, T.C.L. Relaxation and sleep induced by warming of preoptic region and anterior hypothalamus in cats. *Experimental Neurology,* 1969, *25,* 282–294.

Robinson, T.E., Jurson, P.A., Bennett, J.A., and Bentgen, K.M. Persistent sensitization of dopamine neurotransmission in ventral striatum (nucleus accumbens) produced by prior experience with (+)-amphetamine: A microdialysis study in freely moving rats. *Brain Research,* 1988, *462,* 211–222.

Rodin, J., Schank, D., and Striegel-Moore, R. Psychological features of obesity. *Medical Clinics of North America,* 1989, *73,* 47–66.

Roffwarg, H.P., Muzio, J.N., and Dement, W.C. Ontogenetic development of human sleep-dream cycle. *Science,* 1966, *152,* 604–619.

Rogers, M.P., Trentham, D.E., McCune, W.J., Ginsberg, B.I., Rennke, H.G., Reike, P., and David, J.R. Effect of psychological stress on the induction of arthritis in rats. *Arthritis and Rheumatology,* 1980, *23,* 1337–1342.

Roland, P.E. Metabolic measurements of the working frontal cortex in man. *Trends in Neurosciences,* 1984, *7,* 430–435

Rolls, B.J., Rowe, E.A., Rolls, E.T., Kingston, B., Megson, A., and Gunary, R. Variety in a meal enhances food intake in man. *Physiology and Behavior,* 1981, *26,* 215–221.

Rolls, E.T. Feeding and reward. In *The Neural Basis of Feeding and Reward,* edited by B.G. Hobel and D. Novin. Brunswick, Maine: Haer Institute, 1982.

Rolls, E.T. Neuronal activity related to the control of feeding. In *Neural and Humoral Controls of Food Intake,* edited by R. Ritter and S. Ritter. New York: Academic Press, 1986.

Rolls, E.T. Visual information processing in the primate temporal lobe. In *Models of Visual Perception: From Natural to Artificial,* edited by M. Imbert. Oxford, England: Oxford University Press, 1989.

Rolls, E.T., and Baylis, G.C. Size and contrast have only small effects on the responses to faces of neurons in the cortex of the superior temporal sulcus of the monkey. *Experimental Brain Research,* 1986, *65,* 38–48.

Rolls, E.T., Baylis, G.C., Hasselmo, M.E., and Nalwa, V. The effect of learning on the face selective responses of neurons in the cortex in the superior temporal sulcus of the monkey. *Experimental Brain Research,* 1989, *76,* 153–164.

Rolls, E.T., Murzi, E., Yaxley, S., Thorpe, S.J., and Simpson, S.J. Sensory-specific satiety: Food-specific reduction in responsiveness of ventral forebrain neurons after feeding in the monkey. *Brain Research,* 1986, *368,* 79–86.

Rolls, E.T., Rolls, B.J., Kelly, P.H., Shaw, S.G., Wood, R.J., and Dale, R. The relative attenuation of self-stimulation, eating and drinking produced by dopamine-receptor blockade. *Psychopharmacologia,* 1974, *38,* 219–230.

Rose, G.A., and Williams, R.T. Metabolic studies of large and small eaters. *British Journal of Nutrition,* 1961, *15,* 1–9.

Roselli, C.E., Handa, R.J., and Resko, J.A. Quantitative distribution of nuclear androgen receptors in microdissected areas of the rat brain. *Neuroendocrinology,* 1989, *49,* 449–453.

Rosenfield, M.E., and Moore, J.W. Red nucleus lesions disrupt the classically conditioned membrane response in rabbits. *Behavioural Brain Research,* 1983, *10,* 393–398.

Rosenthal, D. A program of research on heredity in schizophrenia. *Behavioral Science,* 1971, *16,* 191–201.

Rosenthal, N.E., Genhart, M., Jacobson, F.M., Skwerer, R.G., and Wehr, T.A. Disturbances of appetite and weight regulation in seasonal affective disorder. *Annals of the New York Academy of Sciences,* 1986, *499,* 216–230.

Rosenthal, N.E., Sack, D.A., James, S.P., Parry, B.L., Mendelson, W.B., Tamarkin, L., and Wehr, T.A. Seasonal affective disorder and phototherapy. *Annals of the New York Academy of Sciences,* 1985, *453,* 260–269.

Rothman, S.M., and Olney, J.W. Excitotoxicity and the NMDA receptor. *Trends in Neurosciences,* 1987, *10,* 299–302.

Rothwell, N.J., and Stock, M.J. A role for brown adipose tissue in diet-induced thermogenesis. *Nature,* 1979, *281,* 31–35.

Routtenberg, A., and Malsbury, C. Brainstem pathways of reward. *Journal of Comparative and Physiological Psychology,* 1969, *68,* 22–30.

Roy, A., De Jong, J., and Linnoila, M. Cerebrospinal fluid monoamine metabolites and suicidal behavior in depressed patients. *Archives of General Psychiatry,* 1989, *46,* 609–612.

Rubin, B.S., and Barfield, R.J. Priming of estrous responsiveness by implants of 17B-estradiol in the ventromedial hypothalamic nucleus of female rats. *Endocrinology,* 1980, *106,* 504–509.

Rudy, J.W., and Sutherland, R.J. The hippocampal formation is necessary for rats to learn and remember configural discriminations. *Behavioural Brain Research,* 1989, *34,* 97–109.

Rumelhart, D.E., McClelland, J.L., and the PDP Research Group. *Parallel Distributed Processing: Explorations in the Microstructure of Cognition.* Cambridge, Mass.: MIT Press, 1986.

Rusak, B., and Groos, G. Suprachiasmatic stimulation phase shifts rodent circadian rhythms. *Science,* 1982, *215,* 1407–1409.

Rusak, B., and Morin, L.P. Testicular responses to photoperiod are blocked by lesions of the suprachiasmatic nuclei in golden hamsters. *Biology of Reproduction,* 1976, *15,* 366–374.

Russell, M.J. Human olfactory communication. *Nature,* 1976, *260,* 520–522.

Russell, M.J., Switz, G.M., and Thompson, K. Olfactory influences on the human menstrual cycle. Paper presented at the meeting of the American Association for the Advancement of Science, San Francisco, June 1977.

Ryback, R.S., and Lewis, O.F. Effects of prolonged bed rest on EEG sleep patterns in young, healthy volunteers. *Electroencephalography and Clinical Neurophysiology,* 1971, *31,* 395–399.

Saayman, G.S. Aggressive behaviour in free-ranging chacma baboons (*Papio ursinus*). *Journal of Behavioral Science,* 1971, *1,* 77–83.

Sachar, E.J., and Baron, M. The biology of affective disorders. *Annual Review of Neuroscience,* 1979, *2,* 505–518.

Sachs, B.D., and Meisel, R.L. The physiology of male sexual behavior. In *The Physiology of Reproduction,* edited by E. Knobil and J. Neill. New York: Raven Press, 1988.

Sackheim, H.A. Lateral asymmetry in bodily response to hypnotic suggestion. *Biological Psychiatry,* 1982, *17,* 437–447.

Sackheim, H.A., and Gur, R.C. Lateral asymmetry in intensity of emotional expression. *Neuropsychologia,* 1978, *16,* 473–482.

Sackheim, H.A., Paulus, D., and Weiman, A.L. Classroom seating and hypnotic susceptibility. *Journal of Abnormal Psychology,* 1979, *88,* 81–84.

Saffran, E.M., Marin, O.S.M., and Yeni-Komshian, G.H. An analysis of speech perception in word deafness. *Brain and Language,* 1976, *3,* 209–228.

Saffran, E.M., Schwartz, M.F., and Marin, O.S.M. Evidence from aphasia: Isolating the components of a production model. In *Language Production,* edited by B. Butterworth. London: Academic Press, 1980.

Sahu, A., Kalra, P.S., and Kalra, S.P. Food deprivation and ingestion induce reciprocal changes in neuropeptide Y concentrations in the paraventricular nucleus. *Peptides,* 1988, *9,* 83–86.

Sakai, F., Meyer, J.S., Karacan, I., Derman, S., and Yamamoto, M. Normal human sleep: Regional cerebral haemodynamics. *Annals of Neurology,* 1979, *7,* 471–478.

Sakai, K. Some anatomical and physiological properties of pontomesencephalic tegmental neurons with special reference to the PGO waves and postural atonia during paradoxical sleep in the cat. In *The Reticular Formation Revisited,* edited by J.A. Hobson and M.A. Brazier. New York: Raven Press, 1980.

Sakai, K., and Jouvet, M. Brain stem PGO-on cells projecting directly to the cat dorsal lateral geniculate nucleus. *Brain Research,* 1980, *194,* 500–505.

Sakuma, Y., and Pfaff, D.W. Facilitation of female reproductive behavior from mesencephalic central grey in the rat. *American Journal of Physiology,* 1979a, *237,* R278–R284.

Sakuma, Y., and Pfaff, D.W. Mesencephalic mechanisms for integration of female reproductive behavior in the rat. *American Journal of Physiology,* 1979b, *237,* R285–R290.

Sakuma, Y., and Pfaff, D.W. Convergent effects of lordosis-relevant somatosensory and hypothalamic influences on central gray cells in the rat mesencephalon. *Experimental Neurology,* 1980a, *70,* 269–281.

Sakuma, Y., and Pfaff, D.W. Excitability of female rat central gray cells with medullary projections: Changes produced by hypothalamic stimulation and estrogen treatment. *Journal of Neurophysiology,* 1980b, *44,* 1012–1023.

Salamone, J.D. Dopaminergic involvement in activational aspects of motivation: Effects of haloperidol on schedule-induced activity, feeding, and foraging in rats. *Psychobiology,* 1988, *16,* 196–206.

Sananes, C.B., and Campbell, B.A. Role of the central nucleus of the amygdala in olfactory heart rate conditioning. *Behavioral Neuroscience,* 1989, *103,* 519–525.

Sapolsky, R. Glucocorticoid toxicity in the hippocampus: Reversal by supplementation with brain fuels. *Journal of Neuroscience,* 1986, *6,* 2240–2244.

Sapolsky, R.M., Krey, L.C., and McEwen, B.S. The neuroendocrinology of stress and aging: The glucocorticoid cascade hypothesis. *Endocrine Reviews,* 1986, *7,* 284–301.

Sassenrath, E.N., Powell, T.E., and Hendrickx, A.G. Perimenstrual aggression in groups of female rhesus monkeys. *Journal of Reproduction and Fertility,* 1973, *34,* 509–511.

Sato, M. Acute exacerbation of methamphetamine psychosis and lasting dopaminergic supersensitivity—a clinical survey. *Psychopharmacology Bulletin,* 1986, *22,* 751–756.

Sato, M., Chen, C.-C., Akiyama, K., and Otsuki, S. Acute exacerbation of paranoid psychotic state after long-term abstinence in patients with previous methamphetamine psychosis. *Biological Psychiatry,* 1983, *18,* 429–440.

Schenck, C.H., Bundlie, S.R., Ettinger, M.G., and Mahowald, M.W. Chronic behavioral disorders of human REM sleep: A new category of parasomnia. *Sleep,* 1986, *9,* 293–308.

Schenkel, E., and Siegel, J.M. REM sleep without atonia after lesions of the medial medulla. *Neuroscience Letters,* 1989, *98,* 159–165.

Scherschlicht, R., Polc, P., Schneeberger, J., Steiner, M., and Haefely, W. Selective suppression of rapid eye movement sleep (REMS) in cats by typical and atypical antidepressants. In *Typical and Atypical Antidepressants: Molecular Mechanisms,* edited by E. Costa and G. Racagni. New York: Raven Press, 1982.

Schiffman, P.L., Westlake, R.E., Santiago, T.V., and Edelman, N.H. Ventilatory control in parents of victims of the sudden infant death syndrome. *New England Journal of Medicine,* 1980, *302,* 486–491.

Schleifer, S.J., Keller, S.E., Camerino, M., Thornton, J.C., and Stein, M. Suppression of lymphocyte stimulation following bereavement. *Journal of the American Medical Association,* 1983, *15,* 374–377.

Schuster, C.R., and Balster, R.L. The discriminative stimulus properties of drugs. *Advances in Behavioral Pharmacology,* 1977, *1,* 85–138.

Schwartz, D.H., McClane, S., Hernandez, L., and Hoebel, B.G. Feeding increases extracellular serotonin in the lateral hypothalamus of the rat as measured by microdialysis. *Brain Research,* 1989, *479,* 349-354.

Schwartz, M.F., Marin, O.S.M., and Saffran, E.M. Dissociations of language function in dementia: A case study. *Brain and Language,* 1979, *7,* 277-306.

Schwartz, M.F., Saffran, E.M., and Marin, O.S.M. The word order problem in agrammatism. I. Comprehension. *Brain and Language,* 1980, *10,* 249-262.

Schwartz, W.J., and Gainer, H. Suprachiasmatic nucleus: Use of ^{14}C-labelled deoxyglucose uptake as a functional marker. *Science,* 1977, *197,* 1089-1091.

Schwartz, W.J., Gross, R.A., and Morton, M.T. The suprachiasmatic nuclei contain a tetrodotoxin-resistant circadian pacemaker. *Proceedings of the National Academy of Sciences, USA,* 1987, *84,* 1694-1698.

Schwartz, W.J., Reppert, S.M., Eagan, S.M., and Moore-Ede, M.C. In vivo metabolic activity of the suprachiasmatic nuclei: A comparative study. *Brain Research,* 1983, *274,* 184-187.

Schwarzkopf, S.B., Nasrallah, H.A., Olson, S.C., Coffman, J.A., and McLaughlin, J.A. Perinatal complications and genetic loading in schizophrenia: Preliminary findings. *Psychiatry Research,* 1989, *27,* 233-239.

Sclafani, A., and Aravich, P.F. Macronutrient self-selection in three forms of hypothalamic obesity. *American Journal of Physiology,* 1983, *244,* R686-R694.

Scoville, W.B., and Milner, B. Loss of recent memory after bilateral hippocampal lesions. *Journal of Neurology, Neurosurgery and Psychiatry,* 1957, *20,* 11-21.

Sedvall, G., Fyrö, B., Gullberg, B., Nybäck, H., Wiesel, F.-A., and Wode-Helgodt, B. Relationship in healthy volunteers between concentrations of monoamine metabolites in cerebrospinal fluid and family history of psychiatric morbidity. *British Journal of Psychiatry,* 1980, *136,* 366-374.

Selye, H. *The Stress of Life.* New York: McGraw-Hill, 1976.

Selye, H., and Tuchweber, B. Stress in relation to aging and disease. In *Hypothalamus, Pituitary and Aging,* edited by A. Everitt and J. Burgess. Springfield, Ill.: Charles C. Thomas, 1976.

Shaikh, M.B., and Siegel, A. Naloxone-induced modulation of feline aggression elicited from midbrain periaqueductal gray. *Pharmacology, Biochemistry, and Behavior,* 1989, *31,* 791-796.

Shallice, T. Phonological agraphia and the lexical route in writing. *Brain,* 1981, *104,* 413-429.

Sharp, P.E., McNaughton, B.L., and Barnes, C.A. Spontaneous synaptic enhancement in hippocampi of rats exposed to a spatially complex environment. *Society for Neuroscience Abstracts,* 1983, *9,* 647.

Shavit, Y., Depaulis, A., Martin, F.C., Terman, G.W., Pechnick, R.N., Zane, C.J., Gale, P.P., and Liebeskind, J.C. Involvement of brain opiate receptors in the immune-suppressive effect of morphine. *Proceedings of the National Academy of Sciences, USA,* 1986, *83,* 7114-7117.

Shavit, Y., Lewis, J.W., Terman, G.W., Gale, R.P., and Liebeskind, J.C. Opioid peptides mediate the suppressive effect of stress on natural killer cell cytotoxicity. *Science,* 1984, *223,* 188-190.

Sherry, D.F., Vaccarino, A.L., Buckenham, K., and Herz, R.S. The hippocampal complex of food-storing birds. *Brain, Behavior and Evolution,* 1989, *34,* 308-317.

Shik, M.L., and Orlovsky, G.N. Neurophysiology of locomotor automatism. *Physiological Review,* 1976, *56,* 465-501.

Shock, N. Systems integration. In *Handbook of the Biology of Aging,* edited by C. Finch and L. Hayflick. New York: Van Nostrand Reinhold, 1977.

Sidman, M., Stoddard, L.T., and Mohr, J.P. Some additional quantitative observations of immediate memory in a patient with bilateral hippocampal lesions. *Neuropsychologia,* 1968, *6,* 245-254.

Siegel, J.M. Behavioral functions of the reticular formation. *Brain Research Reviews,* 1979, *1,* 69-105.

Siegel, J.M. A behavioral approach to the analysis of reticular formation unit activity. In *Behavioral Approaches to Brain Research,* edited by T.E. Robinson. New York: Oxford University Press, 1983.

Siegel, J.M., and McGinty, D.J. Pontine reticular formation neurons: Relationship of discharge to motor activity. *Science,* 1977, *196,* 678-680.

Silver, J.M., Shin, C., and Md Md Md McNamara, J.O. Antiepileptogenic effects of conventional anticonvulsants in the kindling model of epilepsy. *Annals of Neurology,* 1991, *29,* 356-363.

Simpson, J.B., Epstein, A.N., and Camardo, J.S. The localization of dipsogenic receptors for angiotensin II in the subfornical organ. *Journal of Comparative and Physiological Psychology,* 1978, *92,* 581-608.

Sinclair, D. *Mechanisms of Cutaneous Sensation.* Oxford, England: Oxford University Press, 1981.

Sitaram, N., Moore, A.M., and Gillin, J.C. Experimental acceleration and slowing of REM ultradian rhythm by cholinergic agonist and antagonist. *Nature,* 1978, *274,* 490-492.

Sitaram, N., Weingartner, H., and Gillin, J.C. Human serial learning: Enhancement with arecholine and choline and impairment with scopolamine. *Science,* 1978, *201,* 271-276.

Slater, B., and Shields, J. Genetical aspects of anxiety. *British Journal of Psychiatry Special Publication No. 3, Studies of Anxiety.* Ashford, Kent: Headley Bros., 1969.

Smith, C. Sleep states and learning: A review of the animal literature. *Neuroscience and Biobehavioral Reviews,* 1985, *9,* 157-168.

Smith, G.P., Gibbs, J., and Kulkosky, P.J. Relationships between brain-gut peptides and neurons in the control of food intake. In *The Neural Basis of Feeding and Reward,* edited by B.G. Hoebel and D. Novin. Brunswick, Maine: Haer Institute, 1982.

Snyder, F. Towards an evolutionary theory of dreaming. *American Journal of Psychiatry,* 1966, *123,* 121-136.

Snyder, S.H. *Madness and the Brain.* New York: McGraw-Hill, 1974.

Solomon, G.F. Psychoneuroimmunology: Interactions between central nervous system and immune system. *Journal of Neuroscience Research,* 1987, *18,* 1-9.

Solyom, L., Turnbull, I.M., and Wilensky, M. A case of self-inflicted leucotomy. *British Journal of Psychiatry,* 1987, *151,* 855-857.

Sperry, R.W. Brain bisection and consciousness. In *Brain and Conscious Experience,* edited by J. Eccles. New York: Springer-Verlag, 1966.

Spiegel, D., Bloom, J., and Yalom, I.D. Group support for patients with metastatic breast cancer. *Archives of General Psychiatry,* 1981, *38,* 527-533.

Spiegel, D., Bloom, J.R., Kraemer, H.C., and Gottheil, E. Effect of psychosocial treatment on survival of patients with metastatic breast cancer. *Lancet,* 1989, *2,* 888-891.

Spoendlin, H. The innervation of the cochlear receptor. In *Basic Mechanisms in Hearing,* edited by A.R. Møeller. New York: Academic Press, 1973.

Spyraki, C., Fibiger, H.C., and Phillips, A.G. Attenuation by haloperidol of place preference conditioning using food reinforcement. *Psychopharmacology,* 1982a, *77,* 379–382.

Spyraki, C., Fibiger, H.C., and Phillips, A.G. Dopaminergic substrates of amphetamine-induced place preference conditioning. *Brain Research,* 1982b, *253,* 185–193.

Squire, L.R. Stable impairment in remote memory following electroconvulsive therapy. *Neuropsychologia,* 1974, *13,* 51–58.

Squire, L.R., Shimamura, A.P., and Amaral, D.G. Memory and the hippocampus. In *Neural Models of Plasticity: Experimental and Theoretical Approaches,* edited by J.H. Byrne and W.O. Berry. San Diego: Academic Press, 1989.

Sørensen, T.I.A., Price, R.A., Stunkard, A.J., and Schulsinger, F. Genetics of obesity in adult adoptees and their biological siblings. *British Medical Journal,* 1989, *298,* 97–90.

Stanley, B.G., Magdalin, W., and Leibowitz, S.F. A critical site for neuropeptide Y-induced eating lies in the caudolateral paraventricular/perifornical region of the hypothalamus. *Society for Neuroscience Abstracts,* 1989, *15,* 894.

Stanley, B.G., Schwartz, D.H., Hernandez, L., Hoebel, B.G., and Leibowitz, S.F. Patterns of extracellular norepinephrine in the paraventricular hypothalamus: Relationship to circadian rhythm and deprivation-induced eating behavior. *Life Sciences,* 1989, *45,* 275–282.

Stanley, B.G., Schwartz, D.H., Hernandez, L., Leibowitz, S.F., and Hoebel, B.G. Pattern of extracellular 5-hydroxyindoleacetic acid (5-HIAA) in the paraventricular hypothalamus (PVN): Relation to circadian rhythm and deprivation-induced eating behavior. *Pharmacology, Biochemistry, and Behavior,* 1989, *33,* 257–260.

Staubli, U., Larson, J., Thibault, O., Baudry, M., and Lynch, G. Chronic administration of a thiol-proteinase inhibitor blocks long-term potentiation of synaptic responses. *Brain Research,* 1988, *444,* 153–158.

Stebbins, W.C., Miller, J.M., Johnsson, L.-G., and Hawkins, J.E. Ototoxic hearing loss and cochlear pathology in the monkey. *Annals of Otology, Rhinology and Laryngology,* 1969, *78,* 1007–1026.

Steen, S.N., Oppliger, R.A., and Brownell, K.D. Metabolic effects of repeated weight loss and regain in adolescent wrestlers. *Journal of the American Medical Association,* 1988, *260,* 47–50.

Stein, L., and Belluzzi, J.D. Operant conditioning of individual neurons. In *Quantitative Analyses of Behavior. Vol. VII. Biological Determinants of Reinforcement and Memory,* edited by M. Commons, R. Church, J. Stellar, and A. Wagner. Hillsdale, N.J.: Lawrence Erlbaum Associates, 1988.

Steinmetz, J.E., Lavond, D.G., and Thompson, R.F. Classical conditioning in rabbits using pontine nucleus stimulation as a conditioned stimulus and inferior olive stimulation as an unconditioned stimulus. *Synapse,* 1989, *3,* 225–233.

Steinmetz, J.E., Logan, C.G., Rosen, D.J., Thompson, J.K., Lavond, D.G., and Thompson, R.F. Initial localization of the acoustic conditioned stimulus projection system to the cerebellum essential for classical eyelid conditioning. *Proceedings of the National Academy of Sciences, USA,* 1987, *84,* 3531–3535.

Stellar, J.R., Kelley, A.E., and Corbett, D. Effects of peripheral and central dopamine blockade on lateral hypothalamic self-stimulation: Evidence for both reward and motor deficits. *Pharmacology, Biochemistry, and Behavior,* 1983, *18,* 433–442.

Stephan, F.K., and Nuñez, A.A. Elimination of circadian rhythms in drinking activity, sleep, and temperature by isolation of the suprachiasmatic nuclei. *Behavioral Biology,* 1977, *20,* 1–16.

Stephan, F.K., and Zucker, I. Circadian rhythms in drinking behavior and locomotor activity of rats are eliminated by hypothalamic lesion. *Proceedings of the National Academy of Sciences, USA,* 1972, *69,* 1583–1586.

Sterman, M.B., and Clemente, C.D. Forebrain inhibitory mechanisms: Cortical synchronization induced by basal forebrain stimulation. *Experimental Neurology,* 1962a, *6,* 91–102.

Sterman, M.B., and Clemente, C.D. Forebrain inhibitory mechanisms: Sleep patterns induced by basal forebrain stimulation in the behaving cat. *Experimental Neurology,* 1962b, *6,* 103–117.

Sternbach, R.A. *Pain: A Psychophysiological Analysis.* New York: Academic Press, 1968.

Stevens, J.R. Neurology and neuropathology of schizophrenia. In *Schizophrenia as a Brain Disease,* edited by F.A. Henn and H.A. Nasrallah. New York: Oxford University Press, 1982.

Stevens, J.R. Schizophrenia and multiple sclerosis. *Schizophrenia Bulletin,* 1988, *14,* 231–241.

Stevens, S.S., and Newman, E.B. Localization of actual sources of sound. *American Journal of Psychology,* 1936, *48,* 297–306.

Stewart, W.B., Kauer, J.S., and Shepherd, G.M. Functional organization of the rat olfactory bulb analysed by the 2-deoxyglucose method. *Journal of Comparative Neurology,* 1979, *185,* 715–734.

St. George-Hyslop, P.H., Tanzi, R.E., Polinsky, R.J., Haines, J.L., Nee, L., Watkins, P.C., Myers, R.H., Feldman, R.G., Pollen, D., Drachman, D., Growdon, J., Bruni, A., Foncin, J.-F., Salmon, D., Frommelt, P., Amaducci, L., Sorbi, S., Piacentini, S., Stewart, G.D., Hobbs, W.J., Conneally, P.M., and Gusella, J.F. The genetic defect causing familial Alzheimer's disease maps on chromosome 21. *Science,* 1987, *235,* 885–890.

Stoyva, J., and Metcalf, D. Sleep patterns following chronic exposure to cholinesterase-inhibiting organophosphate compounds. *Psychophysiology,* 1968, *5,* 206.

Stricker, E.M., and Zigmond, M.J. Recovery of function after damage to central catecholamine-containing neurons: A neurochemical model for the lateral hypothalamic syndrome. *Progress in Psychobiology and Physiological Psychology,* 1976, *6,* 121–188.

Stunkard, A.J., Sørensen, T.I.A., Harris, C., Teasdale, T.W., Chakraborty, R., Schull, W.J., and Schulsinger, F. An adoption study of human obesity. *New England Journal of Medicine,* 1986, *314,* 193–198.

Sturup, G.K. Correctional treatment and the criminal sexual offender. *Canadian Journal of Correction,* 1961, *3,* 250–265.

Suddath, R.H., Christison, G. W., Torrey, E. T., Casanova, M.F., and Weinberger, D.R. Anatomical abnormalities in the brains of monozygotic twins discordant for schizophrenia. *The New England Journal of Medicine,* 1990, *322* 789–794.

Sutherland, R.J., and Rudy, J.W. Configural association theory: The role of the hippocampal formation in learning, memory, and amnesia. *Psychobiology,* 1989, *17,* 129–144.

Suzdak, P.D., Glowa, J.R., Crawley, J.N., Schwartz, R.D., Skolnick, P., and Paul, S.M. A selective imidazobenzodiazepine antagonist of ethanol in the rat. *Science,* 1986, *234,* 1243–1247.

Svare, B. Psychobiological determinants of maternal aggressive behavior. In *Aggressive Behavior: Genetic and Neural Approaches,* edited by E.C. Simmel, M.E. Hahn, and J.K. Walters. Hillsdale, N.J.: Lawrence Erlbaum Associates, 1983.

Svare, B. Recent advances in the study of female aggressive behavior in mice. In *House Mouse Aggression: A Model for Understanding the Evolution of Social Behavior,* edited by S. Parmigiani, D. Mainardi, and P. Brain. London: Gordon and Breach, 1989.

Svare, B., Betteridge, C., Katz, D., and Samuels, O. Some situational and experiential determinants of maternal aggression in mice. *Physiology and Behavior,* 1981, *26,* 253–258.

Svare, B., and Gandelman, R. Postpartum aggression in mice: The influence of suckling stimulation. *Hormones and Behavior,* 1976, *7,* 407–416.

Svensson, T.H., Grenhoff, J., and Aston-Jones, G. Midbrain dopamine neurons: Nicotinic control of firing patterns. *Society for Neuroscience Abstracts,* 1986, *12,* 1154.

Swaab, D.F., and Fliers, E. A sexually dimorphic nucleus in the human brain. *Science,* 1985, *228,* 1112–1115.

Swaab, D.F., and Hofman, M.A. Sexual differentiation of the human hypothalamus: Ontogeny of the sexually dimorphic nucleus of the preoptic area. *Developmental Brain Research,* 1988, *44,* 314–318.

Swanson, L.W., Mogenson, G.J., Gerfen, C.R., and Robinson, P. Evidence for a projection from the lateral preoptic area and substantia innominata to the "mesencephalic locomotor region" in the rat. *Brain Research,* 1984, *295,* 161–178.

Swedo, S.E., Schapiro, M.B., Grady, C.L., Cheslow, D.L., Leonard, H.L., Kumarn, A., Friedland, R., Rapoport, S.I., and Rapoport, J.L. Cerebral glucose metabolism in childhood-onset obsessive-compulsive disorder. *Archives of General Psychiatry,* 1989, *46,* 518–523.

Szymusiak, R., and McGinty, D. Sleep-related neuronal discharge in the basal forebrain of cats. *Brain Research,* 1986a, *370,* 82–92.

Szymusiak, R., and McGinty, D. Sleep suppression following kainic acid-induced lesions of the basal forebrain. *Experimental Neurology,* 1986b, *94,* 598–614.

Takahashi, Y. Growth hormone secretion related to the sleep waking rhythm. In *The Functions of Sleep,* edited by R. Drucker-Colín, M. Shkurovich, and M.B. Sterman. New York: Academic Press, 1979.

Talairach, J., Bancaud, J., Geier, S., Bordas-Ferrer, M., Bonis, Z., Szikla, G., and Rusu, M. The cingulate gyrus and human behaviour. *Electroencephalography and Clinical Neurophysiology,* 1973, *34,* 45–52.

Tamminga, C.A., Burrows, G.H., Chase, T.N., Alphs, L.D., and Thaker, G.K. Dopamine neuronal tracts in schizophrenia: Their pharmacology and *in vivo* glucose metabolism. *Annals of the New York Academy of Sciences,* 1988, *537,* 443–450.

Tanabe, T., Iino, M., Ooshima, Y., and Takagi, S.F. An olfactory area in the prefrontal lobe. *Brain Research,* 1974, *80,* 127–130.

Tanabe, T., Iino, M., and Takagi, S.G. Discrimination of odors in olfactory bulb, pyriform-amygdaloid areas, and orbitofrontal cortex of the monkey. *Journal of Neurophysiology,* 1975, *38,* 1284–1296.

Tanner, C.M. The role of environmental toxins in the aetiology of Parkinson's disease. *Trends in Neurosciences,* 1989, *12,* 49–54.

Teitelbaum, P., and Stellar, E. Recovery from the failure to eat produced by hypothalamic lesions. *Science,* 1954, *120,* 894–895.

Terenius, L., and Wahlström, A. Morphine-like ligand for opiate receptors in human CSF. *Life Sciences,* 1975, *16,* 1759–1764.

Terry, R.D., and Davies, P. Dementia of the Alzheimer type. *Annual Review of Neuroscience,* 1980, *3,* 77–96.

Tetrud, J.W., and Langston, J.W. The effect of deprenyl (Selegiline) on the natural history of Parkinson's disease. *Science,* 1989, *245,* 519–522.

Thompson, R.F. Neural circuit for classical conditioning of the eyelid closure response. In *Neural Models of Plasticity: Experimental and Theoretical Approaches,* edited by J.H. Byrne and W.O. Berry. San Diego: Academic Press, 1989.

Thornton, S.N., de Beaurepaire, R., and Nicolaïdis, S. Electrophysiological investigation of cells in the region of the anterior hypothalamus firing in relation to blood pressure and volaemic changes. *Brain Research,* 1984, *299,* 1–7.

Tordoff, M.G., and Friedman, M.I. Hepatic control of feeding: Effect of glucose, fructose, and mannitol. *American Journal of Physiology,* 1988, *254,* R969–R976.

Torrey, E.F., Torrey, B.B., and Peterson, M.R. Seasonality of schizophrenic births in the United States. *Archives of General Psychiatry,* 1977, *34,* 1065–1070.

Träskmann, L., Åsberg, M., Bertilsson, L., and Sjöstrand, L. Monoamine metabolites in CSF and suicidal behavior. *Archives of General Psychiatry,* 1981, *38,* 631–636.

Triandafillou, J., and Himms-Hagen, J. Brown adipose tissue in genetically obese *(fa/fa)* rats: Response to cold and diet. *American Journal of Physiology,* 1983, *244,* E145–E150.

Turner, S.M., Beidel, D.C., and Nathan, R.S. Biological factors in obsessive-compulsive disorders. *Psychological Bulletin,* 1985, *97,* 430–450.

Tyrell, J.B., and Baxter, J.D. Glucocorticoid therapy. In *Endocrinology and Metabolism,* edited by P. Felig, J.D. Baxter, A.E. Broadus, and L.A. Frohman. New York: McGraw-Hill, 1981.

Ungerleider, L.G., and Mishkin, M. Two cortical visual systems. In *Analysis of Visual Behavior,* edited by D.J. Ingle, M.A. Goodale, and R.J.W. Mansfield. Cambridge, Mass.: MIT Press, 1982.

Uno, H., Tarara, R., Else, J.G., Suleman, M.A., and Sapolsky, R.M. Hippocampal damage associated with prolonged and fatal stress in primates. *The Journal of Neuroscience,* 1989, *9,* 1705–1711.

Vaccarino, F.J., Bloom, R.E., and Koob, G.F. Blockade of nucleus accumbens opiate receptors attenuates intravenous heroin reward in the rat. *Psychopharmacology,* 1985, *86,* 37–42.

Valenstein, E.S. *Great and Desperate Cures: The Rise and Decline of Psychosurgery and Other Radical Treatments for Mental Illness.* New York: Basic Books, 1986.

Valverius, P., Crabbe, J.C., Hoffman, P.L., and Tabakoff, B. NMDA receptors in mice bred to be prone or resistant to ethanol withdrawal seizures. *European Journal of Pharmacology,* 1990, *184,* 185–189.

Vandenbergh, J.G., Witsett, J.M., and Lombardi, J.R. Partial isolation of a pheromone accelerating puberty in female mice. *Journal of Reproductive Fertility,* 1975, *43,* 515–523.

van de Poll, N.E., Taminiau, M.S., Endert, E., and Louwerse, A.L. Gonadal steroid influence upon sexual and aggressive behavior of female rats. *International Journal of Neuroscience,* 1988, *41,* 271–286.

van der Lee, S., and Boot, L.M. Spontaneous pseudopregnancy in mice. *Acta Physiologica et Pharmacologica Néerlandica,* 1955, *4,* 442–444.

Van Eekelen, J.A.M., and Phillips, M.I. Plasma angiotensin II levels at moment of drinking during angiotensin II intravenous infusion. *American Journal of Physiology,* 1988, *255,* R500–R506.

Verney, E.B. The antidiuretic hormone and the factors which determine its release. *Proceedings of the Royal Society of London, B.,* 1947, *135,* 25–106.

Voci, V.E., and Carlson, N.R. Enhancement of maternal behavior and nest behavior following systemic and diencephalic administration of prolactin and progesterone in the mouse. *Journal of Comparative and Physiological Psychology,* 1973, *83,* 388–393.

Voeller, K.K.S., Hanson, J.A., and Wendt, R.N. Facial affect recognition in children: A comparison of the performance of children with right and left hemisphere lesions. *Neurology,* 1988, *38,* 1744–1748.

Vogel, G.W., Buffenstein, A., Minter, K., and Hennessey, A. Drug effects on REM sleep and on endogenous depression. *Neuroscience and Biobehavioral Reviews,* 1990, *14,* 49–63.

Vogel, G.W., Neill, D., Hagler, M., and Kors, D. A new animal model of endogenous depression: A summary of present findings. *Neuroscience and Biobehavioral Reviews,* 1990, *14,* 85–91.

Vogel, G.W., Thurmond, A., Gibbons, P., Sloan, K., Boyd, M., and Walker, M. REM sleep reduction effects on depression syndromes. *Archives of General Psychiatry,* 1975, *32,* 765–777.

Vogel, G.W., Vogel, F., McAbee, R.S., and Thurmond, A.J. Improvement of depression by REM sleep deprivation: New findings and a theory. *Archives of General Psychiatry,* 1980, *37,* 247–253.

Vold, J.M. Expériences sur les rêves et en particulier sur ceux d'origine musculaire et optique. *Revues Philosophiques,* 1896, *42,* 542. (Cited by Hobson, 1988.)

Volpe, B.T., LeDoux, J.E., and Gazzaniga, M.S. Information processing of visual stimuli in an extinguished field. *Nature,* 1979, *282,* 722.

vom Saal, F.S. Time-contingent change in infanticide and parental behavior induced by ejaculation in male mice. *Physiology and Behavior,* 1985, *34,* 7–15.

vom Saal, F.S., and Bronson, F.H. *In utero* proximity of female mouse fetuses to males: Effect on reproductive performance during later life. *Biology of Reproduction,* 1980, *22,* 777–780.

von Békésy, G. *Experiments in Hearing.* New York: McGraw-Hill, 1960.

Walsh, L.L., and Grossman, S.P. Dissociation of responses to extracellular thirst stimuli following zona incerta lesions. *Pharmacology, Biochemistry, and Behavior,* 1978, *8,* 409–415.

Ward, I. Prenatal stress feminizes and demasculinizes the behavior of males. *Science,* 1972, *175,* 82–84.

Warrington, E.K., and James, M. Visual apperceptive agnosia: A clinico-anatomical study of three cases. *Cortex,* 1988, *24,* 1–32.

Warrington, E.K., and Shallice, T. Word-form dyslexia. *Brain,* 1980, *103,* 99–112.

Webb, W.B. *Sleep: The Gentle Tyrant.* Englewood Cliffs, N.J.: Prentice-Hall, 1975.

Webb, W.B. Some theories about sleep and their clinical implications. *Psychiatric Annals,* 1982, *11,* 415–422.

Webster, H.H., and Jones, B.E. Neurotoxic lesions of the dorsolateral pontomesencephalic tegmentum-cholinergic cell area in the cat. II. Effects upon sleep-waking states. *Brain Research,* 1988, *458,* 285–302.

Weinberger, D.R., and Wyatt, R.J. Brain morphology in schizophrenia: *In vivo* studies. In *Schizophrenia as a Brain Disease,* edited by F.A. Henn and H.A. Nasrallah. New York: Oxford University Press, 1982.

Weingarten, J.P., Chang, P.K., and McDonald, T.J. Comparison of the metabolic and behavioral disturbances following paraventricular-and ventromedial-hypothalamic lesions. *Brain Research Bulletin,* 1985, *14,* 551–559.

Weintraub, S., Mesulam, M.-M., and Kramer, L. Disturbances in prosody: A right-hemisphere contribution to language. *Archives of Neurology,* 1981, *38,* 742–744.

Weiskrantz, L., and Warrington, E.K. Conditioning in amnesia patients. *Neuropsychologia,* 1979, *17,* 187–194.

Weiskrantz, L., Warrington, E.K., Sanders, M.D., and Marshall, J. Visual capacity in the hemianopic field following a restricted occipital ablation. *Brain,* 1974, *97,* 709–728.

Weiss, J.M. Effects of coping response on stress. *Journal of Comparative and Physiological Psychology,* 1968, *65,* 251–260.

Weitzman, E.D. Sleep and its disorders. *Annual Review of Neuroscience,* 1981, *4,* 381–418.

Welle, S.L., Nair, K.S., and Campbell, R.G. Failure of chronic β-adrenergic blockade to inhibit overfeeding-induced thermogenesis in humans. *American Journal of Physiology,* 1989, *256,* R653–R658.

Wernicke, C. *Der Aphasische Symptomenkomplex.* Breslau, Poland: Cohn & Weigert, 1874.

Whipple, B., and Komisaruk, B.R. Analgesia produced in women by genital self-stimulation. *Journal of Sex Research,* 1988, *24,* 130–140.

Whitehead, R.G., Rowland, M.G.M., Hutton, M., Prentice, A.M., Müller, E., and Paul, A. Factors influencing lactation performance in rural Gambian mothers. *Lancet,* 1978, *2,* 178–181.

Whitehouse, P.J., Price, D.L., Struble, R.G., Clark, A.W., Coyle, J.T., and DeLong, M.R. Alzheimer's disease and senile dementia: Loss of neurons in the basal forebrain. *Science,* 1982, *215,* 1237–1239.

Whitten, W.K. Occurrence of anestrus in mice caged in groups. *Journal of Endocrinology,* 1959, *18,* 102–107.

Wiener, S.I., Paul, C.A., and Eichenbaum, H. Spatial and behavioral correlates of hippocampal neuronal activity. *Journal of Neuroscience,* 1989, *9,* 2737–2763.

Wiesner, B.P., and Sheard, N. *Maternal Behaviour in the Rat.* London: Oliver and Brody, 1933.

Wilska, A. Eine Methode zur Bestimmung der Horschwellenamplituden der Tromenfells bei verscheideden Frequenzen. *Skandinavisches Archiv für Physiologie,* 1935, *72,* 161–165.

Winans, S.S., and Powers, J.B. Olfactory and vomeronasal deafferentation of male hamsters: Histological and behavioral analyses. *Brain Research,* 1977, *126,* 325–344.

Winn, P., Tarbuck, A., and Dunnett, S.B. Ibotenic acid lesions of the lateral hypothalamus: Comparison with electrolytic lesion syndrome. *Neuroscience,* 1984, *12,* 225–240.

Winslow, J.T., Ellingoe, J., and Miczek, K.A. Effects of alcohol on aggressive behavior in squirrel monkeys: Influence of testosterone and social context. *Psychopharmacology,* 1988, *95,* 356–363.

Winslow, J.T., and Miczek, J.A. Social status as determinants of alcohol effects on aggressive behavior in squirrel monkeys *(Saimiri sciureus). Psychopharmacology,* 1985, *85,* 167–172.

Winslow, J.T., and Miczek, J.A. Androgen dependency of alcohol effects on aggressive behavior: A seasonal rhythm in high-ranking squirrel monkeys. *Psychopharmacologia,* 1988, *95,* 92–98.

Wise, R.A. Psychomotor stimulant properties of addictive drugs. *Annals of the New York Academy of Sciences,* 1988, *537,* 228–234.

Wise, R.A. Opiate reward: Sites and substrates. *Neuroscience and Biobehavioral Reviews,* 1989, *13,* 129–133.

Wise, S.P., and Rapoport, J.L. Obsessive compulsive disorder: Is it a basal ganglia dysfunction? *Psychopharmacology Bulletin,* 1988, *24,* 380–384.

Wolkowitz, O.M., Bertz, B., Weingartner, H., Beccaria, L., Thompson, K., and Liddle, R.A. Hunger in humans induced by MK-329, a specific peripheral-type cholecystokinin receptor antagonist. *Biological Psychiatry,* 1990, *28,* 169–173.

Wong, D.F., Wagner, H.N., Tune, L.E., Dannals, R.F., Pearlson, G.D., Links, J.M., Tamminga, C.A., Broussolle, E.P., Ravert, H.T., Wilson, A.A., Toung, J.K.T., Malat, J., Williams, J.A., O'Tuama, L.A., Snyder, S.H., Kuhar, M.J., and Gjedde, A. Positron emission tomography reveals elevated D_2 dopamine receptors in drug-naive schizophrenics. *Science,* 1986, *234,* 1558–1563.

Wong-Riley, M. Personal communication, 1978. Cited by Livingstone and Hubel, 1982.

Wood, D.M., and Emmett-Oglesby, M.W. Mediation in the nucleus accumbens of the discriminative stimulus produced by cocaine.

Pharmacology, Biochemistry, and Behavior, 1989, *33,* 453–457.

Wood, P.L. Actions of GABAergic agents on dopamine metabolism in the nigrostriatal pathway of the rat. *Pharmacology and Experimental Therapeutics,* 1982, *222,* 674–679.

Woodruff, R.A., Guze, S.B., and Clayton, P.J. Anxiety neurosis among psychiatric outpatients. *Comprehensive Psychiatry,* 1972, *13,* 165–170.

Woods, S.W., Charney, D.S., Goodman, W.K., and Heninger, G.R. Carbon dioxide-induced anxiety. *Archives of General Psychiatry,* 1988, *45,* 43–52.

Woodworth, R.S., and Schlosberg, H. *Experimental Psychology.* New York: Holt, Rinehart and Winston, 1954.

Wu, J.C., and Bunney, W.E. The biological basis of an antidepressant response to sleep deprivation and relapse: Review and hypothesis. *American Journal of Psychiatry,* 1990, *147,* 14–21.

Wyatt, R.J., Kirch, D.G., and DeLisi, L.E. Biochemical, endocrine, and immunologic studies of schizophrenia. In *Comprehensive Textbook of Psychiatry,* 5th ed., edited by H.I. Kaplan and B.J. Sadock. Baltimore: Williams and Wilkins, 1988.

Wysocki, C.J. Neurobehavioral evidence for the involvement of the vomeronasal system in mammalian reproduction. *Neuroscience and Biobehavioral Reviews,* 1979, *3,* 301–341.

Yamamoto, T., Yuyama, N., and Kawamura, Y. Central processing of taste perception. In *Brain Mechanisms of Sensation,* edited by Y. Katsuki, R. Norgren, and M. Sato. New York: John Wiley & Sons, 1981.

Yeo, C.H., Hardiman, M.J., Glickstein, M., and Steele-Russell, I. Lesions of cerebellar nuclei abolish the classically conditioned nictitating membrane response. *Society for Neuroscience Abstracts,* 1982, *8,* 22.

Young, W.G., and Deutsch, J.A. Intragastric pressure and receptive relaxation in the rat. *Physiology and Behavior,* 1980, *25,* 973–975.

Zarbin, M.A., Innis, R.B., Wamsley, J.K., Snyder, S.H., and Kuhar, M.J. Autoradiographic localization of cholecystokinin receptors in rodent brain. *Journal of Neuroscience,* 1983, *3,* 877–906.

Zeki, S. The construction of colours by the cerebral cortex. *Proceedings of the Royal Institute of Great Britain,* 1984, *56,* 231–257.

Zeki, S., and Shipp, S. The functional logic of cortical connections. *Nature,* 1988, *335,* 311–317.

Zeki, S.M. The representation of colours in the cerebral cortex. *Nature,* 1980, *284,* 412–418.

Zhang, S.P., Bandler, R., and Carrive, P. Flight and immobility evoked by excitatory amino acid microinjection within distinct parts of the subtentorial midbrain periaqueductal gray of the cat. *Brain Research,* 1990, *520,* 73–82.

Zola-Morgan, S., Squire, L.R., and Amaral, D.G. Human amnesia and the medial temporal region: Enduring memory impairment following a bilateral lesion limited to field CA1 of the hippocampus. *Journal of Neuroscience,* 1986, *6,* 2950–2967.

Zvolsky, P., Jansky, L., Vyskocilova, J., and Grof, P. Effects of psychotropic drugs on hamster hibernation: Pilot study. *Progress in Neuropsychopharmacology,* 1981, *5,* 599–602.

Name Index

Subject Index